A SELECTION

FROM THE

DESPATCHES, MEMORANDA, AND OTHER PAPERS

A SELECTION

FROM THE

DESPATCHES, MEMORANDA, AND OTHER PAPERS

OF THE

MARQUESS WELLESLEY, K.G.

DURING HIS GOVERNMENT OF

INDIA

EDITED BY

SIDNEY J. OWEN

GYAN

Published by

Gyan Publishing House
5, Ansari Road
Daryaganj, New Delhi-110002
Phone: 011-47034999, 9811692060
E-mail: books@gyanbooks.com

Distribution Network
gyanbooks.com
India, USA, Canada, UK, Australia

ISBN: 978-93-6780-193-2 (PB)

First Published, 1880

2nd Impression 2024

Printed at: Gyan Press, Delhi.

A SELECTION FROM THE DESPATCHES, MEMORANDA, AND OTHER PAPERS

Editor: SIDNEY J. OWEN

A SELECTION

FROM THE

DESPATCHES, TREATIES, AND OTHER PAPERS

OF THE

MARQUESS WELLESLEY

S. J. OWEN

A SELECTION

FROM THE

DESPATCHES, TREATIES, AND OTHER PAPERS

OF THE

MARQUESS WELLESLEY, K.G.

DURING HIS GOVERNMENT OF

INDIA

EDITED BY

SIDNEY J. OWEN, M.A.

Reader in Law and History, and Tutor at Christ Church
Reader in Indian Law and History in the University of Oxford
Formerly Professor of History in the Elphinstone College, Bombay

WITH AN APPENDIX, A MAP OF INDIA, AND EIGHT PLANS OF BATTLES AND SIEGES

'REDIT A NOBIS AURORA, DIEMQUE REDUCIT'

Oxford

AT THE CLARENDON PRESS

M DCCC LXXVII

PREFACE.

NEARLY twenty years ago, the Rise of the British Empire in India was suggested as a subject of special study in the combined Honour School of Law and Modern History at Oxford.[1] Several causes for some time retarded the adoption of this suggestion. About eleven years since, Orme's great work was substituted for Mr. Mill's history, which had been previously recommended; and I tried the experiment of lecturing upon it to a very small class. This was so far successful, that when, in 1868, the original Teachership of Indian Law, intended for the Selected Candidates for the Indian Civil Service, and which had been for some time renewed from year to year, was established provisionally for a longer period, the claims of British India in the Law and History School were recognized; and the Vice-Chancellor of the day, in his official speech at the close of the Academical year, noticed the appointment of a Reader[2] in Indian Law and History. From that time I lectured regularly on Orme, and the class grew more numerous.

When, on the rearrangement of our University examination system, the Schools of Law and History were separately constituted; and the Historical Board, acting under the

[1] This suggestion was, I believe, due to Mr. Boase, to whose extensive knowledge and untiring zeal the cause of Modern History in the University is so deeply indebted. By a curious coincidence, I was about the same time introducing the study of Thucydides (in Dale's translation) among the Brahmins, Purvoes, and Parsees of Bombay.

[2] I did not discover, until some years later, that, in the Latin Statute, the word equivalent to *Reader* had only been inserted in one place. Thus my legal *persona* is still rather equivocal. *Reader*, however, has always been the name adopted in the English proceedings of Congregation and Convocation, previous to the Decree of last year, which was ambiguous.

New Statute, proposed a group of subjects for special and minute study; British India, from 1784 to 1806, formed one of those subjects. Lord Wellesley's Despatches accordingly became an essential part of this course. But though a portion only of what he wrote, or even published, on his Indian administration, the contents of the five bulky volumes edited by Mr. Montgomery Martin were far too voluminous for the student; and those volumes had long been out of print. Copies however were to be found at the Bodleian, and in some College Libraries; and the increasing demand for them produced 'second hand' copies through the booksellers. The Board did me the honour of entrusting to me the task of specifying those documents with which the student ought to be familiar. An official list of these was accordingly published in the *University Gazette,* and incorporated into the official pamphlet on the Examination Statute and the instructions of the Boards of Studies. But both examiners and students experienced and complained of the inconvenience attending this arrangement; and frequently expressed a wish to have the papers required in a more accessible, compact, and systematic form. Such is the origin of this undertaking.

But though primarily intended to supply a local want, it is hoped that it will serve also a more general purpose. Like Wellesley himself, it goes forth from Oxford; but like him, it is intimately connected with the interests and the pursuits of the great world without. Not only the historian and the Indian administrator, but the statesman, the diplomatist, the soldier, the political economist, the 'educationalist,' even the student of English literature, are—or *ought* to be—all interested in the conduct and the utterances of

> 'the majestic Lord,
> 'That broke the bonds of'

Tippoo and the Mahratta in the East; and prepared the way for breaking those of the Corsican in the West; saved, extended, and organized British India; struck a fatal blow at the trading monopoly of the Company; instituted the magnificent scheme of Fort William College; and expounded and vindicated his measures in State Papers, which as literary compositions, designed for a practical purpose, are models of such handiwork, and the study of which is in itself a manifold and invaluable training for the young aspirant to distinction in a School of Modern History.

The responsibility involved in the task of selection is by no means a light one. It is, indeed, often far easier to determine what to adopt, than what to reject. So rich in lessons of political wisdom, and in able and instructive discussions of great problems, are the compositions of Lord Wellesley; that in spite of the bulk of this volume, I am inevitably reminded of Lord Clive's strong exclamation, when taxed with helping himself too freely to the treasures of the Nawab of Bengal. I can at least say, that no pains have been spared to make these *disjecta membra* of a great and scholarly statesman as representative as possible; and by the omission of minor, occasional, and personal matters, tentative measures, and reduplicated instructions, to gain space for exhibiting the administration in its broader bearings, mature form, and natural sequence.

A careful reperusal of the entire correspondence has led to the rejection of a few pages included in the former list, and to the insertion of many short but important extracts, which, on reconsideration, it seemed undesirable to sacrifice.

The documents have been arranged, for clearness and facility of reference, under distinct heads. To each paper has been prefixed a very short note of its contents; and a running analysis, along the top of the pages, has been added, indicating at once the chief subject of each page, and the general and connected drift of the whole paper. Thus, an Index, which must have either added unduly to the size of the volume, or caused the omission of valuable matter, has been avoided; though it may be well to add that this was not an afterthought, but was designed before the selection was made.

The Appendix is intended to illustrate the Despatches, partly by supplying additional accounts of events; but more by the quotation of thoughtful and critical passages, which delineate the Governor General's policy, either as a whole, or in some of its details, according to the estimate of those, whose opinions, on various accounts, are well worth attention.

By the great kindness of His Grace, the present Duke of Wellington, I have been thus enabled to enrich this collection with the terse and masterly Paper, which forms the Introduction, and with many other documents, the interest and value of which will be seen at a glance; and which, as well as the Map of India, are all taken, by His Grace's permission, from the Supplementary volumes of the Wellington Despatches. Such extracts might, with obvious advantage, have been much more numerous. And I hope hereafter to give a fuller explanation of the great part played by the hero of Assye, as right-hand councillor of the Governor General, and as an administrator in Mysore.

In the Survey, prefixed to the Selections, an attempt has been made to exhibit the policy of Lord Wellesley in its true relations with the circumstances of the time, both in India and in Europe. How baseless is the hazy fancy, which represents Indian history as a stream apart from the main current of world story, will appear in the course of the Survey, and in many other parts of the volume. Such a fancy ought not to be entertained by readers of the Bible, Herodotus, or Gibbon. And it is productive of very mischievous results, both intellectually and politically. But besides a knowledge of the state of Europe in Wellesley's day; a general acquaintance with the condition and revolutions of India, from the rise of Sivaji onwards, is essential to one, who would view the Governor General's conduct (especially as regards the Mahrattas) in its proper light. I accordingly delivered, and soon afterwards published, a course of Lectures introductory to the British Period,[1] to which I venture to refer those who may be disposed to complain, that I have taken for granted much, which ought to have been established on historical evidence, and made enigmatical allusions, where detailed explanations would have been more appropriate. Those Lectures

[1] *India on the Eve of the British Conquest.* Allen & Co. 1872.

indeed ended with an account of the battle of Paniput, in 1761. But the interval between that time and Wellesley's, so far as native history is concerned, has been spanned, in a very interesting volume, by Mr. H. G. Keene.[1] In another course of Lectures I have traversed the corresponding space of Anglo-Indian History; and should it seem worth while to print them, they will, I trust, be found to justify many remarks in the Survey, which may at present seem obscure or questionable.

To His Grace the Duke of Wellington my warmest acknowledgments are due, for the very liberal permission to incorporate in the present volume both the excellent historical Map of India, and the Papers from the Supplementary Despatches; as well as to the Marquess of Salisbury, Secretary of State for India, who kindly allowed the use of all public documents relating to Lord Wellesley's administration, so far as the rights of Government over them extend; also to Alfred Montgomery, Esq., for his most obliging offer to place at my disposal all the Marquess's papers in his possession; and to the Principal Librarian and Mr. E. A. Bond at the British Museum, and to Dr. Rost and Mr. Waterfield at the India Office, for their kind and ready assistance in instituting a search after missing papers. I am beholden also to Mr. Murray, of Albemarle Street, for his courtesy in causing the Plate, from which the Map of India was originally engraved, to be promptly hunted up.

It would not be right to conclude without one more explanation. The lamentable want of interest in the affairs of India which, in spite of our great stake in that country, and the constant residence there of so many of our friends and relatives, notoriously prevails throughout all classes of educated Englishmen, is, I have long been convinced, mainly due to the systematic exclusion of Indian history, as a branch of general study. While, on the other hand, many years experience of its attractiveness (when the really valuable parts of it are carefully brought under their notice) not only to young men, but to both boys and girls, is, to my mind, a very hopeful and encouraging circumstance.

---

[1] *The Fall of the Moghul Empire.* By Henry George Keene. Allen & Co. 1876.

But among the objections to its introduction at Oxford was the question :—How are you to find examiners willing and competent to test your pupils? I had myself no fears, at the time, on this ground. And the sequel has amply justified my confidence. The New Statute empowers examiners to call in assessors, to adjudicate upon out-of-the-way subjects. But, in this case, it has only once (I believe) been necessary to do so. And the character of the papers during the last four years, with which I have had absolutely nothing to do, proves that, whatever may be said of the examiners by ill-informed and captious critics, they have recognized and well fulfilled their obligations; risen with the new emergencies of their position; and taking even more trouble than the Statute required them to do, have placed Indian history on its proper footing, and in its due relations to other subjects.

CONTENTS.

ERRATA.

Page 27,	line 13.	*For* 'practical' *read* 'practicable'
" 126,	" 8.	*Insert* 'Major-General Baird' to &c.
" "	" 30.	*For* 'on' read 'in'
" 129,	" 1.	*For* 'Merriott' *read* 'Marriott'
" 226,	" 26.	*For* 'valuable' read 'vulnerable'
" 319,	" 2.	*Read* 'Omrao'
" "	" 36.	*For* 'measure' *read* 'measures'
" 515,	" 13.	*Before* 'Resident' *insert* 'Acting'
" 529,	" 10.	*For* '1803' *read* '1804'
" 531,	" 20.	*Before* 'Lake' *insert* 'Lord'
" 584,	" 7.	*For* 'appears' *read* 'appear'
" 603,	" 32.	*For* 'rest' *read* 'rests'
" 609,	" 1.	*For* 'employments' *read* 'employment'
" 755,	" 16.	*For* 'means of' *read* 'means by'
" 769,	" 4.	*Before* 'Wellesley' *insert* 'Arthur'

NOTE.—The motto in the title-page, applicable to Marquess Wellesley's administration, as a whole, was (I understand) placed by him on Fort William College.

SURVEY OF

LORD WELLESLEY'S ADMINISTRATION.

(BY THE EDITOR.)

I. MYSORE.

Mahometan Mysore had been for more than thirty years a constant source of alarm and danger to the Madras Government, and of perplexity and expense to Calcutta and Leadenhall Street. Indeed, Hyder and Tippoo were names of fear to the British nation itself. The most conscientiously pacific of Governors-General had been compelled to make war upon the Sultaun. And the policy which, when the turbulent Mysorean had been virtually conquered, and was at our mercy, had spared him, and allowed him to resume his place among the Princes of India, had been much canvassed at the time. His hereditary leaning to the French, and his readiness to throw in his lot with them, were as decided and notorious as his irreconcileable and fanatical hatred of Englishmen. When, in the course of the long agony of Pitt's miserably conducted war on the Continent, it appeared that Tippoo was preparing, with French aid, to resume hostilities against us, and that Buonaparte was on his way to Egypt with a view to co-operate in conquering England in India; the calmest and most constant mind might well entertain misgivings, and be inclined to applaud the prompt and vigorous initiative of the Governor-General against a local enemy, who might otherwise turn out to be an imperial danger of no trifling importance.

The elaborate establishment, in the Governor-General's Minute, of the *casus belli;* the comparatively moderate and defensive nature of the demands which, in the first instance, it was proposed to extort from the Sultaun; his patent and coarse devices to evade the issue and stultify our preparations, till the chapter of accidents might befriend him, and bring the French in force to his assistance; the panic fear at Madras of even attempting to concert defensive measures; the Governor-General's lucid and forcible exposition of our 'critical, not alarming' state; the ability, energy, and rapidity, with which he rehabilitated our alliance with the Nizam, completed the arrangements for a war, in which the army was to be, to a great extent, its own base, and should be enabled, in the Napoleonic fashion, to strike at once at the enemy's capital, and end the contest by 'a single, distinct, and definite operation'; the cordial and useful co-operation of the Nizam's forces, reformed on Wellesley's model, and directed by his military brother; the two victories of Seedasere and Malvelly; the uninterrupted and comparatively expeditious progress of the vast armaments to the scene of their 'certain triumph'; the steady and methodical conduct of the siege; the swift and completely successful assault; the absence of unnecessary carnage; the fortunate death of the Sultaun; the prompt submission of his family, his servants, and of the country generally; the consummate skill with which the delicate and difficult problem of the partition and settlement of the conquered territories was solved, stated, and executed; lastly, the obvious, signal, and at the moment unqualified advantages resulting from the whole undertaking:—all combined to win golden opinions at home from every class of critics in favor of such an achievement on the part of one so recently entrusted with so novel and arduous a charge. Lord Mornington himself plainly conceived that he had herein gained no ignoble *spolia opima*. Again and again he reverts to the conquest of Mysore, as Cicero did to the suppression of Catiline's conspiracy. And the just pride which he felt in the reduction of Tippoo's power, and the confidence with which he counted on public approval in England, appear most clearly in the fact that, when doing what he feels will be most unpalatable to the Directors, he appeals to them by the memory of this event. He dates the Regulation for the establishment of Fort William College on the anniversary of the capture of Seringapatam. His classical mind might revert to Manlius. If you are inclined to condemn me for betraying your commercial constitution, remember—I saved you from Tippoo!

How much he was indebted for his success to the counsels and co-operation of his brother Arthur may be inferred from a paper in the Appendix, and is illustrated at large in the Duke of Wellington's Despatches. Colonel Wellesley's animated description of the order of march is also a valuable historical document, full of local colouring. And, as a ridiculously mythical narrative was circulated of the check which the Colonel sustained in the night attack at Seringapatam, it was thought well to give the authentic accounts of that incident. The pith of the matter is summed up in the following characteristically simple and straightforward words:—'As I could not find out the post which it was desirable I should occupy, I was obliged to desist from the attack, the enemy also having retired from the post.'

The Governor-General's Minute deserves attention, not only with reference to its immediate occasion, but as the starting point of a new policy, and the manifesto and justification of that policy. The sense of insecurity, and the positive expense entailed by the constant fear of war in India; the double peril of French aggression from within and without; the necessity of rescuing the Nizam from the Mahrattas, and placing him permanently under British protection; the exposed condition of our North-West frontier, and the imminence of Afghan invasion; the formidable power of Scindia, and the desirableness of counteracting his influence at Poona, perhaps even of coercing him by arms; the policy of attempting to bridle the whole Mahratta League through the medium of a more intimate and predominant alliance with the Peishwa; the hopeful prospect of a pacified India, regulated and controlled by a wise and 'moderate' British Power:—such are the chief features of the more general view thus early matured in the mind of the Governor-General, and expounded with his usual clearness, and with perhaps some unconsciousness of the obstacles to its realization. The subjoined passage seems to contain the key to his whole system of dealing with native States; and though its full import might not be at once apparent, it at least gives no uncertain sound as to the obvious tendency of his wishes and exertions[1]. How much, as regarded the Mahrattas, he counted without his host, will appear in the sequel. But, by the very announcement of such a scheme, he gave a pretty clear indication that a Mahratta war was by no means unlikely to follow a successful one with Tippoo.

---

[1] 'While we prevent our allies from weakening themselves by repeated contests, we may expect that such an interference in the disputes of the native powers, so far from tending to foment divisions, and to occasion war, will prove the best security for the general tranquillity of India, as well as the most solid pledge of our disposition to preserve that blessing from interruption. However comprehensive and intricate the proposed system may appear at the first view, it will soon be evident to all the powers of India, that the fundamental principle of our policy is invariably repugnant to every scheme of conquest, extension of dominion, aggrandisement, or ambition, either for ourselves or for our allies. Consistently with this principle, it is our right and duty to restore the vigour and efficiency of our defensive alliances; but beyond the limits of this principle, we entertain no project of altering the condition, of reducing or of raising the power of any established state in India. On the other hand, the same principle justifies and demands our firm resistance to the intrusion of any foreign power which shall attempt to acquire a preponderant influence in the scale of Indian politics, to the prejudice of our defensive alliances, and of our just interests. The establishment of our subsidized force at Poonah and Hyderabad will afford effectual means of guarding, not only against any such intrusion, but against the undue growth of any native power. While we possess so formidable a force in the centre of India, no such event can happen without our knowledge and consent.'

II. THE NIZAM.

A rebellious offshoot of the Mogul Empire, the Nizam's power had always been overshadowed and threatened by the Mahrattas. Nizam-ul-Mulk himself had been more than once humiliated by the Peishwa, and had been all along his tributary. Protected for awhile by Bussy's brilliant ascendancy in the Dekkan; allied at a later period with the English, though for a short time their opponent in the first war with Hyder; the Nizam had never been able to throw off the Mahratta claim to *choute*, a convenient pretext for indefinite fiscal exaction and political interference.

The exigencies of the war with Tippoo had induced Lord Cornwallis to strain his conscience so far as to write a letter, which was to have the binding force of a Treaty, to allay the fears of the feeblest member of the Tripartite Alliance, lest he should be devoured by the Mahrattas while engaged against the common enemy. Sir John Shore's non-intervention policy almost occasioned this disastrous result, and brought about the dominant influence of a French corps at Hyderabad. Lord Mornington's first Treaty with Nizam Ally, and the skilfully combined and energetic measures that followed in execution of it, averted the latter danger, and converted the Nizam into a really serviceable ally in the Mysore war. But the second Treaty went much further, and sounded the warning note of still more momentous changes in our political relations. It formally undertook the defence of the Nizam against all enemies, including the Mahrattas; and in consideration of large territorial cessions, it omitted the previous restrictions against the employment of the subsidiary force on minor occasions of internal trouble.

It could hardly be expected, considering the antecedents, that the Mahrattas, whoever might wield the effective power at Poonah, would ever peaceably agree to forego the claim to *choute*. Nor, whatever may have been the case as to the mode and results of its exaction, could it be called in itself an unjust one, as the Duke of Wellington seems to imply in his answer to Lord Castlereagh. Thus, though on general and over-ruling grounds its abolition might be necessary; such a demand almost unavoidably involved a war with the Mahrattas, whenever that people should have the courage to undertake one. But Wellesley hoped that they would not; and that *thus* British mediation might befriend our ally, and deliver him permanently from a burden which was not only humiliating, but grievous and dangerous. In this hope he was deceived, as he had been in Tippoo's case, and as Europeans are very apt to be when they count confidently on natives acting in accordance with what we conceive to be their obvious interest.

III. THE CARNATIC.

Much what Ireland was to the English Government, the Carnatic had long been to the Anglo-Indian rulers ;—a scene of perpetual misgovernment, oppression, and discord ; a constant source of danger ; a tempting prize to our enemies ; a scandal to the English name ; a slough of despond, which, in a series of wars, absorbed treasure and troops, without corresponding advantage, or any assured prospect of permanent improvement. The cessation of the double government, and the annexation of the province by the Company, had long been recommended, and was much desired by the Directors and the Ministry, as Mr. Dundas's letters testify. But this the Nabob, backed by his European advisers and creditors, stoutly resisted, appealing to Treaties, and taking his stand on his technical right to the *status quo*. This was a dangerous line, under the circumstances, to adopt towards Lord Wellesley, who slew him—or rather his successor—with his own weapon. However little the papers discovered at Seringapatam may satisfy Mr. Mill's severe tests ; they clearly enough proved both a technical breach of Treaties, and a violation of their spirit and object. And besides the intolerable nuisance of such a state of affairs as prevailed in the Carnatic, and for which the Company was indirectly responsible ; there could be no reasonable doubt that Mahomed Ali, who was in fact our creature, and not even the eldest son of the family, had played treacherously and most mischievously into Hyder's hands in our earlier wars ; or that his son only followed the traditional practice in associating himself with our most determined enemy. Whatever shortcomings there may have been in the later administration of the Carnatic by the English, the measure which the Declaration (prepared by Lord Wellesley, though issued by Lord Clive) announces and justifies, is broadly distinguishable both in principle and policy from cases which, though liable to be confused with it, may be freely condemned without disputing the propriety or necessity of this change.

IV. OUDE.

Of all Lord Wellesley's proceedings, his dealings with the Nabob Vizier of Oude are apt, at first sight, to seem most harsh and arbitrary. A careful consideration of the circumstances may much modify, if not altogether remove, the impression. The distressing voluminousness of the materials is undoubtedly a difficulty in the way of the enquirer. The present object has been to supply such documents as are requisite to place the matter, in its essential characteristics, fairly and with sufficient fulness, before the reader. That the Nabob was an independent Sovereign, cannot be maintained in the face of the facts of history. The

Duke of Wellington's short Memorandum in the Appendix shews the vital importance to the Company's Provinces of the defence of Oude, and the origin and character of this obligation on the part of the English Government. Sir James Craig shews that, in the opinion of the responsible military authority, while the danger of invasion was great, the Nabob's own army was not only a heavy drain on his exchequer, but a real and formidable peril to our Government. Mr. Dundas strongly recommends the dispersion of these rabble corps. The most doubtful point perhaps was the claim to increase the subsidiary corps indefinitely, at the discretion of the English Government. The increasing probability of a rupture with the Mahrattas, while it might be a plea for the liberal exercise of this pretension, might also make that exercise practically ruinous to Oude. The Treaty, of course, settled this as well as other points; but only after the resort to very severe pressure, the mission of Mr. Henry Wellesley, a controversy which it is painful, even in the light of later events, to read, and the obstinately resisted and ineffectual endeavour to accomplish what had been done in the Carnatic. The rectification of our military frontier, and the territorial isolation of the Nabob, were not only parts of a larger scheme, but in themselves measures of obvious importance, especially at such a crisis. The Nabob continued to amass treasure. But the English intervention cannot be said to have much improved, in the long run, the condition of the country. The dissatisfaction of the Directors with Mr. Henry Wellesley's appointment was a chief cause of the alienation between them and Lord Wellesley.

V. MAHRATTAS.

We now enter on the most memorable and characteristic chapter of Lord Wellesley's administration. The Mysore war was the closing act of an old drama. The Treaty of Bassein was the prelude to a new tragedy. That we took up arms against Tippoo to ward off serious, inveterate, and imminent perils, was sufficiently obvious, and was generally admitted in England. The expediency, and still more the necessity of the Treaty of Bassein, even apart from its almost immediate consequence, the war with Scindia and the Rajah of Berar, was a matter of grave question, and deep misgivings. The rapid and uniformly brilliant course of the contest exactly conformed to the Governor-General's carefully elaborated plan, fully justified his anticipations, enhanced his reputation and that of the British troops, and thus half-disarmed the critics of his previous policy. But it did not prevent them from hesitating to admit the advantages of the general result, or from adverting to the total change of our position in India which it involved, the magnitude and complication of the new obligations which we had contracted, and the difficulties and dangers that must beset even the attempt to fulfil them at all adequately.

And when the war with Holkar followed close on the pacification with the other Mahratta chiefs; and he who had so lately been represented as a needy and desperate adventurer inflicted upon our arms the greatest humiliation they had experienced since the destruction of Baillie's corps; and in spite of the heroic defence of Delhi, the great victory of Deeg, the breathless cavalry chase along the Doab, and the rout of Ferruckabad, contrived to alienate from us our recent and spontaneous ally, the powerful Rajah of Bhurtpore; and with his aid prolonged the contest, and rekindled anew, far and wide, the smouldering embers of disaffection and predatory licence, thus producing a series of sporadic encounters of a petty and inglorious, but perplexing, wearisome, and in their general tendency dangerous character; when, moreover, four vehement assaults by Lake's victorious army were successfully resisted at Bhurtpore, and Scindia shewed an unmistakeable disposition to try once more the fortune of war against us:—then was the feast of croakers! Then Lord Wellesley's supporters waxed faint; and the vehement tide of public opinion in England condemned the rash, ambitious, and war-loving statesman; and floated out the good old nobleman who had first broken Tippoo's power, to die in the futile attempt to reverse an order of things, which he had himself materially, however involuntarily, contributed to bring about.

The fact is, the line which Wellesley pursued in his Mahratta negotiations was a bolder and more original one than had ever been adopted, or probably conceived, by any European statesman in India, Dupleix perhaps excepted. Though it naturally commended itself to his capacious mind and sanguine and benevolent temper, it was also, to a considerable extent, forced upon him by recent circumstances: he was led on from step to step by the course of events, and the falsification of his too confident hopes of the efficacy of his pacific expedients. The objections to his policy were obvious, plausible, and weighty. In working it out he was confronted, and driven at times to over refinements, by embarrassing facts, deeply rooted prejudices, mistimed or misinterpreted restrictions. He was hastily judged, and condemned by the event of a partial and temporary collapse. He was weakened and discouraged at last by the consciousness of hesitating and half-hearted support from the Ministers, virulent and vulgar opposition in the Court of Directors, and ill-informed public clamour; and, acting on his brother Arthur's advice, he threw up the game when on the point of winning it, lest the cards should be rudely snatched out of his hands. His work was mutilated; but it could not be effaced. And when the stress of the Napoleonic war was over, and local anarchy had produced a counterpart of the state of affairs around the shores of the Levant in Pompey's days, Lord Hastings resumed and completed his great predecessor's interrupted task.

I shall endeavor to justify these remarks, and to exhibit, as fairly as possible, the principal considerations which seem to have influenced the views of Lord Wellesley and his opponents respectively.

On the one hand, there was a strong and not unnatural prejudice against a close connexion with the Mahrattas. They were at once turbulent, warlike, unscrupulous, and notoriously jealous of our interference in their concerns. They had played us false more than once; and though the Peishwa was pledged to help us against Tippoo, so far from doing so on the last occasion, he had behaved, according to Wellesley, almost as an enemy. Now that Tippoo was no more, what had we to gain by an alliance with this people? We need hardly fear their attacking us; and if they were disposed to do so, they were quite capable of forgetting friendly professions, and ignoring Treaty stipulations. While to associate ourselves intimately with the Court of Poona, the home of a Prince at once weak, wily, treacherous, and exorbitant in his latent pretensions; the focus of interminable political intrigues, the scene of incessant revolutions, would be the surest way to become hopelessly entangled in 'the labyrinth of Mahratta politics,' and to be compelled to take a side, and thus plunge into war. And with what result? There was an unpleasant memory of the perplexities and disasters of our former hostilities with the same people in Warren Hastings' time. And we could not be sure, that in spite of the subsequent increase of our power, we might not again be unsuccessful, at least for a time. For Mahadajee Scindia had assiduously developed his military resources, and the reputation of his disciplined battalions and formidable artillery was great. While the old awe of the Mahratta cavalry had by no means passed away from the general mind. To side with one party would probably unite the rest against us; other States might join them; and they might call in the French to their assistance. If, on the contrary, we waged successful war, we might be hardly less endangered by our very triumph. Might we not overtax our strength and our resources in endeavoring to secure and administer our conquests, and to keep watch and ward over the restless ocean which we had for awhile dominated? *Mole sua ruit Roma*, was not to be forgotten. And might not we too come to resemble the Oriental river, that loses itself in the sands? Especially as both the nature of the case, and the voice of experience attested, that once launched on such an indefinite career of intervention and consequent hostility, it was by no means clear, where we might be able to stop. Might it not be our case to 'find no end, in wandering mazes lost?' Thus much as to the abstract question.

But special and contemporary facts also gave much additional force to such reasoning. The Peishwa only concluded the alliance in the prescribed form at the eleventh hour, and then as a *pis aller*, in his dire extremity. And could we trust him to abide by it? If it was not necessary to us, for self-defence, still more, if it involved the issues of war and probable conquest, was it not, though the Court might save the letter of the law by authorizing it, still a breach of the spirit and intention of the Act of Parliament? Was not the Company already heavily in debt, and bent on retrenchment and liquidation? Must not even a short and successful war, over so vast an area, be a very costly one? And though the Company had too often been dragged into hostilities, and become a sort of Sovereign against its will; did not this circumstance tell in favor of abstaining from connexions that might lead to a repetition of such a diversion of its energies from their original and proper destination, and of its resources from their imperative object of squaring the account, and paying a good dividend? Lastly, was this a time to occasion extraordinary demands for money and men, when every shilling and every soldier were most urgently required to rescue the British Empire itself from impending ruin? When cash payments were suspended, and Buonaparte was threatening invasion? Such was one side of the case, by no means (it may be thought, even when thus sketched) a weak one.

On the other hand, it is impossible to appreciate justly Lord Wellesley's Mahratta policy without estimating how far he was influenced by the lessons of the past, the political circumstances of the time, and the remoter and more general considerations which his combined utterances indicate. Like Dupleix, he knew that whatever might be thought or said in favor of the Company's commercial privileges, its trade, apart from the salt and opium monopoly, was a losing concern. Like Dupleix, he assumed office when the finances of his employers were embarrassed, and when war must embarrass them, for the time, still further. Like Dupleix again, he sought by the exercise of political influence, by the sagacious, steady, and commanding ascendancy of cultivated genius, by the reputation of European character and established warlike fame, both to throw a magic and irresistible spell over the native mind, to strengthen the position of the Company as an Asiatic power, and to relieve its finances by making the native Princes themselves defray the expenses of the troops by which they were to be overawed. But unlike Dupleix, he was no mere bold and fundamental revolutionist in this course. The British Empire in India was already a great fact, and a substantive portion of the Empire at large; and Wellesley, though bound to attend to trade, not only maintained frankly, forcibly, and consistently, that trade could not flourish unless his political duties were fully discharged, but esteemed the latter altogether paramount, and held that his chief business was to defend, consolidate, and improve the British Indian Empire—as an integral and vitally important part of the parent State. This consideration seems to me really the key to his whole policy—as a statesman; though as a man, (if a distinction may be drawn in thought where in the application of the motives there was none) the claims of humanity, and the duty of pacifying, and ameliorating the social condition of India generally, were powerful ancillary influences in determining his course.

Now, as to the past, he knew too well that British India had been constantly endangered both by the restless and unprincipled ambition of native powers, of recent origin and alarmingly sudden development; by the abstinence of the Company's Government from timely intervention, or by equally casual, awkward, violent, and abortive attempts to check this danger; by the frequent interposition of the French, long after Coote had conquered Lally; by the isolated position and straggling frontiers of the Company's territories, or of others which they were bound to defend; by the extent of seaboard that was still in native hands, and invited a landing hostile to us; and by the impossibility of ensuring, at all times, the command of the sea, so as to prevent such a landing and co-operation with our native enemies. A Mahratta confederacy against us was always on the cards; and after the destruction of Tippoo, both the removal of one whom they had always feared and hated, and our own aggrandisement through that event, gave additional incentives to such a stand against our growing and now singly menacing power.

The complex, fanatical, and irreconcileable antagonism of England and revolutionary and Napoleonized France, the prodigious and alarming progress made by the latter power towards subduing Europe, the military genius and intriguing spirit of Napoleon, and his fixed idea of conquering England in India, together with the French faction already so powerful in Scindia's dominions, and their control over Shah Allum, whom Buonaparte would delight *more suo* to use as a political tool, presented at the time a combination of dangers, which, but for Wellesley's vigilance then, and Trafalgar and the French Emperor's Spanish policy afterwards, might well have proved overwhelming. The expense of guarding against these dangers must have been enormous; and Wellesley knew too well what had happened more than once, when we were caught unprepared in the tornado of Indian warfare, reinforced by Gallic blasts. His orderly mind meanwhile was disturbed, his humane spirit vexed, by the spectacle of the prodigal waste of life, the artificial sterility, and the infinite social misery, resulting from the perpetual anarchy of native India, since the strong hand of the Mogul Emperors had been paralyzed by the establishment and expansion of Mahratta predatory power. Thus various motives combined to induce him to interpose, and attempt to apply, if possible, a peaceful, if not a short and sharp, but in the end effectual remedy for disorders of such magnitude, whether actual or contingent. Security, humanity, economy itself, were all to be provided for by the same means.

The details of the arrangements which commended themselves to his mind necessarily differed, to a certain extent, with circumstances. But the general idea of a strict alliance with the Peishwa was tempting on many accounts, and promised at least alternative advantages of the greatest consequence. While it must not be forgotten, that it was part of a more extensive scheme, he undoubtedly regarded it as the principal, and (so to speak) parental agent in that scheme. Poona and its vicinity would no longer be a battlefield of contending Mahratta factions. Thence would not again go forth, with all the authority of 'the executive head of the Mahratta confederacy,' a decree and an armament for the repetition of the Kurdlah performance, the political extermination of the Nizam, and the establishment of Mahratta influence, if not direct rule, on our Carnatic frontier. The long Mahratta western seaboard would be closed against the French. We should be peaceably strengthened in Guzerat, where a French landing had been pronounced by General Stuart even more dangerous than at Fort William itself. And in Bundlecund we might thus obtain a footing, which would turn the flank of Scindia and Perron in Hindostan, fortify our exposed frontier on the North West, and secure our water communications. The moral influence of the Peishwa's alliance also would be considerable, though Wellesley undoubtedly overrated it. Technically it was of great value. And though it did not in the end prevent the great chieftains standing out against our influence; it materially propitiated many smaller chiefs, and conciliated the Mahratta population of the Peishwa's territories, even when he was himself disposed to resent the too dictatorial tone of his new friends. If it was important to preclude the French from turning to account the Emperor's name, not less important was it to avail ourselves of the Pundit Purdhan's more real authority.

Wellesley seems to have hoped, that his own activity, the divisions and mutual jealousies of the Mahratta chiefs, the fear of the English arms, the impossibility of their obtaining timely and effectual aid from France, his solemn warnings, and perhaps, to a certain extent, even his ingenious argumentations, might avert an actual appeal to arms. And, in such a case, he would probably, by successive Treaties and repeated strokes of diplomatic dexterity, have greatly improved the original position, and effectually trammelled the other chiefs in a network of stipulations tending to disarm them by degrees, establish over them the peaceful supremacy of the British Government, and enclose British India in a cordon of subsidized forces. But if this expedient failed, and war was to be the word, he did not shrink from the issue. For while the question of expediency was determined by considerations already mentioned, the justice of a war which he regarded as ultimately defensive, he did not doubt; and he felt perfectly confident of the rapid and complete success of our arms. And victory would give him at once what must otherwise be the tardier fruit of diplomacy. His own repeated and emphatic statements belie the idea that he expected war from the first. But he must all along have contemplated it as a not very improbable contingency. When war became certain, he drew a plan, the comprehensiveness of which, as a scheme of occupation and conquest, startled Lord Castlereagh, and made him almost despair of our ability to meet its military requirements. But Wellesley felt, that it was both easier, safer, and more economical to garrison permanently even this large area, than to keep up, at our own cost, a force adequate to cope with the augmented and united power of enemies, whom our inaction had fostered, emboldened, and combined.

I have said that the proposed subsidiary alliance with the Peishwa was part of a more general scheme of diplomatic connexion with the native States, for the pacification of India under British hegemony. Though the three greatest Mahratta chiefs declined to be thus reduced, without a struggle, to a practically dependent condition; it must not be forgotten, that Wellesley had with him the sympathies, not only of a vast part of the population which had long groaned under Mahratta extortion, but especially of the older and more regular powers, notably the Rajputs, who had been submerged (so to speak) in the deluge, of which Sivaji had first opened the flood-gates. *They* were only too happy to be comprised in any plan, which should promise their restoration to the peaceful, flourishing, and half-independent state, in which they had long lived under the Mogul Empire. Bhopal, Gohud, and other petty principalities were equally desirous of English protection. The Nizam, the Guikwar, Mysore, and Coorg, were already enjoying it. Travancore was indebted to it for preservation; and has since presented a favorable specimen of the good effects of Wellesley's system, when judiciously carried out. The smaller Sikh States were anxious to be guaranteed against the Mahrattas on the one hand, and the Afghans on the other, and already had reason to fear the rising ambition of their own great tribesman. A similar disposition was shown in Bundlecund, and in the Rajah of Berar's eastern territories. And the Jat Rajah of Bhurtpore himself was fain to enter into the system; and though tempted to abandon it by the arts of Holkar, and the unwonted spectacle of a serious English reverse, he soon reverted to his original mind.

Thus, though it might be feared lest the cords of alliance should be snapped by their very extension; they were, in fact, strengthened as they advanced, and were half-woven beforehand in the hearts of both chiefs and peoples.

Several strong objections, however, were urged at the time, or afterwards, against Wellesley's policy both in Mahratta affairs, and in its more general application.

The charge, that in concluding a Treaty which led directly to war, he broke the law, may be dismissed very briefly. Castlereagh fully acquits him of this charge. As to the letter, the previous sanction of his proceedings by the Directors settles the matter, and satisfies the Act. And though their later tone, and that of the Secretary of the Board of Control, was to a certain extent opposed to this sanction, such retractations came too late; and being based upon general reasonings, inconclusive in themselves and inapplicable to the circumstances, naturally had little weight with him, and neither did nor could undo the past, nor arrest the swift march of events. Especially as the Governor-General had acted with the full concurrence of his Council, and *mirabile dictu!* considering his later line, Sir George Barlow had volunteered a detailed argument in favor of the propriety and necessity of concluding the Treaty, which will be found in its place in these Selections. As to the spirit and intention of the Act, another paper, by the Governor-General himself, also printed in this volume, will be seen to throw much light on the matter, though it refers more to earlier transactions. And though he had no desire to violate that spirit (for I believe him to have been perfectly sincere in his disclaimer of 'irregular ambition'), yet he felt bound to interpret the Act freely, and with reference to altered circumstances; he had given early intimation that such was his view and intention; and he held, that he could neither defend British India, nor secure to the country generally that eventual exemption from the evils of war, which the Act was intended to promote, unless he asserted that supremacy which events had forced upon us, and which his brother, in the Introductory Paper, openly claims as already our own.

If, again, he may seem to have been too careless of the cost of such a widespread contest, however this suspicion may have affected the close of his administration, and the views and conduct of his successors, it must be remembered first, that both wars were, in his eyes, inevitable, and that those could hardly deem them otherwise, who had maintained the necessity of war with France in 1793, into which Pitt himself had been driven by the great Philo-Indian, Edmund Burke; secondly, that Wellesley, like Pitt, did not anticipate a long war, and that much of the cost of the Holkar campaign would have been spared, had the Governor-General's instructions been more exactly followed; thirdly, that he looked to increased and permanent resources to retrieve the temporary sacrifices incurred in obtaining them; and lastly, as I have already observed, that his aim was, by spending freely but not recklessly at the moment, to save the much more serious expense of constant defensive armaments, and a more formidable and costly contest in the end.

Again, it has been maintained that he underrated his enemy, at least in the case of Holkar. The truth is, as before, he anticipated prompt success, and his admirable arrangements justified the anticipation. But besides Fawcett's inexcusable carelessness and consequent mishap, at the outset, Monson's disaster disturbed all the Governor-General's plans. And that disaster was obviously due, in a great measure, to the neglect of his provident and explicit counsels. He disapproved of detached corps, each too weak to defend itself, or force a junction with the other.

Thus the proportions of Monson's corps, and that officer's advance beyond the Mokundra pass, were both distinctly opposed to this wise recommendation. He urged that Monson should be reinforced with European infantry. And the want of such a reinforcement was certainly one of the principal causes of the catastrophe. The Rajah of Bhurtpore's defection, the renewed disturbances elsewhere, and the disposition of Scindia to resume hostilities, were the natural consequences of this really great reverse, though not so great as natives were inclined to pronounce it. But Wellesley, from first to last, fully understood the nature of the case, and never wavered in his estimate of it. India could not be pacified at one stroke. But the first had been mortal to Mahratta military *prestige.* The second was turned aside for a moment, but for a moment only. Deeg, Ferruckabad, and the defence of Delhi, though they did not at once produce their full effect on minds preoccupied with Monson's failure, were eloquent facts. Lake's precipitate and over-confident attempts to scramble into Bhurtpore without proper appliances, regular approaches, the systematic taking off of the defences, and a feasible entrance, were most unfortunate, and drew forth renewed cautions from the clear-sighted Governor-General. But they also opened the Rajah's eyes, and led him to give up the contest and dismiss Holkar. And *he* was rapidly run down in the Punjab, without daring again to look the English army in the face, as indeed he never had dared to do. The waiters on Providence could not be blind to such lessons, though the master spirit of the war no longer animated the Government, and the hasty and timid pacification ignored the completeness of the reduction of Holkar's power. But in one of his last Despatches, Wellesley was able to show that, in spite of all drawbacks, the defensive alliance system had answered, on the whole, well, in the course of his second Mahratta war, and had both diverted from Holkar, and converted to our use, a considerable proportion of the military resources of the country. This is the best answer to Mill's strictures.

Another objection is raised by Castlereagh, and no doubt occurred to many other English statesmen. However ingenious the conception of the system in the mind of the original projector, however skilful its manipulation by the master's hand, however vigilantly supervised by his penetrating and indefatigable scrutiny, how would it fare in other hands? Would it be easy, or even possible, to secure not only one successor, but a series of Governors-General capable of appreciating and carrying on so artificial and delicate an arrangement? Could it dispense with that rare combination of qualities, which made the character and administration of Lord Wellesley so remarkable? Breadth of view and firm grasp of details, untiring devotion to business, fortitude, readiness, and tact, nice discrimination, and lofty impartiality in the selection of agents, strong moral ascendancy over them, combined with a rare faculty for organization and luminous exposition? If such a man, or a series of such men, could be found, would the changes and chances of English political life, and the narrow prejudices of the Directors, admit of their employment? And what would become of the system in *un*able hands? This was a grave consideration; nor can it be said that it has been proved to have been the offspring of a visionary fear. Wellesley, no doubt, felt that sufficient unto the day was its own evil; that his plan, as conducted by himself, was at least a timely palliative, if not a radical cure, for immediate and urgent evils. If later dangers required its readjustment, later wisdom must resolve the new problem. Meanwhile, though in such a case it could not be said, *ce n'est que le premier pas qui coute*, he had at least done much to consolidate and perpetuate his scheme, and to clear the way for his successors. The two great difficulties of native connexion were, the delicacy of the Resident's position and functions, and the tendency of the subsidy to fall into arrears, and thereby necessitate undue interference on our part, and the ruinous expedients to which the native Prince was apt to resort, in order to meet the demand. As to the second point, the territorial cessions, granted once for all in lieu of subsidy, made the arrangement self-acting, and averted the danger. As to the first point, not only did he, by precept and example, impress the existing generation with his own conceptions of the appropriate mode of exercising the functions in question, but he relied on the College of Fort William to train a race of civilians, who should be equal to the task. Nor in leaving India did he renounce the charge of watching over the destinies of the Empire he had done so much to extend and strengthen. His antecedents, his abilities, his knowledge, and his position at home, might well justify a sanguine hope, that his influence would avail much to maintain the vitality and healthy action of the system which he had instituted. Other urgent cares indeed soon engrossed his attention in Europe. But he never lost his interest in India. And his 'school' sustained his credit, and continued his work, with good effect, in the East.

Lastly, a still more serious, fundamental, and permanent objection, was urged against the subsidiary alliance system, which comes to us endorsed by the high authority, and expounded in the forcible language of Sir Thomas Munro. The native Prince being guaranteed in the possession of his dominions, but deprived of so many of the essential attributes of sovereignty, sinks in his own esteem, and loses that stimulus to good government, which is supplied by the fear of rebellion and deposition. He becomes a *roi fainéant*, a sensualist, an extortionate miser, or a careless and lax ruler, which is equivalent in the East to an anarchist. The higher classes, coerced by external ascendancy, in turn lose their self-respect, and degenerate like their master: the people groan under a complicated oppression which is irremediable. Thus, in spite of the Resident's counsels and attempts to secure good government, the back of the State, so to speak, is broken; the spirit of indigenous political life has departed; the native community tends to dissolution; and annexation is eventually the inevitable remedy for its helplessness and chronic disorders.

Or again, the Prince resents his dependent condition: he kicks against the pricks; he violates some or other of the stringent conditions under which he occupies the musnud; he intrigues against the English government, or he murders its officers, or envoys from other States, whose safety it has guaranteed; and he must be punished. His consequent irritation presently expresses itself in fresh acts of contumacy; and he must be coerced anew. And thus again, little by little, or at one fell stroke, his dominions are annexed, and his subjects pass directly under British rule. This, it will be obvious, is by no means a fancy picture: while, though it would be most unfair to assume, that Wellesley deliberately contemplated such a general consummation, it cannot be supposed that he could shut his eyes to the possibility of its occurrence. Probably while he devised and applied the system as an indispensable remedy for actual evils, he regarded it as an important experiment, which he hoped might answer its ends better than the objection assumes it was capable of doing; but which, if it did not, might eventually be replaced by immediate and avowed English dominion. He had a strong sense of the actual degradation and personal demerits of too many native Princes: he saw little hope of their ever becoming good rulers, or of their people enjoying peace and prosperity, without his aid: license either party might have, but hardly manly energy or virtuous enterprise. He had also strong faith in the possibilities of English control in improving the administration, though he was hopeless of it in some cases, where inveterate maladies seemed to defy all remedial appliances. If the native Governments, then, *were* remediable, and capable of being trained into tolerable working instruments for political and social purposes,—good! If not, sooner or later, but not until the experiment had been fairly tried, and circumstances, and public opinion in India *and in England* were ripe for the change, let them give place to our better organized, better principled, and more beneficent sway.

There was, however, one means, as pointed out by Sir Thomas Munro, which might postpone, if not avert, this consummation—the appointment of a native Dewan. And this expedient Wellesley gladly adopted, where he could find such an agent duly qualified. Poornca he at once employed in Mysore, and with good effect. The Nizam's Minister he cordially supported. And, on the other hand, he did his utmost to replace Scindia's infamous father-in-law by a more constitutional and respectable adviser. But at that time, and under the circumstances of the day, such advisers were not too plentiful. The Sir Salar Jungs, the Sir Madhava Raos, and other eminent and enlightened native statesmen are the growth of a state of things, which had not then arisen, though Wellesley did much to hasten its advent. And, after all, though history confirms too strongly the reasonableness of Munro's fears; they were at least exaggerated. In spite even of the free handling of native States by Lord Dalhousie, the Nizam, Mysore, three of the greater Mahratta Powers, the Rajput States, Bhopal, Travancore, and many more, which were less intimately connected than these with Wellesley's history, still survive, and are destined, it may be hoped, to a career of indefinite improvement, as integral but unannexed, and to a certain extent self-governing members of the great Anglo-Indian Empire.

But Munro's remarks suggest, or rather require, a few more words of explanation. When, after predicting, half a century beforehand, the Sepoy mutiny, as the result of the general establishment of our pacific sway, he adds:—'But even if we could be secured against every convulsion, and could retain the country quietly in subjection, I doubt much if the condition of the people would be better than under their Native princes';—his words may well startle us, but should neither be misunderstood, nor received too implicitly, nor assumed as conclusive of what would have been his own view at the present day. That a political machinery which supplied, however imperfectly, a career for honest official exertion, and thus sustained the self-respect and active powers of the office holders, was preferable so far to one, which, by excluding the citizen of a whilom native State from office, tended to debase and asservilize him, was one side of the question. But there was another side. And Munro would hardly have denied, that the liberty to do only evil continually was a questionable advantage over a state of peaceful industry and external prosperity, though associated with a timid and cringing temper. And that Mahratta ascendancy amounted to little else, that but for the English it tended to become universal, and that there was no hope of any constructive, wise, and beneficent political development from such a quarter, are indisputable truths, confirmed by the express testimony of the highest authority on Mahratta history and character, Captain Grant Duff. The Rajputs were a fine, manly, chivalrous race. But was it the English rule which, in their case, depressed the spirit of Princes and people alike, and drove them to cry in agony for a paramount Power to curb the oppressor, and let them freely enjoy their patriarchal life and institutions? Was not the appeal made to the English against the Mahrattas? The 'Moguls' were a proud people at Hyderabad. But did either the Nizam or his subjects escape political and social degradation from the same organized anarchy, until Wellesley came to their assistance? What had happened to the Rana of Gohud and his subjects, and to so many more victims of the pestilent enterprise and devastating power of this political *pieuvre?* this herd of lean kine, which devoured everything, yet itself remained ever meagre and moribund?

Again, if the population in the British provinces was debased and servile, other causes than the character of British rule had long previously contributed to produce this result. Munro judged chiefly, in all probability, from Bengal, which though less familiar to him was notoriously the seat of such a race, and from the Carnatic, with which he was intimately acquainted. As to the former, it would be a waste of words to do more than refer to Macaulay's well-known picture, and to add, that the village system, the best guarantee of native independence and self-respect, had long been undermined there. As to the Carnatic, no one who knows its history, and the character of Mahomed Ali's rule, will much wonder at the want of an elastic and enterprising spirit among its miserable inhabitants.

But Wellesley's aim was to introduce a better state of things. And though he was not hopeful of native agency in high places then, and would hardly have coincided now with the extreme view, which favors the introduction of representative institutions and popular government; yet he undoubtedly anticipated a great improvement in the character of the people; and by the lofty and beneficent spirit of his administration, by his judicial institutions, by his elaborate provision for the education of the civilians, (whereby sympathy with native life, customs, and character would be promoted, and would create corresponding and elevating sympathy on the other side), by encouraging Christian missions as far as his position permitted him, by causing the Scriptures to be translated into native languages, and by other means, he certainly pursued a course well calculated in time to exalt the people above 'this mere animal state of thriving in peace'; though he knew too well, that man must live before he can live such as he ought to be; and that there is a time for all things, among others, even for the too obtrusive ascendancy of a dominant race.

VI. DEFENCE OF THE INDIAN EMPIRE.

I have ventured to say, that the key to Wellesley's whole policy seems to have been, his sense of the necessity of securing and consolidating the Anglo-Indian Empire, as an integral and very vulnerable part of the British Empire at large. The papers arranged under this head will, it is hoped, fully bear out that view, which is further illustrated in other parts of this volume. The Governor-General's first task, both in time and in urgency, was to reduce the power of Tippoo, and to prevent the combination of his forces with those of the French. And this required his arrangements with the Nizam, and the attempt to enlist the Peishwa in the same cause. The fall of Tippoo was shortly followed by the annexation of the Carnatic Payen Ghaut; which, together with the corresponding treatment of Tanjore (in which Lord Mornington only obeyed orders from home), gave us the full command of the Coromandel seaboard, and so diminished the danger of a hostile landing on that coast. Our exposed frontier towards Oude, noted by the Duke of Wellington in his short Memoir on the Vizier's dominions; the relaxed discipline of the troops, and the hopeless misrule, of the same Prince; the power and doubtful disposition of Scindia; the ambition, the military strength, and the wide-spread influence of Perron; the turbulent feebleness of the Sikhs; the restless enterprise and avowed designs of the Afghan Sovereign, and the memory of the Paniput campaign:—all combined to make the Governor-General anxious on the subject of our North-West confines. His apparently harsh conduct towards the Nabob Vizier is, as has been already said, mainly explicable on this ground.

But though he thus turned the danger close at hand into a bulwark, it was not in his nature to 'rest and be thankful' at such a stage, or to await passively more remote perils. He did not at that time succeed in prevailing upon Scindia to return to Hindostan, for the defence of his ill-cemented and disturbed territories there, or in effecting a cordial league with him against the common enemy beyond the Attok gorge. But, adopting a policy analogous to that which Gibbon ascribes to the Byzantine Emperors, he dissipated the storm which was gathering on the Afghan mountains by a diplomatic discharge through the medium of Mehdi Ali Khan; and, following this up by Malcolm's Persian mission, he both secured India from a repetition of the Abdali inroads, and obviated the more distant contingencies of invasion from Central Asia, Russia, or France. How, besides breaking the military power of the Mahrattas, and gaining the moral advantage of the Peishwa's alliance, he acquired by virtue of that alliance the control of the Western seaboard from Goa (which he garrisoned by friendly arrangement with the Portuguese Government) to the Nerbudda; strengthened the position of the Company in Guzerat; and occupied Bundlecund; and how his first Mahratta war gave him Cuttack, the only part of the coast not in our hands, or under our influence [1]; has been already stated.

The *euthanasia* to which he sought to consign the Emperor and his latent but formidable claims, will demand a few words later on. Before we leave the coast of India, and follow him in the more distant perspective of his provident care for the thorough accomplishment of his main object, three other illustrations of his many-sided activity may be properly noticed. First, the regular and constant supply of an adequate amount of European troops, he, of course, felt to be most essential. In estimating that amount, he seems certainly to have overstated it, as resulting from the principles which he laid down, or rather the facts which he assumed as the basis of his calculation. But both his own statements, a letter

---

[1] Canara had been acquired when Mysore was conquered, and Travancore was our dependent ally.

of Lake's (here reproduced), on the newly-conquered territory in the North-West, and other circumstances shew, that he did not exceed the estimate proposed by his military advisers. And, on the other hand, it is notable, that however freely he sanctioned, in the stress of the Mahratta war, the temporary enrolment of irregular troops; and however embarrassing (as Lord Cornwallis states in his letters to Lake and the Directors) were the financial demands thus caused; he steadily refused to tolerate the employment of Pindaries; and would, no doubt, had he remained to superintend the fortunes of a thoroughly pacified India, have devised expedients for economising the charge of our European army. Secondly, in his various Treaties and partitions of territory, he took great pains, both by disentangling the intricacies of joint or commingling holdings among the native chiefs, and by the abatement of Mahratta *choute*, &c., to avert the occasions of renewed quarrels and disturbance; and he rectified frontiers, in a military sense, with minute care, so as to make both us and our staunch dependents as defensible as possible, and to give no advantage either to an open enemy, or to a doubtful and treacherous ally. Thirdly, with his usual thoroughness and foresight, he explored and expounded, in a long letter to Lord Hobart, a variety of ways in which French influence, if not blocked at once by diplomatic stipulations and legal provisions, might again insinuate itself into India. This document is interesting, and very characteristic of the writer, and his point of view. But its length has reluctantly compelled me to give only its conclusion, which however will be found very suggestive.

But Wellesley's defensive and anti-French precautions were not confined to the Indian Continent. Given the assumption, that 'Ceylon was a bulwark of our Indian Empire,' it was as natural that he should claim full authority over our settlement there, as that the commandant of a threatened stronghold should insist upon the control of an adjacent, though detached outwork. In his double capacity he argues the matter, of course, upon commercial and administrative, as well as on purely political and military grounds. But it is obvious that the latter class of considerations was uppermost in his mind. And much as circumstances have since changed, it may still be a practical question whether, in view of our extended dominion along the Eastern and Buddhist shores of the Bay of Bengal, his reasoning is even now out of date.

The islands of Mauritius and Bourbon had been, from the time of Labourdonnais to Tippoo's last quest of assistance from that quarter against us, the advanced base of our European enemies in their warfare on the Indian Continent, as well as in the Indian seas. Even when destitute of the means of assailing efficiently our established power, their inhabitants had done a brisk and profitable business in the way of privateering, as the Governor-General's figures shew. Long before his time, I find in a valuable military memoir of our last war with Hyder Ally by Captain Innes Monro, a scheme for reducing these islands. Wellesley himself suggested such an operation at an early date. That, from the Admiral's objections, and the long delay in advancing them, he was afterwards prevented from executing such a plan, was a matter of serious concern to him, and an occasion of severe argumentative remonstrance with the gallant, but narrow-minded sailor. As that remonstrance is not confined to Indian grounds, but rests directly upon imperial considerations, and the general conduct of the Anglo-French war all over the world, it has been placed under a separate head. And it tends to confirm the idea, that the Empire at large was Wellesley's constant care, and India as an integral portion of that Empire. The Government, I may add, sided with him against the Admiral in this matter.

Again and again he shews clearly how strong was his conviction, that the Governor-General of an Empire essentially maritime in its origin, in so large a part of its frontier, and in the requirements for its preservation, ought to have the disposition of the fleet in the Eastern waters. One of his sharpest rebukes to the Madras Government is on occasion of their presuming to interfere with his provisional initiative, and exclusive power of suggestion, as to the movements of the ships. He directs General Harris's attention, with evident complacency, to the fact that, unlike Cornwallis, he can, during the Mysore war, rely upon the presence of the fleet off the Western coast, the result of such a suggestion, approved by the Admiral.

Wellesley's plan for the occupation of the French islands and the Cape is further worthy of note, as an illustration of his habit of not only devising and recommending expeditions in a general way, but carefully weighing the details of their prosecution. Thus, while the Cape was to be conquered from England, the Mauritius and Bourbon, like Abyssinia in our own time, were to be assailed from India; which in fact was the course eventually adopted in the respective cases.

Foiled in his design upon the islands, the indefatigable and far-sighted ruler turned to another scheme, which also he had previously recommended, a scheme, unlike the others, of co-operation with a Western force. And this, the 'Red Sea Expedition,' actually took place. Mr. Goldwin Smith, indeed, has said that it did nothing. From his immediate point of view, and so far as martial achievements on the spot were concerned, this is, of course, literally true. But Mr. Goldwin Smith would probably be the first to admit, that as an indication of our diffusive energy and confidence in the East, and as a counterblast to Buonaparte's vapouring letter to Tippoo and gasconading demeanour in Egypt, Baird's meanderings with a sepoy army in that country, were by no means an idle military promenade; and were well calculated to impress strongly not only the Oriental, but the French, and especially the Gallo-Corsican imagination. A gun may not be fired in time; but it is nevertheless a formidable weapon. Reserved strength, as the ex-Professor of Modern History at Oxford well knows—and exemplifies—is no small element of reputation and influence.

Cicero's speeches do not differ more in style from Cæsar's plain narrative, than the sonorous periods and elegant phraseology of Lord Wellesley from the masculine simplicity and strong common sense of Wellington's Memoirs. But, as the Governor-General constantly adopted, adorned with literary skill, and executed with congenial determination, the views of his illustrious brother; so, in this case, General Stuart's unpretending but most important and suggestive paper seems to have supplied and justified, in the Governor-General's mind, the combination of measures which have now been reviewed. It thus forms, by anticipation, an epitome of Wellesley's general programme for the defence of our Indian Empire. And it is the best answer to the imputation that, in working out this programme, he was indulging in what he himself happily calls 'irregular ambition'; and again, that however regular as well as fixed was his design of averting serious and manifold dangers, *that* amounted to a gratuitous passion for domination.

As regards the Emperor, and the danger of his pretensions being employed against us by our enemies, especially by the French, the Governor-General carefully considered his course, and has fully explained the grounds and the details of his final determination. His reasons are plausible. But in a Lecture delivered and published last year[1], I ventured to doubt whether, on the whole, that determination was the best that could have been adopted. I shall not here repeat what was then urged. But I may add, that the connexion of Tippoo's family soon afterwards with the Vellore mutiny might have shewn the danger of leaving such a state prisoner enthroned in the Mogul capital[2]; and that the letter of Sir Thomas Munro in the Appendix, on the subject of the Peishwa, tends to confirm the view, that the Company should have either assumed the office of the Emperor, or taken a commission from him.

---

[1] *Anglo-Indian Rule Historically Considered.* James Parker and Co., Oxford and London.

[2] Since the Lecture was printed, I have been favoured with the copy of a letter written by a military officer, in high political employment at the time, to the Governor-General, Lord Ellenborough, warning that nobleman of the danger of allowing the 'King of Delhi' to reside in the imperial city. The warning was disregarded; and the natural and disastrous consequence in due time followed.

VII. MISCELLANEOUS DESPATCHES.

The papers included in this section refer to subjects commented on elsewhere. But it seemed better to give them entire, and as they were written, than to cut them up, and relegate the fragments to their several heads. Speaking generally, they may be regarded as the connecting link, and the informal and confidential line of communication, between the Council Chamber of Calcutta and the Board of Control. Thus they consist partly of Dundas's personal approval, no doubt with Pitt's assent, of the Governor-General's measures; partly of suggestions which were the germ, and the anticipatory sanction of arrangements, carried out according to circumstances, and with modifications and developments, by the Governor-General; partly of expositions and vindications of his own more original proceedings; and occasionally, as in the excursive disquisition on the Supreme Court and its influence, and in the statement of facts militating against the hope of much increasing the revenue by direct taxation or by remittances, of friendly antagonism to Dundas's views. Without reverting to the separate topics, one general circumstance may be here noticed and exemplified, which is very prominent throughout these letters. This is, the Governor-General's readiness to accept responsibility, his independent mode of acting, his resolve to be, though an accountable ruler in the end, still in the meantime a ruler indeed, and not an ornamental figure-head of the State-ship, or a pliant instrument of misgovernment.

Thus he asks the question—How is he to understand the principle previously laid down, that the landing of a *considerable* French force would justify war with Tippoo? But he does not await Dundas's reply, though it turns out to be in entire accordance with his own interpretation of the words. Again, he requests Dundas's sentiments on the projected annexation of the Carnatic. But he frankly adds:—'I shall not wait for the communication' of those sentiments, 'if the season should appear to me to be favorable for the great measure, &c.' He introduces the Bengal institutions into the Circars, though his correspondent thinks the time not ripe for them; and he does not hesitate to establish the Permanent Settlement on the Coromandel Coast, 'without previous reference to the Court of Directors.' So too, he demolishes without mercy, in the last letter of these Selections, the Admiral's alleged scruples against engaging in an expedition to reduce the French islands, without previous instructions from England. Thus again, satisfied of the expediency of the step, and relying on the intimations in the original framework of the Supreme Government, that such a change was contemplated as desirable in the future, he separates its ordinary judicial functions from that Government, and constitutes the Sudder Courts as a distinct institution, and on a scale adequate to the occasion. In like manner he reorganizes the administrative machinery of the Supreme Government, and substitutes for ill-paid and inferior clerks of departments an imposing and costly, but also a really efficient Secretariat.

But he goes further in the same direction. To improve the system would avail little, unless the men who were to work it were properly qualified, and selected according to their respective capacities. There was no fear that he would fail to employ and place judiciously the best men that he could find for each task; and experience abundantly proved how penetrating was his scrutiny, how impartial his choice, how animating his example and countenance, how formidable and judicially just and appropriate was his censure. But in spite of all that Cornwallis had effected for its purification and improvement, the Civil Service was still encumbered with no inconsiderable proportion of inefficient, and with some corrupt men. Seniority and actual position had their natural and conventionally too forcible claims. Men who had done good service once, were unwilling or unable to retire when no longer useful. Others, in the Madras Presidency, were, on the contrary, worth more, and could earn more, if they quitted the service, than its local rules allowed them. The civilians generally were below the standard of cultivation requisite for the difficult, delicate, and diversified political functions arising out of the development of the Anglo-Indian Empire; and too many who aspired to be statesmen were, in training and proficiency, but dull traders. And lastly, in spite once more of Cornwallis's constant and uncompromising protests against such practices, there was too much disposition at home, both among the Directors and the Ministry, to interfere with the patronage of the service, and thus both directly to impair its efficiency by blind favor at a distance instead of calm and discriminating local selection according to merit and proved capacity, and to discredit and enfeeble the authority of the Indian Governments, more particularly that at Calcutta.

For all these evils, except the last, which to a mortifying extent baffled even *his* endeavours, and to which his early determination to resign was not a little due, Wellesley devised prompt and trenchant remedies, most unpalatable to his employers, and which combined with other circumstances to make them desire his resignation or recall. Vigilantly to superintend future appointments was, of course, his primary expedient. Nor was he the man to whom—as even to Cornwallis—the Prince of Wales himself seems to have dared to propose jobs, or to recommend obviously incompetent persons. Thus, by a process of exhaustion, the specific gravity of the inefficient would gradually deposit them below their betters; or leave them, at least, stranded and shelved at such a moderate elevation as seniority claims, hopes of their improvement, and some consideration for their original disadvantages, might combine to procure for them.

But Wellesley was not disposed to leave them long in peace even there. He announces to Dundas a plan, which he is determined to adopt at once, for buying them out, and compelling them to retire, as Cornwallis had recommended in the case of officers in the army—to England. Besides the mere cost of this proceeding, which however he suggests will be more than saved in the end, the narrow views and sordid temper of those, who had first inflicted them on the service, are thus visited upon the pockets of the Directors and the Proprietors. Their original sin finds them out. The 'curse' of nepotism 'comes home to roost.' And thus, again, a significant warning and a salutary check are transmitted from beyond sea, well calculated to diminish bad nominations of 'writers,' and to irritate the disappointed and alarmed patrons.

To propose a general scheme of retiring pensions for the whole service, and to extend to Madras Cornwallis's system of higher regular salaries and stricter prohibitions against irregular sources of emolument, were obvious corollaries from the previous measures, and not less unacceptable to many of the Directors.

It may be remarked incidentally, that the determined exclusion of all Englishmen, not in the service, from Oude, for which Wellesley incurs the wrath of Mill, was not only connected with the contemporary objection to European colonization (partially explained on political grounds by the Duke of Wellington, in the Memoir on Bengal, and previously by Cornwallis); but was intended to prevent the recurrence there of such scandalous transactions between the Government and unofficial Englishmen, as had long embarrassed the Anglo-Indian Government, and had precipitated the annexation of the Carnatic.

If the arrangements for increasing the efficiency of the Civil Service which have already been noticed were likely to be unwelcome to his employers; what had the Governor-General to expect in the case of the comprehensive and costly project of the College at Fort William? Confidently as he writes, he probably anticipated something of the reception which awaited that great design. And thus, besides his forcible, enlightened, and exhaustive pleading, his bold *tour de force* in pressing into the service the sermonizing and inquisitorial passage from the Directors' own Despatch (conceived in so widely different a spirit), the almost sentimental challenge of their approval by the memory of the Conquest of Mysore, and his endeavor to obviate the financial objection, in the first instance, by taxing the Service itself for the institution, from which it was to reap so many benefits; he again steals a march by establishing the College at once; and thus, moreover, when the time comes for suspending and controverting the orders for its suppression, he is able to appeal to the experience of its good working, as a strong argument for its preservation and integrity.

In the matter of the Private Trade, again, he made a temporary experiment almost coincidently with Dundas's advocacy in England of the same step. This reaching the ears of the shrewd Scotchman in an unofficial manner, he urges Wellesley to persevere and repeat the experiment, in the teeth of the Directors and in defiance of their counter-orders, and promises support from the Board of Control. This it will be seen Wellesley does; and follows up the blow by another exhaustive battery of statistics and arguments, such as could hardly fail to flutter the Volscians of Leadenhall Street.

Reverting to political examples of the same tendency to insist upon the initiative, and realize the technical nomenclature of his Government as 'Supreme,' his communications with Lord Clive, and the distinction which he draws between public and private correspondence, are important. He will tolerate no disobedience, no cavilling, no remonstrance, or even hesitation as to the exact execution of his behests, in the public and officially recorded letters. But he is not only ready and anxious to explain his plans and the reasons for them privately to the Governor of Madras; but he will esteem reciprocal private communications of Lord Clive's views a favor. Very similar is his tone in omitted letters to General Harris, when in charge of the same Government, and to Sir J. Craig. And while he was much angered by the transmission to himself of Mr. Webbe's Memorial, written for General Harris, and treats it with lofty and scornful *incuria;* this did not prevent his employing that useful officer in important charges, when he became more conformable, nor his attesting warmly the value of his services on his rather sudden death.

Again, he is emphatic on the propriety of abolishing the very semblance of any authority on the part of the *Supreme* Court 'over the person of the Governor-General.' He says expressly, 'No power in India should appear to be co-ordinate with the Government, and still less to rival or to control it.' At the same time he dwells much, as will be mentioned presently, on the constitutional checks otherwise imposed on the power of the Governor-General.

The subsequent formation of the Indian navy at once obviated and justified his claim to control the operations of the fleet in the East. But this was not the only case in which he felt his position, as a Company's officer, disadvantageous. Great as had become the name of the Company, the name of the King was still greater. Hence he found it necessary, as Cornwallis had already done, to protest against the mischievous consequences of Royal interposition in the affairs of India, not only in the matter of embassies, but in the correspondence of the Prince of Wales with the Nabob of the Carnatic, and the irregular and adventitious importance given to individuals by their being supposed to reflect, in some measure, the beams of Royal favor. He also insists that, though a civilian, he ought to bear a military commission from the

Crown; and the Captaincy-General of the Royal troops was accordingly conferred on him.

Lastly, it may be observed, that his exposition to Governor Duncan, of the latter's relations to his Council, is at once characteristic—*mutatis mutandis*—of the tendency which I have been tracing as his own principle of action; and is perhaps neither more nor less disputable, than the propriety of his equally characteristic delegation of his own actual or assumed powers, independent of *his* Council, successively to Harris, to General Wellesley, and to Lake; a proceeding which, in the second case, the Directors so strongly resented.

VIII. SUPREME AND LOCAL GOVERNMENTS.

The first of the papers included in this section is one of the most notable and characteristic of the whole series. Its exordium is typical both of the writer, and of the position which the Merchant Princes had now attained, and which Wellesley was determined to compel them to recognise in all its amplitude and onerousness. 'We have not hesitated,' he says, 'to consider the extensive and valuable possessions to the Government of which the Company have succeeded, as a great Empire. To view those possessions in any other light, must, we are persuaded, always lead to the most erroneous conclusions as to the principles of policy by which they ought to be governed.'

Thus, without ignoring commercial interests, and in the very act of specifying his duty of supervising trade and providing the investment as one department of his diversified charge, he lays down at starting what may be called a political premiss, which boldly challenges, and sweeps away at a stroke as irrelevant, all such objections to the measures which he is about to announce, as are grounded on purely mercantile considerations.

Next, we have here a clear and impressive account of the Supreme Government, and the several functions which it at that time discharged or controlled. Not less interesting and valuable is the historical retrospect, suggested rather than worked out; the significant hints, so to speak, of the various phases which that Government had, according to the circumstances of successive periods, assumed, and the gradual construction of the complex and somewhat unwieldy engine.

We here also see a new and striking illustration of the Governor-General's turn for organization and systematic development. Here, as elsewhere, he is engaged in unravelling a tangled skein, and weaving it into a symmetrical and abiding pattern. He is steadily bent on getting rid of confused and therefore inadequately discharged duties, and haphazard expedients, and on making all parts of the State machine work effectively, because their functions are duly ascertained and appropriately distributed. So it is with him throughout. He loves not to trust to the chapter of accidents, or the fortunate contingencies of exceptional ability and energy. Whether in amending the terms of native alliances, in disentwining the co-ordinate and conflicting claims of native Princes over the same area, in rectifying our own military frontiers, in ascertaining the principles which were henceforth to regulate the treatment of the French in India, in discussing the Admiral's obligations to co-operate in Indian expeditions, the Governor-General's proper mode of dealing with local Governors, or theirs with their Councils, or in urging the removal of every plea for setting up the Royal authority against that of the Company and its supreme officer;—the same tendency to certification, explicit adjustment, systematic arrangement on general and permanent principles, is observable.

Again, the reforms specified and justified in this Despatch are, as I have already said, very sweeping and fundamental, and well calculated to stereotype the quasi-sovereign character of the Company in India. The Constitution of the Sudder Courts, the development of the Secretariat, the institution of a provisional pension list, in declared anticipation of a more general measure, the rudimentary plan of the College shortly afterwards established, must have fallen upon Dundas himself like so many thunderclaps. And it is curious, and not unamusing, to compare the calm and authoritative tone of conviction, in which the Governor-General insists upon the immediate urgency of these great measures, with the pointed language of the Secretary of the Board of Control, deprecating the vehement and costly reformatory ardor of his enthusiastic correspondent[1].

Far deeper, of course, was the dissatisfaction, decided henceforth and unremitting the hostility, of many of the Directors. But Wellesley did not shrink from the issue. And though the indirect and unmagnanimous revenge, by which they sought to drive him to resign, galled him to the quick, and drew forth his long and able protest to Mr. Addington; and though, but for the Mahratta crisis, he would have gratified his opponents sooner than he did by quitting their service: yet he was justified in assuming that the circumstances of the case, the course of events, and the obvious advantages resulting from the operation of his institutions, would

[1] 'I am well aware,' says Dundas, 'that valuable improvements may still be made upon many of our Indian concerns, and I know that many of those improvements will likewise lead to expense. I am likewise aware that it is natural for men of ardent minds to wish the rapid execution of improvements which they reckon to be valuable and important, but in the present state of our finances, I have no hesitation in being of opinion that we had better for some time remain stationary and postpone for a while even desirable improvements, if they are to lead to immediate expense. In short, my present creed with regard to India is, that nothing new is to be attempted without weighing well every rupee it will cost.'

(except in the case of the College on its original scale) vindicate him in the end, and tend to perpetuate his arrangements.

But the most remarkable feature of this Despatch remains to be considered. This is the bold and ingenious representation of the Supreme Government of India as not only pervaded by the spirit, but assimilated to the form, of the British Constitution. It is, of course, easy to establish particular, if more or less fortuitous, analogies between them both in their history, and in their character. Thus, Arnold described the Norman domination in England as that of an army of occupation in a conquered country. And the similar origin and nature of our hold on the Indian Provinces of the Company naturally tended to reproduce the high-handed proceedings and unscrupulous arrogance of the Anglo-Norman Kings and Barons. While, in each case, the lapse of time, and the accession of rulers whose enlightened talent for civil organization and desire to improve the condition of the people led them to soften the harsher aspects of the *régime*, alike favored the advent of 'the reign of law.' Then came Acts of Parliament in the one case; and in the other, Regulations were multiplied. The establishment of the Courts at Westminster may be not inappositely compared to Wellesley's constitution of the Sudder Courts, offshoots from the Anglo-Indian Council, as the former were from the *Curia Regis*. As again, diplomatic relations with foreign States were so long and so jealously guarded by the English Government from direct popular interference, and as the prerogative of peace and war was tenaciously affected by the personal Sovereign even after the Revolution; so Wellesley insists on the Governor-General in Council exercising such a prerogative, unimpaired by native intervention. And the popular complaints and Parliamentary petitions of early days in England are, in a way, comparable to the proposals for remedial Regulations, which the local magistrates are to lay before the Supreme Government, as the result of careful enquiry in their respective districts. And Parliament secures responsible government at home, as the Governor-General is obviously responsible to more than one controlling authority.

All this is true enough. And much more might be added in the same strain. And though some of his less favorable critics might be inclined to think, that Wellesley indulged in such an analogical vein less for the sake of extenuating the rule of the sword, than for the purpose of enhancing his own importance, and investing himself in a quasi-kingly majesty; still such a disposition was not ill calculated to deepen the sense of moral responsibility, and to steady the steps of the Ruler in the exercise of his inevitably large discretion.

But how completely the analogy failed—and still fails—in the most essential particulars, I have attempted to shew in a Lecture already referred to. A single sentence of this Despatch is enough to prove how superficial was the resemblance between the two political structures, and how, after all, Wellesley's specific for India was one which in the West certainly sounds essentially despotic—'Everything for the people, nothing by them.' He says:—'There is no change in our situation in this country, which can be supposed, in which it would be expedient to admit any part of our native subjects to participate in the legislative authority with the Governor-General in Council.'

It is impossible to determine how far such an opinion might have been modified by later experience. Probably Wellesley would have contemplated with heart-felt satisfaction a great federation of Native States, enjoying considerable freedom of internal administration, under the presiding control of a Viceroy, the representative of British Imperialism. He would also probably have pronounced the opening of the Civil Service to natives, regularly educated in our own way, both a just and a politic proceeding. Nor would he probably have hesitated to admit into its higher grades carefully selected and well tested native gentlemen of ability and integrity. But I cannot conceive that he would have regarded the attempt to set up popular institutions, after the English pattern, otherwise than as political suicide on our part, and as a short cut to anarchy, and the revival of the state of things, from which he toiled so long and so hard to deliver India.

IX. FINANCE AND TRADE.

Some remarks, which properly belong to this section, have been made elsewhere. Others, which naturally occur, would require more space than can here be afforded. But a few circumstances seem to demand mention. In particular, it does not appear easy to determine, in some cases, how far Wellesley's language expresses, I will not say exactly his true, but his independent and full sentiments. As Dean Milman shows that the orthodox scholastic philosophy displayed great mental activity within a prescribed area, and on the condition of not contravening certain foregone conclusions; so the Governor-General appears to take for granted important points, which would be now denied, and which were not beyond question in his own day. Thus, that the Company's exclusive privileges, generally speaking, ought to be continued, European colonization to be prevented, and a sinking fund maintained for liquidating the Indian debt, sound somewhat strange in our modern ears, and would not have received by any means universal recognition at the time.

In these and similar cases he may have simply written as he thought. Or again, he may have accepted these *data* only provisionally; and pending his advocacy of what would now be pronounced by political economists more enlightened measures. For, again to compare him to the scholastics, it will be seen that not only does he appeal to the tribunal of reason, and so indirectly prepare the way for the subversion of mere authority and precedent; but he directly and deliberately attacks certain parts of the established system; and by the tendency of his arguments, and the obvious import of his facts, may seem, by a sort of lime-juice writing, to have invalidated much which he does not repudiate, and to have gone far towards shaking the whole fabric. Thus his objections to European colonization, like his brother's in the Memoir on Bengal, are political rather than commercial. And while he talks of the sinking fund, it is pretty clear, both that he regarded the alarm about the growth of the Indian debt as needless and extravagant; and that he looked to the stimulus to be imparted to commercial enterprise by a more liberal treatment of private traders, to the extension of our commercial relations both in and out of India, and to the increased resources of the Government through his conquests and subsidiary alliances, for diminishing the debt, and turning the deficit into a surplus in the end. And as to the monopoly itself, not only did his Private Trade regulations seriously interfere with it; but if, as his brother says, and he does not deny, the Company traded at a loss; and if, as he shews, the Company is quite unable either to absorb the homeward trade of Calcutta, or to accommodate the independent merchants with British shipping, while it prohibits the employment of Indian vessels for that purpose; it does seem as if, whatever he says about the impropriety of infringing the exclusive privileges of the Merchant Princes, he leaves them much in the unenviable position of the dog in the manger.

Elsewhere, indeed, he goes further, and speaks very plainly, though not to the Directors. Unless, he argues, they are prepared to sink mere mercantile considerations, and administer the country as enlightened and beneficent Sovereigns; the Company's dominions ought to be transferred directly to the Crown. Such a statement is quite in accordance with the general and paramount view which I have said he took of his own position; and is silently implied in the opening passage already quoted from his Despatch on the Supreme Government. And considering how little he conceived the Directors capable of doing what he insisted upon, he may seem to be practically advocating, or at least preparing the way for, the destruction of the Company altogether. This, however, would probably be pressing his words too far, even as to government. While, as to trade, there was a contemporary view, which Cornwallis in offering suggestions on the renewal of the Charter combats, but which Wellesley might have accepted, that the Company should be deprived of its territories, but should be allowed to subsist on its older footing, as a privileged trading institution. Whatever may have been his sentiments on the general subject, he certainly dealt a very effectual blow at particular restrictions, which had hitherto been deemed inseparably connected with the Company's chartered rights. His encouragement of India-built shipping, his statistics on that subject, and his reasons for allowing the independent merchants and shipowners to adjust their mutual relations, unimpeded by the irritating and wasteful intervention of the Company's officers, were hardly reconcileable with his professed desire to preserve the essence of the old order of things. As in politics, so in commercial matters, not without reason but still in fact, he revolutionizes under the guise of conservative readjustment.

Though the Duke of Wellington argues strongly in favor of the course adopted by his brother as to the Private Trade (if he did not first suggest it); there is, it will be observed, a characteristic difference of detail between them. While the Governor-General, with an eye to Indian commerce and finance, emphatically represents the duties on Indian sugars as much TOO HIGH; the soldier-statesman, on imperial and professional grounds, takes the opposite view. As the West Indies are a better nursery for seamen than the East, he thinks that West Indian sugars ought to have the preference over those imported from India Proper. On the other hand, the Governor-General, in urging the necessity of licensing Indian shipping, insists, as usual, on the importance of defending the country, and obviating the political risks connected with foreign vessels. Such vessels are far less under the control of the Government than those of British Indian subjects; and dangerous persons are more likely to be imported in foreign bottoms.

Want of space has compelled the omission of Mr. Dundas's papers on the above subject, as well as of the Debate upon it at the India House, which was reported very copiously, and published, by Mr. Woodfall. This Debate is, in a historical point of view, not only a curious, but an interesting and instructive document.

X. EDUCATION OF CIVIL SERVANTS.

The '*Notes*' on the College of Fort William is certainly one of the most remarkable of Lord Wellesley's compositions. The beauty of the style, unimpaired, in this case, by the amalgam of infusible Orientalisms; the orderly development of the subject; the earnest and dignified pleading for high culture and diversified attainments as indispensable for the competent discharge of important political functions; the impressive picture presented to the imagination of so vast and varied an aggregate of 'peoples, nations, and languages,' so diverse in character and institutions, controlled and administered by a comparatively small number of strangers from the Isles of the West; the not less striking picture of the education of these men for their great task by the union of archaic Eastern lore, fresh from its indigenous sources, and the advanced studies, and severer intellectual processes of Europe, with the novelty of the moral discipline of an Oxford College on the banks of the Hoogly; the pervading impression that one of Oxford's greatest sons is here advocating what he feels and shews has gone far to make him what he would fain make others; the modern aspect of many questions raised in the course of the discussion, which renders it no inappropriate or unprofitable study at the present juncture; the magnificent scale on which the whole plan is conceived, and the confidence with which it is announced and fashioned: —all these circumstances invest the Despatch with a peculiar interest, and may even arrest the attention of that far too numerous class of educated Englishmen, who are well content to remain studiously ignorant of most Indian topics.

Turning to details, for reasons which are partly stated, partly assumed, the 'writers' are still to go out to India at an early age. On this point the Governor-General and his employers were well agreed, though not altogether for the same reasons. While both parties were of opinion, that one who was to spend so much of his life in the East should lose no unnecessary time in entering on his career, and should not be hampered by ties and habits calculated to abate his zeal for a life of struggles, adventures, and even of hardship and peril, and to foster nostalgia; the Directors and their connexions were, no doubt, only too glad to be discharged, as quickly as possible, of the frequently perplexing burden of their young friends, and were ready enough, as Macaulay says, to ship them off—to make a fortune, or die of a fever. Wellesley, on the other hand, was anxious to secure fresh and malleable 'material,' rather than overformed or misformed agents, whose confirmed faults it might be difficult to correct.

But, it will also be observed, he is equally decided in fixing the general termination of the period of service earlier than might have been expected. If the civilian is to go out at sixteen or eighteen, and to be free after twenty-five years' service, he will, as far as age goes, return home in the prime of life, and if his health stand, with the option of many years of good work before him. A certain proportion would, of course, remain in the higher branches of the service. Others would enter the Direction, or go into Parliament, or do both.

But Wellesley may have contemplated the possibility of thus partly supplying a great want in England. He may have aimed at creating betimes the nucleus of a body of well-informed and authoritative public opinion at home on Eastern affairs, which might co-operate with his own influence, contribute to sustain his institutions, and counteract both the dead-weight of general ignorance and indifference, the fussy charlatanism and *doctrinaire* zeal of ambitious sciolists, and, worst of all, the Philistine party spirit which was too apt, then as now, to make an Indian Debate a great field-day for the irrelevant, splenetic, and mischievous display of political rivalry.

Again, both in arranging the retiring pension plan, and in precluding the use of the College staff for the purpose of educating English families in India, the Governor-General finds a new opportunity for discouraging European colonization. He makes, it will be seen, no allusion to the peculiar and rather hard case of those, who have been somewhat affectedly called 'Eurasians.'

And the same desire to make the patronage of the service dependent on local decision, which is defended at length in the Extract from his letter to Mr. Addington, leads him to suggest, that the Presidential designation of the young civilian should be left to the Governor-General, instead of being settled beforehand in England; and that, on emerging from the College, the fledgling should (as at Woolwich) take rank according to the impartial award of the educational authorities.

It is clear that the old and early famous Etonian strongly prefers the preparation of a public school to the ordinary alternative of those days; and that, not only because the distinctive acquirements of the 'commercial academy' are out of date, and inappropriate to the case, but from the superior collateral advantages of the former institution. Learning apart, the celebrated and too often misapplied saying, attributed to his brother Arthur, about the playing fields of Eton, will here occur to many minds.

What he would have thought of the present arrangements for the education of the Civil Servants, is an interesting speculation. Assuming the age at which the Candidates are now admitted, and that they are to remain two or three years at home afterwards, to pursue their studies and prepare for the active work of their profession, there can be little doubt that he would have advocated a University education, and that he would have hesitated to place their residence in London. As to the subject-matter of their studies, the entrance examination now disposes of much that would have been originally comprised in the courses and examinations at Fort William College. But thus much may be said as to the later and more distinctively Indian *curriculum*. In each of the great branches of Law and History, materials have vastly accumulated since his time; and criticism has done much to dispose and elucidate those materials.

But, on the one hand, the study of pure law is undoubtedly distasteful, and apt to seem 'dry,' that is repulsive, to a large proportion of young minds. While the lapse of a very few years, and the exigencies of practical life, present it in a very different point of view, when its details can be mastered much more easily and profitably, because more willingly. On the other hand, historical studies, worthy of the name, I mean *in extenso*, and such as reveal, in due detail and with genuine local colour, the peculiar and influential physical features of the Italy of Asia, the memorable and stirring associations of particular localities, the life, character, and institutions of peoples, the critical phases and secret history of revolutions, the striking individuality, great conceptions, and, dramatic career of statesmen, the silent but unmistakeable and endlessly diversified action of the general causes that overrule personal aims, and amidst all its circumstantial varieties, give a real unity and continuity to the long story of humanity in the East:—such studies are not only more attractive to the young, but, properly directed, are peculiarly adapted to create and rapidly mature that breadth of view and depth of human sympathy, in short that development of the whole man, intellectual and moral, which it was Wellesley's object to promote, and which is the best preparation for the work of a British administrator among an Indian population. Such studies are best calculated to dispel the strong provincial prejudices, and to abate the dangerous *caste* pride of John Bull; to awaken, from the first, a lively and intelligent interest in the places and the people among whom his lot is cast; to identify his aspirations with his local task, and counteract the increasing tendency to live, to a needless extent, as a stranger and a pilgrim in India. Thus they may greatly help to diminish the inevitable perils of foreign domination and arbitrary government; and to multiply and strengthen moral ties, which may, in some measure, supersede the crude terrors of the sword. Hence Lord Wellesley would, I believe, in the case of the Selected Candidates of our own day, have laid greater stress on the study of history, and less on that of pure[1] law, than is now done.

---

[1] *Pure* Law I say advisedly. For he would certainly have hailed with peculiar satisfaction, in such works as those of Sir Henry Maine, a new and invaluable *Organon.* For nowhere else will the student see so powerfully revealed, and so felicitously employed, the discerning, catholic spirit, which it was his study to cultivate; and which has made the dry bones of ancient law and custom live again, for the common edification and mutual sympathy of races superficially so different, but here proved to have so many ancestral pretensions to fraternity, and such indefeasible charters of association.

SYNOPSIS

OF

THE DESPATCHES, APPENDIX, AND PLANS.

'To the eventful and brilliant period of your Lordship's Government, the Court look back with the feelings common to their countrymen; and anxious that the minds of their Servants should be enlarged by the instruction to be derived from the accumulated experience of eminent Statesmen, they felt it a duty to diffuse widely the means of consulting a work unfolding the principles upon which the supremacy of Britain in India was successfully maintained and enlarged under a combination of circumstances, in the highest degree critical and difficult.'—*The Chairman and Deputy Chairman of the Honourable Court of Directors to the Marquess Wellesley.* October 6th, 1836.

'That the authentic record of the principles on which I acted, during the most critical and difficult exigency of the affairs of the British Empire in India, should be deemed by the Court of Directors to contain an instructive and useful lesson for their Servants, is a testimony most glorious to the memory of my Services.'—*The Marquess Wellesley to the Chairman of the Honourable Court of Directors.*

SYNOPSIS.

No.	Date.	Reference to original Edition.	From and to Whom.
	1806	IV, 1893.§	Sir Arthur Wellesley, K.B. **(Introduction.)**
			I. MYSORE.
1.	**1798** June 18.	I, 16.†	The Secret Committee of the Court of Directors, to the Governor-General in Council of Bengal. [Received in Sept. 1798.] (Extract.)
2.	July 6.	I, 21.	Mr. Josias Webbe, Secretary to the Government of Madras. For General Harris.
3.	Aug. 12.	I, 48.	Minute of the Governor-General in the Secret Department.
4.	Nov. 8.	I, 96.	The Earl of Mornington to Tippoo Sultaun.
5.	Dec. 18.	I, 114.	Tippoo Sultaun to the Earl of Mornington. [Received at Fort St. George, Dec. 25, 1798.]
6.	**1797** April 2.	V,* pages 2–6.	Tippoo Sultaun the Victorious to the Representatives of the People, residing in the Isles of France and of La Reunion.
7.	**1798** Jan. 30.	I, pages viii–x.	Proclamation at the Isle of France.
8.	Sept. 20.	I, pages 414–417.	Letter from Sultaun Selim to the Indian Sovereign, Tippoo Sultaun; delivered to Mr. Spencer Smith, his Britannic Majesty's Minister Plenipotentiary, &c.
9.	**1799** Feb. 13, [received.]	I, 136.	From Tippoo Sultaun to the Right Hon. the Governor-General.
10.	Feb. 10.	V,* pages 24–31.	Translation of the Draft of a Letter from Tippoo Sultaun to the Grand Seignior.
11.	Feb. 22.	I, 139.	The Earl of Mornington to his Excellency Lieut.-General Harris.
12.	Feb. 22.	I, 140.	Declaration of the Right Hon. the Gov.-Gen. in Council, &c., on behalf of the Honourable the East India Company, his Highness the Nizam, and the Peishwa.

§ The Wellington Supplementary Despatches.

† The Roman numerals in this column refer to volumes; the Arabic, when pages are not specified, to the number of the document in the original work.

* Supplement, Mysore War.

SYNOPSIS.

I. MYSORE. (*Continued.*)

No.	Date.	Reference to original Edition.	From and to Whom.
13.	1799 Feb. 23.	[Life of Lord Harris, pages 251–256.]	The Governor-General to General Harris.
14.	March 20.	I, 161.	The Earl of Mornington to the Honourable the Court of Directors.
15.	April 20.	I, 177.	The same to the same.
16.	May 11.	I, 198.	The same to the same.
17.	March 8.	I, 154.	Lieut.-General Stuart to the Earl of Mornington.
18.	March 27.	I, 163.	Lieut.-General Harris to the Earl of Mornington.
19.	April 5.	I, 168.	The same to the same.
20.	April 7.	I, 170.	The same to the same.
21.	April 10.	I, 174.	Major-General Floyd to the Earl of Mornington.
22.	May 7.	I, 194.	Lieut.-General Harris to the Earl of Mornington.
23.	May 6.	I, pages 697–699.	Major-General Baird to Lieut.-Gen. Harris, Commander-in-Chief, &c.
24.	May 19.	I, 207.	The Earl of Mornington to the Secret Committee of the Court of Directors.
25.	Aug. 3.	II, 26.	The same to the Honourable Court of Directors.
26.	July 13.	II, pages 43–48.	Subsidiary Treaty of Seringapatam.

II. THE NIZAM.

No.	Date.	Reference to original Edition.	From and to Whom.
27.	1798 Sept. 1.	I, pages 682–685.	Treaty of Hyderabad.
28.	1800 Oct. 12.	II, pages 709–714.	Treaty of General Defensive Alliance.

III. THE CARNATIC.

No.	Date.	Reference to original Edition.	From and to Whom.
29.	1801 July 27.	II, pages 553–561.	Declaration on the Annexation of the Carnatic.

I. MYSORE. (*Continued.*)

II. THE NIZAM.

III. THE CARNATIC.

IV. OUDE.

No.	Date.	Reference to original Edition.	From and to Whom.
30.	1799 Nov. 28.	II, 45.	The Earl of Mornington to the Secret Committee of the Honourable Court of Directors.
31.	1800 Feb. 9.	II, 64.	The Earl of Mornington to the Nabob of Oude.
32.	1801 Jan. 22.	II, 109.	The Marquess Wellesley to Lieut.-Colonel William Scott, Resident at Lucknow.
33.	Nov. 14.	II, 163.	The Marquess Wellesley to the Honourable the Secret Committee of the Honourable the Court of Directors.

V. MAHRATTAS.

No.	Date.	Reference to original Edition.	From and to Whom.
34.	1802 Dec. 24.	III, 2.	The Marquess Wellesley to the Secret Committee of the Honourable Court of Directors.
35.	1803 Feb. 10.	III, 13.	The same to the same.
36.	April 19.	III, 20.	The same to the same.
37.	1802 Dec. 31, 1803 Dec. 16.	III, pages 627–632.	Treaty of Bassein.
38.	July 12.	III, 46, and Enclosure.	The Hon. G. H. Barlow, Esq., to the Marquess Wellesley.
39.	1804 March 4.	V,* pages 302–318.	Lord Castlereagh, President of the Board of Controul, to the Marquess Wellesley.
40.	March 6.	IV, 49, Enclosure.	The Secret Committee of the Honourable Court of Directors of the East India Company to the most noble the Governor-General in Council, Bengal.
41.	Nov. (?)	V,* pages 318–337.	Major-General Wellesley's Observations on the policy of the Treaty.

* Supplement, Mahratta War.

IV. OUDE.

V. MAHRATTAS.

1. English Intervention.

2. Policy of the Treaty of Bassein.

V. MAHRATTAS. (*Continued.*)

No.	Date.	Reference to original Edition.	From and to Whom.
42.	1803 June 26.	III, 34.	The Marquess Wellesley to the Hon. Major-General Wellesley.
43.	July 27.	III, 50, and	The Marquess Wellesley to his Excellency General Lake, Commander-in-Chief, &c.
	July 22.	2nd Enclosure.	N. B. Edmonstone, Esq., Secretary to Government, to Græme Mercer, Esq.
44.	June 3.	III, 31.	N. B. Edmonstone, Esq., Secretary to Government, to Colonel Collins, Resident at the Court of Dowlut Rao Scindiah. (Extract.)
45.	June 20.	III, 33.	The Marquess Wellesley to the Secret Committee of the Court of Directors.
46.	Aug. 1.	III, 60.	The Governor-General in Council to the Honourable the Secret Committee of the Court of Directors.
47.	July 31, [received.]	III, 57.	Dowlut Rao Scindiah to the Marquess Wellesley.
48.	Aug. 6.	3rd Enclosure in III, 63.	Translation of a letter from the Hon. Major-General Wellesley, to Dowlut Rao Scindiah.
49.	Sept. 25.	III, 100.	The Governor-General in Council to the Honourable the Secret Committee of the Honourable the Court of Directors. (Extract.)
50.	Oct. 31.	III, 126.	The same to the same.
51.	Dec. 28.	III, 158.	The same to the same.
52.	Sept. 11, 7.30 P.M.	III, 84.	Lieut.-General Lake to the Marquess Wellesley. [Received at Fort William, Sept. 23, 1803.]
53.	Sept. 12.	III, 86.	The same to the same.
54.	Sept. 13.	III, 87.	The same to the same. [Received at Fort William, Sept. 25, 1803.]
55.	Sept. 17.	III, 93.	The same to the same.
56.	Sept. 24.	III, 96.	The Hon. Major-General Wellesley to the Marquess Wellesley. [Received Oct. 30, 1803.]
57.	Nov. 2.	III, 130.	Lieut.-Gen. Lake to the Marquess Wellesley. [Received Nov. 15, 1803.]
58.	Nov. 30.	III, 144.	The Hon. Major-General Wellesley to the Marquess Wellesley. [Received Dec. 25, 1803.]

3. War with Scindiah and the Rajah of Berar.

V. MAHRATTAS. (*Continued.*)

No.	Date.	Reference to original Edition.	From and to Whom.
59.	1803 Dec. 11.	III, 149.	The Marquess Wellesley to the Hon. Major-General Wellesley. (Extract.)
60.	Dec. 17.	III, pages 633–634.	Treaty of Deogaum.
61.	Dec. 30.	III, pages 634–636.	Treaty of Surje Anjengaum.
62.	1804 June 10.	IV, 30.	The Marquess Wellesley to the Honourable the Secret Committee of the Honourable the Court of Directors.
63.	July 13.	IV, 33.	The Governor-General in Council to the Secret Committee of the Honourable the Court of Directors. (Extract.)
64.	Feb.	III, pages 582–586.	Governor-General's reply to an address from the British inhabitants of Calcutta.
65.	May 21.	IV, 49.	Lord Castlereagh to the Marquess Wellesley. [Received Oct. 14, 1804.]
66.	June 15.	IV, 31.	The Governor-General in Council to the Honourable the Secret Committee of the Court of Directors.
67.	July 28.	IV, 35.	Marquess Wellesley's Notes on the War with Holkar. (Extract.)
68.	1805 March 24.	IV, 90, V,* pages 135–155.	The Governor-General in Council to the Honourable the Secret Committee of the Honourable the Court of Directors. (Extract.)
69.	May 31.	V,* 3.	The same to the same. (Extract.)
70.	1804 Sept. 8.	IV, 40,	Lieut.-General Lake to the Marquess Wellesley.
	Sept. 2.	Enclosure I.	Hon. Colonel Monson to Lieut.-General Lake.
	Aug. 31.	Enclosure II.	Captain Nicholl to the Hon. Brigadier-General Monson.
71.	1805 July 1.	V,* pages 283–292.	Lieut.-General Lake to the Marquess Wellesley. (Extract.)
72.	1804 Nov. 14.	IV, 51.	Hon. Brigadier Monson to the Marquess Wellesley.
73.	Nov. 17.	IV, 52.	Lieut.-Gen. Lake to the Marquess Wellesley.
74.	1805 Jan. 10.	IV, 67.	The same to the same.

* Supplement, Mahratta War.

4. Pacification and Results of the War.

5. War with Holkar.

V MAHRATTAS. (*Continued.*)

No.	Date.	Reference to original Edition.	From and to Whom.
75.	**1805** Jan. 21.	IV, 68.	Lieut.-General Lake to the Marquess Wellesley.
76.	Feb. 21.	IV, 76.	The same to the same.
77.	Feb. 22.	IV, 81.	The same to the same.
78.	March 9.	IV, 81.	The Marquess Wellesley to Lieut.-General Lord Lake.

VI. DEFENCE OF THE INDIAN EMPIRE.

No.	Date.	Reference to original Edition.	From and to Whom.
79.	**1800** July 13.	II, 88.	The Marquess Wellesley to the Right Hon. Henry Dundas.
80.	Dec. 30.	V, Supt. Miscellaneous 1.	The Right Hon. Henry Dundas to the Marquess Wellesley.
81.	Jan.	V, Supt. Miscellaneous 2.	Copy of a private Paper written by General Stuart prior to his leaving India in January 1800, and submitted to the Right Hon. Henry Dundas, on his arrival in England, in July in that year.
82.	**1804** Feb. 20.	III, pages 663, 664.	Enclosure in a Letter from the Acting Resident at Poona. Received March 11, 1804.
83.	**1803** June 20.	III, page 656.	The Marquess Wellesley to Lord Hobart. (Extract.)
84.	March 16.	III, 43.	The Right Hon. Lord Castlereagh to the Marquess Wellesley. [Received July 6, 1803.]
85.	July 25.	III, 58.	Marquess Wellesley to Right Hon. Lord Viscount Castlereagh.
86.	**1798** Sept. 16.	I, 64.	The Earl of Mornington to Major-General Sir James Henry Craig, K.B.
87.	Oct. 6.	I, 75.	Major-General Sir James Henry Craig to the Earl of Mornington.
88.	Oct. 13.	I, 79.	The same to the same.

5. War with Holkar. (*Continued.*)

VI. DEFENCE OF THE INDIAN EMPIRE.

1. European Army.

2. General Policy, especially against the French.

3. North-Western Frontier.

VI. DEFENCE OF THE INDIAN EMPIRE. (*Continued.*)

No.	Date.	Reference to original Edition.	From and to Whom.
89.	1801 Sept. 28.	II, 151.	The Marquess Wellesley to the Honourable the Secret Committee of the Honourable the Court of Directors.
90.	May 10.	II, 130.	The Marquess Wellesley to the Right Hon. Henry Dundas.
91.	1803 Nov. 30.	III, 145.	The Marquess Wellesley to Lord Hobart. (Extract.)
92.	1801 March 19.	II, pages 471–473.	The Marquess Wellesley to the Shereef of Mecca, the Imaum of Senna, and the Sultaun of Aden.
93.	1804 July 13.	IV, 33.	The Governor-General in Council to the Secret Committee of the Honourable the Court of Directors. (Extract.)
94.	1805 June 2.	IV, 115.	The same to the same. (Extract.)

VII. MISCELLANEOUS DESPATCHES.

No.	Date.	Reference to original Edition.	From and to Whom.
95.	1799 March 18.	I, 217.	The Right Hon. H. Dundas to the Earl of Mornington. [Received Aug. 5, 1799.]
96.	March 21.	II, 28.	The same to the same. [Received at Fort William, Aug. 5, 1799.]
97.	1800 March 5.	II, 69.	The Earl of Mornington to the Right Hon. Henry Dundas.
98.	1803 Dec. 15.	III, 153.	The Marquess Wellesley to Lord Castlereagh.

VIII. SUPREME AND LOCAL GOVERNMENTS.

No.	Date.	Reference to original Edition.	From and to Whom.
99.	1800 July 9.	II, 85.	The Governor-General in Council to the Honourable Court of Directors.
100.	1798 July 29.	I, pages 230–232.	The Earl of Mornington to Lord Clive. (Extract.)

4. Persia.

5. Ceylon.

6. Red Sea Expedition.

7. The Emperor.

VII. MISCELLANEOUS DESPATCHES.

VIII. SUPREME AND LOCAL GOVERNMENTS.

VIII. SUPREME AND LOCAL GOVERNMENTS. (*Continued.*)

No.	Date.	Reference to original Edition.	From and to Whom.
101.	1802 Jan. 10.	III, pages xiv–xvii.	The Marquess Wellesley to the Right Hon. Henry Addington. (Extract.)
102.	1800 April 16.	II, 74.	The Earl of Mornington to the Hon. Jonathan Duncan. (Extract.)

IX. FINANCE AND TRADE.

No.	Date.	Reference to original Edition.	From and to Whom.
103.	1799 March 18.	II, 27.	The Right Hon. Henry Dundas to the Earl of Mornington. [Received at Fort William, Aug. 5, 1799.]
104.	1800 Sept. 30.	II, 94.	The Marquess Wellesley to the Honourable the Court of Directors.

X. EDUCATION OF CIVIL SERVANTS.

No.	Date.	Reference to original Edition.	From and to Whom.
105.	1800 July 10.	II, 86.	The Governor-General's Notes with respect to the foundation of a College at Fort William.
106.	July 10.	II, 87.	Regulation for the College at Fort William.
107.	1798 May 25.	II, pages 738–740.	Extract from a public Letter from the Court of Directors of the East India Company to Bengal.

XI. THE FLEET.

No.	Date.	Reference to original Edition.	From and to Whom.
108.	1801 Feb. 5.	II, pages 755–758.	The Marquess Wellesley to his Excellency Vice-Admiral Rainier, &c., &c., &c. (Extract.)

VIII. SUPREME AND LOCAL GOVERNMENTS. (*Continued.*)

IX. FINANCE AND TRADE.

X. EDUCATION OF CIVIL SERVANTS.

XI. THE FLEET.

*

APPENDIX.

No.	Date.	Reference to original Edition.	From and to Whom.
1.	1801 Nov. 10.	Wellesley Despatches. II, pages 600–602.	Lord Wellesley's Oude Treaty. (Extract.)

THE WELLINGTON SUPPLEMENTARY DESPATCHES.

No.	Date.	Reference to original Edition.	From and to Whom.
2.	1798 Oct. 26.	I, 46.	'Reflections upon the plan for having the army in the Carnatic at all times in a state of preparation.'
3.	1799 March.	I, 112.	'Draft of the Description of our march to Major-General St. Leger.'
4.	April 5.	I, 114.	To the Earl of Mornington. (Extract.)
5.	April 18.	I, 115.	To the same. (Extract.)
6.	May 8.	I, 119.	To the same. (Extract.)
7.	Undated.	II, 983.	'Memorandum on Oude.'
8.	1797 or 98	I, 10.	'Memorandum on Bengal.'
9.	1803 Nov. 1.	IV, 1681.	To Lieut.-Colonel Munro. (Extract.)
10.	1804 1805 Sept. Jan. 1805 July 3.	(α) IV, pages 465, 466, & 480. (β) IV, page 511.	Extracts from General Wellesley's Correspondence.

SIR THOMAS MUNRO'S CORRESPONDENCE in his Life by Rev. G. R. Gleig.

No.	Date.	Reference to original Edition.	From and to Whom.
11.	1803 Nov. 28.	III, pages 182–184.	To General Wellesley.
12.	1804 March 6.	III, pages 192–193.	To Colonel Read.
13.	Undated.	III, pages 201, 202.	To his Father.

APPENDIX.

THE WELLINGTON SUPPLEMENTARY DESPATCHES.

SIR THOMAS MUNRO'S CORRESPONDENCE
in his Life by Rev. G. R. Gleig.

SIR THOMAS MUNRO'S CORRESPONDENCE. (*Continued.*)

No.	Date.	Reference to original Edition.	From and to Whom.
14.	1818 April 23.	III, pages 247, 248.	To the Honourable M. Elphinstone.
15.	1817 Aug. 12.	I, pages 461–467.	To his Excellency the Governor-General.

MISCELLANEOUS EXTRACTS.

No.	Date.	Reference.	Authority.
16.	1806	Pages 55, &c.	Anonymous. A Vindication of the justice, &c., of the late Wars, &c.
17.	1841	V, pages 134–136.	Barchou de Penhoën. Histoire de l'Empire Anglais, &c.
18.	1805 Aug. 30.	III, page 544.	Marquis Cornwallis to the Right Hon. Lord Lake. Cornwallis Correspondence.
19.	1806	Pages 1–11.	Mr. T. C. (later Lord) Metcalfe. Kaye's Metcalfe Papers.
20.	1814 December.	Pages 145, 146.	The same Writer, and Work.
21.	1868	1st Edition, pages 32, 33.	Colonel George Chesney. Indian Polity.

MAP AND PLANS.

1.	1858	I.	Wellington Supplementary Despatches.
2.	1840	Page 522.	Lushington's Life of Lord Harris.
3.	1800	Page 169.	Beatson's War with Tippoo Sultaun.
4.	1804	Page 94.	Wellesley's Notes on Transaction in the Mahratta Empire.
5.		Page 105.	The same Work.
6.		Page 67.	The same Work.
7.	1830	I, page 188.	Welsh's Military Reminiscences.
8.	1818	Page 408.	Thorn's Memoir of the War in India.
9.		Page 415.	The same Work.

SIR THOMAS MUNRO'S CORRESPONDENCE. (*Continued.*)

MISCELLANEOUS EXTRACTS.

MAP AND PLANS.

EXPLANATION OF THE PLANS.

Mallavelly (page 117).—The following is given in Lord Harris's *Life*, to explain the Plan reproduced from that work in this volume:—

'References. Red, denotes the 1st position of the English army. Blue, the 2nd ditto. Purple, the 3rd ditto. Yellow, Tippoo's, the 1st ditto. Green, the 2nd ditto. Orange, shows the encampment of the army after the action.

A. A large body of the enemy's horse kept in check by the 25th regiment of light dragoons. B. A party of the horse and rocket boys driven off by the picquet. C. A small party of the enemy's horse charging the 1st, or European brigade, and repulsed. D. The 2nd regiment of cavalry advancing to charge, but halted on the European brigade beginning to fire. E. A large body of the enemy which retreated on the party C being repulsed. F. A party of the enemy's infantry engaged with the left of the European brigade, and obliged to retreat. G. Another party that attacked the 33rd regiment, the head of Colonel Wellesley's division. H. Retreat of the party G charged by the 33rd regiment. I. Charge of three regiments of cavalry, under General Floyd, on the fugitives H. K. Two brass 18-pounders on a high spot, cannonading the enemy while the line formed. L. Ditto advanced to some commanding rocks, from which they opened on the enemy as the line advanced.'

Seringapatam (*ad finem*).—This plan is taken from Lieut.-Colonel Beatson's *War with Tippoo Sultaun*; and that of the Battle of Argaum (page 409) from Colonel Welsh's *Military Reminiscences*. Both will, it is hoped, sufficiently explain themselves, and the events to which they relate.

The Governor-General's *Notes Relative to Transactions in the Mahratta Empire* has supplied the Plans of the Battles of Delhi (page 395), Lasswary (*ad finem*), and Assye (page 401). The following details on the first and third result from a comparison of that work with Major Thorn's *Memoir of the War in India*.

Battle of Delhi.—A. First position of the English army. P. Grand guard and advanced picquets. B. Cavalry reconnaissance, under Lake in person. C. English infantry, and D. do. cavalry, advancing to the attack. N. English cavalry detached against Seik do. H. First battn., 2nd N. Infantry, and K. four guns, appuyed on O., the village. E. Enemy's infantry in array. G.G. English infantry attacking, and S.S., do. pursuing the enemy. Q. The Mahrattas in flight. M. English cavalry dislodging a body of the enemy from a village.

Battle of Lasswary.—The explanatory matter in the margin of the plan is not, as it there stands, very explicit. But the following, which is given at the end of the volume, supplies this deficiency, and corresponds, sentence by sentence, to the letters, which are here accordingly repeated:—

'REFERENCES.

AAA.

First position of the enemy, when attacked by the British cavalry on the morning of the 1st November. The right upon the village of Lasswary, their left extending to the fortified village of Mohaulpoor, with 72 pieces of cannon, arranged in divisions in front of the centre and flanks.

BBBB. . . . . . two white lines

Second position of the enemy at noon drawn up in two lines, with their guns in front. The enemy took up this position on the arrival of the British infantry.

D	E	F
H.M. 27 Drs.	H.M. 8 Drs.	H.M. 29 Drs.
	1st N. Cavy.	2d N. Cavy.
6 N. Cavy.	3d N. Cavy.	4th N. Cavy.

Disposition of the British cavalry (with two batteries of their galloper guns advanced, and covered each by a squadron, K. 1. & K. 2.) in order to divide the enemy's attention in front, and to attack them as soon as the column of British infantry should turn their flank.

C.C.C.C.

Third position of the enemy, in discovering the movement of the columns of British infantry to turn their flank.

H.H.H.H. . . . . . .

Route of the columns of infantry led by H. M.'s 76th regiment; to turn the enemy's right flank, but not being able to turn it, advanced upon their lines C C C, which they broke and routed, taking their guns, &c. &c. The British infantry then drove the enemy off, towards a small mosque . . . . in the rear of the village, about which the enemy were met and charged by the British cavalry in various directions l. m. n. o. . . . red lines.

G.G.G. . . . .

H. M.'s 29th light dragoons who advanced and charged the enemy's cavalry at S on the left flank of the column of British infantry.

. . . . X

A column of the enemy's baggage, infantry, &c. &c. going off, but turned by the charge of the British cavalry, l. m. n. o.

RRRR.

Shows the enemy completely broken and routed in various directions. Two thousand of the enemy finding it impossible to succeed in their attempt to escape, threw down their arms and surrendered themselves prisoners, with baggage and every thing belonging to the enemy's camp.

A Flag. (*See Map.*) Encampment of the British army after the action. Left of the line of infantry at Lasswary; right at Impury, or Sengrah, with the cavalry thrown back on the right towards the Nullah, and facing the hills. A battalion of infantry left in charge of the prisoners of war, who were all collected at the village of Sajepoorah.'

Battle of Assye.—A. English army advancing to the ford. 1, 2, 3, Nizam's and Peishwa's cavalry. X. The left of the enemy's infantry line, in its original position, which it was proposed to attack. B., B., Second position of the enemy's infantry (first line), and of the English army confronting it. D. Enemy's second line of infantry, after its re-formation. C. English army pursuing the enemy's routed first line. E. Mahratta cavalry charging the 74th regiment. F. Countercharge of the English cavalry. G. General Wellesley's charge with the 78th regiment and 7th regiment N. C. H. Position of the General and these troops, after the charge.

The Plans of the Battle and Siege of Deeg (p. 544), and of the Siege of Bhurtpore (p. 547), are given from Major Thorn's *Memoir*.

Battle of Deeg.—A. Goverdown, whence the English reconnoitred and approached. B. A village round which they marched. K. Position of the enemy, when first seen. D. English army advancing to the attack. C. Native cavalry, keeping F., the enemy's cavalry in check. E. E. E. Progress of the English army. I. Enemy's infantry and guns. G. H. English detachment hemming in a body of the enemy. L. A part of that body driven into the marsh. M. Position of the English camp after the battle. O. A cavalry picquet, on a height, to watch the enemy's motions after the battle. The small letters refer to the details of the siege, which is related at large in the *Memoir*.

Siege of Bhurtpoor.—The Plan will, it is hoped, elucidate, sufficiently for the present purpose, the scene and the operations. The letters relate mostly to the successive batteries, breaches, and defences, and are explained in the Major's narrative, to which it may be enough to refer those who wish to study professionally the *minutiæ* of the affair.

INTRODUCTION.

MEMORANDUM ON MARQUESS WELLESLEY'S GOVERNMENT OF INDIA.

By The Duke of Wellington.[1]

IN order to understand the merits or demerits of Marquess Wellesley's government in India, it is necessary to review the state of that country when his Lordship assumed its government in May, 1798, and that in which it was left in April, 1806, which was the close of the official year in which Marquess Wellesley resigned the government. This subject is large, and will require a minute detail of many measures, of the causes which led to them, and of their consequences. But this paper shall be made as short as possible; and nothing shall be inserted in it which is not necessary for the elucidation of the subjects on which it is written.

The first intelligence which reached Marquess Wellesley, upon his arrival in India, was that the ancient Native enemy of the Company had formed an alliance with the French at Mauritius, for the purpose of attacking the British nation in India; and that, in consequence of this alliance, a body of Frenchmen had already been landed at the port of Mangalore on the coast of Malabar, and had marched to Seringapatam. Shortly after the receipt of this intelligence, it was known in India that Buonaparte, with a large French army, had landed and taken possession of Egypt, and that the avowed object of this expedition was to invade India by that route.

The state of warfare which was to be expected in consequence of the intelligence of these measures and movements of the enemies of the British government, rendered necessary a review of its situation in all its branches; and what follows is the result of that review, and of the measures which were adopted to apply a remedy to the inconveniences and evils which were found to exist.

---

[1] Then (1806) Major-General, Sir A. Wellesley, K.B.

The Company were found to have a revenue of 8,059,880*l.*, a sum less than that which they had been found to have in 1793, at the renewal of their charter, by 165,748*l.* The debt amounted to 10,866,588*l.*, having increased since 1793; and the interest was annually 746,933*l.*, having increased since 1793. The total amount of the charges of the government in India, including the interest of the debt, was 8,178,626*l.*; and the deficiency of the revenues, in comparison with the charges, at a time of profound peace in India, was 322,530*l.* At the same time the Company's credit was at the lowest ebb. Money could not be borrowed in Bengal at 12 *per cent.* interest; the Company's bonds and securities at that rate were circulated at such a discount, as well at that Presidency as at Madras and Bombay, as to amount nearly to a stagnation; and with this great war in expectation, the Company's financial servants in India were entirely at a loss to find the means for supporting and carrying on the ordinary operations of the government in time of peace. The Company's armies, although in a high state of discipline, and maintained, that of Fort William at the expense of 1,996,487*l.*, that of Fort St. George at the expense of 1,868,498*l.*, and that of Bombay at the expense of 641,469*l.*, were not in a state of preparation and efficiency to perform the operations which the crisis of the Company's affairs was likely to require from them. The Commander-in-Chief and Adjutant-General of Fort St. George reported that six months would be required to prepare for service the army serving under that Presidency, upon which the brunt of the contest was likely to fall; and the government of that Presidency were apprehensive of the consequences of drawing the attention of the enemy by making the smallest preparation for defence against the attack which they well knew he had meditated. The army of Bombay, on which naturally the task would have fallen of co-operating in the contest with that of Fort St. George, was necessarily scattered in the disaffected provinces under the government of Bombay; and the army of Bengal was stationed principally in the Vizier's territories, with a view to keep them in tranquillity, and to defend them from the expected invasion of the King of Caubul.

Those powers on whom experience of former wars with Tippoo had shown that the Company ought to rely for assistance were the Nizam, the Peshwah, the Nabob of the Carnatic, and the petty rajahs and zemindars on the coast of Malabar. Since the peace of 1792 with Tippoo, which had attained the object of the alliance between the first two and the Company, the situation of these powers had been considerably changed. The Nizam, by the result of an unfortunate state of hostility with the Mahrattas, which ended in battle, and a peace, or rather capitulation, concluded at Kurdlah in the year 1795, had fallen from the state of a great and leading power in Hindustan to that of a tributary to the Mahrattas. His ministers were appointed by the Mahrattas; his army was disbanded; and the only support of his authority was a corps consisting of about 14,000 men, trained, disciplined, and commanded by French officers. These officers had possession of a considerable portion of the Nizam's territories, from the revenues of which they were to pay their troops; and by the power which they acquired by this possession, and by the state of confusion of the government of the Mahrattas at Poonah, the weakness of that of the Nizam, and the supine indifference of that of the Company, they were becoming a French state in the peninsula of India. By their power and violence they overawed the Nizam's councils, and precluded all hope of his cooperation in the war which was expected with Tippoo and his French allies in the year 1798.

The Mahratta government of Poonah, which had afforded such material assistance to the British government in the war which had ended in 1792 by the treaty of Seringapatam, was become equally incapable with the Nizam of affording any aid in that which was expected in 1798. After the peace of Kurdlah in 1795, the Peshwah, Mahdoo Rao Narain, threw himself from a window in his palace at Poonah, and died upon the spot. A contest then ensued for the possession of the power of that government, in which all the principal Mahratta chiefs were engaged, and which, having lasted with various success during the years 1796 and 1797, had ended by placing all the power at Poonah in the hands of Dowlut Rao Scindiah. This chief already possessed the Mahratta territories upon the Jumna and Ganges bordering upon those of the English and the Nabob of Oude, and the actual sovereignty of all those situated to the northward of the rivers Nerbudda and Taptee. By the gain of the influence over the government of the young Peshwah, Bajee Rao, he extended his power to the northern frontier of Tippoo's dominions in Mysore; thus holding in his own hands all the different Mahratta states.

In 1798 this extended power was but feebly established, and would have been unequal to the exertion to be made in the expected contest with Tippoo, even if it could be supposed that Scindiah's policy would have led him to enter into it. But when that chief became the sole head of the Mahrattas, his policy would have led him to support Tippoo rather than the English in the impending contest, supposing his power to have been in that state to enable him to enter into it. He must have been aware that, with respect to him, the English were the most formidable of the two powers; and that his objects would have been forwarded by their defeat. Besides this, Scindiah's principal force consisted in a body of infantry, raised, disciplined, and commanded by French officers; and although the influence of these officers over the government of Scindiah was by no means of the description of that exercised by those in the service of the Nizam over the government of that prince, it was still sufficiently strong to prevent Scindiah from adopting a measure which was contrary to his obvious policy, as the sole possessor of all the Mahratta power from the Ganges to the Toombuddra.

Thus, then, nothing was to be expected from the two powers which had been the principal allies of the Company in the former war with Tippoo; and as the French were likely to be actively and personally engaged in this expected war, it was to be apprehended that they would derive assistance from the force commanded by Frenchmen in the service of those powers who had formerly been considered as the firm allies of the British government.

Since the peace of 1792 the Nabob Mahomed Ali of the Carnatic had died, and had been succeeded by his son, Omdal ool Omrah. This prince, who was very unpopular in his territories, showed every disposition to impede rather than to forward the operations of the British army. He gave them no assistance; and it was afterwards found at Seringapatam that he was in correspondence with the Company's enemy.

As for the rajahs of Malabar, they (with the exception of the Rajah of Koorg) had been in a state of hostility with the Company from the conclusion of the peace of 1792 till the year 1798, and had kept a considerable proportion of the Bombay army in constant hostile operations against them. No assistance was to be expected from them; but, on the contrary, every thing which was in their power to annoy and harass the army and to aid the enemy.

Add to this representation of the state of our affairs in India at this period, that a revolution had just been effected in Oude by Lord Teignmouth; that the government of the reigning Prince Saadut Ali was most unpopular, and by no means firmly established throughout the country; that his army was mutinous and disaffected; that an invasion of his country was expected from Zemaun Shah, the King of Caubul, against which it was necessary to provide by the assembly of a large force in Oude under the command of Sir J. Craig; and that, in this emergency of affairs in Oude, such was the state of mutiny and disaffection of the Nabob's troops, that His Highness could not trust to them the guard of his person, but was obliged to call for British troops to preserve him from the effects of their treachery; and Sir J. Craig, to whom was intrusted the defence of Oude, considered these troops in the light of an enemy's fortress in his rear.

Another circumstance which embarrassed government in India at all times, and was a considerable source of embarrassment at the period under consideration, was the nature and state of the alliances between the British government and its dependent and tributary states.

These alliances had always been formed in a moment of extreme weakness, and generally after the Native and dependent state had been conquered. The principal stipulation was uniformly protection by the British government, in consideration of subsidy to be paid by the Native state, and in other respects the Native state was declared or was considered to be independent in the management of all its internal concerns.

The Native states having in every instance contracted these alliances in a moment of weakness, in which, of course, all the powers of their governments were paralysed, they have invariably been under the necessity of calling for the assistance of the British protecting government for the support of their authority in the management of their internal concerns.

The system of government in India, the foundations of authority, and the modes of supporting it and of carrying on the operations of the government, are entirely different from the systems and modes adopted in Europe for the same purposes.

The foundation and the instrument of all power there is the sword; and when these alliances have been formed, the sword, or, in other words, the army of the East India Company, became the only support and the only efficient instrument of authority of the protected Native states.

This position of affairs, which was the result of the principle of government long established in the East, and of the weakness of the Native state, was attended by a stipulation in some cases, or an understanding in others, that the Native state should be *independent* in all the operations of its internal government; and at the very moment in which this stipulation was made, the interference of the British government was required, and all the internal concerns of the Native state submitted to its judgment, in order that its agents might see whether the cases in which its interference was called for were of a nature to justify it.

Here, then, the door was necessarily opened to the interference of the British government in every concern; and the result was increased weakness in the Native state, jealousy of this interference, and disunion bordering upon treachery.

These evils had long appeared to require a remedy; and they must have been felt particularly at the moment in which the British government was likely to be involved in a most extensive warfare with the most formidable of the Native powers, assisted by the French.

This having been the state of India at the time Marquess Wellesley assumed the government in the year 1798, the measures adopted to apply a remedy to the evils which existed will form an epitome of the history of his Lordship's administration. I shall detail them in that order which is most likely to make them clear to the understandings of those who will read this paper.

The objects which pressed most upon his Lordship's attention in May and June, 1798, were to place the army of Fort St. George in a situation to resist the expected hostility of the enemy, to relieve the finances from the difficulties under which they laboured, and to bring back the allies of the Company to the state in which they had been left by the peace at Seringapatam in 1792, so that the allies might be able to render the assistance in the war which they were capable of affording.

The measures of finance which were at that time successfully adopted laid the foundation of the system which was subsequently acted upon, and which will be fully considered in another part of this paper.

Effectual measures were immediately adopted to put in a situation to enable them to defend themselves the whole disposable force of Fort St. George, and eventually to perform the service which might be, and was afterwards, required from them.

The army of Fort St. George was reinforced by European troops from Bengal, and preparatory measures were adopted to enable government to reinforce it still further with Native troops, when the most favourable season for transporting them by sea should come round.

But the principal measure of those days, that which gave a turn to the state of the Company's affairs in India, and to the general sentiment of the people of that country respecting the British government, was the negotiation at Hyderabad, which ended by the substitution of a British for a French force at the capital of the Nizam.

The Nizam had long been connected with the British government, and by the treaty of 1789 it had been stipulated that he should have the assistance of two British battalions when he should call for them. This article of the treaty had not been performed till the war broke out with Tippoo, which ended by the peace of 1792, when Lord Cornwallis made a new treaty [1790] with the Nizam, and attached to his army two British battalions, which acted with them during that war. At the same time two British battalions were attached to the Mahratta army under Pursheram Bhow.

The services of these battalions stationed with the Nizam, as will be observed by the treaty, were to be confined to operations against foreign enemies and domestic rebels; but not to be directed against the Mahrattas, and in particular not against certain tributaries of the Nizam stationed upon the Mahratta frontier, who were likewise tributaries of the Peshwah.

After the defeat and capitulation of the Nizam at Kurdlah in 1795, which has been above referred to, the Mahrattas had obliged His Highness to send these battalions back into the Company's territories; but during the disputes at Poonah for the succession to Madhoo Rao, His Highness had taken advantage of the momentary weakness of the Mahratta government, and had recalled these battalions to his capital.

The object of the negotiation which Marquess Wellesley commenced with the Nizam was to prevail upon His Highness to perform the defensive treaty of Hyderabad, 1st Sept. 1798; and as it appeared that His Highness was unable to perform it on account of the power which the French officers and their faction had over his councils, it was proposed to His Highness that he should dismiss them and their troops from his service for ever; and an offer was made to supply British troops to enable His Highness to accomplish this object, and to remain thereafter at Hyderabad as substitutes for the troops under the command of the French officers.

A treaty was concluded on this basis with the utmost secrecy and despatch, which contained all the restraining articles for the service of the troops which had been in the treaty of 7th May, 1798; and a body of British troops entered the Nizam's territories, and had made some marches towards Hyderabad before the French officers were aware of their fate. This body of troops, having joined those already at Hyderabad, performed the service on which they were sent without bloodshed; and the Nizam was thus restored to the power of performing his defensive engagements with the Company, and one of the great and fruitful sources of the evils impending over us in 1798, which has been already described, was removed by a timely, well-contrived, and able exercise of the power of the British government.

This negotiation at Hyderabad was accompanied by another at Poonah, with a view to the same objects. But this failed, for reasons which will be reviewed hereafter. In the course of this negotiation all the circumstances attending that carrying on at Hyderabad were described to the Peshwah, with a view to prevent the jealousy which might otherwise have been expected upon the renewal of the ancient alliance between the Company and the Nizam.

After one of the principal allies of the British government had thus been placed in a situation to be enabled to perform his treaty of alliance, a negotiation was opened with Tippoo Sultaun, the object of which was to bring that Prince to an early decision, whether he should be at peace or at war with the Company. It was obvious that the assistance which he had hitherto received from his allies, the French, was small in comparison with that which he might expect from them; and that it was not of an extent and description to be very formidable to the British government, particularly as its alliance with the Nizam had been renewed, and the source of danger in that quarter had been removed. All that was required from Tippoo, therefore, was a renunciation of this offensive alliance, and such an unequivocal proof of it as should be satisfactory to the whole world; and the adoption of arrangements which should facilitate the usual friendly communications between states not in hostility with each other.

These negotiations were attended by military preparations which were calculated to secure early success and a speedy termination to the war, which it was determined should be the consequence of Tippoo's refusal to give the allies the reasonable satisfaction which they had required. The wisdom of these early preparations was soon proved; for on the very day that Tippoo, after a delay of some weeks beyond the period fixed for his answer to the remonstrance of the British government, despatched his answer, and desired that a British officer might be sent to negotiate with him, he commenced his march to attack the Bombay army, which was assembled in the territories of the Rajah of Koorg.

In this review of the measures of Marquess Wellesley's government, it is not intended to detail the movements or the actions of the different armies. The result of the well-prepared and well-combined operations of the war against Tippoo was the capture of his capital, with all his arsenals, treasure, &c.; his own death, on the 4th May, 1799; and the subsequent reduction and submission of all his territories to the allied governments.

The army of the Nizam, with the subsidiary force as formed by the late Treaty of 1798, co-operated in this war with the British army; and His Highness's government shared equally with the British government in the advantages arising from its successful termination. The territories of the Company were increased by the addition of those belonging to Tippoo, situated upon the sea coast of Malabar, and those which gave possession of important military positions. The Nizam received an equivalent, contiguous to his frontier; and a portion was reserved for the Peshwah, to be given on the condition that His Highness should become a party to the alliance between the other governments, and should accede to certain stipulations which were proposed to him, and which will be discussed in a subsequent part of this paper. His Highness having refused to accept these conditions, this portion was divided between the Company and the Nizam.

The principal and all the centre part of the territories of Tippoo were given to a descendant of the ancient Rajahs of Mysore, in whose person a state was formed under the immediate influence and protection of the British government. This state was connected by a treaty of alliance with the Company, which was bound to defend it on condition of the payment of a stipulated tribute. As alliances of this description, by conferring a nominal independence on the Princes connected by them with the Company, had been found in other instances to be attended with many inconveniences, to render necessary a constant interference by the protecting government in the internal affairs of the

Native subordinate state, and to occasion internal weakness, jealousy of the protecting power, and a waste and embarrassment of the resources of the government, it was thought best, in the treaty of alliance with the government of Mysore, to provide for the interference of the British government in all its concerns when such interference might be necessary; and the state in which this government is found to be at this moment, the cordial and intimate union which exists between the government of Mysore and the British authorities, and the important strength and real assistance which it has afforded to the British government in all its recent difficulties, afford the strongest proofs of the wisdom of this stipulation of the treaty.

Thus, then, in less than one year from the period at which the perils which I have above described threatened the existence of the British government in India, our principal ally, the Nizam, was restored to us, the French state growing in the peninsula of India was destroyed, our formidable Native enemy, Tippoo, the certain ally of the French in India, was subdued, and in his place was established in Mysore a government calculated to afford, and which has afforded, the most substantial assistance to Great Britain in all her difficulties.

The Governor-General having now relieved the peninsula of India from the danger by which it was threatened, and affairs in that quarter having been placed on foundations of strength calculated to afford lasting peace and security, turned his attention to the great and increasing cause of the weakness of the north-west frontier of the Bengal provinces. These provinces were covered in that quarter by the territories of the Nabob Vizier of Oude, who was connected with the Company by a treaty of alliance, by which, in consideration of a subsidy amounting to a sum not exceeding 50 lacs sicca rupees *per annum*, the Company were bound to defend him; and with this view to maintain at all times at least 10,000 men in his territories; and in case this number should for any cause be increased beyond 13,000 men, the Nabob was to pay the actual expense incurred by the Company. This treaty was attended by the usual stipulation of the independence of the Nabob in his internal concerns; which stipulation had been uniformly frustrated by the necessary and uniform interference of the Company in all those concerns for the support of the Nabob's authority, for the preservation of tranquillity in the country, and for the security of the funds from which the Company derived so important a portion of the resources applicable to the payment of their military establishments.

For some years previous to 1798 apprehensions had been entertained that Zemaun Shah, the King of Caubul, would carry into execution an old and favourite plan of the Affghan government to invade Hindustan; and these apprehensions had appeared so well founded in 1798 that the Governor-General, Marquess Wellesley, had found it necessary to assemble a large British army in Oude, under the command of Sir J. Craig, for the protection of the Nabob's territories against this expected invasion, notwithstanding the difficulties under which the government laboured at the same period in the peninsula of India.

At the close of the year 1797 the Nabob, Azof ool Dowlah, died, and was succeeded in his government by his supposed son, Vizier Ali. This usurper had been formally deposed by the authority of the British government under Lord Teignmouth, after a full examination of the justice of his claim; and Saadut Ali had been placed in the government of Oude.

This prince was very unpopular with the army, and was not generally agreeable to his subjects. His disposition was parsimonious, and his habits were not of a nature to conciliate the affections of his turbulent subjects.

When the preparations were making to resist the expected invasion of Zemaun Shah, the Nabob, Saadut Ali, although fully convinced of the necessity of collecting the largest force upon the frontier, called for a detachment of the British troops to attend and guard his person against his own turbulent and disaffected troops. He declared repeatedly that these troops were not to be trusted in the day of battle, or on any service; and after viewing their state of discipline and equipment, and obtaining a knowledge of their principles and attachment to the cause of the allied governments, Sir J. Craig considered these troops as worse than useless, as dangerous, and of the nature of an enemy's fortress in his rear; and he actually left a detachment of British troops to watch them, and the turbulent inhabitants of Rohilcund, the frontier province of Oude to the north-west.

The Governor-General, by his negotiations at the court of Persia, had drawn the attention of the King of Caubul to the defence of his own western frontier; and availed himself of the certain tranquillity which he had obtained on the frontiers of Oude to arrange the affairs of that country on a basis better calculated to give it permanent security and tranquillity, and to increase the strength of the British government on its north-west frontier, which was one of its weakest points.

Towards the close of the year 1799 the Governor-General called upon the Nabob of Oude to dismiss his expensive, useless, and dangerous troops, and to fill their places by increased numbers of the Company's troops. The Nabob had desired the assistance of the Governor-General in the reform of the different establishments of his government; but the British government had a right, under the article of the treaty of 1798, to require that this reform should be made. After some difficulties, arising principally from the defective principle on which the military establishments were formed, paid, and commanded, this great object was effected; and arrangements were made for introducing into the Vizier's territories 3000 additional British troops, at the expense to the Nabob Vizier of 76 lacs of Oude sicca rupees *per annum*.

In order to improve the security of Oude still further, a reform of the civil administration of the government was necessary; and this reform was pressed upon the attention of the Nabob. But while the negotiations for this purpose, and for the final arrangement of the military establishments, were going on, the Nabob plainly declared that he was not able to pay the expense of the troops which had been stationed in his country for its defence at the time of the expected invasion of Zemaun Shah, or the expense of the additional troops which had been necessarily stationed in his country upon the occasion of the reform of his military establishments, although he was bound by treaty to defray the whole of these charges.

A demand was then made upon him to give territorial security, according to the 11th article of the treaty of 1798; and, after a long negotiation, a treaty was concluded on the 10th Nov. 1801, by which, in commutation for subsidy, and for the perpetual defence of his country, the Nabob ceded to the Company the territory of Rohilcund, the Dooab, and Gorruckpoor; the two former being his frontier provinces towards the Mahrattas, the Seiks, and Affghans, and the latter bordering upon the Company; and he engaged, further, to introduce a better system of management into the territories which remained in his hands.

By the whole of this arrangement the Company gained,

1st. The advantage of getting rid of a useless and dangerous body of troops stationed on the very point of their defence, and ready at all times to join an invading enemy:

2ndly. The advantage of acquiring the means of placing upon this weak point additional numbers of the British troops, and thereby increasing its strength, and the general security of the provinces in their rear:

3rdly. Ample territorial security for the regular and perpetual payment of these funds for the support of their military establishments in Bengal:

4thly. By the introduction of their own system of government and management into the countries ceded to them, and the employment of their own servants in the administration, they secured the tranquillity of those hitherto disturbed countries, the loyalty and happiness of their hitherto disaffected and turbulent inhabitants; and, above all, they acquired the resources of those rich but hitherto neglected provinces for their armies, in case of the recurrence of the necessity for military operations upon that frontier.

These advantages, the full benefit of which, as will be seen hereafter, was felt in a very few years, were gained without incurring any disadvantage whatever; in particular, that was not incurred which appears most likely to weaken a great continental power, such as the Company is in India, viz. the frontier was not increased. The Company were equally bound to defend, and had actually defended, this same frontier in 1798 and 1799, when the country was governed by the Nabob; so that all was gain and strength, without the smallest degree of disadvantage or weakness.

But the advantages in this arrangement were not gained by the Company only; those of the Nabob were at least equal to those of the Company. Whatever increased the security of the Company manifestly increased his security likewise; and here he acquired a great advantage. But this was not all. It is known that the Nabob of Oude had never collected from the countries ceded, and realised in his treasury, even the sum of 76 lacs of Oude sicca rupees, being the old subsidy paid under the treaty of 1798; much less had he realised the increased sum which he was obliged to pay in consequence of the increase of the number of troops stationed in his country. His pecuniary gain was the difference between the annual sum he realised and that which he was bound to pay. Under the new treaty of Nov. 1801, the Company were bound to defend the territories of the Nabob under all circumstances; and no new demand could be made upon him on any account, whatever might be the extent of the service, or of the expense incurred in their defence. The Nabob has already felt the full advantage of this stipulation.

Besides these advantages of a pecuniary nature, the Nabob derived others from the arrangement. The cession of the provinces had been preceded by the discharge of a large proportion of his troops; and those which remained in his service scattered over the whole surface of his enlarged territories, were unequal to the performance of the duties required from them. These duties could not, with convenience, be performed by the Company's Native troops, commanded as they are by European officers, as the civil government remained in the hands of the Nabob's Native servants. Both the Company's government and the Nabob suffered inconvenience; the former from the frequent calls of the Nabob for the service of their troops in the detail of the collections of the revenue; and the latter from the want of habit of these troops in duties of this description, and the difficulties of performing them through the agency of European officers directed by Native servants. When the provinces were ceded to the Company, the Nabob had the means and advantage of employing in a reduced territory the troops which had been found insufficient for the conduct of the administration of one of greater extent; and these troops, being more immediately under his inspection, and within the reach of his authority, were kept in better order.

Thus then, upon the whole, this arrangement has been advantageous, and has proved satisfactory, to both the parties to it, whatever may have been the difficulties in settling it; and Marquess Wellesley removed by it all the inconveniences and weakness felt upon the north-west frontier of Bengal, and added considerably to the resources of the British government.

The evil to which Marquess Wellesley next directed his efforts was the nature of the British alliances with its tributary states in general, and particularly with the Nabob of Arcot. The alliance between the Company and the family of this prince had commenced in the infancy of the British power in the peninsula of India, and the terms of it had been altered at different periods. The general purport of them, however, at all times, had been protection of the Carnatic by the Company, on the condition of the regular monthly payment of a stipulated subsidy by the Nabob; that the Nabob should have no political communication with any foreign power, excepting through the intervention or with the consent of the Company; that the

Company should not interfere in the internal concerns of the Nabob's government; and the last treaty of 1792 provided particularly that, in case of failure in the payment of the stipulated subsidy, certain countries should be ceded to the Company.

One of the great evils in this alliance, as in all those of this description which had been formed in India, was that it provided that the Company should not interfere in the internal concerns of the Nabob's government, at the same time that the interference of the Company in every possible case was absolutely and essentially necessary for the support of the Native government, and was practised on every occasion.

Another evil which affected this, as well as every alliance of the same description, was that the amount of the subsidy to be paid to the Company was to be realised from the country by the Nabob; and that this subsidy necessarily bore so large a proportion to the revenues which the country could afford, that it was scarcely possible to realise it so as to make the regular monthly payments required by the nature of the Company's service and stipulated in the treaty. The consequence was that the Nabob was obliged to borrow money, at large interest, to make his payments at the stipulated periods; and as the Natives were unable or unwilling to come forward to lend their money upon these occasions, the loans were made from the Company's civil and military servants, and the European inhabitants of Fort St. George and its dependencies.

The interest upon these loans was usually 3 *per cent. per mensem;* and the security for the payment of the interest, as well as the principal, was generally a tuncaw, or order, or assignment, from the Nabob, upon the revenues of certain portions of his territories. It is obvious that the tuncawdar, or holder of these orders, could have no interest in the prosperity of the country of which he was thus appointed by the Nabob the temporary collector, excepting to recover from it as he could, and at the earliest possible period, the sums supposed to be due. Here, then, was established a system which tended not only to the oppression of the inhabitants of the country, to the impoverishment of the Nabob, and to the destruction of the revenues of the Carnatic, but it was carried into execution by the Company's civil and military servants, and by British subjects.

In this view of the evil it was of enormous magnitude. The practice of lending money to the Native powers by British subjects had been repeatedly forbidden by the Company, and the continuance of it, therefore, was a breach of their most positive orders; but it was so general, and the profits so large, that no government had been found sufficiently strong entirely to prevent it. But the evil did not consist only in the ruin of the Nabob and his country, and in this breach of order and discipline, but it established at Madras, and in the subordinate territories, a body of men in the service of the Company, or living under its protection, whose interests and objects, as relative to the Nabob of the Carnatic, were different from those of the Company. On all occasions, whether trifling or important, of difference between the Company and the Nabob, the latter was certain of the advice, assistance, and active exertions of this description of men; and he never failed to succeed in his objects. It is not astonishing, therefore, that a Prince whose views were directed to an increase of his political power, and whose vanity was flattered by the services performed and court paid to him by so many Europeans of the first rank and consequence in that country, should have promoted every object which could have a tendency to continue this system, and should have set his face against every measure calculated to restrain it, although it was evidently ruinous to his finances, to the revenues of his country, and to his real interests and independence.

The countries which by the treaty of 1792 had been assigned as security to be assumed by the Company, in case of the failure in the regular payment of the subsidy, were among the richest of all those under the government of the Nabob; and it had been particularly provided by the treaty that tuncaws should not be granted upon these districts. Those who lent His Highness their money, however, had no objection to take these countries as their security; and it was natural that the Nabob should feel a slighter degree of interest in the permanent prosperity of those countries than in that of the other provinces subject to his authority. Accordingly, tuncaws were generally granted, contrary to treaty, upon these provinces assigned by treaty for the Company's security; and in aggravation of the accumulated evils of this system, the Company's governments abroad had the mortification to observe the daily and increasing ruin of the resources of Fort St. George, and the deterioration of the prosperity of the provinces allotted as their security by the means of their own servants and those living under their protection. Not a month elapsed that did not afford matter of speculation whether the Nabob could continue to pay his stipulated subsidy; and not one in which he did not procure the money by loan at a large interest, by means which tended to the destruction of the country.

From the time the operation of the treaty of 1792 was observed, every Governor had endeavoured to prevail upon the Nabob to consent to an alteration of it, by which the Company's resources should be secured, and the evils above described should be prevented. The endeavours, however, of Lord Buckinghamshire, Marquess Wellesley, and Lord Powis, equally failed in prevailing upon the Nabob to consent to a modification of the treaty; and when the war broke out with Tippoo, the country was labouring under all the accumulated disadvantages of the system, its resources were ruined, and its inhabitants, from long oppression, disaffected.

Besides these evils, there was a manifest indifference, or rather disaffection, in the Nabob, Omdal ool Omrah, himself, to the cause of the British government and its allies, the meaning of which was not discovered till Seringapatam was taken, and the papers of Tippoo had fallen into the hands of the British government. Among them were found all the written communications and correspondence which had been carried on between the Nabob Mahomed Ali and the Nabob Omdal ool Omrah, his son, and Hyder Ali and Tippoo Sultaun, without the knowledge of the Company's government.

The fact of the existence of the correspondence alone was a breach of the treaties by which the Nabobs of the Carnatic had been allied to the British government; but in addition to this fact it was found that the correspondence referred to objects under discussion by the different parties to it, and entirely inconsistent with the principle of the connexion between the British government and the Nabobs of the Carnatic, with the terms of the treaties by which that connexion had been formed, or the existence of friendly intercourse between any states in any part of the world.

As soon as Marquess Wellesley had ascertained all the circumstances attending these communications, by an examination of the persons who had been instrumental in carrying them on, he referred the whole subject to the authorities in England, and stated in detail his sentiments on the conduct of the Nabob, and on the measures which it would be advisable to adopt. These sentiments having been approved, his Lordship proceeded to carry into execution the measures which he had proposed to adopt.

His Lordship's principles on this question were, generally, that the Nabobs, by their communications with Hyder Ali and Tippoo Sultaun, had broken their treaties of alliance with the Company; and that in consequence of this breach of treaty the Company had a right to act in the manner that best suited their own interest. That which best suited their own interest was, to take into their own hands the entire management of the civil and military government of the Carnatic; giving to the Nabob, for the support of himself and his family, such a proportion of the revenues as should be sufficient for those objects, provided His Highness would acquiesce in the arrangements which should be carried into execution. These principles were considered to apply equally to the son, or supposed son, of the Nabob Omdal ool Omrah, as it was obvious that he could claim to inherit the authority of his father in the Carnatic, and the advantages derived from the connexion with the Company, only under the treaties between the Company and his family, all of which had been broken by the correspondence carried on with Hyder Ali and Tippoo Sultaun, by Mahomed Ali and Omdal ool Omrah.

When the orders from Marquess Wellesley upon this subject reached Madras, the Nabob Omdal ool Omrah was in such a state of health as to be incapable of attending to business; and soon afterwards he died. The supposed son was then apprised of the discoveries which had been made at Seringapatam, of the sentiments of the British government in consequence of these discoveries, and of the measures which they proposed to adopt in the Carnatic. But he refused to accept the situation held out to him under the new arrangement. As the claim of this Prince to succeed to his father, supposing that circumstances had allowed of the succession, was by no means clear, and as it was desirable for the peace of the Carnatic that the Nabob's family should adopt the arrangement, Lord Clive (now Earl of Powis) determined to set aside Ali Hussein entirely, and to propose it to Azeem ool Dowlah, the eldest legitimate son of Ameer ool Omrah, who was the second son of the Nabob Mahomed Ali, and brother of the late Nabob Omdal ool Omrah. This Prince having agreed to the arrangement, a treaty was concluded by which the whole of the civil and military government of the Carnatic was transferred for ever to the Company; and the Nabob Azeem ool Dowlah, and his heirs, were to preserve their title and dignity, and to receive one fifth part of the net revenues of the country.[1]

Thus was this important arrangement concluded in a peaceable manner, by which a remedy was provided for all the evils which had attended the former connexion between the Company and the Nabobs of the Carnatic; additional security was given to the British government, and an addition of 800,000*l.* *per annum*, value of 20 lacs of star pagodas, was made to their pecuniary resources. This improvement in their situation was not attended by any extension of their frontier (for the Company was bound before, both by treaty and positive interest, to defend the same line of country), or any circumstance which tended to weaken the British government in the Carnatic.

The arrangement, the nature of which I shall next discuss, is the treaty of 1800, with the Nizam. It will be recollected that the treaty of 1798, which had been a remedy for some of the inconveniences existing at that time in the connexion between the Company and the Nizam, had been directed principally to the object of enabling His Highness to perform his part of the triple alliance of 1790, formed against the power of Tippoo Sultaun, in which object it had completely succeeded. But in reference to the Nizam, there were objects in contemplation also at that moment, which could not be carried into execution; and some inconveniences had grown out of the treaty of 1798 for which it was necessary to provide an early remedy. Between the years 1792 and 1798 the power of the government of the Nizam had fallen under the influence of the Mahrattas. This power had large claims upon His Highness; some founded upon the treaty or capitulation of Kurdlah, which claims had been afterwards modified and given up by other treaties; and others founded upon the general principle of overbearing extortion of the Mahratta government.

As will appear in a subsequent part of this paper, the Governor-General had endeavoured, in 1798, to prevail upon the Peshwah to become a party to the treaty made that year with the Nizam, and to allow the British government to arbitrate in the Mahratta claims on the Nizam's government, but without success; and the Mahrattas continued to bring forward these vexatious and groundless claims, and at different periods, as well

[1] Unless the revenue exceeded the sum of 25 lacs of star pagodas, in which case the 5th part of the excess was to be applied to purposes of military defence.

during the war against Tippoo as subsequently, Scindiah, who at that time possessed the power at Poonah, had collected armies upon the Nizam's frontier for the purpose of enforcing them.

Another evil which had existed in 1798 affecting the Nizam's government, and for which the treaty of 1st Sept., 1798, had been no remedy, was the state of the Nizam's government in relation to its tributaries, who were likewise tributaries to the Mahrattas. A considerable proportion of the pecuniary resources of the Nizam was derived from this source; but the Nizam was unable to enforce payment of his just demands, which the tributaries were encouraged by the Mahrattas to withhold from His Highness.

Under the treaty of 1st Sept., 1798, the Nizam was not entitled to the assistance of the British troops stationed in his country, either to defend him against the Mahrattas, or to assist him in overawing those of his tributaries who were likewise tributaries to the Mahrattas; and after the conquest of Mysore the British government, which by that event had become paramount in India, was obliged to determine the precise nature of the relation in which it would stand, as well to the Nizam's as to the Mahratta government, and that in which those powers should stand to each other.

It was obvious that the Mahrattas would continue to make, and would at length enforce, their unjust demands upon the Nizam's government to the length of replacing affairs at Hyderabad in the situation in which they had been left by the treaty of Kurdlah in 1795, when a Mahratta minister had governed the Nizam's territories. But this was not the only danger. The Nizam's government could not proceed unless its tributaries were brought under subjection. This measure was necessary as well on account of the pecuniary relief which it would afford to the Nizam, as because the rebellion of these tributaries was a dangerous example of insubordination to the governors and collectors of the revenue of the distant provinces of the Nizam's territories. The existence of rebellion and insubordination in any country must always be formidable to its neighbours; but it is particularly so in India: and in the years 1799 and 1800 the existence of these evils was peculiarly inconvenient to the British government, and impeded the settlement of the new government of Mysore and the conquered provinces.

After the peace of Seringapatam, therefore, the British government were compelled to advert to the means of strengthening the government of the Nizam. Those which occurred were first to encourage and aid the Nizam in raising an army, to be disciplined and commanded by European officers. It would have been impossible to provide the number of English officers which His Highness's service would have required, even if all the persons of this description who might have been prevailed upon to go to India could have been depended upon, and if the national policy in respect to India had allowed of the emigration to that country of such a large body of persons. These European officers must therefore have been foreigners, all of whom have been invariably found to be inimical to the British interests, and principally Frenchmen. Here, then, the evil would have been revived, of which the inconvenience and danger had been felt previous to 1798, and for which the treaty of 1798 had been a remedy.

The second mode which occurred was to encourage the Nizam to raise a Native army. From the treachery of the Native chiefs, from their habits of correspondence and communication with the Mahrattas, and the superiority which this nation had acquired over them in a long series of contests, nothing effectual was to be expected from this measure, and it would have led directly to place the Nizam in a state of subjection to the government of Poonah. The Mahrattas would thus have been brought to the Company's frontier in the Northern Circars, the Carnatic, and to the boundaries of the new government of Mysore. The power of the Poonah state was at that time exercised by Scindiah, who was in his own right in possession of all the Mahratta power in Hindustan. Thus one Mahratta would have had in his hands all the power from the Ganges and Indus to the frontiers of the Carnatic and Mysore; touching the Company's frontier on the whole line, and possessing the means of attacking it where he should think proper. Such a power has never appeared in India, and it is to be hoped never will!

The third mode was to extend the basis of the treaty of 1st Sept., 1798; to make it generally defensive against all powers; and, in fact, to take the Nizam under the protection of the British government.

Adverting to the state of the government of the Nizam, to the fact that it was incapable from weakness of carrying on its ordinary operations over the countries and people submitted to His Highness's authority, excepting by the assistance of a Gallo-Indian army, by means which would have subjected His

Highness to the Mahrattas, or by the assistance of the British government; and that in either of the former cases it would have fallen into the hands of our rivals or enemies, and would have been exercised to our disadvantage, there is no man who will doubt of the propriety of the arrangement made by the treaty of 1800.

But this treaty was preceded and attended by other circumstances, which, as a political measure, rendered it more necessary. It has already been stated that, since the peace of Kurdlah in 1795, the Mahrattas had never ceased to make vexatious demands upon the Nizam, supported generally by the assembling of armies upon his frontier. The remonstrances and negotiations of the British government had prevented the invasion of His Highness's territories, with a view to enforce the payment of these demands; and there is no doubt that any symptom of an intention to withdraw from his support would have been followed by their immediate conquest, in the same manner as the omission of the British government to interfere between the two powers in 1795 had been the occasion of the war, and the disasters which were followed by the capitulation of Kurdlah.

Here, then, is a new view of the case—a Mahratta conquest made of the Nizam's territories, in consequence of our moderation at least; and the conqueror placed upon our frontier.

If there had been no treaty with the Nizam, if the British had no interest in his preservation excepting what related to themselves, they would have been bound to interfere to prevent this evil.

But besides the great views of policy which rendered the alteration of the treaty of 1798 desirable, as far as related to the employment of the forces, there were other circumstances, of inferior importance certainly, which rendered expedient the other alterations made by the treaty of 1800.

Under the treaty of 1798 the British government had been bound to furnish the Nizam with a certain force, for the payment of a stipulated sum of money monthly. As was usual in all these cases, this subsidy fell in arrear; and the records of the Presidency are filled with accounts of the complaints made of the existence of these arrears, and of the measures adopted to secure their liquidation. These arrears gave rise to complaints and remonstrances from the British government, which of course must have tended to weaken the good understanding which ought to have existed between the Nizam and them; and they were equally prejudicial to the interests of both powers. The grant of territorial security for the payment of the subsidy removed all these causes of misunderstanding.

The territory which was granted to the Company was that which had been under the government of Tippoo Sultaun, and had been ceded to the Nizam by the treaties of Seringapatam of 1792 and 1799. The authority of the Nizam had never been firmly established in those countries; and the state of confusion in which they were in 1799–1800 was highly prejudicial to the British interests in Mysore, and in the Company's recently acquired countries. The Nizam's treasury had never received any thing from those countries; and His Highness had supported the Company's subsidiary troops by funds acquired from other parts of his territories. It was hoped that the introduction of a better system of government would have produced order and regularity among this hitherto turbulent people, a hope which has been completely fulfilled; and this territory now yields a revenue of , a sum fully equal to pay the expenses of the subsidiary force stationed with the Nizam, and of the administration of government in the provinces which His Highness ceded.

Under this arrangement the Company's frontier is defined by the course of the Toombuddra to its junction with the Kistna; and then by the course of the Kistna to its entry into the province of . The provinces acquired under this treaty cover the Mysore country to the northward; and have removed the source of danger to be apprehended to that newly established government, from the neighbourhood and example of a turbulent and disaffected people, paying no revenue or obedience to the government under which it is placed.

From the general view which has been given of this arrangement, it will readily be believed that the Nizam wished to accomplish it much more eagerly than the British government did. In fact, His Highness felt that before this arrangement was made his government was not in a state of security; and it will be observed that the security of His Highness's government was the principal object and motive of this treaty. Other objects were connected with this principal motive, equally interesting and advantageous to both the parties to the treaty; and upon the whole it may be said that it does not contain an article or an arrangement in which both parties were not equally interested.

The next subject to which I shall advert is the arrangement made with the Peshwah by the treaty of Bassein. It will be recollected that the Mahratta government of Poonah had been connected with the British Government by a treaty made by Lord Cornwallis on 1st Sept. 1798, commonly called the Treaty of Triple Alliance, against Tippoo Sultaun. Under this treaty His Highness was bound to assist the British government and the Nizam, in case either of these powers was attacked by Tippoo.

After the peace of Seringapatam, in 1792, the Mahrattas attacked the Nizam, and the war ended by a peace or capitulation concluded at Kurdlah, by which the Nizam ceded half his territories, placed the remainder under the influence of the Mahrattas, paid a large sum of money, gave up his minister as a prisoner, and appointed other ministers nominated by the Mahrattas. Shortly after this peace the Peshwah, Mahdoo Rao Narain, died. A contest ensued among the different Mahratta chiefs for the succession to the office of Peshwah, and the possession of the influence and power of the government, which, after various success, ended in the establishment of the present Peshwah, Bajee Rao, and the possession of all the power and influence of the government by Dowlut Rao Scindiah.

This chief already had, by right of succession to his relative Mahdajee Scindiah, all the Mahratta territories in Hindustan, situated between the rivers Nerbudda and Taptee, and the Ganges and Indus. The principal support and instrument of his government was an army disciplined and commanded by French officers, with a formidable train of artillery; and, by his influence at Poonah, he had now acquired that part of the power of the Mahratta government which was not already in his hands.

This was the general state of Mahratta affairs in the year 1798, when Marquess Wellesley assumed the government. But this power of Scindiah's was by no means consolidated. A formidable rebellion prevailed in his territories north of the Nerbudda, which was directed and encouraged by the female relations of his predecessor: and the confusion in the southern parts of the empire which had attended the progress of the contest for the possession of the power at Poonah, had not subsided upon its establishment in the hands of Scindiah.

Besides these causes of disquietude, Scindiah was not uninterested in the invasion of India by Zemaun Shah, at that time expected. The first effects of that invasion would have been felt by Scindiah; and his only hope of safety was in the assistance which he might derive from the British government.

It appears that, from this state of affairs, the Governor-

General, Marquess Wellesley, endeavoured to derive additional strength and security to every part of the British empire in India. His first object was to procure the assistance of the Peshwah in the war against Tippoo Sultaun, which was impending, according to the stipulations of the Treaty of Triple Alliance; and with this view he endeavoured first to prevail upon Scindiah to return to Hindustan for the protection of his northern frontier against Zemaun Shah; and secondly, he acquainted the Peshwah with the course of measures he was pursuing for the restoration of the power and activity of the other party to the alliance, the Nizam; and offered to adopt similar measures for the establishment and support of the power of the Peshwah.

With the object of obtaining the assistance of the Mahrattas in the war against Tippoo, was connected another equally important to the permanent interests of Great Britain in India. I have already related the effect which the existence of the Mahratta claims upon the Nizam, and the mode in which they had been enforced, had produced upon the strength of His Highness's government, and upon the general strength and efficiency of the Triple Alliance formed against Tippoo Sultaun, in 1798.

In the view which the British government must have taken of the probable issue of their discussions with Tippoo in 1798, they naturally considered the continuance of that alliance and the strength of all the parties to it as essential to the preservation of the peace of India; and in any event, even if they could have anticipated that which occurred in May, 1799, they must have considered the security of the Nizam's government to be essential to the peace and security of the British territories in the peninsula of India.

The propositions made to the Peshwah, with a view to obtain his assistance in the war, were accompanied by offers to arbitrate in the Mahratta claims on the Nizam, and were attended by a negotiation with Scindiah, to induce him to return to his territories in Hindustan, for their defence against the invasion of Zemaun Shah.

The influence of Scindiah, however, occasioned the failure of this negotiation, and the war against Tippoo was carried on and concluded without the assistance of the Peshwah.

After this event, which ended in the death of Tippoo, the destruction of his power, and the transfer of it to the British government and the allies, the principal object of the Triple Alliance of course existed no longer. The other objects of the alliance with the Peshwah, viz., the independence of his power in relation to Scindiah, and the arbitration and settlement of the Mahratta claims in his name on the government of the Nizam, still existed. The British government therefore repeated the offers which it had made to the Peshwah, accompanied by others, to allow His Highness to participate in the advantages resulting from the war, which were likewise rejected by the influence of Scindiah.

The negotiation was renewed by the Peshwah at different periods, particularly in the year 1800, when his power and the safety of his person were threatened by Scindiah ; but their object was always defeated by the influence and violence of that chief, and by the apprehension of the Peshwah of their effects in the period which must elapse between the moment in which Scindiah might become acquainted with the negotiation and that at which the British troops would be in a position to protect the Peshwah.

At length the confusion which had existed in the northern parts of Scindiah's territories from the period of the death of Mahdajee Scindiah came to a crisis towards the close of the year 1800, which drew Scindiah's attention, and required his presence in that quarter ; and here commenced a new scene in Mahratta affairs, which led immediately to the treaty of Bassein, and the subsequent transactions in which the British government have been engaged.

It has already been noticed that the female relations of the predecessor of Dowlut Rao Scindiah were at the head of a party in Hindustan, who were in rebellion against the authority of Scindiah's government. When the contest had lasted for some time, the Mahratta chief, Tuckajee Holkar, who had been next in rank and power to Scindiah, died in the year 1797; and the sons of that chief came to Poonah to arrange with the Peshwah the succession of one of them to the territories of their father. Scindiah's objects in this arrangement were to procure the succession for Cashee Rao Holkar, the legitimate son most likely to favour the pretensions and objects of Scindiah in the Mahratta empire. The wishes of the family were for Mulhar Rao Holkar, with whom were connected his illegitimate brothers, Jeswunt Rao Holkar and Vittojee Rao Holkar.

While the negotiations were going on at Poonah between these different branches of the Holkar family and the Peshwah, Scindiah, on the night of the   Sept. 1797, attacked the camp of Mulhar Rao Holkar, put him to death, seized his widow, and dispersed all his adherents, including his illegitimate brother. Vittojee Rao Holkar was soon afterwards taken in rebellion against the Peshwah, and was put to death at Poonah. Jeswunt Rao Holkar fled first to Hyderabad, and then to Nagpoor, the capital of the Rajah of Berar, where, by the influence of Scindiah, he was put in confinement; and, after a short time, having made his escape from Nagpoor, he fled into Hindustan, where he joined the army of the rebels against the authority of Scindiah's government, assembled under the influence of the female relations of his predecessor. In a short time Holkar acquired considerable influence in the councils and the army of these females, which he soon turned to his own advantage; and he suddenly attacked and plundered them, and placed himself at the head of their troops. He then increased his forces to the utmost extent that was practicable, and on the 17th and 18th July, 1801, made an attack upon a large detachment of Scindiah's regular infantry stationed at Ougein, the capital of Scindiah's government, which detachment he defeated with great slaughter, particularly of their European officers; and he plundered the city of Ougein. This event drew Scindiah's serious attention to the situation of affairs in Hindustan; and he removed from Poonah with his army in the month of Dec. 1800. [1801. Ed.] His agents, however, still conducted the operations of the Peshwah's government. His Highness's prime minister had been appointed by Scindiah; and, although His Highness's person and his councils were in some degree relieved from the previous constraint under which they had laboured for some years, no act of the government could be carried into execution without the consent of Scindiah's servants.

When Scindiah arrived in Hindustan with his army the contest between him and Holkar continued with increased violence; and at length Holkar was defeated in a great battle, which was fought at Indore, the capital of the possessions of the Holkar family, on the [14th October, 1801]. After this battle, Holkar was obliged to withdraw from Hindustan into the hilly countries between the Nerbudda and the Taptee, into which Scindiah was unable to carry the war, as his attention was still taken up by the settlement of his government in the north of Hindustan, and his armies were not re-united sufficiently from the loss sustained in the different battles which had been fought. Holkar took advantage of this respite to carry the war across the Taptee into the Peshwah's country. In the course of the year 1802 he had several engagements with the Peshwah's troops in Candeish and on the Godavery, in which he was uniformly successful, and at length, in the month of October, 1802, he approached Poonah. Scindiah had sent a small detachment of his regular infantry and a body of cavalry to join the remnant of the Peshwah's army; and on the 25th October, 1802, a great battle was fought between these armies, almost within sight of the city of Poonah, which ended in the complete defeat of the troops of the Peshwah and Scindiah. After this battle the Peshwah fled from Poonah into the Konkan, or low country on the sea-coast between Bombay and Goa. Having been pursued by Holkar's troops, he embarked at Severndroog, on board a ship which was sent from Bombay for his accommodation, and he arrived at Bassein, opposite to the Island of Salsette, on the 16th December; and Holkar remained in possession of the authority of the government of Poonah.

During the progress of Holkar in his invasion of the Peshwah's territories, His Highness the Peshwah renewed the negotiations, which had been so frequently broken off, for the assistance of the British government. These negotiations, however, were not brought to a close on the day of the battle near Poonah; and after the result of that day was known, and immediately previous to his flight, His Highness signed a paper, by which he engaged to perform all the material stipulations required by the British government as the conditions on which they would consent to give him the assistance for which he asked. These were, principally, that His Highness would allot a territorial security for the payment of the troops which the Company would detach into his country; that those troops should occupy a position within his territories; that the Company should arbitrate on the differences between him and the Nizam; and that the Peshwah should not enter into any treaty or correspondence with any foreign power excepting with the knowledge and consent of the Company.

When the Governor-General received this paper from Poonah, it was necessary that he should revise all the proceedings in the negotiations at Poonah, and all the reasonings which had led to and operated upon them; and that he should decide according to the new appearance which affairs had taken in the Mahratta empire since the late revolution.

The principle on which the negotiations at Poonah had turned since the death of Tippoo Sultaun, on the 4th May, 1799, had been, the necessity of introducing the arbitration of the British government in the disputes and claims which existed between the Peshwah and the Nizam. It was obvious that unless the British government should interfere, the Nizam must fall under the power of the Mahrattas; and for this reason the treaty of 1798 with the Nizam had been made generally defensive against all powers whatever by the treaty of October, 1800. When this treaty was concluded there existed a necessity for continuing to urge the Peshwah to admit of the arbitration of the British government in the Mahratta claims; or the British government must have been prepared for, and must have expected, war with the Mahratta nation, whenever these claims should be made, and the Mahrattas should find themselves in a condition to enforce them. The attainment of this political object, therefore, was the only one likely to ensure the peace of the peninsula of India.

The introduction of the British troops into the Peshwah's territories was a mere military question, and turned exactly upon the chance of being able to support the Peshwah's power, and of giving him sufficient authority in his own government to enable him to perform his treaty with the Company in favour of the Nizam.

The cession of territory for subsidy was the best mode of avoiding the disputes and inconvenience which had invariably attended these subsidiary alliances in other instances; and the article respecting the intercourse of the Peshwah with foreign states was rendered necessary by the nature of the constitution of the two governments, the alliances by which each was bound, and the laws which regulated their intercourse with foreign states. The necessity for this connexion with the head of the Mahratta Empire was rather increased by the successful invasion of the Peshwah's territories, and by the usurpation of His Highness's authority by Jeswunt Rao Holkar; and the circumstances which existed at the close of the year 1802, and in the commencement of 1803, afforded the fairest prospect of effecting this great object without hostilities.

Immediately after the flight of the Peshwah from Poonah, Holkar took upon himself the government of the Peshwah's territories; but finding that this arrangement was not popular, and gave offence to the chiefs in the southern parts of the empire, he appointed the son of Amrut Rao, who was the adopted son of the father of the Peshwah, Bajee Rao, to be the new Peshwah;

and Amrut Rao to be his minister, and himself to be the head of his armies. He endeavoured to obtain the consent and acknowledgment of the Nizam and of the British government to this arrangement; and while the negotiations were going on upon this subject, it is well known that he was collecting about his person all the pretenders to authority, and the disaffected subjects of the Company and their allies, that could be found; and he was preparing the documents on which he intended to found the vexatious claims of the Mahratta government on the Nizam, the territories of Mysore and Arcot. He was at the same time urging the British government to acknowledge his new dynasty at Poonah, and to interfere in the settlement of the Mahratta affairs. Scindiah, who had been informed by the Governor-General of the progress of the Peshwah's negotiations with the British government in the year 1802, and who must have been aware of the engagement which the Peshwah had signed upon his departure from Poonah, earnestly urged the British government to interfere in the Mahratta affairs, as the only mode of settling their actual confusion.

The animosity between Scindiah and Holkar still existed with the greatest violence; and in the operations which must be carried on to relieve the Peshwah and to restore his authority, there was every reason to expect that Holkar would find himself exposed singly to the hostility of all the great powers in India, and that he would withdraw from the Peshwah's territories.

Orders were therefore issued for the conclusion of a treaty with the Peshwah, upon the basis of the paper which had been delivered by His Highness to the Resident at Poonah on the day preceding his flight; and the treaty was concluded accordingly on the 31st Dec. 1802. Scindiah's minister, who, as was before related, was the Peshwah's dewan, was privy to the whole transaction; and he on the part of Scindiah, and   on the part of Cashee Rao Holkar, engaged to make good to the Peshwah a part of the expense which he should incur in procuring the interference and assistance of the British government.

The treaty having been concluded on the 31st Dec. 1802, and all the preparatory arrangements made, the British troops marched from the frontiers of Mysore on the 12th March. They were joined on their march by the principal of the Mahratta chiefs and of the Peshwah's officers in the southern parts of the Mahratta empire. The detachments of Holkar's army, which had been upon the Kistna and Godavery, successively fell back;

and the British troops formed a junction with the Nizam's army and the subsidiary British troops in His Highness's service on the 15th April, within 100 miles of Poonah. Nearly about the same time Holkar withdrew from Poonah to the northward, and left that city to be occupied by the British army. A communication was immediately opened with the Peshwah, who was at Bassein, under the protection of a detachment of the army of Bombay, and His Highness entered Poonah and took upon himself the government of his country on the 13th May.

In this manner this great arrangement was effected without the loss of a man. By a skilful and ready application of the forces and resources of the government, and by taking advantage of opportunities, the ally of the Company was restored to his dignity and to the exercise of his authority; the usurpation of a most rapacious freebooter was destroyed; and this dangerous neighbour was removed from the frontier of the Company's allies. At the same time an arrangement was made which was calculated to preserve peace between the Company's allies, and secure the weak government against the unjust claims of the strong; and, by preserving all in the relative situation in which they were at the moment the arrangement was made, to strengthen all the powers of India against the attacks of a foreign invader, and to secure its internal tranquillity.

From the knowledge which the British government possessed that Scindiah was aware of all the circumstances of the negotiations which the Peshwah was carrying on, that he had earnestly desired their interference in the Mahratta affairs, and, above all, because he must have known that they had acquired a most formidable position for their armies in the peninsula, of which nothing could deprive them excepting great military success, it was confidently expected that this arrangement would not have occasioned any subsequent hostilities.

But these were not the only grounds on which this expectation of the continuance of peace was founded. Scindiah had, in point of fact, no right to interfere in an arrangement between the Company and the Peshwah, particularly in one concluded under all the circumstances which had attended the treaty of Bassein.

The Mahratta empire has at times been considered as an institution, in some degree, of the same description with the Empire of Germany; at others it has been considered as the union of a number of chiefs possessing territory and power, acknowledging the Peshwah as their nominal head; and at others, the Peshwah has been considered as the real head of a government of which Scindiah and others were only the powerful officers. Arguments have been drawn from the supposed existence of all these imaginary forms of government to prove that the Peshwah had no right to enter into the treaty of Bassein without the consent of Scindiah and other chiefs of the Mahratta empire.

Admitting the existence of all, or any, of these forms of government (and excepting the similarity to the Empire of Germany, all have in reality existed at different periods of the Mahratta history), the fact is, and cannot be denied, that the Peshwah has frequently made treaties, not only to which none of the Mahratta chiefs consented, but to which some of them objected. For instance, the Treaty of Triple Alliance, in 1798, was objected to by Mahdajee Scindiah and Tuckajee Holkar. The treaty of peace in 1792, at Seringapatam, and of partition, was not consented to by any of the Mahratta chiefs. But if it be true that the Peshwah, who is acknowledged by those who reason upon all these different forms of government to be either the real or the nominal head of what is commonly called the Empire, cannot make a treaty without the consent of Scindiah and the other chiefs, it may be presumed that Scindiah and the other chiefs, who are supposed to be of the second rank, cannot make a treaty without the consent of the Peshwah. How is this fact? They make war and peace in their own names against whom they please, when they please, and as they please; and never use the Peshwah's name, or refer to its authority, excepting as a last subterfuge in the discussions which may attend their negotiations. In point of fact, Scindiah, instead of being a powerful subject, and in that light a party to be consulted in an agreement to be entered into by the Peshwah with the British government, was himself the guarantee of the treaty of Salbye between the same parties.

In this very capacity of guarantee of a treaty he must have been considered, and must have been in fact, independent of the two powers contracting it. Before he became a guarantee, the history of those times shows that he was independent of the Peshwah. But this very act of guarantee has always been considered important in India, particularly by the Native politicians, as it afforded complete evidence of the division of the Mahratta power.

The hopes of the continuance of peace, then, were founded as well upon the right of the Peshwah to conclude the treaty of Bassein, as upon the circumstances which attended its negotiation and its execution.

A new party, however, came forward upon this occasion, through whose means and by whose exertions a peace was patched up between Scindiah and Holkar, on which was founded a confederacy against the British government.

The Rajah of Berar had not been engaged in hostilities since the year 1780, when he had marched to the British frontier of Bengal, and had received a sum of money to desist from his hostilities, excepting during the short campaign of 1795, in which he had co-operated with the other Mahrattas against the Nizam. He was the oldest of the chiefs of the present day, and was renowned among them for his wisdom and political knowledge and skill. He had claims upon the power of the state of Poonah, from his relationship to the Rajahs of Sattarah; and he was known to have entertained serious designs of forming an union of all the Mahratta powers against the British government.

When he perceived the advantage which the British government had taken of the existence of the disputes among the Mahratta chiefs, he saw that he must become the victim of the arrangement. Holkar had been obliged to retire to the northward in front of the British troops; but he could not venture to cross the Taptee, as he would then have been exposed to Scindiah's hostility. Holkar would have been unwilling to discharge his army; he could not remain in the Peshwah's territories, or invade those of the Nizam; and his only resource to provide for their subsistence would have been to enter Berar.

The Rajah, who clearly perceived this consequence (and who has since acknowledged this motive for his conduct), determined to endeavour to organise a confederacy of the Mahrattas against the British government.

Whatever might have been the claim of Scindiah to the possession of the power of the Peshwah's government, and the degree of encouragement he gave to the conclusion of the treaty of Bassein, there is no doubt that he lost solid power by the arrangement, which he could not hope to recover. He had nothing to gain by the continuance of hostilities against Holkar; and the sacrifices which he made, and which he intended should be only nominal, were more than compensated by the advantages which he hoped to acquire from the confederacy, in which, from the efficiency and the general state of his power, he must act the principal part. Holkar could hope nothing from the continuance of his hostilities with Scindiah. The latter had driven him from Hindustan; and in the course of the years 1801, 1802, in which he had settled his government in the northern parts of India, he had acquired additional strength which he could apply in his contest with Holkar, if it should continue.

A combination of all the Mahratta chiefs, with their forces, had long been an object with the Mahratta politicians; and the plan flattered the national vanity, although it was impracticable, unless attended by great and important military successes at its outset. The Rajah of Berar, therefore, succeeded in patching up a peace between Scindiah and Holkar, none of the important articles of which were performed by either party.

Before I proceed to the relation of the events which followed the treaty of Bassein, it will be proper to discuss the justice and policy of the British government in entering into the treaty of Bassein, on the ground that they must have expected the event which followed it.

I have already pointed out the objects of the treaty, the favourable circumstances under which it was negotiated, and the probability which existed that its arrangements would be carried into execution without a war, and that it would secure the permanent peace of India. But the faithless nature of the Mahratta character, and the habits of the councils of all the chiefs, are so well known, that it may be admitted that the British government ought to have contemplated the chance of a confederacy of the Mahratta chiefs to oppose the arrangement.

Considering the nature of the materials of which that confederacy was to be formed; that the two most powerful of the chiefs entertained the most rooted and inveterate animosity against each other; that after they had signed their treaty of peace their hostilities continued, and they could not trust each other so far as to place their armies within reach of attack; that none of the chiefs trusted the other; and that the pride of all prevented them from placing the management of the affairs and the command of the armies of the confederacy in the hands of one; the British government had but little to apprehend from this confederacy, provided vigorous measures were adopted at an early period of time to oppose it effectually, and to prevent it from acquiring strength and consistency by success.

The arrangements which had been made by Lord Wellesley,

viz. the treaty with the Nabob of Oude, the treaty with the Guickowar, the arrangement at Surat, the arrangements in Mysore, the treaty with the Nizam, of October, 1800, and above all, the treaty of Bassein, afforded the most efficient means of opposing the confederacy with success. If the troops did their duty with their usual bravery, its early dissolution became certain; and by the advanced position in which the treaties of Hyderabad and Bassein placed the British troops, the evils of the war would be removed to a distance from the British territories, the seat of the resources of the government.

But it is not clear that the omission to conclude the treaty of Bassein would not have led equally to a war with all the powers of the confederated Mahratta states, under circumstances of increased disadvantage. The removal of Holkar from Poonah was absolutely necessary on every ground of justice, policy, and good faith; and if the treaty of Bassein had not been made, the British government must have aided Scindiah in effecting that object. Holkar's armies would have been defeated, and the power of his rival, Scindiah, would have been established in full vigour at Poonah. He would thus again have been in possession of all the Mahratta power from the Ganges and the Indus to the Toombuddra; and his situation would have been so far more advantageous, as in the course of the years 1801 and 1802 he had overcome the rebellion which had till then prevailed in his northern dominions, and had completely established the authority of his own government in those rich countries. His first demand would have been upon the Nizam; and here at once the Company would have come in contact with a Mahratta confederacy, but under very different circumstances of strength from that with which they were engaged in 1803. In this contest Scindiah would have been really, as well as nominally, at the head of the confederacy; he would have had no rival, or rather actual enemy, in Jeswunt Rao Holkar, and would have been able to direct all his forces against the British government. He would have had on his side, instead of against him, all the strength of the Peshwah, including, what is of no small importance, all the strength of the southern chiefs situated on the frontier of Mysore. The Company, on the other hand, would have been obliged to engage with this more formidable confederacy with diminished means and resources, as they would not have had the Peshwah and the southern chiefs on their side. But their principal loss would have been the position for their armies which the treaty of Bassein gave them. By adopting this position in the Deccan in 1803, the armies were enabled immediately to render offensive the operations of a war which had been undertaken solely for defence. In the war which must have been expected if the treaty of Bassein had not been concluded, the operations must have been defensive upon a frontier extending above a thousand miles, assailable in all its parts; and the seat of the war would have been either the heart of the territories of the Nizam, or those of the Rajah of Mysore.

Upon the whole, then, I conclude that the treaty of Bassein was a wise, just, and politic measure; that none of the chiefs had any right to interfere in it or question its stipulations; and that it was concluded under circumstances and at a time which promised that it would be followed by lasting tranquillity. If it should be contended that the British government ought to have expected, as a consequence of the treaty, the confederacy and war which happened in 1803, I answer that, with the military and political advantages they acquired by the treaty of Bassein, they had nothing to fear from that confederacy; and that if they had not concluded the treaty of Bassein they would in a few months afterwards have been involved in a war with the same power, much increased in strength and resources, and possessing superior advantages, while those of the Company, in every point of view, would have been diminished.

As soon as the British government was made acquainted with the measures which had been adopted by the Rajah of Berar to arrange a confederacy of the Mahratta chiefs against the Company, the Governor-General directed that measures should be taken to make the Rajah of Berar and Holkar acquainted with the stipulations of the treaty of Bassein, and to point out to all the chiefs the innocent and defensive nature of the treaty, and the arrangement contained in the article which provided for the security of all their rights. They were at the same time called upon to declare the nature and object of their negotiations, and their views in marching to join each other in a station at so great a distance from the Nizam's frontier. In answer to these representations, Scindiah declared that he could not say whether there would be peace or war till he should meet the Rajah of Berar. After Scindiah and the Rajah of Berar had joined their troops in a position which enabled them in one march to enter the Nizam's territories, letters were presented to them from the Governor-General, in which the nature and objects of the treaty of Bassein were fully discussed and explained. Scindiah and the Rajah of Berar wrote the following answers to these letters. In the mean time the peace between Scindiah and Holkar had been signed, although but one article of it had been carried into execution, viz. that which stipulated that Hindoo Rao Holkar, the infant and posthumous son of Mulhar Rao Holkar, should be delivered over by Scindiah to Jeswunt Rao Holkar. The object of Scindiah and the Rajah of Berar in writing these answers to the Governor-General's letter was to gain time, to allow the season of the rains to pass over, to conciliate the confidence and receive the co-operation of Jeswunt Rao Holkar, and to complete their preparations for attack on all parts of the frontier of the Company and the allies. Early measures, however, had been adopted by the British government to resist their hostilities, and their armies were completely prepared in the middle of July, 1803. It was an object of importance to bring the confederates to a decision whether there should be peace or war before the season of the rains should pass over, before they should have time to complete their preparations, and to conciliate the confidence of Holkar. Accordingly the following letter was written to them by the commanding officer in the Deccan, in answer to their letters to the Governor-General. They refused to comply with the reasonable demand contained in this letter, and the British Resident quitted the camp of Dowlut Rao Scindiah on the 3rd Aug. and hostilities immediately commenced.

It is useless to follow the operations of the British armies. It is sufficient to state, that owing to the preparations which were made, the positions which they had taken, and the favourable season in which the military operations were commenced, they were uniformly successful; the result was, the early dissolution of the confederacy, in which Holkar never joined, and that in less than two months the confederates sued for peace.

Treaties were concluded with Scindiah and the Rajah of Berar in the end of December, 1803, by which the allies gained an acknowledgment of the treaty of Bassein. The Company acquired from the Rajah of Berar the district of Cuttack, &c., by which they insured the defence of a weak part of the frontier of Bengal, and the continuity of their possessions, and the certainty of a communication at all times between the Presidency of Fort William and Fort St. George. On the north-west frontier they acquired from Scindiah all his possessions on both banks of the Jumna; by which they got that river for a frontier, and secured its navigation, an object of infinite importance to the commerce of that part of the country. They also acquired from Scindiah the town, port, and territory of Baroach, in Guzerat, by which they secured the government of the Guickowar and all the Company's interests in that quarter. Scindiah was also obliged to relinquish the influence which he had exercised over the person and power of the Mogul; and to admit the independence of all the petty states in the north of India, who, during the war, had connected themselves by treaty with the Company. By this arrangement, which affected the Rajpoot state of Jeypoor, and all the petty Rajahs to the northward of that state, the Mahrattas were removed to a distance from the Company's frontier, which was surrounded and guarded by these petty states.

The Nizam acquired by these treaties an exemption from all demands of all descriptions on his territories by the confederates. He also acquired on the side of Scindiah a defined boundary, and all the territories belonging to Scindiah which were within that boundary.

From the Rajah of Berar, the Nizam acquired the province of Berar, with the river Wurda and the hills to the northward as a frontier; by which cession he gained an addition of revenue amounting to 800,000*l.* annually.

The Peshwah acquired from Scindiah the fort and territory of Ahmednuggur, and, by an arrangement made with Amrut Rao at the commencement of the war, he had acquired the jaghire of this chief upon the Godavery. By these arrangements his territories became compact; the city of Poonah was rendered more secure, and the pretext of posting troops in the neighbourhood for the purpose of collecting the revenues of territories in that quarter was annihilated.

Besides these advantages acquired by each of the allies by this war, the British government destroyed entirely the corps in the service of the enemy, which was commanded and officered by Frenchmen, and took from them not less than 823 pieces of ordnance. The advantages resulting from these military successes will be best understood by reflecting on the difficulties and losses sustained in gaining them, and on the reputation for bravery and other military qualities acquired by our officers and troops.

During this war with the confederacy the conduct of Holkar

had been rather favourable than otherwise to the British government. This chief had employed his army in levying contributions in the countries under the government of Scindiah situated north of the Nerbudda, and in endeavours to establish the authority of his infant nephew in the jaghire of the Holkar family. When Scindiah was obliged to collect a body of troops at Ougein, in consequence of the progress made by the army in Guzerat towards that capital, Holkar proceeded to the northward, and began to plunder the Rajpoot states. Shortly afterwards, peace was concluded between the British government and the other members of the confederacy.

SELECTIONS

FROM THE

WELLESLEY DESPATCHES.

I. MYSORE.

1. Extract of Letter from the Secret Committee of the Court of Directors, to the Governor-General in Council of Bengal, dated 18th June, 1798.

Instructions on occasion of Tippoo's reported alliance with the French against the English in India.

'WE take the earliest opportunity of acquainting you that we have received information from His Majesty's ministers that a very large armament of ships, troops, military stores, &c. has been lately fitted out at Toulon, and that it sailed from thence on the 19th ult. Although the ultimate object of this armament has not been ascertained, it is not improbable, from many circumstances that have transpired, and from the spirit of daring adventure by which the French have been actuated during the present war, that its destination may be for India, either (having first taken possession of Egypt) by way of the Red Sea, or by Bussora. His Majesty's ministers have therefore informed us, that immediate measures will be taken for a considerable augmentation of the European force in the East Indies; you may therefore expect that not less than 4,000 seasoned and disciplined troops, and perhaps a larger number, may be sent to the Company's settlements with all possible expedition, part of which will, we trust, reach India not many months after the receipt of this despatch. Should the expedition, notwithstanding the measures taken by His Majesty's Government to intercept and defeat it in the Mediterranean, reach Egypt, and be destined for India by either of the routes we have mentioned, a part of His Majesty's fleet, consisting of two men of war and probably a sloop, now under dispatch for India, will be ordered to be stationed in the Straits of Babelmandel, and in the Gulph of Persia, for the purpose of intercepting any force that may be proceeding to India that way.

'A copy of a Proclamation, issued at the Mauritius in the month of March last, has been transmitted to our several presidencies by Mr. Pringle, the Company's agent at the Cape of Good Hope. We are unable to judge whether this Proclamation be in reality what its import declares it to be, and Tippoo has really conceived any hostile designs against the British empire in India, or intended merely as a feint, with a view to embroil us with that prince. Our respective Governments will, of course, have taken such precautionary measures in consequence as appeared to them necessary and applicable to existing circumstances.

'Our empire in the East has ever been an object of jealousy to the French, and we know that their former Government entertained sanguine hopes of being able to reach India by a shorter passage than round the Cape of Good Hope, and we have no doubt that the present Government would risk a great deal, and even adopt measures of a most enterprising and uncommon nature, for the chance of reducing, if not annihilating, the British power and consequence in that quarter of the world. To effect this, without the aid and previous concert of one of the Indian Powers, seems almost impossible, and would scarcely be attempted. In the present situation of India, Tippoo appears to be the fittest instrument to be employed in the furtherance of such ambitious projects.

'It is highly improbable that Tippoo should have entered into any league with the French without some apparent preparation on his part of an hostile nature in furtherance of their designs. If such, therefore, shall have been the case, it would be neither prudent nor politic to wait for actual hostilities on his part. We therefore recommend, that if you shall not have adopted the necessary measures for bringing Tippoo to a satisfactory explanation before the receipt of this despatch, that you should immediately take the proper steps for so doing, accompanying this inquiry with such a disposition of your force as may give effect to it; and should you judge, either from his answers, or from the steps he is taking, that his designs are such as the French Proclamation represents, and that he is making preparations to act hostilely against us, we think it will be more advisable not to wait for such an attack, but to take the most immediate and most decisive measures to carry our arms into our enemy's country, not failing at the same time to make known to the Powers in alliance with us the necessity of such measure, and that we have not in view a wanton attack upon our inveterate enemy with a design to augment our own power, but a necessary and justifiable defence of our own possessions, and calling upon them for the assistance they are under engagements to furnish us.

'But although we have thus recommended energy, firmness, and decision in your conduct towards Tippoo, we rely upon your using the latitude allowed you in the preceding paragraph with the utmost discretion, that we may not be involved in a war in India without the most inevitable necessity, of which necessity we leave you to be the sole judges. And as it is impossible for us to conjecture, should either the Proclamation circulated at the Mauritius be founded, or the force now in the Mediterranean be really destined for India, what measures the implacable revenge and rash enterprise of the French may induce them to undertake against the British power in India; we can only exhort our several Governments to be constantly upon their guard, and watchful against surprise, by not only keeping the troops in perfect order for action, and our forts and garrisons in constant preparations of defence, but if it shall appear necessary, by encouraging military associations amongst our civil servants and others, as in this country, which may be prepared to act on any emergency; and in carefully keeping in view every channel through which it may be possible for France to get an European force out to India, and taking precautionary measures to prevent it.

'We have transmitted copies of this despatch to our Governments of Madras and Bombay.'

2. From Mr. Josias Webbe, Secretary to the Government of Madras.

Danger of a rupture with Tippoo.

6th July, 1798.

Memorandum for General Harris, in consequence of his late conversation upon the possibility of an early rupture with Tippoo Sultaun.

That M. Malartic's Proclamation is genuine I have no doubt, because it is a termination perfectly consistent with an intrigue which, from respectable intelligence at the time, there was reason to believe on foot previous to the departure of his ambassadors for the Mauritius; but whether we should take measures at this period for punishing or preventing the effect of this negotiation, is the most momentous question which can be proposed in this place. Upon this question it is certainly my duty to state my ideas; but the shortness of time does not admit of any arrangement.

As all questions of national war should, I suppose, be determined by the national interest, it is natural to advert to the state in which India was placed by the Treaty of Seringapatam, because that state was considered at the time we had the means of changing it, as most advantageous to the British interests. The principle of our policy then was, the preservation of Tippoo as a Power of India, and the balance between him, the Mahrattas, and the Nizam by our superior influence and force. Whether this principle has been superseded by other notions in Europe I know not; but whether any attempt can now be made to introduce a new order of things without a greater danger of evil than a chance of good, I doubt.

Tippoo, if he has not advanced in actual strength, has certainly the vantage ground: the three other Powers have certainly receded from the condition they were in at the Treaty of Seringapatam. The shock which the balance between the Nizam and the Mahrattas sustained from the warfare that was allowed to terminate in the Treaty of Kurdlah has driven him from his position, and the distractions which have since prevailed at Poonah incapacitate them from holding their ordinary sphere, while the force of the English is checked and retarded by the pressure of the French war.

In the discussions which took place upon the political state of India, when the expedition against Manilla was under contemplation, it was, I believe, acknowledged that the confusion at that time in the Mahratta empire was such as to render any exertion of their strength improbable, or at least not formidable. The subsequent confinement of Nana Furnavees, the eccentric irregularity of young Scindia, and the want of power in the Peishwa, certainly corroborated that notion, which, if it then left us little to apprehend from their enmity, can now give us little to expect from their friendship. The only respectable part of the Nizam's force is under the uncontrolled command of the French party: that influence has increased, and whether our inertion during the contest between his Highness and the Mahrattas may have alienated the disposition which his ministers once manifested towards ours, whether it is the natural consequence of a prevailing interest inimical to us, we have much reason, from Captain Kirkpatrick's late correspondence, to apprehend that our weight at Hyderabad is not great. The Nizam's irregular troops proved, during the last war, one of our serious impediments: his efficient force could hardly be employed, certainly not trusted, under the command of Perron. In respect to ourselves, a very large proportion of the coast army is detached, our means of resource curtailed by the war in Europe, and our credit in this country, at least upon this coast, bankrupt. If, therefore, with all the advantages we possessed in the year 1790, with the hearty and effectual co-operation of the Mahrattas, and with the friendship of the Nizam, our operations against Tippoo were not made successful without the greatest difficulty, I am fearful that, under the general change of circumstances which I have mentioned, and which I believe to be correct, an attack upon him now is more likely to end in discomfiture than victory.

But let us descend to more particular considerations. Although we have every reason to be satisfied that Tippoo's army has been kept in a state efficient and prepared to meet the events, which there might be reason to expect from the general appearance of convulsion throughout India, yet in the same discussions on the subject of the Manilla expedition, both Sir J. Shore and Lord Hobart were of opinion that he was not likely to hazard a rupture without a very large reinforcement from the French. Whatever may be the object of Tippoo's embassy to the Mauritius, or whatever may be the event of it in Europe, the late intelligence from the islands, which leaves us no room to doubt that the military have been sent to France, and the French marine dispersed, satisfies me that no immediate co-operation can take place; and consequently, that no rupture is to be apprehended but by our own provocation.

This argument I urge in the perfect conviction that during this unprecedented contest in Europe, peace in India is indispensably necessary, and that it ought not to be risked without the prospect of positive advantage. If, however, it should be argued, that this very conjunction of circumstances which I have mentioned, should impel us to make an immediate effort against Tippoo, I answer that all our former united and unexampled exertions were made against Tippoo single, and unsupported by the French; but, single and unsupported as he was, except by the natural obstacles which oppose our progress, the exertions of the allies were only successful. For this I refer to the chance by which Bangalore fell, to the condition of Lord Cornwallis's army before the junction of the Mahrattas, in May 1791, to the difficulty with which the battering train was advanced to Seringapatam in the second campaign, to the condition of the Bombay army, and to the state in which our own army returned after the conclusion of peace. With the war well advanced, with our preparations and arrangements on foot for twelve months before, and with such a combined alliance as may be now despaired of, it still cost Lord Cornwallis two campaigns before he could besiege Seringapatam.

From the intrigues at Seringapatam, and the consequent embassy to the Isle of France, I have no doubt that the French emissaries were employed in persuading Tippoo to hostilities with us, under promises of immediate assistance. This the Sultan appears to have considered insufficient ground to provoke a war; but if he should be provoked to war by us, I conceive there would be a material difference of circumstances; for though the French might find great difficulty in persuading him to war, from the great difficulty of furnishing the force he requires, yet if he should be absolutely plunged into a war, they would find it easily practicable to foment and keep it alive. Hostility with Tippoo, if it should be known before the conclusion of peace, would inevitably tend to protract the war in Europe, or even to revive it if peace should have been made. The French, despairing perhaps of any successful attempt upon England itself, would leave nothing unattempted to subvert, or at least curtail, our

Indian empire. This argument is of the more force, because a very small increase of French soldiers is a very material addition to Tippoo's strength.

In the event of hostility, I take it for granted the object will be to make it a war of alliance against Tippoo. I doubt that it is practicable to obtain the assistance of the Mahrattas: the present disunion of the chiefs renders a hearty co-operation impossible. The assistance of any party, if even it could be persuaded to risk the danger of absence from its own territories, might have the natural effect of throwing its adversaries into the opposite scale. If such an event should take place, the Mahrattas would remain, as they now are, balanced against each other, while Tippoo, freed from the apprehension of their united force, would be at liberty to employ his whole cavalry against us. It is known to every officer in the field, that during the last war the Nizam's cavalry were a heavy incumbrance to us; and if, notwithstanding the apparent change in Azim ul Omrah's dispositions towards us, we should be disposed to rely on the fidelity of his Royal Highness's infantry under the command of M. Perron, it is not extravagant to anticipate an event which has already happened, that marching into the Mysore country with his Highness in alliance, we were compelled to march back again with his Highness in alliance against us. In respect both to the Mahrattas and the Nizam, I think there is no reasonable ground to expect effectual assistance from either until we should strike some signal blow. Neither of them were hearty in the cause during the last war before the fall of Bangalore.

Not to dwell upon the possible predicament in which we should be placed by a refusal of the allies to execute their engagements, let us look to our own means of equipping a force sufficient to support a remonstrance to Tippoo upon his embassy to M. Malartic. It must never be forgotten that the army under General Medows in the month of November, 1790, consisted of about 5,500 European and 18,400 native *seasoned* men, and that even this army was augmented by troops from Bengal before it marched against Bangalore. By the returns you have now received, a body of about 14,000 men can be drawn together, including Lascars and pioneers; a force so inadequate to an offensive war, that you could not venture to quit the Carnatic. From Ceylon you could draw no reinforcements; but, on the contrary, might be called upon to increase the force on that island in the event of our army invading the Mysore country. The whole reinforcement must be sent from Bengal; of what extent it could be we have no means of judging, but it is obvious that it must be so large as to place its arrival here at a very remote distance. The superiority of Tippoo in cavalry, and the greater rapidity with which he moves, would render it impracticable to proceed to the attack of Seringapatam without establishing a systematic chain of posts for depôts of stores and provisions. That he has endeavoured to frustrate this is evident from his policy in the destruction of Ossoor and Bangalore, and in making Seringapatam his only or principal fortification. By the former it is his intention to increase the difficulty of our approach by lengthening the line of our operation, and by the latter to oppose such impediments as to make the capture of Seringapatam impracticable in the course of one campaign. The Cauveryporam pass is yet unexplored; but I understand that the route from thence to Seringapatam lies through a barren country, so much interspersed with jungle as to be extremely adverse to the march of an army. The Gugulhelts pass is no longer thought of. As nothing therefore short of the capture of Seringapatam can justly be considered as striking an effectual blow against Tippoo, the achievement of any immediate success appears to me to be utterly impracticable.

This idea, then, of striking an immediate blow being abandoned, let us look to the slow and regular equipment of an army for the invasion of Mysore. The different corps could, I believe, be assembled at Walajahbad in about two months from the time of their being ordered to march. The equipment of bullocks for the army, with its train of field artillery, could not, according to my estimation, be accomplished before the month of January; but in respect to a train of battering guns, sufficient for the siege of Seringapatam, I can form no notion; nor do I believe Mr. Cockburn can, of the time when it could be furnished with cattle. This period of the season (January) is, by the experience of Lord Cornwallis's campaign, too late for the establishment of a depôt at Bangalore and the siege of Seringapatam in the same season; for though we should be able to put Bangalore in a state to admit of its becoming a depôt, we could not avoid being overtaken at Seringapatam by the monsoon, which sets in in May. Hence the necessity of a second season, and probably of a second equipment of bullocks, before an efficient army could invest Seringapatam. Supposing it however there, and joined by the Bombay army (the difficulty of which it is here unnecessary to consider), I doubt whether there are any well-grounded expectations that they could feed themselves. The experience of Lord Cornwallis's army proves that we were unable to supply ourselves, or to open our rear for the admission of Brinjaries until we had been joined by the Mahratta army, and the whole country embraced.

At present there is no grain at Arnee or Vellor, and I believe no considerable quantity could be stored in the forts of the Bara-Mahal before the harvests of November. The vessels which bring grain from the northern ports and from Bengal do not arrive here before the months of September and October.

Upon the whole there are sufficient grounds for concluding that the whole of the coast army which could be assembled would be incapable of offensive operations, and that they could not be put in motion before the month of January. How far, and at what period, they may be in a condition to make a serious attack upon Tippoo must depend upon the extent and time of reinforcements from Bengal; and as nothing of consequence could be undertaken without them, the time of our making any serious impression must be proportionably delayed.

Meanwhile the movement of our troops and military preparations could not escape the vigilance of Tippoo: his resources are always more prompt than our own; and, as great part of his army is said to be in a state of field equipment, our attempt to strike a blow at him is likely to produce an invasion of the Carnatic before we are in a situation to resist him; for, as Tippoo can, in my opinion, have nothing to apprehend from the Mahrattas, his whole attention will be directed to us. A comparison between his own and his father's wars, with the late experience of his own misfortunes, has taught him that our strength depends upon our supplies. The crops of the Bara-Mahal would be his first object; and the consequences of such a policy, which he has manifested by the demolition of Bangalore and Ossoor, might fix the war in the Carnatic, until by the consumption of our supplies, and the failure of our resources, we should be compelled to accept his terms of peace.

When the war of 1790 begun, the funded debt of this Presidency was 17 lacks of pagodas, the Company's credit high, and the rate of interest low. Very large subscriptions were in consequence made within the course of a few days to a 12 per cent. loan; large supplies of dollars brought hither in the Canton ships, and intended for the China investment, were converted to the purposes of the war, and immense remittances were made from Bengal, as well in specie as by bills. At present the funded debt of this Presidency is 51 lacks of pagodas; the Company's credit so low, that their eight per cent. paper bears a discount of 18 and 20 per cent.; and the scarcity of money so great, that their 12 per cent. bonds do not pass but at a discount of 4 per cent. Every mode has been tried without effect to raise money at this Presidency: our only means of supply is from Bengal. The bills which we have in consequence been long compelled to substitute for ready money payments have overstocked the market, and consequently pass at a discount. After repeated and urgent applications for money, we have been disappointed for want of funds in Bengal; and at this very moment, when the expenses of the military establishment for the ensuing months cannot be provided for without specie from thence, the only sum which we can confidently expect is, as I understand, immaterial in comparison with our wants.

The deficit in the present resources of this government is at least 18 lacks of pagodas; the expense of an army of 14,000 men in the field is, pag[s] , and the expense of providing carriage for them, pag[s] 34,700 per month.

Nothing can be more urgent than our representations to Bengal upon the state of our finances, except the necessities which produced them. It is a fact. that without assistance in money from thence, our military expenses, upon the peace establishment, cannot be provided for beyond the month of September. I am afraid, therefore, that far from being in a state to equip an army for the field, we shall scarcely have the means of marching the different corps to Walajahbad, while the state of the treasury renders it utterly impracticable to make any suitable advance for draft and carriage cattle.

I have not studied to exaggerate any part of this memorandum; but seeing that our resources have, by the mere operation of the war in Europe, been reduced to a state of the greatest embarrassment, and having no hope of effectual relief but in peace, I can anticipate none but the most baneful consequences from a war with Tippoo. If this war is to be a vindication of our national rights, it is clear that we cannot undertake it in less than six months; and this delay, with a reference to our national interests, may probably admit of its being postponed till we attain sufficient strength to prosecute it with vigour. But if war is inevitable, and the present are judged the most advantageous circumstances under which it can commence, I fear that our situation is bad beyond the hope of remedy.

This memorandum only reaches to that period at which your military inquiries commence, they will require no less serious reflection, and must occupy the thoughts of those who are to direct as well as of those who are to execute the operations of the war. For myself, I ought to apologize for the freedom of these opinions, but the desultory manner in which they are stated, will acquit me of all premeditated intention to give offence, and time does not admit of any amendment.

J. WEBBE.

3. Minute of the Governor-General in the Secret Department.

'Casus Belli' against Tippoo. Reasons for delay. Defensive alliance system explained and vindicated. Proposed conduct of the Anglo-Indian Government towards the Sultan.

The Governor-General. Fort William, August 12, 1798.

In communicating to the Board an authentic copy of the proclamation issued by the Governor-General of the Isle of France, during the residence of the Ambassadors of Tippoo Sultaun in that island, I informed the Board that I would prepare the detail of such measures, as appeared to me most advisable, for the purpose of frustrating the united efforts of Tippoo Sultaun and of France. Accordingly I have laid before the Board, for that necessary purpose, a number of propositions, connected in their principle as well as in their object, and I have endeavoured to carry the proposed system of measures into execution with every practicable degree of diligence and despatch. When it is remembered that I did not take charge of this Government until the 18th of May, that the proclamation did not make its first appearance at this Presidency until the 8th of June, and was not authenticated here until the 18th of June, I trust it will appear that I have proceeded with as much expedition as was compatible with the due consideration of the various and important questions which demanded my decision. Although the leading objects of the several propositions which have been adopted by this Government may be collected from my late correspondence with the Governments of Fort St. George and Bombay, and with the Residents at Poonah and Hyderabad, it may be useful to review, with more particularity, the circumstances which have suggested this system of measures to my judgment. My present intention, therefore, is to explain and illustrate the principles upon which that system is founded, the means by which I hope to carry it into effect, and the ends which I expect to accomplish by its ultimate success and permanent establishment. In this retrospect of my conduct, I shall disclose, without hesitation or reserve, the whole train of reflections which has passed in my mind during the agitation of this intricate and extensive subject; and I shall avow, without disguise, every successive variation of my opinion, and every instance in which I have reluctantly submitted my unaltered judgment to the pressure of practical difficulties; nor shall I deny that I have ultimately pursued a course, far within the limits of that, to which the sense of my own duty and character, the clearest principles of justice and of policy, the unquestionable rights and interests of the Company, and the honour of the British name in India, would have directed me, if the obstacles to my progress had not appeared absolutely insurmountable.

The various considerations which have successively engaged my attention may be stated in the following order:—

First,—The nature and character of the recent proceedings of Tippoo Sultaun.

Secondly,—The rights and interests of the Company, and the principles of my duty arising out of those proceedings.

Thirdly,—The circumstances which might suspend or limit the actual exercise of those rights, the immediate and complete establishment of those interests, and the satisfactory discharge of that duty.

Fourthly,—The intermediate precautions which might be adopted during the suspension of more effectual measures, and the securities which might now be provided against the return of our actual danger.

The first consideration required an attentive examination of the proclamation issued at the Isle of France, together with all the collateral circumstances accompanying that extraordinary publication. The proclamation made its first appearance at Calcutta in a newspaper of the 8th of June.

Upon the first view of the subject, I was much inclined to doubt the authenticity of the proclamation. It seemed incredible that, if the French really entertained a design of furnishing aid to Tippoo, they would publicly declare that design, when no other apparent end could be answered by such a declaration, excepting that of exposing the project in its infancy to the observation of our Governments, both at home and in India, and of preparing both for a timely and effectual resistance. It did not appear more probable that Tippoo (whatever might be his secret design) would have risked so public and unguarded an avowal of his hostility; however, even under these circumstances, I thought it advisable to transmit a copy of the proclamation to the Governor of Fort St. George, in a private letter of the 9th of June, apprising him that, if the proclamation should prove authentic, it must lead to a serious remonstrance from this Government to Tippoo, the result of which remonstrance must be uncertain; my letter, therefore, directed him to turn his attention to the means of collecting a force upon the coast, if necessity should unfortunately require such a measure.

The first regular authentication of the proclamation which I received was contained in the letter from Lord Macartney, of 28th of March, and in that from Sir Hugh Christian of the same date, received on the 18th of June. It could now no longer be doubted that the proclamation actually had been issued by the Governor-General of the Isle of France. Still, however, it might have remained a question whether this step might not have been taken without the concurrence of Tippoo Sultaun, and for the promotion of some separate object of the French Government, unconnected with his interests and unauthorized by his consent. From the accounts which I had received of the state of the Isle of France, I was led to believe that the object of Mr. Malartic might have been to clear the Island of the adherents to the cause of the present Government of France, rather than to afford any effectual assistance to Tippoo. It appears, however, from a more accurate investigation of evidence, that the ship (which first conveyed to the Isle of France those accounts of the last revolution in France, and of the violent measures projected against the Isles of France and Bourbon, which occasioned the late disturbances at Port Nord Ouest, and the expulsion of the French national troops from thence) did not reach the Isle of France until Tippoo's Ambassadors had departed from thence on their return to Mangalore. The assistance afforded to Tippoo cannot therefore have been connected with the recent commotions in the Isle of France. However, I do not apprehend, unless some new revolution shall happen in the Isle of France, that Tippoo Sultaun will be able to derive any considerable aid from that quarter. But whatever may have been the motives of Monsieur

Malartic in this transaction, the object of Tippoo Sultaun was always plain and clear, although, fortunately for our interests, his success has not yet been answerable to the extent of his design. Of the object of that design, I soon possessed ample proof, arising from the best evidence which the nature of the case could admit. In the first place it appeared, by the general tenor of the letters from the Cape, as well as by every public account which had been given of the transaction, to be an undisputed fact, that Tippoo despatched two Ambassadors to the Isle of France, and that the proclamation in question was published subsequently to their arrival and during their residence in that island. These facts would perhaps have been sufficient, without further inquiry, to warrant a strong presumption that this proclamation, purporting to declare the object of the embassy, must have been framed with the consent and knowledge of the Ambassadors of Tippoo, then on the spot, and must have corresponded with their instructions from their sovereign, whose orders they would scarcely have ventured to exceed in a matter of such serious consequence as the conclusion of an alliance, offensive and defensive, with the French. In order, however, to obtain the most accurate information with respect to the circumstances attending the reception of the embassy, the publication of the proclamation, and the conduct of the Ambassadors, I examined, upon oath, some respectable persons who were present in the Isle of France during the residence of the Ambassadors at Port Nord Ouest. From the concurrent testimony of these persons, since corroborated by intelligence from various quarters, I obtained a connected account of the whole transaction.

Tippoo despatched two Ambassadors, who embarked at Mangalore for the Isle of France, and arrived there at the close of the month of January 1798. They hoisted Tippoo's colours upon entering the harbour of Port Nord Ouest, were received publicly and formally by the French Government with every circumstance of distinction and respect, and were entertained during their continuance on the Island at the public expense. Previously to their arrival, no idea or rumour existed in the Island of any aid to be furnished to Tippoo by the French, or of any prospect of a war between him and the Company. The second day after the arrival of the Ambassadors, an advertisement was published of the same purport as the proclamation, and immediately afterwards the proclamation was fixed up in the most public places, and circulated through the town. One of the

Ambassadors was perfectly conversant with the French language. A person accompanied the embassy from Mangalore, who was habited in the Turkish dress, who spoke French and English with uncommon correctness and fluency, and who appeared to possess considerable knowledge and talents, and to be well acquainted with most of the country languages of India. This person had been known at Bussorah by the name of Abdoolah, at Surat by that of Derwish, and in the Isle of France passed under that of Talamas, under which last name he had also passed in Bengal, where he resided for some years. The Ambassadors (far from protesting against the matter or style of the proclamation) held, without reserve, in the most public manner, the same language which it contains with respect to the offensive war to be commenced against the British possessions in India; they even suffered the proclamation to be publicly distributed at their own house. Talamas's conversation, though with more caution and mystery, corresponded in substance with theirs. In consequence of these circumstances, an universal belief prevailed in the Island, that Tippoo would make an immediate attack upon the British possessions in India, which opinion had gained so much force, that the persons who gave this evidence, and all those who arrived at that period in India from the Isle of France, expected to find us at war with Tippoo, but they all concurred in declaring, that the temerity of Tippoo's design had excited general ridicule in that Island. The Ambassadors were present in the Island when the French Government proceeded to act under the proclamation in question, and they aided and assisted the execution of it, by making promises in the name of Tippoo for the purpose of inducing recruits to enlist; they proposed to levy men to any practicable extent, stating their powers to be unlimited with respect to the numbers of the force to be raised. The Ambassadors aided and assisted in the levy of 150 officers and privates for the service of Tippoo, under the terms and for the purposes of the proclamation. Few of the officers are of any experience or skill, and the privates are the refuse of the lowest class of the democratic rabble of the Island. Some of them are volunteers, others were taken from the prisons and compelled to embark, several of them are Caffres and people of half-cast. With such of these troops as were volunteers, the Ambassadors entered into several stipulations and engagements in the name of Tippoo.

On the 7th of March, 1798, the Ambassadors embarked on

board the French frigate *La Preneuse*, together with the force thus raised, and they publicly declared an intention of proceeding to the Isle of Bourbon, with the hope of obtaining more recruits for the same service.

The proclamation, therefore, originated in the arrival of the Ambassadors at the Isle of France, was distributed by their agents, was avowed in every part by their own public declaration, and finally was executed according to its tenor by their personal assistance and co-operation.

The proclamation itself furnished the most powerful internal evidence of the concurrence of the Ambassadors in all its essential parts, the principal facts stated therein are—

'That Tippoo Sultaun, through two Ambassadors despatched for the purpose to the Isle of France, had addressed letters to the colonial assembly of the Isle of France, to all the Generals employed there, and to the Executive Directory of France, and had made the following propositions:—

'1st. That he desired to form an alliance, offensive and defensive, with the French, and offered to maintain at his expense, during the continuance of the war in India, whatever troops should be furnished by the French, and to supply (with the exception of certain stores) every necessary for carrying on the war.

'2d. That he had given assurances that all his preparations were already completed, and that the generals and officers would find everything necessary for carrying on a species of war, to which Europeans have not been accustomed in their contests with the Native Powers in India.

'3d. That he only waited for the succour of France to declare war against the English, and that it was his ardent desire to expel the English from India.'

Upon the ground of these facts, the proclamation recommends a general levy of men for the service of Tippoo; and it concludes by assuring 'all the citizens who shall enlist, that Tippoo will give them an advantageous rate of pay and allowances, *which will be fixed by his Ambassadors*, who will also engage, in the name of their sovereign, that the Frenchmen who shall have enlisted in his army, shall never be detained there after they shall have expressed a desire of returning to their native country.'

The avowed purport of this proclamation is to acquaint the inhabitants of the Island with the propositions made by Tippoo

Sultaun, through his Ambassadors then on the spot. It enumerates those propositions with a particularity of detail which could never have been hazarded in the presence of the Ambassadors if the facts stated had not been correctly true, or if the propositions enumerated had varied in substance from those communicated by the Ambassadors under the orders of their sovereign. But the last paragraph of the proclamation connected with the conduct of the Ambassadors as already described, establishes in the clearest manner their participation in the whole transaction. That paragraph contains a direct reference to the powers of the Ambassadors, and engages on their behalf that they shall enter into certain stipulations in the name of their sovereign with respect to the pay and final discharge of such French subjects as shall enlist in his army under the conditions of the proclamation. The accounts which I have received from the Isle of France concur in stating, that the Ambassadors openly acted under this part of the proclamation, and in the name of Tippoo entered into engagements and stipulations with the recruits according to the assurances specified in the proclamation. Monsieur De Bue, now master attendant at Mangalore, stated to one of the witnesses whom I examined, the whole substance of the engagements which had passed personally between him and the Ambassadors, all of which engagements referred immediately to Tippoo's intention of commencing war upon the Company, with the aid of the French force then about to be levied; and it is certain that without some such engagement not a man would have been raised in the Isle of France for the service of Tippoo. It appears from the evidence which I have collected, that the Ambassadors had not brought to the Isle of France a supply of treasure sufficient for advancing bounty money to the recruits. It was stated that an apprehension of the English cruizers had prevented the embarkation of treasure for this purpose, and no doubt was entertained that if the Ambassadors had been better provided with money, they might have raised a much greater number of men, who refused to engage on the mere security of promises in the name of Tippoo.

The Ambassadors, together with the force thus collected during the time of their mission in the Isle of France, landed from the frigate, *La Preneuse*, at Mangalore, on the 26th of April, 1798. Accounts vary with respect to the exact number of the force landed; the most probable are that it did not exceed 200 persons. Tippoo (far from manifesting the least symptom of disapprobation of the conduct of his Ambassadors in any part of the transaction) formally received them, and the officers and leading persons so landed with public marks of honour and distinction. One of his Ambassadors resided for some time with the French recruits in a fortress near Mangalore, and the Sultaun has admitted the whole levy of officers and men into his service. Referring, therefore, to the conduct of the Ambassadors in the Isle of France to their arrival at Mangalore with the force levied in consequence of their mission, and finally to the reception of the Ambassadors and of the French recruits by Tippoo Sultaun, the following conclusions appeared to me to be incontrovertibly established:—

First,—That the Ambassadors despatched by Tippoo Sultaun to the Government of the Isle of France proposed to that Government an alliance, offensive and defensive, against the British possessions in India, which alliance was accepted by that Government, and its acceptance formally notified by a public proclamation.

Secondly,—That the Ambassadors were charged with letters from Tippoo Sultaun to the Executive Directory of France, which letters were stated to contain the same proposition, and that the Ambassadors delivered these letters to the Governor-General of the Isle of France for the purpose of transmission to France.

Thirdly,—That the Ambassadors, in the name of Tippoo Sultaun, gave public assurances that he had actually completed the necessary preparations for commencing immediate hostilities, and that he only waited the arrival of succours from the French to declare war against the Company, for the express purpose of expelling the British nation from India.

Fourthly,—That the Ambassadors demanded unlimited military succour from the French, and levied a military force in the Isle of France with the declared object of commencing immediate war against the British nation in India.

Fifthly,—That this force has been actually landed in Tippoo's country, and publicly admitted into his service with signal marks of approbation; and that the Ambassadors have been received with similar distinction.

Sixthly,—That Tippoo Sultaun (by receiving with public marks of approbation his Ambassadors, who had concluded in his name an offensive and defensive alliance with the French; and by admitting into his service the military force raised for effecting the objects of that alliance) has personally ratified the engagements contained in the proclamation of the Governor-General of the Isle of France, and has proceeded to act under those engagements conformably to the tenor of that proclamation.

Seventhly,—That although the succour actually received by Tippoo Sultaun under his offensive alliance with the French is inconsiderable, yet the tenor of the proclamation, the proposition made to the French Government for unlimited military aid, &c. &c., and the declarations of the Ambassadors prove, that it was the intention of Tippoo Sultaun, to receive into his service the largest force which he could obtain, for the purpose of commencing a war of aggression against the Company in India.

Having thus entered into offensive and defensive engagements with the enemy, having proceeded to collect in conjunction with the enemy, a force openly destined to act against the possessions of the Company, having avowed through his public Ambassadors, that he has compleated his preparations of war for the express purpose of attempting the entire subversion of the British Empire in India, and having declared that he only waits the effectual succour of the French to prosecute offensive operations; Tippoo Sultaun has violated the treaties of peace and friendship subsisting between him and the Company, and has committed an act of direct hostility against the British Government in India.

Before I proceeded to apply the principles of the law of nations to the conduct of Tippoo Sultaun, it appeared proper to enquire what had been the conduct of the Company towards him for some years past, and whether he had received any provocation to justify or to palliate his late proceedings.

Since the conclusion of the Treaty of Seringapatam, the British Governments in India have uniformly conducted themselves towards Tippoo Sultaun, not only with the most exact attention to the principles of moderation, justice, and good faith; but have endeavoured by every practicable means to conciliate his confidence, and to mitigate his vindictive spirit. Some differences have occasionally arisen with respect to the boundaries of his territory bordering upon the confines of our possessions on the coast of Malabar; but the records of all the British Governments in India will shew, that they always manifested the utmost anxiety to promote the amicable adjustment of every doubtful or disputed point; and that Tippoo Sultaun has received the most unequivocal proofs of the constant disposition of the Company to acknowledge and confirm all his just rights, and to remove every cause of jealousy, which might tend to interrupt the continuance of peace.

The servants of the Company in India have not however been ignorant of the implacable sentiments of revenge, which he has preserved without abatement since the hour of his last defeat. It has always been well understood, that Tippoo Sultaun's resentment was not to be appeased by any conciliatory advances on our part, nor by any other means than the recovery of his lost power, the disgrace of the British arms, and the ruin of the British interests in India. With such views it was expected that he would eagerly embrace the first favorable occasion of striking a blow against our possessions; and his intrigues at the Courts of Hyderabad and Poonah, together with his Embassy to Zemaun Shah, (although managed with such a degree of caution as to avoid the appearance of direct acts of aggression,) were sufficient indications of an hostile mind. But none of these circumstances have in any degree affected the conduct of the Company's servants towards him, and the correspondence between him and the late Governor-General, and the letters from Bombay on the subject of the district of Wynaad, furnish ample proofs of a sincere desire to bring that question to a fair issue, '*with the consent and knowledge of both parties,*' according to the tenor of the 7th article of the treaty of Seringapatam; I appeal to the letter which I despatched to him soon after my arrival in Bengal, proposing an amicable adjustment of the same question, as well as of his recent claims upon certain parts of the district of Coorga, for a testimony of the pacific spirit which has marked my first communication with him; although, perhaps, a less mild representation might have been justified, by his unwarrantable precipitation in stationing a military force on the frontier of Coorga, before he had made any trial of the prescribed and regular channels of negociation. Tippoo Sultaun cannot therefore alledge even the pretext of a grievance to palliate the character of his recent acts; he has indeed alledged none, but has constantly professed the most sincere desire to maintain the relations of amity and peace with the Company. In his letters to Sir John Shore (written a short time before the return of the Mysorean Ambassadors from the Isle of France, and received at Fort William on the 26th April,

1798, the day on which the French force landed at Mangalore) Tippoo declares, 'that his friendly heart is disposed to pay every regard to truth and justice, and to strengthen the foundations of harmony and concord established between the two states.' And he signifies his desire that 'Sir John Shore would impress Lord Mornington, with a sense of the friendship and unanimity so firmly subsisting between the two states.'

This is not the language of hostility, nor even of discontent. From what disposition in the friendly heart of Tippoo these amicable professions have proceeded, how they are connected with a regard to truth and justice, or calculated to strengthen the foundations of harmony and concord, and to impress me with a sense of the Sultaun's friendship, can now admit of no question, since it is now proved, that these letters were written at the very moment, when Tippoo was in anxious expectation of the hourly arrival of that military succour, which he had solicited from the enemy for the express purpose of commencing a war of aggression against the Company's possessions.

The motive therefore of Tippoo Sultaun, was no other than that avowed in his correspondence with the enemy, and published under the eyes of his own Ambassadors, '*an ardent desire to expel the British nation from India.*'

It appears highly probable, that he was instigated by the promises and exhortations of the Government of France, (whose emissaries have reached his councils) to hasten the execution of a project, in which every consideration of interest, and every sentiment of passion would induce the French to embark with a degree of zeal, ardour, and rancour not inferior to his own.

The importance of these possessions to all the most valuable interests of Great Britain, has pointed the particular attention of the Government of France to the destruction of our empire in India. The prosperity of our settlements in India, has long been the primary and undisguised object of the jealousy of France, avowed by all her ministers in every negociation, and by all her rulers in every stage of her innumerable revolutions; Tippoo therefore might reasonably hope, that if the cessation of hostilities on the continent of Europe, should at any time enable the French Directory to turn their views to the disturbance of the peace of India, such an adventure would be among the earliest of their operations.

The conclusion of a peace upon the continent of Europe, the weak state of the internal Governments of Poonah and

Hyderabad, the existing dissentions, apparently precluding all co-operation and concert between those two powers, added to the growing strength of a French faction in every part of India, may have appeared both to Tippoo and to the French to offer a favorable opportunity for the prosecution of their joint design. The premature disclosure of this design may perhaps be imputed rather to the policy of M. Malartic, than to the imprudence of Tippoo; whether the scope of that policy was to involve us in a war with Tippoo, or to expose his treachery to our view, is yet a matter of doubt; but whatever circumstances occasioned the premature disclosure of the design, whether the design was wisely or rashly conceived; whether it has partially succeeded, or entirely failed, are questions, the solution of which in no degree affects the offensive nature of an aggression so unprovoked, and of a violation of faith so flagrant and unqualified. The history of the world scarcely furnishes an instance, in which any two powers have united in confederacy or alliance precisely with the same motives. The party proposing an offensive alliance against the Company, cannot be absolved from the consequences of such an act, by any apparent or real indifference in the party accepting such a proposal. The conduct of Tippoo Sultaun, therefore, cannot be correctly estimated by reference to the supposed motives of Monsieur Malartic. From the application of the acknowledged principles of the law of nations to the facts of this case, I formed my judgment of the rights of the Company, and of my own duties with reference to the aggression of Tippoo. The course of reasoning which I pursued may be stated in the following manner.

The rights of states applicable to every case of contest with foreign powers, are created and limited by the necessity of preserving the public safety; this necessity is the foundation of the reciprocal claim of all nations to explanation of suspicious or ambiguous conduct, to reparation for injuries done, and to security against injuries intended.

In any of these cases, when just satisfaction has been denied, or from the evident nature of circumstances cannot otherwise be obtained, it is the undoubted right of the injured party to resort to arms for the vindication of the public safety; and in such a conjuncture, the right of the state becomes the duty of the Government, unless some material consideration of the public interest should forbid the attempt.

If the conduct of Tippoo Sultaun had been of a nature which

could be termed ambiguous or suspicious; if he had merely increased his force beyond his ordinary establishment, or had stationed it in some position on our confines or on those of our allies, which might justify jealousy or alarm; if he had renewed his secret intrigues at the Courts of Hyderabad, Poonah and Cabul, or even if he had entered into any negociation with France, of which the object was at all obscure; it might be our duty to resort in the first instance to his construction of proceedings, which being of a doubtful character, might admit of a satisfactory explanation. But where there is no doubt, there can be no matter for explanation. The act of Tippoo's ambassadors, ratified by himself, and accompanied by the landing of a French force in his country, is a public, unqualified and unambiguous declaration or act of war, aggravated by an avowal, that the object of the war is neither explanation, reparation, nor security, but the total destruction of the British Government in India. To affect to misunderstand an insult and injury of such a complexion would argue a consciousness either of weakness or of fear; no state in India can misconstrue the conduct of Tippoo; the correspondence of our Residents at Hyderabad and Poonah sufficiently manifests the construction which it bears at both those Courts; and in so clear and plain a case, our demand of explanation would be justly attributed either to a defect of spirit or of power, the result of such a demand would therefore be, the disgrace of our character, and the diminution of our influence and consideration in the eyes of our allies, and of every power in India. If the moment should appear favourable to the execution of Tippoo's declared design, he would answer such a demand by an immediate attack; if, on the other hand, his preparations should not be sufficiently advanced, he would deny the existence of his engagements with France, would persist in the denial until he had reaped the full benefit of them; and finally, after having completed the improvement of his own army, and received the accession of an additional French force, he would turn the combined strength of both against our possessions, with an alacrity and confidence inspired by our inaction, and with advantages redoubled by our delay. In the present case the idea therefore of demanding *explanation* must be rejected, as being disgraceful in its principle, and frivolous in its object. The demand of *reparation*, in the strict sense of the term, cannot properly be applied to cases of intended injury, excepting in those instances, where the nature of the reparation demanded may be essentially connected with security against the injurious intention.

Where a State has unjustly seized the property, or invaded the territory, or violated the rights of another, reparation may be made by restoring what has been unjustly taken, or by a subsequent acknowledgment of the right which has been infringed; but the cause of our complaint against Tippoo Sultaun, is not that he has seized a portion of our property which he might restore, or invaded a part of our territory which he might again cede, or violated a right which he might hereafter acknowledge; we complain, that, professing the most amicable disposition, bound by subsisting treaties of peace and friendship, and unprovoked by any offence on our part, he has manifested a design to effect our total destruction; he has prepared the means and instruments of a war of extermination against us; he has solicited and received the aid of our inveterate enemy for the declared purpose of annihilating our Empire; and he only waits the arrival of a more effectual succour to strike a blow against our existence.

That he has not yet received the effectual succour which he has solicited, may be ascribed either to the weakness of the Government of Mauritius, or to their want of zeal in his cause, or to the rashness and imbecility of his own Councils; but neither the measure of his hostility, nor of our right to restrain it, nor of our danger from it, are to be estimated by the amount of the force which he has actually obtained; for we know that his demands of military assistance were unlimited; we know that they were addressed not merely to the Government of Mauritius, but to that of France, and we cannot ascertain how soon they may be satisfied to the full extent of his acknowledged expectations. This, therefore, is not merely the case of an injury to be repaired, but of the public safety to be secured against the present and future designs of an irreconcileable, desperate and treacherous enemy: against an enemy of this description, no effectual security can be obtained otherwise than by such a reduction of his power, as shall not only defeat his actual preparations, but establish a permanent restraint upon his future means of offence.

To this species of security our right is unquestionable, upon the grounds already stated. But it cannot be supposed that Tippoo Sultaun will voluntarily concede to us a security of this nature against the effects of his own resentment, treachery and ambition, and against the success of the most favorite projects of his mind.

Since, therefore, the principles of justice and of the law of nations entitle us to such a security, and since we cannot possibly obtain it by the voluntary concession of Tippoo Sultaun, it is the right of the Company to compel him to yield it; and it is equally my duty to use that compulsion without delay, provided the interests of the Company committed to my charge be not more endangered by the attempt, than by the unrestrained progress of his preparations for war.

In proportion to the continual progress of Tippoo's preparations, he will acquire more decisively the advantage of holding in his hands the issues of peace and war, together with the power of selecting the time and mode of his long meditated attack upon our possessions. He has not yet obtained any formidable accession of strength from his alliance with France, nor is it probable that any such accession will reach his country within a short period, certainly not before the close of the monsoon on the coast of Malabar; while he shall retain the ready means of intercourse by sea with the French Government, it cannot be doubted that they will use every endeavour to assist him with military aid, and to instigate him to war. The arrival of one or two French regiments would probably induce Tippoo to commence offensive operations, and the assistance even of so small a body of Frenchmen might become alarming in the actual state of the native armies of India. The systematic introduction of French officers into the service of all the native powers, is described by Mr. Wickham as the fixed policy of France, adopted with a view of establishing the most certain means of subverting the foundation of our power. This system has been pursued in the armies of the Nizam, of Scindiah, and of many other inferior powers with unremitting assiduity, and extensive success. If Tippoo should be allowed to derive from France such succour as would induce him to act offensively against us, his earliest movements would probably be seconded by the general insurrection of the various bodies of French adventurers, who are incorporated in the service of the several native powers, and who maintain a concert and correspondence in every quarter of India. Under such circumstances, it would be prudent to take advantage of the actual crisis, in which the hostile design of Tippoo has been clearly manifested, but the means of accomplishing it have happily disappointed the ardor of his hopes. In this moment of his comparative weakness, of his disappointment, and of his probable dejection, no policy could be more wise than to strike such an instantaneous blow against his possessions, as should effectually frustrate his preparations for war, and should render him unable to avail himself of the aid of France whenever it may arrive.

The inconsiderable amount of the force which he has already received from France, while it cannot limit our just right to reduce his power, affords a strong argument of policy in favour of an immediate attack.

It is therefore evident that the rights and interests of the Company concur to demand from this Government every practicable effort to anticipate the execution of his projects of vengeance by attacking him on all sides without delay. In this train of reasoning I was confirmed by adverting to the general tenor of the orders of the Court of Directors, and of the proceedings of this Government with reference to the contingency of a French force landing at any time in the territories of Tippoo Sultaun.

The orders of the Court of Directors uniformly enjoin that the landing of a French force in Tippoo's country should be 'the signal for our attack upon him.' The construction of those orders by the late Governor-General in his instructions to the President in Council of Fort St. George of 12th September, 1796, appears to have been, that the number of the French force should be *considerable* in order to justify our attack. But I am persuaded that the real intention of the late Governor-General in those instructions, could not have been to declare, that the justice or policy of attacking Tippoo was hereafter to be measured solely by the magnitude of any French force landed in his country.

It is certainly true that, on the one hand, the landing of a considerable French force in Tippoo's country would be an unquestionable indication of his hostile intentions against the British power, while on the other hand the landing of a few French officers and privates, and even their admission into the service of Tippoo, might, under certain circumstances, be supposed to manifest nothing more than a disposition to improve the general discipline of his armies, without implying any formed design of war against the Company or their Allies. This, I am persuaded, is the only view in which the late Governor-General in Council could consider the magnitude of the French force landed in Tippoo's country as the foundation of a rule for limiting the discretion of the Company's governments in such a contingency. On the present occasion, the hostile intentions of the Sultaun are unequivocally manifested by the proclamation, by the declarations and conduct of his Ambassadors, and by their demand of French troops to an unlimited extent. Connected with these circumstances, the landing and admission into the Sultaun's armies, even of a less considerable force than that which he has received, would be deemed, under the just construction of the opinions both of the Court of Directors and of this Government, 'a signal for our attack upon him.'

My determination, therefore, was fixed to attack Tippoo with every degree of practical despatch.

The objects which appeared to me the most desirable, as well as the most easily attainable, were,—First, To seize the whole maritime territory remaining in his possession below the Ghauts on the coast of Malabar, in order to preclude him from all future communications by sea with his French allies.

Secondly, By marching the army from the coast of Coromandel directly upon his capital, to compel him to purchase peace by a formal cession of the territory seized on the coast of Malabar.

Thirdly, To compel him to defray our whole expense in the war, and thus to secure the double advantage of indemnifying us for the expense occasioned by his aggression, and of reducing his resources with a view to our future security.

Fourthly, To compel him to admit permanent Residents at his Court from us and from our Allies, a measure which would enable us at all times to check his operations, and to counteract the intricacies of his treachery.

Fifthly, That the expulsion of all the natives of France now in his service, and the perpetual exclusion of all Frenchmen, both from his army and dominions, should be made conditions of any treaty of peace with him.

With this plan in view, I directed that the army upon the coasts of Coromandel and Malabar, and at Bombay, should be immediately assembled; and I entertained a very sanguine hope that active operations might have been commenced so early as, with the co-operation of his Majesty's squadron on the coast of Malabar (which Rear-Admiral Rainier had promised), might have secured the effectual reduction of Tippoo's power before any assistance could have reached him from France. But I never proposed to undertake any attack upon him, of which the success could be doubtful in the judgment of those whose opinions must always govern my discretion in every question of military detail.

The avowed designs of Tippoo, the state of his preparations for war (which, notwithstanding his late disappointment, was certainly forward as far as regarded his own troops), the uncertainty of the motives which might impel the violence of his temper to action, and my knowledge of the indiscreet zeal with which he has frequently pursued his favourite object of revenge against the British power, all concurred to urge the necessity of placing ourselves in a state of preparation for war at least equal to that of his army. These measures appeared to me not matters of choice, but of indispensable duty. I could not suffer the security of the Carnatic to rest on so precarious a foundation as the forbearance of Tippoo Sultaun and of his French allies. To resume the power of meeting him in the field, and to replace in our hands the option which he then possessed, of accommodating the time of attack to circumstances and events, appeared to me to be the most prudent step which could be immediately adopted, whatever might hereafter be the service to which our force might be applied. The orders, therefore, which I gave for assembling the army (although pointed more particularly at the execution of the plan of operations, which I have just now detailed) were founded upon principles independent of the practicability of that plan, and were connected not only with the immediate defence of the Carnatic, but with other comprehensive measures of permanent precaution and security, to which my views have been extended at every period of this crisis.

When I submitted my ideas of the time and objects of the proposed attack upon Tippoo to those military authorities, which I shall always consider with respect, it seemed to be their opinion, that the state of our army admitted no doubt of the ultimate success of the plan which I had proposed. If its speedy accomplishment had appeared to them as certain as its ultimate success, I should not have hesitated a moment in directing the commencement of offensive operations; but I found that, instead of deriving to the interests of the Company the inestimable advantages of a sudden and rapid reduction of Tippoo's means of offence, the result of such an attempt was likely to lead to a tedious, protracted, and expensive, although ultimately successful, war. The obstacles which arose were of a nature not to be surmounted by any degree of present activity or resolution, although they originated in causes which I trust may be removed by future diligence and perseverance.

The result of my earliest enquiries convinced me that radical defects existed in the military establishments on the coast of Coromandel, which would render it impossible to put our army in that quarter in motion soon enough to effect the object which I proposed. The opinions which I received from military authorities here, with respect to the impossibility of making any sudden or speedy military movement on the coast of Coromandel, were afterwards confirmed by the concurrent testimony of the Governor of Fort St. George, and of the Adjutant-General of that establishment. I have entered into a particular consideration of this testimony in a Minute recorded in the Secret Department of the 20th July, to which I desire to refer on this part of the subject. The letter of the Government of Fort St. George of the 10th of July proceeds far beyond the limits of any opinion which I had ever formed or heard with respect to the difficulty of restraining the hostility of Tippoo; in that letter the President in Council even deprecates the ordinary precautions of defence, lest they should draw down the resentment of the Sultaun upon our unprotected possessions.

The expense of a protracted war, and the evil effects which such a calamity must produce on the trade of the Company, upon their pecuniary affairs at home, upon the welfare of their subjects in India, and upon the general state of the public revenue and credit of Great Britain, now pressed with great weight upon my mind, and the embarrassment of our finances aggravated all the difficulties of my situation. The question was now entirely changed; the plan which I had originally had in contemplation was nothing more than a military expedition of short duration, of no heavy expense, and of certain success, with the additional advantage that success would certainly exonerate our finances, and throw the whole expense of the undertaking upon the enemy, who had provoked it. But it now appeared that I could not hope to effect any of my proposed objects without encountering the expense and inconvenience of a long war.

In this state of the question, the condition of our Allies occurred as an insuperable obstacle to our progress. Although the assistance of the Peishwa and of the Nizam might not have been deemed indispensable in an expedition of the nature which I have described; I have always been apprized that an offensive war of any long duration in Mysore would be difficult, if not impracticable, without the effectual aid of the Peishwa and of the Nizam, in facilitating the supplies of provision to our army in the field.

The state of the Courts of Hyderabad and of Poonah afforded no hope of their early co-operation with us; and although I had determined to take the most expeditious measures for restoring both our Allies to the power of fulfilling their defensive engagements with us, I could not expect to derive any benefit from those measures for a considerable period of time; and it would have been imprudent to have undertaken offensive operations, with the prospect of a continued war, until the efficiency of our alliances had been previously secured. Under the accumulated pressure of all these difficulties, I felt, with the utmost degree of disappointment and regret, that the moment was unfavourable to the adoption of the only measure which appeared to me sufficient to satisfy the rights and interests of the Company and the exigencies of my own duty; I was therefore compelled to relinquish the idea of striking an immediate blow against the possessions of Tippoo Sultaun. But the circumstances which thus suspended the actual exercise of the rights and the immediate establishment of the interests of the Company, could not absolve me from the duty of providing, without delay, every degree of intermediate security which might now be attainable, by adopting such a system of preparation and defence as might enable us to repel any attack which Tippoo might make upon us, or to support any demand of satisfaction, which we may eventually deem it advisable, in concert with our Allies, to make to him.

The sense of this duty induced me to propose to the Board the several orders and instructions which have been forwarded to the Governments of Fort St. George and Bombay, and to the Residents at Poonah and Hyderabad, from the 8th of July to the present time.

The principles upon which these instructions and orders are founded will be best illustrated by referring to the nature of our actual danger, as well as to the causes which have contributed to produce it.

No comprehensive or satisfactory view can be taken of this subject without adverting to the whole system of our defensive alliances with the Native States, and to the various circumstances which have effected or which now influence the general balance of power in India.

The primary objects of the Treaties of Poonah and Paungul, combined with the Treaty of Seringapatam, were to diminish Tippoo Sultaun's means of future aggression, by reducing his resources and territory, and to provide an efficient defence against him by strengthening the Peishwa and the Nizam, by uniting their interests with ours, and by securing their co-operation in any future war with Mysore. On the other hand, a part of the policy of the Treaty of Seringapatam seems to have been to preserve to Tippoo Sultaun that degree of power which might enable him to maintain a balance with the Mahrattas and the Nizam in such a manner that the interposition of our force might always turn the scale.

It is evident that the policy of this system has been entirely frustrated by the course of recent events, and that neither the Peishwa, the Nizam, nor Tippoo Sultaun now retain the same relative position which they held at the conclusion of the Treaty of Seringapatam, either with respect to one another or to our interests.

Since the conclusion of the peace of Seringapatam, the power and resources of the Court of Hyderabad have been constantly declining. The disgrace which fell upon the Nizam's arms in the unfortunate contest with the Mahrattas at Kurdlah reduced the military character of the Court of Hyderabad to the lowest point of degradation. The treaty in which that defeat terminated completed the humiliation of the Nizam; he was compelled to sacrifice a large portion of territory, to engage to pay a fine of three crores of rupees, and to submit to the captivity of his minister, Azim ul Omra, who was carried a prisoner to Poonah. Azim ul Omra resided at Poonah during the late convulsions in the Mahratta Government; and, although a prisoner, bore a very distinguished part in supporting Nana through the various revolutions which followed the sudden death of the Peishwa, Mahda Row. For these services Nana agreed to relinquish all the benefits acquired by the Peishwa against the Nizam, under the Treaty of Kurdlah.

But the Peishwa, Bajee-row, having called in the assistance of Scindiah to check the overgrown power of Nana, Scindiah persuaded the Peishwa to violate the engagements concluded with Azim ul Omra; and the event has been, that the Peishwa has insisted upon and obtained from the Nizam a cession of one-fourth part of the territory, and the payment of one-fourth part of the fine stipulated by the Treaty of Kurdlah.

In addition to so heavy a loss, both of power and honour, the internal resources of the Nizam's Government have not yet recovered the derangement occasioned by the rebellions of Ali Jah, and the son of Darah Jah; by the unfortunate contest with the Mahrattas; and by the detention of Azim ul Omra at Poonah.

The effect of these causes has necessarily been to reduce the consideration of the Nizam in the scale of the neighbouring states; and in this weak and degraded condition he has been for some time past menaced by the army of Scindiah, stationed in the neighbourhood of Poonah. But the most striking feature of change in the state of the Nizam's affairs since 1793, is the alteration which has taken place in his military establishment. The Nizam, since the peace of Seringapatam, has greatly reduced his cavalry and other troops, and considerably augmented the body of infantry commanded by French officers, and known by the name of Raymond's corps.

The corps of Raymond had been in the service of the Nizam before the last war with Tippoo Sultaun, and in 1792, when it served with Lord Cornwallis's army, its strength was not greater than 1,500 men at the highest estimation, and its discipline very defective. At the battle of Kurdlah, in 1795, its strength amounted to about 11,000 men. During the rebellion of Ali Jah, and in a variety of service in which the corps has since been employed, it has acquired experience and skill, and it is now composed of thirteen regiments of two battalions each, amounting in the whole to upwards of 14,000 men. Its discipline, according to every recent account, is very considerably improved, insomuch that, although inferior to our native force, it is said to be superior, in nearly an equal proportion, to the ordinary scale of the infantry in the service of any of the Native Powers. Besides field pieces to each regiment, a park of 40 pieces of ordnance, chiefly brass, from 12 to 36 pounders, with a well-trained body of artillery men (including a number of Europeans) is attached to the corps. A foundation has also been laid for raising a body of cavalry to act with the corps of infantry. The chief officers of this corps are all Frenchmen of the most virulent principles of jacobinism; many of the privates served originally with the French native force at Pondicherry, and the whole corps constitutes an armed French party of great power, zeal, and activity. The efforts of this party are continually employed to magnify the power, resources and success of France, and to depreciate the character, force, and credit of Great Britain in the eyes of the Court at Hyderabad; and it appears by authentic intelligence, that wherever any detachment of this corps has been stationed for any considerable time, a most unfavourable impression has been produced against the character of the British nation.

The death of Monsieur Raymond, which happened a few months past, appeared likely to impair the influence of this corps at the Court of Hyderabad; and accordingly Azim ul Omra took that opportunity to resume the large Jaghire which had been allotted for the pay and maintenance of the corps, but another Frenchman of the name of Peron has succeeded to the command: his disposition is described to be violent and brutal; and his principles do not appear to differ essentially from those of Raymond. The corps, as now constituted, forms the most considerable and only efficient part of the Nizam's military establishment, and retains such a degree of ascendancy over the councils of the Nizam, as to be an object of serious alarm to Azim ul Omra.[1] This corps has been recruited, in the proportion of one-third of its total numbers from our territories, and from those of the Nabob of Arcot, and partly from deserters abandoning our service.

Distinct proof has been given of the assiduity and success of the emissaries employed by Monsieur Baptiste (the second in command to Monsieur Peron, and stated to be of a very designing and artful character) for the purpose of exciting mutiny and sedition, and of inviting desertion amongst our sepoys stationed on the frontier of the Nizam's dominions. A considerable desertion of our troops took place in that quarter some time ago, and nearly 500 men, with several native officers, who deserted on that occasion, are now serving in Monsieur Peron's corps. The repeated applications of our Resident for the surrender of these deserters have hitherto been frustrated by the prevailing influence of Monsieur Peron and of his army, and by the weakness of the Nizam's Government, which Azim ul Omra has declared to be unable to control the overbearing spirit and

[1] In addition to the command of this corps, M. Raymond had the entire conduct of the Nizam's Ordnance, with an allowance of 50,000 rupees monthly; the Ordnance has since been placed under the command of M. Peron, and he derives great influence from so important a charge.

formidable power of the French faction. After a protracted negociation, Azim ul Omra has at length, with much difficulty, and by an extraordinary effort, obtained the surrender of two Subadars, who were the principal contrivers of the desertion.

Monsieur Peron and his officers maintain a correspondence with a faction at the Nizam's Court denominated the Paugah party, being composed principally of the officers of his Highness's body guard of cavalry.

The Paugah party has long been connected with Tippoo Sultaun, and is entirely adverse to Azim ul Omra, and to all the friends of the British interests at the Court of Hyderabad.

It must not be forgotten, that in the year 1796, during the detention of Azim ul Omra at Poonah, the French faction, with the assistance of the Paugah party, prevailed upon the Nizam to dismiss the British detachment, and took such measures in concert with Tippoo (a large body of whose army marched in this crisis to the frontier of the Nizam's dominions) as would have enabled them to dispose of the succession to the Musnud according to their pleasure, if the Nizam's death had happened in that critical conjuncture. At this period of time, the French contrived to obtain the grant of the large Jaghire, since resumed; this grant (which comprized the district of Maiduck, containing[1] 2,142 square British miles, situated to the northward of Hyderabad, and producing an annual revenue of eighteen lacs of rupees) may be considered as the first step towards the establishment of a territorial revenue; and there can be no doubt that it would have led to that necessary foundation of European power in India, if the death of Monsieur Raymond had not enabled Azim ul Omra to frustrate the project. The French officers at Hyderabad maintain a direct correspondence with their countrymen in the service of Tippoo Sultaun, and of Scindiah. The latest accounts from the Resident at Hyderabad state, that French officers and adventurers arrive continually at Hyderabad to reinforce Monsieur Peron's corps, although the routes by which they gain access to the Deccan are as yet unknown.

This French party, connected as it is with the prevailing factions in the Court of the Nizam, corresponding with Tippoo Sultaun, zealous in the cause of France, and actuated by a spirit

[1] The Company's Jaghire in the Carnatic contains 2,436 square British miles.

of intrigue, which would lead it to mix in every distraction of the State, if not to originate internal confusion, must be considered as a circumstance of positive weakness in the frame of the Government of Hyderabad. Azim ul Omra is fully aware of the magnitude of this evil, and dreads the growth of a party which he can no longer restrain within any bounds of moderation, and which already threatens to subvert his power, and to disturb the regular order of succession, if not to destroy the throne itself. With respect to our interests, and to the value of our defensive alliance under the treaty of Pangul, the change in the Nizam's military establishments places him in a condition worse than that of absolute inefficiency, and renders the Court of Hyderabad a source of additional strength to our enemies, rather than of useful assistance to any branch of the Triple Alliance. The dangers to be apprehended from the existence of Peron's corps are not to be estimated merely by the actual state of its discipline, of its numbers, or of its influence over the councils of the Nizam: our views of this danger must be extended beyond the present moment. The French army at Hyderabad must be considered not only as a powerful aid to the cause of France in the present crisis, but as the basis of a permanent French faction in India; on which, according to the opportunities of fortune, and the variation of circumstances and of events, the activity of the enemy may establish a strength of the most formidable kind, either in peace or war.

It requires no labour of argument to prove the benefits which must be derived to the cause of France, even in time of peace, from the establishment of an army of 14,000 men, commanded by natives of France, in the heart of the dominions of one of our principal allies, in the vicinity of our most active enemy among the native powers, and on the borders of a vulnerable part of our own dominions. In the event of peace, no more convenient channel could be provided for the intrigues of France, no more useful point of union for the numerous adherents to her principles, and emissaries of her designs. And it cannot be doubted, that the natural effect of the unchecked and rapid growth of such an army at the Court of the Nizam must be, to detach that Court from our interests, and to fix it absolutely in those of our enemy.

But in the event of a war with Tippoo Sultaun, or in the still more aggravated case of a war with him, aided by a French force, what assistance can we expect from the Nizam, the main body of whose army is commanded by the correspondents of Tippoo, natives of France, distinguished by their zeal in the cause of that country, and united with the whole body of French adventurers now established in India?

Under such circumstances, the force of the Nizam would become useless and even dangerous to us, precisely in proportion to the exigency of the case, in which we should require its services.

If the French troops of the Nizam did not afford Tippoo open assistance, at least they could not be brought into the field against him without the utmost danger to our cause; nor could they be suffered to remain in the Deccan during the continuance of the contest, unless checked by the presence of an equally powerful force, which must, in that case, be diverted from the objects of the war, and must operate as a positive diminution of our effective strength in the field. It appears however nearly certain, that in the present weak state of the Nizam's Government, the French corps in his service would openly join Tippoo Sultaun, and by a sudden blow, endeavour to seize the Nizam's territories, and to secure them to the dominion of France, under an alliance offensive and defensive with Tippoo Sultaun. This danger is aggravated by the present position of Scindiah's army, and by the disposition and present views of that Chief; he now entertains a large body of infantry in his service under the command of a French officer; and it might be expected that he would readily engage with Tippoo Sultaun (with whom he is supposed to have lately opened a negociation) and with the French, upon the conditions of a partition of the territories and authority of the Peishwa and of the Nizam. The junction which might thus be effected by the French officers in the several armies of the Nizam, of Scindiah, and of Tippoo, might establish the power of France in India upon the ruins of the States of Poonah and of the Deccan. Under all these circumstances therefore it is evident, that the Court of Hyderabad in its present condition (whatever may be its disposition to use every effort for our assistance) is not only disqualified from co-operating with us as an ally against Tippoo, but furnishes him with powerful means of prosecuting his designs against us, and offers every temptation to the ambition of France.

Such being the condition of the Nizam, it will be found that the Peishwa, who forms another branch of the triple alliance against Tippoo Sultaun, is not more able to fulfil his defensive engagements with us.

The precise situation in which the Mahratta Empire stood after the peace of Seringapatam, was the most favourable to our interests: the several co-estates were then so equally balanced as to prevent any danger of that degree of union which might concenter the formidable force of the whole in one consolidated mass, either against the British possessions, or against any other established power in India; nor had any one member of the Empire attained such a degree of strength as to be able singly to encounter our force. On the other hand, the Peishwa, the acknowledged and constitutional head of this extensive confederation, aided by the abilities of his Minister Nana Furnavese, possessed a sufficient influence over several of the leading Chiefs to render him a respectable ally, and to furnish him with the means of bringing a considerable force into the field.

From the period of the peace of Seringapatam to that of the death of Mahda Row, the danger appears to have been, that the address of Nana might have drawn too great a weight into the scale of the Peishwa's power, and have enabled the Government of Poonah to wield the united force of the whole Mahratta Empire. At the battle of Kurdlah the Peishwa was assisted against the Nizam by the contingents of most of the confederate chieftains of the Mahratta Empire; and the power of the Nizam was greatly endangered in that state of the Peishwa's authority and force. But Nana's ambition or jealousy having induced him, upon the sudden death of Mahda Row, to attempt the disturbance of the regular order of succession by intruding an adopted child upon the throne, opened the way to those successive intrigues and revolutions which for some time past have distracted the Mahratta Empire. Without pursuing the various changes and convulsions of the Government of Poonah during the period described, it is sufficient to observe, that their progress naturally tended to weaken the Sovereign power, and has terminated in the imprisonment of Nana, in the ruin of his influence, and in the suspension of the power and authority of the reigning Peishwa, under circumstances which menace the abolition of his office.

Scindiah, who in this changeable scene has alternately taken part with the present Peishwa and with Nana, has at length overpowered both, and has been for some time past so far master of the Government of Poonah, that the Peishwa could not, in his present condition, command the co-operation of any considerable body of the Mahratta chieftains, nor afford us any assistance against Tippoo Sultaun.

During the course of the events which have contributed to weaken and degrade the Governments of Poonah and Hyderabad, their mutual animosities and opposition of interests have risen to such a height as to render all co-operation between them utterly impracticable. The efficiency of our system of defensive alliance against Tippoo Sultaun has therefore been impaired, not only by the respective weakness of each of our allies, but by the difficulty of uniting them in any common view or joint operation.

In the meanwhile Tippoo Sultaun has enjoyed a state of internal tranquillity nearly uninterrupted. While our allies have been distracted and exhausted by faction, rebellion, revolution and war, he has been employed in improving the discipline of his armies, and in repairing the vigour of his resources; he has alternately endeavoured, but without success, to gain the Peishwa and the Nizam to his cause; he however possesses a considerable influence at the Court of Hyderabad, in consequence of his connections with the corps of Râymond, and with other factions adverse to the British interests at that Court. It is also known, that he despatched an embassy to Zemaun Shah, whose design of invading Hindostan has been recently announced in a formal manner to this Government, and to the Nabob Vizier.

That Zemaun Shah really entertains the romantic project of invading Hindostan cannot admit of a doubt; this was the opinion of the late Governor General, in which I entirely concur.

It has been supposed that Zemaun Shah, in his late march towards Hindostan, was recalled from Lahore into his own dominions, either by some domestic dissention, or by the apprehension of an attack from some of the States in the neighbourhood of his Kingdom. And it was hoped that the same causes might for some time obstruct the execution of his declared project, but the last despatches from the Acting Resident at the Court of Scindiah state a report, that Zemaun Shah is now relieved from all apprehensions, either of internal rebellion or of foreign invasion; and his inclination as well as his ability, to move his army towards the frontier of Hindostan, at the close of the rainy season, are now universally credited. It must be recollected, that upon a recent occasion, Zemaun Shah advanced to Lahore without meeting any formidable opposition from the Seiks; although it had formerly been asserted, that the country of the Seiks would always prove an insuperable obstacle to his progress. Between the country of the Seiks and the frontier of Oude no barrier exists to check the motions of the Shah, excepting the power of Scindiah. The dominions of Scindiah at present are so weakened by internal dissentions as to be in a state nearly defenceless, while Scindiah continues at Poonah with the main body of his army, and while his tributary Chiefs, remaining in Hindostan, are notoriously disaffected to his cause, and are prepared to seize any favourable opportunity of annihilating his power.

Zemaun Shah cannot be ignorant of these advantages, and if they should tempt him to invade Hindostan, the diversion of our force which would be occasioned by such an event, would offer the most favourable opportunity to an attack from Tippoo upon the Carnatic. It is not improbable that the object of the intercourse between Tippoo and Zemaun Shah was, (on the part of the former at least) some such plan of joint operation.

The present position of Dowlut Rao Scindiah's army, operates as a double advantage to the cause of Tippoo. The absence of Scindiah from his dominions in Hindostan, invites the invasion of Zemaun Shah and favours its success; while the presence of Scindiah's army at Poonah holds both our allies in check. The weight of Tippoo's power in the general balance, must therefore be considered to have received an augmentation, not only by the declared projects of Zemaun Shah, and by the possibility of their (at least limited) success, but by the operations of Scindiah in addition to all the other events which have concurred to impair the efficiency of our defensive alliance.

In the mean while, the Government of Fort St. George, whose peculiar duty it is to watch the operations of Tippoo Sultaun, and to communicate to me every circumstance relating to the growth of his power, have distinctly stated in their letter of the 10th of July, that 'his resources are more prompt than our own, and that a great part of his army is supposed to have long been in a state of field equipment.' So sensible indeed is the Government of Fort St. George to the terror of Tippoo Sultaun's arms, as to be apprehensive of making any effort for resisting their progress, lest Tippoo should anticipate the tardiness of our preparations by the rapidity of his own, and should overrun the Carnatic, before our army could even move for its defence.

It is difficult to describe the pain and regret, which that letter from the Government of Fort St. George occasioned in my mind; nor can I conceive that it is calculated to raise any other emotions in the mind of any friend to the prosperity of the British interests, or to the honour of the British name in India. If the facts and arguments stated in that letter be correct, it must now be admitted, that the glorious successes of the last war in Mysore, the wisdom which balanced the relative interests and forces of the belligerent powers at the conclusion of Peace, and finally the great expense incurred by the Company in the progressive increase of their military establishments on the coast, have terminated in no better result, than to render Tippoo's power absolutely invincible, and to place the disposal of our fate in his hands. For if the sentiments of the Government of Fort St. George, be founded upon a just estimate of the relative conditions of Tippoo Sultaun and of the Company in India, he possesses the ready means of attack, while we cannot venture to resort even to those of defence; but, with a full knowledge of his hostility, of his offensive alliance publicly concluded with the enemy, and of his continual and advanced preparations for war; we must submit to remain unarmed, because any attempt to counteract his design might possibly accelerate its execution. This argument against the prudence of preparing for our defence would become stronger every day in proportion to the progress of Tippoo's hostile preparations; until at length, we should be reduced to the alternative either of implicit submission, or of incurring a much greater risk than any, which can now be apprehended from assembling our defensive force. Although I am not disposed to adopt the sentiments of the Government of Fort St. George on this subject, I acknowledge with great concern those defects in the military establishments on the coast, which will not admit any large proportion of that army to move for several months; those defects certainly constitute so many additional advantages in the scale of Tippoo's power; and in this view, they become objects of the most serious consideration, and form a principal feature of the danger which it is the duty of this Government to avert, by counsels of another spirit, than that of despondency, and by measures of another character, than that of inaction, or of implicit submission to the will of the enemy.

I have now examined the principal causes of that danger, as they are to be traced in the variable course of events since the peace of Seringapatam; the nature of our actual situation, arising from the combined effects of these causes, will best appear, by a summary review of the facts which I have already enumerated in detail.

Tippoo Sultaun having manifested the most hostile intentions towards us, possesses an army of which a considerable portion is now in readiness to take the field for purposes of offence; he has increased the number of his French officers, and has solicited, and may possibly receive further assistance from the French; he may also receive assistance from the several corps commanded by French officers in the service of the Nizam, of Scindiah, and of many other native powers. He may be assisted by the invasion of Zemaun Shah, and by the direct co-operation of Scindiah. On the other hand, our protecting force upon the coast of Coromandel cannot be put in motion within a shorter period than three, (or according to the Adjutant General Lieutenant Colonel Close, than six) months, even for the purpose of defending the Carnatic; our allies in the mean while, are utterly unable to fulfil their defensive engagements with us; the Peishwa being depressed and kept in check by the intrusion of Scindiah, and the Nizam by the vicinity of that chieftain's army, and by the overbearing influence of an army commanded by French officers, and established in the centre of the Deccan. While we remain in this situation, without a soldier prepared to take the field in the Carnatic, and without an ally to assist our operations in the event of an attack from Tippoo, we leave the fate of the Carnatic to the discretion of Tippoo; we suffer the cause of France to acquire hourly accessions of strength in every quarter of India; we abandon our allies the Nizam and the Peishwa to the mercy of Tippoo and of Scindiah in conjunction with the French; and we leave to France the ready means of obtaining a large territorial revenue, and a permanent establishment in the Deccan, founded upon the destruction of our alliances.

Under all these circumstances the situation of the British empire in India is, without doubt, extremely critical, but in my opinion, by no means alarming. For in the very difficulties of our actual situation are to be found the means, not only of averting the danger of the present moment, but of providing permanent security against the future return of a similar crisis. A common apprehension of the designs of Scindiah has fortunately produced an union of interests between the Governments of Poonah and Hyderabad; and notwithstanding some occasional symptoms of that spirit of duplicity and intrigue which marks the character of every Asiatic Court, Azim ul Omra and the ministers of the Peishwa seem to be sincerely convinced, that a renewal of amicable engagements between the Peishwa and the Nizam is equally necessary to the safety of both. On the one hand it appears, that the Peishwa cannot expect to be speedily emancipated, or effectually defended from the undue influence of Scindiah, without the assistance of the Nizam; and on the other hand, it is evident, that the restoration of the just power and authority of the Peishwa would operate as a constant restraint on the designs of Scindiah, of Tippoo, and of the French against the independence of the Court of Hyderabad. Under these circumstances it appeared to me that neither the Peishwa nor the Nizam would be likely to view with jealousy any assistance which we might think it advisable to afford to either, for the purpose of reviving the triple alliance against Tippoo on its original basis, and of enabling the contracting parties to fulfil their respective engagements. This expectation constituted a fundamental principle of my instructions to the Residents at Poonah and Hyderabad, of the 8th of July. Their subsequent correspondence has furnished abundant proof, that my view of the disposition of the two courts was not erroneous; since it appears, that while I was occupied in framing a system of measures for uniting the Nizam and the Peishwa upon the firm ground of their reciprocal interests, a treaty was actually concluded between those two powers at Poonah, with a view to the same object; the ratification of this treaty on the part of the Nizam, has been delayed by Azim ul Omra; but there appears every reason to hope, that the interposition of our arbitration will accommodate every point of difference. Our arbitration has already been earnestly solicited by both parties, and I am persuaded that it will be both acceptable and efficacious whenever it shall be interposed.

The increasing alarm excited at the Court of Hyderabad, by the intemperate conduct of M. Piron and of the French army, would dispose Azim ul Omra to receive with gratitude any offer of assistance towards the destruction of so powerful and dangerous a faction; and the existing jealousies between the French officers, would facilitate the dismission of the corps. Azim ul Omra has recently expressed in the strongest terms his wish of being enabled, by our assistance, to accomplish this most desirable measure. The only obstacles which appear likely to occur to a general accommodation, are the impetuosity and violence of Dowlut Rao Scindiah, whose continuance in his present position would operate as an effectual assistance to Tippoo, and would preclude the possibility of restoring either the Peishwa or the Nizam to any degree of efficiency or consideration. But the absence of Scindiah from his own dominions, and the ungovernable excesses of his temper, (however to be lamented as having contributed to those events which have impaired the power of our allies,) have at the same time weakened the sources of his own power, have occasioned a spirit of faction and revolt in his own dominions, and have disgusted all the ancient friends and connections of his family, together with every respectable adherent to his cause. His violence towards the female relations of his family has raised a considerable party against him amongst his own followers; and his signal treachery in the imprisonment of Nana, from which he hoped to derive the free use of Nana's treasure, has terminated in rendering that resource inaccessible to him, at the very moment when it is most indispensable to his necessities. He is therefore now surrounded by an army clamorous for pay, is destitute of pecuniary resource, and is unsupported by any one respectable friend. His principal minister, a person of considerable experience, and bearing the highest character of any of his followers, has expressed to the Resident at Poonah in the most distinct terms an entire disapprobation of Scindiah's late conduct, and an earnest wish for an accommodation between Scindiah and the Peishwa through our mediation, and for the peaceable return of Scindiah to his dominions in Hindostan; Scindiah himself has manifested no disinclination to receive the advice of the Resident at Poonah; whose discretion has hitherto limited the extent of his interference; but from what has already passed, it is reasonable to hope, that Scindiah, in the present distressed state of his affairs, will give a favorable attention to any just and moderate proposition, urged with the full authority of his Government. In the mean while, the threatened invasion of Zemaun Shah offers a new motive to recal Scindiah to the protection of his own dominions, and he must be sensible not only that his security, in the event of such an invasion, must depend in a great measure on the co-operation of the British troops, but that in the present disturbed condition of his possessions and of his army, we hold his fate in our hands.

In this posture of affairs, any opposition to our interference for the re-establishment of our alliances, would be equally ineffectual and unjustifiable on the part of Scindiah; and various considerations of policy and interest will concur to render him cautious of taking any step, which might afford us just cause of offence. The last despatches from Poonah afford a hope that Nana Furnaveese and the Peishwa may find it their interest to forget their mutual animosity; any accommodation between them would lead greatly to facilitate an arrangement, embracing the respective interests of the Peishwa, of Scindiah, and of the Nizam.

Such are the circumstances of the present moment, which appear to me to favor the execution of that comprehensive system of precaution and defence demanded by the exigency of our actual situation. The mode in which I have endeavoured to carry this system into effect has been suggested by the following considerations. The Court of Hyderabad has repeatedly and earnestly solicited an increase of the British detachment in the service of the Nizam, under an assurance that the French corps of Piron would be dismissed from his Highness's service immediately upon the arrival of the additional British force. This proposition has hitherto been embarrassed by conditions of a nature incompatible with our engagements at Poonah, and the late dissentions between the Nizam and the Peishwa have precluded all hope of any amicable adjustment of this difficulty. It was therefore thought advisable by the late Governor-General in Council to resort to the expedient of encouraging the introduction of British adventurers into the service of the Nizam, for the purpose of counterbalancing in some measure the influence of the French army at Hyderabad. With this view, the corps commanded by Mr. Finglass has received the protection and encouragement of the Acting Resident, and has been augmented to the number of 8,000 men.

The policy of this expedient always appeared to me very doubtful, and I have entertained serious apprehensions that the measure might ultimately furnish additional recruits to the cause of France, instead of counteracting her influence. In the most favorable view, however, this expedient could only be considered as a palliative of the evil: it could not be expected that such a force as that of Mr. Finglass would enable the Nizam to disband the corps of Piron; it must therefore have been evident at all times, that nothing less than a considerable and permanent increase of our regular subsidiary force at Hyderabad could empower the Nizam to extricate himself from the hands of the French faction, so solidly established in his dominions.

I have already stated my reasons for thinking that the increase of the British detachment at Hyderabad would no longer afford any cause of jealousy to the Peishwa; and under all these circumstances, I have availed myself of the late conduct of Tippoo and of Scindiah, to propose that measure, subject in the first instance to the previous consent of the Court of Poonah: I have accompanied this proposition with a condition, that the arbitration of this Government shall be accepted for the final adjustment of the points of difference still remaining between the two Courts. These points are now so few, and the requisitions of the Court of Hyderabad of a nature so just and moderate, that I entertain a confident expectation of effecting an accommodation upon principles equally advantageous to both parties.

I have already observed that one of the most dangerous circumstances attending the establishment of the French party at Hyderabad, is the influence which they are likely to possess in directing the succession to the throne, whenever it shall become vacant by the death of the Nizam.

Secunder Jah, the eldest son of the Nizam, would be the natural successor, unless the regular order of succession should be disturbed by domestic faction, foreign intrigue, or force; for, although priority of birth may not be considered to give the same absolute and exclusive right to succession in India as it does in Europe, it is invariably deemed the strongest title, and is rarely superseded excepting in case of disaffection, or of positive disqualification. So far from these or any other objections being applicable to the title of Secunder Jah, it is well known that the Nizam has given the strongest indications of his favorable intentions towards Secunder Jah, by entrusting that Prince with the custody of his Seal, and by empowering him to perform certain acts which are reserved exclusively for the Sovereign. This admission to the personal exercise of a portion of the sovereign authority during the life of the Nizam is deemed equivalent to a virtual nomination to the throne; and there is no reason to suppose that the Nizam will nominate any of his younger sons to the exclusion of the heir apparent, unless his Highness should be prevailed upon in the weakness of his last moments to commit an act of such flagrant impolicy and injustice.

Secunder Jah is connected by marriage with the family of

Azim ul Omra, and his establishment upon the throne would give great additional security to the British interests at the Court of Hyderabad: on the other hand, none of the younger sons can hope to reach the throne by any other assistance than that of the French party, and of Tippoo Sultaun. Sufficient proof has been stated of the interest which Tippoo and the French take in the exclusion of Secunder Jah, and of the attempts which they have already made to interfere in governing the succession. These attempts may be renewed, and their success would necessarily involve the destruction of Azim ul Omra and of Secunder Jah, together with the consequent annihilation of the British influence at Hyderabad; all hope of re-establishing the balance of power in India as it existed at the peace of Seringapatam, would then be precluded; the countries of the Nizam would in such an event become in effect a dependency of France, and the partizans of that nation, in conjunction with Tippoo, and with the body of their countrymen lately received into his pay, would have the means of endangering the British power in India.

Under all these circumstances, the same principles which suggested the necessity of increasing the British detachment at Hyderabad, demanded that it should be employed to support the succession of Secunder Jah, as being essentially connected with the permanency of our influence at Hyderabad, and with the effectual exclusion of the interference of Tippoo and of France.

I have therefore authorised the Resident at Hyderabad to employ the British troops in this service, if their assistance should hereafter become necessary; but I am persuaded that the mere presence of our force, accompanied by the knowledge of my firm determination to support the regular order of succession, will preclude every movement either of foreign or domestic opposition.

The arrangements proposed for the service of the Nizam will be very incomplete, unless connected with the restoration of the Peishwa to a due degree of authority and power, and preceded by the cordial approbation of the Court of Poonah. But the great danger to be averted is the growth of the influence of Tippoo and of France in India. It is therefore evident, that the failure of the proposed plan at Poonah would increase the necessity of providing for the safety of the Nizam, and of destroying the French party at his Court. If, therefore, the

Peishwa should either refuse his assent to the propositions to be made to him, or if from the success of Scindiah's operations, or from any other cause, those measures which relate to the Court of Poonah should be frustrated, I have still deemed it advisable to direct the Acting Resident at Hyderabad to carry into effect the increase of the British detachment, and such other parts of my instructions as may appear practicable, reserving always to the Peishwa the power of acceding hereafter to any treaty which we may conclude with the Nizam, and continuing with that view the restrictive terms of our present subsidiary engagements with the latter, as far as they relate to the interests of the Peishwa. The dismission of the French corps at Hyderabad would not fully answer the views with which I have proposed that measure, if the officers or European privates were permitted to enter into the service of any other native power, although I should think them less dangerous in any service than in that of the Nizam. I have endeavoured not only to secure the expulsion of the French from Hyderabad, but also their immediate return to their native country. I have therefore required that the French officers and privates should be delivered up to the Government of Fort St. George, in order that they may be immediately conveyed to Europe; the Nizam is under no engagements either with the Government of France or with the French officers to continue them in his service, and he possesses the full right to dismiss them whenever he shall think fit. The exorbitant power which M. Piron and his army have acquired at Hyderabad, as well as their immoderate abuse of it, will justify the Nizam in taking whatever measures may appear most effectual for the purpose of securing himself against a faction so formidable not only to the independence of his Government, but to the safety of his own person, and to the existence of his throne. With the same view, I have made it a preliminary condition of the whole plan, that the Nizam, his heirs and successors shall for ever exclude the French from their armies and dominions.

The corps of Mr. Finglass, after the establishment of a considerable British force at Hyderabad, will no longer be liable to the full force of the objections which I have stated against the policy of encouraging such a body of adventurers in the service of the Nizam; this question, however, does not require an immediate decision; we shall possess ample means of deciding it according to our discretion, if our propositions to the Court of

Hyderabad should be attended with success. The consent of the Nizam to such parts of the proposed arrangements as relate to the re-establishment of the Government of Poonah is required as a necessary preliminary to the increase of the British detachment at Hyderabad; my intentions being to take no step in the first instance at either Court without the full knowledge and concurrence of the other; a principle, the strict observance of which to every degree of practicable extent, appears to me to be the only effectual mode of removing all causes of jealousy, of uniting the confidence of both parties, and of bringing them to a dispassionate consideration of their mutual interests.

The parts of the proposed arrangement which relate to the re-establishment of the Government of Poonah were suggested by Colonel Palmer's letter of 1st of June, in which he states 'that the authority of the Peishwa would be restored by the appearance of a strong British force at Poonah, and that Scindiah, under the circumstances of Tippoo's recent aggression, could on no just pretence object to such a movement of our troops, nor in his present condition be able to oppose it.'

The whole tenor of the subsequent advices from Poonah tended to confirm this opinion: for while it appeared evidently impossible that the authority of the Peishwa could be restored otherwise than by foreign assistance, there seemed to be every rational ground of expectation, that the mere appearance of our troops would induce all the leading Chieftains of the Mahratta empire to unite in support of the Peishwa, and that such an event would not be unacceptable even to the followers of Scindiah. The Peishwa himself has earnestly solicited the aid of a body of our troops, and has expressed the fullest sense of the necessity, as well as reliance on the efficacy of such a measure for the restoration of his authority and for the protection of his person.

On the other hand, the danger of the Peishwa increased from day to day; the assistance which he had solicited from the Nizam was not likely to reach him before his fate had been decided; and the expectation even of any assistance from the Court of Hyderabad, notwithstanding the conclusion of the late treaty, appeared to rest on a very precarious foundation. In this situation, the direct interposition of this Government by moving a detachment of troops to Poonah was the only measure on which we could rely with any degree of certainty for averting the immediate destruction of our interests at that Court.

The Resident at Poonah was therefore authorized to require

a detachment of troops from Bombay, but previously to so decided a step, it was deemed proper that the Resident should require of the Peishwa his consent to the increase of the British detachment at Hyderabad, his acceptance of our arbitration between the Courts of Poonah and Hyderabad, and his exclusion of the French from his armies and dominions.

With a view of securing the lasting benefit of this arrangement at the Court of Poonah, it is intended that a proposal shall be made to the Peishwa to enter into permanent subsidiary engagements with us of a similar nature and extent with those which shall be concluded at the Court of Hyderabad.

With the same view, the Resident at Poonah has been directed to take such measures as may appear to him most likely to interest Nana Furnaveese in the success of this general arrangement of the affairs of the two Courts.

The last despatches from Poonah afford every reason to hope, that the abilities and experience of Nana may be successfully employed by Colonel Palmer in effecting the return of Scindiah to his own dominions, and the consequent restoration of the Peishwa.

The impediments which Scindiah opposes to the success of this arrangement will probably disappear whenever the union of the two Courts, cemented by our interposition, shall become a matter of public notoriety.

The treasure of Nana is the only resource in which Scindiah can find the means of appeasing the clamours of his discontented army; and Colonel Palmer will avail himself of any favourable opportunity of connecting the interests of Nana with those of Scindiah and of the Peishwa, in such a manner as shall enable Scindiah to retire with safety into his own dominions, without affording him the power of effecting any other military movement.

Being desirous of conciliating the real interests of all parties, I have instructed Colonel Palmer to make the most amicable propositions to Scindiah, and to urge the policy of his return to his own dominions by pointing out their actual danger during his absence, by offering our co-operation against the menaced invasion of Zemaun Shah, and our mediation with the Courts of Poonah and Hyderabad; and I have made the consent of those Courts to our mediation of their respective differences with Scindiah an indispensable preliminary of the arrangements which regard the restoration of their own independence. Scindiah cannot reject our propositions on any ground which would not immediately place him in the rank of a declared enemy to us, and of an avowed auxiliary to Tippoo Sultaun.

In this case, therefore, we must have recourse to compulsion; and I have authorized the Resident at Poonah to use it in the last and, I trust improbable, extremity.

Such are the measures which I have proposed, with a view to restore the efficiency of our alliances, and to check the growth of the French party in the Deccan.

I have already stated the reasons which convinced me (against the opinion of the Government of Fort St. George) that the assembling the army on the coasts of Coromandel and Malabar, and at Bombay, was absolutely indispensable to the defence of the Carnatic, under the circumstance of Tippoo's declared designs and acknowledged preparations for war.

The fatal policy of neglecting to keep pace with the forwardness of the enemy's equipments has been felt more than once on the coast of Coromandel, and, I repeat it, I cannot, consistently with any sentiment of duty, consent to rest the security of the Carnatic, in the present crisis, on any other foundation than a state of active and early preparation for war. But if I had looked only to the success of those measures which are now depending at the Courts of Poonah and Hyderabad (measures essentially involving our present and future means of checking the implacable enmity of Tippoo), I should on that ground alone have proposed to assemble the army upon the coast of Coromandel, at Bombay, and upon the coast of Malabar.

It is impossible to suppose that Tippoo would not employ every effort to prevent the revival of our defensive alliances; and it would, therefore, be nearly certain that his advanced state of preparation for war, and his renewed connection with the French, would tempt him to interfere in the affairs of the Nizam and of the Peishwa, and to assist the views of Scindiah at Poonah, and of M. Piron's army at Hyderabad. It therefore became necessary to check the motions of Tippoo Sultaun, by assembling an army upon his frontier during the continuance of our negociations with our allies.

I have adverted, in the course of this Minute, to those defects in the constitution of the army upon the coast which have impeded its early movement in the present critical conjuncture. The measures which I have proposed for the correction of those defects are absolutely necessary, in my judgment, to our future security in the Carnatic. The detail of those measures will appear in my Minute in the Secret Department of the 20th July, and in the letter to the Government of Fort St. George of the same date.

I am fully aware of the expense to be incurred in establishing any improved system, which shall enable the army on the coast to keep pace with the promptitude of Tippoo's resources, and to move with an alacrity and expedition equal to his.

If, however, the proposed increase of our subsidiary engagements at Hyderabad should take place, it is my intention that the whole detachment, consisting of three regiments, should be furnished from the establishment of Fort St. George. The force thus stationed at Hyderabad will afford an effectual security to the northern Circars against Tippoo Sultaun, or against any other foreign enemy. The duty of the Circars will then require no larger a proportion of troops than may be sufficient to maintain the internal police and good order of the country. It will not therefore be requisite, in the event of peace, to raise more than one regiment at Fort St. George, to replace those serving with the Nizam. This arrangement will operate as a saving of the expense of two regiments upon the establishment at Fort St. George, and will furnish a fund at least adequate to the permanent charges of the new establishments of artillery, draft cattle and grain, which our recent experience has proved to be indispensable for the purpose of enabling the army on the coast to take the field expeditiously, on any sudden emergency.

In this view, the restoration of our defensive alliances against Tippoo is essentially connected with the improvement of our system of defence in the Carnatic; and the assistance afforded to the Nizam will become (without any increase of expense) the source of additional vigour and activity to our army upon the coast.

Deeply as I lament the obstacles which have prevented us from striking an instantaneous blow against the possessions of Tippoo, I expect to derive considerable advantage from the success of that system of precaution and defence which I have been compelled to substitute in place of an immediate war.

The enlargement of our subsidiary engagements at the Court of Hyderabad, combined with the establishment of similar engagements at the Court of Poonah, will become a great augmentation of our strength, attended by no increase of charge, and possibly by a diminution of our military expenses.

The two detachments will form a considerable army, stationed on the most vulnerable part of Tippoo Sultaun's frontier, in a position which will at all times facilitate our approach to his capital, by securing the protection of our convoys of provisions. A force so stationed will operate as a perpetual restraint upon any movements which Tippoo might be disposed to make towards the frontier, either of the Carnatic, of the Northern Circars, or of Malabar. It will also impede any co-operation between the armies of Scindiah and of Tippoo; and will induce the former to remain within his own dominions, where his motions will again be checked by the vicinity of our army on the frontier of Oude.

In such circumstances, it must always be the interest of Scindiah to cultivate our friendship in preference to that of the French, or of any native power. Thus he may become an useful ally to us in the event of Zemaun Shah's approach to the frontier of Hindostan; and the prospect of that event must render him anxious to secure our protection. On the other hand, the success of his present ambitious and unjustifiable views against the Peishwa would fix him in the interests of Tippoo Sultaun and of France, with the accession of whatever strength he might be able to collect from the remnants of the empire which he would have overthrown.

The influence which we shall naturally derive, both at Hyderabad and Poonah, from the presence of so large a body of our troops, will enable us to prevent any aggression on either side, by the constant interposition of our good offices with both parties, to restrain every symptom of a revival of their former spirit of jealousy and contention.

Our endeavours may then be successfully directed to the desirable object of preserving unimpaired the strength and resources of the two powers, on whose co-operation we must rely for assistance in the event of any war with the state of Mysore; and while we prevent our allies from weakening themselves by repeated contests, we may expect that such an interference in the disputes of the native powers, so far from tending to foment divisions, and to occasion war, will prove the best security for the general tranquillity of India, as well as the most solid pledge of our disposition to preserve that blessing from interruption.

However comprehensive and intricate the proposed system may appear at the first view, it will soon be evident to all the powers of India, that the fundamental principle of our policy is invariably repugnant to every scheme of conquest, extension of dominion, aggrandisement, or ambition, either for ourselves or for our allies. Consistently with this principle, it is our right and duty to restore the vigour and efficiency of our defensive alliances; but beyond the limits of this principle, we entertain no project of altering the condition, of reducing or of raising the power of any established state in India. On the other hand, the same principle justifies and demands our firm resistance to the intrusion of any foreign power which shall attempt to acquire a preponderant influence in the scale of Indian politics, to the prejudice of our defensive alliances, and of our just interests. The establishment of our subsidized force at Poonah and Hyderabad will afford effectual means of guarding, not only against any such intrusion, but against the undue growth of any native power. While we possess so formidable a force in the centre of India, no such event can happen without our knowledge and consent.

The last question which remains for consideration is, what shall be the nature and extent of that demand of satisfaction which we shall make from Tippoo Sultaun, whenever we shall have completed the system now depending at the Courts of our Allies, and shall have brought our army in the Carnatic to a state of preparation for the field?

It is evident from the facts which have come under my observation in the course of this discussion, that our safety requires a further reduction of the relative power of Tippoo Sultaun.

The policy of the Treaty of Seringapatam certainly was not to maintain Tippoo's power upon such a scale as should leave him a constant object of alarm and apprehension to the Company. That he has been so for some years past cannot be denied by any person acquainted with the records either of this Government or of that of Fort St. George. The present is the second crisis within the last two years, in which this Government has thought it necessary to assemble the army on the coast, for the sole purpose of checking his motions.

The vague and inaccurate nature of our intelligence with respect to the extent of his force and to the state of his preparations, added to the facility which he possesses of receiving emissaries and succours from France by sea, have contributed to increase the anxiety of the Company's Governments; and our intercourse with him has been of an unsettled and ill defined character, destitute of the advantages either of peace or of war. Under such circumstances, the continuance of Tippoo's power in its actual state, must prove to the Company a perpetual source of alarm, vexation and expense.

The reduction of his means of offence might be effected, either by a positive diminution of his territory and resources, or by a proportionate increase of power and efficiency on our side of the balance, accompanied by such additional securities as might enable us to ascertain at all times the nature of his intentions, as well as his power of carrying them into effect, and to restrain, if not wholly to preclude, his intercourse with Franee.

The diminution of his territory on the coast of Malabar, would certainly be the most effectual mode of precluding his intercourse with France, as well as of preventing his movements towards the Carnatic. But it does not appear probable that this most desirable security can ever be obtained by the mere terror of our arms. It must be purchased at the expense and hazard of war. Any considerable reduction of his resources must probably be purchased at the same price.

I have already stated the nature and tendency of those steps which have been taken, for confining the power of Tippoo within narrower limits by the operation of the proposed system of alliance, of subsidiary engagements, and of improvement of our defences in the Carnatic.

The success of this system will unquestionably operate as an effectual restraint upon the power of Tippoo, and will so strengthen our barriers against him as to afford a rational expectation, that we may be enabled to obtain from him without incurring the hazard of war, a very considerable augmentation of security with respect to all those points, which now form the most alarming features of his power.

I have already stated those points to be, the secrecy of his operations; his continual intercourse with the French, and constant state of equipment for war.

Our demand of satisfaction for his late infraction of treaty, should be so framed as to apply correctives to each of these evils; and such a demand might be founded on principles of moderation and justice so clear and indisputable, as would place the refusal of Tippoo in the most odious light, and in that event prove to all India the necessity of our resorting to arms.

We might distinctly state to Tippoo, that we entertain no view of encroaching upon his territory or of diminishing his resources; and we might appeal to the late restoration of the district of Wynaad, for an unequivocal proof of this disposition.

We might declare, that after a most unprovoked violation of treaty on his part, we do not intend to demand any cession of dominion or payment of money; but will content ourselves with obtaining those ordinary pledges of an intention to abstain from hostilities, which all civilized nations in a state of peace, are in the established habit of requiring reciprocally from one another; we might insist on an unequivocal and final explanation of the real nature of our relation with him; declaring. that we will no longer submit to that ambiguous and anxious state, in which the allies have been placed by his conduct for some years past; we might signify our determined resolution, either to establish with him a real and effectual peace, accompanied by the customary intercourse, by the mutual exchange of good offices, and by all other securities which maintain the continuance of that blessing, or to wage war upon him, until we have removed the causes of our apprehension and danger by the entire destruction of his power.

This declaration might be made jointly by all the allies, and it might be followed by requiring Tippoo to receive at his Court an established Ambassador from each of the allies, according to the practice of all civilized nations in a state of peace, offering at the same time to admit Ambassadors from him on equal terms.

The force levied by him under his offensive alliance with France, having been raised for the express purpose of aggression upon the Company, can be considered in no other light than that of a signal of hostility, while it shall remain in his service. He must therefore be required to disband it without delay, and to remove it from his dominions.

The anxious desire of the French to destroy the British power in India, the nature of Tippoo's acknowledged connection with them, and the interest which they must always feel in instigating him to war, demand the further requisition, that he should enter into an engagement for himself, his heirs and successors, to exclude the French from his armies and dominions for ever.

The advantages resulting from these concessions on the part of Tippoo, would be very considerable.

The residence of an Ambassador at his Court would not only restrain the execution of any hostile designs which he might hereafter form, but would provide an authentic source of intelligence, from which we might always derive timely information of his motions. This measure might also ultimately lead to the establishment of an amicable intercourse with Mysore; for Tippoo may perhaps at length be convinced, that his wisest policy would be to rest satisfied with the undisturbed possession of his present dominions, rather than to risk the loss of what he still retains, by attempting to regain what he has lost.

The dismission of the French corps raised at Mauritius would discourage other adventurers of that nation from attempting to engage in the service of the Sultaun; and with a British Ambassador on the spot, it would be difficult for him to evade the engagements by which he would have bound himself to exclude the French from his armies and dominions.

The combined effect of these two measures would therefore be, if not wholly to preclude, at least to embarrass to a very great degree his intercourse with our enemy. He may also at length perceive that he never can hope to make any lasting impression upon the British power, without the aid of a large French force; and that he never can admit such a force into his dominions, without the utmost danger to his own independence.

The revival of our alliances, the appearance of our armies in the field, and the presence of a part of the British squadron on the coast of Malabar, will probably incline Tippoo to listen to requisitions of this nature. He will soon perceive that we possess ample means of annihilating his military force, and I trust he will also be convinced, that we have no object in view beyond our own security, and that we are really desirous of maintaining the relations of amity and peace with him, as long as he shall rest contented with his present dominions, and shall relinquish his vindictive projects against ours.

If Tippoo should accede to the substance of the requisitions which I have suggested, I entertain a sanguine hope, that with the efficiency of the triple alliance not only restored but considerably strengthened, with a large army at Hyderabad, and another at Poonah, with a Resident established at Seringapatam, and with the exclusion of the French from the dominions of Tippoo Sultaun, of the Nizam, and of the Peishwa, we may be enabled to look confidently to a long continuance of tranquillity in India. The growth of the French power in India, would no longer be a matter of apprehension, Scindiah (or whoever shall succeed to his dominions in Hindostan) would become an useful auxiliary against the threatened irruption of Zemaun Shah; the military charges on the coast of Coromandel, might then safely admit of reduction; this Government would not then be perpetually alarmed with rumours of Tippoo's equipments, and of impending invasions of the Carnatic. We should no longer suffer in time of peace all the solicitude, and hazard, and much of the expense of war; and the continuance of tranquillity would be ensured not more by the predominance of our power, than by the moderation manifested in using it for the sole purpose of obtaining permanent security, and genuine peace.

I am, &c. MORNINGTON.

4. The Earl of Mornington to Tippoo Sultaun.

Proposal to send an envoy to compose the quarrel.

Fort William, 8th November, 1798.

It affords me sincere satisfaction to learn that you have nominated two persons of integrity and honour to meet and confer with the Deputies appointed, under my orders, by Mr. Duncan (the Governor of Bombay), for the purposes of investigating the question regarding the Talooks of Ameera and Soulea. It is only by means of regular enquiry, and amicable discussion, that such questions can be adjusted among independent powers. My determination, in the case of Wynaad, was dictated by those principles of justice and moderation, which always direct the Company's Government, nor shall my scrupulous adherence to the same principles be less manifest in my decision on your claim to the districts at present in question, the possession of which shall not be withholden from you for an instant if, after full investigation, I shall be satisfied of the justice of your title to them.

It is a well known truth, that they are always the most ready to respect the just rights of others who are the most vigilant and resolute to maintain their own.

I have understood your sentiments concerning the 'turbulent disposition of interested men, who, by nature, are ever seeking opportunities of sowing the seeds of dissension.' For the happiness of mankind it is to be lamented that these authors of confusion are too numerous, assiduous and successful, in all parts of the world. In no age or country were the baneful and insidious arts of intrigue cultivated with such success as they are at present by the French nation. I sincerely wish that no impression had been produced on your discerning mind by that dangerous people; but my situation enables me to know that they have reached your presence, and have endeavoured to pervert the wisdom of your councils, and to instigate you to war against those who have given you no provocation.

It is impossible that you should suppose me to be ignorant of the intercourse which subsists between you and the French, whom you know to be the inveterate enemies of the Company, and to be now engaged in an unjust war with the British nation. You cannot imagine me to be indifferent to the transactions which have passed between you and the enemies of my country; nor does it appear necessary or proper that I should any longer conceal from you the surprise and concern with which I perceived you disposed to involve yourself in all the ruinous consequences of a connection, which threatens not only to subvert the foundations of friendship between you and the Company, but to introduce into the heart of your kingdom the principles of anarchy and confusion, to shake your own authority, to weaken the obedience of your subjects, and to destroy the religion which you revere.

Immediately after my arrival at Bengal, I read your correspondence with the late Governor-General, Sir John Shore, and with the Acting Governor-General Sir Alured Clarke; and I perceived with great satisfaction, that in all your letters you constantly professed a disposition to strengthen the bonds of sincere attachment, and the foundations of harmony and concord established between you and the Honourable Company. I received particular pleasure from reading your last letter to Sir John Shore, in which you signified your amicable desire that he should impress me with a sense of the friendship and unanimity so long subsisting between the two States. Your subsequent letters to me have abounded with professions of the same friendly nature.

Combining these professions of amity on your part with the proofs which the Company's Government have constantly given of their sincere disposition to maintain the relations of friendship and peace with you; and adverting, at the same time, to your reputation for wisdom and discernment, it was natural for me to be extremely slow to believe the various accounts transmitted to me of your negociations with the French, and of your military preparations; but whatever my reluctance to credit such reports might be, prudence required both of me and of the Company's allies, that we should adopt certain measures of precaution and self-defence, and these have accordingly been taken, as you will no doubt have observed. The British Government and the allies, wishing nevertheless to live in peace and friendship with all their neighbours, entertaining no projects of ambition, nor any views in the least incompatible with their respective engagements, and looking to no other objects than the permanent security and tranquillity of their own dominions and subjects, will always be ready, as they now are, to afford you every demonstration of their pacific disposition.

The Peishwa, and his Highness the Nizam, concur with me in the observations which I have offered to you in this letter; and which, in the name of the Company, and of the Allies, I recommend to your most earnest consideration; but as I am also desirous of communicating to you, on the behalf of the Company, and their allies, a plan calculated to promote the mutual security and welfare of all parties; I propose to depute to you, for this purpose, Major Doveton, who is well known to you, and who will explain to you more fully and particularly the sole means which appear to myself, and to the allies of the Company, to be effectual for the salutary purpose of removing all existing distrust and suspicion, and of establishing peace and good understanding on the most durable foundations.

You will, I doubt not, let me know at what time and place it will be convenient to you to receive Major Doveton; and as soon as your friendly letter shall reach me, I will direct him to proceed to your presence.

I shall expect your answer to this letter, with an earnest hope that it may correspond with the pacific views and wishes of the allies; and that you may be convinced that you cannot in any manner better consult your true interests than by meeting, with cordiality, the present friendly and moderate advance to a satisfactory and amicable settlement of all points on which any doubt or anxiety may have arisen in the minds either of yourself or of the allies.

A true Copy, N. B. Edmonstone,
Persian Translator to Govt.

5. Tippoo Sultaun to the Earl of Mornington.

Evasive reply to the above. False account of the mission to the Mauritius.

18th Dec. 1798.
(Received at Fort St. George, 25th Dec. 1798.

I have been made happy by the receipt of your Lordship's two friendly letters, the contents of which I clearly comprehend, (vide those written 4th and 8th November). The particulars which your Lordship has communicated to me, relative to the victory obtained by the English fleet over that of the French near the shores of Egypt, nine of their ships having been captured and two burnt, on one of which of the latter was their Admiral, have given me more pleasure than can possibly be conveyed by writing. Indeed I possess the firmest hope that the leaders of the English and the Company Bahauder, who ever adhere to the paths of sincerity, friendship, and good faith, and are the well wishers of mankind, will at all times be successful and victorious; and that the French, who are of a crooked disposition, faithless, and the enemies of mankind, may be ever depressed and ruined. Your Lordship has written to me with the pen of friendship, 'that in no age or country were the baneful and insidious arts of intrigue ever cultivated with such success as they are at present by the French nation. Would to God that no impression had been produced on my mind by that dangerous people; but that your Lordship's situation enables you to know that they have reached my presence, and have endeavoured to pervert the wisdom of my councils, and to instigate me to war against those who have given me no provocation. That it is impossible that I should suppose your Lordship ignorant of the intercourse which subsists between me and the French, who I know to be the inveterate enemies of the Company, and to be now engaged in an unjust war with the British, and that I cannot imagine your Lordship indifferent to the transactions which have passed between me and the enemies of the English.'

In this Sircar (the gift of God) there is a mercantile tribe, who employ themselves in trading by sea and land. Their agents purchased a two-masted vessel, and having loaded her with rice, departed with a view to traffic. It happened that she went to the Mauritius, from whence forty persons, French, and of a dark colour, of whom ten or twelve were artificers, and the rest servants, paying the hire of the ship, came here in search of employment. Such as chose to take service were entertained, and the remainder departed beyond the confines of this Sircar (the gift of God); and the French, who are full of vice and deceit, have perhaps taken advantage of the departure of the ship to put about reports with the view to ruffle the minds of both Sircars.

It is the wish of my heart, and my constant endeavour, to

observe and maintain the articles of the agreement of peace, and to perpetuate and strengthen the basis of friendship and union with the Sircar of the Company Bahauder, and with the Sircars of the Maha Rajah Saheb, Sree Munt Peishwa Bahauder, and his Highness the Nabob Asuph Jah Bahauder. And I am resident at home, at times taking the air, and at others amusing myself with hunting at a spot which is used as a pleasure ground. In this case, the allusion to war in your friendly letter, and the following passage, namely 'that prudence required that both the Company and their allies should adopt certain measures of precaution and self-defence,' have given me the greatest surprize.

It was further written by your friendly pen, that as your Lordship is desirous of communicating to me, on the behalf of the Company and their allies, a plan calculated to promote the mutual security and welfare of all parties; your Lordship proposes to depute to me for this purpose Major Doveton, who formerly waited upon me, and who will explain to me more fully and particularly the sole means which appear to your Lordship and the allies to be effectual for the salutary purpose of removing all existing distrust and suspicion, and of establishing peace and good understanding on the most durable foundations; and that therefore your Lordship trusts I will let you know at what time and place it will be convenient to me to receive Major Doveton. It has been understood, by the blessing of the Almighty, at the conclusion of the peace, the treaties and engagements entered into among the four Sircars were so firmly established and confirmed as ever to remain fixed and durable; and be an example to the rulers of the age; nor are they nor will they ever be liable to interruption. I cannot imagine that means more effectual than these can be adopted, for giving stability to the foundations of friendship and harmony, promoting the security of states, or the welfare and advantage of all parties.

In the view of those who inspect narrowly into the nature of friendship, peace and amity are the first of all objects, as indeed your Lordship has yourself written to me that the allied Sircars look to no other object than the security and tranquillity of their own dominions, and the ease and comfort of their subjects. Praise be to God, that the sum of my views and the wish of my heart are limited to these same points. On such grounds then a just and permanent observance of existing treaties is necessary; and these, under the favours of God, daily acquire new strength and improvement by means of amicable correspondence. Your Lordship is a great Sirdar, a firm friend, and the rectifier of all things, and you possess an enlightened judgement. I have the strongest hope that the minds of the wise and intelligent, but particularly of the four states, will not be sullied by doubts and jealousies, but will consider me from my heart desirous of harmony and friendship.

Continue to allow me the pleasure of your correspondence, making me happy by accounts of your health. What more shall be written.

Dated the 9th of Rujub, 1213, of the Hegirah, (answering to the 18th December.)

A true Translation, N. B. EDMONSTONE,
Persian Translator to Govt.

6. Tippoo Sultaun the Victorious to the Representatives of the People residing in the Isles of France and of La Reunion.

Proposals for an alliance against the English in India.

Seringapatam, 2nd of April, 1797.

Citizens Representatives,

You cannot be ignorant of the friendship which my father and myself have ever entertained for the French. I sought every opportunity of proving it during your former government, *and I have done all in my power since the commencement of your revolution to make known to you the sentiments of my heart.* From want of opportunity and of intercourse with persons acquainted with your customs and manners, I have not been able before this time to inform you of my intentions. A fortunate chance has sent me Citizen Ripaud (one of your officers) who at my request has answered all the questions which I put to him. I consider him to be worthy of my confidence, and from what he has told me, I perceive *it is now the moment for me to revive the friendship which I have always entertained for your nation;* I acknowledge the sublimity of your constitution, and as a proof of my sincerity *I propose to your nation and to you a treaty of alliance and fraternity, which shall be for ever indissoluble, and shall be founded on republican principles, of sincerity and good faith; to the end that you and your nation with myself and my people may become one Family; that the same oath may bind us for life or for death; that your enemies may be mine and those of my people; and that my enemies may be considered as yours.* Thus do I wish henceforth to treat with my allies. You now see my disposition towards your country; when I shall receive a proof of yours, I will fulfil my promises; but, Citizens Representatives. I will not fulfil these engagements with you until I see your forces as well naval as military actually arrive in India. During the last war (it is with regret that I am obliged to recall to your memory the disasters which my friendship for the French nation has brought upon me) I maintained with zeal and courage, all the pretensions of the French. The English, the ambitious English, not having sufficient confidence in their own strength and courage to attack me singly, formed an alliance with the Mahrattas and the Nizam, and attacked me in every quarter. At the very moment when I was on the point of conquering them, the French army under the command of M. de Cossigny, received an order from M. de Bussi to abandon me, though I had paid them well, and they were in want of nothing; but what filled me with indignation was, that those orders extended to M. de Lally, who commanded a body of French in my pay, to withdraw himself with his party; this I opposed, and on just grounds. From that moment, my army became disgusted. Reduced singly to my own resources, and abandoned by my allies, I was compelled to make peace, with the loss of half of my dominions, and three Crores and thirty thousand rupees in specie. Behold what have been my losses, Representatives! What is past is past. I have cited these truths in order to apprize you, that if I should declare war against your enemies, I will not be deserted, nor shall you have the power of making peace without my previous consent, nor without including myself and my people in the treaty. For the security of our reciprocal friendship and good faith it is necessary to stipulate one preliminary condition. It is this, that as my people are ignorant of the customs of the French republicans, and as the republicans are equally unacquainted with the customs of my country, if one of the citizens of either party should violate the customs of the other, he shall be reprimanded immediately by his own superior, without any interruption of the good understanding and harmony, which ought to subsist between good allies. I insert this clause, although Citizen Ripaud has assured me, that the observance of the most severe discipline and of respect for the laws exists in the republican army: mine shall always be conducted in the same manner. I require also that the commanding officer shall always consult me on every measure which he may undertake for the destruction of our common enemy, because I am acquainted with the country, its customs and manners. This is a reservation that he cannot consider as offensive. *Happy moment! the time is come when I can deposit in the bosom of my friends the hatred which I bear against these oppressors of the human race. If you will assist me, in a short time not an Englishman shall remain in India; you have the power and the means of effecting it by your free negroes; with these new citizens (much dreaded by the English) joined to your troops of the line, we will purge India of these villains. The springs which I have touched have put all India in motion, my friends are ready to fall upon the English; for everything here rely on my discretion. Your enemies, as I have apprized you, shall be mine.* Now you are apprized of my designs, delay not to inform me of yours, but make no promises which you cannot perform. I have retained Citizen Ripaud to answer your letters, and I will give him a salary worthy of the situation which he holds near my person. I entreat you not to be offended with him, but on the contrary to approve of what he has done, and to quiet his apprehensions of being considered as a deserter of his country and of his colours, (a laudable motive which interests me for his welfare). I request you to authorize him to remain in his present station with me for the service of his country, of your colonies, and of myself. *I detained him, nor did he consent to remain till after much solicitation*, being extremely attached to the Island of Bourbon, to which he belongs. In case you should consent to my propositions, it is necessary that you should know the extent of my power to assist the French Republic and its army.

Article 1. I engage, immediately on the arrival of the French troops on the coast, to victual both the land and sea forces, (European liquors excepted) and I will furnish all necessaries, such as flour, rice, meat, wood, &c.

Article 2. I engage also to make advances of money for all the wants of the land and sea equipments.

Article 3. I engage to provide all the bullocks necessary for the artillery of the republican troops, as well as the bullocks, camels, and Lascars, for carrying the baggage of the officers and soldiers.

Article 4. I engage to provide palanquins for the Generals, and horses for the officers, of the troops of the Republic.

Article 5. In case the French army should happen to be in want of gunpowder, or other ammunition, I engage to supply it.

Article 6. As soon as the French army shall have disembarked, I engage to march with my troops; which shall in the first instance consist of 30,000 cavalry, and 30,000 infantry and artillery, well disciplined, with arms, ammunition, and everything necessary for the success of our enterprize.

What I require on the part of France is as follows:

Article 1. That the French Republic shall not, under any pretence whatever, conclude peace, but with the consent of me and my people, nor without including us in such treaty.

Article 2. That as the troops of the Republic will derive such advantages from me, the Generals in command shall undertake nothing without first consulting me, to ensure the success of the common cause, and of our respective armies.

Article 3. Should the French General or Republican troops detect traitors in my country, or should I or my troops come to the knowledge of any such in the French army, the chief of the party wherein the traitor may be found, shall cause him to be seized and executed, upon authentic proofs of his guilt, without prejudice to our mutual friendship; since engaged in the same cause, our interests are the same.

Article 4. As I propose to make the advances, and furnish the necessary supplies of money to the French Republic, both for the land and the sea forces, it is just that I should be reimbursed at the end of the war, from the sums of money which may be taken from our common enemy.

Article 5. Every capture made from our common enemy, as towns, forts, territory, money, merchandize, ships, ammunition, &c. shall be equally divided at a fair valuation, fraternally between the troops of the Republic, me, and my people.

Article 6. As I have suffered greatly in supporting the cause of the French in the last war, when I lost the best part of my country, I require that all the towns, forts, territories, or contributions, which I may be able to seize within my former boundaries, be exempted from the 4th Article, that they shall become mine by *right*, and that the republican troops shall have no pretensions or claims thereto. I claim this act of justice from my brethren.

Article 7. If the fortune of war shall put us in possession of Goa and Bombay, the port of Bombay and the territories dependent on it, belonging to the English, shall belong of right to the French; but Goa and its dependencies shall be mine.

Article 8. I demand that all male and female prisoners, as well English as Portuguese, which shall be taken by the republican troops or by mine, shall be treated with humanity, and with regard to their persons, that they shall (their property becoming the right of the allies) be transported at our joint expence, out of India, to some place far distant from the territories of the allies.

Article 9. As the towns, ports, forts, and territories stipulated in the 6th article, are to be divided between the allies, they shall be garrisoned as they may fall into our hands, and the stipulations of that article, shall be afterwards arranged by the French general and myself, with a discretion, if circumstances require it, to blow up any fort which may be deemed useless.

Article 10. In order to achieve the conquest of the English and Portuguese possessions, and those of their allies, it is necessary that I should be assisted with from five to ten thousand regular troops or national guards, and from twenty-five to thirty thousand of your *new citizens*, (if you have put the decree into execution;) selecting the most *subtle and best instructed* of them; *those, in short, who are likely to disturb the peace in your own colonies;* I will answer for our quick and easy success.

Article 11. To facilitate the attack and capture of Goa, a port essential for your squadron and your transports, it will be necessary to disembark at my port of Onore, situated in latitude 14.35 N. and 70 longitude.

Article 12. That I may be apprized whether you accept or reject my propositions, I request, that after having fully considered them, you will despatch a packet-boat to Mangalore, to inform me of your decision as expeditiously as possible. That nothing may be wanting on the arrival of your squadron, a French officer will be stationed at Mangalore, to afford the necessary assistance, and to advise me of your intentions. To avoid any surprize or doubt, the ship, during the time she may remain at anchor in the roads, shall hoist American colours, with the national flag at the main-top-mast head, over that of the Sultaun, which my envoys carry for that purpose. I am desirous, and therefore particularly request that Citizen Aubaigne may be appointed to command this packet boat, as he knows my harbours, and is acquainted with the customs of my country.

Article 13. I depute four of my chiefs who have proved themselves worthy of my confidence, to treat in my name on the articles which I transmit to you; but should you neither have the power of accepting them altogether, nor of carrying them into effect without an order from the executive government of your mother country, I request you to despatch three of my chiefs in one of your best vessels for France, and to join with them some citizen whom your wisdom may select, to guide and to advise them in France. I despatch these chiefs for this express purpose: they are charged with a packet, and with orders to explain my intentions to the executive power; I cannot send my ship thither without giving the English reason to suspect some hostile designs on my part; if you send a squadron, send with it the remaining one of the four chiefs and also my ship, which I request may be coppered, and we will arrange matters accordingly. If, however, you think that the ship cannot be coppered without delaying the voyage of the convoy, you will send the ship back at the proper season, with a captain and two officers, whom I will pay.

Article 14. We will commence hostilities against the English and Portuguese; when, in case the Nizam and the Mahrattas should join them, we will make war against them also, for it will then be necessary to subjugate them also, and to render them tributaries to us.

These, Representatives, are my intentions; do not let my attachment to your nation expose me to the same calamity which I formerly suffered; I entreat you to reflect well before you return an answer, or you may expose me to great anguish of heart, since I shall act according to the tenor of your answer. I offer up my vows for the success of our enterprize, for the continuation of prosperity to the arms of the French Republic, one and indivisible, and for a speedy answer. I swear an inviolable friendship for your nation.

TIPPOO SULTAUN.

(A true Copy.) C. MACAULAY, Secretary.
(A true Translation.) G. G. KEBLE, French Translator.

7. Proclamation at the Isle of France.

Liberté. Egalité.	Liberty. Equality.
REPUBLIQUE FRANCAISE, Une & indivisible.	THE FRENCH REPUBLIC, One and indivisible.
PROCLAMATION.	PROCLAMATION.
Anne Joseph Hyppolite Malartic, General en Chef, Governeur-general des Isles de France & de la Re-	*Anne Joseph Hyppolite Malartic, Commander in Chief and Governor-General of the Isles of France*

union, & Commandant-general des Etablissements Français, a l'Est du Cap de Bonne Esperance.

CITOYENS,

Connaissant depuis plusieurs années votre zèle & votre attachment pour les interèts & la gloire de notre République, nous sommes tres empressés & nous nous faisons un devoir de vous donner connaissance de toutes les propositions que nous fait Tippoo Sultaun, par deux ambassadeurs qu'il nous a dépéchés.

Ce prince a écrit des lettres particulières á l'Assemblée Coloniale à tous les Généraux qui sont employés dans ce gouvernement, & nous a addressé un paquet pour le Directoire Executif.

1°. Il demande à faire une alliance offensive et défensive avec les Français, en proposant d'entretenir à ses frais, tant que la guerre durera dans l'Inde, les troupes qu'on pourra lui envoyer.

2°. Il promet de fournir toutes les choses nécessaires pour faire cette guerre, excepté le Vin & l'Eau de Vie, dont il se trouve absolument dénué.

3°. Il assure que tous les préparatifs sont faits pour reçevoir les secours qu'on lui donnera, & qu'à l'arrivée des troupes, les Chefs & Officiers trouveront toutes les choses

and Reunion, and of all the French establishments to the eastward of the Cape of Good Hope.

CITIZENS,

Having for several years known your zeal and your attachment to the interests, and to the glory of our Republic, we are very anxious, and we feel it a duty to make you acquainted with all the propositions which have been made to us by Tippoo Sultaun, through two ambassadors whom he has despatched to us.

This prince has written particular letters to the Colonial Assembly; to all the generals employed under this government; and has addressed to us a packet for the Executive Directory.

1. He desires to form an offensive and defensive alliance with the French, and proposes to maintain at his charge, as long as the war shall last in India, the troops which may be sent to him.

2. He promises to furnish every necessary for carrying on the war, wine and brandy excepted, with which he is wholly unprovided.

3. He declares that he has made every preparation to receive the succours which may be sent to him, and that on the arrival of the troops, the commanders and officers will

nécessaires pour faire une guerre a laquelle les Européens sont peu accoutumés.

4°. Enfin il n'attend plus que le moment ou les Français viendront à son secours, *pour déclarer la guerre aux Anglais, désirant avec ardeur pouvoir les chasser de l'Inde.*

Comme il nous est impossible de diminuer le nombre des soldats des 107e. & 108e. regimens, & de la garde soldée du Port de la Fraternité, à cause des secours que nous avons envoyés à nos alliés les Hollandais ; nous invitons tous les citoyens de bonne volonté, à se faire inscrire dans leurs municipalités respectives, pour aller servir sous les drapeaux de Tippoo.

Ce prince désire aussi avoir des citoyens de couleur, libres, & nous invitons tous ceux qui voudront aller servir sous ses drapeaux, à se faire aussi inscrire.

Nous pouvons assurer tous les citoyens qui se feront inscrire, que Tippoo leur fera des traitements avantageux qui seront fixés avec ses ambassadeurs qui s'engageront en outre, au nom de leur souverain, à ce que les Français qui auront pris parti dans ses armées, ne puissent jamais y être retenus quand ils voudront rentrer dans leur patrie.

find every thing necessary for making a war, to which Europeans are but little accustomed.

4. In a word he only waits the moment when the French shall come to his assistance, *to declare war against the English, whom he ardently desires to expel from India.*

As it is impossible for us to reduce the number of soldiers of the 107th and 108th regiments, and of the regular guard of Port Fraternité, on account of the succours which we have furnished to our allies the Dutch ; we invite the citizens, who may be disposed to enter as volunteers, to enrol themselves in their respective municipalities, and to serve under the banners of Tippoo.

This prince desires also to be assisted by the free citizens of colour, we therefore invite all such who are willing to serve under his flag, to enrol themselves.

We can assure all the citizens who shall enrol themselves, that Tippoo will allow them an advantageous rate of pay, the terms of which will be fixed with his ambassadors, who will further engage in the name of their sovereign, that all Frenchmen who shall enter into his armies, shall never be detained after they shall have expressed a wish to return to their own country.

Fait au Port Nord-Ouest, le 10 Pluviose, l'an six de la République Française, une & indivisible.	Done at Port North West, the 30th January, 1798.
(Signé) MALARTIC.	(Signed) MALARTIC.

8. Letter from Sultaun Selim to the Indian Sovereign, Tippoo Sultaun, dated Constantinople, 20th September, 1798; delivered to Mr. Spencer Smith, his Britannic Majesty's Minister Plenipotentiary, &c.

An exhortation to abstain from assisting the French against the English in India. The French faithless, and enemies of the Faith.

We take this opportunity to acquaint your Majesty, when the French Republic was engaged in a war with most of the powers of Europe within this latter period, our Sublime Porte not only took no part against them, but regardful of the ancient amity existing with that nation, adopted a system of the strictest neutrality, and shewed them even such acts of countenance as have given rise to complaints on the part of other Courts.

Thus friendly disposed towards them, and reposing a confidence in those sentiments of friendship which they appeared to profess for us, we gave no ear to many propositions and advantageous offers which had been made to us to side with the belligerent powers, but pursuant to our maxims of moderation and justice, we abstained from breaking with them without direct motive, and firmly observed the line of neutrality; all which is notorious to the world.

In this posture of things, when, the French having witnessed the greatest marks of attention from our Sublime Porte, a perfect reciprocity was naturally expected on their side, when no cause existed to interrupt the continuance of the peace betwixt the two nations, they all of a sudden have exhibited the unprovoked and treacherous proceedings, of which the following is a sketch.

They began to prepare a fleet in one of their harbours, called Toulon, with most extraordinary mystery, and when completely fitted out and ready for sea, embarked a large body of troops, and they put also on board several people versed in the Arabic language, and who had been in Egypt before; they gave the command of that armament to one of their generals, named

Buonaparte, who first went to the Island of Malta, of which he took possession, and thence proceeded direct for Alexandria, where being arrived the 17th Muharem, all of a sudden landed his troops, and entered the town by open force, publishing soon after manifestoes in Arabic among the different tribes, stating, in substance, that the object of their enterprize was not to declare war against the Ottoman Porte, but to attack the Beys of Egypt, for insults and injuries they had committed against the French merchants in time past; that peace with the Ottoman empire was permanent, that those of the Arabs who should join, would meet with the best treatment; but such as shewed opposition, would suffer death: with this further insinuation, made in different quarters, but more particularly to certain Courts at amity with us, that the expedition against the Beys was with the privity and consent of our Sublime Porte; which is a horrible falsity. After this they also took possession of Rosetta, not hesitating to engage in a pitched battle with the Ottoman troops, who had been detached from Cairo to assist the invaded.

It is a standing law amongst all nations, not to encroach upon each other's territories, whilst they are supposed to be at peace. When any such events take place as lead to a rupture, the motives, so tending, are previously made known between the parties; nor are any open aggressions attempted against their respective dominions until a formal declaration of war takes place.

Whilst, therefore, no interruption of the peace, nor the smallest symptom of misunderstanding appeared between our Sublime Porte and the French Republic, a conduct so audacious, so unprovoked, and so deceitfully sudden on their part, is an undeniable trait of the most extreme insult and treachery.

The province of Egypt is considered as a region of general veneration, from the immediate proximity of the noble city of Mecca, the Kebleh of the Mussulmen, (the point of the compass to which all Turks turn their face in performing their prayers) and the sacred town of Medina, where the tomb of our blessed prophet is fixed; the inhabitants of both these sacred cities deriving from thence their subsistence.

Independent of this, it has been actually discovered from several letters which have been intercepted, that the further project of the French is to divide Arabia into various republics; to attack the whole Mahommedan sect, in its religion and country; and by a gradual progression, to extirpate all Mussulmen from the face of the earth.

It is for these cogent motives and considerations, that we have determined to repel this enemy, and to adopt every vigorous measure against these persecutors of the faith; we placing all confidence in the Omnipotent God, the source of all succour, and in the intercession of him who is the glory of prophets.

Now it being certain that, in addition to the general ties of religion, the bonds of amity and good understanding have ever been firm and permanent with your Majesty, so justly famed for your zeal and attachment to our faith; and that more than once such public acts of friendly attention have been practised between us, as to have cemented the connection subsisting between the two countries, we therefore sincerely hope, from your Majesty's dignified disposition, that you will not refuse entering into concert with us, and giving our Sublime Porte every possible assistance, by such an exertion of zeal, as your firmness and natural attachment to such a cause cannot fail to excite.

We understand that, in consequence of certain secret intrigues carried on by the French in India, (after their accustomed system) in order to destroy the settlements, and to sow dissensions in the provinces of the English there, a strict connection is expected to take effect between them and your Majesty, for whose service they are to send over a corps of troops by the way of Egypt.

We are persuaded, that the tendency of the French plans cannot, in the present days, escape your Majesty's penetration and notice, and that no manner of regard will be given to their deceitful insinuations on your side: and whereas the Court of Great Britain is actually at war with them, and our Sublime Porte engaged on the other hand in repelling their aggressions, consequently the French are enemies to both; and such a reciprocity of interests must exist between those Courts, as ought to make both parties eager to afford every mutual succour which a common cause requires.

It is notorious, that the French, bent upon the overthrow of all sects and religions, have invented a new doctrine, under the name of Liberty; they themselves professing no other belief but that of Debrees; (Epicureans, or Pythagoreans) that they have not even spared the territories of the Pope of Rome, a country, since time immemorial, held in great reverence by all the European nations; that they have wrested and shared, with others, the whole Venetian State, notwithstanding that fellow republic had not only abstained from taking part against them, but had rendered them service during the course of the war, thus effacing the name of the republic of Venice from the annals of history.

There is no doubt that their present attempt against the Ottomans, as well as their ulterior designs (dictated by their avaricious view towards oriental riches) tend to make a general conquest of that country, (which may God never suffer to take effect!) and to expel every Mussulman from it, under pretence of annoying the English. Their end is to be once admitted in India, and then to develope what really lies in their hearts, just as they have done in every place where they have been able to acquire a footing.

In a word, they are a nation whose deceitful intrigues and perfidious pursuits know no bounds. They are intent on nothing, but on depriving people of their lives and properties, and on persecuting religion, wherever their arms can reach.

Upon all this, therefore, coming to your Majesty's knowledge, it is sincerely hoped, that you will not refuse every needful exertion towards assisting your brethren Mussulmen, according to the obligations of religion, and towards defending Hindostan itself, against the effect of French machinations. Should it be true, as we hear, that an intimate connection has taken place between your Court and that nation, we hope that, by weighing present circumstances, as well as every future inconvenience, which would result from such a measure, your Majesty will beware against it, and in the event of your having harboured any idea of joining with them, or of moving against Great Britain, you will lay such resolution aside. We make it our especial request, that your Majesty will please to refrain from entering into any measures against the English, or lending any compliant ear to the French. Should there exist any subject of complaint with the former, please to communicate it, certain as you may be of the employment of every good office on our side, to compromise the same; we wish to see the connection above alluded to, exchanged in favour of Great Britain.

We confidently expect that, upon consideration of all that is stated in this communication, and of the necessity of assisting your brethren Mussulmen in this general cause of religion, as well as of co-operating towards the above precious province being delivered from the hands of the enemy, your Majesty will employ every means, which your natural zeal will point out, to assist the common cause, and to corroborate, by that means, the ancient good understanding so happily existing between our empires.

A true Copy, N. B. EDMONSTONE,
Persian Translator to Govt.

9. From Tippoo Sultaun to the Right Hon. the Governor General.

Formal acknowledgment of the receipt of the above. Ambiguous consent to treat.

Received 13th February, 1799.

I have been much gratified by the agreeable receipt of your Lordship's two friendly letters, the first brought by a camelman, the last by hircurrahs, and understood their contents. The letter of the Prince, in station like Jumsheid; with angels as his guards; with troops numerous as the stars; the sun illumining the world of the heaven of empire and dominion; the luminary giving splendour to the universe of the firmament of glory and power; the Sultaun of the sea and the land; the King of Rome (i. e. the Grand Signior); be his empire and his power perpetual! addressed to me, which reached you through the British Envoy, and which you transmitted, has arrived. Being frequently disposed to make excursions and hunt, I am accordingly proceeding upon a hunting excursion. You will be pleased to despatch Major Doveton (about whose coming your friendly pen has repeatedly written) slightly attended (or unattended).

Always continue to gratify me by friendly letters, notifying your welfare.

A true Translation, N. B. EDMONSTONE,
Persian Translator to Govt.

10. Translation of the Draft of a Letter from Tippoo Sultaun to the Grand Seignior.

Private reply to Sultan Selim's letter. The English in India faithless, and enemies of the Faith.

In the Name of the Most Merciful God!

[After the customary invocation to the Deity and the Prophet, and a series of pompous titles, addressed to the Grand Seignior, the letter proceeds as follows:]

Your Highness's august letter, written on the 11th of Rubbee oossaunee 1213 of the Hedjree (*answering to the 23d September,*

1798) which was conveyed through the English[1], honoured me by its gracious arrival, was the means of glory and distinction, and the productive source of boundless favour. Its contents added strength and firmness to the foundations of union and attachment; and its gracious expressions gave stability to the fabric of friendship.

With respect to what your Highness wrote, of the invasion of the venerated land of Egypt by the devoted French, by treachery and deceit, notwithstanding the observance of long subsisting friendship on the part of your Highness.. The objects of that irreligious, turbulent people; the determination of the Ottoman Porte to employ the most vigorous measures to repel that rebellious race; of my assisting and joining my brethren Musselmans in the general cause of religion, and defending the regions of Hindostan from the machinations of this enemy; that I would communicate to your Highness whatever subject of complaint I might have against the English, when, by the aid of God and your Highness's good offices, those complaints should be removed to my satisfaction, and the grounds of opposition and estrangement be exchanged for the desirable objects of harmony and union. This, which your Highness did me the honour to write, has been understood.

By the favour of God, and the benevolence of the prophet, all the followers of the faith hold fraternity in religion: particularly the exalted Ottoman State and the Khoodadaud Sirkar (between which, regard and attachment are established firmly as columns, and of which friendship and union, repeated tokens have been interchanged) are aiding and assisting each other. As this labourer in the way of the Lord, is a brother in the faith, is obedient to your Highness's all powerful will, and does not conceive any difference to exist between us; I beg you will communicate to me what your Highness's exalted mind conceives will be conducive to the welfare and interests of the followers of the faith. As the French have made themselves your Highness's enemies, they have made themselves so to all the followers of the Faith—God is the protector and defender of the land of Hindostan; next to him, this suppliant at the Almighty Throne, does not and will not neglect the defence and service of the people. I am fully confident that your Highness will be disposed to afford your assistance and support, in all matters, to us Labourers. All Hindostan is over-run with infidels and polytheists, excepting the dominions of the Koodadaud Sirkar, which like the Ark of

[1] Over this word is written, '*The Governor of Madras.*'

Noah are safe under the protection and bounteous aid of God. It is my hope, from the supreme king of kings, that as at the appearance of a second Adam, the religion of Islaum will obtain exclusive prevalence over the whole country of Hindostan, and that all the sinful heretics will with the utmost ease become the prey of the swords of the combatants in the cause of religion. Be it known to those who stand at the foot of the imperial throne, that the treachery, deceit, and supremacy of the christians in the regions of Hindostan, are beyond the power of expression. A summary elucidation of this, will be found as follows:

A person, by name Da-ood Khaun, an Afghaun, was appointed to the Soobadarry of Arcot, on the part of the Emperor of Delhi. About that time, the French and English, each with one of their detested ships, and a few Kaufers (*Infidels*) on board, came to the coast, expressly for the purpose of trade; bringing with them some of the products of their country, such as knives, scissors, needles, china and glass-ware, for sale. After presenting several articles to the deluded Soobadar, as a Nuzzer (*or offering, expressive of submission*) they requested the grant of a spot of ground, sufficient for a single house, for their residence, in order that they might import the products of Europe, paying the proper duties, and there remain with a dozen of their people. The Soobadar complied with their request; and there the English resided for some time.

It happened, that the exalted Firmaun of Behaudur Shah, Son of Aulumgeer, Emperor of Shahjehaun-abaud (*Delhi*) addressed to Da-ood Khaun, arrived, directing him to leave a trusty Dewan (*Manager*) in Arcot, and repair himself to the presence. In conformity to the Emperor's summons, Da-ood Khaun repaired to Delhi, leaving Saadut-oolla Khaun as his deputy. Owing to the negligence and folly of the ministers at Delhi, Saadut-oolla Khaun became a traitor, and usurped the dominion of the country. About that period, the English and the French applied to the Soobadar for the grant of a little ground round about their houses; to which the Soobadar, from his want of foresight, and from his innate folly, consented; and accordingly granted them the ground which they asked. After this, both these nations erected small forts, and stationed about a hundred men to garrison them, (*verses*) 'Where a country is abandoned by its prince, every village becomes a principality.' The relations and followers of Saadut-oolla Khaun, each took possession of Taalooks (*districts*) and erecting fortresses, established their abode. At the same time, the French and English, taking with them some of the products of Europe, repaired to the districts of the relations and followers of Saadut-oolla Khaun, and contracted friendship with them; and under this cover, obtaining a complete insight into their characters, their mode of living, the structure of their forts, the administration of their territories, and the condition of their forces, they entertained from four to five hundred men of that country and waited their opportunity. In the mean time Saadut-oolla Khaun died. After his death his relations and adherents, who were very numerous, quarrelled among themselves, and one of them, by the name of Sufder Alli Khaun, entered into an intrigue with the infidels of Poonah, and solicited military succours. Agreeably to his request, an army of the Poonah infidels, consisting of 50,000 horse, under the command of Rugghoo Futteh Sing, invaded the province of Arcot; where Sufder Alli Khaun suffered his father Alli Doast Khaun to be slain in battle by the infidels of Poonah. After this, these infidels seeing the dissensions which prevailed amongst the adherents and relations of Sufder Alli Khaun, plundered all the inhabitants of that country, without discrimination of friend or foe; carried off a hundred thousand men and women prisoners to their own country, and sold them to slavery: they also took prisoner Hoossain Doast Khaun, known by the name of Chunda Khaun, who was the husband of Sufder Alli Khaun's sister, and carried him to Poonah. In the meantime, Mortiza Khaun, the governor of Vellore, and husband of another sister of Sufder Alli Khaun, enticed the latter to his house, and put him to death. After this event, Nizam-ool Moolk the Vizier of Delhi, who had made himself master of the Deccan, arrived in the province of Arcot, and appointing Anwar-oo-deen Khaun, Soobadaur of that province, on his own part gave in charge to him the two infant sons of the late Sufder Alli Khaun, with injunctions to protect and educate them, and then returned to the Deccan. After this, Anwar-oo-deen Khaun incited the Afghauns to murder one of the children. A short time after, Chunda Khaun, who was in confinement at Poonah, bribing the infidels with a sum of money, obtained his release, and arrived in the province of Arcot, whence he proceeded to Pondicherry, a factory belonging to the French, where he took refuge: he there procured a body of French troops, with which he marched against Anwar-oo-deen Khaun, with a view to reduce the province of Arcot. In the mean time, Anwar-oo-deen Khaun sought the assistance of the English, who then held a factory at Cheenaputtun (*Madras.*) Accordingly the English joined him with a body of troops. In proof of the words 'He who afforded assistance to the oppressor, shall fall under subjection to the very man he assisted,'—both these persons becoming the objects of the divine anger, sought assistance from these two infidel tribes, and proceeded to hostilities. It was so decreed, however, that Anwar-oo-deen Khaun fell by the hand of Hoossain Doast Khaun. After this, Mohummud Alli Khaun, son of Anwar-oo-deen Khaun, giving up both his worldly and spiritual concerns, to the direction of the English, and making them his protectors, prepared for hostilities against Chunda Khaun. In the mean time, Nizam-ool-Moolk died, and was succeeded by his son Naussir Jung; whom Mohummud Alli Khaun invited to join him: but before his arrival, Naussir Jung's nephew, Hidauyet Mohee-oo-deen Khaun, fled with a small body of troops to Pondicherry; and the French collecting a force which consisted of about a thousand men of their own nation, and about four thousand sepoys, proceeded with the troops of Hidauyet Mohee-oo-deen Khaun, against Naussir Jung; who joined with Mohummud Alli Khaun, after sustaining repeated engagements with the French, laid siege to the fortress of Gingee, which is situated on a hill, and was then in the possession of the French. The latter entering into a collusion with the Sirdars of Naussir Jung's army, attacked it in the night. After the alarm was given, Naussir Jung mounted his elephant; when a man, named Behauder Khaun, an Afghaun in his service, had the baseness to kill him by a musket shot, and causing his elephant to be driven close to that of Naussir Jung, cut off his head and stuck it on the point of a spear. Upon this event, the French set up Hidauyet Mohee-oo-deen Khaun as his successor, and, accompanied by a body of their own troops under the command of an officer named Bussy, directed his march towards Hyderabad. In the course of their march, they halted at the fort of Raychota, where the traitor Behauder Khaun, and the French troops commanded by Bussy, quarrelled about the division of the plundered treasure and jewels, and an engagement took place, in which Behauder Khaun, and the other cursed Afghaun chief, were slain, and precipitated to hell. Hidauyet Mohee-oo-deen Khaun, also fell in this engagement by a musket shot. The French then conferred the succession on the worthless Salibut Jung, second son of Nizam-ool-Moolk, and proceeded with him to Hyderabad;

whereby the whole of the Deccan may be said to have come under the authority of the French at Hyderabad. The French christians (who amounted to near 1,200 men) in a state of intoxication, in open day, entered the houses of the votaries of Islaum, and violated numbers of their women. Many of the females of the nobles ripped up their own bellies, and threw themselves into wells. Hence all the inhabitants of Hyderabad conceived enmity against the French.

In the mean time Nizam Alli Khaun, son of Nizam-ool-Moolk, imprisoned his elder brother Salibut Jung, and established himself in his room. A short time afterwards, when the utmost disagreement had taken place between the people of Hyderabad and the French, the worthless Bussy marched from that city with his troops and returned to Pondicherry. During these transactions Mohummud Alli Khaun, in conjunction with the English, carried on the war against Chunda Khaun, who was cordially the friend of the French. The armies of both the infidel nations contended for the province of Arcot, and after many battles and much bloodshed, the English and Mohummud Alli Khaun, having pledged their faith to him, and under that sanction made him their prisoner, put him to death, and obtained possession of the whole of the Arcot province, yielding a yearly revenue of near four crores of rupees.

When the English had thus established themselves in Arcot, they turned their views to the conquest of Bengal. To this end, with the same treachery and deceit which has been above described, they applied to the viceroy of Bengal also for a spot of ground; and having obtained possession of sufficient for a single house, they there stationed their people as for the purposes of trade, and waited their opportunity. About this time the viceroy of Bengal died, and contentions arose among his children and relations. The English taking part with the one, they subdued the other; and rendering that other entirely dependent upon them, obtained possession of the whole dominion of Bengal, a territory consisting of four Soobahs, and yielding an annual revenue of twenty crores of rupees. Not far from thence is a place called Lucknow, the ruler of which was Mirza Amauni (*Assof-oo-Dowlah*) son of Shujah-oo-Dowlah. By intrigue and chicane with him, they (*the English*) intruded themselves into that country also. What is more extraordinary is this: lately Mirza Amauni sent an ambassador to Zemaun Shah, the king of Caubul. This circumstance coming to the knowledge of the English (*Governor*) General[1] who resides at Calcutta, he proceeded thence on a visit to Mirza Amauni, and having leagued with the ministers of that country, caused Mirza Amauni to be poisoned, violated the chastity of his widow, and plundered his house of money and jewels, to the amount of twenty crores of Rupees. Throughout the territory of Bengal, wherever there were men of learning, science, and rank, the English have forcibly taken prisoners wives and daughters, violated their chastity, and carried them off to their own islands and country; seizing the youths of the class of Syuds, devotees, and learned men, and obliging them to eat the flesh of swine, proclaimed it by beat of tomtom. In the country of Bengal, and in all other places where their authority prevails, they set up swine butchers, and cause them to sell the flesh of hogs publicly in the streets and markets.

All this power and authority have the English acquired in the space of forty years.

About twenty years ago, during the life-time of my late revered father Hyder Alli Khaun, disputes occurring among the worthless Sirdars of the Poonah infidels, Roggoo-naut Rao, the uncle of Narrain Rao, the head of the Poonah state, treacherously murdered his nephew: the turbulent spirit of the chiefs, however, obliged him to seek refuge at Bombay, a place in the possession of the English.

The English, obtaining from him money and jewels to a large amount, detached an army with Roggoo-naut Rao for the reduction of Poonah. The Poonah ministers, deceitfully selected a child of two or three days old from their own class, proclaimed him as the genuine offspring of the murdered Narrain Rao, and as the successor to the Musnud (*throne*) and assembling an army, marched to oppose the English and Roggoo-naut Rao. Finding themselves unable to cope with the English, they repeatedly sent letters by ambassadors of rank to the presence of his late Highness (*Hyder Ali*) soliciting his assistance. His Highness prudently considering, that although it is declared 'Heretics are impure,' yet that it was more advisable to afford than refuse his assistance to the infidels belonging to the country (because the supremacy of the English was the source of evil to all God's creatures)—with a view to the aid of Poonah, marched to Madras with a vast army. Many engagements ensued, and many places fell, and Madras itself was near being taken; when

---

[1] Sir John Shore.

it pleased God that his Highness should end his days in that expedition, and he died in the vicinity of Arcot. After this event, I continued the war; and after many victories, and the capture of numberless prisoners, the English sent their ambassadors, humbly, and by engagement and oath, to sue for peace. Although I was not myself disposed to grant them peace, yet by the earnest advice of the nobles of the Khoodadaud Sirkar, I consented. Four or five years after, when ambassadors from the Khoodadaud Sirkar, arrived at the Sublime Porte; and after representing the sentiments of friendship, returned to the presence. The English, receiving information of this circumstance, with hearts inflamed, immediately conceived that all the tribe of Islaum were about to league together for their destruction. They knew too, that they had given your Highness proofs of their evil disposition, and therefore, uniting to themselves Nizam Alli Khaun, and the infidels of Poonah, they waged war against the Khoodadaud Sirkar for four years. At length, near a hundred thousand of the followers of the faith, had determined to slay their wives and families with their own hands, and rushing upon the infidels, drink the cup of martyrdom, and plunge the infidels into hell. The counsellors, the Lords, and the respected sages of Islaum, all agreed that this attack upon the dominions of the Khoodadaud Sirkar was in consequence of the deputation of ambassadors with letters to the Sublime Porte, and therefore that it was advisable by any means to accommodate matters for the present; to communicate to your Highness all that occurred, and joined with your Highness's aid, proceed to exterminate the infidels. I approved the representation of my faithful servants, and surrendering three crores and thirty lacs of rupees in treasure, and half my country (which was all a dead loss to me) put an end to the contest.

The English having adopted a determined resolution to subdue the whole of Hindostan, and to subvert the Mussulman religion, and having united to themselves Nizam Alli Khaun, and the infidels of Poonah, have for five years past been devising the means; accordingly they have lately written in plain and undisguised terms, that it is their intention to destroy the religion of Islaum—'evil designs return upon the heads of the inventors.' The infidels of Poonah, in consequence of the disagreements prevailing among the ministers at Delhi, have subverted that country, and having destroyed its houses, have erected their own temples on their ruins—they have possessed themselves entirely of that kingdom, whilst a poor sightless individual of the royal family of Delhi, whose servants put out his eyes, is seated in his house in a state the most abject. The resources of his maintenance are fixed from the sale of the fruits of his gardens; and he is obliged to pay the price (*of that maintenance*) by paying adulation to those treacherous infidels. Near five hundred thousand of the infidels of the district of Calicut, Nuzzurabaud, Zufferabaud, and Ashrufabaud, who were wavering on the precincts of obedience, have been converted at different times. Praise be to God, that the whole energy of the well-directed mind of this labourer in the way of the Lord, on whose forehead is engraved the motto 'They dread not the terrific day of judgment,' is continually exerted to support the Religion of Mohummud. Accordingly, having lately been informed of the excessive commotions excited by the son of Abdool Wahaub in the neighbourhood of Mecca the holy, I immediately addressed letters to the supreme minister Yoosuf Vizier, to the Shereef of Mecca, and the servants of the holy receptacle (*meaning the place at Medina where Mohummud is buried*) purporting, that it was my intention to send a considerable force under the command of one of my approved sons, and desiring them to write to me a particular account of the situation of affairs in that quarter. For the illustrious Kaaba is the object of veneration to the followers of truth, and the object of the regard of the All Powerful; and to do services thereunto is productive of blessings, both in this world and the world to come.

The respected and accomplished Syuds, Syud Alli Mohummud and Syud Modaur-oo-deen, are now nominated and deputed with this friendly letter to represent various points of great importance, and to communicate the sentiments of my mind, and with instructions to remain in attendance on your Majesty during three years. I trust that they will be honoured by admission to your Highness's presence, and have an opportunity of a personal conference, and of stating to you my sentiments, and that their representations will obtain full credit with your Highness. May the victorious banners of Islaum be ever prevalent, and every trace of heresy and infidels be wiped away!

[A letter to the same effect as the foregoing, was also written to Zemaun Shah; several alterations, however, which were necessary to adapt the letter to the situation of Zemaun Shah, are inserted in the margin of the draft.]

(A true translation.)

N. B. Edmonstone, P. T. to the Government.

11. The Earl of Mornington to his Excellency Lieutenant-General Harris.

Instructions for the political *conduct of the War with Tippoo.*

Fort St. George, Feb. 22nd, 1799.

Sir,

I have reason to believe that many of the tributaries, principal officers, and other subjects of Tippoo Sultaun, are inclined to throw off the authority of that Prince, and to place themselves under the protection of the Company and of our allies. The war in which we are again involved, by the treachery and violence of the Sultaun, renders it both just and expedient that we should avail ourselves, as much as possible, of the discontents and disaffection of his people. It is, therefore, advisable, to arrange a plan for the regular conduct of all negotiations connected with this object.

Being apprehensive that your more important avocations will not admit of your taking any part in the details of this business, I hereby direct you to constitute a commission for this purpose, to consist of the Honourable Colonel Wellesley, Lieutenant-Colonel Close, Lieutenant-Colonel Agnew, and Captain Malcolm, assistant to the Resident at Hyderabad; with Captain Macaulay, to act as secretary to the commission.

The commissioners are to act constantly in communication with you, and to obey whatever directions you shall think proper to signify to them.

They are to report their proceedings to me as frequently and as regularly as circumstances shall permit.

They will correspond with the commissioners in Malabar on such points as shall be connected in any respect with the objects of this commission: and for this purpose you will be pleased to furnish them with a copy of the Company's cypher, No. 11.

Their duty is to consist, generally, in receiving and considering all such overtures from the subjects of Tippoo Sultaun (of whatever class), as may either be referred by you to the commissioners, or may be addressed to them through other channels.

In cases which may not admit of reference to me, they will decide, under your authority, on the degree and nature of the encouragement proper to be given to such persons as may propose to place themselves under the protection of the Company. The following extracts from my instructions to the commissioners in Malabar (which you will be pleased to communicate to the officers named in the present commission), will explain the general principles by which their conduct is to be regulated.

'I now authorize you to avail yourselves, without reserve, of the overtures made some time since to Mr. Uthoff and to Captain Mahony, by Shehab-ud-Dein Khan, to whatever extent you may judge practicable and useful. You will also receive and encourage from any other of the chiefs, or public officers of Tippoo Sultaun, on the coast of Malabar, any advances which shall appear to you to promise assistance to the Company, in the prosecution of the war against that Prince.

'I am not at present in possession of any information which enables me to judge with sufficient certainty of the general disposition and temper of the inhabitants of Tippoo's remaining dominions on the coast of Malabar. If, however, they should manifest an inclination to revolt against his authority, and you should think it expedient to encourage them, I leave it to your discretion to offer them such support and protection as the state of the British force on your coast may enable you to afford. I also authorize you to give to all tributaries, or others, renouncing their allegiance to Tippoo, and acting heartily in our favour, the most positive assurances, in the name of the Company, that I will use my utmost efforts to compel that Prince to relinquish all claims upon their allegiance, and to agree to their becoming the dependents and subjects of the Honourable Company, on such terms as shall hereafter be arranged under my orders.'

The enclosure No. 1 contains an account of the overtures from Shehab-ud-Dein Khan, referred to in the foregoing extract.

It will be obvious, however, that the instructions apply more particularly to tributaries, or zemindars, possessing or claiming such districts on the borders of the Company's territory as may be annexed to it, in the favourable event of a further reduction of the Sultaun's power, and of a partition of his present dominions.

The commission will communicate with Meer Allum, with respect to all such proposals as may appear likely to concern the interests of the Nizam. Any overtures which may be made by tributaries, or other subjects of the Sultaun, adjacent to the present frontier of his Highness, will be considered with Meer Allum's assistance; the necessary encouragement and assurances to such persons being, more properly, to be adjusted by the powers to whom their allegiance may eventually be transferred.

The same principle must be applied to any offers which may

proceed from districts bordering on the present Mahratta dominions. Should a Mahratta force hereafter join your army, the commissioners will (in the cases to which I now refer), consult with the commander of that force, as well as with the commanding officer of any British detachment from Bombay which may be acting with the Mahrattas.

But, although in the two last cases, authoritative assurances and encouragement would most properly proceed from our allies respectively, it is not improbable that, on some occasions, the guarantee of the Company may be required to such engagements, and even be made an indispensable preliminary condition by the parties proposing to abandon the cause of Tippoo.

It is desirable to avoid all such engagements of the nature of a guarantee, the commissioners, therefore, will be careful not to guarantee any engagements which the allies may be inclined to form with persons renouncing their allegiance to Tippoo Sultaun, excepting in cases where the proposed advantage shall be important to the common cause, and evidently unattainable without a formal guarantee. In general, therefore, such contracts must be avoided; but if a case of peculiar exigency should arise, without a possibility of a previous reference to me, the commissioners will regulate their conduct as nearly as possible on the principles which I have already established, for cases more immediately affecting the particular interests of the Company.

The firm foundation on which our connexion with the Court of Hyderabad is now happily placed, disposes me to guarantee, with less hesitation, any engagements which the Nizam, or Meer Allum, on his Highness's behalf, might be willing to form with the tributaries of the enemy on the side of his Highness's frontier than prudence would require in any similar transaction under the Mahratta power.

With respect to overtures proceeding from the more central parts of the enemy's country, and, therefore, from persons whose possessions are not likely, in any event, to be transferred to any of the allies, it is evident that such overtures cannot be received or encouraged in the same manner as those which have been already considered. To offers of this description, the commission must return merely such assurances of aid and support (whether military or pecuniary), as it may be immediately practicable to afford; avoiding, carefully, any engagements which might ultimately embarrass a negotiation for peace. With regard to pecuniary aids, I authorize you to give your sanction to such advances of money as the commissioners may deem essentially necessary to promote the objects of these instructions; apprizing you, however, that these advances of money must be confined within the limits of moderation, and with due attention to economy.

With these instructions you will receive copies, in Persian and English, of a declaration which I propose to publish for the purpose of justifying to the powers of Hindostan the measures which the conduct of Tippoo Sultaun has compelled the Company and their allies to adopt. You will communicate this document to the commissioners, who are to prepare and publish, in your name, such proclamations as shall appear to them to be best adapted to the state of the different parts of the enemy's country through which you may pass, or with which you may open any intercourse, conforming the general tenor of all such proclamations to the principles and spirit of the declaration.

You have already been furnished with copies in Persian and English, of my correspondence with Tippoo Sultaun, as well as with translations in Persian, of the Grand Signior's manifesto, and of his Highness's letter to the Sultan; you will communicate these papers to the commissioners. Those passages of the correspondence, and of the documents received from Constantinople, which expose the character of the French republic, and the outrages committed by the French against the acknowledged head of the Mahommedan church, may, in particular, be employed to produce an useful impression on all the Mussulman inhabitants of Mysore. The commissioners will make any further use of these documents which may appear advisable.

I also enclose (No. 2) copies, in Persian and English, of an agreement which has been lately concluded, under my direction, with certain chiefs of the Ghyre Mehdy sect of Mussulmans. For an account of the banishment of these sectaries from the dominions of Tippoo Sultaun, I refer you to the accompanying extract of a letter from the Resident at Hyderabad, under date the 4th of January last, making the inclosure No. 3. Among these exiles are many persons who formerly held situations of great trust under the government of the late Hyder Ali Khan, as well as under that of Tippoo Sultaun; and it is obvious that all these persons must be intimately acquainted with the country of the enemy. It will be the business of the commissioners, under your orders, to consider how the knowledge and probable connexions of these people, may be best applied to the promotion of the objects of their commission. It appears that the Sirdars, whom, together with 400 Sillahdar horse, I have agreed to entertain for the present (principally with a view to the advantages which may be derived from their local knowledge and connexions) possess the means, as well as the inclination, of levying for our service a considerable body of cavalry, consisting of their exiled associates, now dispersed throughout the dominions of the Peishwa and of the Nizam. To employ their whole force in the field would be extremely burthensome, and I trust we shall never be under the necessity of resorting to such assistance beyond the extent of the arrangement already concluded with Jaffier Khan and Syed Yacoob.

The commission will be confidentially informed by Captain Malcolm of the progress which may have been made in a certain secret negotiation which has been opened by Meer Allum, in communication with Captain Malcolm since the conduct of Tippoo Sultaun compelled me to adopt the resolution of attacking his territories. It is impossible for me, in the present stage of this negotiation, to give the commission any precise instructions for the regulation of their proceedings with relation to this very peculiar and important case, and, therefore, I must leave the management of it to their discretion, aided by that of Meer Allum. If, however, they should be able to transmit to me any report on this delicate point before the communication between the army and this Presidency shall become precarious or difficult, it is my desire that they should write to me in cypher, a caution which they must always observe in their correspondence with me, from any position which may render their despatches liable to be intercepted.

The enclosure No. 4, consists of a memorandum of a most secret and delicate nature, relating to the family which governed Mysore previously to the usurpation of Hyder Ali Khan.

It is obvious that no advantageous negotiation can be opened with any of the surviving branches of this family under any other circumstances than a determination, accompanied by undoubted power, to effect the total removal of the ruling dynasty. Such a determination in the present stage of our contest with Tippoo Sultaun would be premature, and incompatible with the principles on which my instructions to you of the 3rd instant were founded. My orders for the march of the army being grounded on the necessity of providing for our own indispensable security and reasonable indemnity, and being strictly limited to those justifiable objects. There is, besides, no reason to suppose that any of the persons mentioned in the accompanying memoir could be rendered useful (in any material degree) in the prosecution of the war.

The commissioners must, therefore, confine their proceedings on this subject to enquiries into the state of parties in Mysore, with a view to the practicability of restoring that family with or without the consent of the principal Mussulman chiefs at present in authority in the country. The commission will readily perceive that these enquiries must be conducted with the utmost caution and prudence; for if their object were to transpire, the discovery might check, if not prevent, many advances which would otherwise be made from persons attached to the Mussulman Government.

The personal safety of the surviving adherents of the ancient family of the Rajahs of Mysore, and even of the Rance herself, also requires peculiar discretion and secrecy in the conduct of this part of the business of the commission. The most dreadful scene of vengeance and slaughter would be the probable consequence of Tippoo's receiving the slightest intimation of the contents of the accompanying memoir, which, therefore, after being attentively perused by the commissioners, must be destroyed.

You will direct Captain Macleod, of the intelligence department, to communicate, from time to time, to the commission whatever intelligence he may receive of a nature connected with the objects of the commission, with which I authorize you to make him fully acquainted.

I am, &c.

MORNINGTON.

12. Declaration of the Right Honourable the Governor General in Council, for all the forces and affairs of the British nation in the East Indies, on behalf of the Honourable the East India Company and the allies of the said Company there, his Highness the Nizam and the Peishwa.

Declaration of the occasion of the War with Tippoo.

Fort St. George, 22d Feb., 1799.

A solemn treaty of peace and friendship was concluded at Seringapatam, between the Honourable Company and the

Nabob Asoph Jah and the Peishwa on the one part, and the Nabob Tippoo Sultaun on the other part; and from that day all commotion and hostility ceased. Since that day, the three allied states have invariably manifested a sacred regard for the obligations contracted under that treaty with the Nabob Tippoo Sultaun. Of this uniform disposition, abundant proofs have been afforded by each of the allies. Whatever differences have arisen with regard to the limits of the territory of Mysore, have been amicably adjusted without difficulty, and with the most exact attention to the principles of equity, and to the stipulations of treaty. Such has been the solicitude of the allies for the preservation of tranquillity, that they have viewed with forbearance, for some years past, various embassies and military preparations on the part of Tippoo Sultaun, of a tendency so evidently hostile to the interests of the allies, as would have justified them, not only in the most serious remonstrances, but even in an appeal to arms. On the part of the British Government every endeavour has been employed to conciliate the confidence of the Sultaun, and to mitigate his vindictive spirit, by the most unequivocal acknowledgment and confirmation of his just rights, and by the removal of every cause of jealousy which might tend to interrupt the continuance of peace. These pacific sentiments have been most particularly manifested in the Governor General's recent decision on Tippoo Sultaun's claim to the district of Wynaad, and in the negotiation opened by his Lordship with regard to the districts of Amerah and Souleah. In every instance the conduct of the British Government in India towards Tippoo Sultaun, has been the natural result of those principles of moderation, justice, and good faith, which the legislature of Great Britain and the Honourable the East India Company have firmly established as the unalterable rule of their intercourse with the native princes and states of India.

The exemplary good faith and the pacific disposition of the allies, since the conclusion of the treaty of Seringapatam, has never been disputed even by Tippoo Sultaun. Far from having attempted to alledge even the pretext of a complaint against their conduct, he has constantly acknowledged their justice, sincerity, and good faith; and has professed, in the most cordial terms, his desire to maintain and strengthen the foundations of harmony and concord with them.

In the midst of these amicable professions on the part of Tippoo Sultaun, and at the moment when the British Government had issued orders for the confirmation of his claim to Wynaad, it was with astonishment and indignation that the allies discovered the engagements which he had contracted with the French nation, in direct violation of the treaty of Seringapatam, as well as of his own most solemn and recent protestations of friendship towards the allies.

Under the mask of these specious professions, and of a pretended veneration for the obligations of treaty, Tippoo Sultaun despatched ambassadors to the Isle of France, who, in a period of profound peace in India, proposed and concluded, in his name, an offensive alliance with the French, for the avowed purpose of commencing a war of aggression against the Company, and consequently against the Peishwa and the Nizam, the allies of the Company.

The ambassadors, in the name of Tippoo Sultaun, demanded military succours from the French, and actually levied a military force in the Isle of France, with the declared view of prosecuting the intended war.

When the ambassadors returned, in a French ship of war, from the Isle of France, Tippoo Sultaun suffered the military force, which they had levied for the avowed purpose of making war upon the allies, to land in his country; and finally, he admitted it into his army: by these personal acts ratifying and confirming the proceedings of his ambassadors.

This military force, however, was not sufficiently powerful to enable him immediately to attempt his declared purpose of attacking the Company's possessions, but in the meanwhile he advanced his hostile preparations conformably to his engagements with the French; and he was ready to move his army into the Company's territories whenever he might obtain from France the effectual succours which he had assiduously solicited from that nation.

But the providence of God, and the victorious arms of the British nation, frustrated his vain hopes, and checked the presumptuous career of the French in Egypt at the moment when he anxiously expected their arrival on the coast of Malabar.

The British Government, the Nizam, and the Peishwa, had not omitted the necessary precaution of assembling their forces for the joint protection of their respective dominions. The strict principles of self-defence would have justified the allies at that period of time in making an immediate attack upon the territories of Tippoo Sultaun; but even the happy intelligence of the glorious success of the British fleet at the mouth of the Nile did not abate the anxious desire of the allies to maintain the relations of amity and peace with Tippoo Sultaun. They attempted, by a moderate representation, to recall him to a sense of his obligations, and of the genuine principles of prudence and policy; and they employed every effort to open the channels of negotiation, and to facilitate the means of amicable accommodation. With these salutary views, the Governor General, on the 8th November, 1798, in the name of the allies, proposed to despatch an ambassador to Tippoo Sultaun, for the purpose of renewing the bonds of friendship, and of concluding such an arrangement as might afford effectual security against any future interruption of the public tranquillity; and his Lordship repeated the same proposal on the 10th December, 1798. Tippoo Sultaun declined, by various evasions and subterfuges, this friendly and moderate advance on the part of the allies, and he manifested an evident disposition to reject the means of pacific accommodation, by suddenly breaking up, in the month of December, the conferences which had commenced with respect to the districts of Amerah and Souleah, and by interrupting the intercourse between his subjects and those of the Company on their respective frontiers. On the 9th January, 1799, the Governor General being arrived at Fort St. George (notwithstanding these discouraging circumstances in the conduct of Tippoo Sultaun) renewed with increased earnestness, the expression of his Lordship's anxious desire to despatch an ambassador to the Sultaun.

The Governor General expressly solicited the Sultaun to return an answer within one day to this letter; and as it involved no proposition either injurious to the rights, dignity, or honour of the Sultaun, or in any degree novel or complicated either in form or substance, it could not require a longer consideration. The Governor General waited with the utmost solicitude for an answer to the reasonable and distinct proposition contained in his letter of the 9th January, 1799. Tippoo Sultaun, however, who must have received this letter before the 15th of January, remained silent, although the Governor General had plainly apprized that prince, that dangerous consequences would result from delay. In the meanwhile the season for military operations had already advanced to so late a period, as to render a speedy decision indispensable to the security of the allies. Under these circumstances, on the 3rd of February (eight days having elapsed from the period when an answer might have been received from Seringapatam to the Governor General's letter of the 9th January) his Lordship declared to the allies, that the necessary measures must now be adopted, without delay, for securing such advantages as should place the common safety of the allies beyond the reach of the insincerity of Tippoo Sultaun, and of the violence of the French. With this view, the Governor General, on the 3rd of February, issued orders to the British armies to march, and signified to the commander of his Majesty's squadron, that the obstinate silence of the Sultaun must be considered as a rejection of the proposed amicable negotiation.

At length, on the 13th of February, a letter from Tippoo Sultaun reached the Governor General, in which the Sultaun signifies to his Lordship, 'that being frequently disposed to make excursions and hunt, he was accordingly proceeding upon a hunting excursion;' adding, 'that the Governor General would be pleased to despatch Major Doveton to him, unattended or slightly attended.'

The allies will not dwell on the peculiar phrases of this letter; but it must be evident to all the states of India, that the answer of the Sultaun has been deferred to this late period of the season, with no other view than to preclude the allies, by insidious delays, from the benefit of those advantages which their combined military operations would enable them to secure. On those advantages alone (under the recent experience of Tippoo Sultaun's violation of the treaty of Seringapatam, and under the peculiar circumstances of that prince's offensive alliance with the French) can the allies now venture to rely for the faithful execution of any treaty of peace concluded with Tippoo Sultaun.

The allies cannot suffer Tippoo Sultaun to profit by his own studied and systematic delay, nor to impede such a disposition of their military and naval force, as shall appear best calculated to give effect to their just views.

Bound by the sacred obligations of public faith, professing the most amicable disposition, and undisturbed in the possession of those dominions secured to him by treaty, Tippoo Sultaun wantonly violated the relations of amity and peace, and compelled the allies to arm in defence of their rights, their happiness, and their honour.

For a period of three months, he obstinately rejected every

pacific overture, in the hourly expectation of receiving that succour which he has eagerly solicited for the prosecution of his favourite purposes of ambition and revenge. Disappointed in his hopes of immediate vengeance and conquest, he now resorts to subterfuge and procrastination; and, by a tardy, reluctant, and insidious acquiescence in a proposition which he had so long and repeatedly declined, he endeavours to frustrate the precautions of the allies, and to protract every effectual operation, until some change of circumstances and of season shall revive his expectations of disturbing the tranquillity of India, by favouring the irruption of a French army.

The allies are equally prepared to repel his violence, and to counteract his artifices and delays.

The allies are, therefore, resolved to place their army in such a position as shall afford adequate protection against any artifice or insincerity, and shall preclude the return of that danger which has so lately menaced their possessions. The allies, however, retaining an anxious desire to effect an adjustment with Tippoo Sultaun, Lieutenant General Harris, Commander-in-Chief of his Majesty's and the Honourable Company's forces on the coast of Coromandel and Malabar, is authorized to receive any embassy which Tippoo Sultaun may despatch to the head quarters of the British army, and to concert a treaty on such conditions as appear to the allies to be indispensably necessary for the establishment of a secure and permanent peace.

Dated Fort St. George, 22nd February, 1799, by order of the Right Honourable the Governor General in Council,

JOS. WEBBE.

A true Copy, N. B. EDMONSTONE,
Persian Translator to Govt.

13. From the Governor-General to General Harris.

Advantageous circumstances under which the War was undertaken.

(Private.) Fort St. George, February 23, 1799.

My dear General,

'Having answered all your public and private letters, adopted every arrangement suggested in your several minutes, and furnished you with detailed instructions applicable to every contingency for which I can provide, I now proceed to communicate to you without reserve my private sentiments with regard to your own situation, and to my expectations of the result of the important expedition which I have entrusted to your charge. The army of the Carnatic immediately under your command is unquestionably the best appointed, the most completely equipped, the most amply and liberally supplied, the most perfect in point of discipline, and the most fortunate in the acknowledged experience and abilities of its officers in every department, which ever took the field in India. It comprises a more numerous and better appointed corps of cavalry than any European power in India ever brought into action. The army on the coast of Malabar appears by all accounts to be in an equally efficient state, and the command on that coast never before was lodged in such able hands. All the departments relating to supplies from that quarter promise to afford a far more effectual assistance than was derived from thence during the last war. The powerful force which is destined to co-operate from the southward is an advantage not possessed in the last war, and which will become doubly useful under the conduct of Lieutenant-Colonel Brown; and in the Baramahl, Lieutenant-Colonel Read has already contributed the fruits of his experience in the collection of supplies, and every measure has been taken to secure the earliest benefits from his exertions. The appearance of so large a fleet on Tippoo's coasts is a circumstance of advantage not possessed in the last war, and which cannot fail to aid your operations, by intimidating the enemy and by encouraging defection among his subjects. With regard to the allies, the Nizam's force has appeared in the field at a much earlier period than in the last contest with Tippoo; and the cordial zeal of the court of Hyderabad for our success (which was so questionable during the last war) now admits of no doubt.

The Mahrattahs have accepted a detachment from Bombay; and during the siege of Seringapatam there is no reason to apprehend that the Peishwa will not make every effort to assist you with a large body of cavalry. You are invested with powers fully adequate to the management of these extraordinary and numerous advantages, and you are surrounded by a staff appointed in the most liberal manner, and uniting every species of knowledge and ability which can tend to give additional force to the efforts of your own experience and zeal. The object of your operations is single, distinct, and definite, and the means of attaining it have been the continual study of yourself, and of those acting under your orders. The enemy's country, the nature of his resources, the strength of his defences, and the character of his force, are subjects perfectly familiar to the whole of your staff, and to most of your principal officers. He cannot make a movement which they will not anticipate, nor is any contingency likely to arise against which they will not have provided. On the other hand, Tippoo Sultaun's army is known to have suffered essentially both in numbers and discipline since the last war. His finances are in great disorder; he no longer possesses the confidence of his army, his councils are distracted by a variety of contending factions, and his spirits are dejected and broken by the disappointment of his hopes of French assistance, by the retreat of Zemaun Shah, by the failure of his intrigues at the courts of Poonah and Hyderabad, and by the unexampled vigour, alacrity, and extent of our military preparations. You possess, therefore, every advantage which the most sanguine mind could expect, or the most anxious could desire, in the strength of your own army, in the cordiality of the allies, in the comparative weakness and dejection of the enemy, in the efficiency of your power, in the support of the Government under which you are to act, in the ability of the counsels which you can command, and in the unity and simplicity of the object which you are directed to pursue. Under such circumstances, it is not presumption to expect the most decisive success. With a full confidence that you will make a just use of the unprecedented and unlimited advantages of your present enviable and commanding situation, and with a persuasion that you will conduct your army with a degree of vigour and alacrity proportioned to that with which you have equipped it, I cannot entertain the smallest doubt that (under Providence) the issue of the expedition will be as speedy and prosperous as the means which you possess are abundant and unexampled. I am, however, aware that, in all great enterprises, difficulties will occur; but where previous measures have been well combined, and every seasonable precaution provided, a manly firmness will surmount obstacles even of a formidable appearance, and the trivial ordinary embarrassments of detail are conquered the moment they are despised. Recollect the difficulties which opposed the detachment of a large portion of the central army to accomplish an arduous undertaking at the court of the Nizam; you encountered every impediment with resolution and spirit, and within two months you saw the happy effects of your own firmness in the complete and easy success of that important measure, and you now feel those effects in the great accession of strength which has resulted from that measure to the common cause of the allies.

Recollect that the equipment of the very army which you now command was long represented to be utterly impracticable within the present season; and that difficulties absolutely insurmountable were supposed to preclude the possibility of raising the necessary funds for carrying on the present campaign. Every impartial mind must *now* admit that a more striking example of the efficacy of perseverance and resolution in overcoming practical obstacles of detail cannot be exhibited than that which appears in the actual state of your order of battle, and of your tumbrils. These reflections will naturally animate you to an unremitting exertion of the same spirit of alacrity and promptitude, which has brought your army to its present unrivalled and admirable condition. The magnitude of the enterprise, and the means which you possess of commanding its success by a vigorous use of your extensive powers, will raise your mind above the consideration of all temporary inconveniences, will enable you to overcome every delay, and will accelerate the rapidity of your progress towards that object, which however great and valuable is easily attainable by diligence, fortitude and despatch. With these sentiments, my dear General, I take my leave of you (I trust for a very short period of time), in the firm conviction, that, within a few weeks, I shall have the satisfaction of congratulating you on the prosperous issue of a service, combining more solid advantages and more brilliant distinctions than the favour of fortune, season, and circumstances, ever placed within the reach of any British subject in India, from the earliest success of our arms to the present day.

Believe me, my dear General,
With the greatest regard and good wishes,
Your faithful friend and servant,
MORNINGTON.

14. The Earl of Mornington to the Honourable the Court of Directors.

Vindication and plan of the Mysore War.

Fort St. George, 20th March, 1799.

Hon. Sirs,

My separate despatch, under date the 21st November, forwarded by the *Eurydice*, will have apprized your Honourable Court of the measures which I took for the purpose of restoring to his Highness the Nizam the power of fulfilling his defensive engagements with the Company.

At the same time my endeavours were employed with equal assiduity to give vigour and effect to the treaties subsisting with his Highness the Peishwa. The return of Nana Furnaveese to the administration afforded for some time a just expectation that our alliance with the Mahrattas would speedily be restored with additional vigour and advantage, but the increasing distractions of the Mahratta empire unfortunately frustrated the wise counsels of that experienced and able statesman, and disappointed my views at the Court of Poonah. I had, however, the satisfaction to ascertain that the disposition of that Court, under the administration of Nana, continued perfectly favourable to the British interests, and that want of power would be the sole cause of its inaction in the event of a war with Tippoo Sultaun.

From the moment of my arrival at Fort St. George all the inhabitants of this settlement, and every officer, civil and military, appeared to be animated by an unanimous determination to discharge their respective duties with a degree of cheerfulness and ardour correspondent with the exigency and importance of the occasion; and I was soon satisfied that the disposition, of which I lamented the appearance in the months of July and August, had either been subdued by the just exercise of authority, or corrected by reflection, and by the more full disclosure of the views of the enemy. The zeal, alacrity, and public spirit of the bankers and commercial agents at Madras, as well as of the most respectable of your civil servants at this Presidency, enabled me, within a few weeks, to raise a large sum of money, by loan, for the public service. Previous to my departure from Bengal, I had remitted twenty lacs of rupees in specie for the use of this Presidency; I now despatch the *Sybille* to Calcutta for a further supply; and the extraordinary exertion of his Excellency the Vice-President in Council, assisted by the diligence and ability of Mr. Thomas Myers, the Accountant-General of Bengal, furnished me with an additional aid of twenty lacs within so short a time, that the movement of the army was not delayed for an instant on account of a deficiency of treasure, and Lieutenant-General Harris was provided with a sufficient supply of specie to maintain his army in the field until the month of May.

Tippoo Sultaun remaining silent for a considerable time, after the receipt of my letter of the 9th of January, I concluded that his object must be to delay his answer until the season should be so far advanced as to render the capture of Seringapatam impracticable during the present year.

In the mean while the advices from Bussorah, Bagdad, Constantinople, and Bombay were of so uncertain a nature as to leave me still in doubt with respect to the condition of the French army in Egypt; the only safe conclusion which could be drawn from those advices being, that the French still maintained the possession of that country with a large army.

No intelligence had been received from the Red Sea respecting the arrival of any of his Majesty's ships on that station, nor had I been able to ascertain, with any degree of accuracy, what means the French might either have provided, or might find on the spot to enable them to reach the Sultaun's dominions.

In addition to these circumstances, I knew that, while Tippoo Sultaun had declined to receive an ambassador from the Honourable Company, and had omitted to answer my late letters, he had despatched native vakeels from Seringapatam, who, together with M. Du Buc, (one of the leaders of the French force, raised in the Isle of France under M. Malartic's proclamation,) were on the point of embarking at Tranquebar with an avowed mission from the Sultaun to the Executive Directory of France.

On the 3rd of February I had received no answer from the Sultaun to my letter of the 9th of January; although the communication between Seringapatam and Fort St. George does not require, at the most, a longer time than eight, and is sometimes effected in four, days.

In order, therefore, to defeat the object of the Sultaun's silence, and to avail myself of the actual superiority of our force, and of the advantages of the present season, before the French could effect any junction with him, I determined to commence hostilities without delay, and to suspend all negotiation, until the united forces of the Company and of their allies should have made such an impression on the territories of Mysore, as might give full effect to our just representations.

With these views, on the 3d of February, I directed Lieut.-General Harris to enter the territory of Mysore with the army assembled under his command; and on the same day I issued orders to Lieut.-General Stuart, to be prepared to co-operate from Malabar, and I signified to Rear-Admiral Rainier, and to the several allies of the Company, that I now considered the British Government in India to be at war with Tippoo Sultaun.

At length, on the 13th of February, I received from Tippoo Sultaun the letter marked No. 7, informing me, that, 'being frequently disposed to make excursions and hunt,' he was, 'accordingly, proceeding upon a hunting excursion,' and desiring that I would 'despatch Major Doveton slightly attended;' or 'unattended.'

But the season for negotiation, through the pacific channels, so often offered by me, was now elapsed. After mature deliberation, on the grounds already stated, I had directed the advance of the army into the territory of the Sultaun, and I had signified to the allies my determination to proceed to hostilities. To have delayed the advance of the army, would at once have thrown the advantages which I then possessed into the hands of Tippoo Sultaun, and have rendered the siege of his capital impracticable during the present season. On the other hand, an embassy, combined with the hostile irruption of our army into Mysore, would have been liable to the imputation of insincerity towards Tippoo Sultaun, and while it bore the appearance of indecision in the eyes of the allies, would have promoted, and perhaps, warranted a similar degree of instability in their councils and operations.

The design of this tardy, reluctant, and insidious assent to the admission of an embassy from the British Government could be considered in no other light than that of a new artifice for the purpose of gaining time, until a change of circumstances and of season might enable the Sultaun to avail himself of the assistance of France. This conclusion was now confirmed by my knowledge of the actual embarkation of M. Du Buc and two native vakeels on an embassy from Tippoo to the Executive Directory of France, an event which took place at Tranquebar on the 7th of February.

I, therefore, replied to the letter of Tippoo Sultaun in the terms of the enclosure, No. 8, in which I have declared Lieut.-General Harris to be the only person now authorized by me to receive and to answer whatever communications the Sultaun may think fit to make, with a view to the restoration of peace on such conditions as appear to the allies to be indispensably necessary to their common security. This letter I directed

General Harris to forward to the Sultaun, on the day on which the army under his command should pass the frontier, and at the same time I instructed him to issue, in the name of the allies, the accompanying declaration marked No. 9.[1]

---

[1] The declaration is as follows:—

The Proclamation of Lieut.-General George Harris, Commander-in-Chief of all his Majesty's and the Honourable Company's forces on the coasts of Coromandel and Malabar, to the Zemindars or Poligars, Desmooks, Despondies, Canoongoes, Naurgours, Potails, Shambogues, and to all Aumuldars, Serishtadars, Kelladars, and other inhabitants of Mysore, who shall receive the Company's Cowle.

Whereas Tippoo Sultaun having concluded an offensive alliance with the French, the inveterate enemies of the English, the Peishwa, and the Nizam of Decan rejected all overtures on their part for effecting an accommodation, and giving proofs that he only waited the arrival of the French to involve all India in a war; the allies have sent their armies into this country, under my command, to frustrate his ambitious designs, and to secure their possessions against the future attempts of such insidious enemies.

These being the views of the allies, I come not to make war upon the defenceless inhabitants of this country, but to receive you under their protection, and promise you perfect security under their government. To facilitate the carrying these intentions into execution, Lieut.-Colonel Alexander Read, the same officer under whose administration you experienced last war the benefits of a British Government, is again appointed to superintend the affairs of all the districts dependent on Mysore that may be reduced by the armies of the English; and as a further indication thereof, cowle flags shall be distributed over the country, and safe-guards sent to all the villages in the vicinity of the armies, to secure the inhabitants from depredation.

These measures being taken, and the allied armies sufficiently powerful to afford all the districts in their rear effectual protection, you will remain in your villages, proceed in the cultivation of your lands, and enjoy all the blessings of profound peace.

Benefitting so considerably by the liberal policy of the allies, it will become a duty on your part to merit their protection by serving them as obedient subjects, and rendering them the dues of the Sirkar, in the exaction of which will be evinced that moderation and justice, which distinguish the British from all the other nations of Europe in their conduct towards natives of India.

The general good of the people under them being the study of their Government, it evidently follows, that, whoever shall render them parti-

The Nizam's contingent consists of above 6000 of the Honourable Company's troops subsidized by his Highness, of about the same number of his own infantry, (including a proportion of M. Peron's sepoys, now commanded by British officers,) and of a large body of cavalry.

This force, under the general command of Meer Allum, formed a junction with the British army on the 19th February: and it is with the greatest satisfaction that I remark to your Honourable Court the beneficial effects which the Company has already derived from the recent improvement of our alliance with the Court of Hyderabad. The Nizam's contingent actually arrived in the vicinity of Chittoor, in a state of preparation for the field, before General Harris was ready to proceed on his march from Vellore.

I have annexed to this despatch the last return of Lieut.-General Harris's army, previous to his passing the frontier; an army more completely appointed, more amply and liberally supplied in every department, or more perfect in its discipline, and in the acknowledged experience, ability, and zeal of its officers, never took the field in India. The army on the coast of Malabar is in an equally efficient and respectable condition, and the extraordinary efforts which have been made by Lieut.-General Stuart and Major-General Hartley, seconded by the cordial attachment and unremitting assiduity of the Rajah of Coorga, have collected within a very short period of time a supply so abundant, that I am induced to transmit the particulars of it to your Honourable Court, as a testimony of the distinguished merits of those valuable officers, and of the loyalty and active exertion of that faithful tributary of the Honourable Company.

A considerable force, under the command of Lieut.-Colonels Read and Brown, will co-operate with Lieut.-General Harris in the southern districts of the Carnatic and Mysore.

Under these circumstances, General Harris entered the terri-

---

cular services during the present war, such as aiding Colonel Read in ascertaining the sources of the public revenue, in regulating the police, in procuring supplies for the army, or in giving intelligence of the enemy's designs, may be sure of rewards suitable to the importance and success of their endeavours.

Written at Head Quarters,
5th March, 1799.

GEORGE HARRIS.

-tory of Mysore on the 5th of March, with orders to proceed directly to Seringapatam.

Having thus submitted to your Honourable Court, according to the order of dates, a detailed relation of the events which have led to the war in which we are actually engaged, and having declared to you the motives and objects of my conduct in every stage of this important transaction, I must request your permission to conclude this despatch, with such reflections as arise in my mind from the review of my past measures, and from the prospect of their ultimate consequences and permanent effects.

From the first disclosure of the nature and object of Tippoo Sultaun's embassy to the Isle of France, every principle of justice and policy demanded from your Government in India that an instantaneous effort should be made to reduce his power and resources before he could avail himself of the advantages of the alliance which he had concluded. The defect of means is the sole consideration which can justify me for not having made that effort at the early period when its success would have placed the security of your possessions on a foundation, which the invasion of India by a French force could not have impaired. For without the aid of some native power it is scarcely possible that the French should ever make any permanent impression on your empire in India; and no native power (excepting Tippoo Sultaun) is so infatuated as to be disposed to assist or receive a French army.

The progress of events since the date of my orders of the 20th of June, 1798, has not only confirmed the principles of justice and policy, by which an attack upon the Sultaun was at that time demanded, but has manifested, that the designs of France as well as of the Sultaun, were of a much more extensive and formidable nature, than any which have ever been attempted against the British Empire in India, since the hour of its first foundation.

While the magnitude and danger of these designs were gradually disclosed, I had the satisfaction to feel, that the means of averting them were augmenting in a proportion nearly equal by the success of the negotiations at Hyderabad, and by the progress of the military preparations which I had ordered throughout your possessions.

At the commencement of the month of February the crisis arrived in which I was called upon to form my ultimate decision on the important question at issue with Tippoo Sultaun, and to determine the final result of the whole system of my measures.

On the one hand, the apparent establishment of the French army in Egypt, and the uncertainty of the state of our naval power in the Red Sea, rendered the danger still urgent from that quarter; while Tippoo Sultaun's repeated evasions of my proposals for negotiation, combined with his embassy to the Executive Directory of France, under the conduct of M. Du Buc, appeared to preclude all hope of detaching the Sultaun, from his recent alliance with the enemy. On the other hand, I now possessed ample means of frustrating the most dangerous effects of that alliance, by a seasonable application of the powerful force which the treachery and aggression of the Sultaun had compelled me to collect at a heavy expense to your finances.

Your Honourable Court will determine whether in this state of affairs my orders of the 3rd of February were premature; and whether I should have been justified on the 13th of February in recalling those orders, for the purpose of admitting at that late period a negotiation, which would have enabled Tippoo Sultaun to defeat every object of the armament of the allies for the present season, and would have afforded him ample time to reap the full benefit of his connection with France before the season for besieging his capital should return.

In deciding these important questions, you will necessarily consider, what degree of reliance could be placed on the sincerity of the Sultaun's disposition to conclude an amicable adjustment with your Government at the very moment, when he had actually despatched on an embassy to the Executive Directory of France the commander of the French troops, raised in the Mauritius and admitted into the Sultaun's service for the express purpose of carrying on a war of aggression against your possessions in India.

The admirable condition of your armies on both coasts, and the unequalled perfection of their equipment in every department, added to the extraordinary spirit and animation with which the campaign has been opened, afford every reason to hope that the issue of the war will be speedy and prosperous, and that it must terminate in a considerable reduction of Tippoo Sultaun's resources and power.

The wisdom of your Honourable Court will anticipate the extensive benefits which must result to your interests from an event now become essential to the peace and security of your possessions in India.

The policy of the treaty of Seringapatam certainly was not to maintain Tippoo Sultaun's power in such a state as should leave him a constant object of alarm and apprehension to the Company. That he has been justly so considered for some years past, cannot be doubted by any person acquainted with the records of any of your Governments in India. The present is the second crisis, within the last three years, in which the Government General has thought it necessary to assemble the army on the coast of Coromandel for the sole purpose of checking his motions; and the apprehension of his intentions has obstructed our operations against our European enemies in India during the course of the present war.

The continuance of Tippoo's power on its actual scale, and under such circumstances, must have proved to the Company a perpetual source of solicitude, expense, and hazard. But the engagements which he has contracted with the French, the public proofs which he has given of his eagerness to receive in Mysore as large a force as they can furnish, combined with the prodigious magnitude of their preparations, and the incredible progress of their army, evidently directed to the destruction of the British power in India, form new and prominent features in our political situation in this quarter of the world.

Admitting the wisdom of that policy which dictated the preservation of Tippoo Sultaun's power, at the close of the last war with Mysore, the spirit of our present Councils must be accommodated to the variation of circumstances, and to the actual position, character, and views of our enemies.

In such a conjuncture of affairs I am persuaded that your honourable Court will be of opinion, that no object can be deemed so urgent, or so necessary to the safety of your possessions, as the effectual reduction of the only declared ally of France now existing among the native powers of India.

If Tippoo Sultaun had been disposed to content himself with the quiet possession of his present dominions, if he could have been brought to a sense of his own peril in forming a connection with the French, the representations which I addressed to him would have produced an early and salutary impression; whatever speculative opinions might have been entertained with respect to his interests, views, and power, the justice and moderation of the British Government would never have disturbed his tranquillity. But he resolved to attempt the recovery of his lost dominions at the hazard of those which he still retains; and, in the ardour of his passionate pursuit, he overlooked not only the certain destruction of his own independence (the inevitable consequence even of the most prosperous success of any alliance with France;) but also the predominant influence of the English East India Company, and the vigilance of its Governments, which would probably detect his treachery, and turn against his own empire the ruin which he had meditated against theirs.

The secrecy of his councils, the promptitude of his resources, his constant and active state of equipment for war, added to the facility of his intercourse with the French through his remaining territories on the coast of Malabar, are the most dangerous circumstances in the actual condition of his power and dominion, and constitute his principal means of offence.

If success should attend your arms in this war, I entertain a firm confidence that those dangers will either be wholly averted, or so considerably diminished, as to afford to your government in India the prospect of durable security, and genuine peace.

I cannot close this letter without repeating to your honourable Court the cordial expression of my entire satisfaction in the zealous and honourable co-operation of Lord Clive, as well as of all the Members of this Government. The beneficial effect of their cheerful and ready concurrence in forwarding all my views, is manifest in the rapid progress and perfect completion of the equipments of the army in the field, and furnishes a striking and salutary example of the inestimable advantages of unanimity and concord among your servants in India.

I have the honour to be,
Honourable Sirs, with the greatest respect,
your most obedient and faithful Servant,
MORNINGTON.

15. The Earl of Mornington to the Court of Directors.

Progress of the War.

Fort St. George, 20th April, 1799.

Honourable Sirs,

I now proceed to submit to you a detail of the operations of the armies in Mysore.

The army of Bombay, under the command of Lieutenant General Stuart, marched from Cananore on the 21st of Feb., arrived at the head of the Poodicherrum Ghaut on the 25th of the same month, and took post at Sedapore and Sedasere on the 2nd of March, for the protection of the large supplies which had been collected at Verajunder Pett, in the district of Coorga. From these positions, on Lieutenant-General Harris's approach, Lieutenant-General Stuart intended to form a junction with the army of Madras.

The army of Madras, under the command of Lieutenant-General Harris, entered the territory of Mysore on the 5th of March, and its operations commenced by the reduction of several forts upon the frontier. Some of these forts surrendered without any resistance, and none of them were defended with spirit, although the Sultaun appears, from the improved establishment on which he had placed their garrisons, to have provided as well as he could for a different result.

The progress of the army of Madras, owing to its ample equipments in every department, particularly in that of the ordnance necessary for the siege of Seringapatam, was unavoidably slow. Its movements, however, were but little impeded by the enemy. Considerable bodies of horse hovered about its line of march, but without any other effect than that of rendering the communications with the Company's territories extremely difficult. Some parties of horse attacked the Nizam's contingent, and his Highness's cavalry are reported by General Harris to have conducted themselves with great spirit, a circumstance which may partly be attributed to the improvements recently introduced into the discipline and establishments of his Highness's cavalry at the recommendation of the British Resident under my instructions.

At the period when the army of Madras entered Mysore, Tippoo Sultaun was supposed to be encamped in the vicinity of Maddoor, and to be preparing to move in the direction of Bangalore for the purpose of opposing the progress of the Madras army, in the event of Lieutenant-General Harris actually passing the frontier. But it soon appeared that although the Sultaun had so recently affected a disposition to admit an embassy from the British Government, he had probably no other view than to conceal the design which he had formed of striking a sudden and early blow against the army of Bombay. For without allowing me the same time to answer his last letter which he had taken for replying to those addressed by me to him, and without waiting to hear of the actual commencement of hostilities on the part of the British Government, he came to the resolution of attacking the army of Bombay then assembled beyond the line of his frontier, in the district of Coorga, under the command of Lieut.-General Stuart.

For this purpose Tippoo, taking with him the flower of his army, appears to have marched from his camp near Cenapatam, on the 28th of February, (when General Harris was still within the Company's territories,) and moving rapidly in the direction of Periapatam, to have arrived there on the morning of the 5th of March, (being the same day on which Lieut.-Gen. Harris entered Mysore on the eastern frontier).

On the 6th of March Tippoo Sultaun passed his own frontier, and attacked a detachment of the army of Bombay, under the command of Lieut.-Gen. Stuart, the total strength of whose entire army did not amount to more than 6,000 fighting men. The attack of the Sultaun's force was resisted by a body not exceeding 2,000 men, and the Sultaun's army was finally defeated and totally dispersed, before General Stuart could collect the whole of his divided force. It is with infinite satisfaction that I enclose for the information of your honourable Court the paper marked No. 1, containing Gen. Stuart's account of this brilliant and important action which took place at Sedasere on the 8th of March.

After this signal defeat, Tippoo retreated precipitately to his camp at Periapatam, and remained there until the 11th of March without making any further attempt to molest the army. The loss sustained by Tippoo's army on the 6th of March appears to have amounted to near 2,000 killed, wounded, and prisoners, which included several officers of rank, and some of considerable distinction. That sustained by the army of Bombay will appear in Lieut.-Gen. Stuart's letter.

Adverting to the great disproportion of numbers, and to other circumstances of disadvantage, I am confident that your honourable Court will be of opinion, that the conduct and success of the army of Bombay on that day has seldom been equalled, and never surpassed in India.

Under this impression I take the liberty of recommending to your favourable notice the several officers and corps named by Lieut.-Gen. Stuart, in his letter of the 8th of March, and I am anxious to request your particular attention to the distinguished conduct of Lieut.-General Stuart and Major-General Hartley, as well as of Lieut.-Colonel Montresor and of Lieut.-Colonel

Dunlop. Major-General Hartley had already received a public testimony of my particular approbation of his extraordinary merit in collecting stores and provisions in the district of Coorga, previously to the arrival of General Stuart on the coast of Malabar.

Tippoo returned from Periapatam to Seringapatam, and arriving at the latter place on the 14th of March, moved from thence immediately to meet Lieut.-Gen. Harris and the army of Madras.

Lieut.-General Harris had advanced on the 26th of March to a position between Sultanpetta and Malavelly, having met with no considerable impediment from the enemy. The enemy made their appearance in force on that day, but without attempting to disturb our army. On the 27th of March, when the army reached its ground at Malavelly, Tippoo opened a distant cannonade upon it, which, though at first disregarded by Lieut.-General Harris, ultimately led to a general engagement, in which the enemy was completely defeated, and driven from every post which he attempted to maintain: our loss on this occasion was very inconsiderable, only seven rank and file being killed, and a few men (including four officers) wounded, while that of the enemy is supposed to have amounted to near 700.

I refer your honourable Court to Lieut.-General Harris's letter of the 27th of March, which forms part of the enclosure No. 1, for a more particular account of this important victory, requesting also your attention to the merits of the several officers and corps distinguished by the notice of Lieut.-General Harris.

General Harris marched on the 28th a few miles to the southward of Malavelly, without the least interruption from the enemy, from whence it may be inferred that Tippoo Sultaun was considerably dispirited by the defeat which he had sustained on the preceding day, added to the previous success obtained over him by the army of Bombay.

On the 29th of March General Harris happily accomplished a movement which must have greatly astonished and disconcerted the enemy: instead of proceeding in the direction of Arakerry and Karagat, Lieut.-Gen. Harris suddenly turned towards the River Cavery, where finding a ford at some distance above the junction of the Cavery and Copany, he immediately crossed the Cavery with a part of his army, and occupied strong positions on both banks of that river, at the distance of about fifteen miles from Seringapatam. This movement was also made without the least opposition on the part of the enemy, who indeed does not seem to have entertained the most distant suspicion of the British General's design.

Lord Cornwallis, at a more advanced period of the year, having in vain sought for a practicable ford to the southward of Seringapatam, Tippoo probably concluded that Lieut.-Gen. Harris would have pursued his Lordship's route to the ford of Caniambaddy, northward of Seringapatam, for the purpose of effecting a junction from thence with the army of Bombay. It is difficult to account otherwise for Tippoo's inaction while General Harris executed this arduous and important movement.

The advantages of the position thus acquired by General Harris must prove considerable. In addition to the immediate acquisition of cattle and forage, it must facilitate the junction with the army of Bombay; it must afford additional security to the abundant magazines which have been formed in the Coorga country, and favour the safe approach of our convoys from the southern districts, and from the Barramahl by the pass of Coveriporam; and it promises to open to our army that range of forage, situated to the southward of Seringapatam, which Tippoo seems to have reserved for the consumption of his own army.

Lieut.-Gen. Harris, with his whole army, having crossed the Cavery on the 30th of March, halted near the village of Soselly on the 31st; on the 1st of April he moved towards Seringapatam, and on the 5th encamped two miles south-west of that city, having experienced no opposition from the enemy since the 27th of March. On the morning of the 6th of April, after an engagement in which the enemy appears to have made considerable resistance, Lieut.-General Harris took possession of Sultanpetta and an adjacent tope or grove, and about the same time Major-General Floyd, with a strong detachment, was sent to effect a junction with the army of Bombay: on the morning of the 6th of April Lieut.-General Stuart received at Sedapore a note from Lieut.-General Harris, announcing the arrival of the latter at Seringapatam, and also signifying that Major-General Floyd was to be detached from the army of Madras on the 6th of April for the purpose already stated. In consequence of this intelligence, Lieut.-General Stuart had determined to march from Sedapore to Sedasere on the 7th of April, and it is probable that the junction of the army of Bombay with the detachment under the command of Major-General Floyd was effected on the 8th in the neighbourhood of Periapatam. The last accounts received by me from General Harris are dated on the 7th instant, when he states that he had taken up his position for the siege of Seringapatam.

Tippoo Sultaun, on the 7th of April, had not returned any answer to my letter of the 22nd of February, nor had he manifested any disposition to propose a negotiation. Lieut.-General Harris is instructed to propose preliminary articles of peace to the Sultaun before the British batteries shall be opened against Seringapatam.

While General Harris was advancing towards Seringapatam, Lieut.-Colonel Read was employed in reducing the country to the northward of Ryakottah. His operations were intended to have embraced a wide range, and he had made considerable progress in them, when the more urgent service of convoying to the army the large supplies which were collected in the Barramahl, made it necessary for him to change the direction of his march. He is now drawing together in the vicinity of Coveryporam the numerous brinjarries and other supplies intended for the army encamped before Seringapatam, which place it is hoped he may be able to reach early in May.

To the southward of the Carnatic and of Mysore, Lieut.-Colonel Browne, at the head of a respectable detachment, began his operations by the reduction of Carroor, which surrendered to him, without any serious resistance, on the 5th of April. On the 8th he sent a detachment against Errode, and marched himself on the 9th to reduce Aravacourchy. He would, however, be obliged to suspend his intended operations in the district of Coimbatoor, and to unite his detachment to that of Colonel Read, with the view of forming a force sufficiently strong to give due protection to the large and important supplies proceeding to Seringapatam.

Aravacourchy, which had been considerably strengthened since last war, surrendered to Lieut.-Colonel Brown on the 10th instant.

I have the honour to be, &c.

MORNINGTON.

P.S. 22nd April, 1799.—After closing my letter I had the satisfaction to receive despatches from Generals Harris and Stuart.

I congratulate your honourable Court on the successful junction of the detachment under General Floyd with the army of

Bombay, The final junction of the whole army of Bombay with the army before Seringapatam was expected to take place about the 13th instant. It may be safely affirmed not to be in the power of Tippoo, even materially, to retard this junction, which, when effected, must excite a serious alarm in the mind of the Sultaun for the safety of his capital if not of his person.

Your honourable Court will perceive that Lieut.-General Harris, in his progress to Seringapatam, encountered the same difficulties which were experienced by Lord Cornwallis from the failure of the cattle provided for the service of the army, which, although amply sufficient in point of number at the commencement of the expedition, appear to have rapidly decreased on the entrance of the army into Mysore; the climate and water of that country are represented to be extremely unfavourable to the cattle of the Carnatic. The delay which arose from this unavoidable contingency seems to have been considerable; but your honourable Court will, no doubt, view with satisfaction the spirit and firmness with which this difficulty was met by the Commander-in-Chief, and the zealous exertion of the whole army by which he was enabled to proceed on his march.

16. The Earl of Mornington to the Court of Directors.

Conclusion of the War.

Fort St. George, 11th May, 1799.

Honourable Sirs,

No particular comment is required from me to illustrate the numerous advantages which cannot fail to flow from the brilliant and decisive atchievement announced to your Honourable Court in the despatch of the Governor-General in Council of this date. But I cannot refrain from offering to you my separate and most cordial congratulations on an event, the glory of which has never been surpassed (if it has ever been equalled), in the history of the military transactions of the British nation in India.

The fall of Seringapatam, under all the circumstances which accompanied that event, has placed the whole of the kingdom of Mysore, with all its resources, at the disposal of your Government; and the only power in India to which the French could look for assistance, or which could be deemed formidable to your interests, is now deprived of all vigour, if not entirely extinct. When your Honourable Court recollects that these advantages have been acquired within four months from the date of my arrival at this Presidency, and within two from the period of the army's entrance into Mysore, I trust you will be of opinion that your servants have not been deficient in alacrity or diligence.

When Lieutenant-General Harris took the field, I thought it my duty to invest him with the most efficient and extensive powers which it was possible for me to delegate; and he has carried with him to the gates of Seringapatam the full vigour and energy of your supreme Government. To the judicious exercise of this ample authority, combined with the liberal supplies which had been provided for the army, may be ascribed in a great measure the unparalleled rapidity and promptitude of its operations. I have the further satisfaction to add that the particular detail of those operations, which I shall hereafter submit to your Honourable Court, will furnish the most brilliant examples of judgment, skill, discipline, firmness and valour, under many trials of all those distinguished qualities.

The dreadful fate of Tippoo Sultaun cannot be contemplated without emotions of pain and regret; but I trust it will serve as a salutary lesson to the native Princes of India, and will prove the danger of violating public engagements, and inviting foreign invasion for the prosecution of schemes of ambition and hatred against the British power. He was interred within his own capital on the day following its capture, in the mausoleum of his father, with the honours of war, paid to his remains by the British army. I am persuaded that your Honourable Court will derive peculiar satisfaction from the intelligence that his family and palace suffered no insult or violence during the heat of the assault, and have since been protected with the utmost care.

I have the honour to be, &c.

MORNINGTON.

17. Lieut.-General Stuart to the Earl of Mornington.

Battle of Seedasere.

Seedapore, 8th March, 1799.

My Lord,

I had the honour to address your Lordship on the 20th ultimo, and having marched from Cananore on the following day, agreeably to my intimation of that date, I arrived at the top of Poodiacherrim Ghaut, on the 25th of the same month.

I informed your Lordship, that it was my intention to assume a defensive position close to the frontiers, and there await, in conformity to General Harris's instructions under the 24th of December, his further orders.

In pursuance of this plan I moved the corps successively forward, and placed them in such situations, as might enable me the most promptly, to form the proposed junction with the principal army.

On the 2nd instant, the right brigade consisting of three native battalions under the command of Lieutenant-Colonel Montresor, took up their ground at Seedasere, the boundary of the Coorga country, and about seven miles distant from Periapatam.

The main body of the army, with the park and provisions, remained at Seedapore and Ahmootenaar; the first eight miles and the latter twelve, from the advanced position.

It may be necessary to inform your Lordship, that I was in some measure compelled from the nature of the country, which is every where covered by thick jungle, to place the army in several divisions; but I had a further view in occupying the post at Seedasere, in order to preserve a more ready communication with General Harris, as this was the only spot from whence the signals established between the two armies could be observed. Although I had no reason to apprehend any immediate attack, I thought it advisable to adopt the precaution of encamping the corps at such short distances, as would either enable me to move without much loss of time into the enemy's territory, or to support, if occasion should require it, any quarter that might stand in need of assistance.

In the course of the morning of the 5th, an extensive encampment was unexpectedly observed to be forming on this side of the fort of Periapatam. This circumstance was discovered at 10 o'clock in the forenoon, as the enemy were taking up their ground, by a party of observation on the summit of the high hill of Seedasere, which commands a view of the Mysore almost to the environs of Seringapatam. Before the evening, this encampment assumed a very formidable appearance and covered a great extent of ground.

We were able to count from 3 to 400 tents, amongst the number some of large dimensions were distinguished, and particularly one of a green colour, that seemed to denote the presence of the Sultaun. However much the probability of this circumstance might be strengthened by the respectable appearance of the encampment, it was contradicted by the evidence of two hurcarrahs, who had recently arrived from Seringapatam. These men generally reported, that Tippoo had marched with all his forces on the 20th ultimo, to oppose the progress of the Madras army, and that the Benky Nabob commanded the only force in the field, that remained in the neighbourhood of Seringapatam. This force was represented to be encamped at Cancambaddy and to consist of 5000 Piadas or irregular infantry, who were said to be intended as a covering party to 7000 Brinjaries, and directed to bring as much provisions, as they could collect about Periapatam to the capital.

In this state of uncertainty, I thought it prudent to reinforce Lieut.-Colonel Montresor's brigade with an additional battalion of Sepoys, and waited for more correct intelligence, which I expected hourly, to act with the whole of my forces as affairs might render necessary.

On the morning of the 6th, Major-General Hartley went forward to reconnoitre, and at break of day from the hill of observation, the whole of the enemy's army was discovered to be in motion; but their movements were so well concealed by the woodiness of the country and the haziness of the atmosphere, that it was impossible to ascertain their object, nor in fact was this discovered, until they had penetrated a considerable way in the jungle, and commenced an attack upon our line, which happened between the hours of 9 and 10.

The enemy pierced through the jungles with such surety and expedition, that they attacked the rear and the front of our line almost at the same instant. This despatch prevented more than three of our corps being engaged, as the fourth, which was posted two miles and a half in the rear, was unable to form a junction, from the enemy having cut in between them and Seedasere. The communication was effectually obstructed by a column, which, according to the reports of our prisoners, consisted of upwards of 5000 men under the command of Baber Jung.

Fortunately before the enemy had accomplished their purpose, Major-General Hartley had time to apprise me of their attack, and remained himself to give any assistance that might be necessary. The best position was assumed for repulsing the enemy, and in this alarming situation the corps defended themselves with so much resolution, that the Sultaun's troops were unable to make any impression. The brigade was on every side completely surrounded, and had to contend against a vast disparity of numbers, besides other discouraging circumstances.

As soon as I received intelligence of the perilous situation of the right brigade, I marched to their assistance with the two flank companies of his Majesty's 75th regiment and the whole of the 77th. I arrived about half-past two in sight of the division of the enemy, who had penetrated into the rear, and possessed themselves of the great road leading to Seedasere. The engagement lasted nearly half an hour, when after a smart fire of musketry on both sides, the enemy were completely routed, and fled with precipitation through the jungles to regain their column, which still continued the attack in front. On arriving at Lieut.-Colonel Montresor's post, I found his men exhausted with fatigue, and their ammunition almost expended. At 20 minutes past 3 the enemy retreated in all directions.

For this decisive, and, I hope your Lordship will allow, brilliant success, considering the small number of troops who engaged, under very great disadvantages, probably the flower of Tippoo Sultaun's army, I feel myself peculiarly indebted to the judicious disposition for defence made by General Hartley. He embraced the opportunity of observing the motions of the enemy from the hill, I have above mentioned, and was thus enabled to advise Lieut.-Colonel Montresor of the best method for defeating them. I beg leave also to inform your Lordship, that my best thanks are due to Lieut.-Colonel Montresor for his very active exertions, and to the officers and men, including the artillery of his brigade, for their gallant and steady behaviour throughout the whole of this arduous affair. Lieut.-Colonel Dunlop and the European division under his command, are likewise entitled to my particular approbation for their spirited conduct, which finally routed the enemy.

Our loss on this occasion is far less than could reasonably have been expected, and I have the honour to enclose for your Lordship's information a return of this circumstance.

It was impossible to ascertain the exact loss sustained by the enemy; but it must have been heavy, as in the course of so long an action they were often exposed in crowds to the fire of grape shot and vollies of musquetry. Several men of distinction were killed, and some wounded officers have been made prisoners. I have the honour to enclose the information of Mozdin Khan Bhukhshy and the Commander of a Kutchery, the prisoner of greatest rank, who has fallen wounded into our hands; but concurring reports state that Meer Ghofar is amongst the slain.

As the arrival of General Harris at Seringapatam will not happen at so early a period, as he first intended, the immediate possession of the post of Seedasere was no longer an object of such consequence, and to retain it, while Tippoo continued in force at Periapatam, became an affair of serious difficulty. The secrecy and expedition, with which he had planned his late enterprise, and the correct intelligence, that the leaders of his columns appeared to have obtained of the private routes through the Coorga jungles, led to an opinion, that he would not remain satisfied with this abortive attempt, but might endeavour to penetrate by another direction to the southward, still more open than the passage of Seedasere, where he would only be opposed by Coorgs. This consideration derived a greater weight, as if he succeeded in forcing this entrance, it would throw him into our rear and put him in all probability in possession of the great depôt of rice collected by the Coorga Rajah. These motives have induced me to relinquish the post at Seedasere, and to collect the whole of my force at this place. I have accordingly made a disposition, either to defend my position against the Sultaun, if he should again adventure to attack it, or to move in defence of any part of the Coorga Rajah's territories that the enemy may threaten, provided it shall endanger our magazine of provisions; otherwise I shall remain on the defensive, until I receive advice from General Harris.

Since the action of the 6th, the enemy have continued in their camp at Periapatam, nor have I any intelligence either of the Sultaun's designs, or of the motives, that induced him to undertake his present enterprise. It is not likely that he will remain longer in this neighbourhood, than after he receives intelligence of General Harris having entered the Mysore.

As my communication with General Harris is become insecure, I must take the liberty of requesting your Lordship to inform him of such part of these particulars as may appear to you necessary.

I have the honour to subscribe myself most respectfully,

My Lord, your Lordship's

Most obedient humble servant,

J. STUART.

P.S. By some prisoners, who have been just now brought in by the Coorga Rajah's people, I am informed, that the loss of the

SKETCH of the ACTION near MALLAVELLY, 27th March, 1799.

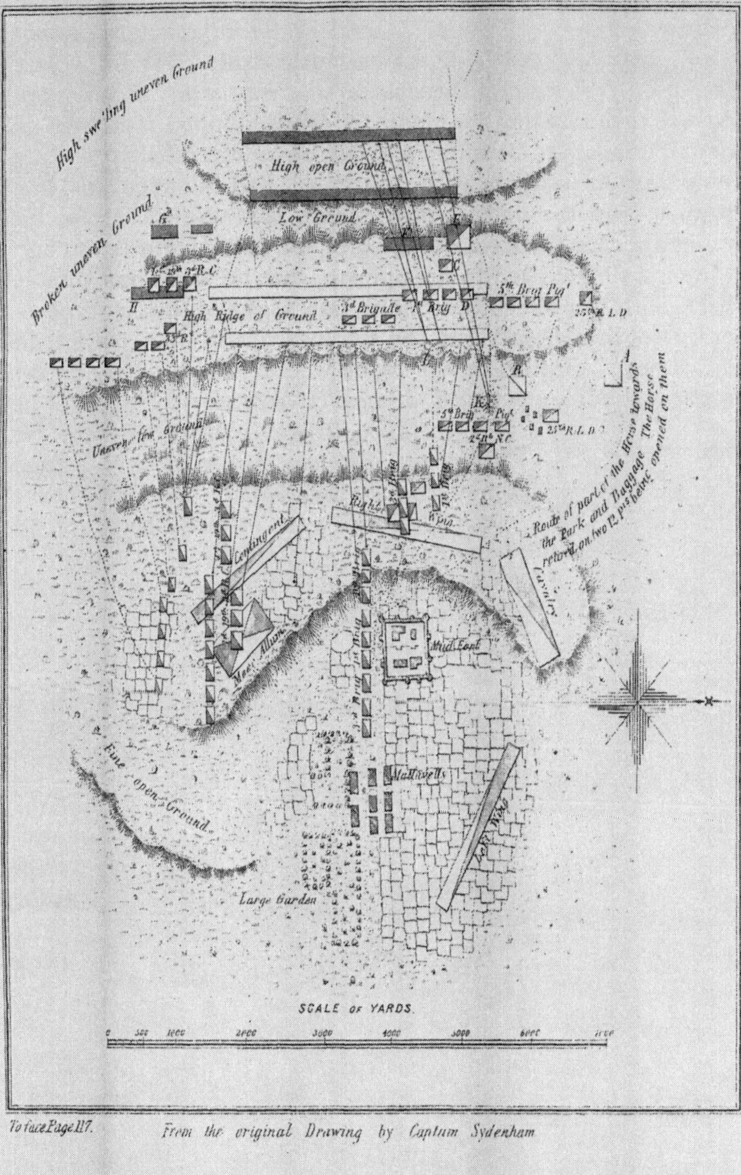

To face Page 117.

From the original Drawing by Captain Sydenham

enemy was very great, and that many men of the first distinction fell. They mention Seyed or Meer Ghofâr and the Binky Nabob, who led the center attack, among the killed. It is added, however, that the Sultaun is collecting more forces and is determined to make a second attack.

18. Lieut.-General Harris to the Earl of Mornington.

Battle of Malvelly.

Camp at Malvelly, 27th March, 1799.

My Lord,

The army marched this morning, many horse were seen as it approached Malvelly, and a large force appeared posted on a high commanding ridge, three miles beyond that place. The ruins of the fort were occupied by a part of our advanced guard, when at 10 o'clock A. M. Tippoo Sultaun opened a cannonade from several heavy guns, so distant, that I paid it little attention, and ordered the ground to be marked for encampment; the shot, however, falling in our lines, and horse menacing our picquet, the 1st European brigade, and two cavalry corps, were ordered to support it on the right, while Colonel Wellesley's division advanced on our left; this brought on a general action, in the course of which, a small body of horse charged the 1st European brigade, some individuals piercing the line, but most of them falling before it. Colonel Wellesley's division turning the right flank of the enemy, gave occasion to General Floyd, with three regiments of cavalry, to disperse a cutchery of infantry, cutting many of them in pieces. The enemy retired about one o'clock, having been driven completely from every position he attempted to maintain. It was my wish to have encamped on the ground he quitted, but a total want of water obliged me to return to the ground I had first taken up at Malvelly. The whole of the enemy's force was, I believe, in the field; their loss I cannot ascertain; ours is trifling. The conduct of the troops on this occasion was such as I could not but approve; our baggage was, during the action, well secured by the left wing of the army, under Major-General Popham. I shall hereafter have the honour to transmit accurate returns of the small amount of our loss. I shall march tomorrow morning to a large tank in the direction of the Cavery, to secure water by approaching the river.

Captain Kinnedy, of the 19th dragoons, Leonard and Strachan, native cavalry, Moore, 74th, are wounded. Part of his Highness the Nizam's horse were engaged, and behaved extremely well.

I have the honour to be, &c.

GEORGE HARRIS.

19. Lieut.-Gen. Harris to the Earl of Mornington.

Malvelly, and March to Seringapatam.

Camp before Seringapatam, April 5th, 1799.

My Lord,

I have particular satisfaction in reporting to your Lordship that the army under my command, encamped this morning before Seringapatam; taking up the position, which with little variation it will be expedient to occupy, till the Division under General Stuart joins me. A strong detachment, commanded by Major General Floyd, marches to-morrow morning to facilitate the junction, and I take the occasion of addressing your Lordship, by what I consider as a safe channel of communication, to report generally what I have by various hircarahs attempted to transmit to your Lordship as the Army advanced on its march.

I left Killamungalum on the 10th of March; and our first movement shewed a very serious deficiency in the Bullock department, particularly in those attached to the Commissary General of Stores. The succeeding march of the 12th, although short and with an intermediate day of halt, marked this deficiency more strongly; crippled in our movements from this cause, our marches have been tedious though short; our halts have been frequent and our progress has been slow, unremitting attention to every species of arrangement by which the store department could be assisted or lightened, was indispensably necessary: some losses were daily sustained. The zeal of individuals was called forth with considerable advantage, and we have succeeded in surmounting these difficulties, and taking our position before the capital of Mysore, with an ordnance equipment which I hope is amply sufficient for its reduction.

The army marched by the route of Anicul, Talgautporam, Cagliaporam, Kankanhilly, and Sultanpett to Malavelly where I arrived on the morning of the 27th of March: The army of Tippoo Sultaun occupying the heights beyond the town from which at about 10 o'clock he commenced a distant cannonade; some shot falling in the line marked for our camp, and a body of horse menacing the picquets of our right, it became necessary to advance corps for their support, which led to a general action. The Infantry line of the Enemy was on commanding ground in rear of his artillery. His Cavalry advanced under cover of his cannon, and a cutcherie or Brigade of Infantry was pushed forward in front of each flank of his Line, mixed with many rocket men. The right wing of the army under my command formed on the picquets of the right; Colonel Wellesley's division, advanced from a considerable distance on the left to attack the right flank of the enemy, and Major General Floyd with the 19th and two regiments of native cavalry moved between these corps. The 25th dragoons and a native regiment keeping in check a body of the enemy's cavalry, which had assembled on our right, while the left wing of the army and a regiment of native cavalry remained halted to protect our stores and baggage. The weak state of the artillery bullocks considerably retarded the advance and formation of our line, with which they were unable to keep pace. A small body of horse, profiting by this circumstance, made a daring charge on the 1st European brigade; they were received with firmness, and repulsed with considerable loss; their infantry in front of our right, being at the same time driven from their position. On the left, the corps of infantry called the *Kerim Ketcherie* advanced on Colonel Wellesley's column. His Majesty's 33rd regiment which opposed soon put them in confusion, and the cavalry under Major General Floyd advancing at this moment to the charge, cut them to pieces. Six colours were taken. The retreat of the enemy soon became general; their cannon were drawn off, and at two o'clock the action had entirely ceased; our line halting on the heights whence theirs had been driven: a total want of water preventing our encamping there, the line returned to the ground originally marked for its encampment at Malavelly. The loss of the enemy as collected from various accounts received since the action, amounted to near two thousand killed and wounded; a return of the casualties of this army is enclosed.

At an early period of our march it had occurred to me, that if it were possible to cross the Cavery, at a ford some distance below Seringapatam, the measure might be attended with considerable advantage, by embarrassing the motions of the enemy, defeating the preparations he might have made to oppose us on the Northern side of the river, and facilitating our communication with the army of Malabar and the force under Colonel

Brown and Read. In addition to these inducements the ford was said to be easy; we had reason to hope the country was still undestroyed, and the southern part of Seringapatam was considered as the least capable of defence. The destruction of the tanks on the road from Malvelly to Arakeery, rendered an oblique movement towards the Cavery less liable to suspicion than it might otherwise have been, and we arrived on the 29th of March at Sosilly on the Cavery, before any measures had been taken to oppose our movement, by destroying forage, or driving off cattle, of which we here procured a considerable supply. The army crossed the river the next day without difficulty, and after halting on the 30th to arrange our departments, marched on the succeeding morning towards Harwelly, the weak state of our cattle, the barren nature of the soil, the total destruction of forage, which immediately followed our passage of the river, and the necessity for regulating our marches by the situation of water, the road leaving the river at some distance on the right, obliged us to make five marches from Sosilly to our present camp, three of which have been in sight of Seringapatam. Numbers of horse have daily watched our motions, but, although the ground was favourable, no attempt has been made to oppose our progress.

The detachment with Major General Floyd consists of H.M. 73rd regiment, three Bengal and two coast battalions of Sepoys with their guns, and one regiment of European and three of native cavalry, with their galloper guns; and a party of the Nizam's horse. During the absence of this party, I shall be employed in preparing materials for the more active operation of the siege, which will commence with the junction of General Stuart's force; and I am happy to add that on this side of the river, I apprehend no want of materials for the siege. We have a sufficient stock of provisions to subsist the troops beyond the time, when the union of our forces, from the opposite coasts may enable me to spare an army of sufficient force, to cover our communication with the stations, whence our supplies are prepared to join us; the cattle now with the camp must in the mean time suffer greatly, but this is no longer an object of consequence.

Numbers of people are employed on this side of Seringapatam, in repairing the fort. It seems to us to require all their labour, appearing to be in a very imperfect state.

I cannot conclude without expressing to your Lordship, in

the strongest terms, the obligations I feel myself under to Meer Allum Bahadur, for the promptitude with which he has in every instance met my wishes in the co-operation, required from the forces of His Highness the Nizam. Their aid in transporting the shot, has been of the greatest use, and it is an act of justice due to Captain Malcolm, to report to your Lordship that his unceasing zeal, in pointing out the manner in which the contingent could promote the common cause of the allies, has been equalled only by the cheerful readiness shewn by Meer Allum, in adopting his suggestions.

I have the honor to be,
My Lord,
Your Lordship's most obedient
and faithful Servant,
GEORGE HARRIS.

20. Lieut.-Gen. Harris to the Earl of Mornington.

Colonel Wellesley's Repulse.

Camp before Seringapatam, April 7, 1799.

My Lord,

After crossing the Cauvery on the 30th ultimo at Sosilly, where the army halted the next day, I advanced by easy marches to this place, and took up my position within two miles south-west of Seringapatam without opposition. On the 5th of this month, wishing to occupy the post where Gen. Abercromby's picquets were attacked in 1792, and the large tope and village of Sultanpetta, both were attacked the night of our arrival, but owing (in great measure) to the darkness of the night, the attack on the first only was partially successful. We sustained some loss from the fire of the enemy, which continued heavily till late next morning, when the posts were again attacked with perfect and rapid success. They give this army a very strong position, and greatly confine that of the enemy. Major Colin Campbell, of the 1st native regiment; Lieutenant George Nixon, and Tulla, of the 12th; and Fitzgerald, of the 33rd, were killed; in these attacks Lieutenants R. Nixon and King of his Majesty's 12th regiment, and Brooke of Bengal artillery, wounded. Gen. Floyd marched on the morning of the 6th to join General Stuart, with his infantry and four cavalry corps, twenty field-pieces, and a body of the Nizam's horse. This force I consider superior to any thing that can be opposed to it by the enemy. The army has now taken up its position for the siege.

GEORGE HARRIS.

21. Major-General Floyd to the Earl of Mornington.

Battle of Malvelly, and Colonel Wellesley's Repulse.

Camp at Periapatam, April 10th, 1799.

My Lord,

As it is possible General Harris's despatches may not have reached you, I beg leave to give a short statement of events, as far as have come to my knowledge.

On the 27th of March the enemy was seen, in force, on the high ground west of Malavilly. General Harris, with the right wing, attacked the enemy in front. Two regiments of cavalry supported. Colonel Wellesley, with the Nizam's army, took a most judicious situation on the enemy's right flank, and attacked it, and threw it into confusion. I was observing, with three regiments of cavalry, between the right flank of Colonel Wellesley and the left of General Harris, and charged and destroyed a great number of the enemy's infantry, taking six stands of colours. About the same period, a number of the enemy's horse had charged the European brigade of the right wing; several of them were killed, and the rest fled; the infantry also were repulsed by ours, and the whole retired out of our reach. It seems, from subsequent accounts, that about 500 wounded men reached the enemy's camp, and that their loss was about 2000 men. Our loss amounted to about 7 or 8 killed, and about 40 wounded—and about 45 horses killed and wounded. No officer killed, and four only wounded. I have no copy of the return by me.

On the 29th March the army encamped at Sosilly, on the bank of the Cavery. Here we found a great collection of inhabitants, and cattle, and rice, and a good deal of paddy and other grain. The army was considerably refreshed.

30th of March, the army had all crossed the river at a good ford.

5th of April, the army took its situation before Seringapatam at the west point of the fort. That night Lieut.-Colonel Shawe took possession of a post between seventeen and eighteen hundred yards from the fort. An attack was also made by Colonel Wellesley on a tope, but the troops were withdrawn on our part—a spent ball, as I have heard, struck the Colonel on the knee, but it did not prevent his walking.

6th April, early in the morning, I marched off for Periapatam with four regiments of cavalry, one regiment European (73d), and five battalions native infantry, and about 2000 of the Nizam's horse. All last night, and most of this day, there was a continued peal of small arms, and, occasionally, heavy guns. We still hear heavy guns at intervals, but I have no account whatever since we left the army.

8th April, I encamped at Periapatam. My signals were answered, and I had communication with General Stuart that night.

9th April, I rode over to General Stuart, and after some arrangements, returned to camp; immediately a considerable number of the enemy's horse appeared, and hovered round most of the day without effecting anything, but with some slight loss on their part.

10th April, General Stuart joined me this day, with rice and some other articles for between 30 and 40 days for his army, and a quantity of military stores. We proceed to-morrow to join the army at Seringapatam, and shall probably reach it in five marches. Having no cypher I refrain from some particulars; the troops are, in general, healthy, and in high spirits, and full of good-will.

I have the honour to be,
with great respect, my Lord,
your most obedient and humble Servant,
J. FLOYD, M. G.

On my marching from hence to-morrow, the communication will be entirely closed on this side.

22. Lieut.-Gen. Harris to the Earl of Mornington.

Storming of Seringapatam.

Seringapatam, 7th May, 1799.

My Lord,

On the 4th instant I had the honour to address to your Lordship a hasty note, containing in few words the sum of our success, which I have now to report more in detail.

The fire of our batteries, which began to batter in breach on the 30th of April, had, on the evening of the 3rd instant, so much destroyed the walls against which it was directed, that the arrangement was then made for assaulting the place on the following day, when the breach was reported practicable. The troops intended to be employed were stationed on the trenches early on the morning of the 4th, that no extraordinary movement might lead the enemy to expect the assault, which I had determined to make in the heat of the day, as the time best calculated to ensure success, as their troops would then be least prepared to oppose us.

Two flank companies of Europeans, taken from those regiments necessarily left to guard our camps and out-posts, followed by the 12th, 33rd, 73rd, and 74th regiments, and three corps of grenadier sepoys, taken from the troops of the three Presidencies, with 200 of his Highness the Nizam's troops, formed the party for the assault, accompanied by 100 of the artillery, and the corps of pioneers, and supported in the trenches by the battalion companies of the regiment De Meuron, and four battalions of Madras sepoys. Colonel Sherbrooke, and Lieut.-Colonels Dunlop, Dalrymple, Gardner, and Mignon, commanded the several flank corps, and Major-General Baird was entrusted with the direction of this important service.

At one o'clock the troops moved from the trenches, crossed the rocky bed of the Cavery under an extremely heavy fire, passed the glacis and ditch, and ascended the breaches in the Fausse Braye, and rampart of the fort, surmounting in the most gallant manner every obstacle which the difficulty of the passage, and the resistance of the enemy presented to oppose their progress. Major-General Baird had divided his force for the purpose of clearing the ramparts to the right and left; one division was commanded by Colonel Sherbrooke, the other by Lieut.-Colonel Dunlop; the latter was disabled in the breach, but both corps, although strongly opposed, were completely successful. Resistance continued to be made from the palace of Tippoo for some time after all firing had ceased from the works; two of his sons were there, who, on an assurance of safety, surrendered to the troops surrounding them, and guards were placed for the protection of the family, most of whom were in the palace. It was soon after reported that Tippoo Sultaun had fallen. Syed Saheb, Meer Saduc, Syed Gofar, and many others of his chiefs were also slain; measures were immediately adopted to stop the confusion, at first unavoidable, in a city strongly garrisoned, crowded with inhabitants, and their property in ruins, from the fire of a numerous artillery, and taken by assault. The princes were removed to camp.

It appeared to Major-General Baird so important to ascertain the fate of the Sultaun, that he caused immediate search to be made for his body, which, after much difficulty, was found late in the evening in one of the gates under a heap of slain, and placed in the palace. The corpse was the next day recognised by the family, and interred with the honours due to his rank, in the mausoleum of his father,

The strength of the fort is such, both from its natural position and the stupendous works by which it is surrounded, that all the exertions of the brave troops who attacked it, in whose praise it is impossible to say too much, were required to place it in our hands. Of the merits of the army I have expressed my opinion in orders, a copy of which I shall forward to-morrow; and I trust your Lordship will point out their services to the favourable notice of their king and country.

I am sorry to add, that on collecting the returns of our loss it is found to have been much heavier than I had at first imagined. An accurate statement shall be sent to-morrow.

On the 5th instant Abdul Khalic, the elder of the princes, formerly hostages with Lord Cornwallis, surrendered himself at our outposts, demanding protection. Kerim Saheb, the brother of Tippoo, had before sought refuge with Meer Allum Behadur. A Cowl Namah was yesterday despatched to Futteh Hyder, the eldest son of Tippoo, inviting him to join his brother. Purneah and Meer Cummer ul deen Khan have also been summoned to Seringapatam. No answers have yet been received, but I expect them shortly, as their families are in the fort.

This moment Ali Reza, formerly one of the vakeels from Tippoo Sultaun to Lord Cornwallis, has arrived from Meer Cummer ul Deen Khan to ask my orders for 4000 horse, now under his command. Ali Reza was commissioned to declare that Meer Cummer ul Deen would make no conditions, but rely on the generosity of the English. He desired merely to state, that his claim to the Jaghire of Gurramconda was well known, as was his family and character. If these and his connexion with the unfortunate family of Tippoo Sultaun should give him a claim to this ancient possession of his house, his sense of obligation would bind him ever to the British interests. If this could not be granted to him, he hoped he might obtain permission to retire with his family to Hyderabad. On this subject

I have promised to ask your Lordship's pleasure; he will shortly arrive, and as the army of the late Sultaun look up chiefly to him, I hope through his means to be enabled at once to restore tranquillity. Monsieur Chapuy and most of the French are prisoners. They have commissions from the French Government.

I have the honour to be, &c.
GEORGE HARRIS.

23. To Lieut.-General Harris, Commander-in-Chief, &c.

Same Subject.

Sir,

Having in obedience to your orders taken the command of the troops ordered for the assault of the Fort of Seringapatam, consisting of a corps of six companies of European flankers from the Bombay army, under Lieut.-Colonel Dunlop; a corps of four companies of European flankers from the Scotch brigade, and the Regiment de Meurone, under Colonel Sherbrooke; his Majesty's 12th, 33rd, 73rd, and 74th regiments; ten companies of Bengal sepoy flankers, under Lieut.-Colonel Gardener; eight companies of coast sepoy flankers, under Lieut.-Colonel Dalrymple; six companies of Bombay sepoy flankers, under Lieut.-Colonel Mignan; one hundred artillerymen, with a proportion of gun lascars, under Major Bell; the European and Native pioneers under Captain Dowse;—amounting as per enclosed return of men actually under arms at the assault, to—

Firelocks	Europeans . .	2,494	Total . 4,376:
	Natives . .	1,882	

I have now the honour to report to you the measures I took to secure the success of the important object entrusted to me, and the result, and to enclose a return of the killed and wounded on the assault.

Having received your instructions to make the capture of the ramparts my first object, as the force under my command was not deemed sufficient to assault the ramparts and town at the same time, when defended by Tippoo's whole army, I directed Lieut.-Colonel Dunlop, with six companies of Bombay European flankers, supported by his Majesty's 12th and 33rd regiments, and ten companies of Bengal sepoy flankers, with fifty artillerymen, to assault the North ramparts, and to push on with the

European flank companies until he met the South attack, under Colonel Sherbrooke, consisting of the flank companies of the Scotch Brigade and Regiment de Meurone, reinforced by the Grenadier companies of his Majesty's 73rd and 74th regiments, in consequence of the vigorous resistance, there was reason to apprehend at the several heavy batteries on the south face of the fort, and supported by his Majesty's 73rd and 74th regiments, eight companies of coast native, and six companies of Bombay native flankers, with fifty artillerymen, when the whole were directed to form on the East face, until arrangements were made for the attack of such of the cavaliers as might not already have been seized on, or for proceeding to the attack of the body of the place, if with the force remaining such a measure should be deemed advisable.

The assault commenced, in obedience to your orders, at one P.M. Colonels Sherbrooke and Dunlop were directed on no account to quit the inner rampart previous to their junction, for any other object but that of seizing on the cavaliers in the neighbourhood of their respective attacks, and to lose no time in regaining their situation on the ramparts, as soon as that object should be attained, and every cavalier or post on the rampart, which it might be deemed essential to secure, were immediately to be occupied by a battalion company or companies from the supporting European regiments, so that the whole of the ground once captured might be secured, and the flankers on their junction be in full force to follow up their success, by an attack on any of the cavaliers which had not fallen in their way, or by an assault on the body of the town and the palace of the Sultaun.

In the success of every part of this plan my warmest wishes were gratified; the whole of the ramparts, and every cavalier in the fort, were in a vigorous assault of a few hours, in the possession of our troops, who were too well acquainted with the value of their conquest to render the retaining it against the whole of Tippoo's army at all doubtful. The place, therefore, being so securely our own, I was not anxious, by an immediate attack on the palace, to bring on a fresh and unnecessary slaughter; and indeed the exhausted state of the gallant flankers rendered it expedient for me to halt a short time before I proceeded to the attack of the palace, which, if Tippoo was in it, there was every reason to suppose would be, if possible, as gallantly defended as attacked.

During this halt, two fresh battalions of sepoys arrived, and trusting that by this time the Sultaun would see how fruitless any further resistance must prove, I requested Major Allen, Deputy Quarter-Master-General, who had just arrived from camp, and who, from his knowledge of the language, was well qualified to execute the duty, to proceed with a flag of truce to the palace, and offer Cowle to Tippoo Sultaun, and every person in his palace, on his immediate and unconditional surrender of himself and family to me; at the same time informing him, if there was the smallest hesitation in acceding to this offer, that an immediate assault on the palace would take place, and every man in it be put to the sword. The Grenadiers, and part of the 12th regiment under Major Craigie, with the 2nd battalion of the 9th regiment of sepoys, accompanied Major Allen to put this threat into immediate execution, if necessary; and I prepared the flankers, now a little recovered from their fatigues, to follow to the attack of the palace on the first signal of hostilities having recommenced (for the firing had ceased on all sides for upwards of an hour). In the mean time I received intelligence from one of the prisoners, of whom I caused enquiry to be made as to the place where the English soldiers, who had been taken in the different assaults on the enemy's outposts during the siege were confined, that they had all been put to death about ten days before in the most barbarous manner, by having nails driven through their skulls. On this I immediately advanced with the flankers of the 74th regiment and the light infantry, and remaining part of the 12th regiment, resolved, if Cowle had not already been granted, and the dreadful accounts of the fate of our fellow soldiers were confirmed, to sacrifice the tyrant to their manes.

On reaching the palace, Major Allen came out to me, and informed me he had been with Tippoo's two youngest sons, who were ignorant where their father was, but were disposed to surrender themselves and the palace on a promise of protection. Anxious, if possible, to discover Tippoo, who I had been informed was certainly in the palace, I hesitated to agree to these conditions unless they would inform me where their father was, and threatened to search the most secret recesses of the palace if he was not instantly produced; but not being able to learn from them where the Sultaun was, and wishing to get them out of the fort before it was dark, after giving them every assurance of protection and kind treatment, I sent them off to you, under charge of Lieut.-Colonel Agnew, your public Secretary, and

Captain Merriott, your Aid-de-Camp, escorted by the light infantry company of his Majesty's 33rd regiment. The palace was then taken possession of without opposition. I now proceeded to the search of the palace, accompanied by Lieut.-Colonel Close and Major Allen, taking care, however, to avoid the Zenana, round which I had posted a sufficient force to make his escape from it impracticable. In the palace we found a man who, on being severely threatened, said that the Sultaun was killed in attempting to escape through the Northern Sally Port, and offered to conduct us to the body. We accordingly proceeded thither, and under a slaughtered heap of several hundreds, many of whom were men of consequence in his service, had the pleasure to discover the body of the Sultaun. He had been shot through the head and body, and was quite dead. I caused him immediately to be put into a palanquin, and conveyed to the palace, where the body was identified by some of the principal men who had fallen into our hands, and by two of the eunuchs belonging to his Haram.

I now proceeded to give such protection to the inhabitants as was in my power, and although it was by this time dark, as I have heard no complaints of outrage or insult being offered to any after the conflict ceased, I may venture to say the natives of India will be satisfied that the British soldiers are not more brave than humane.

Early the next morning Abdual Cawlic, the second son of Tippoo, and the elder son of the two who were delivered to Lord Cornwallis as hostages at the conclusion of the last war, was met by Lieut.-Colonel Dalrymple coming from the island to deliver himself up. He was immediately assured of protection and the most liberal treatment, and I went to meet him to show how much satisfied I was with the confidence he placed in us by thus delivering himself into our hands when the means of escape were perfectly in his power.

Having been led to expect you in the fort yesterday morning, I waited with Abdual Cawlic to deliver him into your own hands. But on being relieved by Colonel Wellesley, I proceeded with him to camp, and delivered him over to you. I perceive, in the general orders of yesterday, that no mention is made of Colonel Sherbrooke. This, I perceive, is owing to that order being published before I had time to make my report to you of the conduct of the troops under my command on the assault, which was highly exemplary throughout, and if, where all behaved nobly, it is proper to mention individual merit, I know no man so justly entitled to praise as Colonel Sherbrooke, to whose exertions I feel myself much indebted for the success of the attack.

I make no doubt but Lieut.-Colonel Dunlop, who commanded a party of equal force with that of Colonel Sherbrooke, would have merited equal praise for his exertions had he not most unfortunately been disabled by a wound very early in the assault, a circumstance I most sincerely regretted, as from the well known character of that officer, and the clear manner in which he understood the instructions I gave him relative to the attack he was to lead, I put the greatest confidence in the success of the attack.

I have the honour to be, Sir,
Your most obedient, humble Servant,
DAVID BAIRD, Major-General.

Camp at Seringapatam,
6th May, 1799.

24. The Earl of Mornington to the Secret Committee of the Court of Directors.

Documents, illustrative of Tippoo's French alliance, found at Seringapatam.

Fort St. George, 19th May, 1799.

Honourable Sirs,

The accidental detention of the *Sarah Christiana* packet enables me to forward to your honourable Committee, by this despatch, documents of great importance, explanatory of the nature of the connexion between Tippoo Sultaun and the French republic.

These papers were found in the palace of Seringapatam, and were transmitted officially to my military secretary by the secretary of the commission appointed to assist Lieut.-General Harris in all matters of a political nature.

The paper No. 1 is a letter from Tippoo Sultaun to the Executive Directory, and appears to be an attested copy of that which was despatched by M. Dubuc with two native vakeels of the 7th of February, 1799. The letter, however, is dated the 20th of July, 1798, at which time the military preparations in the Carnatic had scarcely commenced.

Your Honourable Committee will observe, that, Tippoo Sultaun, in the most distinct manner, states the nature of his late embassy to the Isle of France to have been the same which I have described in my minute of the 12th of August, and in my letter to Tippoo Sultaun of the 8th of November, notwithstanding that he had endeavoured to put a different colour on the transaction in his letter to me of the 18th of December, 1798, received at Fort St. George the 25th of the same month.

It is equally remarkable that he does not attempt to allege against the British Government any ground of complaint since the conclusion of the last war.

The object of his offensive and defensive alliance with France appears to have been not merely the recovery of his former dominions, but the expulsion of the English from all their rich possessions in India, and the utter annihilation of their power in Asia.

You will further observe, that he declares it to be his intention to commence the attack on the first favourable occasion ; and on the whole, that he professes to make common cause with France, under the most solemn protestations of fidelity and zeal to the republic.

The paper, No. 2, is a note of the demands which Tippoo Sultaun's ambassadors were authorized by him to make upon the Executive Directory at Paris. They correspond in substance with the requisitions announced in M. Malartic's proclamation at the Mauritius.

In the articles 5 and 6 you will perceive that the Sultaun intended to commence his operations in the heart of the Carnatic, in concert with a French army to be landed at Porto Novo, and that he did not propose to wait the actual arrival of the French force, but was resolved to make himself master of the coast of Coromandel as soon as he should find it convenient, after having received notice of the motions of the French.

In article 7 it appears that the Portuguese colonies in this quarter of India were to have been divided between Tippoo Sultaun and the French. All the articles of this paper demand particular attention, as tending to prove, in the most conclusive manner, the entire devotion of this infatuated Prince to his alliance with France. This paper also is dated on the 20th July, 1798; both documents are signed in the Sultaun's own handwriting, according to the abbreviated form of signature, which he was accustomed to use in all his letters and other official documents. This mode of signature is usual among the natives of Hindostan, and no doubt can be entertained of the authenticity of the papers.

Your Honourable Committee will observe, that the letter from Tippoo Sultaun to me, which was received at Fort St. George on the 13th of February, must have been written subsequently to the despatch of the papers now enclosed, as M. Dubuc, with the Sultaun's two vakeels, embarked at Tranquebar on the 7th of February.

I have the honour to be, &c.

MORNINGTON.

25. The Earl of Mornington to the Honourable Court of Directors.

Partition and Settlement of Mysore. Treatment of the Sultaun's family. Results of the War.

Fort St. George, 3d August, 1799.

Honourable Sirs,

My last separate letter to your Honourable Court, was dated on the 6th of June, at which period I informed you, that I was occupied in framing a general settlement of the conquered territories of the late Tippoo Sultaun. In this despatch, I shall submit to your Honourable Court, a summary abstract of the principles by which my conduct has been governed in framing this settlement, and of the means which I have employed for carrying it into effect.

From the justice and success of the late war with Tippoo Sultaun, the Company and the Nizam derived an undoubted right to the disposal of the dominions conquered by their united arms. This right of conquest entitled the Company and the Nizam, to retain the whole territory in their own hands; the cession of any portion of it to any other party, might be a consideration of policy or humanity, but could not be claimed on any ground of justice or right.

The Mahrattas, whatever might have been their disposition, having taken no share in the war, had forfeited every pretension to participate in the advantages of the peace. The numerous progeny of Tippoo Sultaun (even if it had been possible to adjust their several pretensions to the succession,) could plead no title which had not been superseded by the conquest of the kingdom; nor was it possible in estimating their claims, to forget the usurpation of Hyder Alli, and the sufferings of the unfortunate family, expelled by his crimes from the throne of Mysore. A lineal descendant of the ancient house of the Rajahs of Mysore, still remained at Seringapatam; but, whatever might be the hopes of his family, from the moderation and humanity of the conquerors, this young Prince could assert no right to any share of the conquered territory.

To the free and uncontrouled exercise of the right of conquest thus vested in the Company and the Nizam, no obstacle existed in the internal state of the kingdom of Mysore. The whole body of the people had manifested the most favourable disposition to submit to our authority; the commanders of most of the principal fortresses had surrendered, or expressed their readiness to surrender to our arms; and within a few days after the fall of Seringapatam, I was satisfied that no difficulty would arise from the influence of the Mahommedans introduced into Mysore, under the usurpation of Hyder Alli and Tippoo Sultaun. It had been the uniform policy of the latter to destroy every vestige of hereditary right, established office, or territorial possession among his subjects, and to concentre not only the whole authority of the State, but the whole administration of the Government in his own person; during his reign, therefore, his numerous Mahommedan chiefs possessed neither individual weight, nor collective force; many of them had fallen at Malavelly, Sedasere, and Seringapatam, during the course of the war; and most of the survivors, together with their families, were actually in the fortress of Seringapatam, subjected to our discretion, and confiding in the clemency of the British Government, without union, spirit, or strength to resist its power. The inclination and temper, both of the surviving chiefs and of the people, were also most happily disposed to receive any new settlement, which might promise to secure them against the revival of a despotism, the barbarity and caprice of which have never been surpassed even by any of the Mahommedan conquerors of India.

In regulating the exercise of our right of conquest, it appeared to me that no principle could more justly be assumed, than that the original objects of the war should constitute the basis of the peace, and of the general settlement of our territorial acquisitions. These objects had been repeatedly declared by the Allies to be a reasonable indemnification for our expence in the war, and an adequate security against the return of that danger, which originally provoked us to arms.

With a view to each of these just and necessary objects, it was requisite that the Company and the Nizam should retain a large portion of the conquered territory; but it required much consideration to determine the precise extent of that portion, as well as the just rule of partition. The war had not been undertaken in pursuit of schemes of conquest, extension of territory, or augmentation of revenue. In proportion to the magnitude and lustre of our success, it became a more urgent duty to remember, that a peace founded in the gratification of any ambitious or inordinate view, could neither be advantageous, honourable, nor secure.

The approved policy, interests, and honour of the British nation therefore required, that the settlement of the extensive kingdom subjected to our disposal, should be formed on principles acceptable to the inhabitants of the conquered territories, just and conciliatory towards the contiguous native States, and indulgent to every party, in any degree affected by the consequences of our success.

To have divided the whole territory equally between the Company and the Nizam, to the exclusion of any other State, would have afforded strong grounds of jealousy to the Mahrattas, and aggrandized the Nizam's power beyond all bounds of discretion; under whatever form such a partition could have been made, it must have placed in the hands of the Nizam many of the strong fortresses on the northern frontier of Mysore, and exposed our frontier in that quarter to every predatory incursion; such a partition would have laid the foundation of perpetual differences, not only between the Mahrattas and the Nizam, but between the Company and both those powers.

To have divided the country into three equal portions, allowing the Mahrattas, (who had borne no part in the expence or hazard of the war,) an equal share with the other two branches of the triple alliance, in the advantages of the peace, would have been unjust towards the Nizam, and towards the Company; impolitic, as furnishing an evil example to our other Allies in India, and dangerous, as effecting a considerable aggrandizement of the Mahratta empire at the expence of the Company, and of the Nizam. This mode of partition also, must have placed Chitteldroog, and some of the most important northern fortresses, in the hands of the Mahrattas, while the remainder of the fortresses in the same line, would have been occupied by the Nizam, and our unfortified and open frontier in Mysore, would have been exposed to the excesses of the undisciplined troops of both powers.

The Mahrattas unquestionably had no claim to any portion of the conquered territory, and any considerable extension of their empire was objectionable, especially when accompanied by the possession of strong fortresses bordering on the line of our frontier. It was, however, desirable to conciliate their goodwill, and to offer to them such a portion of territory as might give them an interest in the new settlement without offence or injury to the Nizam, and without danger to the frontier of the Company's possessions. On the other hand, it was prudent to limit the territory retained in the hands of the Company and of the Nizam within such bounds of moderation as should bear a due proportion to their respective expences in the contest, and to the necessary means of securing the public safety of their respective dominions.

For the information of your Honourable Court, I have annexed to this despatch a comparative statement of several plans for the partition of Tippoo Sultaun's dominions, drawn up under my instructions with a view to the relative interests and power of the Nizam, the Mahrattas, and the Company; to the nature, produce, and geographical boundaries of the country, and to the position and strength of the several fortresses and passes; an attentive investigation of every comparative view of these important questions terminated in my decision that the establishment of a central and separate government in Mysore, under the protection of the Company, and the admission of the Mahrattas to a certain participation in the division of the conquered territory, were the expedients best calculated to reconcile the interests of all parties, to secure to the Company, a less invidious, and more efficient share of revenue, resource, commercial advantage, and military strength, than could be obtained under any other distribution of territory or power, and to afford the most favourable prospect of general and permanent tranquillity in India.

Having decided these leading principles of the new settlement, I proceeded to determine the rule of distribution for the respective shares of the Company, the Nizam, and the Mahrattas, to fix the most eligible position for the cessions to be made to each party, and to define the limits of the new government of Mysore.

To the Company's share naturally fell the Province of Canara, the Districts of Coimbatoor and Daraporam, with all the territory lying below the Ghauts between your possessions in the Carnatic, and those in Malabar. These acquisitions appeared the most eligible, not only on account of their intrinsic value in point of produce, but as securing an uninterrupted tract of territory from the coast of Coromandel to that of Malabar, together with the entire sea-coast of the Kingdom of Mysore, and the base of all the eastern, western and southern Ghauts. To these I thought it necessary to add the forts and posts forming the heads of all the passes above the Ghauts on the Table Land. The possession of the base of the Ghauts alone formed no effectual barrier for the inhabitants of the Low Lands against an enemy possessing the summits of those mountains; and I, therefore, considered the acquisition of all the entrances of the Passes situated above the Ghauts, to be an essential object of security, against every possible approach of danger from the Table Land. This acquisition derived a further importance in my opinion, from the means which it appeared to afford of curbing the refractory spirit of the Polygars, and of all other turbulent and disaffected subjects in the Carnatic, and on the coast of Malabar; I also considered the district of Wynaad to be an useful possession with a view to the tranquillity of your territories on the latter coast. The last addition which I deemed it necessary to make to your share of the conquered dominions, consisted of the fortress, city and island of Seringapatam, the possession of which would effectually secure the communication between your territories on both coasts, and consolidate all your lines of defence in every direction.

To the Nizam, it appeared most expedient to allot the districts of Gooty and Gurrumcondah, bordering on the cessions which he acquired by the peace of 1792, together with a tract of country, the frontier of which should be drawn nearly along the line of Chitteldroog, Sera, Nundydroog, and Colar, leaving, however, these fortresses to the southward to form the frontier of the new Government of Mysore. The Nizam certainly could not assert any just claim to an equal participation with the Company in the advantages of the peace. The operation of the 6th Article of the Treaty of Paungul, respecting an equal division of conquests, was limited to the war which terminated in 1792. Since the peace of Seringapatam, the 10th is the only Article of the Treaty of Paungul which can be considered to continue in force; and no subsequent engagements had been contracted with the Nizam which could entitle him to any advantages in the present peace exceeding his relative proportion in the expences and exertions of the allied force during the late war. It was, however, desirable that the territorial revenue retained in sovereignty by the Company (after deducting whatever charges might be annexed to the tenure) should not exceed the Nizam's portion, and accordingly I determined that this principle should be observed in the partition; reserving, however, to the Company, as a just indemnification for their superior share in the expences and exertions of the war, the principal benefit of whatever advantages might flow from any engagements to be contracted with the new Government of Mysore.

For the Mahrattas, I resolved to reserve a portion of territory, the revenues of which should not exceed two-thirds, nor fall short of one-half, of the portions retained in sovereignty by the Nizam and the Company respectively, after deducting their respective charges: considering that any cession to the Peishwa must be viewed as a matter of mere favour, it appeared to me that the share to be allotted to him was amply sufficient; it would contain Harponelly, Soonda above the Ghauts, Annagoondy, part of the district of Chitteldroog, part of Bednore above the Ghauts, and other districts, but the frontier fortresses of Chitteldroog and Bednore would remain for the protection of the new Government of Mysore. I also determined that no portion of territory should be ceded to the Peishwa unconditionally, and that the cession should form the basis of a new treaty with the Mahratta empire.

The territory remaining unoccupied by this partition could be bounded to the northward by a strong line of hill forts and posts, forming a powerful barrier towards the southern frontiers of the Nizam and of the Mahrattas, from Punganoor on the line of the eastern, to Bednore on that of the western Ghauts, and would be entirely surrounded to the east, west and south, by the territories of the Company above and below the Ghauts, the Company also holding the Fort of Seringapatam in the centre of the Table Land.

The necessity now occurred of determining in what hands the new Government of Mysore should be placed, and although no positive right or title to the throne existed in any party, it seemed expedient, that my choice should be made between the pretensions of the family of Tippoo Sultaun, and those of the ancient house of the Rajahs of Mysore.

The claims of humanity on both sides rendered the decision a painful and ungracious task. No alternative remained, but to depose the dynasty which I found upon the throne, or to confirm the Mahommedan usurpation, and with it the perpetual exclusion and degradation of the legitimate Hindoo sovereigns of the country. The usurpation, although not sanctioned by remote antiquity, had subsisted for such a length of time as to have nearly extinguished the hopes of the Hindoo family, and to have accustomed them to the humility of their actual fortunes, while the sons of Tippoo Sultaun, born in the state of royalty, and educated with the proudest and most exalted expectations of sovereignty and power, would be proportionably sensible to the sudden change of their condition, and to the unexpected disappointment of their splendid prospects. In this view of the subject it would have been more grateful to my mind (securing a munificent provision for the ancient family of Mysore) to have restored that of Tippoo Sultaun to the throne; if such a restoration could have been accomplished without exposing Mysore to the perpetual hazard of internal commotion and foreign war, and without endangering the stability of the intended settlement of your interests and those of your allies in this quarter of India.

Since the peace of Seringapatam, and more especially since the year 1796, the destruction of the British power in India has formed the favourite and unremitting object of Tippoo Sultaun's hopes and exertions. His haughty mind never could be reconciled to the sacrifices which he was compelled to make for the purchase of peace in 1792; and his increasing eagerness to recover the extensive portion of his dominions, then ceded to the allies, urged him to pursue a systematic course of intrigue against the British power among all the native states, and to revert to his ancient and hereditary connection with France, as the only effectual means of gratifying either his ambition or revenge.

The proofs which I had obtained, previous to the war, of the nature and objects of his machinations, were sufficient to satisfy my judgment; they have since been corroborated by the voluminous records discovered in the Palace of Seringapatam; it is now incontestable that Tippoo Sultaun's thoughts were perpetually intent upon the ruin of the British power, that he trusted to have accomplished our expulsion by instigating the French to invade India; and that he prosecuted this unalterable purpose with all the zeal and ardour of passionate resentment and vindictive hate, as well as with the steadiness of a deliberate maxim of state.

Perhaps the most wise policy which Tippoo Sultaun could have pursued would have been to have rested satisfied with the dominions remaining in his hands after the peace of 1792. But a policy of so moderate and pacific a spirit being utterly incompatible with the impetuosity of his temper, with the principles of his religious faith, and with the military character of his government, it might be at least a matter of rational speculation, whether a close alliance with France (however dangerous in its remote consequences) was not his true interest, in the actual state of his immediate views and pursuits. The possession of his lost dignity, wealth, and power could not be recovered without the conquest of a great part of the Company's territory, nor effectually secured without the total subversion of the British interests in India;—a French army was the only instrument by which such an enterprize could be attempted;—an alliance with France was, therefore, the necessary consequence of Tippoo Sultaun's restless, but natural desire to restore his empire to its former splendour and strength. In addition to his correspondence with the French at Tranquebar, with those at the Isle of France, and with the executive Directory at Paris, his embassy to Zemaun Shah, his intrigues at Poonah and Hyderabad, and his correspondence with Mons. Raymond, (all which transactions appear distinctly in the records discovered at Seringapatam) furnish abundant evidence that his antipathy to the English was the ruling passion of his heart, the mainspring of his policy, the fixed and fundamental principle of his councils and government.

The heir of Tippoo Sultaun must have been educated in the same principles, and encouraged to indulge in the same prejudices and passions, and instructed to form the same views of the interests and honour of the throne of Mysore. These sentiments would necessarily acquire additional force in his mind from the issue of the late war. Our unexampled success had subverted the foundations of his father's empire, and transferred to our possession every source of the civil or military power of Mysore. Placed on the throne by our favour, and limited by our controul, he would have felt himself degraded to a state of humiliation and weakness so abject as no Prince of spirit would brook. Under such an arrangement our safety would have required us to retain at least all the territory which we now hold by the partition Treaty of Mysore. Whatever we retained must have been considered by the prince as a new usurpation upon his royal inheritance, and an additional pledge of his degradation and disgrace. In proportion to the reduction of his territory and resources he would have less to lose and more to regain in any struggle for the recovery of his father's empire; nor does it seem unreasonable to suppose that the heir of Hyder Alli and Tippoo Sultaun, animated by the implacable spirit and bold example of his parents, and accustomed to the commanding prospect of independent sovereignty, and to the splendour of military glory, might deliberately hazard the remnant of his hereditary possessions in pursuit of so proud an object, as the recovery of that vast and powerful empire, which for many years had rendered his ancestors the scourge of the Carnatic, and the terror of this quarter of India.

In the most narrow view of the subject, it must be admitted that the son of Tippoo Sultaun must have felt a perpetual interest in the subversion of any settlement of Mysore, founded on a partition of his father's dominions, and on a limitation of his own independence. If, therefore, a prince of this race had been placed on the throne of Mysore, the foundations of the new settlement would have been laid in the very principles of its own dissolution. With such a prince no sincere alliance, no concord of sentiments, or union of views could ever have been established; the appearances of amity or attachment must have been delusive, even his submission must have been reluctant, if not treacherous; while all his interests, his habits, prejudices, and passions, his vices, and even his virtues must have concurred to cherish an irreconcilable aversion to our name and power, and an eager desire to abet the cause, to exasperate the animosity, and to receive the aid of every enemy of the British nation. Whatever degree of influence or strength might have been left to the native Government of Mysore in such hands, would always have been thrown into the scale opposed to your interests. The hostile power of Mysore would have been weakened, but not destroyed; an enemy would still have remained in the centre of your possessions, watching every occasion to repair the misfortunes of his family at your expense, and forming a point of union for the machinations of every discontented faction in India, and for the intrigues of every emissary of France.

Under these circumstances, the same anxiety for the security and repose of your possessions, which originally compelled me to reduce the power of Tippoo Sultaun, now appeared to require that I should provide effectually against the revival of any degree of a similar danger, in the person of his son.

On the other hand, the restoration of the descendant of the ancient Rajahs of Mysore was recommended by the same course of reasoning which excluded the heir of the Mahomedan usurpation.

The indignities which the deposed family of Mysore had suffered, especially during the cruel and tyrannical reign of Tippoo Sultaun, and the state of degradation and misery to which they had been reduced, would most naturally excite a sentiment of gratitude and attachment in their minds towards that power, which had not only delivered them from oppression, but had raised them to a state of considerable affluence and distinction. Between the British Government and this family, an intercourse of friendship and kindness had subsisted in the most desperate crisis of their adverse fortune. They had formed no connection with your enemies. Their elevation would be the spontaneous act of your generosity, and from your support alone could they ever hope to be maintained upon the throne, either against the family of Tippoo Sultaun, or against any other claimant. They must naturally view with an eye of jealousy, all the friends of the usurping family, and consequently be adverse to the French, or to any state connected with that family, in its hereditary hatred of the British Government. The heir of the Rajahs of Mysore, if placed on the throne, must feel that his continuance in that state depended on the stability of the new settlement in all its parts. His interest must therefore be to unite with cordiality and zeal in every effort necessary to its harmony, efficiency, and vigour. The effect of such an arrangement of the affairs of Mysore would not be limited to the mere destruction of the hostile power which menaced our safety. In the place of that power, would be substituted one, whose interests and resources might be absolutely identified with our own, and the kingdom of Mysore, so long the source of calamity and alarm to the Carnatic, might become a new barrier of our defence, and might supply fresh means of wealth and strength to the Company, their subjects, and allies.

In addition to these motives of policy, moral considerations, and sentiments of generosity and humanity, favoured the restoration of the ancient family of Mysore. Their high birth, the antiquity of their legitimate title, and their long and unmerited sufferings, rendered them peculiar objects of compassion and respect; nor could it be doubted that their government would be both more acceptable and more indulgent than that of the Mahomedan usurpers, to the mass of the inhabitants of the country, composed almost entirely of Hindoos.

These considerations induced me to adopt the resolution of preferring the descendants of the Rajahs of Mysore to the heir of Tippoo Sultaun.

I determined at the same time to grant to the families of Hyder Ali and Tippoo Sultaun a more magnificent maintenance than either had enjoyed during the late reign, and to provide with the same liberality for the principal Mahomedan officers and chiefs of the state, who had survived the Sultaun, and for the families of all those who had fallen in the course of the war.

For the accomplishment of a settlement founded on the principles which I have had the honour to detail to your Honourable Court in the preceding paragraphs, I issued a special commission on the 4th of June, appointing Lieutenant-General Harris, The Honourable Colonel Wellesley, The Honourable Henry Wellesley, Lieutenant-Colonel William Kirkpatrick, and Lieutenant-Colonel Barry Close, commissioners for the affairs of Mysore, with the ample powers specified in the commission; and I named Captains Malcolm and Munro to be secretaries, and Mr. Edward Golding and Lieutenant Charles Pasley assistant secretaries to the commission. As the favourable state of the country has rendered my presence at Seringapatam unnecessary, I accompanied the commission with instructions directing the commissioners to proceed without delay to lay the foundations of the new arrangement, and for the purpose of precluding the intrigues of the natives, and of all the great interests which were in suspense, I enjoined the commissioners and their secretaries to take an oath of secrecy, in order that no part of my plan might transpire until the arrangements for the whole had been completed.

The commissioners assembled at Seringapatam on the 8th of June, and under my instructions, their first act was to make provision for the principal surviving officers and chiefs of the late Sultaun, and for the families of those slain during the campaign. I am happy to inform your Honourable Court, that this measure produced the most salutary effect in tranquillizing the minds of the principal Mahomedans remaining in Mysore, and in placing the clemency and generosity of the British Government in the most conspicuous and honourable light. It was determined, that Meer Kummur ud Deen should be settled at Gurrumcondah, with a jaghire from the Nizam, and another from the Company. This arrangement having been concluded, Kummur ud Deen departed from Seringapatam on the 19th of June, with many expressions of gratitude towards the Company's Government. The Brahmin Poorneah, who had been the principal financial minister of the late Sultaun, having given satisfactory proof of his readiness to serve the new Government in the same capacity, it was determined that he should be appointed Dewan to the young Rajah of Mysore.

The next proceeding of the commissioners, in pursuance of my directions, was to undertake the painful, but necessary task of removing the families of Hyder Ali and Tippoo Sultaun from Seringapatam to the Carnatic.

I had previously given orders that the fortress of Vellore should be prepared for the reception of the families, and I had appointed Lieutenant-Colonel Doveton to the command of that fortress, and had also entrusted him with the payment of the stipends allotted to both families, directing him to spare no reasonable expense in providing for their accommodation, on a scale suitable to their former rank and expectations. The four princes, Futteh Hyder, Abdul Khaulik, Moyez oo Deen, and Moyee oo Deen, with their families, arrived at Vellore on the 13th of July; they expressed their satisfaction in the accommodations provided for them. The remainder of the families of Hyder Ali and Tippoo Sultaun will be removed as soon as may be practicable.

Previously to the departure of the princes from Seringapatam, the commissioners had cautiously abstained from all intercourse with the family of the Rajah of Mysore; but as soon as the four elder sons of the late Sultaun had left the capital, the commissioners paid a visit to the young Rajah, whom they found with others of this persecuted family, in a condition of poverty and humiliation, which excited the strongest emotions of compassion; it was determined to fix the residence of the Rajah in the ancient town of Mysore, as being the most eligible situation for the seat of his government.

On the 5th of June I had furnished the commissioners with the first draft of a treaty between the Company and his Highness, the Nizam, for the partition of Mysore, and having received the fullest communication of their sentiments and of those of Meer Allum, on the subject, I made such alterations as appeared to be advisable. On the 22nd of June this treaty was executed by the commissioners and Meer Allum, at Seringapatam, and ratified by me in council at Fort St. George, on the 26th of the same month, and by his Highness the Nizam, at Hyderabad, on the 13th of July. A copy of this treaty is annexed to this despatch under the title of the Partition Treaty of Mysore.

On the 30th of June the Rajah of Mysore was formally placed on the musnud, by the commissioners, assisted by Meer Allum.

On the 8th of June I had forwarded to the commissioners the first draft of the subsidiary treaty, to be concluded between the Company and the Rajah of Mysore. After an ample discussion with the commissioners who had communicated the whole arrangement to the Brahmin Poorneah, and conciliated his co-operation; and after the adoption of several alterations, this treaty was executed in the fortress of Nuzzerbah, near Seringapatam, by the commissioners, and certain proxies on the part of the young Rajah, on the 8th of July, and ratified by me in council on the 23rd of July, under the title of the Subsidiary Treaty of Seringapatam.

In framing this engagement, it was my determination to establish the most unqualified community of interests between the Government of Mysore and the Company, and to render the Rajah's northern frontier in effect, a powerful line of our defence. With this view, I have engaged to undertake the protection of this country, in consideration of an annual subsidy of seven lacs of star pagodas; but recollecting the inconveniences and embarrassments which have arisen to all parties concerned under the double Governments and conflicting authorities unfortunately established in Oude, the Carnatic, and Tanjore, I resolved to reserve to the Company the most extensive and indisputable powers of interposition in the internal affairs of Mysore, as well as an unlimited right of assuming the direct management of the country (whenever such a step might appear necessary for the security of the funds destined to the subsidy), and of requiring extraordinary aid beyond the amount of the fixed subsidy, either in time of war, or of preparations for hostility.

Under this arrangement I trust that I shall be enabled to command the whole resources of the Rajah's territory, to improve its cultivation, to extend its commerce, and to secure the welfare of its inhabitants. It appeared to me a more candid and liberal, as well as a more wise policy, to apprize the Rajah distinctly, at the moment of his accession, of the exact nature of his dependance on the Company, than to leave any matter for future doubt or discussion. The right of the Company to establish such an arrangement, either as affecting the Rajah or the allies, has already been stated in this despatch.

I entertain a sanguine expectation that the Rajah and his ministers being fully apprized of the extensive powers reserved to the Company, will cheerfully adopt such regulations as shall render the actual exercise of those powers unnecessary. Much indulgence will be required at the commencement of the new Government, and it is my intention to abstain from any pressure upon the Rajah's finances, which by embarrassing them, might tend to the impoverishment of the country, and to the distress of the people.

Soon after the enthronement of the Rajah, the Brahmin Poorneah was appointed by the commissioners to be his Highness' Dewan.

The eminent talents and integrity of Lieutenant-Colonel Close, added to his extraordinary skill in the country language, and his experience in the manners, customs, and habits of the natives of India, induced me to select him for the important charge of resident with the Rajah of Mysore. He was accordingly appointed to that office immediately after the Subsidiary Treaty of Seringapatam had been signed; and the commission was then dissolved on the 3rd of July.

Although your Honourable Court will perceive in the commission the names of two persons, of whose merits it may be difficult for me to form an impartial judgment, I feel it to be my duty to recommend the conduct of the commissioners to your most public and distinguished approbation.

The conclusion within one month of two treaties, so extensive in their consequences, and complicated in their details, together with all the subordinate arrangements connected with this important settlement, will appear the most extraordinary effort of diligence and ability, when it is remarked, that reference was necessarily made to me at Fort St. George, in every stage of the business. It will also be satisfactory to your Honourable Court to observe, that the whole arrangement has been conducted at Seringapatam, with a spirit of humanity and liberality, which cannot fail to conciliate the good will of the inhabitants of Mysore.

The command of Seringapatam will remain in the hands of Colonel Wellesley; it is a trust of great delicacy and importance, which it is my duty to repose in a person of approved military talents and integrity, and to superintend with peculiar vigilance and care.

Although I shall deem it prudent to detain the army in the field for a short period of time, I have the satisfaction to assure your Honourable Court, that far the greater part of the dominions of Tippoo Sultaun is now in a state of perfect tranquillity.

A detachment from the army of Bombay took possession of Mangalore on the 4th of June, and the province of Canara, with the exception of the fortress of Jemaulabad, appeared disposed to submit cheerfully to our authority. I have little doubt that the commanding officer of Jemaulabad will soon be induced to surrender to the Company's arms; in any event, however, the fort will be reduced without difficulty. In this confidence, a collector has been appointed for the province of Canara.

The remainder of the territory allotted to the Company in Çoimbatoor, has passed into our hands without any difficulty, and collectors have been appointed for the administration of the revenue. The fort of Gurrumcondah is in the possession of his Highness the Nizam, and those of Sera and Chitteldroog are now garrisoned by the British troops. Some disturbances have taken place in Bidnoor, in which province an adventurer had assembled a banditti, which had distressed the inhabitants of the country; a division of the army being now on its progress towards Bidnoor, I have every reason to expect that the commotions in that quarter will speedily be quelled.

Since the fall of Seringapatam, the conduct of the Mahrattas has been of the most conciliatory nature; it would be premature at present to enter into any detail on the subject of the negociations depending at Poonah; but I have the satisfaction to assure your Honourable Court that no interruption to the settlement of Mysore is likely to proceed from the Mahrattas. Whatever may be the secret inclination either of the Peishwa or of Scindiah, their mutual weakness and reciprocal jealousy are sufficient securities against any danger from that quarter.

The advantages resulting to your interests from the recent settlement of Mysore, are sufficiently obvious, as they appear in the preceding parts of this despatch, and in the papers which accompany it. It may not, however, be useless to submit to your Honourable Court, in a connected form, a general view of the whole of this important question, together with the reflections which have arisen in my mind from an anxious and assiduous attention to every branch of the subject.

Since the first war with Hyder Ali, the tranquillity of your possessions has been continually menaced by the power of Mysore. Even in the intervals of peace, which have succeeded to the several wars in which the Company has been engaged with Hyder Ali and Tippoo Sultaun, your security in the Carnatic has ever been precarious. During the cessation of actual hostilities, the designs of the Sovereign of Mysore have still continued uniformly hostile, and his means of executing them have always remained considerable, while the degrees of your safety have fluctuated with the state of your military establishments and preparations, and with the distribution of your force.

The baneful effects of this perpetual state of uncertainty and solicitude, have been felt not only in the decay of agriculture, and of the arts of peaceful industry on the coast of Coromandel, and in the rebellious spirit of certain descriptions of your subjects on that coast, and on the coast of Malabar, but occasionally throughout all India, in the diminution of the British influence and consideration at foreign courts, in the rising hopes of the turbulent and disaffected, and in the decline of public and private credit, shaken by repeated rumours of war, and by the constant necessity of guarding against a surprise from the sudden aggression of an enemy, whom no clemency or moderation could conciliate, and no faith could bind.

The reduction of Tippoo Sultaun's power and resources effected by the treaty of Seringapatam in 1792, had weakened, but not extinguished the cause of these complicated evils. Soon after the conclusion of peace, this cause and its effects appear to have recovered a considerable degree of activity and vigour, until in the year 1796, the intrigues and military movements of Tippoo Sultaun compelled the Government General to assemble the army on the coast of Coromandel, and in the Autumn of 1797, such apprehensions were justly entertained of his designs and power, as induced the Government of Fort St. George to abandon the prosecution of an expedition ably planned, intimately connected with your interests, and which had already brought a heavy charge on your finances.

Judicious indeed, and provident was the policy which dictated the relinquishment of that enterprise, since subsequent discoveries and events have manifested the great probability, if not the absolute certainty, that the departure of the large force destined for Manilla would have proved a signal to the watchful vengeance of Tippoo Sultaun to invade the Carnatic, or to attack the dominions of the Nizam, even without waiting for succours from France, the assistance of which might not, perhaps, have appeared to him necessary during the absence of so considerable a portion of our army.

But the apprehension of the designs and movements of the power of Mysore had never, perhaps, been more anxiously or more justly entertained, than between the months of June and September, 1798. It cannot be denied that during that period, your interests were menaced by a combination of the most serious dangers. The anxiety and fears hitherto entertained with regard to the designs of Tippoo Sultaun, were now confirmed by a certain knowledge of his having actually proposed to the French projects of the most extensive hostility against your possessions in India. The alarm, as well as the danger, was considerably aggravated by the formidable preparations of the French in the Mediterranean, by the apparently desperate state of our alliances in the Deccan: by the peculiar situation of the Court of Hyderabad, subjected to the will of a powerful French army and French faction; by the menacing declarations and probable views of Zemaun Shah; by the dispersed and defective condition of the army of Fort St. George; and above all, by the general persuasion, that an early attempt to assemble or to move that army, would serve only as a provocation to the enemy to invade and desolate the Carnatic, without furnishing the means of repelling the invader.

The situation of our allies at this period of general despondency, is now well known to your Honourable Court. It will therefore be sufficient in this place to observe, that the degree of danger with which the Nizam and the Peishwa were threatened by the impending storm, exceeded that which menaced our possessions in the same proportion, as the distractions and weakness of the Governments of Poonah and Hyderabad rendered them less able than the Company to counteract the machinations or to repel the assault of the enemy. It is true, that Tippoo Sultaun's views against the Courts of Poonah and Hyderabad, were ostensibly limited to the recovery of the cessions made by him to those powers in 1792. But it cannot be doubted, that his ambition and rapacity would have augmented with the progress of his victories, and his revenge was not of a temper to be mitigated by success.

Your Honourable Court is apprised of the changes which successively and rapidly took place in the condition of our alliances and of our army, substituting at Hyderabad in place of a French faction and a French army, British influence and a considerable British force, and producing ultimately the happy restoration of confidence and energy among your servants at Fort St. George. It is therefore unnecessary to dwell on that part of the subject; but it may be expedient to advert to the state of the general expectations at different periods of time previous to the war, and to compare our actual situation with those expectations, as well as with our position in the month of June, 1798.

At that time, even the most sanguine dispositions, and those least affected by the prevalent panic, would probably have been content to have detached Tippoo Sultaun from his alliance with the French nation; in the hope that, without the aid of a French force, he would not attempt to disturb the tranquillity of the Carnatic.

Even at a later period, when the subversion of the French party at Hyderabad, the restoration of the Nizam to the condition of an efficient ally, and the advanced state of our military preparations had inspired a general spirit of confidence and zeal, the most confident and zealous would have deemed the issue of the approaching contest prosperous as well as honourable, if it had effected a considerable reduction of the power and resources of Tippoo Sultaun, and had obtained a reasonable indemnity for the expenses of the allies.

The entire destruction of Tippoo Sultaun's power, or the absolute transfer of his resources to any hand, less inimical or less violent, would have been deemed a glorious termination even of a long and expensive contest.

But the success of your arms in the short period of the late campaign has not merely excluded the French from Mysore, provided an ample indemnity to you and your ally for the charges of the war, destroyed the hostile power of Tippoo Sultaun, and effectually precluded its revival, but has transferred the sword of your implacable enemy into your own hands, and turned to your use the main springs of his wealth and strength.

By the partition treaty of Mysore you have acquired an augmentation of direct territorial revenue to the annual amount of about star pagodas 6,47,641,10, (£259,056 sterling.)[1] By the subsidiary treaty of Seringapatam, you have secured an annual subsidy of star pagodas 7,00,000, (£280,000 sterling), making together, with your new territorial revenue, the sum of star pagodas 13,47,641,10, (£539,056 sterling), and leaving (after deducting the provision allotted for the families of Hyder Ali Khan and Tippoo Sultaun) an annual increase of your funds in this quarter of India, equal to star pagodas 11,47,641,10, (£459,056 sterling). But a reasonable expectation is entertained, that the territory acquired by the Company, under the treaty of Mysore, will yield, in the course of a few years, a sum not less than, star pagodas 14,78,698, (£591,479 sterling). If such an advance in the nominal revenue of the acquired districts should actually be realized, the positive augmentation of your available annual resources, in consequence of the late settlement of Mysore, will amount nearly to 20 lacs of star pagodas, (£800,000 sterling). But in estimating the increase of your annual available resources since the month of June 1798, the augmentation which took place in the subsidy payable by the Nizam, is not to be omitted. By the treaty of Hyderabad, concluded on the first of September 1798, the annual subsidy was augmented from Arcot rupees 6,44,556, to Arcot rupees 24,17,100, making an increase annually of Arcot rupees 17,72,544, or star pagodas 5,64,982, (£225,992 sterling). Thus, the total augmentation of your available annual resources since June 1798, in this quarter of your possessions, amounts actually to, star pagodas 17,12,623, (£685,048 sterling), and, if the increased revenue of the newly-acquired territory should be realized, (according to just expectation), it will amount to star pagodas 25,43,680 (£1,017,472 sterling).

Against these acquisitions must be placed the expense of whatever additions it may be found necessary to make to your military force, either in consequence of the extension of your territory, or of the subsidiary engagements which have been contracted with the Nizam and with the Rajah of Mysore.

The subsidiary force at Hyderabad must be considered as a part of your efficient strength prepared for your service on any emergency, and ready to aid you in any future war, as

---

[1] Calculating the star pagoda at 8*s*.

it has aided you in the last. It does not appear to me probable that it will be necessary to make any considerable addition to the military establishment of Fort St. George, in consequence of the treaty of Hyderabad, nor do I apprehend that the requisite increase of that establishment, and of the army of Bombay, in consequence of the two treaties annexed to this despatch, will bear any proportion to the increase of your revenue and resources. For it must never be forgotten that, while your territory has been extended, your frontier has been contracted and strengthened, your principal enemy utterly destroyed, and an ally, and dependant of the Company, substituted on his throne.

I do not yet possess the means of stating with sufficient accuracy to your honourable Court, either the amount of the charges incurred in consequence of the various measures of preparation and precaution, which became necessary on the discovery of Tippoo Sultaun's hostile designs in June 1798, or the amount of the expense which is to be placed to the account of the operations of the late war. The accumulated charges both of our preparations and of the war must be considerable; but whenever a statement of the expenses of the late war can be submitted to your honourable Court, your wisdom and justice will necessarily distinguish the charges incurred for the purpose of assembling an effective army in the field, from those actually belonging to the operations of your armies in Mysore, and to the siege of Seringapatam.

From the moment that Tippoo's negotiations had transpired, it became an indispensable duty to place the Carnatic in a posture of complete defence. The experience of former wars with Mysore, the nature of the frontier of the Carnatic, exposed in various points by its almost innumerable passes to the incursion of the enemy, the actual state of affairs in India and in Europe, all concurred to convince me, that the only rational system of defence against Tippoo Sultaun was to assemble your armies on the coasts of Coromandel and Malabar, in such force, in such a state of equipment, and in such a position, as should excite in the mind of the Sultaun a just alarm for the safety of his capital; no other plan was calculated to secure the Carnatic against the ravages of his numerous cavalry; because no other plan would have compelled him to concentrate his forces within his own territories, for the defence of the vital point of his empire. His capital was not only the object of his pride, but the centre of his power; it was his strongest fortification, the principal granary of his army, his only arsenal, the repository of his treasure, and the prison of the legitimate claimant of his throne, as well as of the families of all his great chieftains; whose obedience he secured, by retaining the objects of their reverence and affection within the walls of the fortress of Seringapatam. On the preservation of that fortress, therefore, depended the fate of his kingdom, and (although I did not neglect any practicable precaution against a contrary course of events) my judgment was always decided, that he would never abandon the defence of Seringapatam, but with his life.

The success of the plan (founded on this opinion) fully answered its primary purpose; since no part of the Sultaun's force ventured to enter the Company's possessions in the Carnatic during the late hostilities. It also fully answered the secondary purpose of enabling your armies (when our pacific negotiations had failed) to act offensively with promptitude, vigour, and effect.

Neither the expense of the magazines of grain and other stores on either coast, nor of the battering train, with its equipment of cattle, ought therefore to be charged to the account of the war; for every expense incurred previous to the 3rd of February 1799 (the day on which Lieutenant-General Harris received orders to march) must, and would have been incurred, if no war had taken place; and ought to be charged to the account of the indispensable defence of your possessions, according to the only plan, which could provide effectually for that object.

The expenses of moving the battering train to Seringapatam, as well as of maintaining the army in Mysore, cannot have much exceeded the charges which must have been continued if the whole had remained within your frontier; and when it is considered that, if the army, with the battering train, had not moved to Seringapatam, the expensive, but necessary, system of defence already explained, must have been protracted until all dangers from Tippoo Sultaun's connection with the French should have been averted; your honourable Court will probably sanction my decided opinion, that the rapid movement of the British forces towards the scene of their certain triumph, was not only the most effectual, but the most economical measure which could have been adopted, to frustrate the views of the enemy, and to secure the tranquillity of your possessions.

For, on the one hand, no prospect appeared of any practicable reduction in the expense of a defensive system, during the continuance of the war between Great Britain and France; while every hour of delay in the movement of our army afforded to Tippoo Sultaun the means of increasing his strength, of receiving succours from the French, and consequently of aggravating to the Company, both the expense and hazard of the impending contest.

On the other hand, the state of our army, the arrangements which had been made for its equipment and supply in every department, and the period of the season, left no doubt that the great object of the war would be attained in one short campaign. Nor did this calculation prove to have been in any degree sanguine; for although an alarm of a deficiency of grain prevailed in the army before Seringapatam on the 16th of April, it appeared soon after, upon an accurate examination, that at that time (exclusive of the immense depôt established in the district of Coorga) a quantity of grain remained in camp sufficient to maintain the whole of the fighting men of the army, at half allowance, until the 20th of May; and on the 13th of that month, Major-General Floyd returned to Seringapatam with the large supplies, which had been forwarded from the Carnatic, under the care of Lieutenant-Colonels Read and Brown. It may also be useful to remark in this place, that if any accident had protracted the operations of the siege beyond the 4th of May, ample time would still have remained for the reduction of the place previous to the rising of the Cauveri; since the four eldest sons of Tippoo Sultaun, with an escort of 1500 men, and a considerable train of attendants, crossed that river on the 18th of June, on which day the water was nearly as low as on the day of the assault.

Reviewing all these circumstances, your honourable Court will hereafter compare the expense incurred by the movement of the army to Seringapatam, with the probable charges of any other practicable plan of policy, or of military operation; in any view of the subject it will probably appear, that the increase of your revenue and pecuniary resources obtained by the issue of the war, far overbalances the combined expense of the preparations for your defence, and of the operations of the late campaign.

But in addition to this positive indemnification for your expenses, your honourable Court will also consider the augmentation of your commercial and military resources arising from the conquest of Mysore.

Hitherto, all traffic between your subjects or dependants and those of the late Sultaun has been nearly prohibited, by the restraints to which his hatred of the British Nation, or his ignorance and prejudice had subjected the communication with your possessions. These restraints being removed, and every proper encouragement to commercial intercourse being substituted in their place, it may reasonably be expected that the neighbouring, and now united countries of the Carnatic and Mysore, will mutually consume a considerable portion of their respective productions and manufactures; and that even a proportion of British commodities will soon find a market in Mysore. My information with regard to the articles produced, manufactured, or consumed, in the countries acquired by the Company, and by the Rajah of Mysore, is at present too imperfect to enable me to form any accurate calculation of the imports from the coast of Malabar to Europe; but it appears probable, that your investment in the article of pepper, may soon be augmented to any extent, which you may deem advisable.

Your military resources may be considered to have received a great augmentation, not only from the additional supplies of grain, provisions and cattle, which your connection with Mysore places at your disposal, but from the new channels, which it opens for recruiting the native force, both of the Presidencies of Fort St. George and Bombay; under this head may also be considered the superiority of the climate of Mysore, to any in this quarter of India, and the means which it affords of preserving the health and consequent efficiency of European troops.

Highly as I estimate these immediate and direct advantages of revenue, and of commercial and military resources, I consider the recent settlement of Mysore to be equally important to your interests, in its tendency to increase your political consideration and influence among the native powers of India, together with your means of maintaining internal tranquillity and order among your subjects and dependants, and of defending your possessions against any enemy, either Asiatic, or European.

These are principles of substantial and durable security, the operation of which must be felt throughout every part of your possessions, and in every branch of your affairs both in India and Europe.

The balance which it was the policy of the treaty of Seringapatam in 1792, to establish between the native powers of India, was soon deranged by the course of events; our influence in the general scale proved insufficient, not only to maintain peace between our allies, but to check either the rapid decline of their respective resources and strength, or the growing ascendancy of the French faction at Hyderabad, or the systematic machinations of Tippoo Sultaun. Experience has manifested that the power preserved to that infatuated and restless Prince, must always have been thrown into the scale opposed to our interests, and that in no possible combination or conflict of the views of the courts of Poonah, and Hyderabad, could the interposition or neutrality of Tippoo Sultaun become favourable to our security. If he menaced war, or sought alliance with either, or with both those states, his uniform object was our disturbance. If he remained neuter either in their dissentions or union, it was in order to preserve his own strength unimpaired and unembarassed for that contest with ours, which formed the favourite scope of all his views. In no case, has his power been brought into action, or remained at rest, without a hostile design, and an injurious effect upon our influence and consideration. The balance is now in our own hands, we now possess the irresistible power either of concentrating the most efficient part of the resources of Mysore in one mass, for our single defence against any possible combination; or of throwing the same weight into that scale, which shall appear to require such an aid for the preservation of the general tranquillity, on the solid basis of moderation and justice.

If the Nizam or the Mahrattas, notwithstanding their real interest in maintaining the new order of things, should harbour a disposition to disturb it, our means of defence, as well as of offence with regard to both those states, are become so powerful, as well from the advancement and strength of our frontier, as from the other relative considerations already stated in this despatch, that the internal union of all the divided feudatory chiefs of the Mahratta Empire, or even a confederacy between the Peishwa and the Nizam, could no longer be formidable to your possessions; and your honourable Court is apprized, that the first of these events is highly improbable, and the latter nearly impossible—on the other hand, it is evident that, having annihilated the power of Tippoo, no injury can result to us from the interminable feuds of the Mahratta Empire, or from the mutual jealousy of the Peishwa and the Nizam.

The connexion between the Nizam and the French is entirely dissolved, under circumstances which, I trust, will render its renewal impracticable, at least, for many years.

It is certainly true, that an alliance between the Mahrattas and the French, might prove highly injurious to the British power in India; but it is well known, that whatever may be the disposition of the Mahrattas towards us, it would require a most violent exercise of injustice and oppression, on our part to dispose the suspicious and cautious councils of the Court of Poonah, to favour the progress of a French force in India.

But, although we have nothing to apprehend from the Nizam, or from the Mahrattas, danger may still perhaps be apprehended from an invasion of Oude by Zemaun Shah. I am not disposed to undervalue this danger, but I am satisfied that it is less formidable now, than it has been at any former time. The loss of such an ally as Tippoo Sultaun, must materially affect the hopes of Zemaun Shah; and it is obvious, that although he should persist in his threatened invasion, our means of repelling it are greatly increased; since the army of Fort St. George, in a case of exigency, might now co-operate against Zemaun Shah with that of Bengal. Even during the late alarm of invasion from Zemaun Shah, (although war with Tippoo Sultaun was apprehended, and 3000 native volunteers with a considerable force of artillery, had been detached to the coast of Coromandel) we still were able to maintain an army of at least 20,000 men, on the frontier of Oude.

The intrigues of Tippoo Sultaun among the Rajahs inhabiting the coast of Malabar, among the Poligars in the Carnatic, and among every other description of your disaffected or refractory subjects, were the sources of continual commotion within your territories, while the vicinity of the hostile frontier of Mysore, offered refuge and impunity to every offender against your authority, and to every disturber of the public peace. It may reasonably be expected, that the establishment of your influence in Mysore, will operate as a powerful check on the spirit of disorder in your own possessions, and by removing the causes of internal weakness, will enable you to oppose every foreign attack with greater confidence and vigor.

With regard to any danger from the designs of France, it is evident that the probability of her making any effort to disturb the tranquillity of India, will be greatly diminished from the moment that the intelligence of Tippoo Sultaun's fate shall reach Europe. Perhaps it is not too sanguine a view of our situation, to consider the annihilation of the only native ally of France in India, as the final ruin of all her ambitious and vindictive projects against this great source of the wealth and power of Great Britain. The aid and co-operation of some native State must always be indispensably necessary to any European force, in attempting a serious impression on your possessions in India; without such aid, it seems impossible that any European army should be able to advance from the sea-coast, or even to maintain itself wherever it might land. If, however, contrary to every reasonable expectation, France should still persist in her projects against the peace of India, she will have to contend unsupported by the arms, and (what is of more importance) by the resources of any Indian ally, with a British army, animated by recent success unembarrassed either by any native enemy in Mysore, or by any French faction at Hyderabad, and free to act on any point which France might venture to assail.

Such appear to me to be the consequences of the late settlement, as they relate more immediately to the interests of the Honourable Company; but it will be proper to consider them also as they affect our allies.

Although the advantages offered to the Peishwa by the treaty of Mysore, may not be calculated to satisfy the rapacious character of the Mahratta State, it is reasonable to suppose, that under all the circumstances of the case, they will be received as a distinguished testimony of our amicable disposition towards the Court of Poonah; and that they will tend to appease its characteristic jealousy, if not to conciliate its cordial attachment.

The establishment of an Hindoo State in Mysore, with the restoration of the temples and endowments of that religion, must be grateful to the Government of Poonah, independently of the advantages arising from the substitution of a power of the same religion, and of pacific views, in the place of an odious Mahommedan usurpation, scarcely less hostile to the Mahratta than to the British nation.

With regard to the Nizam, his ambition would also have been more gratified with an arrangement, which should have thrown into his hands a larger share of territory and power; and the distribution of the property captured at Seringapatam, among the British troops and those of his Highness, disappointed his private expectations of appropriating a large portion of that property to his own use. The solid and permanent benefits however, which have resulted to his Highness from the recent improvement of his connection with the Company, and particularly from the new settlement of Mysore, are so obvious and considerable, that they may reasonably be expected to overbalance any temporary disappointment of his avarice or ambition. The existence of his throne was saved by the destruction of the French party at Hyderabad, in October, 1798. The formidable power of Tippoo Sultaun, which perpetually menaced his Highness's possessions, and filled his Court and dominions with intrigues and treason, has been annihilated, and a friendly and allied state established in Mysore. His Highness has received a large increase of territory, revenue, and power; together with several important fortresses tending greatly to secure the tranquillity of his dominions. His expenses in the war have been inconsiderable; and if a comparison were to be instituted of the advantages accruing to him, and to the Company from the whole arrangement, those obtained by his Highness would probably be found to preponderate; for, the danger from which he has been delivered was even more imminent than that which menaced the Company's possessions; and while his expenses have borne no proportion to ours, he has attained equal benefits both of indemnification and security. The collateral benefits derivable by the Company from its connexion with the Rajah of Mysore, will necessarily extend to the Nizam, and be scarcely less felt by him than by us, while he shall remain faithful to his alliance with the Company; and the advantages which his Highness would receive from the proposed mediation of the Company between him and the Mahratta empire, are highly estimated by all those who understand the interests of the Court of Hyderabad. If that mediation should fail, his Highness will receive an increase of territory beyond the amount of the proportion acquired by the Company, in the general partition; I have the satisfaction to know, that although his Highness's extravagant expectations have not been gratified to the full extent, his most able and experienced counsellors are fully sensible of the extensive and solid benefits acquired by his Highness, under the general operation of the late treaties. I am, therefore, persuaded, that his Highness's just sense of the permanent interests of his state, will command his cordial co-operation in the maintenance of the new settlement.

The interests of the Rajah of Mysore, being identified with those of the Company, and the safety, prosperity, and honor of the Peishwa, and of the Nizam, being amply secured by the treaties of Hyderabad and Mysore, and by the subsidiary treaty of Seringapatam; I entertain a confident expectation, that the recent settlement of the dominions of Tippoo Sultaun will prove not less durable, than I trust, it will be found equitable in its fundamental principles, beneficial in its general operation, and conformable in every point of view, to the liberal character of the English East India Company, and to the just and moderate policy prescribed by parliament, for the Government of the British empire in the East.

I am, &c.

MORNINGTON.

26. Subsidiary Treaty of Seringapatam.

A Treaty of Perpetual Friendship and Alliance, concluded on the one part by his Excellency Lieutenant-General George Harris, Commander-in-Chief of the forces of his Britannic Majesty, and of the English East India Company Bahaudur in the Carnatic and on the Coast of Malabar, the Honourable Colonel Arthur Wellesley, the Honourable Henry Wellesley, Lieutenant-Colonel William Kirkpatrick, and Lieutenant-Colonel Barry Close, on behalf, and in the name of the Right Honourable Richard Earl of Mornington, K.P. Governor-General for all affairs, Civil and Military, of the British Nation in India, by virtue of full powers vested in them for this purpose by the said Richard Earl of Mornington, Governor-General; and on the other part by Maha Raja Mysore Kistna Rajah Oodiaver Bahaudur, Rajah of Mysore.

Whereas it is stipulated in the Treaty concluded on the 22nd June, 1799, between the Honourable English East India Company Bahaudur, and the Nabob Nizam ud Dowlah Asoph Jah Bahaudur, for strengthening the alliance and friendship subsisting between the said English East India Company Bahaudur, his Highness Nizam ud Dowlah Asoph Jah Bahaudur, and the Peishwa Row Pundit Purdhaun Bahaudur; and for effecting a settlement of the territories of the late Tippoo Sultaun, that a separate government shall be established in Mysore, and that his Highness Maha Rajah Mysore Kistna Rajah Oodiaver Bahaudur shall possess certain territories specified in Schedule C, annexed to the said Treaty, and that for the effectual establishment of the government of Mysore, his Highness shall be assisted with a suitable subsidiary force, to be furnished by the English East India Company Bahaudur.

Wherefore, in order to carry the said stipulations into effect, and to increase and strengthen the friendship subsisting between the said English East India Company and the said Maha Rajah Mysore Kistna Rajah Oodiaver Bahaudur, this treaty is concluded by Lieutenant-General George Harris, Commander-in-Chief of the forces of His Britannic Majesty, and of the said English East India Company Bahaudur in the Carnatic, and on the Coast of Malabar; the Honourable Colonel Arthur Wellesley, the Honourable Henry Wellesley, Lieutenant-Colonel W. Kirkpatrick, and Lieutenant-Colonel Barry Close, on the part, and in the name, of the Right Honourable Richard Earl of Mornington, Governor-General aforesaid; and by his Highness Maha Rajah Mysore Kistna Rajah Oodiaver Bahaudur, which shall be binding upon the contracting parties as long as the sun and moon shall endure.

Article 1st.—The friends and enemies of either of the contracting parties shall be considered as the friends and enemies of both.

Article 2nd.—The Honourable the East India Company Bahaudur agrees to maintain, and his Highness Maha Rajah Mysore Kistna Rajah Oodiaver Bahaudur agrees to receive, a military force for the defence and security of his Highness's dominions. In consideration of which protection his Highness engages to pay the annual sum of seven lacs of star pagodas to the said East India Company. The said sum to be paid in twelve equal monthly instalments; his Highness further agrees, that the disposal of the said sum, together with the arrangement and employment of the troops to be maintained by it, shall be left entirely to the Company.

Article 3rd.—If it shall be necessary for the protection and defence of the territories of the contracting parties, or of either of them, that hostilities shall be undertaken, or preparations made for commencing hostilities against any state or power, his said Highness Maha Rajah Mysore Kistna Rajah Oodiaver Bahaudur agrees to contribute towards the discharge of the increased expense incurred by the augmentation of the military force, and the unavoidable charges of war, such a sum as shall appear to the Governor-General in Council of Fort William, on an attentive consideration of the means of his said Highness, to bear a just and reasonable proportion to the actual net revenues of his said Highness.

Article 4th.—And whereas it is indispensably necessary that effectual and lasting security should be provided against any failure in the funds destined to defray either the expense of maintaining the permanent military force in time of peace, or the extraordinary expense described in the 3rd article of the present treaty; it is hereby stipulated and agreed between the contracting parties, that whenever the Governor-General in Council of Fort William in Bengal shall have reason to apprehend such failure in the funds so destined, the said Governor-General in Council shall be at liberty, and shall have full power and right either to introduce such regulations and ordinances as he shall deem expedient for the internal management and collection of the revenues, or for the better ordering of any other branch and department of the government of Mysore; or to assume and bring under the direct management of the servants of the said Company Bahaudur, such part or parts of the territorial possessions of his Highness Maha Rajah Mysore Kistna Rajah Oodiaver Bahaudur as shall appear to him, the said Governor-General in Council, necessary to render the said funds efficient and available either in time of peace or war.

Article 5th.—And it is hereby further agreed, that whenever the said Governor-General in Council shall signify to the said Maha Rajah Mysore Kistna Rajah Oodiaver Bahaudur that it is become necessary to carry into effect the provisions of the 4th Article, his said Highness Maha Raja, Mysore Kistna Rajah Oodiaver Bahaudur shall immediately issue orders to his Aumils, or other officers, either for carrying into effect the said regulations according to the tenor of the 4th Article, or for placing the territories required under the exclusive authority and controul of the English Company Bahaudur; and in case his Highness shall not issue such orders within ten days from the time when the application shall have been formally made to him, then the said Governor-General in Council shall be at liberty to issue orders by his own authority, either for carrying into effect the said regulations and ordinances, or for assuming the management and collection of the revenues of the said territories, as he shall judge most expedient for the purpose of securing the efficiency of the said military funds, and of providing for the effectual protection of the country, and welfare of the people; provided always, that whenever and so long as any part or parts of his said Highness's territories shall be placed, and shall remain under the exclusive authority and controul of the said East India Company, the Governor-General in Council shall render his Highness a true and faithful account of the revenues and produce of the territories so assumed; provided also that in no case whatever shall his Highness's actual receipt or annual income arising out of his territorial revenues, be less than the sum of one lac of star pagodas; together with one-fifth of the net revenues of the whole of the territories ceded to him by the 5th Article of the treaty of Mysore, which sum of one lac of star pagodas, together with the amount of one-fifth of the said net revenues, the East India Company engages at all times, and in every possible case, to secure and cause to be paid for his Highness's use.

Article 6th.—His Highness Maha Rajah Mysore Kistna Rajah Oodiaver Bahaudur engages, that he will be guided by a sincere and cordial attention to the relations of peace and amity now established between the English Company Bahaudur and their allies; and that he will carefully abstain from any interference in the affairs of any state in alliance with the said English Company Bahaudur, or of any state whatever; and for securing the object of this stipulation it is further stipulated and agreed, that no communication or correspondence with any foreign state whatever shall be holden by his said Highness without the previous knowledge and sanction of the said English Company Bahaudur.

Article 7th.—His Highness stipulates and agrees, that he will not admit any European foreigners into his service without the concurrence of the English Company Bahaudur; and that he will apprehend and deliver up to the Company's Government all Europeans of whatever description who shall be found within the territories of his said Highness, without regular passports from the Company's Government, it being his Highness's determined resolution not to suffer, even for a day, any European foreigners to remain within the territories now subjected to his authority, unless by consent of the said Company.

Article 8th.—Whereas the complete protection of His Highness's said territories requires that various fortresses and strong places, situated within the territories of his Highness, should be garrisoned and commanded, as well in time of peace as of war, by British troops and officers; His Highness Maha Raja, Mysore Kistna Rajah Oodiaver Bahaudur engages that the said English Company Bahaudur shall at all times be at liberty to garrison, in whatever manner they may judge proper all such fortresses and strong places within his said Highness's territories as it shall appear to them advisable to take charge of.

Article 9th.—And whereas in consequence of the system of

defence which it may be expedient to adopt for the security of the territorial possessions of his Highness Maha Rajah Mysore Kistna Rajah Oodiaver Bahaudur, it may be necessary that certain forts and strong places within his Highness's territories shall be dismantled or destroyed, and that other forts and strong places should be strengthened and repaired; it is stipulated and agreed, that the English East India Company Bahaudur, should be the sole judges of the necessity of any such alterations in the said fortresses; and it is further agreed, that such expenses as may be incurred on this account shall be borne and defrayed in equal proportions by the contracting parties.

Article 10th.—In case it shall become necessary for enforcing and maintaining the authority and government of his Highness in the territories now subjected to his power that the regular troops of the English East India Company Bahaudur should be employed, it is stipulated and agreed, that upon formal application being made for the service of the said troops, they shall be employed in such manner as to the said Company shall seem fit; but it is expressly understood by the contracting parties that this stipulation shall not subject the troops of the English East India Company Bahaudur to be employed in the ordinary transactions of revenue.

Article 11th.—It being expedient for the restoration and permanent establishment of tranquillity in the territories now subjected to the authority of his Highness Maha Raja, Mysore Kistna Rajah Oodiaver Bahaudur, that suitable provision should be made for certain officers of rank in the service of the late Tippoo Sultaun, his said Highness agrees to enter into the immediate discussion of this point, and to fix the amount of the funds (as soon as the necessary information can be obtained) to be granted for this purpose in a separate article to be hereafter added to this treaty.

Article 12th.—Lest the garrison of Seringapatam should at any time be subject to inconvenience from the high price of provisions and other necessaries, his Highness Maha Rajah Mysore Kistna Rajah Oodiaver Bahaudur agrees that such quantities of provisions and other necessaries as may be required for the use and consumption of the troops composing the said garrison, shall be allowed to enter the place from all and every part of his dominions free of any duty, tax, or impediment whatever.

Article 13th.—The contracting parties hereby agree to take into their early consideration the best means of establishing such a commercial intercourse between their respective dominions as shall be mutually beneficial to the subjects of both governments, and to conclude a commercial treaty for this purpose with as little delay as possible.

Article 14th.—His Highness Maha Rajah Mysore Kistna Rajah Oodiaver Bahaudur hereby promises to pay at all times the utmost attention to such advice as the Company's Government shall occasionally judge it necessary to offer to him, with a view to the economy of his finances, the better collection of his revenues, the administration of justice, the extension of commerce, the encouragement of trade, agriculture, and industry, or any other objects connected with the advancement of his Highness's interests, the happiness of his people, and the mutual welfare of both states.

Article 15th.—Whereas it may hereafter appear that some of the districts declared by the treaty of Mysore to belong respectively to the English Company Bahaudur, and to his Highness, are inconveniently situated with a view to the proper connection of their respective lines of frontier, it is hereby stipulated between the contracting parties that in all such cases they will proceed to such an adjustment, by means of exchange or otherwise, as shall be best suited to the occasion.

Article 16th.—This treaty, consisting of sixteen articles, being this day, the 8th of July, A.D. 1799 (corresponding to the 3rd of Suffer, anno Hegere 1214, and to the 7th of the month Assar of the 1221st year of the Salluwunt æra), settled and concluded at the Fort of Nuzzabar, near Seringapatam, by his Excellency Lieutenant-General George Harris, Commander-in-Chief of the forces of his Britannic Majesty, and of the Honourable Company in the Carnatic, and on the Coast of Malabar, the Honourable Colonel Arthur Wellesley, the Honourable Henry Wellesley, Lieut.-Colonel William Kirkpatrick, and Lieutenant-Colonel Barry Close, with the Maha Rajah Mysore Kistna Rajah Oodiaver Bahaudur, the aforesaid gentlemen have delivered to the said Maha Rajah one copy of the same in English and Persian, sealed and signed by them; and his Highness the Maha Rajah has delivered to the gentlemen aforesaid another copy, also in Persian and English, bearing his seal, and signed by Luchuma, widow of the late Kistna Rajah, and sealed and signed by Purneah, Dewan of the Maha Rajah Kistna Rajah Oodiaver; and the aforesaid gentlemen have engaged to procure and deliver to the said Maha Rajah, without delay, a copy of the same, under the seal and signature of the Right Honourable the Governor-General, on the receipt of which by the said Maha Rajah, the present treaty shall be deemed complete and binding on the Honourable the English East India Company Bahaudur, and on the Maha Rajah Mysore Kistna Rajah Oodiaver Bahaudur respectively, and the copy of it now delivered to the said Maha Rajah be returned.

Ratified at Fort St. George, by the Right Honourable the Governor-General in Council, on the 13th day of July, A. D. 1799.

II. THE NIZAM.

27. Treaty of Hyderabad.

An enlarged perpetual subsidiary treaty between the Honourable United English East India Company and his Highness the Nawaub, Nizam ul Mulk Asoph Jah Behadur, Subadar of the Deccan, his children, heirs, and successors, settled by Captain James Achilles Kirkpatrick, by virtue of the powers delegated to him by the Right Honourable Richard Earl of Mornington, Knight of the most illustrious order of St. Patrick, one of his Britannic Majesty's most Honourable Privy Council, Governor General in Council, appointed by the Honourable the Court of Directors of the said Honourable Company, to direct and control all their affairs in the East Indies.

Whereas his Highness Nizam ul Mulk Asoph Jah Behadur, has from the greatness of existing friendship, expressed a desire for an increase of the detachment of the Honourable Company's troops at present serving his Highness, the Right Honourable the Earl of Mornington, Governor General, has taken the proposals to that effect into his most serious consideration, and the present juncture of affairs, and the recent hostile conduct and evil designs of Tippoo Sultaun (as fully evinced by his sending ambassadors to the Isle of France; by his proposing to enter into a treaty offensive and defensive with the French Republic against the English nation; and by actually receiving a body of French troops into his dominions and immediate pay), rendering it indispensably necessary that effectual measures for the mutual defence of their respective possessions, should be immediately taken by the three allied powers, united in a defensive league against the aforesaid Tippoo Sultaun, the aforesaid Governor General has, in consequence, empowered Captain James Achilles Kirkpatrick, Acting Resident at the court of his Highness the Nizam, to enter in behalf of the Honourable United English East India Company, into certain engagements with his Highness Nizam ul Mulk Asoph Jah Behadur, for a permanent increase of the Honourable Company's troops in his Highness's pay, in the proportion and on the conditions specified in the following articles, which must be understood to be of full validity, when this treaty shall be returned, signed and sealed by the Governor General :—

Article 1st.—Such parts of the letter from Earl Cornwallis to his Highness the Nizam, dated 7th July, 1789 (and which has always been considered in the light of a treaty), as relate to the stationing of troops with his Highness, are to be considered as in full force, that the services of the new permanent subsidiary force are to be regulated precisely by the same restrictive clauses that operate on the present detachment, unless the Peishwa shall hereafter consent to any alterations in those conditions, and his Highness likewise approve of the same.

Article 2d.—Agreeably to the practice in the Company's service, the new subsidiary force shall be subject to reliefs, either partial or entire, as often and in such manner as the Company's Government may require, provided withal, that no diminution takes place by such means in the stipulated number to be stationed with his Highness.

Article 3d.—The proposed reinforcement of subsidiary troops shall be in the pay of this state from the day of their crossing the boundaries. Satisfactory and effectual provision shall be made for the regular payment of this force, which, including the present detachment, is to amount to 6000 sepoys, with firelocks, with a due proportion of field pieces, manned by Europeans, and as at the monthly rate of two lacs, one thousand four hundred and twenty-five rupees, the yearly amount of subsidy for the aforesaid force of 6000 men, with guns, artillery-men, and other necessary appurtenances, is twenty-four lacs, seventeen thousand one hundred rupees. The said sum shall be completely discharged in the course of the year by four equal instalments, that is, at the expiration of every three English months, the sum of six lacs, four thousand two hundred and seventy-five rupees, in silver of full currency, shall be issued without hesitation or demur from his Highness's treasury. And should the aforesaid instalments happen to fall at any time the least in arrears, such arrears shall be deducted, notwithstanding any objections thereto, from the current kist of Peishcush, payable to his Highness on account of the Northern Sirkars. Should it, at any time, so happen, moreover, that delay were to occur in the issue of the instalments aforesaid, at the stated periods, in such case, assignments shall be granted on the collections of certain districts in this state, the real and actual revenue of which shall be adequate to the discharge of the yearly subsidy of the aforesaid force.

Article 4th.—The duties on grain and on all articles of consumption, as well as on all necessaries whatever, for the use of the new subsidiary force, shall be commuted agreeably to the practice that obtained with the former detachment. A place likewise shall be fixed on as the head quarters of the said force, where it shall always remain, except when services of importance are required to be performed; and whenever either the whole, or part of the said force, is to be employed in the business of the state, a person of respectability, and who is a servant of this Sirkar, shall be appointed to attend it. The commanding officer and officers of the said subsidiary force shall be treated in all respects in a manner suitable to the greatness and dignity of both states.

Article 5th.—The said subsidiary force will at all times be ready to execute services of importance, such as the protection of the person of his Highness, his heirs and successors, from race to race, and the overawing and chastizing all rebels or exciters of disturbance in the dominions of this state; but it is not to be employed on trifling occasions, nor like Sebundy, to be stationed in the country to collect the revenues thereof.

Article 6th.—Immediately upon the arrival of the aforesaid subsidiary force at Hyderabad, the whole of the officers and serjeants of the French party are to be dismissed, and the troops composing it, so dispersed and disorganised, that no trace of the former establishment shall remain. And his Highness hereby engages for himself, his heirs and successors, that no Frenchman whatever shall ever hereafter be entertained in his own service, or in that of any of his chiefs or dependants, nor be suffered to remain in any part of his Highness's dominions. Nor shall any Europeans whatever be admitted into the service of this state, nor be permitted to remain within its territories, without the knowledge and consent of the Company's government.

Article 7th.—The whole of the European and sepoy deserters from the Company's service, that may be in the French or any other party of troops belonging to this state, are to be seized and delivered up to the British resident; and no persons of the above description are to be allowed refuge in future in his Highness's territories, but are (on the contrary) to be seized without delay, and delivered up to the British resident. Neither shall any refuge be allowed in the Company's territories to sepoy deserters from the service of his Highness, who shall, in like manner, be seized and delivered up without delay.

Article 8th.—Whereas his Highness the Nizam, from considerations of prudence and foresight, and with a view of avoiding manifold evils, has determined on dismissing the French from his service, and on dispersing and disorganising the troops commanded by them, as specified in the 6th Article, and on entertaining a perpetual standing force, of the Honourable Company's, in their room, subject to the limitations and restrictions prescribed by Earl Cornwallis's letter to the Nizam, mentioned in the 1st Article; it is therefore hereby agreed, with a view to the mutual benefit of his Highness and the Peishwa, and the happiness of their respective subjects, that the Company's government will use their best endeavours to have inserted with the consent and approbation of both, in the new treaty in contemplation between the three allied powers, such a clause as shall set each at ease with regard to the other. Should the Peishwa, however, not accede to a proposal so highly advantageous and profitable to both governments, and differences hereafter arise between the two states, namely, that of the Nawaub Asof Jah Behadur, and of the Rao Pundit Perdhaun, in such case, the Company's government hereby engage, that interposing their mediation, in a way suitable to rectitude, friendship and union, they will apply themselves to the adjustment thereof, conformably to propriety, truth and justice. The Nawaub Asof Jah Behadur accordingly hereby engages, never to commit on his part any excess or aggression against the Sirkar of Rao Pundit Perdhaun; and in the event of such differences arising, whatever adjustment of them the Company's government, weighing things in the scales of truth and justice, may determine upon, shall without hesitation or objection, meet with full approbation and acquiescence.

Article 9th.—All former treaties between the Honourable East India Company and the governments of the Nawaub Asof Jah and the Peishwa, remain in full force. Should hereafter the Rao Pundit Perdhaun express a desire to enter into subsidiary engagements, similar to the present, with the Honourable Company, the Nawaub Asof Jah will most readily give his concurrence.

Article 10th.—This enlarged subsidiary treaty, consisting of Ten Articles, being this day settled by Captain James Achilles Kirkpatrick, with the Nawaub Asof Jah Behadur, Captain Kirkpatrick has delivered one copy hereof in English and Persian, signed and sealed by himself, to the Nawaub, who, on his part, has also delivered to Captain Kirkpatrick one copy of the same, duly executed by himself; and Captain Kirkpatrick hereby engages to procure and deliver to his Highness, in the space of fifty days, a ratified copy from the Governor General, in every respect the counterpart of the one executed by himself; and on the delivery of such copy, which will then have become a full and complete instrument, the treaty executed by Captain Kirkpatrick shall be returned. In the mean while, no time shall be lost in writing for the advance of the proposed reinforcement.

Signed, sealed, and exchanged at Hyderabad,
1st September, A.D. 1798, or 19th Rubby
ul-awul, A.H. 1213.

J. A. KIRKPATRICK.

Separate article appertaining to the perpetual subsidiary treaty concluded between the Honourable English East India Company and his Highness the Nawaub Asof Jah Behadur, on the 1st of September, A.D. 1798, or 19th of Rubby-ul-awul, A.H. 1213.

Whereas in conformity to a wish expressed by his Highness the Nizam, the stipulation in the 6th Article of the Subsidiary Treaty respecting the delivering up of the French is agreed to be made a separate one, his Highness hereby engages, that after the arrival of the Company's troops at Hyderabad, the whole of the French officers and soldiers in his service shall be apprehended in such way as Captain Kirkpatrick may point out, and be delivered up to him, or for a time be kept in confinement in an habitation belonging to this Sirkar, but in the custody of the Company's troops, and upon the reorganisation of the party lately under the command of the aforesaid French officers, they, the said French officers and soldiers shall, within the space of two months, be delivered up to the British resident. Strict orders shall, moreover, be issued to all talookdars on the frontiers, and to those in charge of all fords and passes, to seize any Europeans whatever, attempting to pass their respective stations, and send them immediately with all due precaution, prisoners to Hyderabad, where they shall instantly be delivered up to the British resident. On the above condition it is hereby agreed that the Frenchmen thus delivered up, shall not be common prisoners of war, nor be in any respect maltreated. They shall be conveyed at the Company's expense, and with as little restraint as possible to England, and from thence be sent by the first favourable opportunity to France, without being detained for a cartel or exchange of prisoners.

Signed, sealed, and exchanged, at Hyderabad, 1st September, A.D. 1798, or 19th Rubby-ul-awul, A.H. 1213.

Separate article appertaining to the perpetual Subsidiary Treaty concluded between the Honourable English East India Company and his Highness the Nawaub Asof Jah Behadur, on the 1st September, A. D. 1798, *or* 19*th Rubby-ul-awul, A. H.* 1213.

No correspondence on affairs of importance, shall, in future, on any account, be carried on with the Sirkar of Rao Pundit Perdhaun, or with any of his dependants, either by the Nawaub Asof Jah Behadur, or by the Honourable Company's government, without the mutual privity and consent of both contracting parties. And whatever transactions, whether of great or small import, may in future take place with the aforesaid Rao Pundit Perdhaun, or his dependants, a reciprocal communication of the same shall be made to the other contracting party, without delay and without reserve.

Signed, sealed, and exchanged, at Hyderabad, 1st September, A.D. 1798, or 19th Rubby-ul-awul, A.H. 1213.

Ratified by the Right Honourable Richard Earl of Mornington, Knight of the most illustrious order of St. Patrick, &c. &c. &c. Governor General in council.

Fort William,
18*th day of September*, 1798.

28. Treaty of Defensive Alliance.

Treaty of perpetual and general defensive alliance, between the Honourable the English East India Company and his Highness the Nabob Nizam ul Mulk Asoph Jah Behauder, Soubahdar of the Decan, his children, heirs, and successors; settled by Captain James Achilles Kirkpatrick, Resident at the Court of his Highness, by virtue of the powers delegated to him by the most noble Richard Marquess Wellesley, &c. &c. &c.

Whereas, by the blessing of God, an intimate friendship and union have firmly subsisted for a length of time, between the Honourable Company and his Highness the Nabob Nizam ul Mulk Asoph Jah Behauder, and have been cemented and strengthened by several treaties of alliance, to the mutual and manifest advantage of both powers, who with uninterrupted harmony and concord, having equally shared the fatigues and dangers of war and the blessings of peace, are, in fact, become one and the same in interest, policy, friendship, and honour. These powers, adverting to the complexion of the times, have determined, on principles of precaution and foresight, and with a view to the effectual preservation of constant peace and tranquillity, to enter into a defensive alliance, for the complete and reciprocal protection of their respective territories, together with those of their several allies and dependants, against the unprovoked aggressions, or unjust incroachments, of all or of any enemies whatever.

ART. 1. The peace, union, and friendship, so long subsisting between the two states, shall be perpetual; the friends and enemies of either shall be the friends and enemies of both; and the contracting parties agree, that all the former treaties and agreements between the two states, now in force, and not contrary to the tenor of this agreement, shall be confirmed by it.

ART. 2. If any power or state whatever shall commit any act of unprovoked hostility or aggression against either of the contracting parties, or against their respective dependants or allies, and, after due representation, shall refuse to enter into amicable explanation, or shall deny the just satisfaction or indemnity which the contracting parties shall have required, then the contracting parties will proceed to concert and prosecute such further measures as the case shall appear to demand.

For the more distinct explanation of the intent and effect

of this agreement, the Governor-General in council, on behalf of the honourable Company, hereby declares, that the British Government will never permit any power or state, whatever, to commit with impunity, any act of unprovoked hostility or aggression against the rights or territories of his Highness the Nizam, but will, at all times, maintain the same, in the same manner as the rights and territories of the honourable Company are now maintained.

ART. 3. With a view to fulfil this treaty of general defence and protection, his highness the Nabob Asoph Jah agrees, that two battalions of Sepoys and one regiment of cavalry, with a due proportion of guns and artillerymen, shall be added, in perpetuity, to the present permanent subsidiary force of six battalions of Sepoys, of one thousand firelocks each, and one regiment of cavalry, five hundred strong (with their proportion of guns and artillerymen), so that the whole subsidiary force furnished by the Honourable East India Company to his Highness shall henceforward consist of eight battalions of Sepoys (or eight thousand firelocks) and two regiments of cavalry (or one thousand horse) with their requisite complement of guns, European artillerymen, Lascars, and pioneers, fully equipped with warlike stores, and ammunition; which force is to be stationed in perpetuity, in his Highness's territories.

ART. 4. The pay of the above-mentioned additional force shall be calculated at the rate of the pay of the existing subsidiary force, and shall commence from the day of the entrance of the said additional force into his Highness's territories.

ART. 5. For the regular payment of the whole expense of the said augmented subsidiary force (consisting of eight thousand infantry, one thousand cavalry, and their usual proportion of artillery) his Highness the Nabob Asoph Jah hereby assigns and cedes to the honourable East India Company, in perpetuity, all the territories acquired by his Highness, under the treaty of Seringapatam, on the 18th March, 1792, and also all the territories acquired by his Highness, under the treaty of Mysore, on the 22nd June, 1799, according to the schedule annexed to this treaty.

ART. 6. Certain of the territories, ceded by the foregoing article to the honourable Company, being inconvenient, from their situation to the northward of the river Toombuddrah, his Highness the Nabob Asoph Jah, for the purpose of rendering the boundary line of the honourable Company's possessions a good and well defined one, agrees to retain the districts in question, namely, Copul, Gujjinderghur, and others (as marked in the annexed schedule) in his own possession; and, in lieu thereof, assigns and cedes, in full and in perpetuity, to the honourable Company, the district of Adoni, together with whatever other territory his Highness may be possessed of, or is dependant on his Highness's Government, to the south of the Toombuddrah, or to the south of the Kistnah, below the junction of those two rivers.

* * * *

ART. 12. The contracting parties will employ all practicable means of conciliation to prevent the calamity of war; and, for that purpose, will, at all times, be ready to enter into amicable explanations with other states, and to cultivate and improve the general relations of peace and amity with all the powers of India, according to the true spirit and tenor of this defensive treaty. But if a war should unfortunately break out between the contracting parties and any other power whatever, then his Highness the Nabob Asoph Jah engages, that, with the reserve of two battalions of Sepoys, which are to remain near his Highness's person, the residue of the British subsidiary force (consisting of six battalions of Sepoys, and two regiments of cavalry, with artillery) joined by six thousand infantry and nine thousand horse of his Highness's own troops, and making together an army of twelve thousand infantry, and ten thousand cavalry, with their requisite train of artillery, and warlike stores of every kind, shall be immediately put in motion, for the purpose of opposing the enemy; and his Highness further engages to employ every further effort in his power, for the purpose of bringing into the field, as speedily as possible, the whole force which he may be able to supply from his dominions, with a view to the effectual prosecution and speedy termination of the said war, the honourable Company, in the same manner, engaging on their part, in this case, to employ in active operations against the enemy, the largest force which they may be able to furnish, over and above the said subsidiary force.

ART. 13. Whenever war shall appear probable, his Highness the Nabob Asoph Jah engages to collect as many Benjarries as possible, and to store as much grain as may be practicable in his frontier garrisons.

ART. 14. Grain, and all other articles of consumption and provisions, and all sorts of materials for wearing apparel, together with the necessary quantity of cattle, horses, and camels, required for the use of the subsidiary force, shall, in proportion to its present augmentation, be as heretofore, entirely exempted from duties.

ART. 15. As by the present treaty the union and friendship of the two states are so firmly cemented, as that they may be considered as one and the same, his Highness the Nizam engages neither to commence nor to pursue, in future, any negotiations with any other power whatever, without giving previous notice, and entering into mutual consultation with the honourable East India Company's Government; and the honourable Company's Government, on their part, hereby declare, that they have no manner of concern with any of his Highness's children, relations, subjects, or servants, with respect to whom his Highness is absolute.

ART. 16. As, by the present treaty of general defensive alliance, mutual defence, and defence against all enemies, are established, his Highness the Nabob Asoph Jah consequently engages, never to commit any act of hostility or aggression against any power whatever; and in the event of differences arising, whatever adjustment of them the Company's Government, weighing matters in the scale of truth and justice, may determine, shall meet with full approbation and acquiescence.

ART. 17. By the present treaty of general defensive alliance, the ties of union, by the blessing of God, are drawn so close, that the friends of one party will be henceforward considered as the friends of the other, and the enemies of the one party as the enemies of the other; it is therefore hereby agreed, that if, in future, the Shorapoor or Gudwall Zemindars, or any other subjects or dependants of his Highness's Government, should withhold the payment of the Sircar's just claims upon them, or excite rebellion or disturbance, the subsidiary force, or such proportion thereof as may be requisite, after the reality of the fact shall be duly ascertained, shall be ready, in concert with his Highness's own troops, to reduce all such offenders to obedience. And the particular interests of the two states being now, in every respect, identified, it is further mutually agreed, that if disturbances shall, at any time, break out in the districts, ceded to the honorable Company by this treaty, his Highness the Nabob Asoph Jah shall permit such a portion of the subsidiary force as may be requisite, to be employed in quelling the same, within the said districts. If disturbances shall, at any time, break out in any part of his Highness's dominions, contiguous to the Company's frontier, to which it might be inconvenient to detach any proportion of the subsidiary troops, the British Government, in like manner, if required by his Highness the Nabob Asoph Jah, shall direct such proportion of the troops of the Company, as may be most conveniently stationed for the purpose, to assist in quelling the said disturbances within his Highness's dominions.

ART. 18. Whereas, by the favour of Providence, a perfect union, harmony, and concord, have long and firmly subsisted between the Honourable East India Company, his Highness the Nabob Asoph Jah, his Highness the Peshwah Rao Pundit Purdhaun, and Rajah Rhagojee Bhoosillah, therefore should his Highness, Rao Pundit Purdhaun, and Rajah Rhagojee Bhoosillah, or either of them, express a desire to participate in the benefits of the present defensive alliance, which is calculated to strengthen and perpetuate the foundations of general tranquillity, the contracting parties will readily admit both, or either of the said powers, to be members of the present alliance, on such terms and conditions as shall appear just and expedient to the contracting parties.

ART. 19. The contracting parties being actuated by a sincere desire to promote and maintain general tranquillity, will admit Dowlut Rao Scindiah to be a party to the present treaty, whenever he shall satisfy the contracting parties of his disposition to cultivate the relations of peace and amity with both states, and shall give such securities for the maintenance of tranquillity, as shall appear to the contracting parties to be sufficient.

ART. 20. This treaty, consisting of twenty articles, being this day settled by Captain James Achilles Kirkpatrick with the Nabob Asoph Jah Behauder, Captain Kirkpatrick has delivered one copy thereof, in English and Persian, signed and sealed by himself, to the said Nabob, who, on his part, has also delivered one copy of the same, duly executed by himself; and Captain Kirkpatrick, by virtue of special authority given to him on that behalf by the most noble the Governor-General in council, hereby declares the said treaty to be in full force from the date hereof, and engages to procure and deliver to his Highness, in the space of thirty days, a copy of the same from the Governor-General in council, in every respect the counterpart of that executed by himself; and on the delivery of such copy, the treaty executed by Captain Kirkpatrick shall be returned, but the additional subsidiary force, specified in the third article, shall be immediately required by his Highness the Nizam, and furnished by the honourable Company, and all the other articles shall be in full force from this time.

Signed, sealed, and exchanged, at Hydrabad, on the 12th October, Anno Domini 1800, or 22nd Jemmadee ul Awul, Anno Higeræ 1215.

(Signed) J. A. KIRKPATRICK, Resident.

(A true copy.) THOMAS SYDENHAM,
Secretary to the Residency.

Separate and Secret Articles.

ART. 1. The Peshwa, Rao Pundit Purdhaun, shall be admitted to the benefits of this general defensive alliance on the following conditions:

First. Rao Pundit Purdhaun shall accept the mediation of the honourable Company's Government, for the amicable adjustment on the basis of the treaty of Mah, of all claims or demands of Choute, and of all other claims or demands whatever, on the territories or government of his Highness the Nabob Asoph Jah.

The British Government will also take into consideration the claims of his Highness the Nabob Asoph Jah to a total exemption from Choute, and will arbitrate, on the principles of justice and equity, any question now existing, or which shall hereafter arise, relative to the same, between Rao Pundit Purdhaun and the Nabob Asoph Jah, provided Rao Pundit Purdhaun shall agree to accept the said arbitration, and Rao Pundit Purdhaun shall not be admitted to the benefit of this general defensive alliance, until he shall have agreed to accept the arbitration of the British Government, with respect to the said claims of the Nabob Asoph Jah to a total exemption from Choute.

Secondly. Rao Pundit Purdhaun shall give full satisfaction to the honourable East India Company, on the various points depending between him and the British Government in India.

Thirdly. If Rao Pundit Purdhaun shall agree to the foregoing conditions, the honourable East India Company and his Highness the Nabob Asoph Jah will assist him in the restoration of his just authority in the Mahratta empire.

Fourthly. For this purpose, Rao Pundit Purdhaun shall agree to subsidize, in perpetuity, such a body of the said Company's troops, as shall hereafter be judged necessary for the restoration and maintenance of his authority.

ART. 2. Rajah Rhagojee Bhooslah shall be admitted to the benefit of this general alliance on the following conditions:

First. Rajah Rhagojee Bhooslah shall accept the Honourable Company's arbitration of all unadjusted points between his Highness the Nabob Asoph Jah and the said Rajah, according to the tenor of subsisting treaties.

Secondly. Rajah Rhagojee Booslah shall agree to such equitable interchanges of territory with the honourable East India Company, as shall be judged necessary to complete or improve their respective frontiers, or to such cessions of territory (in consideration of a just pecuniary equivalent) as shall be judged necessary to the same purpose.

ART. 3. If contrary to the spirit and object of this defensive treaty, war should hereafter appear unavoidable (which God avert!) the contracting parties will proceed to adjust the rule of partition of all such advantages and acquisitions as may eventually result from the success of their united arms.

The contracting parties entertain no views of conquest or extension of their respective dominions, nor any intention of proceeding to hostilities, unless in the case of unjustified or unprovoked aggression, and after the failure of their joint endeavours to obtain reasonable satisfaction, through the channel of pacific negotiation, according to the tenor of the preceding treaty. It is however declared, that in the event of war, and of a consequent partition of conquests between the contracting parties, his Highness the Nabob Asoph Jah shall be entitled to participate equally with the other contracting parties, in the division of every territory which may be acquired by the successful exertion of their united arms, provided his Highness the Nabob Asoph Jah shall have faithfully fulfilled all the stipulations of the preceding treaty, especially those contained in the twelfth and thirteenth articles thereof.

Signed, sealed and exchanged, at Hydrabad, on the 12th October, Anno Domini 1800, or 22d Jemmadee ul Awul, Anno Higeræ 1215.

J. A. KIRKPATRICK, Resident.

N. B. The omitted articles provide for details of little historical interest, and, together with the schedule of ceded districts, are left out to save space. The seventh article is substantially identical with the last clause of the fifth in the Treaty of Bassein, i. e. from 'the territories to be assigned'—*ad finem:* the ninth and tenth correspond to the seventh and eighth in the same Treaty of Bassein.

III. THE CARNATIC.

29. Declaration on the Annexation of the Carnatic.

Declaration of the Right Honourable the Governor in Council of Fort St. George, by and with the authority of His Excellency the Most Noble the Governor-General in council of all the British possessions in India.

July 27th, 1801.

An alliance of the most intimate union and friendship has long subsisted between the Honourable English East India Company, and the family of their Highnesses Mahomed Ali and Omdut ul Omrah, late Nabobs of the Carnatic Payen Ghaut. By the aid of that alliance, his late Highness the Nabob Mahomed Ali was enabled under Providence, to support his pretensions to the possession of the Carnatic at the death of his illustrious father; to defeat the power of his enemies in arms, and finally to establish his authority in the Government of Arcot, and of its dependencies, on the foundations of the British power. For the defence and protection of the valuable possessions thus acquired by the united arms of the English Company, and of the Nabob of Arcot, various treaties and obligations have been established, by which it was intended that the interests, security and power of both parties in the Carnatic Payen Ghaut, should be cemented and identified. In conformity to the faith and spirit of those engagements the honourable Company has invariably employed not only the resources derived from that alliance, but the whole power of the British empire in India, to maintain the government of the late Nabobs of the Carnatic against all their enemies, and has caused them to be acknowledged by foreign states as the allies of the British nation. By these means, and by the unabated exertion of its whole power, the English nation was enabled during the war which continued from the year 1780 to the year 1783, to support the pretensions of the Nabob Mahomed Ali, and to rescue his dominions from the violence of Hyder Ali Khan, and of his successor Tippoo Sultaun, who, by the assistance of the French nation had been enabled to conquer a considerable part of the Carnatic, and to establish their authority over the greatest portion of the territorial possessions of the said Nabob.

To support the authority of the Nabob Mahomed Ali, and to secure the British interests in the Carnatic, it became expedient for the contracting parties to enter into specific engagements for the maintenance of an adequate military establishment. The English Company accordingly bound itself by a treaty, bearing date in the month of February, 1787, to maintain the whole military force required for the protection of the territories of the allies; in consideration of which engagement, the Nabob Mahomed Ali agreed, among other conditions, and under certain penalties therein specified, to pay an annual subsidy amounting to fifteen lacs of pagodas.

According to the further stipulations of that engagement, rendered necessary by experience for the mutual safety of the contracting parties, the English Company in the year 1790, charged itself with the administration of the civil government in addition to the military defence of the Carnatic, in a critical juncture of affairs, when the ambition and implacable enmity of the late Tippoo Sultaun compelled the British Government in India, to resort to arms for the support of its rights, and for the protection of its allies.

At the conclusion of the war, in the year 1792, (the successful and glorious termination of which tended in the most direct manner, to secure the safety and prosperity of the possessions of his Highness the Nabob of the Carnatic) the British Government restored the civil government of the Carnatic to his Highness, thereby manifesting the strictest adherence to the stipulations of the existing engagement of 1787; but the British Government did not confine itself to the mere discharge of the stipulations of its existing engagements; its views were extended to an enlarged and liberal consideration of the principles of the alliance subsisting between the Company, and the Nabobs of the Carnatic.

At that period of time the Nabob Mahomed Ali, relying on the friendly disposition of the British Government, represented in the most urgent manner to the Marquess Cornwallis, the inadequacy of his Highness's resources to discharge the pecuniary engagements of the treaty of 1787; and the Governor-General, acting in conformity to the spirit of the alliance and friendship so long subsisting between the Nabobs of the Carnatic, and the English Company, relieved his Highness from the burthensome terms of that engagement; thereby surrendering the pecuniary rights, acquired by the Company under the treaty of 1787, for the purpose of promoting the tranquillity, comfort and interests of the Nabob Mahomed Ali.

With this liberal view of the principles of the connexion established between the British Government and the Nabob of Arcot, an indulgent modification of the treaty of 1787 was framed, and by a subsequent treaty, bearing date in the month of July, 1792, the pecuniary contribution of his Highness the Nabob of the Carnatic towards the general defence and protection of the rights and possessions of the allies was diminished from fifteen to nine lacs of star pagodas. The spirit of moderation by which the British councils were guided, in respect to this alliance, was unequivocally manifested by a further stipulation for the purpose of securing to the Nabob Omdut ul Omra, the son and presumptive heir of the Nabob Mahomed Ali, the succession to the territories of his father, on the terms and conditions of the treaty of 1792.

In return for this relinquishment of a considerable portion of its pecuniary resources, the English Company obtained no other advantages than an extended renewal of the territorial security, already provided by the treaty of 1787, for the performance of the Nabob Mahomed Ali's pecuniary engagements, and a repetition of his Highness's previous obligation not to contract alliances, nor to enter into correspondence with any European or native power, without the knowledge and concurrence of the British Government. Conformably therefore to this indulgent modification of the treaty of 1787, the government of the Carnatic was restored to the Nabob Mahomed Ali. On the death of his Highness the Nabob Mahomed Ali, in the year 1795, the Nabob Omdut ul Omra succeeded to the possession of his father's territories, according to the provision of the treaty of 1792.

The Nabob Mahomed Ali, as well as his son and successor, had repeatedly granted tuncaws and assignments of revenue on the districts pledged to the Company, in direct violation of the treaty of 1792, and to the manifest injury of the territorial security provided by the Company, for its interests in the Carnatic. The British Government however, continued to extend to their Highnesses the indulgent operation of the beneficial conditions of the treaty of 1792, by abstaining from the exercise of the just rights acquired against their Highnesses, under the express stipulations of that engagement, and under the acknowledged interpretation of the law of nations.

Under these circumstances, the British Government might

justly have required from the house of Mahomed Ali, not merely the exact and rigid observation of the treaty of 1792, but a zealous and cordial attachment to the spirit of an engagement, under which the Nabobs of the Carnatic had found the most ample protection, accompanied by the most indulgent and liberal construction of every stipulation favourable to their separate interests, and by the most lenient relaxation of those penal articles, the obligation of which their Highnesses had respectively incurred by violating the article of the treaty of 1792, relative to the grants of tuncaws, or assignments of revenue, on the districts pledged to the Company.

It is with the deepest concern, that the Governor in council is compelled to declare, that these ancient allies of the Company, the Nabobs Mahomet Ali, and Omdut ul Omra, have been found not only deficient in every active duty of the alliance, but unfaithful to its fundamental principles and untrue to its vital spirit.

In the full enjoyment of the most abundant proofs of the moderation, indulgence and good faith of the Honourable Company, the Nabob Mahomed Ali, and the Nabob Omdut ul Omra, actually commenced and maintained a secret intercourse with Tippoo Sultaun, the determined enemy of the British name, founded on principles, and directed to objects, utterly subversive of the alliance between the Nabob of the Carnatic and the Company, and equally incompatible with the security of the British power in the Peninsula of India.

After the fall of Seringapatam, the British Government obtained possession of the original records of Tippoo Sultaun ; the correspondence of that Prince's ambassadors, during their residence at Fort St. George, in attendance on his sons, the hostage princes, in the year 1792, and 1793, established sufficient grounds of apprehension, that their Highnesses, the late Nabob Mahomed Ali, and the late Nabob Omdut ul Omra, had entered into a secret intercourse with the late Tippoo Sultaun, of a nature hostile to the British interests in India. The enquiries of the British Government have been since directed to ascertain a fact so intimately connected with the security of its rights in the Carnatic. The result has established the following propositions by a series of connected written and oral testimony.

First. At the very period of time when the Nabob Mahomed Ali appealed to the generosity of the British Government for an indulgent modification of the treaty of 1787, his Highness had already commenced a secret negotiation for the establishment of an intimate intercourse with the Nabob Tippoo Sultaun, without the knowledge of the British Government, and for purposes evidently repugnant to its security and honour.

Secondly. The Nabob Omdut ul Omra (who was empowered by the Nabob Mahomed Ali to negotiate the treaty of 1792 with the British Government, and who actually negotiated that treaty for himself and for his father) was actually employed at the same period of time under his father's authority, in negotiating for himself and for his father the terms of the said separate and secret intercourse with Tippoo Sultaun.

Thirdly. The tendency of the said intercourse was directed to the support of Tippoo Sultaun in victory and triumph over all his enemies.

Fourthly. In the month of December 1792, the Nabob Mahomed Ali imparted secret information to Tippoo Sultaun regarding the sentiments and intentions of the British Government in India with relation to the hostile views and negotiations of Tippoo Sultaun at the Courts of Poonah and Hyderabad; and on the first intelligence of the war between Great Britain and France in the year 1793, the Nabob Mahomed Ali imparted secret information to Tippoo Sultaun respecting the views and power of France in India and in Europe, and respecting the intended operations of the British forces against the French possessions in the Carnatic; and the Nabob Mahomed Ali conveyed to Tippoo Sultaun secret admonitions and friendly advice respecting the most favourable season and the most propitious state of circumstances for the violation of Tippoo Sultaun's engagements with the Honourable Company.

Fifthly. The Nabob Omdut ul Omra was employed by his father as one of the agents to convey secret intelligence, friendly admonition, and seasonable advice to Tippoo Sultaun, through the confidential agents of Tippoo Sultaun, who were furnished with instructions from the said Sultaun of Mysore to receive such communications from the said Nabob of the Carnatic, and from the Nabob Omdut ul Omra.

Sixthly. A cypher was composed and actually introduced into the separate and secret correspondence between the Nabob Mahomed Ali and Tippoo Sultaun. The original key of the said cypher, discovered among the records of Seringapatam, is in the handwriting of the confidential Moonshee (or secretary) of the Nabob Mahomed Ali, and of the Nabob Omdut ul Omra; and the said cypher was delivered by a confidential agent of the Nabob Omdut ul Omra to the ambassador of Tippoo Sultaun for the express purpose of being transmitted to Tippoo Sultaun.

Seventhly. The terms employed in the said cypher, particularly those intended to designate the British Government and its allies, the Nizam and the Mahratta State, united in a defensive league against Tippoo Sultaun, contain the most powerful internal evidence that the communications proposed to be disguised by the said cypher, were of the most hostile tendency to the interests and objects of the said alliance, and calculated to promote the cause of Tippoo Sultaun in opposition to that of the said allies.

Eighthly. The Nabob Omdut ul Omra, in his own handwriting, in the month of August, 1794, corroborated the evidence of his intention to complete the purposes herein described of the secret intercourse which he had negotiated with Tippoo Sultaun; and the continuance of the same intention is manifested by letters from the Nabob Omdut ul Omra, and from his confidential agent, addressed to the supposed agent of Tippoo Sultaun in the year 1796, subsequently to the Nabob Omdut ul Omra's accession to the government of the Carnatic under the treaty of 1792.

Ninthly. At the commencement, and during the progress of the late just, necessary, and glorious war with the late Tippoo Sultaun, the Nabob Omdut ul Omra to the utmost extent of his means and power, pursued the object of his secret intercourse with Tippoo Sultaun by a systematic course of deception with respect to the provision of the funds necessary to enable the British troops to march into Mysore, as well as by a systematic and active opposition to the supply and movement of the allied army through different parts of the said Nabob's dominions.

Tenthly. The stipulations contained in the fifteenth article of the treaty of 1787, and the tenth article of the treaty of 1792, by which the Nabobs of the Carnatic were bound not to enter into any political negotiations or correspondence with any European or native power or state without the consent of the Government of Fort St. George or of the Company, formed a fundamental condition of the alliance between the said Nabob and the Company, and the violation of the said stipulations necessarily involved the entire forfeiture on the part of the Nabob of all the benefits of the said alliance.

Eleventhly. The Nabob Mahomed Ali and the Nabob Omdut

ul Omra have violated the said stipulations, and have thereby forfeited all the benefits of the said alliance; and the Nabob Mahomed Ali, and the Nabob Omdut ul Omrah having violated the said stipulations for the express purpose of establishing an union of interests with Tippoo Sultaun, thereby placed themselves in the condition of public enemies to the British Government in India.

It is manifest, therefore, that the intentions of the Nabobs Mahomed Ali and Omdut ul Omra have been uniformly and without interruption hostile to the British power in India; and that those intentions have been carried into effect to the full extent of the actual power possessed by their Highnesses respectively at the several periods of time in which they have acted in pursuance of their system of co-operation with the enemy.

By acting on these principles of conduct, the Nabobs Mahomed Ali and Omdut ul Omra not only violated the rights of the Company, but by uniting their interests with those of the most implacable enemy of the British Empire, the Nabobs Mahomed Ali and Omdut ul Omra actually placed themselves in the relation of public enemies to the British Government, dangerous to the extent of their respective power, and active according to the means and opportunities afforded to them by the circumstances of the moment, and especially by the most severe exigency and pressure of war. Every principle of public law, therefore, released the British Government from the intended obligations of the treaty of 1792, and every consideration of self-defence and security authorized the Company to exercise its power in the manner most expedient for the purpose of frustrating the hostile councils of the late Nabob of the Carnatic, modelled upon the artful example, actuated by the faithless spirit, and sanctioned by the testamentary voice of his father.

In proceeding to exercise this right it was painful to the British Government to be compelled to expose to the world all these humiliating proofs of the ingratitude and treachery of the Nabobs Mahomed Ali and Omdut ul Omra towards the power which has uniformly proved their guardian and protector; but in acting from the impression of this sentiment, the British Government was more desirous of consulting its own dignity than of admitting any claims on the part of those infatuated princes to its generosity and forbearance.

In conformity to this spirit of temperance and moderation, it was the intention of the British Government to have made a formal communication to the Nabob Omdut ul Omra of the proofs which had been obtained of his Highness's breach of the alliance, with the view of obtaining, by the most lenient means, satisfaction for the injury sustained by the British Government, and security against the future operation of the hostile councils of the Nabob Omdut ul Omra.

Circumstances of expediency, connected with the general interests and policy of the British Government, interrupted the communication of this demand to the Nabob Omdut ul Omra: the intermediate illness of his Highness protracted the execution of that intention, and his subsequent death frustrated the wish of the British Government, to obtain from that Prince satisfactory security for the rights pledged to the Company in the Carnatic.

The death of the Nabob Omdut ul Omra has not affected the rights acquired by the British Government under the discovery of his breach of the alliance. Whatever claim the reputed son of the Nabob Omdut ul Omra may be supposed to possess to the Company's support of his pretentions to the Government of the Carnatic, is founded on the grounds of the rights of Omdut ul Omra himself: the right of the Nabob Omdut ul Omra to the assistance of the Company in securing his succession to the Nabob Mahomed Ali in the government of the Carnatic was founded on the express stipulations of the treaty of 1792: the result of the propositions stated in this declaration has established abundant proof that the fundamental principles of the alliance between the Company and the Nabob Omdut ul Omra, as well as the express letter of the treaty of 1792, had been absolutely violated and rendered of no effect by the Nabobs Mahomed Ali and Omdut ul Omra, previously to the ostensible conclusion of that instrument. It is manifest, therefore, that the Nabob Omdut ul Omra could derive no rights from the formal ratification of that treaty, the vital spirit of which had already been annihilated by the hostile and faithless conduct of his Highness; and that the Nabobs Mahomed Ali and Omdut ul Omra, by forming an intimate union of interests with Tippoo Sultaun had actually placed themselves in the relation of public enemies to the British empire in India.

Whatever claim to the Company's protection and support the reputed son of Omdut ul Omra may derive from his supposed father had been utterly destroyed by the hostile conduct of Omdut ul Omra: it follows, therefore, that the reputed son of Omdut ul Omra has succeeded to the condition of his father, which condition was that of a public enemy, and consequently that, at the death of Omdut ul Omra, the British Government remained at liberty to exercise its rights, founded on the faithless policy of its ally, in whatever manner might be deemed most conducive to the immediate safety and to the general interests of the Company in the Carnatic.

Before the British Government proceeded to exercise this right, founded on the violation of the alliance and on the necessity of self-defence, it was desirous of manifesting its attention to the long established connection between the Company and the house of Omdut ul Omra, by sacrificing to the sentiments of national magnanimity and generosity the resentment created by his Highness's flagrant breach of the alliance. In the spirit of those councils, therefore, with which it had been the intention of the British Government to demand satisfaction and security from Omdut ul Omra, and to avoid the publication of facts so humiliating to the family of that Prince, the British Government communicated to the reputed son of Omdut ul Omra, knowledge of the proofs now existing in the possession of the Government of Fort St. George, of the violation of the alliance; at the same time the British Government manifested a consistent adherence to the principles of moderation and forbearance by opening a latitude to the reputed son of Omdut ul Omra to afford, by means of an amicable adjustment, that satisfaction and security which the hostile and faithless conduct of his supposed father had entitled the British Government to demand, and which the dictates of prudence and self-defence compelled it to require.

The reputed son of Omdut ul Omra, by and with the advice of the persons appointed by his father's will to assist his councils, has persisted in opposing a determined resistance to this demand, thereby exhibiting an unequivocal proof that the spirit which actuated the hostile councils of the Nabobs Mahomed Ali and Omdut ul Omra, has been transmitted with unabated vigour to the supposed son of Omdut ul Omra, secured in its operation under the sanctimonious forms of their testamentary injunctions, and preserved with religious attachment by the ostensible descendant of that Prince.

Frustrated in the hope of obtaining from the reputed son of Omdut ul Omra reparation for its injuries and security for its rights, the British Government is now reluctantly compelled to publish to the world the proofs of this flagrant violation of the most sacred ties of amity and alliance by the Nabobs

Mahomed Ali and Omdut ul Omra, and the hereditary spirit of enmity manifested by the reputed son of Omdut ul Omra to the interests of the British Government. The duty and necessity of self-defence require the British Government, under the circumstances of this case, to exercise its power in the attainment of an adequate security for its rights. Justice and moderation warrant that the family of Omdut ul Omra shall be deprived of the means of completing its systematic course of hostility; wisdom and prudence demand that the reputed son of Omdut ul Omra shall not be permitted to retain the possession of resources dangerous to the tranquillity of the British Government in the Peninsula of India.

Wherefore, the British Government, still adhering to the principles of moderation, and actuated by its uniform desire of obtaining security for its rights and interests in the Carnatic by an arrangement founded on the principles of the long subsisting alliance between the Company and the family of the Nabob Mahomed Ali, judged it expedient to enter into a negotiation for that purpose with the Prince Azim ul Dowlah Bahadur, the son and heir of Ameer ul Omra, who was the second son of the Nabob Mahomed Ali, and the immediate great grandson by both his parents of the Nabob Anwer ud Deen Khan, of blessed memory; and his Highness the Prince Azim ul Dowlah Bahadur having entered into engagements for the express purpose of reviving the alliance between the Company and his illustrious ancestors, and of establishing an adequate security for the British interests in the Carnatic, the British Government has now resolved to exercise its rights and its power, under Providence, in supporting and in establishing the hereditary pretensions of the Prince Azim ul Dowlah Bahadur in the soubahdarry of the territories of Arcot and of the Carnatic Payen Ghaut.

And for the more full explanation of the grounds and motives of this declaration, the Right Honourable the Governor in Council by and with the authority of his Excellency the most noble the Governor-General in Council has caused attested copies and extracts of several documents discovered at Seringapatam to be annexed hereunto, together with an extract from the Treaty of 1792.

By command of the Right Hon. the Governor-in-Council.

J. WEBBE,

Chief Secretary to Government.

IV. OUDE.

30. The Earl of Mornington to the Secret Committee of the Honourable Court of Directors.

Projected military reforms in Oude. Nabob's alleged intention of abdicating.

Fort William, 28th Nov. 1799.

Honourable Sirs,

I. According to the latest accounts dated on the 2nd of November, the affairs of Mysore were in the most favourable condition. The whole of the country (including Sondah and the rest of the reserved territory, now about to be divided between the Company and the Nizam) having been completely settled, with the exception of the inconsiderable possessions of the Polygar of Bullam, against whom a small detachment had been sent, the army in Mysore was on the eve of being distributed in garrisons and cantonments.

Under the disadvantages resulting from the recent military operations throughout the country, Purneah had discharged the first monthly kist of the subsidy stipulated by the late treaty of Seringapatam, namely, that for the month of July, and had announced his intention of soon paying the kists for August and September.

I have very great satisfaction in informing your honourable Committee that the measures which I concerted with Lord Clive, previously to my departure from Fort St. George, for the purpose of reducing the southern Polygars to order and legal government have been executed with the greatest ability and success by Major Bannerman, and that the military power of that refractory race of people is now completely extinct.

The settlement of Tanjore has been arranged with the same happy success. Previously to my departure from Fort St. George, with Lord Clive's assistance, I framed the outlines of a new treaty between the Rajah and the Company vesting the entire and exclusive administration, civil and military, of that country in the Company's government. This treaty was ratified by me in council on the 26th instant.

II. The affairs of Oude have occupied a considerable share

of my attention. No probability existing that Zemaun Shah will be able in the course of the present season to renew his hostile attempts against Hindostan, and a conjuncture so favourable coinciding with our successes in Mysore, the most eligible opportunity appeared to be opened for carrying into execution such a reform of the Nabob Vizier's military establishments as should secure us from all future danger on the frontier of Oude, and should enable me to introduce a variety of necessary improvements in the government of that country. With this view it was my intention to establish a considerable augmentation of our troops in Oude without delay, and to induce the Vizier to disband, under certain regulations, a proportional part of his own useless and dangerous force. I had accordingly given orders to the Resident at Lucknow to commence a negotiation with his Excellency for this desirable purpose, and had also directed the movements of several bodies of troops in the provinces to be so arranged as to enable me, before the expiration of the cold season, to increase our force in Oude considerably. Before, however, the Resident at Lucknow could open the proposed negociation with the Vizier, or had disclosed to him any part of my intended plans, his Excellency, of his own accord, made a proposition to the Resident which necessarily supersedes every other arrangement.

III. For several months past his Excellency had intimated to the Resident from time to time an earnest desire to communicate to me an improved system for the government of Oude. But whenever the Resident had pressed his Excellency for a more full explanation of the nature of the proposed arrangement in order that it might be transmitted to me, his Excellency had evaded the discussion with evident symptoms of agitation of mind. At length on the 12th of November, at an interview which his Excellency had himself desired (and it is important again to remark that at this period no proposition had reached his Excellency from the Resident or from me with relation to the increase of the force in Oude), his Excellency signified an anxious desire and a fixed determination to abdicate altogether the government of Oude, and requested the Resident to draw, for the purpose of being forwarded to me, the enclosed paper which I received last night.

IV. His Excellency appears to have adopted the resolution of abdicating the government upon the maturest deliberation. Your honourable Committee will observe that his Excellency declares this resolution to have originated in the reciprocal aversion subsisting between himself and his subjects (an aversion, which, on his part, he declares to have grown into absolute disgust), and in his sense of his own incompetency from various other considerations, to administer the government either with satisfaction to himself or advantage to his people. But although such considerations may in some degree have influenced his Excellency's determination, I am inclined to believe that the principal causes are to be traced in the timidity and the avarice of his disposition; for it is proper to apprize your honourable Committee that he has intimated an expectation of being permitted to retire with the treasures which he may have amassed.

V. Your honourable Committee will remark that the Resident has used several arguments, but without effect, to dissuade his Excellency from the proposed abdication. If therefore his Excellency should ultimately persevere in this declared intention, it must be deemed entirely and absolutely his own voluntary act.

VI. Whatever may have been the motives, or whatever shall be the ultimate decision of his Excellency on this occasion, it is my intention to profit by the event to the utmost practicable extent; and I entertain a confident hope of being able either to establish, with the consent of the Vizier, the sole and exclusive authority of the Company within the province of Oude and its dependencies, or at least to place our interests in that quarter on an improved and durable foundation.

VII. It occurs to me to be necessary to add in explanation of the close of the third paragraph of this letter, that although the necessity of a reform of the Vizier's military establishments had been for a considerable time under discussion between his Excellency and me, and had even been fully admitted by his Excellency, no detailed measures with a view to the execution of such a plan had yet been suggested, nor had my intention of immediately augmenting our force in Oude been communicated to his Excellency when he opened his mind to the Resident at Lucknow.

I have the honour to be, &c.

MORNINGTON.

31. The Earl of Mornington to the Nabob of Oude.

Necessity of carrying out the military reforms. Exposure of Nabob's inconsistency in opposing them. Stern warning.

Fort William, 9th February, 1800.

The duty imposed on me by my public station, and the concern which I take in your Excellency's personal honour and welfare, as well as in the prosperity and happiness of the inhabitants of Oude, compel me to communicate to you, in the most unqualified terms, the astonishment, regret, and indignation which your recent conduct has excited in my mind.

In order to apprize your Excellency in the most unequivocal manner of the causes and objects of this letter, I propose to state my observations with reference to the following distinct propositions in your Excellency's correspondence with me, and in your declarations made to the British Resident at Lucknow.

1st. Your Excellency, since my arrival in India, has repeatedly complained of the ruinous condition of your internal government, and earnestly solicited my direct interference, as being indispensably necessary for the purpose of effecting a complete reform in your affairs, and especially in your military establishments.

2nd. After having received from me a plan for the reform of your military establishments, you expressed, in the most deliberate and unqualified terms, your approbation of the same, and your hope that it would be carried into effect.

3rd. You have recently declared to Lieut.-Colonel Scott, that this same plan for the reform of your military establishment never, in any measure, met with your approbation or acceptance, or was deemed expedient by you.

4th. You have attempted, by various means, to delay, and ultimately to frustrate the execution of the plan above mentioned, of which you had, after full deliberation, expressed your entire approbation.

5th. The means which your Excellency has employed for this purpose are calculated to degrade your character, to destroy all confidence between your Excellency and the British Government, to produce confusion and disorder in your dominions, and to injure the most important interests of the Company to such a degree as may be deemed nearly equivalent to positive hostility on your part.

In the beginning of August, 1798, your Excellency informed

me, by letter, that the organization of your government, which had for a long period of time been very loose and confused, was become in the last degree ineffective and irregular, adding a request that I would instruct Mr. Lumsden (the Company's Resident at Lucknow) to afford your Excellency his effectual aid in establishing your authority on a *new basis*. A variety of circumstances having rendered it impossible for me to give immediate consideration to your Excellency's representation, your Excellency in a subsequent letter, written in June, 1799, revived the subject, observing, 'it will be impossible to remove the embarrassment under which I labour until I shall have carried into effect the retrenchment of superfluous expenses, and shall have established a systematic settlement of the country, and of the *military* (*which is indispensable*) for promoting the security and ease of the ryots, the prosperity of the country, and the tranquillity of the people.' Your Excellency added 'although I have been informed by Mr. Lumsden that your Lordship has written to him upon this subject; yet nothing regarding it has been written by your Lordship to me; and I therefore hope you will repeat your orders to the Resident to be aiding and assisting me in all matters, so that I may *concert with him* the means of *removing my embarrassments*, and *with his assistance, carry on the affairs* of my government in a manner to produce ease and satisfaction to my mind.' Your Excellency concluded by declaring, 'I rely on your Lordship for support and assistance in everything.'

Such forcible representations of the disordered state of your Excellency's government in its military as well as civil branches, combined with my own intimate knowledge of the actual existence of the evils so repeatedly and emphatically described by your Excellency, authorized a full confidence in the sincerity of your Excellency's reiterated wishes for my active interference in your affairs, and for my assistance in remedying the defects of which you so justly complained. I therefore determined to adopt, without delay, those measures now apparently not less requisite for the ease and satisfaction of your Excellency's mind, than they had long been manifestly essential to the safety of your person and to the security and prosperity of your dominions. Under this impression, while yet occupied by most important affairs at Fort St. George, I appointed Colonel Scott to reside with your Excellency, furnishing him at the same time with such instructions as appeared to me to be best calculated to enable him to accomplish the apparently earnest wishes of your Excellency for establishing an improved system of civil and military government within your dominions.

In considering the course of measures best adapted to this salutary purpose, I became satisfied that it was absolutely necessary to commence with that reform of your Excellency's military forces, which your Excellency had declared to be indispensable. I was originally led to this conclusion by a review of the correspondence and negotiations which had passed between your Excellency and Mr. Lumsden in consequence of the advance of Zemaun Shah to Lahore, towards the end of the year 1798; and I was further confirmed in my opinion by a retrospect of the events which had followed the rebellion and flight of Vizier Alli.

The conduct of different corps of your Excellency's army had in several instances previously to the approach of Zemaun Shah, abundantly manifested that no reliance could be placed either in their fidelity or discipline. Many of them had mutinied, and were prevented from proceeding to acts of open violence against your Excellency's person by the presence of the Company's troops. Your Excellency, when consulted by Sir James Craig and by Mr. Lumsden on the measures of defence to be adopted against the threatened invasion of Zemaun Shah, declared that 'no confidence was to be placed in your troops,' and you not only avowed your military force to be inadequate to contribute any assistance towards the defence of your dominions, but required the presence of part of the British army within your capital for the express purpose of protecting your person and authority against the excesses of your own disaffected and disorderly troops, in the same moment when the services of the whole of the British army were most urgently demanded upon your Excellency's frontier to resist the approach of Zemaun Shah. Hitherto, however, the fidelity and utility of your Excellency's troops had been distrusted principally on grounds suggested by their repeated contumacy and disobedience. That they were actually capable of betraying the interests of your Excellency in a crisis of positive danger, was subsequently proved beyond a possibility of doubt by their treacherous conduct during the commotions excited by Vizier Alli.

The necessity of commencing the general improvement of your Excellency's government by a radical reform of your military establishment being then manifest, Lieut.-Colonel Scott, together with a letter which Sir Alured Clarke addressed to your Excellency, by my desire, delivered to you such further explanations of the proposed measure as the occasion required. It is remarkable that the delivery of Sir Alured Clarke's letter to your Excellency had been preceded within the short space of five days by repeated complaints on the part of your Excellency of the turbulent and disorderly state of your troops.

In the plan of reform for your military establishment presented to your Excellency at that period of time, I proposed that the greatest part of your useless and dangerous forces should be disbanded, and should be replaced by a suitable number of the Company's troops. The reception which your Excellency gave to the proposition corresponded with the expectations which your Excellency's repeated declarations and applications to me had led me to form. Your Excellency perused the letter of Sir Alured Clarke *with satisfaction, and declared your thorough concurrence in the sentiments which it contained.* Your Excellency also, at a subsequent conference with the Resident on the 5th of September, observed, of your own accord, that the proposed measure *was not impracticable, but such as you hoped might be accomplished.*

It is of importance to remind your Excellency in this place that, soon after the opening of these discussions by Lieut.-Colonel Scott, a fresh mutiny broke out among your Excellency's troops, which your Excellency was enabled to quell solely by the assistance of the British Resident at Lucknow.

Having in a letter to your Excellency dated the 26th of September, 1799, expressed my satisfaction in your ready concurrence in the expediency of the measure which had been generally proposed in the letter of Sir Alured Clarke, and particularly explained by Lieut.-Colonel Scott, and having at the same time earnestly exhorted your Excellency not to suffer any consideration to delay for a moment the necessary alterations in your military establishment (referring to the plan which had been minutely detailed to you by Lieut.-Colonel Scott), your Excellency in reply declares 'the benefits, both immediate and future, of such a reform are even more strongly impressed upon my mind than they have been described by your Lordship; *a year before this time, under a sense of the benefits in question*, and of the evils arising from the failure of my resources, and the increase of my expences, I planned, *of my own accord*, in my mind, a *reform of the system*, and was *the first to propose it.*'

To the observation which I had submitted to your Excellency relative to the possible return, in a more formidable shape, of the dangers which had already threatened the safety of your Excellency's person and dominions, your Excellency answers, in the same letter, 'please God, by introducing a reform in the *military system*, all dangers and all apprehension of disturbance will be removed.'

These extracts from your Excellency's own letters, and from Colonel Scott's reports of your verbal communications noted and recorded at the time, warrant me in declaring that your Excellency, in the most direct terms, originally solicited me to prepare a plan for the reformation of your military establishment, and that you afterwards positively approved the plan prepared and submitted to you at your own request. I leave it to your Excellency to judge with what emotions I now learn from Lieut.-Colonel Scott, that you have not hesitated to assert that this identical plan framed at your own suggestion, and approved by your deliberate sanction, *had never, in any measure, met with your approbation or acceptance, or been deemed expedient by you.*

In this place it may not be inexpedient to observe, that even if your Excellency had not professed your approbation of the plan in question, it would have been equally my duty and right to have required your Excellency's adoption of a measure, the execution of which is indispensably necessary to enable the Company to fulfil their engagement 'of defending your dominions against all enemies.'

In my letter to you of the 5th of November last I have sufficiently established the right of the Company to augment their forces within your Excellency's dominions to whatever extent the British Government in India may judge requisite to the permanent security of the common interests. I have also explained in what manner your Excellency is bound by the 7th Article of the Treaty concluded between your Excellency and Sir John Shore, to defray the expense of any force which the British Government shall deem necessary for the effectual protection of your dominions. The right of the British Government to make such an augmentation, even against your Excellency's consent, in the event of an invasion of your dominions, or of any sudden or temporary alarm either of domestic or foreign danger, has never been disputed by your Excellency; but I understand that you have expressed to Lieut.-Colonel Scott an intimation, that the same right does not extend to a permanent increase of the standing army of the Company in Oude. Can your Excellency then suppose that the treaty was intended to provide against dangers merely of a temporary and transient nature, and that it did not embrace the permanent and perpetual security of your dominions, and the lasting interests of that party which has bound itself to protect them against every danger, whether existing or contingent? If a danger shall exist, permanent in its nature, but of which the immediate approach to your Excellency's dominions may be so sudden and rapid as to preclude the possibility of providing against it by any other means, than a consistent and permanent system of preparation and precaution; shall it be contended that the legitimate protector and guardian of your dominions is not bound by every principle of duty to provide such a system without delay? and is not the season of peace and tranquillity the most favourable for the establishment of external security and internal order?

It is certain that the resources of your Excellency are inadequate to the double burthen of the proposed additional force of the Company, and of your own existing military establishment. But if your resources could bear this accumulated pressure, I should still feel myself bound to require that your Excellency should reduce your own disorderly troops. The expediency of disbanding as large a proportion of your own troops as can possibly be dispensed with in the business of the revenue collections, and in the purposes of ceremony and state, does not rest solely on the inefficiency of your troops in a military view, but also on their disaffection, and insubordination, and on the danger with which such a body of armed men must ever menace your person, and the public tranquillity in time of peace; a danger infinitely aggravated in the season either of domestic convulsion, or of foreign attack. The dismission therefore of the troops in question, is not only recommended by considerations of economy, but indispensably requisite by the soundest maxims of prudential policy. So long as these troops shall be entertained, a large proportion of the Company's force must be constantly employed to maintain the peace of the Country; and in the event of an invasion of your Excellency's dominions by a foreign enemy, the necessity of diverting a still more considerable part of the British army from the defence of your frontier, for the purpose of controlling your own licentious and disaffected soldiery, would increase exactly in proportion to the magnitude and imminence of external danger. It must therefore be obvious to your Excellency, that the continuance of these dangerous troops in your service, instead of leading to a diminution of the requisite amount of the British force in Oude, would require a far more considerable augmentation of that force than any hitherto proposed.

Your Excellency always professing the utmost anxiety for the reform of your own troops, having however delayed to concert the necessary arrangements for that purpose with Colonel Scott, it became my duty to accelerate the adoption of those measures for the defence of your Excellency's dominions, which daily became more urgent. It would have been highly gratifying to me, if your Excellency's activity on this occasion had been proportioned to the exigency of the case, or to the earnestness and apparent candour of your own declarations; but the responsibility in this case attaching, according to the stipulations of treaty, solely on the Company I could not have been justified by any consideration, in suspending the measures incumbent on the Company's Government.

On these grounds I determined early in the month of November last, to introduce immediately into your Excellency's dominions as great a proportion as possible, of the force which I deemed necessary to their effectual and permanent defence, in addition to the Company's troops already stationed in Oude.

I communicated this determination to your Excellency, in a letter written on the 5th of November, and forwarded by me to Lieutenant-Colonel Scott.

Before Lieut.-Colonel Scott could deliver this letter, your Excellency had made a proposition to him, which, as he conceived, precluded the necessity of presenting any letter to you; and accordingly it was not delivered until your Excellency thought proper to recall the proposition in question.

In the meanwhile the additional troops which I had determined to send into your Excellency's dominions, continued to assemble for that purpose; because in every event the necessity of the intended reinforcements must have remained unalterable.

The proposition of your Excellency, to which I have adverted was, that you should abdicate the government of your dominions, and, appropriating to your private use all the treasures of the state, retire from Lucknow. You signified at the same time, a desire that one of your sons should be substituted on the Musnud.

Lieutenant-Colonel Scott remonstrated against your Excellency's declared resolution to abdicate the government; but your Excellency persisted, and finally enjoined him to communicate it to me, as the result of your deliberate consideration.

This unexpected determination of your Excellency, although it induced Lieutenant-Colonel Scott to withhold my letter of the 5th of November, until further orders from me, did not prevent him from occasionally pressing upon your consideration the subject of the reform of your military establishment. Your Excellency however, invariably evaded the discussion by declaring, that under the resolution which you had announced of abdicating the government, it was totally unnecessary to proceed at present in the proposed reform.

Your Excellency has been in possession for some time past, of a formal and detailed answer from me (authenticated by my signature) to your declaration of your resolution to abdicate the sovereignty of your dominions. To the arguments by which I endeavoured to modify your Excellency's original plan of abdication, and to the terms on which I declared myself willing to facilitate your retirement from the cares of your government, (the administration of which you have acknowledged yourself to be utterly unequal to conduct,) your Excellency has not yet returned any reply; you have deemed it sufficient to signify to Lieutenant-Colonel Scott, that under my determination not to admit your Excellency's proposition in the terms stated by yourself, you were ready to abandon your design of retirement, and to retain the charge of the government; supporting this apparently new resolution on general grounds of justice to your family. I will not at present enquire whether means might not still be devised for securing ample justice to your family, without reducing your Excellency to the painful and dangerous necessity of continuing in a station, the duties of which you have declared yourself to be incompetent to fulfil, and of governing a people whom you have declared 'neither pleased with you, nor you with them; with whose evil dispositions, enmity, disobedience and negligence, you are disgusted; and from whose government your mind is utterly withdrawn.'

Having requested your Excellency to return a formal and precise answer to my detailed observations and proposals, in consequence of your Excellency's declared wish to abdicate the government, I shall abstain from entering into any minute examination of the nature of the subsequent change in your Excellency's mind, until I shall be furnished in a regular manner, with an explicit statement of the motives which induced that change. I must however remark, that every circumstance accompanying your Excellency's conduct, which has hitherto fallen under my observation, on this extraordinary occasion, appears to me to indicate that your Excellency never previously entertained the design of abdicating your government, however convinced of the truth of those incontestible facts which you alleged as the motives of your abdication, but that you professed such a design with the sole view of defeating by delay, the long meditated measure of a reform of your military establishment.

It is most painful to be compelled to state a charge of so serious a nature, against a person of your Excellency's high rank and exalted dignity; but what other conclusion can I draw from your Excellency's conduct, when Lieutenant-Colonel Scott informs me, that after you had engaged his attention and mine for nearly two months, by your ostensible intention to abdicate the government, you suddenly relinquished that intention, and at the same moment declared for the first time, that if 'the reform of your military establishments were to be adopted on the principles proposed, it would annihilate your Excellency's authority in your own dominions,' although not only the general principles, but all the material details of that reform, to which you now object, had been repeatedly approved by your Excellency, as being essential to the maintenance of your authority, and indispensable to the peace and safety of your dominions.

But your Excellency has proceeded to other measures of a tendency infinitely more dangerous, utterly incompatible with all your professions, and repugnant to the fundamental principles of your connection with the Company, and to every duty of friendship and honourable alliance.

Lieutenant-Colonel Scott informs me, 'that your Excellency, instead of affording any cordial assistance for devising and carrying into execution a plan for the dismission of your battalions, has thrown every possible impediment in the way of that measure, by endeavouring to restrict the additional British force to one position and by delaying to furnish Lieutenant-Colonel Scott with the statements of your military establishments repeatedly required, and absolutely necessary to the commencement of the undertaking.'

Lieutenant-Colonel Scott informs me, that your Excellency is equally desirous of *impeding the progress of the additional*

British troops, by exposing them to difficulties in obtaining supplies of provisions; to prove this intention on the part of your Excellency, Lieutenant-Colonel Scott states, that although he had repeatedly applied to your Excellency for the necessary purwannahs to your several aumils, your Excellency had not yet issued a single purwannah; the consequence of which was likely to prove not only seriously distressing to the British troops destined to the protection of your dominions, but dangerous to the peace of the country through which those troops proposed to march.

It is impossible for me to express in terms of sufficient force, the sentiments which this intelligence has occasioned in my mind.

The conduct of your Excellency in both instances stated, but more flagrantly in the last, is of a nature so unequivocally hostile, and may prove so injurious to every interest, both of your Excellency and of the Company, that your perseverance in so dangerous a course, will leave me no other alternative than that of considering all amicable engagements between the Company and your Excellency to be dissolved, and of regulating my subsequent proceedings accordingly. I am however, always inclined to hope that your Excellency may have been inadvertently betrayed into these imprudent and unjustifiable measures by the insidious suggestions of evil councillors, and being ever averse to construe your Excellency's actions in such a manner as must compel me to regard and to treat you as a Prince no longer connected with the Company, by the ties of amity and of a common interest; I trust that my next accounts from Lieutenant-Colonel Scott, may enable me to view your Excellency's conduct in a more favourable light, but lest my wishes in this respect should be disappointed, it is my duty to warn your Excellency in the most unreserved terms, that your Excellency alone will be responsible for all the evils which cannot fail to result from any further perseverance in the fatal and imprudent course of measures which you have recently pursued. I also think it necessary to entreat your Excellency not to delay for a moment, whatever further steps may be pointed out to you by Lieutenant-Colonel Scott, as necessary to effect the two urgent and indispensable objects; namely, the reform of your military establishment, and the provision of funds for the regular monthly payment of all the Company's troops in Oude.

The least omission or procrastination in either of those important points, must lead to the most serious mischief.

MORNINGTON.

32. The Marquess Wellesley to Lt.-Col. William Scott, Resident at Lucknow.

Project of partial- or total-cession of the Nabob Vizier's territories to the Company.

Fort William, January 22nd, 1801.

Sir,

1. Having reviewed the series of your correspondence since the commencement of the reform of his Excellency the Vizier's military establishments, my attention has been particularly directed to the declaration made by his Excellency in his letter to you of the 29th of Jummad us Sani, relative to a probability of a failure on his Excellency's part, in providing the necessary funds for the regular payment of the additional troops furnished within the last year for the defence of his Excellency's dominions.

2. If the alarming crisis be now approaching in which his Excellency can no longer fulfil his public engagements to the Company, this calamity must be imputed principally to his Excellency's neglect of my repeated advice and earnest representations. The course of your correspondence manifests that the exertion of his Excellency in the reform of his own useless, dangerous, and expensive military establishments, especially of his cavalry, has by no means kept pace with my efforts, to place the security of his Excellency's person and government beyond the reach of foreign and domestic danger. The augmented charges arising from the additional British force specified in the despatch to you from the Secretary in the Secret Department of the 5th of November, 1799, would have been amply provided for by the amount of the reductions which might have been effected in his Excellency's establishment, if his Excellency had vigorously and cordially co-operated with me in the salutary and economical measure of disbanding his own undisciplined, licentious, and disaffected troops.

3. I am perfectly satisfied that every exertion has been employed by you to accelerate the execution of my orders, and that his Excellency's systematic counteraction is the sole cause of the

delays which have arisen; his Excellency having, to my knowledge, used every means within his power to frustrate the progress of a reform which he himself had invited, and which he had declared to be indispensable to the security of his person, and to the prosperity of his dominions.

4. The natural consequences of such a policy on the part of the Vizier are now necessarily felt by his Excellency; and it is now become the duty of the British Government to interpose effectually for the protection of his interests, as well as those of the Company, which are menaced with common and speedy destruction by the rapid decline of the general resources of his Excellency's dominions.

5. The Vizier is already apprized that I have long lamented the various defects of the system by which the affairs of his Excellency's Government are administered. Conscious of the same defects, his Excellency has repeatedly expressed a wish to correct them by the assistance of the British Government. I have never been indifferent to his Excellency's wishes on this subject, or insensible of the urgent necessity of an effectual change in the administration of the affairs of Oude; but circumstances, well known to you, have hitherto prevented me from executing all the dictates of my duty with respect to that distressed country, and have compelled me to limit my efforts to a partial reform of his Excellency's military establishments; providing for the security of his Excellency's dominions and government to the extent of furnishing an efficient and respectable force for their defence and support, and of commencing a proportionate reduction in his Excellency's military establishments.

6. It was always evident that these precautions must prove fruitless if the defects in the civil administration of Oude should be suffered progressively to impair the fundamental resources of the state. The continuance of the present system for a much longer period of time will not only render his Excellency unable to discharge the subsidy on account of the additional troops, but will exhaust the resources of the country to such a degree as to preclude the possibility of realizing the former subsidy.

7. The causes of this increasing defalcation of revenue are manifest, and daily acquire new strength. Had the territories of Oude been subject to the frequent or occasional devastations of an enemy, had they been visited by unfavourable seasons, or by other calamities which impair the public prosperity, the rapid decline of the Vizier's revenues might be imputed to other causes

than a defective administration; but no such calamitous visitations have afflicted the province of Oude, while, in consequence of the protection which it derives from the presence of the British forces, it has been maintained, together with all the Company's possessions on this side of India in the uninterrupted enjoyment of peace. A defective administration of the government is, therefore, the only cause which can have produced so marked a difference between the state of his Excellency's dominions and that of the contiguous territories of the Company. While the territories of the Company have been advancing progressively during the last ten years in prosperity, population, and opulence, the dominions of the Vizier, although enjoying equal advantages of tranquillity and security, have rapidly and progressively declined.

8. The operation of these evils has not commenced with the government of Saadut Ali; they necessarily flow from the system of administration which existed at the period of his Excellency's accession to the Musnud. But none of these evils have been diminished under his Excellency's government; on the contrary, their daily increase and aggravation are notorious, and must be progressive, to the utter ruin of the resources of Oude, unless the vicious system of the native administration of the country be immediately abandoned. In place of inveterate and growing abuses must be substituted a wise and benevolent plan of government, calculated to inspire the people with confidence in the security of property and of life; to encourage industry; to protect the fruits of honest labour; and to establish order and submission to the just authority of the State, on the solid foundations of gratitude for benefits received, and expectation of continual security.

9. The Vizier must now be prepared for the active and decided interference of the British Government in the affairs of his country. His Excellency has repeatedly complained to me, and to the British Resident at his Court, of the ruinous condition of the internal government of Oude; he has repeatedly and earnestly solicited my direct interference, and has declared such interference to be indispensably necessary for the purpose of effecting a complete reform in his affairs. In the month of November, 1799, his Excellency was so convinced of the incurable defects of his government and of his own utter inability to administer it, that he signified to me, in the most formal manner, his deliberate determination to descend from the

Musnud, and to return into private life. He solemnly avowed (not in a moment of temporary anxiety and vexation. but after the most deliberate reflection) 'that his mind was utterly withdrawn from the government of a people who were neither pleased with him nor he with them, and with whose evil dispositions, enmity, disobedience, and negligence he was completely disgusted.' This resolution, so deliberately adopted, was suddenly abandoned, but the cause of so sudden a change in his Excellency's resolution cannot, unfortunately, be traced to any improvement in the general administration of his affairs, to any augmentation of his means of conducting the Government, or to the consequent establishment of reciprocal confidence and attachment between his Excellency and his people. Could any other fact be alleged to favour such an inference it would be totally precluded by his Excellency's recent statement of the condition of his revenues, and by recent and aggravated symptoms of the most alarming disaffection towards his person and government.

10. His Excellency's life has been lately attempted under circumstances of the most formidable description. Active and general support has been afforded by his subjects to the impostor who lately assumed the name of Vizier Ali; and the acknowledged temper of his Excellency's people, combined with the state of his government, exposes his situation every hour to increased anxiety, embarrassment, and hazard.

11. Having maturely considered these circumstances with the attention and deliberation which the importance of the subject requires, I am satisfied that no effectual security can be provided against the ruin of the province of Oude, until the exclusive management of the civil and military government of that country shall be transferred to the Company, under suitable provisions for the maintenance of his Excellency and of his family. No other remedy can effect any considerable improvement in the resources of the state, or can ultimately secure its external safety and internal peace.

12. Under this conviction, and with a view to the preservation of the common interests of the Company and of the Vizier, I have determined to propose to his Excellency a new treaty and arrangement similar to that concluded in November, 1799, between the Company and his Highness the Rajah of Tanjore; and also conformable to the plan of the treaty proposed to his Excellency by me, in my letter of the 9th of February, 1800, at the period of his Excellency's proposed abdication of the

Government. A copy of the treaty with the Rajah of Tanjore is enclosed ; I desire that you will frame from the articles of that treaty, and from the treaty submitted to the Vizier in the month of December, 1799, the plan of such an arrangement, as, while it shall effectually secure all the political benefits described in the eighth paragraph of this despatch, shall also consult, as far as may be compatible with that primary object, the inclinations and prejudices of the Vizier. Having framed such a treaty, you will submit it to his Excellency, and at the same time you will earnestly exhort him to consider the propositions contained in the new arrangement with calm and dispassionate deliberation.

13. If his Excellency should manifest a disposition to adopt the general frame of the proposed arrangement, but should appear desirous of introducing any particular modifications into the proposed treaty, you will receive whatever propositions his Excellency may offer for that purpose, and you will communicate them to me without delay, adding such observations as may occur to you for my further information.

14. On the other hand, if his Excellency should unfortunately be persuaded by the interested councils of evil advisers absolutely to reject the proposed treaty, you will then proceed to inform his Excellency in firm, but respectful language, that the funds for the regular payment of the subsidy to the full extent of the augmented force must be placed, without a moment of delay, beyond the hazard of failure.

15. For this purpose you will require his Excellency to make a cession to the Company in perpetual sovereignty of such a portion of his territories as shall be fully adequate, in their present impoverished condition, to defray those indispensable charges. This cession must be framed upon the same principle which has formed the basis of the late treaty between his Highness the Soubahdar of the Deccan and the Company, by which his Highness has ceded to the Company in full sovereignty, a country rated at the annual revenue of sixty-two lacs of rupees in commutation for a subsidy of about forty lacs of rupees.

16. With respect to the countries to be ceded, it is sufficiently evident that no other portion of the Vizier's dominions possesses so many political advantages as would be derived to the Company from the possession of the Doab. The cession of that province, including the tribute from Furruckabad, must therefore be required in the first instance. In selecting the other districts which may be necessary (after deducting the charges of collection)

to complete the amount of the augmented subsidy it will be advisable to regulate the demand in such a manner as shall place the Vizier beyond the reach of foreign connections and foreign dangers. For this purpose the new possessions of the Company should be so arranged as to surround whatever territory may remain to his Excellency. With this view, the country to be required, in addition to the Doab, must be Rohilcund. The cession of these two provinces may be made with less violence to the pride and prejudices of the Vizier, inasmuch as they were actually added to the possessions of his family by the British arms. In this respect the arrangement proposed to the Vizier is similar to that concluded with the Nizam. The greater part of the countries ceded to the Company by the Nizam having been originally acquired from the power of Mysore by the assistance of the Company.

17. If the present produce of these two provinces, after deducting the charges of collection, should be deemed unequal to the amount of subsidy to be defrayed, the deficiency must be sought in the countries bordering on the district of Juanpoor; and for this purpose either Azimghur or Goruckpoor, or both, must be required.

18. Under such an arrangement, the territories which would remain to the Vizier would probably be sufficiently protected by the position which the Company's troops would necessarily occupy for the defence of the ceded countries; and no division of military force would be required for the express purpose of protecting the Vizier's territory. The continuance, however, of a regiment of native infantry at Lucknow might be expedient as a protection to the person of the Vizier, and a security for the peace of the City. If at any time the state of his Excellency's remaining territories should require the presence of any part of the British force, you would be empowered to issue the requisite orders for that purpose.

19. If the Vizier should manifest a disposition to accede to the first proposal, contained in the eleventh paragraph of this despatch, the transfer of the government will be considerably facilitated by the early adoption of effectual measures for the purpose of conciliating the minds of all persons whose interests or personal consideration may be affected by the dissolution of the existing government. With this view, it will be proper that suitable stipends or pensions should be settled on the principal nobles and officers at present dependent on the Court of Luck-

now, as well as on all military officers of rank and particularly on those of the cavalry, who may lose their employments in consequence of the change of government, or of the reduction of the actual military establishments of Oude. Accordingly you will state for my information and ultimate orders your sentiments with regard to the persons for whom it may be expedient and just to provide; and you will suggest the amount and mode of the provision to be made for the several classes or descriptions of claimants. In the meanwhile, if the state of the negotiation with the Vizier for the relinquishment of the civil and military administration of his dominions, according to the plan of the Treaty of Tanjore, should require your attention to the object of providing for individuals before you can receive any detailed instructions from me on the subject, you will promulgate, in the most distinct manner, such general and particular assurances, in the name of the British Government, as shall appear to you calculated to tranquillize the minds of those affected by the change of the administration.

20. In considering the measures to be adopted with the views stated in the preceding paragraph, it will occur to you that no proceeding can be more calculated to conciliate all descriptions and classes of people, than a liberal attention to the religious establishments and charitable foundations of the country. I accordingly authorize you in the case supposed to take the necessary steps for affording to the people of Oude the most ample satisfaction on this subject; and I desire that you will furnish me with a statement of such public endowments, of both the Hindoo and Mahommedan religion as you may propose to confirm or to extend.

I am, &c.
WELLESLEY.

33. To the Honourable the Secret Committee of the Honourable the Court of Directors.

Advantages secured by the Treaty with the Nabob Vizier. Appointment of the Hon. Henry Wellesley as temporary Commissioner in Oude.

On the Ganges, near Benares,
November 14, 1801.

Honourable Sirs,

1. I have the honour to transmit to you a copy of a treaty concluded by Mr. Henry Wellesley, and Lieut.-Colonel Scott,

with his Excellency the Nawaub Vizier, on the 10th instant, at Lucknow, and ratified by my authority on this day.

2. The various discussions which have taken place during the administration of my two immediate predecessors relative to the state and condition of the interests of the Company in Oude, combined with the documents which have already been submitted to your honourable Committee, on the same subject during my administration, will render the general policy and objects of this treaty sufficiently manifest to your wisdom and experience. It is however my intention, by the Mornington Packet now under despatch to transmit to you a detailed statement of the means which I have employed to accomplish this important arrangement, and of the beneficial consequences which I expect to derive from it to various branches of your affairs.

3. By the present despatch, I shall content myself with requesting your attention to some of the leading advantages obtained by the successful issue of this measure.

4. The treaty effectually secures the reduction of the Nawaub Vizier's military establishments within such limits as may be deemed sufficiently contracted to effect the entire extinction of his military power.

5. Your honourable Committee is already apprized that a considerable progress has been made during the past year in the reduction of his Excellency's army; the third article of this treaty will accelerate the completion of that salutary reform, while it will afford perpetual security against the revival of a similar danger.

6. In the place of his Excellency's irregular and precarious military power, is substituted such a British force as may be deemed adequate to our defence in that quarter in India, while the operation of this treaty exonerates the British Government from the obligation of maintaining any definite or specified number of troops in the province of Oude, the Company being charged with the general defence of the Vizier's dominions, and being relieved from all special engagement with regard to the description or amount of the force to be employed for that purpose.

7. A considerable augmentation is made in the amount of the subsidy for the purpose of embracing the expenses of the army to be maintained on our north-western frontier, in the ceded districts, and in those reserved to the Vizier as well as the charges of administering justice, and of managing the revenue through the channel of the Company's servants.

8. The payment of the subsidy no longer rests on the faith of the native government of Oude, nor is subject to be affected by the corruption, imbecility and abuse of that vicious and incorrigible system of vexation and misrule.

9. The security of the subsidy is now established on the solid foundation of territorial possession, and the result of all accounts which I have been able to obtain, warrants a confident expectation, that under the wise and benevolent administration of the British Government, the territories ceded by this treaty will prove more productive, in a considerable degree than they are represented to be in the statement of Jummah, contained in the first article of the treaty.

10. In addition to these advantages, your honourable Committee must derive great satisfaction from reflecting that the British Government under this treaty will become the instrument of restoring to affluence and prosperity one of the most fertile regions of the globe, now reduced to a condition of the most afflicting misery and desolation by the depraved administration of the native government of Oude.

11. Since my departure from the Presidency, I have enjoyed frequent opportunities of contemplating the benefits diffused by the operation of the British system of government, over every part of the flourishing and happy provinces which I have visited. I can, therefore, declare my conscientious conviction, that no greater blessing can be conferred on the native inhabitants of India, than the extension of the British authority, influence and power.

12. The authority of the Nawaub of Oude was sustained exclusively by his connection with the Company's government, and the reputation and honour of the British nation in India, were deeply involved in the operation of that authority on the welfare and happiness of those countries over which it was upholden by the terror of our name, or exercised by the immediate force of our arms. Your honourable Committee will, therefore, deem it natural, that, having frequently been reduced to the painful necessity of applying the influence of the British name, and the power of the British sword to the maintenance of a system so disgraceful in its principles, and ruinous in its effects, I should feel a considerable degree of satisfaction in substituting for such an administration, the salutary influence of those regulations and laws, of which I have recently witnessed and admired the practical wisdom and extensive benevolence.

13. Your honourable Committee will further remark that by the operation of the sixth article of the treaty, the Company's government has reserved the positive right of interference in the internal management of that part of the country retained by the Nabob Vizier, and you may be assured of my unremitting endeavours to exercise this right to such an extent as shall afford every practicable degree of security for the lives and properties of the Vizier's remaining subjects, and shall preclude any disturbance of the peace and good order of our dominions from the vicinity of his Excellency's administration.

14. It is my intention to proceed immediately to vest the administration of the ceded districts in the hands of the Company's civil servants. This measure appears to me to be indispensably necessary for the purpose of securing all the important objects of the new arrangement. I shall not however attempt to form any settlement of the revenues, or to introduce any special code of regulations and laws, until sufficient time shall have been afforded for ascertaining the resources of the country, and for investigating the local customs, usages, manners and dispositions of its inhabitants. The immediate introduction of the Company's civil servants in the administration of all the details of the government in all its branches will operate as an effectual control upon such native officers and agents as it may be necessary to retain provisionally, and will facilitate the acquisition of that knowledge which must constitute the foundation of a permanent settlement of the country.

15. The peculiar character of the people of the ceded districts, and the obstacles which the artifice and treachery of the Vizier or his dependants may be expected to oppose to the final settlement of the country under the British Government, will require the constant presence of an active and vigorous authority, until the foundations of the new arrangements shall be firmly established. It is, therefore, my intention to place Mr. Henry Wellesley in the ceded districts for some time, with the most ample powers, for the purpose of settling the country, with the aid and assistance of such of the Company's Civil servants as I have selected to co-operate with him in this arduous and salutary task.

16. The discretion, temper, judgment, and firmness which Mr. Wellesley has manifested, in the principal conduct of the negotiation with the Vizier have been the most efficient cause of its speedy, prosperous, and tranquil issue. These qualities, combined with the authority which he naturally derives from his near

connexion with me, have induced me to consider him to be the most useful instrument which I can employ on this occasion. In the course of a year, or possibly within a shorter period of time, I trust that the settlement of the ceded districts may be so far advanced as to enable me to withdraw Mr. Wellesley, and to leave the administration of the country nearly in the same form as that of Benares, with such differences as may be required by the greatly superior magnitude of the dominion ceded by this treaty.

17. In the progress of the important arrangement which I have introduced into Oude, I have frequently had occasion to applaud the zeal, diligence, and address of Lieut.-Colonel Scott. Since Mr. Wellesley's arrival at Lucknow, Lieut.-Colonel Scott's unremitting exertion of the same qualities has had its full share in the success of the negotiation: and Mr. Wellesley has, in an official letter to me, stated his high sense of Lieut.-Colonel Scott's merits and his public acknowledgment of his eminent services. I therefore propose to leave Lieut.-Colonel Scott in the Residency at the Vizier's Court, in which situation considerable talents, knowledge, and vigilance, will be required for the purpose of securing the timely accomplishment and continued effect of the stipulations of the treaty relative to the territories retained in the Vizier's hands.

I have the honour to be,
Honourable Sirs, your's, &c.
WELLESLEY.

V. MAHRATTAS.

1. ENGLISH INTERVENTION.

34. The Marquess Wellesley to the Secret Committee of the Honourable Court of Directors.

The Crisis at Poonah, and the Governor-General's views and action in consequence.

Fort William, Dec. 24, 1802.

Honourable Sirs,

1. Your honourable Committee will receive by the ships which remain to be despatched to England from Bengal in the course of the present season, a detailed narrative of the events

and transactions in the Mahratta empire, which have terminated in a crisis of affairs among the Mahratta powers, highly interesting to the political relations of the British power in India. The same conveyance will furnish you with a detail of the negotiations conducted by the resident at Poonah, under my authority, with a view to the accomplishment of the important object of comprehending the Mahratta states in the general system of defensive alliance with the honourable Company and its allies, on the basis of the treaty concluded with his Highness the Nizam, in the month of October, 1800. Your honourable Committee will also receive by the same channel every document relative to the system of measures which I have deemed it necessary to adopt for the security and promotion of the British interests in the present crisis of the affairs of the Mahratta empire.

2. I am anxious, however, to submit to your honourable Committee, at the earliest practicable period of time, a summary view of these important occurrences, of the principles by which I have been governed in the course of policy which I have pursued, and of my expectations with regard to the final result of the actual crisis of affairs in India.

3. The annexed copy of the instructions of the Governor-General in council, to the resident at Poonah, under date June 23, 1802, (A.) contains a review of the conduct and disposition of the State of Poonah towards the British Government, since the commencement of my administration, down to that period of time.

4. Under those instructions, the resident at Poonah renewed the negotiations for the conclusion of an improved system of alliance with that Court. The increased distractions in the Mahratta state, the rebellion of Jeswunt Row Holkar (illegitimate son and successor of the late Tuckojee Holkar) against the combined forces of the Peishwa and Scindiah, appeared to constitute a crisis of affairs favourable to the success of our negotiations at Poonah.

5. In the course of the discussions which ensued between the Resident and the court of Poonah, the Peishwa manifested a solicitude to contract defensive engagements with the honourable Company, under circumstances of more apparent sincerity than had marked his conduct on any former occasion. The Peishwa, however, continued to withhold his consent to any admissible modification of the Governor-General's propositions, until Jes-

wunt Row Holkar, at the head of a formidable army, actually arrived in the vicinity of Poonah. The superiority of Jeswunt Row Holkar's troops in number and discipline to those of the Peishwa and Dowlut Row Scindiah, rendered the issue of any contest nearly certain. The Peishwa, however, anticipated equal difficulty and hazard, and equal disgrace to his authority, in the success of either party. Nor was the menaced usurpation of Jeswunt Row Holkar more formidable to the Peishwa than the alternative, of the revival and confirmation of the ascendancy of Scindiah; whose troops composed the greater proportion of the army destined to oppose the progress of Jeswunt Row Holkar.

6. Under these circumstances the Peishwa, on the 14th of October, despatched his principal minister to the British Resident, charged with definitive proposals for the conclusion of defensive and subsidiary engagements with the British Government. Those proposals are detailed in the annexed memorial marked B. During the discussions which ensued on the basis of those propositions, the evasive conduct of the Peishwa excited considerable doubts of his sincerity, even at that stage of the negotiation; and on the 24th of October, when the army of Jeswunt Row Holkar had arrived within a few miles of Poonah, the Peishwa despatched a deputation to that chieftain with distinct proposals for an accommodation, which Jeswunt Row Holkar rejected. At the instance of the Peishwa, Suddasheo Bhow, the commander of the combined forces of the Peishwa and Scindiah, had previously marched with the army under his command from Poonah, and had occupied a position in the vicinity of Jeswunt Row Holkar's camp. On the morning of the 25th the two armies engaged, and on the same day, with a view to be prepared for every event, the Peishwa moved from Poonah at the head of his remaining troops; and at the moment of marching sent his minister to the British Resident with a paper, of which a translation is annexed to this despatch (C). The minister Ragonath Row offered to the British Resident the fullest assurances of the Peishwa's intention and meaning, that a general definitive alliance should be concluded and carried into effect at the earliest practicable period of time, between his Highness and the honourable Company, on the fundamental principles, and in conformity to the system of operation detailed in the paper to which this paragraph refers.

7. In consequence of this transaction, the British Resident judged it to be expedient to suggest to the Right Honourable

the Governor of Fort St. George, and to the Honourable the Governor of Bombay, the necessity of preparing a body of troops, under the authority of those presidencies respectively, for the eventual support of the Peishwa's government, and for the protection of his person. The Resident at Poonah transmitted a similar application to the Resident at Hyderabad, for the eventual services of a considerable detachment from the subsidiary force stationed with his Highness the Nizam.

8. The engagement between the combined army of the Peishwa and Scindiah, and that commanded by Jeswunt Row Holkar terminated in the total defeat of the combined army, with great loss. At the close of the action, the Peishwa retired with a small body of cavalry to a fortress in the vicinity of Poonah, whence he prosecuted his march towards the Concan. The city of Poonah remained in the charge of an officer in the service of the Peishwa, while Jeswunt Row Holkar continued to occupy a camp at the distance of four miles from Poonah. The primary object of Jeswunt Row Holkar was to obtain possession of the Peishwa's person, and to compel his Highness to establish such an administration as might secure Jeswunt Row Holkar's ascendancy in the state, to the exclusion of Dowlut Row Scindiah's influence. If this plan should fail, the next project of Jeswunt Row Holkar was to invite to Poonah, Amrut Row (son of the late Rugghoonaut Row, or Ragobah,) to place the son of Amrut Row on the musnud, and to invest Amrut Row with the office of prime minister, while Jeswunt Row Holkar should assume the general command of the troops of the state.

9. This crisis of affairs appeared to me to afford the most favourable opportunity for the complete establishment of the interests of the British power in the Mahratta empire, without the hazard of involving us in a contest with any party. The power of Jeswunt Row Holkar possessed no solid foundation in the justice of his cause, in popular opinion, or in the extent of political or military resource. It could not be doubted that Scindiah would employ every effort to retrieve the disgrace, and to avert the danger of his recent defeat. The continuation of the contest between those chieftains would probably weaken the power, and impair the resources of both, and would afford to the British Government an opportunity of interposing its influence and mediation for the restoration of the Peishwa's just authority, under terms calculated to secure our relations with the Mahratta empire, on the basis of a general defensive alliance and

reciprocal guarantee, both with the Peishwa and with Dowlut Row Scindiah, according to the principles of the treaty of Hyderabad, concluded in October, 1800. No reasonable apprehension existed that the progress of this system of policy would be obstructed, either by the union of the contending parties, or by the decisive success of either chieftain; nor indeed could I apprehend any combined or separate opposition from either in the prosecution of my views.

10. Under these considerations, I confirmed the engagement concluded between the Peishwa and the Resident at Poonah, on the day on which I received it, and I accordingly instructed the Resident to signify to his Highness my ratification of that engagement, and my resolution to employ every effort of the British power for the restoration of his authority. The British Resident was also instructed to direct his attention to the improvement of the terms of the proposed alliance, by endeavouring to obtain the Peishwa's consent to those stipulations, which his Highness had hitherto rejected, and to such additional concessions as appeared to be expedient for the better security and improvement of the British interests in that quarter of India; and the Resident was further directed to avail himself of the earliest opportunity of reducing the proposed conditions of alliance to the form of a definitive treaty. At the same time I transmitted instructions to the Governors of Fort St. George and Bombay, and to the resident at Hyderabad, confirming the requisition of the Resident at Poonah, for assembling troops at the proposed stations, with a view to fulfil the engagements concluded with the Peishwa. Desirous of comprehending the principal branches of the Mahratta empire in a general system of defensive alliance and guarantee, on the basis of the engagements so happily concluded with his Highness the Nizam, in October, 1800, I determined to combine with the measures to be adopted for the restoration of the Peishwa, the renewal of my invitation to Dowlut Row Scindiah to partake the benefits of the defensive alliance; and I accordingly instructed the Resident at Scindiah's Court to proceed from Futtehgur to that chieftain's camp with the utmost practicable expedition, for the purpose of concerting with Scindiah the means of restoring the Peishwa to the musnud, and of proposing to Scindiah the terms under which that chieftain might be admitted to the benefit of the general defensive engagements concluded with the Peishwa.

11. The details of the measures to be adopted for the completion of our engagements to the Peishwa were necessarily confided to the direction and judgment of the Resident at Poonah; but that officer was instructed to adopt every practicable precaution to preclude every risk of hostilities between the British troops and those of Jeswunt Row Holkar, and to endeavour to secure the accomplishment of our views by the means of amicable negotiation.

12. In the actual state of the affairs of the Mahratta empire, it would have been a measure of indispensable precaution to have assembled a considerable army of observation upon the frontier of the Mahratta territories. This important consideration, combined with the communication which the right honourable the Governor of Fort St. George had received from the Resident at Poonah, of the progress of our negotiation with the Peishwa, had induced his Lordship to issue orders for assembling a considerable army within the ceded districts, without awaiting the arrival of my instructions for that purpose. The honourable the Governor of Bombay pursued the same wise and salutary course of vigilance and prudence, by placing in a state of preparation, for immediate service, the disposable force at that Presidency. A considerable detachment of the subsidiary force at Hyderabad was also directed by the Resident at Hyderabad to be prepared for eventual service in the field in conformity to the requisition of the Resident at Poonah.

13. By advices received subsequently to the despatch of my instructions to the Resident at Poonah, and to the Governors of Fort St. George and Bombay, I was informed that the Peishwa had effected his retreat to Mhar, a fort situated on the river of Bancoote in the Concan; and that Holkar now despaired of the success of his endeavours either to obtain the Peishwa's voluntary return to Poonah, or to seize his Highness's person, that Holkar had detached a force to Jejoory (a fort situated in the vicinity of Poonah, and being the actual residence of Amrut Row), and had brought Amrut Row to Poonah with the intention of investing Amrut Row with the general administration of affairs, and of placing the son of Amrut Row on the musnud, while Jeswunt Row Holkar proposed to assume the general command of the army of the state. To this arrangement I was further informed that Amrut Row was not disposed to accede; I also received advice that the Peishwa had signified to the Government of Bombay, through the officers stationed at Ban-

coote, a desire of eventually seeking an asylum at Bombay, and that his Highness had solicited the Government of Bombay to direct a ship to be prepared at Bancoote for his Highness's conveyance to Bombay or to Bassein, if such a measure should appear to be necessary for the safety of his person. The honourable the Governor of Bombay complied with the latter application, by directing the ship *Herculean* to proceed to Bancoote, and to be prepared for the Peishwa's eventual accommodation. The Resident at Poonah being apprized of these circumstances suggested to the Governor of Bombay the expediency of discouraging the Peishwa from seeking an asylum within the British territory, until my sentiments and intentions with respect to the affairs of the Peishwa should be made known, and the Resident recommended that the Peishwa should be advised to maintain his position at Mhar to the latest possible period of time consistently with the safety of his Highness's person.

14. Under the determination which I had adopted of employing every effort for the restoration of the Peishwa's authority, and in the actual situation of the Peishwa's affairs, it appeared to me to be extremely desirable that the Peishwa should immediately place himself under the protection of the British power by retiring to Bombay. I considered that this measure would preclude all hazard of precipitating hostilities with Jeswunt Row Holkar, by any advance of the British troops for the protection of the Peishwa's person, and would enable the British Government to open a negotiation with Jeswunt Row Holkar for the restoration of the Peishwa to the musnud of Poonah, under every circumstance of advantage. This event would also enable us to combine with our other measures, under great advantage, the proposed negotiation with Scindiah for the conclusion of defensive arrangements. It was obvious, also, that the Peishwa's arrival at Bombay would afford the most favourable opportunity for the adjustment of the terms of the definitive alliance with the Peishwa on the basis of my original propositions, with the addition of such stipulations as might appear to be expedient with reference to the actual crisis of affairs.

15. With these sentiments, I transmitted instructions to the Government of Bombay for the reception and accommodation of the Peishwa at that Presidency, and for regulating the conduct of that government in conformity to the measures which I had resolved to adopt.

16. Since the despatch of those instructions, I have received

advices from Poonah stating, that, although Amrut Row continues to be adverse to the arrangement proposed by Jeswunt Row Holkar, the affairs of government are conducted under the authority of Amrut Row's name, and that a considerable force had been detached to the Concan with a view to seize the person of the Peishwa. By advices from Bombay it appeared that the Peishwa had availed himself of the offer of the ship *Herculean*, and had proceeded on that ship to a strong fort in the Concan, named Severndroog, where his person might probably be secure against the attempts of the usurper.

17. The despatches from Bombay further state that the Peishwa had formally recognized the engagements concluded between him and the British Resident, and had applied for a detachment of British troops in part of the stipulated subsidiary force, for the immediate protection of his person.

18. By the latest accounts it appears that Dowlut Row Scindiah is collecting his forces with a view of opposing Jeswunt Row Holkar, and that Scindiah has actually commenced his march from his capital of Ougein towards Poonah.

19. Both Jeswunt Row Holkar and Amrut Row have employed every endeavour to induce the Resident at Poonah to continue at that city, manifestly with the view to obtain the countenance of the British Government in sanctioning the projected revolution in the government of the Mahratta empire. The Resident has prudently rejected every advance of this nature, and has persisted in his resolution to retire to Bombay, for which presidency he with difficulty obtained permission to depart on the 28th ultimo.

20. At the conferences holden by the Resident with Amrut Row and Jeswunt Row Holkar, on the eve of the Resident's departure from Poonah, both those chieftains expressed their solicitude for the preservation of the friendship of the British Government, and directly and earnestly appealed to the Resident for his advice in the present situation of affairs. Jeswunt Row Holkar expressly intimated a wish for the mediation of the Resident, for the express purpose of effecting an accommodation with the Peishwa. The Resident informed Jeswunt Row Holkar that for this purpose it was indispensably necessary that both parties should consent to refer their differences to the mediation of the British Government: but that the Resident could not undertake such mediation without the orders of the Governor-General. The Resident at the same time advised Amrut Row

and Jeswunt Row Holkar to explain their views by a direct application to the Governor-General. At the Resident's final interview with Amrut Row, that chieftain delivered three letters to my address, one from himself, and the others from the persons who at present exercise the functions of ministers of the State. The purport of those letters is to solicit the countenance and support of the British Government by the appointment of a Resident in the place of Colonel Close, whose departure from Poonah to Bombay is represented by Amrut Row and his Ministers to be an abdication of his station of representative of the British Government at the Court of Poonah.

21. I have also had the satisfaction to receive from Dowlut Row Scindiah a letter soliciting the continuance of the friendship of this Government towards his state and that of the Peishwa, and containing a request that I will act in concert with him in the present crisis of affairs at Poonah.

22. This appeal to the British power from all parties concerned in the actual commotions of the Mahratta states, affords the most favourable opportunity for our successful and pacific mediation.

• 23. In the present conjuncture of the affairs of the Mahratta empire, your honourable Committee will remark that the British Government must either persevere in its pacific and equitable efforts for the restoration of the Peishwa's authority, or must abandon all hope consistently with our faith, honour, or permanent interests of concluding with any of the Mahratta states, those defensive engagements, which are essential to the complete consolidation of the British empire in India, and to the future tranquillity of Hindostan. •

24. Reviewing the general state of affairs in the Mahratta empire, I entertain a confident expectation of the complete accomplishment of all our views, and of the restoration of tranquillity within the Mahratta dominions, by the means of amicable negotiation. It appears probable that Scindiah will cordially co-operate with the British Government in the restoration of the Peishwa's authority, and will consent in the actual state of his own affairs to become a party in the proposed system of defensive engagement. It cannot be supposed that Jeswunt Row Holkar will reject any reasonable proposals of accommodation supported by the combined power and influence of the British Government and Scindiah. The intentions of the Rajah of Berar appear to be uncertain. That chieftain

now ostensibly favours the cause of Jeswunt Row Holkar; but I have every reason to believe that the Rajah of Berar is actuated entirely by the cautious policy of apparently favouring the cause of the successful party. His Highness the Nizam is disposed to concur in any course of measures which the British Government may adopt for the success of our mutual views of defensive alliance with the Mahratta states.

25. Since the commencement of this despatch I have received advices from Bombay, notifying the embarkation of the Peishwa, under convoy of the ship *Herculean* from Severndroog for Bassein, and the arrival of Colonel Close from Poonah at Bombay on the 3rd instant.

26. These events will probably accelerate the conclusion of defensive engagements with the Peishwa, and will enable Colonel Close immediately to open a negotiation with Amrut Row and Jeswunt Row Holkar.

27. I have directed Colonel Close and the Governor of Bombay to apprize your honourable Committee of the existing state of affairs at the time when this despatch shall pass through Bombay.

I have the honour to be,
with the greatest respect,
honourable Sirs,
your most obedient and faithful servant,
WELLESLEY.

35. The Marquess Wellesley to the Honourable the Secret Committee of the Court of Directors.

The same subject. Conclusion of the Treaty of Bassein.

Fort William, February 10, 1803.

Honourable Sirs,

In my despatch to your Honourable Committee dated 24th December, 1802, forwarded overland, I had the honour to submit to you a statement of the late transactions in the Mahratta empire, and to explain to your Honourable Committee the system of policy which I considered it to be my duty to pursue for the security and improvement of the British interests in India, in the actual crisis of affairs at Poonah.

I am apprized by the Honourable the Governor of Bombay that in conformity to my instructions, it was his intention to forward to your Honourable Committee with that despatch a continuation of the narrative of events and proceedings in that quarter to the latest period of time. That narrative will comprehend the occurrences of a date subsequent to my last advices from Bombay; I shall therefore confine the present despatch to a statement of my general sentiments on the actual situation of affairs in the Mahratta empire, and of the course of policy which I propose to pursue.

Your Honourable Committee will be apprized by that despatch of the Honourable the Governor of Bombay to which the preceding paragraph refers, of the actual conclusion of a definitive treaty of defensive alliance between the British Government and his Highness the Peishwa.

The terms of that treaty being strictly conformable to the tenor of my original propositions to his Highness, and to the spirit of my subsequent instructions to the Resident at Poonah, I have not hesitated to ratify and confirm the treaty. A copy of the treaty is annexed to this despatch. The conclusion of this important arrangement promises to establish the British interests in the Mahratta empire on the most solid and durable foundation, and to afford additional security for the permanent tranquillity and prosperity of the British dominions in India.

The complete operation of this beneficial arrangement is however still subject to doubt.

It has always been sufficiently manifest that the principal branches of the Mahratta state, are averse to an alliance between the British Government and the sovereign power of the Mahratta empire. The distractions prevailing among the feudatory chieftains afforded the most favourable prospect for the conclusion of such an alliance. It is also evident that his Highness the Peishwa has been induced to conclude the treaty with the British Government by his conviction that no other means existed of recovering any portion of his just authority, or of securing the tranquillity of his dominions.

The knowledge of our arrangements with the Peishwa may induce Dowlut Row Scindiah and Holkar, to compromise their differences and to offer to the Peishwa proposals for restoring His Highness to the Musnud of Poonah, which His Highness may be disposed to accept, notwithstanding the actual conclusion of engagements for that purpose with the British Government. In such an event it is not my intention to attempt to compel the Peishwa to adhere to the faith of his engagements, at the hazard of involving the Company in a war with the combined Mahratta States.

. . . . .

If however the Peishwa should adhere to the faith of his engagements, and if the majority of the Mahratta Jageerdars and Chieftains, subject to His Highness's authority, should concur in the restoration of the Peishwa's authority under the treaty with the Company, I shall consider it to be my duty to proceed, without regard to any partial opposition on the part of Scindiah, or of Holkar, either singly or united.

No reason, however, exists to justify an apprehension that in the event supposed, Scindiah would proceed to such an extremity; nor is any such desperate course of proceeding to be apprehended from the Rajah of Berar. Uncombined with the power of Scindiah, Holkar will not probably venture to resist the Peishwa. Holkar has also anxiously solicited the arbitration of the British Government with respect to his claims.

Your honourable Committee will be apprised by the Government of Bombay of the state of affairs in Guzerat, where, I trust, an establishment is now formed, from which great advantages may be derived to the political, military, and commercial interests of the Company, in that quarter of India.

I have the honour to be, &c.

WELLESLEY.

Feb. 14, 1803.

P.S.—Since the date of this letter I have received advices from the resident at Poonah to the 23rd ultimo; the general tenor of these advices appears to me to be of the most favourable description.

His Highness the Peishwa has despatched two of his principal officers to Dowlut Row Scindiah for the express purpose of reconciling that chieftain to the arrangement which his Highness has concluded with the British Government.

His Highness the Peishwa has addressed letters to the several Mahratta chieftains subject to his Highness's authority, who occupy the districts situated between Poonah and the river Kistna, apprising them of his alliance with the British Government, and directing them to join and co-operate with the British forces. These circumstances have considerably diminished my apprehensions with regard to the possibility of the Peishwa's departure from the faith of his engagements.

Dissensions have arisen between Amrut Row and Jeswunt Row Holkar, which may be expected to produce a separation of interests between those chieftains. Jeswunt Row Holkar is extremely embarrassed by the want of money for the payment of his troops, and is endeavouring to supply the failure of his resources by levying oppressive contributions from the inhabitants of Poonah. That chieftain has repeated his propositions in a modified form to the Resident, for an accommodation with the Peishwa, and has solicited the mediation of the Resident, and of the Peishwa, for the satisfaction of his demands upon Dowlut Rao Scindiah. As a proof of his sincerity, Jeswunt Rao Holkar has signified his intention of sending the females of the Peishwa's family to his Highness at Bassein. Jeswunt Rao Holkar has been equally earnest in soliciting the mediation of his Highness the Nizam.

The situation of affairs justifies a confident expectation of the speedy and happy conclusion of the late arrangements with his Highness the Peishwa, and of the amicable adjustment of the differences existing among the Mahratta chieftains, through the mediation and influence of the British power.

36. The Marquess Wellesley to the Secret Committee of Directors.

The same subject. Restoration of the Peishwa to Poona by Major-General Wellesley.

Fort William, April 19, 1803.

Honourable Sirs,

On the 10th of February, 1803, I had the honour to submit to your honourable Committee, my sentiments respecting the situation of affairs in the Mahratta empire, and the course of policy by which I expected to accomplish the objects of the treaty lately concluded with his Highness the Peishwa, without the hazard of involving the British Government in a war with the Mahratta power; and your honourable Committee has been apprized by a despatch from the Government of Bombay, transmitted in conformity to my directions, of the occurrences in the Mahratta state to the 19th of January last.

Colonel Close will receive my directions to transmit to your honourable Committee, a narrative of the events which have occurred since the date of my last advices from the Peninsula, and he will relate to you the actual state of affairs at the time when this despatch shall reach Poonah and Bombay.

No event of importance has occurred at Bassein since the date of the latest communications to your honourable Committee from that quarter. The Peishwa has uniformly continued to manifest unequivocal proofs of his disposition to adhere to the faith of the engagements which he has contracted with the British Government. His Highness has demonstrated the most implicit confidence in the protection of the British power, and has not appeared to entertain any disposition to accept the invitation of Scindiah to proceed to that chieftain's camp. On the 18th of March, his Highness received the treaty of Bassein, ratified by the Governor-General in council, with demonstrations of the highest satisfaction.

Your honourable Committee has been informed, that Dowlut Rao Scindiah had arrived at Indore with a considerable body of his forces; having prosecuted his march from that station, Dowlut Rao Scindiah crossed the Nerbuddah, on the 4th of February, and arrived in the vicinity of Burhaunpoor, on the 23d of that month.

Colonel Collins arrived at the camp of Dowlut Rao Scindiah, on the 27th of February. The advices which I received from that officer, and from other quarters, induced me to entertain suspicions, that Dowlut Rao Scindiah (notwithstanding his original application for the aid of the British Government in restoring order to the Mahratta empire) meditated an accommodation with Jeswunt Rao Holkar, and a confederacy with that Chieftain, and with the Rajah of Berar, for the purpose of frustrating the success of the arrangements concluded between the British Government, and the Peishwa, without however intending to proceed to the desperate extremity of provoking a contest with the British arms. This suspicion was corroborated by the artifices practised at the camp of Scindiah upon the arrival of Colonel Collins, with a view of eluding the communication of the propositions, with which Colonel Collins was charged under my authority, and the appearance of Scindiah's intentions became still more unsatisfactory from the evasive and indirect, or vexatious replies which Colonel Collins received to my propositions, after he had at length obtained access to Dowlut Rao Scindiah.

Your honourable Committee will not fail to contrast these systematic delays and evasions, with the solicitude previously expressed by Scindiah for the early arrival of Colonel Collins, and for a full communication of my views and intentions in the present crisis. This perverse course of policy, habitual to all the states of India, is the favourite practice of the Mahratta powers. The most effectual mode of frustrating the objects of such a system of artifice and deceit, is to pursue a direct and steady course with firmness and temper, avoiding every deviation which can tend to divert the counsels or arms of the British Government, from their destined purposes either of peace or war. This principle constitutes the spirit and tenor of all my instructions to the British Residents at the courts of the several native powers; experience has proved that a direct and steady course of policy is not less advantageous to our interests, than it is manifestly consistent with our dignity and honour. With the greatest satisfaction, I request the attention of your honourable Committee to a recent instance of the distinguished success of this system of proceeding at the Court of Scindiah.

Colonel Collins having endeavoured, without success, to obtain from Dowlut Rao Scindiah's ministers explicit replies to the propositions which he had offered to that Chieftain's acceptance in my name, at length demanded a private audience of Scindiah.

By the judgment, firmness, and ability, which Colonel Collins exerted on that occasion, an explicit declaration was obtained from Scindiah himself, disclosing in the most distinct and direct terms the views of that Chieftain.

Scindiah plainly declared to Colonel Collins, that, until the communications of the agent despatched to his Court, by his Highness the Peishwa, (for the purpose of explaining the nature and extent of the engagements concluded between his Highness, and the British Government) should be received, Scindiah could not return a decided answer to the propositions which had been stated to him on the part of the British Government, with regard to his accession to the treaty of Bassein as a contracting party. Scindiah accompanied this declaration with a positive assurance, that he had no intention whatever to obstruct the completion of the arrangements concluded between the Peishwa and the British Government, and that it was his wish to improve the friendship at present subsisting between the Peishwa, the British Government, and his own State.

Of the sincerity of Scindiah's declaration, I entertain no doubt, because the course of policy which he has signified his intention of pursuing is manifestly the most consistent with his interests.

The security of Scindiah's dominions, and of his state among the powers of India, cannot be placed on a permanent basis, unless it shall be connected with the restoration of order in the Mahratta empire, under the sanction and defence of the British Government. The interposition of our influence and protection has already rescued Scindiah from destruction, has prevented the accumulation of the whole force of the Mahratta empire in the hands of a desperate and needy adventurer, and has preserved the balance of power between the respective feudal States, by maintaining the paramount authority of the Peishwa. The extreme hazard to which Scindiah's power has been recently exposed by the success of the insurgents at Poonah, may have opened a more distinct view of his real interests, which are entirely consistent with those of the British Government in the present crisis. Scindiah however, may have been desirous of recovering the exorbitant ascendancy which he had acquired at Poonah, and may apprehend a permanent diminution of his influence in the Peishwa's counsels, under the operation of the treaty of Bassein. But the influence of Scindiah at Poonah had actually been subverted, by the success of the insurgents previously to the interposition of the British mediation, and the existence of Scindiah's Government had been greatly endangered by the same event. In this situation therefore, the regret with which he may view the probable diminution of his influence at Poonah, may be sufficiently counterbalanced by his confidence in the security of his dominions, under the protection of the British Government. On the other hand, from the moment that the intentions of the British Government had been avowed, it became the interest of Scindiah to avoid every measure tending to expose him to the jealousy of a power, which commands the frontier of the most valuable portion of his dominions.

The sincerity of Scindiah's declaration is further confirmed by his continuance at Burhaunpoor, in a state of inaction, until the season, together with the progress of our forces, had advanced so far, that no exertion on his part could have enabled him to occupy Poonah, previously to the arrival of the British troops at that capital.

This view of the subject is not inconsistent with Scindiah's desire to delay his accession to the treaty of Bassein, and to the propositions immediately affecting his separate interests, until he shall have received a direct communication from the Peishwa. Scindiah may wisely and justly withhold his assent to any new system of engagement, until he shall have ascertained the real sentiments of the Peishwa on the subject of the late treaty, together with the precise extent of the stipulations which that instrument contains.

Nor is the sincerity of Scindiah's declaration incompatible with the project of a confederacy between Scindiah, Holkar, and the Rajah of Berar for purposes of a defensive nature, which I consider to be the extreme object of Scindiah, in negotiating such a confederacy, without any views whatever of hostility towards the British power.

Jeswunt Rao Holkar has continued to manifest an anxious desire for the accommodation of his differences with the Peishwa and with Dowlut Rao Scindiah, by repeated applications to Lieut.-Colonel Close for the arbitration of the British Government, and by the despatch of an agent of rank to Hyderabad, charged with a statement of the demands of Jeswunt Rao Holkar and of Amrut Rao, and vested with authority to negotiate, through the combined mediation of his Highness the Nizam and of the British Government, the adjustment of his demands on the Peishwa and on Dowlut Rao Scindiah. The demands of Holkar, however, have not been materially abated.

Colonel Close has endeavoured to persuade his Highness the Peishwa to offer to Holkar such concessions as might induce Holkar to compromise the subsisting differences, and to admit his Highness's peaceable return to his capital. His Highness, however, manifested an insuperable aversion to offer any concessions to Holkar, whom he considered to be a rebel against the legitimate authority of the sovereign power of the Mahratta empire.

Colonel Close, therefore, deemed it advisable to address a letter to Jeswunt Rao Holkar, communicating to that chieftain my sentiments on the subject of his demands, assuring him that the influence of the British Government would be exerted for the satisfactory adjustment of his claims on Dowlut Rao Scindiah, and that the British Government would guarantee any adjustment which Holkar might be able to effect of his demands on the Peishwa, and expressing an expectation that Holkar would refrain from any opposition to the establishment of a British force within the Peishwa's dominions.

A negotiation appears to have been opened directly between Holkar and Scindiah for the accommodation of their differences, but no certain accounts have hitherto been received of its conclusion or progress.

Holkar has continued to exercise the utmost degree of violence and outrage upon the inhabitants of Poonah, for the purpose of extorting money for the relief of his exigencies. This proceeding appears to have excited universal disgust, and to have confirmed the resolution of the majority of the Jageerdars and inhabitants of the Peishwa's dominions to support his Highness's cause.

Considerable bodies of Holkar's army have moved in different directions without any other apparent objects than those of observing the movement of the troops assembled on the several frontiers of the Peishwa's dominions, and of facilitating the subsistence of the soldiers and followers of Holkar's camps.

By the latest advices it appears that Holkar has actually evacuated Poonah, and has marched with the main body of his army in a northerly direction towards Burhaunpoor. The probable object of that movement is, either to accelerate the issue of his negotiations with Scindiah, or to facilitate the means of acting offensively against Scindiah, and at the same time to avoid the hazard of hostilities with the united arms of the British Government, the Nizam, and the Peishwa, and to maintain a position favourable to an amicable negotiation with the allied powers.

This movement admits the uninterrupted march of the combined forces of the allies to Poonah. Holkar must, therefore, have abandoned his hopes of effecting a revolution in the government of Poonah, and of seizing a share in the administration. The force of Holkar is stated to amount to 40,000 cavalry and 30,000 infantry, with 180 guns.

The intelligence which I have received from the Court of the Rajah of Berar, indicates that chieftain's dissatisfaction at the conclusion of defensive engagements between the British Government and his Highness the Peishwa.

Whatever may be the aversion of the Rajah of Berar to the interposition of the British Government in the affairs of the Mahratta empire, any attempt on the part of that chieftain to obstruct the execution of the treaty of Bassein, would be inconsistent with the systematic caution of his character and imprudent in the actual state of his military power, and in the exposed situation of his territories. His just rights cannot be endangered, and may receive additional security by the restoration of a regular authority at Poonah, under the protection of the Company.

In conformity to the plan of operations which I determined to adopt for the restoration of his Highness the Peishwa to the musnud of Poonah, the whole of the subsidiary force stationed with his Highness the Nizam marched from Hyderabad towards the western frontier of his Highness's dominions at the close of the month of February. The troops of his Highness assembled for the purpose of co-operating with the subsidiary force, consist of nearly 6,000 infantry and 9,000 cavalry. The subsidiary force under the command of Lieut.-Colonel Stevenson consists of six battalions of native infantry or 6,000 men, two regiments of native cavalry, and sixteen field pieces.

These combined forces reached Paraindah, a station on the western frontier of the Nizam's dominions, situated at the distance of 116 miles from Poonah, on the 25th of March.

I have great satisfaction in stating to your honourable Committee that the conduct of his Highness the Nizam, during the whole course of the late transactions in the Mahratta state, has been uniformly consistent with the obligations of his alliance with the British Government, and that his Highness has manifested a sincere desire to co-operate with the British Government in the measures adopted for the restoration of order in the Mahratta state. His Highness has rejected every overture of the ruling authority at Poonah, and of the Rajah of Berar, for the adjustment of the affairs of the Mahratta empire through any other channel than that of the British Government.

By my instructions of the 2nd of February, Lord Clive (aided by the judgment of Lieut.-General Stuart, and regulated by contingent events) was empowered to determine the actual period of time at which it might be proper for the British troops to advance into the Mahratta territory, and the amount of the force to be detached from the main body of the army for that purpose.

Adverting to the expediency of securing the early arrival of the British troops at Poonah, and of confirming the favourable disposition which had been manifested by the Jageerdars in the southern territories of his Highness the Peishwa, as well as to the actual march of the subsidiary force towards the Nizam's western frontier, and to the necessity of terminating the depending negotiations at the earliest practicable period of time, Lord Clive was of opinion that the time was actually arrived at which it was necessary for the British troops to enter the Mahratta territory, and his Lordship accordingly, on the 27th February, instructed his Excellency Lieut.-General Stuart (then present with the army on the frontier of Mysore) to adopt the necessary measures for that purpose.

In consequence of the absence of Lieut.-General Stuart from the presidency of Fort St. George, Lord Clive deemed it to be necessary that the extent of the force to be detached from the main body of the army should be determined exclusively by the judgment of Lieut.-General Stuart, and his Lordship accordingly referred that point to Lieut.-General Stuart's discretion, under an additional reference to the general spirit of my instructions of the 2nd of February.

The extensive local knowledge and influence possessed by the honourable Major-General Wellesley, the personal intercourse established between Major-General Wellesley and the Mahratta chieftains on the frontier of Mysore, and the confidence reposed by those chieftains in the approved talents, firmness, temper, and integrity of that officer, rendered him peculiarly qualified to discharge the complicated duties of the command of the detachment destined to proceed to Poonah. That important command required the united exertion of considerable military skill, and of great political experience and discretion, Lord Clive accordingly desired that Major-General Wellesley might be appointed to the command of the advancing detachment, and requested his Excellency the Commander-in-Chief to furnish Major-General Wellesley with instructions for the regulation of his conduct according to the spirit of my instructions to his Lordship of the 2nd of February.

In conformity to the foregoing directions, the Commander-in-Chief appointed a detachment from the main body of the army assembled at Hurryhur for the purpose of advancing into the Mahratta territory. The detachment consists of one regiment of European and three regiments of native cavalry, two regiments of European and six battalions of native infantry, with a due proportion of artillery, amounting altogether to 1500 cavalry and 6,800 infantry; and to that force was added 2,500 of his Highness the Rajah of Mysore's horse. Lieut.-General Stuart appointed the honourable Major-General Wellesley to the command of that detachment, in conformity to Lord Clive's suggestion.

Lieut.-General Stuart directed the Honourable Major-General Wellesley—

1st. To encourage the southern Jageerdars to declare in favor of the Peishwa's cause; to employ every means to reconcile their mutual animosities, and to induce them to unite their forces with the advancing detachment for the purpose of re-establishing his Highness's government.

2dly. To proceed to Meritch and form a junction with the Peishwa, or if the Peishwa's march to that station should be deemed unadvisable or impracticable, to unite with such of his Highness's chieftains and troops as might be there assembled.

3dly. To open a communication and to form a junction with the subsidiary force advancing from Hyderabad, and with the contingent of his Highness the Nizam.

4thly. To proceed eventually to Poonah, and to establish an order of things in that capital favourable to the return of the Peishwa, and to the accomplishment of the objects of the treaty lately concluded between his Highness and the British Government.

It is a most grateful part of my duty to express to your Honourable Committee in the strongest terms, my entire approbation of the zeal, alacrity, and ability, with which the right Honourable Lord Clive and Lieut.-General Stuart have commenced the execution of my orders. I entertain the highest estimation of the judgment, skill, and promptitude manifested by his Lordship and by Lieut.-General Stuart, in regulating the details of the arrangements for the successful accomplishment of the objects to which my instructions were directed.

The conduct of Lord Clive on this occasion, corresponds with the uniform tenor of that exemplary spirit, public zeal, and honourable co-operation with the supreme authority in India, which have animated every act of his Lordship's administration. Repeated experience has inspired me with a deliberate confidence in the prosperous issue of every important measure entrusted to his Lordship's immediate execution. In the exigency of every public crisis, and in various and extraordinary difficulties and dangers, the exertions of Lord Clive in the service of the Company, under my orders, have been employed with hereditary energy and success. My gratitude, respect, and affection, must ever attend his character and fame; and it would be a desertion of the most sacred duty of my station to omit any opportunity of recommending Lord Clive's eminent public services to the deserved gratitude of the East India Company, and to the justice and favor of his Sovereign and of his country.

A long course of useful and honourable services has repeatedly obtained my public testimony to the distinguished merits of Lieut.-General Stuart, and has established the reputation of that revered and respectable officer with great lustre in the high esteem of the Company and of the nation. On all occasions of service, I have derived the utmost possible advantage from the zealous application of the numerous qualifications which Lieut.-General Stuart possesses. In the present instance, his extraordinary solicitude to execute my orders according to their true spirit, the judgment, skill, and temper which have marked all his proceedings and operations, and the ardent zeal which he has displayed for the success of the service entrusted to his discretion, demand my most cordial approbation.

If the important arrangements now in progress should terminate with success, you will be indebted in a great degree to Lieut.-General Stuart for the happy accomplishment of a plan, which promises a most powerful augmentation to the security of the British possessions in India, nor can I conceive a more glorious termination of a long and illustrious career of public service.

The detachment under the command of Major-General Wellesley commenced its march from Hurryhur on the 9th ultimo. By the latest accounts it appears that the detachment had advanced to a station near Meritch, with the cordial support and co-operation of the majority of the southern Jageerdars, and with every appearance of general satisfaction among the inhabitants of the Mahratta territory. It was expected that the detachment would arrive at Meritch on the 3rd of April.

The Honourable the Governor of Bombay will communicate to your honourable committee the progress of events in the province of Guzzerat to the period of time when this despatch shall reach Bombay.

By the latest accounts from that quarter it appears that the rebels, after having sustained several defeats by the combined army of the British Government and the Guicowar, had evacuated Guzzerat under circumstances which justify a confident expectation of future permanent tranquillity in that province.

This situation of affairs in Guzzerat is highly favourable to the successful issue of the measures now in a course of operation for the restoration of the Peishwa to the musnud of Poonah. The arrival, at Bombay, of his Majesty's 78th regiment, which embarked from Fort William for that presidency, on the 10th of February, has probably coincided with the period of time when it might be expedient that his Highness the Peishwa should commence his march towards Poonah.

Reviewing all the circumstances connected with the state of the Mahratta empire, I trust that your honourable committee will receive by this despatch intelligence from Poonah and Bombay, of the pacific settlement of affairs in the state of Poonah, and of the establishment of a British subsidiary force in the service of the Peishwa.

Your honourable committee will appreciate the importance of the successful accomplishment of the proposed arrangements at Poonah in its relation to the maintenance of peace, and to the general security of our interests in India, and in its particular reference to the exclusion of the interests and influence of France from the Mahratta empire.

The importance of this object is considerable, with a view to the contingency either of peace or war between Great Britain and France, in India. In order to improve our relations with the Peishwa, and to oppose in the present crisis every attainable barrier to the progress of France in India, I deemed it necessary to issue instructions to Lieut.-Colonel Close, directing his attention to the improvement of that article of the late treaty with the Peishwa, which provides for the eventual exclusion of Europeans, subjects of any state which may be at war with Great Britain, from the territories of the Peishwa.

I have the honour to be,
with respect,
Honourable Sirs,
your most obedient and faithful servant,
WELLESLEY.

37. Treaty of Bassein.

Treaty of perpetual and general defensive alliance, between the Honourable English East India Company and his Highness the Peishwa Badjee Rao Ragonaut Rao Pundit Purdhaun Bahauder, his children, heirs and successors, settled by Lieutenant Colonel Barry Close, Resident at the Court of his Highness, by virtue of the powers delegated to him by his Excellency the Most Noble Richard Marquis Wellesley Knight of the most illustrious order of Saint Patrick, one of his Britannic Majesty's Most Honourable Privy Council, Governor General in Council, appointed by the Honourable Court of Directors of the said Company to direct and controul all their affairs in the East Indies.

Whereas, by the blessing of God, the relations of peace, and friendship, have uninterruptedly subsisted for a length of time between the Honourable English East India Company and his Highness Rao Pundit Purdhaun Bahauder, and have been confirmed at different periods, by treaties of amity and union; the powers aforesaid adverting to the complexion of the times have determined, with a view to the preservation of peace and tranquillity, to enter into a general defensive alliance, for the complete and reciprocal protection of their respective territories, together with those of their several allies and dependants, against the unprovoked aggressions or unjust encroachments of all or any enemies whatever.

ARTICLE 1st. The peace, union and friendship, so long subsisting between the two states, shall be promoted and increased by this treaty, and shall be perpetual. The friends and enemies of either, shall be the friends and enemies of both, and the contracting parties agree, that all the former treaties and agreements between the two states, now in force, and not contrary to the tenour of this engagement, shall be confirmed by it.

ARTICLE 2nd. If any power or state whatever, shall commit any act of unprovoked hostility or aggression against either of the contracting parties, or against their respective dependants or allies, and after due representation, shall refuse to enter into amicable explanation, or shall deny the just satisfaction or indemnity, which the contracting parties shall have required, then the contracting parties will proceed to concert and prosecute such further measures, as the case shall appear to demand.

For the more distinct explanation and effect of this agreement the Governor General in Council on behalf of the Honourable Company, hereby declares, that the British Government will never permit any power or state whatever to commit with impunity, any act of unprovoked hostility or aggression against the rights and territories of his Highness Rao Pundit Purdhaun Bahauder, but will at all times maintain and defend the same, in the same manner as the rights and territories of the Honourable Company, are now maintained and defended.

ARTICLE 3rd. With a view to fulfil this treaty of general defence and protection, his Highness Rao Pundit Purdhaun Bahauder agrees to receive, and the Honourable East India Company to furnish, a permanent subsidiary force of not less than six thousand regular native infantry, with the usual proportion of field pieces, and European artillery-men attached, and with the proper equipment of warlike stores and ammunition, which force is to be accordingly stationed, in perpetuity in his said Highness's territories.

ARTICLE 4th. For the regular payment of the whole expence of the said subsidiary force, his Highness Rao Pundit Purdhaun Bahauder hereby assigns and cedes in perpetuity to the Honourable East India Company, all the territories detailed in the schedule annexed to this treaty.

ARTICLE 5th. As it may be found that certain of the territories ceded by the foregoing article to the Honourable Company, may be inconvenient from their situation, his Highness Rao Pundit Purdhaun Bahauder, for the purpose of rendering the boundary line of the Honourable Company's possessions, a good and well defined one, agrees, that such exchanges of talooks or lands shall be made hereafter, on terms of a fair valuation of their respective revenues, as the completion of the said purpose may require, and it is agreed and covenanted, that the territories to be assigned and ceded to the Honourable Company by the 4th article, or in consequence of the exchange stipulated eventually in this article, shall be subject to the exclusive management and authority of the said company and of their officers.

ARTICLE 6th. Notwithstanding the total annual expence of the subsidiary force is estimated at 25 lacs of rupees, his said Highness hath agreed to cede by article 4th. lands estimated to yield annually the sum of 26 lacs of rupees, the additional lac being intended to meet possible deficiencies in the revenues of the said lands, and save the Honourable Company from loss.

ARTICLE 7th. After the conclusion of this treaty, and as soon as the British Resident shall signify to his Highness Rao Pundit Purdhaun Bahauder, that the honourable Company's officers are prepared to take charge of the districts ceded by article 4th. his Highness will immediately issue the necessary Purwannahs or orders to his officers to deliver over charge of the same to the officers of the honourable Company, and it is hereby agreed, and stipulated that all collections made by his Highness's officers, subsequently to the date of this treaty, and before the officers of the honourable Company shall have taken charge of the said districts, shall be carried to the credit of the honourable Company; and all claims to balance from the said districts, referring to the periods antecedent to the conclusion of this treaty, shall be considered null and void.

ARTICLE 8th. All forts situated within the districts to be ceded as aforesaid shall be delivered to the officers of the honourable Company with the said districts: and his Highness Rao Pundit Purdhaun Bahauder engages, that the said forts shall be delivered to the honourable Company without being injured or damaged, and with their equipment of ordnance stores and provisions.

ARTICLE 9th. Grain and all other articles of consumption, and provisions and all sorts of materials for wearing apparel together with the necessary numbers of cattle, horses and camels, required for the use of the subsidiary force shall be entirely exempted from duties, and the commanding officer, and officers of the said subsidiary force shall be treated in all respects in a manner suited to the dignity and greatness of both states. The subsidiary force will at all times be ready to execute services of importance—such as the protection of the person of his Highness, his heirs and successors, the overawing and chastisement of rebels, or exciters of disturbance in his Highness's dominions, and due correction of his subjects or dependants, who may withhold payment of the sircar's just claims; but it is not to be employed on trifling occasions, nor like sibundy to be stationed in the country to collect the revenues, nor against any of the principal branches of the Mahratta Empire, nor in levying contributions from Mahratta dependants in the manner of Moolkgeery.

ARTICLE 10th. Whereas much inconvenience has arisen from certain claims and demands of the Mahratta state, affecting the city of Surat, it is agreed, that a just calculation shall be made of the value of the said claims by his Highness Rao Pundit Purdhaun Bahauder and the government of Bombay; and in consequence of the intimate friendship now established between the contracting parties, his Highness Rao Pundit Purdhaun Bahauder agrees for himself, his heirs and successors, to relinquish for ever, all the rights, claims, and privileges of the Mahratta state affecting the said city of Surat, and all collections on that account shall cease and determine from the day on which this treaty shall be concluded; in consideration of which act of friendship, the Honourable East India Company agrees, that a piece of land yielding a sum equal to the estimated value of the said claims of the Mahratta state, shall be deducted from the districts ceded by article 4th. And on the same principle, and from similar considerations, his Highness further agrees, that the amount of the collections made for the Poonah state, under the title of Nagabundy, in the Purgunnahs of Chourassy and Chickly shall be ascertained, by an average taken from the receipts of a certain number of years, or by such other mode of calculation as may be determined on; and his said Highness doth further agree, for himself, his heirs, and successors, to relinquish for ever the Nagabundy collections aforesaid, and they shall accordingly cease from the conclusion of this treaty, and it is agreed and stipulated that a piece of land yielding a sum equal to the amount of the said Nagabundy collections, shall be deducted from the districts ceded by article 4th. in the same manner as stipulated in regard to the Choute of Surat.

ARTICLE 11th. Whereas it has been usual for his Highness Rao Pundit Purdhaun Bahauder to enlist and retain in his service Europeans of different countries, his said Highness hereby agrees and stipulates, that in the event of War breaking out between the English and any European nation, and of discovery being made that any European or Europeans in his service belonging to such nation at war with the English, shall have meditated injury towards the English, or have entered into intrigues hostile to their interest, such European or Europeans, so offending, shall be discharged by his said Highness, and not suffered to reside in his dominions.

ARTICLE 12th. Inasmuch as, by the present treaty, the contracting parties are bound in a general defensive alliance, for mutual defence and protection against all enemies, his Highness Rao Pundit Purdhaun Bahauder consequently engages, never to commit any act of personal hostility and aggression against his Highness the Nabob Asoph Jah Bahauder, or any of the Honourable Company's allies or dependants, or against any of the principal branches of the Mahratta Empire, or against any power whatever, and in the event of differences arising, whatever adjustment the Company's Government, weighing matters in the scale of truth and justice, may determine, shall meet with full approbation and acquiescence.

ARTICLE 13th. And whereas certain differences, referring to past transactions, are known to subsist between the Sirkar of his Highness Rao Pundit Purdhaun Bahauder and the Sirkar of his Highness the Nabob Asoph Jah Bahauder, and whereas an amicable adjustment of those differences must be highly desirable for the welfare and benefit of both the said Sirkars, his Highness Rao Pundit Purdhaun Bahauder with a view to the above end, agrees, and accordingly binds himself, his heirs, and successors, to fulfil and conform to the stipulations of the treaty of Mahr;

and his Highness Rao Pundit Purdhaun Bahauder further agrees, that on the basis of the fulfilment of the said treaty of Mahr, and of the claims of his Highness the Nabob Asoph Jah Bahauder, to be totally exempted from the payment of Choute, the Honourable Company's Government shall be entitled to arbitrate and determine all such points, as may be in doubt or difference between the Sirkars of their Highnesses above mentioned; and his Highness Rao Pundit Purdhaun Bahauder further agrees, that in the event of any differences arising between his government and that of his Highness the Nabob Asoph Jah Bahauder, at any future period, the particulars of such differences shall be communicated to the Honourable East India Company, before any act of hostility shall be committed on either side, and the said Honourable Company interposing their mediation, in a way suitable to rectitude, friendship, and union, and mindful of justice and established usage, shall apply themselves to the adjustment of all such differences, conformable to propriety and truth, and shall bring the parties to a right understanding. And it is further agreed, that whatever adjustment of any such differences the Company's Government, weighing things in the scale of truth and justice, shall determine, that determination shall, without hesitation or objection, meet with the full approbation and acquiescence of both parties. It is however agreed, that this stipulation shall not prevent any amicable negotiations which the Honourable Company and the Courts of Poonah and Hyderabad, respectively, may be desirous of opening, provided no such negotiation shall be carried on between any of the three parties, without full communication thereof to each other.

ARTICLE 14th. Whereas a treaty of friendship and alliance has been concluded between the Honourable Company and Rajah Anund Row Guickwar Bahauder, and whereas the said treaty was mediated and executed, without any intention that it should infringe any of the just rights or claims of his Highness Rao Pundit Purdhaun Bahauder affecting the Sirkars of the said Rajah, his said Highness adverting thereto, and also to the intimate alliance now established between the contracting parties, doth hereby formally acknowledge the existence of the said treaty between the Honourable Company and Rajah Anund Row Guickwar Bahauder; and inasmuch as, by reason of certain unfinished transactions, the conclusion of which has been suspended from time to time, various demands and papers of accounts are found to subsist between the Government of his Highness Row Pundit Purdhaun Bahauder and the Sirkar of the Rajah aforementioned, his said Highness, placing full reliance on the impartiality, truth, and justice of the British Government, doth hereby agree, that the said government shall examine into, and finally adjust, the said demands and papers of accounts; and his said Highness further stipulates and binds himself, his heirs, and successors, to abide by such adjustment as the British Government shall accordingly determine.

ARTICLE 15th. The contracting parties will employ all practicable means of conciliation to prevent the calamity of war, and for that purpose will, at all times, be ready to enter into amicable explanations with other states, and to cultivate and improve the general relations of peace and amity with all the powers of India, according to the true spirit and tenor of this defensive treaty. But if a war should unfortunately break out between the contracting parties and any other power whatever, then his Highness Row Pundit Purdhaun Bahauder engages, that with the reserve of two battalions of Sepoys, which are to remain near his Highness's person, the residue of the British subsidiary force, consisting of four battalions of Sepoys with their artillery, joined by six thousand infantry and ten thousand horse of his Highness's own troops, and making together an army of ten thousand infantry and ten thousand cavalry, with the requisite train of artillery and warlike stores of every kind, shall be immediately put in motion, for the purpose of opposing the enemy: and his Highness likewise engages to employ every further effort in his power, for the purpose of bringing into the field, as speedily as possible, the whole force which he may be able to supply from his dominions, with a view to the effectual prosecution and speedy termination of the said war. The Honourable Company, in the same manner, engage on their parts, in this case, to employ in active operations against the enemy, the largest force they may be able to furnish, over and above the said subsidiary force.

ARTICLE 16th. Whenever war shall appear probable, his Highness Rao Pundit Purdhaun Bahauder engages to collect as many Brinjaries as possible and to stow as much grain as may be practicable in his frontier garrisons.

ARTICLE 17th. As, by the present treaty, the union and friendship of the two states is so firmly connected, that they may be considered as one and the same, his Highness Rao Pundit Purdhaun

Bahauder engages neither to commence nor to pursue in future, any negotiations with any other power whatever, without giving previous notice, and entering into mutual consultation, with the Honourable East India Company's Government: and the Honourable Company's Government, on their parts, hereby declare that they have no manner of concern with any of his Highness's children, relations, subjects, or servants, with respect to whom his Highness is absolute.

ARTICLE 18th. Inasmuch as, by the present treaty of general defensive alliance, the ties of union are, with the blessing of God, so closely drawn, that the interests of the two states are become identified, it is further mutually agreed, that if disturbances shall at any time break out in the districts ceded to the Honourable Company by this agreement, his Highness Rao Pundit Purdhaun Bahauder shall permit such a proportion of the subsidiary troops, as may be requisite, to be employed in quelling the same within the said districts. If disturbances shall, at any time, break out in any part of his Highness's dominions contiguous to the Company's frontier, to which it might be inconvenient to detach any proportion of the subsidiary force, the British Government, in like manner, if required by his Highness Rao Pundit Purdhaun Bahauder, shall direct such proportion of the troops of the Company, as may be most conveniently stationed for the purpose, to assist in quelling the said disturbances within his Highness's dominions.

ARTICLE 19th. It is finally declared, that this treaty, which, according to the foregoing articles, is meant for the support and credit of his said Highness's Government, and to preserve it from loss and decline, shall last as long as the sun and moon shall endure.

Signed, sealed, and exchanged, at Bassein, the 31st of December, Anno Domini 1802, or the 5th of Ramzaun, Anno Higeræ 1217.

A true Copy,

B. CLOSE,
Resident at Poona.

Ratified by the Governor General in Council
11 February 1803.

Schedule of the Territories ceded in perpetuity, by His Highness Bajee Rao Ragonaut Pundit Purdhaun Bahauder to the Honourable English East India Company, agreeably to the fourth Article of the annexed Treaty.

1st. From the province of Guzerat and territories south thereof: Dundooka, together with Chooia, Komapoor, and Gogo,	1,05,000
Cambay, Choute, and Nassoor,	60,000
South of the Taptie. Purnair, 27,000; Bootseer, 6,200; Banwanny, 8,800; Balsur, 85,000; Parchole, 1,07,000; Soopa, 51,000; Sarbaun, 30,000; Wallow, 30,000; Bamdoo Kusbah, 7,900; Waunsda Choute, 7,000; Durumpoory do. 9,000; Surat do. 42,100; Customs, 83,000.	
Between the Taptie and Nerbuddah. Oolpah, 3,16,000; Hansood, 85,000; Octisier, 78,000; Nundary, 65,000. Total south of the Taptie, and between Taptie and Nerbuddah, 10,38,000. Deduct twenty per cent. on account of decrease of revenue, 2,07,600	8,30,400
Nahabundy of Chourassy and Chickley, 20,000; Phoolparra, Coomarria Cattergom, 5,000.	25,000
2d. From the territories near the Toombuddrah; Savanore, 26 Talooks, 10,22,838; from Bankapoor, 5,56,762.	15,79,600
Grand Total	26,00,000

Signed, sealed, and exchanged at Bassein,
31st December, Anno Domini 1802, or
the 5th Ramzan, Anno Higeræ 1217.

A true Copy, B. CLOSE.

Supplemental to the Treaty of Bassein, 1803.

A treaty, consisting of nineteen articles, was concluded at Bassein, between the Honourable English East-India Company Bahauder and his Highness the Paishwa Badjee Rao Ragonaut Pundit Purdhaun Bahauder. The following articles of engagement are now agreed on and settled, as supplemental to the said Treaty, by Lieutenant-Colonel Barry Close, on the part of the said Honourable Company, and Anund Rao Vakeel, on the part of the said Rao Pundit Purdhaun Bahauder, under full power and authority granted to them respectively for the purpose.

ARTICLE 1st. That of the territory ceded in perpetuity to the Honourable East India Company by the said treaty of Bassein, the country of Savenore, and Taalooks of Buncapoor, in the Carnatic, yielding an annual revenue of sixteen lacks of Rupees, shall be restored, in perpetuity, to the Sircar of the said Rao Pundit Purdhaun Bahauder.

ARTICLE 2nd. That of the territory ceded in perpetuity to the English East India Company by the treaty of Bassein, the Purgunnah of Oolpah, in Guzerat, yielding a revenue annually of three lacks and sixteen thousand Rupees, shall likewise be restored, in perpetuity, to the Sircar of the said Rao Pundit Purdhaun Bahauder, in order that it may be restored to Nursing Khundy Rao, who has served the Sircar with fidelity and attachment.

ARTICLE 3rd. That a regiment of native cavalry, of the same strength and complement as the cavalry regiments belonging to the Hyderabad subsidiary force, shall be added to the British Poona subsidiary force.

ARTICLE 4th. In the fifteenth article of the treaty of Bassein it is stipulated, that ten thousand cavalry and six thousand infantry, with a due proportion of ordnance and military stores, shall be furnished by the said Rao Pundit Purdhaun Bahauder, and in addition thereto, such further force as the Sircar of the said Rao Pundit Purdhaun Bahauder should be able to bring into the field. This stipulation is now annulled, and, in lieu thereof, it is agreed and covenanted, that in time of war the said Rao Pundit Purdhaun Bahauder shall appoint and furnish five thousand cavalry and three thousand infantry, with a due proportion of ordnance and military stores, and, in addition thereto, such further force as the said Rao Pundit Purdhaun Bahauder shall be able to bring into the field.

ARTICLE 5th. That a corps of Mahratta cavalry, amounting to five thousand, shall be maintained by the British Government during the present war, for the service of the Poona State, under the orders of the British Government; of which five thousand horse, two thousand shall serve with his Highness the Paishwa, and the remaining three thousand with the British army in the field; and in the said five thousand Mahratta cavalry are not to be included the Mahratta troops serving with the British army under the chieftains Bapoojee, Gunneis Punt Goklah, and Sudojee Rao Nimalcar, which troops shall continue to be subsisted at the charge of Rao Pundit Purdhaun Bahauder.

ARTICLE 6th. By the first and second articles of this agreement, territory, yielding an annual revenue of 19,16,000 rupees, is restored to the Sircar of Rao Pundit Purdhaun Bahauder; in lieu thereof, and for the purposes hereafter mentioned, the said Rao Pundit Purdhaun Bahauder agrees and stipulates to cede, in perpetuity, to the honourable English East India Company, from the province of Bundelcund, conquered for the Poona State by Ali Bahauder, territory yielding an estimated annual revenue of 36,16,000 rupees, agreeably to the following detail:

1. In lieu of the country of Savenore, and Taalooks of Buncapoor, in the Carnatic, and the Purgunnah of Oolpah, in Guzerat, a tract of territory, yielding an annual revenue of 19,16,000 rupees.

2. On account of the stated high value of Oolpah, a tract of territory, yielding an annual revenue of 50,000 rupees, in excess for that Purgunnah.

3. To bear the entire expence of the regiment of cavalry mentioned in article III., a tract of territory, yielding an annual revenue of 7,50,000 rupees.

4. To serve as an equivalent for the expence to be incurred by the British Government, in paying and maintaining, during the present war, the five thousand cavalry mentioned in article V., a tract of territory, yielding an annual revenue of 5,00,000 rupees, and lastly, a tract of territory, yielding an annual revenue of 4,00,000 rupees, to meet the extraordinary expence which the British Government must be subject to, in establishing its authority in Bundelcund, which is disturbed and ravaged by rebels, who must be subdued and punished.

Total ceded from Bundelcund 36,16,000 rupees.

ARTICLE 7th. The whole of the foregoing territory, ceded, as above, from Bundelcund to the honourable English East-India Company, shall be taken from those quarters of the province most contiguous to the British possessions, and in every respect most convenient for the British Government.

ARTICLE 8th. Inasmuch as the Purgunnah of Oolpah was particularly valuable to the honourable Company's Government, by reason of its proximity to the city of Surat, in the prosperity of which the British Government bears an anxious concern, it is accordingly agreed and stipulated, that the said Purgunnah of Oolpah shall be so managed and governed, at all times, by the Mahratta authority, as to conduce to the convenience of the said city, by attention to the rules of good neighbourhood, and the promotion of an amicable and commercial intercourse between the inhabitants of both sides. And inasmuch as the sovereignty of the river Taptee doth belong to the British Government, it is accordingly agreed and covenanted, that the Mahratta authority in Oolpah shall have no right or concern whatever in the wreck of any vessel that may be cast upon any part of the Oolpah territory, connecting with the said river Taptee, but be bound, in the event of any such wreck, to render the vessel all practicable aid, for which the parties assisting shall be entitled to receive from the owners of the wreck a just and reasonable compensation.

Signed, sealed, and exchanged, at Poona,
the 16th December, Anno Domini 1803,
or the 1st Ramzaun, Anno Higeræ 1218.
Ratified by the Governor General in Council, the
7th January, 1804.

2. POLICY OF THE TREATY OF BASSEIN.

38. The Honourable G. H. Barlow, Esq. to the Marquess Wellesley.

Approval of the policy of the Treaty.

(Private.) July 12, 1803.

My Lord,

I do myself the honour of enclosing the draft of a note to your Excellency, which I had prepared this morning. I trust you will excuse my sending it in an almost illegible state, and on scraps of paper. I had intended to copy it fair, but it has extended to a greater length than I had expected; and not being very well, I do not feel myself quite equal to the task. In its present state, it will, I trust, answer equally well the purpose of conveying to your Excellency what has occurred to me on the subject of the question discussed yesterday.

I have the honour to be, with the highest respect,
your Excellency's most faithful, and obedient servant,
G. H. BARLOW.

(Enclosure.)

Conceiving it may be satisfactory to your Lordship to know what has occurred to me on a deliberate consideration of the important question discussed yesterday, I shall do myself the honour of stating the result. No doubt was entertained, as far as related to the question of right and justice, that the British Government was at full liberty to prosecute the present plan of measures, or to declare the alliance with the Peishwa void. If any difficulty existed with regard to this branch of the question, it was to assign reasons for declaring the alliance at an end without hazarding an impeachment of our good faith.

It only remained, therefore, to determine whether good policy required our persevering or withdrawing, under the unexpected circumstances of the total inability of the Peishwa to fulfil his part of the engagements, of the probability of hostilities with France, of the part taken by the Rajah of Berar, and the confederacy formed between Scindiah, the Rajah of Berar, and Holkar, of the certainty of the approaching dissolution of the Nizam, and of the nature of the orders received from England.

If we abandon the alliance, and withdraw our forces, (whatever may be the reasons we may assign for the measure,) no other construction will be given, both by friends and enemies, to this change of policy but this; that we were at least doubtful of the success of the impending military operations. They will never believe that in the present advanced stage of the business, and after all the declarations which have been made by our ministers at the Mahratta courts, that we should abandon a plan which has been pursued with unremitting perseverance for a course of years, and the advantages of which to our interests are so obvious, but from an apprehension of our inability to repel the opposition which has been raised to the consolidation of our alliance with the Peishwa. What will be the effect of this impression on the minds of our friends and enemies? Our friends will no longer entertain their present implicit confidence in our power and protection, and our enemies will make all India resound with shouts of triumph at our having yielded the field to them. The mischievous consequences which must be produced by this change in the sentiments of the states of India with respect to the British power, cannot be calculated.

But is it certain, in the event of our withdrawing our forces, that we should be allowed to retain the countries ceded to us by the Peishwa to indemnify us for the expense of the measures undertaken for his support? Is it not to be apprehended that the power which might succeed in usurping the authority of the Poonah Government, would endeavour to compel us to relinquish those countries, by committing continued depredations in them, in the confidence that the same motives which induced us to avoid war when our armies were in the field, and in the most advantageous positions, would influence us still more strongly, when we had to collect those armies again, and which the operations of the most successful campaign could not be expected to place in their present advantageous positions? There is no conjecturing to what lengths the presumptuous character of the Mahrattas might impel them under such circumstances. Thus we might be compelled to go to war under the disadvantages of loss of national character, and of limited means, and probably after having afforded to the French an opportunity of connecting themselves as auxiliaries with some of the Mahratta states.

Should this be the result, the Government would incur a heavy load of responsibility in England. Its conduct would be first censured for engaging in the alliance, next, for withdrawing from it, and lastly, for placing itself in a situation which reduced it to the alternative of engaging in a war under the disadvantages above stated, or of sacrificing the national character by relinquishing the retained territories.

With respect to the expected death of the Nizam, supposing the Mahrattas, or any of the disaffected members of the Nizam's family, to have it in contemplation to take advantage of that event to destroy our connection with the Court of Hyderabad, our armies in the Deccan could not be more favourably stationed than they are at present for the purpose of frustrating any such designs. If such designs are entertained, I am persuaded it would have been your Lordship's duty to have called the same armies into the field, supposing no alliance had been concluded with the Peishwa.

With respect to the French, supposing the present questions in Europe not to lead to an immediate rupture, we are now certain that the whole course of their policy has for its object the subversion of the British empire in India, and that at no distant period of time they will put their plans into execution. It is absolutely necessary for the defeat of these designs, that no native state should be left to exist in India, which is not upheld by the British power, or the political conduct of which is not under its absolute control. The restoration of the head of the Mahratta empire to his Government through the influence of the British power, in fact, has placed all the remaining states of India in this dependent relation to the British Government. If the alliance with the Peishwa is maintained, its natural and necessary operations would in the course of time reduce Scindiah (the power which may already be said to be in the interests of France) and the Rajah of Berar, to a state of dependence upon the Peishwa, and consequently upon the British power, even if they had acquiesced in the treaty of Bassein. But their unjust opposition to this treaty affords us an opportunity of at once reducing their power to a state that will remove every obstacle to the consolidation of the alliance with the Peishwa, and to the attainment of all its advantages. When can we hope for another opportunity equally favourable, or (under all the probable consequences of withdrawing from the alliance,) when can we hope to have all India again at our command? With respect to the chiefs combined against us, have we any reasonable ground to apprehend that we shall not prevail in the contest? The Guicowar state (always considered to form a considerable part of the strength of the Mahratta empire,) is actively employed in our support. The Peishwa, although unable from imbecility of character, to command with effect the resources at his disposal, is with us. We have the aid and countenance of his authority, and his territories to the south of the Godavery friendly to our cause, at least more so than to that of our enemies. Scindiah, therefore, is the only chief who possesses the means of making any serious opposition. We know that the Rajah of Berar possesses neither military knowledge nor military resources. We also know that Holkar's army consists of a body of plunderers, and that he has no means of maintaining a contest of any duration. Our army, well equipped, has established itself within the heart of the dominions of these chiefs, and within a few marches of their camp, where they are collected without money, resources, or provisions, and where there is every prospect we shall destroy or disperse their whole force at one blow. It is scarcely possible that their military power could be placed in circumstances more favourable for our effecting its destruction.

With respect to the solicitude expressed in England for carrying into effect the plan for paying off the debt in the next six years, we can estimate with tolerable accuracy to what degree the execution of that plan is likely to be interrupted by a perseverance in the present course of measures in the Mahratta empire. This interruption is likely to be less in extent and duration than that which may be expected from abandoning the alliance with the Peishwa, if there is any foundation for the conjectures which I have stated as to the probable consequences of that measure. Every year would probably produce some of those calamities which would inevitably attend our declining power and influence, and we cannot conjecture what would be our situation at the expiration of six years. On the other hand, if we persevere in the present measures, and succeed, we are certain, not only that the existing debt, with the addition to it which may be occasioned by the prosecution of the present measures, will be extinguished within the expected time, but that the British power will be established throughout India, in prosperity, glory, and security.

The conviction of the justice and wisdom of the line of policy which your Excellency has pursued with respect to the Mahratta empire, is more strongly impressed on my mind in proportion as I consider it in all its relations. I am confident that the line of policy is entitled to this character, whether considered with reference to the discharge of the debt, to the augmentation of the investment, or the other objects which the authorities in England have in view, to the true interests of the Mahratta chiefs, to the happiness of the millions of wretched people who inhabit the countries subjected to their power, to the exclusion of the French, to the honour and reputation of our national character, or to the stability of the British empire in India.

39. Lord Castlereagh, President of the Board of Controul; to the Marquess Wellesley.

Strictures on the Policy of the Treaty.

(Most Secret.)

Whitehall, March 4th, 1804.

My dear Lord,

The Bombay letters of the 28th July, announcing the probability of a rupture with the Mahrattas, induced me to read over carefully our negotiations with the Court of Poonah, for a series of years, which from a variety of other important subjects pressing upon my attention, I had till then omitted to do.

The outline of the opinion I have been led to form upon this subject will be conveyed to your Lordship in a despatch through the Secret Committee, but I should not feel satisfied in differing from your Lordship on some points of policy, as connected with the late treaty, if I did not put you in possession of the grounds upon which my opinions are founded; I am induced therefore without attempting to throw the substance into the form of a letter, to send you without reserve, my sentiments in the precise form in which they were first thrown together, trusting to their being not less acceptable to your Lordship so conveyed, than if transmitted in a more formal shape.

I have the honour to be,
My dear Lord, with great regard,
Your faithful and obedient servant,
CASTLEREAGH.

[*Enclosure in Lord Castlereagh's letter to the Marquess Wellesley of the 4th of March*, 1804.]

The question now depending between the British power and the Mahrattas is one of great difficulty and importance.

What directions it may be expedient ultimately to give from home must depend on the precise issue of the present discussions, whatever might have been originally wise as a rule of conduct may now require modification, with reference to *events*, to *engagements*, and to the *collateral effects* to be apprehended from any particular course we may take.

The next advices from India will probably ascertain whether the discussions have ended in actual war; in a jealous truce, still requiring the presence of a British army; or, in that apparent acquiescence on the part of the Mahrattas, which may lead the Governor-General to consider that the professed objects of the treaty have been accomplished, and induce him to return the troops (with the exception of the subsidizing force) to their respective cantonments.

It may be expedient in the meantime to examine—1st. The abstract policy of what has been aimed at. 2ndly. How far it has been judiciously pursued; and 3dly. Whether the Governor-General has exceeded his legal authority, or gone beyond the instructions, under which, if his own authority were inadequate, his powers were derived.

1st. As to the policy of a connexion with the Mahrattas:

In considering this question it is material to *ascertain precisely* what the *nature* of the connexion is, at which we have aimed. The professed end in view is, a *defensive alliance* and *guarantee* connecting the Mahrattas with the Nizam and the Company, and through that league *preserving the peace* of *India*.

Although the apprehension of remote danger from French influence, acting through the Mahratta confederacy, is stated as a collateral object to be thus provided against, yet the main policy of the system, as relied upon, is, its *pacific tendency*.

On this ground it must principally be tried, the British power in India is too firmly consolidated at this moment, and the prospect of attack from any quarter too remote to justify us in prudence in risking a war, with a view of providing against a danger merely speculative.

The British empire in India may be considered (including allies and dependents) as comprehending nearly every thing in Hindostan (the Mahratta possessions excepted). In addition to our old possessions in Bengal, and on the coast, recently strengthened by the treaties which have placed the whole of the Carnatic, and a large proportion of Oude under our immediate administration, we have by two wars, equally just and successful, bound up the entire of Mysore in our dominions, and by a negotiation conducted with great ability and wisely undertaken, expelled French influence from Hyderabad, and connected the Nizam indissolubly with our interests.

Whatever questions may have been hitherto raised *on the justice* of our conduct towards certain dependent states, upon the *policy* of our measures (always assuming them to be founded in justice) so far as concerns the consolidation of our authority in the Carnatic, in Tanjore, and in Oude, the reduction of the power of Tippoo, and the intimate connexion established with the Nizam, no well founded doubt can be entertained.

Considering this as the well established sphere at this day of the British power in India, the next step towards a close connexion with another power, and that power necessarily involved in the complicated relations of the Mahratta confederacy, is a question of critical and delicate policy.

The idea upon which the treaty of Bassein was concluded, seems originally to have arisen out of, and to have been founded upon the connexion subsisting, previously to the conquest of Mysore, between the Company, the Mahrattas and the Nizam, by the treaty concluded 1790, at Poonah.

The object of this league was to watch and guard against the power of Tippoo. The treaty was defective, inasmuch as it did not specify, except with respect to the war then existing, the amount of force which the allies were bound to furnish to each other; nor did it *in terms* bind their heirs and successors, which led to cavils on the part of the Peishwa.

It gave us however, in Lord Cornwallis's war ending in 1792, the advantage of considerable succours both from the Nizam and the Peishwa against Tippoo.

Upon the peace of Seringapatam, Hurry Punt pressed Lord Cornwallis to let the Peishwa subsidize in future a corps of British troops in like manner as the Nizam then did. Whether he was so authorized by the Peishwa is not known.

Lord Cornwallis, although the Mahratta General urged it strongly (stating that to refuse was acting towards them with less friendship than towards the Nizam) declined the proposal; thinking it hazardous to mix ourselves in the unsettled policy of the Mahratta states, and that the principles, upon which it had been thought wise to connect ourselves with the Nizam (regard being had to the resources and position of his dominions, and also to the hazard of his being thrown into the hands of Tippoo, if not connected with the Company) did not apply to the state of Poonah; neither did he at that time think it essential to our general security, having materially reduced the power of Tippoo, to aim at establishing a commanding influence at Poonah.

Whether an acquiescence in Hurry Punt's proposal would have guarded against the decay of the Peishwa's power, which afterwards happened, it is difficult now to determine; but we find that, previously to the war of 1798-9 against Tippoo, both the Peishwa and the Nizam were so reduced in authority, the former by the ascendancy of Scindiah; the latter by a strong French faction in his army, as to render it very little probable, that the Company, in the event of a rupture with Tippoo, could hope to derive any efficient aid from the alliance.

The object of the Company was then to strengthen its allies, in order that they might be in a situation to fulfil their engagements; Scindiah's purpose was to weaken the Peishwa, and to get the power at Poonah into his own hands. Hence arose a jealousy between Scindiah and the Company, which produced a proportionate union of interest between him and Tippoo. The number of French officers in the armies of Scindiah, of Tippoo, and of the Nizam, rendered the danger very serious of a formidable combination of the native powers against us supported by France.

In this state of things, Lord Wellesley wisely determined to use every expedient to revive our influence and authority both at the courts of Poonah and Hyderabad. A British force was offered the Peishwa to protect his person and re-establish his government, and an augmentation of the subsidiary force was proposed to the Nizam.

Under a variety of pretences, evidently resulting from a jealousy of our power, as well as that of Scindiah, our offer was declined by the Peishwa. What then occurred is noticed here principally to mark *the jealousy* which even then disinclined the Peishwa to place himself in our hands, as well as to point out the strong defensive policy, which warranted us to risk much for the purpose of giving vigour and consistency to the only alliance, on which we could reckon, against the hostile confederacy with which we were threatened.

The result was, that we derived no support from the Mahrattas in the last Mysore war; our connection with the Nizam was improved, the French force in his Highness's service finally destroyed, and a commanding British corps established in its room.

The termination of the war in the conquest of Mysore, and the absolute extinction of French influence in that quarter of India, as well as at Hyderabad, placed the Mahratta question entirely on new grounds.

Hitherto, a connection with the Mahrattas had been sought as a defence against Tippoo and the French influence generally. The fall of Tippoo and the extinction of the French party in Mysore and Hyderabad, leaving only what was to be found in Scindiah's army, as any object of jealousy, put an end to the importance as a means of necessary and immediate security of a connection with the Mahrattas.

From this time it could not be argued to be of *pressing necessity.* The most that could be contended for was, its being desirable on grounds of general expediency, and as tending to guard against remote and contingent dangers, we were certainly justified in risking less to accomplish it.

It was reasonable also to suppose, that in proportion as our power had been increased and consolidated, and as that of Tippoo was absolutely extinguished, the Mahrattas would entertain additional jealousy of any subsidiary connection with us.

We find accordingly, after the peace, that upon the Peishwa being invited to accede to the treaty of Hyderabad, upon which condition we should have deemed him entitled to a certain share in the conquered territories, he declined the proposal evidently from indisposition to receive a British force within his dominions.

Between that period and the treaty of Bassein, several attempts were made by us to induce him to enter into subsidiary engagements with us. The same was proposed to the Rajah of

Berar, and an opening left in the treaty of Hyderabad of 1800, for Scindiah to accede on certain terms; but the connection was declined by all.

The Peishwa, when most oppressed and in danger from Scindiah, proceeded considerable lengths in entertaining the proposition of a subsidiary alliance, but always resisted the idea of the subsidiary force being stationed *within his dominions.* Even with this qualification, our connection was an alternative which the Peishwa never latterly shewed any disposition to adopt, but under the pressure of extreme embarrassment, and it is even doubtful whether he was ever really sincere in the propositions he made, as his system invariably was to play off Scindiah and us against each other, and his overtures were generally accompanied by some stipulation which he had reason to suppose would not be acceded to by the Governor-General.

If the connection, after the fall of Tippoo, became of less pressing necessity, doubts may be entertained of the policy of appearing to pursue the object with such unremitting anxiety. It will be necessary hereafter to examine under what circumstances a Mahratta alliance would or would not be desirable; but if the early conclusion of it was not of urgent importance to our immediate security, it might perhaps have been more successfully accomplished under a system of *more reserve* on our part.

The eagerness with which we appeared to press our connection upon all the leading states in succession, might naturally lead them to apprehend that we meant more than we avowed, that our object was ultimately to be masters instead of allies, and that, having obtained either possession of, or absolute influence over every state, except the Mahrattas, with whom we had been in connection, our object was to obtain a similar influence over *their* councils.

Under whatever estimate of our views it may have been formed, the fact is indisputable, that a general repugnance to the British connection on the terms proposed universally prevailed amongst the great Mahratta powers. It was avoided by all as long as they had any choice. It was only embraced by the Peishwa, when an exile from his dominions; and the jealousy of it was such as to have since led Holkar and Scindiah to forget their animosities, and to appear disposed to league with the Rajah of Berar against the Company and the Peishwa. How long the Peishwa will continue faithful to engagements which were contracted from necessity and not from choice, in opposition to the other Mahratta states, is yet to be seen.

The practical question to be considered is, whether an alliance formed under such circumstances can rest upon any other foundation than mere force, and if not, whether the means by which it is to be upheld, are not destructive of its professed advantages.

Supposing Holkar, Scindiah, and the Rajah of Berar adverse, and the Peishwa acquiescent, but in his heart not cordially satisfied, can we expect that the subsidiary force alone will enable us to maintain our influence at Poonah?

If such be the *unqualified feeling* of the Mahratta states to a connection with us upon the principles on which the present has been formed, unless we are prepared to establish ourselves by conquest in that quarter of India, it seems necessary either to abandon the connection (if it can be abandoned consistent with a due regard to our engagements), or to modify it (should such be practicable) so as to reconcile at least a proportion of the Mahratta states.

It appears hopeless to attempt to govern the Mahratta empire through a feeble and perhaps disaffected Peishwa. The military power of the state of Poonah is at present inconsiderable.

It may be said the military power of the Peishwa under our protection may be consolidated and restored, and other states may be gradually reconciled to the alliance. Both these results may be possible; but the true question is, whether they are probable in such a degree, and whether they are likely to occur within such a reasonable period of time, and to be accomplished with so little hazard of expence as to make it politic to persevere against present opposing difficulties? Is the future effect likely to add so much to our prospects in point of security and tranquillity as to counterbalance the immediate inconveniences of war with the several Mahratta powers?

In examining this, the motive to alliance must be reverted to. Whatever may be the disposition amongst the Mahratta states to plunder each other, they have hitherto respected our territory. They have seldom even levied contributions on the Nizam, notwithstanding the disputed claims for Choute, &c. since his close connection with us.

The Mahrattas have never in any instance commenced hostilities against us. When, by taking part in their internal disputes we have been at war with any of the Mahratta states, they have always availed themselves of the first opening for peace, and have shewn forbearance and humanity to a British army, more than once, when in difficulty. So far then as past experience goes, there seems no special ground to apprehend future danger from the Mahrattas. The French officers in Scindiah's army are just objects of jealousy, and their mixing themselves in the affairs of the native powers must be watched, and be matter of alarm in proportion to the degree in which it takes place, and as those states are *near* to, or *remote* from our possessions; but this alone cannot render the alliance prudent, nor is this danger at present of a magnitude to call for the adoption of a system, otherwise of dubious policy.

As far as the Mahratta interests are concerned, what motive can they have in acquiescing in the ostensible head of their empire being placed in our hands?

Whatever we may hold out to reconcile the Peishwa to the alliance, and however we may profess to respect his independence in the management of his own internal affairs, we cannot deny that in fact as well as in appearance, whilst a British army is at Poonah, he can be considered in no other light than as *politically dependent on us.*

The Mahratta contentions between the leading states have been chiefly for influence at Poonah. To obtain this, Holkar attacked Scindiah. Having been deprived of this, Scindiah abandoned the Peishwa, and seems prepared to join his greatest enemy. The same motives which before opposed them to each other now oppose them both to us, and the Berar Rajah, perhaps with views to supplant the Peishwa, and with common feelings of jealousy, joins the confederacy.

What will reconcile them to a different course? To talk to them of the advantage of our guarantee for preserving the peace of Hindostan, assumes that the genius of their government is *industrious* and *pacific*, instead of being *predatory* and *warlike;* nor is it to be expected that independent states, especially of the description in question, can feel any disposition to make us, or any other great power, an arbiter of their destiny.

We not only place the Peishwa as a prey out of their reach, but we declare our purpose is to prevent them from plundering each other. They wish to be unrestrained in carrying their arms wherever they can derive advantage. Temporary distress may make them in their turn accept our support. Were it given as a temporary assistance it would frequently *be sought* for, and, as far as their means would go, *paid for;* but when it is to be given *permanently*, or not at all, it will only be accepted when no other resource remains. It will be avoided by each state exempt from the pressure, when the danger is gone by it will be disrelished by the state which has submitted to it, and ultimately we must either alter the genius of the various states, or rely upon our arms alone for the preservation of our authority.

To aim at a connection with the Mahratta powers on these grounds is, to say the least, extremely hazardous. It is evidently against the grain. It may be difficult and expensive to be established, not less so to be maintained, and as it must, when accomplished, rest *on our authority and arms,* rather than the disposition of our allies, it must practically operate as an extension of our own dominions.

Such a result we disavow as our object. In principle, as well as in policy, we are bound by the laws of the land to abstain from it, and it certainly would be a hazardous project to embark in the management of this half-civilized people, in addition to the widely extended empire of which we are now possessed. If we are not prepared to contemplate such a purpose, we should avoid being gradually led into a course of measures, the tendency of which leads to such a result as their natural consequence.

Is there then no connection with any of the Mahratta states, at which in policy we should aim?

It does not follow because an alliance, which places a British force in immediate contact with a weak Mahratta power, and that power the supreme head of the empire, in opposition to the will of all the stronger states, is unwise and dangerous, that no relation can be established between the British power and certain states of that empire, which may have a tendency to protect our interests against such dangers as might otherwise arise *from*, or operate *through*, that confederacy.

It may, however, be asserted, that to be either safe or useful, it must be formed on a broader basis than the present, and as the British power, from its magnitude, must now have become a more natural object of jealousy to the Mahratta states than any other, it is not probable that any considerable portion of the Mahratta confederacy will be disposed to connect themselves with us, unless we can present to them that connection in a shape less inconsistent with their natural propensities and independence than the late treaty.

When jealousy is once strongly aroused, any arrangement is become of more difficulty. Whether it might have been feasible, must remain matter of speculation, but I can conceive, if Holkar and Scindiah had been suffered to reduce each other, before a treaty had been proposed to the Peishwa, that a broader connection might have been formed; especially if the introduction of the British force to be subsidized *into the dominions* of our allies had not been made a *sine quâ non.*

It may be said, if the treaty had not been pushed with the Peishwa when at Bassein, he might have refused it afterwards; possibly so; but it may be doubted whether the treaty so obtained was a benefit.

The benefit as well as the necessity of a Mahratta connection has for the last four years been in my conception always overrated. The importance of not taking the whole of the burthen upon ourselves of restoring the Peishwa, appears to have been strongly felt by Lord Wellesley, and he accordingly after the conclusion of the treaty wished to hold back, and leave Holkar and Scindiah to weaken and reduce each other; but as the treaty could not be concealed from Scindiah and the other powers, the success of this course depended upon their sentiments with respect to the treaty itself. Our troops, however, were moved forward by Lord Clive's orders, before the result could be distinctly ascertained.

Perhaps our safest line would have been to have received the Peishwa hospitably, to have professed a disposition to assist the other Mahratta powers in repressing Holkar's rebellion, and restoring the Peishwa to the Musnud, provided we found his Highness and his allies were disposed to connect themselves in interest with us.

Had we remained with our army on the frontiers, pledged to neither party, and in a position to assist either, our aid must have been an object of competition to both.

Neither had any claim upon us, and consequently neither (whatever might be our opinion of the merits of their cause) had any right to expect our assistance without an equivalent. In postponing any negociation with the Peishwa, till he could treat in conjunction with Scindiah, we should have been able more correctly to estimate the grounds upon which we were proceeding.

It is probable the Peishwa and Scindiah united, could not have dislodged Holkar from Poonah without our aid. If so, it lay upon them to offer terms to us. But then, in treating with the Peishwa and Scindiah conjointly, we left the Peishwa in Scindiah's hands as before. And why not? Our motive for interference was not any principle of attachment to the Peishwa or any claim he had upon us. It was with a view of establishing an influence in the Mahratta empire, calculated to improve our general security and preserve the tranquillity of India. This could alone be effectually accomplished by a substantial and not a nominal connection, which Scindiah and the Peishwa united might amount to, but not the Peishwa singly.

The mistake appears to have been, the following up too strictly the policy acted upon before the fall of Tippoo. Then we were obliged to endeavour to take the Peishwa out of Scindiah's hands, inasmuch as the latter, with a view of strengthening himself at Poonah, leant to Tippoo and against us. Had we on the present occasion not manifested any particular jealousy of Scindiah, but expressed a willingness to *receive proposals* for connecting ourselves *with both*, and limited our views to what would *strengthen us*, without either *in appearance* or *in fact* making them instruments in our hands, I see no reason (if practicable at all) why a treaty with both might not have been made.

The main advantage of the treaty of Bassein I take to be, the increased footing it gives us in the Guzerat. Our position at Poonah, abstractedly considered, appears to me more calculated to weaken our influence over the other states than to strengthen us by the power to be found there, and I should (as at present informed) much prefer having the subsidiary force stationed at certain positions within our own territories than stationed in those of our ally.

Had we concluded subsidiary engagements with both the Peishwa and Scindiah, obtaining the Iaidad as now in the quarter of Guzerat, the troops never to be moved into the territories of either state, except *upon requisition*, we should have obtained an increase of force and territory in our weakest quarter. The right to call for this force would have raised these states in the scale of the Mahratta powers, without exposing them to our unsolicited interference, and as all our subsidiary engagements have been made with a reserve as to the application of the troops against certain powers named, we should have possessed a salutary influence in the councils of our allies not incompatible with their independence.

The history of our own connections in India affords instances of both descriptions of alliances. By the treaty of 1768 with the Nizam, explained by Lord Cornwallis's letter in 1789, we were bound to furnish to his Highness two battalions of Sepoys, and six pieces of cannon, when called upon so to do, but not otherwise. The treaty of 1798 encreased the subsidiary force to six battalions, and that of 1800 to eight battalions, to be *stationed within* the Nizam's *dominions.*

The former principle of connexion appears most suited to *remote* and *independent* states. The latter to a power which circumstances have nearly incorporated in policy and interest with our own.

The former appears to me to be alone applicable to any portion of the Mahratta empire, consideration being had to its composition and nature, and also to *our position* with respect to it. The latter under the circumstances was wisely applied to the Nizam, substituting British in the room of French influence, and throwing the shield of our authority over that state, incapable in itself of preserving its territories against the continual incursions of the Mahrattas.

It may be said, had the Peishwa and Scindiah met, they would have declined all permanent connection with us. Supposing this to have been the case, there were other courses open to us, without supporting an usurper in opposition to the Peishwa. We might either in conjunction with the Rajah of Berar have offered a *disinterested mediation*, and thereby dispelled much of the alarm that had grown up, as to *our* views; or, if we preferred co-operating with Scindiah in the restoration of the Peishwa without any permanent alliance, we might have obtained, I have no doubt, an ample territorial indemnity in the quarter of Guzerat for our *services*, as well as our *expences.* At all events, in preserving an army of observation on the frontier, and not mixing ourselves in Mahratta politics, except upon sure grounds, if we gained no more than securing our own territory, as well as that of our ally the Nizam from insult, we escaped war, whilst the Mahratta powers wasted their strength.

I cannot but doubt the policy of our making from the outset the Peishwa our only, or even our main object. The determination to take him out of the hands of Scindiah was, from the first apparent, if not avowed; and from that moment, if Scindiah could save himself by negociation with his opponents, he had every inducement to throw himself into the scale against us.

His doing so, rendered our success without a war extremely

doubtful, and more than any other circumstance rendered the Peishwa's fidelity to our alliance precarious.

It remains to be considered whether, as has been suggested, the Governor-General has exceeded his powers, and lastly, what instructions should now be given from hence for the future regulation of his conduct.

The first question depends on his powers.—1st. Under the 42nd section of the act of 1793. 2ndly. Under his instructions from home of the 10th of September 1800, and 4th of December of the same year.

The law clearly gives him no authority to conclude any treaty binding the Company to guarantee the territories of any state, except that state shall at the same time bind itself to support the Company in a war then actually existing, or in the case of preparations then making for war against the Company. It has not been alledged that Holkar, when this treaty was made, had either committed, or meditated hostilities against us or our *allies;* the treaty of Bassein was therefore clearly not within the scope of the 42nd clause.

The next question is under his instructions. The instructions were necessarily general. The precise course pursued in acting upon them may in policy be questioned, but I think the Governor-General, as far as powers go, is clearly borne out in what he has done, regard being had to the tenor of those instructions, coupled with the recorded proceedings of his negotiations at the court of Poonah, of which the Government at home were from time to time put in possession, and which when acquiesced in, might be fairly considered by him as approved of, and consequently illustrative of those orders.

The orders specifically approved of a subsidiary treaty with the Peishwa similar to that of the Nizam.

They enjoined a large subsidiary force as indispensable, and assumed that the Peishwa must *tacitly renounce his independence.*

In the letter of the 4th of December it is stated, that if by any arrangement *not likely to lead to hostilities*, the Peishwa could be relieved from the influence of Scindiah, it would be highly desirable, &c. &c.

In that of the 10th of September, the Governor-General's plan for establishing a subsidiary force at Poonah is approved of. *Caution* is recommended in *renewing* the *negotiation*, except at the instance of the court of Poonah, or at a *crisis*, when there can be no doubt of the proposition being accepted.

Now, although the alliance under a *reasonable apprehension of hostilities* is not authorized, yet it would be too much to suppose that it could be concluded without *any risk* being incurred, particularly as it was declared and clearly understood, that nothing but the *last necessity* would induce the Peishwa to sign such a treaty, and the object being to dispossess Scindiah of his influence at Poonah, his opposition could not but be expected.

In July 1800, the Peishwa fearing that his person might be seized by Scindiah, vested certain persons with the power of signing a treaty for him.

In this event of the flight or seizure of the Peishwa, Lord Wellesley ordered the Resident to conclude a subsidiary treaty with him, or those authorized on his part, also the British troops to occupy the Mahratta districts south of the Kistna.

This was a stronger case of risk than the present, as Scindiah then must have been forcibly driven from Poonah, whereas the state of his own affairs lately afforded some prospect of his cooperation, and the chance of a rupture was more with Holkar an adventurer than with the established feudatories of the Mahratta empire.

Early in May of the same year, Lord Wellesley authorized the Resident at Poonah to conclude a secret treaty with the Peishwa, in which the Company were to engage to *compel Scindiah* to remove from the Deccan, and also to bind themselves to maintain the Peishwa *in his just rights and authority* over that chief, and over the other acknowledged feudatories of the empire, the Nizam and Rajah of Berar, to be at liberty to accede.

The latter is even a stronger proceeding. In both these cases Scindiah was to be necessarily opposed. In the latter absolutely forced. Whereas previously to the treaty of Bassein our interference was solicited by all parties.

It is not here the question whether the negotiation was judiciously conducted, or whether the treaty in itself was the most advisable one that could have been framed under the circumstances. It is only meant in this part of the argument to state, that in the position wherein the Mahratta states then were placed with relation to each other, no *crisis* could have been found more propitious to the formation of a connexion if under any circumstances it were attainable.

It is also contended, that under the words of his instructions and the mode in which he had acted under them on the above occasions with the acquiescence of the Government at home Lord Wellesley might reasonably consider himself as authorized to pursue the course he took.

Whatever therefore there may be to criticize in respect to the policy aimed at, or the management of the negotiations, it cannot well be contended that Lord Wellesley's conduct should be called in question, as having acted in breach of the instructions sent him.

Before we proceed to apply the principles heretofore laid down to the existing case, or to consider what orders it may be advisable to send from hence, it is material to mark, that the objections above-stated are not against any and every description of Mahratta connexion but against that which gives us the Peishwa alone, whilst it commits us in hostility with the three greatest military powers of the empire.

It is also considered that no alliance which does not give us a majority of the preponderating chiefs of the confederacy in cordial connexion with us can in the long run prove of advantage, inasmuch as such an alliance will occasion frequent recurrence to arms, and place the discontented states more in a situation to be tampered with by France.

That there is no reason, certainly none from experience, to suppose an alliance can ever be formed with the Mahrattas by a European power on principles destructive of the independence of any leading state; but more especially of the ostensible head of the Mahratta confederacy, without making all the other powers enemies, and even occasioning the fidelity of the allied state to be precarious.

That the Mahratta confederacy, though the power of the Peishwa is imperfectly defined, and feebly maintained, is yet so far a body politic as to make the acts of each member a matter of common concern to all.

That Lord Wellesley when he looked to treat secretly for the expulsion of Scindiah from Poonah in terms recognized a paramount power to reside in the Peishwa over Scindiah and the other Mahratta chieftains. This paramount authority as head of the empire, and not his individual strength, could never have *suggested the policy* of looking principally to the Peishwa's connexion.

If that be the case, it is impossible to contend that the Peishwa can treat and act as a separate and independent state; and whilst he retains and asserts his authority over the Mahratta feudatories, submit himself in the management of his external concerns in a great degree to a foreign power. If he does so act, he must do it at his peril, and the other states will naturally consider how those acts are likely to affect their security or independence.

An alliance with the Peishwa and Scindiah jointly under the circumstances which took place subsequent to the defeat of the confederate forces before Poonah, perhaps might have been formed upon the basis of stationing the subsidiary force within our own territories, liable to be called on under certain conditions by each power in proportion as it contributed the funds towards its maintenance and support, not restricting either to a communication with us, before he *concluded any treaty;* for such stipulation where it is not *reciprocal*, is upon the face of it an abrogation of independence; but trusting *that* and every other question which might touch our interests to the legitimate influence gradually arising out of a connexion framed with a view to support and not extinguish the authority of the other contracting party, and also to the known and acknowledged power of the British arms, which it could never be their wish or their interest to provoke.

If an alliance framed on principles compatible with the feelings of a large proportion of that empire could not be formed under the circumstances which then prevailed, when so many parties had the strongest motives for cultivating our support, it may be doubted whether a Mahratta connexion is to be accomplished on any grounds short of subjugation. To subdue the Mahratta empire would be (if at all practicable) to charge ourselves with an incumbrance, and to bring ourselves in contact with neighbours much more troublesome, it would be sacrificing a tolerable barrier for one infinitely more precarious; and it must never be forgot, that were our object accomplished, of placing a subsidiary force of equal strength with that which the Peishwa is to receive under the treaty of Bassein, in the dominions of each of the four great military chieftains of the confederacy, we should be only permanently extending our native force to the amount of 24,000 men, without any assurance that the empire at home can spare us, *that additional proportion of European* force, which, whether actually making a part of the subsidiary corps or not, ought always invariably to accompany every encrease of our Indian army.

Success therefore whether in war, or in negotiation, so long as we are *forcing*, and not *inviting this alliance*, however, for the time it may give a lustre to our authority, can only embark us in difficulties, from which it may be embarrassing to recede.

The British empire in India contains above fifty millions of inhabitants, it produces a revenue of above thirteen millions sterling a year, encreasing with the general prosperity of the country at this moment rapidly advancing under the mild and beneficent administration of the Company. Our regular army native and European, on its peace establishment amounts to 115,000 men, a force capable of immediate extension in time of war. With such an empire a Mahratta connexion may be a very good thing, if it can be had without mixing us too deeply in their internal disturbances, or leading to an extension of dominion beyond our purpose, but we are too strong *to require it.* Our wisest policy is to place our dependence in that quarter, on the consolidation and improvement of what we already possess. On the steady application of our resources to the reduction of our debt, and approaching every native power possessed of and valuing its independence, with offers of alliance and connexion (when any such are to be made) on grounds really compatible with that independence, trust to the friends which such a course of conduct will make for us in the hour of trial, it being little probable that any competitor for eastern dominion can deprive us of our share of alliances when the danger is at hand, unless we ourselves by a mistaken course of policy lay the grounds before he approaches.

It has not been a matter of choice, but of necessity, that our existence in India should pass from that of traders to that of sovereigns. If we had not, the French would long since have taken the lead in India to our exclusion.

In the various contentions for power, in which our security was at the same time really involved, we have risen to an extent of possession and authority which can no longer be safely permitted to rest on any other foundation than our own intrinsic strength. Events have latterly accelerated our progress so much as in itself (the rather as most political transactions will admit of question) to give an impression, with respect to our policy, which, *if heightened*, may be productive of serious embarrassment to our interests both at home and abroad. Without being disposed to admit, or in truth feeling, that the tenor of our administration in India has been otherwise than highly honourable to the national character, I think it is material, having already accomplished so much in point *of power* and glory, that we should now be studious to give to our councils a complexion of moderation and forbearance, trusting, as we may safely do, the preservation of our Indian possessions to the resources abundantly contained within our present limits.

In determining what it may be advisable to do, under present circumstances, it is necessary to decide to what extent we are bound and prepared to support the treaty of Bassein.

Lord Wellesley from the outset declared his determination not to persevere in the connection if the Peishwa's conduct was such as to prove him averse and faithless to the alliance.

His Lordship also resolved not to force the restoration of the Peishwa contrary to the feelings and inclinations of the majority of the immediate jaggeerdars and feudatories of the Poonah state.

Should the conduct of the Peishwa have become such as to induce the Governor-General to consider the alliance dissolved under the treaty of Bassein, the British Government will have an undoubted claim to retain the territories ceded by his Highness till he shall have fully discharged the extraordinary expense incurred in replacing him on the musnud.

In case the Peishwa shall have performed his part of the treaty, he is entitled to our support, and having guaranteed his dominions in good faith and character, we are bound to defend and maintain him on the musnud.

The treaty itself may be considered as consisting of two parts, the first affecting the immediate interests of the Peishwa, the second principally affecting our own; the former, unless modified with his Highness's concurrence, we are bound to adhere to; the relaxation of the latter depends principally on ourselves, and can meet with little difficulty on his part.

The 3rd and 17th articles are obvious points of jealousy to all the Mahratta states, and from former experience of the Peishwa's reluctance to the receiving *a subsidiary force within his dominions*, the third article is not likely to be in truth more acceptable to him.

The 12th article also deserves consideration which binds the Peishwa to accept our arbitration in all disputes with the other powers. If the reasoning contained in the former part of these notes is right, doubts may be entertained of the policy of a connection with the Poonah state, which is necessarily calculated to mix the British Government so intimately in Mahratta politics, and must in appearance render the Peishwa absolutely dependent on us.

As far as relates to arbitrating the differences between the Nizam and the Peishwa as allies of the Company, we were bound to contend for it under the treaty of Hyderabad of 1800, but beyond this, having provided that our troops were not to be employed *against any of the principal branches of the Mahratta empire*, it would perhaps be better not to stipulate for a right, which being general, may alarm other states, and cannot be very acceptable even to the Peishwa himself, but rather to rely for the means of regulating his conduct upon pacific principles on the grounds we shall have to withhold the subsidiary force in cases where the Peishwa may be deemed the aggressor, than upon a positive right of arbitration in all cases binding upon him.

Without therefore failing in the spirit of our obligations to the Peishwa, we have the means of altering so far the character of the treaty as to restore his Highness to a state of more *ostensible independence*, and to give to the alliance less the aspect of aiming at an interference in Mahratta affairs.

Much of my doubt upon the policy of any Mahratta connection, however modified, arises from an apprehension of its tendency to involve us too much in the endless and complicated distractions of that turbulent empire. Much of my difficulty would be removed by our connection being so far simplified as to confine it to a mere support upon requisition, and that claim of support necessarily qualified by the principles which strictly belong to every *defensive* alliance. We should then always have a good plea for keeping out of discussion, which appeared to us foreign to the principles of our alliance; we should equally derive all the advantages connected with the late cessions, and being less pledged to interference, we should perhaps be in a situation to exercise a more beneficial influence than we can do by making ourselves *absolute parties*, in which light we must be considered so long as the subsidiary force is at Poonah and the Peishwa actually in our hands.

The object of the late treaty has been to obtain a complete and commanding influence: to render this at all secure from interruption and contest, our authority must be introduced upon similar principles into other leading Mahratta states. The accomplishment of this seems little probable if desirable, and the reasons for not thinking it desirable have been already stated.

The objections to forming a subsidiary connection with the

Mahratta states upon the modified plan herein proposed appear less serious, as it throws less weight of management and interference upon us, whilst in its nature it is less calculated to excite the resentment and jealousy of powers not included in the alliance; the stipulations may be fulfilled without so large an extension of our native force, but even upon this principle it ought not to be carried beyond what appears *absolutely requisite* to unite some proportion of the confederacy in interest with us, as I am satisfied the limited number of men that can be obtained in Europe for general service in the present state of our manufactures and commerce, and the extended scale on which it will be thought necessary hereafter to provide for our home defence, renders it hopeless to aim at obtaining for India a larger establishment of King's troops.

In any modification of the treaty of Bassein upon the principles above suggested, it is of great importance to guard against any impression calculated to make the Nizam discontented with the treaty of Hyderabad of 1800.

This cannot be difficult to manage. The Nizam has a direct interest in the subsidiary force being so stationed as effectually to cover his dominions from Mahratta incursions; it will be easy to make him feel the policy of modifying our connection with the Court of Poonah, the head of the Mahratta confederacy, so as to occasion less jealousy in the other states; and as war always augments his expenses, as our ally, he will have the same interest in the adoption of measures tending to allay the uneasiness of the other Mahratta powers which we ourselves have.

The object to be aimed at should be, to place the alliance with the Court of Poonah, as nearly as may be, on the footing of our connection with the Nizam previous to 1798, retaining however the assigned lands as a permanent provision for a permanent force to be held always disposable for the protection of the Peishwa, although not stationed within his dominions; and it appears to me that so far from encouraging or wishing the Peishwa to order this force frequently and without adequate necessity to enter his territory, that the object of the Resident at Poonah should be to discourage as much as possible his applying for it, when its services can be dispensed with, and whenever the service is performed on which it is required, that it should be *our endeavour* to have it returned to its station with the least possible delay.

Such is the course of management which appears to me best calculated to strengthen our influence not only at Poonah, but in the other Mahratta Courts. Between this, and a system of authority founded on force, and not likely to be effected without continual struggles, I apprehend there is no safe medium.

Whether this alteration of our engagements with the Peishwa had better be made a matter of general negotiation at the peace with the Mahratta states, or at once settled between the Peishwa and the Company, must be judged of on the spot; in the former case, it may lead to some equivalent arrangements on the part of our enemies; in the latter, it would bear less the complexion of a concession, whilst it would probably narrow materially the points at issue with the other powers.

Our first object then seems to be, to fulfil our engagements to the Peishwa; our second, to alter to a certain degree the nature of our connection with that state. A third consideration is, what steps we are called upon to take in consequence of the part which the other Mahratta powers have acted on the present occasion, particularly Scindiah and the Berar Rajah, Holkar by the last accounts not having as yet joined the confederacy.

Whatever might have been their natural motives of jealousy, their conduct has throughout been marked by the utmost duplicity. They appear to have taken their measures for war whilst they were professing friendship.

They did not remonstrate against the treaty of Bassein; on the contrary, Scindiah disclaimed any purpose of disturbing it, and declared he did not consider it to contain any stipulation inconsistent with his interest; the evidence we had of orders given by Scindiah to his chiefs on the Bengal frontier clearly marks that his interview with the Berar Rajah, and the menacing posture taken by their united forces immediately on the Nizam's territories, was a prelude to hostilities.

Not having demanded *explanation*, nor made any attempt to settle the question by amicable negotiation, but having on the contrary pursued a course of equivocation and deceit, we are warranted in considering them as aggressors.

In this case we are entitled to demand from them (subject to prudential considerations) indemnity for the expenses incurred by us and our allies in the war; in the application however of this right, it would be highly unadvisable to protract the war in the hope of obtaining such retribution.

Pecuniary compensation is very much out of the question

with such states; they have little treasure and less credit, and any security given on lands is only keeping alive a question of litigation between them and us if our successes are such as to place within our reach any concession on their part without protracting the contest. Better take it in some absolute and unqualified surrender than any thing connected with a protracted settlement; and if the surrender is of a territorial description, it is desirable that it should be some point of value rather as a means of security to our existing possessions than selected with a view to their extension.

The expelling the French now in the service of Scindiah is certainly a considerable object, and one to which the Governor-General's attention appears already earnestly directed. As far as my means of information go I should conceive Baroach in the Guzerat belonging to Scindiah, and Cuttack to the Rajah of Berar, would be the points of most importance to insist on, as tending to deny to European intrigue their best channels of intercourse with the native powers.

The object however of *most importance* will be, to bring the war to an end as early as is consistent with our good honour and good faith. Extension of territory not being our purpose, we have nothing to gain from the contest, whilst it suspends all our views to the reduction of debt, &c.

CASTLEREAGH.

40. The Secret Committee of the honourable Court of Directors of the East India Company to the most noble the Governor-General in Council, Bengal.

Strictures on the Policy of the Treaty. Propriety of relaxing some of its Articles.

East India House, London, 6th March, 1804.

We have received despatches from our Presidency of Bombay, dated the 8th September, 1803, announcing to us the actual commencement of hostilities between our forces and certain of the Mahratta powers.

The successes with which the campaign has opened by the immediate reduction of Ahmednuggur and Broach, in a manner so highly creditable to the British arms and to the officers who directed those operations, could not fail to afford us the highest satisfaction. But as it was always our wish to avoid a connection with the Mahrattas at the expense or even at the serious risk of a war with any of the leading members of that confederacy, we deeply regret that such has been the result of the treaty concluded with the Peishwa at Bassein, and we feel it necessary in consequence thereof at this early period, to convey to you our sentiments upon the present posture of affairs.

Removed as we are from the immediate scene of action, much must necessarily at all times be left to the discretion of our governments on the spot, in applying the principles which we may think it necessary to prescribe for the direction of their conduct to the precise state of circumstances under which they may be called upon at the moment to act. We shall, therefore, confine ourselves in the present despatch, to a statement of the general considerations by which we desire your conduct may be governed.

Whilst we are prepared to make every exertion which is due to the good faith, and which the character and honour of our government may require, we do not, as a measure of policy, attach that value to the provisions of the treaty in question, which would lead us to wish that it should be maintained at all hazards in its present form, if by any modifications of the stipulations therein contained, our connection with the state of Poonah can be rendered a measure of less alarm and jealousy to the other Mahratta powers, being firmly persuaded that no alliance with a Mahratta power, but more especially with one in military rank not standing higher than the third or fourth in the empire, can in the long run be consistent with our interests, unless the preponderating majority of the confederacy can be reconciled to that connection.

The most prominent grounds of jealousy entertained by the Mahratta states of the late treaty, appear to arise out of the third and seventeenth articles, the former introducing and permanently stationing a commanding British force in the Peishwa's dominions, the latter binding his Highness without the stipulations being reciprocal, not to commence any negotiation with any other power without previous communication with the British Government, which two stipulations they consider as tending to place under our control and guidance the legitimate head of their Empire.

Under a strong conviction of the embarrassment which must arise from our mixing ourselves too intimately in the complicated politics of this distracted empire, our wish is to confine the purposes of the treaty strictly to the support and defence of the Peishwa in the quiet possession of his own immediate dominions, and to avoid not only in fact but in appearance every thing which can be construed to affect the independency of the Mahratta confederacy through its legitimate head, or which can create distrust and jealousy between the Peishwa and the other great powers of the empire. We are therefore desirous whilst the support to which his Highness is entitled under the treaty of Bassein (so long as he shall remain faithful to his engagements), is afforded to him in the fullest manner, that we should not hesitate to relax in such stipulations as were introduced into that treaty rather for our, than for his Highness's accommodation. When we refer to the Peishwa's former reluctance to the introduction of a subsidiary force within his dominions, and when we couple this with the decided repugnance which undoubtedly exists to the arrangement lately concluded, on the part of the other states, we cannot doubt that a relaxation of this condition of the treaty will prove highly satisfactory to his Highness, and we also flatter ourselves that by this relaxation a material objection in the feelings of the other states may be removed. In order more distinctly to mark that our object is sincerely to support and by no means to infringe the independency of our ally, our wish is that it should be expressly stipulated in an additional article to the treaty that the subsidiary force shall hereafter be stationed within the Company's territories, in such a position as shall enable it to act on the shortest notice in support of the Peishwa, but that it shall upon no account, except upon a formal requisition from the Peishwa, (unless restraint should be put upon his Highness's person) enter his dominions. We also are willing to abandon the seventeenth article, and to rely on the interest his Highness will have in cultivating a good understanding with the British for his fidelity to the general stipulations of the alliance in any connections he may form with other powers. It is material further to call your attention to the twelfth article of the treaty. Having in conformity to the treaty of Hyderabad stipulated in article thirteen for a right of arbitrating all the differences subsisting between the Nizam and the Peishwa, we entertain great doubts whether it is desirable, regard being had to the character and complexion which it is our object to give to the alliance, to stipulate for a general right of arbitration as between the Peishwa and other states. Such a right must in itself create much jealousy, and we are inclined to think that it would be on the whole better not to push our claim of arbitrating so far. This course seems the less hazardous as the treaty of Bassein is not only guarded by the general principles which appertain to all defensive alliances, but is also specifically restricted with reference to certain states therein named. In thus conveying our instructions upon this important subject we think it due to the Governor-General in Council to state, that the objections which attach upon the treaty of Bassein in its present form did not when this subject was last under consideration in the months of September and December 1800, as circumstances then stood, impress themselves upon our minds with equal force. We therefore desire to be understood, as not attaching blame to the conduct of our government abroad with respect to the form of the treaty itself, however subsequent events may have convinced us of the hazard of aiming at so close a connection with the court of Poonah. We cannot close this despatch without adverting to the late proceedings of the other Mahratta chiefs. Whilst we are ready to admit that states jealous of their independency might naturally entertain some alarm at stipulations capable of being represented to them as placing the head of the empire under the immediate control of a foreign power, we cannot avoid noticing the deceitful and disingenuous conduct pursued by Scindiah and the Rajah of Berar previous to the rupture. Instead of openly avowing their sentiments and endeavouring by amicable explanation to obtain relief from any stipulations of the treaty which could be supposed to affect their interests, they in terms disclaimed any ground of objection, and disavowed any intention of obstructing this connection. Whilst such was their language it appears they were intent upon gaining time with a view of arranging a confederacy and of acting hostilely against the Company and its allies so soon as their measures were ripe for execution and the season favoured their operations. Such having been the conduct of these chieftains, the Company are clearly entitled to consider them as aggressors and (as far as prudential considerations will justify them in asserting the claim) to demand from the enemy a reasonable indemnity for the expences of the war. But you are to understand, however indisputable this claim in strictness may be, that it is our positive direction the war may by no means be protracted in pursuit of such an object. Upon the whole our wish is that a modification of the treaty should at all events take place in conformity to the above instructions, not on the ground of concession but upon a deliberate consideration of the system of policy which appears to us to be the best adapted to the genius and the character of this people. Determining to support the Peishwa on the Musnud unless his Highness by some act of his shall have dissolved the alliance, as also the treaty of Bassein, upon the modified plan herein described, whenever the powers we are opposed to shall be disposed to recognize our rights and those of our ally the Peishwa as under the treaty so amended, we see no adequate motive for continuing the war, and should the success of our arms be such as under all the circumstances appear to you in prudence to warrant a demand of some concessions from our opponents, we desire that the demand be framed upon principles of great moderation and with a view to the improvement of the military security rather than the extension of our present dominions.

We must however impress most strongly on your minds that the early termination of the war is the object to which we desire your efforts may be most earnestly directed, and although we have thought it right to advert to the possible expediency of requiring certain sacrifices in the nature of reparation from our opponents, you are by no means to consider such suggestions as controlling your conduct in case you should be of opinion under all the circumstances that peace is likely to be more firmly established and future causes of dissension more effectually obviated by an entire restoration of all our conquests.

We are your affectionate friends,

JACOB BOSANQUET,
JOHN ROBERTS,
W. DEVAYNEZ.

41. Major-General Wellesley's Observations on the policy of the Treaty.

Reply to Lord Castlereagh's strictures and proposals.

As the author of observations on Mahratta affairs does not appear to me to have viewed the policy of the treaty of Bassein in the light in which I have viewed it, and as I conceive that much of his reasoning upon the subject is to be attributed to his erroneous view in my opinion of the political state of India at the time the treaty was made, I deem it necessary to advert shortly to the political situation of the great powers in India at different periods in which any important change has taken place since the peace of Seringapatam, before I proceed to consider the amendments to the treaty of Bassein which have been proposed.

In the consideration of all questions of Indian policy, it is necessary to extend our views beyond those powers immediately possessing territory. It is well known that the French have never ceased to look to the re-establishment of their power in India; and although they possess no territory themselves on the continent, they have at all times had some influence in the councils of the different native powers, and sometimes great power by means of the European adventurers introduced into native armies. There can be no doubt but that the French government would avail themselves of an instrument, such as the influence or the power of these adventurers would give them, to prosecute their favourite plan in India; and it is equally certain, that whether at peace or at war with Great Britain, the object of every French statesman must be to diminish the influence, the power, and the prosperity of the British Government in India. I therefore conclude, that in the consideration of every question of Indian policy, or in an inquiry into the expediency of any political measure, it is absolutely necessary to view it, not only as it will affect Indian powers, but as it will affect the French.

When I establish this principle, I don't mean that the assertion 'that the French interest has been affected,' is to be admitted in justification of every political measure of the government. It is necessary only that it should be recollected by those who are to judge of political affairs in India, that French power and French influence are important parts of every political discussion by the governments abroad; and it will appear by the view which I shall take of the political situation of the great powers in India at different periods, that French influence was powerful, that to have omitted to guard against the French would have been ruinous to the Company, and that the necessity of guarding against French influence was one of the principal causes of the treaty of Bassein.

In order thoroughly to understand the relations in which the different powers of India stood to each other at the period at which the treaty of Bassein was concluded, and to be able to comprehend the objects and benefits of that treaty, it is necessary to advert to the situation in which they stood at the peace of

Seringapatam in 1792, and to trace their progress from that period.

The three great powers, the English, the Peishwa, and the Nizam, having each received injuries from Tippoo Sultaun, joined in the war, the result of which was that peace; and the object of the British Government was if possible to preserve the power of each in the situation in which it was left by the pacification. Lord Cornwallis, who foresaw the difficulties and dangers to which the alliance would be exposed from the claims of the Mahrattas upon the Nizam, endeavoured to establish the alliance upon a more firm basis, by interposing the arbitration of the British Government in their disputes; but the Mahrattas who knew that their claims were without foundation, that they depended entirely upon their superior strength, and that the result of an arbitration by the British Government must be unfavourable to them, declined to accept the offer made by Lord Cornwallis.

I conceive this to be the real history of the refusal of Lord Cornwallis to allow the Mahrattas to subsidize two British battalions as mentioned by the anonymous observer, if such a proposal was ever made to him. His Lordship found that without giving the British Government any additional strength or security, the Peishwa's general wished to have the assistance of the British troops in the support of the Peishwa's internal government; and his Lordship was not desirous of being involved in the internal disputes of the Mahrattas, without having some corresponding political advantage.

The result of the refusal of the Mahrattas to allow the arbitration of the British Government was exactly what his Lordship had foreseen. In the course of very few years the Mahrattas attacked the Nizam for the purpose of enforcing their unjust claims. The British Government of that day did not interfere, and the Nizam was obliged, in a treaty signed at Kurdlah, on the   to cede half his territories, to pay a great sum of money, and to give up to the Mahrattas his prime minister Musheir-ool Mulk, and to appoint another minister, recommended by the enemies who had reduced his power to that low state. His Highness was also obliged to consent to send out of his territories the two British battalions which had continued with him since the peace of Seringapatam.

In the contest which had just taken place between the Mahrattas and the Nizam, the troops principally employed, and whose gallantry had been most conspicuous, were the corps of infantry in the service of Scindiah on the one side, and those in the service of the Nizam on the other. Both these corps were commanded, and in general officered by Frenchmen and other foreigners. The corps in the service of the Nizam in particular, commanded by M. Raymond, had distinguished itself in an extraordinary manner, although unsuccessful.

After the experience of the war, which had just terminated, the Nizam, seeing that he could not rely upon the assistance of the British Government against the Mahrattas, determined to increase the corps of infantry, officered by Frenchmen and other foreigners, to the greatest extent that his finances would admit, and to render it as efficient as was possible. With this view, a large territory was granted in Jagheer to M. Raymond, from the revenues of which he was to pay the troops under his command; and the number of troops and French officers to command them was vastly increased.

In a short time after the peace of Kurdlah, the Peishwa Madoo Rao Narrain died, and a scene of intrigue and confusion ensued at Poonah, the object of which was the succession to the Musnud of the Peishwa, and the possession of the power of the Poonah state.

It is useless to the consideration of the question under discussion to endeavour, and would be impossible to succeed in detailing the events which occurred upon that occasion; the result was the establishment, in the hands of Dowlut Rao Scindiah, of all the power of the Peishwa.

The predecessor of this chief had conquered the territories in the Doab of the Jumna and Ganges, and those on the right of the Jumna; he was in possession of the person of the King, and of his power, by virtue of his office of Vakeel ul Muluck; and thus was established in the hand of one Mahratta, all the territory and all the power on the west side of India, extending from Hurdwar to the Toombuddra, along the frontiers of the Company, the Nabob Vizier, the Nizam, Tippoo Sultaun, &c. I have already observed that Scindiah had in his service a corps of infantry, commanded and generally officered by Frenchmen. This corps had conquered the territories in Hindostan, had rendered essential service in the war which preceded the peace of Kurdlah, and had been the principal instrument in the establishment of Scindiah's power at Poonah. This corps, therefore, commanded and officered by Frenchmen, may be fairly stated to have been the principal instrument and support of the enormous power thus established in the western side of India.

On the other hand a similar corps, officered in a similar manner, was the principal, indeed the only support of the state of the Nizam. The difference between the two was, that that of Raymond was the most powerful; and Raymond had the most influence in the councils of the Prince whom he was serving, owing to the destruction of the power and authority of the Nizam in his own territories, occasioned by the disgrace suffered at Kurdlah.

In this situation, the Governor-General, Lord Wellesley, found political affairs when he assumed the government in the year 1798.

As Lord Cornwallis had foreseen, the state of the Nizam was nearly destroyed by the Mahrattas; the policy of the British Government had obliged the Nizam to support his tottering authority by the service of a body of troops commanded by French officers, in whose hands was the only power in the state.

The Peishwa's power was lodged by another train of events in the hands of Scindiah, who possessed besides all the power of the north and west of India, and whose principal support and instrument was a corps of a similar description, likewise commanded by Frenchmen.

It is useless to detail the measures adopted by Lord Wellesley to remedy the evils which resulted from this state of the governments of the allies of the Company in the war with Tippoo Sultaun, of which he saw the probability in the year 1798. It is sufficient here to observe, that his Lordship relieved the Nizam from the state of dependence in which he was held by the commanding officer of the French corps in his service. The French officers were dismissed; British troops were subsidized in lieu of the corps which the French officers had commanded; and the British Government enjoyed the advantage of the assistance of the Nizam in the war which ensued with Tippoo Sultaun.

The measures by which the Governor-General proposed to relieve the government of the Peishwa from the state in which it was held by Scindiah failed to produce their effect. His Highness's Government was in Scindiah's hands, and the British Government derived no assistance from this branch of the alliance:

After the destruction of the power of Tippoo Sultaun, on the 4th of May, 1799, a new combination of politics appeared in

India. The native power, against whose enmity it had been necessary to provide, by an alliance with the Peishwa and the Nizam was no more, and the Governor-General was to determine the relation in which the British Government should stand in respect to the powers which remained. These were that of the Nizam, and that of the Mahrattas.

It was obviously the interest of the British Government that the power of the Nizam should continue to exist in a state of independence. If there had been any reasonable ground for hope that his Highness's state could continue in independence, there might possibly have been no occasion for an alteration of the treaty by which the Company was then allied with his Highness. But it could not exist in that state, unless the Peishwa should consent to admit the mediation and arbitration of the British Government in the questions or claims which his Highness had upon the Nizam. The Governor-General therefore offered to allow the Peishwa to participate in the acquisitions made by the destruction of the power of Tippoo Sultaun, provided his Highness would admit the arbitration of the British Government in his disputes with the Nizam, and would receive a subsidiary force. The Peishwa declined to accept this offer; and the acquisitions made in the war were divided between the parties concerned in carrying it on.

The state of the Nizam's government however, after this refusal of the Peishwa, must still have pressed upon the consideration of the Governor-General.

By the treaty of 1798, his Highness was precluded from the employment of the British subsidiary troops against the Mahrattas, or against certain tributaries of his, likewise tributaries of the Peishwa; and it was obvious that however advantageous the treaty of 1798 had been to his government in many respects, his Highness was still in the situation in respect to the Mahrattas, in which he had been in the year , with this difference, however, that he had no longer the support and service of the corps commanded by the French officers. It became necessary therefore for the Governor-General to decide respecting the Nizam's government, whether he would allow it to fall into the hands of the Mahrattas; whether he would allow it to revert into the hands of the French adventurers from whom he had relieved the Nizam in the year of 1798; or whether he would by an alteration of the treaty of 1798 extend the objects of the alliance, and render it defensive against all powers whatever, and in this manner undertake the defence of the Nizam, against the vexatious claims which it was certain that the Mahrattas would make upon him.

It is scarcely necessary that I should advert to the consequences which would have resulted from the first. The Mahrattas would shortly have exercised the power of the Nizam's government, whose territory at that time extended to the southward of the Kistna and Toombuddra, along the frontier of the newly established government of Mysore. They would soon have found the means of making claims in his name, or in that of the Peishwa, on the Rajah of Mysore, or the Nabob of the Carnatic, or even the Company, and the consequence would have been a war with that restless power, of which the seat would have been the territories of the Company or their allies, and the sources from which the means to carry on the war were to be drawn.

The second mode would have been in direct contradiction to the opinion of parliament and the nation, and of every man who had given an opinion on the Governor-General's conduct in his transactions with the Nizam's government in the year 1798. It would have introduced Frenchmen, French influence, interests and power into the heart of India, after they had been expelled by the Governor-General.

There remained then only to take the Nizam under the protection of the Company; and this measure was adopted by the general defensive treaty of 1800, although every man who knew anything of the politics of India foresaw that the consequence of this measure might be sooner or later a war with the Mahrattas.

The probability of such a war was foreseen by the former Governor-General Sir John Shore, in a minute in which he discussed the question regarding a closer alliance with the Nizam; and it is supposed that Lord Wellesley saw clearly that the only mode of avoiding that war, was to induce the Peishwa to become a party to the alliance, and to submit his claims to the arbitration of the British Government. Consistently with this opinion, it was the duty of the Governor-General to repeat his offers of alliance as frequently as opportunities might occur; and accordingly they were repeated upon different occasions.

I cannot agree in opinion with the anonymous observer, that the offers to admit the Peishwa as a party to the general defensive alliance were not accepted, because the Governor-General insisted that a body of British troops should be posted in his Highness's territories.

In the first place it does not appear that the Governor-General insisted upon that object as a *sine quâ non*. He may, for reasons into which I will enter hereafter, have thought it desirable that a body of British troops should be at Poonah; but he did not insist upon it. However, I shall consider this point upon the facts stated by the anonymous observer.

Till the end of the year 1800, Scindiah was at Poonah with an army; it was obvious that he would not willingly consent to the defensive treaty because it would put an end to all his projects of ambition in the Deccan; and the Peishwa could not consent to it, because he would have been exposed to the tyranny of Scindiah from the time at which he would sign the treaty to that at which the British troops would arrive at Poonah.

When circumstances obliged Scindiah to quit Poonah with his army, he appointed the Peishwa's ministers, who still continued to negotiate with the British Resident; and it is a fact well known that the Peishwa did not know even of the existence of a negotiation, much less the nature of the objects offered to his acceptance, and refused by his servants.

The result of this statement and reasoning is, that the policy of a connection with the Mahrattas did not 'arise from the connection subsisting previously to the conquest of Mysore, between the Company, the Mahrattas, and the Nizam, by the treaty concluded in 1790 at Poonah;' but subsequently to the conquest of Mysore; it originated, 1st. In the necessity of preserving the state of the Nizam in independence. 2ndly. In the unjust claims of the Mahratta nation on the Nizam. 3rdly. In the certainty that those claims would be asserted in arms, and that the Nizam must submit unless he should protect himself by raising an army to be officered by European adventurers, particularly Frenchmen. 4thly. In the necessity of preventing the Nizam from entertaining those adventurers, and of affording him protection at least equal to that which he would have procured for himself by those means, even at the risk of a war with the whole Mahratta nation.

In this view of the question I have entirely omitted the enlarged considerations which must be obvious to every statesman who discusses it. I have likewise omitted to advert to the peculiar situation of the British power in India, which requires that the funds applicable to the defence of the country should be applied to commercial purposes, and therefore renders it necessary that the local government should derive means of supporting armies different from those usually resorted to; I have considered nothing but that which was absolutely necessary for security in the first instance, and for peace in the second.

There can be no question about the Mahratta claims, or that they would have been enforced with arms, or that the Nizam must have yielded unless supported by the French, or by the Company. The question is, whether the best mode of preventing the war was to prevail upon the Peishwa to become a party to the defensive alliance.

It is not necessary that I should consider the particular circumstances of the times at the different periods at which proposals were made to the Peishwa to become a party to the defensive alliance. It will be sufficient for the purpose under consideration to state, that the consequence of the conclusion of the defensive arrangements with the Peishwa at any period since the year 1799, must have been to join against Scindiah a great proportion of the Mahratta nation. It is possible that under these circumstances Scindiah might have acquiesced in the arrangement, but supposing that he should have gone to war to oppose it, the war would have been one of far less extent and difficulty than that in which the Company must sooner or later have been involved with the whole Mahratta nation, by the necessity of supporting the Nizam. The seat of it would have been the territories of our enemies instead of our own, and the sources from which we were to draw the means of carrying it on.

But the question is not properly referable to the admission of the Peishwa to the defensive alliance, at any period antecedent to the treaty of Bassein, but to that treaty itself.

In order to be able to form a judgment whether the circumstances under which it was negotiated afforded the best chance of preserving the peace of India, it is necessary to advert to the situation of Mahratta affairs from the years 1798–9.

Dowlut Rao Scindiah appears to have possessed the power to which I have referred in the former part of this memorandum, from the time at which he placed the Peishwa Bajee Rao on the musnud. He was involved however in a contest in Malwa with the females of the family of his predecessor Madhajee Scindiah; and after the death of Tuckojee Holkar, he was desirous of influencing the disposal of the succession of that chief, in such a manner as to forward his own political objects. In pursuance of these views, he murdered Mulhar Rao (the son of Tuckojee

Holkar) at Poonah. Jeswunt Rao Holkar, the natural son of Tuckojee Holkar, fled upon that occasion, and after a variety of adventures in the territories of the Nizam and of the Rajah of Berar, he first joined the Bhyes, and then plundered them. He afterwards, in the year 1800, attacked and defeated a detachment of Scindiah's army at Oujein.

These events obliged Scindiah to quit Poonah. Towards the end of that year, he defeated Holkar in a pitched battle fought at Indore; and in 1801 and 1802, drove him out of Malwa into the Deccan. Holkar then attacked the Peishwa, and having a large body of troops defeated the united armies of Scindiah and the Peishwa at Poonah. In the month of October 1802, the Peishwa fled, and took refuge under the Company's protection at Bassein, having previous to the battle at Poonah signed an agreement, which contained all the principal objects of the treaty of Bassein.

In this crisis, all the Mahratta powers pressed the Governor-General to interfere in their affairs. Scindiah repeatedly urged the Governor-General to settle the Peishwa's affairs; and begged that his Highness and himself might enjoy the benefit of the Company's friendship.

I believe it might be proved that Scindiah was fully informed of every point in the negotiation of the treaty of Bassein. His vakeel Ballajee Koonjeer was the Peishwa's dewan at the time, and he knew every thing.

Holkar's declared intention and apparent object was to establish a new government at Poonah under one of the sons of Amrut Rao as Peishwa.

The government at Poonah would under this arrangement have been administered in its military branch by Holkar; and in its civil, by Amrut Rao. These persons both repeatedly requested the Company's countenance for themselves; and in fact the arrangement failed because Amrut Rao saw that the British Government was determined to oppose it, and to support Bajee Rao. At all events, Holkar and Amrut Rao requested the Company's mediation of their disputes with the Peishwa, and urged the Governor-General to interfere to settle the affairs at Poonah.

Although it cannot be asserted that the Peishwa is a powerful prince, there is a large party in the empire attached to his person, all of whom were anxious in the expression of their wishes that the British Government should interfere in his affairs. The Peishwa's right to the musnud is universally acknowledged, although his authority is from circumstances imperfect, and his orders but ill obeyed; and his cause supported by the British Government was certainly popular in the southern parts of the empire.

The southern chiefs who are the principal support of the government of Poonah had not submitted to Holkar; they were in arms waiting for the arrival of the British troops, as the instruments of the interference of the British Government in the Peishwa's affairs; and they joined the British army when it arrived in their neighbourhood. There was no probability that Holkar would make any serious opposition to the march of the British troops to Poonah. He had not made his peace with Scindiah, indeed neither party thought of it, and he would have opposed himself singly in an unpopular cause, to all the great powers in India.

Under all these circumstances, and allowing for the treachery of the Mahratta character, there was every reason to believe, that the close of the year 1802 was the most favourable period that had ever occurred, or that would occur, for the admission of the Peishwa as a party to the defensive alliance without a war.

I have already stated my reasons for thinking that this measure was the only one that could be devised to avoid a war which sooner or later must have occurred with all the Mahratta powers, in the support and defence of the Nizam; and the anonymous observer has pointed out with great truth and accuracy, the sentiments of the Court of Directors, and of the Government at home, on the subject of the admission of the Peishwa to the defensive alliance. It is true that the Court of Directors do not appear to have had a very distinct knowledge of the objects of the defensive alliance; and like the anonymous observer, supposed that it was founded upon the triple alliance of the year 1790, to defend the allies against Tippoo, who was no more. However, whatever may have been the reasons of the approbation of the Court of Directors, and of the authorities at home, they approved the measure, and ordered the Governor-General, according to the anonymous observer, to carry it into execution. Surely it will not be denied that if the Governor-General had passed over the opportunity which offered at the end of the year 1802, he would have been guilty of the most flagrant disobedience of orders, and dereliction of his own principles and measures repeatedly reviewed by himself and by the first authorities in India and in England.

If the Governor-General had omitted to take advantage of the opportunity which presented itself at the close of the year 1802, I think the most probable result would have been a war with the Poonah state under the government of Holkar and Amrut Rao, and it is not improbable but that the war might have extended to the whole of the Mahratta states.

The British Government might on this plan of proceeding have collected their armies, and have remained upon the frontier to watch the course of proceedings as recommended by the anonymous observer, or they might have passed over, as unworthy of notice, every thing that was doing at Poonah; and have delayed to take any steps till the moment when they or their allies should be attacked. I cannot exactly discern the object in assembling the army upon the frontier, if it was to do nothing. The most expensive article in India is an army in the field; and the most useless is one destined to act upon the defensive. An army in a state of preparation to act offensively when opportunity will offer is indeed useful, and I believe no army ever seized so favourable an opportunity as that which marched to Poonah in March and April, 1803.

But the anonymous observer says, that we ought to have concerted our arrangements with Scindiah; that we ought to have offered a disinterested mediation, and to have acted in concert with Scindiah at one time, and at another with the Rajah of Berar.

I have already shewn, and the anonymous observer acknowledges that the British Government were encouraged, nay, strongly urged, by all the principal Mahratta powers, amongst others by Holkar himself, to interfere in the settlement of the Peishwa's affairs. In respect to a concert, the anonymous observer forgets the difficulty and length of every communication with the chief who was to be party to the concert. Supposing that it had been possible to bring Scindiah into our measures, the direct object of which was to take the Nizam out of his reach, and to deprive him of all objects of ambition in the Deccan, it would still have taken six months before the Commander-in-Chief of the army could receive the orders of the Governor-General to advance to Poonah, even if the diplomatic agent charged with the negotiations with Scindiah should have had occasion to make but two references to the Governor-General. But in this case the objects of the British Government, of Scindiah, and of the Rajah of Berár would have been entirely different. That of the British Government would have been to restore the Peishwa to the exercise of his authority, independently of any of the feudatory Mahratta chiefs, in order that his Highness might perform his treaty with the Company, in favour of the Nizam. That of Scindiah would have been to restore the government of the Peishwa, in order that he might usurp and exercise its authority, and revive the old claims and objects of ambition in the Deccan. As far as it is possible to form a judgment of the course of politics of any Mahratta, the Rajah of Berar favoured Holkar's usurpation at Poonah, and the establishment of the new government to be founded upon it.

Supposing that it had been possible, by placing the treaty of Bassein upon a broader basis, as proposed by the anonymous observer, to induce Scindiah to agree to its only important stipulation, viz., that of the mediation and arbitration of the Mahratta claims in the Peishwa's name made upon the Nizam, it would have become a question of considerable importance to the British Government to decide whether that chief should be allowed to resume his situation at Poonah, and to usurp all the power and authority of the Peishwa's government.

It must be recollected that Scindiah's resumption of his power must have been preceded by the defeat of Holkar's army in the Deccan. Scindiah's power was already established in the whole of Hindostan and Malwa. The reduction of Holkar's force, and the re-establishment at Poonah of Scindiah's power would have replaced Mahratta affairs in the situation in which they had been since the death of Madhoo-Rao-Narrain, from which they had been relieved by a variety of unforeseen events. One powerful Mahratta chief, with a French force as his principal support, would have possessed all the territory, influence and power, from the sources of the Ganges to the Toombuddra; the situation which all Indian politicians have deprecated since the British nation have had any thing to do with Indian politics.

It is therefore very probable that the British Government and Scindiah would not have agreed in a detailed concert for the settlement of the Peishwa's government; and it is certain that they would not have agreed with the Rajah of Berar.

In this diversity of opinions and objects the negotiations would have been protracted possibly more than a year.

In all military operations, but particularly in India, time is every thing; and I am decidedly of opinion, that if we had not seized the opportunity which was taken, the march to Poonah would never have been effected.

If the British Government had hesitated in the measures which it should adopt, Amrut Rao would have consented to the arrangement proposed for his son. This boy would have been placed upon the musnud with the title of Peishwa. The southern chiefs would soon have submitted to Holkar. They are generally connected with Amrut Rao, and that party in the state which favours his pretensions, and Holkar had already detached troops and adopted other measures to reduce them; and would have extended his authority to the frontiers of Mysore.

We should then have seen at Poonah the Peishwa's government administered by the ablest Mahratta in the civil affairs of the empire, and served by a formidable army commanded by the most enterprising chief. This army, however, would have had no means of support; for the revenues of the Peishwa's country are already assigned to the Jagheerdary chiefs in the southern districts, who, if they had not been certain of British assistance, would have submitted to Holkar, and would have joined his army with their troops. Holkar would have been under the necessity of keeping his army together; and after the southern chiefs would have submitted, he must have attacked the Nizam or the Company, in order to support his troops.

It is well known that when he was at Poonah, he was collecting documents to enforce the claims of the Poonah state upon the Nizam; and that every discontented pretender of every description from the territories of the Company or the Company's allies was received with distinction, and encouraged to hope for the assistance of Holkar's armies in enforcing his pretensions to portions of these territories.

While the British Government would have been wasting its time and resources, according to the plan of the anonymous observer, with an army upon the frontier, and in a vain attempt to frame a concert with Scindiah or the Rajah of Berar, Holkar would have attained the greatest degree of strength.

We have seen that the Rajah of Berar favoured Holkar's usurpation at Poonah. Scindiah certainly was adverse to it, but I doubt much whether Scindiah would have done any thing against Holkar.

Scindiah certainly could have done nothing excepting he could bring his brigades to Poonah: the country had been already destroyed in a great measure by Holkar, and the destruction would have been completed if Scindiah had attempted to move. It may be said that he moved his brigades afterwards into the Deccan, for the purpose of opposing the British Government, and that he might equally have moved them to Poonah to destroy the power established by Holkar's usurpation ; but in answer I observe that an operation of this description is very different when opposed by British troops, and when opposed by such an army as Holkar's. The former don't, and indeed have not the means of destroying the country; to destroy the country is the only mode of warfare of the latter, and it is certain that this mode would have been adopted by Holkar to prevent Scindiah from entering the Deccan.

If it be true, as I have supposed, that the concert proposed by the anonymous observer could not have been formed, if the Rajah of Berar favoured Holkar's usurpation at Poonah, and if Scindiah could not have advanced his troops into the Deccan, it is my opinion that the result of the negotiations would have been a combination of all the Mahratta states to attack the Company and the Nizam.

In the negotiations for the proposed concert the British Government must have kept aloof from the new government at Poonah. Neither our principles or our practice permit us to encourage by marks of favour or kindness an usurpation, while we are negotiating with other powers the means of destroying it. But in this instance the state of our negotiations must have been known to those against whom they were to be directed. There is no secret in a Mahratta Durbar ; and it may be depended upon that this secret above all others would have transpired.

Then would have commenced a counterplot conducted by certainly the ablest Mahratta in the empire ; I mean Amrut Rao.

In considering a question of this kind, respecting the remote consequences of any particular line of policy which never was adopted, it is not possible to do more than to state the general principles and opinions of the parties concerned, their conduct upon other occasions, and to draw from these premises a conclusion respecting their conduct in the supposed case.

There can be no doubt whatever that the great object of every Mahratta statesman has been to combine their force to attack the British Government ; and if they had ever been free from disputes among themselves, they would have carried that plan into execution.

The person who I believe of all the Mahrattas to have been

the most determined enemy of the British Government, and who was the soul of this plan, was the Rajah of Berar. This person would have been the centre of the negotiations for the concert, supposing that the Governor-General had adopted the plan of the anonymous observer; and on the other hand, he would have been the instrument of Amrut Rao's counterplot to support his own usurped authority.

We have seen the Rajah of Berar, under circumstances very unfavourable, negotiate a peace between Scindiah and Holkar for the purposes of a combination against the Company. The question is whether, supposing the British Government had not brought back the Peishwa to Poonah, and had followed the plan of the anonymous observer, he would not have had in his hands materials which would have enabled him to effect that pacification with greater ease than he effected that under which the combination was formed in the summer of 1803.

The loss which Scindiah sustained by the subversion of the Peishwa's government was power and influence. He lost no territory in consequence of Holkar's victories. Those which he had in the Deccan remained with him till he went to war with the Company.

On the other hand, Holkar had claims to the possessions of his family in Malwa, and to certain portions of the territories which Madhajee Scindiah had conquered in Hindostan. In the pacification which was effected through the mediation of the Rajah of Berar in the summer of 1803, with the view to the combination against the Company, all these territories and claims were ceded by Scindiah to Holkar.

We have already seen that Scindiah would have found himself unable to do any thing against Holkar in the Deccan singly; and on the other hand, the British Government, according to the plan of the anonymous observer, would do nothing excepting in concert with Scindiah or the Rajah of Berar. We have seen Scindiah's object in restoring the Peishwa's government would have been to usurp its authority again, and to assert its claims and revive the old plans of ambition in the Deccan. Ours would have been to make the Peishwa so independent of all the Mahratta powers as that he would have been able to perform his treaty with the Company in favour of the Nizam. That of the Rajah of Berar would have been to support the new government, established by Holkar's and Amrut Rao's usurpation. These discordant views were to be reconciled by negotiation before the British Government could have taken any step to overcome Holkar; and these negotiations must have been attended by all the tediousness which is the usual consequence of references to Calcutta, on account of the distance.

Amrut Rao and the Rajah of Berar would in the meantime have endeavoured to bring about a peace on the basis of Holkar's cession of his territories and claims in Malwa, &c., and of Scindiah's acknowledgment of the new Peishwa and the state of affairs established at Poonah, and of a combination of the whole Mahratta nation to enforce their claims upon the Nizam, the Nabob Vizier, and the Company.

We have seen that the negotiations for the concert with Scindiah would have turned upon the degree of power which Scindiah was to have at Poonah after the Peishwa's government should be restored: the object of the British Government would have been, that the Peishwa should be independent; that of Scindiah to have the whole power of the state in his hands; and he would have been aware that the British Government would never consent to that arrangement.

In this state of affairs he would have had to choose whether he would co-operate with the British Government in restoring the Peishwa's government, in rendering it independent of himself, and in renouncing all its vexatious claims upon the Nizam; or whether he would leave the power at Poonah in the hands of Holkar and Amrut Rao, keeping peaceable possession of what he had in Malwa, Hindostan, and the Deccan.

In either case the power at Poonah would have been lost to him, and he would have derived no advantage from the arrangement with the British Government, excepting the gratification of his enmity against Holkar. On the other hand, by the pacification with Holkar and the combination against the British Government, he would have adopted a favourite and popular plan of policy among the Mahrattas, in the execution of which he would have played the principal part; and if it had been successful, he would have been the greatest gainer.

I have no doubt respecting the choice which Scindiah would have made, and I declare that I conceive that peace between Scindiah and Holkar, and a combination upon the basis supposed, would have included more interests, and would have been more practicable than that which was formed in the summer of 1803.

If the British Government had remained unarmed, and a tacit

spectator of events in the Mahratta empire, the result would possibly have been the same. Holkar would certainly have been obliged to spread his armies into the Nizam's country for subsistence, and we must eventually have been at war. But as we should not have been actively employed in negotiations for a concert against the new government at Poonah, it is possible that Amrut Rao might not have thought it necessary to commence his administration by combining all the Mahrattas against us. Nothing however would have been able to destroy the new government; and whenever the peace between Scindiah and Holkar would have been effected, the British Government and its allies would have been attacked.

In the consideration of this part of the question I have omitted purposely to introduce any reference to the French. It must not be forgotten however, that at the time that the Governor-General decided on the part which he would take in the Mahratta affairs at the end of the year 1802, he had every reason to expect the French in India; and I leave those who will peruse this memorandum to judge how much this event would have increased the difficulties of a protracted and complicated negotiation, against which one of the parties would have been plotting with Amrut Rao and Holkar.

I may therefore conclude that the treaty of Bassein and the measures adopted in consequence of it, not only afforded the best prospect of preserving the peace of India, but that to have adopted any other measures would have rendered war with Holkar nearly certain, and war with the whole Mahratta nation more probable than it could be under any other course of events.

Having now considered the general policy of admitting the Peishwa as a party to the treaty of general defensive alliance, and the policy of concluding the treaty of Bassein, at the time at which it was concluded, and of the measures which were adopted in consequence of that treaty, I come to consider the particular articles of that treaty to which the anonymous observer objects, and the nature of his objections to them.

I have already pointed out that the object of the Company in concluding any arrangement with the Peishwa was to secure the Nizam against the vexatious claims which might be made upon him either by the Peishwa or by one of the great chiefs acting in his name, and under the authority of the government of Poonah. It is obvious that the Company's object could not have been gained unless the Peishwa should agree either to give up the claims upon the Nizam entirely, or to admit the mediation and arbitration of the Company in deciding on the justice of those claims.

To have insisted on the Peishwa's relinquishing his claims entirely, would have been an unjust and arbitrary proceeding, and would probably have occasioned the loss of the whole treaty. The only mode, therefore, which remained was to insist upon establishing the mediation and arbitration of the Company, as the mode of deciding all questions, disputes, and claims between the two powers.

The Company were bound to the Nizam to settle the questions and claims existing on the part of the Peishwa, or his Highness's government.

It does not appear practicable for the Company to be bound in a defensive alliance with both governments without stipulating to arbitrate their disputes; and this will appear more clearly when the events are recollected which have occurred since the year 1792.

In respect to the article by which it is required that a body of troops should be stationed within the territories of the Peishwa, this will appear the more necessary when the situation of the Peishwa's government in relation to the other great Mahratta powers is considered.

The object of these powers, as stated by the anonymous observer, was to get possession of the power of the Peishwa's government at Poonah. The attainment of this object, it is very evident, must have defeated the great view which the British Government must have had in admitting the Peishwa at all to become a party to the general defensive alliance.

As soon as Scindiah or Holkar would have established themselves at Poonah they would immediately have revived the old claims upon the Nizam; and the Peishwa without power would have been unable to execute his own treaty.

The question then upon this part of the subject comes to be whether the Peishwa is more likely to be able to maintain his independence in relation to the other great chiefs of the empire by having the British troops stationed in his territories, or by having the force subsidized by himself stationed in the territories of the Company.

Upon this point I have to observe, that as in order to defend the Peishwa, against the attempts of either of those chiefs to establish an influence at his Durbar by means of an armed force, it would be necessary to bring the troops from a great distance; and they would have to arrive and operate in a country in which no magazines or establishment would have been formed for them. I can have no doubt respecting the expediency, as a military question, of establishing the subsidiary force within the Peishwa's territories.

As a political question, I consider that inasmuch as the subsidiary troops being on the spot, would provide a force ready at all times to support the Peishwa's power, to have them in that situation would be more likely to prevent attempts to influence his Durbar by force of arms which must occasion war, than to station them in the Company's territories.

In respect to the notion of the anonymous observer, that by extending the basis of the treaty of Bassein, it might be hoped to include some of the other great Mahratta powers, I have to observe that the object is to make the Peishwa powerful in his own government so that he may be able to keep his treaty with us.

I have already shewn that there was no ground for hope that any of the great chiefs would consent to any arrangement which would place the power at Poonah out of their reach, and nothing short of such an arrangement would answer our purpose.

It would not be desirable that any of them should become parties to the defensive alliance if the great object of our policy should be defeated by that measure.

In this view of the question, it is scarcely necessary to advert to the assertion of the anonymous observer, that a subsidiary alliance, such as that formed in the year 1768 with the Nizam, is most applicable to the situation of the Peishwa and of his territories. The independence of the Peishwa's power is an object, and that we must effect by whatever means we may have in our hands; but if it were necessary to the argument, I could point out to the anonymous observer that the Peishwa is a power much nearer to us, and who touches us upon many more important points, than the Nizam does.

When considering this objection to the 4th article of the treaty of Bassein, it is necessary that I should advert to the objection of the anonymous observer, that by placing the troops in the territories of the Peishwa it is necessary to increase the number of European troops in India; and that Great Britain cannot afford to supply the number of European troops required for the service in India.

The 4th article does not specify that European troops shall be stationed in the Peishwa's territories, and therefore the objection does not apply to the treaty of Bassein.

It is perfectly true that in the important services in which the Company's troops may be engaged on the part of the Peishwa, European troops may be necessary; but as those services must equally have been performed, if the troops had been stationed in the Company's territories, European troops would equally be necessary.

But the anonymous observer has not supposed that an increase of European troops would be required on the ground that their services might be necessary in the Peishwa's territories, but on a general calculation of certain proportions of European to native troops in India in general.

In the first place the increase of European troops would be necessary on this ground also, whether the subsidiary force were stationed in the territories of the Peishwa or not; the native army must still have been increased (unless indeed it should be proposed to take the Peishwa's subsidy and not furnish him with any troops) and the number of European troops must likewise have been increased in order to keep up the due proportion; but in the second place, this calculation of proportions of European to native troops is certainly erroneous, and does not exist in the mind of any man who has ever conducted or considered the details of the service in India. If the proportion does exist, on what calculation is it founded? In what part of India is it practically carried into execution?

In almost all services in India it is certainly necessary that there should be some European troops; but the number in proportion to the native troops employed on the same services must vary according to the nature of the service required, and the description of the enemy against whom it is directed.

For instance, in the wars against Tippoo Sultaun, the proportions of European to native troops were about one-third in the first, and one-fourth in the second. In the late war against the Mahrattas the number of Europeans employed in proportion to natives, was not more than one-tenth or one-eleventh.

I certainly agree with the idea of the anonymous observer so far, that a body of 8 or 10,000 native troops ought never to be assembled without some Europeans, for very obvious reasons; but as there are few such collections of troops in India, I should conceive that I founded my calculations upon very erroneous principles, and deceived those to whom I should communicate them, if I should upon this opinion state that the European troops ought to be in the proportion of one-eighth or one-tenth to the native troops throughout the Indian establishments. Thousands of native troops must necessarily be employed in garrisons in the interior and on various duties, in which it would be very inconvenient to employ Europeans; and on the other hand Europeans are absolutely necessary in certain garrisons and stations and services, in some cases in equal proportions, in others one-third of the number of natives.

The only safe mode therefore of forming an opinion respecting the number of European troops required in India is to call for and examine details; and if this mode should be adopted, it will be found that the treaty of Bassein does not add, and does not render it necessary to add one European infantry soldier to the establishments in India.

In respect to the increase of the European troops in general, it is my opinion that it will be found that they are not more numerous at this moment than they were in the years 1790, 91, and 92. According to the detailed distributions which I have seen, the number of regiments of European infantry now required for the continent of India is twenty, including three of the Company's regiments, viz. six for Bengal, ten for Madras, including one for the subsidiary force at Hyderabad, and four for Bombay, including one for Goa. This is the peace establishment.

In the years 1790, 91, and 92, there were of King's infantry in India nine regiments, two regiments of Hanoverians, six Company's regiments in Bengal, four at Madras, and two at Bombay; making altogether twenty-three regiments. The artillery at the different Presidencies were nearly of the same strength with the artillery at present.

At all events if an increase of European troops is necessary, which in my opinion it is not, beyond twenty regiments complete to 1000 rank and file, the necessity of this measure must not be attributed to the treaty of Bassein.

In respect to the proposal that the treaty of Bassein should be altered in this article, viz. that the troops should be removed from the Peishwa's territories, I have reason to know that his Highness would be exceedingly alarmed if the proposal were made to him; and that it is more than probable he would move with the troops.

I have now to consider the objection of the anonymous

observer to the 12th and 17th articles of the treaty of Bassein, by the former of which, the Peishwa is bound to abide by the Company's mediation and arbitration in all cases, and by the latter not to commence any negotiation with any power without giving previous notice to the Company's government.

In order to understand clearly the object of these articles, it is necessary to consider the nature and constitution of the contracting parties; to examine their political objects and systems, to see by what rules or systems of policy they are respectively bound, and in what manner affected by their respective connections with other sovereign authorities. European governments were till very lately guided by certain rules and systems of policy, so accurately defined and generally known, that it was scarcely possible to suppose a political event in which the interests and conduct of each state would not be as well known to the corps diplomatique in general as to the statesman of each particular state.

The Asiatic governments do not acknowledge, and hardly know of such rules and systems. Their governments are arbitrary, the objects of their policy are always shifting, they have no regular established system, the effect of which is to protect the weak against the strong; on the contrary, the object of each of them separately, and of all of them collectively, is to destroy the weak; and if by chance they should by a sense of common danger be induced for a season to combine their efforts for their mutual defence, the combination lasts only as long as it is attended by success; the first reverse dissolves it; and at all events it is dissolved long before the danger ceases, the apprehension of which originally caused it.

There cannot be a stronger proof of this defect of policy in the Asiatic governments than the dissolution of the combination of the year 1790, between the English, the Mahrattas, and the Nizam, by the attack of the Mahrattas on the Nizam in the year 1795.

These observations apply to the government of the Mahrattas more than to any other of the Asiatic governments. Their schemes and systems of policy are the wildest of any: they undertake expeditions not only without viewing their remote consequences upon other states or upon their own; but without considering more than the chance of success of the immediate expedition in contemplation.

The Company's government in India, the other contracting

party to this alliance, is one bound by all the rules and systems of European policy.

The Company's power in India is supposed to depend much upon its reputation; and although I do not admit that it depends upon its reputation as distinguished from its real force, as appears to be contended by some, I may say that it is particularly desirable for a government so constituted as the Company's, never to enter upon any political object, the probable result of which should not be greatly in favour of success. Besides this, the Company's government in India is bound by acts of Parliament not to undertake wars of aggression; not to make any but defensive alliances, and those only in cases in which the other contracting party shall bind itself to defend the possessions of the Company actually threatened with hostilities.

The Company's government in India is also connected with his Majesty's Government, and as an Asiatic power is liable to be involved in wars with European powers possessing territories in India, whenever his Majesty shall be at war with those powers.

The picture above drawn of the state of politics among Asiatic powers proves, that no permanent system can be adopted which will preserve the weak against the strong, and will keep all for any length of time in their relative situations, and the whole, in peace; excepting there should be one power, which, either by the superiority of its strength, its military system, or its resources, shall preponderate, and be able to protect all. This is proved by the history of the last fourteen years.

The Company has been the preponderating power, and by the 2nd article of the treaty of Bassein has in so many words taken the Peishwa under its protection.

I might contend that the stipulations of the 12th and 17th articles are only consequences of the protection promised, and really offered. But in my opinion these stipulations are the necessary consequence of the alliance between a power such as the Peishwa's, and one such as the Company's, bound by rules of policy, acts of Parliament, and by the acts of his Majesty's Government.

It would be impossible to define the various claims, and grounds for war, existing not only between the Peishwa and the Nizam, but between the Peishwa and all the other powers of India.

The Mahrattas claim the choute of all India; and all the

claims of this description centre in the Peishwa's authority. Besides this general claim, there are others of various descriptions and denominations upon every power, of all which there are records at Poonah; and it is a mistake to suppose that the Peishwa, however weak in point of troops and resources, will not find persons in the Mahratta empire ready and willing to enforce these claims in his name.

All the warfare which would be the consequence of bringing forward these claims will be prevented by the stipulation that the Company shall mediate and arbitrate in every case.

But the anonymous observer says, that the benefit to be derived from the 12th article ought to have been left to the operation of the British influence in the Peishwa's councils, and ought not to have been the subject of a treaty. To this objection to the article in question, the best answer is to state the fact, viz. that notwithstanding the right which we have acquired by treaty to mediate between the Peishwa and other powers, and the influence which we have in his councils, by that stipulation and a variety of events which have occurred since the treaty of Bassein was concluded, it is not so easy as the anonymous observer imagines, at all times to prevent the evils which must result from the Peishwa's enforcing these claims.

The anonymous observer says, that if the Peishwa should contrary to our advice and opinion, commence an unjust war, he ought not to be supported by the British Government. This is perfectly true; but the object of the 12th article is to prevent the possibility of unjust wars, and to preserve the Peishwa's government from the destruction which must be the consequence of his entering into any war without the Company's assistance.

This article is the bond of peace to India. It is this which renders the treaty really defensive, and makes the Governor-General really responsible for every war in which the British Government may be engaged. If this article were not in the treaty, the Peishwa would be the responsible person.

If the general mediation on the part of the Company be necessary to ensure peace, there is certainly no occasion that the Peishwa should be in communication with other independent powers. All his foreign affairs must be transacted and eventually settled by the Company; and any other communication must be intended only for sinister purposes.

The stipulation of the 17th article is necessary in order to enable the British Government to have a knowledge of, and stop at once any intrigues which have a tendency to war. Those who have seen the course of proceedings of a Mahratta Durbar will not be at a loss to find reasons for this stipulation; and in fact even this stipulation cannot entirely check the intrigues which are its constant operation.

But the mode in which it will operate most beneficially will be by checking intrigues with European powers; and surely this cannot be deemed an inconsiderable object by the anonymous observer.

The principle and foundation of the treaty of Bassein, which is protection from the Company's government to that of the Peishwa, would prevent the stipulation of the 17th article from being reciprocal. The Company's government must have communication with some powers with which the Peishwa never had any; and it would be very inconvenient to be obliged to lay these communications before the Peishwa's Durbar.

But it must be recollected that the Company are constantly liable by the acts of his Majesty's prerogative, to be at war, or hold communications with European nations having territories in India; and it would be a curious proceeding to lay these communications before the Peishwa's Durbar. This measure would be necessary, if the stipulations of the 17th article were made reciprocal.

ARTHUR WELLESLEY.

3. War with Scindiah and the Rajah of Berar.

42. The Marquess Wellesley to the Honourable Major-General Wellesley.

Delegation to General Wellesley of extraordinary powers for the conduct of the Mahratta War, &c.

(Secret.)

Fort William, June 26th, 1803.

Sir,

The present state of affairs in the Mahratta empire, and the security of the alliance lately concluded between his Highness the Peishwa and the British Government require, that a temporary authority should be constituted at the least possible distance from the scene of eventual negotiation or hostilities, with full powers to conclude upon the spot whatever arrangements may become necessary either for the final settlement of peace, or for the active prosecution of war. In such a crisis, various questions may arise of which the precise tendency cannot be foreseen, and which may demand a prompt decision. The issue of these questions may involve the result of war or peace, and in either alternative the delay of reference to my authority might endanger the seasonable despatch and the ultimate prosperity of the public service.

The success of the military operations now placed under your directions may depend on the timely decision of various political questions which may occur with relation to the interests and views of the several Mahratta Chiefs and Jaggeerdars, and of their Highnesses the Peishwa and the Nizam; on the other hand, the issue of every political arrangement now under negotiation with the powers of Hindostan, or the Deccan, must be inseparably blended with the movements of your army.

It is therefore necessary during the present crisis to unite the general direction and control of all political and military affairs in Hindostan and the Deccan under a distinct local authority, subject to the Governor-General in Council. These powers could not be placed with advantage in any other hands than those of the general officer commanding the troops destined to restore the tranquillity of the Deccan.

Your approved ability, zeal, temper, activity, and judgment, combined with your extensive local experience, your established influence, and high reputation among the Mahratta Chiefs and States, and your intimate knowledge of my views and sentiments concerning the British interests in the Mahratta empire, have determined me to vest these important and arduous powers in your hands.

The nature of your military command under the orders of his Excellency Lieut.-General Stuart is not likely to admit any doubt, or to lead to any embarrassment. In order, however, to obviate all possible difficulty on this point, I hereby appoint you to the chief command of all the British troops, and of the forces of our allies serving in the territories of the Peishwa, of the Nizam, or of any of the Mahratta states or chiefs, subject only to the orders of his Excellency Lieut.-General Stuart, or of his Excellency General Lake.

I further empower and direct you to assume and exercise the general direction and control of all the political and military affairs of the British Government in the territories of the Nizam, of the Peishwa, and of the Mahratta states and chiefs.

The instructions addressed to the Resident at Poonah convey to you full authority to carry into complete effect all the measures therein provisionally prescribed, as far as the accomplishment of those measures may depend upon your proceedings, without previous reference to my authority.

I hereby confirm that authority, and I further vest you with full powers to decide any question which may arise in the prosecution of the measures prescribed by those orders, according to the general spirit of my views and intentions concerning the affairs of the Mahratta state, directing you however to refer to me in all cases in which a previous reference to my authority may not appear to hazard the public interests. Under the same reservation, I authorize and empower you to commence and conclude negotiations with any of the Mahratta Chiefs and Jaggeerdars on the part of the British Government, for the purpose of promoting the general objects of the alliance lately concluded with his Highness the Peishwa, or of that subsisting with his Highness the Nizam.

This general authority especially empowers you either directly or through the representatives or officers of the British Government to negotiate and conclude any engagements with Dowlut Rao Scindiah, with the Rajah of Berar, or with Jeswunt Rao Holkar, which may induce those chieftains to retire with their forces within the limits of their respective dominions, or to afford any other satisfactory pledge of their respective pacific intentions towards the British Government and its allies. You will be careful to form any such engagements on principles conformable to the dignity, honour and interests of the British Government and of its allies, and to the spirit and tenor of our subsisting treaties. You are also authorized under this instruction to arbitrate on the part of the British Government the terms of any convention between his Highness the Peishwa and those chieftains respectively, for the settlement of mutual differences or demands, or for the adjustment of relative pretensions, and to pledge the guarantee of the British Government for the observance of those terms by the contracting parties. You are also empowered to arbitrate and guarantee the terms of accommodation between Scindiah and Holkar, if any points should yet remain unadjusted between those chieftains; and to frame, negotiate, and guarantee any terms between those chieftains jointly or separately, and the Rajah of Berar. It is my particular intention by these instructions to enable you to conclude such arrangements with any of those chieftains either separately or combined, as may preclude or frustrate any confederacy, or other measures directed to the subversion of the treaty of Bassein, or to the injury of our rights and interests, or those of our allies.

You are also empowered to conclude such engagements with any subordinate chieftains of the Mahratta state as may appear to you to be expedient for the purpose of securing their co-operation in the event of hostilities between the British Government and Scindiah, the Rajah of Berar, Jeswunt Rao Holkar, or any other power. You are authorized further to adopt the necessary measures for conciliating the obedience of the subordinate chiefs to the Peishwa's authority.

In the actual relation of the British Government to the Peishwa we possess the right of securing to the Chiefs and Jaggeerdars of the Mahratta empire the satisfaction of their just and equitable claims, even independently of any direct act of the Peishwa's Government. The exercise of that right becomes a duty in proportion to the danger with which the tardy, infirm, or erroneous proceedings of the Peishwa's Government may menace the security of the alliance, and the stability of his Highness's legitimate authority.

The policy of the treaty, and my inclination, would induce me to limit our interference in the internal affairs of the Peishwa's Government within the most moderate bounds. I am determined, however, to pursue that course which shall lead most directly and speedily to the full restoration and establishment of his Highness's authority on a permanent basis, and to the efficient operation of the benefits of the alliance. If the imbecility of his Highness's councils, the defects of his personal character, or the intrigues of his servants should tend to frustrate or to retard the accomplishment of those salutary objects, the provisional interference of the British power must be seasonably and firmly applied to rescue his Highness from the immediate effects of evils which cannot be suffered to operate for a moment, without the hazard of every interest which the treaty of Bassein was destined to restore and to confirm.

You will, therefore, proceed without delay to conclude all such arrangements with his Highness's jaggeerdars and servants of all descriptions as may appear to you to be necessary to enable you to meet the exigencies of the present crisis; and you will not abstain from the most direct and even ostensible interposition of the British authority, which may in your judgment be requisite to secure the exertions, to animate the zeal, or to reward the services of the Peishwa's subjects and servants in the common cause of his Highness and of his allies. Whatever immediate expence may be necessary for this purpose will be defrayed at present by the British Government, and will hereafter become a charge against the Peishwa, as being inseparably connected with his Highness's restoration and establishment.

All such engagements as you may conclude with his Highness the Peishwa, and with any of the Mahratta chiefs and jaggeerdars, or other powers, will be confirmed by me under the limitations and restrictions herein prescribed.

In exercising the powers hereby entrusted to your sole discretion, I direct you to hold the most unreserved and confidential intercourse with the Residents at Poonah, at Hyderabad, and at the camp of Dowlut Rao Scindiah, and also with the Resident in the territory of the Guicowar; and you will regularly correspond with Lord Clive and with Mr. Duncan.

You will necessarily continue to receive the orders of his Excellency Lieut.-General Stuart, and to submit a full view of all your operations to the direction of his Excellency. I particularly enjoin you to submit to his Excellency the earliest information of your proceedings of a political nature under these instructions.

If circumstances should render it necessary for his Excellency Lieut.-General Stuart to unite the whole force of the army in the field, and to assume in person the general command in the Deccan, in that case I hereby vest the authority conveyed to you by this despatch in his Excellency Lieut.-General Stuart, under the fullest confidence that he will exercise it with the same advantage to the public service, which I have uniformly derived from the exertion of his Excellency's distinguished talents, experience, and virtues.

In the case supposed I empower his Excellency to delegate the whole or any part of the said authority to you; and I desire that in exercising the said authority or any part thereof in his own person, his Excellency will be pleased to communicate fully with you, and to receive your advice and opinion.

In the execution of these instructions I authorize and direct you to employ any additional military staff, and to require the services of any civil officers; whose assistance you may deem necessary to the despatch of the arduous affairs connected with the subject of this order.

I have the honour to be, &c.

WELLESLEY.

43. The Marquess Wellesley to his Excellency General Lake, Commander-in-Chief, &c.

Necessity, Objects, and Plan of the War in Hindostan; and Principles to be observed in negotiating with M. Perron and the native Chiefs.

(Secret.)

Fort William, July 27th, 1803.

Sir,

1. The necessity of providing for the event of hostilities with Scindiah and the Rajah of Berar has already induced me to transmit to your Excellency, in the form of private notes, such suggestions as have appeared to me to be requisite for the purpose of enabling your Excellency to frame a plan of military operations, connected with the political considerations which have ultimately compelled me to engage in war against those chieftains, and with the objects which I deem most important to secure by the success of our arms in the final settlement of peace.

2. These private communications from me have been answered by your Excellency in the same form, and I have hitherto deemed it to be expedient to return my observations upon your Excellency's propositions through the channel of private correspondence. It is now expedient to adopt the regular course of official correspondence with your Excellency in the Secret Department, and I shall accordingly henceforth address you in the form observed in this letter, or through the secretary in the Secret Department, according to the nature of the subject under discussion.

3. In this despatch I propose to state to your Excellency my views and intentions with regard to the following important points.

First. The objects which appear to me to be the most desirable to be attained in the prosecution of hostilities against Scindiah and the Rajah of Berar on the north-western frontier of Hindostan.

Secondly. The general plan of military operations by which

these objects appear to be attainable with the greatest degree of expedition and security.

Thirdly. The course of political arrangements and negotiations which I propose to pursue under your Excellency's superintendance, for the purpose of facilitating the operations of your army, and of ensuring the stability of peace under the most favourable conditions to the British interests.

4. With a view to render the statement of my sentiments on these questions more clear and distinct, I have annexed to this despatch copies of the documents enumerated in the margin.

5. To every person conversant with the true nature of the British interests and power in India, the north-western frontier of Hindostan must have appeared to present the most vulnerable point of our extensive empire.

6. The condition of the power of the Seiks, as well as of that of the Mahrattas and of the Rajpoots, and other petty states, offers considerable advantage to an invading enemy from the more remote north-western countries of Asia, or from the banks of the Indus; and it is unnecessary to remark to your Excellency's judgment, experience, and knowledge, that the enterprizing spirit of France, or the ambition of Russia, or even the violence and rapacity of the Afghan tribes, or of other Asiatic nations inhabiting the northern and western countries of Asia might have pursued projects of invasion in that quarter which might have occasioned considerable embarrassment to the British power in India.

7. A sense of this danger concurred with other motives to induce me to conclude those arrangements with the Nabob Vizier, which terminated in the treaty of Lucknow, and which secured a considerable augmentation of the military, political and financial resources and power of the British nation on the north-western frontier of Oude.

8. The result of that happy settlement has certainly afforded a great accession of security against the dangers which menaced the stability of our empire on that side of India.

9. But the local position of Scindiah's territories, the condition and nature of Scindiah's military force in Hindostan, and the corrupt and profligate councils of that weak, arrogant, and faithless chief, still constitutes a serious danger to the British interests. The territories of Scindiah between the Jumna and the Ganges interrupt the line of our defence in that quarter; and some of his

principal posts are introduced into the centre of our dominions, while the possession of Agra, Delhi and of the western and southern bank of the Jumna enables him to command nearly the whole line of our north-western frontier.

10. In the event of any considerable accession to Scindiah's power, or in the event of his forming any connection with France, or with any other enemy to the British interests, the actual position of his territories and forces in Hindostan would furnish great advantages to him in any attack upon the Company's dominions.

11. Formidable as the power of Scindiah might have become in the event of any accession to his strength, a danger more urgent and more direct in all its consequences has grown out of the decline of Scindiah's local authority in Hindostan, and has recently assumed a more alarming aspect in proportion to the accumulated embarrassment of Scindiah's circumstances in the Deccan, and to the general decay of his resources and power.

12. The regular infantry in the service of Scindiah under the command of European officers, is supported by funds derivable almost exclusively from the territorial possessions of that chief situated between the Jumna, the Ganges and the mountains of Kumaon.

13. A considerable portion, if not the whole of this territory has been assigned to M. Perron, a French officer, who has succeeded Mr. Duboigne in the chief command of Scindiah's regular infantry.

14. M. Perron has formed this territory into an independent state of which Scindiah's regular infantry may be justly termed the national army. That force is now stated to amount to 8,000 infantry and an equal number of cavalry.

15. The inhabitants of the districts comprehended in M. Perron's Jagheer, consider that officer as their immediate sovereign, while the troops supported from the revenues of the country regard M. Perron as the immediate executive authority from which the army is to receive orders, subsistence and pay. Possessing such means M. Perron dictates with the authority of a sovereign state of a superior rank, and with the vigour of efficient military power to the petty states occupying the countries to the southward of the Jumna, and by the terror of his name and arms holds in abject submission the Rajpoot states of Jyenagur and Jodpore, together with the Jauts and the state

of Gohud, extending his influence even to Bundelcund and to the country occupied by the Seiks.

16. Scindiah retains no efficient control over M. Perron or over his regular troops. Various instances must be familiar to your Excellency's knowledge in which M. Perron has either openly disobeyed, or systematically evaded the orders of Scindiah especially in the late crisis of that chief's affairs.

17. M. Perron has for some time past manifested a systematic disposition to remove all British officers from the command of Scindiah's regular infantry, and to introduce French officers under his own immediate patronage.

18. M. Perron is supposed to have amassed a considerable fortune, and your Excellency is intimately acquainted with his anxious desire to retire to Europe, and to dispose of his actual command, and of his territorial possessions to some person of the French nation.

19. To these considerations it is important to add that M. Perron is in possession of the person of the unfortunate Emperor Shah Allum, and consequently is master of the nominal authority of that unhappy prince. M. Perron therefore may transfer this valuable possession together with his property of any other description to any French adventurer, or officer, who may be enabled to complete such a purchase.

20. Thus the coincidence of various extraordinary and uncontrolable accidents, the weakness of Scindiah's personal character, the rapacity and profligacy of his ministers, (who have engaged him in pursuits of aggrandizement, avarice, and ambition, at a distance from Hindostan, in the Deccan, at Poonah, and in the southern provinces of the Mahratta empire)—the treachery of many of his chiefs whose interests consist in diverting his attention from the affairs of Hindostan to those of the Deccan, and the recent shock which his power has received from Holkar, have contributed to found an independent French state on the most vulnerable part of the Company's frontier.

21. Under the influence of a succession of French adventurers, this state must be exposed to every intrigue of the French in India, and even to the ambition and hostile spirit of the person who now rules the French nation; nor could an instrument of destruction more skilfully adapted to wound the heart of the British empire in India, be presented to the vindictive hand of the Chief Consul of France.

22. This French state actually holds possession of the person

and nominal authority of the Moghul, maintains the most efficient army of regular native infantry, and the most powerful artillery now existing in India, with the exception of the Company's troops, and exercises a considerable influence over the neighbouring states, from the banks of the Indus to the confluence of the Jumna and the Ganges.

23. In the supposition of the most intimate and established connection of amity and alliance between Scindiah and the British power, and in the event even of Scindiah's accession to the treaty of Bassein, and to the general defensive alliance with the Company, the Nizam and the Peishwa, it is impossible to suppose that this French state would co-operate with cordiality in support of the British interests. The aid of this state could be least expected in the case which would most urgently demand it, and which would require the most active operation of the principles of the general defensive alliance.

24. In the event of an attack from France upon the British dominions or power in India, it would not be expected that a French state erected under the nominal and ostensible auspices of Scindiah in Hindostan, would afford any substantial aid to the ally of the British power in a contest against France, even if that ally should be disposed to assist us in such a crisis.

25. On the other hand no doubt exists that Scindiah would receive the most zealous aid from the same state in any attempt which he might be disposed to make either for the reduction of the British or for the aggrandizement of the French power in India.

26. In addition to these remarks, your Excellency is apprized that the vicinity of M. Perron's regular infantry, operates as a constant drain upon the population of the Company's provinces, and diminishes the sources of our agriculture, manufactures, commerce, and revenue as well of our recruits for the army in that quarter.

27. In the present crisis when every circumstance announces the probability of a renewal of the war with France, and urges the necessity of resorting to every practicable measure of precaution and security, the safety of the British dominions requires the reduction of M. Perron's military resources and power, independently of any question which might exist between Scindiah and the British Government.

28. In a state of profound peace and even of alliance with Scindiah, the necessity of providing for our own security would

justify a formal demand for the removal of a danger, so imminent, from the frontier of our dominions. The refusal of Scindiah to comply with such a demand would afford a just ground of war against that chief; and any true or false plea of inability on the part of Scindiah to control the movements or to reduce the power of this French state, would authorize and require the British Government to assume the protection of its own territories, and to remove with his own hand the proximate cause of insecurity and alarm. Your Excellency will therefore be pleased to understand that the most desirable object in prosecuting hostilities against Scindiah on the north western frontier of Hindostan appears to me to be the entire reduction of M. Perron's regular corps. This operation necessarily includes the capture or destruction of all his artillery and military stores and especially of all arms of European construction.

29. Connected with this object and with every principle of security bearing relation to it is the occupation of the whole tract of country forming the Doab between the Jumna and Ganges to the mountains of Kumaon. And similar considerations will require the occupation of Delhi and Agra and of a chain of posts on the western and southern bank of the Jumna from the mountains of Kumaon to Bundelcund sufficient to secure to the British power the free navigation of the Jumna and the possession of both banks of that river. It is not my desire to extend the actual possessions of the Company beyond the line of the Jumna including Agra and Delhi, with a continued chain of posts to the westward and southward of the Jumna for the purpose already described.

30. Within the described line my wish and intention is to establish the system of the Company's Government in all its branches, but whatever connections may be formed beyond that line to the westward and southward of the Jumna must be regulated on the principle of defensive alliance or tributary dependence in such manner as shall form between the actual possessions of the Company and the Mahrattas, a barrier of petty states exercising the internal government of their respective dominions in alliance with the Company and under the protection of our power.

31. In drawing this line I am aware of the position of the Jagheers of Sumroo's Begum situated between the Jumna and the Ganges. For this special case I have accordingly provided in my instructions to Mr. Mercer. It is certainly necessary that

the Jagheers of Sumroo's Begum should ultimately be brought under the immediate government of the Company.

32. It is highly important to secure the possession of the person and nominal authority of the Moghul against the designs of France. The Moghul has never been an important or dangerous instrument in the hands of the Mahrattas, but might become a powerful aid to the cause of France in India, under the direction of French agents.

33. The person and authority of that unhappy monarch have been treated by the Mahrattas and by M. Perron with the most barbarous indignity and violence, and it would contribute to the reputation of the British name to afford an honourable and tranquil asylum to the fallen dignity and declining age of the King of Delhi. It would also be necessary to extend our protection to his majesty's heir apparent and to any of the royal family who might otherwise fall into the hands of France.

34. The reduction of M. Perron's force would afford us the means of forming alliances with all the inferior states beyond the Jumna for the purpose of enabling us in the first instance to prosecute the war with the greatest advantage and finally by forming a barrier composed of these states, to exclude Scindiah and the Mahrattas altogether from the northern districts of Hindostan.

35. It is extremely desirable that Bundelcund should ultimately be placed under the immediate authority of the British Government. Such an arrangement would afford great additional security to the rich province and city of Benares and would effectually check whatever power might remain to the Rajah of Berar or to any other Mahratta chief in that quarter.

36. Reviewing these statements your Excellency will observe that the most prosperous issue of a war against Scindiah and the Rajah of Berar on the north-western frontier of Hindostan would in my judgment comprize,

1st. The destruction of the French state now formed on the banks of the Jumna together with all its military resources.

2dly. The extension of the Company's frontier to the Jumna, with the possession of Agra, Delhi and a sufficient chain of posts on the western and southern banks of the Jumna.

3dly. The possession of the nominal authority of the Moghul.

4thly. The establishment of an efficient system of alliance with all the petty states to the southward and westward of the Jumna from Jyenagur to Bundelcund.

5thly. The annexation of Bundelcund to the Company's dominions.

37. The result of such an arrangement would destroy the influence of the French and of the Mahrattas in the northern districts of Hindostan, and would enable us to commence the foundations of such an intercourse with the Seiks and with the tribes inhabiting the Punjab and the banks of the Attock, as might furnish sufficient means of frustrating any attempt of an invading enemy from the western side of the Indus.

38. In stating to your Excellency my sentiments with regard to the general plan of military operations by which the proposed objects appear to be attainable with the greatest degree of expedition and security, your Excellency will be pleased to understand that it is not my intention either to limit the free exercise of your discretion, or to interpose any ideas, which may not meet the full approbation of your Excellency's superior judgment, experience and professional skill.

39. I have however deemed it to be my duty under this restriction to communicate to you in my private correspondence such opinions on this branch of the subject as have appeared to me to merit consideration; and with the same view I have transmitted to your Excellency my observations on the plans which I have received from you. I shall therefore proceed to state without further reserve in this official form such conclusions as I have drawn from a review of the documents and suggestions which have been brought under my examination.

40. The first object of the campaign must be to destroy the military force and resources of M. Perron; and it is extremely important that this object should be accomplished previously to the close of the rainy season.

41. It is therefore necessary that the main body of the army should be assembled at the point most favourable for the attack of M. Perron's force, and in the state of preparation and of equipment which may be deemed by your Excellency most advantageous for the speedy execution of that service.

42. Your Excellency will have observed from the whole tenor of every communication which you have received from me, that I not only concur entirely with you in deeming the destruction of M. Perron's force to be the primary object of the campaign, but that the most deliberate consideration of the actual state of affairs between his Majesty and France would have induced me

to have undertaken this service even independently of any contest with Dowlut Rao Scindiah.

43. I shall therefore readily sanction any augmentation which your Excellency may think fit to make to the strength of the main army to be directed against M. Perron, by suspending the operations of the several proposed detachments or by concentrating the movements of those detachments with a view to the principal object of the campaign, which is comprized in the '*early and effectual demolition of the French state erected by M. Perron on the banks of the Jumna.*'

44. With this observation I desire that your Excellency will compose the main army and regulate the strength and operations of the several detachments in the manner which shall appear to your judgment to afford the most absolute security for the '*complete destruction of M. Perron's force previously to the conclusion of the rains.*'

45. The point of most urgent importance connected with the destruction of M. Perron's force is in my opinion the security of the person of the Moghul, and of the heir apparent, and it is therefore my earnest wish that early measures should be taken for that purpose. The operations of the detachment proposed to cover Rohilcund, and eventually to invade Saharunpore might probably effect this object, and at the same time might tend to promote the success of the movements of the main army against M. Perron.

46. I trust that the powers already furnished to your Excellency for the augmentation of the regular corps to the war establishment, and for raising such temporary and local corps as may be requisite for the maintenance of the internal tranquillity of the provinces, will enable you to provide effectually against internal commotion during the continuance of the war. But any temporary inconvenience of that nature must be hazarded if the security of the great objects of the campaign should require you to incur such a danger. The early success of the army in the field will enable you to suppress without difficulty every effort of our domestic enemies whose number cannot be considerable and whose power is extremely contemptible.

47. I consider the operations of the detachment stationed in the direction of Delhi to be next in importance to those of the main army.

48. After the destruction of M. Perron's power shall have been effected and the person of the Moghul shall have been

protected beyond the possibility of hazard, the operation of greatest importance will be the reduction of the fortress of Agra. Your Excellency will form the most correct judgment in deciding the time and mode of undertaking this service. Whether it would be possible either to blockade or to seize Agra during the time of the movements of the main army against M. Perron, or whether the siege of Agra should be postponed until the main army shall be at liberty to act against Agra, are points which I submit implicitly to your Excellency's determination, it is however important that Agra should be reduced previously to the close of the rainy season.

49. The occupation of Bundelcund is the object next in importance to those already stated, and it appears to me that the detachment to be assembled at Allahabad and the detachment to be assembled for the purpose of covering Benares will effect that object in sufficient time to afford additional countenance to the operations of the main army.

50. The effectual protection of Benares is a point of considerable importance and your Excellency appears to have taken sufficient precautions for that purpose.

51. It has appeared to me to be prudent to adopt a systematic and comprehensive plan of defensive measures on the whole line of the frontier from Mirzapore to Midnapore, and I have directed the Chief Secretary to transmit to your Excellency a copy of the orders which I have issued on that subject.

52. The occupation of the passes from the southward and westward of the Jumna to the Deccan, is an object which has already engaged your Excellency's attention. If you should be enabled to bring the main body of M. Perron's force to action, or should find it practicable to secure that force in any other manner, it appears improbable that Scindiah's troops can occupy those passes in any considerable strength.

53. Major General Wellesley may be expected to commence operations against Scindiah in the Deccan at the close of this month, and I entertain a firm confidence of the complete success of those operations in the entire defeat of Scindiah's forces and of those of the Rajah of Berar in that quarter. It is however an object of importance and of prudent precaution, to secure the passes between Hindostan and the Deccan previously to the close of the rains.

54. The expediency of occupying the post of Gwalior previously to the defeat of M. Perron, must depend upon local

circumstances upon which your Excellency will exercise your discretion, after having considered the tenor of my instructions to Mr. Mercer.

55. Mr. Duncan has received my orders for the seizure of Scindiah's sea-port of Baroach, and of all his other possessions in Guzerat; which objects will probably be effected whenever General Wellesley shall seize the important fortress of Ahmednugger. The loss of these possessions will deprive Scindiah of the most efficient portion of his military resources in the Deccan.

56. An expedition from Calcutta and Ganjam will occupy Cuttack in the month of August.

57. It may be reasonably expected that these combined attacks will leave no other enemy opposed to your Excellency's force during the rainy season than M. Perron's troops, and whatever force may have been assembled at Calpee: and I confidently expect that before the close of the rains, a material impression will have been made on every branch of the Mahratta power. It is however possible that M. Perron may have induced some of the Seik chiefs to aid him by predatory incursions into the Company's northern territories, and it will therefore be necessary for your Excellency to advert to that possible danger.

58. The objects proposed to be attained in this campaign, and the general plan of military operations which I have described, will limit the movement of the main army to the Doab between the Ganges and the Jumna, with the addition of a narrow tract of country on the western and southern branch of the Jumna.

59. No detachment of the army will probably be required to move beyond Gwalior before the close of the rains. It may therefore be expected that your Excellency will not experience any considerable difficulty either in the supply or movements of the armies; and that you will be enabled during the course of this campaign to establish such depôts of provisions, stores and other supplies, as may facilitate your advance into Berar, towards the Deccan, or towards the territories of the Rajpoot chiefs, if such movements should become necessary in another campaign.

60. Your Excellency has provided with great prudence for the maintenance of tranquillity and order within the reserved territories of his Excellency the Nabob Vizier, by leaving a respectable force in that quarter. I entirely approve that precaution, leaving it, however to your discretion to vary the description or strength of the force stationed in the Vizier's reserved territories

according to your judgment, and to the state of local circumstances.

61. I have written to the Vizier, desiring his Excellency's assistance in the supply of elephants and cattle, and as I have engaged to defray the whole expense of whatever assistance the Vizier may contribute, I entertain a sanguine hope that his Excellency will be desirous of making an effort to manifest his zeal and attachment on this important occasion.

62. In stating these observations to your Excellency, I have purposely avoided all details relative to the disposition of corps, to the strength of the main army, or of the several detachments, to the formation of the staff, or of the different constituent parts of the army in the field. The regulation of all questions of this description, is more properly your Excellency's peculiar duty, and I entertain the most firm confidence that your Excellency will form your arrangements with that ability, public spirit, and honourable zeal for the service, which have distinguished your conduct in the various arduous situations, to which you have been called by the confidence of your Sovereign and of your country.

63. With these sentiments, I am particularly anxious to abstain from any interference of my authority which might tend to contract the sphere of your Excellency's approved talents, activity, and integrity. It will be my constant endeavour to apply my authority in such a manner, as shall afford the most effectual support to your Excellency in the display of those eminent qualifications, during a crisis, which demands their unrestrained exertion, and which promises to augment the reputation and honour of your Excellency's name, together with the glory of the British arms, and the security of the British power.

64. With regard to the political negotiations and arrangements connected with the operations of your Excellency's army, I have addressed to you on this day a letter, vesting you with special powers of the same nature as those which I have entrusted to Major-General Wellesley, and eventually to Lieut.-General Stuart in the Deccan. That letter connected with my instructions to Mr. Mercer, and with my separate letter to your Excellency of this date respecting the situation of his Majesty Shah Allum, will sufficiently apprize you of the course of political measures which your Excellency is empowered to pursue, with a view of facilitating your military operations.

65. It may, however, be convenient to state in this place, the general principles by which I am desirous of regulating your Excellency's proceedings, under the powers committed to your management.

66. It will be highly desirable to detach M. Perron from Scindiah's service by pacific negotiation. M. Perron's inclination certainly is, to dispose of his power to a French purchaser; but I should not be surprized if he were to be found ready to enter into terms with your Excellency, provided he could obtain sufficient security for his personal interests. I desire your Excellency, however to abstain from any negotiation which may afford M. Perron the opportunity of gaining time, or of preserving, by escape, or by any means, any part of his force, especially of his artillery, or ordnance.

67. I therefore request your Excellency not to commence any negotiation with M. Perron, until the success of the force to be employed against him shall appear to be perfectly secure, or until you shall be fully satisfied that the negotiation cannot afford to M. Perron any means of defeating the objects of the armament.

68. Under these precautions, I empower your Excellency to conclude any agreement for the security of M. Perron's personal interests and property, accompanied by any reasonable remuneration from the British Government which shall induce him to deliver up the whole of his military resources and power, together with his territorial possessions, and the person of the Moghul, and of the heir apparent, into your Excellency's hands.

69. The same principle applies generally to M. Perron's European officers, and the proclamations with which I have furnished your Excellency, will enable you to avail yourself of the first proper opportunity of offering propositions to those officers, or to the several corps under M. Perron's command.

70. It is probable that the blockade of Agra would enable your Excellency to obtain immediate possession of that place by offering favourable terms to Mr. Hessing and his garrison. You will act in this matter according to your judgment.

71. This despatch together with those which you have already received from me, will relieve your Excellency from any difficulty with regard to the suspension of the question of war or peace. You are now in possession of my final determination '*to reduce the power of the French state in Hindostan without delay*,' and to liberate the neighbouring chiefs and Rajahs from the yoke of that state, and of the Mahrattas, for the purpose of establishing

an effectual barrier against the revival of a similar danger in Hindostan.

72. My instructions to Mr. Mercer contain every detail which can be requisite to guide your Excellency's judgment in forming engagements with those chiefs, either for the purpose of securing their assistance during the war, or of establishing a permanent system of alliance at the conclusion of peace.

73. The general objects of the war, as described at the commencement of this despatch, sufficiently indicate the nature of the final settlement by which it is my desire to terminate hostilities, and to secure peace.

74. Your Excellency will be pleased to fix your attention upon those objects as stated in the 36th paragraph of this despatch, and to frame every permanent arrangement with the native Chiefs and Rajahs, in conformity to the general principles of excluding the influence of the French and Mahrattas from the northern provinces of Hindostan, of extending the British territory to the Jumna, and the British influence to the borders of the Deccan, and of engaging the petty chiefs and states to strengthen the proposed system by their aid and co-operation under the assurance of the protection of the British arms, and of the secure and free enjoyment of their respective rights, authorities, and possessions, within the limits of their respective territories.

75. The principles by which your Excellency will regulate your conduct towards the Moghul, are stated in my separate despatch of this date.

I have the honour to be, Sir,
Your Excellency's most faithful servant,
WELLESLEY.

N. B. Edmonstone, Esq., Secretary to Government, to Græme Mercer, Esq.

Instructions for negotiations in Bundelcund, with Rajpoots, and Sumroo's Begum.

(Most Secret.)

Fort William, July 22nd, 1803.

Sir,

1. I am directed by his Excellency the most noble the Governor-General in Council to inform you that in consequence

of a probable rupture with Dowlut Rao Scindiah and other Mahratta chieftains who have manifested a disposition to form a confederacy with that chief against the interests of the British Government, his Excellency in Council has deemed it expedient to appoint a special agent for the purpose of conducting certain political negotiations with the several states bordering on the western frontier of the British provinces under the Presidency of Bengal, and of forming defensive alliances with those states on the part of the British Government against the hostile designs of the Mahratta chieftains.

2. His Excellency in Council, in consideration of the local knowledge which you have obtained of the state of those countries, and having a firm reliance in your zeal, ability, and discretion, has been pleased to nominate you as his special agent for the purposes abovementioned, and to direct that you will immediately proceed to Allahabad with all practicable expedition, where you will enter upon the duties of the charge entrusted to you, under the following instructions.

3. You are already apprized of the proposals made some time since by Himmut Behâdur to the honourable Henry Wellesley, through Mr. John Messelbeek at Allahabad, for the transfer of the province of Bundelcund to the authority of the Honourable Company.

4. The importance which his Excellency in Council attaches to the possession of this province, as covering the Company's possessions from the inroads of a hostile force from Berar, has been considerably increased by the information received from Mr. Ahmuty, the Collector of Allahabad, that Dowlut Rao Scindiah has actually despatched a considerable body of his forces to the north-western frontier of the Company's dominions, and has addressed letters to Himmut Bahâdur, instigating those chieftains to commit depredations in the Company's dominions contiguous to Bundelcund; and that Shumshere Bahâdur, the eldest son of the late Ali Bahâdur, has arrived in the province, and assumed the authority over it, under a sunnud from Amrut Rao, and supported by a force in the service of Jeswunt Rao Holkar.

5. Under these circumstances, the immediate interposition of the British Government in the affairs of Bundelcund has become necessary, as a part of the general system of defence against the meditated designs of Dowlut Rao Scindiah and his confederates the Rajah of Berar and Jeswunt Rao Holkar.

6. His Excellency has, therefore, determined to enter into a negotiation with Himmut Behâdur for his aid and influence in establishing in the province of Bundelcund an arrangement calculated to afford to the British Government the military and political advantages of the local situation of that province in the present crisis of affairs, and his Excellency has accordingly addressed a letter to that chieftain, stating, in general terms, his Excellency's views with respect to the province of Bundelcund, and requesting him to despatch to Allahabad a confidential agent for the express purpose of conferring with you on the details of the proposed arrangement. Copies of this letter, and of the detailed proposals which Himmut Bahâdur has lately transmitted through Mr. Ahmuty, are enclosed for your information.

7. During the progress of the negotiation you will be enabled to ascertain more precisely than has hitherto been done, the means which Himmut Bahâdur may possess of effectually supporting the interests of the British Government in the province, and will accordingly be enabled to submit to his Excellency the claims which he may possess to a recompense from the Government for his co-operation.

8. It appears from the former communication with Himmut Bahâdur that his objects are the attainments of a Jaghire in the Company's provinces within the Dooab, and the release of his relation Omrao Geer, from confinement at Lucknow.

9. The first of those objects his Excellency authorizes you to engage for on the part of the Government; the extent of the Jaghire to be hereafter proportioned to the means he may possess of forwarding the views of Government; and to the zeal and activity he may shew in the application of those means to the desired object.

10. Omrao Geer was put into confinement on a suspicion of his having been engaged with the adherents of Vizier Ali in a conspiracy against the government of the Nabob Vizier. As the British Government is exclusively responsible for the protection of the dominions and government of the Nawaub Vizier, his Excellency is of opinion that an application from the British Government to the Nawaub Vizier for the release of Omra Geer would be acceded to on proper measures being taken to obviate the risk of any future attempts on the part of Omrao Geer to disturb the tranquillity of the Vizier's Government. This might, perhaps, be most effectually guarded against by rendering Him-

mut Bahâdur responsible in his person and Jaghire for the future conduct of Omro Geer.

11. Our imperfect knowledge of the internal state of Bundelcund and of the relative situations of the several chiefs of the Bundelahs possessing power or influence in that province, precludes the practicability of determining at the present moment the specific arrangements which it may be advisable and practicable to enter into with them for the attainment of the object in view. Those arrangements must be regulated by the information you may be enabled to acquire on those points after your arrival at Allahabad, and by the general spirit of his Excellency's views and intentions. General assurances may be given to those chiefs who may be inclined to support the British interests of a liberal attention on the part of Government to their rights and interests; and the advantages which they will individually obtain from an emancipation from the yoke of the Mahrattas, may be urged in favour of their ready co-operation with the British troops for that purpose.

12. His Excellency has been informed that the strong forts of Calinger and Damounie in Bundelcund are still possessed by dependants of the former Bundelah Rajahs, and that the determined resistance which has been shewn by those people to the Government of Ali Bahâdur and the present Regency, has arisen from the dread that, notwithstanding any engagements to the contrary, the very considerable property they possess would be plundered by the Mahrattas on their resigning the possession of those forts. As it is probable that an engagement on the part of the British Government for the security of their persons and property would induce those dependants of the former Bundelah Rajahs to resign the possession of these forts to the British Government, you are authorized to enter into engagements with them for that purpose, on the condition of their ready submission to the Government. This, however, is to be considered as a secondary object, and you will attempt a negotiation of this nature only in the event of your deeming it in no measure inconsistent with the general conciliatory measure to be pursued with the inhabitants of the country.

13. His Excellency the Commander-in-Chief will be requested to take the necessary measures to support the arrangements which may be formed by the application of a military force to act in conformity to them.

14. The province of Boghelcund or Rewah Mackunpore,

situated to the south-east of Bundelcund, is considered by his Excellency as tributary to the latter. As no permanent conquest of this province has, however, been made by Ali Bahâdur, and as Rajah Ajeet Sing, the hereditary chief of the province, is in actual possession, it is his Excellency's wish that every endeavour should be made to conciliate that chief to the interests of the British Government, and the necessary assistance granted him, if required, to defend the province from the inroads of the Berar Mahrattas, by sending a detachment to assist him in securing the principal passes into his country from Nagpore.

15. The countries adjoining to Bundelcund, on the north-west, formerly possessed by the Ranah of Gohud and other Jaut chiefs, are now, with the exception of Kalpee, (a Jaghire, held under the sunnud of the Peishwa,) exclusively under the dominion of Dowlut Rao Scindiah. It is understood that those chiefs are very generally averse to the authority of the Mahratta chieftain, and that they would readily embrace any effectual means which might be proposed to them for the purpose of obtaining an emancipation from that authority.

16. As a co-operation on the part of those chiefs would essentially forward the military operations which it may be found expedient to prosecute in those countries, his Excellency directs me to furnish you with the following observations on the general principles which it is his Excellency's wish to adopt in forming arrangements with those chiefs.

17. In the event of a war with Dowlut Rao Scindiah, the security of the British possessions in the Dooab against the future designs of that chief, would seem to demand the total abolition of his authority and interference in the north-western provinces of Hindostan.

18. As it is not his Excellency's intention, however, in the event of a successful war with Scindiah, to extend at present the British regulations beyond the Dooab, with the reservation of Bundelcund and of such cities, forts, or districts, on the western banks of the Jumna, as may serve effectually to secure the safe navigation of that river, and to protect the frontier of the Dooab, it appears to his Excellency that engagements with those chiefs, formed on the basis of mutual security and support, and excluding all interference on the part of the British Government in the internal regulation of their respective possessions, would most effectually secure their co-operation, and present the strongest barrier to the efforts of Scindiah to regain an influence in that quarter.

19. Upon this principle engagements may be entered into with those chiefs, securing to them the undisturbed possession of their hereditary tenures on the condition of their zealous and ready co-operation with the British Government, to the extent of their respective means, in expelling the troops of Dowlut Rao Scindiah from that quarter of Hindostan, and preventing any future attempts on the part of that chieftain, or of any other foreign power, to establish an authority in those provinces.

20. The ancestors of the Ranah of Gohud possessed the principal authority and influence amongst the Jaut chiefs to the westward of the Jumna, and although the authority and property of the present Ranah have been completely subjugated by Dowlut Rao Scindiah, yet his influence amongst the Jaut tribes is supposed to be still considerable, and might, perhaps, be advantageously used to assist in expelling the troops of Dowlut Rao Scindiah from the provinces of Hindostan.

21. The poverty of the Ranah might, however, render it necessary that he should be supplied with sufficient funds to enable him to exert this influence to the effectual support of the British interests.

22. If upon more minute and local information of the state of the Ranah's circumstances, and of the influence which he may possess amongst the Jaut tribes, you should be of opinion that he is inclined to co-operate with the British forces in the expulsion of the troops of Dowlut Rao Scindiah from the country of Gohud, and that an advance of money from the British Government might enable him to give useful support to the military operations of the British forces in that country, his Excellency directs me to authorize you to grant him such advance as you may deem immediately necessary for the purpose of enabling him to collect his adherents, not to exceed the amount of rupees, 100,000, without receiving the further authority of his Excellency in Council. The enclosed letter addressed by his Excellency to the Ranah of Gohud (a copy of which is enclosed for your information) will be forwarded by you only in the above event of your conceiving that his co-operation may be advantageously exerted.

23. To complete the system proposed by his Excellency of defensive alliance against the future encroachments of Dowlut Rao Scindiah or other foreign powers into the north-western provinces of Hindostan, his Excellency attaches much importance to securing the accession of the Rajpoot chiefs of Jypore

and Jodepore to the plan above laid down, of mutual security and support.

24. Enclosed are copies of letters which his Excellency has with this view addressed to the Rajahs of Jypore and Jodepore, which sufficiently explain the principles on which it is his Excellency's intention to form arrangements with those chiefs. The original letters have been forwarded through his Excellency the Commander-in-Chief, and duplicates have been delivered to the Vakeels of those chiefs at the Presidency for transmission to their principals.

25. His Excellency considers it a desirable object to be attained in the negotiation with the Jaut and Rajpoot chiefs, that their frontiers should be secured by a subsidiary force from the British Government proportionate to the extent of their possessions and means respectively. This will more particularly be desirable with the Ranah of Gohud and the Rajahs of Jypore and Jodepore, the amount of whose revenues his Excellency conceives would easily admit of a subsidy being paid to the British Government for the defence of their possessions.

26. From the enclosed copy of a letter, addressed to Zeib ul Nissa Begum, you will observe that his Excellency the Governor-General is inclined to extend the protection and favour of the British Government to the Begum. As the Jaghire possessed by the Begum is within the Doab, his Excellency is desirous that in any engagement entered into on the part of the British Government, such conditions may be inserted as may facilitate the introduction of the British regulations into the Jaghire in the event of a settlement of the adjoining parts of the Doab being formed upon the system of government established in the British possessions.

27. His Excellency the Commander-in-Chief has already been furnished with the instructions of his Excellency the most noble the Governor-General, in regard to the measures to be pursued for dissolving the force under the command of M. Perron, and in the service of Dowlut Rao Scindiah.

28. A general political authority will also be vested in his Excellency the Commander-in-Chief by his Excellency in Council, founded on the spirit of these instructions, a copy of which will be forwarded to his Excellency, and subject to such further secret instructions as his Excellency the most noble the Governor-General may deem expedient to forward to the Commander-in-Chief.

29. As it will be of the utmost importance that the details of the measures, directed by the above general instructions, should be conducted under the inspection and with the sanction of his Excellency the Commander-in-Chief, his Excellency in Council desires that so soon as you may deem the negotiation in regard to Bundelcund, in such a state of forwardness as to admit of your proceeding to join his Excellency the Commander-in-Chief, you will entrust the further prosecution of the arrangement adopted for putting the British troops in possession of that province, to Mr. R. Ahmuty, the collector of Allahabad; and proceed yourself to the head quarters of the army, under the command of his Excellency, where you will be furnished with such further instructions as may be deemed necessary, through the medium of his Excellency the Commander-in-Chief.

30. To enable you to discharge the varied and extensive duties now entrusted to you with promptitude and effect, his Excellency the Commander-in-Chief will be requested to authorize one or more of the military officers under his Excellency's command, who may be spared from their military duties, and who may be otherwise qualified, to be employed under your direction in carrying into effect the political arrangements committed to the general superintendence of his Excellency the Commander-in-Chief.

31. The collectors of Allahabad, Cawnpore and Etawah, will be directed to honour your drafts on his Excellency the most noble the Governor-General for such sums as you may require for the purposes of the public service.

32. You will be pleased to correspond with the Secretary to the Government in the Secret Department on all points connected with the objects of your mission, transmitting for the information of his Excellency the most noble the Governor-General, a regular detail of your proceedings, and you will communicate copies of all your letters to the Secretary to his Excellency the Commander-in-Chief.

I am, &c.

N. B. EDMONSTONE,
Secretary to Government,
Secret and Political Department.

44. N. B. Edmonstone, Esq., Secretary to Government, to Colonel Collins, Resident at the Court of Dowlut Rao Scindiah.

Argument against the right of the Confederated Chieftains to object to the conclusion, or to obstruct the execution, of the Treaty of Basscin.

(Extract.)

Sir, Fort William, June 3rd, 1803.

* * * * * * * *

You will be prepared to oppose any arguments founded on Scindiah's alleged rights and privileges, as a branch of the Mahratta empire, by which Scindiah may contest the right of the Peishwa to conclude political engagements with the British Government, or with any foreign power, without the previous consent and concurrence of the feudatory chieftains, or may endeavour to justify his interference in the late arrangements, or assert a right to participation in the future administration of the Peishwa's affairs.

Under the instructions of his Excellency the Governor-General you have already successfully combated the principle assumed by Dowlut Rao Scindiah that, as guarantee to the treaty of Salbye, his previous consent to the engagements between the British Government and the Peishwa should have been obtained. No such principle can, in his Excellency's judgment, be maintained by any arguments derived either from the original constitution of the Mahratta empire, or from the actual practice of the several chieftains composing the Mahratta confederacy. The exclusive right of concluding treaties and engagements with foreign states, not of a nature to compromise the separate rights and interests of the feudatory chieftains of the empire, must be considered to be inherent in the supreme executive authority of the Mahratta state, and it may be a question whether the Peishwa, acting in the name and under the ostensible sanction of the nominal head of the empire, might not conclude treaties which shall be obligatory upon the subordinate chiefs and feudatories without their concurrence. But even under a contrary supposition, it would be absurd to regulate any political question by the standard of a constitution which time and events have entirely altered or dissolved. The late Mahajee Scindiah and his successor Dowlut Rao have uniformly exercised the powers of independent dominion by making war on the neighbouring states, by concluding engagements with them, and by regulating the whole system of their internal administration without the participation or previous consent of the Peishwa, whose supremacy, however, both Mahajee Scindiah and Dowlut Rao Scindiah have uniformly acknowledged.

Dowlut Rao Scindiah, therefore, cannot, even on the supposed principles of the original constitution, deny the right of the Peishwa to conclude his late engagements with the British Government independently of his concurrence, without impeaching the validity of his own proceedings and those of his predecessor; nor can he, according to the more admissible rules derived from practice and prescription, justly refuse to admit the exercise of those independent rights of dominion on the part of the Peishwa, which both Scindiah and his predecessor assumed in a condition of acknowledged subordination to his Highness's permanent authority.

The Rajah of Berar is known to entertain pretensions to the authority of the Sahoo Rajah, and on the accession of a Peishwa, he is admitted to the privilege of investing the Peishwa with a khelaut. Under these circumstances, the Rajah of Berar's acknowledgement of subordination to the paramount authority of the Peishwa may be doubted. But while the Peishwa continues to exercise that authority in his capacity of representative of the Sahoo Rajah, the Rajah of Berar cannot possess the right of controlling the Peishwa's actions.

In proportion as the Rajah of Berar disclaims the supremacy of the Peishwa, he has less right to interfere in any degree in the Peishwa's concerns. The Peishwa must be considered by the Rajah of Berar, either as the representative of the Rajah of Berar's paramount Sovereign, or as an independent state, in amity with the Rajah of Berar, or as a power acknowledged by every other state in India, but which it is the secret design of the Rajah of Berar to subvert, with a view to supersede its authority for his own aggrandizement. In any of these cases, and more especially in the last, the other powers of India cannot admit the right of the Rajah of Berar to control the Peishwa's intercourse with other states, unless the Peishwa shall attempt to injure the independence of the Rajah of Berar.

The arguments stated in the preceding paragraphs are equally applicable to Dowlut Rao Scindiah's assumption of a right to interfere in any manner in the arrangement concluded between the British Government and the Peishwa, or in the future administration of his Highness's affairs; such interference is incompatible with the complete and effectual operation of our engagements with his Highness, and the right to secure their due operation, is necessarily combined with the right to contract them.

Scindiah cannot justly deny the right of the Peishwa and of the British Government to conclude the terms of a defensive alliance without his previous consent, nor claim the right of interfering in the arrangement or in the future administration of the Peishwa's affairs on the grounds of his having employed his arms and resources in the support of the Peishwa's cause.

Scindiah did not originally take up arms for the defence of the Peishwa. He had long been engaged in a contest with Jeswunt Rao Holkar, whose frequent successes and increasing power menaced the security of Scindiah's dominion, and the unsuccessful resistance which the forces of Dowlut Rao Scindiah opposed to those of Holkar in the vicinity of Poonah was merely a continuation of the contest. The efforts of Scindiah to check the progress of Holkar's arms were necessary for the preservation of his own power, and the object of his exertions was not changed by the danger to which the state of Poonah was exposed by the approach of Holkar to that capital. The preservation of Scindiah's usurped ascendancy in the state of Poonah, and the security of his own dominion, which would have been more than ever endangered by the establishment of Holkar at the capital of Poonah, rendered the protection of the person and government of the Peishwa an object of individual interest to Scindiah, and the same motives must be supposed to have influenced his subsequent operations. His exertions, however, have not contributed in any degree to the Peishwa's restoration. Aware of the doubtful issue of a further contest with the arms of Holkar, Scindiah solicited the co-operation of the British power, and continued in a state of inactivity at a considerable distance from the scene of action. The energy, promptitude, and power of the British Government were the exclusive causes which compelled Jeswunt Rao Holkar to abandon his design of subverting the dominion of the Peishwa and of establishing his own authority upon its ruins, and to retire from Poonah; deprived him of the means of supporting his military power, and secured the restoration of the Peishwa to his capital and government; and to these seasonable and arduous exertions of the British power, Scindiah is absolutely indebted for the present secure possession of his dominion.

The combined result of all these facts and arguments is, that the interposition of the British power for the restoration of the Peishwa, and the conclusion of the late alliance with the state of Poonah, is not only warrantable upon every principle of justice, and the law of nations, but indispensably necessary for the preservation of the integrity of the Mahratta empire, and to the security of the legitimate rights and interests of its respective branches, and especially of Scindiah. That those rights and interests are effectually secured by the terms of the alliance, and consequently that any attempt on the part of any state or chieftain, to disturb the operation of the treaty of Bassein, may justly be considered to be an act of hostility against the British Government.

Under all these circumstances we possess an undoubted right to require that Dowlut Rao Scindiah should afford the most unequivocal proofs of his resolution to abstain from the adoption of any measures, which we may deem to be calculated to impede the accomplishment of the late arrangements in the Mahratta state.

* * * * * * * * *

I have the honour to be, &c. N. B. EDMONSTONE,
Sec. to Government.

45. The Marquess Wellesley to the Secret Committee of the Court of Directors.

Progress of Mahratta affairs. In spite of rumours and appearances, the Governor-General thinks war will not ensue.

Fort William, June 20th, 1803.

Honourable Sirs,

In my despatch of the 19th of April, 1803, forwarded overland, I had the honour to communicate to your honourable Committee the progress of transactions on the western side of the peninsula, to the period of my latest advices, and to state my sentiments respecting the situation of affairs in the Mahratta empire. The Resident at Poonah, in conformity to my instructions, has transmitted to your honourable Committee a narrative of occurrences in the Mahratta state to the 15th of May.

The intelligence of the important event of his Highness the Peishwa's restoration to the exercise of his just authority in the Mahratta state, under the protection of the British power, must have afforded great satisfaction to your honourable Committee. Every circumstance connected with that prosperous event justifies a confident expectation of the complete and pacific accomplishment of the beneficial objects of the late alliance with the Peishwa.

It is my duty, on this occasion, to express to your honourable Committee the high sense which I entertain of the distinguished ability manifested by the honourable Major-General Wellesley in conducting the British detachment, under his command, from the frontier of Mysore to Poonah.

The documents forming the enclosures to this despatch, and transmitted by the *Devaynes*, will afford to your honourable Committee a full view of the considerable military skill with which Major-General Wellesley surmounted the difficulties of his long and arduous march; and combined the various arrangements requisite to secure the supply and movement of his army, and the co-operation and junction of the troops from Hyderabad and Bombay. Your honourable Committee will also observe with pleasure the prudence, address, and temper with which Major-General Wellesley conciliated the Mahratta states occupying the countries through which he passed, and you will approve the signal success with which he composed the various animosities and dissensions of the several Mahratta chiefs, and united that discordant and turbulent race in the common cause of the Peishwa and of the British Government.

The particular attention of your honourable Committee will be directed to the judgment, humanity, and activity manifested by Major-General Wellesley in saving the city of Poonah from destruction by the rapid march and seasonable arrival of the British troops. This happy event impressed the inhabitants of that city with the most favourable opinion of the British power. It is a circumstance equally honourable to our character, and propitious to our interests in that quarter of India, that the first effects of the British influence in the Mahratta dominions should have been displayed in rescuing the capital of the empire from impending ruin, and its inhabitants from violence and rapine.

It will be satisfactory to your honourable Committee to be informed that his Highness the Peishwa has expressed the utmost degree of admiration in observing the promptitude, energy, and success of those exertions to which his Highness is indebted for his restoration to his government and dominions; and that the conduct of Major-General Wellesley, and of Lieut.-Colonel Close, on this occasion, has apparently established in his Highness's mind the most implicit confidence in the good faith, justice, and power of the British Government, and in the valour, skill, and integrity of its officers, with a high sense of the benefits which his Highness must derive from the operation of the late alliance on every branch of his interests and affairs.

From the enclosed copy of my latest advices from the Resident at Poonah, your honourable Committee will observe the disposition of the Peishwa to conform to the advice and recommendation of the British Government, in the adoption of every measure necessary to consolidate his Highness's authority, and to accomplish the objects of the treaty of Bassein; and you will find that his Highness's confidence in the British Government has been increased, and has received additional confirmation by every event which has occurred since his Highness has resorted to our protection for the recovery of his rights.

Although the information contained in Lieut.-Colonel Close's address to your honourable Committee, and the tenor of my latest advices from the courts of Dowlut Rao Scindiah and the Rajah of Berar tend to countenance the rumours of a projected confederacy between those chieftains and Jeswunt Rao Holkar, the existence of any such confederacy is still a subject of considerable doubt. If any such combination has been formed, its object is probably restricted to purposes of a defensive nature, without involving any views of hostility towards the British power. The local situation and comparative power and resources of Scindiah and Ragojee Bhoousla preclude the apprehension of any attempt of those chiefs to subvert the Peishwa's government, or the treaty of Bassein, at the desperate hazard of a war with the British power. The situation of Holkar is precarious and accidental; the instability of the resources of that adventurer reduces the continuance of his power to the utmost degree of uncertainty, and absolutely deprives him of the means of opposing any systematic or formidable resistance to the operation of our alliance with the state of Poonah. With a view, however, to anticipate every possible contingency, I have framed and despatched the instructions and letters which are annexed to this despatch, and are noted in the margin.

Anxious to furnish the Resident at Poonah and Major-General Wellesley with instructions for the regulation of their conduct immediately after the return of the Peishwa to Poonah, I have transmitted directions to those officers, in a despatch to the former of which a copy is enclosed.

That despatch contained a general statement of the principles on which the late treaty with the Peishwa is founded, of the objects to which it is directed, and of the measures necessary to be pursued for securing the complete operation and stability of the alliance between the Company and the Mahrattas, I, therefore, deem it sufficient to refer your honourable Committee to that document for information on those important points.

With a view to aid the effect of the representations which Lieut.-Colonel Close was instructed in that despatch to address to his Highness the Peishwa, I deemed it to be expedient to address a letter to his Highness, a copy of that letter is also annexed to this despatch for the information of your honourable Committee.

Your honourable Committee was informed by Lieut.-Colonel Close of the exactions levied by Jeswunt Rao Holkar upon his Highness the Nizam's city of Aurungabad. No reason exists to countenance an apprehension that these depredations on the Nizam's territory are connected with the supposed confederacy between Holkar and Scindiah. Destitute of any permanent resources, Holkar is compelled to supply his exigencies by indiscriminate plunder. It is probable that Holkar has been induced to levy contributions from Aurungabad by the treacherous suggestions of the Nizam's officer commanding at that station, who is believed to have participated in the booty.

Major-General Wellesley, however, deemed it to be proper to direct Lieut.-Colonel Stevenson to advance with the whole of the Nizam's subsidiary force towards Aurungabad for the eventual protection of his Highness's dominions. I have lately received information that Holkar has retired with his army from the Nizam's frontier towards the northward.

The judicious arrangements which Major-General Wellesley has effected for the disposition of the troops under his command is calculated to meet every exigency of affairs, even under the improbable supposition that Scindiah, the Rajah of Berar, and Jeswunt Rao Holkar have really entertained designs of a hostile nature against the British Government or its allies. Our early state of preparation, and the formidable force which Major-General Wellesley has opposed to every possible operation on the part of any or of all those chieftains, must effectually deter them from the prosecution of war. In the same spirit of seasonable precaution Lieut.-General Stuart has judged it to be expedient to advance the army under his immediate command to a position which may enable him to co-operate with the troops under Major-General Wellesley and Colonel Stevenson.

My instructions to Colonel Collins, of the 5th of May, and to Lieut.-Colonel Close, of the 7th of May, together with my letter of the 15th of May, to the Rajah of Berar, have probably already produced an arrangement of a pacific nature with all the chiefs of the Mahratta empire, whose formal accession to the treaty of Bassein has not yet been signified to me. The Peishwa having actually resumed his government, the stipulations of the treaty have been notified to Scindiah, and to the Rajah of Berar. The terms of the treaty must also have been known to Jeswunt Rao Holkar, and as the articles of the treaty provide a more effectual security for the possessions of Holkar and Scindiah than either could have attained under any other arrangement compatible with the existence of the Peishwa's power, it may be expected that a sense of their own interests will induce those chiefs to acquiesce in the settlement which has been effected at Poonah.

The depredations which have been committed by Holkar on the territories of the Nizam, unquestionably would furnish a just ground of war against that adventurer, if he were to be considered in the situation of an established power in India. But as the exactions at Aurungabad appear to have been levied with the concurrence of the Nizam's officers, whose faith had been long suspected, and as no principle of justice or policy requires the acknowledgment of Holkar among the states of India, I propose to view this transaction as the combined offence of two unfaithful servants of the states of Poonah and Hyderabad; and I shall not attempt to prosecute hostilities against Holkar, unless he shall endeavour by force to obstruct the operation of the treaty of Bassein. It will not be difficult to obtain sufficient satisfaction for the Nizam by pacific accommodation with Holkar, after the latter shall have submitted, formally, to the legitimate authority of the Peishwa.

At the date of my latest advices from the Resident with Dowlut Rao Scindiah, that chieftain had not proceeded beyond the frontier of his own territory. The Resident describes Dowlut Rao Scindiah to be personally disposed to pursue measures of an amicable nature towards the British Government, although it is possible that Scindiah may have been induced to signify a reluctant consent to the formation of the projected conspiracy by the urgency of his principal ministers.

This circumstance is confirmed by the communications which

Colonel Collins has received from Ballajee Koonjur, the officer despatched by his Highness the Peishwa to Scindiah, for the purpose of explaining to that chieftain the detail of the engagements concluded by his Highness with the British Government.

I have received intelligence that the Rajah of Berar had entered his tents with a view of commencing his march from Nagpore, for the purpose of meeting Scindiah, but that the information of the arrival of the British troops at Poonah, which reached the Rajah of Berar soon after he entered his tents, would probably deter that chieftain from advancing.

Under all these circumstances, any opposition from the Mahratta chieftains to the complete accomplishment of the stipulations of the treaty of Bassein, appears to be improbable, and I entertain a firm hope that the British Government will be speedily relieved from the danger which menaced our possessions in the Peninsula during the recent commotion in the Mahratta empire, and that tranquillity will be permanently established on our frontier by the operation of the alliance happily concluded with his Highness the Peishwa.

[1]* * * * * * * * *

In closing this despatch, it will be satisfactory to your honourable Committee, that I should add my expectation that the necessary expense of the late military operations in the Peninsula is not likely to occasion any derangement in the general prosperity of the finances of the Company in India, or in the accounts or services of the present year.

I have the honour to be, &c.

WELLESLEY.

46. The Governor-General in council to the Honourable the Secret Committee of the Court of Directors.

Unsatisfactory negotiations with Scindiah and the Rajah of Berar. War now appears probable, for which the Governor-General is well prepared.

Fort William, 1st August, 1803.

Honourable Sirs,

The Governor-General has had the honour of communicating to your honourable Committee, in his several despatches of the

[1] The omitted passage contains a high eulogy of Lieut.-Colonel Close, and his recent diplomatic services.

24th of December, 1802, 10th of February, 19th of April, and 20th of June, 1803, the progress of transactions in the Mahratta empire, and of stating to your honourable Committee the measures which his Excellency deemed it necessary to pursue for the security and improvement of the British interests, as connected with that empire, and his general sentiments with respect to the actual state of affairs at those several periods of time.

The Governor-General in council now deems it proper to continue the narrative of events from the date of the Governor-General's latest communication to your honourable Committee, a duplicate of which accompanies this despatch overland.

At a conference between Dowlut Rao Scindiah, and the Resident at the court of that chieftain, holden on the 28th of May, the Resident communicated to Dowlut Rao Scindiah the representations which he was instructed to make in conformity to the notes of instruction, of which a copy formed an enclosure in the Governor-General's address to your honourable Committee of the 20th of June.

The Resident began the conference by imparting to Dowlut Rao Scindiah the whole of the treaty of Bassein, of which he also delivered a copy to that chieftain, agreeably to the directions of the Governor-General. After some discussion with regard to particular parts of that treaty, the Resident called on Dowlut Rao Scindiah to declare whether it appeared to him to contain any stipulations injurious to his just rights. In reply to which, that chieftain candidly acknowledged that it contained no such stipulations. The Resident then adverted to the reported confederacy between Dowlut Rao Scindiah, the Rajah of Berar and Jeswunt Rao Holkar, and to the actual approach of the Rajah of Berar, for the purpose of meeting Dowlut Rao Scindiah, and in conformity to the Governor-General's instructions, required that chieftain to state the nature of the late negotiations between those Mahratta chiefs, and to disavow any intentions of confederating with the Rajah of Berar, and with Jeswunt Rao Holkar, for the purpose of obstructing the completion of the arrangements established by the treaty of Bassein.

The Resident enforced these demands by every argument which the nature of the case suggested, and by the declaration, which he was instructed to make, of the determined resolution of the British Government to resist any attempt on the part of any state or power to obstruct the complete execution of the treaty of Bassein, and the Resident apprized Dowlut Rao Scindiah, that in the event of his refusing to afford the just and reasonable explanations and assurances which the Resident has demanded, and of his continuing to prosecute military operations in opposition to the Resident's remonstrances, the British Government would be compelled to adopt measures of precaution on every boundary of that chieftain's dominions. The Resident added, agreeably to the Governor-General's instructions, that certain intelligence of the accession of Dowlut Rao Scindiah to any confederacy against the British power would produce immediate hostility on all parts of his frontier.

These representations however, failed to produce the desired effect; Dowlut Rao Scindiah repeatedly declared to the Resident, that he could not afford the satisfaction demanded until a meeting should have taken place between that chieftain and the Rajah of Berar, whose arrival was expected in the course of a few days, and Dowlut Rao Scindiah closed the discussion by stating to the Resident, that immediately after his interview with the Rajah of Berar, the Resident should be informed 'whether it would be peace or war.'

This unprovoked menace of hostility, and the insult offered to the British Government by a reference of the question of 'peace or war,' to the result of a conference with the Rajah of Berar, who, at the head of a considerable army, had reached the vicinity of Dowlut Rao Scindiah's camp, together with the indication which it afforded of a disposition on the part of those chieftains to prosecute the supposed objects of their confederacy, rendered it the duty of the British Government to adopt without delay, the most effectual measures for the vindication of its dignity, and for the security of its rights and interests, and those of its allies, against any attempt on the part of the confederates, to injure or invade them.

The Governor-General accordingly issued private instructions to his Excellency the Commander-in-Chief at Cawnpore, to make the necessary arrangements for assembling the army on the north-west frontier of the Company's possessions, and the Governor-General at the same time directed his attention to the formation of a plan of operations for the British army in that quarter, and to the accomplishment of a system of political arrangement with the neighbouring states and chieftains, calculated to diminish the power and resources of the enemy, and to facilitate the success of the British arms in the event of our being compelled to proceed to measures of hostility against the power and possessions of Dowlut Rao Scindiah.

The course of measures which the Governor-General deemed it advisable to adopt for those purposes, is described in the enclosed paper of notes, which was transmitted to the Commander-in-Chief for his immediate information and guidance.

[1] * * * * * * * * *

The Governor-General in council now proceeds to state the progress of the negotiations and transactions on the western side of India.

Although the answer which Dowlut Rao Scindiah returned to the just and reasonable demands of the Resident, on the 28th of May, would have justified the Resident in immediately quitting the camp of that chieftain, the Resident in conformity to the desire expressed by the Governor-General to employ every practical endeavour to effect a pacific accommodation of subsisting differences, properly resolved to postpone his departure until a meeting should have taken place between Scindiah and the Rajah of Berar.

On the 3d of June, the Rajah of Berar arrived within one march of Scindiah's camp, and was met by the latter chieftain on the following morning. On the 5th the Resident despatched his native Secretary with a complimentary message to the Rajah of Berar, who received him with distinguished attention. The Rajah of Berar expressed with apparent sincerity, his solicitude to maintain the relations of friendship which had so long subsisted between the British Government and the state of Berar, and informed the Resident's emissary that he had received the Governor-General's letter of the 13th of May, and that he should speedily return a reply.

The two chieftains having held a private conference on the 8th, the Resident despatched a message to Dowlut Rao Scindiah, on the following day, intimating that the intended interview between Dowlut Rao Scindiah, and the Rajah of Berar, having taken place, it was incumbent on Dowlut Rao Scindiah to return an immediate and explicit answer to the demands, which the Resident had stated on the 28th of May. To this message, Dowlut Rao Scindiah returned an evasive reply. The Resident being of opinion, that Dowlut Rao Scindiah systematically post-

---

[1] The passage here omitted explains the object and character of the special powers vested in Major-General Wellesley, as printed elsewhere.

poned a decisive reply with a view to gain time, and being aware of the necessity of bringing the question of peace or war to an immediate decision, addressed a memorial to that chieftain. In reply to this memorial, the Resident received a verbal message, purporting that the required explanation should be afforded in the course of two or three days. On receiving this message, the Resident signified to Dowlut Rao Scindiah that he considered that reply to be final, and apprized that chieftain of his intention to quit his camp without further delay. On the 14th the Resident received a reply to his memorial, containing excuses for the delay of a specific answer on the subject of the question depending, and soliciting the Resident to postpone his departure.

Dowlut Rao Scindiah having declared, that the decision of the question of peace or war rested with the Rajah of Berar, and the latter chieftain being equally concerned in the progress and issue of the depending negotiations, the Resident deemed it expedient to communicate with that chieftain, in the hope that the Governor-General's letter of the 13th of May, might have induced the Rajah of Berar to manifest a disposition more conformable to the dictates of policy and justice, than that which appeared to actuate the conduct of Dowlut Rao Scindiah. The Resident accordingly despatched his native secretary to the Rajah of Berar with instructions to ascertain whether that chieftain had prepared any reply to the Governor-General's letter of the 13th of May, and to apprize him of the contents of the memorial which the Resident had addressed to Dowlut Rao Scindiah. This message produced no other result than a continuation of the same system of evasion, and delay, which the Resident had already experienced from Dowlut Rao Scindiah. The Resident therefore addressed another memorial to Scindiah, respecting his determination to quit the camp on a specified day. The memorial produced a correspondence between the Resident and Dowlut Rao Scindiah, which terminated in a resolution on the part of the Resident to postpone his departure for a few days, in the expectation which he was induced to entertain of a change of conduct on the part of those chieftains.

It is impracticable to comprise within the compass of a despatch overland the detail of the subsequent negotiations between the Resident and the confederated chieftains to the date of our latest advices from the Resident. Those details will be communicated to your honourable Committee by a sea conveyance. The particulars already stated will enable your honourable

Committee to form a judgment of the spirit which has actuated those chieftains in the late important discussions. It is sufficient to add, that although they continued to practise the same artful evasions, the Resident was induced, by their promises and persuasions, to protract the period of his actual departure from the camp of Dowlut Rao Scindiah, with a view to afford an unequivocal proof of the anxiety of the British Government to maintain the relations of amity and peace with those chieftains, and to render them exclusively responsible for the consequences of their perseverance in a system of conduct inconsistent with those relations, and repugnant to every principle of justice and good faith.

[1] * * * * * * * * *

Your honourable Committee is apprized of the grounds on which the Governor-General founded his reasonable expectation of the pacific accomplishment of the arrangements concluded between the British Government and the Peishwa. Every argument deducible from the just and amicable nature of those arrangements, from the equitable and moderate course of proceeding adopted by the British Government towards the Mahratta states, and from the relative power and resources of the British Government, and the confederated chieftains in the actual situation of their respective forces, favour that expectation. If, under the peculiar disadvantages with which those chieftains must now undertake a contest with the British power, they should continue to withhold the proofs which the Governor-General has demanded of their pacific intentions, it must be obvious to your honourable Committee that any delay in the prosecution of offensive operations against the power and possessions of those chieftains would hazard the security of the British interests by enabling those chieftains to pursue their hostile designs at a future period of time under circumstances more favourable to their success.

The Governor-General in council confidently expects that under the powers vested in the honourable Major-General Wellesley, that officer will have required the Resident with Dowlut Rao Scindiah to quit that chieftain's camp within a specified period of days, unless Scindiah and the Rajah of Berar shall

---

[1] The omitted passage contains a justification of the Governor-General's conduct in insisting on his ultimatum, at the risk of war. It is repeated, and given, elsewhere.

previously separate their forces, and commence their return to their respective territories.

By the latest accounts the united armies of Dowlut Rao Scindiah and the Rajah of Berar occupied a position within a few days' march of the pass of Adjuntee, one of the principal passes on the western frontier of his Highness the Nizam's dominions. The subsidiary force under the command of Lieut.-Colonel Stevenson, together with his Highness the Nizam's contingent, was encamped at a short distance from Aurungabad.

The honourable Major-General Wellesley marched from Poonah with the main body of the forces under his command on the 4th of June, and by the latest advices was encamped within a few marches of Ahmednuggur, a strong fort belonging to Dowlut Rao Scindiah, at the distance of about eighty miles from Poonah. The army under the command of Major-General Wellesley is accompanied by an inconsiderable portion of the contingent of troops which the Peishwa is required to furnish by the treaty of Bassein. There is no reason, however, to ascribe this deficiency to any want of inclination on the part of his Highness to adhere to the faith of his engagements with the British Government.

By the latest advices, Jeswunt Rao Holkar occupied a position with the main body of his army on the north side of the Taptee river. The endeavours of Dowlut Rao Scindiah and the Rajah of Berar to induce that chieftain to join them, appear to have been unsuccessful. It is not probable that Jeswunt Rao Holkar will ever be induced by any concessions cordially to connect his interests with those of Dowlut Rao Scindiah.

The Governor-General has great satisfaction in assuring your honourable Committee that in the event of hostilities between the British Government and the confederated chieftains, we shall enter upon the contest under every circumstance of advantage arising from the season of the year, from the superiority of our troops, and from the relative position of the British forces.

The character of Major-General Wellesley, the extent of our force, and the approved valour, steadiness, and discipline of our troops, afford a prospect of the speedy and complete success of our arms on the western side of India, if the conduct of the Mahratta states should ultimately compel us to resort to hostility.

The extent and efficiency of the British forces on the north-western quarter of the Company's dominions under the command of his Excellency the commander-in-chief, and his Excellency's approved skill, activity, perseverance and prudence constitute a just foundation of confidence in the success of our military operations against the possessions of Dowlut Rao Scindiah in that quarter of Hindostan.

The Governor-General is employed in framing the necessary arrangements for the occupation of the province of Cuttack in the event of hostilities, and the Governor-General in council entertains no doubt of the speedy success of the expedition which will be directed to that quarter in the event of hostilities between the British Government and the confederated Mahratta chieftains.

The necessary measures have been adopted for defending the whole line of frontier from Allahabad to Midnapoor from the incursions of predatory bodies of the enemy's troops.

No events have occurred at Poonah of a nature to produce any change in the sentiments which the Governor-General has had the honour to state to your honourable Committee with respect to the stability and the benefits of the alliance concluded between the British Government and the Peishwa.

The accounts which the Governor-General in council has received of the state of his Highness the Nizam's health, lead to an apprehension of that prince's immediate decease. Measures have long since been adopted for securing to his Highness's eldest son, Mirza Secunder Jah, the succession to the Soobahdarry of the Deccan on the decease of his father, and the Governor-General in council has no reason to apprehend that the decease of his Highness the Nizam will occasion any commotion at Hyderabad, or in any degree operate prejudicially to the political interests of the British Government in India.

We have the honour to be,
Honourable Sirs,
your most obedient and faithful servants,

WELLESLEY,
G. H. BARLOW,
G. UDNY.

Examined,
W. B. Bayley, Assistant.

47. Dowlut Rao Scindiah to the Marquess Wellesley.

Conditional assent to the Treaty of Bassein.

Received July 31st, 1803.

I have received your Lordship's friendly letter notifying the conclusion of new engagements between his Highness the Peishwa and the English Company at Bassein, together with a copy of the treaty; and I have been fully apprized of every word of its contents, which have also been fully communicated to me by Colonel Collins.

Whereas the engagements subsisting between the Peishwa and me are such, that the adjustment of all affairs and of the concerns of his state and government, should be arranged and completed with my advice and participation, by the favour of God! through a regard to what is above stated, the degrees of mutual concord have so increased, that to this time no interruption or derangement of them has occurred on either side. Notwithstanding this, the engagements which have lately been concluded between that quarter (British Government) and the Peishwa have only now been communicated; and on the part of the Peishwa, to this time of writing, *nothing*. Therefore, it has now been determined with Rajah Ragojee Bhoosla, in presence of Colonel Collins, that confidential persons on my part and the Rajah's, be despatched to the Peishwa, for the purpose of ascertaining the circumstances of the (said) engagements. At the same time no intention whatever is entertained on my part to subvert the stipulations of the treaty consisting of nineteen articles, which has been concluded at Bassein, between the British Government and the Peishwa, on condition that there be no design whatever on the part of the English Company and the Peishwa to subvert the stipulations of the treaty, which, since a long period of time, has been concluded between the Peishwa's Sircar, me, and the said Rajah and the Mahratta chiefs.

Further particulars will be communicated by the letters of Colonel Collins. Let the receipt of friendly letters continue to be the means of gratification to me.

A true translation.
N. B. Edmonstone,
Persian Sec. to Government.

48. Translation of a letter from the Honourable Major-General Wellesley, to Dowlut Rao Scindiah, dated 6th of August, 1803.

Declaration of War.

I have received your letter [the writer here repeated its substance].

You will recollect that the British Government did not threaten to commence hostilities against you; but you threatened to commence hostilities against the British Government, and its allies; and when called upon to explain your intentions, you declared that it was doubtful whether there would be peace or war; and in conformity with your threats, and your declared doubts, you assembled a large army in a station contiguous to the Nizam's frontier.

On this ground I called upon you to withdraw that army to its usual stations, if your subsequent pacific declarations were sincere; but instead of complying with this reasonable requisition, you have proposed that I should withdraw the troops which are intended to defend the territories of the allies against your designs, and that you, and the Rajah of Berar, should be suffered to remain with your troops assembled in readiness to take advantage of their absence.

This proposition is unreasonable and inadmissible, and you must stand the consequences of the measures which I find myself obliged to adopt, in order to repel your aggressions.

I offered you peace upon terms of equality and honourable to all parties, you have chosen war, and are responsible for all the consequences.

(A true Copy.) R. BARCLAY, Dep. Adj.-General in Mysore.

49. The Governor-General in Council to the Honourable the Secret Committee of the Honourable the Court of Directors.

'Casus Belli' against Scindiah and the Rajah of Berar. Vindication of the Governor-General's policy. Earlier operations of the War. Death of Nizam Ali. Quiet accession of Secunder Jah.

Honourable Sirs, Fort William, Sept. 25th, 1803.

[1] * * * * * * * * * *

50. The preceding detail affords a convincing proof of the justice, moderation, and forbearance which have regulated the

---

[1] The omitted paragraphs contain a tedious detail of abortive negotiations, the result of which is summed up in what follows.

conduct of the British Government during the course of the late important discussions with Scindiah and the Rajah of Berar, and will satisfy your honourable Committee that the conduct of those chieftains has been actuated by a systematic design to employ the resources of their combined power and influence for the subversion of an arrangement founded on principles of undisputed equity and of acknowledged security to the rights and independance of those chieftains, at the hazard of a contest with the united power of the British Government and its allies; and that the object of their professions of amity, and their disavowal of any design to obstruct the execution of the treaty of Bassein, was to induce the British Government to abandon the arrangements and preparations necessary for the security of our rights and interests, or to suspend the prosecution of them until a change of season, and an accession of force should enable those chieftains to pursue their unwarrantable designs, with improved advantages and a better prospect of success.

51. The belief that those chieftains entertained designs hostile to the British Government at the earliest stages of negotiation between the Resident and Dowlut Rao Scindiah, is supported by the information which the Governor-General has from time to time received of the proceedings of that chieftain.

52. In a letter from the Resident dated 28th of February, and received on the 22nd of March, the Resident apprized the Governor-General in council that Ambajee Inglia (one of Dowlut Rao Scindiah's principal ministers) had informed one of the Resident's native agents, that orders had been issued to General Perron directing him to place the army under his command in a state of preparation for the field, with a view to an eventual rupture with the British Government.

53. At that time Ambajee Inglia was supposed to possess the greatest influence over the mind of Scindiah, whose proceedings were said to be principally regulated by the councils of that chieftain; it appeared highly improbable, therefore, that Ambajee would have communicated these orders to the Resident's agent if they had really been issued.

54. This circumstance induced the Governor-General to discredit the despatch of those orders, and to believe that the object of the communication was merely to discover the views and intentions of the British Government with respect to Dowlut Rao Scindiah.

55. Adverting also to the established power and ascendancy of the British Government in India, to the comparative weakness

even of the combined power of Dowlut Rao Scindiah and of the Rajah of Berar, and to the peculiar disadvantages under which those chieftains must enter upon a contest with the British arms, it could not reasonably be supposed that Dowlut Rao Scindiah meditated any hostile designs against the British Government, and this obvious consideration induced the Governor-General to discredit the rumours which at that time prevailed of the confederacy which that chieftain and the Rajah of Berar have since actually formed, for purposes hostile to the interests of the British Government. These indications of an hostile disposition on the part of those chieftains, therefore, did not appear to the Governor-General to be sufficiently manifest to warrant the immediate adoption of corresponding measures of precaution on the part of the British Government.

56. The concurrent testimony of facts, and the state of M. Perron's military force, however, which have subsequently been ascertained, induced the Governor-General to give entire credit to the information which the Resident communicated in the month of March respecting the despatch of orders to General Perron to the effect above described, even at that early stage of our negotiations with Dowlut Rao Scindiah.

57. In a letter from the Resident dated the 14th of June, and received on the 6th of July, the Resident transmitted a paper of intelligence from his agent at Delhi, stating that messengers from Dowlut Rao Scindiah had lately come to the Rohilla chieftain, Gholaum Mahomed Khan, who resides at Nadown, and letters had been received by that chieftain from General Perron inviting him to proceed with his followers towards the station of General Perron's army by the way of Suharunpore, for the purpose of exciting commotions in the Jaghire of Rampore, and assuring him of ample support both from Scindiah and General Perron, and that General Perron had clandestinely addressed letters to the principal persons residing in the Jaghire, and other places, urging them to employ their exertions in disturbing the tranquillity of the Company's possessions.

58. Notwithstanding Scindiah's solemn disavowal of the orders said to have been issued by his authority to the commanding officer of the body of horse despatched from Scindiah's camp to the north-western frontier of the Company's territories, and to the Peishwa's officers in Bundelcund for the prosecution of hostile operations against the British territories, as noted in the 3rd paragraph of this letter, the Governor-General in council is

induced, by the many instances of insincerity manifested by that chieftain, by the general tenor of his conduct, by the authenticity of the source of the Governor-General's information upon those subjects, and by circumstances which have subsequently been ascertained, to give entire credit to the intelligence originally received relative to those acts of aggression on the part of Scindiah.

59. Those facts were communicated to the collector of Allahabad by the express direction of Himmut Bahâdur (one of the Peishwa's officers in Bundelcund) to whom the letters of Scindiah were said to have been addressed, and who had previously transmitted proposals to the Governor-General for the transfer of that province to the authority of the British Government. The intelligence of the invitation to Gholaum Mahomed Khan from Dowlut Rao Scindiah and General Perron was corroborated by information repeatedly received and communicated to the Governor-General by the Resident at Lucknow and the agent of the Governor-General in the ceded provinces of Oude of the preparations of Gholaum Mahomed Khan for the avowed purpose of complying with the suggestions which he had received from Scindiah and General Perron to excite disturbances in the district of Rampore, and to disturb the tranquillity of the Vizier's and the Company's dominions; and on the 26th of July copies of letters from Dowlut Rao Scindiah to Gholaum Mahomed Khan and Bumboo Khan (the son of the late Nujeeb ou Dowlah, who occupies a territory in the vicinity of Suharunpore) declaring the intention of Scindiah to commence a war of aggression against the British power, and instigating that chieftain to cooperate with the forces of General Perron against the British possessions, were received by the Governor-General from Mr. Leycester, the collector of Moradabad, to whom they had been transmitted by Bumboo Khan.

60. A translation of those documents is enclosed for your honourable Committee's notice.

61. Combining the tenor of those documents with the facts and arguments above stated, the Governor-General in council entertains no doubt of the actual despatch of letters, in the terms of those documents, to the chieftains to whom they are stated to have been addressed by Dowlut Rao Scindiah. The Governor-General has, however, deemed it proper to adopt measures for the purpose of procuring the originals of those important papers.

62. Your honourable Committee will observe that these documents tend to confirm the original information received of the actual transmission of instructions from Scindiah to the Peishwa's officers in Bundelcund, and the communication of orders to Dhurrum Rao to the effect described in the third paragraph of this despatch. Those documents also state the nature of the directions issued by Scindiah to General Perron for the prosecution of hostilities against the British possessions.

63. It appears from a passage in those documents that the letters of Scindiah to Gholaum Mahomed Khan and Bumboo Khan, were written subsequently to the march of Dowlut Rao Scindiah from Boorhaunpore on the 4th of May; but the despatch of messengers to Gholaum Mahomed Khan and the transmission of the instructions to General Perron, under which that officer addressed letters to the principal persons in Rampore and other places as noticed in the 57th paragraph, must be referred to an earlier period of time. The complete state of preparation in which the army of General Perron was actually placed, is a corroborative evidence of the actual transmission of orders to that officer to the effect described in the 52nd paragraph of this letter.

64. These facts reciprocally confirm each point of the evidence of Scindiah's hostile projects, and combined with information at various times communicated by the Resident with Dowlut Rao Scindiah, of the proceedings of that chieftain with the repeated rumours of the formation of an hostile confederacy between Dowlut Rao Scindiah and the Rajah of Berar and Jeswunt Rao Holkar, and with the tenor and result of the Resident's negotiations, must be considered to amount to full proof of the alleged design of subverting the alliance formed between the British Government and the Peishwa.

65. These proceedings of Dowlut Rao Scindiah indicate not merely the resolution of that chieftain to oppose the execution of the treaty of Bassein by force of arms, but collectively and separately constitute acts of hostility against the British Government.

66. At no period of time since the departure of the Peishwa from his capital have the transactions of the British Government been such as to justify even precautionary measures of military preparation on the part of Scindiah. From those transactions no argument could arise to justify the adoption of measures either of hostility or precaution on the part of the confederated chieftains, unless such an argument could be deduced from a denial of the right of his Highness the Peishwa to contract de-

fensive engagements with a foreign state without the participation of the feudatory chieftains of the Mahratta empire, or from a conviction that the engagements actually concluded with his Highness were injurious to the acknowledged rights of those chieftains.

67. Various precedents might be adduced of the exercise of that right by his Highness the Peishwa in his negotiations with the British Government, and the uniform course of the political and military proceedings of Dowlut Rao Scindiah and of his predecessor Mahdajee Scindiah, affords numerous instances of the exercise of a similar right on the part of those chieftains, independently of the Peishwa, to whose authority they have invariably acknowledged obedience.

68. This question has been fully discussed in the Governor-General's instructions to the Resident with Dowlut Rao Scindiah, dated the 3d of June.

69. The treaty of Bassein is purely defensive, and not only contains no stipulations injurious to the rights of the feudatory Mahratta chieftains, but provides additional security for those rights.

70. In the course of the negotiations between the Resident and Dowlut Rao Scindiah, that chieftain maintained that in his capacity of guarantee to the treaty of Salbye, he ought to have been consulted previously to the conclusion of engagements with the Peishwa. The Resident successfully opposed that operation by the arguments stated in the Governor-General's instructions of the 11th of February, and maintained the right of the Peishwa to conclude engagements without the participation of the feudatory chieftains, upon the obvious principles of acknowledged supremacy, and approved and established precedent; and at a conference between Scindiah and the Resident on the 23d of March, on the subject of the engagements concluded with the Peishwa, Dowlut Rao Scindiah abandoned that ground of argument, and merely contended that the Peishwa ought to have apprized that chieftain of the terms of the treaty concluded between his Highness and the British Government.

71. At that period of time the details of the treaty of Bassein had not been communicated to Dowlut Rao Scindiah, but he was informed that it was purely of a defensive nature, and on that occasion Scindiah assured the Resident, in the most unequivocal terms, that he had no intention to attempt the subversion of any engagements concluded between the British Government and the

Peishwa, yet measures of decided hostility against the British Government were adopted by Dowlut Rao Scindiah in the ensuing months of April and May.

72. No military preparations founded on a distrust of that chieftain's pacific disposition were commenced on the part of the British Government, until the close of the month of June, and even the army under the command of Major-General Wellesley, did not commence its march from Poonah until the beginning of that month.

73. It is manifest therefore, that the hostile measures pursued by Dowlut Rao Scindiah against the British Government, have been adopted on grounds distinct from any denial of the Peishwa's right to contract his late engagements with the British Government, from the alleged existence of any stipulation in those engagements injurious to the rights of the Mahratta feudatories, and from any apprehension of the effect of any measures either of precaution, or of apparent hostility on the part of the British Government.

74. The conduct of Dowlut Rao Scindiah towards the Peishwa during a long course of time antecedent to the Peishwa's degradation from the musnud of Poonah, and the views which that chieftain and the Rajah of Berar are known to have entertained, with respect to the supreme authority of the Mahratta state, afford the means of forming a correct judgment of the motives which may have rendered those chieftains desirous of subverting the treaty of Bassein, although they had admitted that treaty to be equitable in its general principle, and to furnish additional security for the just rights of the feudatory chieftains of the Mahratta empire, and especially for their own.

75. The whole course of Dowlut Rao Scindiah's proceedings, since his accession to the dominions of Mahdajee Scindiah, has manifested a systematic design of establishing an ascendancy in the Mahratta state upon the ruins of the Peishwa's authority.

76. The government in the person of the Peishwa had long been placed under a degrading subjection to the oppressive control and unwarrantable usurpation of Dowlut Rao Scindiah, who had remained with a numerous army in the vicinity of the Peishwa's capital for a considerable period of time.

77. The usurpation of Scindiah existed in full force at the commencement of the last war between the Company and Tippoo Sultaun, and the undue influence of Scindiah in the Mahratta empire in that crisis, not only deprived the British

Government of every benefit from the nominal alliance of the Peishwa at the commencement and during the progress of the war, but afforded positive encouragement to the cause of Tippoo Sultaun, and menaced the Nizam's dominions previously to the expulsion of the French from Hyderabad in October, 1798, and subsequently in 1799 while the Nizam's contingent was actually employed with the British army in the common cause of the triple alliance against Tippoo Sultaun.

78. At that time Scindiah was restrained from the actual invasion of the Nizam's dominions by the direct interposition of the British Government; his influence however, and the terror of his violence and supposed power continued to rule the Court of Poonah, and to alarm the Court of Hyderabad, until the exigency of his affairs in the north of Hindostan, occasioned principally by the successful progress of Jeswunt Rao Holkar's arms, compelled Dowlut Rao Scindiah to retire from Poonah for the protection of his own territories.

79. The complete establishment of Holkar's authority at Poonah by the defeat of Scindiah's troops required the utmost exertion of Scindiah's power against that active and successful enemy.

80. Had Scindiah succeeded in subverting the power of Holkar, it cannot be doubted that he would have taken advantage of that success for the complete establishment of his own undue authority in the state of Poonah. He would probably have reinstated the Peishwa Bajee Rao in the government or would have raised another to the musnud, to be the pageant of his own power, or would have usurped the supreme ministerial authority in his own name, if the disposition of the other chieftains of the Mahratta empire should have encouraged an expectation of their acquiescence in that ambitious project.

81. The uniform tenor of Dowlut Rao Scindiah's conduct, the invariable principles of Asiatic policy, and the personal character, habits and disposition of Dowlut Rao Scindiah, preclude the supposition that he would have abandoned the absolute power which he would have acquired by the subversion of Holkar's usurpation, and would have adopted the liberal policy of restoring the exiled Peishwa to the exercise of the established authority of the empire.

82. In the moment of alarm which succeeded the signal success of Jeswunt Rao Holkar, Dowlut Rao Scindiah indirectly solicited the co-operation of the British Government, under the

pretext of restoring the Peishwa's authority. He probably expected that the aid of a detachment of British troops would have insured his success against Holkar, without controlling his project of restoring his own undue ascendancy at Poonah on a more secure and extensive basis. It now appears that the active and powerful exertions employed by the British Government at the express solicitation of his Highness the Peishwa, for his Highness's complete restoration to the musnud of Poonah, were neither desired nor expected by Dowlut Rao Scindiah. The actual re-establishment of the Peishwa in the government of Poonah under the exclusive protection of the British power and the conclusion of engagements calculated to secure to his Highness the due exercise of his legitimate authority on a permanent foundation, deprived Dowlut Rao Scindiah of every hope of accomplishing the objects of his ambition, injustice and rapacity, so long as that alliance should be successfully maintained.

83. This statement of facts sufficiently explains the anxiety of Dowlut Rao Scindiah to effect the subversion of an arrangement, the justice and equity of which he was compelled to acknowledge, and that chieftain's unprovoked prosecution of hostile designs against the British Government and its allies.

84. Adverting to the manifest design of Dowlut Rao Scindiah to aggrandize his power by annexing the dominion and resources of the Peishwa to his own, your honourable Committee will concur in the expediency of supporting an arrangement calculated to preclude the dangerous consolidation of the power and resources of two rival branches of the Mahratta state, in the hands of an ambitious and enterprizing chieftain, whose disposition is hostile to the British Government, and whose dominion has been established and maintained on the most vulnerable part of our north-western frontier in Hindostan, by a formidable military force under the exclusive command of French officers.

85. The motives which must be supposed to have influenced the Rajah of Berar in combining his power with that of Dowlut Rao Scindiah for the subversion of the alliance concluded between the British Government and the Peishwa, were manifestly similar to those which actuated the conduct of Dowlut Rao Scindiah.

86. The Rajah of Berar has always maintained pretensions to the supreme ministerial authority in the Mahratta empire, founded on his affinity to the reigning Rajah of Satara, and in the course of a conference with the native Secretary of the

Resident with Dowlut Rao Scindiah on the 10th of June, the Rajah of Berar distinctly avowed those pretensions.

87. Convinced that the permanency of the defensive alliance concluded between the British Government and the Peishwa, would preclude all future opportunity of accomplishing the object of his ambition, the Rajah of Berar appears to have been equally concerned with Dowlut Rao Scindiah in the subversion of that alliance.

88. Although the views ascribed to those chieftains were manifestly incompatible with the accomplishment of their respective designs, the removal of an obstacle which would effectually preclude the success of either chieftain in obtaining an ascendancy at Poonah, constituted an object of common interest to both. It appears also to be highly probable that those chieftains, sensible that the combination of their power afforded the only prospect of subverting the alliance concluded between the British Government and the Peishwa, agreed to compromise their respective and contradictory projects, by an arrangement for the partition of the whole power and dominion of the Mahratta state.

89. But whatever may have been the specific objects of Scindiah and the Rajah of Berar, the operation of the treaty of Bassein was evidently calculated to preclude the accomplishment of any ambitious projects on the part of those chieftains, and to confine their power and authority within the just limits of their respective dominions.

90. Under this view of the subject, a sufficient cause will be discovered of the hostile conduct of those chieftains, although no just ground of complaint should even have been alleged by them against the British Government, nor any design imputed to us in any degree injurious to the security of the acknowledged rights and independence of Scindiah and the Rajah of Berar.

91. The inability of those chieftains to allege any ground of complaint against the British Government or its allies, affords the most unequivocal proof of the justice and moderation of our proceedings.

92. The mere junction of the armies of Scindiah and the Rajah of Berar upon the frontier of the dominions of our ally, for any purpose unconnected with the security of the rights of those chieftains, would have compelled the British Government to demand the removal of those armies from that menacing position, and would have required the adoption of measures of precaution on our part; and the refusal of those chieftains to

comply with that demand, would have justified an appeal to arms, for the security of our interests and those of our allies. Under actual circumstances, no other security for the pacific conduct of those chieftains could have been accepted, than such as should deprive them of the power of prosecuting with success the designs which they manifestly entertained against the rights and interests of the British Government and its allies.

93. The Governor-General in Council deems it proper in this place to state, in a distinct and connected form, the leading facts of the late transactions, which have terminated in a dissolution of the relations of amity between the British Government and the confederated chieftains, Dowlut Rao Scindiah and the Rajah of Berar.

94. When his Highness the Peishwa had been compelled by the violence and usurpation of a subject of his Government to abandon his capital, his Highness solicited and obtained the aid of the British power for the restoration of his authority, and concluded engagements with the British Government calculated to secure his Highness's rights and independence against the hostile designs of any foreign or domestic enemy. Those engagements not only contained no stipulations injurious to the just rights of the feudatory chieftains of the Mahratta empire, but provided additional security for the unmolested exercise of those rights.

95. After Dowlut Rao Scindiah had distinctly expressed his concurrence in the propriety of the measures adopted by the British Government for the restoration of the Peishwa's authority, and had been assured by the Resident, in the name of the British Government, that those engagements were merely of a defensive nature; and after Dowlut Rao Scindiah had abandoned the untenable assertion that the Peishwa did not possess the right to conclude such engagements without the concurrence of the Mahratta feudatories, that chieftain persisted in soliciting the junction of the Rajah of Berar with the whole body of his forces, for the purpose of eventually employing their united power and resources to subvert the arrangements concluded between the British Government and the Peishwa; and in conformity to Dowlut Rao Scindiah's solicitation, the Rajah of Berar commenced his march for the purpose of effecting the proposed junction of their numerous armies in a menacing position on the frontier of the ally of the British Government.

96. Your honourable Committee will not fail to observe, that

these measures were not adopted by those chieftains with a view to the defence of their rights and interests, against any apprehended design on the part of the British Government to injure or invade them, nor to the protection or internal settlement of their possessions in the vicinity of the Nizam's dominions. Those measures were avowedly concerted for the express purpose of enabling those chieftains to carry into effect their eventual resolution, to undertake a war of aggression against the British Government and its allies.

97. Under these indications of hostility on the part of those chieftains, the British Government merely required that they should retire with their armies to their usual stations in Berar and the north of Hindostan, proposing that the British army in the Deccan should also retire in a similar manner.

98. At the moment when Dowlut Rao Scindiah, after being apprized of all the stipulations of the treaty of Bassein, acknowledged that it contained no provisions injurious to the rights of the feudatory chieftains, that chieftain publicly declared to the Resident, that the question of peace or war with the British Government, depended upon the result of a conference with the Rajah of Berar, whose arrival at the head of the whole body of his forces in the vicinity of Scindiah's camp, was then daily expected.

99. The Governor-General in council requests your honourable Committee's attention to the hostile and insulting nature of this declaration. Occupying a position with the whole body of his forces near the frontier of our ally, Scindiah publicly declared in open Durbar, to the representative of the British Government, that he awaited the arrival of the Rajah of Berar at the head of a numerous army on the frontier of the dominions of our ally, for the purpose of deciding whether the united arms of those confederated chieftains should be employed in the prosecution of a war of aggression against the British Government and its allies. The armies of these chieftains effected the proposed junction, and the chieftains met for the purpose, avowed by Scindiah, of deciding 'whether it should be peace or war with the Company.' After the junction of their armies, those chieftains continued by systematic delays and evasions, to withhold any declaration with regard to the nature of their designs during a period of two months, and although at the expiration of that period of time, the confederated chieftains disavowed all intention of obstructing the complete execution of

the treaty of Bassein, they refused to abandon the arrangement avowedly adopted and the position occupied for the eventual prosecution of hostilities against the British Government.

100. It is proper to observe, that during the whole course of the negotiation between the Resident and Dowlut Rao Scindiah, that chieftain and the Rajah of Berar employed their most assiduous endeavours to induce Jeswunt Rao Holkar to unite in the confederacy, and to form a junction with the allied armies; and those chieftains even assigned the depending negotiation with Jeswunt Rao Holkar as a cause for maintaining their united armies in the position from which they were required to retreat.

101. From the preceding detail the following facts are established—

First. That according to the evidence of facts, and to the distinct avowal of Dowlut Rao Scindiah, and the Rajah of Berar, those chieftains had no cause of complaint against the British Government, nor any reason to apprehend that their just rights and interests were exposed to hazard, by the arrangements concluded between the British Government and the Peishwa.

Secondly. That the junction and continuance of the armies of those chieftains on the frontier of the Nizam, was avowedly unnecessary for any purpose connected with the security of their rights, or with the protection or internal arrangement of any part of their territorial possessions.

Thirdly. That the general conduct and language of those chieftains indicated designs of an hostile nature against the British Government and its allies, the Peishwa and the Nizam; and that Scindiah had distinctly declared, that he and the Rajah of Berar meditated eventual war.

Fourthly. That those chieftains assembled their armies in a menacing position on the frontier of our ally the Nizam, for the purpose of enabling them eventually to carry those designs into execution.

Fifthly. That those chieftains proceeded to acts of direct hostility, by a public and insulting menace of war against the British Government, and by various preparations and arrangements, hostile to the British Government and its allies, not only without any cause of complaint deducible from the measures and proceedings of the British Government, or of its allies, but under a distinct acknowledgment of the inoffensive nature of our arrangements with the Peishwa, and an avowed conviction of our pacific intentions.

Sixthly. That the hostile nature of the proceedings of those chieftains and their repeated violation of public faith, precluded all reliance on their promises and professions, and rendered it the duty of the British Government to require the separation and return of their armies to their respective territories, as the only security to the rights and interests of the British Government and its allies, against the meditated designs of those confederated chieftains.

Seventhly. That this requisition was accompanied by a proposal to withdraw the British army from its advanced and commanding position at Ahmednuggur in the Deccan, and that such a proposal was not only an incontrovertible proof of the just and pacific views of the British Government, but furnished ample security to the confederated chieftains against the possibility of any danger which could be apprehended by them from their compliance with our requisition.

102. The preceding statement sufficiently demonstrates the equity of the arrangements concluded with the state of Poonah, and the justice and moderation manifested by the British Government in carrying those arrangements into effect. It may however, be expedient to submit to your honourable Committee, some observations with regard to the general policy of the alliance which has been concluded between the British Government and the Peishwa, and to the period of time, at which that important arrangement was accomplished.

103. The grounds on which the policy of concluding subsidiary engagements with the state of Poonah, similar to those which were concluded with the Nizam on the 1st of September 1798 is founded, were originally stated in the Governor-General's instructions to the Resident at Hyderabad, under date the 8th of July 1798 of which a copy was transmitted to your honourable Committee with our despatch of the 23d of August 1798; and that subject was resumed in our despatch of the 18th of January 1800 which communicated to your honourable Committee the details of the unsuccessful negotiations between the British Government and the Peishwa, for the conclusion of subsidiary engagements after the termination of the war with Tippoo Sultaun; and those principles were further detailed in the Governor-General's separate letter to your honourable Committee, under date the 9th of June 1800.

104. Your honourable Committee on various occasions has intimated to the Governor-General in council, your concurrence in the principles of that policy, and in the 22d paragraph of your honourable Committee's despatch of the 10th of September 1800, your honourable Committee expressed your approbation of the basis of the proposed arrangements with the state of Poonah. Your honourable Committee on that occasion signified to the Governor-General in council your opinion, that with a view to secure the important objects of those arrangements, the subsidiary force stationed at Poonah, should not be less than 6,000 regular infantry, with the usual proportion of artillery.

105. The Governor-General's acceptance of the propositions of the Court of Poonah in 1799, for subsidizing a force consisting of two battalions of native infantry, was founded on the expectation that such an arrangement must necessarily lead to the introduction of a subsidiary force on a more enlarged scale.

106. The extent of the subsidiary force actually stationed with his Highness the Peishwa, is conformable to the intimation of your honourable Committee; and at the express desire of the Peishwa, the amount of the subsidiary force to be stationed at Poonah, has been augmented since the conclusion of the treaty of Bassein, by the addition of a regiment of cavalry; it will be desirable to augment the detachment at Poonah still further, until it shall be equal to that at Hyderabad, which now consists of one regiment of European infantry, six battalions of native infantry, and two regiments of native cavalry.

107. The general defensive engagements concluded with the Nizam, in the year 1800, and subsequently proposed to the acceptance of the Peishwa, were founded on the same principles, and were calculated to provide improved means of accomplishing the original objects of the projected system of alliance between the British Government and the states of Hyderabad and Poonah.

108. The detail of the improved arrangements at Hyderabad, was communicated to your honourable Committee in our despatch of the 31st of August, 1800.

109. Although the Governor-General in council has not been honoured by any intimation of your honourable Committee's sentiments on the subject of the arrangements concluded at Hyderabad in October 1800, your honourable Committee's previous concurrence in the principles, on which those arrangements were founded, and in the importance of the objects to

which they were directed, has satisfied the Governor-General in council, that your honourable Committee would approve the resolution of the Governor-General, to avail himself of any favourable opportunity of reviving the negotiation for the conclusion of defensive and subsidiary engagements with the state of Poonah, similar to those which were concluded with the Nizam in the month of October, 1800.

110. The progress of events both in Europe and in Asia since that period of time, has tended to urge the expediency of the proposed alliance with his Highness the Peishwa, and the endeavours of the Governor-General have accordingly been assiduously employed for the accomplishment of that desirable arrangement.

111. The Governor-General's instructions to the Resident at Poonah, of the 23d of June, 1802, a copy of which accompanied the Governor-General's despatch to your honourable Committee of the 24th of December 1802, contains a review of the various unsuccessful attempts of the British Government to engage the Peishwa's consent to the proposed alliance; and of the considerations, which rendered the improvement of our political connection with the state of Poonah, an object of essential importance to the complete security of the British empire in India.

112. The justice of those considerations was confirmed, and the policy of accomplishing the proposed alliance, was augmented by the events which subsequently occurred in the Mahratta empire.

113. After the power of the Peishwa had been annihilated by the success of Holkar against the united arms of the Peishwa and Dowlut Rao Scindiah, it could not be expected that his Highness would have been restored to the efficient exercise of his authority, either by Jeswunt Rao Holkar, or by Dowlut Rao Scindiah.

114. The design of the former chieftain to engross the whole power and authority of the state of Poonah, was demonstrated by his actual usurpation, and by the project which he formed and endeavoured to accomplish, of placing on the musnud of Poonah a new Peishwa, or of restoring Bajee Rao to the musnud, under circumstances which would have secured to Holkar the whole military power, and civil authority of the state. It cannot be doubted, that motives of ambition and of inveterate enmity against Dowlut Rao Scindiah would in that event have induced Jeswunt Rao Holkar to direct his arms against the possessions

of Dowlut Rao Scindiah, and the accession of military power and resources which Holkar would have acquired by the permanent establishment of his authority in the state of Poonah, would probably have enabled him to prosecute his views of conquest with success.

115. If the arms of Dowlut Rao Scindiah had ultimately triumphed over those of Holkar, the power and resources of the state of Poonah, together with those of Holkar, would have been added to his own.

116. Adverting to the consideration stated in the preceding paragraph, your honourable Committee will not fail to appreciate the peculiar danger to which the British interest would have been exposed, by such an accession of power in the hands of Dowlut Rao Scindiah.

117. No ultimate issue of the distractions at that time existing in the Mahratta empire could reasonably be supposed, which would not have consolidated under one head, a degree of power and dominion dangerous to the British Government, to the extent in which the balance of contending interests in the Mahratta empire should have been disturbed, and in proportion to the means which a power so consolidated would possess, of eventually co-operating with the Government of France in hostile designs against the British empire in India.

118. Those convulsions in the state might possibly have continued for some time, and might have afforded a temporary security to the British Government against any hostile designs on the part of the Mahrattas, either singly or united with an European power. But the effects of such confusion must speedily have extended to the contiguous dominions of our ally the Nizam, and ultimately to those of the Company, and would have compelled the British Government to engage in the contest.

119. The establishment of Holkar's power at Poonah, would probably occasion demands on the part of that chieftain upon his Highness the Nizam; but even under a contrary supposition, it is demonstrable from the state of the country, that Holkar could not long have maintained an army in the Deccan, without invading the dominions either of the Nizam, or of the Company.

120. The territory around Poonah, to a considerable extent, having been entirely desolated by the troops of Holkar, that chieftain would have been compelled to invade the territories of

the Nizam, or to penetrate into the country situated to the southward of the river Kistna for the subsistence of his numerous troops and followers.

121. The adoption of the latter alternative would have retarded for some time the predatory incursions of Holkar's troops into the territory of the Nizam or of the Company. But when the immediate resources of the Peishwa's southern provinces should have been exhausted, Holkar would have been compelled to draw the means of subsistence for his troops from the plunder of the Company's contiguous territories, on the resources of which we must principally have depended for the supply of our troops in the contest which that irruption would have rendered inevitable. If, therefore, the British Government had not adopted measures for the restoration of the Peishwa's authority, either the Company's territories, or those of our ally the Nizam, would have been exposed to all the evils of war, while neither the Company nor the Nizam under such circumstances could have possessed the means which both now command, of averting the war from their own dominions, and of accelerating its prosperous conclusion by a vigorous system of attack upon the enemy.

122. The restoration of the Peishwa, therefore, under the protection of the British power, was a measure indispensably requisite for the defence, not only of the territories of our allies, but of our own possessions bordering the Mahratta dominions in the peninsula of India.

123. The continuance of the existing convulsions in the Mahratta empire would have afforded a favourable opportunity to the Government of France for the successful prosecution of its favourite object of establishing a dominion within the peninsula of Hindostan, by the introduction of a military force to aid the cause of one of the contending parties; and the views of France would have been favoured by the strength of M. Perron's forces established in the Doab of the Jumna and Ganges, at Agra, Delhi, and in the Punjab, and by the facility of communicating with the maritime possessions retained by Scindiah in Guzzerat. The security and tranquillity of the British empire in India, therefore, might ultimately have been endangered, as much by the effects of a protracted warfare in the Mahratta state, as by the immediate consolidation of a dangerous extent of power and dominion in the hands of one of the contending parties.

124. While the views of the Government of France shall be

directed to the establishment of its authority within the peninsula of Hindostan, it is manifestly the policy of the British Government to accomplish such a system of alliances with the powers of India as may preclude the occurrence of those internal convulsions which would afford to France the most favourable opportunity of effecting her ambitious purpose. Independently of this consideration, the prosecution of such a system of alliance is prudent and advisable in the degree in which the tranquillity and prosperity of our dominion is endangered by the disturbed and distracted condition of neighbouring states.

125. The restoration of the Peishwa, therefore, to the just exercise of his authority under the protection of the British Government, and the conclusion of defensive and subsidiary engagements with his Highness, afforded the only means of precluding the dangers to be apprehended, either from the consolidation of a formidable power, or from the continuance of the distractions in the Mahratta empire.

126. In a letter which the Governor-General addressed to the honourable the Court of Directors, under date the 3d of August, 1799, containing a review of the interests, the power, and disposition of the several states of India under the change produced in the relative condition of those states by the conquest of Mysore, the Governor-General expressed his opinion that a consolidation of the powers of the Mahratta empire was highly improbable, and that it would require a most violent exercise of injustice and oppression on our part to dispose the suspicious and cautious counsels of the Court of Poonah to favour the progress of a French force in India.

127. That opinion was amply justified by the situation of affairs in the Mahratta empire at that period of time; since that time, however, the internal condition of the Mahratta empire has suffered a material change.

128. The ascendancy which Scindiah had then established in the state of Poonah was not such as to menace the actual dissolution of the constitutional form of the Mahratta empire, or to produce a civil war amongst its component branches; and the contending interests of the several feudatory chieftains appeared to afford a sufficient security against any dangerous consolidation of the Mahratta power.

129. Since that time a new power has arisen in the Mahratta state, under the direction of Jeswunt Rao Holkar, which acquired sufficient strength to endanger the stability of all the

principal feudatory states, and was actually directed to the subversion of the constitutional form of the empire.

130. If the progress of the contest which ensued between that chieftain, the Peishwa, and Dowlut Rao Scindiah, had not been checked by the seasonable interposition of the British power for the restoration of the Peishwa's legitimate authority, it is reasonable to conclude that in the moment of extreme danger the Peishwa, or either of those chieftains, would have been disposed to accept the aid of a French force for the support of his cause, and that the contest would either have terminated in the consolidation of a formidable power in the Mahratta state, accompanied by the complete establishment of the authority of France in the peninsula of India, or would have required the interposition of our arms after the aid of the French had actually strengthened one of the belligerent powers, and had consequently increased the difficulty, expense, and hazard of the war.

131. The security, therefore, which the British Government might be supposed to derive from a balance of power and interests among the Mahratta states, and from the jealousy which the Mahratta nation has uniformly entertained of the influence and ascendancy of any European power, ceased to exist, and that security has been still further diminished by the augmented solidity and actual independence which the French force in the service of Dowlut Rao Scindiah has gradually acquired since the termination of the war with Tippoo Sultaun.

132. After the expulsion of the Peishwa from his capital, not only the Peishwa, but Dowlut Rao Scindiah and Jeswunt Rao Holkar afforded the most unequivocal proof that the characteristic jealousy of the Mahratta states would not have deterred those chieftains from having recourse to the aid of France, if an opportunity should have occurred in any crisis of affairs in which their danger or their interest should have suggested the expediency of such a measure.

133. The Peishwa directly solicited and obtained the aid of the British power for the restoration of his authority, Dowlut Rao Scindiah indirectly invited our co-operation ostensibly for the same purpose, and Jeswunt Rao Holkar in his own name and in that of Amrut Rao signified his consent to the terms of alliance which had been proposed to the Peishwa on the condition of our support.

134. If the danger or the interest of those chieftains was

so urgent as to induce them to seek the aid and alliance of an European state, of which the established power, extensive dominion, and unrivalled ascendancy in India had been the peculiar object of the jealousy and apprehension of the Mahratta states, it may reasonably be supposed that in such a crisis of affairs any of those chieftains would have been still more disposed to accept the aid of a military force from the French, who, being destitute of any regular establishment in India, could not in the same degree with the British Government be an object of jealousy and apprehension to the native powers, and especially to the Mahrattas.

135. If, therefore, the British Government had refused to the Peishwa the aid which he solicited, it is reasonable to conclude that his Highness would have availed himself of any opportunity which might have occurred for obtaining the assistance and co-operation of a French military force, and the peace existing at that time with France, might have afforded a favourable opportunity to the French power in India for aiding the Peishwa or any of the contending parties in the Mahratta empire. Admitting, however, that the characteristic jealousy of the Mahratta nation might deter any of the Mahratta chieftains from accepting the aid of a considerable body of European troops furnished by the Government of France, it cannot be doubted that in a situation of emergency any of those chieftains would be disposed to receive into their service a number of French adventurers to be employed in improving the discipline of their armies, and in augmenting the strength and efficiency of their military establishments. The evils which have arisen from the employment of French officers in the service of the native powers have been abundantly manifested in the gradual establishment of the formidable French force in the dominions of his Highness the Nizam, which was happily dissolved under the operation of the treaty concluded with his Highness in the year 1798, and in the growth and extension of the force lately under the direction of M. Perron.

136. In the actual situation of affairs no argument unfavourable to the policy of our engagements with the Peishwa could justly be deduced from the jealousy with which the other Mahratta states might be expected to contemplate the establishment of the British influence in the state of Poonah. The dangers which eventually menaced the security of the British dominion in India under the circumstances above described, far exceeded

any which could be apprehended from the effects of that jealousy, and could only have been averted by the interposition of the British power for the restoration of order and tranquillity in the Mahratta state.

137. From the preceding remarks it appears that the acknowledged policy of contracting defensive and subsidiary engagements with the state of Poonah was never so urgent as at the moment when those engagements were actually concluded, and the course of recent transactions in the Mahratta empire (as detailed in the several despatches from the Governor-General to your honourable Committee) combined with the relative power of the British Government and of the confederated chiefs, with the commanding position of our armies, and with the exposed condition of the territories of Scindiah and the Rajah of Berar at that period of time, constituted a crisis of affairs apparently favourable to the pacific accomplishment of that arrangement, or to the complete success of our arms in the event of opposition on the part of Scindiah or the Rajah of Berar.

138. The Governor-General in council now proceeds to state to your honourable Committee the progress of the British arms in the contest in which this Government has been unavoidably involved with the confederated Mahratta chieftains.

139. The compass of this despatch will not admit the immediate communication to your honourable Committee of the detailed instructions issued by the Governor-General to his Excellency the commander-in-chief on the several points of political arrangement described in the Governor-General's despatch to his Excellency of the 27th of July. Those details will be transmitted to your honourable Committee by a sea conveyance: it is sufficient to state on the present occasion that every measure has been suggested and adopted which the judgment of the Governor-General in council could devise for the successful accomplishment of those arrangements.

140. On the 7th of August his Excellency the commander-in-chief commenced his march with the main body of the British army in the ceded provinces from Cawnpore.

141. On the 28th of August the commander-in-chief received a letter from General Perron indicating a desire on the part of that officer to effect an arrangement which might preclude the necessity of an actual contest between the British forces and those under the command of General Perron. It is proper to apprize your honourable Committee that General Perron had

some time before preferred an application to the British Government for permission to enter the British territories, in prosecution of his intention to retire from the service of Dowlut Rao Scindiah, with which application the Governor-General immediately complied. Subsequent events, however, prevented General Perron from availing himself of that permission. The commander-in-chief replied to General Perron's letter by desiring him to despatch a confidential agent to his Excellency for the purpose of conferring on the subject of General Perron's letter. A person on the part of M. Perron accordingly met the commander-in-chief on the morning of the 29th of August, but having evaded the propositions of the commander-in-chief for the surrender of M. Perron, he departed without effecting any arrangement.

142. On the 29th of August the British army arrived in the vicinity of Coel, the principal station in the territory under the authority of General Perron. The forces of General Perron were drawn up in a strong position near the Fort of Allyghur, and were immediately attacked by the British army with the utmost degree of skill, gallantry, and spirit. This vigorous attack compelled the enemy to retreat, after a very slight resistance.

143. On the 4th of September the fort of Allyghur, hitherto deemed impregnable, was attacked and carried by assault, by a detachment from the British army.

144. Your honourable Committee will unite with the Governor-General in council in applauding the extraordinary activity, valour, and perseverance displayed by the British troops on this memorable occasion.

145. To enable your honourable Committee to form a judgment of the importance of this acquisition, we have the honour to annex to this despatch copies of letters which were found in the fort after its capture.

146. On the 7th of September the commander-in-chief received a letter from General Perron, renewing his application for permission to retire within the Company's territories, with which application the commander-in-chief, with his usual judgment and promptitude, deemed it proper immediately to comply.

147. The Governor-General considered the retirement of General Perron in the present crisis of affairs to be an event highly favourable to the success of the British arms, and to the interests of the British Government in India. The defection of

that officer, may be expected to relieve the surrounding states and chieftains, from the dread which they entertained of his power, and to encourage them to manifest the desire which they are generally believed to entertain, of emancipating themselves from the control of the Mahratta power, by co-operating with the British forces. This event must also diminish the confidence which the native powers of India, have been accustomed to repose in the fidelity of their French officers.

148. On the 8th of September the Fort of Koorja, which the commander-in-chief represents to be of considerable strength, was evacuated.

149. The Governor-General in council has the highest satisfaction in transmitting to your honourable Committee the accompanying printed copies of letters from his Excellency the commander-in-chief, dated the 11th, 12th, and 13th of September, containing the important intelligence of the entire defeat of the Mahratta army under the command of M. Louis, in the vicinity of Delhi. The glory of this most brilliant and decisive victory has not been exceeded by any of the numerous achievements which have established the reputation of the British arms in this quarter of the globe.

150. By this distinguished success the French force established in the dominions of Dowlut Rao Scindiah may be considered to be completely destroyed. Your honourable Committee will not fail to appreciate the importance of this event under the actual renewal of war between Great Britain and France.

151. The Governor-General in council has the further satisfaction of apprizing your honourable Committee that the inhabitants of the Mahratta territory through which the British army has passed, have uniformly testified the utmost joy at the success of our arms, and have been active in furnishing supplies and provisions to the British troops.

152. Several of the chieftains, subjects or tributaries to the Mahratta Government, have expressed to the commander-in-chief their desire to place themselves under the protection of the British Government, and to co-operate with the British forces; and every reason exists to justify an expectation that their example will be followed by many of the Seik chieftains and others, whom the power and ascendancy of General Perron in that quarter of India had compelled to yield a reluctant acquiescence in the requisition of that officer for the aid of their respective forces in the present contest.

153. Rajah Runjeet Sing, the Rajah of Lahore and the principal amongst the Seik chieftains, has transmitted proposals to the commander-in-chief for the transfer of the territory belonging to that nation south of the river Sutledge, on the condition of mutual defence against the respective enemies of that chieftain and of the British nation.

154. His Majesty Shah Allum has manifested the utmost solicitude to avail himself of the protection of the British power, and your honourable Committee will anticipate from the contents of the commander-in-chief's despatch of the 12th of September, the probability that his Majesty's person and authority will speedily be entrusted to the defence of the British power, and that the honourable Company will soon obtain in the eyes of all the native states of India, the distinguished honour which must attend the deliverance of that aged and unfortunate monarch from a condition of the utmost degree of misery and degradation, and his restoration under the protection of the British Government to a state of dignity, competency and comfort.

155. The Governor-General in council is happy to inform your honourable Committee that no event has occurred to counterbalance these brilliant successes. Five companies of sepoys under the command of Lieut.-Colonel Coningham, occupied a small frontier post at Shekohabad. That inconsiderable body of troops was attacked on the 2nd of September by a numerous detachment of cavalry under the command of a Frenchman named Fleury, and succeeded in compelling the enemy to retreat, but being again attacked on the 4th of September by the same superior force, and having nearly expended its ammunition, the party of British troops capitulated to the enemy. On the receipt of this intelligence his Excellency the commander-in-chief detached a considerable body of cavalry and infantry to oppose the Mahratta troops under the command of M. Fleury, and the Governor-General in council has since had the satisfaction to learn that the approach of that detachment, combined with the fall of the fortress of Allyghur, induced M. Fleury to retire precipitately with the troops under his command across the Jumna; those troops have since dispersed.

156. The Governor-General in council now proceeds to communicate to your honourable Committee the course of military operations on the western side of India.

157. The honourable Major-General Wellesley who occupied a position within one march of Dowlut Rao Scindiah's fortress of

Ahmednuggur, having received intelligence of the issue of the Resident's negotiation, commenced his march towards that fortress on the 8th of August, and the same day attacked and carried by escalade the fortified town of Ahmednuggur. On the 10th of August the batteries of the British army opened against the fort, which was surrendered on the 12th instant. For the details of this brilliant and important success, the Governor-General in council has the honour to refer your honourable Committee to the enclosed publication, issued by the authority of the Governor-General in council, and the accompanying printed copy of Major-General Wellesley's despatch to the Governor-General of the 12th of August.

158. The possession of this fortress is of peculiar importance to the prosecution of our military operations, by securing the communication with Poonah, and by affording a depôt for supplies of provisions and military stores.

159. In the interval of time between the 12th and 21st of August, the date of the latest advices from that officer, Major-General Wellesley took possession of all the districts dependent on Ahmednuggur, yielding an estimated annual revenue of six lacs, thirty-four thousand rupees; those districts were placed under the temporary management of a British officer.

160. On the 21st of August, a part of the force under the command of Major-General Wellesley had crossed, and the remainder was crossing the river Godaveree, on its march towards the enemy, and eventually to form a junction with the subsidiary force of Hyderabad under the command of Colonel Stevenson, which occupied a position near Jafirabad.

161. By the latest advices from the armies of the confederated chieftains, it appears that those chieftains had despatched their heavy baggage to Boorhanpore, and were moving towards the Budowlee pass, one of the passes into the territories of the Nizam.

162. The following is the amount of the respective forces of the Rajah of Berar, and Dowlut Rao Scindiah, assembled near the Nizam's frontier on the 5th of July—

Forces of Scindiah.—Cavalry, 18,500; infantry, 11 battalions, matchlock men, 500; heavy ordnance, 35; field pieces, 170.

Forces of the Rajah of Berar.—Cavalry, 20,000; infantry, 6,000; field pieces, 35; rocket men, 500; camel guns, 500.

163. The foregoing statement includes troops of every description. The Governor-General in council has reason to believe,

that the number of the confederated forces has been considerably diminished by desertion, in consequence of the scarcity of provisions.

164. The force under the immediate command of Major-General Wellesley, consists of 1,731 European and native cavalry[1], 6,999 infantry[2], exclusive of European artillerymen, and 653 pioneers, of the establishment of Fort St. George, 2,400 cavalry belonging to the Rajah of Mysore, and about 3,000 Mahratta horse. Two battalions of sepoys were detached in the month of July with a large convoy of treasure, bullocks, and grain, from the army under the command of his Excellency Lieut.-General Stuart, to the army of Major-General Wellesley. The British force remaining at Poonah for the protection of that capital, consists of 1,778 infantry and artillery[3].

165. The forces under the command of Colonel Stevenson, consist of the whole of the subsidiary force, amounting to 7,920 infantry, cavalry, and artillery[4]; and about 16,000 men, cavalry and infantry of his Highness the Nizam's troops.

166. The Resident at Poonah will receive instructions to communicate to your honourable Committee, the progress of the operations of the British armies to the date of his latest advices, at the period of time when this despatch shall reach Poonah.

167. The most active measures have been adopted under the orders of the Governor-General, for the occupation of Dowlut Rao Scindiah's sea-port of Baroach; and the Governor-General

---

[1] Cavalry.—H. M.'s 19th light dragoons, 384; 4th, 5th, and 7th, regiments native cavalry, 1347—total 1731. Artillery, 173.

[2] Infantry.—H. M.'s 74th regiment, and H. M.'s 78th regiment, 1368; first battalion 2nd, N. I.; first battalion 8th, N. I.; second battalion 12th, N. I.; second battalion 18th, N. I.; and third regiment N. I., 5631.—Total 8903. With 357 Madras artillery lascars, and 653 Madras pioneers.

[3] H. M.'s 84th regiment, five companies, 470; European artillerymen, 93; native infantry, 1215.—Total 1778. With 117 Bombay lascars, and a small park of artillery,

[4] Cavalry.—3rd, and 6th, regiments native cavalry, 909; artillery, 120. Infantry.—H. M.'s Scotch brigade, 778; second battalion 2nd, N. I., first battalion 6th, N. I., second battalion 7th, N. I., second battalion 9th, N. I., and 11th, regiment N. I., 6113.—Total 7920. With 276 gun lascars, and 212 pioneers.

in council confidently hopes, that the information from Bombay of the capture of that important place will accompany this despatch.

168. By the latest advices it appears, that Jeswunt Rao Holkar still maintained his position between the rivers Taptee and Nerbuddah; there is no reason to believe that the Rajah of Berar and Dowlut Rao Scindiah, have succeeded in their endeavours to obtain the co-operation of that chieftain.

169. In our despatch of the 1st of August the Governor-General in council informed your honourable Committee, that the attention of the Governor-General was directed to the formation of an arrangement for the occupation of the province of Cuttack. For this purpose a part of the northern division of the army under the Presidency of Fort St. George, commanded by Lieut.-Colonel Campbell, was ordered to be holden in readiness to proceed on that expedition from Ganjam[1], and a detachment consisting of two companies of his Majesty's 22nd regiment of foot, and a part of the 20th Bengal regiment was despatched from Bengal, to reinforce the troops under Lieut.-Colonel Campbell's command; the whole of that force consists of 565 Europeans of his Majesty's and the honourable Company's troops, 2,200 sepoys, and a party of native cavalry consisting of fifty men.

170. The Governor-General also directed a detachment consisting of 500 Bengal volunteers, and twenty-one artillerymen, with four six-pounders to proceed by sea, under the command of Captain Morgan, for the purpose of occupying Balasore; and another detachment has been formed at Jelasore, under the command of Lieut.-Colonel Ferguson, consisting of 835 sepoys, and eighty-four men of the Governor-General's body-guard, for the purpose of advancing into the province of Cuttack, and forming a junction with the detachment at Balasore, when the state of the intermediate country, or the progress of the main army shall favour that movement. This detachment is supported by a force of 1,400 sepoys, assembled at Midnapore under the command of Lieut.-Colonel Fenwick.

171. It is proper to inform your honourable Committee, that in consequence of a severe illness which prevented Lieut.-Colonel Campbell from proceeding with the army, the Governor-General despatched Lieut.-Colonel Harcourt, of his Majesty's

[1] The detail, here given in a note, is omitted, to save space.

12th regiment, his Lordship's Military Secretary, to Ganjam, for the purpose of taking the command of that army.

172. On the 8th of September, the troops under the command of Lieut.-Colonel Campbell commenced their march from Ganjam. On the 11th of September, Lieut.-Colonel Harcourt arrived at Ganjam and took the command of the troops, Lieut.-Colonel Campbell continuing in a state of health which rendered him unable to move with the expedition.

173. On the 14th instant, the British troops conducted by Lieut.-Colonel Harcourt, took possession of Manikapatam without any resistance on the part of the Mahratta troops, who fled on the approach of our army.

174. From that station Lieut.-Colonel Harcourt despatched a letter to the principal Bramins of the pagoda of Juggernaut encouraging them to place the pagoda under the protection of the British troops.

175. On the 16th instant, a favourable answer was received from the Bramins, and a deputation was sent to the British camp to claim the protection which had been offered by Lieut.-Colonel Harcourt.

176. On the 18th instant, the army encamped at Juggernaut; the Mahratta troops which were there stationed fled on its approach.

177. The inhabitants of the country subject to the Mahratta Government through which the British troops have passed, have manifested the utmost degree of satisfaction at their approach.

178. On the 21st instant, the detachment under the command of Captain Morgan landed at Balasore, and succeeded in occupying that station after a very slight resistance on the part of the enemy.

179. From the accounts which have been received with regard to the troops of the Rajah of Berar in the Province of Cuttack, there is no reason to suppose that these troops are either numerous or formidable, nor is it probable that they can receive any considerable reinforcements from Berar, while Major-General Wellesley's operations engage the attention of the Rajah for the defence of his person and of his capital; at all events it may be expected, that the introduction of any additional force into the Province of Cuttack will be effectually prevented by the previous occupation of the passes leading into that province, either by the British troops, or by the chieftains occupying the territory on the frontier of Cuttack, whom we may

be enabled to conciliate to the interests of the British Government.

180. The Governor-General in council entertains a hope that the officers of the Rajah of Berar, may be induced to surrender the possession of that province to the British power without a contest; and the Governor-General has adopted measures calculated to produce that desirable event; under any probable circumstances, however, the Governor-General in council confidently anticipates the complete and speedy success of the expedition against the province of Cuttack.

181. In our despatch of the 1st of August, the Governor-General in council apprized your honourable Committee of the expected death of his Highness the Nizam.

182. The event took place on the 6th of August; his Highness's eldest son Mirza Secunder Jah was immediately proclaimed successor to the Soobahdary of the Deccan; on the 7th of August, Mirza Secunder Jah formally took his seat on the musnud, to which he was conducted by the Resident at Hyderabad, and by Rajah Ragotim Rao, the deputy of his late Highness's prime minister Azim ul Omra, and received the congratulatory presents of all the principal officers of his government at Hyderabad.

183. On that occasion, the Resident at Hyderabad was received by his Highness with the most distinguished honours as the representative of the British Government in India, and his Highness publicly delivered to the Resident an instrument under his Highness's seal, acknowledging the obligation of the treaties subsisting between the British Government, and the state of Hyderabad.

184. The Governor-General had previously directed the Resident to require from Secunder Jah the delivery of an instrument to that effect, as the first act of that Prince's Government, and his Highness assented to that requisition with the utmost readiness.

185. Rajah Ragotim Rao on that occasion, suggested the demand of a corresponding engagement on the part of the British Government, which suggestion the Resident properly rejected. The Governor-General in council however, being of opinion that a voluntary act of recognition on our part, would tend to conciliate the confidence of Secunder Jah, and would produce an impression on the minds of his subjects, and of the several princes and chieftains of India, and particularly on the

mind of his Highness the Peishwa, highly favourable to the credit of our justice, moderation, and public faith, deemed it expedient to execute an engagement in terms corresponding with the instrument delivered by Secunder Jah, and an instrument to that effect was accordingly executed by the Governor-General in council under the seal of the honourable Company, and transmitted to the Resident, with directions to deliver it to his Highness the Soobahdar in the most public and formal manner.

186. The Governor-General in council has great satisfaction in stating to your honourable Committee, that the event of his Highness the Nizam's death has not occasioned any interruption of the public tranquillity, and that the accession of Mirza Secunder Jah has been generally and cheerfully acknowledged by the younger sons of his late Highness, and by all the officers and subjects of his Highness's Government.

187. The preservation of tranquillity at this crisis must be ascribed principally to the position of our armies, under the command of Major-General Wellesley and Colonel Stevenson, and of a considerable detachment from the army, under the personal command of his Excellency Lieut.-General Stuart, which his Excellency, under the orders of the Governor-General despatched towards the southern frontier of the Nizam's dominions, for the purpose of eventually proceeding to Hyderabad, if the situation of affairs should render such a movement expedient or necessary for the preservation of tranquillity, or for securing the regular order of succession on the death of the Nizam.

188. Adverting to the known designs and proceedings of the confederated chieftains with relation to the British Government, to the intrigues which they had long carried on at the Court of Hyderabad, with a view to dissolve the connection subsisting between the British Government and the state of Hyderabad, and to the position of their united armies on the frontier of the Nizam's dominions, it can scarcely be doubted that unless the movements of their armies had been checked by the position of the British troops, those chieftains would have taken advantage of the event of the Nizam's decease, to excite commotions in the state of Hyderabad, and to disturb the regular order of succession by affording the aid of their troops in support of the known pretensions of Ferreedoon Jah, (the younger brother of Secunder Jah) to the musnud of Hyderabad.

189. The expected event of his Highness the Nizam's decease,

and the opportunity which that event might afford to the confederated chieftains in the actual position of their armies to prosecute their injurious designs, furnished an additional reason for requiring those chieftains to withdraw their armies from the menacing position which they occupied on the frontier of the Nizam's dominions.

190. The Governor-General in council deems it proper to transmit to your honourable Committee, an extract from a despatch from the Resident at Poonah, detailing propositions on the part of his Highness the Peishwa, for the transfer to the honourable Company of a part of his Highness's possessions in the Province of Bundlecund, yielding an estimated annual revenue of thirty-six lacs of rupees, in lieu of the territory ceded by his Highness in the southern quarter of his dominions, and of a part of the cessions in the vicinity of Surat, and other proposed modifications of the treaty of Bassein.

191. The Governor-General in council considering those proposed modifications of the treaty of Bassein to be a considerable improvement of the terms of that treaty, with reference to the interests of the British Government, has assented to the Peishwa's propositions.

192. Your honourable Committee will observe with satisfaction, that these propositions from the Peishwa afforded an unequivocal proof of the sincerity of his Highness's disposition to adhere to the principles and spirit of the alliance happily concluded between his Highness, and the British Government.

193. In conformity to the plan of operations and political arrangements contained in the Governor-General's instructions to his Excellency the Commander-in-Chief, of the 27th of July, (of which a copy accompanied our despatch of the 1st of August,) a considerable detachment of British troops was assembled near Allahabad, for the purpose of co-operating with the force under the command of Himmut Bahâdur (one of his Highness the Peishwa's principal officers in Bundlecund) in the occupation of that province, agreeably to the proposals which that officer some time since transmitted to the British Government, as noted in the 59th paragraph of this despatch; and the Governor-General has received information that the detachment has crossed the river Jumna, and entered the province of Bundlecund.

194. The Governor-General in council has every reason to expect the pacific introduction of the Company's authority into the province of Bundlecund, and the late cession of a part of the

Peishwa's possessions in Bundlecund may be expected greatly to facilitate the accomplishment of that object.

195. Adverting to the brilliant success and rapid progress of the British arms in the present contest with the confederated Mahratta chieftains, to the accumulated and seasonable pressure of an active and skilful system of military operations on all the most vulnerable points of their resources and dominions, and to the probable issue of the various political arrangements adopted on this occasion for the purpose of securing the co-operation, or neutrality of the several states and chieftains, whose power and resources might be employed in support of the enemy's cause, the Governor-General entertains a confident expectation of the early conclusion of peace with those chieftains on terms, which shall deprive them of the means of disturbing the tranquillity of our possessions, and of impairing the efficiency and stability of our alliances.

196. Under the prosperous issue of such a general pacification, we expect that with a considerable augmentation of the lustre and glory of the British arms in India, we shall witness the accomplishment of a comprehensive system of alliances and political connection in Hindostan and the Deccan, calculated to promote the general tranquillity of India, and to secure on the most permanent foundations the interests and dominions of the honourable Company, against the hostile attempts of any native or European power, and especially to protect the north-western frontier of Oude, and to destroy the last remnant of French influence in India.

We have the honour to be,
Honourable Sirs,
with the greatest respect,
Your most obedient and faithful servants,
WELLESLEY.
G. H. BARLOW.
G. UDNY.

50. The Governor-General in Council to the Honourable the Secret Committee of the Honourable the Court of Directors.

Progress of the War. First attempts at negotiation.

October 31, 1803.

Honourable Sirs,

The unavoidable delay in the despatch of the *Packet* over-land, enables the Governor-General in council to communicate to your honourable Committee, by the present opportunity, the accounts which we have received of the progress of our arms, since our last address to your honourable Committee.

On the 12th of September, the army, under the personal direction of his Excellency the Commander-in-Chief, commenced crossing the river Jumna. In consequence of the total defeat of the army under the command of M. Louis Bourquain on the 11th of September, the whole of the French and Mahratta force dispersed, leaving to the British troops the undisputed passage of the Jumna.

Conformably to the permission granted to General Perron, that officer attended by his secretary, Mr. Beckett, and by Mr. Fleury, passed into the Company's territories, and has since arrived at Lucknow, whence he will shortly proceed to the Presidency. General Perron was attended by his body-guard consisting of near 400 horse. On the 14th M. Louis Bourquain, and four of his officers, surrendered themselves prisoners of war to the Commander-in-Chief at Delhi.

On the 16th, his Excellency the Commander-in-Chief attended by the principal officers of the British army waited on the unfortunate Emperor Shah Allum, at the royal palace, in the Fort of Delhi.

On that occasion his Majesty's eldest son, Mirza Akber Shah, proceeded to the British camp, and conducted his Excellency the Commander-in-Chief to the presence of his Majesty, who received his Excellency seated on his throne.

His Majesty and the whole of his court testified the utmost joy at the events which have placed his Majesty and the royal family, under the protection of the British Government.

The attention of the Governor-General is now directed to the formation of a permanent arrangement for the future maintenance of the dignity and comfort of his Majesty and the royal family, on principles calculated to provide for the exigency with the least practicable inconvenience to the honourable Company, and with the greatest advantage to the reputation of British justice, and liberality, and to secure the important benefits to be derived from the connection which will now be renewed between his Majesty, and the British power in India.

The Governor-General having received from his Excellency the Commander-in-Chief, returns of the ordnance captured in the Fort of Alygur on the 4th of September, and of the artillery taken on the field of battle near Delhi, on the 11th of September, which completed the official statement of the military operations conducted under the personal command of his Excellency the Commander-in-Chief, from the 29th of August, to the 18th of September, the Governor-General in council issued general orders, under date the 1st of October, expressing the sentiments of applause and admiration with which the British Government has contemplated the rapid and brilliant success of the British arms, under the distinguished conduct of his Excellency the Commander-in-Chief, and the extraordinary valour and exertions of the officers and troops by which that success was atchieved.

On the 24th of September, his Excellency the Commander-in-Chief marched from Delhi with the army under his command in the direction of Muttra and Agra, leaving Lieutenant-Colonel Ochterlony to attend the person of the Emperor Shah Allum; and for the protection of Delhi one complete battalion and five companies of infantry, together with a corps of Mahrattas, then raising under the superintendance of two officers, British subjects, who quitted the service of Scindiah at the commencement of the war.

On the 30th of September, M. Dodernique, a French officer in the service of Dowlut Rao Scindiah, commanding a brigade of Scindiah's troops, surrendered himself to Colonel Vandeleur, who had arrived at Muttra with a detachment of British troops from Futtygur. M. Dodernique was accompanied by a British subject, and by a French officer in Scindiah's service. His Excellency the Commander-in-Chief received notice on the 1st of October, of the intention of Mr. Brownrig, and of three more officers, British subjects belonging to the corps under the command of Mr. Brownrig, to surrender themselves at the earliest opportunity.

The Governor-General in council has the satisfaction to inform your honourable Committee, that no French officers of any consideration now remain in the service of the confederated Mahratta chieftains.

On the 2d of October, the army under the command of his Excellency General Lake arrived at Muttra. The Governor-General in council deems it to be a testimony due to the exemplary discipline and good conduct of the British troops, to insert in this place an extract from his Excellency the Commander-in-Chief's letter to the Governor-General, of the 2d of October, describing the impression produced on the minds of the inhabitants of the country between Delhi and Muttra, by the order and regularity of the troops during their march through that territory.

"*It is with a mixed sentiment of pride and pleasure that I inform your Lordship, that all the inhabitants of this place, who for a time fled, returned to their habitations last night, on perceiving that no ravages had been committed by the troops, which I attribute to the particular attention payed by Colonel Vandeleur to this circumstance.*"

"*I am informed from all quarters that the inhabitants behold with astonishment, this proof of the discipline and good conduct of the army. All declare that hitherto it has been unknown in Hindostan that a victorious army should pass through a country without destroying by fire, and committing every excess the most injurious to the inhabitants; but on the contrary from the regularity observed by us, our approach is a blessing, instead of bringing with it as they at first feared all the horrors of war attended by rapine and murder; that their cattle remain in their fields without being molested, and the inhabitants in their houses receive every protection.*"

"*I cannot find words to express to your Lordship the pleasure I have received from this account. The favourable opinion the inhabitants have formed of us from these circumstances cannot fail of producing the most beneficial consequences.*"

On the 9th of October his Excellency the Commander-in-Chief concluded a treaty of general defence and guarantee with the Rajah of Bhurtpoor, one of the principal chieftains of the tribe of Jauts whose country is situated in the vicinity of Muttra and Agra.

The Governor-General in council having entirely approved the terms of that treaty, has ratified it; a copy is enclosed for your honourable Committee's information.

In consequence of the conclusion of this engagement the Rajah of Bhurtpoor has despatched to the British camp, a detachment of 1,200 cavalry to co-operate with the British army.

The character and influence of that chieftain in the north-western quarter of Hindostan, render his alliance an object of considerable importance to the interests of the British Government.

The Governor-General in council entertains a confident expectation, that the Rajpoot and other chieftains in that quarter will shortly be induced to connect their interests with those of the British Government, and if necessary to co-operate with the British troops against the enemy.

On the 4th of October the army under the command of his Excellency General Lake, arrived before Agra; a summons was immediately sent demanding the surrender of the fort to which no answer was returned. The Mahratta officers in the fort had confined all the Europeans stationed there, and the greatest confusion was said to prevail within the fort. A body of the enemy's troops consisting of seven battalions being encamped under the walls of the fort, it became necessary to dislodge that force before the operations of the siege could be commenced. The Commander-in-Chief accordingly appointed a detachment of British troops under the command of Brigadier General Clarke for that duty, and on the 10th of October, the British detachment attacked and completely defeated the force of the enemy.

By this success, the British troops obtained possession of the town of Agra, and were enabled to commence operations for the siege of the fort.

On the 12th of October the battalions of the enemy which were opposed to the British troops on the 10th of that month surrendered to the Commander-in-Chief; their number amounted to about 2,500.

On the following day, the Governor of the Fort of Agra solicited a cessation of hostilities for the purpose of negotiating the terms of capitulation, and despatched an European officer to the British camp, with a letter signed by the principal officers in the fort, stating the conditions on which they were disposed to surrender it; his Excellency the Commander-in-Chief immediately despatched a British officer into the fort for the purpose of finally adjusting the terms of the capitulation, but while that officer was actually engaged in the negotiation the firing from the fort recommenced, and the British officer returned to camp.

On the 17th the breaching batteries opened against the fort with great effect, and on the evening of the same day the garrison capitulated and surrendered the celebrated Fort of Agra to the British troops.

The acquisition of the important fortress of Agra, added to our possession of Delhi and Muttra, has completed the reduction of the territory of Scindiah situated on both banks of the Jumna.

The enemy being entirely repulsed on the north-western frontier of Oude, no event has occurred to disturb the tranquillity of our possessions since the incursion of the detachment under the command of Mr. Fleury, of which the details were communicated in our despatch to your honourable Committee of the 25th of September. Some internal disturbance has arisen in consequence of outrages committed by the Zemeendar of Tutteea, who has for some time been in a state of rebellion against the British Government; these disturbances however were entirely quelled, and several of the rebels were in custody for trial by the civil power on the 21st of October.

Gholaum Mahomed Khan the Rohilla chief, who, at the invitation of Scindiah and of M. Perron, had advanced with a body of troops to Coonjpoorah, a town situated on the river Jumna to the northward of Delhi, with the intention of crossing that river and of proceeding towards Rampore, on receiving intelligence of the battle of Delhi, and the total defeat of the army under the command of M. Louis Bourquain, immediately retreated with the utmost expedition, and was deserted by a considerable part of the troops which he had collected.

The Governor-General in council deems it proper in this place to insert an extract from a letter from Mr. A. Seton, the political agent of the Governor-General in the ceded provinces, dated the 18th of September, describing the impression produced on the minds of the inhabitants of our north-western provinces by the brilliant victory obtained by the army under the command of his Excellency General Lake, over the troops conducted by M. Louis Bourquain on the 11th of September in the vicinity of Delhi.

"*It is impossible to express the astonishment which has been raised amongst all ranks of natives by the brilliant success of his Excellency the Commander-in-Chief on the 11th instant; at first the intelligence was not believed, and when confirmed was only believed to be admired. The beneficial effects of so glorious and so complete a victory gained under circumstances of such difficulty, must be almost beyond calculation. The language of the natives is that their admiration is divided between two objects, and that they know not which to extoll most,—British valour, or British humanity.*"

The Governor-General in council now proceeds to communicate to your honourable Committee, the progress of operations in the province of Cuttack, which we have the satisfaction to inform your honourable Committee have terminated by the capture of the town and fort of Cuttack, and the consequent subjection of the whole of that valuable province to the British authority.

Our despatch of the 25th of September, contains the communication of the progress of the British army under the command of Lieutenant-Colonel Harcourt from Ganjam to Juggernaut, and of the occupation of that place by the British troops.

The inundated state of the country prevented the march of the army under the command of Lieutenant-Colonel Harcourt from Juggernaut, until the 24th of September. During the first day's march, the advanced corps of the army were several times engaged with parties of the enemy's troops who were repulsed with loss.

An action subsequently took place between an advanced detachment of the British troops and a party of the enemy near Muckundpore, in which the latter was defeated with considerable loss.

No further resistance was opposed to the progress of the British army until its arrival at Cuttack on the 10th of October, but the inundated state of the country and the rise of the rivers greatly retarded the march of the troops.

The town of Cuttack was immediately occupied by the British troops without opposition.

Our despatch of the 25th of September, also contains the information of the occupation of Balasore by a detachment of troops which proceeded from Fort William by sea, under the command of Captain Morgan.

On the 30th of September, Captain Morgan detached two companies under the command of Lieutenant Slye, towards Soorong twenty miles south of Balasore, for the purpose of dislodging a party of the enemy stationed near that place, and of opening the communication in the direction of Cuttack.

On the 1st of October the detachment under the command of Lieutenant Slye, attacked and defeated the enemy which was posted at a village a short distance north of Soorong, and the troops of the enemy stationed at Soorong, subsequently retreated to the southward. The detachment under Lieutenant Slye having been reinforced by another company from Balasore, occupied Soorong on the 3d of October without further opposition.

In our despatch of the 25th of September, the Governor-General in council has communicated to your honourable Committee, the formation and destination of a detachment under the command of Lieut.-Colonel Fergusson, at Balasore.

On the 4th of October the whole of the detachment under the command of Lieut.-Colonel Fergusson arrived at Balasore without any opposition.

On the 10th of October the detachment under the command of Lieut.-Colonel Fergusson marched from Balasore in consequence of orders from the Governor-General, directing that officer to proceed for the purpose of forming a junction with the army under the command of Lieut.-Colonel Harcourt at Cuttack; and on the 15th of October that detachment arrived near Budruck, a village situated near half-way between Balasore and Cuttack.

The inhabitants of the province of Cuttack afforded every assistance to the British troops on their march, and expressed the utmost satisfaction at the prospect of being speedily relieved from the oppressions to which they had uniformly been subjected by the Mahratta Government, and of being placed under the protection of the British power.

On the 19th of October the Governor-General received the satisfactory intelligence of the capture of the strong fort of Barrabutty, or Cuttack, on the 14th, by assault.

The Governor-General in council contemplates with sentiments of the highest approbation the distinguished zeal and ability of the British officers, and indefatigable perseverance and alacrity of the British troops in surmounting the extraordinary difficulties which the nature of the country of Cuttack, and the inclemency of the season opposed to the progress and operations of an invading army.

The Governor-General in council desires to offer to your honourable Committee his congratulations on the success of the British arms in the province of Cuttack, by which the whole of that valuable and highly productive province has been annexed to the honourable Company's dominions, the frontier of Bengal materially strengthened, and the continuity of your possessions between the presidencies of Bengal and Fort St. George, ultimately secured.

On the 3rd of October the Governor General in council had the satisfaction to receive despatches from Bombay, notifying the assault and capture of the important seaport of Baroach, on the 29th of August, by a detachment under the command of Lieut.-Colonel Woodington.

By the capture of this important seaport, its dependant territory estimated to yield an annual revenue of more than eleven lacks of rupees, has been subjected to the authority of the British Government.

The Governor-General has had the satisfaction to receive advices from the honourable Major-General Wellesley, containing the important intelligence that on the 23rd of Sept. an action took place near the Adjuntee Pass, in the Deccan, between the forces under the command of the honourable Major-General Wellesley, and the main body of the combined army of the confederated chieftains. After a most severe engagement the enemy was completely defeated, and ninety-eight pieces of canon were taken on the field of battle by the British troops at the point of the bayonet; our loss in this signal and splendid victory has been great.

The Governor-General in council solicits the particular notice of your honourable Committee, and of the honourable Court of Directors, to the distinguished merits of the honourable Major-General Wellesley, and of the officers and troops under his command in that extraordinary exertion of British discipline, valour, and skill.

The satisfaction with which the Governor-General in council contemplates the late rapid and glorious success of the British arms in every direction in which they have been opposed to the enemy's forces, is augmented by the reflection, that under the pressure of accumulated defeat, with aggravated loss of resources, power, reputation, military strength, and dominion in every quarter of India, the confederate chieftains must speedily be compelled to accede to such reasonable terms of pacification as shall sufficiently provide for the safety of our allies, for the future security of the honourable Company's possessions, and for the permanent establishment of tranquillity in Hindostan and the Deccan.

The Governor-General in council cannot close this despatch without expressing to your honourable Committee in the strongest terms the sentiments of high respect, admiration, and gratitude, with which he contemplates the energy and perseverance, the military skill, judgment, and invincible intrepidity manifested by his Excellency General Lake, commander-in-chief, under extraordinary difficulties, in preparing the army of Bengal for the field, in conducting it by a rapid succession of glorious victories to the complete defeat of a powerful enemy, and in maintaining the honour of the British name in India by a humane attention towards the inhabitants of the conquered provinces, and by a due respect and reverence towards the unfortunate representative of the house of Timur, and towards his Majesty's royal family.

The glory of this uninterrupted success is not surpassed by any recorded triumph of the British arms in India, and has been attended by every circumstance calculated to elevate the fame of British valour, to illustrate the character of British humanity, and to secure the stability of the British empire in the east. The Governor-General in council therefore earnestly recommends the conduct of General Lake to the most distinguished approbation and applause of the East India Company, and to the gracious favour of his Majesty; nor has any officer in the most brilliant periods of our history in India displayed the high qualifications requisite for the arduous station of commander-in-chief, with more honour to the military reputation, or with more advantage to the political interests of the British nation in the east.

The public duty of the Governor-General in council also demands a testimony of justice to the conduct of the honourable Major-General Wellesley. The attention of your honourable Committee has already been solicited to the merits of Major-General-Wellesley in conducting the British troops from the frontier of Mysore to Poonah, in establishing his Highness the Peishwa upon the musnud, and in the reduction of the important fortress of Ahmednuggur. The conduct of Major-General Wellesley in the exercise of the extensive political and military powers, vested in him by the Governor-General in council, also deserves the highest approbation of your honourable Committee, and of the honourable the Court of Directors.

At the close of a campaign of the most brilliant success, and glory, in every quarter of India, the transcendent victory obtained at Assye in the Deccan, on the 23d of September, appeared to the Governor-General in council to demand a testimony of public honour, equal to any which the justice of the British Government in India has ever conferred on the conduct of our officers and troops in the most distinguished period of our military history.

The Governor-General in council highly approved the skilful plan formed by Major-General Wellesley on the 21st of September, for precluding the escape of the enemy, and for reducing their combined army to the necessity of hazarding a general action.

His Excellency in council also signified his most cordial approbation of the magnanimity, promptitude, and judgment with which Major-General Wellesley determined upon the instantaneous attack on the enemy on the 23d of September.

During the severe action which ensued, the conduct of Major-General Wellesley united a degree of ability, of prudence, and of dauntless spirit, seldom equalled and never surpassed.

The important benefits resulting from the triumph of our arms in the battle of Assye, are not inferior to the splendour of the action. The immediate consequences derived from the exertions of that day have been the complete defeat of the combined army of the confederate chieftains; an irreparable blow to the strength and efficiency of their military resources, especially of their artillery, in the Deccan; the expulsion of a predatory and hostile army from the territory of our ally the Soubahdar of the Deccan; and a seasonable and effectual check to the ambition, pride and rapacity of the enemy.

Under these circumstances the Governor-General in council is induced to recommend the conduct of the honourable Major-General Wellesley to the particular approbation of the honourable Court of Directors, and to the gracious notice of his Majesty.

In the course of an extensive and complicated system of military operations, the glorious success of our arms since the commencement of this war has been uniform in every part of India. The able and gallant officers and troops of his Majesty's service, and of the several establishments of the three Presidencies have been actuated by equal sentiments of public spirit and honour, and have co-operated with equal ardour and success, in an united effort to accomplish the just objects of the allies. The Governor-General in council confides in the justice of our cause, in the unanimous zeal of the three Presidencies, and in the continued co-operation of their respective resources and power, that the views of the confederate chieftains will be speedily frustrated by the complete restoration of peace and tranquillity to the provinces of Hindostan and the Deccan, which have been disturbed by the ambition and violence of the enemy.

We have the honour to be, &c.

WELLESLEY.

G. H. BARLOW.

G. UDNY.

P. S. The Governor-General has received on this day, a despatch from the honourable Major-General Wellesley, under date the 6th of October, containing intelligence that on the 5th of October Major-General Wellesley had received a letter from the enemy's camp signed by Ballajee Koonjur, requesting that Major-General Wellesley would despatch a British officer, together with an officer of the Soubahdar of the Deccan to the enemy's camp, for the purpose of negotiating terms of peace between the allies and the confederated Mahratta chieftains.

Ballajee Koonjur was originally despatched by his Highness the Peishwa from Bassein, to Dowlut Rao Scindiah, for the purpose of explaining to that chieftain the nature of the engagements concluded between the Peishwa and the British Government; but with the accustomed versatility and treachery of a Mahratta politician Ballajee Koonjur has subsequently attached himself to the service of Dowlut Rao Scindiah.

Major-General Wellesley judged it to be expedient to decline a compliance with this request for the despatch of a British officer, and of an officer of the Soubahdar of the Deccan to the camp of the confederates; first, because in the application of Ballajee Koonjur no reference is made to the authority, either of Dowlut Rao Scindiah or the Rajah of Berar, and consequently it is not certain that the application proceeds from either of those chieftains, either or both of whom might hereafter disavow the act of Ballajee Koonjur; and secondly, because the presence of a British officer in the enemy's camp at that moment, would have tended to raise the spirits of the enemy's troops, and to prevent their dispersion, and would have been represented by the enemy as an attempt on our part to sue for peace.

The Governor-General in council entirely approves the judgment and prudence manifested by Major-General Wellesley in refusing to comply with the request of the enemy, and is satisfied that the duplicity and debased art of the Mahratta councils would have perverted the acquiescence of Major-General Wellesley in this insidious proposition, to the purpose of impairing the reputation of our arms and power.

The Governor-General in council however, is inclined to believe that the ambition, pride, and rapacity of the confederate chieftains have received such a check, as must compel them to abstain from the prosecution of their inordinate designs; and we therefore expect to receive early intelligence of the disposition of the confederate chieftains to despatch directly from their respective authorities, to the British camp, an embassy, duly authorized to negotiate the terms of peace conformably to Major-General Wellesley's proposition.

WELLESLEY.
G. H. BARLOW.
G. UDNY.

51. The Governor-General in Council to the Honourable the Secret Committee of the Court of Directors.

Progress of the War, and of negotiation.

Fort William, December 28, 1803.

Honourable Sirs,

On the 31st of October, the Governor-General in council had the honour to communicate to your honourable Committee the progress of transactions connected with the operations of the war in which the British Government is engaged with the Rajah of Berar and Dowlut Rao Scindiah, to the latest date of our advices.

The Governor-General in council has now the honour to continue the narrative of the transactions and operations of the war.

After the glorious victory obtained at Assye on the 23d of September, under the command of the honourable Major-General Wellesley, over the forces of the Rajah of Berar and Dowlut Rao Scindiah, the confederates having collected the remains of their broken armies, moved to the westward along the bank of the Taptee, with a view to proceed to the southward by the Caserbary Ghaut, and to prevent General Wellesley proceeding northward against Scindiah's city of Boorhanpoor, and the strong and important fortress of Asseerghur.

This movement induced General Wellesley to remain to the southward with the division of the British army under his immediate command, in order to check the operations of the confederates in that direction. General Wellesley however determined to prosecute his original plan of operations against the fortress of Asseerghur, and accordingly directed Colonel Stevenson, who on the 25th of September had descended the Adjuntee Ghaut in pursuit of the enemy, to continue his march to the northward, and to attack Boorhanpoor and Asseerghur.

As soon as the confederates found that although General Wellesley remained with the division of the army under his immediate command to the southward of the Adjuntee Pass, he had detached a sufficient force for the reduction of Scindiah's important possessions to the northward of that pass, they altered their plan of operations. They separated their armies, the Rajah of Berar proceeded towards Chandore and Scindiah made a movement to the northward, for the purpose of interrupting Colonel Stevenson's operations against Asseerghur. General Wellesley therefore on the 16th of October marched again to the northward, and on the 19th descended the Adjuntee Ghaut. Scindiah halted as soon as he heard of General Wellesley's movement to the northward, and afterwards moved in an easterly direction towards Berar by Mulkapoor, and through the valley formed by the Taptee and Poorna rivers.

In the meanwhile General Wellesley received authentic accounts that the Rajah of Berar had passed through the hills which form the boundaries of Candeish, and had moved towards the river Godavery. General Wellesley therefore ascended the Adjuntee Ghaut on the 25th of October, and continued his march to the southward on the 26th, and passed Aurungabad on the 29th of that month.

Colonel Stevenson with the subsidiary force, serving with the Soubadar of the Deccan, marched to Boorhanpore, a city belonging to Scindiah, and the capital of the district of Candeish. That city was evacuated on Colonel Stevenson's approach, and was occupied by the British troops on the 15th of October. On the 17th Colonel Stevenson advanced to Asseerghur, and on the 18th attacked and gained possession of the Pettah. On the 19th preparations were made for the siege of the fortress of Asseerghur belonging to Scindiah, the key of the Deccan. A flag of truce with a summons to surrender the fort had been previously sent to the officer in command, who returned an equivocal reply. The operations against the fort were therefore continued, and on the 20th the batteries were opened; in the course of an hour a signal was made from the fort indicating the Commandant's acceptance of the terms which Colonel Stevenson had offered to the garrison. Those terms were that the garrison should be permitted to march out with their private property, and that their arrears should be discharged to the amount of 20,000 rupees. On these terms the Fort of Asseerghur was surrendered to the British arms on the 21st of October. The number of killed and wounded of the troops under the command of Colonel Stevenson during the operations against Asseerghur was inconsiderable.

Previously to the occupation of Boorhanpore nine officers and four serjeants, subjects of France and other European states surrendered themselves to Colonel Stevenson, under the proclamation of the Governor-General in council of the 29th of August.

Subsequently to the capture of Asseerghur Colonel Stevenson proceeded with the subsidiary force, and the contingent of his Highness the Soubadar of the Deccan to the eastward in pursuit of Dowlut Rao Scindiah, and Colonel Stevenson was directed by the Honourable Major-General Wellesley to prosecute his march as far as the fortress of Gavilghur the principal fortress in the possession of the Rajah of Berar, and to lay siege to that place.

In the despatch of the 31st of October, the Governor-General in council informed your honourable Committee that on the 6th of October, the Honourable Major-General Wellesley received a letter from the enemy's camp, requesting that Major-General Wellesley would despatch a British officer, together with an officer of the Soubadar of the Deccan to the enemy's camp, for the purpose of negotiating the terms of peace between the allies and the confederated Mahratta chieftains; the motives which had induced Major-General Wellesley to refuse compliance with that request, were also stated to your honourable Committee on the 31st of October. The Governor-General in council at the same time expressed his expectation of the early receipt of intelligence of the disposition of the confederate chieftains to despatch to the British camp an embassy duly authorized to negotiate the terms of peace.

Subsequently to the despatch of Major-General Wellesley's reply to the letter from the camp of the enemy, Major-General Wellesley received various letters and messages on the subject of a pacification through different channels. All these communications however proceeded from persons unauthorized by official situation under the government of Dowlut Rao Scindiah to open negotiations on the part of that chieftain. In the first week of the month of November, a person of considerable rank named Jeswunt Rao Goorparah and another person of inferior rank named Naroo Punt Nana arrived from Dowlut Rao Scindiah's camp, in the camp of Major-General Wellesley, declaring themselves to be authorized by Scindiah to negotiate the terms of peace.

At the first conference which Major-General Wellesley held with Jeswunt Rao Goorparah and Naroo Punt Nana on the 10th of November, those persons could not produce powers from

Scindiah to prosecute the negotiation. Major-General Wellesley therefore referred Jeswunt Rao Goorparah and Naroo Punt Nana to Scindiah for full powers, in the meanwhile permitting those persons to remain in the British camp.

Subsequently to the date of Major-General Wellesley's conference with those persons, Major-General Wellesley received a letter from Dowlut Rao Scindiah by which it appeared that Scindiah intended to appoint a person named Mahomed Meer Khaun to negotiate the peace, and that Scindiah disavowed Jeswunt Rao Goorparah and Naroo Punt Nana. On the receipt of that letter Major-General Wellesley sent for Jeswunt Rao Goorparah and his colleague, and held a conference with them on the 20th of November. The result of this conference confirmed Major-General Wellesley in the opinion which he had previously entertained, that notwithstanding the letter of Scindiah disavowing Jeswunt Rao Goorparah and Naroo Punt Nana, those persons had actually been sent to the British camp, by the authority of Scindiah. Major-General Wellesley deemed it to be probable that full powers would be transmitted to Jeswunt Rao Goorparah as soon as Scindiah should have been apprized of the amicable reception of that agent in Major-General Wellesley's camp.

Major-General Wellesley therefore considered it to be advisable to state to that agent, and to his colleague, the dangers to which they were exposed by the defect of the necessary credentials, and the moderation and favour which had been manifested towards them by permitting them to remain with impunity in the British camp, rather than to dismiss them with disgrace.

They accordingly retired from the conference of the 20th of November highly satisfied with the treatment which they had received from Major-General Wellesley, and greatly disgusted with the evasive and equivocal conduct of their employer. On the same day, in the course of two hours, Naroo Punt Nana returned to Major-General Wellesley with a letter from Dowlut Rao Scindiah, which was written by that chieftain in consequence of the reference made to him after the conference of the 10th of November, conveying powers to Jeswunt Rao Goorparah and Naroo Punt Nana, to negotiate with Major-General Wellesley.

The Governor-General in council will hereafter communicate to your honourable Committee the detail of the intrigues which appear to have prevailed in the camp of Dowlut Rao Scindiah, with a view to direct the negotiations for peace through various channels. These intrigues suggested doubts of the authenticity of the mission of Jeswunt Rao Goorparah and Naroo Punt Nana.

It is manifest that various persons at the Durbar of Dowlut Rao Scindiah have respectively endeavoured to become the channel of negotiation; and Major-General Wellesley is of opinion that Jeswunt Rao Goorparah has succeeded by exaggerated reports of the solicitude of Major-General Wellesley for the conclusion of peace, and by encouraging an expectation that Major-General Wellesley would be induced to despatch a British officer for that purpose to the camp of Dowlut Rao Scindiah.

The course of the negotiations for peace, and the general plan of pacification in Hindostan and the Deccan, will form the subject of a separate despatch to your honourable Committee by an early opportunity, when the further progress of the conferences and negotiations now pending shall have enabled the Governor-General in council to submit to your consideration a full view of his proceedings in the conduct of those important affairs. At present, it appears to be sufficient to inform your honourable Committee that, at the conference held with Jeswunt Rao Goorparah and Naroo Punt Nana, on the 20th November, after the verification of their general powers from Scindiah, it appeared that those powers were still defective in the essential point of enabling the ambassadors to conclude any of the several territorial compensations to the Company and the allies, which must form the basis of the peace with Scindiah. Major-General Wellesley, therefore, with great judgment, referred the ambassadors again to their chief for distinct powers to negotiate those compensations. At this conference, Scindiah's ambassadors earnestly solicited Major-General Wellesley's consent to a suspension of hostilities with Scindiah and the Rajah of Berar, which that officer granted to Scindiah exclusively.

Your honourable Committee will observe, that by the terms of the armistice, the Rajah of Berar was expressly excluded from the benefit of it; it being obviously prudent not to allow either of the confederates to treat for the other, and the Rajah of Berar not having yet despatched any ambassador to the British camp, or manifested any inclination to conclude peace.

The Governor-General in council entirely approved the conduct of Major-General Wellesley in refusing the proposed armistice to the Rajah of Berar, and in granting it to Scindiah.

These transactions justified an expectation of the dissolution of the confederacy between Dowlut Rao Scindiah and the Rajah of Berar, and of the conclusion of a separate peace with the former of those chieftains. A despatch, however, was received on the 23rd December, from the Hon. Major-General Wellesley, under date the 30th Nov., communicating the intelligence that, on the 29th of November, an action had taken place between the combined armies of the confederated chieftains and those of Major-General Wellesley and Colonel Stevenson, which had terminated in the total defeat of the enemy, with the loss of all their artillery, amounting to thirty-eight pieces of ordnance, with ammunition, baggage, &c. with the slaughter of great numbers of their troops.

The annexed copy of Major-General Wellesley's despatch of the 30th November, contains the detail of this signal victory, and of the insidious artifices by which Dowlut Rao Scindiah had evaded the first conditions of the armistice, and had united the remnant of his forces with those of the Rajah of Berar in a position close to Major-General Wellesley's army; in consequence of which act of treachery, General Wellesley had given notice to Scindiah's ambassadors, previously to the day of the action, that the armistice was inadmissible, and that the British army would act against both of the confederates without delay.

The Governor-General in council is happy to find that this decisive success has been obtained with inconsiderable loss on our side.

The Governor-General in council confidently trusts that the ultimate objects of the war will be more speedily and completely obtained, in consequence of this signal defeat of the combined armies of the confederates, than could have been expected even by the conclusion of a separate treaty of peace with Dowlut Rao Scindiah.

In the despatch of the 31st October, the Governor-General in council communicated to your honourable Committee the intelligence of the occupation of the seaport of Baroach, and of its dependent territory, by the British troops under the command of Lieutenant-Colonel Woodington, on the 29th of August. After the capture of that place, Lieutenant-Colonel Woodington proceeded to reduce the district of Champaneer, which was the only territory remaining to Scindiah in Guzzerat; and subsequently attacked the fort of Powanghur, a strongly-fortified hill, with the town of Champaneer attached, situated about twenty-five miles east of Brodera, on the western confines of the province of

Malwa. The town of Champaneer was attacked and carried by assault, with little loss on the part of the British troops; and the fort was summoned to surrender. The Killedar having refused to comply with the summons, preparations were immediately made for the attack of the fort, which was to have been stormed on the 17th of September, when the fort capitulated, and was immediately occupied by the British troops. This success was followed by the reduction of the district of Godra, a territory belonging to Scindiah, in the province of Malwa, and contiguous to the district of Champaneer. Colonel Murray, who commands the British forces stationed in Guzzerat, has since been employed in settling the revenues of the district of Godra.

The capture of Boorhanpoor and Asseer-ghur was followed by the subjection of Scindiah's territory in Candeish, of which Boorhanpore is the capital; and that territory has for the present been delivered into the hands of the officers of his Highness the Soubahdar of the Deccan.

These successes have completed the conquest of the whole of Dowlut Rao Scindiah's territorial possessions situated in Guzzerat and south of the Nerbudda.

The Governor-General in council has now the honour to communicate to your honourable Committee the progress of the military operations and political arrangements in Hindostan, under the direction of his Excellency the Commander-in-Chief, subsequently to the reduction of Agra on the 17th of October, of which event information was transmitted to your honourable Committee in the despatch of the Governor-General in council of the 31st of October.

The British army marched from Agra on the 27th of October in pursuit of a force of the enemy, composed of fifteen of Monsieur Perron's regular battalions (which had been detached by Scindiah from the Deccan, in the early part of the campaign, under the command of Monsieur Duderneg), and of two battalions which had effected their escape from Delhi after the battle of the 11th of September. During the siege of Agra, this force occupied a position about thirty miles in the rear of the British army, but made no attempt to interrupt the siege of that important fortress. It appears that these battalions of the enemy were destined to proceed towards Delhi for the purpose of attempting the recovery of that important post; and the existence of so considerable a force of the enemy in Hindostan alarmed those native chieftains who were disposed to unite with the

British government, and encouraged all those who might be adverse to our interests. The destruction of this force, therefore, became an object of the utmost importance.

On the 31st of October, the British army made a march of twenty miles, and arrived and encamped at a short distance from the ground which the enemy had quitted the same morning. Possessed of this intelligence, the Commander-in-Chief determined to make an effort to overtake the enemy with all the cavalry of the army, intending to delay the enemy by a light engagement until the British infantry should be able to effect a junction with the cavalry in advance, and if any confusion should be occasioned by this attack, to seize the enemy's guns and baggage. With this view, the Commander-in-Chief, with the whole of the cavalry, marched at twelve o'clock, on the night of the 31st of October, and after a march of twenty-five miles, came up with the enemy at day-break, on the morning of the 1st of November, notwithstanding the difficulties which are opposed by the climate of India to the rapid movements of European troops. The distance marched by the army under General Lake, in the mornings of the 30th and 31st of October, exceeded forty miles, making a total distance marched by the army in forty-eight hours upwards of sixty-five miles. Previously to the march of the British cavalry, orders were given for the infantry to march at three o'clock in the morning.

On the 1st of November, in the morning, when General Lake with the British cavalry overtook the enemy, the enemy appearing to be on his retreat, and in great confusion, the Commander-in-Chief was induced to try the effect of an attack with the cavalry alone, without awaiting the arrival of the infantry. The cavalry succeeded in breaking the enemy's line, and in taking possession of some of the enemy's guns; but the fire of the enemy's numerous and well-served artillery rendered it necessary to withdraw the cavalry out of the reach of the guns until the British infantry could approach. The British cavalry accordingly retired in perfect order, retaining possession of part of the enemy's artillery.

On the arrival of the infantry, a general attack was made on the enemy, who, after a long and vigorous resistance, were completely defeated, with the loss of all their bazars, camp equipage and baggage, a considerable number of elephants, camels and bullocks, seventy-two pieces of cannon, five thousand stand of arms thrown down on the field of battle, forty-four stands of colours, sixty-four tumbrils, completely laden with ammunition, together with three tumbrils of money, fifty-seven carts laden with matchlocks, muskets, and stores. Two thousand prisoners were taken and numbers slain.

The resistance opposed by the enemy on this memorable occasion was more determined than any which the army under General Lake had experienced since the commencement of the campaign.

The victory must principally be attributed to the admirable skill, judgment, heroic courage, and matchless activity of the Commander-in-Chief, whose magnanimous example, together with the recollection of his achievements at Coel, Alligurh, Delhi, and Agra, inspired general confidence and emulation.

In the morning, General Lake led the charge of the cavalry, and in the afternoon conducted in person, at the head of his Majesty's 76th regiment, all the different attacks of the enemy's line.

The Commander-in-Chief displayed not only the most resolute fortitude and ardent valour, but the utmost degree of professional ability and knowledge, availing himself with admirable promptitude of every advantage presented by the enemy, and frustrating every effort of the enemy's obstinacy and boldness.

The Governor-General in council desires to offer to your honourable Committee his congratulations on this most splendid and important victory, which has completed the subversion of Scindiah's hostile power and formidable resources in Hindostan.

Your honourable Committee will contemplate, with sentiments of the highest admiration, the unexampled rapidity and success of the British arms in every part of India since the commencement of hostilities.

From the 8th of August, the day on which hostilities commenced, to the 29th of November, the date of the battle of Argaum in the Deccan, the British army has conquered all the possessions of Scindiah in Guzerat, the city of Boorhaunpoor in Candeish, together with all the territorial possessions of that chieftain situated to the southward of the Nerbuddah, the province of Cuttack in Orissa, the Mahratta dominions between the Jumna and the Ganges, the city of Delhi and the right bank of the Jumna, the city of Agra and the adjoining territory; has reduced by storm the fortified town of Ahmednuggur, the forts of Allyghur, Baroach, and Cuttack, and by capitulation, after having opened the batteries, the forts of Ahmednuggur, of Powanghur and Champaneer, the forts of Asseergurh and Agra, and has defeated the enemy in four general engagements—at Delhi, on the 11th of September; at Assye, on the 23rd of September; at Laswaree, on the 1st of November; and on the plains of Argaum, on the 29th of November.

The defeat of the formidable force of the enemy assembled at Laswaree, has tended in a considerable degree to promote the success of his Excellency the Commander-in-Chief's negotiations with the chiefs and states of Hindostan.

The Commander-in-Chief has accordingly made considerable progress in the various political arrangements connected with the exclusion of the Mahratta power from the Company's frontier in Hindostan.

The Commissioners appointed for the affairs of Cuttack have proceeded successfully in the settlement of that province, and have already realized a proportion of its revenues.

The progress of our military operations and political arrangements, down to the date of this despatch, connected with the war in which the British government is engaged, has been uniformly prosperous and successful in every quarter of India, and the speedy termination of hostilities may be expected to place the interests and security of the British empire in India on a basis of improved strength and power.

We have the honour to be, &c.

WELLESLEY.
G. H. BARLOW.
G. UDNY.

52. Lieut.-General Lake to the Marquess Wellesley.

Battle of Delhi.

Head Quarters, Camp opposite Delhi,
half-past Seven P.M. Sept. 11, 1803.
[Received at Fort William, Sept. 23, 1803.]

My Lord,

I have the satisfaction to inform your Lordship, that after a march of eighteen miles this morning, I learnt that the enemy in great force under Mr. Louis, had crossed the Jumna from Delhi, with the intention of attacking us.

When we had encamped, we found our outposts were attacked by a body of the enemy. On reconnoitring to our front, I found

To face Page 395

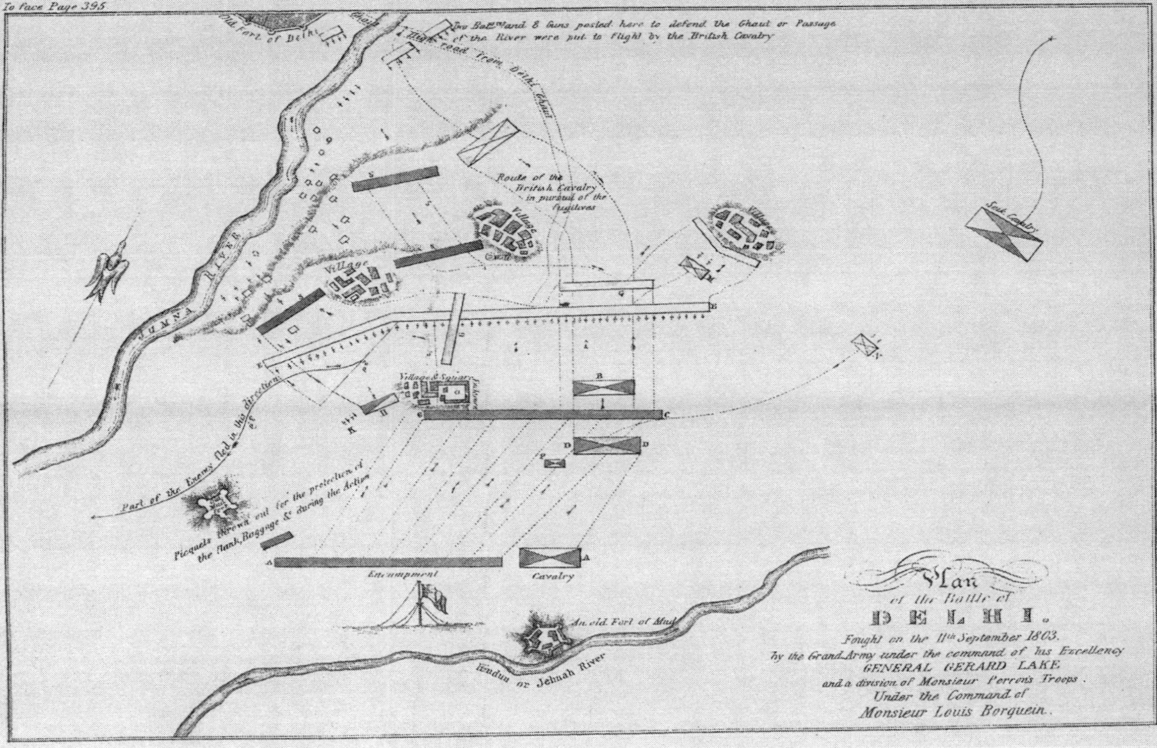

Plan of the Battle of DELHI.

Fought on the 11th September 1803.

by the Grand Army under the command of his Excellency GENERAL GERARD LAKE

and a division of Monsieur Perron's Troops.

Under the Command of

Monsieur Louis Borguein.

that the enemy's whole army were drawn up in order of battle, I immediately ordered out the whole line, and advanced to attack them in front.

The enemy opposed to us a tremendous fire from a numerous artillery, which was uncommonly well served, and caused us considerable loss in officers and men, but I have the satisfaction to add, that our advance under a most heavy cannonade, and actual charge of the enemy, at about one hundred paces distant, caused a most precipitate retreat, and left in our possession the whole of their artillery.

The cavalry pursued the fugitives to the Jumna, making great havock, and numbers were drowned in attempting to cross.

In short, I have only to express my entire approbation of the gallantry of the troops under my command during the whole of this most brilliant action, and shall have the honour to detail it more particularly to-morrow, which the lateness of the hour prevents me doing at present.

The whole army was under arms from three this morning till this moment.

I have the honour to be, my Lord,
Your Lordship's
Most faithful humble servant,
G. LAKE.

53. Lieut.-General Lake to the Marquess Wellesley.

Battle of Delhi. Reasons for advance thither.

My Lord, September 12th, 1803.

It is with the most heartfelt satisfaction that I now congratulate you upon the attainment of your wishes. The action of yesterday was so decisive and proved our superiority so completely, that I have not a doubt all the chieftains will come in to our standard. Louis having plundered Delhi with the few troops he had left, and taken himself and all his vagabonds off this morning, will I trust, destroy all confidence in Frenchmen. Where he is gone I know not, but I rather believe towards Agra. I imagine that the few men he has with him will go to their own homes. I really do think the business was one of the most gallant actions possible; such a fire of cannon has seldom been seen if ever, against which our men marched up within one hundred yards without taking a firelock from off their shoulders, when they gave one volley, charged instantly and drove the enemy; then they opened ranks and let the cavalry through, who did their duty in the most gallant and judicious manner possible; indeed their conduct was remarkable throughout the day. From having detached so large a body of troops to the ceded provinces, we were yesterday most considerably outnumbered, but his Majesty's 76th regiment did set such an example that could not fail of inspiring every creature with zeal, energy, and spirit. I do not think there could have been a more glorious day, but as I may be thought partial, I will say no more, but leave it to others to relate the fact, exaggerate I think they cannot.

Now my dear Lord, I hope you will agree with me that the destruction of Perron's troops and power was the first object. Added to which, allow me to state my reasons for coming on to Delhi, which were as follow—I had certain information that Louis was making all the use possible of the King's name, and of his royal prerogative, and I thought it most probable that many persons with the concealed design of taking advantage of the present times, but absolutely in obedience to the King's mandate, might either join Louis or spread over the Company's provinces for the sake of plunder. Another reason for coming to Delhi, was considering the character of Mr. Louis more active, and perhaps more zealous than Mr. Perron, and considering also his personal connection with the Seiks, I was decidedly of opinion, that the crushing of these political intrigues, and the subversion of his French connection were primary objects, and that nothing would be so likely to accomplish the above objects as the sudden appearance of the army at the capital of Delhi, and I am happy to say, that my conjectures were not ill-founded, as is clearly proved by the flight of Mr. Louis, the departure of the Seiks, and the strong desire of his Majesty for our troops to march into Delhi that he may be placed under our protection. The army will pass the moment the boats come from the other side. Another consideration was, that if the enemy were active, vigorous, and enterprising, our provinces are much at his mercy; the movement of my army to Agra might save the lower part of the Doab, but the upper part, together with Rohilcund, would have been exposed to the depredations of Louis's detachment, and as he possessed Saharunpore, and probably expected co-operation from the Rohillas, he would probably have overrun Rohilcund with greater facility than Perron could carry his depredations to any considerable extent.

It so happens that from all I can learn, and by a letter just received from Mr. Leycester, I do not believe at this moment any commotion is likely to take place, particularly after the event of yesterday. I shall most undoubtedly see the King of Delhi this night or to-morrow morning, when I understand he intends going through the form of delivering the country over to the British Government. Your Lordship may depend upon my attending to your instructions respecting his Majesty. Mr. Mercer is not yet arrived, but I imagine soon will, as by a letter this day received from him, his negotiation seems in a most forward state.

I have this moment learnt, that the remaining part of Louis's army have dispersed in different directions, and that the country people are so enraged at their plundering them, that they have retaliated by plundering them since they have separated, and killed a great many of them.

I cannot, my dear Lord, avoid saying in the most confidential way that, in the event of a foreign foe coming into this country, without a *very great addition of force in Europeans*, the consequences will be fatal, as there ought always to be one European battalion to four native ones, this at least I think necessary. I have seen a great deal of these people lately, and am quite convinced without King's troops very little is to be expected, in short the infantry of this army as well as cavalry should be new modelled, as I will convince your Lordship when I am so fortunate as to conduct you to Delhi, which I sincerely hope will be very shortly. I am not clear which way I shall move next, but rather think it may be toward Agra, which place must fall upon our approach. I apprehend the Seiks if assured of our not interfering with their government, will enter into a treaty of amity with us, and would ensure the capture of the fort called Hansi, late George Thomas's, provided we would promise to destroy it, which in my opinion would be a good thing; I believe at present there are a great many of Perron's guns in it, which might be got by this means, and which I shall endeavour to do without trouble or difficulty.

I trust all your endeavours will be crowned with success, and remain,

My dear Lord,
Your faithful and attached servant,
G. LAKE.

54. Lieut.-General Lake to the Marquess Wellesley.

Statistics of the Battle of Delhi.

Head Quarters, Camp, near Delhy Ghaut, Sept. 13th, 1803.
[Received at Fort William, Sept. 25th, 1803.]

My Lord,

For your Lordship's information, I have the honour to enclose a list of the killed and wounded, officers and men, of the army under my command, in the action of the 11th instant.

Your Lordship will perceive that our loss has been very great; but when I consider that we moved on against an immense artillery, of nearly one hundred pieces of cannon, and many of a very large calibre, under as heavy a fire as I have ever been witness to; and that this fire was directed against a line, consisting, on the most correct calculation, of not more than four thousand five hundred men, including cavalry, artillery and infantry; and that we were opposed by upwards of four times that number; it is no longer a matter of surprize.

It is necessary to remark, that we had only one brigade of cavalry, consisting of the 27th light dragoons, and the 2d and 3d regiments of native cavalry; the other brigades being detached for the protection of our own provinces.

The more I reflect on the glorious affair of the 11th, the more forcibly I feel the bravery and intrepidity displayed by every individual composing my army. I cannot find words to express my feelings on this occasion, nor can I sufficiently lament the loss of many brave fellows who have fallen.

I have the honour to be, my Lord,
Your Lordship's most faithful humble servant,
G. LAKE.

55. Lieut.-General Lake to the Marquess Wellesley.

Military requirements in the conquest territory.

Delhi, Sept. 17th, 1803.

My Lord,

Yesterday was passed according to the usual forms in waiting upon the King, making and receiving presents from his Majesty, when every thing was properly conducted on both sides.

The crossing our troops is a most tedious operation from the scarcity of boats, and will prevent my moving towards Agra before the 22d instant, on which day, or the day after, I shall hope to begin my march, and when that fort is taken I shall have little to do but to settle the country, at present of course we must adjust some little disorders in different parts; however, they are so trifling that they are easily checked.

The want of rain must make the collections very uncertain, and if we have not some, the consequences will be fatal, as a famine is to be apprehended.

I have engaged some irregular force this day under some Sirdars lately in the service of Perron; two of them are of high character in that line, and I believe to be depended upon, at least as much if not more than any we can get. The state of the case my dear Lord is, the immense tract of territory we have gained requires a great, I may say, a very great force to keep, and at this time it must be supposed there are numbers of people that will avail themselves of the unsettled state of the country to sow dissensions, and endeavour either to throw the country into confusion, or take possession of land and property of others, besides various reasons they may have for committing depredations, such as a dislike to any change of government, or old jealousies and animosities towards their neighbours. All these considerations render a very large force necessary, and as from my little army it is impossible for me to detach any more into the interior of the now acquired part of the Doab, it becomes necessary to arrange matters for the protection and tranquillity of it, and I see at present no substitute for supplying the place of our troops, but having that description of people which are most likely to keep the people in order. You may depend upon it I will not have one man more than is necessary.

The rapidity of our march and loss in action, will with wounded and sick have weakened my army very considerably, many of which cannot be replaced, and those men that are to be got in this country, Sepoys I mean, will require time to be made soldiers. I really think when peace is restored, and we have nothing to think of but internal arrangements that our army is not by any means equal to the number of posts that ought to be occupied to prevent depredations, which we are always liable to and which must be guarded against.

After this is done, there ought always to be a disposable force, and I would have that respectable and not very small; if your Lordship comes to see your new territories, which I sincerely hope you will, I am convinced you will see the necessity of always keeping a very large army upon this frontier. I entreat your Lordship if possible, to come up this season if all is quiet enough to allow you to leave Calcutta. I perceive by the letter from the Court of Directors, that they still incline to reduce two regiments of native cavalry, when in my opinion they ought to raise several more, they also talk of one regiment of European cavalry for Bengal, in my opinion, two *at the least* is necessary, and my firm opinion is, that five regiments of English infantry is necessary in the Bengal army, and those kept complete; I have seen the good effects of the King's troops, and am most thoroughly convinced that without a large proportion of them in this army, our possessions in this country cannot be secure.

When I have a little leisure, I will if your Lordship chooses it, write an official letter upon the subject, though perhaps it may be better to delay it till I can exactly ascertain the number of points we ought to have posts at.

I think we can have but little dependance in the Sebundy corps; here and there from the exertion of a particular man commanding them they will exert themselves, but in general I fear they imagine themselves stationary, get into habits of their own, and get connected too much with the inhabitants; but although I have said thus much, I should be sorry if any alteration took place respecting these corps till I can have some private conversation with your Lordship. I think it is possible the new plan of your Lordship in forming provincial battalions may prove much more useful from being under martial law, but the same objection still exists in the men becoming too intimately connected with the natives of that country in which they are raised.

I suspect nothing but regular battalions will answer the purpose of keeping the country in order, and they, as I told you in a former letter, require much alteration in their system which is radically bad.

I imagine Agra will cause us but little trouble, and if I dared to divide my army, it would not be necessary for me to go there, but I have so many reasons which I shall not commit to paper, but keep them for your private ear, for being with them that I am determined not to separate them.

The army, I am happy to say, are in high spirits, and I flatter myself ready to do anything I ask of them. Their good humour, patience, and readiness to obey any orders of mine is delightful

To face Page 401

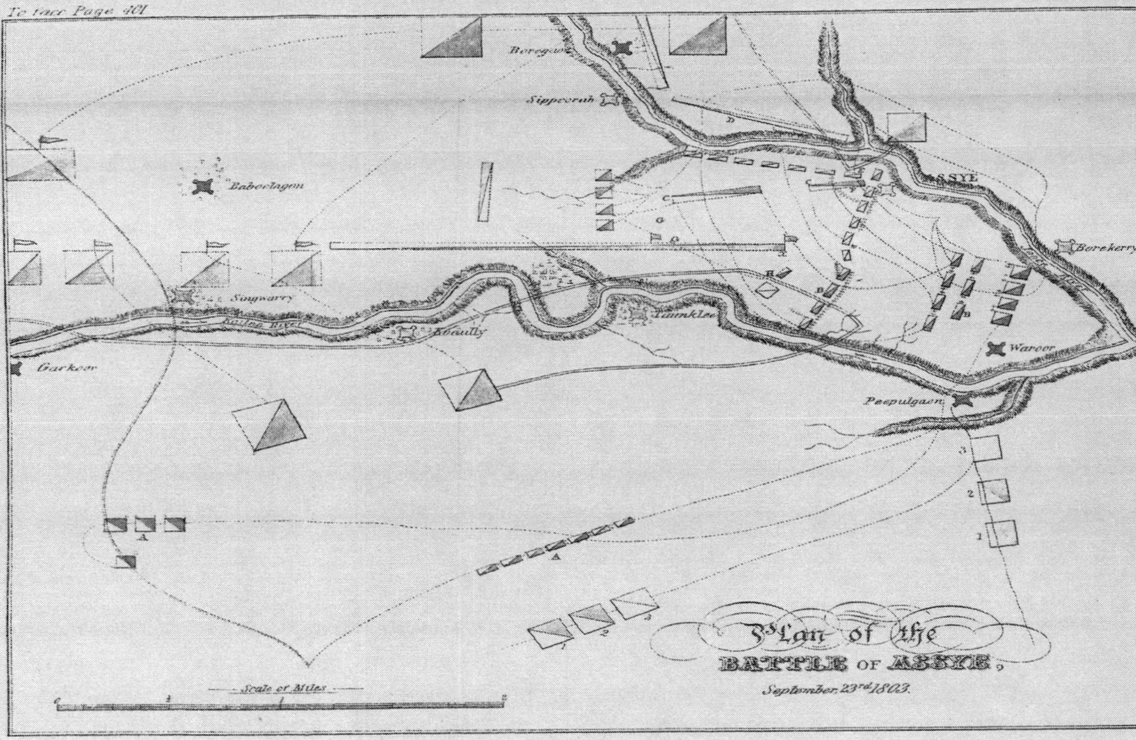

and most satisfactory, and gives me the greatest confidence in them.

I hear Monson is going on well, he is a most excellent man and incomparable officer. I cannot express how much I admire his conduct at Alighur.

If we could get hold of those brigands from the Deccan, not a Frenchman would be left in the country.

Believe me, my dear Lord,
With real attachment most truly yours,
G. LAKE.

I forgot to say, that I looked upon the strong fort at Hansi to be ours, as there are very few persons in it, and the person who commands has sent to say, he will give it up to me if I can send troops, which will be difficult, he therefore will keep it, as the people he has in it are entirely his.

56. The Hon. Major-General Wellesley to the Marquess Wellesley.

Battle of Assye.

Camp at Assye, Sept. 24, 1803.
[Received Oct. 30, 1803.]

My Lord,

I was joined by Major Hill with the last of the convoys expected from the river Kistna on the 18th, and on the 20th was enabled to move forward towards the enemy, who had been joined in the course of the last seven or eight days by the infantry under Colonel Pohlman, by that belonging to Begum Sumroo, and by another brigade of infantry, the name of whose commander I have not ascertained. The enemy's army was collected about Bokerdun, and between that place and Jaffierabad.

I was near Colonel Stevenson's corps on the 21st, and had a conference with that officer, in which we concerted a plan to attack the enemy's army with the divisions under our command on the 24th in the morning, and we marched on the 22nd, Colonel Stevenson by the western route, and I by the eastern route round the hills between Budnapoor and Jalna.

On the 23rd I arrived at Naulniah, and there received a report that Scindiah and the Rajah of Berar had moved off in the morning with their cavalry, and that the infantry were about to follow, but were still in camp at the distance of about six miles from the ground on which I had intended to encamp.

It was obvious that the attack was no longer to be delayed; and having provided for the security of my baggage and stores at Naulniah, I marched on to attack the enemy.

I found the whole combined army of Scindiah and the Rajah of Berar encamped on the bank of the Kaitna river, nearly on the ground which I had been informed that they occupied. Their right, which consisted entirely of cavalry, was about Bokerdun, and extended to their corps of infantry, which were encamped in the neighbourhood of Assye. Although I came first in front of their right, I determined to attack their left; as the defeat of their corps of infantry was most likely to be effectual; accordingly I marched round to their left flank, covering the march of the column of infantry by the British cavalry in the rear, and by the Mahratta and Mysore cavalry on the right flank.

We passed the river Kaitna at a ford beyond the enemy's left flank, and I formed the infantry immediately in two lines, with the British cavalry as a reserve in a third, in an open space between that river and a nullah running parallel to it. The Mahratta and Mysore cavalry occupied the ground beyond the Kaitna on our left flank, and kept in check a large body of the enemy's cavalry which had followed our march from the right of their own position.

The enemy had altered the position of their infantry previous to our attack; it was no longer, as at first, along the Kaitna; but extended from that river across to the village of Assye upon the nullah, which was upon our right. We attacked them immediately, and the troops advanced under a very hot fire from cannon, the execution of which was terrible. The picquets of the infantry, and the 74th regiment, which were on the right of the first and second lines, suffered particularly from the fire of the guns on the left of the enemy's position near Assye. The enemy's cavalry also made an attempt to charge the 74th regiment at the moment when they were most exposed to this fire, but they were cut up by the British cavalry, which moved on at that moment. At length the enemy's line gave way in all directions, and the British cavalry cut in among their broken infantry; but some of their corps went off in good order, and a fire was kept up on our troops from many of the guns from which the enemy had been first driven, by individuals who had been passed by the line under the supposition that they were dead.

Lieut.-Colonel Maxwell, with the British cavalry, charged one large body of infantry, which had retired, and was formed again, in which operation he was killed; and some time elapsed before we could put an end to the straggling fire, which was kept up by individuals from the guns from which the enemy were driven. The enemy's cavalry also, which had been hovering round us throughout the action, was still near us. At length, when the last formed body of infantry gave way, the whole went off, and left in our hands ninety pieces of cannon.

This victory, which was certainly complete, has, however, cost us dear. Your Excellency will perceive by the inclosed return, that our loss in officers and men has been very great; and in that of Lieut.-Colonel Maxwell and other officers, whose names are therein included, greatly to be regretted.

I cannot write in too strong terms of the conduct of the troops; they advanced in the best order, and with the greatest steadiness, under a most destructive fire, against a body of infantry far superior in numbers, who appeared determined to contend with them to the last, and who were driven from their guns only by the bayonet; and notwithstanding the numbers of the enemy's cavalry, and the repeated demonstrations they made of an intention to charge, they were kept at a distance by our infantry.

I am particularly indebted to Lieut.-Colonel Harness, and Lieut.-Colonel Wallace, for the manner in which they conducted their brigades; and to all the officers of the staff for the assistance I received from them. The officers commanding brigades, nearly all those of the staff, and the mounted officers of the infantry had their horses shot under them.

I have also to draw your Excellency's notice to the conduct of the cavalry commanded by Lieut.-Colonel Maxwell, particularly that of the 19th dragoons.

The enemy are gone off towards the Adjuntee Ghaut, and I propose to follow them as soon as I can place my captured guns and the wounded in security.

I have the honour to be, my Lord,
with the greatest respect,
your Excellency's most obedient,
and faithful humble servant,
ARTHUR WELLESLEY.

Colonel Stevenson arrived this morning at Bokerdun, and I imagine that he will be here this evening.

57. Lieut.-General Lake to the Marquess Wellesley.

Battle of Lasswary.

Head Quarters, Camp near Lasswary, Nov. 2, 1803.
[Received Nov. 15, 1803.]

My Lord,

In my despatch of yesterday's date, I did myself the honour to state for your Lordship's information, some particulars of the march of the army from Agra to the camp it now occupies, together with the general result of the action which took place yesterday. I now have the honour to send your Excellency a more detailed account of that affair.

After a forced march of twenty-five miles, which was performed by the cavalry in a little more than six hours, I came up with the enemy, who appeared to be upon their retreat, and in such confusion, that I was tempted to try the effect of an attack upon him with the cavalry alone. By cutting the embankment of a large reservoir of water, the enemy had rendered the road very difficult to pass, which caused a considerable delay in the advance of the cavalry; of this the enemy had availed himself to take an advantageous post, having his right upon a rivulet, which we had to cross, and his left upon the village of Lasswary; the whole of his front was amply provided with artillery. I was prevented from discovering this change in the situation of the enemy by the quantity of dust which, when once clear of the water, totally obscured him from our sight; I therefore proceeded in the execution of my design, by which I hoped to prevent his retreat into the hills, and secure his guns; directing the advanced guard and first brigade commanded by Colonel Vandeleur, upon the point where I had observed the enemy in motion, but which proved to be the left of his new position; the remainder of the cavalry I ordered to attack in succession, as soon as they could form after passing the rivulet.

The charge of the advanced guard under Major Griffiths, and that of the first brigade led by Colonel Vandeleur, was made with much gallantry; the enemy's line was forced, and the cavalry penetrated into the village; they still, however, continued to be exposed to a most galling fire of cannon and musketry, which, as it was impossible under such circumstances to form the squadrons for a fresh attack, determined me to withdraw them. The guns which had fallen into our hands could not be brought away from the want of bullocks. In this charge Colonel

Vandeleur fell, mortally wounded; in him the service has lost a most valuable officer.

The attacks of the other brigades were conducted with the same spirit, but after taking several of the enemy's guns, being still fired upon without being able to discover the enemy, they retired in good order, retaining possession of a part of the artillery. In the performance of this service, the third brigade, consisting of his Majesty's 29th regiment, and the 4th regiment of native cavalry, under the command of that meritorious officer, Colonel Macan, met my entire approbation.

The infantry having marched at three A.M. arrived upon the banks of the rivulet about eleven o'clock. After so long a march it was absolutely necessary to allow some time for the men to refresh themselves, during which time the enemy sent in to say that if certain terms were allowed them, they were willing to surrender their guns. Anxious to prevent the further effusion of blood, I directed a letter to be written, acquiescing in their proposals, and allowing them an hour to decide; in the mean time the several columns for the attack were formed. The infantry formed in two columns upon the left; the first, composed of the right wing under the command of Major-General Ware, was destined to gain the enemy's right flank, which he had thrown back since the morning, leaving a considerable space between it and the rivulet, and to assault the village of Lasswary; the second, composed of the left wing, under Major-General St. John, was to support the first column. The third brigade of cavalry under Colonel Macan was to support the infantry; the second brigade under Lieut.-Colonel Vandeleur was detached to the right, to be ready to take advantage of any confusion in the enemy's line, and to attack him upon his retreat; the brigade under Colonel Gordon composed the reserve, and was formed between the second and third brigades. As many of the field pieces as could be brought up, with the gallopers attached to the cavalry, formed four different batteries.

At the expiration of the time which I had allowed the enemy to decide, I ordered the infantry to advance: as soon as they became exposed to the enemy's guns, the four batteries commenced their fire, and continued to advance, though opposed by a great superiority, both in number and weight of metal.

When the 76th regiment, which headed the attack, had arrived at the point from which I intended to make the charge, they were so much exposed to the enemy's fire, and losing men so fast, that I judged it preferable to proceed to the attack with that regiment, and as many of the native infantry as had closed to the front, to losing time in waiting until the remainder of the column should be able to form, the march of which had been retarded by impediments in the advance.

As soon as this handful of heroes were arrived within reach of the enemy's canister shot, a most tremendous fire was opened upon them. The loss they sustained was very severe, and sufficient alone to prevent a regular advance; at this moment the enemy's cavalry attempted to charge, but were repulsed by the fire of this gallant body; they, however, rallied at a short distance, and assumed so menacing a posture, that I thought it advisable to order them to be attacked by the cavalry; this service fell to the share of his Majesty's 29th regiment, commanded by Captain Wade, (Major Griffiths having at that instant been unfortunately killed by a cannon shot,) and was performed with the greatest gallantry, and in a manner which entitles Captain Wade, and every officer and soldier in the regiment to my warmest acknowledgments. The remainder of the first column of infantry arrived just in time to join in the attack of the enemy's reserve, which was formed in the rear of his line, with its left upon the village of Lasswary, and its right thrown back.

About this time Major-General Ware fell dead, his head being carried off by a cannon shot. He was a gallant officer, and one whose loss I deeply lament. On his death the command of this column devolved upon Colonel Macdonald, who, though wounded, continued to acquit himself in this important command very much to my satisfaction.

The enemy opposed a vigorous resistance to the last, and it was not until he had lost his guns that he abandoned his post. Even then his left wing did not fly, but attempted to retreat in good order; in this, however, they were frustrated by his Majesty's 27th regiment, and the 6th regiment of native cavalry, under the command of Lieut.-Colonel Vandeleur, who broke in upon the column, cut several to pieces, and drove the rest in prisoners, with the whole of the baggage.

Severe as the loss has been which we have sustained in the achievement of this complete victory, that of the enemy has been far greater. With the exception of upwards of 2,000, who have been taken prisoners, (of which number I have only detained the principal officers, amounting to forty-eight), I have reason to believe that very few escaped the general slaughter.

It would be a violation of my feelings were I to close my despatch without bearing testimony to the gallant conduct of Major Macleod, and Captain Robertson, of his Majesty's 76th regiment, and of every officer and soldier of that inestimable corps, in the attack of the village of Lasswary. Major Gregory, too, at the head of the second battalion of the 12th regiment of native infantry, in the same service, displayed a conduct highly meritorious.

In the list of those officers who particularly distinguished themselves, I cannot omit the names of Lieut. Wallace, of his Majesty's 27th regiment, who was entrusted with the command of a battery of gallopers, nor that of Lieut. Dixon, of the 6th regiment of native cavalry, who was employed in the same service.

The whole of my staff upon this, as upon every former occasion, are entitled to a large share of praise, and to my warmest gratitude. The zeal which they displayed upon this memorable day is too plainly proved by the enclosed returns of the killed and wounded. I have sustained a great loss by the death of Major William Campbell, the deputy quarter-master-general, and by that of my aid-de-camp, Lieut. Duval, of his Majesty's 19th Light Dragoons, who was a young man of great promise.

Herewith I have the honour to enclose returns of the ordnance and colours which were captured upon this occasion.

I have the honour to be, my Lord,
Your Lordship's most faithful,
and humble servant,
G. LAKE.

PS. In the hurry which I wrote my despatch of yesterday's date, I fear I did not explain to your Lordship, that the enemy's corps which we have defeated, comprised the whole of the fifteen regular battalions which had been sent from the Deccan under the command of Monsieur Duderneg, and two battalions of the same description which had escaped from Delhi. I therefore have the satisfaction of congratulating your Excellency upon the annihilation of the whole of the regular force in Scindiah's service, commanded by French officers.

G. L.

58. The Hon. Major-General Wellesley to the Marquess Wellesley.

Battle of Argaum.

Camp at Parterly, Nov. 30th, 1803.
[Received Dec. 25th, 1803.]

My Lord,

Having found that the Rajah of Berar was moving towards his own territories, that the body of troops he had with him was but small, and decreasing in numbers daily, and not likely to do much mischief to the territories of the Soubah of the Deccan, I descended the Ghauts by Rajoora on the Sindpauna in order to support and cover Colonel Stevenson's operations against Gawilghur in Berar.

Colonel Stevenson had equipped his corps at Asseer-Ghur for the siege of that fort, and had marched to Ballapore, where he was joined on the 24th by the Brinjarries, and other supplies which had been saved from the enemy by Captain Baynes's affair at Amber; and he marched forward on the 26th.

Your Excellency has been informed, that on the 23d I had consented to a suspension of hostilities with the troops of Dowlut Rao Scindiah, in this quarter and Guzerat. The condition on which this agreement depended, viz. that Scindiah should occupy a position twenty coss to the east of Elichpour had not been carried into execution; and Scindiah was encamped at Sersooly, about four miles from the camp of Munnoo Bappoo, which was at this place. The army of the former consisted only of cavalry; that of the latter was cavalry, a great part, if not the whole of Ragojee Bhooslah's regular infantry, and a large proportion of artillery.

In the course of the 28th, the vakeels from Dowlut Rao Scindiah urgently pressed me not to attack these troops; but I informed them repeatedly, that there was no suspension of arms with Ragojee Bhooslah; and none with Scindiah till he should comply with the terms of his agreement: and that I should certainly attack the enemies of the Company wherever I should find them.

Colonel Stevenson's division and mine both marched to this place yesterday; the Colonel having with great prudence and propriety halted on the 28th at Hattee Andorah, to enable me to co-operate in the attack of the enemy. We found on our arrival that the armies of both chiefs had decamped; and I could perceive, from a tower in Parterly, a confused mass, about two

To face Page 409.

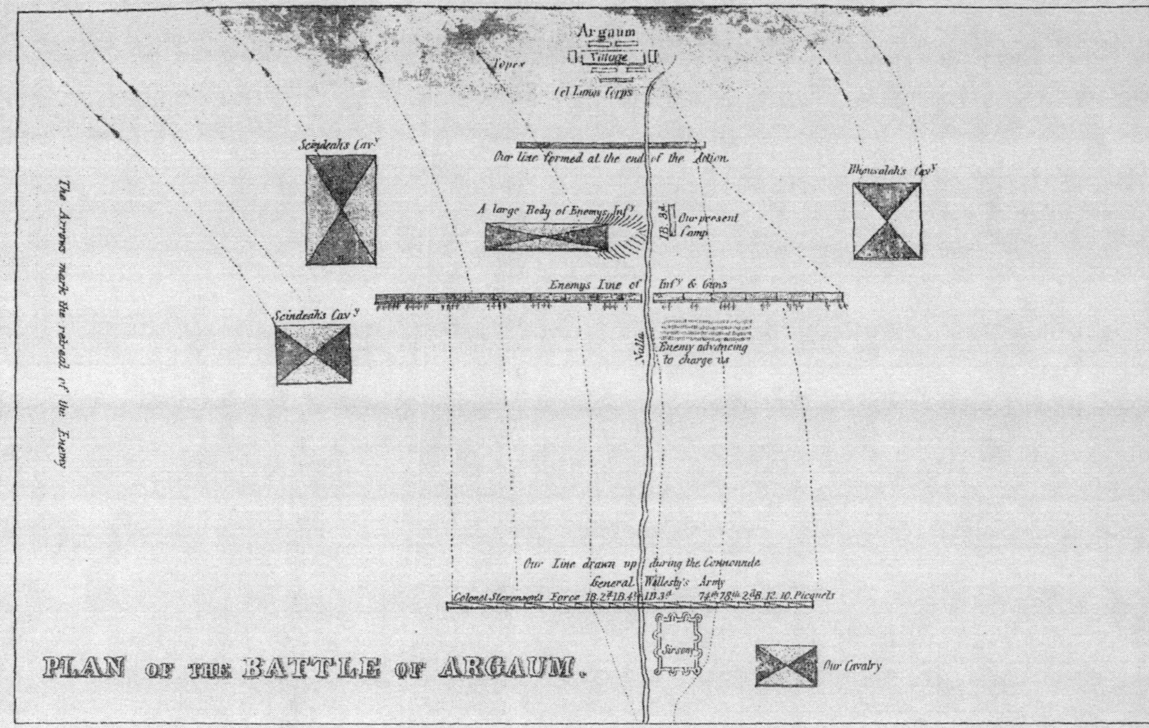

miles beyond Sersooly and Scindiah's old camp, which I concluded to be their armies in march.

The troops had marched a great distance on a very hot day, and therefore I did not think it proper to pursue them, but shortly after our arrival here, bodies of horse appeared in our front, with which the Mysore horse skirmished during a part of the day; and when I went out to push forward the picquets of the infantry, to support the Mysore cavalry, and to take up the ground of our encampment, I could perceive distinctly a long line of infantry, cavalry, and artillery, regularly drawn up on the plains of Argaum, immediately in front of that village, and about six miles from this place, at which I intended to encamp.

Although late in the day, I immediately determined to attack this army. Accordingly I marched on in one column, the British cavalry leading, in a direction nearly parallel to that of the enemy's line; covering the rear and left by the Mogul and Mysore cavalry.

The enemy's infantry and guns were in the left of their centre, with a body of cavalry on their left. Scindiah's army, consisting of one very heavy body of cavalry, was in the right, having upon its right a body of Pindaries and other light troops. Their line extended above five miles, having in their rear the village and extensive gardens and enclosures of Argaum, and in their front a plain, which however was much cut by water-courses, &c. &c.

I formed the army in two lines: the infantry in the first, the cavalry in the second, and supporting the right; and the Mogul and Mysore cavalry the left, nearly parallel to that of the enemy; with the right rather advanced to press upon the enemy's left. Some little time elapsed before the lines could be formed, owing to a part of the infantry of my division which led the column having got into some confusion. When formed, the whole advanced in the greatest order; the 74th and 78th regiments were attacked by a large body (supposed to be *Pathâns*) and all these were destroyed. Scindiah's cavalry charged the 1st battalion 6th regiment, which was on the left of our line, and were repulsed; and the whole line retired in disorder before our troops, leaving in our hands thirty-eight pieces of cannon and all their ammunition.

The British cavalry then pursued them for several miles, and destroyed great numbers, and took many elephants and camels, and much baggage. The Mogul and Mysore cavalry also pursued the fugitives, and did them great mischief. Some of the latter are still following them; and I have sent out this morning all of the Mysore, Mogul, and Mahratta cavalry, in order to secure as many advantages from this victory as can be gained, and complete the enemy's confusion.

For the reasons stated in the commencement of this letter, the action did not begin till late in the day, and, unfortunately, sufficient day-light did not remain to do all that I could have wished; but the cavalry continued their pursuit by moon-light, and all the troops were under arms till a late hour in the night.

I have the honour to enclose a return of our loss in this action. The troops conducted themselves with their usual bravery. The 74th and 78th regiments had a particular opportunity of distinguishing themselves, and have deserved and received my thanks. I am also much indebted to Colonel Stevenson, for the advice and assistance I received from him; to the honourable Lieut.-Colonel St. Leger for the manner in which he led on the British cavalry; and to Lieut.-Colonels Wallace, Adams (who commanded Lieut.-Colonel Harness's brigade, the latter being absent on account of severe indisposition), Haliburton, Macleane, Pogson, and Major Huddlestone, who commanded brigades of cavalry and infantry; to Major Campbell commanding the 94th regiment; to Captain Beauman commanding the artillery with the division under my immediate command; to Captain Burke commanding the artillery with the subsidiary force; and to the officers of the staff with my division, and belonging to the subsidiary force.

I have also to inform your Excellency, that the Mogul cavalry under Salabut Khan, and the Mysore cavalry under Bistnapah Pundit, distinguished themselves. The former took a standard from Scindiah's troops.

The Mahratta cavalry were not engaged, as the person who went to them with orders, missed his road. Amrut Rao was not in the action, as he had encamped some distance in my rear on the 28th, and he could not march the whole distance to Parterly yesterday morning; but he sent for orders as soon as he heard that I intended to attack the enemy.

I propose to march to-morrow towards Gawil-ghur, and I shall lose no time in attacking that place.

I have the honour to be, my Lord,
your Excellency's most obedient
and faithful humble servant,
ARTHUR WELLESLEY.

4. PACIFICATION AND RESULTS OF THE WAR.

59. The Marquess Wellesley to the Honourable Major-General Wellesley.

Occasion and results of the war, and consequent character of the pacification.

Extract.

(Secret and Official.) Fort William, Dec. 11, 1803.

Sir,

14. The just, necessary, and attainable conditions of peace will be clearly ascertained by examining the causes, objects, and result of the war, together with the situation of the enemy at the present time.

15. The immediate cause of the war was the refusal of the confederates to separate and withdraw to their usual stations within their respective territories the armies which they had assembled and united on the frontier of our ally the Soubadar of the Deccan, after having declared that the intention of that junction was to decide, whether there should be peace or war with the British Government and its allies.

16. Under these circumstances the continuance of the confederate army in the position which the chieftains appeared determined to maintain, was a manifest indication of a design to frustrate by hostilities, or by the terror of their arms, the operation of the alliance concluded between the British Government and the Peishwa, and to disturb the tranquillity of the dominions of the Nizam, and ultimately of the Company. The union of the confederate forces and their commanding and menacing position, afforded every advantage to the chieftains in prosecuting the hostile design which they had manifested, and enabled the confederated chieftains to hold the issue of peace and war in their hands, and to arbitrate the fate of the Deccan according to their interests or caprice.

17. At the same time the position and state of Scindiah's forces, under the command of his French officers in Hindostan, and the machinations of M. Perron with the adjoining states and with the subjects of the Company, and of the Vizier, manifested additional proofs of the hostile designs of the confederates, and furnished those chieftains with additional means of prosecuting such designs.

18. The primary object of the war originating in these causes, was to deprive the confederates of the means which they possessed

of prosecuting their unwarrantable designs, and the general plan of military operations, connected with a corresponding system of political arrangement, was calculated to preclude the confederates from reviving the sources of that military and political power, which they had employed to disturb the security of our alliances, dependencies and dominions.

19. The power of Dowlut Rao Scindiah considered with relation to his means of affecting the security of the British empire in India, may be described to have consisted at the commencement of the war in the following branches of military and political resource:

First. The efficient state of Scindiah's military establishment, under the direction of European officers, and particularly the formidable condition of his regular infantry and artillery under the command of those officers.

Secondly. The possession of an extensive and rich territory and of various strong forts, magazines, founderies and arsenals, with considerable supplies of ammunition and military stores, deposited in convenient stations upon our frontier, contiguous to the most vulnerable part of the British dominions in Hindostan.

Thirdly. The establishment of a large and well disciplined body of troops, with a formidable train of artillery, under the command of French officers within that territory in Hindostan.

Fourthly. The actual assignment of that territory in Hindostan to the French officer holding the chief command of those troops.

Fifthly. The possession of the person of his Majesty Shah Aulum, under the immediate power of the forces commanded by French officers in the service of Dowlut Rao Scindiah, and the exercise of the nominal authority of the Moghul through those French officers.

Sixthly. The ascendancy established by the agency of the French officer in command of Scindiah's troops in the north-west of Hindostan over the Rajpoot chieftains of Jynagur and Jodepoor, and other states and chieftains in the northern and western provinces of Hindostan, and over many of the Seik chiefs and others, occupying the territory from the Jumna to the banks of the Indus, and the facility afforded by the advanced posts of M. Perron's army towards the Indus of aiding the invasion of the British dominions through that quarter.

Seventhly. The facility which the possession of the sea-port of Baroach afforded to Scindiah of improving his military establishment, by the accession of French or other European officers, of military supplies and stores, &c. and even of a body of French or other European troops.

Eighthly. The power of disturbing the tranquillity of the possessions of the Guickowar, and of the Company in the province of Guzerat, by means of Scindiah's intermixed territories and fortresses in that province, and by his claims and influence in that quarter.

Ninthly. The power of disturbing the tranquillity of the state of Poonah, and the stability of our alliance with the Peishwa by Scindiah's intermixed territories and fortresses in the vicinity of Poonah, and to the southward of the river Taptee, especially the fortress and territory of Ahmednuggur, and by Scindiah's various claims upon the state of Poonah, and by his influence at that court.

Tenthly. Scindiah's intermixed and bordering fortresses and possessions which enabled him to menace and disturb the dominions of the Soubadar of the Deccan, and to impair the efficiency of the British alliance with that prince, and Scindiah's various claims upon the Soubadar of the Deccan, and consequent influence at Hyderabad.

Eleventhly. The general magnitude, wealth and strength of Scindiah's dominions and army, and the reputation of his military power from which he derived a general influence and ascendancy at Poonah and over all the Mahratta states, and even at Hyderabad, which influence and ascendancy had been uniformly directed to injure the British power.

20. Under this view of the condition of Dowlut Rao Scindiah's power at the commencement of this war, it was dangerous to the British empire:

First. By the facilities which it afforded to the French of injuring the British interests in India, either in co-operation with Scindiah, or through the independent aid of his French and other European officers.

Secondly. By maintaining against the British Government a rival and hostile influence throughout every native state in India, and especially amongst our most important dependents and allies on the western side of India.

21. The danger arising from the condition of the Rajah of Berar's power with reference to the same considerations, appeared to be at the commencement of the war:

First. A military force greatly inferior to Scindiah's, in point of discipline, numbers, and artillery, but furnishing a considerable accession to the general strength of the confederacy against the British Government.

Secondly. The possession of an extensive territory and several strong forts, commanding the dominions of the Company and the Soubadar of the Deccan, in several vulnerable points.

Thirdly. The possession of the province of Cuttack by which the Rajah of Berar was enabled to interrupt the communication between our northern and southern possessions, to facilitate the invasion of Bengal and of the northern Circars, and to obtain the aid of French, and other European officers, or troops, to be landed in the province of Cuttack.

Fourthly. The intermixture of the Rajah of Berar's possessions with those of the Soubadar of the Deccan, and his vexatious claims upon the Court of Hyderabad, and his consequent influence at that court.

Fifthly. The Rajah of Berar's pretensions to the Government of Poonah, and the ascendancy and influence which he derives from his descent, connected with the general magnitude of his dominions and resources, with his supposed wealth, and with the hostile spirit which has been manifested by the state of Berar for many years in counteracting the interests of the British empire in India.

22. It is not necessary to advert to the state of Holkar's power, as he has not hitherto been considered to be a party in the war.

23. It would also be superfluous to enumerate the special objects of the war, as they have been sufficiently described in the view which the preceding paragraphs contain of the condition of the enemy's power at the commencement of the war.

24. The progress of the war and the glorious success of our arms in Hindostan and the Deccan, in Guzerat, and Orissa, have actually accomplished every requisite object with respect to the reduction of Dowlut Rao Scindiah's military and political power, have materially affected the Rajah of Berar, and have placed in our hands the means of establishing the security of the British interests against Dowlut Rao Scindiah, and the Rajah of Berar, on foundations, which appear to promise considerable duration.

25. At the date of your last despatch, you could not have been apprized of the extent of Scindiah's loss, and of our success against his power in every quarter in which it has been attacked. These considerations however must form the basis of the con-

ditions which we are empowered to require from Scindiah at the conclusion of peace.

26. The French force under the immediate command of M. Perron in Hindostan has been completely destroyed, nearly the whole force of Scindiah's regular battalions in Hindostan, and the Deccan, has been destroyed or dispersed by the victories obtained under the personal command of his Excellency General Lake at Delhi on the 11th of September, and at Laswaree on the 1st of November, and under your personal command at Assye on the 23d of September, and nearly the whole of Scindiah's artillery has been taken or destroyed. The greater part of Scindiah's European officers is now placed under the protection of the British power. The territory formerly possessed by Dowlut Rao Scindiah, in the Doab of the Jumna and Ganges, and assigned to M. Perron for the payment of the French force in Scindiah's service has been subjected to our authority. Scindiah has lost the Forts of Delhi, Muttra and Agra, with the adjoining territory on the right bank of the Jumna, and a considerable sum of money (twenty-four lacs of rupees) taken in the Fort of Agra, and five lacs of rupees at Delhi, with further sums of money taken at Allyghur, and in other places, and immediately divided by the troops after the several actions. The person of his Majesty Shah Aulum and the royal family have been placed under the protection of the British power. Scindiah has been deprived of the means of availing himself of the connexion with the Seiks, with the Rajpoots and with all the chiefs and states in the north of Hindostan, and the alliance of several of those chieftains has been transferred to the British Government. Begum Sumroo has placed herself under the protection of the British Government, and has recalled her battalions in the Deccan from Scindiah's service. From the state of the negotiation with Rajah Ambajee, at the date of our latest advices from his Excellency the Commander-in-Chief, it may be expected that Scindiah is now deprived of that portion of his territorial possessions in Hindostan, which was placed under the authority of Ambajee, and that Scindiah has altogether lost the support of Ambajee's power. The sea-port of Baroach and its dependent territory, the Forts of Champaneer and Powanghur, with the whole of Scindiah's territory in the province of Guzerat, situated to the northward of Baroach, have been subjected to our authority. The district of Godra has been occupied by our

troops. The fort and territory of Ahmednuggur, with the city of Boorhanpore, and the Fort of Asseerghur, have also been subjected to the authority of the British Government, and the fort and district of Jalnapore, with other districts in the Deccan, have been occupied by the combined armies of the British Government, and the Soubadar of the Deccan.

27. The loss sustained by the Rajah of Berar, must be considered separately in any negotiation with that chief. It is proper however to state that loss in this place, because it has diminished the power of Scindiah as a confederate against the British Government and our allies, in the further prosecution of the war.

28. From the Rajah of Berar all the intermixed Mahratta territories within the frontier of the Company on the side of Midnapore, have been taken and annexed to the British dominions, and the valuable province of Cuttack has also been subdued, and nearly settled. The loss of Juggernaut must deeply affect the consideration of the Rajah of Berar in the eyes of all the native powers. It is also reasonable to suppose that the military force of the Rajah of Berar must have suffered considerably at the battle of Assye, and during his subsequent unsuccessful operations, until the period of his disgraceful retreat to his own territories.

29. Under these circumstances the power and dominion of Dowlut Rao Scindiah must be considered to have suffered a degree of reduction nearly amounting to total ruin; and the Rajah of Berar with such reduction as he has suffered in his separate resources, appears to be at the mercy of the British Government for the remainder of his possessions, without any further hope (in the event of a continuance of the war) than that which he may found on the existing remnant of Scindiah's power.

* * * * * * * * *

40. The restoration to Dowlut Rao Scindiah of any part of the territories conquered from that chieftain is therefore to be viewed as an act of mere concession, and liberal clemency on the part of the British Government, proceeding from those principles of moderation and prudence, which constitute the foundations of our policy in India.

41. It would neither be just, humane, nor honourable to insist upon the reduction of Scindiah's power to any extent unnecessary to secure the just objects of the war, together with the safety of the British power and its allies. The British Government will

never deem any course of policy to be consistent with its wisdom and true interests, which is repugnant to the genuine dictates of justice, humanity and honour.

42. My duty requires me to employ every effort to reduce the power of the enemy within the bounds prescribed by the security of the interests committed to my charge, but it would be equally injurious to the glory and power of this government to prosecute war for the purposes of vengeance, and to urge the fall of a conquered enemy beyond the limits of our own safety and self-defence.

60. Treaty of Deogaum.

Treaty of Peace between the Honourable English East India Company and their Allies, on the one part, and Senah Saheb Soubah Ragojee Bhooslah, on the other, settled by Major-General Wellesley, on the part of the Honourable Company and their allies, and by Jeswunt Rao Ramchunder, on the part of Senah Saheb Soubah Ragojee Bhooslah; who have each communicated to the other their full powers.

ART. 1. There shall be perpetual peace and friendship between the honourable Company and their allies on the one part, and Senah Saheb Soubah Ragojee Bhooslah, on the other.

ART. 2. Senah Saheb Soubah Ragojee Bhooslah cedes to the honourable Company and their allies, in perpetual sovereignty, the province of Cuttack, including the port and district of Balasore.

ART. 3. He likewise cedes to the honourable Company and their allies, in perpetual sovereignty, all the territories, of which he has collected the revenues, in participation with the Soubahdar of the Deccan, and those of which he may have possession, which are to the westward of the river Wurdah.

ART. 4. It is agreed, that the frontier of Senah Saheb Soubah, towards the territories of his Highness the Soubahdar of the Deccan, shall be formed, to the west, by the river Wurdah, from its issue from the Injardy hills, to its junction with the Godavery. The hills on which are the forts of Nernallah and Gawulghur, are to be in the possession of Senah Saheb Soubah, and every thing south of those hills, and to the west of the river Wurdah is to belong to the British Government and their allies.

ART. 5. Districts amounting to four lacs of rupees per annum, contiguous to, and to the south of the forts of Nernallah and Gawulghur, are to be given over to Senah Saheb Soubah. Those districts are to be fixed upon by Major-General Wellesley, and delivered over to Senah Saheb Soubah at the same time with the forts.

ART. 6. Senah Saheb Soubah, for himself, his heirs and successors, entirely renounces all claims of every description on the territories of the British Government and their allies, ceded by the 2d, 3d, and 4th Articles, and on all the territories of his Highness the Soubahdar of the Deccan.

ART. 7. The honourable Company engage, that they will mediate and arbitrate according to the principles of justice, any disputes or differences that may now exist, or may hereafter arise, between the honourable Company's allies, Secunder Jah Bahaudur, his heirs and successors, and Rao Pundit Purdhaun, his heirs and successors respectively, and Senah Saheb Soubah.

ART. 8. Senah Saheb Soubah engages never to take or retain in his service, any Frenchman, or the subject of any other European or American power, the government of which may be at war with the British Government; or any British subject, whether European or Indian, without the consent of the British Government. The honourable Company engage on their part, that they will not give aid or countenance to any discontented relations, Rajahs, Zemindars, or other subjects of Senah Saheb Soubah, who may fly from, or rebel against, his authority.

ART. 9. In order to secure and improve the relations of amity and peace hereby established between the governments, it is agreed, that accredited ministers from each shall reside at the court of the other.

ART. 10. Certain treaties have been made by the British Government with feudatories of Senah Saheb Soubah. These treaties are to be confirmed. Lists of the persons with whom such treaties have been made, will be given to Senah Saheb Soubah, when this treaty will be ratified by his Excellency, the Governor-General in council.

ART. 11. Senah Saheb Soubah hereby renounces, for himself, his heirs and successors, all adherence to the confederacy formed by him and Dowlut Rao Scindiah, and other Mahratta chiefs, to attack the honourable Company and their allies. He engages not to assist those chiefs if the war with them should still continue.

ART. 12. This treaty of peace is to be ratified by Senah Saheb

Soubah within eight days from this time, and the ratification is to be delivered to Major-General Wellesley; at which time the orders for the cession of the ceded territories are to be delivered and the troops are to withdraw. Major-General Wellesley engages that the treaty shall be ratified by his Excellency the most noble the Governor-General in Council, and that the ratification shall be delivered in two months from this date.

ARTHUR WELLESLEY, Major-General.
JESWUNT RAO RAMCHUNDER, on the part of SENAH SAHEB SOUBAH.

Done in Camp at Deogaum, this 17th December 1803, answering to the 2d Ramzaun 1213 Fusslee.

61. Treaty of Surje Anjengaum.

Treaty of Peace between the Honourable English East India Company and their Allies on the one part, and the Maharajah Ali Jah Dowlut Rao Scindiah on the other; settled by Major-General Wellesley on the part of the Honourable Company and their Allies, and by Eetul Mahadeo, Moonshee Kavel Nyn, Jeswunt Rao Goorparah Ameer-ool-Omrah, and Naroo Hurry, on the part of the Maharajah Dowlut Rao Scindiah, who have each communicated to the other their full powers.

ART. 1. There shall be perpetual peace and friendship between the honourable Company and their allies, on the one part, and the Maharajah Ali Jah Dowlut Rao Scindiah on the other.

ART. 2. The Maharajah cedes to the honourable Company and their allies in perpetual sovereignty, all his forts, territories, and rights in the Doab or country situated between the Jumna and Ganges; and all his forts, territories, rights and interests in the countries which are to the northward of those of the Rajahs of Jeypoor and Joudpoor and of the Ranah of Gohud; of which territories, &c. a detailed list is given in the accompanying schedule. Such countries formerly in the possession of the Maharajah situated between Jeypoor and Joudpoor, and to the southward of the former, are to belong to the Maharajah.

ART. 3. The Maharajah likewise cedes to the honourable Company and their allies in perpetual sovereignty, the fort of Baroach and territory depending thereon, and the fort of Ahmednuggur and territory depending thereon; excepting those lands which it is agreed by Article 8th of this treaty, that the Maharajah is to retain.

ART. 4. The Maharajah likewise cedes to the honourable Company and their allies, all the territories which belonged to him previous to the breaking out of the war, which are situated to the southward of the hills, called the Adjuntee hills, including the fort and district of Jalnapore, the town and district of Gandapore, and all other districts between that range of hills and the river Godavery.

ART. 5. The Maharajah Ali Jah Dowlut Rao Scindiah, for himself, his heirs and successors, hereby renounces all the claim to the forts, territories, rights and interests, ceded by the 2d, 3d, and 4th articles; and all claims of every description upon the British Government, and their allies the Soubahdar of the Deccan, the Peishwa, and Anund Rao Guikwar.

ART. 6. The fort of Asseerghur, the city of Boorhanpore, the forts of Powanghur and Dohud, and the territories in Candeish, and Guzerat, depending on these forts, shall be restored to the Maharajah Dowlut Rao Scindiah.

ART. 7. Whereas the Maharajah Dowlut Rao Scindiah has represented that his family have long held in Enaum as a gift from the kings of Hindostan, the districts of Dhoolpoor-Baree, and Rajah-Kerrah, which are situated to the northward of the countries of the Rajahs of Jeypoor and Joudpoor, and of the Ranah of Gohud, and that lands in Hindostan, ceded by the 2d Article of this treaty to the honourable Company and their allies, are held in Jaghire by persons of the family of the late Madhajee Scindiah, and others by principal Sirdars in his service, all of whom would suffer distress, if deprived of the advantages they enjoy in those countries: it is agreed, that the Maharajah shall continue to hold and enjoy in Enaum the lands of Dhoolpoor-Baree, and Rajah-Kerrah; and that Bala Baye Sahib, and Munsoor Sahib, Moonshee Kavel Nyn, Boogajee Jamdah, Amrajee Jadhoo, and Wirdah Charie, shall continue to hold their lands in Jaghire, under the protection of the honourable Company: and further, in order that no individual may incur loss or suffer distress in consequence of this arrangement, it is agreed, that the honourable Company shall either pay pensions, or grant lands in Jaghire, according to the option of the British Government, to certain other Sirdars and others to be named by the Maharajah, provided that the total amount of the sums paid, or Jaghires granted or held, does not exceed seventeen lacs of rupees per annum, including the annual value of the lands, which it is agreed by this Article that Bala Baye Sahib, Munsoor

Sahib, Moonshee Kavel Nyn, Boogajee Jamdah, Amrajee Jadhoo, and Wirdah Charie, are to continue to hold; and provided that no troops in the service of the Maharajah are to be introduced into Dhoolpoor-Baree and Rajah-Kerrah, or the other lands held in Jaghire, under the pretence of collecting the revenue, or any other pretence whatever.

ART. 8. Whereas the Maharajah Dowlut Rao Scindiah has represented that his family have long held in Enaum certain lands, villages, &c. in the territories of Rao Pundit Purdhaun, viz. Chomargoondee Pergunna, Jamgaum, Ranjingaum, half of Seo Gaum Pergunna, six villages in Umber Pergunna, five villages in Pytun Pergunna, five villages in Niwaz Pergunna, five villages in Kurla Pergunna, six villages in Poonah Pergunna, two villages in Wahy Pergunna, six villages in Patutood Pergunna, five villages in Pandipeergaum Pergunna, five villages in Pagood Pergunna, two villages in Parnyra Pergunna, which have lately been taken possession of by the British Government and their allies; it is agreed, that those lands and villages shall be restored to him, provided that no troops shall ever be introduced into those lands and villages, under pretence of collecting the revenues, or any other pretence whatever.

ART. 9. Certain treaties have been made by the British Government with Rajahs and others heretofore feudatories of the Maharajah Ali Jah Dowlut Rao Scindiah. These treaties are to be confirmed, and the Maharajah hereby renounces all claims upon the persons with whom such treaties have been made, and declares them to be independent of his government and authority, provided that none of the territories belonging to the Maharajah, situated to the southward of those of the Rajahs of Jeypoor and Joudpoor, and the Ranah of Gohud, of which the revenues have been collected by him or his Aumildars, or have been applicable as Surinjamee to the payment of his troops, are granted away by such treaties. Lists of the persons with whom such treaties have been made will be given to the Maharajah Dowlut Rao Scindiah, when this treaty will be ratified by his Excellency the Governor-General.

ART. 10. No person whatever is hereafter to be molested on account of the part which he may have taken in the present war.

ART. 11. It is agreed that the rights of his Highness the Peishwa to certain lands in Malwa, and elsewhere, shall be established as heretofore, and in case any difference should arise respecting those rights, it is agreed that the honourable

Company shall mediate, arbitrate, and decide according to the principles of justice between his Highness and the Maharajah, and whatever shall be thus decided, will be agreed to by both parties, and will be carried into execution.

ART. 12. The Maharajah Dowlut Rao Scindiah hereby renounces all claims upon his Majesty Shah Alum, and engages on his part to interfere no further in the affairs of his Majesty.

ART. 13. The Maharajah Ali Jah Dowlut Rao Scindiah engages never to take or retain in his service any Frenchman, or the subject of any other European or American power, the Government of which may be at war with the British Government; or any British subject, whether European or native of India, without the consent of the British Government.

ART. 14. In order to secure and improve the relations of amity and peace hereby established between the Governments, it is agreed, that accredited ministers from each shall reside at the court of the other.

ART. 15. The honourable Company being bound by treaties of general defensive alliance with his Highness the Soubahdar of the Deccan, and his Highness Rao Pundit Purdhaun, to which the Maharajah Ali Jah Dowlut Rao Scindiah is desirous of acceding, he is to be admitted to the benefits thereof; and the honourable Company, with a view to the future security of the Maharajah's territories, engage in the event of his agreeing to the treaty above-mentioned, in two months to furnish him with a force consisting of six battalions of infantry, with their complement of ordnance and artillery, and usual equipments of Military stores, &c. and the expense of this force is to be defrayed out of the revenues of the lands ceded by the 2d, 3d, and 4th Articles. But it is agreed, that in case it should suit the interests of the Maharajah's Government to decline to enter into the treaty above-mentioned, such refusal shall not affect any of the stipulations of this treaty of peace, which are in every respect to be binding on the contracting parties, their heirs and successors.

ART. 16. This treaty is to be ratified by the Maharajah Dowlut Rao Scindiah in eight days from this time, and the ratification is to be delivered to Major-General Wellesley.

Major-General Wellesley engages that it shall be ratified by his Excellency the most noble the Governor-General in Council, and the ratifications shall be delivered to the Maharajah in three months, or sooner, if possible.

The orders for the cession of the territories shall be delivered to Major-General Wellesley at the same time with the ratification of the treaty of peace; but the forts of Asseerghur, Powanghur, and Dohud, are not to be delivered up, till accounts will have been received that the territories ceded, have been evacuated by the Maharajah's officers and troops.

ARTHUR WELLESLEY,
EETUL MAHADEO,
KAVEL NYN,
JESWUNT RAO GOORPARAH,
NAROO HURRY.

Done in Camp at Surje Anjengaum, this 30th of December 1803, answering to the 15th Ramzaun 1213 Fusslee.

62. The Marquess Wellesley to the Honourable the Secret Committee of the Honourable the Court of Directors.

Partition of Mahratta Conquests.

Fort William, June 10, 1804.

Honourable Sirs,

At the earliest practicable period of time, after the conclusion of peace with the confederated Mahratta chieftains, the attention of the Governor-General in Council was directed to the important object of establishing the general principle which should regulate the partition of our late acquisitions (under the treaties of peace with Dowlut Rao Scindiah and the Rajah of Berar,) between the British Government and its allies, and of applying that principle to the circumstances of those states which were to be considered as allies in the war, and the Governor-General in Council now deems it his duty to communicate to your honourable Committee the sentiments and resolutions of the Governor-General in Council on that important subject.

With a view to determine and to apply the principle of partition of conquests, it was necessary to decide, 1stly, what states of India should be considered as the allies of the British Government in the late war; 2dly, what states possessed a positive right to participate in our conquests; and 3dly, whether it was expedient to admit the participation of any of the allies, who might not be considered to possess a positive right to participate in our conquests, and to what extent the admission of such participation might be deemed politic and just.

The Governor-General in Council was decidedly of opinion that the only states which could properly be considered as allies of the British Government in the late war were those of the Peishwa, and the Soubahdar of the Deccan. The nature of the relations and the engagements subsisting between the British Government and the states of Mysore and of the Guickwar (the troops of which, particularly of the former, were employed in the prosecution of the war) is not such as to place them in the condition of the allies designated by the treaty of peace with Dowlut Rao Scindiah and the Rajah of Berar, nor was it probable that the governments of either of those states entertained any expectation of benefiting by the result of the war in any other manner than by acquiring an additional degree of security in the peaceable enjoyment of their respective rights and possessions.

The Governor-General in Council, however, was decidedly of opinion that none of the states of India claiming to be allies of the British Government, could justly found a right to participate in the conquests of the war, merely on the declaration contained in the treaties of peace, that the cessions were made generally in favour of the British Government and its allies.

This declaration was introduced into the treaties of peace with reference, first, to the engagements actually subsisting between the British Government and the Soubahdar of the Deccan, by which that Prince is entitled, under certain considerations, to participate equally with the British Government in the conquests of joint war. 2dly. To the declared intention of the Governor-General to admit the Peishwa also to a participation in the conquests of the late war, in such a proportion and in such a manner as should appear to be expedient on the conclusion of a general peace. That declaration was not intended to convey to any of the allies any right of participation which they did not possess on other grounds.

If a contrary principle were admitted, a right of equal participation on the part of the allies could not justly be denied, and that right must have been recognized independently of the conduct of the allies during the war, and with respect to the Soubahdar of the Deccan, independently of his fulfilment of those conditions, on which alone his right of equal participation is stipulated by positive treaty to depend. This could not be supposed to have been in the contemplation of either of the contracting parties at the conclusion of the treaties of peace.

The states of Hyderabad and Poonah, therefore, being the only states which could be considered as allies of the British Government in the late war, it became necessary to determine whether either or both of those states possessed a right to participate in our conquests; and under the defect of right, whether either or both those states should be admitted, on principles of expediency and policy, to a participation.

By the 3d of the secret and separate articles of the treaty of Hyderabad concluded in October 1800, his Highness the Soubahdar of the Deccan is entitled to participate equally with the British Government in the conquests of joint war on certain conditions. With a view, therefore, to determine whether his Highness possessed a right to participate in the conquests of the late war, it was necessary to examine in what degree his Highness had fulfilled the conditions on which that right was stipulated to depend.

It is declared in the 3d of the separate and secret articles of that treaty, that 'in the event of war, his Highness shall be entitled to participate equally with the other contracting parties in the division of any territory which may be acquired by the successful exertions of their united arms, provided his Highness the Nawaub Asaph Jah shall have faithfully fulfilled all the stipulations of the preceding treaty, especially those contained in the 12th and 13th articles thereof.'

The obligation imposed upon his Highness the Soubahdar of the Deccan by the 12th and 13th articles is, that in the event of war, his Highness shall furnish a force of 6,000 infantry and 9,000 cavalry, to act with the subsidiary force; that his Highness shall also employ every further effort in his power for the purpose of bringing into the field, as speedily as possible, the whole force which he may be able to supply from his dominions, and that his Highness shall collect as many Bunjarrahs as possible, and shall store as much grain as may be practicable in his frontier garrisons. In other words, his Highness is required to unite cordially with the British Government in the prosecution of the supposed war, and to combine with the exertions of the British power, all the force and resources of his own state, as the condition of his being entitled to participate equally with the British Government in the territories which may be acquired by the war.

Although the conduct of the state of Hyderabad, during the late war with the confederated Mahratta chieftains, is described in the course of the narrative of transactions contained in our despatch to your honourable Committee of the 12th of April, the Governor-General in Council deems it proper with a view to trace distinctly the grounds of his decision on the question of his Highness's right of participation to repeat on this occasion the leading facts of the case.

After long and urgent solicitation on the part of the Resident at Hyderabad, a body of his Highness's troops, amounting nearly to the number stipulated by treaty, joined the subsidiary force, and the general conduct of those troops was consistent with the obligations of the treaty. In other respects, however, the state of Hyderabad altogether failed in the discharge of the duties of an ally, and the conduct of his Highness's officers was of a nature actually hostile to the British Government.

At an early period of the war Major-General Wellesley was invested by his late Highness the Nizam with a general power of control over the officers of his Highness's government on the western frontier of his dominions. That power of control, however, proved entirely nugatory. The orders of Major-General Wellesley were utterly disregarded; every exertion on the part of his Highness's officers in facilitating the movement and supply of the British troops, and in opposing those of the enemy, was insidiously withheld or directly refused, and his Highness's officers not only neglected to store grain in the frontier garrisons for the service of the combined troops in conformity to an express stipulation in the treaty of Hyderabad, but refused to furnish any supplies, and even to permit the purchase of grain in his Highness's territory for the use of the British army.

His Highness's officer commanding the fort of Dowlutabad refused admission to the sick and wounded of the British troops engaged in the battle of Assye. The Killadar of Dharore refused to give protection under the guns of his fort to a convoy proceeding with supplies to the army, without orders for that purpose from the Court of Hyderabad, and the Killadar of Budnapore actually fired upon a detachment of British troops on its march to join Major-General Wellesley.

Although the conduct of his Highness's officers may be ascribed in a great measure to the weakness of his government, yet the sentiments which his Highness Secunder Jah himself is stated to have declared upon that occasion, justify a suspicion that their hostile conduct was encouraged by his Highness. The Governor-General in Council here refers to a declaration of his Highness to Azim Ool Omrah, reported by that minister to the Resident of Hyderabad, and communicated in a despatch from the Resident of the 13th October 1803, that it was not necessary for him to attend to all the remonstrances of the British Government on the subject of the conduct of his officers; that 'no apprehension should for instance be entertained on the representations that had lately been made to him regarding the Killadar of Dharore and others, for that it was not stipulated in any part of his engagements that British officers and their troops should positively be admitted within the forts of his government, and that it was a matter of equal indifference whether the Killadars did or did not admit them.'

These unwarrantable sentiments, and those which his Highness is stated by the Resident to entertain generally with regard to the alliance subsisting between the British Government and the state of Hyderabad, accompanied by the several acts enumerated in the preceding paragraph, are manifestly inconsistent with a due attention to the obligations of the alliance.

In addition to these facts, it was manifest that his Highness did not, agreeably to the spirit of his engagements, combine with the exertions of the British power all the force and resources of his own state for the prosecution of the war, and consequently did not fulfil the conditions on which he would be entitled to participate equally in the conquests which have resulted from the war.

The conclusion of any engagements between states necessarily supposes the ability, as well as the disposition of both parties, to fulfil the obligations of them. Admitting therefore that the conduct of his Highness's officers originated in causes wholly independent of his Highness's control, and that his Highness was precluded by the inherent vices and defects of his Government, from applying the resources of the state to the promotion of the common cause, his Highness could not consistently with the acknowledged principles of reciprocity, be permitted to claim the benefit of this argument, and to found a right to an equal participation of conquests on his inability to fulfil the conditions on which alone that right was admitted to exist.

Independently of these considerations, however, his Highness's claim to an equal participation is precluded by the tenor of the 15th article of the treaty of peace with Dowlut Rao Scindiah, combined with the actual conclusion of defensive and subsidiary engagements between the British Government and Dowlut Rao Scindiah on the basis of that article.

It is stated in that article that if Dowlut Rao Scindiah shall consent to the conclusion of a subsidiary treaty, the charges of the subsidiary force consisting of six battalions of infantry, with their complement of ordnance and artillery, and usual equipment of military stores, &c., shall be defrayed out of the revenues of the lands ceded by the 2d, 3d, and 4th articles of the treaty of peace; his Highness therefore could not justly claim an equal share in the lands on which are charged the expense of the subsidiary force to be furnished by the British Government to Scindiah, and the Governor-General in Council is decidedly of opinion, that under a just construction of the 15th article of the treaty of Serji Anjengaum, combined with the provisions of the subsidiary engagement lately concluded with Dowlut Rao Scindiah, his Highness the Soubahdar could not claim any portion of the territory ceded by the 2d, 3d, and 4th articles of the treaty of Serji Anjengaum, because the British Government being pledged by the subsidiary and defensive engagements concluded with Dowlut Rao Scindiah, eventually to employ the whole power and resources of the state for the defence of that chieftain's rights and possessions, the lands on which are charged the expense of the subsidiary force, may be justly considered to be assigned for all the actual and contingent charges of fulfilling that obligation of our defensive engagements. It was also evident that those territories are subject to other charges connected with the general principles of the pacification, and that from the revenues arising out of those territories must be defrayed the expense of providing for Scindiah's principal officers and chiefs, and certain branches of his family, as well as for the charges incidental to our engagements with several chiefs and states in Hindostan, and for the maintenance of the king and the family.

It follows from this statement, that if his Highness the Soubahdar of the Deccan had maintained a claim to an equal participation of conquests, he must also be subjected to an equal share of the charges incidental to the security of those conquests, and resulting from the general principles of the pacification. If, therefore, the estimated value of all the cessions made to the allies by the peace were opposed to the necessary charges of the whole arrangement, there can be no doubt that his Highness the Soubahdar's share of the profits of the war would be greatly inferior to that which has actually been assigned to him, added to the positive gain which his Highness has acquired by the total abrogation of the claims of the Rajah of Berar and Dowlut Rao Scindiah on his Highness's government under the distinct provisions of an article in the treaties of peace with each of those chieftains.

Although his Highness the Soubahdar of the Deccan cannot be considered to possess on any ground a right to an equal participation in the territories acquired by the late war, a question may be supposed to exist, whether his Highness was not entitled to a share of the conquests proportioned to the degree in which he contributed the aid of his troops in the prosecution of the war. On this subject it may be observed, 1st, that the conditions on which his Highness's right of participation depends are absolute, and that the engagement does not state any obligation on our part dependent on a partial execution of those conditions on the part of his Highness, and 2dly, that no definite principle of comparison can be established between the benefit which our cause may have derived from the co-operation of his Highness's troops, and any precise proportion of territory to be assigned as an equivalent to his Highness.

Under the circumstances above stated, the only points connected with the interests of the Soubahdar of the Deccan which remained to be decided were—

1st. Whether his Highness the Soubahdar of the Deccan should be admitted to any share of the conquered territory? and if this question were decided in the affirmative:

2dly. Whether without reference to the conduct of his Highness's government during the war, such territory should be assigned to his Highness on the ground of his Highness's right to participate in the conquests of the war, or simply as a gratuitous cession on the part of the British Government, on grounds distinct from any question of a right to participation of conquests?

3dly. What territory should be assigned to his Highness if he should be permitted to retain any part of the conquered countries?

With regard to the first point the Governor-General in Council was of opinion that, adverting to considerations of a political nature, and to the local position of a considerable part of the conquered territory, it was expedient to assign a certain portion of it to his Highness the Soubahdar.

On the 2d question, as the Soubahdar possessed no positive right to any precise portion of our conquests, it appeared to be just and expedient that the territory to be assigned to the Soubahdar of the Deccan should be considered as a gratuitous cession to his Highness on the part of the British Government, and not surrendered to his Highness on the ground of his right to participation in the conquests effected during the war.

The territories which it was expedient to cede to his Highness the Soubahdar of the Deccan, were obviously those which were intermixed with his Highness's present possessions, or were contiguous to them.

Those territories are, 1st, the districts, of which the Rajah of Berar collected the revenues in participation with the Soubahdar of the Deccan, and generally all the territory formerly in the possession of the Rajah of Berar, situated to the southward of the hills, on which are the forts of Narnulla and Gawilghur, and to the westward of the river Wurdah, ceded by the 3d and 4th articles of the treaty of Deogaum, excepting only such districts as are stipulated by the 5th article of that treaty to remain in the possession of the Rajah of Berar.

2dly. The districts ceded by the 4th article of the treaty of peace with Dowlut Rao Scindiah, viz. those which are situated to the southward of the Adjuntee hills, including the fort and district of Jalnapoor, the town and district of Gondapore, and all other districts formerly belonging to Dowlut Rao Scindiah, situated between that range of hills and the river Godavery.

These territories had already been placed under the charge of his Highness's officers by the honourable Major-General Wellesley, under an express declaration on the part of that officer that his Highness's permanent appropriation of those territories must be subject to the future resolution of the Governor-General in Council.

Upon the grounds detailed in the preceding part of this letter, the Governor-General in Council resolved to annex those territories permanently to the dominions of the Soubahdar of the Deccan.

The Governor-General in Council now proceeds to state to your honourable Committee his sentiments with regard to the question of a right to participate in the acquisitions of the late war, as applicable to our ally the Peishwa, and the arrangements which the Governor-General in Council finally adopted in favour of his Highness under the acquisitions resulting from the successes of the war.

The treaty of Bassein is framed on the basis of the treaties concluded with the Nizam in October, 1800. It stipulates for the aid of a certain portion of the Peishwa's troops in the event of a war, but does not provide for his Highness's participation in any conquests which may be achieved by the war.

Admitting, therefore, that the Peishwa had furnished the stipulated number of troops for the prosecution of the late war, he would have acquired no right to participate in the conquests which have resulted from it. It was unnecessary, therefore, to enter into any discussion on the question of his Highness's right of participation, founded on the consideration of his having contributed to the support of the common cause in the degree in which the weakness and confusion of his Highness's government admitted of his co-operation. The peculiar circumstances of his Highness's situation rendered such a pretension in the highest degree exorbitant and unreasonable.

The war originated in the measures adopted by the British Government for the restoration of his Highness from a state of exile and of personal danger to his legitimate dominions, and to a condition of comparative dignity and permanent security.

The utmost limit of the Peishwa's just and reasonable expectations was attained in the preservation of his dominion, by the result of the war, from the violence and ambition of external and domestic enemies. His Excellency in Council, therefore, could discern no ground of claim on the part of the Peishwa, to a participation of conquests effected in the defence of his Highness's rights and possessions by the exertions of the British arms and the wisdom of British councils, not only unaided by any efforts on the part of his Highness, but in some points impeded by the unaccommodating and vindictive spirit of his Highness's policy.

The Peishwa could not in the judgment of the Governor-General in Council establish any pretension to participate in the territories acquired by those arduous exertions of the British arms, to which his Highness was exclusively indebted for the existence of his power.

The restoration of the Peishwa's legitimate authority, together with the recovery of the dominions which he possessed previously to his expulsion from Poonah, and with the provisions established for securing his Highness in his state and actual possessions, appeared to the Governor-General in Council to constitute an ample participation in the success of the war, and in the benefits of the peace.

Considerations of policy, however, suggested the expedience of admitting the Peishwa to a participation in our late conquests.

The jealousy with which the Peishwa contemplated an intimate connexion with the British Government prevented his acceptance of our proposals for the conclusion of a defensive alliance until the successful rebellion of Jeswunt Rao Holkar had subverted his government, and had compelled him to abandon his capital.

The Peishwa has experienced the benefits of that alliance by his restoration to the exercise of his legitimate authority, under the protection of the British arms and of the British power.

The Governor-General in Council, however, was of opinion that the characteristic jealousy of the Peishwa could not be completely eradicated until he should be satisfied by a further experience of the moderation and liberality of our proceedings under the alliance, that it is our object rather to augment than to impair the power and resources of his government. The assignment of a portion of our recent conquests to the Peishwa, under the total defect of his Highness's right to participate in them, founded either on the obligations of treaty or on the aid which his Highness contributed in the prosecution of the war, was calculated in the judgment of the Governor-General in Council to impress upon his Highness's mind the most favourable opinion of the equity and liberality of the British Government, to encourage his confidence in its public faith and honour, and to fix his attachment to the alliance, as well as to elevate the fame and character of the British Government in the judgment of every state in India.

For these reasons his Excellency in Council deemed it advisable to assign to the Peishwa as large a portion of our late territorial acquisitions as could be conveniently annexed to his dominions, consistently with the security of our own rights and possessions, and with the arrangements which the Governor-General in Council had resolved to accomplish in favour of our ally the Soubahdar of the Deccan.

His Excellency in Council accordingly resolved that the city and province of Ahmednuggur, excepting such portion of the latter as was restored to Dowlut Rao Scindiah by the terms of the treaty of peace, should be annexed to the Peishwa's dominions.

Upon the basis of the observations and resolutions stated in the preceding part of this despatch, instructions were transmitted to the Residents at the courts of Hyderabad and Poonah, under the date the 30th of March, 1804, directing those officers to communicate to their Highnesses the Soubahdar of the Deccan and the Peishwa respectively, the territorial arrangements which the Governor-General in Council had resolved to adopt in favour of their Highnesses, and to be prepared to oppose any assumption on the part of their Highnesses of a right to participate in the conquests of the war. The Resident at Poonah was especially directed to endeavour to impress upon the mind of the Peishwa a just sense of the liberality of the British Government in assigning to his Highness so valuable a portion of our recent conquests, under the total defect of his Highness's right to participate in them, founded either on the stipulations of the treaty, or on the aid afforded by his Highness in the promotion of the common cause.

The draft of a treaty of partition framed in conformity to the resolutions above described, was at the same time transmitted to the Residents at Hyderabad and Poonah respectively, with directions to obtain the seals and signatures of their Highnesses the Soubahdar of the Deccan and the Peishwa to separate treaties to be prepared in conformity to that draft.

The Governor-General in Council deeming the period of adjusting the participation of conquests to be the fittest opportunity for obtaining their Highnesses the Soubahdar's and the Peishwa's ratification of the treaties of peace concluded with Dowlut Rao Scindiah and the Rajah of Berar, transmitted with his instructions to the Residents on the subject of a partition of conquests, copies of those treaties directing the Residents to present to their Highnesses the Soubahdar of the Deccan and the Peishwa respectively, copies of those treaties, in order that their Highnesses might affix their seals to each of those treaties in testimony of their recognition of the terms of the pacification, and the Residents were further instructed to return those treaties so attested for the purpose of being deposited among the records of Government. It was at the same time signified to the Residents that the Ratification of the treaties of peace must precede the execution of the treaties of partition.

On the 28th of April the Resident at Hyderabad waited upon his Highness the Soubahdar of the Deccan for the express purpose of obtaining his Highness's ratification of the treaties of peace, and his execution of the treaty of partition.

His Highness, after an attentive perusal of the treaties of peace, affixed his seal and signature to those documents. The Resident then delivered to his Highness the proposed treaty of partition, which, after being attentively perused, was executed by his Highness without the slightest hesitation. The Resident at the same time delivered a counterpart of that treaty to his Highness the Soubahdar. Immediately after the exchange of those instruments, the minister, Azim Ool Omrah, in the presence of his Highness, expressed to the Resident his Highness's entire satisfaction at the amicable and liberal spirit of the territorial arrangements for which the treaty of partition provided.

In the course of the conversation, the Resident took occasion to intimate to the minister that the assignment of territory to his Highness, prescribed by the treaty of partition, must be considered as gratuitous on the part of the British Government, and not as surrendered on the ground of his Highness the Soubahdar's right to participation in the conquests of the war. But no pretensions having been advanced by his Highness to an equal share of conquests, the Resident judged it unnecessary to press the discussion of that question upon the court of Hyderabad.

The treaty of partition, executed by his Highness the Soubahdar of the Deccan, was received at Fort William on the 13th of May, and was ratified by the Governor-General in Council on the following day.

Adverting to the extent and value of the cessions to the Soubahdar of the Deccan under the treaty of partition, and to the benefits which his Highness derives from the renunciation on the part of the Rajah of Berar and of Dowlut Rao Scindiah of all claims of every description on the state of Hyderabad, the Governor-General in Council is decidedly of opinion that under the treaty of partition the Soubahdar of the Deccan has acquired a share in the conquests and advantages of the war greatly exceeding the proportion in which his Highness contributed to its success, and not inferior to that which his Highness must have received under an admission of his right to an equal participation of conquests.

The court of Poonah on this occasion manifested a spirit of cavil and of inordinate pretension, wholly unbecoming the relative situation of his Highness the Peishwa, and unsuitable to the nature of the obligations imposed upon his Highness by the arduous exertions of the British Government for the re-establishment of his authority, and by the liberality of its conduct in resolving to assign to his Highness a portion of the conquered territory under the total defect of his Highness's claim to such a participation.

When the Resident submitted to his Highness the Peishwa copies of the treaties of peace for ratification, apprizing him that when his Highness should have ratified those documents, the Resident would communicate to his Highness an arrangement for the cession of the fort and territory of Ahmednuggur to the state of Poonah, his Highness refused to ratify those treaties with his seal and signature, justifying his refusal by claims and pretensions of a most extravagant and unreasonable nature.

The instructions of the Governor-General in Council, however, enabled the Resident to oppose with success the exorbitant demands and expectations of the Peishwa, who finally consented to recognize the provisions of the treaties of peace by affixing his seal to the copies of those treaties presented to him for that purpose by the Resident.

The Resident then proceeded to submit the treaty of partition to his Highness's acceptance. Upon this occasion the Peishwa renewed his unreasonable claims, and even advanced pretensions to participate equally with the British Government in the conquests of the war. The Resident found no difficulty, however, in demonstrating to his Highness and his ministers the absurdity of these pretensions, and after some further discussion his Highness consented to withdraw his unreasonable claims and to affix his seal and signature to the treaty of partition.

Accordingly on the 14th of May the Resident at Poonah waited on his Highness the Peishwa, who on that occasion affixed his seal to the treaties of peace concluded with Dowlut Rao Scindiah and the Rajah of Berar, and duly executed the proposed treaty of partition.

The treaty of partition, as concluded with his Highness the Peishwa, has also been ratified by the Governor-General in Council.

Copies of the treaty of partition, as concluded with their Highnesses the Soubahdar of the Deccan and the Peishwa, are also annexed to this despatch for your honourable Committee's information.

We have the honour to be, honourable Sirs,
your most faithful humble Servants,
WELLESLEY.
G. UDNY.
G. H. BARLOW.

63. The Governor-General in Council to the Secret Committee of the Honourable the Court of Directors.

Advantages resulting from the War.

(Extract.)

Fort William, 13th July, 1804.

Honourable Sirs,

139. The Governor-General in Council deems it proper to close this despatch by a general recapitulation of the benefits which the British Government in India has derived from the operations of the war, and the combined arrangements of the pacification, including the treaties of peace, of partition, and of defensive alliance and subsidy. Those benefits may be enumerated under the following heads:—

The reduction of the military power and territorial resources of Dowlut Rao Scindiah, and the Rajah of Berar, within the limits indispensably necessary for the security of the British Government in India and of its allies.

The destruction of the French territorial power established by M. Perron, on the most vulnerable part of the frontier of the British possessions in India, under circumstances of internal strength, military resource, and political influence, which menaced the British Government with great and extensive dangers.

The barriers opposed by the stipulations of treaty, to the revival of the French power and influence in any quarter of India.

The annexation to the British possessions of the territory formerly occupied by the French force under M. Perron. Under this accession of territory, our north-western frontier has been strengthened by being advanced to the banks of the Jumna, and by the occupation of the several important posts and fortresses, which command that river, and from the source of former danger we now derive additional security to the British possessions in India.

The augmented sources of revenue and commerce acquired by the annexation to the British territories of the fertile countries situated in the Doab of the rivers Jumna and Ganges (in which the authority of M. Perron had been established) combined with the complete command over the navigation of the Jumna.

The deliverance of the Emperor Shah Allum from the control of the French power, established in the north-western quarter of Hindostan; by which the government of France has been deprived of a powerful instrument in the eventual prosecution of its hostile designs against the British Empire in India, and the British Government has obtained a favourable opportunity of conciliating the confidence, and securing the applause of surrounding states, by providing a safe and tranquil asylum for the declining age of that venerable and unfortunate monarch, and a suitable maintenance for his numerous and distressed family.

The establishment of the British influence in the north-western division of Hindostan, and the additional security acquired by the conclusion of treaties of defensive alliance with the Rajpoot state of Jyenagur, and the petty states in the vicinity of our possessions in that quarter. Those states under the operation of the alliances concluded with them, constitute a barrier between the British territories and the Mahratta states; which arrangement, with other stipulations of the pacification, secures the permanent exclusion of the influence and control of the Mahrattas from the north-western quarter of Hindostan.

The commanding position which the British Government has secured by the possession of the strong fortress of Gwalior, and by the establishment of a subsidiary force within the territory of the Ranah of Gohud, under the conditions described in the 48th paragraph of this despatch. This branch of the general arrangements of the peace contributes in a particular degree to maintain the tranquillity of Hindostan, and to consolidate the barrier established for the exclusion of the Mahratta power and influence from that quarter of India. The same arrangements also connect our possessions in Bundlecund with those to the northward of the province of Gohud, and provide additional security to the navigation of the Jumna, and additional protection to our valuable possessions in the Doab, from the hostile attempts of any regular state, or from the predatory incursions of any enterprizing adventurer.

The additional means of defence acquired by the established system of our external relations in the north-western quarter of Hindostan, against any attempt on the part of the northern powers of Asia, or of the French Republic, through the aid of those powers, to disturb the security of the British possessions in India.

The augmented security which the British Empire derives from the annexation of the valuable province of Cuttack, including the sea-port of Balasore, and all the dependencies of that province to the British dominion. By establishing between the province of Midnapore, and the northern Circars, a continuation of the British dominion and authority, and thereby completing the line of connexion between the territories under the immediate government of Bengal, and those under the authority of Fort St. George. By depriving the government of France of the facilities which the province of Cuttack while in the possession of a foreign power, afforded for the prosecution of intrigues, injurious to the British interests, and for the invasion of the British territories, either singly, or in co-operation with a native power. By the advantages which our possession of the province of Cuttack would afford to us in the event of a contest with the state of Berar; and by the augmented sources of revenue and commerce opened to the British Government by that fertile and valuable province, and by the influence and reputation to be acquired throughout India, from the possession of the great temple of Jaggernaut, and from the just and benevolent administration of the affairs of that temple with relation to the innumerable pilgrims, who frequent it from every part of India.

The acquisition of the port and territory of Baroach, and of the sea-ports belonging to Scindiah on the western side of India, which afforded to Scindiah, and to the French officers in his service, the means of intercourse with the government of France, and to the French an easy access to the Mahratta states, in a quarter where our military power was less formidable, and our political influence less firmly established than in other parts of India.

The degree of security afforded by the possession of the sea-port and territory of Baroach against any attempt on the part of France, to supply by that channel any native state with arms and military stores, or with officers for the purpose of disciplining their armies, and against the prosecution of any intrigues between the government of France and any native state, by means of the facility of communication which the sea-port and territory of Baroach might afford while in the hands of a Mahratta power, to the indefatigable zeal of French emissaries.

The additional security which our possessions and interests in Guzerat must derive from the possession of the port and territory of Baroach, and from Dowlut Rao Scindiah's renunciation of all claims on our ally the Guikwar.

The augmented sources of revenue and commerce, acquired by the possession of the port of Baroach and its district.

The improved state of our alliances with the Soubahdar of the Deccan and the Peishwa, under the provisions of the treaties of peace and of partition. By the combined operation of those treaties the power, territory, and resources of the Peishwa and the Soubahdar of the Deccan have been encreased and consolidated, and their means of discharging the duties of alliance have been consequently augmented. The confidence of those allies in the power, justice, and moderation of the British Government has been confirmed and encreased by their experience of the advantages of the alliance in the prosecution of the war, and in the ultimate arrangements of the peace.

The stipulations of the treaties of peace have in a considerable degree removed the causes of dissension, and the means of political intrigue between our allies and the Mahratta states, by precluding the future intermixture of their territories, and the consequent collision of their authorities; by requiring from Dowlut Rao Scindiah and the Rajah of Berar, the renunciation of their claims on the Soubahdar of the Deccan and the Peishwa, and by vesting in the British Government a right of arbitration in all cases of difference which may arise between those powers respectively. Thus the influence and ascendancy of the British Government in the councils of Hyderabad and Poonah have been encreased and permanently established, not by limiting the authority, controlling the independence, or reducing the power of those states, but by the operation of arrangements which have confirmed and corroborated their respective rights, authorities and independence, extended their dominion, consolidated their power, and augmented their resources; secured them from the vexatious claims, and litigious and violent interference of other powers, and established the sources of permanent tranquillity and prosperity within the limits of their respective dominions.

Our influence and ascendancy in the councils of those allies are now founded on the solid basis of their entire confidence in the equity and moderation of our views, and in their just reliance on our protecting power.

The elevation of the fame and glory of the British nation in India, by the splendid achievements of the war, and by the clemency, moderation, and public faith, which distinguished the British counsels in the conclusion of the peace.

The conclusion of a defensive and subsidiary alliance between the British Government and Dowlut Rao Scindiah, by which the British influence has been completely established at the court of that chieftain on the foundation of Dowlut Rao Scindiah's deliberate view of the real interests of his government, and by which the most formidable enemy of the British power in the late contest with the confederated Mahratta chieftains, has been rendered an efficient ally of the honourable Company.

The power acquired by the British Government under the general arrangements of the peace and the treaties of partition and subsidiary alliance, of controlling the causes of dissension and contest among the several Mahratta states, and of precluding the restoration of any of those states to a formidable degree of power, their combination for purposes injurious to the British Government or its allies, their communication and co-operation with an hostile European force, and their means of prosecuting dangerous intrigues with allies or subjects of the British Government.

The security afforded to the territories of our allies the Soubahdar of the Deccan, the Guikwar, the Rajah of Mysore, and the honourable Company, from the dangers to which they were exposed by the anarchy and confusion existing in the Mahratta empire, and by the character and habits of the contending Mahratta chieftains.

140. The general arrangements of the pacification combined with the treaties of partition, with the defensive and subsidiary alliance now concluded with Dowlut Rao Scindiah, with the general condition of our external relations, and with the internal prosperity of the British empire, have finally placed the British power in India in that commanding position with regard to other states, which affords the only possible security for the permanent tranquillity and prosperity of these valuable and important possessions.

141. By the establishment of our subsidiary forces at Hyderabad, and Poonah, with the Guikwar, Dowlut Rao Scindiah and the Ranah of Gohud, an efficient army of 22,000 men is stationed within the territories, or on the frontier of foreign states, and is paid by foreign subsidies. That army is constantly maintained in a state of perfect equipment, and is prepared for active service in any direction at the shortest notice. This force may be directed against any of the principal states of India, without the hazard of disturbing the tranquillity of the Company's possessions, and without requiring any considerable encrease to the permanent military expences of the governments of India.

142. The position, extent, and equipment of this military force, combined with the privilege which the British Govern-

ment possesses of arbitrating differences and dissensions between the several states with which it is connected by the obligations of alliance, enables the British power to control the causes of that internal warfare, which during so long a term of years has desolated many of the most fertile provinces of India, has occasioned a constant and hazardous fluctuation of power among the native states, has encouraged a predatory and military spirit among the inhabitants, and formed an inexhaustible source for the supply of military adventurers, prepared to join the standard of any turbulent chieftain for the purposes of ambition, plunder, or rebellion.

143. A general bond of connection is now established between the British Government, and the principal states of India, on principles which render it the interest of every state to maintain its alliance with the British Government, which preclude the inordinate aggrandizement of any one of those states by an usurpation of the rights and possessions of others, and which secure to every state the unmolested exercise of its separate authority within the limits of its established dominion, under the general protection of the British power.

We have the honour to be,

Hohourable Sirs,

Your most faithful humble servants,

WELLESLEY.

G. H. BARLOW.

G. UDNY.

64. Governor-General's reply to an address from the British inhabitants of Calcutta.

Justification of the War, and of the Terms of Peace.

Gentlemen,

The regularity, order, and deliberation with which the proceedings of your public meeting have been conducted, are conformable to the respectable character of this great settlement, and to the magnitude and importance of this happy occasion. The sentiments expressed in your address, are derived from an attentive observation of the events which preceded the commencing of hostilities on the continent of India, and from a correct knowledge of the principles which constitute the basis of the general pacification. You have considered the glory of our victories, and the genuine lustre of our ultimate triumph to be inseparably blended with the original justice of our cause, and with the moderation and clemency exercised in the hour of conquest. Satisfied that the public safety, and the national honour required an appeal to the sword, you have manifested a due sense of the national advantages obtained by the brilliant success of the war, and confirmed by the equitable conditions of the peace.

In this course of proceeding, I recognize with satisfaction and pride, the public spirit of British subjects. To commence or to continue war for purposes of aggrandizement, for the extension of dominion or power, for the gratification of pride, vanity, hatred, or irregular passion, is a species of policy, which no success can sanction, and which every British subject must abhor. Your birth, your education, your attachment to the laws and constitution of our country preclude your admiration of any system of public measures, however adorned by success, which is not founded in the sacred maxims of justice, humanity and honour. I therefore deem it to be a circumstance highly creditable to the character of this settlement, and of my administration, that I should have received from you this unsolicited, deliberate, and public testimony of your sincere and zealous concurrence in the principles of British policy, which have regulated my conduct from the origin to the close of the late memorable war. In the moment of alarm and danger, my duty required me to repel the menaces, insults, and power of the enemy by the most active use of our military force. In the full career of victory, and with the most splendid prospects of unlimited success, the same duty forbad me to prosecute hostilities to the extremity of vengeance, or to urge the fall of a vanquished enemy beyond the just limits of national security, and public faith. With these sentiments I accept this address, not only as a valuable mark of your personal regard, and an unequivocal proof of your honourable attachment to the interests of the public service, but as a solemn pledge of your unanimous determination to maintain in this distinguished settlement, that ardent and active zeal for the glory of our country in which consists the vital principle of the British empire, the source and support of our national fame and power, the origin of our triumphs abroad, the strength of our security at home, and the main bulwark of our defence in every quarter of the globe.

During the crisis which preceded the war I should have

viewed the situation of these possessions with anxiety, if I had not been supported by a firm confidence, that the spirit which you have displayed on this occasion, animated the counsels of this government and those of the governments of Fort St. George and Bombay; and that an equal zeal prevailed amongst the generals, officers and troops charged with the execution of my orders.

With united counsels, with an unrivalled army, with flourishing resources, with powerful alliances, and with a just cause, I was enabled to encounter and to surmount the difficulties which surrounded me, and to witness the rapid and complete effect of our military operations on every point of the enemy's strength. The vast extent, complicated system, and matchless success of the campaigns in Hindostan and the Deccan, cannot be contemplated without emotions of gratitude and admiration. The execution of the plans, which it was my duty to form, corresponded with the renown of an army, accustomed to victory, inured to fatigue and danger, attached to the just principles of discipline and order, animated by the memory of former triumphs, and commanded by generals who possess every qualification requisite to inspire confidence, to excite enterprize, and to ensure success.

Peace is the fairest fruit of victory, the brightest ornament of military triumph, and the highest reward of successful valour. The peace, which has been concluded, comprehends every object of the war, with every practicable security for the continuance of tranquillity. The object of the war was not to accomplish inordinate projects of extravagant conquest; not to subvert ancient and revered authorities; not to desolate flourishing provinces; not to plunder private property; nor to disturb the civil and religious institutions of contiguous states; nor to raise commotion in the bosom of established governments; nor to excite discord among powers connected by the relations of amity and peace. The object of the war was, to vindicate and to secure the just and legitimate rights, interests, and honour of the British government and of its allies against usurpation, violence, and rapine. The restoration of the legitimate authority of our ally the Peishwa at Poonah, the establishment of our ally the Soubahdar of the Deccan in his hereditary rights and dominions at Hyderabad, and the deliverance of the unfortunate and venerable emperor Shah Aulum from the hands of the Mahrattas and French at Delhi, were the earliest effects of the success of our military operations. During the progress of our arms, every endeavour was employed to mitigate the horrors of war, even in the midst of hostilities, and to extend security and protection to the utmost limits compatible with the safety of our armies in the field.

In the termination of hostilities, my solicitude has been directed to the important purpose of effecting a general pacification of India on principles of reciprocal justice and moderation. The power, reputation and dignity of the British empire in India, will derive additional security and lustre from the establishment of peace and good order among the native states. In the decline of intrinsic strength, inferior states may perhaps have gained a temporary safety by fomenting the discord of contiguous powers. In any extremity such a policy is unwarrantable and disgraceful; nor can permanent repose be secured upon such precarious foundations. In the actual condition of this empire, I am happy to declare, that the concord of the established native states, the independence of their separate authorities, the internal peace of their respective dominions, and the tranquillity and happiness of their respective subjects will tend to confirm and to fortify the power and resources of the British government, and must constitute the most desirable objects of British policy in India.

In pursuance of these principles, the treaties of peace provide the means, not only of enlarging and consolidating the resources and power of our allies, but of guarding the less powerful neutral states from oppression; of placing the illustrious house of Timur in a condition of competent affluence, dignity, and honourable repose, and even of admitting our vanquished enemies to the benefits of a general defensive alliance, calculated to secure them in the independent exercise of their actual rights, and in the uncontrolled government of their present dominions; to exclude usurpation, and to limit the several powers of Hindostan and the Deccan to the undisturbed cultivation of their separate resources, within the boundaries of their respective possessions. I trust that the result of this system will prove equally advantageous to our interests and to our honour.

The foundations of our empire in Asia are now laid in the tranquillity of surrounding nations, and in the happiness and welfare of the people of India. In addition to the augmentation of our territories and resources, the peace has manifested exemplary faith and equity towards our allies, moderation and lenity towards our enemies, and a sincere desire to promote the general prosperity of this quarter of the globe. The position in which we are now placed is suited to the character of the British nation, to the principles of our laws, to the spirit of our constitution, and to the liberal and comprehensive policy, which becomes the dignity of a great and powerful empire.

My public duty is discharged to the satisfaction of my conscience by the prosperous establishment of a system of policy, which promises to improve the general condition of the people of India, and to unite the principal native states in the bond of peace, under the protection of the British power.

WELLESLEY.

65. Lord Castlereagh to the Marquess Wellesley.

Doubtful policy of Annexations at the close of the War.

London, 21st May, 1804.
[Received 14th October, 1804.]

My dear Lord,

With respect to the great question to which your Lordship's last despatches principally relate, the pressure of other business has prevented Mr. Pitt from going into the subject in that detail, which he deems to be necessary previous to his forming a conclusive judgment upon it: he feels, however, all the importance of it, and has promised me to apply himself as early as possible to its examination. Until his Majesty's ministers have gone through the various despatches, and come to a decision upon them, and more particularly till I have had an opportunity of conferring deliberately with Mr. Pitt and Lord Melville, I should wish to postpone troubling your Lordship with any very detailed remarks upon this subject, in the new and enlarged shape in which it is now presented to our consideration. Hitherto I have been led to examine it as a question of alliance merely, upon the presumption, that the Mahratta empire was to continue to subsist in the same shape, or nearly so, as it has hitherto done, and in this point of view I own reflection has only served more strongly to impress upon my mind a conviction, that the principles of connection as laid down in the despatch from the secret Committee of February last, is upon the whole the best adapted to states so circumstanced as those composing the Mahratta confederacy, and that which I apprehend would be the most likely sincerely to dispose them towards a connection with us.

Your Lordship's instructions to the Generals Lake and Wellesley of the 27th June and 27th July, take up the question upon a much wider range, and suggest a comprehensive scheme for the partition and new distribution of the greater portion of the Mahratta territory. The splendid and unexampled success of our arms may probably have brought the execution of such a measure within the reach of your Lordship's power, and I am by no means at present prepared to convey to your Lordship a conclusive opinion upon the comprehensive scheme of policy laid down in those instructions; I wish only at present to draw your Lordship's attention to the marked distinction between the two questions. When lately reasoning upon the treaty of Bassein, we were considering how we could best connect ourselves with the state of Poonah, and what plan of alliance was upon the whole the most likely to conciliate, and include some of the other leading states in that connection. Now we are to examine the effects upon our Indian system, not only of that state being occupied by a British force, but of the other leading states materially reduced in territory being almost entirely encompassed either by the possessions, which it is intended should be acquired in direct sovereignty by the Company, or by the Rajpoot states, with whom it is proposed to enter into close alliance. The arrangement in question carries the Company's frontier far to the north and west of Delhi; it adds to their dominions in direct possession, exclusive of introducing their authority over the whole of the Mahratta empire, a territory considerably exceeding in extent the entire of Oude, and brings them in contact with Sikhs and other northern tribes, with whom it is proposed to establish connections throughout the Panjab as far as the Indus.

Such I take to be the question, which may have been presented by the result of the war to your Lordship's decision, and it is impossible not to feel that it is the largest in its bearings, and the most important in its effects upon our Indian system that has ever come into discussion. As an Indian question merely, it involves considerations of the highest moment, two of which I shall only at present slightly glance at. 1st. Whether assuming the whole to be the result of legitimate conquest, it does not in the great extent of direct acquisition, or indirect control thus to be acquired, contravene too strongly the system of policy, upon which the legislature has professed to act, by pushing our dominion beyond what the necessity of the case may fairly appear to warrant. 2nd. Whether it does not swell so largely and so suddenly not only our immediate possessions, but our dependencies necessarily included within the dominion of our army, as to run some risk of rendering the frame of our government complicated and unwieldy in such a degree as to hazard its becoming enfeebled and embarrassed in ordinary hands, and in weighing the latter consideration we should deceive ourselves if we expected to find a successor to replace your Lordship, capable of giving and continuing to the machine of Government that impulse which every department of the state so visibly receives from the mind that now directs it.

It is fair on the other hand to weigh the encreased security resulting from there being no longer any native power capable of contending with us in the field; an advantage, however, which I apprehend will not relieve us (if we may judge from past experience) from the necessity of carrying forward our military establishments, nearly in the proportion in which the sphere of our dominions is extended.

The question is not less serious as applied to the empire at home, not so much from any claims which it may furnish the enemy with, to limit our pretensions at a peace, to preserve in our hands in other parts of the world points of importance to our general security, but as founding our Indian system upon a basis so broad, as to create a doubt, whether such an empire can be fed with its due proportion of European troops from hence. When I recollect that the number of Europeans civil and military governing fifty millions of subjects, do not exceed thirty thousand, I cannot but look with anxiety to the extension of our native population and dependencies, whilst I am unable to see my way through the means of carrying forward, as our empire advances, even this apparently inadequate proportion of the governing principle. At this moment, I regret to observe, that our European is not to our native army more than in the proportion of one to seven; I have always been taught to consider this as too low a proportion, and it has been an anxious, though a fruitless object of my solicitude, since I have been in office, to obtain for India a larger proportion of King's troops. Having hitherto failed of completing an establishment of 24,000 men, which is deficient at this moment nearly six thousand of its complement, I am the less disposed to be sanguine in my expectations that an establishment of 31,000 men can be preserved complete, which is the force specified in your Lordship's second plan, which I take to be that which you conceive to be required for India, should the proposed arrangements in the Mahratta empire be carried into effect. I shall have occasion to address your Lordship more in detail on this subject by another conveyance; in the meantime I must fairly apprize your Lordship, that as it would require above 10,000 men to bring your establishment to the proposed standard, from my past experience of the difficulties which occur at home in raising the amount of force requisite for the public service at large, I wholly despair of such an army being in the first instance supplied, or subsequently kept complete for the service of India.

My object in calling your Lordship's attention to these considerations at the present moment, is not for the purpose of conveying to you by anticipation a decision upon the main question itself, but from a desire that you should be aware of the doubts that are to be well weighed, before it shall be finally decided on.

I cannot close this letter either in justice to your Lordship, or to myself, without acknowledging an error into which the result has proved, I had fallen from defect of information in my former reasonings upon Mahratta affairs. Indeed I believe others who had better means of intelligence were inadequately impressed, as well as myself, with respect to the extent of the regular force in Scindiah's service. It certainly has proved much more formidable than even Mr. Henry Wellesley, from whom I have on all subjects connected with India obtained the most satisfactory and accurate intelligence, conceived it to be; and although it would be doing injustice to the grounds of the war, to state the destruction of this force as being in itself any part of the cause upon which it was undertaken, distinct from the intended hostile application of that force, against the British power; yet I must reckon its dissolution and annihilation as amongst the most valuable services which your Lordship could have rendered; and I look upon the war as carrying with it in this collateral effect, the most solid advantages to our empire in the east. I will only add one remark on this subject, that it will still remain a question, supposing a close connection could have been formed with Scindiah as well as the Peishwa, subsequent to the expulsion of the latter from Poonah, whether the dissolution of this corps, of the leading officers of which, I have understood Scindiah had latterly become exceedingly jealous, might not have been accomplished by more amicable measures.

Believe me, my dear Lord,
with great regard,
yours most faithfully,
CASTLEREAGH.

P.S. Reserving the discussion of the military establishment in a larger sense for a future occasion, it may be satisfactory to your Lordship to be apprized, that in addition to 12 or 1500 recruits, which have already been despatched in the ships of the present season to join their regiments in India, having been completely disciplined and formed previous to their departure; the 17th foot completed to 1000 rank and file is now under orders, and will proceed in the next fleet appointed to sail in the end of June.

Your Lordship will have also learned before this reaches you, that a complete regiment of infantry, I think the 66th, was embarked for Ceylon in March last; exclusive, therefore, of this reinforcement sent to Ceylon, the army on the continent will have received in the course of the present season an addition of 2,500 men, which added to the 12,211 the effective force in December, 1803, will raise the King's infantry, exclusive of Ceylon, to about 14,000 rank and file.

C.

5. WAR WITH HOLKAR.

66. The Governor-General in Council to the Honourable the Secret Committee of the Court of Directors.

Origin of the War with Holkar. General narrative of its earlier operations[1].

15th June, 1804.

Honourable Sirs,

The position of a body of troops under the command of Jeswunt Rao Holkar, and the conduct and language of that

[1] The Governor-General's account of the circumstances under which the war with Holkar was begun is rather complicated. It is hoped that the paragraphs here printed will sufficiently explain the facts, and Lord Wellesley's view, and line of action in relation to them. A postscript, at the end of the Despatch, not relating to Holkar, has also been omitted.

freebooter rendered it necessary for the security of the British interests, and those of our allies, to retain the army under the personal command of his Excellency the Commander-in-Chief in the field for a considerable period of time after the conclusion of peace with Dowlut Rao Scindiah and the Rajah of Berar. The most important considerations of policy, and especially of economy, required that the earliest means should be employed for establishing the British army at the stations which might be fixed for its permanent position in consequence of the peace. And it was therefore necessary to bring Jeswunt Rao Holkar to some definite explanation of his designs, the uncertainty of which might have involved considerable expense by occasioning the protracted detention of the army in the field.

2. The result of these negotiations has finally compelled the Governor-General in Council to adopt the most decisive measures for reducing the power and resources of Jeswunt Rao Holkar.

5. Towards the conclusion of the war, Jeswunt Rao Holkar advanced towards the frontier of our ally the Rajah of Jyenagur, in prosecution of his habits of predatory warfare, and occupied a position with the main body of his forces, which indicated an intention to violate the territories of the Rajah of Jyenagur. Many other indications of an hostile nature were also manifested by Jeswunt Rao Holkar.

6. In the month of December, 1803, Jeswunt Rao Holkar addressed letters to his Excellency the Commander-in-Chief, which, though expressed in the spirit of arrogance, which Jeswunt Rao Holkar assumed upon all occasions, contained assurances of his disposition to cultivate the friendship of the British Government.

7. The conduct of Jeswunt Rao Holkar, however, at this period of time, was wholly inconsistent with these amicable professions. A letter was delivered to the Commander-in-Chief by the Rajah of Macherry, addressed to the Rajah by Jeswunt Rao Holkar, the object of which was to detach that chieftain from his alliance with the British Government. Further correspondence of a nature hostile to the British Government was discovered between Holkar and persons owing allegiance to the British Government. Authentic information was also received that Holkar had barbarously murdered three British subjects in his service on a charge of a correspondence between one of those officers and the Commander-in-Chief.

8. The replies of the Commander-in-Chief to the letters which his Excellency had received from Jeswunt Rao Holkar expressed the wish of the British Government to abstain from the prosecution of hostilities against him, declaring at the same time our determination to resist any attempt on the part of any chief or power to molest the allies, or to invade the rights of the British Government. The tenor of these answers was entirely approved by the Governor-General, who deemed it proper at this time to furnish the Commander-in-Chief with a statement of his views and intentions with respect to Jeswunt Rao Holkar, and with instructions for the guidance of the Commander-in-Chief's conduct with respect to that chieftain.

9. It appeared to the Governor-General to be indispensably necessary either to adopt measures for the reduction of Jeswunt Rao Holkar's predatory force, or to frame some arrangement with him which, without compromising the dignity of the British Government, and without violating the general principles of justice, or the acknowledged rights of other chieftains, might render it the interest of Jeswunt Rao Holkar to abandon his predatory habits, and preclude the necessity of an expensive permanent arrangement for the defence of our territories, and those of our allies against the incursions of that freebooter.

11. * * * The Governor-General in Council therefore ultimately determined to authorize the Commander-in-Chief to conclude an agreement with Jeswunt Rao Holkar, engaging on the part of the British Government to leave Jeswunt Rao Holkar in the unmolested exercise of his authority, provided only that Jeswunt Rao Holkar should engage on his part to abstain from any acts of aggression and hostility against the British Government, and from any invasion of the rights of our allies. For the accomplishment of this arrangement the Commander-in-Chief was instructed to signify to Jeswunt Rao Holkar, either by letter or through the channel of the vakeels whom he might be invited to despatch, that the British Government entertained the most amicable disposition towards him, and harboured no intention of prosecuting hostilities against him, unless compelled to that extremity by acts of aggression on his part against the British Government, or any of its allies. That the British Government was pledged by the obligation of its engagements with various chiefs and states in Hindostan to guarantee them against all exactions and demands unfounded in justice; that we did not admit his claim to tribute of any denomination upon those chiefs or states founded upon

the pretensions of the Holkar family, and that we should therefore be compelled to resist any such demands on the part of Jeswunt Rao Holkar. That with the consent of his Highness the Peishwa, the British Government would be disposed to arbitrate the differences subsisting between Jeswunt Rao Holkar and Cashee Rao Holkar, and to adjust the claims of the several branches of the family on the principles of equity and justice. That we were desirous of preserving peace with Jeswunt Rao Holkar, and that we would abstain from any unsolicited interference in his concerns beyond the limits required for the protection and security of the rights and territories of our allies, and that we merely required that he should manifest a similar conduct by abstaining from all measures and operations of a contrary tendency, by withdrawing his troops from any position which they might at that time occupy menacing to the British Government or to our allies, and by withholding all demands on the states or chieftains with which the British Government was in alliance; adding, that if Jeswunt Rao Holkar should advance any claims on those states in his individual capacity, the British Government would be disposed to arbitrate all such claims on principles of equity and justice.

12. The Commander-in-Chief was desired to exercise his discretion with regard to the degree of security which we might possess under Jeswunt Rao Holkar's acquiescence in the terms of the proposed arrangement; and the Commander-in-Chief was also authorized to employ the British forces against Jeswunt Rao Holkar, if the views of that chieftain should appear to be evidently hostile.

20. On the 16th of March two vakeels from Jeswunt Rao Holkar arrived in the British camp, and on the 18th of that month held a conference with his Excellency the Commander-in-Chief. It appeared that the vakeels possessed no powers to conclude any arrangement, but were simply instructed to state the propositions of Jeswunt Rao Holkar, and to acquaint him with the terms which might be offered by the Commander-in-Chief. The demands which the vakeels brought forward in the name of Jeswunt Rao Holkar at this conference were,

1st. 'That he should be permitted to collect the chout agreeably to the custom of his ancestors.

2d. 'That the ancient possessions formerly held by the family, such as Etawa, &c., twelve Pergunnahs in the Doab, and a Pergunnah in Bundelcund should be granted to him.

3d. 'That the country of Hurriana, which was formerly in the possession of the family, should be given to him.

4th. 'That the country then in his possession should be guaranteed to him, and a treaty should be concluded with him on the same terms as that with Scindiah.'

21. These demands were of a nature so extravagant, and in every point of view so entirely inadmissible, that they were positively rejected by the Commander-in-Chief, who expressed his surprise at the conduct of Holkar in proposing terms utterly incompatible with the propositions of the Commander-in-Chief and inconsistent with the tenor and apparent spirit of his late communications.

22. The Commander-in-Chief referred the vakeels to the former letters of Holkar, containing the terms on which his Excellency was authorized to conclude an arrangement with Jeswunt Rao Holkar, and required as a preliminary to any negotiation, Holkar's immediate return within his own territories. The Commander-in-Chief directed the attention of the vakeels to the promise expressed in Holkar's letter to the Commander-in-Chief, that he would withdraw his troops from their actual position, and asked the vakeels if he might depend on the performance of the promise. They replied in explicit terms, that Holkar would not consider that promise to be binding, unless the demands now brought forward by the vakeels should be complied with. The whole of the conversation on the part of the vakeels during this conference was distinguished by the most offensive spirit of arrogance and haughtiness. They appeared to entertain an expectation of inducing the Commander-in-Chief to accede to their demands by an exaggerated description of Holkar's military power and resources, and by insinuating that Holkar while soliciting the Commander-in-Chief's compliance with his demands possessed ample means of enforcing them.

23. After the conference was concluded, the vakeels conveyed an intimation to the Commander-in-Chief, that although the demands which they had brought forward were conformable to their instructions, they were authorized to recede from those demands and to accept on the part of Holkar any provision in lands or money which the British Government should think proper to assign to him. The Commander-in-Chief replied to this proposal by referring to his former proposition, and by again requiring as an indispensable preliminary to any negotiation, the immediate return of Holkar within his own possessions.

24. Shortly after this conference, the vakeels quitted the British camp on their return to that of Jeswunt Rao Holkar.

27. While the negotiation with Jeswunt Rao Holkar was depending, the Governor-General in Council received a copy of a letter, addressed to the honourable Major-General Wellesley by Jeswunt Rao Holkar, apparently written at the commencement of the month of February, 1804, in which Jeswunt Rao Holkar distinctly demands the cession of certain provinces in the Deccan, stated by him to be the original property of the family of Holkar, as the condition of peace; adding, in terms of insulting menace, that in the event of war, although unable to oppose the British artillery in the field, 'countries of many hundred coss should be overrun and plundered and burnt. That he (meaning the Commander-in-Chief) should not have leisure to breathe for a moment, and that calamities would fall on lacs of human beings in continued war by the attacks of his (Holkar's) army, which overwhelms like the waves of the sea.'

28. The insolent and hostile declarations contained in that letter, combined with the equivocal conduct of Holkar in his negotiation with the Commander-in-Chief, and his detected attempts to create rebellion within the Company's provinces, appeared to require the immediate adoption of measures of extremity against that chieftain.

36. Holkar levied considerable contributions in Ajmere, and attempted, though without success, to obtain possession of the fort. A considerable part of his force, however, remained on the frontier of Jyenagur, after having committed depredations on the territory of the Rajah. This circumstance, combined with the tenor of the letters of Jeswunt Rao Holkar and Bhowanny Shunker, with the renewal of those extravagant and inadmissible demands which had already been positively rejected by the Commander-in-Chief, and the evasive and deceitful conduct of Jeswunt Rao Holkar, throughout his negotiation with the Commander-in-Chief, precluded all expectation of effecting any pacific arrangement with Jeswunt Rao Holkar, on terms compatible with the security of the British interests and those of our allies, or with the honour and dignity of the British name.

47. On the 5th of February a vakeel despatched by Holkar had arrived in the camp of Dowlut Rao Scindiah. The minister of Scindiah intimated to the Acting Resident that the principal object of the mission of Holkar's vakeel was, to engage Scindiah to accommodate his differences with Jeswunt Rao Holkar, and

unite in an attack on the British possessions. The minister stated that Scindiah had signified his refusal to engage in the proposed measure in the most positive terms, adding, that even if he were inclined to violate his faith with the British Government, the character of Holkar and the experience which Scindiah had acquired of his utter disregard of the most solemn engagements, would effectually prevent him from forming any connection with that chieftain. The minister added, that Scindiah had declared to Holkar's vakeel that he had no inclination to attack Holkar, provided he would retire within his own territory, and abstain from committing acts of hostility against Scindiah and his dependants.

48. Adverting to the enmity subsisting between Dowlut Rao Scindiah and Jeswunt Rao Holkar, and to the solicitude of Dowlut Rao Scindiah to induce the British Government to adopt measures of extremity against Jeswunt Rao Holkar, the assertions of the Durbar of Scindiah with respect to the proceedings of Holkar, must be received with distrust. The Governor-General in Council, however, entertains no doubt of the truth of those assertions, the conduct of Holkar being entirely consistent with such a project of combined hostility against the British Government.

54. The ministers of Dowlut Rao Scindiah accompanied this report to Major Malcolm of the negotiations of Scindiah's vakeel at the camp of Jeswunt Rao Holkar, with the communication of a paper which they stated to have been received from the vakeel of Scindiah at Nagpore, containing the concurrent report of messengers despatched for intelligence to the camp of Jeswunt Rao Holkar, with respect to the declared intention of that chieftain to carry on a predatory war against the British possessions.

56. These combined facts demonstrate that such of the possessions of the Company and of our allies, as might be accessible to the troops of Jeswunt Rao Holkar, were the immediate objects of his predatory designs. But even the amicable disposition of Holkar would not have afforded to the British Government or to its allies any security against the predatory incursions of that chieftain's forces. The charges of Holkar's numerous troops greatly exceeded the precarious resources of his usurped dominion, and had hitherto been defrayed by the profits of indiscriminate plunder; and the continuance of the same system of predatory warfare directed against such territories as were most accessible and had not yet been desolated,

afforded to his tumultuous followers the only prospect of relief from the distress to which they were exposed by the inability of Holkar to provide for their subsistence.

57. By the extension of the system of political alliances which had been adopted by the British Government during the war, most of those petty states from whose territories Holkar and other freebooters had been accustomed to derive their plunder, were now connected by alliance with the British Government, which was bound to protect them against all aggressions.

58. The scarcity occasioned by the unusual deficiency of rain during the last rainy season, the operations of the contending Mahratta armies, antecedent to the conclusion of the treaty of Bassein, and the subsequent depredations of the troops of Holkar had spread desolation over the greater part of the Deccan and of the southern provinces of Hindostan. Holkar's predatory force, therefore, must shortly have been compelled for subsistence to violate the territories of the British Government or of states, for whose defence the British Government was bound to provide.

59. The plunder of the opulent city of Jyenagur, which would probably have been the first object of his depredations, would have afforded to Holkar a great accession of pecuniary resource, would have enabled him to retain a formidable force, and would consequently have augmented his means of plunder and devastation; and the employment of our military force for the suppression of Holkar's predatory operations, would ultimately have become indispensably necessary under circumstances of augmented inconvenience, difficulty and expense.

60. The recent peace with Dowlut Rao Scindiah and the Rajah of Berar has deprived of employment numerous bands of irregular troops. Persons of that description would either have been encouraged by the hope of plunder, or impelled by the necessity of obtaining subsistence to unite with Holkar in the plunder of the countries towards which he might direct his force. Under these circumstances, it would have been indispensably necessary either to maintain our army in a state of inactivity in the field upon a scale of expense not inferior to that which would attend the most active operations of war, or to have exposed the territories of the British Government and those of our allies, to the certain ravages of Holkar's troops, until the army could again be placed at a still more burthensome expense in a condition to repel their incursions.

61. The facts and considerations above stated sufficiently demonstrate that the existence of the horde of freebooters which Holkar conducted was hazardous to the tranquillity of our possessions and those of our allies, and that our continued forbearance was calculated to encourage his predatory designs, to augment his means of carrying them into effect within the limits of our own possessions, and to involve the British Government in great additional expense. The reduction of that predatory power therefore was manifestly a measure not only of just policy and necessary security, but of ultimate economy with reference to the finances of the honourable Company.

62. The Governor-General therefore on the receipt of the despatch from the Commander-in-Chief to which the 34th preceding paragraph of this despatch refers, issued orders to the Commander-in-Chief, and to Major-General Wellesley, under date the 16th of April, for the immediate commencement of hostile operations against Holkar in Hindostan and the Deccan. The Governor-General at the same time notified this determination to Major Malcolm, and directed that officer to apprize Scindiah of his Excellency's resolutions. The Governor-General in Council has the honour to enclose for the information of your honourable Committee copies of the instructions to the Commander-in-Chief, Major-General Wellesley, and Major Malcolm, to which this paragraph refers.

63. The Governor-General in Council now proceeds to submit to your honourable Committee a review of the military operations which have been directed to the object of reducing the power and resources of Jeswunt Rao Holkar, and of the success with which they have been attended down to the date of the latest advices which have been received by the Governor-General in Council.

64. On the receipt by Major-General Wellesley of the letter addressed by Holkar to that officer, referred to in the 27th paragraph of this despatch, Major-General Wellesley, judging from the tenor of that letter, and from the advices which he had received of the proceedings of Jeswunt Rao Holkar in Hindostan, that the Governor-General in Council would deem it necessary to direct the immediate prosecution of hostilities against that freebooter, thought it advisable to adopt without delay such measures as should enable him to afford the most effectual support to the operations which might be commenced under the orders of the Governor-General in Council by the

Commander-in-Chief from Hindostan. The principal possessions now occupied by the partisans of Jeswunt Rao Holkar under that usurper's authority in the Deccan are, the fort and territory of Chandore. Jeswunt Rao Holkar's partisans also possessed some territory in Candeish, and a few districts intermixed with the territories of his Highness the Nizam. The capture of the fort of Chandore would deprive Holkar of all those possessions. The siege of that fort therefore was the primary object to which the operations of the British army in the Deccan was to be directed. The state of the country however between Poonah and Chandore, which was suffering under the calamity of a severe scarcity, presented serious obstacles to the advance of an army in that direction, and Major-General Wellesley was apprehensive that unless the commencement of hostilities was postponed until the rainy season, he might not be able to conduct active operations against Holkar's possessions in the Deccan. Major-General Wellesley however proceeded to place the troops under his immediate command in a state of equipment for active service.

65. Major-General Wellesley was of opinion that considerable effect might be produced by the advance of the British troops in Guzerat against the possessions of Holkar in Malwa; and Major-General Wellesley accordingly adopted immediate measures for reinforcing the troops in that quarter with three battalions of native infantry. The probability that it might be the determination of the Governor-General in Council to station in Guzerat the force to be subsidized by Dowlut Rao Scindiah according to the stipulations of the defensive alliance, operated as a farther inducement to General Wellesley to reinforce the troops in Guzerat, which after the addition above stated, amounted to two regiments of European infantry and six battalions of native infantry, one battalion of which was 1,600 strong.

66. These arrangements, together with the sentiments of the honourable Major-General Wellesley on the subject of a general plan of operations against Jeswunt Rao Holkar, were stated by that officer to his Excellency the Commander-in-Chief in a letter dated 23rd April, of which a copy is annexed to this despatch for the information of your honourable Committee.

67. On the receipt of the instructions of the Governor-General, under date the 16th April, Major-General Wellesley issued immediate instructions to Colonel Murray, commanding the British troops in Guzerat, for the guidance of his conduct in the

operations which General Wellesley directed Colonel Murray to adopt without delay against Holkar's possessions in Malwa.

68. Major-General Wellesley, at the same time, directed the Resident at the court of Dowlut Rao Scindiah to require Dowlut Rao Scindiah to employ his arms without delay in the reduction of such parts of the possessions of Holkar as might be accessible to Scindiah's troops. The Resident was also directed to desire that Scindiah would despatch an officer on his part to join the army under the command of Colonel Murray for the purpose of procuring supplies for the use of the army under the command of Colonel Murray, and of taking charge of any districts captured from Holkar, which Colonel Murray might think proper to deliver to his charge. The Resident, with Dowlut Rao Scindiah, was also apprized of General Wellesley's opinion that a detachment of British troops should join Scindiah's army, and was desired to call on Scindiah to provide battering guns for the eventual use of Colonel Murray's army.

69. Dowlut Rao Scindiah had received the notification of the Governor-General's resolution to reduce Jeswunt Rao Holkar, and of his Excellency's intention with respect to the future division of the territory under the usurped authority of Holkar, as stated in the instructions to the acting resident with Scindiah under date the 16th April, a copy of which is annexed to this despatch. With every demonstration of satisfaction Scindiah promised to employ every exertion to co-operate effectually with the British troops against Holkar, and after some discussion with the Resident, consented to adopt the measures recommended by Major-General Wellesley.

70. The Governor-General in Council has the honour to annex to this despatch a copy of the instructions issued by Major-General Wellesley to Colonel Murray. That document, together with the letter from Major-General Wellesley to the Commander-in-Chief to which the 66th paragraph of this despatch refers, will afford to your honourable Committee complete information with respect to the plan of operations against Holkar to be undertaken from the Deccan and Guzerat.

71. The Governor-General in Council now resumes the narrative of the proceedings of his Excellency the Commander-in-Chief in Hindostan under the Governor-General in Council's instructions of the 15th of April.

72. During the negotiation with Jeswunt Rao Holkar the Commander-in-Chief had continued to advance slowly towards

the territories of the Rajah of Jyenagur for the combined purpose of accelerating the progress of the negotiation with Holkar, of protecting the country of Jyenagur from any hostile attempt on the part of Holkar, and of more effectually protecting the dominions of the British Government, and of our allies, against the predatory incursions of any bodies of troops in the direction of the Jumna.

73. A detachment of considerable strength, under the command of Lieut.-Colonel Ball, occupied a position near Canoon, a town situated about eighty miles south-west of Delhi, which was calculated effectually to oppose the attempts of any body of troops to penetrate in that direction into the recently acquired possessions of the British Government.

74. Previously to the receipt of the Governor-General's instructions of the 16th of April, the Commander-in-Chief had judged it to be expedient to adopt some arrangement calculated to arrest the progress of the depredations which Holkar, returning from Adjmeer, had actually commenced within the territories of the Rajah of Jyenagur, where he occupied a position which menaced the security of the capital of that province. Holkar had previously despatched his guns towards Malwa, but remained at the head of a considerable body of horse. With a view to protect the city of Jyenagur, and to give confidence to the government and troops of the Rajah, the Commander-in-Chief formed a detachment of three battalions of native infantry, under the command of the Honourable Lieut.-Colonel Monson, of his Majesty's 76th regiment, which marched towards Jyepore on the 18th of April. The march of the detachment was regulated in such a manner as to enable the Commander-in-Chief eventually to join it in one forced march with the whole army. On the 21st of April, the detachment under the command of Lieut.-Colonel Monson arrived in the vicinity of Jyenagur. The detachment was accompanied by an officer despatched by the Commander-in-Chief, with instructions to confer personally with the Rajah of Jyenagur on the means of opposing the designs of Holkar, and to persuade the Rajah to adopt the most vigorous and decisive measures towards the accomplishment of that object. The march of the detachment to Jyenagur immediately compelled Holkar to retreat. On the morning of the 23rd of April that chieftain suddenly retired from his position within the territory of Jyenagur, and commenced his march with great precipitation

to the southward. Holkar was followed in his retreat by parties of Hindostanee horse, under the command of European officers, who had been detached by the Commander-in-Chief for the purpose of observing Holkar's motions, and harassing his troops on their march.

75. A short halt made by Holkar of two days having induced the Commander-in-Chief to suspect that Holkar's retreat might be intended as a feint, his Excellency thought it proper to advance with his army, directing the detachment under the command of Lieut.-Colonel Monson to precede the main army with the utmost expedition. On the approach of the British troops, however, Holkar resumed his flight with the utmost precipitation, and with every appearance of apprehension and alarm.

76. Holkar continued his retreat with the utmost celerity until he arrived in the vicinity of Kotah, at which place he halted, the rapidity of his flight having placed him at so great a distance from the British troops as to relieve him from the apprehension of any immediate attack. The parties of Hindostanee horse which had been detached by the Commander-in-Chief continued to accompany his retreat, and had opportunities of engaging parties of his troops. Regular information was received by the Commander-in-Chief from the officers commanding the Hindostanee horse employed in the pursuit of Holkar, which described the situation of that chieftain during his flight to be in the utmost degree wretched and distressed. The countries through which he passed had been nearly desolated by his former outrages, and afforded a scanty subsistence for his troops, of whom great numbers deserted.

77. After Holkar's flight the Commander-in-Chief received a letter from that chieftain, recommencing protestations of friendship, and proposing to despatch a vakeel to the Commander-in-Chief. The Commander-in-Chief replied to this overture by referring to the propositions which he had originally offered to Jeswunt Rao Holkar's acceptance. Copies of those documents are annexed to this despatch.

78. The Commander-in-Chief continued the march for some days in the direction of Holkar's flight, the detachment under Lieut.-Colonel Monson still continuing in advance. His Excellency proposed to attack the fort of Rampoorah, belonging to Holkar, the occupation of which by the British troops would deprive that chieftain of his possessions in that quarter of India.

For this service his Excellency detached a force consisting of three battalions of native infantry, one regiment of native cavalry, and a proportion of heavy ordnance and field artillery, under the command of Lieut.-Colonel Don. The detachment arrived before Rampoorah on the . That fort was assaulted by a party of the troops under Lieut.-Colonel Don on the 16th of May, and carried with the greatest gallantry and rapidity. The despatch from the Commander-in-Chief, of which a copy is annexed to this despatch, contains an account of the assault and capture of Rampoorah, which reflects the highest honour on the officers and troops who were engaged on that service.

79. The rapid flight of Holkar, and his distance from the Commander-in-Chief, and from the detachment under Lieut.-Colonel Monson, rendered it highly improbable that any force acting from Hindostan would be able to bring Holkar to action. The improbability of Holkar's return to the upper parts of Hindostan, combined with the advices which the Commander-in-Chief had received of the forward state of preparations in Guzerat, and the conviction that the operations of the British troops in that quarter, in concert with those of Scindiah, afforded during the present season the only prospect of making an effectual impression on the territories of Holkar, appeared to render it expedient to withdraw the main body of the British army from the advanced position which it occupied, and to confine the plan of operations on the side of Hindostan to the adoption of measures for the effectual exclusion of Holkar from that quarter.

80. With this view, his Excellency the Commander-in-Chief directed Lieut.-Colonel Monson to form such a disposition of his force as should completely obstruct the return of Holkar in that direction. The force under Lieut.-Colonel Monson was fully equal to any which it was probable that Holkar would be able to oppose to it before the season for more active operations should arrive. The possession of Rampoorah, and of the territories of Holkar which depended on that fort, also contributed to oppose any attempt of that chieftain to return towards the position from which he had fled.

81. A large body of Scindiah's troops, which had advanced from Ougein to co-operate with the Commander-in-Chief, was instructed to press upon Holkar, and to harass him on his march.

82. The Governor-General entirely approved the arrangement which the Commander-in-Chief had resolved to adopt.

83. In the actual state of affairs, it appeared to the Governor-General in Council to be impracticable to carry on active operations against Jeswunt Rao Holkar until the close of the rainy season, when it might be expected that those countries which had been desolated by the ravages of the predatory troops of the Mahratta chieftains, in the contests which preceded the conclusion of the treaty of Bassein, and by the deficiency of rain during the last season, would afford subsistence to the British troops which might be employed against the territories and resources of Jeswunt Rao Holkar in the Deccan. The Governor-General in Council deemed this to be a favourable moment for withdrawing the British troops in every quarter of India to their usual stations, with the exception of the subsidiary forces which the British Government is bound to furnish to the Peishwa and the Guikwar, to Dowlut Rao Scindiah and the Ranah of Gohud. With this view, the Governor-General, on the 25th of May, issued the notes of instructions of which a copy is transmitted for the information of your honourable Committee.

84. The completion of the arrangements prescribed in the notes of instructions will enable the British Government, at the close of the rainy season, to reduce the power of Jeswunt Rao Holkar within due bounds, without entailing any further expense than that to which the British Government is exposed by the establishment of the subsidiary forces at Poona and with the Guikwar, Dowlut Rao Scindiah and the Ranah of Gohud; for which, however, the most ample resources have been provided by our subsidiary engagements with those states respectively. Your honourable Committee will remark with satisfaction, that the whole of the subsidiary troops in the Deccan, forming a force of upwards of 22,000 men[1], may be employed against

---

[1] *At Hyderabad*—1 regiment Europeans, 6 battalions Sepoys, 2 regiments Native Cavalry, 2 companies Artillery, 1 company Pioneers. *At Poona*—6 battalions Sepoys, 2 companies Artillery, 1 regiment Native Cavalry. *With Dowlut Rao Scindiah*—6 battalions Sepoys, 2 companies Artillery, 1 regiment Native Cavalry. *With the Guikwar*—2 battalions Sepoys, 1 company Artillery. *Total*—1 regiment Europeans, 3 regiments Native Cavalry, 20 battalions Native Infantry, 7 companies Artillery, 1 company Pioneers.

Jeswunt Rao Holkar, or any other disturber of the public tranquillity, without incurring any serious demands on the permanent establishments of your respective presidencies, or without making any considerable addition to the military charges in India. Your honourable Committee will not fail to appreciate the advantages of an arrangement by which the charges of so considerable a proportion of the established military force of India is defrayed by foreign subsidies. Adverting to the constant state of preparation and equipment in which the subsidiary forces must be maintained, your honourable Committee will not fail to estimate the influence and security which the British Government must derive from the establishment in the heart of the Deccan of so formidable a force, in positions calculated at once to repel external aggression and to secure the maintenance of tranquillity within your flourishing and extensive possessions in the peninsula of India.

85. On the   of May last, the Commander-in-Chief commenced his march on his return towards the British possessions, for the purpose of cantoning the troops at their usual stations, with such changes of position as the state of our newly-acquired possessions may demand.

86. It has been stated in the 74th paragraph of this despatch, that the Commander-in-Chief had detached a body of Hindostanee cavalry to accompany the movements of Holkar's troops. That body of cavalry consisted of two parties; one commanded by Captain Gardiner, an officer in the service of the Rajah of Jyenagur, and the other by Lieutenant Lucan, of his Majesty's 74th regiment.

87. On the morning of the 29th of May, Captain Gardiner, with the detachment under his command, arrived at a place called Balloo-Khery, where he received intelligence that a native chieftain, in the interest of Jeswunt Rao Holkar, named Tantia, was encamped with 3 battalions of infantry, 11 guns, 200 Mewattees, and 3,000 horse, at the distance of about 5 miles from Captain Gardiner's position. Captain Gardiner immediately addressed a letter to Lieutenant Lucan, who occupied a position about two miles in the rear, apprizing him of the circumstance, and requesting Lieutenant Lucan's assistance in attacking Tantia's party. Lieutenant Lucan soon joined Captain Gardiner's party, and the two divisions lost no time in advancing towards the enemy.

88. Tantia having before been apprized of the approach of

the force under Captain Gardiner and Lieutenant Lucan, was retreating with his battalions to a strong position, which they reached about nine o'clock on the 29th of May. In this situation they were attacked by the united detachments of Captain Gardiner and Lieutenant Lucan, which had been divided into four parties for the purpose of pressing the battalions on every side and of preventing their escape. At five o'clock P.M. the guns attached to Lieutenant Lucan's division arrived after a march of thirty-five miles, when the native chieftain commanding Tantia's battalions demanded a parley, and agreed to surrender his party on condition of being escorted in safety to the camp of Bappoo Scindiah, the officer commanding the advanced army of Dowlut Rao Scindiah, and of never serving against the British Government. These terms having been acceded to by Captain Gardiner, the battalions (surrounded by parties of Captain Gardiner and Lieutenant Lucan's cavalry) immediately commenced their march to Balloo-Khery. The force of the battalions, including 200 Mewattees, amounts to 2099 effective men. Tantia himself retreated with his cavalry, on the first appearance of the divisions under Captain Gardiner and Lieutenant Lucan.

89. On the 2d of June the Governor-General in Council received information that a body of predatory horse had made an incursion into the province of Bundlecund.

90. Lieutenant-Colonel Fawcett, who, by the illness of Colonel Powell, and the death of Lieutenant-Colonel Polhill, had accidentally succeeded to the command of the British troops serving in the province of Bundlecund, consisting of 450 European infantry, four battalions of sepoys, and two squadrons of native cavalry, had sent a detachment of seven companies of sepoys, a troop of native cavalry, and the park of artillery, under the command of Captain Smith, to attack a fort at the distance of about five miles from Lieutenant-Colonel Fawcett's position at Kooch.

91. On the morning of the 22d of May, the party of predatory horse succeeded in cutting off a part of Captain Smith's detachment, which was posted in the Pettah of the fort. This party consisted of Captain Feade, and Lieutenant Morris of the artillery, with two serjeants, two corporals, four gunners, and forty-one matrosses, and a proportion of Lascars, Mr. Hooper, assistant-surgeon, and two companies of sepoys from the 1st battalion 18th regiment, under Lieutenant Gillespie. The whole

of the party was cut off with the exception of 130 wounded natives, who returned to Lieutenant-Colonel Fawcett's camp on the 24th of May, two howitzers, two 12-pounders, one 6-pounder, and all the tumbrils belonging to the parks were also captured by the party of predatory horse. Captain Smith, with the remaining five companies of sepoys, retreated (with the loss of one man only) to Lieut.-Colonel Fawcett's camp. The party of predatory horse made several attempts to cut off Captain Smith's retreat but without success.

92. The detail of this disaster will be found stated in the annexed copy of a despatch from Lieut.-Colonel Fawcett, under date the 22d of May.

93. The party of predatory horse was originally stated to be fifteen or twenty thousand in number, and to be commanded by Ameer Khaun, formerly a partizan of Jeswunt Rao Holkar. From information, however, subsequently received, there is every reason to believe that this party of predatory horse did not exceed five thousand, that they did not belong to Ameer Khaun, and that the predatory incursion had no connection with the movements of Jeswunt Rao Holkar, but was a mere incursion of vagrant banditti for the purpose of obtaining subsistence by plunder.

94. The same party of predatory horse afterwards attacked the town of Calpee, and attempted to cross the Jumna, but was repulsed by two companies of sepoys under the command of Captain Jones; and was afterwards defeated near Kooch on the 30th of May by Colonel Sheppard, commanding a small party of troops lately in the service of Ambajee Inglia. Since that period of time, the predatory horse have entirely evacuated the province of Bundlecund.

95. Their progress, however, from Eritch to Calpee, and from Calpee to Kooch, the greatest part of which tract of country belongs to the Nana of Calpee, was marked by plunder, cruelty, and devastation.

96. Lieut.-Colonel Fawcett subsequently moved with his detachment in various directions from Kooch to the river Betwah, thence to the Jumna, and ultimately marched to Calpee.

97. In the course of the various marches of the detachment, the troops experienced the utmost degree of distress from the intense heat of the weather, and from the deficiency of forage and provisions, and the lives of several valuable officers and men were lost by the mere effects of excessive heat and fatigue.

98. The conduct of Lieut.-Colonel Fawcett on this occasion appearing to the Governor-General to be in the highest degree censurable, contrary to the positive orders of the Commander-in-Chief, and utterly inconsistent with the duty of Lieut.-Colonel Fawcett, and unworthy of the character of a British officer, the Governor-General directed that Lieut.-Colonel Fawcett should be placed under arrest, and that a judicial investigation into his conduct should be instituted. The Commander-in-Chief, immediately on the receipt of the intelligence of the destruction of the party detached from the force under the command of Captain Smith, had issued orders to Lieut.-Colonel Fawcett, directing that officer to deliver over his command to the officer next in rank with the design of instituting a judicial enquiry into Lieut.-Colonel Fawcett's conduct. The Commander-in-Chief has also placed Captain Smith in arrest, with a view of instituting an enquiry into his conduct, which appears also to have been blameable.

99. At this period of time, Captain John Baillie who conducted on the part of his Excellency the Commander-in-Chief all political and civil duties in Bundlecund, resided at Banda, a place situated to the southward of the river Betwa, and nearly in the centre of that part of the province of Bundlecund, in which the British authority had been established. The force with Captain Baillie consisted only of a small force of cavalry belonging to Shumshere Bahauder, about 200 cavalry belonging to Rajah Himmut Bahauder, and 1000 sepoys, under the command of an European officer in the service of the latter chieftain. Notwithstanding the consternation which had spread throughout the province of Bundlecund on the incursion of the predatory horse, whose numbers had been greatly exaggerated, Captain Baillie deemed it to be his duty to maintain his situation at all hazards, and the Governor-General in Council is satisfied that the preservation of tranquillity in the districts in our possession south of the Betwa is to be ascribed entirely to the confidence inspired, and to the subordination maintained throughout those districts, by the firmness, manly prudence, and fortitude manifested by Captain Baillie on that occasion.

100. On the day after the receipt of the intelligence of the destruction of the party detached from the force under the command of Captain Smith, the Commander-in-Chief marched from the position which he then occupied with the whole of the cavalry with the intention of crossing the Jumna, and

of proceeding through the Doab to the south-east, for the protection of that territory from the eventual incursion of the predatory horse.

101. In consequence of the late occurrences in Bundlecund, the Governor-General deemed it necessary to adopt an arrangement for the complete establishment of the British authority throughout the districts of Bundlecund, ceded to the honourable Company by his Highness the Peishwa, and for the consolidation of the civil and military authorities in that province, and for its future security against any irruption of predatory horse.

102. By the latest accounts, Jeswunt Rao Holkar had retreated to within a short distance of Ougein, still followed by the irregular cavalry, under the command of Captain Gardiner, and whilst the detachment under Lieut.-Colonel Monson occupied a position calculated to preclude the possibility of Holkar's return into Hindostan.

103. It may be reasonably expected that during the course of the rainy season now commencing the situation of Jeswunt Rao Holkar will be arranged in such a manner as to secure the peace of India. In the meanwhile the Company's provinces enjoy a state of perfect tranquillity, and the Governor-General in Council expects to be able to complete all the arrangements connected with the late treaties of peace and subsidy previously to the conclusion of the rains. With a view to accelerate these desirable objects, the Governor-General proposes to proceed by water to the upper provinces in the course of a few days, and hopes to be able to meet the Commander-in-Chief in the course of the month of August; after which event, the Governor-General will have the honour to submit to your honourable Committee a more detailed state of the arrangements connected with the late treaties of peace and subsidy.

We have the honour to be, &c.

WELLESLEY.
G. H. BARLOW.
G. UDNY.

67. Marquess Wellesley's Notes on the War with Holkar.

Necessity of re-inforcing Lieut.-Colonel Monson with European troops.

(Extract.)

Fort William, July 28, 1804.

2. This state of circumstances presents a favourable opportunity for striking a decisive blow against Holkar's power and resources. No expectation can be entertained of any accommodation with Holkar as long as he shall remain in any degree of force. In the actual situation of affairs, a defensive war on our part would be attended with the most serious consequences to our reputation and interests. It does not appear that either of the corps under the command of Colonel Murray, and of Lieut.-Colonel Monson, are sufficiently strong to encounter singly Holkar's force in the field. We must not depend on Scindiah for assistance, and whether his recent conduct proceeds from treachery, or from inability to put his troops into motion, it is evident that no aid will be derived from his co-operation in the prosecution of hostilities against Holkar. It is also evident that as long as Holkar shall be enabled to maintain a superiority in the field, it will be impossible for the detachments under Colonel Murray and Lieut.-Colonel Monson, to effect a junction of their forces, and a protracted and expensive war may be expected to be the consequence of this system of operations.

3. Under these circumstances it appears to be highly expedient to adopt immediate measures for the attack of Jeswunt Rao Holkar. The first step with a view to this desirable object is to reinforce either of the detachments under Colonel Murray or Lieut.-Colonel Monson, to the extent which may be necessary to enable either of those detachments to encounter singly the army of Holkar. The two detachments may then effect a junction, or adopt any other system of operations which may be deemed more advisable.

4. From the distance of Colonel Murray's detachment from the troops in the Deccan, it will be impossible to reinforce him from that quarter; and the force stationed in Guzerat will be required for the protection of that province against predatory incursions. It appears, therefore, to be necessary to reinforce the detachment under Lieut.-Colonel Monson, with a regiment

of European cavalry, and *two*, or if possible *three*, regiments of native cavalry, and with such a proportion of native infantry and European artillery, as shall enable Lieut.-Colonel Monson to advance against Holkar, and to leave a sufficient corps to defend the Mucundra Pass, and to prevent any incursion in that direction into Hindostan. It would be very desirable, if possible, to afford to Lieut.-Colonel Monson a reinforcement of European infantry. The Commander-in-chief knows how far he can rely on our native infantry for the attack of Holkar's artillery, supposing Holkar's artillery to be as formidable as it has been lately described.

5. If the native troops should be deemed unequal to the attack, what arrangement can be immediately adopted for the attainment of that important object? How can an European force be supplied to Lieutenant-Colonel Monson for the attack of Jeswunt Rao Holkar's artillery?

68. The Governor-General in Council to the Honourable the Secret Committee of the Honourable the Court of Directors.[1]

Progress of the War. Operations against Bhurtpore. Critical relations with Scindiah.

Fort William, March 24, 1805.

Honourable Sirs,

In our despatch of the 15th of June, 1804, the Governor-General in Council had the honour to submit to your honourable Committee a statement of the circumstances and considerations which had compelled the British Government to adopt measures for the reduction of the power of Jeswunt Rao Holkar, within such limits as might be consistent with the security of the rights and interests of the British Government and its allies, and of the successful commencement of hostile operations against the troops of that chieftain.

---

[1] A great part of this voluminous despatch does not relate, directly, to the war with Holkar. It has been therefore omitted. But it was thought desirable to insert the passages describing the crisis at Scindiah's Court, which threatened the renewal of hostilities between that Chief and the British Government. Nor was it thought necessary to reproduce the arrangements preliminary to operations in the Deccan, or the tedious and uninstructive detail of detached actions during the latter part of the war with Holkar, in Cuttack, Rohilkund, and Bundlecund.

In that despatch the Governor-General in Council communicated to your honourable Committee the general plan of opera tions originally intended to be pursued for the reduction of Jeswunt Rao Holkar's power. Your honourable Committee will have observed that the basis of that plan was a combination of the movements and operations of the British troops and those of Dowlut Rao Scindiah and the Guickwar, acting against the forces and territories of Holkar from Guzerat, Malwa, and the Deccan, while the main army under the personal direction of his Excellency the Commander-in-Chief pursued the enemy from Hindostan.

It was not expected that the whole of this plan of operations could be immediately carried into effect, and we apprized your honourable Committee in our despatch of the 15th of June, of the insurmountable obstacles opposed to the immediate advance of the army of the Deccan which was destined to occupy the forts and territory of Holkar, south of the Nerbudda, by the desolated state of the country through which that army would have occasion to pass. Until those obstacles, however, should have been removed by the return of the rainy season, we had reason to expect that the operations of the British troops on the side of Hindostan, combined with those of the allied forces from Malwah and Guzerat, would either effect the destruction of Jeswunt Rao Holkar's force, or would circumscribe the movements of the enemy in such a manner as to occasion the dispersion of his forces, or at least to prevent his return to Hindostan after the army of his Excellency the Commander-in-Chief should have compelled him to retire from the position which he occupied within the territory of the Rajah of Jyenagur.

Your honourable Committee has been apprized by our despatch of the 15th of June, that the detachment under the command of Colonel Monson had compelled the enemy to retire from that position. The Governor-General in Council further apprized your honourable Committee of the circumstances, which in the judgment of his Excellency the Commander-in-Chief rendered it expedient to withdraw the main body of the British army from the advanced position which it occupied, and to confine the plan of operations on the side of Hindostan, to the adoption of measures for the effectual exclusion of Holkar from that quarter, until the return of a season more favourable for active operations.

Your honourable Committee will have observed that his

Excellency the Commander-in-Chief judged the strength of the detachment under the command of Lieut.-Colonel Monson to be sufficient for that purpose, and accordingly directed Lieut.-Colonel Monson to form such a disposition of his force as should completely obstruct the return of Holkar into Hindostan.

This arrangement was founded on the following suppositions. 1st. That the army and resources of Jeswunt Rao Holkar had been greatly reduced and were daily diminishing, and that his military reputation had suffered from his precipitate flight. 2ndly. That the British force in Guzerat would be enabled to act offensively against the force of Jeswunt Rao Holkar according to the original plan of operations. 3rdly. That the forces of Dowlut Rao Scindiah were prepared to co-operate with the British troops on the side of Malwah and Guzerat.

The information which had been communicated to his Excellency the Commander-in-Chief, relative to the reduced condition of Jeswunt Rao Holkar's power and resources, was entitled to every degree of credit. The expectation, however, which his Excellency the Commander-in-Chief entertained that the British force in Guzerat would be enabled to carry on offensive operations against Holkar, was not consistent with the information which the Governor-General had received relative to the obstacles opposed to the advance of that force by the general distress of the country in which it would be required to act. Although the Governor-General was not disposed to place any implicit confidence in the aid of Dowlut Rao Scindiah, his Excellency had no reason to doubt either the disposition or the ability of that chieftain to prosecute with energy and effect offensive operations against Jeswunt Rao Holkar.

In our despatch of the 15th of June, the Governor-General in Council apprized your honourable Committee that this state of circumstances appeared to the Governor-General to afford a favourable opportunity for withdrawing the British troops in every quarter of India to their usual stations, with the exception of the subsidiary forces which the British Government was bound to furnish to the Peishwa and the Guickwar, to Dowlut Rao Scindiah and the Rana of Gohud, and for framing a disposition of those subsidiary forces which would enable the British Government at the close of the rainy season to reduce the power of Jeswunt Rao Holkar within due dounds, without incurring any considerable expence.

Your honourable Committee has already been furnished with

a copy of the Governor-General's notes of the 25th of May, prescribing the detail of these proposed arrangements, and your honourable Committee will not fail to observe that those arrangements were not limited to the object of providing for the supposed situation of affairs, but were calculated to meet the exigency of any probable occurrence, or future state of circumstances. Those arrangements were framed on principles calculated to provide not only for the contingency of an erroneous estimate of the reduced power and resources of Jeswunt Rao Holkar, and of Dowlut Rao Scindiah's inactivity, but even for the possible event of a combination of Jeswunt Rao Holkar's forces with those of Scindiah and the Rajah of Berar.

No doubt whatever can be entertained that the completion of the proposed arrangements would have secured the accomplishment of the expectation announced to your honourable Committee in our despatch of the 15th of June, of effecting the reduction of Jeswunt Rao Holkar's power at the close of the rains, without any considerable expence, since the stipulated strength of each of the subsidiary forces, combined with their assigned positions, was such as to render them irresistible by the troops of any native power, and to afford the certain means of pressing with success upon the enemy to whatever point he might direct his forces.

The reports which the Governor-General in Council originally received of the nature and extent of the incursion into the province of Bundlecund, of which the substance is stated in our despatch to your honourable Committee of the 15th of June, rendered it necessary in the Governor-General's judgment to direct the suspension of the arrangements prescribed by the notes of the 25th of May, and the vigorous prosecution of hostilities against Jeswunt Rao Holkar, and accordingly the Governor-General in an official letter, addressed to his Excellency the Commander-in-Chief, under date the 8th of June, 1804, stating the sentiments of the Governor-General relative to the possible consequences of the irruption into Bundlecund, and to the conduct of Lieut.-Colonel Fawcett, who commanded the troops stationed in that province, authorized the Commander-in-Chief to postpone the prescribed arrangements, and to employ every effort to reduce Jeswunt Rao Holkar and the predatory chiefs connected with him or acting upon our frontiers, or within the territories of our allies, in the pursuit of separate schemes of plunder.

Although it appeared by subsequent information that the reports which the Governor-General had originally received with regard to the extent of the force, which had invaded Bundlecund, were greatly exaggerated, that the number of the predatory horse which had entered Bundlecund did not exceed 5000, and that the invaders had abandoned the province, the Governor-General did not think proper to revoke his orders for the prosecution of active measures against Jeswunt Rao Holkar and his adherents, because the success of that predatory force in destroying a detachment of British troops, and in accomplishing its objects of plunder and devastation, and especially the retreat of the British troops, under the command of Lieut.-Colonel Fawcett, might encourage similar attempts on a more extended scale on the part of Jeswunt Rao Holkar, or of other predatory chiefs, and because in the actual positions of the several branches of our military force, the operation of the orders for the prosecution of active measures against Jeswunt Rao Holkar, and other predatory chiefs to a certain extent, was not calculated to prevent or even to retard the ultimate accomplishment of the arrangements prescribed by the notes of the 25th of May, if circumstances should render the immediate prosecution of active measures of hostility unnecessary or inexpedient.

The causes which have protracted the existing disturbances beyond the expected period of time, will be traced in the ensuing narrative of transactions and occurrences.

Your honourable Committee was informed by our despatch of the 15th of June, 1804, that his Excellency the Commander-in-Chief, with the army under his personal command, had commenced his march on his return from the vicinity of Jyenagur to the British possessions for the purpose of cantoning the troops at their usual stations, and in the 101st paragraph of that despatch it is stated, that on the day after his Excellency's receipt of the intelligence of the incursion of a body of predatory horse into the province of Bundlecund, the Commander-in-Chief marched from the position which he then occupied with the whole of the cavalry, with the intention of crossing the Jumna, and of proceeding through the Doab to the south-east for the protection of that territory from the eventual incursions of the predatory horse.

The repulse and retreat of the banditti, however, which had entered Bundlecund, rendered unnecessary the adoption of any extraordinary measures for the protection of the Doab, and his

Excellency the Commander-in-Chief pursued his march to Cawnpore, where the whole of the European cavalry and infantry had arrived before the middle of the month of June. On his march, the Commander-in-Chief cantoned the native troops in different positions on the right bank of the Jumna, and at such stations within the territory of the Doab, as appeared to be best calculated to provide for the security and tranquillity of our possessions in that quarter.

Our despatch of the 15th of June, contained a narrative of the operations of the detachment commanded by the honourable Lieut.-Colonel Monson from the period of its formation until the close of the month of May, the date of the latest advices which had been received at Fort William, relative to the operations of that detachment.

After the capture of the Fort of Rampoora by a detachment under the command of Lieut.-Colonel Don on the 16th of May, as stated in the 78th paragraph of the same despatch, Lieut.-Colonel Don leaving in that fort a sufficient garrison, joined the detachment under the command of Lieut.-Colonel Monson, with the remainder of his force.

With this re-inforcement Lieut.-Colonel Monson moved to the southward in the direction of Kotah, near which place he arrived early in the month of June. Colonel Monson was joined at Kotah by a body of troops in the service of the Rajah of Kotah, who had on many occasions, expressed a decided inclination to obtain the friendship of the British Government, and whose overtures to the Commander-in-Chief for the establishment of a more intimate connection with the British Government were stated to your Honourable Committee in our despatch of the 12th of April, together with the reasons which induced the Governor-General to suspend the negotiation.

Colonel Monson having advanced from Kotah, arrived at the strong pass of Mokundra, situated about 30 miles to the southward of Kotah, and having halted a few days at the pass for the purpose of collecting supplies, he resumed his march on the 28th of June, and on the 1st of July, arrived in the vicinity of the fortress of Hinglaisgurh; this fort, which is represented to be a place of considerable strength, is an ancient possession of the Holkar family, and was at this time, occupied by a garrison in the interest of Jeswunt Rao Holkar, consisting of 800 foot and 300 horse. Jeswunt Rao Holkar, who is said to have attached considerable importance to the possession of Hinglaisgurh, was at this time, encamped about forty-four miles from that fort with his whole force. Lieut.-Colonel Monson states, that these considerations induced him to attack the fort without delay: accordingly on the evening of the 1st of July, Lieut.-Colonel Monson detached a party of the troops under his command against the fort. The party (which was placed under the command of Major Sinclair) consisted of 9 companies of the 2d battalion 2d regiment of native infantry, with 6 six-pounders, and a party of Hindostanee cavalry commanded by Lieutenant Lucan.

On the 2d of July, Major Sinclair, with the force under his command, arrived within a short distance of the fort, which was assaulted on the evening of that day, and carried by the British troops with the greatest gallantry and rapidity, and with inconsiderable loss on our part.

After the capture of Hinglaisgurh, Lieut.-Colonel Monson advanced his position about fifty miles from the Mokundra pass, in which position he was informed that he would be able to procure supplies. Lieut.-Colonel Monson also expected to be able to communicate with Colonel Murray, at that time, on his march, with a considerable detachment of troops, from Guzerat, towards Ougein.

The corps under the command of Lieut.-Colonel Monson at this period, consisted of five battalions of sepoys, with a proportion of artillery, and of two bodies of irregular horse, under the command of Lieutenant Lucan, and of Bapojee Scindiah, amounting to about 3000 men.

On the 7th of July 1804, Lieut.-Colonel Monson received intelligence, that Jeswunt Rao Holkar, (who, since his retreat before the army of the Commander-in-Chief, had occupied a position in Malwa, having the Chumbul river between him and Lieut.-Colonel Monson's corps) had crossed the Chumbul river with the whole of his army and guns. Lieut.-Colonel Monson was desirous of attacking Jeswunt Rao Holkar, and moved towards the place at which it was stated that Jeswunt Rao Holkar had crossed the Chumbul river. It appears, however, that Lieut.-Colonel Monson found, that he had only two days' grain in his camp; part of his corps had been detached to bring up grain; one battalion of his force was on its march to join him from Hinglaisgurh, and he expected to be joined by an escort, with treasure for the use of his detachment. Lieut.-Colonel Monson had also received accounts from Colonel Murray, of that officer's intention to fall back on the Myhie river. This movement, and the causes stated to justify it, are subsequently described in this despatch.

Lieut.-Colonel Monson also received information, that the extent of Jeswunt Rao Holkar's force was such as to render it imprudent to hazard a general engagement. Under these circumstances, Lieut.-Colonel Monson determined to retire to the Mokundra pass. Accordingly, the whole of the baggage and stores, belonging to Lieut.-Colonel Monson's detachment, was sent off at four A. M. on the morning of the 8th of July 1804, to Soonarah, and Lieut.-Colonel Monson remained on the ground of encampment, with his detachment formed in order of battle, until half-past nine. At that hour Lieut.-Colonel Monson commenced his retreat, leaving Lieutenant Lucan and Bappojee Scindiah with the irregular cavalry on the ground, with orders to follow in half an hour, and to send to Lieut.-Colonel Monson the earliest intelligence of Jeswunt Rao Holkar's motions.

The detachment had marched nearly twelve miles, when Lieut.-Colonel Monson received intelligence, that Lieutenant Lucan's party had been attacked, at a considerable distance, in the rear of Lieut.-Colonel Monson's division, by the whole of Jeswunt Rao Holkar's cavalry. On the receipt of this intelligence, Lieut.-Colonel Monson formed his troops in order of battle, and was proceeding to the support of Lieutenant Lucan's detachment, when Bappojee Scindiah joined Lieut.-Colonel Monson's division, bringing intelligence, that the rear guard had been defeated, that many chiefs had been either killed or wounded, and that Lieutenant Lucan, with several chiefs, were taken prisoners. In consequence of this information, Lieut.-Colonel Monson resumed his march in the direction of the Mokundra Pass, where he arrived at noon on the 9th of July, without having been molested by the enemy.

The intelligence of the commencement of Lieut.-Colonel Monson's retreat reached the Commander-in-Chief at Cawnpore on the 18th of July. His Excellency immediately adopted measures for re-inforcing Lieut.-Colonel Monson's detachment, and for supplying it with grain, in the hope of enabling that detachment to maintain its ground against the enemy. His Excellency also made such arrangements as appeared to be best calculated for the security of the British territories against any incursion which the continued retreat or defeat of Lieut.-Colonel Monson's detachment might eventually encourage and enable the enemy to attempt.

Our despatch to your honourable Committee of the 15th of June 1804, represented the condition of Jeswunt Rao Holkar's force, according to the information then before us, to be in the utmost degree wretched and distressed, and his troops to be deserting in great numbers. Upon the ground of this information were partly founded instructions to the Resident with Dowlut Rao Scindiah, under date the 30th June 1804, on the subject of effecting an accommodation with Jeswunt Rao Holkar, through the agency of Dowlut Rao Scindiah, the substance of which will be found stated in that part of this despatch which relates to the transactions at the Court of that chieftain. Before the close of the month of July, however, the Governor-General in Council received information, that in the early part of that month, Jeswunt Rao Holkar had found means, probably from the remains of Scindiah's disbanded forces, to collect a large body of cavalry and infantry, with a large train of artillery, and was posted with the whole of his force in the vicinity of the Mokundra Pass.

The Governor-General in Council is not yet sufficiently informed with regard to the detail of transactions and events in the southern and western provinces of Hindostan, which immediately followed the retreat of Jeswunt Rao Holkar, to be able to explain, with accuracy and precision, the means by which Jeswunt Rao Holkar was enabled so considerably to augment the number, and to revive the spirit of his troops, notwithstanding the precipitation of his flight, the real distress of his army, and the apparently desperate condition of his affairs. The investigation of the conduct and movements of the British detachments employed against the army of Jeswunt Rao Holkar may be expected to elucidate this subject, and to afford the means of explaining in a satisfactory manner the causes of that change in the situation of affairs which produced the necessity of adopting a system of measures and arrangements entirely different from those by which the Governor-General in Council confidently hoped to accomplish the effectual reduction of the power of Jeswunt Rao Holkar.

The Governor-General in Council deems it proper in this place to state to your honourable Committee, the substance of the instructions which the Governor-General issued to his Excellency the Commander-in-Chief, on a consideration of this change in the situation of affairs, and the sentiments on which those instructions were founded.

It did not appear probable that Holkar would again separate the extensive force which he had been enabled to assemble, unless the necessity of his affairs should compel him to adopt that measure. A division of his force would evidently expose some part of it to the hazard of being destroyed by either of the detachments under Colonel Murray, or Lieut.-Colonel Monson, or by the troops of Scindiah, or of some other of the native chiefs.

This state of circumstances therefore, appeared to the Governor-General to present a favourable opportunity of effecting a decisive blow against Holkar's army.

No expectation could be entertained of effecting an accommodation with Holkar, consistent with the honour and interests of the British Government, while he should remain in force, and our perseverance in a system of defensive arrangements, under actual circumstances, was manifestly calculated to injure the reputation of the British power, and to encourage the hopes of the enemy.

Neither of the corps under Colonel Murray, or Lieut.-Colonel Monson acting separately, appeared to be of sufficient strength to contend with success against the whole of Holkar's force; nor while Holkar maintained a superiority in the field, could those two detachments effect a junction. No aid could be expected from Dowlut Rao Scindiah, who had entirely failed in performing the obligation of the alliance, (as stated in a subsequent part of this despatch.)

The immediate attack of Jeswunt Rao Holkar appeared, under these circumstances, to be obviously the most expedient course of policy. It appeared to the Governor-General that this object might be accomplished with most expedition and facility, by re-inforcing the detachment under the command of Colonel Murray, or of Lieut.-Colonel Monson, to such an extent as to enable it to contend singly against Holkar's whole force. It was obvious that when this object should have been effected, the two detachments would be able to effect a junction, or to undertake any other operation which might appear to be advisable.

The distance of Colonel Murray's corps from the station of the British troops in the Deccan, and the necessity of retaining in Guzerat the force stationed in that province, precluded the practicability of strengthening the detachment under the command of Colonel Murray in any material degree. The attention of the Commander-in-Chief was therefore directed to the means.

of re-inforcing Colonel Monson's detachment with a sufficient body of European and native cavalry, infantry, and artillery. The Commander-in-Chief was directed to exercise his discretion with regard to the expediency of placing this force under the orders of an officer of superior rank to either of those who commanded the separate detachments, and of investing the officer so appointed with powers to conclude, under favourable circumstances, a pacific arrangement with Holkar. The Governor-General in Council was still of opinion that great advantage would be derived from an accommodation with Holkar on the terms proposed in the instructions to the Resident with Scindiah of the 30th of June, but the Commander-in-Chief was directed to consider an early and vigorous attack on Holkar's force, and if necessary, the reduction of his power and resources, to be the main object of his attention.

The instructions of which the substance is stated in the preceding paragraphs were prepared before the Governor-General had received information of Lieutenant-Colonel Monson's retreat before the army of Jeswunt Rao Holkar. Previously however to the actual despatch of those instructions, the Governor-General received the intelligence of that event.

Although the retreat of Lieutenant-Colonel Monson's detachment rendered it probable that a necessity might arise for more extended preparations against Holkar than those prescribed by the Governor-General's instructions to the Commander-in-Chief, the Governor-General did not deem it necessary at that moment to issue further orders founded on the tenor of that intelligence. The Governor-General was satisfied that every exertion would be employed by his Excellency the Commander-in-Chief for the relief of Lieutenant-Colonel Monson's detachment; and that every necessary precaution would be adopted by his Excellency to provide against the effects of Lieutenant-Colonel Monson's retreat until his Excellency should receive the Governor-General's instructions, founded on the further information which might speedily be expected with regard to the operations of Colonel Monson's detachment.

The Governor-General in Council now resumes the narrative of the proceedings of Lieutenant-Colonel Monson's detachment.

On the morning of the 10th July, a large body of the enemy's cavalry, under the personal command of Jeswunt Rao Holkar, approached the position of Lieut.-Colonel Monson's detachment, and continued to increase in number until noon of the next day, when Jeswunt Rao Holkar dispatched a letter to Lieut.-Colonel Monson, demanding the surrender of the guns and small arms of the British detachment. This demand being rejected with becoming spirit, Jeswunt Rao Holkar divided his force into three bodies, which at the same point of time attacked the front and flanks of Lieut.-Colonel Monson's corps. The judicious position occupied by Lieut.-Colonel Monson, and the valour and discipline displayed by the troops under his command, enabled the detachment to repel this attack; and after various unsuccessful attempts which continued until evening, Jeswunt Rao Holkar drew off his troops to a position about four miles distant from Lieut.-Colonel Monson's corps, where he was joined by his infantry and guns, and where he encamped with the supposed intention of attacking Lieut.-Colonel Monson's detachment the following morning. The loss sustained by the British troops on this occasion was very inconsiderable.

Lieut.-Colonel Monson in his narrative of the proceedings of the detachment, states that in the position which his detachment occupied at this period of time, he apprehended that the enemy might pass his rear, and cut off his communication with the Mokundra Pass, and with the town of Kotah, which was the only place from which he could expect to derive supplies. Adverting also to the circumscribed nature of his own position, to the reputed strength of Jeswunt Rao Holkar's force, and to the supposed weight and number of Jeswunt Rao Holkar's guns, Lieut.-Colonel Monson did not consider his post at Mokundra to be tenable, and accordingly resolved to retire to Kotah, which place the detachment reached on the 12th July in the morning, after experiencing extreme fatigue from the inclemency of the season, and the inundated state of the country. The conduct of all the troops both in the contest with the force of Jeswunt Rao Holkar and under the pressure of the difficulties which impeded their retreat, is stated by Lieut.-Colonel Monson to have been distinguished by an invincible spirit of gallantry and firmness.

The Rajah of Kotah, alarmed at the near approach of Holkar's force, and fearful of the consequences of affording succour to the English detachment, was unwilling to admit Lieut.-Colonel Monson into the town, and declared his inability to supply the detachment with provisions. Lieut.-Colonel Monson was therefore compelled to continue his march the same day in the direction of a ford on the river Chumbul, distant about seven miles from Kotah; such however was the severity of the weather and the state of the road, that this short march could not be accomplished until the following day.

On the 14th July the detachment halted for the purpose of endeavouring to procure supplies.

On the 15th the detachment attempted to proceed, but the progress of the guns being prevented by the severity of the rain, it became necessary to halt.

On the morning of the 16th July, the guns had sunk so deep into the mud, that it was impracticable with every degree of exertion to extricate them. All the supplies of the detachment being expended, and the neighbouring villages being exhausted, Lieut.-Colonel Monson was induced to spike his guns, and to order the ammunition to be destroyed: at the same time, he wrote to the Rajah of Boondee, desiring him to dispatch people to extricate the guns and to deposit them in a place of security. Lieut.-Colonel Monson then prosecuted his march, and with the utmost difficulty reached the Chumbulee rivulet on the 17th of July. The rivulet was not fordable on the 17th, but on the 18th July the European artillery-men crossed the rivulet on elephants, and proceeded to Rampoorah.

On the 19th of July the rivulet began to rise; at this time the troops were absolutely destitute of provisions, but their immediate distress was relieved by a supply of grain, sufficient for the consumption of the detachment for two days, which was obtained from a village at a short distance by a party detached for that purpose. That party was attacked on its return to camp by a body of the enemy's horse, which was however repulsed with inconsiderable loss on our side.

In the evening of the 21st July, Lieut.-Colonel Monson detached a body of troops, under the command of Captain O'Donnell, to attack a body of the enemy's cavalry encamped at some distance. In this attempt the British detachment was completely successful; having destroyed the enemy's camp, captured several camels and 200 horses, and killed a great number of the enemy's troops.

By means of rafts, which Lieut.-Colonel Monson procured, two of the battalions crossed the rivulet in the course of the 23d and the 24th of July, and Lieut.-Colonel Don, with one battalion, was detached to a ford, a few miles lower down the rivulet, with a view to expedite the passage of the detachment. During the 24th of July, a large body of the enemy's cavalry having approached, Lieut.-Colonel Monson drew up the remainder of his detachment, amounting to about seven hundred men, and maintained a contest with the enemy until sun-set, when the enemy retired with the loss of several men and horses. Of the British troops, about twenty men were killed and wounded.

On the 25th of July, Lieut.-Colonel Monson detached another battalion to join the detachment under Lieut.-Colonel Don; and the rivulet having on that day become fordable, Lieut.-Colonel Monson crossed the remainder of his force, which at this time was totally destitute of provisions. Lieut.-Colonel Monson therefore proceeded with the division which had crossed the rivulet to the fort of Rampoorah, where he arrived on the 27th of July. Lieut.-Colonel Monson immediately adopted measures for supplying the two remaining corps under Lieut.-Colonel Don with provisions, and Lieut.-Colonel Don joined him at Rampoorah on the 29th of July.

At the period of time when the Governor-General in Council received the intelligence of the continued retreat of Colonel Monson's detachment, under circumstances of the utmost distress, and with the loss of guns, camp equipage, and baggage—the Governor-General in Council had also received information with regard to the state of Colonel Murray's detachment at Ougein, and to the conduct of the officers of Dowlut Rao Scindiah's government in Malwa (the details of which will be stated in a subsequent part of this despatch) which precluded the hope of deriving any immediate benefit from the services of Lieut.-Colonel Murray's detachment. In this state of affairs, the Governor-General deemed it necessary to consider, without delay, the most effectual means of resisting the force of Holkar, and of preventing the evils which might be expected to flow from the retreat of the detachment under Lieut.-Colonel Monson. The Governor-General accordingly prepared and transmitted to his Excellency the Commander-in-chief, on the 17th of August, a paper of notes, containing his sentiments and instructions on the course of measures to be adopted in the actual crisis of affairs, and comprising a general view of the objects to be pursued, and the means of attaining them with the greatest practicable degree of certainty and dispatch.

The judgment of the Governor-General was decided, that those objects could not be attained by any system of operations which should be limited to the measure of opposing the force of Jeswunt Rao Holkar by small detachments, neither possessing the component parts of an army, nor the power of moving with celerity. It was obvious, that detachments of this description, unless strongly posted and secure of an ample and constant supply of provisions, would be exposed to the hazard of being compelled to retire before an army of such strength as that which was then commanded by Jeswunt Rao Holkar, and that any partial success on the part of Jeswunt Rao Holkar would increase his reputation, and by the numbers which that success would induce to join his cause, considerably augment his strength, whilst a continuation of the enemy's success might be expected to depress the spirits of our own troops.

The first point stated in the Governor-General's notes of instructions was the immediate preparation of an army in Hindostan, equipped for light movements and of sufficient strength to defeat the main body of Holkar's force, to be commanded by the Commander-in-chief in person, and to be joined by a party of irregular horse, to be furnished by our native allies. The Governor-General suggested that the operations of this army should be directed immediately against the army under the personal command of Holkar, and should pursue Jeswunt Rao Holkar to the last extremity, if it should not be possible to compel him to risk an action; a necessity which it might be expected that he would endeavour by every means in his power to avoid.

It appeared to the Governor-General to be proper that a detachment should be stationed in the neighbourhood of the passes into the British territories in Hindostan, at some position between Agra and Delhi, for the purposes of defending those passes; and that the detachment should be of sufficient strength, both to preserve tranquillity in those territories, and to defeat any part of Holkar's force which might pass in the rear of the Commander-in-chief. The Governor-General observed, that a detachment thus formed and posted, might act as a body of reserve to the army of the Commander-in-chief, and might be strengthened from the garrisons of Agra, Delhi, Muttra, and other places.

The defence of Delhi against an attack from the enemy was stated to the Commander-in-chief to be an object of the greatest importance.

The position of an efficient detachment in Bundlecund was considered and stated by the Governor-General to form an important branch of the general plan of operations.

The Governor-General observed, that the situation of affairs in

Malwa and Guzerat appeared to render it desirable that the corps under the command of Colonel Murray should retire from Ougein towards the frontier of Guzerat, where it might occupy a position for the protection of that province, and co-operate with the main army acting against Holkar, if his march should be directed to that quarter, provided a force could be furnished to supply the place of Colonel Murray's detachment at Ougein.

For this purpose, it appeared to be desirable that the subsidiary force for Dowlut Rao Scindiah should be prepared in Hindostan, and should form a part of the army of the Commander-in-chief; and on his Excellency's advance into Malwa, should march to Ougein to remain in that position prepared to act as the events of the campaign might render advisable. According to this plan, Holkar would have been placed between five separate British armies.

1st. The army under the personal command of the Commander-in-chief.

2d. The detachment to be posted between Delhi and Agra, near the passes.

3d. The detachment in Bundlecund.

4th. The subsidiary force to be stationed at Ougein.

5th. The corps under the command of Colonel Murray to be posted on the frontier of Guzerat.

It appeared to be highly improbable that Holkar should be able to evade the attack of all these detachments; and it was the Governor-General's decided opinion, that the proposed plan of operations was preferable to any system merely defensive.

The speedy conclusion of the war appeared to be of the highest importance in every view of the question, and a vigorous and early attack on the enemy's main force offered the fairest prospect of such a result.

The Governor-General also communicated to the Commander-in-chief some suggestions respecting the mode of supplying his army, under the eventual necessity of pursuing Holkar into Malwa, and of drawing the British army to a distance from the countries from whence it was to derive its supplies.

A copy of these instructions, which, with a view to despatch, were prepared in the form of notes, is annexed for your honourable Committee's information.

The Governor-General in Council now resumes the narrative of the proceedings of Lieut.-Colonel Monson's detachment, which has been interrupted for the purpose of stating in the regular order of transactions, the substance of the instructions issued by the Governor-General to the Commander-in-chief, under the information possessed by the Governor-General at the date of those instructions with regard to the situation of affairs in Hindostan.

On his arrival at Rampoorah, Lieut.-Colonel Monson was joined by two battalions of sepoys, with four 6-pounders, and two howitzers, and a body of Hindoostanee cavalry, under the command of Major Frith, together with a supply of grain, which had been despatched from Agra by the orders of the Commander-in-chief, after his Excellency received the intelligence of Lieut.-Colonel Monson's situation at the Mokundra Pass.

Every practicable exertion was, at the same time, employed by Lieut.-Colonel Monson to obtain additional supplies, but the state of the country, and the vicinity of Jeswunt Rao Holkar's force, precluded all hope of collecting supplies to the extent necessary to enable the detachment to continue at Rampoorah. Lieut.-Colonel Monson therefore determined to prosecute his retreat to Khooshaul Ghur, where he expected to be joined by six battalions and twenty-one guns, under the command of a native commander, named Suddasheo Bhow Bukshee, in the service of Dowlut Rao Scindiah, and where he also hoped to obtain a sufficient supply of provisions, to enable him to keep the field against Jeswunt Rao Holkar. Before his departure from Rampoorah, Lieut.-Colonel Monson made the necessary arrangements for its security. A garrison was left in the fort of Rampoorah, under the command of Captain Hutchinson, of the Bengal artillery, consisting of the 2d battalion 8th regiment, and four companies of the 21st regiment, with four 6-pounders, and a considerable stock of provisions.

On the 22d of August, the remainder of Lieut.-Colonel Monson's detachment, consisting of five battalions and six companies of sepoys, with two howitzers, marched from Rampoorah, and on the morning of the 23d August 1804, reached the Bannas river. That river had risen in consequence of a heavy fall of rain, and was so deep as to be scarcely fordable for the largest elephants.

Three boats were found at the Bannas river, and Lieut.-Colonel Monson perceiving that the river did not fall so rapidly as might be expected, ordered Captain Nicholl, with the six companies of the 2d battalion 21st regiment to cross the river, and to proceed to Khooshaul Ghur, in charge of the treasure of the detachment.

Jeswunt Rao Holkar's cavalry appeared in large bodies in front of Lieut.-Colonel Monson's detachment on the morning of the 23d of August 1804, and encamped at the distance of about four miles from the British detachment.

On the morning of the 24th of August, the river having been found fordable, Lieut.-Colonel Monson began to cross the baggage, and one of the battalions. At the same time the enemy took possession of a large village on the right of Lieut.-Colonel Monson's position; but Lieut.-Colonel Monson attacked this post, and carried it with the loss of a few men. The river having become fordable in many places, the enemy's cavalry began to cross in great numbers, at different places to the right and left of Lieut.-Colonel Monson's position. The greater part of Lieut.-Colonel Monson's baggage had crossed, and Lieut.-Colonel Monson despatched three more battalions and one howitzer for its protection, intending to follow with the remainder of the detachment, when the whole of the baggage and camp followers should have crossed the river.

At four P.M. however, the enemy's infantry and guns arrived, and opened a heavy cannonade on the 2d battalion 2d regiment, and the picquets posted on the south side of the Bannas river. Lieut.-Colonel Monson immediately charged the enemy with this small body of men, and succeeded in carrying some guns. The troops of the enemy, however, encouraged by their superiority of numbers, rallied; and advancing with great celerity in different directions, the picquets and the 2d battalion 2d regiment were overpowered, and compelled to retire, and to abandon the remaining howitzer. Our troops suffered severely in this operation, and with difficulty effected a retreat under cover of the 1st battalion 14th regiment, which advanced to the bank of the river for their support.

The enemy prosecuted the advantage which he had obtained, and Lieut.-Colonel Monson was compelled to abandon his baggage, and to continue his retreat to Khooshaul Ghur, which he reached on the night of the 25th of August.

During the march to Khooshaul Ghur, the enemy's cavalry, supported by guns, made several attacks on Lieut.-Colonel Monson's detachment, but without success; Captain Nicholl, with the treasure placed under his charge, had arrived at that place on the preceding day.

It has been already stated that on his arrival at Khooshaul Ghur, Lieut.-Colonel Monson expected to be joined by a considerable force under the command of Suddasheo Bhow Bukshee, in the service of Dowlut Rao Scindiah. Immediately after the arrival of Captain Nicholl however at Khooshaul Ghur, Suddasheo Bhow Bukshee, with the force under his command, attacked Captain Nicholl's detachment, but was repulsed with considerable loss.

On the morning of the 26th of August, the whole of the enemy's cavalry encamped in separate bodies, surrounding Lieut.-General Monson's detachment. A correspondence was at this period detected between some of the native officers of Lieut.-Colonel Monson's corps and Jeswunt Rao Holkar, the object of which was to encourage among our troops a spirit of desertion. The most vigorous measures were immediately adopted to render these attempts abortive, but notwithstanding every effort on the part of Lieut.-Colonel Monson, and of his officers, nearly two companies from the 1st battalion 14th regiment, and a large proportion of the Hindoostanee cavalry deserted to the enemy.

Disappointed in his expectation of receiving support from the troops of Dowlut Rao Scindiah, and of obtaining supplies at Khooshaul Ghur, and destitute of every species of equipment necessary to enable the detachment to continue at Khooshaul Ghur, Lieut.-Colonel Monson was compelled to prosecute his retreat, and accordingly, on the 26th of August, at seven P.M. Lieut.-Colonel Monson moved from the Fort of Khooshaul Ghur, and formed his detachment into an oblong square, having previously spiked the remaining howitzer.

During the night of the 26th of August, and the greater part of the 27th, the enemy's cavalry, supported as before by guns, attempted several times to penetrate the detachment, but could not make the least impression on this compact body of men. On the night of the 27th of August, Lieut.-Colonel Monson took possession of the ruined fort of Hindown, and at one A.M. on the 28th continued his retreat towards Agra. As soon as the detachment had cleared the ravines near Hindown, the enemy's cavalry charged the detachment with extreme violence in three separate bodies, but was received by the sepoys with determined coolness and bravery. The sepoys reserved their fire until the enemy's cavalry had come almost within reach of the bayonet, and then gave their fire with such signal effect, as to compel the enemy to retire in every direction.

Lieut.-Colonel Monson reached the Biana Pass about sunset on the 28th August. The troops were almost exhausted with fatigue and hunger, and Lieut.-Colonel Monson halted with an intention to remain during the night at the entrance of the Pass. The enemy however succeeded in bringing up some guns and opened a heavy fire, which compelled Lieut.-Colonel Monson to continue his retreat towards Agra. The detachment reached the town of Biana at nine P.M. on the 28th of August. The night was dark, and the camp followers, with such baggage as remained with the detachment having mixed with the line, the troops were thrown into confusion. It was impossible to restore order, and the different corps retreated in great disorder to Agra, which they all reached by the 31st August. The enemy followed as far as Futtypoor, in straggling parties for the purpose of plundering, but made no united attack after the 28th. During the whole of this unfortunate retreat the officers and troops of the detachment displayed the greatest perseverance, fortitude and gallantry; and in the different engagements with the enemy they manifested a degree of courage and determined resolution which, under less adverse circumstances, would have ensured the most distinguished success.

To the retreat of the detachment under the command of Lieut.-Colonel Monson, under circumstances of extreme difficulty and distress, occasioned partly by the state of the country and the unusual inclemency of the season, and partly by the failure of supplies, must be attributed both the necessity of suspending the establishment of the subsidiary forces prescribed by the Governor-General's notes of the 25th of May, and the means which Jeswunt Rao Holkar acquired of maintaining a contest with the British power.

Your honourable Committee will observe from the tenor of those notes, that the security of the detachment under the command of Lieut.-Colonel Monson was a peculiar object of the Governor-General's solicitude; the Governor-General having suggested the necessity either of withdrawing that detachment, or of adding to its strength by a corps of Europeans and a proportion of cavalry. The Governor-General at the same time stated his opinion in favour of the former measure, because no hope could reasonably be entertained of employing that detachment in active operations against the force of Jeswunt Rao Holkar until the close of the rainy season.

The Governor-General in Council is not yet enabled to state

the precise causes which precluded the adoption of one or other of those measures. It is the intention however of the Commander-in-Chief to furnish the Governor-General with detailed information upon this point at the earliest practicable period of time. The Governor-General in Council is also unable at this time distinctly to explain the causes of the retreat of Lieut.-Colonel Monson's detachment under circumstances of difficulty and distress. Those causes must be sought in the conduct and operations of the several detachments actively employed against the forces of Jeswunt Rao Holkar, which the Governor-General in Council is not yet enabled to state with accuracy and precision; the distance of the scene of action, and the necessity of accelerating the operations of the main body of the army, having precluded the possibility of completing any satisfactory investigation of the movements of those detachments. Every effort, however, will be employed to submit to your honourable Committee with the least practicable delay, all the details connected with such transactions as may now appear to be imperfectly related.

If circumstances had admitted the reinforcement of the detachment under Lieut.-Colonel Monson, or its immediate recal in the manner suggested by the Governor-General on the 25th of May, either the return of Jeswunt Rao Holkar's force to the north of Hindostan would have been prevented, or his force would have returned under circumstances which would have facilitated the early reduction of his power. But the retreat of Lieut.-Colonel Monson's detachment, and the disasters which attended it, enabled Jeswunt Rao Holkar to return with the whole body of his forces to Hindostan under circumstances of advantage.

Although no apprehension could reasonably be entertained of any incursion into the provinces of Benares, Behar, Bengal, or Cuttack, the retreat of Colonel Monson's detachment under such disastrous circumstances, and the approach of Jeswunt Rao Holkar's army to the Jumna, rendered it expedient in the Governor-General's judgment upon general principles of prudence, to provide by every practicable arrangement for the protection of the western frontier of those provinces.

With this view, instructions were issued on the 12th of September 1804, to the magistrates of the several districts, extending from Midnapore to Mirzapore, and to the officers commanding at Midnapore, in Ramgurh, and at Benares, renewing the measures of precaution which were adopted during the late war with Dowlut Rao Scindiah and the Rajah of Berar, for the purpose of preventing the irruption of marauders into the Company's possessions, as described in the 618th and following paragraphs of our despatch of the 12th of April 1804. The defence of the province of Cuttack was entrusted to Colonel Harcourt, the officer commanding the forces in that province, and instructions were issued to Colonel Harcourt, under date the 19th of September 1804, directing him to regulate his conduct by the principles stated in the orders which were issued to the officers entrusted with the defence of the frontier during the late war, as far as those principles were applicable to the protection of the province of Cuttack.

Jeswunt Rao Holkar continued to advance with the whole of his cavalry, and having halted some days at Biana, prosecuted his march toward the Jumna, and encamped with the whole of his force at a short distance from Muttra, his cavalry being posted in numerous divisions over the whole of the adjacent territory.

The continued retreat of Colonel Monson's detachment, and the advance of the main body of Holkar's army towards the banks of the Jumna, necessarily occasioned a deviation from the plan of operations prescribed in the Governor-General's notes.

Under the Governor-General's instructions, his Excellency the Commander-in-Chief issued orders for assembling near Agra a large force of native infantry and cavalry, and for placing that force in a state of equipment to take the field. His Excellency also made preparations at Cawnpore for enabling the European cavalry and infantry to move at the earliest practicable period of time.

The march of these corps, however, was unavoidably retarded by the inclemency of the season, but no inconvenience was occasioned by this delay; the state of the Jumna precluding any attempt on the part of the enemy to molest our possessions in the Doab. His Excellency the Commander-in-Chief commenced his march from Cawnpore, with the whole of the European cavalry and infantry on the 3d of September, and on the 22d of that month arrived at Agra. His Excellency immediately proceeded to Secundra, about six miles from Agra, where the troops which had been assembled at the latter place were encamped. The force assembled at Secundra consisted of three regiments of European light dragoons, five regiments of native cavalry, and the horse artillery, his Majesty's 76th regiment of foot, the flank companies of his Majesty's 22d regiment of foot, and ten battalions of native infantry, and the usual proportion of artillery, &c.

The necessity of waiting for supplies prevented the Commander-in-Chief from marching from Secundra until the 1st of October, on which day the army advanced towards the enemy who had remained in the vicinity of Muttra, and had at different periods appeared to entertain the opposite designs of hazarding an engagement in the field, and of retiring from the banks of the Jumna.

On the approach of the British army, the enemy drew off to the north-west along the bank of the Jumna. His infantry and guns appeared to take the direction of Delhi, and his cavalry which remained in the rear, attempted to obstruct the march of the British troops and to cut off the baggage. They did not, however, succeed in effecting any object of importance. The Commander-in-Chief made three different attempts to engage the cavalry of the enemy, commanded by Holkar in person, on the 2d, 7th, and 10th of October, but the dispersed position of the enemy's cavalry, and the celerity of the enemy's retreat on the approach of the British troops, rendered ineffectual his Excellency's utmost endeavours to compel the enemy to maintain an action.

The manifest determination of the enemy's cavalry to avoid an action with the British troops, induced the Commander-in-Chief to suspend his operations against the enemy's cavalry, until by the defeat of the infantry and guns, the cavalry should become the only object of pursuit.

Previously to his march from Secundra, the Commander-in-Chief had detached a force under the command of Captain Worsley into the Doab, for the purpose of preserving tranquillity and of expelling a party of predatory horse which had crossed the Jumna at Muttra and plundered the neighbouring country. On the approach of our troops, the enemy re-crossed the river. Captain Worsley's corps was afterwards stationed at Muttra, where that officer was employed in collecting and forwarding supplies, in maintaining the tranquillity of the neighbouring country, and in protecting the important post of Muttra and the passage of the Jumna against any attempt of the enemy.

In the mean while the infantry and artillery of Holkar continued to advance to Delhi, before which city they arrived on the morning of the 8th of October.

The city of Delhi is of great extent, and its defences consist merely of a high wall, in many places in a ruinous condition. The garrison consisted of only one battalion and four companies of regular sepoys, a battalion of irregulars, and a corps of matchlockmen.

On the day of the enemy's arrival at the city of Delhi, a heavy cannonade was opened upon the walls, but the distance of the batteries rendered it of no effect. On the 9th, the enemy having approached nearer to the walls, opened a battery with considerable effect. Lieut.-Colonel Burn, the officer commanding the garrison, finding that the enemy's fire would soon effect a practicable breach in the walls, resolved to interrupt the operations of the besiegers by a sally from the garrison. Colonel Burn accordingly prepared a party, consisting of 200 men of the battalion under his command, and 150 men of the irregular troops, and placed the whole under the command of Lieutenant Rose.

This party proceeded on the evening of the 10th to storm the enemy's battery, and completely succeeded in obtaining possession of it, and having spiked the guns, returned with little loss; the loss of the enemy is supposed to have been considerable. The enemy's fire was renewed the next morning, but without much effect, being soon silenced by the fire from a battery which had been erected on one of the bastions of the city. The enemy subsequently changed the point of attack, and opened batteries on another part of the wall, in which they speedily effected a breach. By the exertions of the garrison, however, the enemy was prevented from taking advantage of the breach. On the 14th, in the morning, a general assault was made by the whole force of the enemy, but without success, the enemy being repulsed with heavy loss.

On the following day, the enemy despairing of success in his attempts to carry the place, and intimidated by the approach of the Commander-in-Chief, who, on receiving intelligence of the design of the enemy to attack the city of Delhi, advanced with the utmost rapidity to the relief of the garrison, drew off the whole of his infantry and guns, and retired from the vicinity of Delhi.

The Governor-General in Council reflects with sentiments of the highest admiration and applause, on the skill, activity, judgment, and gallantry, which distinguished the conduct of the officers and men of the garrison of Delhi in defending that city under circumstances of such extreme disadvantage, difficulty, and danger, against the efforts of the enemy's whole force of infantry and guns, continued with unremitted exertion during a period of seven days.

On the 18th of October, the Commander-in-Chief, with the army under his personal command, arrived at Delhi. His Excellency entertained a confident expectation of being enabled to pursue the enemy without delay. An unexpected delay in the arrival of supplies, however, compelled the Commander-in-Chief to halt at Delhi for a few days; during this period, the infantry and artillery of Holkar continued their retreat from Delhi, and proceeded by a circuitous route through the hills towards Deig, a strong fort belonging to the Rajah of Bhurtpore, and situated about twenty-five miles in a westerly direction from Muttra.

On the 31st of October, the Commander-in-Chief having received information that Jeswunt Rao Holkar, with the whole body of his cavalry had crossed the Jumna at a ford a short distance above Delhi, determined to divide his force, to detach the infantry and artillery of the army, with two regiments of native cavalry, under the command of Major-General Frazer, the second in command, in the direction of the enemy's infantry and guns, and to proceed in person with the whole of the European dragoons, and three regiments of native cavalry, the horse and artillery and the reserve of the army, consisting of two companies of European and three battalions of native infantry in pursuit of the enemy's cavalry which had entered the Doab.

The object of the Commander-in-Chief by this combined and judicious movement, was, to compel both Holkar's infantry and cavalry to risk an action with the British troops, or to fly from Hindostan, under such circumstances of ignominy and distress as must be attended with the most fatal consequences to the cause of the enemy.

In pursuance of this plan, his Excellency crossed the Jumna on the 1st of November, with the force above described, and followed the direction of the enemy's cavalry. Holkar's first object appeared to be, to cut off a battalion of native infantry, commanded by Colonel Burn, which had been detached into Sehaurunpore after the retreat of the enemy from Delhi, for the purpose of suppressing the disturbances which had been occasioned in that quarter of the Doab, partly by the insurrection of refractory Zemindars, and partly by the incursions of several petty chieftains of the tribe of Seiks, instigated by the intrigues of Jeswunt Rao Holkar, and allured by the hopes of plunder. Holkar attacked the battalion, but was unable to make any impression on it, and was obliged to desist after having sustained considerable loss.

Jeswunt Rao Holkar proceeded for a few days in a northerly direction, with the supposed intention of crossing the Ganges into Rohilcund, at a ford on that river not far distant from Hurdwar. But being closely pressed by the Commander-in-Chief, he suddenly changed his route and proceeded by rapid marches down the Doab. The Commander-in-Chief continued to pursue the enemy with a degree of unexampled rapidity and vigour which prevented the enemy from extending his ravages beyond the narrow limits of his immediate track.

Holkar continued to fly down the Doab by rapid marches, until his arrival at Furruckabad on the 16th of November. On the same day, the Commander-in-Chief who had followed Holkar daily at the distance of one march, in his rear, arrived at Alligunge, distant from Futtyghur thirty-four miles, after a march of more than twenty miles.

The Commander-in-Chief being apprized of Holkar's march in the direction of Furruckabad, resolved to pursue him without delay in the hope of preventing the plunder of that city, and of the cantonments of Futtyghur, and of compelling the enemy to risk an engagement. His Excellency therefore, after halting at Alligunge only a few hours to refresh his men and horses, resumed his march at nine o'clock in the evening of the same day. The success of this most active, able, and enterprizing operation was complete and decisive. The British cavalry arrived in the vicinity of Holkar's camp at day-break on the 17th of November, after a march of fifty-eight miles performed within twenty-four hours, and completely surprized the enemy. After the discharge of a few rounds of grape from the horse artillery, the British cavalry charged the enemy's troops in every direction, and routed them with great slaughter. The British cavalry pursued the enemy for many miles, destroying great numbers, and compelling the survivors to disperse in all directions. The whole of the enemy's cattle and supplies were captured by the British troops. Holkar himself narrowly escaped by an early flight at the first approach of the British troops. Our loss was very small, and no officer was either killed or wounded. Holkar with the remains of his cavalry fled with the utmost precipitation and apparent consternation towards the Jumna, which he forded at Mahoba and proceeded towards Dieg.

Including the pursuit of the enemy on the 17th of November, the British troops marched a distance of seventy miles from their movement on the morning of the 16th, until they took up their ground on the 17th, and had it not been for the accidental explosion of a tumbril, belonging to the British troops, within a few moments before the approach of the Commander-in-Chief to Holkar's position, no doubt can be entertained that Holkar himself would either have been killed, or taken prisoner.

The Commander-in-Chief having halted two days to refresh his men and horses, resumed his march in pursuit of the enemy on the 20th of November. Holkar, however enabled, escaped across the Jumna.

The Governor-General in Council is convinced, that your honourable Committee will contemplate with satisfaction, this decisive proof of the progressive improvement of our cavalry, and of its great superiority to that of the enemy. The result of this extraordinary and successful pursuit has proved, that the most rapid movements, even of the Mahratta horse, cannot avail against the celerity and discipline of our cavalry under its present improved construction. The utmost degree of credit is due to the Commander-in-Chief for his unremitting attention to the improvement of the cavalry of Bengal, and his Excellency's complete success in attaining this important object has been distinguished with splendour and honour on every occasion under his personal command, during the late operations against the Mahratta horse.

While these events were passing in the Doab, Major-General Frazer having been joined at Delhi by the expected convoys of supplies, commenced his march from that city towards the main body of the enemy. On the 11th of November, he arrived at Goberdun, about fourteen miles from Deig, under the walls of which fort the whole of the enemy's infantry and artillery were strongly posted. On the following day, Major-General Frazer marched to within six miles of Deig. Having ascertained exactly in the course of the night, the nature of the enemy's position, Major-General Frazer with the greatest judgment and spirit, determined to attack the enemy's force on the following day.

On the 13th in the morning, the British army advanced to the enemy's position, which was of uncommon strength and defended by numerous batteries of guns, which extended over a space of nearly two miles almost to the walls of the fort.

Led by Major-General Frazer, the British troops attacked the enemy's forces with the utmost gallantry, and after a most severe and arduous contest, completely defeated them, and drove them from their guns into the town of Deig with heavy loss; eighty-seven pieces of cannon, and almost the whole of the ammunition belonging to the enemy, were taken or destroyed on the field of battle on this memorable day. This brilliant, glorious and important victory was not obtained without considerable loss both in officers and men on our part.

The Governor-General in Council laments with the deepest concern the irreparable loss of that gallant and distinguished officer Major-General Frazer, to whose eminent judgment and military skill, and exemplary valour, is principally to be ascribed the signal success of the British arms on this memorable occasion. Major-General Frazer received a severe wound in the leg while in the act of leading his troops to the attack of the enemy's batteries. Even after he had received the wound, Major-General Frazer continued by his voice and action to animate and encourage the exertions of the troops. Having suffered amputation, Major-General Frazer after languishing some days, expired at Muttra, on the 24th of November.

The applause and gratitude of the British Government in India, and of the nation, must ever be connected with sentiments of the deepest regret for the loss of that heroic officer. The established reputation of Major-General Frazer for professional knowledge, gallantry, activity and public zeal, justified the expectation which the Governor-General in Council confidently entertained of deriving from the talents and exertions of Major-General Frazer, the most essential advantages in the prosecution of the war; and the Governor-General in Council deems it a subject of public sorrow, that the British Government in India should have been deprived of the services of that valuable officer at the commencement of his career of glory in Asia, and in the moment of victory.

After Major-General Frazer had been wounded, the command of the army devolved on Lieut.-Colonel Monson, who displayed the utmost activity and courage during the whole of the engagement.

The force of the enemy in this action is stated to have been twenty-four battalions of infantry, with 160 pieces of cannon, and a large body of horse; and a party of the Rajah of Bhurtpore's horse, and three battalions of his infantry were engaged on the side of the enemy, and the British troops suffered greatly by the fire of the guns from the fort of Deig which opened on their approach. After the action, the British army encamped near the field of battle.

It is remarkable that in this glorious action most of the artillery lost by Lieut.-Colonel Monson's detachment, were retaken at the point of the bayonet by the troops, of whom the command had devolved to Lieut.-Colonel Monson.

The Commander-in-Chief having re-crossed the Jumna at Muttra, on the 28th of November, joined the British infantry which had retired to that place from Deig, a few days after the battle. The reasons assigned by Lieut.-Colonel Monson for this movement, are stated in the annexed despatch from his Excellency the Commander-in-Chief, to which the Governor-General in Council has the honour to refer your honourable Committee.

On the 4th of December, the Commander-in-Chief arrived at Keerasamy, about four miles from Deig, and remained at this position until he was joined by the battering train which his Excellency had ordered from Agra for the purpose of commencing the siege of Deig, at which fortress the remains of Holkar's force continued to encamp. This fortress belongs to the Rajah of Bhurtpore, with whom a treaty of alliance had been concluded by the Commander-in-Chief, under the authority of the Governor-General, as is stated in our despatch to your honourable Committee, under date the 31st of October 1803.

* * * * * * *

The hostile conduct of the Rajah of Bhurtpore in the battle of Deig, when his guns opened upon our troops, and his cavalry acted with the enemy, had precluded the practicability of continuing on terms of amity with that chief, and rendered indispensably necessary the vigorous prosecution of measures for the punishment of his gross and flagrant violation of every principle of public faith and honour.

Independently however of these considerations, the change of the condition of Jeswunt Rao Holkar produced by the complete identification of his interests with those of the Rajah of Bhurtpore, rendered the prosecution of hostile operations against the possessions of the Rajah, the most effectual means of extinguishing the remnant of Holkar's military power.

The territorial resources of that chieftain were not at any period of the war applicable to the support of his army, and were at this time completely reduced. Holkar never had ranked among the states of India; he had never risen above the character of an adventurer and freebooter, whose success in some attacks upon detachments of the forces of Scindiah had gained a reputation of military enterprize. Holkar's force was now however greatly reduced by the defeats which his troops had sustained at Furruckabad and Deig. His hopes of support from the native states of India declined with his declining fortune, and he was compelled to depend exclusively upon the Rajah of Bhurtpore for the supply of every branch of military resource.

Under these circumstances, the Commander-in-Chief resolved on the immediate attack of the forts in the Rajah of Bhurtpore's country, upon which the strength and resources of that chieftain principally depended.

On the 20th of December, the Governor-General having reviewed the whole of the Commander-in-Chief's communications on the subject of the Rajah of Bhurtpore, and having taken into consideration the whole tenor of that chieftain's conduct, addressed a despatch to the Commander-in-Chief, approving and confirming his Excellency's proceedings with respect to the Rajah, and containing the expression of the Governor-General's sentiments and instructions on the measures necessary to be pursued against that chieftain, and on other points connected with the prosecution of hostilities against Jeswunt Rao Holkar and his confederates.

The Commander-in-Chief was authorized and directed by those instructions to proceed immediately to reduce the whole of the territories of the Rajah of Bhurtpore, and to annex them to the British dominions.

The Commander-in-Chief was at the same time informed that the Governor-General still considered the destruction of the force attached to the person of Jeswunt Rao Holkar to be the main object of the war, and that the prosecution of operations against the territory of Bhurtpore was to be considered as subordinate to that important object.

The Governor-General also stated his opinion that the subjugation of the territory and power of the Rajah of Bhurtpore was essential to the reduction of Holkar's hostile force, the entire subversion of which the Governor-General considered to be indispensably requisite for the tranquillity of India.

The Commander-in-Chief was further directed to introduce into whatever part of the territory of Bhurtpore which might be conquered, a civil authority for the collection of the revenues, and the administration of civil and criminal justice.

The proceedings to be adopted against the Rajah of Bhurtpore being calculated to serve as an example to all the other petty chiefs and states in that quarter of India, the Governor-General directed the Commander-in-Chief to address letters to all those chiefs, explaining the principles of his conduct towards the Rajah of Bhurtpore, and assuring them of the determination of the British Government to respect the independence of all contiguous states.

The Commander-in-Chief was also directed to circulate a declaration, warning all persons of the consequences of assisting the enemies of the British Government.

The Governor-General took this occasion to furnish the Commander-in-Chief with instructions for the guidance of his conduct towards Bapoojee Scindiah, who commanded the army of Dowlut Rao Scindiah in Malwa, and on the retreat of Lieut.-Colonel Monson's detachment, deserted with his force to the enemy, as is related in a subsequent paragraph of this despatch. Bapoojee Scindiah being not only an officer of Dowlut Rao Scindiah's government, sent expressly to co-operate with the Commander-in-Chief against Jeswunt Rao Holkar under the stipulations of the defensive alliance, but also included in the list of chieftains entitled to jaggeers or pensions from the British Government under the 7th article of the treaty of peace, could not be considered to possess any claim to the rights of war.

The Governor-General therefore desired the Commander-in-Chief to issue a proclamation, ordering Bapoojee Scindiah and his followers to repair to the British camp within a certain time, under the penalty of being considered and treated as rebels and traitors to the cause of the allies, and in the event of their neglecting to appear to bring such of them as might be seized to trial before a court martial, and to carry into effect such punishment as might be awarded by the Court.

A similar course was directed to be pursued towards Sud-dasheo Bhow and his followers, whose defection is stated in a preceding paragraph of this despatch.

On the 12th of December the Commander-in-Chief having been joined by his battering train from Agra, took up the position before Deig, which he intended to occupy during the siege. On the 17th December batteries were opened against a strong out-work, which entirely commanded the town and the works of the fort, and which was flanked by batteries in which was planted all the artillery of Holkar, that remained in his possession after the battle of the 13th November.

On the 23d of December, a practicable breach having been effected in the wall of the out-work, the Commander-in-Chief determined to storm it on that night. This attack was combined with two separate attacks to be made on the enemy's batteries to the right and left of the principal work. The conduct of these combined attacks was committed to Lieut.-Colonel Macrae, of his Majesty's 76th regiment. At the appointed hour, the parties destined to these several attacks advanced, under a heavy fire from the whole of the enemy's batteries, and after a severe and arduous contest, each party completely succeeded in effecting the object of its attack.

Our loss on this occasion was considerable, but not more than the strength of the works to be stormed, and the nature of the attack, rendered probable. The conduct of Lieut.-Colonel Macrae, and of the officers to whose charge the conduct of the attacks on the enemy's batteries were entrusted, and of every officer and soldier engaged in this arduous enterprize, reflects on them the highest honour, and entitles them to the warmest admiration and applause.

In consequence of the success of the attack on the out-works, the garrison abandoned the fort on the night of the 24th, and retired in the direction of Bhurtpore, another strong fortress, situated at the distance of about thirty miles in a southern direction from Deig.

The number of guns captured from the enemy in the lines before Deig, and in the town and the fort, amounted to one hundred.

The Governor-General in Council suspends the narrative of the proceedings of his Excellency the Commander-in-Chief for the purpose of communicating to your honourable Committee the operations against the power of Jeswunt Rao Holkar, which have been conducted on the western side of India.

* * * * * * *

Lieut.-Colonel Wallace marched from Poonah, as has been stated in a preceding paragraph of this despatch, on the 22d of August.

Lieut.-Colonel Wallace crossed the Godavery with his infantry, at Peytun, about the 18th of September, and on the 27th was joined at Forkabad by Lieut.-Colonel Haliburton, whose march as well as that of Colonel Wallace, had been impeded by the severity of the weather; and on the 30th Lieut.-Colonel Wallace was joined by his cavalry, which had proceeded higher up the Godavery than Peytun in search of a ford.

Lieut.-Colonel Wallace was joined by the Peishwa's contingent early in the month of October.

On the 8th of October, Colonel Wallace detached a party for the purpose of taking possession of a small fort belonging to Holkar, called Lasselgong, about twelve miles from Chandore. The party which was despatched on this service, failed in an attempt to storm the fort, and was compelled to retire to the Pettah, or town, which had been previously occupied by the British troops, until a re-inforcement arrived from Colonel Wallace, when the place was stormed with complete success. In accomplishing this service, forty-four men of the British detachment were killed and wounded, and two officers were also wounded.

On the same day, Colonel Wallace arrived before the town aud fortress of Chandore, and took possession of the former without opposition. Preparations were immediately made for the siege of the fort, and a battery was nearly ready to open, when proposals of capitulation were received from the garrison, which were accepted by Lieut.-Colonel Wallace, and the fort was immediately surrendered to the British troops on the 12th. The conditions on which the garrison surrendered were the safety of private property, and permission to the troops composing the garrison, to proceed whither they pleased. Our loss during the siege was inconsiderable. After the capture of Chandore, Lieut.-Colonel Wallace detached a party against another fort, situated in the same range of hills and occupied by a garrison in the interest of Holkar, called Dhoorb, which surrendered on the 14th of October, and several other small forts in the vicinity having been evacuated by the enemy's troops, and occupied by those of the Peishwa, Lieut.-Colonel Wallace marched from Chandore on the 17th.

On the 21st of October, he arrived before Galna, a strong fort belonging to Holkar, and took possession of the Pettah without opposition. On the 23d two practicable breaches having been effected, the garrison surrendered on the conditions of being allowed to march out with their arms and private property; which conditions being accepted by Lieut.-Colonel Wallace, the British troops took possession of the fort.

The possession of these forts deprived Holkar of all his possessions to the southward of the Tapty. The conduct of the troops is represented by Colonel Wallace to have been highly meritorious, and the manner in which these operations have been conducted by Colonel Wallace, entitles that officer to considerable praise.

After having made the necessary arrangements for maintaining these fortresses, and for establishing the authority of his Highness the Peishwa in the country which had been reduced by the success of our operations, Lieut.-Colonel Wallace proceeded to Borenaire, a position from whence he should be able to move in whatever direction the services of his detachment might be required; and in the neighbourhood of which he proposed to remain until he should receive further orders, or until circumstances should require the march of the detachment.

The subsequent movements of this detachment being connected with transactions at the Court of Nagpore, will be stated in another part of this despatch.

Destitute of any other resources than such as he derived from the habits of indiscriminate plunder and exaction, the power of Jeswunt Rao Holkar has been preserved from entire destruction, exclusively by the seasonable application of the military resources of the Rajah of Bhurtpore, with whom the British Government, previously to the conclusion of the late war with the confederated Mahratta chieftains, concluded an alliance, as has been reported to your honourable Committee in our despatch of the 31st of October 1803.

Events have incontrovertibly demonstrated that the arrangements suggested for the speedy and successful termination of the war, which the British Government was compelled to undertake against Jeswunt Rao Holkar were more than adequate to the accomplishment of that object under any occurrences, or any situation of affairs which could reasonably be contemplated; since the British forces acting under circumstances much less favourable than those to which the prescribed arrangements refer, have succeeded in accomplishing the reduction of all the forts and territories of Jeswunt Rao Holkar, in completely defeating his whole assembled army of infantry and artillery, and his entire force of cavalry at the memorable battles of

Deig and Furruckabad, and in capturing the whole of Holkar's numerous artillery.

The complete success of our arms in every contest with the troops of Jeswunt Rao Holkar must have produced the entire destruction of his power, if the resources of the Rajah of Bhurtpore's territory, the aid of his forces and the protection of his forts had not supported the cause of Jeswunt Rao Holkar, and compelled the British Government to direct its arms against the possessions of the Rajah of Bhurtpore.

* * * * * * *

With our despatch to your honourable Committee, under date the 15th of June, the Governor-General in Council had the honour to transmit a copy of instructions issued by the honourable Major-General Wellesley to Colonel Murray, the officer commanding the British troops in the province of Guzerat, for the co-operation of a considerable detachment under the command of that officer, with the army under the immediate direction of his Excellency General Lake, against the forces of Jeswunt Rao Holkar.

The Governor-General in Council now proceeds to state to your honourable Committee the proceedings of that detachment.

After providing for the protection of Surat and Baroda, in the manner suggested by the honourable Major-General Wellesley, the force under the personal command of Colonel Murray amounted to two regiments of European infantry, and five battalions of native infantry, with a due proportion of artillery.

Arrangements were also made for the co-operation of a body of troops in the service of the Guikwar; but those troops did not join the army of Colonel Murray until after its arrival at Ougein.

In the supposition that Jeswunt Rao Holkar (who was then at Ajmere) if pressed by the army of the Commander-in-Chief, might retire in a south-western direction, Colonel Murray was directed by the instructions of the honourable Major-General Wellesley to place his detachment in such a position as would enable it to embarrass and impede Jeswunt Rao Holkar's retreat.

But, in the event (which was deemed more probable) of Jeswunt Rao Holkar's proceeding towards Ougein, Lieut.-Colonel Murray was instructed to endeavour to effect an early junction with Dowlut Rao Scindiah's army; and under any circumstances, to proceed with the utmost practicable expedition in the direction of Holkar's force, and to take advantage of any opportunity of attacking it.

Jeswunt Rao Holkar's troops having subsequently moved in the direction of Ougein, Colonel Murray determined in conformity to the spirit of his instructions, as well as in compliance with the urgent solicitations of Dowlut Rao Scindiah, to proceed with the utmost practicable expedition for the protection of that capital. The advance of Colonel Murray's detachment however, from Baroda to the frontier of Guzerat, was considerably retarded by the difficulty of procuring conveyance in Guzerat; by the exhausted condition of the country, and the consequent difficulty of procuring forage, and by the necessity of previously securing ample supplies of provisions. About the middle of the month of June however, Colonel Murray arrived with the detachment under his command in the vicinity of Dowlut Rao Scindiah's Fort of Dohud.

At the suggestion of Major-General Wellesley, the transmission of orders to the Commandant of that fortress for the reception of the heavy ordnance and stores of the detachment under Colonel Murray's command, had been a subject of repeated urgency on the part of the Resident at the court of Dowlut Rao Scindiah, with that chieftain and his ministers, who explained the delay which occurred in the transmission of those orders, by asserting that the Commandant of that force was in the service of Ambajee, and that orders addressed to him would be of no effect. This subject will be stated more in detail in that part of the present despatch, which relates to the transactions at the court of Dowlut Rao Scindiah. It appears however, that ultimately the Commandant not only consented that the heavy ordnance should be deposited in the fort, but proposed that a British guard should be stationed in it.

On the 30th of June, the detachment under the command of Colonel Murray, arrived at Budnawar on its route to Ougein. At that station Colonel Murray received intelligence which induced him to suspend his advance to Ougein, and to retire to a position behind the river Myhee.

The causes which influenced Colonel Murray's resolution to retire behind the Myhee, appeared to have been principally the information which he received from Lieut.-Colonel Monson of the return of the army under the personal command of the Commander-in-Chief into cantonments, and of the intention of Lieut.-Colonel Monson to halt with his detachment at the Mokundra pass, until he should receive further orders from General Lake, combined with intelligence which Colonel Murray received at the same time, of the intention of Jeswunt Rao Holkar to direct the whole of his force against the detachment advancing from Guzerat.

Colonel Murray stated it to be his opinion, that the detachment under his command was unequal to oppose the whole force of Jeswunt Rao Holkar, without the assistance of the cavalry, with which he expected to be furnished by the Guikwar, and by Dowlut Rao Scindiah, and that by advancing into Malwa, he might not only endanger the safety of his detachment, but afford to Jeswunt Rao Holkar a favourable opportunity for the invasion of Guzerat. In addition to these causes of retreat, Colonel Murray considered his position at Budnawar to be unfavourable to the operations of a body of infantry against a superior force, while the position to which Colonel Murray proposed to retire in the rear of the Myhee, appeared to that officer to possess advantages which would enable his detachment to resist the attack of the whole of Holkar's force. Colonel Murray accordingly on the 1st of July, commenced his retreat towards the Myhee.

On the 5th of that month however, Colonel Murray received intelligence that Holkar had detached a considerable body of his troops towards Hinglaisghur, (the assault and capture of which place by the British troops has already been described,) and that the main body of Holkar's force had marched in a direction north-east of Mundasere. These movements appear to have relieved Colonel Murray from the apprehensions which he entertained with respect to the safety of his detachment, and accordingly on the 5th of July, Colonel Murray resumed his march towards Ougein, at which city he arrived on the 8th of the same month without having encountered any opposition.

At an early period of time after the march of Colonel Murray from Guzerat, that officer communicated to the Resident with Dowlut Rao Scindiah, his anxious desire to be furnished with a body of Scindiah's cavalry, to co-operate with the detachment under his command. Before the arrival of Colonel Murray at Ougein, a vakeel on the part of Antajee Geerdur, the principal officer of Dowlut Rao Scindiah at that capital, had arrived in the camp of Colonel Murray, in consequence of orders issued by Dowlut Rao Scindiah's ministers, in conformity to the urgent application of the Resident (as described in a subsequent part of this despatch). Colonel Murray transmitted through this vakeel also, repeated applications to Antajee Geerdur, urging his immediate advance with a body of Scindiah's cavalry. But this reinforcement though frequently promised, was never despatched, and even after Colonel Murray's arrival at Ougein, every endeavour to obtain the services of an efficient body of Dowlut Rao Scindiah's forces proved unavailing. The expectation also of being joined by Scindiah's forces under the command of Bapoojee Scindiah, having been disappointed by the defection of that chieftain, Colonel Murray submitted to the Resident with Dowlut Rao Scindiah, a plan for securing the services of a considerable body of Pindarree horse, which had formerly been in the service of Dowlut Rao Scindiah, and was then in the neighbourhood of Bopaul. Colonel Murray also proposed to raise a body of Sillehdar horse in Malwa, for the purpose of co-operating with his detachment.

The Resident with Dowlut Rao Scindiah, in reply to Colonel Murray's propositions, explained the various objections to the employment of Pindarries in the service of the British Government, but submitted the decision of the question to the authority of the Governor-General in Council.

The Governor-General in Council concurred entirely in the sentiments expressed by the Resident with Dowlut Rao Scindiah, and signified to Colonel Murray, his Excellency in Council's disapprobation of the employment of troops of that description.

Colonel Murray having submitted to the Governor-General several questions relative to the extent to which he might be permitted to encourage desertion among the adherents of Jeswunt Rao Holkar, and to offer to them employment in the service of the allies, and to what extent he might make pecuniary advances to the servants of Dowlut Rao Scindiah for the purpose of enabling them to act with vigour and exertion, the Governor-General in Council deemed it to be advisable to furnish Colonel Murray with instructions on those several questions. On the first point, the Governor-General in Council stated his opinion to be, that the advantages to be derived by the employment of a large number of deserters from the cause of Holkar would not be adequate to the expence and inconvenience attending that measure. On the question regarding the advance of money to the officers of Dowlut Rao Scindiah, Colonel Murray was referred entirely to the judgment of the Resident at that chieftain's court.

To the disordered condition of the whole frame of Dowlut

Rao Scindiah's government must be ascribed the conduct of his officers in Malwa, in failing to supply an efficient force for the purpose of co-operating with Colonel Murray's detachment; and to the same cause must be ascribed the difficulty which Colonel Murray experienced in obtaining supplies or necessaries for his troops, and in restoring his establishments of carriage-cattle and other equipments which had suffered by the severity of the Monsoon, and Colonel Murray was apprized at an early period of time by the Resident with Dowlut Rao Scindiah, of the necessity of acting without reference to any expectation of useful assistance from the government of that chieftain in the operations of the war.

During the continuance of Colonel Murray's detachment at Ougein, that officer took possession, without any resistance, of the whole of the territory in the occupation of Jeswunt Rao Holkar, situated in that quarter, and of Indore, the capital of the possessions of the family of Holkar. These places were immediately delivered over to the charge of the officers of Dowlut Rao Scindiah.

It has been stated in a preceding paragraph of this despatch, that the troops which had been furnished by the Guickwar to co-operate with Colonel Murray's detachment, did not form a junction with that detachment until after its arrival at Ougein. The body of troops selected by the government of the Guickwar for this service, consisting of 3600 horse and 800 foot, was assembled at Ahmedabad in Guzerat, soon after the Resident at Baroda notified the desire of the British Government, that such a force should be prepared in conformity to the plan of operations prescribed by the honourable Major-General Wellesley.

The disordered state of the Guickwar's finances, compelled the British Government to provide for the pay and subsistence of the troops composing the Guickwar's contingent while in the field, and the Resident at Baroda accordingly, under the authority of the Governor in Council of Bombay, adopted an arrangement for that purpose. A British officer was appointed to reside in the camp of the Guickwar's contingent for the purpose of conducting communications between the commanders of the troops of the Guickwar and the Resident at Baroda and Colonel Murray, and of superintending the payment of those troops. Considerable delay occurred before the troops commenced their march, occasioned by the extravagant demands of the officers commanding the different bodies of men composing the contingent. These difficulties having been at length overcome, the contingent commenced its march, and on the 7th of July arrived at Godra, a possession of Dowlut Rao Scindiah, near the frontier of Guzerat. At this station, the progress of the troops was delayed by the same cause which had retarded the commencement of their march. This obstruction was at length removed by an advance of money on account of the pay of the troops which was made by Captain Williams (the British officer, residing in the camp of the Guickwar's contingent) under authority which he had received for that purpose from the Resident at Baroda. The troops of the Guickwar then resumed their march, but their progress was extremely slow. The disorderly and turbulent habits of the troops and of the commanders of the different parties, were not less conspicuous on their march from Godra than they had been before. The repeated orders of Colonel Murray to the commander on the subject of expediting the march of the troops and on other points of duty connected with the public service, were entirely disregarded.

Being of opinion that these troops might be usefully employed in the protection of a convoy, which was advancing from Guzerat, with a small detachment of British troops, Colonel Murray instructed Captain Williams to require the commander of the Guickwar's troops to join the convoy for the purpose above stated, and in the event of his refusal, to leave the camp and to inform the commander that the services of his corps would not be required. The demand of Captain Williams being refused, he quitted the camp of the Guickwar. The progress of the convoy, however, being accidentally retarded, the Guickwar's contingent joined the convoy a few days after Captain Williams's departure, and advanced to Ougein, at which city the contingent arrived on the 16th of August.

The causes which had unhappily produced a disagreement between Colonel Murray and the officer commanding the troops of the Guickwar, did not cease to operate after the junction of the contingent with the British detachment. With a view to remedy the evils occasioned by the disagreement existing between Colonel Murray and the commander of the Guickwar's contingent, it was determined in concert with the Government of the Guickwar (which had, on all occasions, manifested a sincere disposition to promote the common cause) to supersede the commanding officer of the contingent and the principal member of the Guickwar's Government, prepared to assume the command in person. This arrangement, however, was subsequently abandoned.

In the mean time, the Guickwar's contingent remained at Ougein, and was employed by Colonel Murray in the reduction or occupation of some of the possessions of Holkar, situated in that vicinity. No cordiality however appears to have been established between Colonel Murray and the commander of the Guickwar's contingent, and Colonel Murray continued to transmit to the government of Bombay, and to the Resident at Baroda, complaints of the misconduct of that officer.

On the 18th of October, Colonel Murray having completed the equipments of his troops, which had been nearly destroyed by the violence of the Monsoon, and having collected a sufficient number of cattle, advanced from Ougein, in compliance with the urgent and repeated orders of the Commander-in-Chief, who considered the early advance of this detachment to be an object of the utmost importance in the prosecution of the war; especially in the event of Holkar being compelled to retire towards Malwa on the approach of the army under his Excellency's personal command. Colonel Murray was accompanied on his march by the Guickwar's contingent.

On the 11th of November, Colonel Murray arrived at Mundasere, having occupied the Pergunnahs of Burrowda and Jowrah, belonging to Holkar, through which he had directed his march. Advancing from Mundasere, Colonel Murray took possession of the forts of Narrayn-Gurh and Mulhar-Gurh, which were held by the adherents of Holkar. The next operation performed by the detachment under the command of Colonel Murray, was the attack of Rampoorah, a fortress of some strength, belonging to Holkar, and distinct from the fort of Rampoorah, the assault and capture of which, is stated in a preceding paragraph of our despatch of the 15th of June, and which is still occupied by a British garrison.

This fort was occupied by a party of British troops on the 19th of November, after an able resistance on the part of the enemy. The possession of Rampoorah completed the conquest of the whole of Holkar's territories on the west of the river Chumbul.

* * * * * * *

The Governor-General in Council now proceeds to communicate the sequel of the Acting Resident's negotiations at the Court of Dowlut Rao Scindiah.

The conviction which the Acting Resident entertained of the infamous designs of Serjee Rao Ghautka was corroborated in the Acting Resident's judgment by an occurrence in his camp on the night of the 27th of December. On that night the guard stationed at the tent which contained the public baggage of the Residency was attacked and overpowered by a large body of plunderers, who murdered or wounded every person near the tent, and plundered money and other property to the value of about 12,000 rupees. The most valuable part of the public property however was preserved by the activity of the Resident's escort, which compelled the plunderers to retreat with precipitation. The Acting Resident was induced to suspect that this outrage was instigated by Serjee Rao Ghautka, but of this fact no evidence appears. Dowlut Rao Scindiah expressed the utmost degree of regret upon this occasion, and promised to afford the Resident every practicable satisfaction. The Acting Resident did not suspect that Dowlut Rao Scindiah had any concern in this outrage. That chieftain had previously expressed an earnest desire that the Acting Resident should encamp on the same ground with his army on account of the Pindarries, whom his Highness acknowledged his inability to control. Although the suspicions of the Acting Resident with regard to the designs of Serjee Rao Ghautka were confirmed by this occurrence, the Acting Resident very properly determined not to render it an exclusive cause for quitting the court of Dowlut Rao Scindiah.

Between the 7th and the 9th of January the army of Dowlut Rao Scindiah invested the fort of Saugur for the purpose of realizing the amount of his demand ; in consequence of which, the Acting Resident despatched a message to his Highness, intimating that he had resolved to march the following morning, and desiring passports. To this message the Acting Resident received an answer purporting that Ramchunder Bhasker (the Agent before mentioned) should be despatched to the Acting Resident in the course of the morning, and that all points should be satisfactorily adjusted.

The Acting Resident, however, having repeated his demand for passports, he received a message from Dowlut Rao Scindiah signifying that Ambajee Inglia was expected to arrive in the space of eight days, and that on his arrival, it would be determined whether his Highness should proceed to Ougein, or the Acting Resident should receive his dismission.

This insulting message confirmed the Acting Resident in his

resolution to march the succeeding morning unless Dowlut Rao Scindiah should consent to proceed immediately in the direction of Ougein. This resolution, however, the Acting Resident was subsequently induced to change, after having made preparations for marching by striking all the tents of the British camp and loading the baggage, on receiving from Dowlut Rao Scindiah, through the agency of Ramchunder Pundit, the most solemn assurances of his Highness's determination to march in the direction of Ougein on the 16th of January, and to act in every respect according to the Acting Resident's advice. The delay of six days was required in consequence of the decease of a female of distinction in the family of Dowlut Rao Scindiah.

It is proper to observe in this place that the information which the Acting Resident received with regard to the object of Ambajee's expected visit, was calculated to palliate the hostile and insulting tendency of the message which was conveyed to the Acting Resident upon that subject, as described in a preceding paragraph.

The Acting Resident was informed that repeated and earnest invitations had been transmitted to Ambajee, to proceed to the camp of Dowlut Rao Scindiah, in the hope and expectation that his influence would effect the expulsion of Ghautka. The Acting Resident also stated that in the general opinion Ambajee was decidedly adverse to the renewal of war with the British Government. The arrival of Ambajee therefore was calculated to maintain peace and amity between the two states, although the expectation of it was announced to the Acting Resident in an apparent spirit of hostility and insult.

On the evening of the 15th of January the Acting Resident received a message from Dowlut Rao Scindiah stating, that his Highness's march on the following morning agreeably to his engagement would be attended with considerable inconvenience, and requesting that the Acting Resident would consent to a further delay of two days, promising in the most positive terms to prosecute his march at the expiration of that time, without a halt to Ougein. To this proposal the Acting Resident after some opposition assented, and on the 11th of January Dowlut Rao Scindiah actually commenced his march; but only a small portion of the army accompanied his Highness. The battalions and guns, together with the greater portion of the army, continued to occupy their position in the vicinity of Saugur, and the extent of his Highness's march did not exceed three miles. The

Acting Resident was also informed that it was the intention of Dowlut Rao Scindiah to halt four days where he had pitched his tents.

The Acting Resident having despatched a message remonstrating on his breach of promise, his Highness replied, that in compliance with the Acting Resident's desire, his Highness had considered it to be incumbent upon him to march on the 18th. That his resolution of proceeding to Ougein remained unchanged, but that within the period of thirteen days after the decease of a member of his family, it was inconsistent with established custom to quit the spot where such an event had happened; adding however, that he would positively proceed on the march to Ougein after the four days which the prescribed period of mourning compelled. The Acting Resident considered the whole of this proceeding to be the result of collusion and deceit, but his solicitude to abstain from a measure which in his apprehension would revive the war between the two states, induced him to attend to the promises and professions of Dowlut Rao Scindiah.

* * * * * * *

The Acting Resident's report of his proceedings at the court of Dowlut Rao Scindiah is interrupted by the miscarriage of a despatch to that officer under date the 22nd of January. It appears however, by a despatch from the Acting Resident of a subsequent date, that he had received an insulting message from Dowlut Rao Scindiah's Durbar in answer to his demand for passports, and that the Acting Resident actually marched from Dowlut Rao Scindiah's camp on the 23d of January to the distance of about fourteen miles. Previously to his departure, the Acting Resident received a visit from two of Dowlut Rao Scindiah's officers, the object of which was to persuade the Acting Resident to remain, but those persons not being authorized to vouch for Dowlut Rao Scindiah's march on that day, the Acting Resident resisted their entreaties and commenced his journey towards the camp of the British forces.

On receiving information of the Acting Resident's departure, Dowlut Rao Scindiah despatched an officer of high rank together with Ramchunder Bhasker the agent before mentioned to the Acting Resident's camp, for the purpose of persuading the Acting Resident to return. They arrived at his camp on the evening of the 23d, and on being received by the Acting Resident, solemnly pledged themselves that if he would return to Dowlut Rao Scindiah's camp on the morning of the 24th,

Dowlut Rao Scindiah would commence his march towards his capital on the following day. The Acting Resident however refused to accept this assurance, but being informed by those persons that they were authorized to pledge Dowlut Rao Scindiah's name for the performance of any conditions which could induce the Acting Resident to return; the Acting Resident proposed the following:—

1st. That on the day following the Acting Resident's return to camp, Dowlut Rao Scindiah should commence his march to Ougein, to which place he should proceed without any further halt than the usual and necessary intervals.

2ndly. That Scindiah should act in conformity to the Acting Resident's advice respecting Ambajee without any further delay.

3dly. That Scindiah should comply with the Acting Resident's advice to disavow in a letter to the Governor-General, the conduct of Ambajee and of the vakeel at Hyderabad, and that letters of recall to the latter persons should be delivered to the Acting Resident in order that they might be transmitted through the Resident at that court. The messengers having agreed in the most solemn manner to these conditions, the Acting Resident consented to return to camp, and he accordingly returned on the 24th of January.

On the evening of that day the Acting Resident received information that Dowlut Rao Scindiah had resolved to halt the following day. This resolution being a direct violation of one of the conditions on which the Acting Resident had consented to return to camp, the Acting Resident recommenced his march, but after proceeding a short distance was informed that Dowlut Rao Scindiah had expressed a desire to receive a visit from the Acting Resident, who in consequence of this intimation directed that his baggage should remain at a grove in the vicinity of the encampment of Dowlut Rao Scindiah's regular brigades, and proceeded with Lieutenant Stuart, the officer commanding the escort, to the tents of Dowlut Rao Scindiah. After some endeavour on the part of Dowlut Rao Scindiah to excuse his conduct, he signified his determination to comply that day with all the Acting Resident's demands respecting Ambajee, and to commence his march towards Ougein on the following morning.

The Acting Resident refused to be satisfied unless the letters which he had demanded should be prepared and despatched in his presence. To this his Highness after much discussion consented, and the Acting Resident was requested to retire with some of Dowlut Rao Scindiah's public officers to a separate tent, that the letters might there be prepared in the terms which the Acting Resident should prescribe. The Acting Resident accordingly retired with Lieutenant Stuart while Dowlut Rao Scindiah continued to hold his court. The letters were in a state of preparation, when the Acting Resident was informed that Dowlut Rao Scindiah desired to retire for the purpose of performing his devotions, which had been interrupted by the Acting Resident's visit, and the letters when completed should be carried to him, and if the terms of them should not entirely accord with the Acting Resident's wishes, he might return to his Highness's tents in the evening for the purpose of suggesting the necessary alterations.

The Resident accordingly returned to take leave of Dowlut Rao Scindiah, and immediately despatched orders, recalling the baggage of the Residency. In the mean time, however, the British camp was surrounded and overpowered by the whole body of Dowlut Rao Scindiah's Pindarries, who plundered the whole of the baggage. Lieutenant Greene, who commanded the escort, and Dr. Wise the surgeon of the Residency, were severely wounded, and many of the Sepoys and other persons attached to the Residency were also wounded.

Dowlut Rao Scindiah expressed the utmost horror and regret at this occurrence, and promised to restore the whole of the plundered property. In the mean time the gentlemen of the Residency being deprived by this atrocious violence of all the means of accommodation, were reduced to a situation of extreme distress.

With whatever degree of regret and indignation the Governor-General in Council contemplated this unparalleled outrage, justice requires the expression of our decided opinion, that it was perpetrated without the participation or knowledge of Dowlut Rao Scindiah. The Governor-General in Council even doubts whether that outrage was instigated or abetted by Serjee Rao Ghautka, and deems it most probable that the plunder of the baggage was the exclusive object of this act of violence on the part of some of Dowlut Rao Scindiah's irregular horse and other licentious troops. This occurrence therefore produced no alteration in the sentiments of the Governor-General in Council with regard to the views and dispositions of Dowlut Rao Scindiah as described in preceding paragraphs.

The Governor-General, however, deemed it indispensably necessary to demand from Dowlut Rao Scindiah a full explanation of that extraordinary act of violence and ample reparation

L l 2

and atonement for it, and the Governor-General considered it to be proper to address a letter to that chieftain, stating in general terms the sentiments of the British Government with regard to the whole tenor of his conduct, adverting however in an especial manner to the outrage committed upon the British Representative at his Highness's court, and containing also a demand of reparation and atonement. A copy of that letter is annexed to this despatch for your honourable Committee's information.

* * * * * * *

The Governor-General in Council now resumes the narrative of the proceedings of the army under the personal command of his Excellency the Commander-in-Chief.

The Commander-in-Chief having completed the necessary arrangements at Deig and having left a proper garrison in the fort, proceeded against Bhurtpore, another strong fort belonging to Rajah Runjeet Sing and his usual place of residence.

The Commander-in-Chief directed his march near Muttra for the purpose of favouring his junction with his Majesty's 75th regiment and a large convoy of provisions. His Majesty's 75th regiment and the convoy having joined the main army on the 29th of December, the Commander-in-Chief pursued his march towards Bhurtpore, where the army arrived on the 3rd of January.

The Commander-in-Chief commenced operations against the town of Bhurtpore, and a battery of six 18-pounders was opened against the wall on the 7th of January. On the 9th, the breach being reported practicable, preparations were made to storm it, and Lieut.-Colonel Maitland of his Majesty's 75th regiment was appointed to the command of the storming party.

Extraordinary and unexpected obstacles however opposed the progress of the storming party and occasioned its detention during a considerable period of time in a situation where it was exposed to a heavy fire from the walls of the town, and on reaching the breach, it was unfortunately found to be impracticable. The party was therefore compelled to retire after repeated attempts to ascend the breach with the loss of many officers and men, and of Lieut.-Colonel Maitland whose courage and exertions were eminently conspicuous on this unfortunate occasion. A flanking party, however, which was directed against the enemy's battery at the same time succeeded in gaining the battery, spiked the guns which were found in it and killed a considerable number of the enemy.

The party which endeavoured to storm, retreated in good

order to the batteries of the British army. Although this attempt to storm the breach terminated unsuccessfully, the British troops have on no occasion displayed a greater spirit of gallantry and firmness than in this attack. The failure of this attack must be exclusively ascribed to the insurmountable nature of the obstacles which opposed the progress of the troops.

On the following night a new battery was commenced for the purpose of breaching the wall in a different place and was opened on the 14th with great effect.

On the 21st of January, the breach which had been effected by the fire from the batteries which had been erected after the assault of the town on the 9th appearing to be practicable, the Commander-in-Chief determined upon another attempt to carry the place by storm. On the evening of that day the storming party, which was commanded by Lieut.-Colonel Macrae of his Majesty's 76th regiment, moved out of the trenches. The ditch however which surrounds the town was found to be so broad and deep that every attempt of the storming party to cross it proved unsuccessful, and the party was compelled to return to the trenches. The Commander-in-Chief represents the conduct of the troops on this occasion to have been distinguished by their accustomed steadiness, activity, and valour.

The Governor-General in Council is concerned to add that the heavy fire to which the troops were unavoidably exposed during a considerable time in endeavouring to effect their passage across the ditch and during their return to the batteries occasioned a severe loss.

The failure of these attempts determined the Commander-in-Chief to carry the approaches close to the surrounding ditch, by which means it was his Excellency's expectation that the obstacles which had hitherto prevented our success would be effectually overcome.

His Excellency accordingly stationed the army in a new position on the southern side of the town and recommenced the operations of the siege.

* * * * * * *

On the 11th of February the main body of the army under the command of Major-General Jones, which had advanced from Guzerat, formed a junction with the army of the Commander-in-Chief, and encamped in a position in the vicinity of the ground occupied by the army of Bengal.

The remainder of the force from Guzerat under the command of Lieut.-Colonel Holmes, was advancing with a convoy of treasure and stores by a different route, and at the period of the latest advices was arrived at Rampoorah.

On the 20th of February the advanced state of the operations against the town of Bhurtpore appeared to the Commander-in-Chief to render it advisable to assault the place without further delay. On that day his Excellency made preparations for the attack. The party destined to storm the breach was formed of the greater part of the European infantry belonging to the Bengal army and three battalions of Sepoys under the command of Lieut.-Colonel Don. Another party consisting of 200 men, his Majesty's 86th regiment, and one battalion of Bengal native infantry under the command of Captain Grant of the former corps, was ordered to attack the enemy's trenches and guns on the outside of the town, while a third column composed of 300 men from his Majesty's 65th regiment and two battalions of Bombay native infantry was destined to attack one of the gates of the place which was understood to be accessible. The attack conducted by Captain Grant entirely succeeded, and the British troops obtained possession of the enemy's guns, which were brought into camp. The Governor-General is concerned to state that neither of the other attacks succeeded. The ditch was found to be so deep as to render the approach of the storming party under the command of Lieut.-Colonel Don to the breach impracticable. The troops then attempted to ascend one of the bastions of the town but without success, and after repeated endeavours to ascend, was finally compelled to desist. The column under the command of Lieut.-Colonel Taylor which was intended to attack the gate was detained a considerable time on its march, and was early exposed to a most heavy and destructive fire from the town, which destroyed the ladders and rendered every attempt to succeed by assaulting the gate impracticable. Lieut.-Colonel Taylor, therefore, was compelled to withdraw his men until he received orders to return to camp. The Commander-in-Chief has expressed his opinion of the conduct of Lieut.-Colonel Don and of Captain Grant and the troops under their command in terms of the greatest approbation.

The failure of this attempt to carry the town by assault having been occasioned in a great degree by the occurrence of unexpected accidents and delays, and the Commander-in-Chief having reason to suppose that a few hours more battering would render perfectly practicable the bastion which our troops had attempted to escalade, his Excellency determined to renew the attack on the following day.

The storming party consisted of the whole of the European force and two battalions of Native infantry from the army of Bengal and the greater part of his Majesty's 65th and 86th regiments, the Grenadier battalion and the flank companies, and another battalion of Native infantry from the army of Bombay. The whole was commanded by the honourable Colonel Monson, and moved out to the attack at three o'clock in the afternoon of the 21st of February.

The troops engaged in the attack with the most determined zeal and bravery, but their utmost exertions to gain the top of the breach were unsuccessful, and after successive attempts, which were continued with unabating ardour during two hours, were compelled to retire with a severe loss of officers and men. It is with the deepest concern that the Governor-General in Council announces to your honourable Committee this further failure in the attempt to carry Bhurtpore by assault, and his Excellency in Council extremely laments the loss of the many brave officers and men who have fallen on this occasion. Although the exertions of the troops have not been attended with success, they have not on any occasion displayed a greater degree of gallantry and steadiness, and the Commander-in-Chief has expressed the highest approbation of the conduct of Lieut.-Colonel Monson and of all the troops engaged in the assault.

The causes of the repeated failures in the attempts upon Bhurtpore have not yet been fully stated to the Governor-General in Council, and will require further investigation.

On the 24th of February the Commander-in-Chief took up a new position on the north-east side of Bhurtpore, and his Excellency is prepared to re-commence operations against that place as soon as he shall have received supplies of stores and ammunition which are advancing towards the army from the stations within the Company's provinces at which they had been collected. The Commander-in-Chief expresses a confident hope of obtaining possession of Bhurtpore before the conclusion of the season for active military operations in that quarter of India.

The Rajah of Bhurtpore however, aware that the exertions of the British forces must ultimately be successful and that the utter destruction of his power must be the consequence of our success, despatched on the 25th of February a letter to his Excellency the Commander-in-Chief, proposing an accommodation with the British Government.

* * * * * * *

On a consideration of all the transactions which have been recorded in the preceding narrative, combined with the actual condition of our internal and external relations, the Governor-General in Council has no reason to doubt the accomplishment of the expectations, which in our despatch of the 13th of July the Governor-General in Council has expressed with regard to the benefits to be derived from the general arrangements of the peace concluded with Dowlut Rao Scindiah and the Rajah of Berar. The fundamental principles of that policy which regulated the measures of the British Government in framing those arrangements which must constitute the basis of the power and security of the British Empire in India, cannot be considered to be affected by the circumstances of the existing contest with Holkar and his partizans. The immediate effect of that extended system of political connection which is indisputably requisite for the permanent establishment of general peace and tranquillity throughout India, must necessarily be to deprive of employment that numerous class of military adventurers, who have hitherto derived subsistence from the wars and contests of the various discordant and unconnected powers of India. To the operation of this cause must be ascribed the facility with which Holkar and his partizans have been enabled without any pecuniary or territorial resources to assemble and maintain a numerous horde of freebooters. But the gradual and certain operation of those principles on which is founded the existing system of our political relations, must ultimately tend to subdue the characteristic habits and dispositions of those rude and predatory classes, and to encourage the cultivation of the arts of peace, and industry throughout every state in India.

The power of Jeswunt Rao Holkar is destitute of any solid foundation, and of every element of an established Government; and although under actual circumstances the British Government is still under the necessity of maintaining our armies in the field during an unexpected period of time, no conclusions can be deduced from the present situation of affairs, of a nature to justify a doubt of the ultimate establishment of that system of general peace and security throughout India, to which the views and measures of this government have been uniformly directed.

We have the honour to be,
Honourable Sirs,
Your most faithful humble servants,
WELLESLEY.
G. H. BARLOW.
G. UDNY.

69. The Governor-General in Council to the Honourable the Secret Committee of the Honourable the Court of Directors.

Terms of the Treaty with the Rajah of Bhurtpore. The Defensive Alliance System tested favourably by the War with Holkar.

(Extract.)

Honourable Sirs, Fort William, 31st May, 1805.

The terms to which the Rajah of Bhurtpore has ultimately assented are, that the Rajah shall pay to the honourable Company the sum of twenty lacks of rupees by instalments, the whole to be discharged within the space of four years.

The last instalment however to be remitted, if the intermediate conduct of the Rajah shall be satisfactory to the British Government.

That the Rajah shall assist to the utmost of his power in repelling any attack upon the British possessions, and that the Rajah shall never hold any correspondence with the enemies of the British power, or be in any way connected with them.

That the Rajah will never entertain in his service any subject of Great Britain or France, or any European, without the sanction of the British Government.

That as a security for the performance of the articles of the treaty, one of the Rajah's sons shall constantly remain with the officer commanding the British forces in the Soubahs of Delhi or Agra, and that the fortress of Deig shall continue in the occupation of a British garrison, until the British Government shall be perfectly satisfied of the Rajah's fidelity and attachment.

On the other hand, the British Government engages permanently to guarantee Rajah Runjeet Sing in the possession of his antient territory: the Rajah consenting, as the condition of his right eventually to claim the aid of the British power, to submit to the arbitration of the British Government any difference which may occur between him and any other state or chieftain.

The terms of this treaty do not differ materially from those which were prescribed in the Governor-General's instructions of the 19th of March; and being considered by the Governor-General in Council to be in every respect advantageous and honourable to the British Government, the treaty was ratified by the Governor-General in Council on the 2d of May.

Although the treaty with Rajah Runjeet Sing was not finally executed until the 17th of April, all the stipulations of it were adjusted on the 11th of that month; and on the evening of that day, the Rajah's son arrived in the British camp as an hostage. On the same evening Jeswunt Rao Holkar was compelled by the Rajah to leave Bhurtpore.

* * * * * * *

In concluding this despatch, the Governor-General in Council deems it expedient to submit to your honourable Committee the following observations respecting the effect of the war with Holkar upon the principles of the general system of our defensive alliances, in Hindostan and the Deccan.

The different states of India included in the general system of defensive alliance are, the Peishwa; Soubahdar of the Deccan; Rajah of Mysore; Guikwar; Rajah of Jeypore; Rajah of Bhurtpore; Rajah of Matcherry; Rana of Gohud; Scindiah.

In the prosecution of hostilities against Jeswunt Rao Holkar, we have derived considerable assistance from the Peishwa, the Soubahdar of the Deccan, the Rajah of Mysore and the Guikwar, under the operation of our engagements with those states. That assistance could not have been expected under any other state of circumstances. The troops of these states have actually joined our armies, while the resources of their respective territories have been at our disposal, and have been applied with advantage to the use of our troops in the field.

At this moment the troops of the Peishwa and of the Soubahdar of the Deccan form an useful addition to the army in the Deccan. The troops of the Rajah of Mysore are already prepared for active operations. The troops of the Guikwar have rendered considerable services with the army under the command of Major-General Jones, and have furnished convoy for the extensive supplies, which have been drawn as well from the Guikwar's territories as from the Company's resources for the use of the army.

These advantages could not have been obtained without the operation of the system of alliances established with those states respectively, and it may justly be apprehended that in a different state of circumstances, the resources by which our military operations have been so materially facilitated might have been applied against us. The causes which have precluded the operation of the alliance with Dowlut Rao Scindiah have been fully detailed in the narrative of transactions and events at that chieftain's court, and your honourable Committee will observe that those causes are wholly unconnected with any considerations affecting the general policy of the alliance.

The Rajah of Jeypore has not fulfilled the duties of the alliance against the common enemy. With regard to active exertions, he has observed a strict neutrality. But this conduct on the part of the Rajah must be attributed to the internal state of the politics of that court. The Rajah of Jeypore however has been useful in a certain degree, by assembling his troops and by publicly manifesting a design to co-operate with the British forces. Had the Rajah of Jeypore been unconnected with us, the difficulties of the war in Hindostan would have been increased by the necessity of adopting measures of precaution to guard against the possible effect of intrigues at that court, which we should not then have had the means of controlling.

The Rajah of Matcherry has performed all the duties of defensive alliance with fidelity and zeal.

The Rana of Gohud has been equally faithful, and his troops have been actively employed against the enemy.

With regard to the Rajah of Bhurtpore, it may be observed that a sufficient period of time had not elapsed to give full effect to the alliance, before the advance of Holkar compelled the British power to direct its immediate attention to the prosecution of hostilities against that chieftain. The retreat of Colonel Monson's detachment, followed by the troops of Jeswunt Rao Holkar, favoured the success of Holkar's intrigues at the durbar of the Rajah of Bhurtpore; and the characteristic treachery of the Asiatic durbars combined with an exaggerated impression of Holkar's power, induced the Rajah of Bhurtpore to violate his engagements and to join the cause of the enemy. The experience of the difficulty, danger and distress which have attended his connection with Jeswunt Rao Holkar, has induced the Rajah of Bhurtpore to abandon the cause of that chieftain, and to seek the sources of security and prosperity in the renewal of his alliance with the British power.

It is evident therefore that the war with Jeswunt Rao Holkar has not only not affected the general system of our political relations, but has demonstrated the utility of those relations in their application to the increase of our resources and power against our enemies. Under every possible advantage derived from the exertions of intrigue, from the unsettled state of our conquests, from the internal commotion naturally occasioned by a state of active war on the frontier, from the exaggerated impression of Holkar's power, resources, skill and reputation, the disturbances excited by Holkar have not shaken the great foundations of the alliances established in Hindostan and the Deccan, and it may be reasonably expected that the ultimate consequence of the war with Holkar will tend to confirm the stability of all our alliances, and to secure the tranquillity of all our dominions.

We have the honour to be,
Honourable Sirs,
Your most faithful humble Servants,
WELLESLEY.
G. H. BARLOW.
G. UDNY.

70. Lieut.-General Lake to the Marquess Wellesley.

Monson's Retreat.

My Lord, Head Quarters, Camp near Gunge, Sept. 8th, 1804.

I have now the honour to forward for your Lordship's information, the honourable Colonel Monson's report of the operations of his detachment from the 23d to the 31st of August, the period of the arrival of the detachment at Agra. This with my former despatches will put your Lordship in possession of every information I have received respecting the movements of Colonel Monson's corps since he retreated from Mochundie Ghaut.

Although I cannot sufficiently lament the unfortunate turn affairs have taken with this detachment, or the circumstances which led to them, still I feel it my duty to represent to your Lordship, that both officers and men of the detachment, on every occasion on which they were actually engaged with the enemy, maintained the superiority of British discipline, and showed the utmost steadiness and gallantry; and that should an opportunity occur of leading against the enemy those who remain, I shall place the fullest confidence in their attachment, and approved bravery and experience.

I shall cause every possible enquiry to be made into the apparent disaffection, on the part of some of the corps, who formed the detachment, but I have the pleasure to assure your Lordship, that it does not appear to have been by any means extensive; numbers of the sepoys are daily coming in; and those that are still with the enemy and have been obliged to take service, have sent word to their officers that they will avail themselves of the first opportunity of escaping to return; those who refused to enter the enemy's service, have been most cruelly treated and in general mutilated in the right hand.

I have the honour to be,

My Lord, &c.

G. LAKE.

1st Enclosure.

Hon. Colonel Monson to Lieutenant-General Lake.

Agra, Sept. 2nd, 1804.

Sir,

I had the honour to inform you, in my letter under date the 22nd instant, that I was encamped on the banks of the Banas river, which I was in hopes I should be able to cross the following day, but finding the river did not fall so rapidly as I had reason to expect, I ordered Captain Nicholl with six companies of the 2nd battalion of the 21st regiment to cross in boats and proceed immediately to Khooshall Ghur, in charge of the treasure with my detachment. On the evening of the 23rd the whole of Holkar's cavalry came up, and pitched their camp about two coss from me; on the morning of the 24th at day-light, finding the river fordable, I began to cross my baggage. At eight o'clock A.M. the enemy took possession of a large village on my right, and commenced making embrasures for two guns, I therefore ordered without delay two companies from the 12th regiment and the advanced picquet from the 2nd battalion, 2nd regiment, the whole under the command of Lieutenant Parr of the latter corps, to storm it, which they did with the loss of few men killed and wounded. About twelve o'clock the whole of my baggage with the 12th regiment, 1st battalion 14th, 2nd do. 9th regiment had crossed and one howitzer, the above corps leaving their picquets standing, the 2nd battalion, 2nd regiment remaining to support them, finding any attempt to withdraw my picquets before dark must prove inevitable destruction to them. About four o'clock P.M. Jeswunt Rao Holkar's infantry came up;

in the morning nearly the whole of his cavalry had crossed at a ford three or four miles below me for the purpose of attacking my baggage, which had obliged me to cross my infantry as his cavalry crossed. When his infantry had surrounded my picquets, they opened a heavy cannonade, which obliged the party I had posted in the village we had taken in the morning, to withdraw, and of which the enemy took possession directly, and planted two guns, but our right flank being protected by a high hill, they had no effect; they therefore soon withdrew them more to our left, and after having cannonaded us for nearly an hour, they came down to the attack making a hideous noise. Our troops received them with great coolness and charged; the enemy fled, and we carried a line of guns, but were prevented making use of them, the whole of the ammunition being carried away. The enemy immediately opened a fire extremely heavy from a fresh line of guns, and surrounded us with bodies of infantry and cavalry; most of my troops were now either killed or wounded, and further resistance being vain, I retreated to the Ghaut with the howitzer, the enemy pressing on me very fast; when we reached the river, the confusion was very great. The enemy's horse cut in, and every man that stood by the howitzer was cut down. Our troops now pressed fast into the river endeavouring to make their escape, but the enemy pushed after and many were either killed or drowned. At this instant, while the enemy were making a dreadful slaughter of our troops, Colonel M'Culloch with the 1st battalion 14th regiment, came down to the river on the opposite side, upon which the enemy retired, and enabled a few of our troops to escape, which was scarcely done, when the enemy brought their guns to the Ghaut, and under the cover of their fire began to cross. I immediately formed my troops into an oblong square and commenced my march.

The enemy's cavalry pressing me hard, I found it impossible to save the whole of my baggage; therefore leaving my baggage to make the best of its way, I moved rapidly on, and I reached Khooshall Ghur on the evening of the 25th, the greater part of my baggage having fallen into the hands of the enemy. We had been greatly annoyed the whole of the day, the enemy's horse hanging on the rear, and threatening to charge, which had obliged me to halt and open the howitzer on them, several times. I found Captain Nicholl's detachment encamped in the fort; they had been attacked by the battalions belonging to

Rao Mahdoo Sadishoo Buxy; for the particulars I refer your Excellency to Captain Nicholl's letter which I have the honour to enclose. I was much surprized on my arrival at Khooshall Ghur, not to find five battalions and twenty pieces of cannon belonging to the Rajah of Jeypore, as I understood from that court that I was to be joined by that force on my arrival there, but they had left it some days previous to my arrival. On the morning of the 26th the whole of the enemy's cavalry arrived, and in the evening they encamped in separate bodies all around me. It is with great pain I now inform your Excellency that I discovered during the day a correspondence going forward between some of the native commissioned officers of the 1st battalion 14th and 2nd battalion 9th regiment, with Holkar, respecting those corps going over to the enemy: fortunately a letter from Holkar to a Soubahdar was brought to me, which put it into my power to take some steps towards preventing any thing serious with regard to the safety of the detachment being endangered taking place; however, nearly two companies from the 1st battalion 14th regiment going off, and about 400 of Major Frith's irregular cavalry deserting at the same time, and receiving two verbal summons from Holkar to surrender during the day, made my situation truly alarming, not knowing to what extent the treachery of my troops might exist. I must in justice notice that the exemplary conduct of the 12th regiment, and the six companies of the 2nd battalion 21st regiment during the whole of the campaign, shewed their attachment to the government and their reliance on their officers, and at this period in particular, their steady good conduct was very conspicuous. On the 26th at seven o'clock P.M. I moved out of the fort, and formed an oblong square: finding the howitzer would prove a serious delay to us, I ordered it to be spiked, and commenced my march. The enemy, as soon as they knew we had moved, followed us, and one body charged but were easily repulsed, the guns nearly at the same time belonging to Rao Mahdoo Sadishoo Buxy's battalion opened on us but with no effect. It being so dark they could not distinguish our troops at the distance we were. The enemy's cavalry followed us the whole of the night of the 26th, and during the day of the 27th, harassing our troops by attempting to charge and keeping up a constant fire from three gallopers, but which fortunately did little mischief. In the evening about six o'clock we reached Hindoun, the troops greatly exhausted. I took possession of an old ruined fort and remained until one o'clock A.M. on the 28th, when I commenced my march; at day-light the enemy's horse were in sight, they keeping the high road whilst we marched among the ravines, the guide taking what he said was the best road. We had just cleared the ravines when the enemy's cavalry made a desperate charge in three bodies, which was received by our troops with determined coolness and bravery, the 12th regiment reserving their fire until the enemy were within a few yards of their bayonets, which when delivered did great execution, several Sirdars falling. The enemy finding they could make no impression, wheeled off and made no more attempts to charge during the day.

We reached the Biana Pass about sunset, and finding the troops greatly fatigued, I halted, intending to remain for the night at the entrance of the pass. The enemy's guns at this time came up, and finding I had halted, brought their guns around me and opened a furious cannonade, which obliged me to proceed. We got to the city of Biana about nine o'clock P.M. The night being extremely dark, the baggage had mixed with the line, and thrown the troops into great confusion: however I got the corps together as well as possible and moved on, but they were soon separated again, owing to the darkness of the night and the great cultivation. Finding it impossible to collect the whole together again, each corps made the best of their way to Agra, keeping together as much as possible, where most of the troops arrived by the 30th and the whole by the 31st at day-light.

I beg leave now to assure your Excellency that the coolness and determined bravery shewn by the officers and men of the detachment during this arduous contest, merits my warmest praise; the firmness with which they received the repeated attacks of so superior and powerful an enemy and the patience with which they underwent the greatest hardships, claims my admiration and gratitude, and shewed themselves worthy of the name of British troops. To Lieutenant-Colonels M'Culloch and Ashe, Major Radcliffe, Captains Nicholl, Featherstone, and Fletcher I feel greatly indebted for their exertions. Lieutenant-Colonel Don and Captain O'Donnel, both in a bad state of health, exerted themselves greatly and rendered me essential service.

Your Excellency will perceive, by the enclosed return of killed and wounded, that our loss has been very great. Though I cannot but lament with the deepest regret the loss of so many noble fellows, yet I cannot but observe with some satisfaction, that even in the hour of death, each emulated the other to deeds of glory, and fell as became British soldiers and men.

I have the honour to be, &c.

W. MONSON,
Brig. Com.

2d Enclosure.

Captain Nicholl to the Hon. Brigadier General Monson.

Agra, Aug. 31st, 1803.

Sir,

I take this, the earliest opportunity of detailing the occurrences of the detachment you did me the honour to place under my command on the river Banas.

After crossing the Banas in the evening of the 22nd, with six companies of the 2nd battalion of the 21st regiment, (not exceeding 240 firelocks) I moved from its bank about ten o'clock on the following morning in charge of the treasure, tumbrils, &c., and proceeded according to your instructions on the road to Coossial Ghur. About seven in the evening I halted at a small village to refresh the people; and between three and four of the morning of the 24th, moved with the intention of waiting your arrival at the town of Bebonda agreeable to your directions, but being refused admittance, I hesitated not a moment in pushing for Coossial Ghur, under the supposition that my presence there might favourably operate upon the Mahratta chiefs, with whom I had understood negotiation was carrying on. My approach to the town was arrested by a body of Mahratta cavalry, which I (reluctantly) submitted to upon the principle of moderation, and as we came upon them rather unexpectedly, the military etiquette of stopping our approach to their camp to ascertain the cause of our mission, might not be deemed irregular or improper. After being informed that our arrival was for the express purpose of conciliation, we were permitted to proceed to the Fort, under the walls of which I encamped about 12 o'clock, forming a junction with a company of the 12th regiment which had been there some days. Our arrival seemed to excite a good deal of commotion among the Mahrattas, who immediately got under arms, and in an hour sounded a signal for march; I then advised them again that we had come on terms of friendship, and begged they would persuade themselves to remain where they were until your arrival, which might be expected in all the next day; this, however, had no other effect than producing a declaration, on their part, that they had been deceived, and about 4 o'clock they marched off and encamped a coss distant on the opposite side of the town; at 9 o'clock at night all our picquets were attacked at the same moment by horsemen, &c. With our little line under arms, I directed the picquets to stand their ground, which they did until the morning, when I recalled them and moved into the Fort of Coossial Ghur, having several gates and more openings. Between 7 and 8 o'clock on the 24th I was apprized of the Mahrattas' intention of levying a maumlah upon the town, accompanied with a threat, that if in two hours a certain sum was not paid, they would open a cannonade upon it. Conceiving that in alliance with the Jeypoor Rajah, it was my duty to defend his rights, I wrote to the Mahratta Chiefs, repeating the cause and intention of our arrival, adding that if they were determined to insist upon unjust exactions, I was equally determined under all the circumstances existing to oppose them, to which they replied as enclosed (leaving me no doubts as to my own conduct) in haughty terms demanding all my elephants, treasure, arms, &c., and observing that if I would resign them I should be permitted to retire unmolested wherever I pleased. Not having great confidence in Mahratta faith, and feeling all the indignity annexed to the insolence of such a demand, I of course made no reply, and in an hour they opened a battery of 10 guns, 9 and 6 pounders, which they continued playing until 3 o'clock P.M., when finding they could make no impression, they moved round to the northward. Although their battery had been within musket shot, I treated them with silent contempt, which may have encouraged their attack upon the town in the evening, as about 5 o'clock they recommenced their cannonade (all the towns-people quitting the fort), and their infantry, 6 or 800, entering by the north gate with colours flying and drums beating, but by the brisk gallantry of Lieutenant Harriott with his own company of the 2d battalion of the 12th regiment, followed with equal spirit by about 100 men of the 2d battalion of the 21st regiment, the enemy were beat back under disgrace, leaving several killed, and many must have been wounded. Observing the animated conduct of this spirited detachment, I regretted most seriously that I had not a few more sepoys to have enabled me to take advantage of an exulting moment, but the responsibility of a charge so serious in its nature as the treasure, made me pause, fearful of carrying even gallantry too far, though I had not the smallest doubt of success had I attempted their battery. After repulsing their attack upon the town I had however determined to storm this battery upon the close of day, and had given orders to that effect, but whether the enemy had been apprized of your approach or my determination, they wisely moved off their guns to their camp, where altogether they possessed 24 or 25 pieces of cannon. The spirited conduct of our small body in this little affair does them great credit, and is, in my humble opinion, deserving of praise. The men of the 2d battalion of the 21st followed with animated courage the bright example of the company of the 12th regiment. Lieutenant Brownrigg, who upon this occasion acted as a volunteer, behaved with great spirit.

I have the honour to be, &c.

W. NICHOLL,

Capt. commanding a Detachment.

The Company of the 12th, one Drummer killed.

Do. do. 21st, one Sepoy do.

71. Lieut.-General Lake to the Marquess Wellesley.

Monson's Retreat.

Head Quarters, Muttra, July 1st, 1805.

My Lord,

Soon after the conclusion of the late war with the Mahratta confederates, the attention of Government was directed to Jeswunt Rao Holkar. The armies of that chief occupied a position highly dangerous to our security, and he openly avowed an intention to invade our possessions. He was likewise committing the most destructive depredations on the territories of our allies, and employing the most active means to excite revolt and insurrection in those provinces which had recently been subjected to our dominion.

A consideration of these circumstances induced your Lordship in Council to authorize me to enter into a negotiation with Jeswunt Rao Holkar; and in conformity to the instructions with which I was furnished on this occasion, I employed such means as were deemed consistent with the dignity, honour and interests of government to avert the hostile designs of that chief, and to adjust his various insolent and groundless pretensions.

During the progress of this negotiation, I judged it expedient to move forward with the army, which as your Lordship knows, had remained in the field since the conclusion of the former war. This movement was dictated by the desire of giving weight to the means employed for the purpose of accommodation ; by the necessity of protecting from the ravages of Jeswunt Rao Holkar, those states with whom we were in alliance, and by the advantage of placing my army in a situation from whence it might act with effect and celerity in the event of failure in our pacific measures.

In the course of my communications with Holkar, it gradually became manifest that the relations of peace and friendship could not be established with that chief. His language was arrogant and unconciliating, his demands were extravagant and inadmissible, and his conduct continued menacing and hostile. Under these circumstances I continued slowly to advance forward until your Lordship's final decision should authorize what appeared no longer avoidable, the commencement of military operations.

Holkar's force had occupied a position in the country of Ajmeer, contiguous to the frontier of the Jyepoor possessions, from whence it had extended its depredations to all the surrounding countries. On my arrival at Doussa, I was informed that it had moved into the territories of Jyepoor and advanced so far as to threaten the capital of that state. It became of importance to avert a plan which would be destructive to our ally the Rajah of Jyepoor, and add in a great degree to the resources of a chief whose hostile intentions in regard to the British Government were no longer doubtful. I therefore determined to advance a force for the protection of Jyepoor, which my vicinity to that place would have enabled me to support with the rest of my army if necessary.

The force destined for this service marched from my camp at Doussa, on the 18th of April 1804, and consisted of three battalions of Native infantry, with suitable equipments of artillery, military stores, &c. It was commanded by the honourable Lieut.-Colonel Monson of his Majesty's 76th regiment, whom I instructed, unless compelled for the safety of Jyepoor, to avoid engaging any part of the enemy's force, and to remain within such a distance of my army as might enable me to give him whatever degree of support circumstances might require.

The advance of this detachment, and the situation of my army compelled Holkar to abandon his designs against Jyepoor. He moved slowly off in a southerly direction, destroying the villages and laying waste the country in his neighbourhood.

My proceedings in the course of the negotiation I carried on with Jeswunt Rao Holkar had been transmitted to your Lordship, and produced a conviction of the impossibility of avoiding hostilities with that chief. Your Lordship in consequence was pleased to transmit me instructions to commence military operations with every practicable degree of haste and vigour. The despatch on this occasion under date 16th of April 1804, was received whilst the army was encamped at Doussa, and I commenced without delay to carry into effect the orders it contained.

The enemy having halted in the Jyepoor territories an opportunity seemed to offer of bringing him to a general action, and I accordingly proceeded from Doussa with the greatest expedition towards the position he occupied. My approach however induced him to retreat, and he pursued his course with such celerity in a southerly direction as left no probability that I could compel him to engage my army.

The flight of Holkar, and the inexpediency of pursuing him on account of the advanced period of the season and other causes, induced me to halt the army at Nuahee, a position near the frontier of the Jyepoor country, and at an inconsiderable distance from Tonk and Rampoorah, places which with an extensive country connected to them belonged at this time to the enemy, and of which it was of importance that we should obtain possession.

Tonk, which is a walled town of considerable extent and population, was about this time very gallantly attacked and carried by a body of irregular horse, which I had sent in advance under the command of Lieutenant Lucan of his Majesty's 74th regiment, for the purpose of giving every possible annoyance to the rear of the retreating enemy.

Rampoorah is a fortress deemed by the natives of great strength, I therefore judged it necessary to detach a force from the army properly equipped for taking possession of it. The party intended for this service accordingly consisted of two battalions of Native infantry, the necessary artillery, and a regiment of Native cavalry under the command of Lieut.-Colonel Don of the honourable Company's service.

Lieut.-Colonel Don and his detachment executed this duty with the utmost spirit and success. Having in vain endeavoured to induce the enemy to surrender the place, Colonel Don concerted the necessary measures for attempting to carry it by assault on the 16th of May. This was contrived with so much wisdom, and executed with such spirit and energy, that the attempt completely succeeded. The greatest part of the garrison was destroyed, whilst the loss on our part was extremely inconsiderable.

These rapid and important successes, with the situation of my army, and the advancement of the detachment under the honourable Lieut.-Colonel Monson, appeared to impress the enemy with a great degree of consternation. They fled rapidly across the Chumbul river, and returned towards Malwa, laying waste the country in their progress in that direction.

At this period I was informed from all quarters, that Holkar's pecuniary resources were reduced to the lowest ebb, that his army was filled with terror and dismay, and that his troops who before had been mutinous and discontented were now deserting from him in great numbers. These representations were rendered more probable from the consideration that a successful war is necessary to retain together an army and to support the confidence of troops whose chief band of union is plunder. I therefore gave them considerable credit, although I found it impossible to obtain accurate information, and was aware of the exaggeration which the natives of this country give to all their relations.

This reduced state of the enemy's power and resources, and the great distance to which he had prosecuted his flight, appearing to me in a great measure to have released those states with which we were in alliance from all hazard of future depredation, and to have deprived Jeswunt Rao Holkar of all hopes of success in any future attempt to invade the British territories in Hindostan, I determined without further delay to withdraw the main army to their respective cantonments within the Company's provinces.

Other considerations at the same time concurred to render this measure highly expedient. No advantage could have resulted from remaining in the position I then occupied, and a further pursuit of the enemy was rendered impossible from the nature of those countries in advance, in regard to water and provisions. It was highly desirable too to place my European troops under cover before the approach of the rainy season, which could not fail to be destructive to them in the field.

Before I commenced my march to cantonments, it was of

importance to take every precaution in regard to our future security, and it appeared to me that this object would be completely attained by securing the passes of Boondee and Lakery in that chain of mountains to the southward of Rampoorah. I accordingly directed Lieut.-Colonel Monson with the force under his command, to occupy and maintain a position in their vicinity. Lieut.-Colonel Don was at the same time instructed to place himself under the command of Colonel Monson, with the whole force that had captured Rampoorah, with the exception of a regiment of native cavalry which I ordered to rejoin my army.

Having formed this arrangement, and furnished the honourable Lieut.-Colonel Monson with such instructions as appeared necessary for the guidance of his future conduct, I commenced my march with the main army towards Agra on the 18th of May, and I arrived at that place on the 5th of June 1804.

Though this march was in some degree hastened by unexpected occurrences, which at this time happened in the province of Bundelcund, yet my movements were adapted as much as possible to the extreme heat of the season. Notwithstanding however every precaution that could be taken, I lost a number of Europeans, and my whole army suffered severely from the excessive heat.

I stationed the principal part of my native force at Agra and at Muttra, as well for the purpose of securing tranquillity in the districts contiguous to these places, as with the view of ensuring the fidelity of the neighbouring petty states, and of being in readiness to proceed again to the southward, should circumstances at a future period require their presence in that quarter.

No cantonments for European troops had been constructed on the banks of the Jumna, and I therefore proceeded towards Cawnpore with my European force, which consisted of his Majesty's 8th, 27th, and 29th regiments of light dragoons; two companies of his Majesty's 22d and the whole of the 76th regiment of foot, with two companies of the honourable Company's European regiment. These arrived at Cawnpore about the end of June, a few days previous to the commencement of the rainy season.

The detachment which I had left under the command of the honourable Lieut.-Colonel Monson consisted of five complete battalions of native infantry, a suitable proportion of artillery, and about 4,000 irregular cavalry, who, under the command of Lieutenant Lucan, had been ordered to join Colonel Monson's detachment soon after its arrival at Jyepoor. These troops were in a high state of discipline and had been accustomed to victory, and their equipment and efficiency were rendered perfect by an ample supply of treasure and all kinds of military stores.

The passes near which this detachment was stationed afford the only entrance through the mountains above mentioned from Malwa into Hindostan. Through these the enemy had retreated, and whilst they were defended by our troops, his return appeared to be rendered impossible. The situation of Colonel Monson's corps therefore appeared to secure all the advantages which had been obtained, and to obviate every danger that could accrue to ourselves or to our allies, from the absence of the main army.

It was my intention that the detachment should have remained in this position until the termination of the rainy season, where either alone or strengthened by reinforcements from Hindostan as circumstances might have rendered necessary, it could have advanced into Malwa for the purpose of carrying on offensive operations against the enemy. Unfortunately my views were defeated by Colonel Monson's departure from the plan which I intended him to pursue.

The irregular cavalry belonging to Colonel Monson's detachment were sent in advance to distress as much as possible the rear of the retreating enemy, and their exertions in this service were attended with considerable success. Several small parties of the enemy were cut off. On the 29th of May, Lieutenant Lucan, assisted by Captain Gardiner, who likewise commanded a small body of irregular horse, surrounded three battalions and eleven guns belonging to Tantia, a partizan of Holkar, and after a short engagement, in which these officers displayed great activity and courage, compelled them to surrender.

Unfortunately it appeared to Colonel Monson about this time, that advantage would likewise result from the advance of his main force. It appeared to him that the presence of his detachment would animate to resistance the chiefs of those countries in which Holkar was committing depredations. Such resistance in the present reduced and dismayed state of the enemy might be thought to be attended with important effects, and the promises of support and of supply held out to him by the Rajah of Kotah seemed to obviate every risk of an advanced movement.

As soon as I understood that Colonel Monson had formed the resolution of advancing beyond the position I had assigned to him, I expressed in the strongest terms my disapprobation of such a measure, and my apprehension of the mischiefs that might follow. Before however, he could receive my communications on this subject, he had actually crossed the Chumbul near Kotah, and was proceeding towards Mokundra, (a pass in a more distant range of hills) which appeared to Colonel Monson as defensible and as well calculated to command the future operations of the enemy as those at which he had been originally stationed.

Though the reasons which Colonel Monson assigned for this forward movement did not appear to me satisfactory, yet I was disposed to allow considerable latitude to the judgment of this officer, as well from his being best able to obtain a knowledge of such circumstances as immediately regarded his situation, as from the confidence in his zeal, courage and abilities with which his whole conduct during the former war had inspired me.

Finding therefore that the detachment had occupied the advanced position at Mokundra, it appeared to me that the most desirable measure I could pursue, was to form such arrangements as were calculated to support it in that situation, and point out to Colonel Monson such precautions as were likely to obviate the evils to be apprehended.

All my communications to Colonel Monson at this period had in view to impress him strongly with the danger of advancing; with the importance of being in a situation where his supplies would be liable to no uncertainty; with the advantages to be derived from his conciliating the chiefs of those countries in his neighbourhood, and with the necessity of extreme vigilance in regard to whatever concerned the movements and designs of the enemy.

I likewise directed Colonel Monson to correspond frequently with Colonel Murray, and to keep that officer regularly informed of the nature of his situation and intentions, and of his opinions on such objects as he thought ought to engage their mutual attention and exertions.

Colonel Murray at the commencement of the war had been directed by Major-General Wellesley to move forward from Guzerat into Malwa. The force under his command was of sufficient strength to engage the main body of the enemy, and he had been instructed to use every exertion to accomplish that object. At the present period he was advancing to Oujein, where his presence appeared necessary for the defence of that capital against an attack with which it was threatened by the enemy's force.

My communications to Colonel Murray informed him of the situation of the detachment under the command of Colonel Monson, and instructed him to correspond and co-operate with that officer, in the fullest confidence that two bodies of troops of such strength and efficiency could not only have supported each other, but by availing themselves with judgment of such favourable circumstances as offered, might have had it in their power to accomplish the total overthrow of the enemy.

For reasons which have never been satisfactorily explained to me, Colonel Murray after he had advanced within a short distance of Oujein, formed the extraordinary resolution of retreating behind the Myhee river, and actually fell back for that purpose. This movement gave the enemy confidence; relieved him from any apprehension of an attack on the side of Malwa, and left him at liberty to direct his whole attention to the honourable Colonel Monson's detachment. Colonel Murray after several retrograde marches, again altered his intentions and advanced to Oujein. He was however, either too late to give the necessary support to Colonel Monson ; or he declined affording that degree of assistance and co-operation which seemed to me so much in his power, and which the situation of the latter so much required.

Colonel Monson was at this time unfortunately induced to quit his secure situation at Mokundra. It had appeared to him that the Fort of Hinglaisghur, situated at some distance in advance of that Pass, might greatly tend to strengthen his position, and he resolved to make an effort to gain possession of it. With that view therefore he proceeded forwards, and by an attack concerted with skill and executed with vigour, he carried it by assault on the 2d of July 1804. On this occasion the activity of Colonel Monson, and the gallantry and good conduct of his troops appeared to merit such an expression of my approbation as I had the honour of transmitting to your Lordship.

After the capture of Hinglaisghur, the detachment remained encamped several days in its vicinity, at a place nearly fifty miles in advance of the Mokundra Pass; and whilst they were in this situation, intelligence was received that the main body of the enemy's force was advancing for the purpose of attacking them.

Jeswunt Rao Holkar had occupied a position in Malwa and was now advanced to the vicinity of Rampoorah on the left bank of the Chumbul. During the short period that had elapsed since his retreat, he had been exerting himself to collect his scattered forces; to renew their confidence and their attachment to his cause; and to equip himself in such a manner as would enable him to make a vigorous exertion against the British detachment. How he succeeded in so great a degree as to be enabled to make those exertions which afterwards marked his conduct, my deficiency of information prevents me from explaining.

Colonel Monson's farther progress would have deprived the enemy of his most valuable possessions; and been entirely destructive of whatever confidence or spirit his followers yet retained. These considerations therefore, in the very exposed situation of the British detachment at the present period, formed a sufficient inducement to the enemy to hazard a decisive engagement.

The Chumbul which at that season is a considerable river was interposed between our troops and Holkar's army; and whilst the enemy were crossing it, with their numerous artillery, an opportunity offered to Colonel Monson of attacking him, which appeared to promise success. Success at this period would have secured to Colonel Monson his advanced position; procured him supplies from the neighbouring country, and enabled him afterwards to prosecute whatever plan of operations circumstances might have required. Colonel Monson was aware of these circumstances, and wrote to me that he intended to attack the enemy. Unfortunately, however, he altered these intentions and permitted Jeswunt Rao Holkar's force to cross the river unmolested and to advance upon his detachment.

As another occasion equally favourable for an attack could not occur to Colonel Monson, perhaps the omission should have been repaired by an attack under the most favourable circumstances that could afterwards be obtained. His numbers were certainly inferior to those of the enemy, but he had on his side discipline, approved valour, and the choice of position. A bold effort was likewise evidently necessary to extricate him from his situation, and to avoid the disgrace and misfortunes inseparable from a rapid retreat.

Instead of adopting this plan, Colonel Monson formed the resolution of retreating to the Mokundrah Pass, with the intention as he informed me of making a stand in that situation; and he accordingly moved from his position on the 8th of July, leaving the whole of his irregular cavalry on the ground of his encampment, for the purpose of protecting the rear of the detachment in the event of an attack from the enemy.

Colonel Monson's infantry effected their retreat without suffering any loss; but his cavalry having as he informed me, remained longer behind than he intended, were attacked, and, after an obstinate contest, nearly cut to pieces. The number of these had lately been increased by a body of horse belonging to Bapojee Scindiah, and in this affair amounted to four thousand. Lieutenant Lucan who commanded them signalized himself to an extraordinary degree, till being severely wounded he was made prisoner. He afterwards fell a sacrifice to the inhuman treatment he met with from the enemy.

After the detachment had arrived at the Mokundrah Pass, its out-posts were attacked by bodies of the enemy's horse which had followed in its rear. These were repulsed with very severe loss, but the supposed approach of the enemy's infantry, and the apprehensions entertained by Lieut.-Colonel Monson in regard to his future supplies, determined him after a short halt to prosecute his retreat to Kotah. This he effected on the 12th of July with more precipitation than was necessary; having on his departure from Mokundrah left his camp standing in order to deceive the enemy in regard to his intentions.

At Kotah Colonel Monson's difficulties did not appear to him to be diminished. He stated that he was unable to obtain the necessary supply of provisions; and a misunderstanding with the Rajah having at the same time created some distrust in regard to the disposition and views of the latter, the Colonel determined to re-cross the Chumbul and retire on the fortress of Rampoorah.

On its march from Kotah to Rampoorah, the detachment sustained considerable loss, and was exposed to great inconvenience from the severity of the rains and the want of provisions. Colonel Monson reported to me that the obstacles produced by the very broken state of the roads and the swelling of the rivers, were surmounted with the utmost difficulty, and compelled him to leave behind the whole of his artillery and military stores. These in consequence fell into the hands of the enemy, where they remained until retaken by my army at Deig and Bhurtpore.

Colonel Monson was detained a considerable time at the Chumbulee rivulet, which was much swelled by the rains; and at length found such difficulty in crossing it, that several of his men were drowned. He states, likewise, that he was attacked in this situation by a body of the enemy's horse, which he repulsed with some loss. The detachment arrived at Rampoorah about the 27th of July.

As soon as I was apprized that Colonel Monson had commenced his retreat, I urged him in the most pressing manner to occupy some position in which he could make a stand against the enemy; and I at the same time ordered two fresh battalions with ample supplies of ammunition, provisions and treasure to march from Agra with all possible expedition to his support. These battalions under Colonel M'Culloch and a thousand irregular horse under Major Frith reached Rampoorah a few days after Colonel Monson's arrival at that place.

When I was informed that the detachment joined by this reinforcement was at Rampoorah, I transmitted instructions to Colonel Monson to make a stand at that place, if such a measure appeared to him practicable; but if the enemy could not be opposed with considerable prospect of success, to throw a sufficient garrison with the necessary quantity of provisions and stores into the Fort of Rampoorah, and fall back in a slow and regular manner on the frontier of the British possessions, before the enemy were in a situation to press his retreat.

The honourable Colonel deemed it most advisable to retreat; and he accordingly marched from Rampoorah on the 21st of August, after having garrisoned that place as I had directed. He had, however, waited till the enemy were close upon his rear. On the 22nd of August the detachment arrived at the Bannas river, which was so swelled in consequence of the late rains as to be impassable. This occasioned a halt until the river might subside, during which the whole force of the enemy had assembled in the neighbourhood of the detachment.

The river having become fordable, the detachment was ordered to cross it on the 24th of August, notwithstanding the presence of the enemy; and the precautions taken by Colonel Monson on this occasion were not sufficient to prevent the enemy from availing himself successfully of the opportunity which was offered to him of attacking our troops.

When four battalions of the detachment had crossed the river, the enemy commenced a sharp attack upon the pickets which had not yet been withdrawn. Colonel Monson immediately advanced to their support with a battalion of the second regiment of the native infantry, now the only corps remaining on that side of the river. This party was in consequence exposed to the whole force of the enemy's attack.

The utmost steadiness and intrepidity was displayed in this unequal contest. The battalion above mentioned, not only withstood the utmost efforts of the enemy, but charged and drove them from several of their guns. The great numbers however which had fallen, and the great loss of officers it had sustained, rendered it unable to maintain the advantages it had obtained. It was compelled after an arduous struggle to fall back upon the river; and the obstacles it there met with in crossing exposed it so much to the enemy's attack, that great numbers were destroyed.

Colonel Monson continued his retreat to Khooshalghur, where he arrived on the night of the 25th of August, and joined a party consisting of six companies of sepoys, which he had sent forward under Captain Nicholl with the treasure of the detachment, the day preceding the action at the Bannas river.

A body of troops belonging to Dowlut Rao Scindiah were at this time encamped in the neighbourhood of Khooshalghur, and had resolved to attack the town for the purpose of levying a contribution. The hopes of obtaining possession of the treasure induced them at the same time to commence an attack on Captain Nicholl's party. They were however repulsed with some loss, and afterwards joined the enemy.

A great part of the corps of irregular cavalry, commanded by Major Frith, deserted during the retreat from Rampoorah; and at Khooshalghur some sepoys of the 14th regiment went over with their arms to the enemy. The defection amongst the latter was however more the consequence of extreme fatigue than of disaffection, and never took place to any very alarming extent.

On his route from Khooshalghur, Colonel Monson formed his detachment into an oblong square, which resisted with great steadiness repeated attacks of the enemy, who continued to harrass its march. On the 28th of August, in the neighbourhood of Hindown, the detachment repulsed with severe loss a very vigorous charge made upon it by the whole of the enemy's cavalry.

As the detachment approached our own territories, however, it lost in a considerable degree that regularity which it had hitherto preserved. In this situation several were destroyed; and others, exhausted and dispirited by hunger and fatigue, allowed themselves to fall into the hands of the enemy. The remainder, greatly harrassed and nearly worn out, arrived in a scattered and irregular manner at Agra about the 31st of August.

It is painful to me to reflect on these distressing particulars. It affords however some satisfaction to be assured of the steadiness and attachment of our native troops, even under circumstances of the severest misfortune. The same corps which constituted Colonel Monson's detachment, have served under my immediate command during the whole of this campaign, and they have on every occasion displayed the utmost patience, activity, steadiness and discipline.

The impression made on the public mind by the misfortunes of the honourable Lieut.-Colonel Monson's detachment, was much increased by the ferocious cruelty exercised on those who fell into the hands of the enemy. Europeans of all descriptions were immediately put to death; and such natives as refused to engage in the service of the enemy, were mutilated in a most shocking and inhuman manner. Fortunately, a very small number of the former have suffered; and the latter, as a means of preservation, embraced a cause which they soon afterwards found an opportunity of deserting.

The enemy's cavalry followed close in the rear of the honourable Lieut.-Colonel Monson's detachment; and his infantry and artillery arrived in a few days afterwards, and took up a position in the neighbourhood of Bhurtpore. This rendered necessary the adoption of that system of measures which I shall have the honour of detailing to your Lordship in my next despatch.

I have the honour to be,

My Lord,

Your Lordship's most faithful humble servant,

LAKE.

72. Honourable Brigadier Monson to the Marquess Wellesley.

Battle of Deeg.

My Lord, Camp near Deeg, Nov. 14, 1804.

However proud and happy I may feel in communicating to your Excellency some particulars respecting the brilliant and decided victory, which through the favour of Providence we have obtained over the whole of the infantry and guns of Jeswunt Rao Holkar, commanded by his chief Sirdar, Hernaut Dada; at the same time I cannot sufficiently lament the event which has made it fall to my lot, in consequence of Major-General Fraser having received a severe wound, which obliged him to quit the field. I attribute our decided and glorious victory over the enemy, entirely to the arrangements made for the attack by Major-General Fraser, and to the confidence and enthusiasm with which he inspired the whole army, heading his Majesty's 76th regiment with the most undaunted gallantry.

Your Excellency has already heard from Major-General Fraser the particulars respecting the commencement of the action.

After we had carried the village, we descended the hill, and charged the enemy's advanced party under a most tremendous discharge of round, grape, and chain, from their guns, which they abandoned as we came up to them, retiring to fresh batteries, the whole of which we carried for upwards of two miles, they flying before us in every direction; numbers of them perishing in the swamp which encompasses that angle of the fort at Deeg, and even in the ditch of the fort itself, being pursued by us close up to the very walls. After having carried the different ranges of guns, which extended from the village on their right flank to the south-east angle of the fort, we returned to attack a large body of the enemy drawn up to the eastward of the lower end of the lake, and who kept annoying us with a most destructive fire from 18 and 12 pounders, which until now we had no opportunity of dispersing; these however were kept in check by Major Hammond with the 1st battalion 2nd regiment, and three 6-pounders, who maintained his position with the utmost steadiness and gallantry. I ordered some more 6-pounders to be brought up, and, under cover of their fire, I moved round upon the enemy's left flank, who as we advanced made a precipitate retreat into the lake, where numbers perished, amongst whom were Mohummud Shah Khan and Abdil Khan, two of the principal Sirdars of the Ally-Goles. After this, the enemy made no further opposition, but entirely quitted the field, flying in all directions. Lieut.-Colonel Browne, with the 2nd and 3rd regiments of native cavalry and gallopers, continued to watch the motions of a considerable body of horse during the action, and afterwards moved down to the field of engagement to protect the removal of the captured guns and our wounded, who were unavoidably left there. Lieut.-Colonel Ball at the same time moved down with the 3rd brigade to support the cavalry.

I find it impossible to express my gratitude and obligation for the support I have received from every officer and soldier engaged. Were I allowed to offer my individual thanks, to Lieut.-

To face Page 544

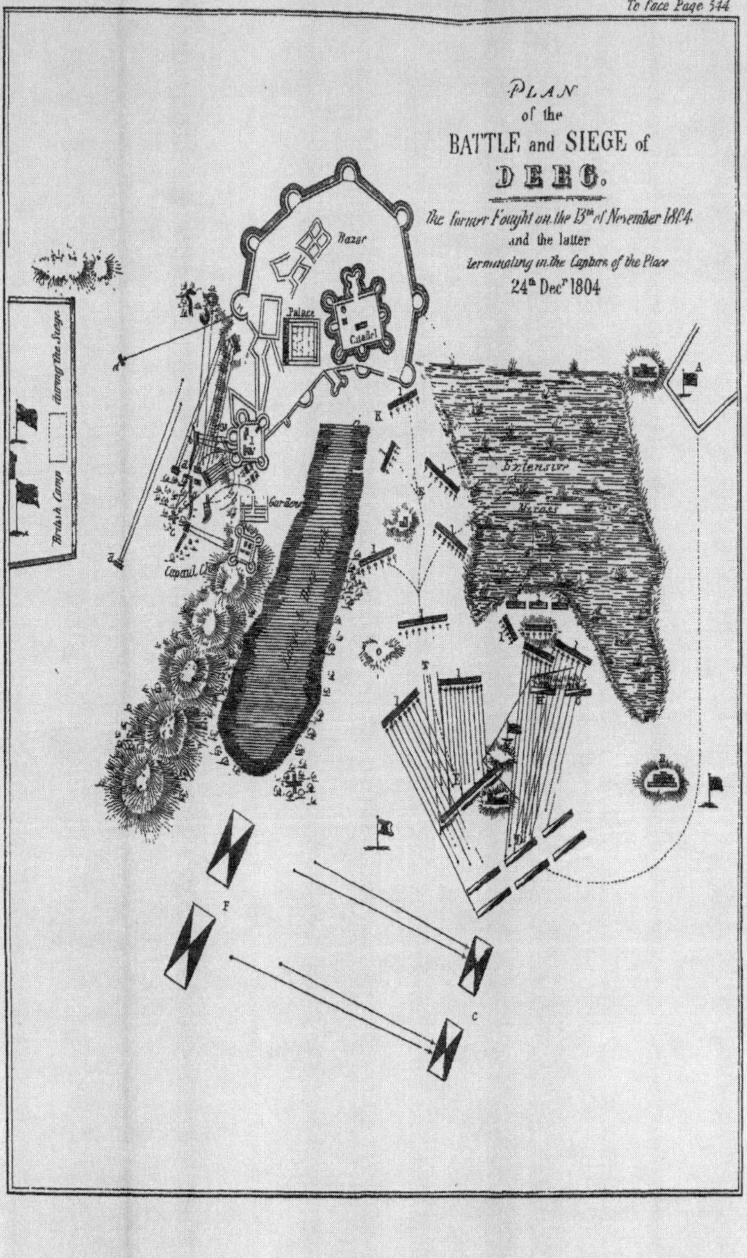

Colonel Horsford, commanding the artillery, and to Lieut.-Colonel G. S. Browne, commanding the 2nd brigade infantry, they are particularly due.

From Brigade Major Menzies, Captains Fraser and Macknight, the officers of Major-General Fraser's staff, I received the most active assistance, for which I feel myself highly indebted. My sincere thanks are also due to my Brigade Major Captain Carr, and to Ensign Bowyer, of the 12th regiment native infantry, who acted as my Aid-de-Camp on this occasion.

I should not be doing justice to my feelings were I not to mention in the most pointed manner the undaunted bravery and steadiness of his Majesty's 76th regiment, which was never more conspicuously displayed than on this day.

I have equal satisfaction in mentioning the conduct of the 1st European regiment, under the command of Lieut.-Colonel Burnet, who showed themselves in every way worthy of the name of British troops.

From the most accurate accounts I can obtain, the enemy's force consisted of twenty-four battalions, a considerable body of horse, and one hundred and sixty pieces of cannon, the greater part of which is already brought to camp. The enemy's loss, as far as I can ascertain, has been very great, and it is supposed near two thousand have been killed and drowned in their efforts to escape. At the same time, glorious as has been the result of this day, I have to lament the death of many a gallant soldier.

The remains of the enemy's army which took shelter in the Fort of Deeg are in the greatest consternation, and are deserting in vast numbers.

I have the honour to enclose a general return of killed, wounded, and missing, of the corps engaged, and a return of ordnance, &c. captured and brought into camp; more guns are hourly discovered. I have the satisfaction to add, that among the captured guns are eleven 6-pounders and two 12-pounders, lost by the detachment under my command.

I have the honour to be, my Lord,
your Lordship's most obedient
and most devoted Servant,
W. Monson.

73. Lieutenant-General Lake to the Marquess Wellesley.

Surprise and rout of Holkar and his cavalry.

Head Quarters, Furruckabad, Nov. 17, 1804.

My Lord,

I have the honour to inform your Lordship, that in pursuance of my intentions expressed in my despatch of yesterday's date, I reached this place this morning with the cavalry before day-break, after a march of upwards of thirty-four miles.

The enemy occupied a position close under the walls of Furruckabad, and I completely succeeded in surprizing them. The consequence has been, that vast numbers of their men and horses have been destroyed, and the whole cattle and baggage taken which they possessed.

Jeswunt Rao Holkar escaped by an early flight, but his troops in the greatest confusion, were pursued and every where cut to pieces by my cavalry. I am happy to add, that we have sustained very little loss either in men or horses.

I have not time at the present moment to express the satisfaction I have derived from the good conduct of all the corps engaged, but I shall have the honour of forwarding to your Lordship my sentiments on this subject as soon as possible.

I have the honour to be, my Lord,
your Lordship's most faithful humble Servant,

G. LAKE.

74. Lieutenant-General Lake to the Marquess Wellesley.

First unsuccessful assault on Bhurtpore.

Head Quarters, Camp before Bhurtpore,
January 10th, 1805.

My Lord,

I have the honour to inform your Lordship, that in consequence of the breach in the wall of the town being reported practicable, I determined on storming the place yesterday evening. I chose this time, in order to prevent the enemy from stockading the breach during the night, which had hitherto been the case.

I am sorry to add, that obstacles of an insurmountable nature were opposed to the storming party, on their arrival at the breach; the water in the ditch was exceedingly deep; this difficulty however was speedily surmounted, and the party gained the foot of the breach; but though every exertion was made by both officers and men, the breach was so imperfect, that every effort to gain

To face Page 517

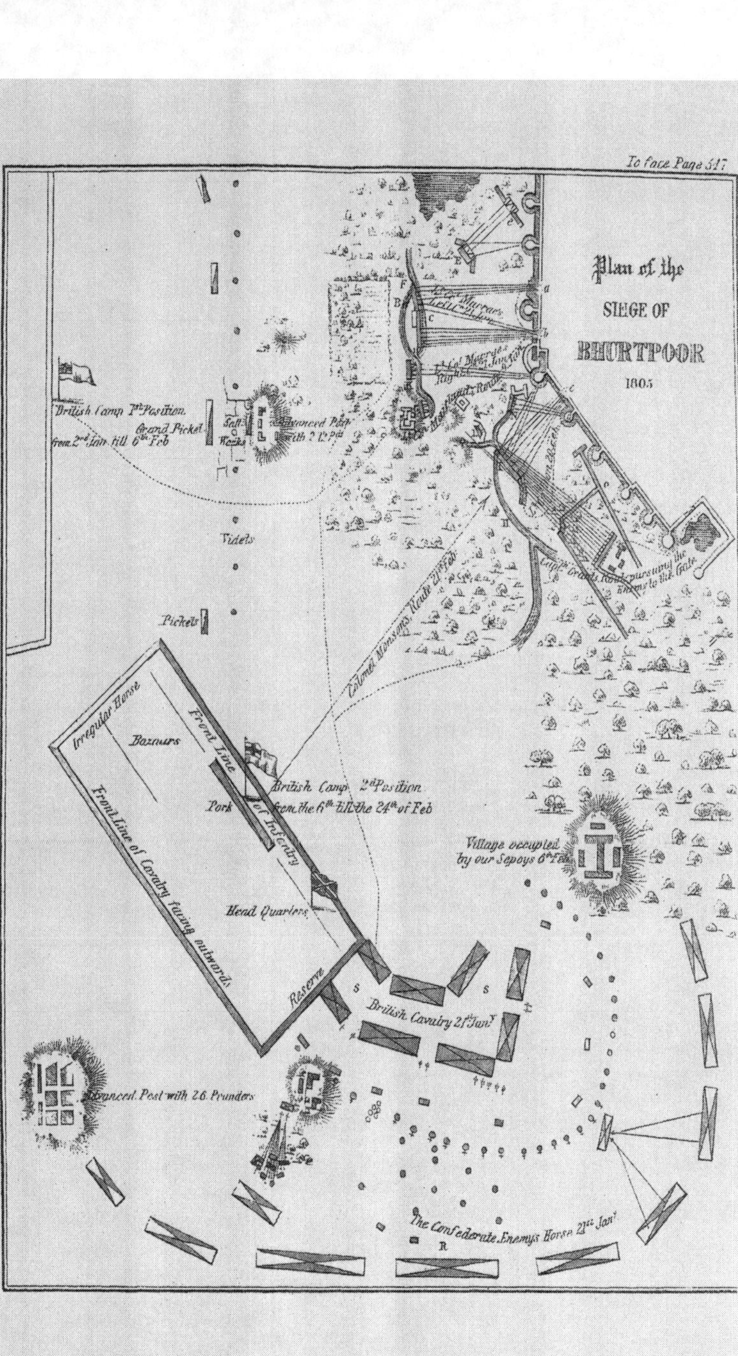

the top proved fruitless, and the column, after making several attempts with heavy loss, was obliged to retire, which they did in excellent order, to our battery.

Among the many brave men who have fallen on this occasion, it is with sincere grief I report the death of Lieut.-Colonel Maitland, of the 75th regiment, who commanded the storming party; his exertions are described by all to have been of a nature the most heroic, and his example animated the men to persevere in their attempts, which nothing but difficulties, of a nature the most unexpected, could have rendered unsuccessful. This gallant officer, though he had received several severe wounds, continued to exert himself until he received a shot in the head, which proved instantaneously mortal.

Although we unfortunately failed in gaining possession of the place, we were not wholly unsuccessful. A flanking column on the right, under the orders of Major Hawkes, gained possession of the enemy's battery, and succeeded in spiking and disabling their guns, and in destroying the greatest part of the enemy who were opposed to them.

I beg to assure your Lordship, that the conduct of our officers and men employed last night, has been as exemplary as on every former occasion; but circumstances, of an unexpected and unfortunate nature, occurred, which their utmost efforts could not surmount: but I hope, in a very few days, their excellent conduct will be rewarded by the possession of the place.

I have the honour to be,
My Lord,
Your Lordship's most faithful humble servant,
G. LAKE.

75. Lieutenant-General Lake to the Marquess Wellesley.

Second unsuccessful assault on Bhurtpore.

Head Quarters, Camp before Bhurtpore,
Jan. 21, 1805.

My Lord,

I have the honour to inform your Lordship, that the breach appearing in a sufficient state of forwardness, I determined to attempt the place again this afternoon.

The storming party moved out of the trenches, where they had been lodged for the purpose, a little before three o'clock. I am sorry to add, that the ditch was found so broad and deep, that every attempt to pass it proved unsuccessful, and the party was obliged to return to the trenches, without effecting their object.

The troops behaved with their usual steadiness, but I fear, from the heavy fire they were unavoidably exposed to, for a considerable time, that our loss has been severe.

I shall have the honour to forward returns of the killed and wounded, as soon as possible.

I have the honour to be, my Lord,
your Lordship's most faithful humble Servant,
G. LAKE.

76. Lieut.-General Lake to the Marquess Wellesley.

Third unsuccessful assault on Bhurtpore.

Head Quarters, Camp before Bhurtpore,
February 21, 1805.

My Lord,

My despatch of the 20th will have informed your Lordship, of our failure on that day, in an attempt to carry Bhurtpore by assault.

I have now the honour to detail for your Lordship's information, the plans that were formed to ensure, if possible, the success of the attempt.

The storming party under the orders of Lieut.-Colonel Don, was formed of the greatest part of the European force belonging to the Bengal army, and three battalions of Sepoys.

One column composed of 200 of his Majesty's 86th regiment, from the Bombay division, and the 1st battalion 8th regiment Bengal native infantry, under Captain Grant, of the former corps, was ordered to attack the enemy's trenches and guns outside the town, whilst a third column composed of 300 men of his Majesty's 65th regiment, and two battalions of Bombay Sepoys, marched to attack the Beem Narain Gate, which from every report I had received was easy of access for guns, &c.

The signal for the storming party to move out was the commencement of Captain Grant's attack on the enemy's trenches, which took place a little before four o'clock in the afternoon.

Captain Grant's column was completely successful, and got immediate possession of the enemy's guns, eleven in number, all of which have been brought into camp. The gallant conduct of Captain Grant and his party merits every praise.

I am sorry to say, that neither of the other columns succeeded.

Lieut.-Colonel Don's was unfortunately delayed by some unexpected circumstances, and on its arrival at the ditch, it was found to contain such a depth of water as to render it impossible to gain the breach. The troops immediately attempted to ascend by the bastion, but the obstacles they met with were of so serious a nature, that their utmost efforts were unsuccessful, though the colours of the 12th native infantry were planted within a short distance of the top.

The column from the Bombay division under Lieut.-Colonel Taylor, notwithstanding every exertion, could not effect their object. They were considerably delayed on their march by a large body of the enemy's horse; and, by a mistake on the part of their guide, were very early exposed to a most heavy and destructive fire from the town, which by destroying their ladders rendered the attempt on the gate impracticable, and obliged Lieut.-Colonel Taylor to draw his men under cover, until he received orders to return to camp.

I feel it my duty to assure your Lordship, that though unfortunately not crowned with success, the exertions of Colonel Don were meritorious and gallant in the extreme, and I feel under infinite obligations to this officer.

I have the honour to be, My Lord,
Your Lordship's most faithful humble servant,
G. LAKE.

77. Lieut.-General Lake to the Marquess Wellesley.

Fourth unsuccessful assault on Bhurtpore.

Head Quarters, Camp before Bhurtpore,
February 22, 1805.

My Lord,

My despatch of yesterday's date will have conveyed to your Lordship intelligence of our want of success, in a fourth attempt made to carry this place by assault.

As it appeared that our failure on the 20th was to be accounted for, in a great measure, by the occurrence of unexpected accidents and delays, as part of the corps who formed the storming party had surmounted the principal difficulty, and had nearly gained the summit of the bastion, where I was informed a few hours more battering would render the ascent perfectly easy, I determined to make another attempt yesterday.

The party for this service consisted of the whole European

force, and two battalions of native infantry of the Bengal army, and the greater part of his Majesty's 65th and 86th regiments, and the grenadier battalion, and flank companies of the 1st battalion 3d regiment, from the Bombay division. The whole moved on to the attack about three o'clock in the afternoon, under the command of the honourable Brigadier Monson.

The troops, most confident of success, commenced the attack and persevered in it for a considerable length of time, with the most determined bravery, but their utmost exertions were not sufficient to enable them to gain the top of the breach. The bastion which was the point of attack was extremely steep, the resistance opposed to them was vigorous, and as our men could only mount by small parties at a time, the advantages were very great on the side of the enemy. Discharges of grape, logs of wood, and pots filled with combustible materials, immediately knocked down those who were ascending, and the whole party, after being engaged in an obstinate contest for two hours, and suffering very severe loss, were obliged to relinquish the attempt, and retire to our trenches.

I have to lament the loss of very many gallant officers and men, as will appear to your Lordship by the accompanying return of killed and wounded on this occasion.

It is with sincere grief I inform your Lordship, that among the killed is my aide-de-camp, Major Menzies, of his Majesty's 80th regiment, who proceeded with the storming party, and fell, whilst, among the foremost, he was making the most heroic exertions to ascend the breach. I feel sincere sorrow for his loss, no less on account of the great regard I entertained for his private worth, than from the high estimation in which I held his merits as an officer.

The Honourable Colonel Monson, to whom the conduct of the attack was entrusted, made every possible exertion, and has received my best thanks for his uncommon gallantry and perseverance on that occasion.

Though the troops were unable to effect their object, I am happy to assure your Lordship that they have on no occasion displayed greater steadiness. Those of the Bengal army supported their former character, and the Bombay division displayed a degree of resolution and discipline which entitles them to my highest praise and approbation.

I have the honour to be, my Lord,
your Lordship's most faithful humble servant,

G. LAKE.

78. The Marquess Wellesley to Lieut.-General Lord Lake.

Unsuccessful assaults on Bhurtpore.

Fort William, March 9th, 1805.

My dear Lord,

In reading over my private communications to your Lordship, I fear that you may be impressed with an opinion that I feel too strong a desire for the early termination of the war, even on any terms. I certainly am most anxious for peace, but I wish your Lordship to understand distinctly that my first object is the vigorous and steady prosecution of the war. With this view I entreat your Lordship not to attempt to accelerate operations at Bhurtpore (if you should resume the siege of that place), in any manner which can expose us to the risk of failure. Time and regular proceeding must ensure the fall of the place if an adequate battering train sufficiently supplied be duly provided and properly directed, with the application also of regular means for taking off the defences of the place. I request your Lordship not to attempt to renew the siege without full and ample means for its prosecution; nor to attempt any assault while the least doubt exists of success. I fear that we have despised the place and enemy so much as to render both formidable.

The resumption of the siege of Bhurtpore previously to the pursuit of Holkar is also a point which I must seriously recommend to your attention. Unless the reduction of the place be absolutely necessary previously to that pursuit, or essential to our honour, I wish your Lordship to consider whether the risk of another failure, and the consequent loss (to say no more), ought to be hazarded. To your superior judgment I commit this important question. The health of the troops must also be most seriously and tenderly considered. A large army must be cantoned on the right bank of the Jumna, and a force must drive Holkar from our frontier.

My advices from Scindiah's camp of the 10th February still leave that chief's views in a painful state of doubt. If he should move towards our frontier your Lordship will march directly against him. His conduct is inexplicable and most vexatious. Your Lordship will judge of my sufferings amidst all the vexations which have fallen upon me in a manner so miraculous and distressing

Ever, my dear Lord,

yours, most affectionately,

WELLESLEY.

VI. DEFENCE OF THE INDIAN EMPIRE.

1. European Army.

79. The Marquess Wellesley to the Right Hon. Henry Dundas.

Reform and increase of the European army.

July 13th, 1800.

My dear Sir,

The representations which I have lately received from Fort St. George, relative to the reduced state of his Majesty's regiments of infantry serving at that Presidency, have suggested such serious considerations to my mind, as render it my indispensable duty to direct your immediate and unremitting attention to this most important subject.

It would be superfluous to detail in a letter to you, the reasons which demonstrate that the security of our interests in India require the European force, which may be deemed necessary for the different establishments in India, to be maintained as complete and efficient as possible. The total number of European troops to be maintained for the general service of India, may admit of a variety of opinions. My own judgment is, that the augmentation of our European force should always bear a due proportion to the increased value and extent of our possessions in India; since in every arduous crisis we must principally depend, for the preservation of those possessions, on our European troops. If, therefore, previous to the late war in Mysore, the European establishment in India did not exceed the requisite proportion, that establishment must be deemed inadequate to our present extended dominions, as well as to the increase which it has been unavoidably necessary to make in the native part of our Indian army. Considerations of prudence as well as of military convenience demand, that every augmentation of our native troops in India should be accompanied by a due augmentation of our European force, artillery as well as infantry. The conquest of Mysore, by diminishing our danger in India from the native powers, may appear to diminish the necessity of augmenting our European force; but if the extension of our dominions, and of our alliances has rendered an increase of our native force indispensable, the same reasons demand a proportionate augmentation of the European part of the army. In addition to these considerations it must be observed that, while the war in Europe shall continue, our empire in India must constantly be exposed to the attempts of the French, although that danger also is certainly much diminished by the fall of Tippoo Sultaun.

It is unnecessary to observe to you, that no augmentation of our European force has taken place since the late war in Mysore. But I desire to call your particular observation to the alarming condition of our European force in India since that period. The casualties of the several corps have necessarily been numerous, and the supply of recruits from Europe has either totally ceased, or been extremely inconsiderable. The number of his Majesty's regiments of infantry in India, continues indeed to be the same; but instead of consisting of 1,200 rank and file, according to the establishment, those employed under the Presidency of Fort St. George, are stated to be reduced to an average of about 500 rank and file fit for duty. The regiments belonging to the establishment of Bombay, and those on the Island of Ceylon, are also very incomplete. His Majesty's three regiments of infantry at this Presidency do not exceed 2,400 rank and file, or about 800 men each. The Company's European artillery are everywhere extremely weak. The fixed establishment of this corps is defective at all the Presidencies; and the numbers wanting to complete even that defective establishment are now so considerable, that I intend without delay to reduce one of the Company's European regiments in Bengal, for the purpose of augmenting the artillery of this Presidency, and I shall probably carry into effect a similar measure at Fort St. George and Bombay.

From a statement which I have received from the Commander-in-Chief it appears that the sixteen King's Regiments of Infantry now in India, consisted on the 1st of May, 1800, of about 11,000 rank and file; the deficiencies amounting to above 8,000 men. The Company's four European Regiments may be reckoned at 2,500 rank and file; the Swiss Regiment De Meuron at about

600, making the total European infantry in India, King's and Company's, about 14,000 rank and file.

But as these numbers include the sick, from this amount must be deducted at least one-fourth in calculating the numbers now ready for service, which would leave the total number of Europeans actually able to take the field in the British empire in India, about 10,500 men.

This European force is far inferior to the strength of that which ought to be constantly maintained in India, in a condition for field service. In Bengal alone 6,000 European infantry should always be ready for active duty; and the establishment of Bengal, in order to be enabled at all times to furnish such a disposable force, ought to consist at least of eight regiments of the present nominal strength, or 1,200 rank and file each.

Eight thousand European infantry should always be ready for service on the Coast of Coromandel including Mysore; and at least 4,000 for the service of Ceylon and Bombay, and the Coasts of Canara and Malabar. To furnish 12,000 efficient men for these different points would require an establishment of at least 20,000 rank and file.

I would therefore propose that the European infantry for India should be fixed at twenty-five regiments of the present establishment of strength 1,200, (making altogether 30,000 rank and file) which number, according to past experience, would be requisite in order at all times to furnish a force of 18,000 men for field service. This calculation however, supposes an improved degree of attention to the regular supply of recruits from Europe.

The whole of this European infantry should consist of King's troops; and the Company's European regiments in Bengal, at Fort St. George and Bombay, should be converted into artillery as far as the men might be found serviceable in that branch of the army. The remainder might either be drafted into his Majesty's regiments, or returned to Europe.

I am not of opinion that it will be necessary that the European regiments of the Company, which I propose to be reduced, shall be replaced by new regiments of native infantry raised merely for that purpose. The course of our subsidiary engagements, and the extension of dominion to which they are likely to lead. by means of the commutation of subsidy for territory, will necessarily require some increase of the native infantry, and consequently afford sufficient means of disposing of the officers belonging to the reduced European corps. But whatever augmentation of the native infantry may hereafter be requisite on account of our new subsidiary engagements, and the augmentation of our territorial resources; you will observe that the expense will not prove any additional burthen to the Company, but will be defrayed either in money or cession of territory by the state, for whose service or protection the additional troops shall have been raised.

An augmentation of our European cavalry in India is scarcely less necessary than that of our infantry. I am of opinion that we ought to maintain at least eight complete regiments of dragoons. Of the additional regiments, two should be stationed in the Peninsula of India, and two in the province of Oude.

I have already stated the alarming deficiency of our artillery throughout India, and the expedient to which I intend to resort for the remedy of this serious evil. But the best remedy which I may be enabled to apply will be insufficient, on account of the great deficiency of officers of artillery; some companies have now no more than one commissioned officer doing duty with them. This deficiency proceeds in a great measure, from the original inadequacy of the establishment in point of commissioned officers; and partly from the neglect of a regular supply of cadets. Of the establishment of officers, defective as it is, nearly one-third are either on furlough, or employed in staff offices which preclude them from the performance of regimental duty. One additional subaltern at least should be posted to every company of artillery; and I most particularly request your attention to the necessity of sending out to India without delay, both an ample supply of private artillery men, and of cadets for the artillery corps.

As connected with the subject of artillery, I beg leave to call your particular attention to the declining state of the foundery at Fort William, which, owing to the ignorance of those in charge of that department, is no longer able to supply the ordnance required for the use of this, and of the other Presidencies. This failure has made it necessary that we should apply to England for a supply of field ordnance, and I earnestly entreat you to adopt the requisite measures for enforcing a complete compliance with the Indent of the military board for this purpose. I also most particularly recommend to your immediate consideration the absolute necessity of sending as soon as possible to Bengal one or more scientific persons properly qualified to conduct the foundery at Fort William, this is an evil which requires the most serious attention, and the most prompt remedy.

Believe me, my dear Sir,
With the greatest regard and esteem, ever
Yours most faithfully,
WELLESLEY.

80. The Right Honourable Henry Dundas to the Marquess Wellesley.

The same subject. Financial and other objections to the proposed scheme. Counter proposals.

Wimbledon, Dec. 30th, 1800.

My dear Lord,

A few days ago brought me your overland despatch in cypher, dated 13th July last, and I conceive it so material to put your Lordship in immediate possession of the impression it has made upon me, that it is my intention to suggest to the Chairman of the East India Company the propriety of despatching this letter by an overland conveyance.

In our various private correspondence I have had occasionally an opportunity of stating to your Lordship the deep importance I attach to the necessity of such a steady and regulated system of economy, as may enable us to reduce the great load of debt, by which our affairs in India are encumbered, and unless we are able to accomplish that important object, all our ideas of boasted prosperity are mere delusion, and the bubble will burst the first moment we are again involved in any severe struggle for the protection or security of our Indian interests. For my part I consider an overgrown and unwieldy load of Indian debt as our only mortal foe: our debt even at its present amount is of so formidable a nature as to blast every prospect of future prosperity, if it is permitted to remain at that amount. I must therefore fight it down, and unless that most dangerous of all enemies is subdued, the fall of Seringapatam and the acquisition of Mysore will only be found ultimately to encrease our weakness, by having extended our establishments beyond our means of maintaining them. From the close of the former Mysore war down to the commencement of the present, I had the satisfaction, year after year, of detailing to the public, through the medium of my Indian exposition, the gradual diminution of our debt, and the gradual amelioration of our Indian concerns at home and abroad. Neither was I in any degree alarmed by the rapid progress of debt, which the late war in India has produced; but my reason for not being alarmed, was, that if our debt in India was not permitted upon the whole to exceed about fourteen millions sterling, I saw clearly before me the means of a rapid reduction of it, the moment that peace was restored in Europe, and there ceased to be any such exigency of affairs at home, as to render any further loans necessary on the part of the public. But every idea I entertain of seeing a rapid reduction of our Indian debt is bottomed on the foundation of believing, that the restoration of peace in India would be productive of such a state of our finances there, as would enable us at least to have a large surplus for the discharge of the principal, and interest of our debts, after defraying every necessary establishment. If such is the state of our finance, we know by experience that the provision of investment, and the discharge of our Indian debt can be made mutually and beneficially subservient to each other, and I have greatly deceived myself if I have not formed a plan, by which, on the restoration of peace in Europe, that system of combining the reduction of debt and the provision of investment may be improved upon in a degree hitherto unpractised; but I repeat again to your Lordship that this plan and every other for the solid and permanent prosperity of India must prove abortive if at that period we shall find the state of our finances in India, such as that our large revenues in that quarter are found inadequate even to the discharge of our establishments.

I have contented myself with giving your Lordship this general sketch of my ideas without troubling you with detailed explanations; because I am so confident in my own opinions, and in the certainty of the propositions and conclusions I have stated, that neither your Lordship, nor any man equally conversant with you in the affairs of India, can entertain a doubt of the truth of any thing I have stated. I have therefore only to refer your Lordship to the facts as they exist, and the application of them is too obvious. I refer you to the statement prepared by Mr. Myers under your own authority, and transmitted by your Lordship for my information. I further refer you to the statement of the India budget as last prepared and transmitted to India for your perusal, and upon examining the statements therein contained, founded upon the data as I thought myself then warranted to assume them, you will perceive how much upon a level our revenues and establishments appear to be, and what a pittance only of surplus revenue is there held out in expectation; but even at that time, additions appear to have been made to the establishments of which I was then ignorant, and which when brought forward into calculation and statement, will be found to absorb and exceed every existing revenue.

With these feelings operating upon my mind, your Lordship will not be surprised, when I profess myself truly alarmed by the extent of establishment which your Lordship's letter of the 13th July recommends to my adoption. I lay entirely out of view all considerations of a collateral nature, and therefore do not enlarge upon the topic how far the population of the country amidst all the other calls upon it, could easily bear such a drain for the maintenance of its European establishment in India. I wish at the present moment to consider the subject merely upon the footing of finance, and in that view I should be without hope indeed, if I could be persuaded, that so great an establishment, especially of a European description, was necessary to be kept up for the security of our Asiatic possessions. I should be without hope because in the present state of our finances or under any near prospect of what they may arrive at, it would be impossible for us to pay such an establishment without having recourse to the finances of this country, and in so far making our Indian Empire a burthen upon the mother country. I am sure your Lordship would be as sorry as I could be, to see such a new circumstance arise out of the events which have recently taken place in India; but it is altogether unnecessary to dwell upon such speculations, for I can venture to assert, that if such a contingency was to occur the disappointment and chagrin of the country would soon put an end to any value they have recently been accustomed to attach to our Indian empire.

In considering this subject, I have made a comparison of the establishment at a former period, with that which would be the amount agreeable to the letter to which I am now replying. With this view I have referred back to the establishment as settled in 1796. This was a period when the establishments underwent a revision, and when the power of Tippoo Sultaun and the danger resulting from it were fully before us; and yet including artillery, cavalry and infantry, European and native, the establishment does not seem to have exceeded eighty thousand men. Since that time, and particularly since the end of the late Mysore war, it has been increasing by rapid strides, and if put upon the scale recommended by your Lordship's letter, it would, notwithstanding the fall of Seringapatam, and the Mysorean power, amount to no less than 142,600 men. The addition of expense is enormous in proportion, and the addition alone which your Lordship recommends of European force, would, as nearly as I can conjecture, upon a rough guess, amount to above £500,000 sterling per annum.

I am sure, when I bring those particulars so pointedly before you, you will consider both your own time and mine as usefully employed, when we enter upon a calm discussion how far there can be a utility, far less a necessity, for such an overgrown establishment.

In the first place I greatly doubt if upon a re-examination of the particulars of your letter, your Lordship will find yourself accurate in the data on which you proceed. You rest your opinion of the European infantry establishment necessary for India on the following principle, viz. that whatever be the number actually borne on the army returns, one fourth must be deducted for the number probably sick, or otherwise unfit for duty. On this principle your Lordship argues, that an effective force for Bengal of 6,000 rank and file will require eight regiments or 9,600 rank and file; and that an effective force for Coromandel, Bombay, Malabar, Ceylon, &c. of 12,000, will require 20,000 rank and file, or seventeen regiments taken together; that to furnish 18,000 effective men will require an establishment of twenty-five regiments of 1200 each, or 30,000 rank and file.

Even if the principle be allowed to be correct, the calculation does not appear to be so; 9,600 men or eight regiments less by one fourth, will leave 7,200 instead of 6,000, or one fifth more than you reckon upon, and 20,400 men or seventeen regiments less by one fourth, will leave 15,300 instead of 12,000, being above a quarter more than you reckon upon. Take both together; 30,000 men or twenty-five regiments as proposed by your Lordship, less by one fourth, will leave 22,500 men, or more than the force wanted by your Lordship's statement by 4,500 or one fourth.

Admitting the principle to be just, viz. that whatever the establishment is, one fourth must be deducted for non-effectives, and that the strength required in effective men is, as stated by your Lordship, 18,000, the number of regiments necessary to furnish that force is twenty, or at 1200 rank and file each, 24,000 men; deduct one fourth, and we have 18,000 the number required, and five regiments less than proposed by your Lordship, will be sufficient for the purpose.

But the deduction of one fourth of the number on the army returns for sick does not correspond with the actual state by the returns from Madras and Bombay in which alone the distinction is made; however, as the greatest number of European regiments are stationed at those Presidencies and their dependencies, (viz. 16 out of 21) it may be sufficient in a general view to take the calculation from those returns.

At the end of 1799 the number of King's infantry rank and file at Madras was 5941, of which sick or invalids 853, little more than 1–7th; the Company's infantry rank and file were 1286, of which sick 109, about 1–12th—both together 7227, sick, &c. 962—rather more than 1–8th.

At Bombay the King's infantry rank and file were 3837, of which sick, &c. 448, not 1–8th—the Company's 754, of which sick 65, not 1–11th; both together 4591, of which sick, &c. 513, or about 1–9th.

Take both establishments together, the total rank and file are 11,818, of which sick, &c. 1475 or 1–8th.

It appears from what is above stated, that an allowance of 1–8th for sick would be sufficient, and the force required to furnish 18,000 effective men, would therefore be about seventeen regiments of 1200 rank and file each, making 20,400, deducting 1–8th leaves 17,850 or 150 short of the complement.

But as the returns from Bengal do not specify the sick, and as they may be more in proportion there, than at the other Presidencies; in order to make an apparently ample allowance let the deduction be stated at 1-6th. In this case, to furnish 18,000 effectives will require 18 regiments of 1,200 each, or 21,600—deduct 1-6th or 3,600, and we have the exact number 18,000.

In the above observations your Lordship will perceive that I have proceeded upon the supposition, that your proposition of having, at all times, a force of 18,000 men for field service was necessary for the security of India. But you have not laid before me any detailed data by which to judge of this as a military proposition. If I judge from past experience and some general maxims which I have often heard stated on that subject, I should be disposed to doubt, if such an extent of European establishment was necessary.

Your Lordship's opinion upon this subject seems to rest upon two general grounds of reasoning. In the first place you state that our establishments ought to increase in proportion to the extent of our territory, and secondly, that our European establishment should increase in proportion as we increase our native.

Upon the first of those propositions, I must beg leave to pause, and to substitute another criterion as more applicable to the subject. The criterion by which that question ought to be decided, is rather, by the relative power of our supposed enemies than by our own extent of territory. I am perfectly aware that the internal peace and the security of a newly acquired territory may require an addition of establishment to a certain extent; but if, at the same moment we acquire that territory, we have narrowed our former frontiers, and subdued a restless hostile and enterprising neighbour, it does by no means follow, that our new territory is to receive an establishment in proportion to our old one. The application of this principle to our present state in India is so obvious, I need not consume your time by an illustration of it.

Your second proposition I admit to be true, in so far as to agree that there must be a certain proportion of European force, corresponding to the number of native troops maintained upon the establishment. But still the question occurs, what that proportion ought to be. Some military men have stated a fifth of the whole to be sufficient. None with whom I have conversed have ever stated more than a fourth to be necessary. When your Lordship examines the extent of European establishment as detailed in the orders, which I hope the Court of Directors will send out without delay, and as more particularly to be stated in the sequel of this letter, I believe that your Lordship will find that the European force, consisting of artillery, infantry, and cavalry, amounts to about a fourth of the whole military establishment, which can, with any attention to economy, be maintained in our possessions in India.

Upon the best consideration, therefore, I can give to the subject, I do not find myself at liberty, consistently with any attention to necessary economy, to authorize an establishment of twenty-five European regiments of infantry. I am satisfied that seventeen is adequate to every purpose, even with a view to our subsidiary treaties, unless in one event, viz. that of a permanent arrangement being made with the Portuguese for retaining the possession of Goa. In that event, two more would be necessary; but even in that case it would be six short of what your Lordship proposes. I would propose six King's regiments at Bengal for the service of our own provinces and the Vizier's country. I would propose six King's regiments at Madras for the purposes of our former territories, together with our new acquisitions upon the coasts of Canara and Malabar, and to enable us to perform our engagements with the governments of Hydrabad and Mysore. I would propose two King's regiments for the protection of Bombay and its dependencies as now regulated.

These upon the whole amount to fourteen regiments, which together with one Company's European infantry regiment at each settlement, would make the whole seventeen regiments.

I have deliberated much in my own mind how far it would not be expedient to urge the Directors at the present moment to give up totally their European infantry, and to rest the whole of their European strength upon their artillery, which I agree with your Lordship ought to be put upon the most respectable footing. I hold a well regulated artillery and a highly disciplined cavalry to form our most solid and permanent pre-eminence for the preservation of our military superiority in India. You will observe that I have proposed to get rid of one regiment of Company's European infantry, in order to make good a part of the expense necessary for the artillery. If I had been to consult my own judgment only, I should have urged the Court of Directors to get rid of their whole European infantry with the view of a still further immediate addition to their artillery, and I feel my reasons for the measure to be so forcible, I think I should have been successful in persuading the Court of Directors to acquiesce in my judgment; but as it has been stated to me from quarters too respectable to be resisted, that it is essential for preserving the strength and connection of their different establishments, that there should be a proportion of European infantry, from which their non-commissioned officers must be drafted for their native troops, I do not feel myself at liberty to be pertinacious in my own opinion; but acquiesce in the propriety of keeping up and recruiting, at each of the settlements, one European regiment of infantry, under the immediate authority of the Company.

I have another objection to the proposal of sending out such a multitude of regiments to India, for if ever any storm should arise in the north of Europe to threaten our Indian possessions, or if ever that menace should become more formidable by a union between any great European power and the northern tribes of India, it is not likely such a confederacy would be so sudden as not to enable us to take the necessary precautions. Against any combination that is not of a tremendous size, I hold the proposed establishment perfectly adequate to our security; but if from any such causes as I have suggested, it should become a necessary policy to increase our European force, your Lordship will agree with me in thinking, that it is always a matter of great importance to study how far you can add to your military strength without increasing the number of officers, which not only from the expense of their establishment, but from the contingent charges attending them, add greatly in proportion to the expense of a military establishment. If, therefore, at any time it should be necessary to add to our European force, it should be done, not by additional regiments with additional field officers, but by additional companies to the 17 I have already mentioned. Two companies to each regiment would at once add an European force of above 3000 men, and so in proportion. Even if four companies were in case of urgency to be added, they could on a short warning be got from the army at home, and would, when added to the fourteen King's regiments established for India, make each regiment consist of not more than two battalions of 800 men each.

By adhering to the system I have mentioned, the expense and inconvenience of sending new and raw regiments would be avoided, and the addition made to your European infantry, when required, would have the advantage of being engrafted on old disciplined well seasoned regiments.

The same principle ought now to be applied to the other parts of the service in so far as there is just ground for the augmentation of any part of it. I entirely agree with your Lordship that the present artillery is inadequate to the great additional services now to be performed by that valuable corps; and I likewise agree with you in thinking, that the great extension of territory and the fulfilment of the subsidiary treaties must render an addition to our cavalry strength absolutely necessary. But in both those cases, it does not appear to me that there is at present any occasion either for new battalions of artillery or for those additional regiments of European cavalry which your Lordship's letter suggests. The Court of Directors, I make no doubt, will approve as a temporary expedient, under a pressing exigency, of the measure you have resolved to adopt of completing your artillery establishments by drafts from their European infantry; but besides completing that corps up to its former establishment, it is necessary to make an addition to it, and for the present this should be done by adding two companies to each battalion, and each company to have an additional Lieut.-Fireworker, and ten additional matrosses.

With regard to the cavalry, there are at present four European regiments, and in place of adding to the number of the regiments, the addition should be made to the strength of the existing regiments. This can be speedily and effectually done by adding two companies and twenty men to each regiment, whereby a very considerable addition of strength would be obtained at a moderate expense of officers, namely, one field officer, and the officers necessary for the additional companies; whereas by additional regiments the expense is enhanced beyond all necessity by an addition of no less than five field officers, besides all the others of inferior rank.

This reasoning equally applies to the native cavalry. By adding two troops to each regiment, you will in like manner, at a moderate expense, comparatively speaking, make an addition to your cavalry strength both at Bengal and Madras of not less than twelve troops at each.

Upon the principles I have detailed, I have resolved to recommend to the Court of Directors a revision of their establishments, making every economical reduction where circumstances will admit of it, and at the same time, making such additions to some branches of their service as necessity dictates; but even in those additions consulting economy in every instance, and adopting that mode, which gives the additional strength at the least possible expense.

In the detail I have given, it will not escape your observation, that I have taken no notice of Ceylon. It is because I have formed a decided opinion that the protection of that island cannot be left as a burthen upon the revenues of India. Indeed, at present those revenues cannot afford it. But independent of that consideration, I am fully satisfied that the measure of connecting the administration of that Island with the governments of India was prematurely and inadvertently adopted. The possession of Ceylon, I conceive to be of the last importance to the permanent security of India; but the principles by which it is to be governed, and the establishments by which its affairs are to be administered, cannot be formed upon the model of our Indian establishments. The European part must be very limited in point of number, and their establishments such as they may be settled, must be upon a scale of expense and allowances, far inferior to the establishments upon the Continent of India. I wish not to dwell upon the mischief which has already happened from blending the service of Ceylon with that of Madras. There may certainly be some exceptions to the observation; but as a general proposition, I am fully satisfied upon a minute examination of the subject for some months past, that as on the one hand it would be unwise and inexpedient to admit only the refuse of the Indian servants to the charge of affairs at Ceylon, so on the other hand, it would be unreasonable to expect that the servants upon the Indian establishment of superior talents would be induced to come to Ceylon with the very limited prospects, which the service there would afford to them.

For these and various other considerations, unnecessary for the present purpose to be detailed, I shall submit to his Majesty my opinion, that Ceylon be restored to the state of a royal government, and administered upon the same principles as the government of the Cape is now conducted.

In the perusal of your Lordship's letter I have not been inattentive to what you state as to the deficiencies in the present establishment of our European force, and the inadequacy of the supply of recruits which latterly have been sent to India, and your observation is true in point of fact, that since the late war in Mysore, no augmentation of our European force has taken place; but your Lordship will recollect that, on the first suspicion which arose in my mind of the probability of a war in India, I sent near 5000 of the flower of the British army to the assistance of our Indian establishments, and that valuable force arrived in due time to perform most important service. And this very circumstance will fully account to your Lordship why there has been such a scanty supply of recruits from that period to the present. The defence of India was to the greatest degree pressing, and therefore the force I have referred to, was sent there in preference of every other service. But your Lordship knows enough of the state of Europe at that time and ever since, and likewise of the state of Ireland and our extended distant possessions, to be aware how sensibly every other pressing service was affected by that great reinforcement sent to India, and therefore, when the immediate danger of India was at an end, and its safety ensured by the brilliant issue of the contest, it was natural and wise to appropriate all the recruits we could collect to supply the deficiencies in other quarters. I have only further to observe, that this inconvenience would not have been remedied if there had existed in India an establishment consisting of the number of regiments which your Lordship's letter suggests. The number of recruits for the service of India could not have been larger than it was, and the only consequence would have been an immense additional expense without any additional strength. I have had a full communication with the Commander-in-Chief upon the subject, and I trust effectual means will be concerted for maintaining complete the European establishments to the amount I have mentioned in this letter, and which will be more accurately detailed in the official orders which will be sent without delay from the War Office and from the Court of Directors.

It only remains for me to advert to the concluding part of your Lordship's letter. I never before heard of the defective state of the foundery at Fort William, which your Lordship describes as no longer able to supply the ordnance required for the use of Bengal and the other Presidencies. Your Lordship may rest assured I shall, without delay, call the attention of the Court of Directors to the subject, and an immediate and radical cure must be administered to so serious an evil.

As your Lordship's letter was confined to the subject of military establishments, my reply is of course confined to the same topics. But I am sure when your Lordship adverts to the foundation of a deep-rooted anxiety, which I entertain upon one branch of our expenditure, you will so far concur with me in that feeling as to extend the same principles to every other species of expenditure. I am well aware that valuable improvements may still be made upon many of our Indian concerns, and I know that many of those improvements will likewise lead to expense. I am likewise aware that it is natural for men of ardent minds to wish the rapid execution of improvements which they reckon to be valuable and important, but in the present state of our finances, I have no hesitation in being of opinion that we had better for some time remain stationary and postpone for a while even desirable improvements, if they are to lead to immediate expense. In short, my present creed with regard to India is, that nothing new is to be attempted without weighing well every rupee it will cost.

I have troubled your Lordship with a long letter; but when you consider the importance and extent of the subject I have been under the necessity of discussing, your Lordship will be satisfied that I could scarcely compress the subject within a narrower compass.

I have the honour to be,
my dear Lord,
your most obedient humble servant,
HENRY DUNDAS.

2. GENERAL POLICY, ESPECIALLY AGAINST THE FRENCH.

81. Copy of a private Paper written by General Stuart prior to his leaving India in January 1800, and submitted to the Right Honourable Henry Dundas, on his arrival in England, in July in that year.

Danger of foreign invasion, by land and sea. Importance of securing the whole sea-board. Commercial policy.

There are some important circumstances respecting Bombay and this side of India, which are neither understood in England, nor in this country.

As it is of consequence to the welfare of the British possessions in this part of the world, and of infinite moment to the interests of a large body of men; I would communicate although in ever so hasty a manner, the opinions which I have been led to form on this subject; connecting them with some more general observations on the state of our relations with India. It seems to be too much the practice to neglect the western parts of India, and to value nothing but the fertile fields of Bengal; while in point of real riches, I am not sure but we excel them. We have a variety of articles fit for commerce, and we occupy a soil fit for every production.

It may be doubted whether the revenue derived in cash from the ground in this country, is in any degree less hurtful in its effects with regard to us, than so much money dug from a mine. It is true, that it enables us to pay our troops, and keep up a formidable appearance; but without some other principle of vigour, this kind of wealth would lead to poverty and indolence, as has happened to the Spaniards in America, and to the Dutch in Asia. The true utility of our establishments in India arises from the commerce they produce, the sailors they maintain, the numbers of people to whom they afford food or labour, the commodities by this means exported, or imported, with the industry and the spirit of adventure thence created.

Commercial pursuits first made us visit India; but a scene of brilliant exploits, little connected with commerce, led to the establishment of an extensive empire, which must now be supported by a just combination of military strength, with objects relating to trade. Hence the encouragement of military and commercial exertion, is the chief object of national concern. By this means we have acquired, and by these means we must maintain our dominion over this country.

Whether or not we do wisely, in extending our possessions to the interior parts of India, further than we have already done, is a question of great political consideration. It is difficult to resist the temptation and allurements of conquest. Nations and individuals are alike insatiable in their desires; and it is rarely, that either know the temperate medium which should bound their acquisitions. Prudent men, and those who have been accustomed to examine on the spot the state of India, and the nature of our connection with it, would rather see us in possession of the coasts, which would secure to us every where the commerce, and which would always be accessible to our fleets. We must at all times support a vast establishment to resist, or keep in awe the great Indian foreign powers; but this will be more formidable by being concentrated, than by an excessive extension of territory, which is more likely to produce weakness, from the necessity in that situation of scattering and dispersing our forces.

The expense of the armies can as well be maintained by territories near the sea, as by those more inaccessible and distant. Their efficiency can be much better supported, as when close to the shore their wants can be more easily supplied, and the connection with the parent state kept alive, an object which distance and time are apt to diminish, and which should therefore never be lost sight of. From the great superiority which we possess in courage and science, our danger from the nations of India, will never probably be very imminent. They have been from the remotest times successively reduced by men of colder regions, partaking of a fiercer and more hardy temperament. In the beginning exposed to the alternate ravages or conquest of the nations of the Caspian Tartary, and Persia; they were only at intervals relieved by the vast distance which separated them from these hordes, and which put a stop for a time to their incursions. It is now upwards of forty years since India was visited by these barbarians: and they are at present supplanted by the English. The facility afforded of reaching this country by ships, and the great ease of transporting men and stores, have obtained us this superiority. An attention to the same means may no doubt long maintain us in this advantage; but an advertency to the former periods of history, and in particular the recent attempts of Zemaun Shah to march by land to India, ought to caution us to keep a watchful eye on this quarter, and not to conclude the danger to be over, because its effects have not been lately felt.

The route by which Alexander, and other conquerors arrived in India, is still open, and the people whose ancestors composed their armies, possess at this moment perhaps an equal degree of courage and adventure as their forefathers. They require but an ambitious or enterprizing leader, to pour forth their uncivilized bands, and to overspread like a torrent, the fertile fields of Hindostan, which, aided by the remembrance of the exploits of their predecessors, holds out a perpetual object of temptation.

But it is easier to resist the unregulated efforts of barbarians, than the constant and systematic attempts of European nations. The superiority which has always attended the people in possession of the commerce, or power of this part of Asia, must ever excite jealousy and raise up opponents. The present interest, the ancient rivalship, and the fixed ambition of the French nation, will perpetually incite them to drive us from this country. Under whatever government they may fall, and whatever diminution their power may sustain in the issue of this war, the principle will be pursued with the same vigour, and the first moment of prosperity, or of opportunity, will be seized to establish themselves in India, or to expel us from it. The first step indeed, will have in view the last.

To effectuate either of these objects, no resources of genius, policy, or activity will be wanting. It is on a return of peace probably, that we shall have to combat the practice of every art, which will, in spite of conventions, or treaties, and in defiance of their import, be resorted to by this enterprizing and unprincipled rival, to obtain a footing in India.

To accomplish this design, the French have in their power other advantages, of which they will not fail to avail themselves. The possession of the Mauritius affords them a safe harbour, a situation where they may concert their plans in secret; and containing a population that would contribute a considerable number of soldiers and sailors towards their success. The French at these Islands possess a colony within the tropics of white men, as active and ardent as the mother country. They are the only European nation in possession of this advantage; for the English colony of St. Helena is too weak to be any assistance; and it is yet to be seen whether the colonists at the Cape, who from their situation are able to give great support to our Indian empire, are more disposed to obstruct than promote the views of Government.

It is not perhaps so much to be imputed, as matter of blame to us, as to the natural consequence of superiority under the most circumspect behaviour, that the French character is more popular in India than ours. This is however very true, and individuals of that nation are always sure of a more favourable reception from the Native Princes. This predilection affords them an opportunity of introducing themselves at the principal durbars, where many of them have acquired great influence, and risen to the first offices of the state. It was chiefly by the degree of personal esteem and favour that they obtained such weight and power at the court of the Nizam. It was by the instrument of force, and the agency of fear, that we succeeded in expelling them from Hyderabad. The imbecility of the Nizam's government, and the need he was in of our protection against Tippoo, made him consent to a measure which otherwise it was his interest and inclination to oppose.

The Mahrattas more independent and with great prejudices, have not yet given themselves up to either nation. It cannot however be doubted, but that they are secretly disposed to the French, and will, whenever occasion may offer, assist their schemes of commerce, or aggrandizement in opposition to us.

In finishing this cursory and imperfect view of the danger to which our possessions in this country stand exposed; as I am of opinion that the greatest peril to them will proceed from the attempts of the French; I would according to that view regulate the distribution of the forces, and the choice of our positions. When we retire into the inland parts of India to collect the revenue of the ground, we are forgetful of our real welfare, our real strength, and the origin of both in this country. The natives of India are ignorant of the value of the sea; trade is not their object; they neither know its importance, nor its principles. They would willingly relinquish a territory bordering on the sea, for one in an inland situation, which should produce a few more rupees per annum. They never would allow the vast benefits that might arise from the ocean, the source of all our greatness, to enter into their calculation. If this observation is a just one, it results from it, that without much difficulty we could secure to ourselves by exchange, every part of the coasts of India. The wealth and power of the interior states would then be equally at our disposal.

The late war with Tippoo Sultaun has shewn us pretty nearly what an Indian enemy can do, and that we have not much to fear from them alone. It cannot be too often repeated, that our danger will arise from a foreign enemy, who could secure alliances in this country. This ought to be the great object of our attention, as it is the true source of any apprehension.

The best way of considering this circumstance, is to take an impartial view of our situation in this country, and examine where we are sufficiently secure, or where we are defective in strength.

We are in the first place in possession of the sea coasts of Ceylon, and may be considered as the sovereigns of the whole Island. This is a possession of the greatest importance to the defence of all our Indian dominions, and in the hands of an active nation, would soon be turned into the most dangerous instrument of power against us. If the Island should be confirmed to us at a peace, it ought to be more strongly fortified, and defended by a large body of Europeans.

At present being in possession of the sea coasts of Ceylon, we have all the strength there that can be required from situation, more especially as there can be little danger from the native Prince of the Island.

The Bengal provinces appear very safe from an external enemy coming by sea to that side of India. The river is a dangerous one, of itself forming a strong defence, and we are in possession of nearly the whole of the coast towards Madras. The part that does not belong to us is savage and fruitless, and would never be thought of as the direction of entrance or attack from without. We have besides a large army in that valuable country; and Fort William, a very strong fortress, must in the first place fall before any invading enemy from the sea could make much progress against us in Bengal. The most immediate danger to these provinces will probably proceed from Zemaun

Shah, or some of the northern states in conjunction with the Seykes and Mahrattas. As these nations are all ignorant of the art of sieges, the interior frontiers of Bengal ought to be strongly secured by fortifications, which would form insurmountable barriers to such enemies: and this is one of the few situations where the construction of forts appears advisable in India, or where it is necessary to keep up a large body of forces inland. The difficulty that an European enemy would have in reaching Bengal, either by land or sea, and of establishing themselves afterwards, seems fortunately to secure it for a long time from any attempt of the kind. Neither have any of the European nations a sufficient footing there to begin upon, and we shall no doubt prevent their forming encroachments on our territories, for every step they advance must be a diminution of our power.

From Madras to the southernmost point of the Peninsula, the whole of the sea coast is in our possession. It is guarded by a powerful army, which if collected, would always overcome any force which could arrive there by sea, as there is no country power here that could lend material assistance to an enemy. The Nizam and the Mahrattas are too remote, and the former is besides watched by a large body of English troops quartered at his capital, who will be able to check the first symptoms of disaffection. Nor can the French have a direct communication with either of these states by sea from this quarter.

The coast is however open to invasion from the ocean, and there should constantly be a great army on foot in the Carnatic. It may therefore be doubted whether we have added to our security by fixing so large a part of the forces in Mysore, where they are at such a distance from the object of attack. The three Presidencies form the basis of our power in India, and an enemy landing on the coast of Coromandel would march directly to Madras, if he was not prevented by a superior army. The best part of a month would be consumed before the troops could collect and move to its succour from Mysore. What may not an enemy do in this time? It may also be asked what imminent danger threatens Mysore, or what particular interest have we there that requires a large force to be maintained in that country?—We must first fight on the sea coast for our empire in India; when defeated there, it may be necessary to retire to the interior holds, and all that should be done in this case is to secure the means of retreat. But when separated from the sea and obliged to seek for an inland posture of defence, our affairs must be in a desperate state.

Although the Carnatic is every where open to attack from the sea, this is certainly not the point where an European enemy will choose to invade India, nor even look for a commercial establishment. Both these objects will be sought for, I apprehend, on the western shores of the Peninsula, and it is now necessary to turn our attention to them.

Since the acquisition of Kanara, we may be considered as possessing the coast on this side from Cape Comorin to Goa, for it is needless to except the country of Travancore; and we may even include Goa while we have so large a body of troops there. By these late arrangements we have acquired an additional degree of safety in this quarter. But from the Carwar to the mouths of the Indus northward, the sea coast, with a few exceptions, is in the possession of the Mahrattas, the most formidable power of Hindostan. The intermediate, that are not in this situation, are the island of Bombay, Salsett, Carranjah, Demaun, Diu, the small settlement of Bancoote, and the City of Surat, the whole belonging either to the English or Portuguese.

The long tract of coast subject to the Mahrattas abounds with harbours where an enemy could easily land, and where in a fertile country he would find himself amply supplied with all he could want for nourishment or war. This is not the place to enquire into the causes that have kept Europeans from acquiring settlements in this rich country; but as this only depends on their forbearance, it may be safely predicted that these valuable and defenceless possessions will not remain much longer neglected.

If a French force were to land in the Conkan or Guzerat with the *goodwill* of the Mahrattas, they surely would not be less formidable than if they were set down at the gates of Fort William. On the contrary, they would be more formidable, for they would have leisure to secure whatever they had not time to bring with them, and to be joined by bodies of their friends. Such a combination is far from being improbable. The storm would fall on Bengal a little later, but not with less violence.

If they should land *without the consent* of the Mahrattas, they might effect an establishment in Guzerat in spite of their opposition, nor would it be difficult to reconcile them to a measure which would serve as a counterpoise to us. Before the reduction of Seringapatam, had the French succeeded in reaching this country, they would have landed in Tippoo's states or at Goa, which is in their neighbourhood, and which they looked on as an easy conquest.

The political change since that event will induce them to seek the same support from the only remaining independent power, the Mahrattas, whom they will conclude from that reason to be in a natural state of opposition to us.

From this circumstance and others which I have pointed out, the French will still be led to direct their designs on India to the western part of the Peninsula, where they can alone hope for an ally, and where an extensive region of fertile country lies open to their enterprize.

There is no individual, I believe, of any observation on this side of India, who does not look with the same apprehension at its defenceless state.

Notwithstanding every provision that has been made in the power of the Bombay government, if a body of French troops were to land at Surat, it must instantly fall into their hands, and laying aside all consideration for the misfortunes of 2 or 300,000 inhabitants which it contains, or the disgrace which would attend its loss to us, it is evident what resources of all kinds such a city and such a country would afford. It would open an immediate means of communication with the Mahrattas, and lay the foundation of a connection that might annihilate our commerce and our consequence in this part of the world.

The forts of Diu and Demaun belonging to the Portuguese are in this neighbourhood. They are both naturally strong, and they are well fortified but weakly garrisoned. These places would almost fall without resistance into the hands of an enemy, and he would thus find himself in possession of forts, than which we have perhaps nothing superior, and requiring only men to defend them. He would obtain this footing in a fertile, and probably too a friendly country. That this is not a needless cause of fear, I beg to call to remembrance that the French actually made an attack within these few years past on Diu, but fortunately with a very insufficient force.

While Tippoo's government existed, and he was holding out offers to the French, it is pretty certain, that if they had been able to come to India, they would have endeavoured to get possession of Goa, or to land thereabouts.

The situation of all things is changed. The only power to

which that nation can now look is the Mahrattas, and the place of attack, especially since we have secured Goa by our troops, will most probably be transferred to some part of the coast, to the northward of Bombay. Here besides easiness of conquest, they would find wealth and every thing necessary to support war.

We should on all these accounts strengthen ourselves not only at Bombay, the coast of Malabar and Surat, but endeavour to procure a part or the whole of Guzerat, which would give us a sufficient influence from Cape Comorin to the mouths of the Indus. The possession of the Guzerat would be attended with military and commercial advantages of the first importance. It is a small country; but it is the richest in India. From it almost all the cotton is brought which is exported from Bombay to China and Europe. The produce of sales at Canton in this article of the private trade alone, amounts to nearly a million a year. This serves to pay for the Company's investments, and makes an annual return of so much property to the mother country: the more valuable, as it is the entire fruit of industry. The landed revenues of Guzerat are also very considerable; and from its peculiar geography, it could be defended by a small number of troops.

When Mr. Hastings ceded Broach and Bassein to the Mahrattas, he certainly diminished the resources of Bombay, whether for its own defence, or the assistance it might afford the Company's finances.

The possession of Guzerat would give us a new bulwark against Zemaun Shah, whose possessions extend to the banks of the Indus. It would secure to us the best manufacture of piece goods; and the command of the cotton market, the most valuable staple of India.

Another evident advantage besides immediate security would arise from our possessing this line of coast. From its different ports all the pirates that infest this part of India are known to issue. It is our duty to protect the fair trader who daily suffers by those robbers: but putting this out of the question, the import trade from Europe can never be considerable while they are allowed to exist. This trade is carried on by boats or small vessels, who distribute to the different ports whatever production or manufacture of Europe is required for the internal consumption of India. The facility of entering rivers and shoal water, the want too of capital, with the necessity of retailing the goods at many different places, confining these vessels to a small size;

they are thereby rendered an easy and constant object of piratical depredation.

What kind of gain will make up for such a risk? The Company have desired to know why their exports of woollens have ceased to some ports? This is the solution of the question: The demand is not sufficient at one place for the cargoes of large ships that could protect themselves, and the smaller craft, that could distribute to a great amount, dare no longer venture to trade. The marine are quite incapable of affording the necessary degree of protection, nor does there appear any other way than by possessing the coast, and subduing the strongholds of the pirates.

But, it will be asked, shall we go to war without a shew of justice, in order to accomplish all those desirable changes?

With respect to the pirates, this question is easily answered, as we are in fact in a state of hostility with them; and we are justly charged with imbecility for not ere now crushing the nests of so many robbers.

In regard to any views on the Guzerat, these will demand a more serious consideration; and we should not certainly go to war when that can be avoided. Something may be amicably settled by exchanging with the Mahrattas our inland territory, for what would be more for our advantage in all respects, and more acceptable to them. But this question of war will soon resolve itself. It may be considered as a thing certain that the time is not far distant when the avarice or ambition of some European state will lead them to form establishments in Guzerat. The bad government of the Mahrattas, the well-known wealth of the country, and the vast commercial advantages which it holds out, are temptations too powerful to be long resisted. The question then really is, whether we shall be the first to possess ourselves of these advantages, or wait until we have to dispute them with others?

To these arguments we may add, that the strongest political motives press us to secure the sea-coast of India, as the only effectual method of excluding Europeans from this country; and of preventing them disturbing its peace, either by their intrigues or their arms.

No native state can ever be very formidable without the assistance of an European ally; and there is but little reason of apprehension from their aggrandizement by an extension of territory, so long as that is confined to the inland countries.

A much greater intercourse seems to have formerly subsisted between the western ports of India and Persia than at present. A great quantity of English goods, particularly woollens, found their way into that country. We obtained in return silks and silver. This formed a considerable branch of commerce, which may be again revived, but which has long since had but a nominal existence.

In a political light our intercourse with Persia deserves attention, for it is in the power of the sovereigns of that country to repress or assist the hosts of barbarians ready at all times to precipitate themselves on India as on a certain prey.

Bombay is our natural emporium with Persia, as well as the Red Sea, which has acquired a new degree of political importance since the attempt of the French to reach India from Egypt. Whatever may be the present success of this attempt, it becomes incumbent on us to watch henceforward this avenue to India. The design is in itself practicable, and would most likely have succeeded, had the Turks either been in alliance with the French, or had the enemy pushed on, immediately after he reached Cairo.

However this may be, if we mean to secure ourselves in India, the evacuation of Egypt will be made the first condition of peace.

The trade to the Red Sea also seems capable of improvement, and may probably defray the expense of the establishments, which it may be found necessary to maintain in that quarter. Piece goods and grain may be made barter for any quantity of coffee. The former and coarse woollens are in demand in Abyssinia.

The East India Company once carried on a considerable commerce with Japan. They lost this advantage by the ill-judged conduct of the Portuguese, and have been prevented regaining it by the intrigues of the Dutch. It is a censure on us that they have alone for such a period enjoyed the profits of this trade, and a reproach on the commercial spirit of the nation, that we have made no attempt to recover our former footing in Japan. The promotion of science should have been a sufficient incitement to the enterprize. The present low state of the Dutch nation would be favourable to this effort. Furs, cotton, piece goods and woollens may be imported into that country. The returns would be chiefly in gold and copper.

J. STUART.

82. Enclosure in a Letter from the Acting Resident at Poona, dated 20th of February.

French incendiary proclamation to the Chiefs of Hindostan.

Received 11th March, 1804.

Translation of the Declaration by his Excellency General Decaen, Captain-General and Governor of the Isles of Mauritius and Bourbon, and of their dependencies, addressed to all the Chiefs of Hindostan.

From the time when the English obtained possession of more than half of Hindostan, they have continually laboured to defame the character of the French, and have endeavoured to persuade you that we are a faithless and a perfidious people. Without noticing the gross falsity of this assertion, I will withdraw the veil with which they have hitherto concealed their cunning.

Be it known unto you, that, at a time when the French nation was convulsed by internal contests, the English endeavoured to extend the flames of civil discord, as they had before done in Hindostan; but they did not accomplish their infernal object. Aware of their treacherous designs, we composed our animosities, and cordially uniting with each other, we attacked them with so much vigour that they were compelled to consent to terms of peace. Of this circumstance you have doubtless been already informed.

You have observed the line of conduct which the English pursue in Hindostan; you have witnessed the treachery by which they obtained possession of Bengal and Behar; you have seen their tyranny and cruelty in expelling Rajah Cheyt Sing from Benares; their savage and unmanly treatment of the unhappy Begums at Fyzabad; their injustice and violence in wresting from their rightful owners the countries of Oude, Arcot, and Surat; their fraud and rapacity in seizing the territories of Tippoo Sultaun; and, lastly, the unjust and aggressive war in which they are now engaged with the Mahratta Chieftains.

Had you opposed their first attack with the same spirit as our selves, they would not have now had it in their power to exercise their tyrannical and oppressive sway over the countries of Hindostan.

A remedy may be found. Your enemies are by no means numerous. In the whole of Hindostan there are only a few thousand; the remainder of their force consists of native soldiers, your own subjects.

Tell those deceived and unfortunate persons, that they will hereafter be accountable to God, the Prophets, and the (Tacoor) deities, for thus drawing their swords against their liege sovereigns.

Ye chiefs, descended from the stock of the ancient kings and rulers of Hindostan, know your own power—you have hearts, and soldiers, and treasures.

Attack them with your united force, and liberate Hindostan from their violence, oppressions, and tyranny.

Farewell! direct your observation to Ceylon; imitate the example which the inhabitants of that island have placed before you, and the plan which they have pursued.

83. The Marquess Wellesley to Lord Hobart.

Precautions against the revival of French power and influence in India.

(Official and Secret.)

(Extract.) Fort William, June 20, 1803.

My Lord,

This letter having necessarily involved a discussion of considerable detail, it may be convenient to your Lordship that I should conclude by recapitulating the principal questions on which I am anxious to obtain your Lordship's instructions.

First. Whether the convention of 1787 has been formally revived between his Majesty and France, or whether the admission of the French to the benefits of that treaty rests absolutely upon his Majesty's indulgence, and cannot be claimed as an obligation of public faith.

Secondly. By what jurisdiction and in what manner civil and criminal justice is to be administered to the subjects of France within the territories and dependencies of the British Government in India.

Thirdly. By what regulations the establishments of the French within the British possessions and dependencies are to be limited or restrained.

Fourthly. Whether the French Government in India is to be considered as a mere commercial establishment, or as a political and military power.

Fifthly. If the French Government in India is to be considered as a political and military power, what are to be the relations of that power towards the British possessions, dependencies, and allies, and also towards the independent and unallied native powers; what is to be the extent of the military power to be maintained by France in India, and what is to be the extent of her right to repair or to construct fortifications, or to strengthen her military resources in India by alliances or by other means.

Sixthly. If the French Government in India is to be considered in the situation merely of a commercial establishment, with relation to all the powers of India, European and native, by what regulations, and by what system of policy, is the local British Government of India to be authorized to enforce the obligations of such a condition upon the French Government, and upon the other powers of India.

Seventhly. What is to be the condition of the Batavian Government in India, with reference to military and political power.

Eighthly. The nature and extent of the naval power of the French and Batavian Governments in India.

Ninthly. Whether the French and Batavian Republics respectively, are to be permitted to interchange their respective territories and possessions, or to make cessions of territories or possessions to each other respectively; or to receive interchanges or cessions of territory from any other European, or native power in India.

In examining the various topics which this despatch embraces, I have omitted to observe to your Lordship, that some of our dependents exercise a local and distinct sovereign authority within their immediate possessions; the Nawaub of Oude, the Rajah of Mysore, and the Nizam, with several other states are of this description. It may become a question whether French subjects or others, residing within the possessions of such princes or states, should be amenable exclusively to the civil and criminal jurisdiction on the spot, or to the Company's, or to any concurrent jurisdiction of these authorities. On this point your Lordship will receive the most correct opinion from the high legal authorities in England. It is desirable that the conduct of European foreigners resident within the immediate territories of our dependent princes should be controlled by some jurisdiction of more just and regular operation, and of more efficacious, certain and speedy effect than can be derived from the arbitrary, corrupt, and precarious administration of any native state in India.

I have the honour to be, &c.

WELLESLEY.

84. The Right Hon. Lord Castlereagh to the Marquess Wellesley.

Impending renewal of war with France. Economy to be combined with military efficiency in India.

London, March 16th, 1803.
[Received July 6th, 1803.]

My dear Lord,

You will probably hear from me, by an overland express, before this despatch may reach you by sea. I shall delay my communication, by the former channel, in hopes that I may be enabled, in the course of a very few days, to apprize you, with more precision than I can do at this moment, of the actual or probable result of the present discussions carrying on with the French Government. It is enough for me at present to say, that his Majesty's ministers felt that the situation, in which we were placed, as well by the importance and delicacy of those discussions, as by the military preparations which have been carrying on for some time past in the ports of France and Holland, destined ostensibly for St. Domingo and Louisiana, was such as to call for active measures of precaution on our part; and accordingly a strong squadron has been ordered to be equipped for sea. Press-warrants have been issued; and the entire of the militia has been called out.

The usual communication has been made to Parliament on this subject, and was received precisely with the temper one could wish. A strong disposition is shewn from all quarters to support the honour and the interests of the country. Opinions naturally withheld till information can be given, but no attempt made to press Government for premature explanation.

The funds, as might be expected, fell on the first alarm, but have since considerably recovered.

In the present state of things we can only furnish your Lordship with intelligence of what is passing, and desire you to wait for the result before you adopt any measure which can be productive of expence. You will receive, through the Secret Committee, a despatch to this effect, coupled with some observations referable to the principles upon which it may be wise to regulate the future measures of your government in the event of a renewal of hostilities.

It is unnecessary for me to press these observations upon your Lordship's particular attention. The discussions which have lately taken place both at home and abroad on the important measure of reducing the debt, now so happily brought to a decision by the plan for that purpose, before transmitted, having received nearly the unanimous sanction both of the Court of Directors and of Proprietors, and the honourable exertions which you have been making by retrenchments of expence, for giving effect to such a measure, will render you amongst the most unwilling to disturb, beyond what the exigency shall absolutely require, those arrangements, on which the success of the plan depends.

I am sure your Lordship will keep in view how much will be gained in positive strength by directing our exertions, even in war, against the debt, so long as there is little appearance of the enemy being enabled to menace India. However jealous France is of our power in the East, and however steady she may be in her purpose of aiming at positions, from which she might one day hope to shake that power, yet I cannot persuade myself that she has, or can have for a length of time, the means to attempt any direct attack against possessions so defended as ours are by the army now on foot.

I wish you, therefore, to consider how, under the smallest possible extension of expenditure, the army can be kept in that state of adequate preparation which belongs to war. For the five first years of the late war, the surplus abroad was as follows, — 1792–3, £1,326,000; 1793–4, £1,683,000; 1794–5, £1,458,000; 1795–6, £977,000; 1796–7, £508,000.

Whatever efforts France may be able to make in Europe, India cannot be considered as more exposed now than in the years 1793–4–5, &c., whilst Tippoo was yet formidable. I must, therefore, indulge a sanguine hope that your Lordship will find it practicable to adopt a system, even in war, which shall be compatible with our financial objects, and that the surplus revenue, as in the years alluded to, will be still applicable in a large amount to the reduction of debt. If peculiar difficulties arise, we must make corresponding exertions; but let us save our means till those difficulties appear, as far as prudence will permit.

I conclude that the several restitutions have ere this been made to the French and Dutch Governments. How we stand at present with respect to the Portuguese settlements, which were garrisoned by us during the war, I cannot ascertain, either from any orders sent from home, or from any intelligence received from abroad. Under present circumstances I have only to request your Lordship, till you hear further from home, to turn your attention to the possible result of the discussions now pending, and to digest previously in your own mind the war system, on which you would propose to act, if hostilities should actually recommence, limiting it within the narrowest bounds in point of expence, which you deem at all consistent with the public safety. In the latter event, you shall receive early instructions from home as to the precise measures to be taken, with respect to the possessions of the several European powers either on the Continent of India, or in the Eastern Seas.

I have the honour to remain,
with great truth and regard,
your Lordship's most faithful and sincere
humble servant,
CASTLEREAGH.

85. Marquess Wellesley to Right Honourable Lord Viscount Castlereagh.

Difficulties of such a combination. Reduction of Mauritius, the Cape, &c. desirable, and how to be effected.

(Secret.)

Fort William, 25 July, 1803.

My dear Lord,

1. I have the honour to acknowledge the receipt of your letter of the 16th March 1803.

2. I return your lordship many thanks for the information communicated in that despatch.

3. Your Lordship may be assured of my utmost endeavours to accelerate the success of the measures adopted in England for the reduction of the Indian debt; and I entertain a confident expectation that the circumstance of a renewal of hostilities with France, unaccompanied by the danger of military operations of the French in India, or by a rupture between the Company and the Mahratta power, would not occasion any material delay in the progress of the system adopted for the liquidation of the Indian debt, provided the Court of Directors shall duly supply treasure from home equal to the prime cost of investment in India.

4. It is however my positive duty to apprize your lordship

that I received the letter from the Secret Committee under date (the 17th March 1803) with sentiments of the utmost concern, as well as of the most serious apprehension.

5. The orders contained in that letter directing the principal attention of this government in the supposed event of a renewal of hostilities with France to the reduction of the Indian debt appears to me to inculcate principles of policy which may prove injurious to the safety of this empire, especially in time of war.

6. The proportion which the Indian debt now bears to our annual revenues, the proportion of our annual charges to our annual revenues, the reduction effected in the rate of interest upon public loans since the year 1798, the amount and operation of the sinking fund established in India, the present high credit of all the securities of Government, and the flourishing and progressive condition of every branch of our resources, must satisfy your lordship that exaggerated apprehensions have been disseminated with respect to the magnitude and pressure of the debt in India; and that its existence cannot be considered to form the principal object of danger to India in a season of war with France.

7. Just economy in time of war is a bulwark of strength against the enemy; and I trust that your lordship will confide in my anxious solicitude to avail myself of this powerful aid as well as of every other means of prosecuting war against France in India. At the same time I am convinced, that your lordship will not suffer commercial prejudice and the eager desire of temporary mercantile advantage to contract the comprehensive scale of our military preparations or to repress the activity of military enterprize in India in the event of a renewal of hostilities with our formidable and implacable foe.

8. My construction of the tenor of the letter of the Secret Committee may I hope prove erroneous: it appears to me to contain orders calculated to abate that spirit of alacrity and forward military preparation which it has been my anxious endeavour to encourage, and on which must ever depend the security of the British possessions in India not only during the existence of war with France, but even in time of peace.

9. In my letter addressed to your lordship under date 20th April 1803, I had the honour to request your attention to the deficiencies in the effective strength of the European force destined for the peace establishment of India. The peace establishment proposed by your lordship if completely main-

tained (with some additions which I shall have the honour of submitting to your lordship's consideration in a separate despatch) would in my opinion answer every ordinary purpose of security; even in time of war.

10. Extraordinary emergencies must be met by adequate efforts; but it is absolutely necessary that the military establishment maintained in India (especially the European troops) even in time of peace with France, should be formed upon a scale calculated to frustrate surprize from the French and to maintain a commanding superiority over the improving military establishments of the Mahratta powers.

11. The degree of danger to be apprehended from the efforts of France in India in time of peace, is stated in a despatch to Lord Hobart (of the 20th June 1803), a copy of which is enclosed for your lordship's information. Your lordship appears to be fully impressed with the necessity of maintaining in India even in time of peace with France an European army equal to all the ordinary exigencies of war: and my opinion, with regard to the amount of the force adequate to that purpose, will not be found at variance with your lordship's judgment to any considerable extent.

12. The reductions which I effected in the strength of our native regiments upon the conclusion of peace with France were expressly founded upon that event, with reference also to the existing state of peace with all the native powers. In referring to my despatch (of the 8th February 1802) to the Commander-in-Chief on that subject, your lordship will observe that I have considered those reductions to be inseparably connected with the continuance of general peace in India and Europe.

13. The degree of danger to be apprehended from France in India during the existence of war is in my opinion inconsiderable in the present state of our power in India, provided that power be duly exerted in maintaining a commanding superiority in these seas, and in preserving our European and native land forces in a state of complete efficiency and strength. It is also essential to the security of these dominions to cultivate the military energy of the government, and to animate its vigilance and zeal, together with the spirit of the army, by encouraging the free and unrestrained course of our exertions against the enemy in India.

14. While the Cape of Good Hope, the Mauritius, Batavia and Amboyna shall remain in the hands of the French and

Batavian Republics, the security of this empire in time of war must rest upon the extent and condition of the naval and military force stationed in India; upon the constant and diligent observation of the enemy's motions, and upon the prompt application of our means of defence to such operations as may frustrate the attempts, which may be expected from those places during the progress of the war.

15. In addition to these considerations it is to be observed that the several forts and settlements of the French, the Dutch, and Portuguese in India in time of war with France must either be garrisoned by British troops or must afford considerable advantage to France in the prosecution of hostile designs against our power. This consideration necessarily requires the employment of a considerable body of our troops either for the purpose of occupying those places, or of observing the movements of any French force which may be stationed in those places respectively, or may menace them.

16. All the possessions of the French and Dutch on the continent of India now remain in our hands, and Goa must be garrisoned by British troops. It would therefore have been necessary with reference exclusively to these circumstances to maintain our European establishment at least upon the full scale of efficiency proposed by your lordship for a peace establishment, and to raise all the native corps to the war establishment.

17. The state of preparation required by the commotions in the Mahratta empire, by the conduct of Dowlut Rao Scindiah, and of the Rajah of Berar, by the position and strength of Scindiah's French corps under the command of M. Perron, has already compelled me to restore the native corps to the war establishment, even previously to the certainty of a renewal of hostilities with France; and the subsidiary engagements concluded in the Deccan have required the addition of three native regiments in Bengal.

18. The orders from the Secret Committee prohibit any attempt against the Mauritius or Batavia, Any such attempt from India in the present state of the Mahratta power would be imprudent. But it is my duty to state to your lordship my conscientious opinion that in the event of a renewal of war with France, the early conquest of the Isle of France would be an object of the utmost importance to the commerce and political security of these possessions.

19. While the French shall retain the Isle of France with the advantage of an amicable communication with the Cape of Good Hope, a force may be maintained between these two settlements which may be employed either in attempting some vulnerable point of our extensive coast, or in endeavouring to aid some native power in effecting conquests of neutral possessions which might enable the French to menace our frontier.

20. Your lordship will observe that this last suggestion relates to the probable designs of France upon the coast of Ava.

21. I shall entertain no apprehension of being enabled to meet the most vigorous attempt which France could probably make on any part of our possessions, provided the military establishments be preserved in complete vigour. But the arrival of a French force on the continent of India (an event which may be expected in the progress of the war if the French should retain the Cape of Good Hope and the Mauritius) and the partial or temporary success of such an invasion would occasion alarm, and might encourage some of our tributaries or dependants to excite disturbances.

22. A French force might be employed from the same settlements against Malacca or Prince of Wales' Island, (if not against any of our continental possessions) and in that case a considerable expense must be incurred for the purpose of expelling it in the probable event of its first success.

23. Under these circumstances all our measures of defence must be adopted with the supposition that the French may assemble at the Isle of France and at the Cape of Good Hope a force adequate to hostile purposes, and your lordship is apprized that at certain seasons of the year no superiority of naval strength can entirely secure all our possessions from attack.

24. The great extent of the coasts of India, and the variety of services which may require the attention of his Majesty's ships, added to the defective authority of the Company's Government with regard to the navy in India, render the naval defences of our Indian empire extremely precarious even with a decided superiority in the number and strength of his Majesty's ships over those of France and Holland.

25. At present the French and Dutch ships in the Indian and Eastern seas exclusive of those at the Cape of Good Hope, are supposed to be superior in number and weight of metal to his Majesty's squadron within the same seas. But I am not apprehensive

of any early junction of these forces. The distance between Batavia, the Isle of France, and the Cape of Good Hope, and the actual position of the squadron which brought M. Decaen, together with the state of all the French and Dutch ships and men, appear to preclude all immediate danger; and I conclude that early reinforcements to the navy and army in India will speedily arrive from England. But in any case the Company's Government must provide for the immediate defence of our ports and of their trade, while the French and Dutch shall retain any possessions or force in those seas.

26. While the French shall remain in possession of the Isle of France, the British Government in India will be subjected to a heavy expense in supporting a separate marine force for these objects and for the protection of the country trade, and of the Company's ships. During the last war with France the captures made in India by privateers fitted out from the Isle of France, are estimated at four millions sterling.

27. This additional expense for maintaining a marine force must be incurred immediately upon the commencement of war with France.

28. During the last war his Majesty's squadron was never equal to all the objects which demand the protection of a naval force on these seas, and the immediate defence of the trade of the ports of Calcutta and Bombay devolved principally on the Company's Government. Similar difficulty must be expected to arise on the renewal of hostilities with France and Holland.

29. The possession of the Isle of France would diminish the danger to our trade and dominions in India which must be expected to arise from the possession of the Cape by the Batavian Republic, if it should not be found convenient or deemed advisable to recover that colony from the hands of the enemy.

30. I have learnt with considerable concern that opinions are entertained by most respectable persons in England tending to undervalue the importance of the possession of the Cape of Good Hope in time of war with France and Holland. I cannot furnish your lordship with a more satisfactory testimony of my opinion on that question, than by requesting your attention to the annexed extract of a letter which I addressed to Mr. Dundas from the Cape of Good Hope in (the month of February) 1798, during my residence in that colony, at which I touched upon my voyage to India.

31. Your Lordship, I trust, will pardon the emotions of zeal for the security of these possessions, which induce me to express an earnest hope that an early attempt may be made to disturb the strength of the enemy either at the Cape of Good Hope or at the Isle of France.

32. The reduction of either of those possessions would afford great additional security to our Indian empire, and it will be obvious to your Lordship that the reduction of either possession would facilitate our operations against the other.

33. It would not be advisable to undertake an expedition against the Isle of France by a combined operation from England and from India. It is always to be apprehended that some branches of the arrangements for a combined operation from such distant points may fail. The season may be lost, and the enemy may easily obtain information of the intended attempt, in time to prepare resistance. Under any state of affairs on the Continent of India no considerable aid in European troops could prudently be afforded from India, even if the peace establishment, proposed by your Lordship, of seventeen regiments, of one thousand men, were completed.

34. In the present state of the European force in India, your Lordship is apprized of the deficiencies which render it unequal to the purposes originally in your Lordship's contemplation.

35. After the reduction either of the Isle of France or of the Cape of Good Hope, it would be a practicable and expedient measure to compose a part of the garrisons of either of those places of native sepoys from India; and in that event, a part of the European force originally sent from England to the Cape of Good Hope, or to the Mauritius, might proceed to India.

36. Any operation against the Cape of Good Hope would, in all probability, appear to his Majesty's ministers to promise most speedy and effectual success by being despatched directly from England, and I would strongly recommend that in any expedition against the Cape of Good Hope no reliance should be placed upon co-operation from India.

37. It would be difficult to despatch an expedition against the Mauritius directly from Europe; if, therefore, any expedition be intended against the Mauritius, it would appear most advisable to commence the operation by a considerable reinforcement of the European troops in India. Those reinforcements might be divided between Madras, Bombay and Ceylon, distributing the largest proportion at Madras and Ceylon.

38. An expedition might then be prepared by the Government of India for the attack of the Mauritius, with the advantage of a short voyage, of the most recent information relative to the defences of the Island, and also with the aid of a proportion of native troops.

39. Your Lordship will remark that most of the contingencies supposed in this letter require an increase of military and marine charges, and that the state of affairs with the Mahrattas has already compelled me to restore the native army to the war establishment, while the subsidiary engagements concluded with the Peishwa and the Guicowar have rendered an increase of the native force in Bengal indispensably necessary.

40. In stating the necessity of these expences, I have not pointed your Lordship's attention to any other opinions than such as I have been enabled to form upon the important question of our military establishments and state of preparation.

41. Entertaining a firm persuasion that I have the honour to possess your Lordship's confidence, I am satisfied that you will give me full credit for the most anxious desire to avoid every increase of expence which is not absolutely essential to an adequate state of preparation for war. If, however, I were to refer your Lordship to the opinions of the Commander-in-Chief General Lake, of Lieut.-General Stuart, and of the Governments of Fort St. George, Bombay and Ceylon, your Lordship would find that the additions which I have made to our military force in consequence of the events to which I have adverted is inferior to the augmentations proposed by those respectable authorities.

42. The Commander-in-Chief General Lake, for whose opinion I entertain the highest respect, concurs with me on the sufficiency of the augmentations made in Bengal, and I trust that if our European establishment be maintained complete, according to suggestions which I shall have the honour to submit to your Lordship in a separate letter, no further increase of our military force can be required, unless with a view to fulfil new treaties of subsidy, which, of course, will include the provision of additional funds.

43. To meet the expences incident to the preparations for war, and to the execution of our treaties with the Peishwa and with the Guicowar, the subsidiary grants of territory from those states will prove an efficient resource.

44. If war should take place with the Mahrattas and Monsieur

Perron, it will probably be attended by the conquest of territories, which will speedily repay our expences.

45. With respect to the account which your Lordship has enclosed of the surplus realized in India from the peace of Seringapatam to the year 1796–7, it is difficult to apply that account to present circumstances without entering into a minute examination of the principles on which the surplus in India was calculated during those years.

46. It would also be requisite to examine whether during that period of time the military establishments in India were maintained in a state of adequate preparation for war. At the time of my arrival in India, I have no hesitation in repeating to your Lordship the opinion which I recorded at that moment, that our Indian empire was not in a state of military or naval preparation in any degree calculated to meet the exigency of war.

47. The destruction of Tippoo Sultaun's power has removed the most formidable enemy of the British power in India, but the actual condition of the Mahratta powers connected with the views of France and the constitution of some branches of Scindiah's military establishment will require the most vigilant and extensive state of military preparation.

48. I entertain no apprehension, however, of meeting the expence incident to these preparations without any material check to the Company's commercial investment, and without any important delay in the operations for the reduction of the debt. My apprehensions of the approaching crisis would be much more serious, if I were not confident that your Lordship will oppose the generosity, vigour and firmness of your mind to the progress of any system of compromise between the conflicting characters of merchant and sovereign, which compose the constitution of the East India Company. While that Company shall represent the sovereign executive authority of the realm in so great, populous, and flourishing a portion of the British empire, its duties of sovereignty must be deemed paramount to its mercantile interests, prejudices, and profits. In time of peace, the happiness of its subjects, the permanent improvement of its dominions, the dignity, purity, and vigour of its government must take precedence of commercial considerations. The sovereignty of the Company is the basis and strength of its commerce; and from the faithful discharge of the duties of empire in India must ever flow the wealth and credit of the trading corporation in London. In time both of peace and of war, the strength and

efficiency of the army, and above all, the military spirit and character of the government in India must be cultivated with uninterrupted assiduity, and determined perseverance. To that spirit and character we owe the origin of this empire; and in preserving the cause of its origin we shall provide the most effectual security for its preservation. The most indispensable duty of the sovereign executive government in India is therefore the maintenance of the military power, without which no security can exist for the mercantile or financial interests of the Company, or even for the tranquillity and welfare of our Indian subjects.

49. I shall have the honour of addressing despatches to Lord Hobart relative to the restitutions to be made to the French and Dutch Governments, to the Portuguese settlements, and generally to the possessions of the several European powers on the Continent of India, or on the Eastern Seas. Copies of these despatches will be transmitted to your Lordship for your information, and I shall hope to receive his Majesty's further instructions, relative to those points, from your Lordship, or from the Secretary of State.

I have the honour to be,
with great respect, my dear Lord, &c.
WELLESLEY.

3. NORTH-WEST FRONTIER.

86. The Earl of Mornington to Major General Sir James Henry Craig, K.B.

Enquiry as to military precautions to be taken against Zemaun Shah's threatened invasion.

Fort William, Sept. 16, 1798.

Sir,

This letter will be delivered to you by Lieut.-Col. Collins, who having been appointed Resident at the Court of Scindiah, is proceeding to take charge of the interests of the British Government at that Court.

The continual reports of the approach of Zemaun Shah to Hindostan engaged my attention at the earliest period of my arrival in Bengal, and I have already taken every step (which appeared to me justifiable in the great uncertainty of the prevailing rumours) for checking the motions of the Shah, in the event of his advancing towards our frontier.

It could not be supposed that such an expedition, as that meditated by the Shah, would be planned without any view to the plunder of the most opulent and flourishing parts of Hindostan; I have, therefore, always considered that he must intend to advance to Lucknow, and to our provinces, if circumstances should favour his progress. And with this opinion, I have thought that his march ought to be opposed at the earliest possible period, and his operations checked at the greatest possible distance from our frontier.

But if I had ever entertained any doubt of the tendency of the Shah's operations, it would have been removed by his own distinct declaration to the Vizier and to me. 'That he should consider our not joining his royal standard, and our not assisting him in the restoration of Shah Allum, and in the total expulsion of the Mahrattas in the light of an act of disobedience and enmity.' As it is utterly impossible for me to aid the Shah in such a project, or to submit the honour and faith of the British Government to such conditions, I must suppose that the Vizier and this Government, will be treated as enemies by him, whenever he shall have an opportunity of bringing his army to act on our frontier. The most useful barrier against this invasion, in the first instance, would be the resistance of the Seiks, of the Rajpoots, especially the Rajahs of Jyenagur and Judpoor, and of Dowlut Rao Scindiah.

My attention has been directed to a system of measures, the effect of which, (if successful) would have occasioned the immediate return of Scindiah to his dominions in Hindostan, and have given us the benefit of a defensive alliance with him against the Shah. I cannot yet ascertain, what the motions of Scindiah are likely to be, or what may be the ultimate turn of his fate. But at all events, it will be necessary to consider the terms of a defensive league to which, whether Scindiah shall be a party or not, the Rajpoots and Seiks must be invited.

The most difficult question in the formation of such a treaty, will be of a military nature. It may be thus stated. What is the extreme limit beyond the frontier of the Vizier, to which the operations of the British force could be advanced, without danger to that frontier, and to the force so advanced. On the one hand, it would certainly be desirable to restrain the operations of our army, as nearly as possible, to the exclusive protection of the

Nabob's and Company's possessions. But on the other hand, it could not be expected, that any efficient or cordial assistance could be derived from any practicable system of defensive alliance, if our army was to be exclusively exempted from any share in the common defence of the dominions of the contracting powers.

I am aware of the difficulty under these circumstances of fixing such a point for the extreme advance of our army, as shall relieve us from both of the embarrassments which I have stated.

But as I am persuaded, that the question which I have proposed in this letter, must frequently have occurred to you in all its military bearings and consequences, I take the liberty of requesting, that you will have the goodness to favour me with your opinion upon it, in order that I may hereafter be enabled to enter upon the consideration of it more advantageously and accurately, whenever it shall become necessary to discuss it with the Commander-in-Chief.

I shall also esteem it as a favour, if you will state your ideas on this subject to Lieutenant Colonel Collins, who will be employed in the negociation of any defensive engagements which it may be deemed advisable to contract.

If any other suggestions, with regard to the defence of our North Western frontier, should appear to you important to the public service, I should be happy to receive them. One defect has necessarily attracted your notice; the useless, or rather the dangerous condition of the Vizier's own army. This subject is at present under my consideration; and I confess I see but one effectual mode of obtaining a serviceable army in the Vizier's pay. The substitution of regular regiments from the Company's service, in place of the Nabob's own troops; or in other words, such an increase of our force in Oude, as would warrant nearly a total reduction of the Nabob's present army. I believe that this measure might be accomplished not only with infinite advantage to the external defence, but also to the internal tranquillity of the Nabob's dominions, to the safety of his person, to the stability of his authority, and to the order of his finances.

I have the honour to be, Sir, with great respect,

Your most obedient and humble servant,

MORNINGTON.

87. Major General Sir James H. Craig to the Earl of Mornington.

Reply to the enquiry. Importance of a Mahratta alliance, military imbecility of Oude, and probable weakness of the Sikhs.

Cawnpore, 6th October, 1798.

My Lord,

I am sure your Lordship will believe that it is not without giving it every attention in my power, that I sit down to lay before your Lordship the various considerations which have presented themselves to my mind, on the subject of the question upon which your Lordship has honoured me with your commands that I should give you my opinion.

In the consequence which your Lordship is pleased to attach to any opinion of mine, your Lordship has certainly manifested that confidence in my judgment which I should have felt to have rested upon a better merited claim had it been applied solely to my ambition of being useful to the service of my country; but whatever may be the sense that I entertain of my capacity to do it fully, I feel at the same time the force of the demand on me which your Lordship has established, that I should make the best return that is in my power to the confidence that your Lordship places in me; and it appears to me that I should ill discharge that obligation were I to confine myself to the considering the question as a mere abstract proposition, and did not enter into it more fully as connected with the probable circumstances of our situation, in the event from whence alone can arise the necessity of your Lordship's decision upon it.

I have already had the honour, on another occasion, to explain to your Lordship my idea upon the nature of our frontier, which I shall request that your Lordship will have the goodness to carry in your mind in what I may now have occasion to offer to your Lordship. It is singularly unfortunate, and surely much to be regretted, that in the thirty odd years that we may be said to have been in possession of this country, it has, I should suppose, never been considered in a military point of view as being within the possibility of attack; hence it arises, that except Allahabad, which hardly yet deserves the name, there is not a single fortress or place of strength in the whole country. It is not necessary to enter into the various inconveniences, and indeed essential circumstances of danger, which may arise from this deficiency.

It is here alluded to principally as connected with and certainly very materially affecting the object in question.

However such as is the natural barrier which limits our frontier, and with every inconvenience which we might experience from the deficiency to which I have adverted, I have not a doubt but that if the army in the field is carried to 20,000 men, the position that I have pointed out in the memoir which is already in your Lordship's hands, and the other measures of precaution that are there recommended to be adopted, would be equal to our security, although I have laid it down as an axiom, that it can be endangered only under circumstances of previous advantage to the enemy, by which his numbers will be increased to almost any extent to which he may wish to carry them; but were we to confine ourselves thus solely to our own defence, however successful we might at present be in that object, I for my own part have scarcely a doubt, that a new and formidable power would establish itself in our nearest neighbourhood, a power which would overset the whole political state of Hindostan, would require an unremitting vigilance and constant state of preparation on our part, attended with an enormous expense, and that at last we should have to contend for our existence, under circumstances of infinitely greater difficulty and embarrassment than those which will now attend our opposition to its first establishment. I ought to apologize to your Lordship for thus obtruding an opinion which has not been called for, but I have been led to it by the view of acceding, most fully, to the wisdom of the measure of a junction with the Mahrattas, and as pointing out the grounds on which I may allude to the expediency of doing it with cordiality and effect.

It appears to me to be impossible to point out any precise bounds at which danger commences to the army that quits a frontier, and to the frontier which is left by it. Its communication, indeed, becomes more and more precarious in proportion as it abandons the country with which it is to be preserved, but in all situations, with respect to action, it is equally liable to the fate of war; and with respect to the frontier, it is impossible, except under local circumstances of peculiar advantage, very rarely to be met with, that it can be covered by any army that is advanced before it. The true question, however, that I think arises is, how far the object in view will justify the possible danger that may attend the movement, and the principal circumstance of consideration should be, to adopt the best measures that human wisdom can devise, to lessen or to meet the danger, with the best means within our command.

The expediency of a defensive alliance with the Mahrattas being admitted, it follows of course that as the object must be their defence as well as ours, the operations of the armies employed must be directed by what appears to be the best means of accomplishing that end. It is not to be supposed that the Mahrattas would sacrifice a part of their country in order to contract the line of defence to what may lessen the danger to ours. Their object will be to meet the enemy on their frontier; and it will scarcely be practicable to make them comprehend that they can receive any advantage from an alliance with us, unless we join them there. Fortunately every step we take to defend their dominions is equally applied to the protection of our own; their frontier becomes, in fact, ours, which is truly and effectually covered by it; and having once quitted the precise line which would be obviously marked out by our confining ourselves solely to our own defence, it matters, I think, very little whether we are 50 miles farther from or nearer to that line.

At the same time that I hazard this idea, for it will, I am persuaded, meet many opponents, I beg your Lordship to be assured that I by no means overlook the consequences that may attend its being adopted in its fullest extent. I am well aware of the difficulty of communication, I am fully sensible of those that may be experienced with respect to subsistence, and I feel all the dangers and hazards that would attend us in the unfortunate event of a defeat, when, unquestionably, every mile we should have advanced would increase the peril of retreat. I am even inclined to give additional weight to these circumstances, because it is my decided and fixed opinion, that our enemies are as numerous as the inhabitants of the country; and I have not a doubt but that a reverse of fortune would exhibit them starting from every tope and from behind every bank. But all these inconveniences and dangers commence, to a certain degree, the moment our army quits the banks of the Ganges. It is to the greater or less extent to which they may be carried that my reasoning applies; and it is under the conviction, that the benefits to be derived from a junction with the Mahrattas will be found to justify and to overbalance them all, that I observe that their being more or less increased by a greater or less distance from our frontier is of no weight when put in competition with the expediency of acting with the strictest cordiality, and in the closest union with those people. It is not to be imagined that they will give up Delhi without a contest: their first position will certainly be beyond it. Their frontier extends to Carnaul, which is 60 coss, perhaps something better than 100 miles from Delhi. I should have no hesitation to recommend that there should be no restriction to our advancing so far in co-operation with them. The only condition that I would annex to the permission would be, that they should put into our hands some place of strength between Anopsheer and the army, to serve as a depôt and magazine. The question, in short, appears to me to be reducible to this: Whether we shall meet the enemy and oppose him, though at a distance, under every advantage of the assistance to be derived from a numerous and powerful body of friends, equally interested in the cause with ourselves, and masters of the intermediate country between our own frontier and the scene of our operations, by which the danger, which might otherwise arise from that distance, will be very considerably lessened; or whether we shall wait to be attacked at home, when we shall be deprived of that assistance, and when our enemy will himself have acquired all the advantage to be derived from increased resources, augmented numbers, and established authority, exerted with the ardour and enthusiasm usual in a career of victory and conquest, and with our own native troops, perhaps, labouring under all the effects of a contrary impression?

But in viewing the subject of the danger attending our advancing, it is necessary that we should advert to the numbers of which the army will consist that may be applied to the defence of our north-western frontier. I have ventured to suppose that that number may be carried to 20,000 men, but as I am entirely ignorant of the services for which, independent of the internal security of our provinces and the necessary attention to Fort William, the remainder of our army may be required, I may err very considerably in my calculation on this subject. One circumstance is, however, clear to me, and that is, that if we cannot command that number at least, independent of the garrison of Allahabad, our means of defence will be scarcely proportionate to the magnitude of the danger with which we are threatened.

After determining the actual strength of the army that can be collected for the whole of the service required, it will then remain to proportion its several parts into the different branches into which that service will divide itself. For if it is judged expedient that the principal corps should be carried beyond the frontier to any distance, that a cordial co-operation with our allies may require, I believe there is no one will doubt the necessity of leaving no very inconsiderable force in these provinces, as well to assist in guarding the passes on the river as to insure to us that command and influence, and those services, that may be indispensable to our safety. Your Lordship judges most rightly that, in its present shape, no sort of service can be expected from the Nabob's army, and I am confident that without a total change in the policy of the Court and the manners of the people, there exists no possible means by which it can ever be rendered such as can merit that the smallest degree of confidence should be placed in it. The money now expended on them is thrown away, and can only be rendered subservient to the object of general defence, by being appropriated to the increase of the Company's army. But I much fear that it is too late to adopt such a measure, with the hope that any troops that would be raised with this view can be of service if the Shah's invasion take place this season. This consideration should, however, only act as a spur to us to begin the attempt as early as possible; and it may perhaps be much facilitated by the possibility of taking into our service some of his battalions entire. They are all, to a certain degree, disciplined, and under the charge of a proper selection of officers, might soon become serviceable. There seems to be little doubt of their willingness to engage.

With respect to the number of which the corps that is to act with our allies should consist, there appears to me to be no medium. It should either be a simple detachment of two or three battalions, such as was that which, under Captain Little from Bombay, accompanied a body of the same people during the Mysore war, and that which was on the same occasion attached to the Nizam's army, or it should consist of the utmost strength that can be collected, with a due regard to other services. I hold it for certain that in all situations in which we are to act with any of the country powers, the whole brunt of the operations will rest with us; nor will our particular safety ever be considered by them as an object that can be put in competition with any danger that a regard to it might entail upon themselves. Our force should, therefore, be such that any misfortune that might befall it could have no sensible influence upon the general state of our affairs; or it should be such as is sufficient for its own defence,—as can, if necessary, act upon the means which it possesses within itself, and as can give us that influence, and entitle us to that pre-eminence, which it is so essential for us on all occasions to preserve. A medium force would only expose us to insult from our arrogant and selfish friends, and to defeat and ruin from our more open enemies, whilst the deficiency which might be occasioned in our general means of defence, by a loss which as such would be considerable, might very materially cripple, perhaps render vain, our further efforts. Could, by any means whatever, the acting army be carried to any thing near the strength I have proposed, and could a corps of five or six thousand men be formed at the same time in these provinces, and provided decisive measures for the tranquillity of Rohilcund be adopted, I should certainly imagine that we might hope to give the Shah such cause to repent his incursion as would secure the future tranquillity of Hindostan, at least from foreign invasion, for some time.

I feel, my Lord, that in what I have hitherto had the honour of offering to your Lordship, I have in some shape departed from the datum upon which your Lordship's questions seem in some degree to be founded. Your Lordship observes, that it will be necessary to consider the terms of a defensive league, to which, whether Scindiah shall be a party or not, the Rajpoots and Seiks must be invited, whereas I have confined myself entirely to the supposition of an alliance and hearty co-operation with the Mahrattas; that is, I presume, with Scindiah, without once adverting to either the Rajpoots or the Seiks.

The truth is, my Lord, that, with all deference to better information, and still greater to better judgment, it does not appear to me that it can be practicable for us to enter into any alliance with either of the Powers mentioned, but through the Mahrattas, if I may use the expression. I mean by it that it is utterly impossible that we can join or co-operate with the former but by the concurrence and in concert with the latter, for we cannot even communicate but through the dominions of Scindiah. Exclusive of the geographical difficulty, there would, I apprehend, be found a much greater in the inveterate hatred that exists between the two people. Any communication between us and the Seiks, without the participation of Scindiah, would excite a jealousy that would, I fear, be fatal to our friendship with the latter. The same circumstances exist with respect to the most powerful of the Rajpoots, the Rajahs on the western frontier of Scindiah's territory. It appears, therefore, to me, that if we cannot form an alliance with Scindiah, it will be difficult, if not impossible, to form any other. If, indeed, we can convince him of his true interests, I believe it will be an easy matter to engage the Rajah of Jynajur, and others whose territories are adjacent to his, for it is impossible that they can be desirous that the Shah should establish himself in these parts. With respect to the Seiks, the task may be more difficult. What advantages can we hold out to induce them to act in co-operation with us? They will naturally ask if we expect that they should abandon their country and possessions to join us, and of what use we can be to them while posted on the frontiers of the Mahratta dominions? The answers to these questions seem difficult.

Another consideration arises, however, upon this subject. Suppose the Seiks were found to be cordially disposed to join in the league, and should the Mahrattas on their part be equally willing, would it be expedient that we should carry our operations to the length of advancing into the country of the former, upon which terms alone it would be possible to bring into action the united forces of the three Powers? I do not, indeed, think the case is likely to occur, in which a decision may be necessary on this question, at least beyond a certain degree. If the Shah carries his intentions into effect, he is probably at this moment on his march, and the fate of the Seik frontier, most likely of Lahore itself, will be decided long before we can possibly be at hand to take a part in the contest. Our movement, therefore, to that extent, cannot in any case be necessary; but the Rajah of Patiala is represented to be a powerful prince, commanding at all times a force of 10,000 horse, and as many footmen, and capable of raising many more in case of necessity. His territories border on those of the Mahrattas: and should the Seiks have remained disunited and separate, or should he by any means have escaped the effects of any defeat which his countrymen may have suffered on the frontier, so that his force may remain entire, and probably increased by the junction of such as may have escaped the Shah's army;—I think such an addition of strength would be an object, and would justify a further advance; but certainly not unless our force were such as would command the respect of both parties, and place us in the light of umpires, capable of enforcing our wishes on either.

I have no doubt of the Mahrattas readily acceding to any alliance your Lordship may propose; and Scindiah's return seems more probable now than it did when your Lordship's letter was written, but even should that event not take place, though it will be a circumstance much to be regretted, as crippling the energy with which his strength might be exerted under his own direction, yet it would appear that the approach of so manifest a danger must unite all parties to avert it, which they would be perhaps more inclined to do under our controlling influence than if they were left to themselves.

I have the honour to be, with great respect,

My Lord,

Your Lordship's most obedient and

Most humble Servant,

J. H. CRAIG.

88. Sir J. H. Craig to the Earl of Mornington.

Same Subject.—English army deficient in training and ammunition. Danger of underrating the enemy.

Cawnpore, 13th October, 1798.

My Lord,

The letter from my Kurnaul correspondent, to which I have alluded in my public letter, is principally on the subject of Gholaum Mahommed, whose motions I have directed him to watch. After, however, mentioning the construction of the bridge over the Attock, he adds—

'A constant intercourse is maintained between the Chiefs of the Sick nation and those of the Mahrattas. The former are all at their stations.'

I have written to him for a further explanation, and have directed him to make particular enquiry, as far as may be in his power, as to the probability of the two people entering into an alliance to oppose the Shah; and more especially as to the disposition of the Seiks, and how far they are united among themselves, for that purpose. I have also written in the same terms, on the latter subject, to my friend at Amrutsir. In the meantime I have forwarded the account to Colonel Collins: as, if these people should really have an intention of entering into a defensive league against the common enemy, it may be much facilitated I think by its being known that your Lordship is willing to be a party in it, whilst that circumstance will undoubtedly have a tendency to inspire them with a little more confidence in the force of any treaty that may take place between them, than is otherwise likely to exist betwixt inveterate enemies, each knowing the other to be capable of every treachery.

Not having the honour to be known to your Lordship, it may now be necessary that I should assure you that I am not apt to obtrude opinions, or to step out of my sphere in the presumption of offering advice. The only merit to which I lay any claim is that of an ardent zeal in the service of my country, but I wish not that it should be intemperate, and if I assume the liberty, on this occasion, of continuing a *private* correspondence with your Lordship, you owe it to the honour which you did me in your first letter: by the frankness of which I was led to believe that it would be received by your Lordship precisely in the light in which alone I can assure you it is ventured upon.

I have not heard from Colonel Collins since he left this for Futtyghur. In the conversation that I had with him here I endeavoured to impress him with a conviction of the necessity of his losing no time in entering into the negociation with which he is charged, and I am sure he was himself sensible of it; but since we have such good reasons for believing that the Shah has actually begun his march, so far as to be on the banks of the Attock upwards of twenty days ago, I now feel it to be of double importance that he should proceed without an instant's delay. I am concerned to have to say, that from all the information I can get, and I have made every inquiry in my power, I am led most firmly to believe that the Seiks, if left to themselves, will not make any opposition at all to the Shah's approach; or if they do, that it will be very feeble. I believe, indeed, that the power of the Seiks rest very much upon opinion, and that in the day of trial the delusion will appear. I neither believe them to be so numerous, or so hardy, as they have been represented, although sufficiently so to lord it over the real inhabitants of the country, for I make no doubt that your Lordship is aware that the Seiks are not the fortieth part of the inhabitants of the district over which they have established their dominion. The mass of these are a mixture of Mussulmen and Hindoos; the former of which from every motive, and the latter in detestation of the oppressions of their present Lords, will rejoice in the Shah's approach. Nothing I believe can produce any important exertion from the Seiks but a junction with the Mahrattas; and giving even credit to the letter from Kurnaul, whatever appearance it may carry of the probability of such an event, I still imagine it will be with difficulty accomplished, but under your Lordship's auspices; but I much doubt the ability of the Mahrattas themselves to assemble in time such a force as will give confidence to the others. There is no appearance of it that I can yet hear of; they are quarrelling among themselves at Delhi, without seeming much to think of the danger with which they are threatened. The Attock is but a little better than 400 coss from Delhi, a space that may with the utmost ease be marched in six weeks, and that without adverting at all to the celerity with which the Shah's army is reported to move. If, (and it is no very improbable supposition) despising the Seiks, whose behaviour in 1796 was no ways such as to give him cause to hold them in high estimation, the Shah should adopt a bold step; and, leaving a corps of troops to keep them in awe, he should move on with rapidity, in the view of anticipating the Mahrattas at Delhi, he may be there in a time, that I almost tremble to think of. It is not utterly impossible, my Lord, that he might anticipate our preparations; though it is indeed hardly to be expected that, entertaining the same opinion of the Mahrattas as that which I have supposed him to do of the Seiks, he should venture to leave them behind in order to attack us, especially before the fords of the Ganges are open. However, I wish to shew the expediency of exertion and activity on our part. The extent to which it is meant to carry the army being ascertained, the troops that are to compose it should be immediately assembled, not in the slow progress of the ordinary relief, when battalion relieves battalion, but the utmost expedition should be used in it. The ordnance and stores should be hurried up in some very unusual way, unless it can be furnished from Chunar, as I have suggested to the Commander-in-Chief; and, above all, some steps should be adopted, with respect to further arrangement, that might preclude the necessity of a daily reference to the present seat of Government.

I know not what to say with respect to the Nabob's troops, I would be content that they should be useless, but I dread their being dangerous, unless some step is taken with regard to them. I should be almost as unwilling to leave them behind me as I should be to leave a fortress of the enemy. The Nabob is highly unpopular, and of all his subjects, I believe he would least expect attachment from his army. I fear much that it is too late to reap any benefit from the arrangement which your Lordship proposes with respect to them; and if we should be called to the frontier I doubt whether it may not be hazardous to attempt to reduce them. We shall have of ourselves too many recruits in our ranks, indeed, a number that will very much weaken the dependence to be placed in our battalions. On this subject I feel that I tread on tender ground; but I write to your Lordship in the confidence of a private communication. Neither the discipline of the army, or the knowledge of the officers, are such as to admit of our being insensible to other disadvantages. We are to expect a numerous and ferocious enemy, undisciplined and disorderly, but impetuous in their attacks, and rapid in their movements,—abounding in cavalry, and acting in a country the most favourable to that arm, where, if we can secure one flank, it will be a fortunate position. Against them our reliance must be on our artillery, and on the steadiness of our infantry,—where discipline should keep them firm in their ranks, and where confidence in their advantages should teach them not to shrink under the impression of a tumultuous charge of cavalry, the circumstance of all others the most likely to affect the mind of a young soldier, while the knowledge of the officers, and the previous training of the corps, should ensure the ability of moving with the utmost precision and rapidity, and of forming in every direction, to resist a surrounding cavalry. Battalions, with full one-third of recruits, are little equal to this description in its first part, and truth compels me to say that I have not yet seen one that came any where near it in the latter.

Your Lordship will do me justice in believing that I do not mean to hold out discouragement by this description. We must act, and we must make the best of the tools in our hands. My view is, that your Lordship may be aware of the true state of the army, which it is at least possible that you may not become through any other channel; three-fourths of them with whom your Lordship may converse do not themselves know it, and the other fourth will not confess it. There is a third class of people which your Lordship may meet,—and it is a numerous one, even in my own profession,—who either do, or affect to, hold in contempt the idea of the necessity of its being otherwise. It is a fact, however, past controversy, that within these four years, and owing to these very circumstances of want of discipline and knowledge, the fate of our Empire in India probably hung by a thread of the slightest texture; since even the impetuosity of the enemy ought naturally to have led to the very advantage which his ignorance would not permit his being sensible of.

Our stores are utterly incompetent to any forward move, such as I have ventured to suggest as justifiable, if co-operation with the Mahrattas can be purchased by it. Our proportion of musquet ammunition is 120 rounds per man, and that for the small arms of the cavalry is 40; with this I most certainly would not venture to stir a step from the Ganges, and how we are to get up more, in the time in which I think it is probable that it may be requisite for us to do so, I know not; I have written in strong terms to the Commander-in-Chief upon the subject. For our artillery we have 300 rounds, but that is, if possible, still less equal to what we ought to have, at least in a depôt, to which we could have a much more ready access than we have to Chunar or Allahabad. The latter should be our grand depôt, in which should be lodged a quantity of stores of every species, equal to every possible emergency; while a field depôt fed continually from it, should move successively from post to post as we advance, and be always at hand to renew our deficiencies. Upon the whole, do not, my Lord, consider it as presumption if I say that I feel a great deal more arrangement to be necessary than appears to me to occur to others as such. It is an easy thing to put the whole upon the issue of one battle, and unfortunately it is the mode which is attended with the least trouble.

I really beg your Lordship's pardon for this long and very free intrusion; but my apology is already offered in the fore part of my letter, and I shall therefore say no more, but that I have the honour to be,

My Lord,

Your Lordship's most obedient and humble Servant,

J. H. CRAIG.

4. Persia.

89. The Marquess Wellesley to the Honourable the Secret Committee of the Honourable the Court of Directors.

Persian embassy and Treaty, and advantages thus secured. Why an European ambassador, in state, was required.

Monghyr, September 28th, 1801.

Honourable Sirs,

Your Honourable Committee has been apprized of the motives which induced me to despatch Captain Malcolm to the Court of Persia, and of the general objects of his mission. I have now the satisfaction to inform you, that Captain Malcolm returned from his embassy in the month of May, after having completely succeeded in accomplishing every object of his mission, and in establishing a connection with the actual government of the Persian Empire, which promises to the British nation in India, political and commercial advantages of the most important description, and of as great a degree of stability as appears compatible with the nature and character of the Persian Government.

2. I have the honour to transmit separate numbers in this despatch, copies of two treaties, the first relating to a political connection, and the second to a commercial arrangement, and a copy of a letter from Captain Malcolm, which accompanied the communication of these treaties from Persia. These treaties have been concluded by Captain Malcolm, between the British Government of India, and the Court of Persia.

3. I likewise transmit copies of the whole of Captain Malcolm's correspondence with this Government from the date of his appointment until his return, from which your Honourable Committee will be informed of all the circumstances attending this interesting and important mission.

4. Notwithstanding the fluctuations which have occurred in the Government of Persia, the power of the reigning Prince appeared to me to have acquired sufficient stability to render it an object of considerable importance to conciliate the attachment of that Prince to the British interests, and to establish with Persia an intimate connection founded on durable and comprehensive principles. The policy which dictated my opinion, was calculated to provide not only against the menaced invasion of Zemaun Shah, but also against the views which other powers

may entertain of attacking the British possessions in India. This object is important in proportion to the hazard to which the British interests would be exposed, by a connection between the Court of Persia, and those European powers, whose views have long been directed to this quarter of the British dominions. Great advantages in a commercial point of view were likewise to be expected from the connection which I proposed to form with the Court of Persia.

5. To accomplish these important objects, it was indispensably necessary that the embassy should be so constituted as to convey to the Court of Persia, and to the inhabitants of that country, a respectable impression of the power, wealth, and dignity, of the British Government in India. To produce this effect upon the minds of a nation peculiarly devoted to outward form and ceremonies, I judged it to be necessary to attach to the embassy, appointments calculated to ensure from the Court of Persia, a reception suited to the dignity of the British Government and to the importance of the mission.

6. From the perusal of the correspondence your honourable Committee will find, that my opinion on this subject was amply justified, and I am satisfied that the extent of the appointments of the embassy, and the liberal manner in which it was conducted, materially contributed to its success, and tended to excite in the minds of the inhabitants of Persia, an exalted opinion of the power and liberality of the Company's government in India.

7. Your honourable Committee in your letter of the 10th of September, 1800, has expressed a doubt of the policy of Captain Malcolm's mission, founded on the accounts which had been received from Bombay, of the success of Mehdi Ali Khan's exertions in a similar capacity.

8. The objects of Mehdi Ali Khan's mission were comparatively of a limited and temporary nature. This mission was neither intended, nor calculated to embrace those important and comprehensive views which I had in contemplation, in furnishing Captain Malcolm with credentials to the court of Persia. The value of Mehdi Ali Khan's services on that occasion was certainly considerable, but he was not in my opinion a proper person to be entrusted with the negotiation of such important objects as those which I had in contemplation at the Court of Persia, in the mission of Captain Malcolm. Independently of any disqualifications applicable to Mehdi Ali Khan, the

objections to the employments of a native of India in such a mission are numerous and insurmountable.

9. It is not consistent with the dignity of the British Government, to employ any native of this country as its representative at a foreign court, nor could the British interests be with any degree of safety confided to any person of that description. Intrigue, falsehood, and collusion, are the uniform characteristics of such of the natives of India, as aspire to the qualifications of statesmen. They are ignorant of the national honour, and insensible to every emotion of public spirit; they are, therefore, ever disposed to sacrifice the public interests to views of private ambition and individual profit.

10. No native of India can possess a sufficient knowledge of the political interests of the British nation, nor of the principles and maxims which regulate its conduct, to qualify him for the arduous duty of superintending an important branch of the political relations of the British empire in India, nor can he assume that degree of consideration at a foreign court, which is indispensably necessary in a situation so distinguished and important as that of the representative of the honourable Company in Asia.

11. The natives of India may occasionally be employed with advantage for the promotion of temporary views of policy, or for the attainment of separate and limited objects. They may sometimes be rendered, in a subordinate situation, successful instruments for opening the way to political systems of a more permanent and comprehensive nature. In both these respects, I consider the services of Mehdi Ali Khan to have merited reward and approbation; but I should have betrayed the important interests committed to my charge, if I had attempted to accomplish views of such magnitude as those which suggested the mission of Captain Malcolm, through the agency of Mehdi Ali Khan, or of any other native agent.

12. I shall now proceed to make some remarks upon the nature and effects of the alliance so happily established with the Court of Persia, for the purpose of enabling your honourable Committee to form a just estimate of the advantages which may be expected to result from the success of Captain Malcolm's mission.

13. A firm and intimate connection has now been established between the British Government and a State, the resources of which are capable of aiding in an essential manner the hostile

views of the enemies of the British nation against our Eastern possessions.

14. The measures which have succeeded in conciliating the ſavourable disposition of the Persian Government towards the British nation, have produced a proportionate opposition in that Court to the views and interests of our enemies, and have opened to us the prospect of commanding those resources and local advantages, which, under a different state of circumstances, might eventually have been employed against us. I entertain the fullest confidence that the Court of Persia, in conformity to its declarations and engagements, will cordially resist any attempts which may be made, either by negotiation, or by force, on the part of our enemies, to obtain any establishment in that country, or to render it in any manner subservient to their views.

15. I consider the unrestrained use of the Persian sea-ports, and the exclusion of our enemies from them, to be an essential advantage. By securing the entire command of the Persian coast, we shall facilitate the means of defeating any attempts on the part of our enemies to establish themselves in that quarter, and as the enemy's cruizers will be deprived of all refuge and assistance in those ports, the commerce of the Persian Gulph, (which, under the operation of the commercial treaty, may be expected rapidly to increase), will in a great measure be free from interruption, and the communication with Europe, by the way of Bussorah, will be less subject to molestation.

16. The active measures adopted by the Court of Persia against Zemaun Shah, which were instigated in the first instance by Mehdi Ali Khan, and subsequently encouraged by Captain Malcolm, produced the salutary effect of diverting the attention of Zemaun Shah from his long projected invasion of Hindostan during three successive seasons. The hostility of Baba Khan unquestionably proved the ruin of Zemaun Shah's power. The assistance afforded by Mehdi Ali Khan under my orders, to the Prince Mahomed Shah, originally enabled that Prince to excite those commotions, which have recently terminated in the defeat of Zemaun Shah, in his deposition from the throne, and in the entire extinction of his power; to the consolidated and active government of Zemaun Shah, has succeeded a state of confusion in the country of the Afghans highly favourable to our security in that quarter. Since the fall of Zemaun

Shah, several competitors for the throne have opposed the establishment of Mahomed Shah, and the Afghan power is broken down by their mutual contentions, while the vicinity of the King of Persia's force, now connected with our interests, operates as an additional cause of weakness to the empire formerly held by Zemaun Shah. The relation which that Prince had formed with Tippoo Sultaun, and the probability of his concurrence in the hostile views, either of Russia, or of France, render the actual state of affairs in Candahar a most favourable contrast with that which existed in the year 1798.

17. The details of the transactions which have led to the fall of Zemaun Shah accompany this despatch.

18. The engagements which Captain Malcolm has lately contracted with the Court of Persia, relative to the Afghans, afford abundant reason to believe, that the provinces of Hindostan will, for a long course of years be effectually relieved from the apprehension of an Afghan incursion.

19. The immediate effect of these arrangements has been to enable me to prosecute with confidence my negotiations at Lucknow, and to relieve me from the necessity of making expensive military preparations on the frontiers of Oude, a measure which, under other circumstances, I should have thought it my duty to adopt.

20. I consider the liberty granted by the Court of Persia to British merchants to settle at any of the ports in the Persian dominions, for the purposes of commerce, to be a valuable concession, calculated to establish the foundation of important benefits to our commercial and political interests in that quarter.

21. The proposed settlement in the Gulph of Persia, which your honourable Committee will observe, is suggested in several parts of Captain Malcolm's correspondence, is a question worthy of the most serious consideration. I shall communicate my sentiments to your honourable Committee on this important subject, in a future despatch.

22. From the perusal of Captain Malcolm's correspondence, your honourable Committee will have the satisfaction to observe, that this important and beneficial alliance with the Court of Persia has been concluded under circumstances, which warrant a perfect confidence in the sincerity of the Persian Monarch, and that the impression, which the embassy has produced upon the minds of the inhabitants of Persia, is so favourable to the interests

of the British nation, as to leave no apprehension of its being effaced by the intrigues of a rival power, or by any internal changes or revolutions in the Persian empire.

23. Your honourable Committee will further have the satisfaction to observe that these important advantages have been obtained without any sacrifice whatever, either of interest or of honour on the part of the British Government. The returns which the British Government is bound to make, are of a nature to improve the advantages acquired by us, and are consistent with every principle of true policy and honour.

24. The issue of Captain Malcolm's negotiation with the Imaum of Muscat, has proved highly advantageous to the interests of the British nation. The importance of cultivating a good understanding with the Government of Muscat, is sufficiently obvious, and the arrangements which have taken place with that government, through the agency of Captain Malcolm, may be expected to ensure all the benefit of which that connection is susceptible.

25. The intercourse which Captain Malcolm held with the Pasha of Bagdad, appears to have produced upon the mind of that Prince, an impression extremely favourable to the British interests, and to have laid the foundation of future essential advantages, intimately connected with the alliance so happily contracted with the Court of Persia.

26. Under these circumstances, adverting to the great public advantages which have already resulted from Captain Malcolm's mission, as well as to those which may be expected to flow from its future consequences, I anxiously solicit the particular attention of your honourable Committee, and of the Court of Directors, to the ability, firmness, temper, and dignity, which have distinguished Captain Malcolm's conduct, through the whole course of the arduous and important duties committed to his charge.

27. Your honourable Committee will observe by Captain Malcolm's letter, under date the 31st of July, that he has transmitted to me the journal of his mission to Persia, which I should have forwarded by this despatch to your honourable Committee, had I not understood from Captain Malcolm that it was his intention, as soon as he should have leisure to arrange the materials which he had collected, to prepare a much more complete and extended work upon this interesting subject.

28. I have the honour to annex to this letter, two documents which I have received from Captain Malcolm, and which contain

discussions serving to illustrate the objects and consequences of his mission.

I have the honour to be, &c.
WELLESLEY.

5. CEYLON.

90. The Marquess Wellesley to the Right Hon. Henry Dundas.

Importance of placing Ceylon under the Indian Government.

Barrackpore, May 10th, 1801.

My dear Sir,

1. The object of this despatch is to intimate to you, my sentiments on the plans which you appear to have in contemplation relative to the permanent government of the Island of Ceylon, if that possession should remain in our hands after the peace.

2. The present civil establishment of Ceylon is certainly a heavy burthen on the finances of the Company in India, and as far as relates to them, it would be a relief to throw the burthen of the civil government of Ceylon on the Crown. With respect to the European force to be maintained for the defence of that island, I think it might be provided without any addition to the number of 18,000 effective infantry, which I proposed in my letter of the 13th July, 1800, for the whole of our present Indian Empire, continental, as well as insular, including Ceylon, the Moluccas, Malacca, and Goa, as a British possession.

3. The revenue of Ceylon is not adequate to the payment of the necessary establishments under a separate royal government; nor can I think, that the revenue of that Island will be found answerable to its necessary expenditure under a separate government, if ever, for many years to come. The deficiency must, therefore, be provided from home, if Ceylon be entirely separated from the general Government of India. To meet this charge at home, the cargoes of cinnamon, and the investment of Ceylon, might possibly be taken by the Crown; still however, an advance must annually be made by Parliament for the expenses of Ceylon, to be balanced by the sale of its investment, as the charges of our colonies in the West Indies may be balanced by the duties levied on the produce of those colonies. But I rather suppose that the Crown would take no direct concern in the commercial investment, but would leave that trade, either to the East India Company, or to private traders under

certain regulations, and that the Crown would levy duties on the trade, as a more natural and proper mode of drawing a resource from the possession of Ceylon.

4. The transfer of the civil and military expense of Ceylon to the Crown, would render that part of our Indian Empire a charge on the public of the United Kingdom, and would be substantially the same measure which you so earnestly deprecate. For the direct operation of such an arrangement necessarily must be to render that part of our Indian Empire a burthen upon the mother country, and to have recourse to the public finances at home, for the payment of that branch of our Indian establishments.

5. In this view of the subject, therefore, the account between the British Islands and India, would stand, precisely the same as if aid were to be granted by Parliament, to a similar extent, in the shape of direct assistance to the finances of the East India Company, holding Ceylon as a territorial possession, and defraying the general charges of that possession, together with those of the continental empire of India.

6. In this case, as in the separate case of Ceylon, if annexed to the Crown, the public would be remunerated by the duties derived from the trade, and by other collateral benefits resulting from the extensive power of Great Britain in the East.

7. It appears to me, however, to be a perfectly just and reasonable statement in taking a general view of the expectations which you have held out at various times to Parliament respecting India, to exclude from the account altogether, the charge of Ceylon, and of our possessions acquired from the Dutch in the Eastern Seas, of Goa, and perhaps of all our acquisitions in the East obtained from European powers during the present war.

8. But the same benefit must in reason and justice be allowed to the Government of India, and to the credit of the Company's finances; and with this allowance, after having excluded the charges of those acquisitions, a large surplus revenue would certainly accrue applicable to the combined purposes of reducing debt, and of maintaining commercial investment.

9. As far as the questions of expense and finance are to be viewed distinctly from other branches of political consideration, I am convinced that the revenue of Ceylon would be infinitely better administered, and more productive, and that its expenses would be much more moderate, if it were permanently annexed

as a province to the Government of Fort St. George, than if it be retained as a separate and distinct Government under the Crown.

10. The permanent annexation of Ceylon to the Crown, while the continent of India shall remain under the Government of the East India Company, is however, a measure more important in my estimation with respect to its political, than to its financial operation.

11. It is essential to the vigour of this Empire, that the administration of all its parts should be uniform, framed upon the same system, combined by similar principles, and directed to similar objects and views. Unity of power, and an invariable correspondence of system and action throughout the whole fabric of our government, are the best securities which can be provided against the dangers to which we are necessarily exposed in India, by the vast extent of our possessions, and by the variety of interests which they embrace. If to the natural principles of division and discord, resulting from the remote position of our provinces, and from the differences of local prejudice and conflicting interests, be added the establishment of distinct authorities, different in substance and in form from the general government of the Empire, and exempt from its control, the weakness of overgrown dominion must ultimately fall upon us, and in every arduous crisis our power will be found inefficient in proportion to its nominal magnitude and extent.

12. Whatever, therefore, may be the nature of that Government which the wisdom of Parliament may permanently establish for India, I hold two principles to be indispensable to its permanent efficiency and vigour.

First, that every part of the empire in India, continental as well as insular, shall be subject to the general control of one undivided authority; which shall possess energy in peace, to maintain order, connection and harmony between all the dispersed branches of our dominion, and to extend equal benefits of good government to every class of our numerous and various subjects; and in war, to direct every spring of action to similar and correspondent movements, to concentrate every resource in an united effort, and by systematic subordination, to diffuse such a spirit of alacrity and promptitude to the remotest extremities of the Empire, as shall secure the co-operation of every part in any exigency which may demand the collective strength of the whole.

Secondly, that the constitution of every branch of the empire should be similar and uniform; and above all, that no subordinate part should be so constituted as in any respect to hold a rivalry of dignity even in form with the Supreme Power.

13. The distinction between the Royal Power and that of the Company is perfectly understood by the natives of India, and more sensibly felt by them than by any class of persons in Europe. Even by Europeans in India a degree of respect is attached to the representation of the Royal Power, which they either boldly refuse, or reluctantly yield to the Company's Government.

14. The application of these principles to the case of Ceylon would lead me to submit most seriously to your consideration the absolute necessity of preserving the control of the Governor-General in Council over the Government of Ceylon entire, and in the fullest efficiency; without this control the possession of Ceylon, instead of being as you justly estimate it, the great bulwark of this Empire, may become nearly as useless to the common cause as if it were in the hands of a neutral power.

15. An independent Governor of Ceylon, acting in the King's name, might prove the source of the most dangerous confusion and distraction in the bosom of our dominions. In the next place, I should feel it to be my duty to represent to you, that if the Governor of Ceylon shall permanently hold a commission, civil and military, from the Crown, the Governor-General should hold a commission, civil as well as military, from the same authority. Without this arrangement, I doubt whether it would be possible permanently to maintain an efficient control over Ceylon when annexed to the Crown.

16. An anxiety for the good government of India being the common sentiment of your mind and of mine, will be my excuse for having submitted these ideas to you, you will use them according to your discretion.

I have the honour to be, &c.

WELLESLEY.

91. The Marquess Wellesley to Lord Hobart.

The same subject.

(Extract.) (Official and Secret.)

My Lord, Fort William, Nov. 30th, 1803.

36. The events however which have passed in Ceylon, have occasioned serious reflections in my mind with regard to the security of that valuable possession, and to the operation of the present constitution of its government upon the general interests of the British empire in India.

37. The separation of the government of Ceylon from the control of the general government of India, always appeared to me to be a measure of the utmost danger to this empire. Accordingly at an early period of time, I submitted my opinion upon the subject to the President of the Board of Commissioners for the affairs of India in a secret letter dated 10th of May 1801, of which I have the honour to enclose a copy for your Lordship's information.

38. The separation of Ceylon from the Government-General, was however deemed advisable; and the consequences which have resulted from that measure appear to me to have confirmed the justice of those apprehensions which I expressed in my letter to the President of the Board of Commissioners in May 1801.

39. Under the new constitution, treaties have been concluded, and a war has been undertaken by the government of Ceylon without the previous knowledge of the Government-General; the expences of that war however, have been supplied in the first instance by the Government-General; and the calamities which have attended the progress of the war, have occasioned demands for troops from the Government-General. Whether the war in Ceylon could have been altogether avoided, whether its commencement could have been postponed to a more convenient season, or whether its conduct could have been improved, and an early and honourable peace established upon permanent foundations, are questions, which it is neither my present duty nor intention to examine; but it is evident that every arrangement connected with these questions might have been formed with greater advantage under the direct authority of the power which must ultimately furnish the supplies for war, and provide the securities for peace. Had the government of Ceylon remained subordinate to this government, the war in that island, if deemed necessary, would have been undertaken after a

deliberate preparation of sufficient resources, and after a full consideration of the most effectual mode of applying them. This government could not have been taken by surprize with respect to the actual commencement of the war, or to its result; and an opportunity would have been afforded of apportioning at an early period of time to the service in Ceylon such aid, as might have appeared on a just comparison of objects and means to be compatible with due attention to other branches of the service in India, or to be indispensably necessary for the safety of Ceylon.

40. The independence of Ceylon has placed all these considerations beyond the reach of the Governor-General in council, who was unapprized of the approach of war in Ceylon until it had actually commenced, and of the probable demand for considerable reinforcements in Ceylon, until a war on the continent of India had limited the means of furnishing them.

41. The operation of treaties and political arrangements concluded by the separate authority of his Majesty's Government of Ceylon may materially affect the general interests of the British empire in India, even in those cases which may not immediately involve the issues of peace and war. His Majesty's instructions together with the Company's charter, and the various acts of regulation, appear to preclude the Governor of Ceylon from the right of concluding treaties, or of making war with any of the continental states of India, or with any state situated beyond the limits of the island of Ceylon. It is perhaps doubtful whether the Governor of Ceylon possesses even within the limits of that island, the same powers relative to peace and war, which are granted by special Act of Parliament to the Governor-General in council within the limits of the Company's charter. These points certainly require full and distinct explanation by the highest authority; but whatever may be the legal right of the Governor of Ceylon with regard to these questions, the practical operation of the new constitution of Ceylon has been amply proved by the experience of the last year.

42. Even if the political powers of the government of Ceylon be limited to the island, the nature of treaties concluded with the King of Candi, or with his ministry, nobility, or other authorities in the island, may be contrary to the general policy pursued by the Company's Government in India, and may therefore prove injurious to the British character and influence on the Continent of India, and among such insular states in these seas as may have formed or solicited connections with the Company.

43. The king of Candi is particularly venerated by the Court of Ava, and a considerable degree of sanctity is attributed in the Burmese dominions to the character of the king of Candi, and to the island of Ceylon, whence the Burmahs derive the source of their mythology, and of their religious institutions. The conduct of the British Government, therefore, towards the king and kingdom of Candi, and the general tenor of the policy pursued in the island of Ceylon, is important to the reputation of the Company's Government on the Continent of India, in proportion to the importance of the Burmese empire in the general scale of Asiatic powers. To your Lordship's intimate knowledge of the affairs of India, it is unnecessary to add more detailed facts or arguments to prove that the operation of any system of treaties, alliances, or political or diplomatic arrangements pursued towards the native states and subjects within the limits of the island of Ceylon, cannot be confined to the coasts of that island, even if such system should exclude the contingency of war in Ceylon.

44. If treaties or political systems concluded with the native states or powers in Ceylon should involve the issue of hostilities, although the theatre of the war may in the first instance be confined to Ceylon, it is evident that even the first and most limited operation of such a war must affect the finances, as well as the general security of the British empire in India.

45. The charges of war in Ceylon must be defrayed from Bengal. If the war should prove unfortunate in Ceylon, troops and every military resource must be supplied from Bengal. Even in the most favourable supposition, troops occupied in hostile operations within the island of Ceylon, (omitting all consideration of the fatality of the climate,) not only become inapplicable to any purposes of general defence on the Continent of India, but are withdrawn from the protection of the coasts and maritime forts of the island. The danger will be aggravated, if, at the same moment, the Company's government shall be engaged in war upon the Continent of India, and shall be unable to supply troops for the support of a war in Ceylon, or for the defence of the forts and coasts of that island, deprived of the aid of its proper military establishments.

46. In the event, therefore, of an existing war with France, Holland, or with any power capable of attacking Ceylon, the existence of an internal war in the island may convert that bulwark of our Indian empire into a powerful instrument of offensive

war in the hands of our enemies; and the consequences of a treaty concluded by a Governor of Ceylon within the limits of that island may endanger the whole fabric of this vast empire.

47. The situation of the Governor-General under the circumstances described will be duly appreciated by your Lordship. Ignorant of the approach or causes of war, he may be suddenly required to furnish resources for its prosecution at a moment when the exigencies of his own government, and the general service of the empire in India may preclude the possibility of affording adequate supplies either of money or men. Without power to direct the conduct, or to check the progress of hostilities, he may be compelled to abide their consequences, and to remain an inactive and helpless spectator of the perils of his own government, of the disgrace of the British name and arms, and possibly of his own reputation and honour, involved in the result of counsels and operations contradictory to his judgment, and exempt from his control.

48. On the other hand, the Governor of Ceylon, by the practical operation of the present constitution of the island, exercises the sole prerogative of making war within that island, but must depend for the means of prosecuting war upon an authority which he cannot control.

49. The legislature has vested in the Governor-General in council, subject to the control in England, the sole power of making war against any native state on the Continent of India. The same principle requires that the Governor-General in council should possess similar powers with regard to war in Ceylon. The wisdom of the legislature has provided an unity of executive power as the most effectual security for the British empire on the Continent of India, and has determined that the authority invested with the sole power of disposing of all the resources necessary for the prosecution of war, should also possess the sole power of making war, and that no provincial, local, or subordinate authority should be enabled to involve the general interests of the empire in the expense and hazard of hostilities.

50. The same principles have been wisely established with regard to the political powers of the Supreme Government on the Continent of India, and it has been determined by Parliament that the Governor-General in council, who alone can be competent to form a comprehensive view of the interests affected by treaties or by wars with the native states, shall alone be competent to conclude treaties, or to make war. But under

the existing constitution of the island of Ceylon, your Lordship will observe that the order and system established for the general government of India are absolutely reversed. The Governor of Ceylon exercises the exclusive authority of concluding treaties, of making war, and of conducting military operations in the island, without the power of furnishing supplies, either of men or money, beyond the fixed establishment of the island; while the Governor-General in council is required to furnish supplies of men and money for the prosecution of war in Ceylon, without possessing any power of controlling the origin, conduct, or progress of the war, which may, however, deeply affect the security, interests and honour of the general government of India.

51. The island of Ceylon, however, cannot be excluded from the general operation of these wise and salutary principles, unless it be also excluded from the general system of the British civil and military government in India. But that island has justly been termed the bulwark of our empire in India; it is therefore an essential part of our strength, and the due administration of its civil and military government is of the utmost importance to the defence of all our dominions in India. No security for that administration can be so effectual as the uniform operation of the same authority which has been extended over every other branch of the British possessions; nor can an argument be adduced to prove the importance of Ceylon, which will not also demonstrate that its interests are inseparably blended with those of the empire on the Continent, and that its government cannot be separated from the general control without hazard to the safety both of that empire, and of the island of Ceylon.

52. The entire military establishment of India ought to be applicable to the general defence of the whole empire. The subdivision of that establishment, and the separation of our general strength into detachments subjected to independent commands, and appropriated to exclusive provincial and local services, must impair the general efficiency of our army, by destroying the unity of our military power.

53. The same principle applies with equal force to the civil authority which, in an empire of such magnitude and extent, cannot be separated from the military power without the hazard of confusion.

54. In reviewing these considerations, your Lordship will

anticipate the regret and concern with which I have learned that not only the civil and military government of the island of Ceylon are to remain independent of the general superintendance and control of the Governor-General in council, but that the military establishments of that island are to be entirely disjoined from the chief command of the forces on the Continent of India; and that the allowances and other regulations respecting the military establishments are to be framed in Ceylon upon principles different from those established at any of the presidencies on the Continent of India.

55. The effect of this arrangement will entirely remove the military establishments at Ceylon from the superintendance and control of the general officer commanding in chief his Majesty's and the Company's forces in India.

56. Every sentiment of public duty requires me to submit to your Lordship my most serious apprehension of the evil consequences which must result to the discipline and efficiency of the military forces in Ceylon, if exempted from the salutary control of the officer holding the chief command in India.

57. Every facility should be afforded to the employment of the military establishment of Ceylon in purposes of general defence in India, whenever the exigency might require such an effort. But the entire separation of the civil and military authorities, and the difference of the regulations and constitutions of the separate military establishments will oppose difficulties nearly insuperable to the employment on the Continent of India of any part of the military establishment of Ceylon, and especially of his Majesty's regiments.

58. On the other hand, the same causes will oppose nearly equal difficulties to the employment of any portion of the military establishments of the Continent of India, and especially of his Majesty's regiments in the island of Ceylon, in the event of any exigency which might demand a reinforcement of the troops on that island. The utmost confusion and disorder might be expected to result from the conflicting authorities which must be mixed in conducting any military operations on that island, which should demand the aid of troops from the Continent of India. It might even become a question whether the Governor-General would be justified in exposing the army destined to defend the British empire in India, to be wasted in the prosecution of petty wars in Ceylon (of which the cause and issue might be equally doubtful), under a system of management calculated

to injure the discipline, to break the spirit, and to destroy the health of the troops. In the present state of the government and military command in Ceylon, it is doubtful whether the governments or commanders-in-chief on the Continent of India could retain any power over troops landed in Ceylon, and whether those authorities could in any degree control the discipline or operations of their own troops within the island, or could limit the objects to which the services of such troops should be applied, or the time or mode of recalling such troops to the Continent of India, or of embarking them for distant service.

59. The independence of the government and military command of Ceylon would considerably embarrass the Government-General in the prosecution of operations against the remaining possessions of the French and Dutch to the eastward of the Cape of Good Hope, or in any eventual expedition against the Cape of Good Hope, or against Egypt, or against various places in these seas, or even in any transfer of troops from the several maritime garrisons in India. Your Lordship is intimately acquainted with the advantages which the ports of Ceylon offer for assembling troops and ships, and for completing every necessary depôt in the preparation of such services. The Government-General repeatedly derived important advantages from the full command of those ports during the last war. In the present state of the island it would not be possible to use its ports and resources with similar effect. A considerable portion of the value of Ceylon in time of war is therefore actually suspended by the existing constitution of the government of that island.

60. Your Lordship is apprized of the nature and extent of the military commission with which his Majesty was pleased to honour me under date of the 7th of August, 1800. By the terms of that commission I have hitherto understood that I possessed the general command over all the land forces serving in Ceylon, as well as over those serving in every other part of the East Indies.

61. The terms of this commission seemed to enable me to issue orders to the troops in Ceylon, but the effect of such orders appeared to me to be entirely frustrated by the independent powers of the civil government of the island, which must be deemed paramount to any powers derived from a mere military commission, unless that commission in express terms had superseded the authority of the civil government.

62. It would be extremely advantageous to furnish me with a distinct rule for my guidance with regard to the operation of my

commission of Captain-general of the land forces over the island of Ceylon.

63. The preceding statements will apprize your Lordship, that if Ceylon be entirely exempted from the control of the general civil and military government of India, and from the command of the commander-in-chief, and of the Captain-general, in India, the military establishments of that island cannot be deemed to constitute an efficient part of our general resources and power in India, excepting only to the extent to which these establishments may be sufficient to prevent the reduction of the island of Ceylon by the forces of any enemy, directed exclusively against that possession.

64. Your Lordship's judgment and experience in the affairs of this quarter of the globe will enable you to decide with facility, whether such a separation and subdivision of powers be preferable to an union of all the British resources and strength in the hands of one supreme authority in India, possessing power to apply every branch of the General Government to the defence of each part, or of the whole; and embracing in one comprehensive view the general welfare and security of the empire, together with the particular and local interests of every province and possession.

65. The despatch addressed to the President of the Board of Commissioners for the affairs of India, under date 10th May, 1801, to which I had the honour to refer in the 37th paragraph of this letter, will convey to your Lordship my sentiments on this important question. These sentiments have been confirmed by the most mature and deliberate reflection, and by every event relating to the affairs of Ceylon which has reached my knowledge since the independence of that government has been established.

66. In one respect only has my opinion undergone any degree of variation. I am now convinced that the most effectual mode of rendering Ceylon a valuable addition to the British possessions in India, and an efficient augmentation of our military and political power would be to annex it, as a province directly to the Supreme Government of Bengal, with orders to the Governor-General in Council to adopt such measures as might appear requisite for regulating the civil and military government and establishments of the island. Such an arrangement would unite considerable advantages in point of economy, with a great improvement of the internal tranquillity, happiness, and prosperity of the island, and with a correspondent increase of its military strength.

67. The government of Ceylon might either be formed upon

the model of that of any of the provinces subject to the immediate government of Bengal, and made the station of a Court of Circuit and Appeal, with establishments for the revenue and commerce of the island, and with one of his Majesty's general officers upon the staff commanding the troops; or the Government of Ceylon might be similar to that of Prince of Wales island, with a Lieutenant-Governor appointed from the civil service of Bengal. In this case also Ceylon should be the station of a general officer on the staff.

68. I am satisfied that, under either of these arrangements, the island of Ceylon would become a more valuable and a more secure possession than it can prove under the present constitution of its civil and military government. Your Lordship will receive these observations as a testimony of my anxiety for the safety and prosperity of this great empire. My opinions are founded upon mature deliberation and practical experience; and it appears to me to be my positive duty to submit them to your Lordship in the most direct and unequivocal language. I request your Lordship, however, to be assured that I offer my sentiments on the subject of this despatch to your judgment, with the highest sense of respect, and with a just impression of my obligations of obedience and subordination to your Lordship's authority. Whatever may be his Majesty's determination with regard to the government of Ceylon, my submission will be implicit and cheerful; and your Lordship may rely on my most earnest endeavours during the present crisis, and at every future exigency, to mitigate the evils which I have respectfully represented, by the most cordial exertion of a sincere public zeal, and by an unfeigned spirit of effectual co-operation in the common cause.

69. I cannot however conclude this despatch without expressing a most anxious hope, that if it should not be deemed expedient to change the entire constitution of the government of Ceylon, his Majesty may at least be advised immediately to issue the necessary orders for subjecting, during the existing war with France and Holland, the civil and military government of Ceylon (including the exercise of all political power, and the command of the army,) to the control of the Governor-General in Council, of his Majesty's Commander-in-Chief, and of his Majesty's Captain-General of the land forces in the East Indies.

70. Without such a control, I shall entertain serious apprehensions, in the event of protracted war with France. Your Lordship however may be satisfied, that while I shall continue

to hold my present charge, no possible combination of difficulties or dangers can abate my zeal for the defence, security, and welfare of every part of the British possessions in India, for the defeat of every project of the enemy, and for the effectual prosecution of every service connected with the execution of his Majesty's commands, with the success of his Majesty's arms, and with the honour and interests of our country in the present arduous contest.

I have the honour to be, &c. WELLESLEY.

6. RED SEA EXPEDITION.

92. To the Shereef of Mecca, the Imaum of Senna, and the Sultaun of Aden.

Summons to join us in expelling the French from Egypt.

Fort William, 19th March, 1801.

The friendship and harmony which during a long course of years has firmly subsisted between the Sublime Porte and his Britannic Majesty, is well known to you; that friendship has been still more closely cemented by the faithless conduct of the French towards the Ottoman Porte; the French are now become the common enemy of both states. That perfidious people, disregarding all the obligations of friendship and the stipulations of treaty have sent forth their armies to invade the peaceful provinces of Egypt, the acknowledged territory of the Ottoman Porte; without urging the slightest pretext to justify this outrage, but on the contrary professing sentiments of perfect friendship and regard, these disturbers of the peace of nations have carried war and desolation into the most fruitful provinces of the empire, the venerated sanctuary of the Mahomedan faith; they have attempted to establish their authority upon the ruins of your religion; they have now unequivocally declared their resolution to maintain by force what they have acquired by the violation of every principle of public faith, and of every maxim of civil and religious obligation.

I entertain too high an opinion of your attachment to the interests and independence of the parent state, and of your zeal for the support of the religion which you revere, to believe that you can have witnessed without indignation and alarm, this unexampled instance of the inordinate ambition and perfidious conduct of the French nation.

I am persuaded you cannot view with unconcern the ambitious and encroaching spirit of the French nation which, unresisted, must inevitably complete the downfall of the Mahomedan authority, not only in Egypt, but in all the neighbouring territories, and must establish the supremacy of the French power in the most sacred seats of the Mahomedan religion.

It has been the uniform policy of the French to endeavour to disarm the resentment of the people, whose country they have invaded, by professing the most amicable intentions, and by pretending that the sole motive of their actions is to mitigate the tyranny of oppressive governments, to establish the independence of oppressed nations, and to secure to mankind the full enjoyment of civil and religious rights. By these insidious arts, the French have succeeded in reducing to their absolute power many of the states of Europe, which they have invaded and ravaged, without the slightest pretext or provocation.

They have employed the same means to reconcile the inhabitants of Egypt to their unprovoked violence and unjust usurpation, and they will endeavour to practice the same perfidious policy for the purpose of subjugating the remaining dependencies of the Ottoman empire in Arabia.

They will labour to impress you with a belief of their amicable disposition, and of their regard for the sanctity of your religion ; under the pretence of establishing your independence, they will endeavour to subvert your government, and to erect their tyrannous misrule upon its ruins.

With the most friendly solicitude, I warn you to take example from the unhappy fate of other states, and to beware of yielding to the insidious professions of a nation, which has forfeited all pretensions to credit by a systematic contempt of the obligations of public faith, and of the established law of nations, especially by their unprovoked and unjustifiable invasion of Egypt.

You have no other security for the preservation of your independence, and for the maintenance of your rights, than a determination to resist the force, and to frustrate the frauds of the French nation.

You are called upon, therefore, by every motive of interest and of self-preservation, by every principle of national honour and religious attachment, to unite your efforts with the combined exertions of the British power, and of the Ottoman state, for the expulsion of the French from Egypt. A formidable army of Turkish troops is already acting with vigour, for the purpose of dispossessing the French of their usurped authority in Egypt, and a numerous body of British troops now co-operates in Egypt with the army of the Porte, in effecting the expulsion of the French from Egypt.

With a view to second the operations of this combined army, I have detached a considerable force of European and native troops from India, to unite in a joint effort for the expulsion of the common enemy. This measure while it favours the success of the operations to be carried on from the side of Syria and the Mediterranean, is calculated to provide for the security of the Mahomedan possessions, on the Arabian side of the Red Sea.

As the existence of the Mahomedan dominion in Arabia, and the interests of the Mahomedan religion are obviously concerned in the expulsion of the French, I cannot doubt that you will employ all the resources of your country, and the influence of your authority in promoting the success of the projected enterprize; I am the more induced to rely upon your exertions by the report which has been made to me by Captain Wilson, and by Lieutenant-Colonel Murray, (who were deputed under my orders to the Red Sea,) of the friendly disposition which you entertain towards the British nation.

I trust you will employ every effort to procure and to facilitate the despatch of provisions, and of stores to the troops employed in the Red Sea, that you will furnish a reinforcement of the troops of your country to act with the British army, and that you will encourage the several chiefs and states in Arabia, and in Egypt, to make common cause against the common enemy of your nation, and of the British power.

Major-General Baird the commander-in-chief of the Indian forces, or a proper person deputed by him, will have the honour to deliver to you this letter, and will present to you a few articles, the produce of Europe, and of this country, as a token of my friendship and regard.

I request your favourable attention to the suggestions and applications which may be made on my part for your assistance in promoting the object of the expedition.

For the rest, believe me anxious for accounts of your welfare &c.

WELLESLEY.

(A true Copy.) N. B. EDMONSTONE,
Secretary to the Government.

7. The Emperor.

93. The Governor-General in Council to the Secret Committee of the Honourable the Court of Directors.

Danger of the French availing themselves of the Imperial pretensions. Importance of placing Shah Allum and his family under British protection.

(Extract.)

Fort William, 13th July, 1804.

Honourable Sirs,

67. Your honourable Committee is aware that the late Mahajee Scindiah, after having rescued the unfortunate representative of the house of Timour from the sanguinary violence of Gholaum Kaudir, obtained from his Majesty the grant of the office of Vakeel ool Mutluck, or executive prime minister of the Moghul Empire, for his Highness the Peishwa, and was himself appointed to execute the functions of that office under the title of deputy, and that Dowlut Rao Scindiah succeeded to the office of deputy Vakeel ool Mutluck, and to the consequent control which his predecessor had established over the person and family of the aged and unhappy monarch of Delhi. By successful intrigue, M. Perron obtained the office of commandant of the fortress of Delhi, which is the residence of the royal family, and thus secured the possession of the person and of the nominal authority of the Emperor.

68. Notwithstanding his Majesty's total deprivation of real power, dominion, and authority, almost every state and every class of people in India continue to acknowledge his nominal sovereignty. The current coin of every established power is struck in the name of Shah Aulum. Princes and persons of the highest rank and family still bear the titles, and display the insignia of rank which they or their ancestors derived from the throne of Delhi, under the acknowledged authority of Shah Aulum, and his Majesty is still considered to be the only legitimate fountain of similar honours.

69. The pride of the numerous class of Mussulmans in India is gratified by a recognition of the nominal authority of the illustrious representative of the house of Timour over the territories which once constituted the extensive and powerful empire of the Moghul, and the Mussulmans are still disposed to acknowledge the legitimacy of pretensions or demands, ostensibly proceeding from the authority of the imperial mandate.

70. Under these circumstances, the person and authority of his Majesty Shah Aulum might form a dangerous instrument in the hands of any state possessing sufficient power, energy, and judgment, to employ it, in prosecuting views of aggrandizement and ambition.

71. The Moghul has never been an important or dangerous instrument in the hands of the Mahrattas, but the augmentation of M. Perron's influence and power and the growth of a French interest in Hindostan, had given a new aspect to the condition of the Moghul, and that unfortunate Prince might have become a powerful aid to the cause of France in India, under the direction of French agents.

72. The views with which the Government of France prepared to resume its possessions in India under the provisions of the treaty of Amiens, were unequivocally manifested by the extent and nature of the staff and equipments which accompanied the officer appointed to exercise the chief authority over all the restored possessions of the French in this country, and additional demonstrations of those views have appeared since the renewal of the war with France. No doubt remained that it was the intention of the Government of France after the conclusion of peace, to establish on the foundation of her possessions in India a political and military state, and to strengthen and augment it by every practicable connection with the native states of India, and by every art of indefatigable intrigue and systematic ambition. The system of introducing French adventurers into the armies of the native states, for the improvement of their discipline and efficiency, had been found to afford the readiest and most effectual means of establishing the influence and authority of the French in the government of those states, and of erecting an independent territorial and military power within the limits of a foreign dominion. The extension and improvement of this system during the continuance of peace, would undoubtedly have constituted a principal object of the attention of the Government of France in India, and adverting to the facilities which would be afforded to the views and projects of the French by the extent of territorial and military power and independence established under the direction of M. Perron in the north-west of Hindostan, it cannot be doubted that under the continuance of peace between his Majesty and France and between the British Government and the Mahratta states, the progress of French intrigue, and the aggrandizement of

the French power in India, would have been most rapid and dangerous to our security. In the prosecution of these views, the French would manifestly have derived essential aid from the possession of the person and family of the Emperor Shah Aulum. The name of that monarch would have been employed to justify exaction, violence and encroachment, and under the plea of restoring his Majesty to his hereditary dominion, the power of France in India might have been directed to the subversion of every state, and to the appropriation of every territory unprotected by alliance with the British nation. The Emperor might have been compelled to constitute the territorial possessions of France in India an independent sovereignty, and under the plea of possessing sovereign authority, the proceedings of the Government of France in India might have proved in the highest degree injurious to the interests and security of the British Empire in this quarter of the globe.

73. If any doubt could be entertained of the views of the French in this respect, that doubt would be removed by the tenor of documents obtained at Pondicherry and Calcutta, and transmitted by the Governor-General to the Right Honourable Lord Hobart, of which copies are now annexed to this despatch.

74. With a view however to submit to your hon. Committee's immediate and particular notice a distinct proof of the projects in the contemplation of the Government of France with respect to the Emperor Shah Aulum, the Governor-General in Council deems it advisable to insert in this place a translation of an extract from one of the documents to which the preceding paragraph refers.

75. That document is entitled a Memorial on the present importance of India, and on the most 'efficacious means of re-establishing the French nation in its ancient splendour in that country.'

76. That document was obtained at Pondicherry from a French officer, named Le Febre, who accompanied General Decaen to India. 'Such has been the treatment received from a company of merchant adventurers by the Emperor of Hindostan, the sole branch of the illustrious house of Timour, so revered throughout the East, that his sovereignty is universally acknowledged although his power is no more, and the English Company derived its own constitutional power from his infinite goodness. It is evident that Shah Aulum ought to be the

undisputed sovereign of the Moghul Empire, as the great grandson of Aurung Zebe, the tenth succession in a direct line from Tamerlane. This great question with respect to the sovereignty of the Empire being decided, it remains to consider whether it is not possible that the branches of this unfortunate family may find at some time protectors, who shall assert their sacred rights and break their ignominious chains. It will be then that a mutual alliance, and a judicious union of powers shall secure the permanent sovereignty of the Emperor, and render his immediate subjects, as well as his tributaries, happy in the enjoyment of personal security, and of that wealth which springs from peace, agriculture and a free trade. The English Company, by its ignominious treatment of the great Moghul, has forfeited its rights as dewan and treasurer of the Empire; the Nabobs of Oude and of Bengal are equally criminal, because they have acted as traitors towards their lawful sovereign: thus the Emperor of Delhi has a real and indisputable right to transmit to whomsoever he may please to select, the sovereignty of his dominions, as well as the arrears due to him from the English. These arrears of the tribute of 26 lacs of rupees, promised by the Company, with the interest of the country added, will amount at this present time to four hundred and fifty-two millions tournois, a sum which greatly exceeds the value of the Company's moveable capital.'

77. The preceding observations may serve to illustrate the importance of placing the person, family and nominal authority, of his Majesty Shah Aulum under the protection of the British Government, and the accomplishment of that arrangement was accordingly considered by the Governor-General to be a principal object, though not a cause of the war, and an indispensable condition of the peace.

78. Independently of the considerations above stated, adverting to the degree of veneration with which the illustrious descendant of Timour is regarded by all classes of people in India, and especially by the class of Mussulmans, and to the state of indignity and misery to which that unfortunate monarch had been reduced under the oppressive control of the Mahrattas and the French, the Governor-General in Council considered among the most important political benefits of that arrangement, the reputation which the British name would acquire by affording an honourable and tranquil asylum to the fallen dignity and declining age of the King of Delhi, and by securing

the means of comfort to his Majesty's numerous and distressed family.

We have the honour to be,
Honourable Sirs,
Your most faithful humble servants,
WELLESLEY.
G. H. BARLOW.
G. UDNY.

94. The Governor-General in Council to the Secret Committee of the Honourable the Court of Directors.

Establishment of Shah Allum as titular King of Delhi.

(Extract.)

Honourable Sirs, Fort William, June 2, 1805.

The Governor-General in Council now submits to your honourable Committee the arrangement which has been adopted by this government for the purpose of providing for the future maintenance of his Majesty Shah Allum and the Royal family, and for the general settlement of his Majesty's affairs, and the principles upon which that arrangement is founded.

It has never been in the contemplation of this government to derive from the charge of protecting and supporting his Majesty, the privilege of employing the Royal prerogative, as an instrument of establishing any control or ascendancy over the states and chieftains of India, or of asserting on the part of his Majesty any of the claims which in his capacity of Emperor of Hindostan his Majesty may be considered to possess upon the provinces originally composing the Moghul empire. The benefits which the Governor-General in Council expected to derive from placing the King of Delhi and the Royal family under the protection of the British Government are to be traced in the statements contained in our despatch to your honourable Committee of the 13th of July 1804, relative to the evils and embarrassments to which the British power might have been exposed by the prosecution of claims and pretensions on the part of the Mahrattas, or of the French, in the name and under the authority of his Majesty Shah Allum, if the person and family of that unhappy monarch had continued under the custody and control of those powers, and especially of the French. With reference to this subject, the Governor-General in Council has the honour to refer your honourable Committee to the contents of the enclosure of our despatch of the 13th of July 1804, marked A., and to the 73d paragraph of that despatch, in proof of the actual existence of a project for the subversion of the British empire in India, founded principally upon the restoration of the authority of the Emperor Shah Allum, under the control and direction of the agents of France. The difficulty of every project of that nature has been considerably increased by the events which have placed the throne of Delhi under the protection of the honourable Company. The Governor-General in Council further contemplated the advantages of reputation which the British Government might be expected to derive from the substitution of a system of lenient protection, accompanied by a liberal provision for the ease, dignity, and comfort of the aged monarch and his distressed family, in the room of that oppressive control and that degraded condition of poverty, distress, and insult, under which the unhappy representative of the house of Timur and his numerous family had so long laboured.

Regulated by these principles and views, the attention of the British Government has been directed exclusively to the object of forming such an arrangement for the future support of the King and the Royal family as might secure to them the enjoyment of every reasonable comfort and convenience, and every practicable degree of external state and dignity compatible with the extent of our resources, and with the condition of dependence in which his Majesty and the Royal family must necessarily be placed with relation to the British power. In extending to the Royal family the benefits of the British protection, no obligation was imposed upon us to consider the rights and claims of his Majesty Shah Allum as Emperor of Hindostan, and the Governor-General has deemed it equally unnecessary and inexpedient to combine with the intended provision for his Majesty and his household, the consideration of any question connected with the future exercise of the imperial prerogative and authority.

The Governor-General in Council has determined to adopt an arrangement upon the basis of the following provisions. That a specified portion of the territories in the vicinity of Delhi, situated on the right bank of the Jumna should be assigned in part of the provision for the maintenance of the Royal family. That those lands should remain under the charge of the Resident at Delhi, and that the revenue should be collected, and justice should be administered in the name of his Majesty Shah Allum, under regulations to be fixed by the British Government. That his Majesty should be permitted to appoint a Dewan and other inferior officers to attend at the office of collector, for the purpose of ascertaining and reporting to his Majesty the amount of the revenues which should be received and the charges of collection, and of satisfying his Majesty's mind that no part of the produce of the assigned territory was mis-appropriated. That two courts of justice should be established for the administration of civil and criminal justice, according to the Mahomedan law, to the inhabitants of the city of Delhi, and of the assigned territory. That no sentences of the criminal courts extending to death should be carried into execution without the express sanction of his Majesty, to whom the proceedings in all trials of this description should be reported, and that sentences of mutilation should be commuted.

That to provide for the immediate wants of his Majesty, and the royal household, the following sums should be paid monthly in money, from the treasury of the Resident at Delhi:—to his Majesty for his private expences, 60,000 sicca rupees; to the heir apparent, exclusive of certain Jagheers, 10,000 do.; to a favourite son of his Majesty, named Mirza Izzut Buksh, 5,000 do.; to two other sons of his Majesty, 1,500 do.; to his Majesty's fifty younger sons and daughters, 10,000 do.; to Shah Newauze Khan, his Majesty's Treasurer, 2,500 do.; to Syud Rezzee Khan, British Agent at his Majesty's court, and related to his Majesty by marriage, 1,000 do.—Total per mensem, 90,000 sicca rupees.

That if the produce of the revenue of the assigned territory should hereafter admit of it, the monthly sum to be advanced to his Majesty for his private expences might be increased to one lac of rupees.

That in addition to the sums specified, the sum of 10,000 rupees should annually be paid to his Majesty on certain festivals, agreeably to ancient usage.

The Governor-General in Council deemed the arrangement proposed by the Resident at Delhi for the establishment of a military force for the protection of the assigned territory and of the north-western frontier of our possessions in Hindostan, to be judicious, and accordingly resolved to confirm those arrangements, with certain modifications calculated to afford a provision for part of the irregular force in the service of the British Government, from the expence of which it was an object of the British Government to be relieved, and also for a proportion of the European officers heretofore in the service of Dowlut Rao

Scindiah, who quitted that service under the proclamation of the Governor-General in Council of the 29th August 1803.

On the basis of this plan of arrangement detailed instructions were issued to the Resident at Delhi, under the date the 23d May, with orders to carry it into effect, with the least practicable delay.

The Governor-General in Council entertains a confident expectation that the proposed arrangement and provision will be satisfactory to his Majesty, and will be considered throughout all the states of India to be consistent with the acknowledged justice, liberality, and benevolence of the British Government.

The Governor-General in Council also confidently trusts that the proposed arrangement will be sanctioned by the approbation of your honourable Committee, and of the honourable the Court of Directors.

We have the honour to be,
Honourable Sirs,
Your most faithful humble servants,
WELLESLEY.
G. H. BARLOW.
G. UDNY.

VII. MISCELLANEOUS DESPATCHES.

95. The Right Hon. H. Dundas to the Earl of Mornington.

Foreign Politics. Relations of Anglo-Indian Government to the Nizam, Zemaun Shah, the Mahrattas, and Tippoo.

Wimbledon, 18th March, 1799.
[Received 5th Aug. 1799.]

My dear Lord,

As the ships at present despatched are under orders to sail, it deprives me of the opportunity of writing to you upon the important subjects treated of in your letters, lately arrived overland. These letters are so voluminous that they are not yet decyphered; and from what is reported to me as to the progress made in decyphering, I have great doubts if these despatches will be ready to be brought under my view before the ships actually sail. From your general letter to the Secret Committee, I perceive that the subjects of those undecyphered papers are of a very interesting nature, and your Lordship may be assured of hearing from me by the first opportunity after I have considered them.

It is my intention, in my present letter, to advert to some of the general topics to which you have referred in your letter of an earlier date, and the subject of which I may not have exhausted in any former communication.

It is impossible for me not to begin with noticing the letter recently received, enclosing the Treaty you have made with the Nizam. Your Lordship has long before this time anticipated the satisfaction I have derived from that transaction, which has been completed in so masterly and effectual a manner. Long before this, I trust, it has been carried into final execution. I have long felt uneasy from the circumstance of the French force in the service of the Nizam; and it was, perhaps, the circumstance of all others which gave me the most uneasiness, when I became satisfied that the powerful armaments under Buonaparte were destined for Egypt, as his best road for the annoyance of our Indian possessions. Your Treaty with the Nizam effectually puts an end to every alarm upon that part of the business, and whether you consider it negatively as removing the French force from our neighbourhood, or positively in respect of the additional strength it affords to ourselves and the aid it gives to our finances, it is a transaction which tells in our favour in a variety of ways, and was well worth accomplishing at any risk, even if the Mahratta powers had been dissatisfied with it. I do not, however, see any real foundation for their being so, and I trust it will not be long before I shall hear that your Lordship has been able, by proper exertions with the Mahrattas, to connect them with the Nizam and us still more closely upon the principles of a common interest of defensive alliance against Tippoo, and every power in alliance with France.

Upon the subject of the Rajah of Berar, it is only necessary for me to say, that in so far as my general knowledge and recollection of Indian affairs enable me at present to decide, it appears to me that he has always been friendly to the British interests in India; and I should conceive that in no respect a close connection with him can be prejudicial to our defensive system, and the desire of preserving the general peace of India, which, if it can be observed with honour, is certainly our wisest system; and as it is most likely to be disturbed by the hostility of Tippoo, it of course follows that every connection which strengthens our power against him must be ultimately beneficial to the Indian interests of Great Britain. This naturally leads me to advert to the views of Zemaun Shah, and the situation of Scindia as connected with that subject.

It was some time ago the fashion, in my opinion, too much to undervalue the menaces of Zemaun Shah respecting India, but I think that opinion is gradually wearing away as it ought to do. You are more in the way of collecting accurate information than I am; but if the French were ever to obtain such a footing as to enable them seriously to distress us, I have long thought that it would be a material point of the plan to obtain the co-operation of Zemaun Shah. And even if Tippoo himself, from any misguided ambition, should be induced to undertake any extensive project against us, I must always believe that his best endeavours would be used to obtain the assistance of Zemaun Shah. I take it for granted, Mr. Jones, at Bagdad, transmits regularly to India the information his situation there enables him to collect; but in case, by any accident it should not have reached you, I herewith send you a copy of the information[1] recently received from him on the subject of Zemaun Shah, and comparing it with others, it strongly confirms me in the belief of his hostile designs, and that we ought to keep a very watchful eye upon the motions of that Prince, whose talents, military force, and pecuniary resources, afford to him the means of being a formidable opponent. It would be too strong for me to state, that under no given circumstances our own forces were to go beyond our own provinces and the territories of the Vizier; but the temptation must be very great, and the advantage very evident, to induce us to do so. The means of resisting any intended aggression on the part of Zemaun Shah appear to be the following. First, to encourage and keep up those distractions and animosities within his own territories, the apprehensions of which must always, to a certain degree, keep him in a state of alarm, and which obliged him to return rapidly from his last attempt to invade Hindostan. Secondly, every encouragement should be given to the Seiks and Rajpoot tribes to harrass and distress him in his progress. But lastly,

---

[1] 'The information alluded to by Mr. Dundas not having been received in time will be forwarded under a separate cover.

W. CABELL.'

what of all others appears most material is, upon the ground of his own danger, to engage Scindia cordially in that defensive system of alliance, which it is our interest, by every means, to strengthen and confirm, with a view to the security of our Indian empire. It is perfectly obvious, that if ever Zemaun Shah gains a material footing in Hindostan, Scindia and his power must fall the first sacrifice to his ambition.

Under these circumstances I do not think your Lordship can do a more essential service to the interests of your country in India than by using your best endeavours to soothe and heal those jarring animosities which annihilate the force of the Government of Poonah, and render them an easy prey to the restless ambition either of Tippoo Sultaun or of Zemaun Shah. Nothing can more effectually tend to secure this object than persuading Scindia to abandon that system of wickedness, perfidy, and intrigue, which he is now pursuing at Poonah, and engaging him to return to the care and protection of his own territories which require his best attention, and must ultimately tend to gratify his ambition, and consolidate his power, more than any advantages he can hope to attain by aiming at more remote or distant objects of ambition. I cannot more strongly convey to your Lordship the importance I attach to the suggestions I have laid before you, than by stating it as my opinion, that if you are able to consolidate in one defensive system the Nizam's power, the Mahratta power, and the power of Great Britain in India, we have nothing to fear in that quarter of the globe from any combinations that can be formed against us.

Upon the subject of Tippoo Sultaun I have little to say in this letter, further than to express my approbation of the line of conduct you have pursued relative to that restless Prince. You will have seen long before this, from the letter I wrote to you in the month of June last, how much the principles upon which you have acted correspond with the suggestions I laid before you at that time, when the object of Buonaparte's expedition was not ascertained, but which for the reasons I then gave, I was satisfied was intended for the prosecution of those objects which afterwards proved to be the case. The first thought which you seem to have entertained, viz., that of attacking Tippoo in consequence of his conduct at Mauritius, was a very natural feeling, and there can be no doubt that the Ambassadors he sent there, and the alliance he appears to have formed upon principles hostile to us, would have fully justified you in any measures you might have thought proper to adopt. His conduct was tantamount to a declaration of war against us, but still I think you judged well in not bringing it to that extremity. By the line of conduct you have pursued towards him, you have asserted the pride and honour of the British name, which must never for a moment be let down; but you have done it in a manner to enable you to review, deliberately, your resources, and to arrange your force in such a manner as will enable you to act with effect, if the humility of his acknowledgments is not adequate to what our power and the justice of our cause entitle us to demand. By this delay, likewise, you have accomplished the important point of strengthening the connexion with the Nizam, and of disbanding that pernicious French force which had grown up within his territory. Besides this you have received the additional confidence naturally resulting from the military force which has been sent to you from this country and from the Cape, and I likewise trust that the bullion which has been sent from this country has reached you before this time, and has tended to enliven your circulation and resources. It shall not be my fault if much more is not done in the same line in the course of the present season, but I do not enlarge upon that subject at present, as I will have occasion to advert to it in a letter upon the trade and finances of India, which I intend to write to you time enough I hope to go by the present conveyance. Neither has the delay been attended with any detriment to your affairs.

It is unnecessary to trouble you with any details with regard to the situation of the French army in Egypt. Our information of what passes there is so slow and tedious, I trust that the means which have been taken to supply you with intelligence from thence have kept you as well and early informed in India, if not more so than we are at home; but from what we have learnt from various quarters, I flatter myself Lord Nelson's splendid victory, and the exertions of our fleet in the Mediterranean, leave us little reason to apprehend any danger at present to India from the French force which has landed in Egypt. I trust that army will find its grave in Egypt, and consequently as Tippoo must be well informed of those circumstances, you will not find that his expectation of a French succour will add much pride or vigour to his communications with you.

As your Lordship is perfectly familiar with the different

points of which I have treated in this letter, I have not thought it necessary to trouble you with minute details on each topic; but I flatter myself I have said enough to make you perfectly acquainted with my sentiments on those leading points of Indian policy. The result of the whole is, that our security rests, primarily, on our own reputation and power; but that in order to render our exertions efficient and permanent, it ought to be our unceasing care to keep the power of the Nizam and of the whole branches of the Mahratta confederacy in a strict amity with us for the purpose of establishing an impregnable barrier against all Asiatic ambition, whether acting separately or in co-operation with European allies; as an essential ingredient of this system, I have no hesitation in stating that your Lordship is warranted to consider the nourishing and maintaining any French force or French men, within any of their territories, as an insurmountable bar against any close connexion with us.

It still remains for me to state to you my opinion upon one or two separate points on which you desire to be advised.

You desire to know what is meant by a considerable French force, which is the expression generally used in the instructions from home on the subject of Tippoo Sultaun receiving French force into his country. The application of the principle to the particular occasion must be left to the exercise of sound discretion, but as a general principle, I have no hesitation in stating that we are entitled under the circumstances of the present times, to consider the admission of any French force into his army, be it greater or smaller, as direct hostility to us.

I remain, my dear Lord,

your's very faithfully,

HENRY DUNDAS.

96. The Right Hon. Henry Dundas to the Earl of Mornington.

'Interior administration of our different settlements,' Bengal, Oude, the Carnatic, Tanjore, the Northern Circars, The Malabar Coast. Indian Taxation.

Whitehall, 21st March, 1799.

[Received at Fort William, 5th August, 1799.]

My dear Lord,

By this conveyance I have troubled your Lordship with a despatch on the general system of alliance, which we ought to pursue with a view to the security of our Indian possessions, and likewise with a despatch on the subject of our Indian finance and commerce. In the present letter, I wish to bring under your view a few observations on the interior administration of our different settlements.

On the subject of Bengal, I have much satisfaction in feeling that I have occasion to say very little. The wise system adopted during Lord Cornwallis's administration, and to which I make no doubt you will adhere, leaves me no reason to apprehend any real danger to the wealth and resources of the valuable provinces under your immediate administration. I think, for the last two years I have observed, that the arrears of land revenue were somewhat larger than they used to be; I trust this has been owing to some accident, and not to any defect in the system of permanent security given to the landowners of India. Among the many other important benefits expected to arise from that beneficent plan, a prominent one was the regularity in payment of the stipulated jumma, and nothing has ever occurred to me, or been stated to me, which had a tendency to lessen the prospect of that benefit resulting from it. I could not however, refrain from bringing the circumstance to which I have referred, immediately under your view.

As we have limited the extent of land revenue in India, by the measure of a permanent settlement, it has sometimes occurred to me to reflect, that the principles which led to the adoption of that system, naturally opened a prospect of other sources of revenue, in so far as it entitled us to expect an increase of the wealth, industry and population of the country. Every circumstance which has since happened, has led to the conviction that these effects have been produced by it. The encreasing produce of the revenue on salt, opium and spiritous liquors, all tend to corroborate this observation. I wish therefore to direct your attention to consider, and report to me, how far in your opinion, there is, either in the articles I have mentioned, or in any others of a similar nature, any prospect of raising more revenue on articles of general consumption among the natives of India. This can never be attempted but with a perfect consideration to their happiness and content; and I am likewise aware that a people whose wants are very limited and simple, do not present to their Government the same various objects of taxation, which exist in other countries differently circumstanced. It appears however, to be a point worthy your consideration, if possible, at all times to insure a revenue in India, equal to all the exigencies, not only of our expensive establishments, but for the payment of a tribute to this country, through the medium of a beneficial and encreasing commerce.

The circumstance connected with the Government of Bengal, to which one can look with the least confidence is the situation of Oude. I trust the late arrangements made by Lord Teignmouth, may enable your Lordship to give further improvement to this essential part of our system. I have nothing very minute to suggest; all I have to say, is comprehended under two general heads. The first is, a just and pure administration by the Vizier of his own country, in which is comprehended an accurate collection of his real revenues, and an economical expenditure of them. The second is, that he could be induced to keep up an efficient military establishment for the security of his own, and our frontier. This object never can be accomplished, but by dispersing his useless rabble, and forming an army to be kept up and disciplined under our immediate superintendance.

Respecting the affairs of the Coromandel coast, I had so full a communication with you before your departure, it is not necessary to add much more at present. I think for some time past the interior administration of affairs there, has considerably improved. Their revenues are encreasing, their estimates are made with more accuracy, and their accounts are kept much more regularly than they used to be; and I have a perfect reliance on the assiduity, talents and integrity of Lord Clive, that the improvement will be progressive. Our chief difficulties in the administration of the Carnatic, are, first—the anomalous connection in which we stand with the Nabob of Arcot. Secondly, a similar inconvenience attending the Government of Tanjore. Thirdly, the insubordination and distractions so frequently prevalent in the northern Circars.

The double government existing in the Carnatic has long been felt as a serious calamity to that country. It enfeebles the natural resources of the country, and above all, tends to continue that system of intrigue and consequent corruption which has been imputed to the Madras Government so much more than to our other settlements. It is singular to remark, that the country of Oude is the other part of India, where the purity of the Company's servants has been most suspected, and that the same circumstance of a double government has always been assigned as the cause. Consistently with our treaties with the Nabob of

Arcot, we cannot at present materially meliorate his government, but must wait favourable opportunities, and embrace such means of conciliation and attention to him, as are most likely to accomplish this desirable object. We must lay our account with being at all times obstructed in our views, by that corruption and intrigue to which I have referred. Nothing will counteract it but a pure and steady government, acting instantaneously against any of the Company's servants, who may be detected in those practices. Lord Hobart's administration was characterized by a very laudable spirit in this respect, and you cannot doubt, that the same purity and spirit will actuate the conduct of Lord Clive, who will have the additional advantage of the newly-established judicature to aid him in the punishment of those offenders. I have always thought, however much it has been the fashion to clamour against it, that the Supreme Judicature at Calcutta, has had very beneficial effects in preserving the purity of the servants under that presidency.

The affairs of Tanjore are more simple in their nature, and less complicated in their administration. It is exposed in a certain degree, to the same inconveniences which have been injurious to the government of the Carnatic; but from the recent transactions which have taken place there, and from the feelings of gratitude which appear to operate on the mind of the Rajah, I flatter myself he will be inclined more and more, to listen to the admonitions of our government, to whose power and justice he is indebted for his situation. If those sentiments regulate his conduct, our part is simple and easy; we have nothing to ask of him, but a pure and virtuous administration of the affairs of his country, the effects of which will be equally felt by him and us, in the respective interests we have in the prosperity of Tanjore.

The northern Circars have certainly never produced to us those advantages which the extent of the country, and the fertility of the soil in many parts, entitle us to expect. I know not to what cause to attribute it, but the inhabitants of some of its higher parts seem to be in a state of very uncivilized society, and this can only be gradually removed by a steady, just and vigorous government. We must not too rapidly apply to that part of our possessions the same principles of government, which have been wisely applied to the more civilized Provinces of Bengal. I believe the same observations may to a considerable degree be made, with regard to some parts of the Circars, that

I shall immediately bring under your view, with regard to the Malabar Provinces.

From the situation of the countries in our possession, on the Coast of Malabar, they are calculated to be either a great security, or a great annoyance to our power in India; and whether they shall be one or the other, depends much on the manner in which they are managed.

I remain, my dear Lord,
Your's most faithfully,
HENRY DUNDAS.

97. The Earl of Mornington to the Right Honourable Henry Dundas.

Foreign and internal politics. Chiefly in answer to the two last. Civil Service reform. Sudder Courts. Supreme Court. Also on Finances, and Commerce.

Fort William, March 5th, 1800.

My dear Sir,

Although most of the points touched in your several despatches have already been anticipated, either by my letters to you, by the communications which I trust you have received through Mr. Wellesley, or by my despatches to the Secret Committee and the Court of Directors, I propose in this letter to reply regularly to such of your communications as have not already been directly answered by me.

HYDERABAD.—I received with the greatest satisfaction your approbation of the treaty of Hyderabad. Subsequent events have abundantly confirmed the justice of the expectations, which you formed upon the first view of that treaty. It was indeed the source of all our recent successes in India; and even if it has in any degree aggravated the characteristic jealousy of the Mahrattas, it has furnished ample compensation in establishing an impregnable barrier against their power. The system on which the treaty of Hyderabad was founded, would certainly be most effectually completed by the conclusion of a similar engagement at Poonah, and I am resolved never to lose sight of that most desirable object.

The various instances in which the jealousy of the Mahratta State has lately been disclosed, are rather to be attributed to the peculiar character of that nation, and to the singular disposition of the present Peishwa, than to any formed aversion to a nearer connection with the British power.

The influence of Scindia has also contributed to frustrate my proposed measures, because their necessary effect must have been to restore the Peishwa to a certain degree of credit and power; and to reduce Scindia in the same proportion. I have no reason to believe that Scindia would be averse to a separate connection with us, but not perceiving any possible advantage which could arise from such a connection under all the circumstances of the present moment, I have taken no steps to cultivate it, while I have avoided any manifestation of an unfriendly disposition.

The distractions of the Mahratta empire must continue to increase, until they shall be checked by foreign interference. No power in India excepting the British now possesses sufficient strength to interpose with effect in these dissentions; and I shall not be surprised if ultimately the subsidiary force, which I am so anxious to establish at Poonah, should be required with equal anxiety by the Mahratta State, as the only means of restoring order, and of saving the whole of that country from plunder and desolation.

Mr. Colebrooke has now resided several months at Nagpoor, and I have every reason to believe, that the Rajah of Berar will prove well inclined to support whatever plan the British Government may ultimately adopt with regard to the affairs of the Mahratta empire.

With respect to the views of Zemaun Shah, the papers found in the palace at Seringapatam have completely justified your opinion of Tippoo's disposition to obtain the assistance of that Prince; and of Zemaun Shah's inclination to afford it.

For some time to come, I trust that Zemaun Shah will be too much occupied at home, to admit of turning his arms against Hindostan; and I am inclined to think that the encouragement of divisions in his own government, and of hostility between the contiguous State of Persia and his dominions, is the system of defence against Zemaun Shah on which it is most safe to rely under the present circumstances of affairs in India.

The profligacy of Scindia's character, the distracted state of his councils and armies, and the distress or rather ruin of his finances preclude the hope of effecting a secure or useful alliance with him.

The establishment of a subsidiary force at Poonah, would

compel Scindia to return to his own dominions; and in that event, it might not be difficult to convince him that his best security would consist in imitating the example of the Nizam and of the Peishwa; and in placing himself under the immediate protection of the British power.

With respect to the general system of policy to be adopted by us in India in consequence of the conquest of Mysore, I shall review all the important considerations connected with that extensive question in a separate despatch, addressed by some future opportunity, either to you or to the Secret Committee.

I conclude, that the power of the French in Egypt is either already extirpated, or that you will continue the war until that indispensable object shall be completely effected. Notwithstanding the present proud and commanding predominance of the British power in India, we cannot expect an uninterrupted continuance of tranquillity while France shall be permitted to maintain a powerful establishment in Egypt.

Since I wrote the preceding paragraph, I have received despatches from Lord Elgin, dated the 22nd December, 1799, by which it appears that Kleber remains in Egypt with 15,000 men, and that Buonaparte is at the head of a new Government in France. Lord Elgin proposes a powerful diversion from India, through the Red Sea, for the purpose of accelerating the evacuation of Egypt by the French; but after a full discussion of this subject with General Stuart, I am satisfied that it would be an useless waste of treasure and blood to attempt such an expedition on a large scale, unless the whole plan of co-operation from the Mediterranean had been previously concerted. Desultory operations against any places retained by the French on the shores of the Red Sea may be advantageous, they would neither be perilous, nor expensive.

You are already apprized of my entire coincidence in your opinion, respecting the importance of Goa; and I trust that you will be enabled to give full effect to the measures which I have adopted for the purpose of rendering that possession an additional source of strength to the British Empire in India. I also consider the possession of Diu to be a most desirable object, particularly with a view to the coercion of the Piratical States on the north-western coast of the peninsula of India.

FINANCES.—Notwithstanding the large import of bullion during the present season, the expences of the war, and the considerable amount of the 12 per cent. securities, coming in course of payment within the current and succeeding year of account, have compelled me to continue the system of adding to the debt in India, in order to secure a considerable commercial investment for the ensuing season. I have however, the satisfaction to assure you, that every symptom has concurred to confirm my opinion, that the debt in India is likely to become more manageable in every succeeding year. The loans which I have opened at this Presidency during the current year, have been made at a rate of interest much more favourable than any which has been raised since the year 1796, as will appear by the terms of the loans of this year. Although the second loan on the same terms is actually open, the state of the public securities is now—

5th March, 1800.

	Buying.	Selling.	
6 per cent.	13 0 0	14 0 0	Discount.
8 per cent.	5 0 0	6 8 0	Discount.
10 per cent.	10 8 0	9 8 0	Premium.
12 per cent.	1 8 0	2 0 0	Premium.

Having been at the corresponding period in the preceding year—

5th March, 1799.

	Buying.	Selling.	
6 per cent.	24 8 0	25 8 0	Discount.
8 per cent.	14 8 0	15 8 0	Discount.
10 per cent.	—	—	Discount.
12 per cent.	0 2 0	0 6 0	Discount.

The distress for specie has gradually vanished, and private credit has proportionably been improved; and I have been enabled to send home with valuable cargoes every regular ship belonging to the Company in India, while on the other hand, I have employed the whole tonnage which the Port of Calcutta could furnish since the month of December, to carry to the Port of London, nearly the whole of the goods of individuals, which had been tendered for exportation previous to that month, over and above the 3,000 tons which the Company is bound by law to furnish.

The finances of the Government of Madras have improved in a still greater proportion than those of Bengal. At that Presidency they have opened a loan, under which they have been enabled to raise a large supply. The great augmentation of the resources of Fort St. George, under the subsidiary treaties of Hyderabad and Seringapatam, and the partition treaty of

Mysore, together with the improvements in the revenues of Tanjore and of the country of the Polygars will render the finances of that Presidency an object of the highest consideration. It may also be expected that industry, population and manufacture, and all the sources of public and private credit will take a new spring in our possessions on the Peninsula of India, in consequence of our increased security in that quarter.

To these causes of progressive prosperity, it is reasonable to add the benefits which cannot fail to accrue from the extension, to that part of our empire, of the system of judicature and revenue, under which these provinces have attained so eminent a degree of opulence and internal tranquillity.

I trust that the 8 per cent. loan now opened in Bengal, will be rapidly filled, and will enable me to provide for all the services stated in my several estimates; I expect hereafter to be able to borrow money at 8 per cent. under the former system of repayment of the public securities according to priority of date.

Notwithstanding these favourable expectations, I am of opinion, that the surplus revenue of India is not likely to afford any considerable or certain resource. The increasing magnitude of our empire in India, and the continual expansion of every branch of our numerous and complicated interests, must preclude any considerable reduction of our permanent charges civil, military, or commercial. More cannot be hoped from the utmost exertion of vigilance, integrity and ability in any persons to whom the government of this empire may hereafter be entrusted than to check, by a seasonable and diligent system of revision, that tendency to excess and abuse which is the inherent vice of all great establishments. On the other hand, it is my decided opinion, that the growing resources of India will keep pace with the demands upon them.

With respect to the resource which you expect to derive in India from bills upon the East India Company under the plan of remittance, the prosperous state of public credit in England and in India will co-operate to render that resource of little avail. The state of the public funds in England will diminish the desire of remitting private fortunes to England from India in proportion to the increase of the public prosperity at home, and the high degree of security which our Indian empire has acquired by the success of the late war against Tippoo Sultaun, has inspired so general a confidence in the stability of the British power in India, that individuals will think their capital equally safe in India, where it will certainly be more productive than in England.

These circumstances, added to the vast increase of the export of goods from India to England will probably detain much capital in this country, and retard the operation of any plan of remittance which could be devised.

Private merchants, for commercial purposes, will always offer more advantageous terms than the Company; and in time of public prosperity the bills of individuals of undoubted capital will be received by many in preference to bills drawn on the Company on terms less favourable.

The same causes will naturally tend to maintain, if not to increase the present high rate of exchange upon bills on England; and while the natural and current rate of exchange shall be so much higher (as it is at present) than that allowed by the plan of remittance through the Company, it is not to be expected, that individuals will resort to that plan to such an extent as shall furnish any important financial resource.

COMMERCE.—That the export of British manufactures to India, under proper regulations, might be extended to the amount of a considerable resource, I entertain no doubt; but I must observe, that before such an effect can be expected an entire reform must take place in the conduct of the East India Company's exports to India.

The leading points which require minute and diligent care in the management of this branch of the Company's affairs appear to me to be, first, that the goods should be of the first quality; secondly, that they should be invoiced at a reasonable and just price; and thirdly, that they should be assorted in a manner suitable to this market, and conformably to the indents sent from hence.

Under the present system the quality of the goods is frequently defective; for the two last years the invoice price has been considerably increased without any correspondent improvement in the quality of the goods, and the assortments have been injudicious and contrary to the indents sent from hence by those officers who are best acquainted with the nature of the market.

As connected with this subject, in one point of view, I desire to call your particular attention to the defective and unserviceable state of the arms annually exported to India for the use of our troops. This is a disgraceful evil, and of a most pernicious tendency. I am apprehensive that the whole system of the Company's exports to India is rendered subservient to private interests at the expense of the public.

Mr. Pitt's Bill for the reduction of the duties upon imports from India has grievously disappointed the expectation of the commercial part of the community. The duty imposed by that bill upon the *Sugars, particularly on the coarser sort, is* much TOO HIGH; and the object of inviting the trade of India to the Port of London, will not, I fear, be effected by the general scale of duties adopted in that bill.

INTERNAL ADMINISTRATION OF BENGAL.—The increasing arrears of the land revenue of Bengal occupied my attention immediately after my arrival in India.

After full consideration I passed a law for the purpose of remedying the increasing evil[1] of accumulating balances. The beneficial effects of it have already been felt to so great an extent as to warrant a confident expectation that the stipulated income will hereafter be paid with great regularity.

My judgment and experience coincide entirely with your opinion, that the system adopted by Lord Cornwallis has proved and must continue to prove a fruitful source of happiness, wealth, industry, and population to this flourishing country. That system, however, has still to encounter some avowed and many secret enemies; nor have its benefits been yet fully realized, it has not been carried into execution with cordiality, zeal, and energy proportioned to its merits; it has received no aid of collateral institutions calculated to furnish a supply of men properly qualified to fill the several stations of judicature and revenue; nor has a due and impartial selection been uniformly made of the persons best qualified in the actual state of the service to fill such stations as have progressively become vacant; nor has the administration of justice throughout the provinces been superintended with a sufficient degree of vigilance and care.

I have nearly matured a plan with a view to these salutary objects. The principal measures on which it will be founded will be, first, the institution of a Court of Sudder Dewannee and Nizamut Adawlut distinct from the Council; but of which the Chief Justice shall be capable of sitting in Council, if appointed from home to a seat in Council. The province of this new Court

---

[1] Regulation No. VII, 1799.

shall be, not only to receive and judge appeals, but also to superintend the administration of justice and the general state of police in all the inferior courts, branches and departments of the judicial institutions.

It is my intention to constitute this court of those persons who bore a principal share in framing the system so happily adopted by Lord Cornwallis. Their talents, integrity, and experience, as well as the peculiar propriety and dignity of their manners render them the fittest to hold this distinguished station, to which it is my intention to annex the highest rank which the law enables me to grant.

The Chief Justice of this new court may hereafter become a member of the Council, in which event he will still continue to preside in the court. In the meanwhile I wish to be empowered by law to give a rank to the Chief Justice of the Sudder Dewannee and Nizamut Adawlut, which shall place him as nearly as possible on a level with the Chief Justice of the Supreme Court of Judicature.

2nd. The institution of a College or University at Calcutta in which the Writers shall be subject to the rules of collegiate discipline for the first two or three years subsequent to their arrival; and shall study the languages, history, laws, manners, and customs of India, the laws enacted by the Governor-General in Council, and such rudiments of the laws of England as are necessary to enable the judges throughout these possessions to administer the laws of India in the spirit of the British constitution.

3rd. I propose to pass regulations subjecting all persons appointed to offices of the judicature or revenue to public examination in the several branches of knowledge requisite in their respective stations, before they shall be entitled to receive the emoluments of the office to which they may have been appointed.

4th. In the several stations of revenue and judicature throughout the provinces many public officers are to be found avowedly incompetent to the due discharge of their duties. Some from ignorance, natural incapacity or fixed habits of indolence and dissipation, others from age and infirmity. Such persons have been suffered to retain their stations under the orders of the Court of Directors, prohibiting the grant of pensions of retreat to the civil service. This prohibition is contrary to true principles of economy. The inevitable operation of it has been to fix incapable persons in stations requiring efficiency; and the loss sustained by their negligencies or errors infinitely overbalances the expense of providing for them at the public charge. The application of this prohibition to persons who have grown old or infirm in the public service is illiberal and cruel, as well as impolitic. On the other hand it may, perhaps, be questioned whether those whose ignorance, natural inability, or other defects disqualify them for the public service, can be entitled to any compensation from the state which has already supported them at a considerable expense, under the presumption of their sufficiency to discharge the duties for which they receive emolument.

But viewing the actual state of the civil service at this Presidency, I know that many persons do not, and never will, render justice to the public in the stations which they now hold, although it would appear an act of great harshness and rigour to remove these persons, without making some provision for them. Their number is not very considerable, it bears no proportion to the mischief occasioned by their evil administration, and by the dangerous example which their conduct affords to the younger branches of the service. My intention, therefore, is (without waiting for orders from home) to remove all persons of any of the descriptions to which I have adverted *from efficient office;* and to provide for them by adequate pensions for life, payable to their agents in India on the condition of their returning to England. The present allowance to the Company's servants out of employment being payable only to such as reside in India would not answer the purpose proposed. Among the servants now out of employment, but residing in Bengal, few, if any, are qualified for efficient office ; the amount of the pensions to be paid under the new plan must bear a just proportion to the period of service as well as to the offices actually enjoyed at the period of removal : it will be for the Government at home to consider whether any permanent plan of pension for civil servants retiring from the service in India shall hereafter be adopted. The measure which I propose to carry into effect, is more immediately applicable to the actual state of the civil service in India ; but the principles on which it is grounded may furnish the foundation of a permanent system, which shall for ever secure this Government against the evils of inefficiency, ignorance, and negligence in the subordinate branches of the executive administration.

TAXATION.—The accounts which you will have received this year of the revenue on salt will be highly satisfactory to you, and you will have observed with peculiar pleasure that the revenue arising from the sale of opium has been completely restored by the improved system of agency, by the extreme care applied to the manufacture of the drug, by the due proportion now preserved between the quantity manufactured and the current demand, and by the measure which I have uniformly carried into effect of publicly destroying all such opium as had been declared to be adulterated. The produce of the two last sales of opium (which included the whole annual quantity for the last season) has exceeded that of the most favourable sales of that drug ever experienced in Bengal, the nett profit to the Company on the two sales in December, 1799, and February, 1800, having amounted to more than 23 lacs of rupees (£287,500 sterling). I have little doubt that this branch of revenue will continue to flourish under the same judicious system, vigilantly administered. The public service is greatly indebted to Mr. Fleming, second Member of the Medical Board, for his careful inspection of the opium, as well as for his various suggestions by which the manufacture has been placed under improved regulations.

You will observe with great satisfaction the considerable increase which has taken place in the Government customs at Calcutta since my arrival in India. This is to be attributed entirely to increased care and vigilance in the business of the custom house. The customs were placed for some time under the management of Mr. Haldane, a Member of the Board of Trade, who was principally aided by a young gentleman of the name of Twining, in restoring order to the business of the custom-house. Mr. Twining has distinguished himself very much in this transaction; he is at present too young in the service to be placed in the enjoyment of a salary adequate to his merits, but I shall take the first practicable opportunity of promoting him; in the meanwhile I have appointed Mr. Dashwood to the collection of the customs. I can rely on his diligence and integrity, and Mr. Twining will act under him.

It is necessary to observe that the right of the Governor-General in Council to raise the duties on goods in the Port of Calcutta is questioned by the lawyers here, in the present indefinite state of our powers of legislation.

An improvement of the tax upon spirituous liquors and intoxicating drugs is now under my consideration, and I have little doubt that this branch of the revenue may be much increased. But here again I feel myself embarrassed by the anomalous constitution of this government. Under the construction given to the laws for the government of the British possessions, it is a received doctrine, that the Governor-General in Council cannot legislate for the town of Calcutta. Therefore the capital City of this empire must be exempt from the operation of any law imposing additional duties on the articles above mentioned, unless I can contrive to pass such a law under the pretext of an improvement of the duties appropriated to the support of the police. I am disposed to hope that sources of just and moderate taxation may be discovered on other articles of general consumption; but this measure must be adopted gradually and with great caution. I must here also observe, that although Calcutta must necessarily be the place of the greatest consumption, as well as that where any new tax would be less sensibly felt than in the country, the supposed restrictions of the law, and the strange conflict of authorities between the Supreme Court of Judicature and the Government, preclude the possibility of my applying any system of taxation on articles of general consumption to the town of Calcutta. I trust you will, without delay, relieve this Government from a predicament so embarrassing.

POLICE.—The Police of Calcutta is now in a deplorable condition, and if speedy measures be not adopted the town will soon relapse into its ancient state of filth and unhealthiness, and will again become fatal to European constitutions. It is my intention immediately to proceed to improve the drains and roads, to widen the streets and avenues, and clear away the jungles, and remove the tanks and other nuisances situated in the neighbourhood of the town. These improvements will necessarily occasion expense; but it is an expense which the Company must incur, or forfeit every title to the character of a wise and munificent sovereign. In aid of this expense it would be just to levy an assessment on the inhabitants of Calcutta; but I have already stated that measure to be impracticable in the limited state of my powers. Various other regulations of police are requisite for the preservation of the peace and order of the town; even these I shall find it difficult to enforce until my right to legislate for Calcutta shall be rendered indisputable by act of parliament.

OUDE.—Of the two general heads, under which you have stated the objects of your anxiety, with regard to the situation of Oude, I trust that the second is now nearly accomplished;

namely, the substitution of an efficient military force under the Company's authority, in place of the Nabob Vizier's dangerous and undisciplined army. This reform has not been effected without great reluctance on the part of the Vizier, whose character has been displayed on this occasion in the genuine colours of Asiatic treachery and falsehood. I have nothing to hope from any other quality in his Excellency's mind, excepting his acknowledged pusillanimity, which I flatter myself will induce him to submit to the introduction of such a portion of the British authority into the management of his country, as is indispensably necessary to the just and pure administration of the Government; to the accurate collection and economical expenditure of his revenues; and to the relief of his people from the extortion, cruelty and oppression, under which they now suffer. I shall hereafter submit to you a detailed view of my proceedings in Oude; at present it may be sufficient to say, that I consider the reform of the Vizier's military establishment to be far advanced, and that in consequence of the success of that preliminary step, I entertain a sanguine hope of being able to carry the same spirit of reform with vigour and effect into every other branch of his affairs.

GOVERNMENT OF FORT ST. GEORGE.—I am happy to be able to express my entire concurrence in your opinion, with regard to the progressive improvement of the administration of affairs at Fort St. George; and I have no doubt that the same system will continue to be pursued by Lord Clive and by the persons who now constitute his advisers at that Presidency. My long residence at Fort St. George, and the cordiality, temper, and honour of Lord Clive have completely identified the two Governments, and I find no more difficulty in governing our extensive possessions on the coast, with all our recent acquisitions of territory and influence, than in regulating any of the collectorships in Bengal. You will observe, by the public proceedings, that I have lately transmitted to Fort St. George detailed orders for introducing into the possessions under the immediate Government of that Presidency, the same system of internal administration, under which these provinces have so happily flourished. I entertain no doubt, that, under the present Government at Fort St. George, my orders will be carried into effect with the utmost degree of honesty, alacrity, and zeal. The execution, however, of those orders must necessarily be imperfect unless accompanied by the application to the civil service at Fort St. George, not only of all those subsidiary improvements still requisite in Bengal, but of other remedies more peculiarly demanded by the state of the service at Fort St. George. My present inclination is to render the Court of Sudder Dewannee and Nizamut Adawlut in Bengal the Supreme Court of Appeal from all the Company's possessions, and to vest in it the general superintendence of the administration of justice and the regulation of police throughout the British empire in India. This arrangement appears to be well calculated to secure uniformity, consistency, and purity in the conduct of all the subordinate courts of justice, and in every institution of police. I do not apprehend that it will be necessary or expedient to establish any intermediate Court of Appeal at Fort St. George between the Sudder Dewannee Adawlut in Bengal, and the ordinary Courts of Circuit and Appeal, to be instituted on the coast of Coromandel. I am also inclined to think that the writers destined for Fort St. George may advantageously pass the two first years of their residence in India at the University of Calcutta; where proper professors may be established for their instruction in the languages peculiar to the territories subject to the immediate Government of Fort St. George.

The adoption of a plan for pensioning public officers incapable of service is required at least as much at Fort St. George as in Bengal. But the peculiar evil now inherent in the constitution of the service at Fort St. George is not only unknown in Bengal, but directly contrary to the fundamental principle on which Lord Cornwallis rested all his plans for amending and purifying the administration of affairs in these provinces. He prohibited all indirect and secret emoluments, and all mixture in pursuits of commerce, or of other affairs incompatible with a due attention to the public service; and he established the allowances of the public officers on so liberal a scale as might enable them not merely to subsist during the period of their public labours, but to realize, with due economy, a competent provision after a moderate period of service.

This system is not founded on any principle exclusively applicable to the characters, habits, or interests of the public servants in Bengal. It is founded in a just and correct knowledge of mankind, for no proposition can be more self-evident, or of more universal application, than that the best security against the temptation of illicit profit, is to annex liberal emolument to honest labour. It is, therefore, difficult to conceive on what ground an expectation can be formed, that the public service at Fort St. George should be as pure and correct as that in Bengal; while the civil servants of Fort St. George shall be permitted to mix in pursuits foreign to their public duties; and while the general scale of the allowances at Fort St. George shall remain so low as to preclude those prospects of honest profit deemed necessary in Bengal for securing the integrity of the public servants. I am aware that this remark does not apply with so much force to the commercial as to other branches of the Company's service at Fort St. George. Some of the commercial allowances have been increased at that Presidency, on the very principle of rendering them so ample as to preclude the temptation of irregular profit; and yet the irresistible application of the same principle to other branches of the service at the same Presidency has never been admitted in practice, however it may have been acknowledged in argument. For it can never be supposed that the Company can deliberately deem it to be a more incumbent duty of Government to secure the honest discharge of its commercial concerns, than to preserve its revenues from peculation, and the administration of its laws from corruption and oppression. It is possible that the limited and precarious condition of the revenues of the Presidency of Fort St. George, and its state of insecurity during the existence of the contiguous hostile power in Mysore, may have retarded the due consideration of this subject. But in the present increased, and, I trust, progressive state of the prosperity and security of that valuable possession, no such obstacle exists to a reform urgently demanded by every principle of humanity, policy, and justice.

I am convinced that the continuance of the present inadequate allowances of the public servants at Fort St. George would prove an insuperable bar to the improvement of the revenues, and to the due administration of justice in that part of our Empire. At present the public servants at Fort St. George, in most of the offices, can find no alternative but poverty or corruption. Is it the part of wisdom or honour in any Government to reduce its servants to such an alternative? During my residence at Fort St. George a most respectable member of the Board of Revenue, Mr. Harrington, resigned his seat at the Board because his salary did not afford him the hope of providing a competent maintenance for his family at the expiration of his service; and he entered into a Commercial House of Agency, withdrawing from the Company's service talents, integrity, and zeal, which had proved highly useful, and might have been exerted with increased benefit to their affairs. I know that Mr. Cockburne, (whose abilities, knowledge, and integrity, are not surpassed by any person in India,) entertains similar intentions of retiring from the Company's service. And it must be evident to your comprehensive view and long experience of public affairs that this evil will be aggravated in proportion to the increased magnitude and importance of the interests entrusted to the management of the public servants at Fort St. George; and that ultimately a service so defective must be deserted by all who are not disposed to take advantage of its abuses.

The consideration of all these circumstances has induced me to call Lord Clive's particular attention to the scale of allowances at Fort St. George; and it is my intention to accompany the institution of the new Courts of Judicature at that Presidency by a general revision of the salaries of their civil service; the result of which will, I trust, enable me to place all the allowances on a proper level.

The delay attendant upon the expectation of orders from home and the urgent pressure of the evil will, I trust, sufficiently justify my determination to apply, with all practicable despatch, such a remedy as shall appear to my judgment to promise the most speedy, beneficial, and permanent effect.

I entertain little doubt that the revenues, under the management of the Government of Fort St. George, will be considerably improved in all their branches; and that the additional expense of providing for the important objects stated in the preceding paragraphs will be far overbalanced by the consequent amelioration of all our resources in that quarter.

CARNATIC.—The double Government of the Carnatic is a difficulty which continues to present the most serious and alarming obstacles to every attempt at reform. The expectation of favourable opportunities of negociation with the Nabob of Arcot, and of the effects of conciliation and attention towards him will, I am convinced, be ever disappointed by the event. You recollect with what sanguine hopes I looked forward to the result of measures adopted in a spirit of mildness and persuasion, but I have found them entirely vain and fruitless; nor can I cherish the slightest ray of hope that such a course can ever prove successful, during the life of the present Nabob. His Highness is surrounded by European advisers of the most dangerous and profligate character, whose interests are deeply involved in the perpetuation of the abuses of his Government, and who (amongst other means of perverting his councils) labour to inspire him with the notion of a distinction of interests and powers between the Royal Government and that constituted by Act of Parliament for the administration of the British Empire in India. In all his conversations and correspondence, he studiously distinguishes his Majesty's Government from that of the Court of Directors; uniformly treating the latter with disrespect, and even with ridicule and contempt. In my last conversation with his Highness he plainly declared to me that he considered his Majesty to be his father, friend, ally, and protector, but that the Court of Directors desired to 'obtain his country any how.'

The principles of this distinction are encouraged in his Highness's mind by the letters and embassies which have occasionally reached him from his Majesty through channels not only unconnected but avowedly at variance with the British Government in India. All such letters and embassies have the most pernicious tendency to withdraw the confidence and respect of the natives from the governments in India, and to fix their attention on his Majesty's naval or military officers, or such persons (of whatever character) as may accidentally be the bearers of his letters. The frequent letters which his Highness the Nabob receives from his Royal Highness the Prince of Wales greatly aggravate the same evil; and it is with the utmost concern that I feel myself bound by my public duty to request that you will take an opportunity of representing to his Royal Highness that his correspondence with the Nabob of the Carnatic has produced an effect entirely contrary to his Royal Highness's wishes, and has been highly injurious to the public service in India.

Few, if any, of the Company's servants at Madras are now directly engaged in the intrigues of his Highness's Durbar. The principal and most mischievous agents and counsellors of his Highness are to be found among persons who have been the bearers of letters to his Highness from England, and among the attorneys and low practitioners of the law, who notoriously conduct his Highness's correspondence with the Government. Nor can I entertain any expectation that the newly established

Judicature at Madras, under its present constitution, will in any degree assist the Government in repressing the intrigues and corruption of the Durbar. My experience during my residence at Fort St. George leads me to believe that the powers of the Court of the Recorder will prove entirely inadequate to the detection and punishment of the usurious and corrupt practices which that Court was intended to repress, while the establishment of such a Court will tend to confirm the audacity of the tribe of pettyfoggers which now infests the Carnatic, and governs the Nabob's Durbar. I confess that I cannot concur with you in ascribing the purity of the service in Bengal to the influence of the Supreme Court of Judicature at Calcutta. The most corrupt period in the history of Bengal, or perhaps in that of any of our foreign establishments, is to be dated from the institution of the Supreme Court to the arrival of Lord Cornwallis, a period of time, during a considerable portion of which that Court exercised its powers to their utmost possible extent. The purity of Lord Cornwallis's personal example, and the integrity and wisdom of his institutions, the increase of the regular and avowed public allowances, the separation of the legislative, judicial, and executive powers of the Government, and the consequent subjection of the Government itself to the controul of its own laws, were the real foundations of the reform at this Presidency. This constitution was the source, and its operation has been the security, of that reform; neither the design nor the execution of the amended system of administration in Bengal was in any degree aided by the co-operation, influence, or example of the Supreme Court. During the administrations of Lord Cornwallis, and of Lord Teignmouth, the Supreme Court teemed with abuses of every description, and would have afforded a much fitter subject than an instrument of reform. Respectable and honourable as the person is who now presides in that Court, and eminent as his public services have been in the detection and remedy of the abuses abetted by his predecessors, I cannot discover in what manner the influence or authority of the Supreme Court now operate to preserve the purity of the service of Government.

The public servants look exclusively to the person in whose hands the Government resides, and to the practical result of that constitution which he is bound to administer. Under that constitution he possesses ample powers of reward and punishment; and the due exercise of those powers constitutes the vital principle of the public service, and the sole spring from which the purity or corruption of the subordinate officers must ever flow. The responsibility of the Governor-General in Council to the Government at home, and the conspicuous station in which he is placed, sufficiently secure the due exercise of his arduous functions.

The Supreme Court possesses no power of rewarding the public servants, and with respect to their punishment, it can never proceed vigorously or efficaciously without the co-operation of Government; even with that co-operation, the powers of the Supreme Court must be limited by the difficulties of obtaining legal proof of malversation; and even where such proofs can be obtained, the species of punishment which the Supreme Court can inflict can neither be so speedy nor so formidable to the public servants as the powers of suspension and subsequent prosecution at home vested in the Government. Whenever punishment in the form of public prosecution may become requisite, I am convinced that it would be much more effectually inflicted, if the prosecution were always to be instituted in England. With regard to petty cases of abuse every useful purpose would be answered by a tribunal, independent of the Government, but placed towards it in the relation of a mere interpreter of the laws of England, modified by such as may be enacted by the Governor-General in Council.

The supposed controul of the Supreme Court over the person of the Governor-General never can be exercised without occasioning a convulsion in the Government; it is, therefore, either useless, or dangerous, and every trace of it ought to be abolished. The extreme cases in which the crimes of the Governor-General may require the controul of a superior authority, cannot be provided against in India without the application of a remedy infinitely more perilous than the supposed evil; the existence of which is scarcely within the verge of possibility. The remedy of such cases should be left on the same ground as it stands on in Ireland with relation to the possible personal crimes of the chief Governor exercising the sovereign executive power. No power in India should appear to be co-ordinate with the Government, and still less to rival or to control it.

I shall hereafter address you more in detail on the present constitution of the Supreme Court of Judicature, (particularly on such parts of it as have proved practical impediments to the exercise of the control of this government over its own native officers, civil and military and native subjects); but it would have been uncandid in me to pass without notice a passage in your correspondence, relating to so important a subject, in which I have the misfortune not to concur in your opinion.

I cannot conclude this subject without adding my cordial testimony in favour of the moderation, discretion and propriety with which the present Court (under the direction of Sir John Anstruther) has uniformly exercised its powers, not only without a symptom of jealousy, but with every possible attention to the dignity, vigour and efficacy of the government; but a power radically dangerous ought not to find protection in the temporary forbearance of those hands in which it is vested.

The duty of communicating to you without reserve, my sentiments on this subject of the utility of the Supreme Court of Judicature, has led me to digress from the actual state of the Carnatic.

I am thoroughly convinced, that no effectual remedy can ever be applied to the evils which afflict that country, without obtaining from the Nabob powers at least as extensive as those vested in the Company by the late treaty of Tanjore. At the death of the present Nabob, such a treaty might easily be obtained from his successor, (if after that event it should be thought advisable to admit any nominal sovereign of the Carnatic, excepting the Company.) A young man resides at Chepauk, who is treated by the Nabob as his Highness's son. This young man is certainly the son of a dancing woman, who was received for some time in his Highness's house; and the Nabob declares himself to be the father. Numerous legitimate descendants of Wallajah are in existence. The whole question of the succession will therefore be completely open to the decision of the Company, upon the decease of the present Nabob. The inclination of my opinion is, that the most advisable settlement would be, to place Omdut ul Omra's supposed son on the Musnud, under a treaty similar to that which was lately concluded with the Rajah of Tanjore: it will however, be expedient that you should immediately consider whether it might not be a more effectual arrangement to provide liberally for every branch of the descendants of Wallajah and Omdut ul Omra, and to vest even the nominal sovereignty of the Carnatic in the Company.

On this subject I request your immediate instructions; which you will frame with reference to the following most important and interesting considerations.

During the whole course of the late war with Tippoo Sultaun, the conduct of all the Nabob's officers without exception, amounted nearly to positive hostility in every part of his territories through which the British army, or that of the Nizam marched, or even in which supplies were ordered to be procured or collected for their use. When complaints were stated to his Highness he promised redress, but never afforded it in any instance.

I was compelled to seize the persons of some of his principal officers, and to bring them down to Fort St. George, from districts in which our force was not sufficiently considerable to furnish an effectual check to their treasonable practices. In all districts so circumstanced his Highness's officers did not scruple to proceed to open violence for the purpose of obstructing our supplies.

During this arduous crisis, his Highness frequently endeavoured to anticipate my complaints by alleging pretended grievances to justify the conduct of his officers, but upon examination his Highness's complaints uniformly appeared to be utterly devoid of foundation.

At the most critical period of our military preparations, when every European and native at Madras, emulated each other in aiding the public service by loan and contribution, his Highness could not be induced to advance, even on account of his acknowledged debts, any assistance to the public treasury. He indeed, with much reluctance, under the apprehension of a cessation of all friendly intercourse between him and me, engaged to advance a sum on account of his new cavalry debt; but after the most solemn protestations of punctuality, he broke his faith with every circumstance of infamy and dishonour, at a moment when this violation of his engagements might have proved fatal to the progress of the army; if I had suffered myself to be so far the dupe of his repeated assurances, as to have relied in any degree on their performance for any pecuniary supply of the troops in the field.

During the whole of this period, I have every reason to be confident that his Highness possessed the ready means of satisfying a much more considerable demand, than I had deemed it expedient to make upon him.

It was perfectly evident during the progress of our success, that his Highness derived no satisfaction from the triumph of our arms; and it is remarkable that he never appeared in public at the celebration of any of the rejoicings occasioned by the glorious termination of the war.

Whatever suspicions of his Highness's personal disaffection to the British Government might have been warranted by all these combined circumstances, I was rather disposed to attribute them to the weakness of his government, or to the corruption and intrigues of his advisers than to any spirit of positive treachery in his own disposition; but the records of the late Tippoo Sultaun, which fell into our hands after the capture of Seringapatam, have furnished me with the most authentic and indisputable evidence that a secret correspondence of a nature the most hostile to the British power, was opened with Tippoo Sultaun by the late Nabob Wallajah towards the close of his life, through the agency of Omdut ul Omra the present Nabob.

Omdut ul Omra appears to have been extremely zealous and forward in the conduct of this secret intercourse during the life of his father, and no question can be entertained that the late Nabob, as a principal, and Omdut ul Omra as an agent, were guilty of a flagrant violation of the treaty of 1792; as well as of the fundamental principle of their connection with the Company. Omdut ul Omra was a party to the treaty of 1792, and on that circumstance founds all his present rights. Sufficient proof appears that Omdut ul Omra, after his accession, manifested a disposition to maintain the correspondence commenced by his father through him; and I entertain no doubt that his objects in that correspondence were of the same hostile and treacherous character, as they had been previous to the death of his father. The proof arising from written documents of his overt acts of hostility since his accession, is not so full and distinct as that which relates to his former agency. But this defect may be supplied by oral testimony, as all the necessary witnesses are alive and in our hands.

No doubt exists in my mind, that the British Government would now be completely justified, in depriving the Nabob of all power over his country, and reducing him to the state of a mere pensioner.

The only questions which remain for decision are the time of carrying this measure into execution, and the amount of the provision to be made for the Nabob, for his descendants, and for those of Wallajah. As soon as you shall have received this letter, I request you to despatch an express to me with your opinion, although mine is so decided, that I shall not wait for the communication of yours, if the season should appear to me to be favourable for the great measure which is now become indispensable on every principle of justice and policy.

TANJORE.—With respect to Tanjore, the treaty which I framed previous to my departure from Fort St. George, and which has since been carried into effect by Lord Clive, will, I trust, place the administration of the affairs of that country on an improved foundation. The difficulties which I encountered in obtaining a correct and consistent account of Tanjore, are scarcely to be described or imagined.

After a most tedious enquiry, I brought the several contending parties to a fair discussion (or rather to a bitter contest) in my presence; and after an argument which lasted three or four days, I proceeded to review the whole case in a regular manner, adverting to every fact and argument on both sides of the question. At length the contending parties unanimously concurred in the expediency and justice of the treaty, in the form in which it has been concluded.

A question will arise with respect to the unregistered debt of the late Rajah of Tanjore. I am inclined to believe that some branches of that debt, as well as that of the unconsolidated debt of the Nabob of the Carnatic, are at least as well entitled to consideration as any part of the debt sanctioned by parliament. The subject merits your attention. I shall not feel myself at liberty to act upon it without orders from home; but I am satisfied that you will find some cases of great hardship among many rather deserving prosecution than payment.

CIRCARS.—The Northern Circars, according to the report of the Board of Revenue at Fort St. George, are now in a state to receive the same principles of government, with some local modifications, which have been applied to Bengal. The new settlement now about to be introduced upon the coast, will therefore include that vast tract of country. It may be convenient to observe to you in this place that my determination to render the new settlement of the land revenue on the coast perpetual, without previous reference to the Court of Directors was founded on intelligence from Mr. Cockburne that the terror of such a reference would render all settlement impracticable, and above all would entirely frustrate the sale of the Havelly Lands.

MALABAR.—The condition of the coast of Malabar has been so entirely changed by the conquest of Mysore, that the principles stated in your despatches to the Government of Bombay, and in General Stuart's letters to you, are no longer applicable to the actual circumstances of that district. The conquest of Mysore will, I trust, enable us to settle Malabar and Canara on a systematic and durable plan of government. The subject is now under my consideration. One principle however, I am persuaded will appear as evident and incontrovertible to your mind as it does to mine ; that whatever may be our ultimate determination with respect to the power of the several Rajahs, it must appear to flow from the generosity, justice and power of the British Government ; and not to be derived from a timid submission to the refractory spirit of any rebellious tributary.

COMMUNICATION WITH ENGLAND.—If the war with France should be protracted, and Buonaparte continue at the head of affairs, I am persuaded that some attempt will be made by France against our Indian empire. A regular monthly despatch overland from London to India will, in that event, be of the utmost importance. Indeed, under any circumstances, a speedy and certain communication between England and India, appears to me to be an object in which the interests of both countries are deeply involved. My opinion is, that, in addition to the despatch overland, monthly packets should be established to sail regularly both from Europe and India. They might carry small cargoes and passengers, which, with the profits of postage on letters, would more than defray their expence.

In reviewing your correspondence, I have not thought it necessary to return any particular replies to your several letters of recommendation. The receipt of them is noted in the annexed memorandum. Being in possession of your principles with respect to recommendations, I do not think any further explanation necessary.

I remain, my dear Sir, &c.

MORNINGTON.

98. The Marquess Wellesley to Lord Castlereagh.

General vindication of territorial acquisitions during Lord Wellesley's administration.

Fort William, Dec. 15th, 1803.

My dear Lord,

Your Lordship has been already apprized of the motives which had induced me to continue in this government beyond the period of the month of January 1803, with a view to the important crisis of affairs which had occurred in the Mahratta empire. Subsequent events have proved that I was not mistaken with regard to the importance of that crisis, and to the nature of my public duties as connected with it.

I received with great satisfaction the determination of his Majesty's ministers, and the Court of Directors upon the late settlement of the Carnatic.

Your Lordship and the public being in full possession of the information upon which my decision respecting the affairs of the Carnatic was formed, I entertain no doubt that a correct judgment will be delivered upon the issue of any public discussion relative to that settlement. Having exercised my judgment upon the question to the best of my ability, my duty appears to me to be completely discharged, and I retain no further solicitude upon the subject than that such an arrangement of the affairs of the Carnatic as may appear to Parliament to be just, wise, and honourable, may be secured upon permanent foundations.

Your Lordship's superior understanding, and your high sense of the public interests and honour, have already led you to draw a just conclusion from the transactions in the Carnatic; and I am satisfied that your sentiments on that subject will be confirmed by further deliberation, and will be maintained with the ability and energy, which have always distinguished your public opinions.

The act of 1793 declares, that the 'pursuit of schemes of conquest and extension of dominion in India, is repugnant to the wish, the honour, and policy of the nation.' This declaratory preamble introduces the regulation of preventing the commencement of hostilities in India, in the conclusion of treaties of guarantee involving the contingency of war, without the express command and authority of the Court of Directors, or of the Secret Committee.

No inference can be drawn from the letter or spirit of the act of 1793, to preclude the extension of the British territories in India, by just and legitimate means, unconnected with schemes of conquest and irregular ambition.

The extension of territory which followed the conquest of Mysore in 1799, might otherwise have been condemned on similar grounds. That conquest as the result of a just and necessary war, and the transfer of the enemy's dominions to our authority, although involving considerable extension of territory, was never deemed for that reason to be inconsistent with the policy of the act of 1793, but was declared to be justified by the same principles which had justified the commencement of the war.

With the Nabob of the Carnatic, and with the Rajah of Tanjore subsidiary engagements were concluded by Lord Cornwallis in 1792, which eventually stipulated for a considerable extension of the territory of the Company, in the contingency of ultimate failure on the part of those princes in the regular payment of the subsidy; but it never yet has been contended that in the event of such failure, it would have been inconsistent with the policy of the act of 1793, to have insisted upon the right of the Company to demand the execution of those articles of the respective subsidiary treaties, which either in direct terms or by manifest implication entitled the Company to an extension of territory in commutation of the subsidiary payments.

The Company on various occasions, with the authority of his Majesty, has expressed great anxiety to commute the subsidies of the Carnatic, and Tanjore, for adequate territorial security. It never has occurred until the present moment, to represent such a commutation as in any degree repugnant to the wish, the honour, or policy of the nation, or to the letter or spirit of the acts of regulation.

On my arrival in India in April 1798, I endeavoured in conformity to my original instructions from the Court of Directors, to obtain a commutation of this nature in the Carnatic. Your Lordship is apprized of my repeated and anxious efforts to effect this object, and you are also informed that in pursuing it I followed the steps of Lord Hobart's government, which had proceeded also under the commands of the Court of Directors.

Lord Hobart and I were equally unsuccessful, but our efforts have received the most unequivocal and frequent testimonies of public and official approbation, nor was an attempt ever hazarded to represent our endeavours for the improvement of the subsisting subsidiary engagements of the Company in the Carnatic, as a systematic violation of the act of 1793; although the success of those endeavours must have been accompanied by an extension of the territory of the Company in India.

In the settlement of Mysore upon concluding subsidiary engagements with the Rajah of Mysore, I have already declared in my letter of the 3d of August 1799, to the Court of Directors, that my express purpose was to facilitate the direct control of the Company over the whole territory of Mysore, with a view to the more effectual security of the subsidy. In fact, the territory governed in the name of the Rajah was actually annexed to the Company's dominion, by that article of the subsidiary treaty of Seringapatam, which empowers the Company at any time to assume the direct management of the whole country. But this treaty has not yet been quoted to prove the existence of a systematic plan of territorial acquisition inconsistent with the policy of the act of 1793.

In Tanjore, I effected in the year 1800, a commutation of subsidy founded on the spirit of my original instructions respecting the Carnatic, and accordingly the territory of Tanjore was annexed to the Company's possessions.

In the year 1800, a new treaty of subsidy was formed with the Nizam; adverting to the uniform policy pursued by the Company since the act of 1793, to the tenor of my instructions respecting the Carnatic, and to my experience of the evils resulting from the existing systems of subsidy in Oude and the Carnatic, I formed the subsidiary treaty with the Nizam upon the principle of obtaining territorial security for the payment of the subsidy, instead of depending for the safety of those funds on the precarious power, and imperfect administration of an Indian Government.

The new treaties with the Rajah of Tanjore, and with the Nizam, have not hitherto been arraigned on the grounds recently stated.

The treaties of Surat, and the treaties with the Guikowar, were founded on similar principles with those of Tanjore and Hyderabad, substituting territorial security for an engagement to pay the amount of the subsidy from the treasury of the state.

The right to conclude a subsidiary engagement with the Guikowar was derived from that stipulation of the treaty of Salbye, which constitutes the Company to be the guarantee of the succession and government of the Guikowar state.

The new subsidiary treaty concluded with the Nabob of Oude in November 1801, rested on the same foundations, and effected a commutation of all the Nabob Vizier's engagements with respect to subsidy and aid in war, for a cession of territory.

The treaty of Bassein recently concluded with the Peishwa proceeds on the same grounds. In renewing the ancient alliance between the Peishwa and the Company, it has constituted that alliance by a subsidiary engagement, and by a territorial cession formed upon the improved plan of policy repeatedly sanctioned by the authority of his Majesty, and of the East India Company, and already effected with other dependent states, in preference to that defective scheme of subsidiary alliance which had produced innumerable evils in various parts of our dependencies in India, which for many years had constituted an annual theme of lamentation for all the governments in India, and for the honourable Court of Directors, and the policy of which appeared to have been exploded by the deliberate wisdom and long experience of that sage body.

The transfer of the civil and military government of the Carnatic to the Company, was warranted by the justice and necessity of that proceeding, founded upon the forfeiture incurred by Mahomed Ali, and Omdut ul Omra, and upon the dangers which menaced the security of the Company's rights on the coast of Coromandel, in consequence of the treachery of those faithless and abandoned characters. The justification of this proceeding rests upon principles similar to those by which war is justifiable against any public enemy, and the extension of territory which accompanied the prosecution of a just and legitimate public right, cannot be condemned upon any principles correctly derived from the act of 1793.

In prosecuting the just rights of the Company against the Nabob of the Carnatic, I resorted to my original instructions respecting the Carnatic; and I framed the new settlement with reference to the acknowledged expediency of effecting commutation of the subsidy for territorial security, and of rescuing the Carnatic from the evils of divided government and conflicting power, by establishing over that province one distinct authority in the hands of the Company, with a liberal provision for the Nabob and his family. I am at a loss to comprehend the application of the act of 1793, to any part of this transaction.

The acquisitions of territory which have been accomplished in India during my administration, have proceeded either from the successful prosecution of war, or from forfeiture in consequence of the violation of dependent alliances, or lastly from the improvement of existing, or the formation of new treaties of subsidy and guarantee. The first description includes those provinces and possessions of Tippoo Sultaun, retained by the

Company under the partition treaty of Mysore. The second description consists of the possessions of Omdut ul Omra in the Carnatic; and the last comprehends the territories commuted for subsidy by the Rajah of Tanjore, by the Nizam, and by the Nabob of Oude, and the territories ceded in payment of subsidy by the Nabob of Surat, by the Guikowar, and ultimately by the Peishwa.

The records of the Company will furnish your Lordship with sufficient evidence that every extension of territory acquired under each of these classes, has originated in principles not only strictly conformable to the act of 1793, but to the general maxims of justice and policy, applicable to our Indian empire.

No extension of territory has been acquired otherwise than by the prosecution of just and necessary war, or of just and legitimate public right; the result of these acquisitions has not involved the necessity of defending any territory, which had not previously furnished increased means of offensive war to our enemies, or which we were not previously bound to defend either by the obligation of positive treaty, or of our own manifest interest. Our means of defence in every case are now greatly augmented, by the annexation of the civil and military government of the territories, from which we derive the military resource applicable to defray the charge of their respective protection and security.

With regard to the question of the floating debts of the Nabob of the Carnatic, I have already intimated my opinion to Mr. Addington, as far as it appeared to me proper to offer any opinion, while the settlement of the Carnatic remains in suspense in Parliament, after a public notification of an intention to subject that settlement to the result of a parliamentary enquiry.

I trust that your Lordship will not recognize any part of the Nabob's unconsolidated debt, without previous investigation under the authority of the legislature. When that authority shall have been furnished, I shall be fully prepared to offer my sentiments on every branch of the subject.

In the meanwhile I have the honour to enclose for your Lordship's notice, extracts of the opinions which I have already communicated to Mr. Addington in a private letter.

I cannot suppose that the condition of the Company with relation to any part of its territorial possessions in India, can be considered to be similar to that of a private individual proprietor of a landed estate. The Company with relation to its territory in India, must be viewed in the capacity of a sovereign power. If any other principle be recognized, and the Company be permitted to hold the nominal sovereignty of India, endless confusion must ensue; in such an extremity no possible remedy could save this country from anarchy and ruin, but the instantaneous assumption of the direct executive power of the British possessions in India, by the Crown of the United Kingdom.

If any accommodation with the Nabob's creditors should be attempted, it appears to me that the proposition which I offered to the Nabob Omdut ul Omra, in my letter of the 24th of April 1799, would form an eligible basis of such an arrangement. But in the present circumstances, it would not be advisable to recognize any part of the debt, without previous enquiry under authority from Parliament to the Court of Directors, and from the Court of Directors to the Government General.

Your Lordship's observations respecting the settlement of Oude, and the conduct of Mr. Henry Wellesley in the negotiation of the treaty with the Vizier, and in the superintendance of the provincial government of that country, have afforded me the highest satisfaction. On this subject your Lordship has received such ample details by the *Swallow* packet, as preclude the necessity of any further remark from me.

It has been a matter of great surprize as well as of considerable satisfaction to me to have found myself enabled within so short a space of time to establish the regular civil authority of the Company, in a country of which the disorderly and lawless state under the government of our ally the Vizier had long afforded occupation to the main body of the army of Bengal; I should have deemed it a reasonable compromise for the Court of Directors, to have secured the settlement of the country, and the regular introduction of their civil servants at the expiration of a military commission of the duration of five or seven years.

I feel however considerable pleasure in assuring your Lordship, that although the tranquillity of that province is not yet completely secured, and although the final settlement of the Doab may hereafter require the employment of authority, great advantages have been derived in the prosecution of the present war, from the improvements already accomplished in the state of Oude, under the operation of the commission over which Mr. Henry Wellesley presided.

With regard to the policy and justice of the treaty of Lucknow, and to the recent settlement of Oude, your Lordship's letter (to which I have now the honour to reply) expresses a sanguine hope that I shall receive the approbation of the honourable Court. On this question, as on the subject of the Carnatic, my duty has been completely discharged, by applying the most assiduous exertion of my judgment to the formation of a settlement on principles which appear to me to be just, expedient, and desirable, and by submitting to the Court of Directors the grounds of my decision. I entertain no further anxiety on any part of this question, than that the public interests in Oude should be saved for my country; and if the honourable Court should be pleased to condemn the arrangements by which I have saved those interests from ruin, I trust that the wisdom and justice of that body will amend my errors, and reform the present government of the ceded provinces.

My correspondence with the Secret Committee upon the subject of Finance, embraces every point stated by your Lordship upon that important question. No doubt can exist that if the prime cost of investment in India be regularly supplied with bullion from Europe for a few years, every object in your Lordship's contemplation will be fully secured.

War with France, unless extended to India by active operations of the French, will not materially retard the progress of your Lordship's plan for the reduction of the debt.

War in India must be expected to produce a temporary delay. The war in which we are now engaged has however been attended with so large and immediate an increase of revenue, that I trust our accounts at the close of the year will appear highly favourable; and as an early peace may be expected on terms of considerable advantage, and of permanent duration, the ultimate result of your Lordship's plan for the reduction of the debt will I trust, be rather accelerated than retarded by the events of the present war.

I cannot close this letter without repeating to your Lordship the sincere expressions of my high respect, and entire confidence. It is due to that confidence to apprize your Lordship, that you will find the primary object of all my views to be, the success of your Lordship's just, and wise plans for the prosperity and honour of this empire.

I have the honour to be,
with great respect and regard,
my dear Lord,
always yours most faithfully,
WELLESLEY.

VIII. SUPREME AND LOCAL GOVERNMENTS.

99. The Governor-General in Council to the Honourable Court of Directors.

Constitution, Functions, and Reform of the Supreme Government.

Fort William, July 9th, 1800.

Honourable Sirs,

The great pressure of the numerous and important duties now performed immediately by the Governor-General in Council, has induced us to take a review of the constitution of the Government-General, considered as the supreme authority in India.

It has been his Lordship's object in this review to determine what duties now executed immediately by the Governor-General in Council ought still to be performed by him; what duties ought to be delegated to other establishments, and lastly to make a permanent provision for the due discharge of those duties which the Governor-General in Council must necessarily retain, as well as of those which it has been deemed advisable he should relinquish.

In the discussion of these important questions we have not hesitated to consider the extensive and valuable possessions to the government of which the Company have succeeded, as a great Empire. To view those possessions in any other light, must, we are persuaded, always lead to the most erroneous conclusions as to the principles of policy by which they ought to be governed.

The early administration of the Company succeeded to the despotic power of the native princes.

Those princes, as in other despotic governments, united in their own persons the whole legislative, executive, and judicial powers of the State, and exercised them according to the dictates of their own discretion.

No form of Government could be so ill adapted to these countries when they became dependent possessions of the British Empire, subject to be governed by persons occasionally deputed from the Mother Country.

Experience of the evils attendant on this form of Government conducted by a delegated British administration, led to the modelling of the Government of Bengal, on principles drawn from the British constitution.

A distribution of the legislative, executive, and judicial powers of the state, analogous to that which forms the basis of the British Constitution, was made the foundation of the new constitution of the Government of Bengal.

Considerations, however, arising out of the nature of our situation in this country demanded that these fundamental principles of the British Constitution should be introduced with a variety of modifications.

The lines between these three authorities were distinctly drawn, but it was obviously necessary that the Governor-General in Council should exercise exclusively the entire legislative authority.

But at the same time that we excluded our native subjects from all participation in the legislative authority, abundant security was afforded to them, that the exercise of that authority would always be directed to their happiness and benefit.

The confirmation of their ancient laws in all matters connected with their religious prejudices, or their domestic relations, formed one of the first acts of the Governor-General in Council under the new constitution.

Provision was also made for ascertaining the sense which the people might entertain of the laws and regulations enacted for the government of the country, by the authority given to the judges of all the Courts of Judicature to propose such general or local laws as, from their intercourse with the natives in the administration of justice, might appear to them necessary to promote the public happiness and prosperity.

As an effectual security against every abuse of the legislative power vested in the Governor-General in Council, it was made a fundamental principle of the new constitution, that he shall print and publish every legislative Act in a form which renders him responsible to his country for the unjust or unwise exercise of that power.

The executive authority was of necessity also exclusively vested in the Governor-General in Council.

No check can be imposed on the Governor-General in Council in the exercise of this authority in the regulation of our connection with the foreign States of India. But as our own interest, and that of our subjects with regard to those connections are necessarily the same, they have the best security that the most effectual means will always be taken to protect the country from foreign enemies.

With regard to all acts of the executive power as they relate to the internal government of the country, the people possess. the same security against any infringement by this power of the rights and principles which have been granted to them by the laws, as is enjoyed under the British Constitution.

It was judged advisable, however, to restrict the controul over the executive authority to cases actually provided for by the regulations. But as legislative provisions are made for all cases not included in the existing laws as such cases arise, the discretionary power which the Governor-General in Council may now exercise in cases of that nature, must in progress of time entirely cease.

As constituting the Courts of Sudder Dewanny Adawlut and the Nizamut, or the chief civil or criminal Courts, the Governor-General in Council also exercises a large portion of the judicial power.

The reasons which originally occasioned the continuance of the entire legislative and executive authority in the Governor-General in Council, are obviously of a permanent nature.

There is no change in our situation in this country, which can be supposed, in which it would be expedient to admit any part of our native subjects to participate in the legislative authority with the Governor-General in Council.

The same principle applies to the executive authority of the Governor-General in Council, as far as regards the relations of the British possessions with foreign states. It can never be expedient that our native subjects should be allowed to interfere in those relations, or that any local restrictions should be imposed on the Governor-General in Council, in the conduct of them.

With regard to the executive authority of the Governor-General in Council, as far as relates to the internal government of the country, this authority can only be vested in him. But the nature of our situation affords additional reasons for subjecting the executive authority in this branch gradually to the complete controul of the law, in the same manner as that authority is restricted by the laws of the British constitution.

While our political security demands that the entire legislative and executive authority should continue to be vested exclusively in the Governor-General in Council agreeably to the principles of the existing constitution: it is at the same time a satisfaction to know, that under the checks which are imposed on the Governor-General in Council in the exercise of these powers, the union of them in his hands, (notwithstanding the objections to which this union may be liable in theory) is perfectly compatible with the ends of good government.

There are no circumstances however connected with our political situation in this country, which require that the Governor-General in Council should continue to exercise any portion of the judicial authority.

It is equally necessary to the happiness of the people, to the prosperity of the country, and to the stability of the British Government, that such laws as the Governor-General in Council may sanction in his legislative capacity, should be administered with ability, integrity, impartiality and expedition.

All the provisions made by the British constitution for precluding the legislative and the executive powers of the state, from any interference in the administration of the laws, are not only applicable to the government of this country, but, if it were possible, demand to be strengthened.

An efficient controul may be exercised from England over the conduct of the Governor-General in Council, in his legislative capacity. But no effectual controul can be exercised over him in the administration of the laws, and he may render the laws altogether nugatory by abuses, omissions, or delays in their administration.

It is essentially necessary that the security of private rights and property should be rendered altogether independent of the characters of those who may be occasionally placed at the head of your affairs in this country. This however, can never be the case, while the Governor-General in Council who makes the law, and whose acts in his executive capacity, as well as those of the long train of officers who exercise authority under him in that capacity also, constitute the chief courts which controul the general administration of justice.

No inconvenience can arise from divesting the Governor-General in Council of all immediate interference in the administration of the laws, while he has the power of altering at his pleasure the law itself.

These objections to the exercise of any judicial power by the Governor-General in Council, are founded on general and established principles of government; but other considerations render this duty incompatible with the proper functions of the Governor-General in Council.

The administration of justice in open court, is one of the principal securities for its due administration.

The constant appearance of the Governor-General in Council in an open court of justice would be incompatible with that dignity which, to render him competent to the conduct of the government, it is essentially necessary that the person invested with the supreme executive and legislative power should maintain, not only in the estimation of the people immediately subject to his government, but also of the foreign powers.

The presence of the Governor-General in Council in open court, would prevent the pleading of causes with becoming freedom. No native pleader would venture to contest his opinions, and the will of the Governor-General, and not the law would be considered as the rule of decision.

As the Governor-General must necessarily be often unacquainted with the languages of the country, this circumstance alone would render it impracticable for him to preside at trials in open court, unless it should be determined that the trials should be conducted in English, and by English pleaders.

In consequence of these circumstances, the Courts of Sudder Dewanny Adawlut, and Nizamut Adawlut are held in the council chamber. Neither the parties nor their pleaders are in any cases present. The proceedings are translated into English, and read to the members of the Court who pass their decision, which the register records.

The necessity of making these translations constitutes the chief cause of the delay in the decision of the causes which are brought before the chief civil and criminal courts. The translations cannot however be dispensed with for the reasons above stated. They are also requisite for record and transmission to England, as they now constitute the only check on the Governor-General in Council in the administration of the law; but for these considerations, no translations of the proceedings on trials would be necessary.

But there is another object, unconnected with any of the above considerations, which is of itself sufficient to establish the necessity of divesting the Governor-General in Council of the judicial authority now exercised by him.

A conscientious discharge of the duties of the Sudder Dewanny Adawlut, and the Nizamut Adawlut, would of itself occupy the whole time of the Governor-General in Council.

The proper duties of these courts are not confined to the determination of the causes which are brought before them. It is also their duty to superintend the conduct of all the other courts, to watch over the general police of the country, and to frame for the consideration of the Governor-General in Council, new laws as cases may arise demanding further legislative provisions.

When your Honourable Court shall advert to the extent of your dominions, to their population, to their growing prosperity, and to the consequent multiplied concerns of individuals, it will at once be evident that it is physically impossible that the Governor-General in Council can ever dedicate that time and attention to the duties of these courts, which must necessarily be requisite for their due discharge.

It is impossible to have the benefit of a regular and systematic government without numerous laws, and for the due administration of those laws, the necessary establishments must be provided.

Of the value of a system of government founded on these principles as connected with your permanent interests, a competent judgment may be formed by a comparison of the present state of your territories in Bengal, with that of your ancient possessions on the coast of Coromandel, as described in the able report of the Board of Revenue at Fort St. George, forwarded to your Honourable Court by this despatch.

These considerations have induced us to determine, under the sanction of the clause of the act, of the year of the reign of his present Majesty, that the Governor-General, and the members of council shall not constitute the Court of Sudder Dewanny Adawlut in future, but that distinct judges shall be appointed to preside in that court, with all the powers and authorities now exercised by the Governor-General and the members of council, as the judges of that court.

We have also determined, that the same judges shall constitute the Court of Nizamut Adawlut, with all the powers now exercised by the Governor-General and members of council, as judges of that court.

The adoption of this arrangement will establish the prosperity of your dominions in Bengal, on the most solid foundations. Your Honourable Court will yourselves be able to exercise the most effectual controul over the Governor-General in Council in his legislative capacity, as his acts printed and published come under your revision. His executive authority as far as regards the internal government, will be subject to the controul of the laws, and the due administration of the laws, will be secured by the courts appointed to administer them being rendered entirely distinct, both from the executive and legislative authority, at the same time that the conduct of the judges of the superior courts, will be subject to the most vigilant controul on the part of the executive power.

The necessity of divesting the Governor-General in Council of the exercise of any judicial authority at some future period was foreseen at the first establishment of the present constitution. It will accordingly appear, that throughout the code of regulations the powers of the Sudder Dewanny Adawlut and the Nizamut Adawlut are so framed, as to admit of these courts being at any time constituted in the manner now proposed. But the cautious spirit which will be found to pervade every part of that constitution, wisely left these judicial powers to be exercised by the Governor-General in Council, until circumstances should dictate the necessity of his relinquishing them.

The establishment of the new Courts of Sudder Dewanny Adawlut and Nizamut Adawlut, providing for the discharge of the judicial duties now exercised by the Governor-General in Council, the only point connected with the subject of this address which remains to be considered, is the permanent provision to be made for enabling the Governor-General in Council to execute the legislative and executive duties which are still to be performed by him.

The duties of the Governor-General in Council in his legislative capacity, are first, the framing of such laws or regulations as may occur to him to be necessary for improving the internal government of the country. Secondly, the consideration of such laws or regulations as may be proposed to him by any of the Courts of Judicature, or other authorities empowered to propose regulations.

In a despotic government the will of the ruling power stands in the place of law; but when it becomes the fundamental principle of a government, to be guided by written and defined laws, every case which occurs, for which no provision is made, and every defect discovered in the existing laws, calls for the interposition of the legislative authority.

Numerous cases now demand that interposition; but it is unavoidably withheld, from the various avocations of the Governor-General in Council, rendering it impossible to give his attention to the several cases, or defects, or to make the necessary legislative provisions for them.

The superintendance of this important duty, on the due performance of which depend the happiness of the people, the extent of your resources, and the stability of your empire, will in future devolve chiefly on the new Court of Sudder Dewanny Adawlut and Nizamut. It will be the province of the Governor-General in Council to determine on the expediency of adopting the regulations which may be submitted to him by these courts, or by the other authorities empowered to propose regulations.

The duties of the Governor-General in Council in his executive capacity consist of—first, his duties as exercising the executive authority of the government of the British possessions in India. Secondly, his duties as the chief representative of the Company in India, in their commercial capacity.

The first-mentioned duties must be considered, as they relate to the conduct of the relations between the British power in India, and Foreign States; and secondly, as they are connected with the internal government of your own possessions.

The glorious termination of the late war in Mysore, and the events which preceded it, have not only widely extended your political relations, but have established the ascendancy of the British power over all the States of India.

The maintenance of this ascendancy, necessarily demands the constant and vigilant attention of the Governor-General in Council.

The public records afford abundant testimony, how great a proportion of the time of the Governor-General in Council must necessarily be occupied by this most important duty.

The executive duties of the Governor-General in Council as connected with the internal government of the British possessions of Bengal, comprise the management of the public revenue, the superintendance of the general finances of India, the regulation of the army, and the infinite variety of miscellaneous business which falls under the cognizance of the executive authority in every government.

The general controul exercised by the Governor-General in Council over the civil and military affairs of the subordinate governments, forms another important branch of these executive duties.

The two subordinate governments may be considered with relation to the supreme government as dependent states. The nature of the controul exercised over those governments, corresponds in many material respects, with that exercised by the Crown, with regard to the American and West Indian possessions.

It is essential that this controul should be extended to all matters in any respect connected with the unity, strength and stability of the British power in India.

The various questions arising out of the settlement of our recent conquests, of our connection with the dependent power established in Mysore, and lastly, the introduction of the constitution of the internal Government of Bengal, into the British territories, subject to the Governments of Fort St. George and Bombay, demand at present a more than ordinary attention of the Governor-General in Council, to the affairs of those governments.

Another branch of the duties of the Governor-General in Council in his executive capacity, is the superintendance of the subordinate settlements, and of our acquisitions from the French and the Dutch.

As the chief representative of the Company in their commercial capacity the Governor-General in Council has the immediate superintendance of their commercial concerns in Bengal, and exercises a general control over the provision of the investment at the other presidencies, including a considerable degree of attention to their affairs in China.

The establishment attached to the Governor-General in Council in his legislative and executive capacity, for the conduct of these various and important duties under circumstances peculiarly arduous and critical, has hitherto consisted of a secretary, and four sub-secretaries. The assistants under these officers are necessarily incompetent to afford them any effectual aid, in their more important duties.

From the constitution of these offices of sub-secretary, these offices were not acceptable to persons of any pretensions in the respective departments, either from their rank in the service, or from their talents. They have accordingly for the most part been filled by junior servants, necessarily incompetent to afford any efficient assistance in the execution of the duties of government.

It is of the greatest importance to the public interests, that the establishments of the several departments immediately connected with the legislative and executive capacity of the Governor-General in Council should be so constituted, as to ensure at the head of the respective departments, the assistance of men of ability, integrity and experience, competent to the due conduct of the ordinary duties of the government.

Establishments so constituted, will form a great check to negligence or misrule; at the same time, that they will always be powerful instruments in the hands of those who are zealous in the promotion of the public interests.

The Governor-General in Council therefore determined to make the situations of the public officers, who are to be his instruments for the conduct of the government of the British possessions in India, offices of high honour, and of the first emolument.

This was the only mode of enabling the Governor-General in Council to command the services of men of the first talents and ability, in the respective departments.

As connected with the principle of relieving the Governor-General in Council from all unnecessary labour of detail, our attention has been drawn to the number of papers which it has been the practice for the Governor-General in Council to attest with his own signature. Much of the time of the Governor-General in Council is occupied unnecessarily in the signature of these papers, and the despatch of the public business is often considerably impeded in obtaining his signature to them.

We have accordingly determined, that all public papers shall be authenticated by the signature of the secretary to the department. From this general rule however, we have of course excepted our addresses to your honourable Court, and to the subordinate Presidencies and all other papers, to which considerations of respect to superior authority, or other circumstances, may render it proper that the signatures of the Governor-General in Council should be affixed. Conformably to this determination, your honourable Court will find the sets of the public proceedings which are transmitted to you, attested by the secretaries of the respective departments, by order of the Governor-General in Council, instead of being signed by the Governor-General and the members of council.

In this review of the constitution of the supreme Government of the Company's possessions in India, it could not escape the Governor-General in council, that the wisest system of government will but imperfectly answer its ends, unless means are at the same time taken for providing persons duly qualified for the conduct of the system.

It would be useless to enter into any argument to prove that the same general qualifications necessary for the first political, judicial, financial and commercial stations in Europe, are equally requisite for the due discharge of the duties of similar situations in India.

Your honourable Court can yourselves form an adequate judgment how far your servants are in general competent to discharge these high offices. You know at what age they are sent from England, and what are at that period their qualifications for the offices to which they are destined. You are also apprized how far the occupations on which the first years of their residence in India are employed, are calculated to give them these qualifications.

Your servants are nominated to the highest stations of civil government, without any test of their possessing the requisite qualifications for the discharge of the functions of these offices. No such test could now indeed be required, none having been prescribed, and no means having been afforded to individuals of acquiring the necessary qualifications for public stations.

In consequence of this serious defect in the system of your government, it has been the practice to transfer your servants from one line of the service to another, with little regard to the qualifications for the offices for which they have been selected. No imputation attaches in this respect to your governments. Among those from whom the selection was to be made, there could not possibly exist any material ground of preference.

It is far from our intention in these observations to reflect on the general talents, character, or integrity of your servants on this establishment. Whatever may be their deficiencies, they are not ascribable to themselves, but to the nature of the service. Great exertions indeed have been made by individuals, and it affords matter of astonishment, that under such disadvantages they should have acquitted themselves with so much ability and success, in situations which in Europe are to be attained only by regular and systematic education and laborious exertions.

It is obvious that an education exclusively European or Indian, would not qualify your servants for the situations which they are destined to fill. The foundation of their education must be laid in England, and it must be completed systematically after their arrival in India.

The Governor-General in Council has, therefore, determined to found an establishment at this Presidency, of the nature of a collegiate institution, for the purpose of enabling the servants of the Çompany to perfect themselves in those acquirements, which form the necessary qualifications for the different lines of the service, in which they may choose to engage. It is our intention that the junior servants shall be attached to this institution for a certain period after their arrival, instead of being employed in the unprofitable occupation of transcribing papers, and abandoned to the dictates of their own discretion, both with regard to their morals and acquirements.

An institution of this description will ensure a succession of men, equal to the support of the great interests of the Company, and of the British nation in India.

The above observations with regard to the education and qualifications of your civil servants in Bengal, for the conduct of civil government apply with equal force to your servants under the other Presidencies. Under our instructions to Fort St. George, of the 31st December last, and the orders which we have it in contemplation to issue to Bombay, the civil servants on those establishments will be shortly called upon to exercise the same important functions, as the civil servants in Bengal.

Whether it will be advisable to bring the junior servants attached to the Establishments of Fort St. George and Bombay to Bengal in the first instance, in order to enable them to acquire the necessary qualifications here, or to found institutions for the purpose at those Presidencies, is a question which will demand further consideration.

When the details of the plan of the intended institution shall have been arranged, we shall lose no time in forwarding it to your honourable Court. As it cannot fail to redound equally to the honour and happiness of the civil servants, as well as to promote the solid and substantial interests of the Company, and of the nation, we feel the strongest conviction that it will meet your approbation.

As connected with the subject of forming the characters of your servants, we cannot omit to notice the state of your religious establishments in this country.

The sentiments which have occurred to the Governor-General regarding these establishments, will hereafter form the subject of a separate address to your honourable Court from his Lordship.

It is of the last importance to the stability of the British power in India, that these establishmonts should be placed on the most respectable footing. Such establishments will cherish in the minds of the servants of the Company, a sense of moral duty, and teach those who fill important stations, that the great public duties which they are called upon to execute in India, are not of a less sacred nature than the duties of similar situations in their own country. In proportion as persons holding such situations are brought to entertain these high and worthy notions of their functions, and to consider themselves as more especially accountable to that Being, whose instruments they are in the government of a large portion of the human race, in the same degree will they discharge their duties with zeal, diligence and integrity.

We feel that it would not only be impolitic, but highly immoral to suppose that Providence has admitted of the establishment of the British power over the finest provinces of India, with any other view than that of its being conducive to the happiness of the people, as well as to our national advantage.

In proportion as the policy and conduct of the British Government shall correspond with these beneficent intentions, we are persuaded that its power will acquire increasing stability.

Impressed with a deep sense of the justice and wisdom of these principles, we are confident that it will always be equally for the interests of the Company, and of the British nation, that they should constitute the basis of the system of our Indian Government; and that consistently with the considerations of a well regulated economy, we ought never to withhold that portion of the resources derived from these valuable possessions, which may be found indispensably necessary for dispensing to them the invaluable blessings of civil order and good government.

We have the honour to be, &c.

WELLESLEY and COUNCIL.

100. The Earl of Mornington to Lord Clive.

Relations of the Supreme to the Subordinate Governments.

(Extract.) (Most Private and Confidential.)

Fort William, July 29th, 1798.

My Lord,

Having troubled your Lordship with so much detail upon the subject of the internal Government of Fort St. George, I shall proceed to state some considerations with regard to the nature of the relation between that Government and the Governor-General in Council of Bengal. Your Lordship is, I doubt not, perfectly conversant with the provisions of the law on this point; I shall therefore advert merely to the practical principles resulting from those provisions; and I am anxious to explain my sentiments to your Lordship upon this head in the earliest period of your government, not only because the greatest inconveniences have resulted to the public service from misunderstandings of the distinct practical duties of the two Governments, but because I know that a faction exists at Madras, whose constant endeavour has been and will be assiduously employed to foment those misunderstandings into a systematic spirit of jealousy and contention.

All measures relating to the general defence and protection of India, to the system of our alliances, and of our negociations or intercourse with the native powers, to the levying war or making peace, to the general administration of the revenues of all the Presidencies, to the employment of the military force, and finally to every point affecting the general interests whether civil, military, or political of the Company's possessions, form the exclusive duties arising out of the superintending power of the Governor-General in Council. For all measures of this description, he alone is responsible; and therefore the duty of the other Presidencies, with regard to such measures, consists in a cordial co-operation in the execution of that, which it is the peculiar province of the Governor-General in Council to determine. The Governor-General being in possession of the whole superintendence and control, as well as of the means of comprehending in one view the entire state of the Company's empire and trade, and of all the various considerations and circumstances which may affect either, must frequently issue instructions, the fundamental principles and final scope of which cannot at first sight be fully understood by the other Presidencies: in such cases (as well indeed as in any of those already described), I am persuaded that your Lordship will concur with me in thinking that the duty of the other Presidencies can never be to mix direct or indirect censures with their formal obedience to the legal authority of the Governor-General in Council: still less can it be their duty, to anticipate his decisions by the premature interposition of their opinions and advice in any quarter, where such interference may counteract the success of his general plans, and may introduce all the mischiefs and confusion of divided councils, and of conflicting authority. The examination of the records of the late Government of Fort St. George, will manifest to your Lordship a constant tendency towards this fatal error; and even since my arrival in Bengal, I have found it necessary to restrain the symptoms of the same disposition in two instances; the one a letter written to Admiral Rainier, without any previous concert with me, suggesting a plan of operations for his Majesty's squadron entirely incompatible with my views for the general protection of our possessions. The other, a letter to me in Council, containing both direct and indirect censures of the orders which I have lately issued for assembling the army on the coast; a measure indispensably necessary, and founded on a variety of reasons, of which the Government of Fort St. George could not at that time comprehend either the nature or extent.

Under your Lordship's administration, I am confident that no such embarrassment can ever occur. With the same freedom which I have used throughout this letter, I will state to you distinctly the mode in which I propose to conduct the intercourse between the two Governments, with a view to secure their cordial co-operation, and to preclude the possibility of distraction. Every endeavour shall be used on my part to communicate to your Lordship the fullest and earliest intelligence of the nature and object of any measure which I may have in contemplation, either with relation to your particular Government, or to the general interests of the whole British Empire in India. These communications will be made to your Lordship through the channel of my private correspondence. On the other hand, I make it my earnest request to your Lordship, that whenever any such communication shall be delayed, you will attribute the delay either to the absolute necessity of the case, or to my views of the public service; and that you will therefore have the goodness to prevent the Government of Fort St. George from proceeding to take any steps upon matters belonging to my exclusive responsibility, without a full previous communication with me, and without being apprised of my concurrence. In your Lordship's private correspondence, I trust that your Lordship will permit me to hope for the advantage of your unreserved opinion, not only with respect to all matters within your own peculiar charge, but to any point which you may think essential to the general interests of the British Empire in India; and I assure your Lordship most sincerely that I shall always receive your private suggestions as personal favours. In regulating your public correspondence, I request that your Lordship will advert to the suggestions contained in this letter, and that you will exclude from the public records every indication of jealousy and counteraction. On my part you will always find a sincere disposition in every transaction, both public and private, to consider your Lordship's authority as a part of my own, and to repel every attempt to disunite the two Governments.

I have the honour to be, &c.

MORNINGTON.

101. The Marquess Wellesley to the Right Honourable Henry Addington.

Serious dangers involved in the direct assumption of Indian patronage by the Directors, or the Board of Control.

(Extract.)

Cawnpore, Jan. 10, 1802.

My dear Sir,

The proper office of the Court of Directors is to superintend and control the local governments of India in the exercise of the power of appointment to the various executive offices of this country, as well as in every other branch of the executive government.

It was not in the contemplation of the legislature, by the act of 1793, to vest in the Court of Directors the direct power of nomination to every office in the local government of India; the power of nomination to such offices, and indeed the whole civil and military government are in distinct terms vested by the act of 1793 in the Governors in Council of the three Presidencies, subject to the local control of the Governor-General in Council, and in Europe to that of the Court of Directors, and of the Board of Commissioners for the affairs of India.

The Court of Directors may certainly issue orders directing the government of India to appoint any particular person to any executive office in India, but the government on the spot ought to possess and to exercise the same free discretion with regard to the execution of such orders, as it possesses and exercises with regard to any other orders from home. It is, however, highly inexpedient to issue any orders from England for the direct nomination of any person to office below the Councils in India; and it is evident, that, under any modification, such orders, although not peremptory, must greatly restrain the discretion of the local government in the choice of its instruments.

If all such orders are to be considered as of a peremptory nature, the whole local patronage of India will, in fact, be disposed of in Leadenhall Street, and the most attentive consideration is due to the probable effects of such a system.

If the King's Commissioners for India and the Court of Directors should at any time agree to co-operate in filling from home all official vacancies which shall occur in India, it is evident that the result of such a combination might be the transfer of the whole local patronage of India, or of a certain share of it to the Crown.

Whatever share of the patronage of India should be obtained by the Crown in this manner, would be exercised in the most dangerous and objectionable form; for as the appointments to office would be made in an indirect manner, and through several successive channels of authority, no direct responsibility would attach to the ministers of the Crown; and the influence of the Crown might become considerably extended through a secret and unobserved course, and without the possibility of public control.

The direct transfer of the whole local patronage of India to the Crown, under a definite and public responsibility, would be infinitely less objectionable than the exercise of such an indirect and indefinite influence. That share of the local patronage of India which, under the arrangement supposed, would be allotted to the Court of Directors, would tend to establish in their hands a species of influence, which could never be regulated by a due control, and which, in a numerous and fluctuating body, subject to the impulse of various interests, and necessarily exempt from individual responsibility, would not often be governed by the exclusive consideration of the prosperity of the public service in India.

The Governor-General, and each of the Governors in India, acts under a severe personal responsibility in every nomination to office; and while the nominations of the respective local governments shall be superintended and controlled by the Court of Directors and by the Board of Commissioners, (neither authority possessing any private interest directly or indirectly in any such nomination,) the system of control would appear to be so complete, as to secure the public interests at home against the growth of any undue influence, and the public service abroad against any material abuse of the local patronage.

But if the Court, or the Board, or both united, are to be considered as the direct sources of the local patronage of India, they will possess a private interest in the decision of every question which can arise concerning the nomination to any office in India; they will be interested to rescind appointments made in India for the purpose of exercising their own patronage from home; and they will become utterly disqualified for the exercise of a pure and impartial superintendence and control of the conduct of the Indian government in the important duty of administering the local patronage of this vast empire.

Such a system would be sufficiently objectionable even in its application to the public and constitutional interests in England; its application to the public service in India is however infinitely more perilous.

It must extinguish all local subordination in India, since no public servant would ever respect the local government, after it should have been deprived of the power of regulating official appointments and removals. All emulation to obtain the approbation of the local government would expire; no public servant would esteem the countenance or even the nomination of the local government to be any security for promotion in the service, or would dread the consequences of its disapprobation or censure. The attention of the whole public service would be withdrawn from the Governor on the spot, and would be fixed on schemes of intrigue and cabal, for the purpose of forming and cultivating interests in England, by which the favour of the Court of Directors or of the Board of Control might be approached.

In such a situation the Governor on the spot would be an useless cypher without power, authority or respect. He might be compelled in every branch of the administration to employ instruments in whose capacity, knowledge or integrity he placed no reliance, and to witness the exclusion from office of the most able, intelligent, and honest servants of the public. For it is impossible to suppose that the Government on the spot should not always possess the best means of ascertaining the relative estimation and value of the characters of the public servants and officers in India, and should not always feel the nearest and most urgent interest in the proper selection of the immediate instruments of the local executive power.

In this respect, a remote authority, constituted as the Court of Directors is, can neither possess equal knowledge, nor feel an equally pressing and sensible interest, nor be restrained by equally powerful ties of responsibility and personal character.

If any Governor be supposed incapable or unwilling to make such a proper selection of public servants and officers, let him be removed; but while he shall be suffered to remain in India, the public service absolutely demands that he shall possess and exercise that decisive influence in the distribution of office which may enable him to maintain due subordination, to excite honourable emulation, and to secure the efficient, pure, and regular despatch of the public business in every department, by employing those in whom he confides, by excluding those whom he distrusts, and by convincing the public servants that his approbation is the certain road to public emoluments and honours, and that his censure is a public disgrace.

All these important objects I have hitherto accomplished, by such a discharge of my duty in the distribution of the patronage committed to my trust, as it will be the happiness and pride of my life to submit to the most severe inspection of Parliament; but I cannot consent to encounter the responsibility of this station, under a system calculated to bind my hands and to frustrate every dictate of my judgment and conscience.

The great and wise object of Parliament in 1793 was, under due control, to impart such a degree of local authority and vigour to the government of India as should enable it to maintain this perilous empire against the hourly vicissitudes which surround it. Where is the security of that object if the government of India shall be thwarted in every subordinate department, deprived of all local influence, and counteracted in every official detail by a remote authority, interfering in the nomination of every public servant and officer? It would be impossible to conduct any government in any part of the world under the weight of such disgraceful chains; but it would be the excess of rashness and insanity to attempt to hold this most arduous charge, in the present crisis, with hands so weakened, and with an authority so embarrassed and impaired.

Believe to be, my dear Sir,
with the most sincere respect and regard your's,
always most faithfully and affectionately,
WELLESLEY.

102. The Earl of Mornington to the Hon. Jonathan Duncan.

Working of the Local Government in the absence of the Governor, within the limits of the Presidency.

(Extract.)

Fort William, April 16th, 1800.

Sir,

While the Governors of Fort St. George or Bombay remain within the limits of their governments, it is evident that the members of the respective councils possess no powers distinct from the Governor, and that they are incompetent to perform any act of government otherwise than in his presence, and even otherwise than with his assent in every case excepting judicial proceedings, and those particularly specified in the Act of Parliament.

If, therefore, the necessity of the occasional absence of the Governor from the Presidency be admitted, either the general administration of the affairs of the Government must be suspended during his absence, or he must exercise, under his separate responsibility, to the extent which circumstances may require, all the powers which are vested in him by law when in council at the Presidency, afterwards recording his acts in council.

The legal incompetency of the council to exercise any portion of the public authority independently of the Governor, is not more evident than the expediency of limiting the exercise of the powers of government, in the case under consideration, to the Governor's hands, and of precluding the members of council, in the absence of the Governor, from exercising any such independent authority. The Governor, by law, under all circumstances, is responsible for the administration of the affairs of the Government. He is not only authorized, but bound to act on his separate opinion distinct from that of the council in all cases of deliberate difference on subjects of importance. A deference to the opinions of the members of council, or an inclination to conciliate their co-operation in the general system of the government, will not justify the Governor in any departure from his own conscientious judgment in any matter affecting the public interests; for the letter and spirit of the law have rendered it not only his right, but his duty to act on his own separate judgment, wherever, in cases of magnitude, it shall be clearly and decisively different from that of the council. If the Governor should submit his opinion to that of the council, he alone is, and ought to be, responsible for the consequences of any act done under such circumstances. The power of acting separately is an active trust in the hands of the Governor, and he must be responsible, not only for its abusive exercise, but for suffering it to lie dormant whenever the public service requires it to be called forth. As long as this responsibility attaches to the Governor, he ought to retain all the powers necessary to the discharge of his duties. Were these powers to devolve to the council during the absence of the Governor, in the case supposed, it is evident that they might be employed during that period, to the subversion of the general system of measures which the Governor might have established.

It is, therefore, my opinion, that during your residence at Surat, no measure of importance should be taken by the members of council at Bombay without your previous sanction, where the case may be such as to admit of the delay of a reference to you; and that all appointments to offices should proceed directly from yourself in the same manner as if you were present at the seat of government.

I also recommend that you direct copies of all the papers of importance to be forwarded to you by the most expeditious conveyance, and that you issue such orders on the subject of them, as you may think proper, under your own separate responsibility.

The members of the council may conduct the ordinary details of government during your absence, and their acts, as well as your own, may be regularly recorded in council on your return to the Presidency.

I have the honour to be, &c.

MORNINGTON.

IX. FINANCE AND TRADE.

103. The Right. Hon. Henry Dundas to the Earl of Mornington.

Necessity and means of 'keeping up a large investment from India.' Encouragement of India-built shipping for Private Trade.

Wimbledon, 18th March, 1799.
Received at Fort William, 5th August, 1799.

My dear Lord,

The financial state of our affairs in India, and the arrangement of them in future, will be the subject of official correspondence from the Court of Directors, by some early conveyance; but the present situation of the finances and commerce of India have suggested to my mind many important considerations, which I would think it wrong to withhold from you in the form of a private communication, as the opinions I shall lay before you may probably operate upon your conduct previous to the period when the same opinions may reach you in the more tedious form of despatches through the medium of the Court of Directors. This mode of earlier communication with you is the more necessary, as I am aware some of the opinions which I hold will be the cause of a difference of opinion among the Directors, and must ultimately be settled by the authority of the Board of Control, a form of proceeding necessarily productive of delay.

If there had been the prospect of the war coming to any speedy conclusion, I should not have been uneasy by the circumstance of a very considerable addition of the debt in India, for the purpose of continuing a large investment from an Indian capital, because from the experience I have already had in extricating their affairs under very unpromising circumstances, I should have felt perfectly satisfied that a few years after the return of peace, would have sufficed, speedily, to wipe off the debt which the mixt exigencies of war and commerce had created. This, however, has its bounds, for if the debt in India is allowed to increase so much as to become unwieldy and unmanageable, we are cut off from the means of extricating our affairs when peace shall have returned. The loans, from being made in times of difficulty, are accomplished at an exorbitant rate of interest, and thereby exhaust the whole of the surplus revenue, which is to operate as the sinking fund for the redemption of the debt after the return of peace. It is the more necessary I should give a particular attention to these considerations, because it is very natural for the Court of Directors to turn their eyes chiefly to the state of their affairs in Leadenhall-street, and both they and the Proprietors are flattered, by the view of sales at home, uncommonly large, and a swelling balance in their coffers at home; while, at the same time, it is obvious to every person who will take a comprehensive view of their affairs, that this flattering delusion, permitted to go on for a very few years, would bring irretrievable ruin upon the finances of India, and totally disable us from maintaining there that pre-eminence of wealth and power which has proved so important to the general interests of the British Empire.

Viewing this subject in all its bearings, I am well aware of the importance of keeping up the means of a large investment from India. This principle is important, not only from the encouragement it affords to the navigation and shipping of the kingdom; from the addition it makes annually to the wealth and capital of the country, and from its being a fruitful source of revenue; but in addition to all these and similar considerations, I must add the necessity of such an investment, as immediately connected with the prosperity of our Indian provinces. *It is to the increased exports from India to Europe, that we are to attribute the increase of Indian prosperity, industry, population, and revenue;* and the manufacturers of that country would be reduced to very deplorable circumstances if any severe check was to be given to the usual investment and exports from India. These considerations necessarily lead to the conclusion of bringing home as large an investment as our means will enable us to do. I see no difficulty in accomplishing this, but it must be done by means of resources which do not lead to the ruin of our finances in India. The same circumstances which have led to putting the whole commerce of the world into the hands of this country, do operate in a proportionable degree to extend beyond the example of all former times, the trade of the East India Company, and the produce of their sales in Leadenhall-street. This ought to be encouraged by every means; but the overflowing balance from thence arising after defraying their necessary burdens at home, ought to be employed in the purchase of bullion, to be consigned to India and China, for the purchase of a large and profitable investment. The times, from the influx of wealth into this country, are highly favourable to such an operation, the beneficial effects of which are obvious in a variety of ways. Your Lordship states, and all the other settlements concur in the same statement, that our Indian possessions are greatly distressed from the want of specie. The measure I have mentioned effectually removes that distress, and is likewise productive of another essential benefit. It is stated that the increase of the loans at so high a rate of interest, checks all private credit, and obstructs all other pecuniary transactions; but this inconvenience would not be found, if the system I have alluded to, was carried into execution.

It is with much satisfaction I observe in some of your Lordship's recent despatches, that you find yourself warranted by the opinions of some of the most intelligent persons upon the spot, in stating, that the export of manufactures from this country may be considerably increased. This is certainly the most desirable of all resources for the supply of a commercial investment from India, and it ought to have no limits, except what are prescribed by the power of selling them in India or China.

Another commercial resource, is what can be got in India upon the foundation of the remittance plan. This, I understand, has likewise received a check, in consequence of the high rate of interest paid for the government loans in India; but if these loans are stopped, and the capital of the debt itself considerably diminished each year by the remittance plan, an effectual cure is administered to this inconvenience, and the commercial resources of the Company materially aided, without the necessity of extravagant loans for that purpose.

These are the outlines of the system which, in my opinion, ought to be pursued during the remainder of the war, and as during its continuance our commerce will remain unbounded, and the wealth of the world continue to be collected here, no inconvenience whatever can arise from the export of bullion to India and China; on the contrary, I understand it would rather be in this point of view, materially convenient. The result, therefore, of what I have stated, is that the investment ought not to be diminished, but kept up at its present standard, and the resources for doing so are,—1st, The surplus revenues in India, after defraying the expense of establishment and the interest of debt. This fund will increase in proportion as the debt is diminished by the plan of remittance. 2ndly, By bills upon the East India Company to the amount of what can be got there, applicable to the reduction of the capital of the debt in India. 3rdly, An increased amount of the export of manufactures from this country, which generally upon an average, has been reckoned for some years past for India, exclusive of China, to amount to about five hundred thousand pounds. And lastly, a remittance of bullion to whatever amount may be necessary, joined to the above mentioned resources, to keep up the usual investments from India.

If this system is adopted, and invariably adhered to, we will be enabled, without any material inconvenience, to continue the war so long as our inveterate enemy shall be disposed, or in a condition to carry on the contest. The many other collateral advantages resulting from such a system, and connected with the prosperity and safety of India, are so obvious, it is unnecessary to trouble your Lordship with detailing them.

Having stated all that appears to be necessary, so far as concerns the finances of India, and the commercial resources of the East India Company, as connected with their finances, I wish now to direct your Lordship's attention to the trade of India, in a more extended point of view.

It is notorious that at no period the capital or commercial powers of the East India Company have been able to embrace the whole, or near the whole of the wealth of India, exported from thence by trade to Europe. This is placed beyond a doubt by a great share of the Indian trade now in the possession of neutral nations, a great part of which rests upon the capital and fortune of the servants of the East India Company. Your Lordship will recollect that at the time I introduced the proposition for renewing the Charter of the East India Company, I endeavoured to remedy this obvious absurdity by obliging the East India Company to allot a certain proportion of tonnage to the purposes of private trade. They agreed to it with reluctance, and it is so managed as to render the provision almost illusory. I need not enumerate to your Lordship the causes which have rendered it of no avail. They appear in the applications made to the Government of India by the resident traders in India, and are recorded in the correspondence between the Board of Trade and Supreme Council in India, so that they must be perfectly familiar to your Lordship. In truth, there is no remedy for this evil but two—1st, Alluring the trade of India to resort to the port of London, by diminishing the expenses of doing so. The 2nd is, By authorising the Government of India to license the *appropriation of India-built shipping to the purpose of bringing home that Indian trade, which the means and capital of the East India Company is unable to bring home.* The first of those ways will, I trust, be effectuated by the Bill which Mr. Pitt has agreed to introduce for the reduction of the duties upon imports from India, and the second must be accomplished by giving to the Government in India that authority to license India-built shipping, to which I have already alluded.

This last measure will, I take it for granted, undergo much discussion before it can be carried into execution, but it must be carried. The whole weight of the shipping interest will be opposed to such a proposition, under a most false and erroneous idea that it is prejudicial to their interests. Nothing but ignorance of the subject could lead them to entertain such an idea. They made an attempt to accomplish it by inflaming the interests of the ship carpenters in the river Thames, at the time of the general mutiny in the navy. It was an unhandsome proceeding upon their part, and was resisted by me in a letter I then addressed to the principal ship-builders in the river. I do not know whether they did not choose to answer it, or whether they found it to be unanswerable; but I never received any reply to it. I have often thought upon the subject since, and the more I have thought upon it, the more I am convinced of the truth of every proposition which that letter contains; I send you a copy of it, and you may rest assured, that no exertion shall be wanting on my part speedily to introduce into practice the system detailed in that letter.

It has not reached me in any authentic form, but I am credibly informed that your Lordship, upon the application of the resident traders in India, has authorized a number of India-built ships to be taken up, for the purpose of bringing home the surplus trade of India. I hope the information is true, both because it is a measure of much wisdom, and because it will bring the point directly to issue, and you need not be under any apprehension as to the result of it.

Although, from the influence I have stated, there may be a contest in the Court of Directors with regard to the subject last mentioned, I do not believe there will be any material objection offered against any of the other measures I have had occasion to treat of in this letter; indeed, one leading principle has already been acted upon to a considerable extent, for the Court of Directors have already sent out to India, bullion to the amount of £759,226, and they have it in contemplation to send more. In short, I make no doubt of their being induced to send out what is requisite for the accomplishment of the commercial plan, I have detailed in the course of this letter.

I have nothing further to trouble you with at present. It is only necessary for me to remind you, that although the opinions I have laid before you, rest for the present merely upon the footing of a private unofficial communication, I trust they, or the substance of them, will speedily be conveyed to you in due official form.

I remain, my dear Lord, your's very faithfully,

HENRY DUNDAS.

104. The Marquess Wellesley to the Honourable the Court of Directors.

Propriety of licensing India-built ships for Private Trade between India and England.

Fort William, September 30th, 1800.

Sirs,

Having deemed it to be my duty to revert during the present season to my plan of the 5th of October, 1798, for the encouragement of the private trade between India and the Port of London, I now have the honour to submit to your Honourable Court, a view of the urgent considerations which have determined me to adopt this temporary arrangement for the current year, and to add the reasons which induce me to hope that your honourable Court will speedily confirm my proceedings by a permanent system of regulation, founded on similar principles.

I entertained a confident expectation, that I should have received at an early period of the season the sanction of your honourable Court for reverting to the plan of October, 1798, or for adopting some arrangement equally calculated to facilitate and encourage the private trade between India and England; but I have been disappointed in my expectation of receiving an early and seasonable notification of your final commands; and the usual season for exportation from this port to Europe, is already opening under such circumstances as absolutely compel me to adopt a resolution, which my duty and inclination would have induced me to delay.

The employment of ships built in India, between this port and that of London, is no longer merely a question of expediency, or of liberal commercial policy; the deficiency of the tonnage expected from Europe reduces me to the absolute necessity of providing a large proportion of Indian tonnage, for the service of the present season, in order to secure the conveyance of the heavy articles of your investment, and to fulfil your legal obligations. The only question, on which I retain the power of exercising a free judgment with relation to this subject, is confined to the mode of obtaining the necessary tonnage for these indispensable purposes.

In forming my decision on this question, it was also necessary to consider what provision should be made for the conveyance to the Port of London of such goods, as might be provided during the current season by private British merchants resident in India, beyond the amount of the statutable tonnage of 3,000 tons; and by what regulation the exportation of such goods should be governed. The importance and urgency of both these considerations were greatly enhanced by the actual state of the foreign trade of this port.

The nature of the case appeared to me to limit my decision to an option between the regulation observed in the season 1799–1800, (conformably to the orders of your honourable Court of the 25th of May, 1798,) and the plan contained in the advertisement, published by the Board of Trade under my orders on the 5th of October, 1798.

I have carefully compared the principles, objects, policy, and practical operation of both systems, and I now have the honour to lay before your honourable Court the result of that comparison.

The orders of your honourable Court of the 25th of May, 1798, were framed with a view of facilitating and encouraging the private trade between India and England. The primary objects of those orders were to protect the merchants, not being proprietors of ships, against any undue enhancement of the price of freight by the proprietors of ships, and to prevent persons, being proprietors of ships, and also merchants, from trading to greater advantage than such merchants as might not unite both capacities.

Your orders of the 25th of May, 1798, were considered by the merchants, for whose benefit they were intended, (particularly by the proprietors of heavy goods) to be extremely prejudicial to their interests.

Those orders were received with equal dissatisfaction by the proprietors of ships, who manifested the greatest reluctance to let their ships unconditionally to the Company, although the rate of freight allowed for the ships was comparatively high.

The proprietors of ships, and the freighters (possessing no property in ships) considered it to be for their mutual advantage, that they should be left to make their arrangements with each other; both parties appearing equally adverse to the intervention of the Company's agency.

Under the plan contained in the advertisement of the 5th of October, 1798, the proprietors of ships were enabled to make a more perfect assortment of the cargoes; to load their ships in the most advantageous and expeditious manner; to despatch them at the most favourable periods of the season; and to prevent the loss, which (under the plan adopted in conformity to your orders of the 25th of May, 1798,) the proprietors of ships sustain by unavoidable delays in the adjustment of accounts, and in the payment of the freight by the Company in England.

The proprietors of ships were enabled, under the plan of October, 1798, to afford the freight at a reduced rate, at the same time that they derived a greater profit on that rate than on the higher rates of freight fixed by the Governor-General in Council in 1799–1800, in conformity to your orders of the 25th of May, 1798.

To the merchant who is not proprietor of a ship, the plan contained in the advertisement of the 5th of October, 1798, affords the most important advantages. He obtains a considerable reduction in the rate of freight; he is enabled to settle his engagements with the proprietor of the ship previously to the purchase of goods; to purchase such goods as may be advantageously invested under the existing rates of freight; and to regulate every consignment and draft according to the quantity of the tonnage engaged, to the period of despatching the goods from India, and to that of their expected arrival in England.

The merchant is embarrassed, if compelled, under any modification, to depend on the Company for tonnage, for the arrangement of the rates of freight, or for the distribution of the cargo. He can neither be secure of the requisite quantity of tonnage, nor of the time of despatching his goods from India, nor of the ship on which they may be laden, nor of the mode in which they may be distributed; and his trade is burthened with an expensive rate of freight, which deprives him of all reasonable expectation of profit.

The quantity of tonnage (exclusive of the goods sent in the privileges of the commanders and officers of ships) annually occupied by private goods, shipped from this Presidency alone, in the several years elapsed subsequent to the Act of Parliament in 1793, is stated in the following account:—

	Tons.		Tons.		Tons.
1794–5 .	2,473	1796–7 .	4,659	1798–9 .	6,223
1795–6 .	5,346	1797–8 .	3,787	1799–1800 .	7,748

The correspondence of the Board of Trade with the Governor-General in Council on the subject of the provision of tonnage has been submitted to the consideration of your honourable Court. The reports of that Board, with the documents annexed to them, afford abundant proof, that a much larger quantity of private goods would have been shipped for England during the seasons enumerated in the preceding account (particularly during the year 1799–1800) if adequate encouragement had been extended to the navigation and commerce of your dominions in ships built in the ports of India, and if the British merchants resident in India had been assured of permanent indulgence to their trade with the port of London.

Upon an average of the six years specified in the preceding account, about 5,000 tons of private goods from Bengal alone were annually exported to England; the amount, therefore, of the private goods exported from Bengal alone, during that period of time, has exceeded by 2,000 tons annually the amount of the tonnage allotted by law for all India. It is to be observed, that a considerable portion of the total amount of these 5,000 tons was annually furnished by ships built in India.

Exclusively of two ships recently engaged, and provided with cargoes, to the amount of 1,500 tons, the port of Calcutta now contains above 10,000 tons of shipping, built in India, of a description calculated for the conveyance of cargoes to England. This tonnage has already been tendered, and is actually at command for that purpose.

From the preceding statement, and from the correspondence of the Governor-General in Council with the Board of Trade, it is evident, that the wise policy which dictated the clauses of the Act of Parliament passed in 1793, with respect to the trade of private merchants between India and England, has been to a great degree frustrated by the insufficiency of the tonnage furnished from England, and by the unavoidable expense and inconvenience attending the terms and manner of its provision.

From the quantity of private tonnage now at command in the port of Calcutta, and from the state of perfection which the art of ship-building has already attained in Bengal, (promising a still more rapid progress, and supported by abundant and increasing supplies of timber,) it is certain that this port will always be able to furnish tonnage to whatever extent may be required for conveying to the port of London the trade of the private British merchants of Bengal.

The considerable amount of tonnage occupied by private goods from Bengal in the years 1795–6, 1798–9, and 1799–1800, compared with the amount occupied by goods of a similar description in the years 1794–5, 1796–7, and 1797–8, affords a satisfactory proof that the permission granted to individuals of providing their own tonnage was equally favourable to the interest of the proprietors and to that of the freighters of the ships.

This conclusion is not affected by the large quantity of goods shipped in 1799–1800, under the arrangement made in conformity to your orders of the 25th of May, 1798; for it is well known, that, under a confident expectation of enjoying the continued advantages of the plan of 1798, the merchants had considerably extended their provision of goods for the European markets. Many from necessity, others from motives of respect to the laws, shipped their goods on the tonnage provided by the Government, while others disposed of their goods to the numerous foreign agents then employed in the port of Calcutta.

The quantity of private goods shipped for England in 1799–1800, affords, therefore, an incontrovertible proof of the eagerness and alacrity with which the British merchants resident in Bengal provided goods, with a view to embrace the expected opportunity of conveying their trade to London on terms of advantage; but no argument can justly be drawn from the same circumstance to prove that the continuance of the regulation adopted in 1799–1800 would afford adequate encouragement to the private trade between India and England.

The preceding considerations satisfied me that the plan of hiring ships, on the part of the Company, and of re-letting them to the proprietors of ships, leaving the proprietors of ships and the merchants at liberty to settle the terms of freight, is more advantageous both to the proprietors and freighters of ships, than the arrangement adopted under your orders of the 25th of May, 1798.

In your letter of the 25th of May, 1798, your Honourable Court appears to have intimated an opinion that persons uniting the capacities of proprietors and freighters of ships may trade from Bengal to the port of London, to greater advantage than merchants possessing no property in ships. It appears to me that the difference between the actual charge incurred by merchants being proprietors of ships, on account of the freight of their goods sent to England in their own ships, and the rate of freight paid by merchants not being proprietors of ships, cannot be deemed a profit derived by the proprietor of a ship on his goods. No person will employ any part of his capital in the purchase of property in ships without the prospect of deriving an adequate profit on the capital so invested. I am satisfied that it would not be practicable for the proprietors of ships in this port to maintain an effectual combination for the establishment of enhanced rates of freight; unless such a combination should be maintained, it is to be presumed that the profits of the proprietors of ships on their capitals invested in ships will never exceed, on an average, a reasonable advantage on the amount of those capitals after defraying all the expenses of their ships. This profit must, therefore, be deemed entirely distinct from the profit which the proprietors of ships may derive on their goods conveyed to England in their own ships; and consequently the proprietors of ships cannot be supposed to possess in the general course and conduct of their trade, in the purchase, transportation or sale of their goods, any material advantage over merchants who are not proprietors of ships.

Various additional arguments, involving consequences of a more complicated and comprehensive description, appeared to me to demand, not only that I should recur without delay to the plan of the 5th of October, 1798, but that I should respectfully represent to your honourable Court, in the most distinct terms, my decided and conscientious conviction, that the permanent establishment of a systematic intercourse between the ports of India and that of London, regulated by principles similar to those adopted by this Government in October, 1798, is become indispensable to the united and inseparable interests of the Company and of the nation in India.

Under the beneficial influence of the British Government in India, combined with the increased demand both in Europe and in America for Indian commodities, the produce and manufactures of the British territories in India have increased to an extent far exceeding the amount which the capital applicable to the purchase of the Company's investment can embrace.

The wise policy, the just pretensions, and the increasing commercial resources and political power of Great Britain in India, claim for her subjects the largest attainable share in the valuable and extensive commerce of such articles of Indian produce and manufacture as are necessarily excluded from the Company's investments.

A large proportion of this valuable trade is already in the possession of foreign nations; and unless means be immediately adopted for depriving those nations of the undue share which they have obtained in that trade, the most serious consequences are to be apprehended to the combined interests of the English East India Company and of the British nation.

The British merchants at this Presidency not having obtained the expected permission to freight their ships to the port of London in the last year, agreeably to the plan adopted in October, 1798; goods to a large amount, originally intended for the port of London, were sold to foreigners in the port of Calcutta, and thus diverted to the channel of the foreign trade.

The nature and extent of that trade have undergone a particular investigation. From the accompanying statements your honourable Court will observe, that the trade of America and Portugal with the port of Calcutta alone in 1799-1800, amounted,—

In Imports, 81,81,005 sicca rupees; in Exports, 71,30,372 sicca rupees.

Being an increase in 1799-1800 of the trade carried on in ships bearing American and Portuguese colours, compared with the average of that trade in the three preceding years,—

In Imports, 63,98,678 sicca rupees; in Exports, 43,92,768 sicca rupees.

On the other hand, the imports of the British subjects in the year 1799-1800 amounted only to 47,87,101 sicca rupees, and the exports to 67,66,649 sicca rupees.

Of the trade carried on in foreign bottoms with the other ports in India, from Europe and America, I possess no sufficiently accurate information. It is, however, known to be conducted on a very extensive scale.

In the present season, the trade conveyed in foreign bottoms, if left unrestrained, promises to increase beyond even the rapid progress of last year. From the accompanying statement, your honourable Court will observe, that the port of Calcutta at this early period of the season contains about 8,500 tons of shipping under American, Portuguese, and Danish colours.

I possess no means of forming an accurate estimate of that proportion of the foreign trade from India to Europe, and to America, which is supported by capital actually belonging to the nations, under whose flags the ships are navigated.

It appears, however, from the statements prepared by the reporter of external commerce, that less than one-fourth of the funds imported by the Americans in 1799–1800, for the purchase of their investments, was brought from America. Of the bullion £200,000 was imported from London, and the remainder from other parts of Europe and from the Island of Madeira. I have not been able to ascertain the proportion of British capital employed in the trade between India and Portugal. Admitting the whole capital employed in the foreign trade with India to belong to the nations under whose flags the ships are navigated, the undue proportion which they have obtained of that trade, to the injury of the British merchants, demands the most serious attention.

The trade conveyed in the foreign ships is conducted with all the advantages of a comparatively low rate of freight; of strict economy in the management of the concern; and of voyages and returns of extraordinary expedition and celerity. The voyage from America to Calcutta is frequently performed in less than four months. In the last season several American ships disposed of their imports, purchased their cargo for exportation, and left the port within twenty-five, and some within twenty, days from the date of their arrival.

Under all the existing impediments, and under the uncertainty which has hitherto embarrassed the trade of the British merchant in India, it is impossible that his goods can reach the markets of the continent of Europe through the channel of the public sales in England, at so low a price as the goods conveyed directly from India to the same markets in foreign bottoms. The Company's sales in England must necessarily be affected by the quantity of Indian goods passing into the markets of the continent of Europe through the channel of the foreign trade, and the profits of the private British merchant, whose goods are disposed of at the Company's sales, must be proportionably diminished.

Although the voyage by which the produce of India is conveyed in foreign ships to Europe may occasionally be circuitous, the superior advantages, enumerated in the preceding paragraphs, enable the proprietors of the goods to dispose of them at a lower price than that for which the same descriptions of goods can be brought to the continental markets of Europe, if exported from India by British merchants under the heavy freight [1], and other incumbrances to which their trade is at present subject.

It must ever be impracticable, if it were justifiable or politic, by any restrictions or penalties on the trade of the British subjects, to prevent the increasing produce and manufactures of India from being conveyed to the markets in Europe, where a demand for such articles shall exist. Such restrictions tend to throw the trade into the hands of foreign nations, and to enable them to supply the markets of Europe on terms which must equally affect the Company's sales in England. If the same goods which now pass to the continent of Europe, through foreign hands, were brought to the Company's sales in England, the effect on the general price of articles exposed to sale at the Company's warehouses would be less prejudicial than that now experienced from the sale of those goods in the markets on the continent of Europe. The Company and the private British merchant would equally feel the advantage in the improvement of the general sales in England, and the private trade of India would become a fertile source of wealth and strength to the

---

[1] The Portuguese and Americans pay only one per cent. on Indian produce imported and re-exported. By the Warehousing Act lately passed in Great Britain, calicoes pay 2½, and muslins 7½, per cent. on the sales, if sold for exportation. All other goods (excepting cotton, spices, bullion, &c., diamonds, precious stones, which pay no duties) pay two per cent. exclusive of the convoy duty, payable by the Importers. A reduction of those duties in England is absolutely necessary to complete the system of drawing the private trade of India to the port of London.

British nation, instead of contributing to the opulence and aggrandizement of foreign powers.

The interests of the Company, and of the British nation, are undivided and inseparable with relation to this important question. Every principle of justice and policy demands the extension of the utmost practicable facility to the British merchants in India, for the export from India to the port of London, of the largest possible proportion of the manufactures and produce of India, not required for the Company's investment. Such advantageous terms of freight and such other benefits should be opened to the British merchants in India as should not only remove every inducement to conduct the trade through foreign channels, but should enable the British merchants in India to enter into a competition in the markets of Europe with merchants trading in goods of similar produce or manufacture provided by foreign capital.

To foreigners the indulgence may safely be extended of purchasing, with their own capital, such part of the manufactures or produce of India, calculated for the European or American markets, as may not be embraced by the capital employed in the purchase of the Company's investment and of the cargoes of the British merchants resident in India.

It is, however, doubtful whether [1] foreign nations would be able to retain any considerable proportion of the trade from India to Europe, were the British merchants in India permitted to avail themselves of their superior means of drawing the whole of the trade to England. Their local knowledge, added to all the advantages necessarily derived from a constant residence on the spot, must always enable them to command a supply of goods, of a better quality, and at a cheaper rate, than foreign merchants can obtain. In the conveyance of Indian goods to Europe rests the foreign merchant's sole advantage over the British. The

[1] The Americans obtain Indian goods so much cheaper by a direct intercourse with India than they could through the circuitous route of Europe, that they will probably continue to deal largely even on their own capital with India. It is now the ordinary practice of the Americans, under the last treaty of commerce, to ship cargoes in India for America, to touch at some port in America, and without transhipping or unloading the goods in America to proceed directly to Europe, and to dispose of their Indian cargo in an European port. This practice is unquestionably contrary to the treaty of commerce with America.

superior facility which the foreign merchant enjoys in this respect gives him so decided a command over the trade, that he is enabled not only to outbid the British merchant in India, but also to undersell him in the markets of Europe.

Were the British merchants in India permitted to provide their own tonnage as occasion might require, every reason exists to justify a belief that they would soon possess themselves of nearly the whole of the private export trade from India to Europe, and would render London the universal mart for the manufactures and produce of Asia.

If the capital of the merchants in India, and the remittance of the fortunes of individuals, should not supply funds sufficient for the conduct of the whole private export trade from India to Europe, no dangerous consequences could result from applying to this branch of commerce capital drawn directly from the British empire in Europe.

Beneficial consequences of the utmost importance would certainly result to the British empire in India from any considerable increase of its active capital, which is known not to bear a just proportion to the productive powers of the country.

The necessary effect of such an increase of active capital in India would be to augment the produce and manufactures of your dominions to the full extent of any possible demand. The high rate of interest on money applied to mercantile purposes, and the charge of the public debt would consequently be diminished in India, while every source, both of public and private credit would be proportionably improved. No possibility appears of any injurious consequences resulting to the British Empire in Europe from an event so advantageous to India. It cannot be supposed that the private trade of India will ever absorb any portion of British capital which can find more advantageous employment at home. If any portion of British capital be now employed in the American, or Portuguese, or Danish trade with India, the general interests of Great Britain will unquestionably be promoted by inviting, under increased advantages, the application of the same funds to the trade of the private British merchants resident within the Company's dominions.

From whatever source the capital of the private British trade in India might be derived, the goods would be obtained in India under the same wise, humane, and salutary regulations now enforced with respect to the provision of every article of produce or manufacture in this country, either by the Company or by private merchants; Great Britain would enjoy all the advantages of that trade which is now a source of increasing wealth and strength to foreign nations, and which tends ultimately to introduce foreign intrigue, to establish foreign influence, and to aggrandize foreign power in India.

It would be equally unjust and impolitic to extend any facility to the trade of the British merchants in India, by sacrificing or hazarding the Company's rights and privileges; by injuring its commercial interests; by admitting an indiscriminate and unrestrained commercial intercourse between England and India; or by departing from any of the fundamental principles of policy, which now govern the British establishments in India.

It may be urged, that if a considerable proportion of the goods now exported from India to the continent of Europe by foreigners, were to be imported into England by the British merchants in India, under rates of freight more advantageous than those now paid by the Company, the demand for the Company's goods would be reduced, and the value of the Company's goods would be impaired.

It has already been observed that the public sales of East India goods in England must necessarily be affected by the aggregate quantity of those goods sold in the continental markets of Europe; and that the effect on the sales in England, would probably be less prejudicial and could not be more so, if a larger proportion of the goods provided in India for the European markets should be imported into England, and sold in the first instance at the Company's sales.

The long establishment of the Company's factories in India, the skill of its servants regularly educated for the conduct of those factories, the habitual confidence of the manufacturers in the good faith and integrity of the Company have secured to the Company so decided a superiority in the provision of the most valuable articles of piece-goods and raw silk, that no private merchant by any practicable reduction of freight can be enabled to rival the Company in these important articles of its investment.

In the first purchase of sugar and other gruff goods, the trade of the private British merchant has more nearly reached that of the Company; nor will the Company ever be able to trade advantageously in these articles, unless the Government in

India shall resort to ships built in India, for the conveyance of such goods; the valuable branches of your investment will, it is supposed, be always conveyed with more advantage in your regular ships.

If the British merchants should be permitted to employ ships built in India under the plan of October, 1798, the Company's gruff goods may also be conveyed to England in ships of a similar description, at rates of freight equally advantageous with those paid by the private merchants. The Company will, therefore, derive a considerable benefit in this branch of trade, from encouraging the trade of the private British merchants in India [1]; at present neither the Company nor the private British merchants can rival foreigners in the markets of Europe in the less valuable articles of Indian produce and manufactures.

It is now evident that the extra tonnage engaged in England by the Company for the service of India can never be rendered a practicable channel through which the British private trade of India can contend with foreign adventure. This observation necessarily applies with more force to the regular ships of the Company, although experience has proved those ships to be admirably calculated for the conveyance of the Company's valuable investment.

The plan contained in the advertisement of the 5th of October, 1798, affords to the British merchants, every necessary facility for the conduct of the private trade from India to England, while the important principles of the trade and government of India are preserved from hazard, and sufficient precautions are provided against all the dangers justly apprehended from an unrestricted commercial intercourse between England and India.

The essential object of preventing the resort to India of persons unlicensed by the Company is not affected. The powers of the Government in India over unlicensed persons remain in full vigour and efficiency. No goods or passengers can be received in the private ships either in India or in England, without the sanction of the Company or of its government; the voyage to England and the return to India, are required to be performed under the instructions and control of the same authority; and as

---

[1] The probable saving to the Company in the present season by the conveyance of their gruff goods in ships built in India may amount to £20,000.

the proprietors of the ships, the commanders and officers, the seamen, (mostly natives of India) and all the persons concerned in the immediate conduct of the trade, are subject to the authority of the British Government in India, it is always in the power of the Company and of its government, to prevent the perversion of an intercourse thus regulated between India and England to any sinister purposes endangering the rights and privileges of the Company, or the interests of the British Empire.

Omitting the difference in the rate of freight, these considerations alone are sufficient to recommend the employment of ships built in India in the private trade between India and Great Britain. Over private ships furnished from England the Company and their government in India, could not exercise an equally efficient control.

It is remarkable that the principle which has hitherto regulated the commercial intercourse between India and England has actually occasioned the very evils which it was intended to avert.

The operation of this erroneous principle has forced the trade between India and Europe from a channel, in which it could have been controlled and regulated without difficulty, into the hands of foreign nations, where it cannot, without considerable difficulty be subjected to any degree of controul, regulation, or restraint: the same mistaken policy has filled the Ports of India with the ships of foreign nations, has enabled those nations to rival the Company both in Europe and in India in many articles of its export and import trade, has invited from Europe and America adventurers of every description; and, by the number and activity of these foreign agents, has menaced the foundations of your commercial and political interests throughout every part of Asia, and even within your own dominions.

If the extension of additional indulgences to the British merchant necessarily involved the admission of numerous British adventurers into India, the wisdom of your honourable Court could not fail to remark that your Government can always with less difficulty control the operations of British, than those of foreign agents; while the danger to be apprehended from the views and designs of foreigners of every description must ever be greater than any which can probably arise from an increased resort of British subjects, under such limitations and restraints as your wisdom may frame, and the vigilance of your government in India may be enabled to enforce.

But it does not appear probable that any increase of the

private British trade of India would necessarily produce a proportional augmentation in the number of British agents resorting to your dominions; the British merchants now resident in India being equal to the conduct of much more extensive concerns, and likely to be employed by persons engaged in commercial concerns at home, who might easily conduct their operations with India through those British subjects actually established within your dominions.

On the other hand, foreigners generally deal directly with the natives, or with foreign houses of agency: the number of these houses (in consequence of the war) is now inconsiderable; the increase of foreign adventurers will, therefore, be a necessary consequence of any considerable increase of the trade in foreign hands. Foreign ships also, being necessarily exempt from the control of the British Government in Europe, offer to every emissary of the enemy, and to every dangerous political adventurer, an easy entrance into India. In proportion to the increased resort of foreign ships to our ports in India, foreign intrigue will find a more ready channel of admission. It is a well-known fact, that those to whom your permission and license to visit India have been refused usually resort to foreign ships, and thus evade your authority. The same channel is also always open to afford refuge and the means of escape to every public defaulter and delinquent from the authority of your government in India.

It is impossible to check the resort of the ships of foreign nations to India, by any other regulation than by rendering the trade unprofitable to foreign adventure. This effect cannot be accomplished otherwise than by enabling the British merchants in India to undersell foreigners in the markets of Europe. A system, which, under due regulation, shall afford to the British merchants in India, the greatest practicable facility of conveying their trade to England, instead of endangering the stability of the trade and power of the Company, and of the nation in India, will, therefore, constitute the most solid basis of security for the preservation of both.

The preceding observations may, I trust, satisfy your honourable Court, that the principles of the plan of the 5th of October, 1798, combine the requisite indulgence to the private trade, with the indispensable precautions necessary for securing your interests in India.

It is not my duty to enter into any detailed discussion of the objections urged by the ship-builders in England, against the admission of ships built in India, to a participation in the trade from India to the port of London; it may not however be useless to add some remarks on this part of the subject.

Experience having proved that tonnage cannot be furnished from England, on terms which would enable the British merchants in India to rival foreigners in the trade between India and Europe, the exclusion of ships built in India from the port of London would not increase the number of British ships hitherto engaged in the Indian trade, in any proportion which could materially benefit the ship-builders in England. This measure, therefore, without any proportional benefit to the ship-builders in England, would perpetuate and aggravate the evils now experienced from the restraints imposed on the private trade between India and England; on the other hand, by admitting ships built in India to partake of the trade to England, the ship-builders and other artists, manufacturers, and traders in England will reap all the benefits arising from the large sums expended in the repair of the numerous ships annually resorting to England from the ports of India. Other interests connected with the building of ships in England will also derive the profit resulting from the great demand for the articles necessary in the construction and outfit of the ships built in the ports of India; the fact being established, that many of those articles must necessarily be brought from England.

On their return to India, these ships from the moderation of their rates of freight will afford a most advantageous mode of conveyance for such of the manufactures of the British Empire in Europe, as may be demanded in India; consequently the facilities granted to the private trade, and to the ships built in India will serve to encourage the exportation of British manufactures to Asia, to whatever extent the demand may be enlarged.

I have thus carefully revised the plan contained in the advertisement of October, 1798, for the encouragement of the trade of the British merchants resident in India with England; I have compared that plan with the arrangement adopted under the orders of your honourable Court of the 25th of May, 1798; I have considered the probable effects of any future attempt to provide for the conveyance of the private trade of India to the port of London, either in the Company's regular ships, or in extra ships hired in England; and I have adverted to the comparative practical operation of the systems adopted by this government in the years 1798, 1799, and 1800, as it appears on the accounts of the exports and imports of the port of Calcutta in each of those years; I have also submitted to your examination a combined view of the motives which induce me to revert to the plan of October, 1798, for the present season, and to form an anxious expectation, that my conduct in this proceeding may meet with your approbation and countenance, and may become the foundation of an improved and durable system of intercourse between India and England under the sanction of your authority.

The rapid growth of the foreign trade during the last season, urgently demanded the immediate interference of your government on the spot. The number of foreign ships actually in the port of Calcutta, the alacrity, enterprize and skill of the foreign agents now assiduously employed in providing cargoes, and the necessary inaction and languor of the British private trade, embarrassed by the restraints of the existing law, created a serious apprehension in my mind, that any further delay in the decision of this momentous question might occasion evils, of which the remedy might hereafter become considerably difficult, if not absolutely impracticable. The unrestrained progress of the foreign trade in the present season, added to its great increase during the last, might have established its predominance over the private trade of British subjects to an extent, which no future regulation might have proved sufficient to limit or restrain. The difficulty of diverting this lucrative commerce from the channel into which it had been forced, would naturally be aggravated in proportion to the length of time during which the trade should continue to flow in that course.

Under these serious impressions, and convinced that a prompt decision was demanded with a degree of exigency equal to the importance of the question at issue, I directed the accompanying notice to be published at Fort William, on the 19th instant, and I ordered the governments of Fort St. George and Bombay, to publish correspondent advertisements at those Presidencies with such modifications, as local circumstances may render indispensably necessary.

It will rest with your honourable Court to determine, whether this plan shall be rendered permanent. A temporary restraint is now applied to the progress of the foreign trade in India, during the present season; and a temporary encouragement is granted, for the same period of time to that of British subjects resident within your dominions, ample time is thus afforded for the deliberate formation of your final judgment; the result of which I shall await with a respectful, but confident hope, that your wisdom may approve and perpetuate the policy which dictated my orders of the 5th of October, 1798, and of the 19th of September, 1800; and that your liberality may confirm to all the interests affected by this important measure, the lasting enjoyment of those commercial and political advantages, which it has been my constant endeavour, under your countenance and favor, to cultivate, to improve, and to extend.

I have the honour to be, honourable Sirs,
with the greatest respect,
Your most obedient and faithful servant,
WELLESLEY.

X. EDUCATION OF CIVIL SERVANTS.

105. The Governor-General's Notes with respect to the foundation of a College at Fort William.

Necessity of a special collegiate training of Civil Servants. Plan of the proposed institution, and its anticipated benefits.

Fort William, 10th July, 1800.

The British possessions in India now constitute one of the most extensive and populous empires in the world. The immediate administration of the government of the various provinces and nations composing this empire is principally confided to the European civil servants of the East India Company. Those provinces, namely, Bengal, Behar, Orissa, and Benares, the Company's Jaghire in the Carnatic, the northern Circars, the Baramahal, and other districts ceded by the peace of Seringapatam, in 1792, which are under the more immediate and direct administration of the European civil servants of the Company, are acknowledged to form the most opulent and flourishing parts of India; in which property, life, civil order, and religious liberty are more secure, and the people enjoy a larger portion of the benefits of good government, than any other country in this quarter of the globe. The duty and policy of the British Government in India therefore require, that the system of confiding the immediate exercise of every branch and department of the government to Europeans, educated in its own service, and subject to its own direct control, should be diffused as widely as possible, as well with a view to the stability of our own interests, as to the happiness and welfare of our native subjects. This principle formed the basis of the wise and benevolent system introduced by Lord Cornwallis, for the improvement of the internal government of the provinces immediately subject to the Presidency of Bengal.

In proportion to the extension of this beneficial system, the duties of the European civil servants of the East India Company are become of greater magnitude and importance: the denominations of writer, factor, and merchant, by which the several classes of the civil service are still distinguished, are now utterly inapplicable to the nature and extent of the duties discharged, and of the occupations pursued by the civil servants of the Company.

To dispense justice to millions of people of various languages, manners, usages and religions; to administer a vast and complicated system of revenue throughout districts equal in extent to some of the most considerable kingdoms in Europe; to maintain civil order in one of the most populous and litigious regions of the world; these are now the duties of the larger proportion of the civil servants of the Company. The senior merchants composing the five Courts of Circuit and Appeal under the Presidency of Bengal exercise in each of those Courts a jurisdiction of greater local extent, applicable to a larger population, and occupied in the determination of causes infinitely more intricate and numerous than that of any regularly constituted courts of justice in any part of Europe. The senior or junior merchants, employed in the several magistracies and Zillah Courts, the writers or factors filling the stations of registers and assistants to the several courts and magistrates, exercise in different degrees, functions of a nature, either purely judicial, or intimately connected with the administration of the police, and with the maintenance of the peace and good order of their respective districts. Commercial or mercantile knowledge, is not only unnecessary throughout every branch of the judicial department, but those civil servants who are invested with the powers of magistracy, or attached to the judicial department in any ministerial capacity, although bearing the denomination of merchants, factors or writers, are bound by law, and by the solemn obligation of an oath, to abstain from every commercial and mercantile pursuit; the mercantile title which they bear, not only affords no description of their duty, but is entirely at variance with it.

The pleadings in the several courts, and all important judicial transactions, are conducted in the native languages. The law which the Company's judges are bound to administer throughout the country is not the law of England, but that law to which the natives had long been accustomed under their former sovereigns, tempered and mitigated by the voluminous regulations of the Governor-General in Council, as well as by the general spirit of the British constitution. These observations are sufficient to prove, that no more arduous or complicated duties of magistracy exist in the world, no qualifications more various, or more comprehensive, can be imagined than those which are required from every British subject, who enters the seat of judgment within the limits of the Company's empire in India.

To the administration of the revenue, many of the preceding observations will apply with equal force; the merchants, factors and writers, employed in this department also, are bound by law to abjure the mercantile denomination appropriated to their respective classes in the Company's service; nor is it possible for a collector of the revenue, or for any civil servant employed under him, to discharge his duty with common justice, either to the state, or to the people, unless he shall be conversant in the language, manners, and usages of the country; and in the general principles of the law, as administered in the several courts of justice. In addition to the ordinary judicial and executive functions of the Judges, Magistrates, and Collectors, the Judges and Magistrates occasionally act in the capacity of Governors of their respective districts, employing the military, and exercising other extensive powers. The Judges, Magistrates, and Collectors, are also respectively required by law to propose, from time to time, to the Governor-General in Council, such amendments of the existing laws, or such new laws as may appear to them to be necessary for the welfare and good government of their respective districts. In this view the civil servants employed in the departments of Judicature and Revenue, constitute a species of subordinate legislative council to the Governor-General in Council, and also form a channel of communication, by which the Government ought to be enabled, at all times, to ascertain the wants and wishes of the people. The remarks applied to these two main branches of the civil service, namely, those of Judicature and Revenue, are at least equally forcible in their application to those branches which may be described under the general terms of the Political and Financial Departments, comprehending the offices of Chief Secretary, the various stations in the Secretary's office, in the Treasury, in the office of Accountant-General, together with all the public officers employed in conducting the current business at the seat of Government. To these must be added the Diplomatic branch, including the Secretary in the political department, and the several residencies at the Courts of our dependent and tributary Princes, or of other native powers of India.

It is certainly desirable, that all these stations should be filled by the civil servants of the Company: it is equally evident, that qualifications are required in each of these stations, either wholly foreign to commercial habits, or far exceeding the limits of a commercial education.

Even that department of this empire, which is denominated exclusively commercial, requires knowledge and habits different, in a considerable degree, from those which form the mercantile character in Europe; nor can the Company's investment ever be conducted with the greatest possible advantage and honour to themselves, or with adequate justice to their subjects, unless their commercial agents shall possess many of the qualifications of statesmen, enumerated in the preceding observations. The manufacturers, and other industrious classes, whose productive labour is the source of the investment, bear so great a proportion to the total population of the Company's dominions, that the general happiness and prosperity of the country must essentially depend on the conduct of the commercial servants employed in providing the investment: their conduct cannot be answerable to such a charge, unless they shall be conversant in the native languages, and in the customs and manners of the people, as well as in the laws by which the country is governed. The peace, order, and welfare of whole provinces may be materially affected by the malversations, or even by the ignorance and errors of a commercial resident, whose management touches the dearest and most valuable interests, and enters into the domestic concerns of numerous bodies of people, active and acute from habitual industry, and jealous of any act of power injurious to their properties, or contrary to their prejudices and customs.

The Civil servants of the English East India Company, therefore, can no longer be considered as the agents of a commercial concern. They are, in fact, the ministers and officers of a powerful sovereign; they must now be viewed in that capacity, with reference, not to their nominal, but to their real occupations. They are required to discharge the functions of Magistrates, Judges, Ambassadors, and Governors of provinces, in all the complicated and extensive relations of those sacred trusts and exalted stations, and under peculiar circumstances, which greatly enhance the solemnity of every public obligation, and aggravate the difficulty of every public charge. Their duties are those of statesmen in every other part of the world, with no other characteristic differences than the obstacles opposed by an unfavourable climate, by a foreign language, by the peculiar usages and laws of India, and by the manners of its inhabitants. Their studies, the discipline of their education, their habits of life, their manners and morals should, therefore, be so ordered and regulated as to establish a just conformity between their personal consideration, and the dignity and importance of their public stations, and to maintain a sufficient correspondence between their qualifications and their duties. Their education should be founded in a general knowledge of those branches of literature and science which form the basis of the education of persons destined to similar occupations in Europe. To this foundation should be added an intimate acquaintance with the history, languages, customs and manners of the people of India, with the Mahommedan and Hindoo codes of law and religion, and with the political and commercial interests and relations of Great Britain in Asia. They should be regularly instructed in the principles and system which constitute the foundation of that wise code of regulations and laws enacted by the Governor-General in Council for the purpose of securing to the people of this empire the benefit of the ancient and accustomed laws of the country, administered in the spirit of the British constitution. They should be well informed of the true and sound principles of the British constitution, and sufficiently grounded in the general principles of ethics, civil jurisprudence, the law of nations, and general history, in order that they may be enabled to discriminate the characteristic differences of the several codes of law administered within the British Empire in India, and practically to combine the spirit of each in the dispensation of justice, and in the maintenance of order and good government. Finally, their early habits should be so formed, as to establish in their minds such solid foundations of industry, prudence, integrity, and religion, as should effectually guard them against those temptations and corruptions with which the nature of this climate, and the peculiar depravity of the people of India, will surround and assail them in every station, especially upon their first arrival in India. The early discipline of the service should be calculated to counteract the defects of the climate and the vices of the people, and to form a natural barrier against habitual indolence, dissipation, and licentious indulgence; the spirit of emulation, in honourable and useful pursuits, should be kindled and kept alive by the continual prospect of distinction, and reward, of profit, and honour; nor should any precaution be relaxed in India, which is deemed necessary in England, to furnish a sufficient supply of men qualified to fill the high offices of the State with credit to themselves and with advantage to the public. Without such a constant succession of men in the several branches and departments of this Government, the wisdom and benevolence of the law must prove vain and inefficient. Whatever course and system of discipline and study may be deemed requisite in England to secure an abundant and pure source for the efficient supply of the public service, the peculiar nature of our establishments in the East, (so far from admitting any relaxation of those wise and salutary rules and restraints,) demands that they should be enforced with a degree of additional vigilance and care, proportioned to the aggravated difficulties of the civil service, and to the numerous hazards surrounding the entrance of public life in India.

It is unnecessary to enter into any examination of facts to prove, that no system of education, study, or discipline, now exists, either in Europe or in India, founded on the principles, or directed to the objects described in the preceding pages; but it may be useful in this place to review the course through which the junior civil servants of the East India Company now enter upon the important duties of their respective stations, to consider to what degree they now possess or can attain any means of qualifying themselves sufficiently for those stations, and to examine whether the great body of the civil servants of the East India Company, at any of the Presidencies, can now be deemed competent to discharge their arduous and comprehensive trusts in a manner correspondent to the interests and honour of the British name in India, or to the prosperity and happiness of our native subjects.

The age at which the writers usually arrive in India is from sixteen to eighteen; their parents or friends in England, from a variety of considerations, are naturally desirous, not only to accelerate the appointment at home, but to despatch the young man to India at the earliest possible period. Some of these young men have been educated with an express view to the civil service in India, on principles utterly erroneous, and inapplicable to its actual condition; conformably to this error, they have received a limited education, confined principally to commercial knowledge, and in no degree extended to those liberal studies which constitute the basis of education at public schools in England. Even this limited course of study is interrupted at the early period of fifteen or seventeen years.

It would be superfluous to enter into any argument to demonstrate the absolute insufficiency of this class of young men to execute the duties of any station whatever in the civil service of the Company beyond the menial, laborious, unwholesome and unprofitable duty of a mere copying-clerk. Those who have received the benefits of a better education, have the misfortune to find the course of their studies prematurely interrupted at the critical period when its utility is first felt, and before they have been enabled to secure the fruits of early application.

Both descriptions of young men, those whose education has been originally erroneous and defective, and those, the early promise of whose studies has been unseasonably broken, once arrived in India, are equally precluded from the means, either of commencing a new and judicious course of study, adapted to their new situation, or of prosecuting that course which had been prematurely interrupted. Not only no encouragement is offered by the present constitution and practice of the civil service to any such pursuits, but difficulties and obstacles are presented by both, which render it nearly impossible for any young man, whatever may be his disposition, to pursue any systematic plan of study, either with a view to remedy the defects, or to improve the advantages of his former education.

On the arrival of the writers in India, they are either stationed in the interior of the country, or employed in some office at the Presidency.

If stationed in the interior of the country, they are placed in situations which require a knowledge of the language and customs of the natives; or of the regulations and laws; or of the general principles of jurisprudence; or of the details of the established system of revenue; or of the nature of the Company's investment; or of many of these branches of information combined. In all these branches of knowledge, the young writers are totally uninformed. They are consequently unequal to their prescribed duties. In some cases, their superior in office experiencing no benefit from their services, leaves them unemployed. In this state many devote their time to those luxuries and enjoyments which their situation enables them to command, without making any effort to qualify themselves for the important stations to which they are destined. They remain sunk in indolence, until, from their station in the service, they succeed to offices of high public trust.

Positive incapacity is the necessary result of these pernicious habits of inaction; the principles of public integrity are endangered, and the successful administration of the whole Government exposed to hazard. This has been the unhappy course of many, who have conceived an early disgust in provincial stations against business, to which they have found themselves unequal, and who have been abandoned to the effects of despondency and sloth.

Even the young men whose dispositions are the most promising, if stationed in the interior of the country at an early period after their arrival in India, labour under great disadvantages. They also find themselves unequal to such duties as require an acquaintance with the languages, or with the branches of knowledge already described. If intensely employed in the subordinate details of office, they are absolutely precluded from reviving any former acquirements, or from establishing those foundations of useful knowledge indispensably necessary to enable them hereafter to execute the duties of important stations with ability and credit. Harassed with the ungrateful task of transcribing papers and accounts, or with other equally fatiguing and fruitless labours of a copying-clerk or index-maker, their pursuit of useful knowledge cannot be systematic; their studies must be desultory and irregular, and their attention to any definite pursuit is still more distracted by the uncertainty of the nature of those employments to which they may hereafter be nominated. No course of study having been pointed out by public institution, no selection prescribed by authority of the branches of knowledge appropriated to each department and class of the service, diligence is lost for want of a guide, and the most industrious are discouraged by the apprehension, that their studies may prove fruitless, and may frustrate instead of promoting their advancement in the public service.

When their rank in the service has entitled them to succeed to offices of importance, the current duties of those offices necessarily engross their whole attention. It is then too late to revert to any systematic plan of study with a view to acquire those qualifications, of which, in the ordinary discharge of their official functions, they feel the hourly want. If, at this late season, they should make an effort to acquire knowledge, it must be sought by the interruption of their current business, to the detriment of the public interests, and to the inconvenience or injury of the individuals subject to their authority.

With respect to the young men attached to offices at the Presidency, their duty consists chiefly in transcribing papers. This duty, if pursued with the utmost diligence and assiduity, affords little knowledge of public affairs, is often prejudicial to health, and would be better performed by any native or Portuguese writer. They attain no distinct knowledge of the public records; because they pursue no regular course of reading, examining, or comparing the documents which compose those records; they have, indeed, scarcely time to understand and digest those papers which they are employed to transcribe; their acquaintance even with the current affairs of the Government must be limited and partial, and must rather tend to confuse than to instruct their minds. At the expiration of the period, during which they usually remain in these situations at the Presidency, their knowledge of public business is necessarily superficial and incorrect. Having had little intercourse with the natives, these young men are in general extremely deficient in the knowledge of the language of the country. In the meanwhile their close and laborious application to the hourly business of transcribing papers has been an insuperable obstacle to their advancement in any other branch of knowledge, and at the close of two or three years, they have lost the fruits of their European studies, without having gained any useful knowledge of Asiatic literature or business. Those whose dispositions lead them to idleness and dissipation, find greater temptations to indulgence and extravagance at the Presidency than in the provinces; many instances occur in which they fall into irretrievable courses of gaming and vice, and totally destroy their health and fortunes. Some succeed, in the ordinary progress of the service, to employments, in which their incapacity or misconduct becomes conspicuous to the natives, disgraceful to themselves and to the British name, and injurious to the State.

All these descriptions of young men, upon their first arrival in India, are now exposed to a disadvantage, the most perilous which can be encountered at an early period of life. Once landed in India, their studies, manners, morals, expenses or conduct are no longer subject to any degree of regulation or direction. No system is established for their guidance, improvement, or restraint; no authority has been constituted with either the duty or power of enforcing any such system; and they are abandoned, at the age of sixteen or eighteen, with affluent incomes to pursue their own inclinations, without the superintendence or control of parent, guardian, or master, often without a friend to advise or admonish, or even to instruct them in the ordinary details and modes of an Indian life.

The practice of consigning the young writers to the care of friends resident in India, affords no adequate remedy to this evil. Those friends are often incompetent to the arduous and delicate task imposed upon them; and it frequently happens that they may be so far removed from the spot at which the young man may be stationed by the Government, that years may elapse before he may have been able even to see the persons appointed by his European friends to superintend his introduction into India.

In earlier periods of our establishment, when the annual incomes of the civil servants were of a more fluctuating nature, and derived from sources more vague and indefinite, the tables of the senior servants were usually open to those recently arrived from Europe; and the young writers, upon their first landing in India, were frequently admitted and domiciliated in the families established at the Presidency or in the provinces.

The objections to this loose and irregular system are numerous and obvious. Without entering upon that topic, it is sufficient to observe, that the definite and regular sources of profit, established in the civil service by Lord Cornwallis, have occasioned a material alteration in the economy of every private family among the civil servants.

Incomes being limited and ascertained, and no other source

of emolument now existing beyond the annual savings from the regulated salaries, the tables of the civil servants can no longer be open to receive the numerous body of writers annually arriving from Europe; still less can these young men be generally admitted to reside habitually in families of which the annual expenses are now necessarily restrained within certain and regular bounds.

Many of the young men, on their first arrival, are, therefore, compelled to support the expense of a table; the result of this necessity is obvious, and forms one leading cause of expense and dissipation.

Under all these early disadvantages, without rule or system to direct their studies; without any prescribed object of useful pursuit connected with future reward, emolument, or distinction; without any guide to regulate, or authority to control their conduct, or to form, improve, or preserve their morals; it is highly creditable to the individual characters of the civil servants of the East India Company, that so many instances have occurred in various branches and departments of the civil service at all the Presidencies, of persons who have discharged their public duties with considerable respect and honour.

It has been justly observed, that all the merits of the civil servants are to be ascribed to their own characters, talents, and exertions, while their defects must be imputed to the constitution and practice of the service, which have not been accommodated to the progressive changes of our situation in India, and have not kept pace with the growth of this empire, or with the increasing extent and importance of the functions and duties of the civil servants.

The study and acquisition of the languages have, however, been extended in Bengal, and the general knowledge and qualifications of the civil servants have been improved. The proportion of the civil servants in Bengal, who have made a considerable progress towards the attainment of the qualifications requisite in their several stations, appears great, and even astonishing, when viewed with relation to the early disadvantages, embarrassments, and defects of the civil service. But this proportion will appear very different when compared with the exigencies of the State, with the magnitude of these provinces, and with the total number of the civil servants, which must supply the succession to the great offices of the Government. It must be admitted that the great body of the civil servants in Bengal is not at present sufficiently qualified to discharge the duties of the several arduous stations in the administration of this empire; and that it is peculiarly deficient in the judicial, fiscal, financial, and political branches of the Government.

The state of the civil services of Madras and Bombay is still more defective than that of Bengal. Various causes have concurred to aggravate, in an extreme degree, at both those Presidencies all the defects existing in the civil service of Bengal, while many circumstances peculiar to those Presidencies have favoured the growth of evils at present unknown in this. The condition of the writers, on their first arrival at either of the subordinate Presidencies, is still more destitute, and more exposed to hazard, than at Calcutta.

The study or acquisition of the languages, and of other necessary attainments, has not been extended in the civil service at Madras or Bombay to any considerable degree. To this remark, eminent and meritorious individual exceptions exist in the civil service at both subordinate Presidencies; but those exceptions are not sufficiently numerous to constitute a general rule. But whatever may be the actual condition of the civil service in its superior classes at any of the Presidencies, if the arduous duties of that service have been justly defined in the preceding pages, if the qualifications requisite for their discharge have been truly described, if the neglected and exposed condition of the early stages of the service has not been exaggerated, it must be admitted, that those stages of the service require additional safeguards, and a more effectual protection. The extraordinary exertions of individual diligence, the partial success of singular talents, or of peculiar prudence and virtue, constitute no rational foundation of a public institution, which should rest on general comprehensive and uniform principles. If the actual state of the higher classes of the civil service were such as to justify a confidence in the general competency of the civil servants to meet the exigencies of their duty, the necessity of correcting the evils stated in the preceding pages would still remain, unless the facts alleged could be disproved. It would still be a duty incumbent on the Government to remove any obstacles tending to embarrass or retard the progress of their servants in attaining the qualifications necessary for their respective stations. The Government is not released from this duty by the extraordinary, or even general exertion of those servants to surmount the early difficulties of the first stages of the service. If the good Government of this empire be the primary duty of its sovereign, it must ever be a leading branch of that duty to facilitate to the public officers and ministers the means of qualifying themselves for their respective functions. The efficiency of the service cannot wisely or conscientiously be left to depend on the success of individual or accidental merit, struggling against the defects of established institutions. A due administration of our affairs can alone be secured by the constant effect of public institutions, operating in a regular and uninterrupted course upon the various characters, talents, and acquirements of individuals. The nature of our establishments should furnish fixed and systematic encouragement to animate, to facilitate, to reward the progress of industry and virtue; and fixed and systematic discipline, to repress and correct the excesses of contrary dispositions.

From these remarks may be deduced the indispensable necessity of providing some effectual and speedy remedy for the defects in the education of the young men destined to the civil service in India. The nature of that remedy will afford matter of serious discussion.

It may, however, be useful, previously to that discussion, to advert to a general topic of argument, which may possibly be adduced to disprove the necessity of any new institution for the improvement of the civil service of the East India Company. It may be contended, that this service, through a long period of years, and in the course of various changes and chances, has always furnished men equal to the exigency of the occasion; that servants of the Company have never been wanting to conduct to a happy issue the numerous revolutions which have taken place in the affairs of the Company in India; and that these eminent personages have ultimately fixed the British empire in India on the most solid foundations of glory, wealth, and power. Why, therefore, should we apprehend, that this source, hitherto so fruitful and furnishing so abundant a supply of virtue and talents, will fail in the present age, and prove insufficient to the actual demands of our interests in this quarter of the globe? The answer to this topic of argument is obvious. Extraordinary combinations of human affairs, wars, revolutions, and all those unusual events which form the marked features and prominent characters of the history of mankind, naturally disclose talents and exertions adapted to such emergencies. That the civil or military service of the East India Company has supplied persons calculated to meet all the wonderful revolutions of affairs in India, is a circumstance not to be attributed to the original or peculiar constitution of either service at any period of time. That constitution has undergone repeated alterations at the suggestion, and under the direction of the great characters which it has produced; and it has still been found answerable to every new crisis of an extraordinary nature. But it must never be forgotten, that the successive efforts of those eminent personages, and the final result of various revolutions and wars, have imposed upon the East India Company the arduous and sacred trust of governing an extensive and populous empire. It is true that this empire must be maintained in some of its relations by the same spirit of enterprize and boldness which acquired it. But duty, policy and honour require that it should not be administered as a temporary and precarious acquisition, as an empire conquered by prosperous adventure, and extended by fortunate accident, of which the tenure is as uncertain as the original conquest and successive extension were extraordinary; it must be considered as a sacred trust, and a permanent possession. In this view its internal government demands a constant, steady, and regular supply of qualifications, in no degree similar to those which distinguished the early periods of our establishment in India, and laid the first foundations of our empire. The stability of that empire, whose magnitude is the accumulated result of former enterprize, activity and resolution, must be secured by the durable principles of internal order; by a pure, upright, and uniform administration of justice; by a prudent and temperate system of revenue; by the encouragement and protection of industry, agriculture, manufacture and commerce; by a careful and judicious management of every branch of financial resource; and by the maintenance of a just, firm, and moderate policy towards the native powers of India. To maintain and uphold such a system in all its parts, we shall require a succession of able magistrates, wise and honest judges, and skilful statesmen, properly qualified to conduct the ordinary movements of the great machine of Government.

The military establishments of this empire form no part of the subject of the present enquiry. It may be sufficient to observe in this place, that their extent, and the spirit in which they require to be governed, must correspond with the magnitude of the empire, and with the general character of our civil policy. In the civil service, we must now seek, not the instruments by which kingdoms are overthrown, revolutions accomplished, or wars conducted, but an inexhaustible supply of useful knowledge, cultivated talents, and well ordered and disciplined morals. These are the necessary instruments of a wise and well regulated Government. These are the genuine and unfailing means of cultivating and improving the arts of peace; of diffusing affluence and happiness, willing obedience, and grateful attachment over every region and district of this vast empire; and of dispensing to every class and description of our subjects the permanent benefits of secure property, protected life, undisturbed order, and inviolate religion. It is not the nature of these inestimable blessings to spring from a turbid source, or to flow in a contracted and irregular channel.

The early education of the civil servants of the East India Company is the source from which will ultimately be derived the happiness or misery of our native subjects; and the stability of our Government will bear a due proportion to its wisdom, liberality, and justice.

From the preceding discussion, it appears, that the actual state of the Company's civil service in India is far removed from perfection or efficiency, and that the cause of this defect is to be found principally, if not exclusively, in the defective education of the junior civil servants, and in the insufficient discipline of the early stages of the service. The facts, which have been reviewed in the course of this discussion, furnish the main principles on which an improved system of education and discipline may be founded with a view to secure the important ends of such an institution.

The defects of the present condition of the civil service may be comprised under the following heads:

First, An erroneous system of education in Europe confined to commercial and mercantile studies.

Secondly, The premature interruption of a course of study judiciously commenced in Europe.

Thirdly, The exposed and destitute condition of young men on their first arrival in India, and the want of a systematic guidance and established authority to regulate and control their moral and religious conduct in the early stages of the service.

Fourthly, The want of a similar system and authority to prescribe and enforce a regular course of study, under which the young men upon their arrival in India might be enabled to correct the errors, or to pursue and confirm the advantages of their European education, and to attain a knowledge of the languages, laws, usages and customs of India, together with such other branches of knowledge, as are requisite to qualify them for their several stations.

Fifthly, The want of such regulations as shall establish a necessary and inviolable connection between promotion in the civil service, and the possession of those qualifications requisite for the due discharge of the several civil stations.

It is obvious, that an education exclusively European, or Indian, would not afford an adequate remedy for such of these defects, as relate to the morals and studies of the East India Company's servants, and would not qualify them for the discharge of duties of a mixed and complicated nature, involving the combined principles of Asiatic and European policy and government. Their education must therefore be of a mixed nature, its foundation must be judiciously laid in England, and the superstructure systematically completed in India.

An important question may arise, with respect to the proportion of time to be employed in that part of the education of the junior civil servants, which should be appropriated to England; and completed previously to their departure for India. It may be contended, that many of the enumerated evils may be precluded by not allowing the writers to proceed to India until they shall have reached a more advanced age, than that at which they now usually embark, and by requiring them to undergo examinations in England, for the purpose of ascertaining their proficiency in the branches of knowledge necessary to the discharge of their duties in India.

To this arrangement various objections of a private, but most important nature, will arise in the mind of every parent, who may have destined his children for India. To attain any considerable proficiency in the course of education and study described in this paper, must necessarily require the detention of the student in Europe to the age of 20 or 22 years; many parents could not defray the expence of such an education in England, even if the other means of prosecuting it now existed, or could hereafter be provided at any school or college at home.

Other objections of a private nature might be stated against this plan; but those which are founded on public considerations appear to be absolutely insurmountable. It is a fundamental principle of policy in the British Establishments in the East Indies, that the views of the servants of the Company should terminate in the prospect of returning to England, there to enjoy the emoluments arising from a due course of active and honourable service in India.

Were the civil servants, instead of leaving England at the age of sixteen or seventeen, to be detained until the age of twenty or two-and-twenty; a great proportion of them must abandon all hope of returning with a moderate competence to their native country.

Remaining in England to this advanced age, many would form habits and connections at home, not to be relinquished at that period of life without great reluctance; and few would accommodate themselves with readiness and facility to the habits, regulations and discipline of the service in India.

While these causes would render the civil servants intractable instruments in the hands of the Government of India, the regular progress through the service would also be retarded. Twenty-five years may be taken as the period within which a civil servant may regularly acquire, with proper habits of economy, an independent fortune in India. Upon this calculation, before the most successful could hope to be in a situation to return to England, they would have attained an age, when many of the powerful affections and inducements, which now attract the servants of the Company to return to their native country, would be greatly weakened if not entirely extinguished.

At that age, many from necessity, and many probably from choice, would establish themselves permanently in India. It is unnecessary to detail the evil consequences which would result to the British interests in India, were such an habit to become general in the civil service.

Detention in England to the age of twenty or twenty-two years would certainly afford the writers an opportunity of advancing their knowledge in the necessary branches of European study; but within that period of time, even in those branches it could scarcely be completed; especially in the important sciences of general ethics and jurisprudence (for how few understandings are equal to such a course of study previously to the age of twenty,) and it would be entirely defective in the essential point of connecting the principles of those sciences with the laws of India, and with the manners and usages of its inhabitants. No establishment formed in England could give a correct[1] practical knowledge of the languages, laws and customs of India, of the peculiar habits and genius of the people, of their mode of transacting business, and of the characteristic features of their vices or virtues. These most essential acquirements would, therefore, remain to be attained after the arrival of the student in India, at an age when the study of languages is attended with additional difficulties, when any prescribed course of study, when any systematic discipline, or regular restraint becomes irksome, if not intolerable. As the East India Company's servants would arrive in India at a period of life too far advanced to admit of subjection to any system of public discipline or control, they must necessarily be left to the dictates of their own discretion with regard to whatever part of their knowledge had been left incomplete in Europe.

The wants and expenses of individuals arriving in India at the age of twenty or twenty-two years would greatly exceed the scale of the public allowances to the junior servants. At this age no restraint could be applied in India to their moral conduct, for the purpose of protecting them against the peculiar depravities incident to the climate, and to the character of the natives.

From the early age at which the writers are now usually sent to India, opportunity is afforded to the government on the spot of obtaining a knowledge of the characters of individuals, before they become eligible to stations of trust and importance. Of this advantage the government would be in a great degree deprived, if the East India Company's servants were all detained in England until the age of twenty or twenty-two: this inconvenience would prove nearly an insurmountable impediment to the important and necessary rule of selecting for public office, those best qualified to discharge its duties with propriety and effect.

The junior civil servants must, therefore, continue to embark for India at the age of fifteen or sixteen, that they may be tractable instruments in the hands of the government of the country; that their morals and habits may be duly formed and protected by proper safeguards against the peculiar nature of the vices and characteristic dangers of Indian society; that they

[1] Sir W. Jones was not intelligible to the natives of India, when he arrived at Calcutta, in any of the oriental languages.

may be enabled to pass through the service before the vigour of life has ceased, and to return with a competent fortune to Europe, while the affections and attachments which bind them to their native country, continue to operate with full force; and lastly, that they may possess regular, seasonable and certain means of attaining the peculiar qualifications necessary for their stations.

Under all these circumstances, the most deliberate and assiduous examination of all the important questions considered in this paper, determined the Governor-General to found a Collegiate Institution at Fort William, by the annexed regulation.

This regulation comprises all the fundamental principles of the Institution. The detailed statutes for the internal discipline and good government of the College will be framed gradually as circumstances may require.

A common table and apartments are to be provided in the College, for all the civil servants who may be attached to the establishment.

The benefits of the establishment are extended to the junior civil servants of Fort St. George and Bombay, who will be directed to proceed to Fort William as soon as the accommodations requisite for their reception shall have been provided.

This arrangement appeared in every respect preferable to the establishment of Colleges at both, or either of those Presidencies. Independently of the considerations of expense and other objections and impediments to the foundation of such Institutions at Fort St. George and Bombay, it is of essential importance, that the education of all the civil servants of the Company should be uniform, and should be conducted under the immediate superintendance of that authority, which is primarily responsible for the government of the whole of the British possessions in India; and which must consequently be most competent to judge of the nature and principles of the education which may be most expedient for the public interests.

It may be expected, that the operation of this part of the new institution will ultimately extinguish all local jealousies and prejudices among the several Presidencies; the political, moral, and religious principles of all the British Establishments in India, will then be derived directly from one common source; the civil service of Bengal is unquestionably further advanced in every useful acquisition, and in every respect more regular and correct, than that of either of the subordinate Presidencies; no more speedy or efficacious mode can be devised of diffusing throughout India, the laudable spirit of the service of Bengal, and of extending the benefit of improvements, which, under the new institution, may be expected to make a rapid progress at the seat of the Supreme Government, than by rendering Fort William the centre of the education and discipline of the junior civil servants in India.

Provision is made for admitting to the benefits of the Institution civil servants of a longer standing than three years (on their making application for that purpose) under such regulations as may be deemed advisable. The Institution may prove highly beneficial to many servants of this description; as many of them will be received on the establishment, as its funds and other considerations may admit.

Provision is also made for extending the benefits of the Institution to as many of the junior military servants, as it may be found practicable to admit from all the Presidencies. Essential benefits will result to the British armies in India, from the annual introduction of a number of young men, well versed in the languages with which every officer, but particularly those belonging to the native corps, ought to be acquainted. It is also of most essential importance to the army in India, that it should be composed of officers attached by regular instruction, and disciplined habits, to the principles of morality, good order, and subordination.

Further regulations are in the contemplation of the Governor-General, for the education of the cadets destined for the army in India, which will be connected intimately with the present foundation.

It cannot be denied that, during the convulsions with which the doctrines of the French Revolution have agitated the Continent of Europe, erroneous principles of the same dangerous tendency had reached the minds of some individuals in the civil and military service of the Company in India; and the state, as well of political, as of religious opinions, had been in some degree unsettled. The progress of this mischief would at all times be aided by the defective and irregular education of the writers and cadets; an Institution tending to fix and establish sound and correct principles of religion and government in their minds at an early period of life, is the best security which can be provided for the stability of the British power in India. The letter of the

Court of Directors, under date the 25th of May, 1798, has been constantly present to the Governor-General's mind; it is satisfactory to know, after the fullest consideration, that many apprehensions stated in that letter, appear to have been conceived with more force than is required by the actual state of any of the settlements in India.

But among other important advantages of the new Institution, it will provide the most effectual and permanent remedy against the evils, (as far as they existed) which it was the object of the orders of the Honourable Court of the 25th of May, 1798, to correct.

The situation of the junior servants on their early arrival in India, has been fully described in this paper. Under the new Institution, they will be immediately received by the Provost, (a clergyman of the church of England ;) they will be provided with apartments in the College, and with a common table; consequently they will be removed from the danger of profusion, extravagance and excess. Every part of their private conduct, their expenses, their connections, their manners and morals will be subject to the notice of the Provost, and principal officers of the College, and (through the collegiate authorities) of the government itself.

While attached to the Institution, the junior servants will have the most ample means afforded to them of completing the European branch of their education, or of correcting its defects; of acquiring whatever local knowledge may be necessary for that department of the service, in which, (after mature reflection on their own inclinations, acquisitions and talents) they may determine to engage; of forming their manners and of fixing their principles on the solid foundations of virtue and religion.

The acquirements, abilities, and moral character of every civil servant may be ascertained before he can be eligible to a public station; and every selection of persons for high and important offices may be made under a moral certainty, that the public expectation cannot be disappointed.

The twenty-fourth clause of the Regulation will afford the foundation of a law which may at all times secure the civil service against the effects of the possible partiality or ignorance of any government.

It is intended that the allowance of every civil servant of less than three years' standing, being a student in the College, should be brought to one standard of 300 rupees per month, without any allowance for a Moonshy.

As a table and apartments will be provided for the students, this allowance will place them in a better situation than any writer of the same standing now enjoys. With these advantages, under the control of the official authorities of the College, and with the benefit of their advice and admonition, aided by statutes for the prevention of extravagance and debt, it may be hoped that many young men will adopt early habits of economy, and will lay the foundations of honest independence at a much earlier period than is now practicable. This advantage will be considerable in every view, in no one more than as it will tend to contract the period of each servant's residence in India, to give a nearer prospect of return to England, and to keep that desirable object more constantly in view.

The discipline of the College will be as moderate as may be consistent with the ends of the Institution. It will impose no harsh or humiliating restraint, and will be formed on principles combining the discipline of the Universities in England with that of the Royal Military Academies of France and of other European monarchies.

It may be expected that the great majority of young men on their arrival in India, will eagerly embrace the opportunities afforded to them by this Institution of laying the foundations of private character, of public reputation, and of early independence. It cannot be supposed that many will be so insensible to their own honour and interests, and so destitute of every liberal feeling and sentiment, as not to prefer the proposed course of studies in the College to the menial labour imposed upon them of transcribing papers in an office where, in the nature of their duty, they are levelled with the native and Portuguese clerks, although infinitely inferior in its execution.

Those young men who may not at the first view discover all the advantages to be derived from the Institution, will soon improve by the example and communications of others. If any individuals should continue insensible to the calls of public duty, and of private reputation, (and it is of importance that persons of this description should be known before an opportunity has been afforded to them of injuring the public interests, by their vices and defects,) the public good will demand that they should be punished by neglect and exclusion from employment. Considering the liberal manner in which the servants of the Company are rewarded for their services, the public may justly insist on submission to whatever regulations may be prescribed by this Institution.

The incitements to exertion being as powerful as the consequences of contrary habits will be ruinous, instances of gross neglect or contumacy will rarely occur. In this respect the Institution possesses peculiar advantages, and it will become a powerful instrument in the hands of the Government in India, which will be enabled thereby to bring the general character of the servants of the Company to such a standard of perfection as the public interests require. To every other inducement, which any Collegiate Institution in the world can supply for the encouragement of diligence, will be added the immediate view of official promotion, increase of fortune, and distinction in the public service.

If it be asked whether it be proper that the whole time of the junior servants, for the first three years of their residence in India, should be devoted to study in the College, and that the Company should lose the benefit of their services during that period, while the junior servants receive a salary?

It may be enquired, on the other hand, what is now the occupation of the civil servants for the first three years after their arrival in India, what benefit the Company now derives from the services of the junior servants during that period, and what, in general, are now the characters and qualifications of those servants at the expiration of that period?

To all these questions sufficient answers have been given in the preceding pages.

Further details respecting the nature of the Institution will be forwarded officially to the Court of Directors at an early period.

The reasons which induced the Governor-General to found the College without any previous reference to England were these;—His conviction of the great immediate benefit to be derived from the early commencement even of the partial operation of the plan.

His experience of the great advantages which had been already derived by many of the young men from their attendance on Mr. Gilchrist, in consequence of the first experiment made on a contracted scale with a view to a more extended Institution.

His anxiety to impart to the very promising young men

arrived from Europe within the last three years, a share of the advantages described in this paper, and his solicitude to superintend the foundation of the Institution, and to accelerate and witness its first effects.

This Institution will be best appreciated by every affectionate parent in the hour of separation from his child, destined to the public service in India. Let any parent (especially if he has himself passed through the Company's service in India) declare, whether the prospect of this Institution has aggravated or mitigated the solicitude of that painful hour—whether it has raised additional doubts and fears, or inspired a more lively hope of the honourable and prosperous service, of the early and fortunate return of his child?

With regard to the funds for defraying the expense of the Institution, the Governor-General does not intend, without the sanction of the Honourable Court of Directors, to subject the Company to any expense on account of the Institution, beyond that which has already received their sanction independently of the Institution.

The Honourable Court have authorized this Government to purchase the Writers' buildings, if they can be obtained on advantageous terms. These buildings cannot be obtained on such terms; nor can they be advantageously converted to the final purposes of the Institution. A sum equal to the just value of the buildings, or to the rent now paid for them, will be applied towards the purchase of a proper spot of ground, and to the buildings requisite for the College.

The ground proposed to be employed is situated on the Garden Reach, where three or four of the present gardens will be laid together, a new road formed, and a large space of ground cleared and drained. This arrangement will improve the general health of the neighbourhood of Calcutta, as well as afford ample room for every accommodation required for the use of the College, or for the health of the students.

The expenses of the Institution will be defrayed by a small contribution from all the civil servants in India, to be deducted from their salaries. This resource will probably be sufficient for all present purposes, with the addition of the fund now applied to the Moonshy's allowance, and of the profits to be derived from a new arrangement of the Government printing-press.

The Governor-General has not deemed it proper, in the first instance, to subject the Company to any additional expense on account of the Institution. The Honourable Court of Directors will, however, reflect, that the Institution is calculated to extend the blessings of good government to the many millions of people whom Providence has subjected to our dominion, to perpetuate the immense advantages now derived by the Company from their possessions in India, and to establish the British Empire in India on the solid foundations of ability, integrity, virtue, and religion. The approved liberality of the Honourable Court will therefore certainly be manifested towards this Institution to an extent commensurate with its importance.

It would produce a most salutary impression in India if the Court, immediately on receiving this Regulation, were to order the Governor-General in Council to endow the College with an annual rent-charge on the revenues of Bengal, and issue a similar order to the Governor in Council at Fort St. George with respect to the revenue of Mysore; leaving the amount of the endowment, on each fund, to the Governor-General in Council.

All those who feel any concern in the support of the British interests in India, and especially those whose fortunes have been acquired in the service of the Company, or whose connections may now or hereafter look to this service for advancement, will undoubtedly contribute to the support of this Institution. Under the auspices of the Court, it is hoped that a large sum might be raised by subscription in Europe. The Governor-General considered the College at Fort William to be the most becoming public monument which the East India Company could raise to commemorate the conquest of Mysore. He has accordingly dated the law for the foundation of the College on the 4th of May, 1800, the first anniversary of the reduction of Seringapatam.

The early attention of the Governor-General will be directed to the Mahommedan College founded at Calcutta, and to the Hindoo College established at Benares. In the disorders which preceded the fall of the Mogul Empire and the British conquests in India, all the public Institutions calculated to promote education and good morals were neglected, and at length entirely discontinued. The Institutions at Calcutta and Benares may be made the means of aiding the study of the laws and languages in the College at Fort William, as well as of correcting the defective moral principles too generally prevalent among the natives of India.

An establishment of Moonshies and native teachers of the languages under the control of the collegiate officers at Fort William will be attached to the new College, and the young men will be supplied from this establishment, instead of being left (as at present) to exercise their own discretion in hiring such Moonshies as they can find in Calcutta or in the provinces.

These arrangements respecting the native Colleges, while they contribute to the happiness of our native subjects, will qualify them to form a more just estimate of the mild and benevolent spirit of the British Government.

In selecting the Garden Reach for the site of the building for the New College, two objects were in the contemplation of the Governor-General; first, that the ordinary residence of the students should be so near that of the Governor-General as that he may have the constant means of superintending the whole system and discipline of the Institution. The distance of fifteen or sixteen miles, in this climate, would often embarrass the communication.

Secondly. That the College should be removed to some distance from the Town of Calcutta. The principle of this object is sufficiently intelligible without further explanation; it is, however, desirable that the College should not be so remote from Calcutta as to preclude the young men from all intercourse with the society of that city. Advantages may be derived from a regulated intercourse with the higher classes of that society. The Garden Reach combines these advantages, with many others of space and accommodation. The situation of the Writers' buildings is objectionable on account of their being placed in the centre of the town. Nor would it have been practicable in that situation (even if the Writers' buildings could have been purchased on reasonable terms) to have obtained an area of ground sufficiently spacious for the new building.

As it will require a considerable time before the new buildings in Garden Reach can be completed, it is intended in the meanwhile to continue to occupy the Writers' buildings, and to hire such additional buildings in the neighbourhood as may be required for the temporary accommodation of the students and officers of the College, for the library, the dining-hall, the lecture-rooms, and other purposes. It will be necessary to make some considerable purchases of books for the foundation of the library. The Governor-General will effect whatever purchases can be made with economy and advantage in India. Lists of books will be transmitted to England by an early opportunity, with a view to such purchases as it may be necessary to make in Europe; and the Governor-General entertains no doubt that the Court of Directors will contribute liberally towards such purchases. That part of the library of the late Tippoo Sultaun, which was presented by the army to the Court of Directors, is lately arrived in Bengal. The Governor-General strongly recommends that the Oriental manuscripts composing this collection should be deposited in the library of the College at Fort William; and it is his intention to retain the manuscripts accordingly, until he shall receive the orders of the Court upon the subject. He will transmit lists of the collection by the first opportunity.

It is obvious that these manuscripts may be rendered highly useful to the purposes of the new Institution, and that much more public advantage can be derived from them in the library of the College at Fort William, than can possibly be expected from depositing them in London.

Such of the manuscripts as may appear to be merely valuable as curiosities may be transmitted to England by an early opportunity.

It is the intention of the Governor-General that the first term of the College should be opened in the course of the month of November; and the lectures on several of the languages, it is hoped, be commenced in the course of the ensuing winter.

With the aid of such temporary arrangements as may be immediately made, it is expected that many other branches of the Institution may be brought into immediate operation, particularly those which relate to the expenses, morals, and general studies of the young men. Fortunately for the objects of the Institution, the Governor-General has found, at Calcutta, two Clergymen of the Church of England, eminently qualified to discharge the duties of Provost and Vice-Provost. To the former office he has appointed Mr. Brown, the Company's first Chaplain; and to the latter Mr. Buchanan. Mr. Brown's character must be well known in England, and particularly so to some Members of the Court of Directors; it is in every respect, such as to satisfy the Governor-General that his views in this nomination will not be disappointed. He has also formed the highest expectations from the abilities, learning, temper, and morals of Mr. Buchanan, whose character is well known in England, particularly to Dr. Porteus, Bishop of London, and to

Dr. Milner, Master of Queen's College, in the University of Cambridge.

With respect to the Professorships, those which relate to the languages will be best filled in India; and the Governor-General entertains little doubt, that he shall soon be able to fill them permanently, in an efficient manner. In the meanwhile, the most laudable zeal has been manifested by such persons in the civil and military service, as are competent to assist the Governor-General in making a temporary provision for the discharge of the duties of these Professorships. The persons properly qualified to fill certain of the other Professorships must be sought in Europe. The Institution will be so framed as to offer strong inducements to such persons; and the Governor-General will endeavour, at the earliest possible period, to secure the assistance of talents, learning, and morals from Europe, adapted to the great purposes of this Institution. It may be useful to observe, in this place, that the Professors and native Moonshies or teachers will be prohibited from instructing any other persons than the students of the College. The object of this regulation is to prevent European parents, resident in India, from attempting to commence or to complete, by means of the new Institution, the regular education of their children in India. It is an obviously necessary principle of policy to encourage the present practice of sending children, born in India of European parents, at an early age, to Europe for education.

The Governor-General means to recommend that the Court of Directors should hereafter nominate all persons destined for the civil service, at any of the Presidencies in India, to be students of the College at Fort William. To each studentship (as has already been observed) will be annexed a monthly salary of 300 rupees, together with apartments and a common table. It will be for the Honourable Court to decide whether the ultimate destination of the student to the Civil Establishment of Bengal, Fort St. George, or Bombay, shall be specified in the original appointment to the studentship at the College of Fort William: it would certainly be more advantageous to the public service, that no such appointment should be made in England, and that the ultimate destination of each student should be determined in India under the authority of the Government on the spot, according to the inclinations and acquirements of the students respectively. The improved state of the Civil Service at Fort St. George, and the indispensable necessity of introducing the same improvements into the service at Bombay, will speedily render the Civil Service at each of those Presidencies no less advantageous and respectable than that of Bengal.

The Governor-General highly applauds the wisdom of the late order of the Court regulating the rank of the cadets for the artillery according to the period of time when they may be respectively reported to be qualified for commissions under the institutions of the Academy at Woolwich. It would be a most beneficial regulation to declare that the rank of all students appointed to the College of Fort William, in the same season, should be regulated according to their respective progress in the prescribed studies of the College, and to the public testimonials of their respective merit, established according to the discipline and institutions of the College.

If the Court of Directors should approve the principles and objects of this Institution, and should accordingly order the Governor-General to endow it with a rent-charge upon the land revenue of Bengal and Mysore, it would be a gracious act to relieve the Civil Service in India from the tax which the Governor-General intends to impose on the public salaries for the support of the College. The tax will indeed be very light, but the Court of Directors may probably be of opinion that such an Institution as the present ought to be supported, rather by the munificence of the Sovereign of the country than by any diminution, however inconsiderable, of the established allowances of the public officers.

WELLESLEY.

106. Regulation for the College at Fort William.

Fort William, July 10th, 1800.

Regulation for the foundation of a College at Fort William in Bengal, and for the better instruction of the Junior Civil Servants of the Honourable the English East India Company in the important duties belonging to the several arduous stations to which the said Junior Civil Servants may be respectively destined in the administration of justice, and in the general government of the British Empire in India.—Passed by the Governor-General in Council, on the 10*th July*, 1800; *corre-*

sponding with the 28th Assar, 1207, Bengal era; the 4th Sawun, 1207, Fussily; the 28th Assar, 1207, Willaity; the 4th Sawun, 1857, Sumbut; and the 17th Suffer, 1215, Higeree; —But by his Lordship's special order, bearing date on the 4th May, 1800, being the first anniversary of the glorious and decisive victory obtained by the British arms at Seringapatam, the capital of the Kingdom of Mysore.

Whereas it hath pleased the Divine Providence to favour the counsels and arms of Great Britain in India with a continued course of prosperity and glory; and whereas, by the victorious issue of several successive wars, and by the happy result of a just, wise, and moderate system of policy, extensive territories in Hindostan, and in the Deccan, have been subjected to the dominion of Great Britain, and under the government of the Honourable the English East India Company, in process of time a great and powerful empire has been founded, comprehending many populous and opulent provinces, and various nations, differing in religious persuasions, in language, manners, and habits, and respectively accustomed to be governed according to peculiar usages, doctrines, and laws; and whereas the sacred duty, true interest, honour, and policy of the British nation require, that effectual provision should be made at all times for the good government of the British empire in India, and for the prosperity and happiness of the people inhabiting the same; and many wise and salutary regulations have accordingly been enacted from time to time by the Governor-General in Council with the benevolent intent and purpose of administering to the said people their own laws, usages, and customs, in the mild and benignant spirit of the British constitution; and whereas it is indispensably necessary with a view to secure the due execution and administration of the said wise, salutary, and benevolent regulations in all time to come, as well as of such regulations and laws as may hereafter be enacted by the Governor-General in Council, that the civil servants of the Honourable the English East India Company exercising high and important functions in the government of India, should be properly qualified to discharge the arduous duties of their respective offices and stations; should be sufficiently instructed in the general principles of literature and science; and should possess a competent knowledge, as well of the laws, government, and constitution of Great Britain, as of the several native languages of Hindostan and the Deccan, and of the laws, usages, and customs of the provinces which the said civil servants respectively may be appointed to govern; and whereas the early interruption in Europe of the education and studies of the persons destined for the civil service of the Honourable the English East India Company precludes them from acquiring, previously to their arrival in India, a sufficient foundation in the general principles of literature and science, or a competent knowledge of the laws, government, and constitution of Great Britain; and many qualifications essential to the proper discharge of the arduous and important duties of the civil service in India, cannot be fully attained otherwise than by a regular course of education and study in India, conducted under the superintendence, direction, and control of the supreme authority of the government of these possessions; and whereas no public institution now exists in India, under which the junior servants appointed at an early period of life to the civil service of the Honourable the English East India Company, can attain the necessary means of qualifying themselves for the high and arduous trusts to which they are respectively destined; and no system of discipline or education has been established in India for the purpose of directing and regulating the studies of the said junior servants, or of guiding their conduct upon their first arrival in India, or of forming, improving, or preserving their morals, or of encouraging them to maintain the honour of the British name in India by a regular and orderly course of industry, prudence, integrity, and religion; The most noble Richard Marquess Wellesley, Knight of the illustrious Order of Saint Patrick, &c. &c., Governor-General in Council, deeming the establishment of such an institution, and system of discipline, education, and study, to be requisite for the good government and stability of the British empire in India, and for the maintenance of the interests and honour of the Honourable the English East India Company, his Lordship in Council hath therefore enacted as follows.

II. A college is hereby founded at Fort William in Bengal for the better instruction of the junior civil servants of the Company, in such branches of literature, science, and knowledge, as may be deemed necessary to qualify them for the discharge of the duties of the different offices constituted for the administration of the government of the British possessions in the East Indies.

III. A suitable building shall be erected for the college, containing apartments for the superior officers, for the students, for a library, and for such other purposes as may be found necessary.

IV. The Governor-General shall be the patron and visitor of the college.

V. The members of the Supreme Council, and the judges of the Sudder Dewanny Adawlut, and of the Nizamut Adawlut, shall be the governors of the college.

VI. The Governor-General in Council shall be trustee for the management of the funds of the college, and shall regularly submit his proceedings in that capacity to the Honourable the Court of Directors.

VII. The Comptrolling Committee of Treasury shall be treasurers of the college.

VIII. The Accountant-General, and the Civil Auditor, shall be respectively accountant, and auditor of accounts, of the college.

IX. The Advocate-General, and the Honourable Company's standing Counsel, shall be the law officers of the college.

X. The immediate government of the college shall be vested in a Provost and Vice-Provost, and such other officers as the patron and visitor shall think proper to appoint, with such salaries as he shall deem expedient. The Provost, Vice-Provost, and all other officers of the college, shall be removable at the discretion of the patron and visitor.

XI. The Provost shall always be a clergyman of the church of England, as established by law.

XII. Every proceeding and act of the Patron and Visitor shall be submitted to the Honourable the Court of Directors, and shall be subjected to their pleasure.

XIII. The primary duties of the Provost shall be to receive the junior civil servants on their first arrival at Fort William; to superintend and regulate their general morals and conduct; to assist them with his advice and admonition; and to instruct and confirm them in the principles of the Christian religion, according to the doctrine, discipline, and rites of the church of England, as established by law.

XIV. The Patron and Visitor shall establish such professorships, with such endowments as shall be judged proper.

XV. Professorships shall be established as soon as may be practicable, and regular courses of lectures commenced, in the following branches of literature, science, and knowledge:

Languages.—Arabic, Persian, Shanscrit, Hindoostanee, Bengal, Telinga, Mahratta, Tamul, Canara; Mahomedan law, Hindoo law, ethics, civil jurisprudence, and the law of nations; English law; the regulations and laws enacted by the Governor-General in Council, or by the Governors in Council at Fort St. George and Bombay respectively, for the civil government of the British territories in India; political œconomy, and particularly the commercial institutions and interests of the East India Company; geography and mathematics; modern languages of Europe; Greek, Latin, and English classics; general history, antient and modern; the history and antiquities of Hindoostan and the Deccan; natural history; botany, chemistry, and astronomy.

XVI. The Patron and Visitor may authorize the same professor to read lectures in more than one of the enumerated branches of study, and may at any time unite, or separate any of the said professorships, or may found additional professorships in such other branches of study as may appear necessary.

XVII. The Provost and Vice-Provost, after having remained in the government of the college for the complete period of seven years, and any professor, after having read lectures in the college for the complete period of seven years, or of twenty-eight terms, and after having respectively received, under the hand and seal of the Patron and Visitor, a testimonial of good conduct during that period of time, shall be entitled to an annual pension for life, to be paid either in Europe or in India, according to the option of the party. The pension shall in no case be less than one-third of the annual salary received by such Provost or Vice-Provost respectively during his continuance in the government of the college, or by any such Professor, during the period of his regular lectures. The pension may in any case be increased at the discretion of the Patron and Visitor.

XVIII. All the civil servants of the Company who may be hereafter appointed on the establishment of the Presidency of Bengal, shall be attached to the college for the first three years after their arrival in Bengal, and during that period of time, the prescribed studies in the college shall constitute their sole public duty.

XIX. All the civil servants now on the establishment of the Presidency of Bengal, whose residence in Bengal shall not have exceeded the term of three years, shall be immediately attached to the college for the term of three years from the date of this regulation.

XX. Any of the junior civil servants of the Company in India, whether belonging to the establishment of this Presidency, or to that of Fort St. George, or of Bombay, may be admitted to the benefits of the institution by order of the Governor-General in Council, for such term, and under such regulations, as may be deemed advisable.

XXI. Any of the junior military servants of the Company in India, whether belonging to the establishment of this Presidency, or to that of Fort St. George, or of Bombay, may be admitted to the benefits of the institution, by order of the Governor-General in Council, for such term, and under such regulations, as may be deemed advisable.

XXII. In the college at Fort William, four terms shall be observed in each year; the duration of each term shall be two months. Four vacations shall also be established in each year; the duration of each vacation shall be one month.

XXIII. Two public examinations shall be holden annually, and prizes and honorary rewards shall be publicly distributed by the Provost, in the presence of the Patron and Governors, to such students as shall appear to merit them.

XXIV. Degrees shall be established, and shall be rendered requisite qualifications for certain offices in the civil governments of Bengal, Fort St. George and Bombay; and promotion in the civil service shall be the necessary result of merit publicly approved, according to the discipline and institutions of the college.

XXV. Statutes shall be framed by the Provost of the college, under the superintendence of the Governors of the college, respecting the internal regulation, discipline, and government of the college; but no statute shall be enforced until it shall have been sanctioned by the Patron and Visitor. The statutes so sanctioned shall be printed according to a form to be prescribed by the Patron and Visitor.

XXVI. The Patron and Visitor shall be empowered, at all times of his sole and exclusive authority, to amend or abrogate any existing statute, or to enact any new statute for the regulation, discipline, and government of the college.

XXVII. A regular statement of all salaries, appointments, or removals of the officers of the college, shall be submitted by the Patron and Visitor of the college at the expiration of each term, to the Governor-General in Council, and by the Governor-General in Council to the Honourable the Court of Directors; printed copies of all statutes enacted by the Patron and Visitor shall also be submitted to the Governor-General in Council, and to the Honourable the Court of Directors, at the same periods of time, and in the same manner.

107. Extract from a public Letter from the Court of Directors of the East India Company to Bengal dated 25th May, 1798.

An objurgation on the character and conduct of the servants of the Company.

70. Conceiving it a duty incumbent upon us to afford our civil and military servants, and all Christians living under our protection, professing the Protestant religion, the means of attending Divine service, in which we trust, those in superior station will set the example, we most cheerfully acquiesce in your proposal for erecting chapels in the progressive manner pointed out in the 63d paragraph of the letter to which we are now replying, such edifices to be as plain and simple as possible, that all unnecessary expense may be avoided.

71. Having thus, as far as depends upon us, provided for the due observance of public worship on the sabbath-day, we cannot avoid mentioning the information we have received, that at the military stations it is no uncommon thing for the solemnity of the day to be broke in upon by horse-racing, whilst Divine worship, (for which the sabbath is especially enjoined to be set apart) is never performed at any of those stations, though chaplains are allotted to them. And we have now before us a printed horse-racing account, by which it appears that not less than eight matches were run at Chinsurah in one day, and that on a Sunday. We are astonished and shocked at this wide deviation from one of the most distinguishing and universal institutions of Christianity. We must suppose it to have been so gradual, that transitions from one step to another have been little observed; but the stage at which it is now arrived, if our information be true, must appear to every reasonable man, highly discreditable to our government, and totally incompatible with the religion we profess.

72. To preserve the ascendancy which our national character

has acquired over the minds of the natives of India, must ever be of importance to the maintenance of the political power we possess in the East, and we are well persuaded that this end is not to be served either by a disregard of the external observances of religion, or by any assimilation to Eastern manners and opinions, but rather by retaining all the distinctions of our national principles, character and usages. The events which have recently passed in Europe, point out that the present is least of all the time in which irreligion should be promoted or encouraged; for with an attachment to the religion which we profess, is found to be intimately connected an attachment to our laws and constitution; besides which, it is calculated to produce the most beneficial effects in society; to maintain in it the peace, the subordination, and all the principles and practices on which its stability and happiness depend.

73. We therefore enjoin that all such profanations of the sabbath, as have been mentioned, be forbidden and prevented; and that Divine service be regularly performed, as in England, every Sunday, at all the military stations; and all European officers and soldiers, unless hindered by sickness or actual duty, are to be required punctually to attend, for which such an hour is to be fixed as shall be most suitable to the climate. The chaplains are to be positively ordered to be regular and correct in the performance of their duty, and if any one of them neglect it, or by his conduct bring discredit on his profession, we direct that he be dismissed from our service.

74. We rely on the ready obedience of the commanding officers at the different stations, in carrying this necessary regulation into execution, and particularly depend on the attention of our Commander-in-Chief, and of our Governor-General for giving it full effect.

75. We are here naturally led to remark, exclusive of what relates to the public institutions of religion, that the general tenor of the Indian newspapers, and periodical publications which come under our inspection, as well as the private informations which reach this country, concur in exhibiting an increasing spirit of luxury and dissipation in our principal settlements, and even at some of the subordinate stations.

76. This suggests to us much matter of very serious concern and apprehension. It points to evils incalculable in their consequences. One inference immediately arising from it is, that either the general scale of allowances and emoluments in our

service is too large, or that by an improvident use of them, a principle of new wants and new desires is kept in too much activity, and thus a tone given to the general manners most contrary to that regulated economy on which so much turns the welfare of governments, and the comfort, independance, and respectability of individuals.

77. It is on the qualities of our servants that the safety of the British possessions in India essentially depends; on their virtue, their intelligence, their laborious application, their vigilance and public spirit. We have seen, and do still with pleasure see, honourable examples of all these; we are anxious to preserve and increase such examples, and therefore cannot contemplate without alarm, the excessive growth of fashionable amusements and shew, the tendency of which is to enervate the mind, and impair its nobler qualities, to introduce a hurtful emulation in expense, to set up false standards of merit, to confound the different orders in society, and to beget an aversion to serious occupations.

78. This taste in a society which, with an exception of the article of commercial gains, a source by no means general, derives its whole income mediately or immediately from the State, is especially to be deprecated. The progressive wealth and prosperity of any country, do indeed too naturally increase luxury and its attendant evils; but where this order is inverted, and luxury increases, whilst the grand source that supplies it remains without proportionate augmentation, as is the case of the land revenue of Bengal, now unalterably fixed in its amount, the consequences must be eventually ruinous, unless a system so preposterous is effectually checked.

79. Believing that the enjoyment of avowed, honourable allowances, would tend to promote, among other beneficial effects, a due regulation of expense, the Company have, from such considerations, strained their own means to put their servants on the most liberal footing; but whilst they feel themselves weighed down by the civil and military charges of their establishments, they are still frequently assailed in one way or another, by new applications for pecuniary concessions; and yet at the same time that we hear of straits and hardships resulting from inadequate allowances, we not only discern evident marks of increasing dissipation in the general habits of European society in India, but in some of them a spirit of gaming publicly shewing itself in lotteries, and the keen pursuits of the turf.

80. We must here mention the information we have received, that some individuals at, and under your Presidency, have lately introduced the pernicious practice of gaming to a very considerable extent, which must be ultimately ruinous to many. As we consider such practices to be totally incompatible with the interest of the Company, we earnestly recommend it to our Governor-General, to endeavour to discover the names of those concerned therein; and if his admonitions should be unavailing in putting a stop thereto, we authorize him to make an example of the person or persons who may be the principal promoters of such licentiousness, by removing them from office, and sending them to Europe.

81. As in this general subject none of our Presidencies on the Continent of India is wholly unconcerned, it will behove our several governments there to bestow a very serious attention upon it, and to consider of the means of which, in the way of regulation, influence, or retrenchment, the growing taste for expensive living, amusements, and display may be repressed; especially we recommend this interesting subject to the care of our Governor-General, to whom we are persuaded it will appear in its just importance, and from whose judgment and example we shall confidently hope for a co-operation with our views.

82. Indeed we are disposed to believe, that many persons give into modes of expense less from inclination than the fear of being singular; and we think it will be worthy of our servants who are honourably distinguished by character, talents, or situation, to be distinguished also for moderation and frugality in their habits of living.

XI. THE FLEET.

108. The Marquess Wellesley to His Excellency Vice-Admiral Rainier, &c. &c. &c.

Propriety of the Fleet in the Indian Seas co-operating, without special orders from England, in expeditions projected by the Governor-General, and not deemed imprudent by the Admiral.

(Extract.) Feb. 5, 1801.

Sir,

1. This letter will contain my reply to your Excellency's despatch marked (most secret B,) of the 20th December, 1800.

2. My sincere personal respect for your Excellency concurs with my sense of public duty, to render that despatch a subject of the deepest regret, and of the most severe disappointment to my mind.

3. Your Excellency has signified to me in the first paragraph of that despatch, that your concurrence in the expedition which I had proposed against the Isle of France, is withholden, because in your decided opinion no such enterprize can with propriety be undertaken, unless by the express command of the King, signified in the usual official form to the British Government of India, and to the commanders of his Majesty's land and sea forces. Admitting, for the present, that your Excellency is required to apply this rule to your own conduct, I cannot admit the force of any such rule to be so great, as to impose on your Excellency the duty of frustrating or impairing the use of such separate means and resources as the British Government in India may possess for the seasonable annoyance of the enemy, without reference to your co-operation, or to the principles by which your discretion may be governed.

8. My experience of your Excellency's uniform zeal and alacrity in the prosecution of the public service, since my arrival

in India, precludes the possibility of my regarding your dissent from the proposed expedition in any other light than that in which you have stated it, as an intended act of duty towards his Majesty. And if your Excellency's objections had been founded on the difficulty of the proposed plan of attack, either in the present, or in any future season, I should have received with respect and consideration the decision of a person whose judgement on that branch of the subject must necessarily be entitled to the utmost degree of attention. But your Excellency, approving the general outlines of the plan of attack, as founded upon the respectable evidence and accurate information furnished by Mr. Stokes, has declared your decided opinion that no such enterprize can with propriety be undertaken, unless by the express command of the King, signified in the usual official manner to me, and to the commanders of his Majesty's land and sea forces.

9. Injurious to the public service as the operation of such a principle must be, even if limited to the present case, its general application appears to me to involve evils of much greater magnitude, and of more dangerous extent.

10. If the ground of your Excellency's dissent from the proposed expedition to the Isle of France, be admitted as a general rule to govern the conduct of the military and naval service in these distant possessions during the existence of war; I apprehend that the greatest advantage must result from thence to the cause of the enemy. It is an established maxim of state, as well as an unqualified principle of public duty, that, in time of war, all public officers should employ their utmost endeavours to reduce the power and resources of the common enemy of the state, and should avail themselves of every advantage which circumstances may present for the advancement of the interests of their country, by the vigorous prosecution of hostilities. In remote possessions the exigency of this duty increases in proportion to the distance from the parent state, and to the consequent difficulty of obtaining from home express and precise orders, applicable to the various emergencies which must arise in the course of war. If no advantage can ever be taken of the temporary or accidental weakness of the enemy's possessions in India, without express orders from England, signified through the usual official channels, not only to the Government of India, but to the commanders of his Majesty's land and sea forces, it is evident that opportunities of reducing the enemy's power and

resources must frequently be lost without the hope of recovery, by reference for formal commands to the source of sovereign authority at home. In the present instance, an extraordinary and fortunate accident had disclosed to me the weak and almost defenceless state of the most important possessions remaining to France in this quarter of the globe. In my judgment, I should have failed in my duty towards my King and country, if I had waited for his Majesty's express commands, or for his orders, signified through the official channels established by Parliament for the government of India, before I had proceeded to take the necessary steps for availing myself of the critical posture of the French interests within the reach of the force entrusted to my controul. The arduous powers vested in me by Parliament are sufficient to render my opinion in India a substitute for the occasional and unavoidable defect of precise and express commands from the sovereign authority of the British empire.

In the exercise of this discretion I am subject to a severe responsibility; but wherever it appears to me to be my duty to exercise my discretion, and to apply for the assistance of his Majesty's naval force in the prosecution of my endeavours against the common enemy, I conceive that his Majesty's naval commander is not only justified in complying with my application, but absolutely required to aid me, unless the condition of his ships shall preclude their co-operation, or unless, in his conscientious judgment, the attempt which I propose may appear to be impracticable, or dangerous to the public service. The want of his Majesty's express commands will never be received either by his Majesty, or by the public, as an admissible justification of the conduct of any public officer for declining to co-operate against the enemy in an attack which appears to be practicable, and which promises advantage to the general cause.

11. Of the rule which I assert, I have furnished an example in my own practice, and if the principle which your Excellency has adopted had governed my conduct, the conquest of Mysoor would not have been achieved.

12. Your Excellency supposes that the express command of his Majesty is necessary to justify your co-operation on the present occasion, because his Majesty's express command had been signified to the commanders of his naval forces on all similar occasions within the compass of your experience.

13. It is undoubtedly the duty of his Majesty's ministers, in time of war, to issue express commands in all cases which can

be foreseen, and to which such orders may be justly applicable. This practice will be more diligently pursued in proportion to the activity and ability of the administration actually in power. But however general such a practice may have been under the administration of his Majesty's present ministers, during the course of this war, no argument of precedent can thence be derived to exempt public officers, stationed in distant possessions, from the indispensable duty of availing themselves, with promptitude and alacrity, of those invaluable occasions and opportunities of reducing the enemy, which remote wisdom cannot foresee, and for which remote authority cannot provide.

14. By issuing express commands for the annoyance of the enemy in India, in particular instances, the wisdom of his Majesty's councils never proposed to render the receipt of his express previous commands in time of war, a necessary preliminary of every important act of hostility, nor to forbid the commencement of any rational enterprize in this quarter of the globe, until the direct notification of his royal pleasure should arrive in an official form. In any case, such a limitation upon the genius and spirit of the public servants in India, could only tend to contract our sphere of action, and to impair the predominant strength of the British power. But in the present war, contending against an enemy of indefatigable activity, of inexhaustible resource, and of the most daring spirit of adventure, this confined policy would weaken all our means of meeting the characteristic advantages of our antagonist, and would leave to him the undisputed possession of the most extensive field for the free exercise of his formidable powers of enterprize, promptitude, and boldness.

15. If this argument could require any additional illustration, it would be furnished by the extent of the injury which the trade and commerce of India have sustained from the activity and boldness with which the inhabitants of the isles of France and Bourbon have employed the limited resources of those islands in the prosecution of hostilities during the present war, under every disadvantage of internal discord, and even of the occasional neglect, if not of the positive enmity of France.

16. In the midst of all these difficulties and embarrassments, the naval force of the French islands has carried into Port Louis British property to the amount of above two millions of pounds sterling, since the commencement of the present war.

17. My intimate personal knowledge of the characters of his

Majesty's present Ministers, as well as my experience of their public conduct, enable me to assure your Excellency, that they will never become the patrons of any system, which in any quarter of the globe shall be calculated to limit the energy of British talents, to discourage the ardour of British spirit, or to open new and secure channels to the enterprizing character of French adventure.

18. Even in the instances in which express orders have been dispatched to India from home in time of war, great latitude has always been afforded to the discretion of the Government on the spot; and while I have had the honour to hold the arduous station in which I am now placed, I have uniformly claimed from his Majesty's Ministers that degree of confidence which, during time of war, should admit of my selecting, in concert with the commanders of the sea and land forces, the time and mode of attacking the possessions of the enemy in India. Without this extent of confidence, it would be impossible for any person in my station to be responsible for the safety of his important charge. On the other hand, I am persuaded that his Majesty's Ministers rely on me, that no practicable opportunity of reducing the enemy's power in India will be neglected, and it shall be my earnest endeavour to justify their confidence in this respect.

I have the honour to be, &c.

(Signed) WELLESLEY.

APPENDIX.

1. Lord Wellesley's Oude Treaty.

Treaty between the Honourable the East India Company and his Excellency the Nawaub Vizier Ool Mumaulick, Yemeen oo Dowlah, Nazim ool Moolk, Saadut Ali Khan Bahauder, Mobaurez Jung, for ceding to the Company, in perpetual sovereignty, certain portions of his Excellency's territorial possessions, in commutation of the subsidy now payable to the Company by the Vizier.

(Extract.)

2. The subsidy, which by the second Article of the treaty of 1798, his Excellency engaged to pay to the Company (now that territory is assigned in lieu thereof and of the expences of the additional troops) is to cease for ever; and his Excellency is released from the obligation of defraying the expences of any additional troops which at any time may be required for the protection of Oude and its dependencies, whether of the countries ceded to the Company, or the territories which shall remain in the possession of his Excellency the Vizier.

3. The Honourable the East India Company hereby engage to defend the territories which will remain to his Excellency the Vizier against all foreign and domestic enemies; provided always, that it be in the power of the Company's Government to station the British troops in such parts of his Excellency's dominions as shall appear to the said Government most expedient; and provided further, that his Excellency, retaining in his pay four battalions of infantry, one battalion of Nejeebs and Mewatties, two thousand horsemen, and to the number of 300 Goolandauz, shall dismiss the remainder of his troops, excepting such number of armed Peons as shall be deemed necessary for the purpose of the collections, and a few horsemen and Nejeebs to attend the persons of the Aumils.

4. A detachment of the British troops, with a proportion of artillery, shall at all times be attached to his Excellency's person.

5. That the true intent and meaning of the first, second, third, and fourth articles of the treaty may be clearly understood, it is hereby declared, that the territorial cessions being in lieu of the subsidy, and of all expences on account of the Company's defensive engagements with his Excellency, no demand whatever shall be made upon the territory of his Excellency on account of expences which the Honourable Company may incur by assembling forces to repel the attack or menaced attack of a foreign enemy, on account of the detachment attached to his Excellency's person, on account of troops which may occasionally be furnished for suppressing rebellions or disorders in his Excellency's territories, on account of any future change of military station, or on account of failure in the resources of the ceded districts, arising from unfavourable seasons, the calamities of war, or any other cause whatsoever.

6. The territories ceded to the Honourable Company by the first article of this treaty, shall be subject to the exclusive management and control of the said Company and their officers; and the Honourable the East India Company hereby guarantee to his Excellency the Vizier, and to his heirs and successors, the possession of the territories which will remain to his Excellency after the territorial cession, together with the exercise of his and their authority within the said dominions. His Excellency engages that he will establish in his reserved dominions such a system of administration (to be carried into effect by his own officers) as shall be conducive to the prosperity of his subjects, and be calculated to secure the lives and property of the inhabitants; and his Excellency will always advise with, and act in conformity to the counsel of the officers of the said Honourable Company.

9. All the articles of former treaties, for establishing and cementing the union and friendship subsisting between the two States, are to continue in full force; and all the articles of the treaty concluded by the late Governor-General Sir John Shore, on the part of the Honourable the East India Company and his Excellency the Vizier in the year 1798, not annulled by this treaty, are to remain in force and continue binding upon both contracting parties.

SELECTIONS FROM THE WELLINGTON DESPATCHES.

2. Reflections upon the plan for having the army in the Carnatic at all times in a state of preparation.

Mobilization and reinforcement of the Madras army, against Tippoo.

26th Oct., 1798.

The first question to be considered is, whether, with any preparation, the greatest army which it is possible for the Company to maintain in the Carnatic can, in co-operation with the army on the Malabar coast, take the field with any prospect of success without assistance in men from Bengal. The object which these armies must have is the siege of Seringapatam, and can they undertake it with any reasonable prospect of success, with the numbers which it is possible for them to bring into the field?

Cavalry:		
Native	1,600	
European	800	
		2,400
Artillery		400
Native infantry		9,000
Europeans		3,500
		15,300

These numbers are according to an enlarged calculation of General Harris, which provides for leaving in Fort St. George, and other necessary garrisons in the Carnatic, a sufficient number of troops to defend them. What the army from the Malabar side would be, it is impossible to say; but I will suppose it 5000 men, composed as usual of European and Native infantry, and of European artillery. Thus the army destined for the siege of Seringapatam would consist of 20,000 men.

It is impossible to decide absolutely whether this army would be sufficient for the siege of Seringapatam without having been at that place, and knowing not only its former but its present situation. We must therefore have recourse to conjecture upon this subject, and must be led by probabilities founded upon the experience of the former war; and we must at the same time take into consideration the circumstances which bear upon the question, and which have occasioned an alteration in our situation since that time. When Lord Cornwallis made his attempt he had about 20,000 men. He had, it is true, a larger number of Europeans than the army would have at present, and a larger proportion of artillery; but I believe the total numbers of his army were not greater than what I have above stated that we should have under the arrangement proposed by General Harris.

There are some circumstances, however, in the relative situation of this army and Tippoo's which are considerably advantageous to us. The first of these is, that we have now a considerable body of regularly disciplined cavalry: at that time we had none. Another is, that he had at that time the frontier: we have it now. He had parties which acted constantly in our rear, which obliged Lord Cornwallis occasionally to detach large bodies not only for the immediate protection of his convoys, but for the safety of the Carnatic, and probably that of his own army: as we have now that iron frontier, the fortresses of which we never had in our possession in the last war, there is no reason to expect that the same detachments which were then necessary will be equally so in any war that we may have in future.

Another consideration is, that in the former war the operations from unavoidable causes took two campaigns. One of these was the necessity of reducing Bangalore. At present Bangalore is destroyed; and although that may by some be reckoned a disadvantage, yet as it is not absolutely necessary to adhere to that route to Seringapatam, the disadvantage of wanting the place as a depôt is more than counterbalanced by the advantage of not being obliged to wait to take it. Either by the route of Cauveryporam or Ryacotta, the communication between Seringapatam and one of our own fortresses is nearly as short as it is between that place and Bangalore; and there is this additional advantage by using one of these last routes, that there will be no necessity to take many of those large and strong hill forts to which Lord Cornwallis laid siege and took in the last war. This will save much time.

Another circumstance of advantage in the destruction of Bangalore is, that, as probably the operations will not linger out to two campaigns, there will not be so much necessity for a junction with the Allies as there was in the last war, and time will not be lost in effecting the junction, and time and troops will be saved in taking the places of which it was necessary to have possession in order to insure their communication with their own country, and all the benefits which we must expect to derive from their co-operation. In every future war the possession of our present frontier will enable us to commence our operations more from the southward, and the measures taken to secure a supply of grain upon the scene of action will enable us to proceed without the immediate assistance of our Allies.

Under these circumstances, then, it appears not only that the army would be as large as that which Lord Cornwallis had, and with which he succeeded, but that this country has many advantages at present which it had not at that time, and which would enable the Government to undertake the operation with a better prospect of success than it had formerly, and of success in a shorter period of time.

Those, however, who know most upon this subject, at least whose official situation enables them to be the best judges, say that this number of men is not sufficient, and that it is impossible to commence the operations against Tippoo Sultaun without assistance in men from Bengal. It becomes therefore necessary to consider the question relating to the state of preparation of this army with a reference to that assertion, supposing it to be well grounded.

The march of a detachment, say of six thousand men, from Bengal, may be supposed to take six months at least. Whether the number of men is six thousand or eight thousand, it is a matter of indifference; but it is certain that, whatever the number may be, it cannot take less than six months, and probably it will take more, to bring them down by land.

If then it will take six months to bring down that which will alone enable the Government to undertake anything effectual against the enemy, why may not the preparations be making during the time that the reinforcement is on its march? Why should the Company be put to the expense of keeping up an immense army of 15,000 men constantly in a state of preparation for the field, when those who are in the command of it, and who propose that it should be kept up to that extent, are of opinion that even then it can do nothing?

The question then is, is it advisable to incur this large expense under these circumstances? Those articles of preparation which will occasion expense are, 1st, an establishment of bullocks for the train; 2ndly, one for carriage; 3rdly, a depôt of grain; 4thly, an augmentation of the Native troops, in order to make the number of those in the centre division in readiness equal to 9,000; 5thly, camp equipage for the officers.

There is no doubt but that bullocks might be provided for the train during the time that the Bengal detachment would be coming down, if it is to come down by land; and therefore that it may be said that the expense of keeping up draught bullocks in time of peace, with a view to their use in war, would not be necessary. However, in answer thereto, it may be said, 1st, that the measures which I shall propose presently may bring the Bengal detachment here in a shorter period than six months; 2ndly, that the draught bullocks which will have been trained for a certain time, will be better than any which are provided just at the moment when they are wanted; 3rdly, not a military, but a political object will be gained by having some bullocks, as it will not be necessary that foreign powers should know the full extent of our preparations, and probably they may have the effect of preventing the execution of any hostile design. I therefore think that at all events it is advisable to have always 1500 draught bullocks ready.

2ndly. The carriage bullocks.

I understand that these are to be had in any number by making advances to the bullock owners or maistries in proportion to the number wanted; that two months will give any number that the army may want;

and that any permanent expense, however great (short of the expense of keeping at all times the entire number wanted), would not produce them in a shorter time. If this is the case, it is not advisable to incur any expense under this head.

3rdly. The expense of a depôt of grain is so trifling, it gives so much ease to all the first movements of the army, and renders its operations so certain, that it ought certainly to be incurred.

4thly. The augmentation of the army.

General Harris proposes that[1] regiments should be added to its present numbers, even supposing that all the regiments were in the Carnatic, &c., and that other means of defence were found for Ceylon and the conquests to the eastward. According to his distribution, there would then be 9000 disposable Native infantry in the centre division, and all the garrisons would be amply provided for. Here will be the great expense; and as even that number of men will not enable this Government to make a forward movement, and as a reinforcement from Bengal must still be waited for, I recommend that no part of it should be incurred.

The number which I think sufficient is from 4000 to 5000 Natives in the centre division; and the number of regiments which therefore ought to be struck off General Harris's account is two. The manner in which I propose to provide the remainder of the men is, 1st. To put the Bengal marine battalion upon the establishment, and make it a regiment of two battalions, or 2000 men, all to be raised at Chittagong. 2ndly. To turn the Calcutta militia into another marine regiment of 2000 men. 3rdly. If the Nawab-Vizier will consent to reduce his establishment of troops, and to take our troops in lieu of them, to raise at Chittagong and upon the sea coast all the regiments which must be added to the establishment in consequence thereof; but at all events to add a third marine regiment of 2000 men to the establishment, even if you should be obliged to reduce one of the high caste regiments at present in the service. These marine regiments should always be kept at Barrackpoor, Midnapoor, Burhampoor, &c. &c., in the neighbourhood of Calcutta: they would answer equally well with the others for doing the duty of those places; and they would not only enable the Supreme Government, in addition to volunteers, to send to this country a large body of troops in a short time at short notice, but they would be a body of troops which might be employed in all parts of India, and would therefore add infinitely to the power of the Company, which is cramped by the prejudices and habits of the Bengal Native troops.

If it should be necessary to add any regiments to this establishment in consequence of the arrangements with the Nizam, they ought to be raised here; as the sepoys of this country are cheaper, and I must say

[1] Blank in manuscript. ED.

better, than any that can be got in Bengal. It may then be said, why not raise in this country any force which must be raised avowedly for the purposes of its defence? It must be observed, however, there will be no additional force, at least a very small one: it will be only an arrangement, making a battalion a regiment, turning militia into regulars, and making a high caste regiment one which will go to sea.

5thly. Camp equipage for the officers.

What has been said upon the subject of carriage bullocks applies equally to the means of conveying camp equipage. It can always be got ready before the army is ready to take the field, but a sufficiency for a very large body of troops ought to be kept in the stores in the centre division.

Having noticed those subjects which General Harris has mentioned, I come now to the consideration of one of which he has taken no notice. It is the repair of the garrisons upon the frontier and in the Carnatic. Both require it, and it will cost some money immediately, as well as annually a certain sum. ARTHUR WELLESLEY.

3. Draft of the Description of our March to Major-General St. Leger.

March of the Army to Seringapatam.

The British grand army and the Nizam's army had joined previous to our entering Mysore, and marched together. The former consisted of about 3000 excellent cavalry, five strong regiments of European infantry, all good, and eleven battalions of sepoys, with about fifty pieces of cannon.

The Nizam's army, under my command, consisted of the 33rd, six excellent battalions of the Company's sepoys, four rapscallion battalions of the Nizam's, which, however, behaved well, and really about 10,000 (which they called 25,000) cavalry of all nations, some good and some bad, and twenty-six pieces of cannon. These armies marched in two columns parallel to each other; one from its right, the other from its left, at the distance of about three miles from each other.

The British cavalry generally led the British column, about 500 of the best of the Nizam's led that of the Nizam; these two generally closed towards each other.

One regiment of British cavalry was generally in the rear of the British column, the whole of the cavalry of the Nizam in the rear of mine, and these rather closed to each other, so that the march of these two armies was almost in the form of a square or oblong, of which the front and rear were formed of cavalry, and about two or three miles in extent; the right and left (owing to the immense space taken up in the column by field-pieces drawn by bullocks) about six or seven miles. In this square went everything belonging to the army, and the whole space was filled excepting what lay between the leading brigade of infantry of each column, which was left clear, lest it should become necessary to form.

You will have some idea of what there was in that space when I state to you the number of bullocks that I know were in the public service, and in the employment of brinjarries or grain merchants, which did not compose one-half of the whole number that were with the army. There were in the department of the commissary of stores about 25,000, in that of the commissary of grain about 20,000, in that of the commissary of provisions about 5000, in that of the camp equipage department about 5000, making in all in the service of the British grand army about 60,000 bullocks, of which about 15,000 were draught, the others carried loads.

The Company's bullock department in the Nizam's army had in it about 3000, divided among different departments. Besides these there were with the grand army about 20,000 bullocks loaded with grain belonging to the brinjarries, about 8000 loaded with gram for the cavalry horses belonging to the gram agents. The Nizam's army (to my constant daily annoyance) had with it 25000 bullocks loaded with grain belonging to the brinjarries. Besides all these, the number of elephants, camels, bullocks, carts, coolies, plunderers, &c. &c., belonging to individuals in the army, particularly in that of the Nizam, was beyond calculation; but as upon one occasion I had an opportunity of seeing one wing of the British army, and the whole army of the Nizam, move light to attack the enemy, that is to say, without anything belonging to the public excepting what was necessary for the field train, and a few days' provisions for the Europeans, I was able to form a judgment of the quantity of private baggage in the army, and I have no scruple in declaring that the number of cattle and people in the employment of individuals was double that in the employment of the public. Yet on that day it is fair that I should mention to you the Nizam's army marched above twenty miles. You may have some idea of the thing when I tell you that when all were together, there was a multitude in motion which covered about eighteen square miles.

We brought forward from Madras to Seringapatam a battering train, and in fact a moving arsenal. The former consisted of 50 pieces of iron cannon, for each gun of which were brought forward 1200 rounds of shot and immense quantities of powder, and every kind of small stores which are used in an arsenal.

Our march was usually as long as those made by large armies in Europe, from ten to twelve miles; we always started at six, and we arrived at our ground about twelve, sometimes later, if there were difficulties on the road. We encamped in two lines fronting different ways, and this heap of baggage between us. What is most extraordinary, by the order of march and encampment above described, we did not lose anything to signify during our whole march, notwithstanding the efforts of the enemy's light troops who constantly attended us, and who are certainly the best troops of that kind that I have ever seen.[1]

WELLESLEY.

4. To the Earl of Mornington.

Battle of Mallavelly.

(Extract.) Camp, 2 miles west of Seringapatam, 5th April, 1799.

My dear Mornington,

In the action of the 27th of March, at Mallavelly, his troops behaved better than they have ever been known to behave. His infantry advanced, and almost stood the charge of bayonets of the 33rd, and his cavalry rode at General Baird's European brigade. He did not support them as he ought, having drawn off his guns at the moment we made our attack, and even pushed forward these troops to cover the retreat of his guns. This is the cause of the total destruction of the troops he left behind him, without loss to us, and of the panic with which we

---

[1] *Return of Tippoo Sultaun's Army at the commencement of the campaign of 1799.*

Names.	Number of Fighting Men.	Monthly Expense. Cant. Pagodas.		
Meer Meerans (Generals)	26	2,800	0	0
Meer Suddoors (Officers in general superintending of Forts)	9	750	0	0
Buckshees, or Commanders of Brigades	101	4,840	0	0
Stable Horse	3,503	25,799	3	0
Silladar Horse (a horse the property of the rider)	9,392	86,800	0	0
Infantry, Regulars	23,483	132,884	9	2
Geish (Armed Militia)	6,209	25,518	8	0
Ashâam (Matchlockmen and Peons)	4,747	12,956	6	8
Total Fighting Men	47,470	292,349	6	10
Mootsuddies, Lascars, Pioneers, Artificers, Establishments, &c. &c.	22,392	67,971	5	12
Total of every description of Persons attached to the Army	69,862	360,321	4	6
Out Garrisons, 27 Principal Forts	14,947	43,338	1	14
" 113 Lesser Forts	14,981	14,955	1	14
Total	29,828	58,293	3	12

have reason to believe all his troops are now affected. His light cavalry, looties, and others, are the best of the kind in the world. They have hung upon us, night and day, from the moment we entered his country to this. Some of them have always had sight of us, and have been prepared to cut off any persons venturing out of the reach of our camp-guards. We came by a road so unfrequented that it was not possible to destroy all the forage, which would have distressed us much; but they did as much, even in that way, as could be expected from them. If Tippoo had had sense and spirit sufficient to use his cavalry and infantry as he might have done, I have no hesitation in saying that we should not now be here, and probably should not be out of the jungles near Bangalore.

Believe me, &c.,
ARTHUR WELLESLEY.

5. To the Earl of Mornington.

Colonel Wellesley's Repulse.

(Extract.)

Camp before Seringapatam,
18th April, 1799.

My dear Mornington,

On the night of the 5th we made an attack upon the enemy's out-posts, which, at least on my side, was not quite so successful as could have been wished. The fact was that the night was very dark, that the enemy expected us, and were strongly posted in an almost impenetrable jungle. We lost an officer killed, and others and some men wounded (of the 33rd); and at last, as I could not find out the post which it was desirable I should occupy, I was obliged to desist from the attack, the enemy also having retired from the post. In the morning they re-occupied it, and I attacked it again at daylight, and carried it with ease and little loss. In the course of the night of the 5th and the day of the 6th the General was enabled to occupy a line of posts which gave complete security to his camp till the Bombay army joined, at the same time that they enabled him to commence his operations for the siege with advantage.

I got a slight touch on the knee, from which I have felt no inconvenience, on the night of the 5th; and I have come to a determination, when in my power, never to suffer an attack to be made by night upon an enemy who is prepared and strongly posted, and whose posts have not been reconnoitred by daylight. We remained in the posts which we occupied on the 6th till the Bombay army joined on the 14th.

Believe me, &c.,
ARTHUR WELLESLEY.

6. To the Earl of Mornington.

Plunder of Seringapatam.

(Extract.) Seringapatam, 8th May, 1799.

My dear Mornington,

It was impossible to expect that after the labour which the troops had undergone in working up to the place, and the various successes they had had in six different affairs with Tippoo's troops, in all of which they had come to the bayonet with them, they should not have looked to the plunder of this place. Nothing therefore can have exceeded what was done on the night of the 4th. Scarcely a house in the town was left unplundered, and I understand that in camp jewels of the greatest value, bars of gold, &c. &c , have been offered for sale in the bazaars of the army by our soldiers, sepoys, and followers. I came in to take the command on the morning of the 5th, and by the greatest exertion, by hanging, flogging, &c. &c., in the course of that day I restored order among the troops, and I hope I have gained the confidence of the people. They are returning to their houses and beginning again to follow their occupations, but the property of every one is gone.

Believe me, &c.,

ARTHUR WELLESLEY.

7. Memorandum on Oude.

The Company necessarily responsible for the defence and internal administration of Oude.

(Undated.)

The province of Oude is situated to the north-west of the provinces of Bengal and Bahar, which are under the Bengal government. It is bounded to the northward by impassable mountains, which separate it from the country of Thibet, the river Ganges forming its western boundary. As the Ganges and Jumna run through it, part of it is on the same side of the former as Bengal and Bahar. To the south-west are Corah, Allahabad, and the Jumna; and to the south the province of Bundelcund, which was possessed by a race of petty Rajahs.

Rohilcund, which lies on the left or east of the Ganges, was not at that period in the possession of the Nabobs of Oude, nor were Corah and Allahabad, commonly called the Dooab, and lying between the Jumna and the Ganges. Benares, however, was tributary to Oude, which province is also situated east, or on the left of the Ganges.

Oude is a fertile country, was at that time well cultivated, and is peopled by a hardy race, who have for a great length of time supplied soldiers to all the states of India.

In this situation it is obvious that the government of Oude must always have been an object of jealousy to that power which possessed the provinces of Bahar and Bengal, which are situated lower down upon the Ganges. In fact, these provinces had no natural barrier against an invasion from Oude, and depended for their security upon their own artificial means of defence.

This was the case not only in respect to the state of Oude itself, but in respect to the Rohillas; to the King,[1] who was at that period of time in some degree of strength; and to the Mahrattas; each of which powers might have found an easy and convenient passage through Oude to an invasion of the Company's provinces of Bahar and Bengal.

On the other hand, by the possession of the provinces under the government of Oude, or an intimate union with the government, a barrier was immediately provided for the provinces under the Bengal government. Nothing remained on the left or east of the Ganges besides the Nabob of Oude and the Company excepting the Rohillas, and this river afforded a strong natural barrier against all invaders. Besides this object, the seat of war, in consequence of the alliance with or possession of Oude, was removed from the Company's provinces, the source of all the means of carrying on war, to those of the enemy, if it should have been practicable to carry on offensive war; or at all events to those of the Nabob, if such supposed war should have been reduced to the defensive.

By the first treaty with the Nabobs of Oude, the Company were bound to assist the Nabob with their troops, on the condition of receiving payment for their expenses. The adoption of this system of alliance is always to be attributed to the weakness of the state which receives the assistance, and the remedy generally aggravates that evil. It is usually attended by a stipulation that the subsidy should be paid in equal monthly instalments; and as this subsidy is generally the whole or nearly the whole disposable resource of the state, it is not easy to produce it at the stipulated moment. The tributary government is then reduced to borrow at usurious interest, to grant tuncaws upon the land for repayment, to take advances from aumildars, to sell the office of aumildar, and to adopt all the measures which it may be supposed distress on the one hand and avarice and extortion on the other can invent to procure the money necessary to provide for the payment of the stipulated subsidies.

As soon as such an alliance has been formed, it has invariably been discovered that the whole strength of the tributary government consisted in the aid afforded by its more powerful ally, or rather protector? and from that moment the respect, duty, and loyalty of its subjects have been

---

[1] i.e. The Emperor. Ed.

weakened, and it has become more difficult to realize the resources of the state. To this evil must be added those of the same kind arising from oppression by aumildars, who have paid largely for their situations, and must remunerate themselves in the course of one year for what they have advanced from those holding tuncaws and other claimants upon the soil on account of loans to government, and the result is an increasing deficiency in the regular resources of the state.

But these financial difficulties, created by weakness and increased by oppression, and which are attended by a long train of disorders throughout the country, must attract the attention of the protecting government, and then these last are obliged to interfere in the internal administration in order to save the resources of the state and to preclude the necessity of employing the troops in quelling internal rebellion and disorder, which were intended to resist the foreign enemy.

ARTHUR WELLESLEY.

8. Memorandum on Bengal.

Influence of the Company's rule upon the resources and prosperity of Bengal. Private Trade Tribute.

In the 'Remarks upon the Present State of the Husbandry and Commerce of Bengal,' several circumstances are adduced in order to prove that that country loses by its connection with Great Britain, as that connection at present exists, through the medium of an exclusive commercial Company.

The grievances principally complained of are the want of due encouragement to the cultivation of its valuable produce; the commercial monopoly of the Company, which, as it raises the price of freight, precludes the possibility of transporting that produce to a valuable market; and the proportion of the revenues of the country which is drawn from it as a tribute to the Company and to the British Government.

Another circumstance of which complaint is made, but which is totally distinct from the abuses of the management of an exclusive Company, is the want of encouragement at home to the raw and to some of the manufactured produce of Bengal, such as sugar, tobacco, raw silk, &c., &c. I shall consider each of these with that impartiality which should always reign in discussions upon subjects of this nature.

The productions of India are grain, indigo, raw silk, tobacco, sugar. It has often been a question whether the total rent which is paid by the inhabitants of Bengal is greater at present than it was during the dynasty of the Moguls or the subsequent government of the native princes; it however seems now to be understood that it is about equal to what it was at those times, and I shall take that for granted.

The sum which is paid to the Government is about equal to that which was paid to the Government of the Moguls, and which appears to have been divided into two parts: the one was applied to pay the expenses of the government in Bengal, the other was sent to the treasury in Delhi. The expenses of the collection of those revenues were about equal to what they are at this moment, and therefore the zemindar or landholder, or under whatever title he might have been known, retained no more of the rent than he does at this moment under the British Government. If the profits of the zemindar are small now, they were equally so formerly, which, in addition to its being a proof that there were formerly no landlords in Bengal, or, in other words, that the zemindars were not proprietors, is a proof that the British Government gives as much encouragement to the cultivation and improvement of land as was given during the time of the best of the native governors.

But the British Government not only have not taken more rent than the native governments, but they have made an engagement that they will not take more than they do at present, by making a permanent settlement and by giving to the zemindars the property of the soil. Therefore, as far as security and permanency give encouragement to agriculture, more encouragement has been given by the British Government than by the natives.

It seems, however, that there are certain articles which are produced in Bengal which require a superior cultivation and a greater expense, which neither the tenants nor the landholders are enabled to advance. Among these, indigo, sugar, tobacco, and silk are enumerated.

In order that these articles may receive the cultivation which they require, and in order that there may be a body of landholders capable of bearing the expense of giving it to them, it is proposed that Europeans should be allowed to purchase and to become proprietors in India.

The first question is, whether the cultivation would be mended by their interference. The husbandry in India is said to be very defective. The simplicity with which all its complex operations are performed is not supposed to be advantageous to it, and it is therefore imagined that superior ingenuity and management would give a larger product at a cheaper rate, and that, in time, the example set by skilful Europeans would be followed throughout the country. Notwithstanding the objections which the Hindoos have to alter any institution which has been handed down to them by their ancestors, many of which are reckoned sacred, it is believed that if the advantages of European or British management could be made clear to them, it would, in time, be universally adopted. It is also true that the expense of clearing and stocking a farm as it ought to be cannot be borne excepting by an

European, and therefore the Europeans ought to be allowed to purchase, if it is wished that the agriculture of the country should be much improved. There are, however, objections to that measure, which arise partly from the character of the natives, and partly from the effect which the climate has upon European constitutions. The natives hold every European in the greatest awe, and therefore it is imagined that, if these were allowed to settle in such parts of the country as they might think fit, they might be induced to tyrannise over the former, who would fear to complain, and thus the British name and character would become an object of detestation to the Hindoos. However, regulations might be adopted to prevent this evil, of which the natives might be made acquainted; and as they have had many opportunities of witnessing the rigour of British justice, even upon British subjects, when they deserve it, it is believed that they would not fear to complain in case of receiving an injury. The climate is a great objection to suffering the unconstrained resort of British subjects to India. Those who have not been in Bengal are not aware of the effects which its climate has upon the European constitution; but they are so great, and those who have been there for any length of time become so enervated, that it is doubted whether those benefits which are expected would result from their residence. A European cannot with safety expose himself to the sun: how then can he hope to superintend the various operations of husbandry with success? His generation, even supposing him to be married to a European woman, dwindles and falls off to such a degree that the third generation from the original settler is but little removed, in manners and disposition, from the old inhabitants of the country; and therefore, excepting by a constant drain from the mother country, the full benefits of this colonization cannot be expected.

The policy of the Company's Government has hitherto been to prevent, as much as possible, the residence of Europeans in India; and it has been grounded upon the necessity of preserving in the minds of the natives a respect for the British name and character, which, it is feared, an unrestrained intercourse would tend to remove, as well as upon the danger which would result were they to become acquainted with the language and character of the natives in their territories, and then to enter into the service of the native princes. If an unrestrained intercourse hitherto would have produced either of these effects, it is equally dangerous at the present moment, even although every British subject should become a proprietor; and from some events which have taken place lately, from the language which has been held in the 'Remarks,' it is more than ever necessary for the Company to prevent the resort of Europeans to Bengal. The circumstance which tended most in the course of the last year to preserve the allegiance of the army to the Company's Government was the desire which every individual had to return to Great Britain, and the certainty that if the violent measures proposed were adopted, or that if encouragement were given to proceed to extremities, the door to his return was shut for ever. To this no individual, particularly none of those who have fortunes sufficiently large to maintain them, could make their minds up; and the consequence was that, at the moment when everything appeared most desperate, all subsided. If Europeans had been settled with their families in India; if these men had, or could have had, their homes in that country, the Company would have lost it, and nothing could ever have regained it.

By the violence of the language and of the sentiments which are held forth in the 'Remarks,' by the bitter complaints which are made of the British Government and connection, the sentiments of the Company's civil servants and of those who reside in India by the Company's licence are very apparent: how much more violent would they be if they were proprietors of a soil for the commercial advantages of whose inhabitants they now so violently contend! It is to be expected that they would likewise make India their home; and thus Great Britain would lose its strongest hold upon their allegiance, their desire to return to their native country. However desirable, therefore, it may be that the natives of India should obtain the advantage of British skill and management in agriculture, it is not advisable that the Company should suffer its servants, or those who reside in India by its licence, to become proprietors of land.

There are other measures, which, although they might not be equally efficacious, might still tend considerably to the prosperity of Bengal, as far as that is connected with its agriculture. Markets might be established throughout the country, which would enable the cultivator at all times to sell his produce without the difficulty and expense attending upon a long carriage. These would likewise insure a uniformity in price, which, above all things, has been found in other countries the most favourable to agriculture; and by enabling one district to profit by the plenty of another, they would insure all parts of Bengal from that worst of evils, with which it has been so frequently afflicted,—a famine.

Good roads should likewise be made at first from the principal place in each district to those in its neighbourhood. These ought to be kept in repair. The inland navigation ought to be encouraged, and every measure ought to be adopted, which, by rendering its use more easy, will make more perfect the communication from one part of this country to the other.

If these measures were adopted, the agriculture of Bengal would not require the assistance of Europeans, in order that it might be brought to a very sufficient state of perfection.

The commerce of Bengal consists at present in an unrestrained intercourse with all parts of India and the Eastern Seas; in the commerce carried on by the Company, and in its intercourse with Europe and America by means of foreign nations, and clandestine trade carried on by the persons resident in India under the Company's licence and by Americans, and likewise the inland trade with the northern parts of India and the Deccan by the water-carriage, caravans, &c. &c. The amount of the whole is four millions and a half.

The freedom of the trade which is carried on with the different parts of India is highly to the honour of the Company; it has more than trebled since the peace of '83.[1] It has suffered in some degree for want of naval protection in the course of this war; but a peace will re-establish it again upon its old footing, and it is probable that, with the same freedom, it will increase in a greater proportion than it has hitherto.

The commerce which the Company carries on with Bengal by means of its monopoly is so little productive, that were it not for the necessity of bringing home the surplus of the revenues through the medium of trade, lest Bengal should be entirely drained of the precious metals, it would be better for them as a commercial body to give up the trade entirely. However, that trade at present amounts to above a million sterling. It consists chiefly in piece goods and saltpetre, and some indigo; but the price of the Company's freight is so high, that the other articles which are produced in India, and which are marketable in Europe, cannot be carried, as their bulk is too great in comparison with their value. Thus, then, the commerce which the Company carries on with Bengal is disadvantageous to itself, and does not tend so much to the advantage of that country as it might were it differently managed, and did the price of freight come more nearly to what it is really worth.

The price which it is fixed the private traders are to pay for the freight they occupy in the Company's ships is 5*l.* per ton out and 15*l.* per ton home, which is liable to an addition in time of war. The Company aver, and, it is believed, with some truth, that their freight costs them more; but what article, besides the expense of insurance, can repay that price? It is certain that the Company have monopolized the exportation of the most valuable articles; but still they are losers; and how much greater must be the loss of the private traders to whom is left the trade in gross produce, and the raw materials of manufacture alone! A considerable trade has long been carried on with Europe from Bengal by American and foreign vessels, and some clandestine trade.

The majority of these American and foreign vessels have belonged

---

[1] Tonnage of the shipping employed in the country trade in . '83 . . 44,865
" " " " '91 . . 175,407
Total number of ships in . . . . '83 . . 128
" " . . . . '91 . . 575

to British subjects resident in India, who thus supply Europe with the produce of Bengal without submitting themselves to the control of the Company, and without paying any duties in London. The amount of this trade is supposed to be one million four hundred thousand pounds.[1]

In order that Government might obtain a control over this trade, that London might become its emporium, and that Great Britain might have the advantage of levying a duty upon the consumption of Europe of Indian articles, the Company were obliged to give 3000 tons, to be increased, when necessary, to the private trade; but the price fixed for that tonnage is very high, because the Company have retained the monopoly of those articles which by their value were most likely to pay the tonnage; and as shipping could be procured at a rate infinitely lower, the foreign or clandestine trade exists to as great a degree at present as it did at the time when the regulation was adopted that the Company should furnish a proportion of tonnage to private traders. These insist that tonnage might be procured at 3*l.* per ton out, and 3*l.* per ton home. However, it seems certain that tonnage can be procured at a much cheaper rate than that at which the Company supply it; and although it may still be necessary that the trade with Bengal should be carried on through the medium of an exclusive Company, there is no good reason why the people of Great Britain should pay the extravagant price of this tonnage for the Indian goods they consume, in addition to the price they pay for the mismanagement natural to an exclusive Company in all its commercial concerns.

Bengal and Great Britain both suffer from the high price of this freight: Bengal, as it is deprived of the British market for much of its produce; and Great Britain, as it pays a high price for all the Indian commodities which it consumes, and as it is deprived of much of the Bengal produce which would be useful in its manufactures, but which, on account of the high price of freight, cannot be transported with any reasonable prospect of profit. Therefore, as far as this high price of freight tends to deprive Bengal of a market for its produce, the inhabitants have reason to complain of want of encouragement in their agriculture; but they have not more reason to complain than the people of Great Britain, who, from the same arrangements, suffer both as consumers and as merchants and manufacturers.

Without at present entering into the question whether it would be advisable or otherwise to lay open the trade entirely, or whether it would be advisable to suffer an unrestrained intercourse between Great Britain and India, it may be said that policy as well as justice requires that

---

[1] Number of ships about . . . 30
Tonnage " . . . 13,000

shipping should be found at the lowest rate, in order that due encouragement may be given to the agriculture and commerce of Bengal, and that the private trade should be left as free as the nature of the Company's government at home and abroad will permit it. If measures are not adopted having these objects in view, it is not to be expected that the clandestine and the foreign trade will not increase; and thus Great Britain will lose not only the advantage of being the carriers of Indian produce for all Europe, but likewise the duties which she would be enabled to levy upon the consumption of Europe upon Indian articles in their transit.

Measures having lowness of freight and freedom of trade in view may be adopted upon two principles: either the commerce with India may be laid open to all England from the port of London, and every man who pleases may adventure thither, or the Company may be the medium of export as well as import. If the former be adopted, the unrestrained resort of British subjects to India must be the consequence, which in another part of this paper I have objected to, and therefore that measure ought to be laid aside; if the latter be adopted, the Company ought to be obliged to find freight at the lowest rate to as great an extent as private merchants might think fit to call for it. These ought to be confined as to the time of calling for it, and they ought to pay for all they call for, even if it is not used. The exportation of British manufactures, excepting of military stores, ought to be free, and private merchants ought to have it in their option to import whatever they might think fit (subject always to the British revenue laws), and all merchandise ought, as at present, to pay the Company's duty, and be exposed to sale at the India House. These regulations would give perfect freedom to the private trade, with cheapness of freight, at the same time that the commerce of Great Britain and Bengal would be under the control of Government. The consequence would probably be the annihilation of the Company's commerce; but as it has been already said that the Company lose by their connection with Bengal, considering it as a commercial concern, no great evil will arise from that circumstance. The Company will be freed from a considerable expense of establishments both at home and abroad, which is incurred at present merely for their commercial concerns; but when the commerce falls into the hands of individuals, and nothing remains to the Company excepting the government, the expenses of the former will be separate from those of the latter, and both will be better and more cheaply carried on.

It has been already said that the Company neither receive more rent from the lands of Bengal, nor do the occupiers pay more under the Company's Government, than the old Governments received, or than the occupiers then paid; but the Company's Government, by taking into their own hands the monopolies of salt and of opium, have raised the revenues upwards of a million sterling, and out of that arises the surplus by means of which the Government are enabled to bring anything home to Europe.

In order to ascertain whether the natives of Bengal have any reason to complain that the surplus of the revenues over the expense is carried to a distant country, it is first necessary to ascertain what proportion is applied to purposes in India, in which Bengal has an immediate concern, and next what proportion goes home; and then the question will arise whether the withdrawing these sums from Bengal through the medium of commerce is unfavourable to that country.

The amount of the revenue received under all heads is . .	£5,033,000
The charges in Bengal amount to	3,127,000
Surplus	1,906,000

It cannot be contested but that the establishments at Madras and Bombay, Bencoolen and Prince of Wales Island, are essentially necessary to Bengal; and even if there were no connection between Great Britain and that country, they ought to be supported. The interest of the debts contracted at Madras and Bombay, as they must be supposed to have been contracted in wars in support of the chief establishment, it ought likewise to pay; and therefore the supplies to those settlements, and the interest of their debts, may be fairly chargeable to Bengal itself, and not to its connection with Great Britain.

The surplus, as already stated, is		£1,906,000
Deduct supplies to Madras and Bombay	£350,000	
" Prince of Wales Island and Bencoolen	50,000	
Interest of debts in India	561,923	
		961,923
The surplus will then be reduced to		£944,077

But it appears that the gross amount of the revenue is made up of sums received upon bills and certificates, and of sums received for sales of goods in Bengal, in addition to the land revenue, the customs, the opium, and salt monopolies. The former, as they may be fairly stated to be received for a value given, ought to be deducted from the amount of the claim, and the account will stand as follows:

Surplus as above		£944,077
Amount of sales	£350,000	
Bills and certificates	126,461	
		476,461
Remaining surplus		£467,616

The amount of sales ought not to be deducted, as it is not included in the gross amount of the revenue:

Surplus as stated	£467,616
Add amount of sales	350,000
Actual surplus	£817,616

Thus then the sum which Great Britain draws from Bengal is 817,616*l.*, and this is drawn away in trade.

If the question were, whether the people of Bengal would not be more happy and comfortable if they did not pay more revenue than is necessary to defray the expenses of their establishments, there could be no doubt upon the subject; and if their own comfort were alone to be considered, the surplus revenue ought to be remitted to them as soon as possible. But, as I shall show hereafter, Great Britain has a right to expect this tribute from them, it is impossible to devise means by which a revenue can be drawn from a people so little to their injury, as that which Great Britain draws is injurious to the natives of Bengal.

If specie were not essentially necessary for all the purposes of commerce, and if a drain to the amount of the surplus above stated would not be felt severely in all transactions of barter and exchange in the country, there would be no harm in sending this revenue home in money. The amount of the demand in Europe of Indian articles remaining the same, the exports from Bengal, the quantity of surplus produce for export, would be precisely equal to what they are at present; with this difference, that they would be paid for in the manufactures or money of Great Britain, instead of in the money raised from the country. As the case stands at present, there is a large revenue raised from this people: it is spent in the first instance in defending them, and in paying the usual expenses of government; in the next, in paying the expenses of their dependencies, which may be called their defence; in the third, in paying the interest of debts contracted for their defence and security; and in the fourth, in a tribute to Great Britain. The three last may be stated to be laid out in the country in encouragement of agriculture and manufactures. Supposing the sums laid out for the support of Madras, Bombay, &c., for the interest of debts, or for the tribute, were remitted in the revenue, and that the tenantry still continue to pay the same sums as at present, which is more than probable, it is doubted whether the proprietors of land, into whose hands they would go, would encourage the agriculture and manufactures of the country to the degree that they are at present encouraged by the present application of the revenue; and in that case if the demand for the produce of Bengal, upon the coast, &c., and in England were to cease, the country would indeed be in a ruinous condition.

Therefore, upon the whole, although the peasants may complain of the amount of what they pay, and that so little is left to them, they have no reason to complain of the manner in which what is taken from them is applied. There is another question upon this part of the subject which has been treated with a considerable degree of asperity in the 'Remarks:' it is whether it is just or right for Great Britain to take any tribute whatever from Bengal? The first question ought to be, whether it is just or right for one country to conquer another? and when the circumstances under which the conquest of Bengal was made are considered, the rights of Great Britain to have made that conquest are very apparent. After a conquest has been made, and the Government is in the possession of the conqueror, it is said in the 'Remarks' he has no right to any advantage but the Government. That would be true in some instances, but otherwise in many others.

Some nations when they have made a conquest gain a barrier to their former dominions, as the French did in their conquests of Alsace, &c., towards the Rhine, and there they have no right to claim any further advantages. Others gain a monopoly of commerce, as all nations in Europe do in the conquest of West India islands, and there likewise they have no right to tribute: others, again, gain the advantage of men and provisions for their armies and fleets, the advantage that the country in question is not connected with another power, such as Great Britain enjoys in her connection with Ireland, from which country, although she defends it, she has no claim to tribute: others get corn at a cheap rate, as Rome did from Egypt, from which country she received no other tribute. But I cannot perceive either a barrier, a useful or necessary monopoly in trade, a connection which gives Great Britain men or provisions for her fleets and armies, or grain at a cheap rate, in Bengal; and therefore I conclude that in return for the protection which that country undoubtedly receives, Great Britain has some right to expect remuneration. In fact, all conquered countries give the conquerors an advantage in some point of view; and Bengal gives none to Great Britain, excepting in tribute, which therefore the latter ought to take.

In the 'Remarks' much is said upon the subject of sugars; great complaints are made that Great Britain, by the high duties she lays upon the importation of sugars from the East Indies, gives an undue preference to the West Indies, to the injury of the former. If the question were abstractedly whether it is proper to pay dearer for a certain commodity when you can get it cheaper, there would be no doubt upon this subject; and there is no doubt but that the preference given to the West India sugars raises a great tax upon the people of Great Britain, and is highly injurious to the natives of Bengal, who undoubtedly deserve every encouragement that can be given to them. But the subject involves questions of greater magnitude than the authors of the

'Remarks' are aware of, and requires the cool and candid judgment of an unbiassed mind to decide upon it, instead of that of persons who may be fairly stated to be interested in the event.

One leading fact is stated, upon which the whole question turns. It is this: that if the East Indian sugars were admitted at the same rate of duty as the West Indian, even at the present high rate of freight, they would undersell them; nay, it may be stated that, owing to the disastrous war which has desolated the West India Islands for the last [1] years, the price of sugars has been raised so considerably, that the Company have found it expedient to import sugars from Bengal, paying the advanced duty and the high freight.

These circumstances being considered, the avowed consequence of admitting Bengal sugars at an equal duty must be the annihilation of the West India Islands.

Before any measures are taken which can have that effect, it will be wise to ascertain the nature and the quantity of property there is in those islands belonging to British subjects there residing, as well as to those who reside in England, all of whom or whose ancestors have purchased, or otherwise obtained and hold them, under the implied faith of the nation that they were to be supported in them at all times during war, and that the commercial policy of the nation in peace was likewise to be directed towards their support.

It will likewise be wise to ascertain what quantity of property and what quantity of shipping are embarked in this trade under the same faith; and after these circumstances will have been nicely ascertained, and that the nation has determined to make good all reasonable losses which individuals may sustain by this change of its commercial policy, it may deliberate upon this question, whether it be more for the advantage of Great Britain to pay this advanced price for the sugars it consumes, and that the natives of Bengal should wait their market for that article; or that it should make compensation to all individuals concerned in the West Indies or in the trade to the islands, for their losses.

Combined with this question there will be others which will claim the consideration of those who are to decide upon the subject. Their attention will be claimed by the importance of the islands in the hands of other powers of Europe at enmity with Great Britain, the importance of the trade to them as a nursery for seamen, and a certain resource to the nation at the commencement of a war. In those points of view, even supposing that the pecuniary considerations were out of the question, they are of the utmost consequence. I have not materials to form a judgment of their political importance to Great Britain supposing them in the hands of other European powers, but as a nursery for seamen, a few facts will show their consequence.

---

[1] Blank in manuscript. ED.

It has been said that the climate of the West Indies is so unwholesome that a residence in it is fatal to most of those who go there.

Without disputing that fact, I may safely assert that it is not more unwholesome or unfavourable to European constitutions than the climate of Bengal. Generally speaking all tropical climates are equally so, and that alone which makes one preferable to another is the difference of the conveniences and luxuries which are in use by the inhabitants to render the climate more bearable. Bengal is more favourable to the higher class of Europeans than other climates, because it is the custom and the fashion there for them to take more care of themselves; but it is not more so to the lower orders of people than other places situated in the tropics, as they have not more means of taking care of themselves, more luxuries and conveniences there, than they have elsewhere. Therefore upon the whole it may be safely said that Great Britain does not lose more seamen in the one country than in the other, considering the proportion of the numbers employed in each.

But the advantage which the West India trade has over that of the East is, that the seamen are a shorter time absent from their own country in the former than they are in the latter. A voyage to the West Indies may be stated at six months, during half of which time only can it be stated that the men are in a bad climate; whereas a voyage to the East Indies always lasts eighteen months, generally two years, and four-fifths of that time are spent in a climate avowedly unfavourable to European constitutions. Therefore supposing the numbers employed in each were the same, it may be concluded that the loss of lives would be greatest in that in which they remained longest. But there is another reason why the West India trade is a preferable employment for seamen. The voyage is so quickly performed that the nation has them always in her power; the fleets can be manned from them in a short space of time: whereas if the seamen from the East India fleet were the only or principal dependence for manning the navy, weeks and months might elapse after a declaration of war before the fleets could put to sea, and the disadvantages thereof might have the most fatal consequences. The seamen employed in the West India trade are generally more expert than those employed in the trade to the East Indies. They navigate seas in which there is a greater diversity of weather than there is in a voyage to the East Indies, during which, if it is commenced at the proper season, there will probably be no occasion to alter the sails once, however long it may be.

Upon the whole, therefore, the West India trade may be stated to be the best school for seamen, and their importance to the welfare, even to the existence of Great Britain, should induce the Legislature to adopt with great caution any measure which can diminish the West India trade in order to give a preference to that with the East.

It is to be observed upon this part of the subject, that it has no relation to the existence of the Company's exclusive privileges of commerce. It is a subject for the consideration of Parliament, entirely distinct from that of their monopoly. The other articles which are stated in the 'Remarks' to labour under the same inconveniences, such as silk, tobacco, &c., as being loaded with high duties on their importation from India, in order that they may not come in competition with similar articles the produce of foreign European nations or of America, must likewise be considered in the same point of view. The necessity of a naval defence for Great Britain causes the necessity of encouraging commerce with all parts of the globe, particularly with those parts which are most contiguous to it. If the commerce of Great Britain were confined to one quarter alone, its sources of wealth might be stopped; the efforts of its enemies, by being directed against that quarter, might at all events do the country the greatest injury in time of war, and in the event of success the country would be entirely ruined. As long as its commerce is directed to all quarters, it must flourish; one source may be cut off, but others will be found.

Having considered the whole of this subject, I conclude, first, that agriculture is considerably encouraged under the administration of the British Government in Bengal; that the measures recommended in the 'Remarks,' viz. to allow Europeans to become purchasers, are impolitic, and ought not to be adopted; but that other measures might be adopted which would give to agriculture all the encouragement it could require.

2. I conclude that it is not advisable to throw open the trade, but that the Company ought to be obliged to furnish private traders with the quantity of tonnage they might require at the lowest rate at which it could be got. That the import of Bengal articles ought to be as free for private traders as for the Company, and the export of British produce (military stores excepted) ought to be the same.

3. That the tribute is not so prejudicial to Bengal as it is stated, and that it is a matter of right, founded upon the policy usually adopted by modern and ancient nations in regard to conquered countries.

4. I conclude that the protection given to West India sugars, and to other articles the produce of Europe and America, to the prejudice of the same produced in Bengal, is necessary on account of the want of seamen for the British navy.

ARTHUR WESLEY.

9. To Lieutenant-Colonel Munro.

Answer to Munro's first criticism on the Battle of Assye.

(Extract.) Camp at Cheesekair, 1st Nov., 1803.

My dear Munro,

As you are a judge of a military operation, and as I am desirous of having your opinion on my side, I am about to give you an account of the battle of Assye, in answer to your letter of the 19th[1] of October, in which I think I shall solve all the doubts which must naturally occur to any man who looks at that transaction without a sufficient knowledge of the facts.

Before you will receive this, you will most probably have seen my public letter to the Governor-General regarding the action, a copy of which was sent to General Campbell. That letter will give you a general outline of the facts. Your principal objection to the action is, that I detached Colonel Stevenson. The fact is, I did not detach Colonel Stevenson. His was a separate corps, equally strong, if not stronger than mine. We were desirous to engage the enemy at the same time, and settled a plan accordingly for an attack on the morning of the 24th September. We separated on the 22nd, he to march by the western, I by the eastern road, round the hills between Budnapoor and Jaulna: and I have to observe, that this separation was necessary; first, because both corps could not pass through the same defiles in one day; secondly, because it was to be apprehended that, if we left open one of the roads through these hills, the enemy might have passed to the southward while we were going to the northward, and then the action would have been delayed, or, probably, avoided altogether. Colonel Stevenson and I were never more than twelve miles distant from each other; and when I moved forward to the action of the 23rd, we were not much more than eight miles apart.

As usual, we depended for our intelligence of the enemy's position on the common hircarrahs of the country. Their horse were so numerous that, without an army, their position could not be reconnoitred by an European officer; and even the hircarrahs in our own service, who are accustomed to examine and report positions, cannot be employed here, as, being natives of the Carnatic, they are as well known as an European.

The hircarrahs reported the enemy to be at Bokerdun. Their right was at Bokerdun, which was the principal place in their position, and gave the name to the district in which they were encamped; but their left, in which was their infantry, which I was to attack, was at Assye, about six or eight miles from Bokerdun.

I directed my march so as to be within twelve or fourteen miles of their army at Bokerdun, as I thought, on the 23rd. But when I arrived at the ground of encampment, I found that I was not more than five or six miles from it. I was then informed that the cavalry had marched, and the infantry were about to follow, but were still on the ground: at all events, it was necessary to ascertain these points; and I could not venture to reconnoitre without my whole force. But I believed the report to be true, and I determined to attack the infantry, if they remained still upon the ground. I apprised Colonel Stevenson of this

---

[1] The letter referred to will be found in Sir Thomas Munro's *Life* by Mr. Gleig, Vol. III. pp. 177–179. It is there dated 14th Oct.

determination, and desired him to move forward. Upon marching on, I found not only their infantry, but their cavalry, encamped in a most formidable position, which, by the by, it would have been impossible for me to attack, if, when the infantry changed their front, they had taken care to occupy the only passage there was across the Kaitna.

When I found their whole army, and contemplated their position, of course I considered whether I should attack immediately or should delay till the following morning. I determined upon the immediate attack, because I saw clearly, that, if I attempted to return to my camp at Naulniah, I should have been followed thither by the whole of the enemy's cavalry, and I might have suffered some loss; instead of attacking, I might have been attacked there in the morning; and, at all events, I should have found it very difficult to secure my baggage, as I did, in any place so near the enemy's camp in which they should know it was: I therefore determined upon the attack immediately. It was certainly a most desperate one, but our guns were not silenced. Our bullocks, and the people who were employed to draw the guns, were shot, and they could not all be drawn on; but some were, and all continued to fire as long as the fire could be of any use.

Desperate as the action was, our loss would not have exceeded one half of its actual amount if it had not been for a mistake in the officer who led the piquets which were on the right of the first line. When the enemy changed their position, they threw their left to Assye, in which village they had some infantry, and it was surrounded by cannon. As soon as I saw that, I directed the officer commanding the piquets to keep out of shot from that village: instead of that, he led directly upon it: the 74th, which were on the right of the first line, followed the piquets, and the great loss we sustained was in these two bodies.

Another evil which resulted from this mistake was the necessity of introducing the cavalry into the cannonade and the action long before it was time; by which the corps which I intended to bring forward in a close pursuit at the heel of the day, lost many men, and its union and efficiency. But it was necessary to bring forward the cavalry to save the remains of the 74th, and the piquets, which would otherwise have been destroyed. Another evil resulting from it was, that we had then no reserve left, and a parcel of stragglers cut up our wounded; and straggling infantry, who had pretended to be dead, turned their guns upon our backs.

After all, notwithstanding this attack upon Assye by our right and the cavalry, no impression was made upon the corps collected there till I made a movement upon it with some troops taken from our left, after the enemy's right had been defeated; and it would have been as well to have left it alone entirely till that movement was made. However, I do not wish to cast any reflection upon the officer who led the piquets.

I lament the consequences of his mistake, but I must acknowledge that it was not possible for a man to lead a body into a hotter fire than he did the piquets on that day against Assye.

After the action there was no pursuit, because our cavalry was not then in a state to pursue. It was near dark when the action was over, and we passed the night on the field of battle.

Colonel Stevenson marched with part of his troops as soon as he heard that I was about to move forward, and he also moved upon Bokerdun. He did not receive my letter till evening. He got entangled in a nullah in the night, and arrived at Bokerdun, about eight miles from me to the westward, at eight in the morning of the 24th.

The enemy passed the night of the 23rd at about twelve miles from the field of battle, twelve from the Adjuntee Ghaut, and eight from Bokerdun. As soon as they heard that Colonel Stevenson was advancing to the latter place, they set off, and never stopped till they got down the Ghaut, where they arrived in the course of the night of the 24th. After his difficulties of the night of the 23rd, Colonel Stevenson was in no state to follow them, and did not do so until the 26th. The reason for which he was detained till that day was, that I might have the benefit of the assistance of his surgeons to dress my wounded soldiers, many of whom, after all, were not dressed for nearly a week, for want of the necessary number of medical men.

I had also a long and difficult negotiation with the Nizam's sirdars, to induce them to admit my wounded into any of the Nizam's forts; and I could not allow them to depart until I had settled that point. Besides, I knew that the enemy had passed the Ghaut, and that to pursue them a day sooner, or a day later, could make no difference.

Believe me, &c.,

ARTHUR WELLESLEY.

10. Extracts from Gen. Wellesley's Correspondence.

Monson's Retreat.

a. Monson's disasters are really the greatest and the most disgraceful to our military character of any that have ever occurred. The detachment had not two days' provisions; was cut off from its resources by many rivers, on which we had neither bridge nor boat; and all measures to supply with provisions the only fort (Rampoora) to which, in case of emergency, he might have recourse, were omitted. To employ the detachment at all was an error; but the common modes of securing its safety have been omitted.

β. You will have heard of Colonel Monson's retreat, defeats, disgraces, and disasters. He is, however, at last arrived at Agra, he and his detachment woful examples of the risk to be incurred by advancing too far without competent supplies, and of the danger of attempting to retreat before such an army as Holkar's is. He would have done much better to attack Holkar at once, and he would probably have put an end to the war. At all events, he might have made a better retreat. This is between ourselves, as I am very unwilling to circulate my opinion of the late transactions to the northward. I only hope that they will not induce our late enemies to break out again.

γ. After Colonel Monson's defeat I acknowledge that I considered the peace with the Mahrattas very precarious; and indeed if the success of Holkar had continued, I consider that we should have had to fight over again not only our battles with the Mahrattas, but those with all the other powers of India, whether considered as our dependants or our allies. I also believe that the Rajah of Berar in particular, and very possibly Scindiah, considered the advantages gained by Holkar to have been much greater than they really were; that they anticipated farther successes, and the former prepared to take advantage of them.

Assaults on Bhurtpoor.

δ. The 4th and 5th failures before Bhurtpoor are disastrous events, of which I apprehend the worst consequences. They must have blundered that siege terribly, for it is certain that, with adequate means, every place can be taken; and —— —— having been so long before the place, adequate means must have been provided, or in his power. The fault lies therefore in the misapplication of them, or, most probably, in the omission to employ all those which were necessary to accomplish the object in view, either through the ignorance of the engineers, or the impetuosity of —— ——'s temper, which could not brook the necessary delay.

Selections from Sir Thomas Munro's Correspondence.[1]

11. To General Wellesley.

Criticism on the Battle of Assye.

(Extract.) Cawderabad, 28th November, 1803.

Dear General,

I have received your letter of the 1st instant, and have read with great pleasure and interest your clear and satisfactory account of the battle of Assaye. You say you wish to have my opinion on your side: if it can be of any use to you, you have it on your side, not only in that battle, but in the conduct of the campaign: the merit of this last is exclusively your own. The success of every battle must always be shared in some

[1] Given in his *Life*, by the Rev. G. R. Gleig.

degree, by the most skilful general with his troops. I must own, I have always been averse to the practice of carrying on war with too many scattered armies, and also of fighting battles by the combined attacks of separate divisions. When several armies invade a country on different sides, unless each of them is separately a match for the enemy's whole army, there is always a danger of their being defeated one after another; because, having a shorter distance to march, he may draw his force together, and march upon a particular army, before it can be supported. When a great army is encamped in separate divisions, it must, of course, be attacked in separate columns. But Indian armies are usually crowded together on a spot, and will, I imagine, be easier routed by a single attack, than by two or three separate attacks by the same force. I see perfectly the necessity of your advancing by one route, and Colonel Stevenson by another, in order to get clear of the defiles in one day; I know, also, that you could not have reconnoitred the enemy's position without carrying on your whole army; but I have still some doubts whether the immediate attack was, under all circumstances, the best measure you could have adopted. Your objections to delay are, that the enemy might have gone off and frustrated your design of bringing them to battle, or that you might have lost the advantage of attack, by their attacking you in the morning. The considerations which would have made me hesitate are, that you could hardly expect to defeat the enemy with less than half the loss you actually suffered; that after breaking their infantry, your cavalry, even when entire, was not sufficiently strong to pursue any distance, without which you could not have done so much execution among them as to counterbalance your own loss; and lastly, that there was a possibility of your being repulsed; in which case, the great superiority of the enemy's cavalry, with some degree of spirit which they would have derived from success, might have rendered a retreat impracticable. Suppose that you had not advanced to the attack, but remained under arms, after reconnoitring at long-shot distance, I am convinced that the enemy would have decamped in the night, and as you could have instantly followed them, they would have been obliged to leave all or most of their guns behind. If they ventured to keep their position, which seems to me incredible, the result would still have been equally favourable: you might have attacked them in the course of the night; their artillery would have been of little use in the dark; it would have fallen into your hands, and their loss of men would very likely have been greater than yours. If they determined to attack you in the morning, as far as I can judge from the different reports that I have heard of the ground, I think it would have been the most desirable event that could have happened, for you would have had it in your power to attack them, either in the operation of passing the river, or after the whole had passed, but before they were completely formed. They must, however, have known that Stevenson was approaching, and that he might possibly join you in the morning, and this circumstance alone would, I have no doubt, have induced them to retreat in the night. Your mode of attack, though it might not have been the safest, was undoubtedly the most decided and heroic; it will have the effect of striking greater terror into the hostile armies than could have been done by any victory gained with the assistance of Colonel Stevenson's division, and of raising the national military character, already high in India, still higher.

Believe me, dear General,

Yours most truly,

THOMAS MUNRO.

12. To Colonel Read.

Rationale of Mahratta defeats.

(Extract.) Punganoor, 6th March, 1804.

Dear Read,

Our constant succession of victories is chiefly to be attributed to the Bengal and Madras armies having had a much greater body of regular cavalry than in any former war, and to the conduct of Generals Lake and Wellesley in availing themselves of this circumstance to make the campaign entirely offensive, to give the enemy no respite, and to push all their advantages to the utmost; but other causes also contributed greatly to favour our operations. The Mahrattas in general were much weakened by their long dissensions, and Scindia in particular had suffered heavy losses in his war with Holkar. The introduction of a great body of regular infantry, with a vast train of artillery, had made his armies unwieldy, and in order to keep up the foot, the cavalry were neglected. They were deficient in number and quality, and as they were considered as only a secondary corps to the infantry, they had lost all their spirit of enterprise. They gave very little support to their infantry in the different battles that were fought, and they attempted nothing alone. They fell in during the campaign with several convoys, and though the escorts were but inconsiderable, they did not cut off one of them. I have heard much said of the excellence of Scindia's battalions, and of the danger to which our power in this country would have been exposed, had he been permitted to go on much longer augmenting them. But my own opinion is the very reverse of this, for I think that he could have had no chance of success, except from his cavalry; and that as he must have reduced them in proportion as he increased his infantry, every addition to that part of his army would only have tended to weaken his real force. Had he been satisfied with Peons instead of battalions, and with a few long field-pieces instead of a cumbersome train of artillery, and had he applied the funds consumed by his infantry to the equipment of his cavalry, his army might not have been so able to meet us in battle, but it would have been much better calculated than it was to have carried on a protracted, harassing, and doubtful war. His infantry was regular enough, but it wanted steadiness, in which it must always be greatly inferior to ours, from the want of a national spirit among its officers, and of the support and animating example of European regiments. At the battle of Assaye, the severest that took place in the course of the war, I do not recollect, among all our killed and wounded officers, one that suffered from a musket-ball or a bayonet, a convincing proof that the Mahratta infantry made very little serious opposition. Its discipline, its arms, and uniform clothing, I regard merely as the means of dressing it out for the sacrifice. Its numerous artillery prevents it from escaping by rapid marches; it is forced to fight, deserted by its cavalry, and slaughtered with very little loss on our side. Scindia, by abandoning the old system of Mahratta warfare, and placing his chief dependence on disciplined infantry, facilitated the conquest of the states of Polligars and Rajahs, whose forts and jungles might have secured them against his horse; but he at the same time disabled himself from maintaining a contest with us, for he reduced the war to a war of battles and sieges, instead of one of marches and convoys. As long as his battalions are not under French influence, by being commanded by officers of that nation, it is more our interest that he should keep them up than that he should disband them and raise horse.

Yours truly,

THOMAS MUNRO.

13. To his Father.

Same Subject.

(Extract.) (Undated.)

Dear Sir,

Plundering horse are not fond of venturing without support into an enemy's country, where they expect to meet with cavalry. They carry on their ravages boldly only when no resistance is looked for, or when they are followed by their main army, and can retire upon it in case of danger; but Scindia never was able to cross the Godaveri, and his irregulars therefore durst not pass into the rear of our armies. Scindia, without infantry, with his cavalry alone, made several attempts to pass that river, in order to carry the war into the Nizam's and Company's territories; but he was always obliged to relinquish his design by General Wellesley's following him closely for several days, because his supplies would have been intercepted or overtaken. A great army of Mahratta horse cannot march so rapidly as is generally supposed; it is encumbered by the tents and baggage, and often by the women of its chiefs, by elephants, camels, and servants, and even when all these are left behind, it must still have a great train of bullocks for the carriage of provisions. It is to no purpose that the cavalry can march thirty or forty miles a day, they cannot find subsistence in an enemy's country, and must at last halt for their grain bullocks, which cannot march so fast as the army which pursues them. The open countries of the Deccan and Mysore, as soon as the harvest is gathered in, present nothing but a naked waste to an invader. The inhabitants are all armed; the villages are all fortified, and cannot be taken without infantry. An army consisting merely of horse can raise very few contributions among them, it must therefore depend chiefly for its subsistence on supplies drawn from its own country.

I am, dear Sir, your affectionate son,

THOMAS MUNRO.

14. To the Honourable M. Elphinstone.

Expediency of the Company's assuming the office of Peishwah.

(Extract.) Camp at Naggurmurly, 23rd April, 1818.

Sir,

The Jageerdars have now, I believe, no expectation of seeing Bajee Row, or any of his relations, at the head of a state; but their zeal for the continuance of the office of Peshwah, even though divested of all real power, is as strong as ever. They retain their own possessions, and feel, therefore, in a much smaller degree the dissolution of the substance of the Mahratta empire than that of its forms. They derive whatever they possess from those forms; they have for generations been accustomed to respect and serve under them, and they regard it as disgraceful to abandon them for others. The easiest way of subduing these prejudices, and of rendering them useful feudatories, would be for the Company to take upon itself the office of Peshwah, and to issue all public acts as coming from the Pundit Purdhan, as under the late Government Investiture might be received, according to custom, from the Rajah of Sattarah. The Company, acting as the Pundit Purdhan, would hold an office which, as in the case of that of the Dewanee in Bengal, would take from it none of its sovereign powers; and its governing the country under this ancient title, would, I believe, reconcile the Jageerdars to the change of masters, and induce them to employ their troops willingly at the call of the British Government. They testify at present great aversion to being summoned as its immediate servants, and propose that they should rather give up part of their Jageers, and hold the rest service free. This objection is possibly exaggerated; but if it can be removed merely by the maintenance of a form, and the substitution of a name, it ought perhaps to be done, more particularly as the preservation of this ancient name would probably be likewise acceptable to Scindia and Holkar, as their ancestors obtained their possessions not from the Rajahs of Sattarah, but from the Pundit Purdhan.

I have the honour to be, &c.

THOMAS MUNRO.

15. To his Excellency the Governor-General.[1]

Ultimate tendency of the subsidiary alliance system.

(Extract.)

Darwar, 12th August, 1817.

There is so little system or subordination in Native governments, that much more energy is required under them, than under the more regular governments of Europe, to give full effect to their resources. Scindiah was never formidable, even in the height of his power. The great means which he possessed were lost in his feeble hands. The exertions of Holkar against Lord Lake were still weaker than those of Scindiah. The power of Scindiah's, as well as of Holkar's government, has so much declined since that period, that it is scarcely credible that either Scindiah or Meer Khan would venture to oppose by force, any measure for the suppression of the Pindarries. But it is still possible that they might act otherwise; for there is sometimes a kind of infatuation about Indian chiefs who have lost a part of their dominions, which tempts them to risk the rest in a contest which they know to be hopeless.

The situation of the British Government with regard to the Native powers, is entirely changed within the last twenty years. It formerly brought very small armies into the field, with hardly any cavalry; and the issue of any war in which it engaged was extremely uncertain. It now brings armies into the field superior to those of the enemy, not only in infantry, but also in cavalry, both in quality and number. The superiority is so great, that the event of any struggle in which it may be engaged is no longer doubtful. It has only to bring forward its armies, and dictate what terms it pleases, either without war, or after a short and fruitless resistance. It may however be doubted whether, after the settlement of the Pindarries, it ought to avail itself of its predominant power, in order to extend the system of subsidiary alliances, by stationing a force in Bhopaul or in any other foreign territory. While the military power of Mysore and of the Mahratta chiefs was yet in its vigour, subsidiary alliances were in some degree necessary for its safety, but that time is now past; and when, therefore, the evils which a subsidiary force entails

[1] The Marquis of Hastings.

upon every country in which it is established are considered, it appears advisable that future security against the Pindarries should be sought by their reduction, and by compelling Scindiah, for his conduct in supporting them, to cede the districts restored to him in 1805–6, rather than by stationing a subsidiary force in Bhopaul. There are many weighty objections to the employment of a subsidiary force. It has a natural tendency to render the government of every country in which it exists, weak and oppressive; to extinguish all honourable spirit among the higher classes of society, and to degrade and impoverish the whole people. The usual remedy of a bad government in India is a quiet revolution in the palace, or a violent one by rebellion, or foreign conquests. But the presence of a British force cuts off every chance of remedy, by supporting the prince on the throne against every foreign and domestic enemy. It renders him indolent, by teaching him to trust to strangers for his security; and cruel and avaricious, by showing him that he has nothing to fear from the hatred of his subjects. Wherever the subsidiary system is introduced, unless the reigning prince be a man of great abilities, the country will soon bear the marks of it in decaying villages and decreasing population. This has long been observed in the dominions of the Peishwah and the Nizam, and is now beginning to be seen in Mysore. The talents of Purneah, while he acted as Dewan, saved that country from the usual effects of the system; but the Rajah is likely to let them have their full operation. He is indolent and prodigal, and has already, besides the current revenue, dissipated about sixty lacs of pagodas of the treasure laid up by the late Dewan. He is mean, artful, revengeful, and cruel. He does not take away life, but he inflicts the most disgraceful and inhuman punishments on men of every rank, at a distance from his capital, where he thinks it will remain unknown to Europeans; and though young, he is already detested by his subjects.

A subsidiary force would be a most useful establishment, if it could be directed solely to the support of our ascendency, without nourishing all the vices of a bad government; but this seems to be almost impossible. The only way in which this object has ever, in any degree, been attained, is by the appointment of a Dewan. This measure is, no doubt, liable to numerous objections; but still it is the only one by which any amends can be made to the people of the country for the miseries brought upon them by the subsidiary force, in giving stability to a vicious government. The great difficulty is to prevent the prince from counteracting the Dewan, and the resident from meddling too much; but, when this is avoided, the Dewan may be made a most useful instrument of government.

There is, however, another view under which the subsidiary system should be considered,—I mean that of its inevitable tendency to bring every Native state into which it is introduced, sooner or later, under the exclusive dominion of the British Government. It has already done this completely in the case of the Nabob of the Carnatic. It has made some progress in that of the Peishwah and the Nizam; and the whole of the territory of these princes will, unquestionably, suffer the same fate as the Carnatic. The observation of Moro Dekshat, in speaking of the late treaty to Major Ford, 'that no Native power could, from its habits, conduct itself with such strict fidelity as we seemed to demand,' is perfectly just. This very Peishwah will probably again commit a breach of the alliance. The Nizam will do the same; and the same consequence, a farther reduction of their power for our own safety, must again follow. Even if the prince himself were disposed to adhere rigidly to the alliance, there will always be some amongst his principal officers who will urge him to break it. As long as there remains in the country any high-minded independence, which seeks to throw off the control of strangers, such counsellors will be found. I have a better opinion of the natives of India than to think that this spirit will ever be completely extinguished; and I can therefore have no doubt that the subsidiary system must every where run its full course, and destroy every government which it undertakes to protect.

In this progress of things, the evil of a weak and oppressive government, supported by a subsidiary alliance, will at least be removed. But even if all India could be brought under the British dominion, it is very questionable whether such a change, either as it regards the natives or ourselves, ought to be desired. One effect of such a conquest would be, that *the Indian army, having no longer any warlike neighbours to combat, would gradually lose its military habits and discipline, and that the native troops would have leisure to feel their own strength, and, for want of other employment, to turn it against their European masters.*[1] But even if we could be secured against every internal convulsion, and could retain the country quietly in subjection, *I doubt much if the condition of the people would be better than under their Native princes.* The strength of the British Government enables it to put down every rebellion, to repel every foreign invasion, and to give to its subjects a degree of protection which those of no Native power enjoy. Its laws and institutions also afford them a security from domestic oppression, unknown in those states; but these advantages are dearly bought. They are purchased by the sacrifice of independence—of national character—and of whatever renders a people respectable. The natives of the British provinces may without fear pursue their different occupations, as traders, meerassidars, or husbandmen, and enjoy the fruits of their labour in tranquillity; but none of them can aspire to any thing beyond this mere animal state of thriving in peace—none of them can look forward to any

---

[1] The Italics are the Editor's.

share in the legislation, or civil or military government of their country. It is from men who either hold, or are eligible to public office, that natives take their character: where no such men exist, there can be no energy in any other class of the community. The effect of this state of things is observable in all the British provinces, whose inhabitants are certainly the most abject race in India. No elevation of character can be expected among men who, in the military line, cannot attain to any rank above that of subahdar, where they are as much below an ensign as an ensign is below the commander-in-chief, and who, in the civil line, can hope for nothing beyond some petty, judicial, or revenue office, in which they may, by corrupt means, make up for their slender salary.

The consequence, therefore, of the conquest of India by the British arms would be, in place of raising, to debase the whole people. There is perhaps no example of any conquest in which the natives have been so completely excluded from all share of the government of their country as in British India.

Among all the disorders of the Native states, the field is open for every man to raise himself; and hence among them there is a spirit of emulation, of restless enterprize and independence, far preferable to the servility of our Indian subjects. The existence of independent Native states is also useful in drawing off the turbulent and disaffected among our native troops. Many of these men belonging to the Madras army, formerly sought service in Mysore.

If the British Government is not favourable to the improvement of the Indian character, that of its control through a subsidiary force is still less so.

Its power is now so great, that it has nothing to fear from any combination; and it is perfectly able to take satisfaction for any insult, without any extension of the subsidiary system being necessary. It will generally be found much more convenient to carry on war where it has not been introduced. This was the case in both the wars with Tippoo Sultan. The conquest was complete, because our operations were not perplexed by any subsidiary alliance with him. The simple and direct mode of conquest from without, is more creditable both to our armies and to our national character, than that of dismemberment from within by the aid of a subsidiary force. However just the motives may be from which such force acts, yet the situation in which it is placed, renders its acting at all too like the movements of the Prætorian bands. It acts, it is true, only by the orders of its own Government, and only for public objects; but still it is always ready in the neighbourhood of the capital, to dictate terms to, or to depose the prince whom it was stationed there to defend.

16. Anonymous.

Lord Wellesley's Policy.

(Extract.)

Could the power and system of the Company continue fixed, when nothing around it was permanent? Could either remain stationary while other powers were rapidly encreasing their resources and their strength?

* * * * * * *

India, like Europe, has undergone changes which, there, as well as here, require a variation in our policy.

Reviewing then our past, and reflecting on our present situation, it may reasonably be assumed that no line of policy could be more fatal to us . . . . than that of suffering any of the more powerful chieftains of India to swallow up the rest, which must be the case, if they are permitted, without restraint, to perfect their knowledge of the art of war, as practised among the nations of Europe, and to direct the acquirement of it to the attack and destruction of their weaker neighbours. Yet this would be the consequence of acting on the notions of the opponents of Lord Wellesley, according to which it would be permitted to these powers, without interruption, to wage war against each other until one more successful than the rest subjugated the whole. To this point was the progress of Tippoo, and Scindiah, more immediately and rapidly tending. A few years more on this system, and India was inevitably lost to Great Britain. The alarming strides these powers were making to liberate the East from our dominion; the new French state, nominally dependent on Scindiah, rising on our weakest frontier; its powerful army and resources; the strong holds in its possession; the communication of its chief with Buonaparte; the danger of a junction of the principal native military forces co-operating in this one object of our expulsion; the interest they had in obtaining severally from France all those means of annoying us which could give effect to their views, and which she could pour in with such facility while the ports of Malabar, Guzerat, and Cuttack were open to her ships; the alluring motives she had for furnishing them, at their call, with these supplies—all presented the most fearful prospect. The vigilance of our cruizers in time of war could not have been equal to the entire blockade of their shores (in peace it was out of the question); and such a combination of military force, with such means of assembling and guiding it, in its growing improvement, would have proved in a few years, thus supported, utterly irresistible. What is the general system of these powers? War, in its vilest aspect. . . . . War is their end. It is the distinctive feature of the government, that the empire always considers itself in a state either of predatory or of vindictive hostility. . . .

To us, war is a calamity, with the Marhattas it is a pursuit. We raise armies to defend ourselves; they, to annoy others. In the difference of systems, let us not overlook the appropriate policy we are invited to observe in our wars and intercourse with a people whose peculiar customs, modes of thinking, and principles of government, bear no similitude with any of the more regular constitutions existing in Europe, but are hostile to all those bases on which the more civilized nations of the Christian world consider national prosperity, the rights of justice, and public happiness to rest. Empires thus constituted seem to be at variance with the justice of Providence, and when they fall, perhaps they yield to his decrees. The awful instance before us at this eventful crisis, too fatally shows whither an unbridled system of military government in the heart of a great continent may lead, if founded in the love of war, and military spoliage. It feeds upon nations; it preys on the independence of all: its existence is their scourge; its destruction is their hope. Such is the overwhelming march of France; and such have been the consuming strides of Marhatta, and Mysorean power. Predatory irruptions, foreign and internal oppressions and exaction, perfidy, domestic murders, public massacres, famine, depopulation, and wide-spreading misery; this is their system: these have been the volcanoes which too long have encircled our possessions, and overflowed the plains of India. To extinguish them is no more than justice to ourselves; to close their crater, the sublimest humanity to the suffering millions who have long been exposed to their ravages. This has been the policy our security demanded: this has been the course to which our glory pointed; and this has been the successful end to which the exertions of Lord Wellesley have tended. To uphold such a system as the one just described is to cherish insecurity; to defend it, is to vindicate rapine and barbarity.

Let us for the moment only look at the sorry policy which is pleaded in favour of the continuance of a system of power so fraught with misery to the human race, and which it is not denied, exposes the finest provinces in India to perpetual convulsions, and the surrounding states to continual danger. . . . Leave these powers to their own intestine feuds—let us tranquilly behold the scene—their wars against each other are beneficial to the Company—the more sanguinary their battles, the more destructive to their power—they are effectually playing our game—every blow given on either side is a victory for us—these struggles enfeeble them reciprocally—in their weakness is our strength—the miseries they spread, and the blood they spill, cement more firmly the empire we possess. This is the course of reasoning pursued by those who arraign the conduct of Lord Wellesley; and a surrounding warfare is the security to which they look for the preservation of the British power in India. This is their system; they see their safety where his Lordship perceives his danger, in the carnage of battle, the embers of desolation, and the smoking ruins of ravaged and depopulated districts. . . . . Such a proceeding resolves itself into the little sentiment of feeling nothing for others, but all for ourselves. . . . Is it nothing in the scale of charity to feel for suffering human nature? Is it nothing on the score of a generous and enlightened policy to limit those torrents of blood which so long have deluged the fertile plains of India, destroyed their population, and convulsed their industry? . . . . It is a contradiction in terms to say that they are not the advocates of war, while they declare themselves friendly to the unfettered existence of a system of power which adopting war for its basis, has even blended it with its system of revenue, and embodied it as it were into the very spine of its constitution.

How different from this limited view of the subject is the more expansive and benevolent survey of it by the comprehensive mind of Lord Wellesley! Ascending from individuals to universals, he sees, in disseminated peace, the springs of general happiness. In the tranquillity of the native states throughout the Deckan and Hindostan, he traces not merely a more solid security for the preservation of our own power; but in the advantages of peace to them he discerns fresh sources of prosperity to ourselves: the condition of society meliorated—our political relations improved—the industry of India reanimated: strife disarmed: jealousy restrained: new channels of commerce opened: the interchange of produce enlarged: the merchants of India journeying in security from one state to another: our home manufactures reaching countries where before they never entered: an improved revenue to the Company and the state: the vast peninsula of India reposing after the convulsion of centuries: its rest secured by judicious alliances, and well-poised power: the warlike tribes which cover it, restrained in their predatory habits, and gradually incited by the sweets of peace, to turn their attention to the happier pursuits of commerce and of agriculture, instead of moistening, as heretofore, their plains with the blood of each other; and lastly, the national character and honour exalted, by the sublime result of so generous and elevated a line of policy. These happy ends he traces as a consequence from the principle of establishing, through a system of well-distributed power, a durable peace among the different states of India, and more immediately of those composing the Marhatta confederacy. In this way he sees, that individual benefit is general good; that the misery of one state is not the happiness of another, but that the prosperity of each increases the felicity of all. This is the system of Lord Wellesley. It embraces peace and repudiates war; it denies that partial misery is public good: it disowns the principle that the blood of one nation is a desirable offering to the prosperity of another: it rejects the doctrine that, to foment their intestine divisions and arm them against each other, is a wise or a dignified line of conduct either morally or politically considered; but it admits, as it seeks to establish that, to resist their encroachments, to crush their exactions, to heal their differences, to stifle their wars, to curb the enlargement of their empire, to balance more justly their power, to uphold the authority of their Peishwah or chief magistrate, and through its stability, to ameliorate equally the condition of the sovereign and the subject, are objects of an enlarged and rational policy; and that the surest way of increasing the prosperity of British India, of strengthening the affections of its inhabitants, and of ensuring to us the general good-will of the great masses composing the subjects of these different states, is, through the medium of a lasting peace guaranteed to them by a commanding power, to make them participate in the tranquillity, security, and happiness, which the Company's possessions enjoy. These are the views of Lord Wellesley, and this is the plan to the complication of which his attention has been directed. It is needless to comment on its quality; its splendour is marked by the shade of its contrast.

* * * * * * * *

It remains only further to observe, that if experience acquired in the school of local knowledge; if an attentive study of the interests and suitable policy of the Company, facilitated by situations held for many years in its service, where the sources of knowledge were immediately before the author's view; if a life devoted to the consideration of these subjects, combined with his interests as a proprietor, can entitle him, without presumption, to form some present opinion on the means best calculated to advance the prosperity of the East India Company, he may then be permitted to observe, that, considering our views of policy to have been at no former period either so comprehensive or so steady as the interests and safety of British India required, he has never till now thought that country a very secure possession. He thinks differently now. He has no apprehension. He sees, at last, the only system realized that can effectually give security to our empire there. The system of Lord Wellesley is the system by which India has been saved. It is the system by which alone it can be preserved to future ages. It is a system which holds up security to the Company, happiness to India, and wealth to the parent state. It rests on humanity, poised by justice, and supported by power.[1]

---

[1] From *A Vindication of the justice and policy of the late Wars carried on in Hindostan and the Deckan, by Marquis Wellesley.* Anonymous, London, 1806. 4to. Printed for John Stockdale, Piccadilly. The copy in the Library at the India Office has, in manuscript, 'L. D. Campbell (?).'

17. Barchou de Penhoën.

Retirement of Lord Wellesley.

Cependant il arrivait dans le gouvernement un changement d'une grande importance. Dès le mois de décembre 1803, Lord Wellesley avait annoncé aux directeurs son intention de retourner en Europe. Les hostilités qui suivirent l'engagèrent à différer l'exécution de cette résolution. Dans le mois de mars 1805, tout en exprimant à la cour des directeurs ses inquiétudes croissantes sur le mauvais état de sa santé, le besoin qu'il éprouvait de la refaire dans un climat plus doux et d'être délivré des soins et des soucis du gouvernement, il énonçait pourtant son intention de ne pas déserter son poste; il était résolu à ne pas quitter l'Inde avant que la paix ne fût assise sur des bases solides et permanentes. Mais des mesures avaient été prises dès cette époque pour un changement d'administration dans l'Inde. Les directeurs et les ministres s'alarmaient depuis quelque temps de l'accroissement de la dette et des difficultés pécuniaires qui entouraient la Compagnie; on commençait à désirer la paix. L'opinion publique, toujours prête à s'en prendre aux hommes des nécessités politiques, voyait dans Lord Wellesley un ambitieux et prodigue administrateur. La plus grande partie de son administration s'était trouvée employée à la guerre, à la conquête. On croyait que cela tenait au caractère de l'homme; on s'obstinait à croire qu'il avait fait naître volontairement la guerre, bien qu'en définitive il se fût seulement borné à en apercevoir de bonne heure l'imminente nécessité. Un grand nombre de gens arrivèrent à penser, à dire que les intérêts britanniques n'auraient jamais de sécurité tant que Lord Wellesley demeurerait à la tête des affaires. Or, un des prédécesseurs de ce dernier, Lord Cornwallis, s'était toujours montré modéré dans sa politique, opposé à la guerre et à tout accroissement de territoire; l'opinion publique, par un de ces engouements qui lui sont familiers, se plaisait à en faire l'homme de la paix. On sait comme la fantaisie populaire est portée à personnifier les idées. En ce moment Lord Cornwallis parut le seul homme capable de faire refleurir la paix dans l'Orient. Courbé sous les ans, glacé par l'âge, gémissant sous le poids des infirmités, étranger depuis long-temps aux affaires de ce pays, Lord Cornwallis n'en sembla pas moins le remède à tous les maux de l'Inde. Il fut nommé gouverneur-général, et arriva à Calcutta le 30 juillet 1805.[1]

---

[1] *Histoire de l'Empire Anglais dans l'Inde,* tome 5me, p. 134–136.

18. Marquis Cornwallis to the Right Hon. Lord Lake.

The political situation, and the Governor-General's intended policy.

Near Caragola, Aug. 30, 1805.

My dear Lord,

I received yesterday with great satisfaction your very kind letter of the 11th instant, and have no doubt that we shall act together with as perfect harmony as we ever have done on former occasions.

You will easily imagine it was no slight cause that urged the Ministers at home to press me to return once more to this country, and that I would not, without seeing very great necessity, have engaged at my time of life in so difficult and, I may say, so rash an undertaking.

The real circumstances are, that it is not the opinion only of Ministers, or of a party, but of all reflecting men of every description, that it is physically impracticable for Great Britain, in addition to all other embarrassments, to maintain so vast and so unwieldy an empire in India, which annually calls for reinforcements of men and for remittances of money, and which yields little other profit except brilliant Gazettes. It is in vain for us to conceal from ourselves that our finances are at the lowest ebb, and that we literally have not the means of carrying on the ordinary business of Government.

If necessity should require it, the armies that are prepared must, at all hazards, be put in action; but I certainly would postpone that measure until the last extremity, as I sincerely believe that if all other necessary payments of Government were suspended, it would scarcely be possible for us to provide for their support.

With regard to any movement of your own, I certainly do not wish that you should submit to any measure of insult or aggression, but I very much deprecate its taking place. The situation of Scindia and Holkar are in a very considerable degree different, and perhaps it would not be necessary to observe exactly the same conduct towards both of them. I cannot easily define, in the multiplicity of cessions and conquests, what may be considered actually, or what may be regarded virtually, as our territory; but wherever our own government has been regularly established, I would promptly resist an invasion by either of them.

From the reports I have received from our Residents, I am sorry to find that the States who are most intimately connected with us, such as the Peshwa and the Nizam, are reduced to the most forlorn condition; that these Powers possess no funds or troops on whom they can depend; that anarchy and disaffection prevail universally throughout their dominions, and that unless the British Residents exercised a power and an ascendancy that they ought not to exert, those Governments would be immediately dissolved.

The Rajah of Berar, and other chiefs who have suffered great deprivations, can certainly entertain no friendly disposition towards us, and unless a very great change can be effected in the minds of the natives of India, and in the ideas they must now harbour of our views, I confess that, under all these impressions, I cannot look forward with any sanguine hope to the establishment, by any means in our power, of that happy and permanent peace, which is so much to be desired, and of which you see so fair a prospect.

I have been indisposed for some time, and the complaint has now fallen into my feet, which puts me to great pain; I cannot therefore, at present, without considerable inconvenience make more use of my own pen than by signing my name to any letters I have occasion to write.

I am, &c.,

CORNWALLIS.

19. Mr. T. C. (later, Lord) Metcalfe.

The Policy of Sir George Barlow.

1806.

Sir George Barlow has determined, from some motives which he designates 'the fundamental principles of his administration,' to withdraw from all connexion and alliance with the states situated west of the Jumna, and to get rid of all our possessions west of the same river, with the reservation of a strip of land along its western bank of a few miles' breadth. This determination has been so powerful as to supersede every other consideration. The advantages of increased resources, the military strength of our frontier, and even our reputation, is sacrificed to it. To every argument that has been urged to dissuade the Governor-General from this determination, the same answer has always been given: 'It is a fundamental principle of my administration, and to this all other considerations must yield.'

If the Jumna was a river of such depth as to form a boundary, some reason might be supposed for making a boundary of it. But the fact is, it is everywhere fordable in all months excepting those during which, in common with it, every rivulet swelled by the rains is impassable. The lands to the west are as fertile, the people under good government would be as quiet, and the states with whom we have alliances are as good as elsewhere. What magic is it which shall make one bank of such a stream the object of dread and aversion, when the other is everything desirable? Why should an alliance on one side be useless, when on the other it is salutary? Why should influence to the right be dangerous, if to the left it is power and safety? Sir George Barlow in his closet, looking at a map, sees a black line marking the course of a river; he draws his pencil along this line, and says, 'Thus far shalt thou go, and no farther;' and this forms a fundamental principle. I can fancy no other cause for his astonishing determination to keep nothing that he can get rid of on one side of the imaginary line. But he may as well set his chair on the sands of the sea, and order the waves to stop; for the influence of Britain will roll in spite of him beyond the Jumna, or else the Atlantic Ocean will be the Jumna which shall separate the states of India from the British Empire. This inflexible rule looks too much like a government of straight lines; it looks like a government which decides political questions by examining maps in a closet, without attention to the knowledge which is to be acquired by an extensive view of the whole field.

Sir George's fundamental principle in this policy is, perhaps, part of that general principle at this moment in favor with our rulers, of withdrawing from all external connexions, and confining our views to the government of our own territories. It is asserted that our force will thus be concentrated, our power compact, and our empire at peace. Would the human body be more vigorous by the application of an axe to its limbs? Would a skilful surgeon, in order to increase its strength, cut off an arm? It is as wise to throw away the power and influence which we actually possess west of the Jumna. That power and influence I believe to be an arm to the British Empire, which may be exercised with important advantage. The treaty of peace with Holkar, bad as it is, has left us in possession of the acknowledged supremacy in Hindostan, and has liberated from Mahratta extortion and oppression those states which are under our protection[1]. The protection of these states against the Mahrattas (and there exists no other power against which we can be called to protect them) can be no encumbrance. The relinquishment of all claims upon them being acknowledged by the Mahrattas in treaties, they would certainly refrain from attacking them unless they were prepared to engage in war with us; and if they are willing to incur this risk, they may as soon make an incursion into our territories as upon our allies, or break any other article of the treaty. Nothing can be easier than to keep those states quiet with each other; say but the word, and they will be still. Of this I have no doubt. Their confirmed habits of restraint and dependence make it certain.

The assertion that these alliances are no benefit to us is not true. They form a large extent between the Mahrattas and us. Under our influence they are good neighbours. They make a good military frontier. In the event of war with the Mahrattas, hostilities are carried far from our territories, and we still enjoy the advantages of a friendly country in

[1] The mischief of this treaty has been completed by the Governor-General's subsequent acts, by the gratuitous cession of Tonk Rampoora, &c., to Holkar, the abandonment of the Rajah of Boondee to Holkar's revenge, and the rupture of the Treaty of Jyepore. [Author's note.]

our rear. These alliances afford us all the benefit which is derived from influence and supremacy. Weak as Holland is, surely France derives advantage from her influence over it. Hers is an influence by usurpation; our influence over these petty states is one of their seeking, and one which they will not resign as long as they can keep it. A proof of this is that the government, in order to get rid of the alliance with Jyepoor, sets up a right, false, I think, and unjust, to dissolve it; and proposes to persuade the Rajahs of Bhurtpore and Macheree to resign their alliances with us by offering considerable territory to them.

The most important advantage to us from these alliances is the preservation of these countries from the Mahrattas, and the consequent diminution of Mahratta power, influence, and resources. India contains no more than two great powers, British and Mahratta, and every other state acknowledges the influence of one or the other. Every inch that we recede will be occupied by them. It is a new species of policy to increase our own strength by increasing the power of our rival and natural enemy. Suppose England to have an established influence over Holland, would Ministers glory in their wisdom if they withdrew that influence and threw Holland necessarily under the oppression of France? What is it that should make political wisdom in this country so opposite to what has been considered wisdom in Europe? I have occasionally heard something of a commercial policy belonging to the Company separate from its interests as a sovereign state. Without entering here into the question how far the Company may have benefited by becoming a potentate, and granting, without discussion, the full justice of all the lamentations which are uttered on this subject by many worthy directors and proprietors, I must be allowed to say that it cannot now be helped—the evil is done. Sovereigns you are, and as such must act if you do not mean to destroy the power of acting at all, to demolish your whole corporation, your trade, and your existence. Execrate the memories of Clive and Watson, and those who first brought you from the state of merchants. Burn them in effigy, hang their statues, and blast with infamy those malefactors. Your progress since has been inevitable, and necessary to your existence. 'To stop is dangerous, to recede is ruin,' said Lord Clive at an early stage of our power. We have arrived now at that pitch that we may stop without danger, but we cannot recede without serious consequences. We have been made so strong that the idea of ruin cannot enter into my mind, and we may lose considerable strength without immediately feeling the loss. This, however, does not make it wisdom wilfully and wantonly to incur that loss, and to impair that strength. This does not make it wisdom to give power and resources to those who are our rivals, and will be again, if strengthened, our enemies. I find that I have entered on a subject that is too extensive for the purpose with which I commenced these notes.

I repeat, you are, in spite of yourselves, sovereigns, and must be guided by those rules which the wisdom of the world has applied to the government of empires.

I have heard much of the vicious consequences of the spirit of ambition and aggrandisement which has sullied our character; I have heard, I say, much of this, but have seen nothing either of the vicious consequences, or imaginary causes. That our power, reputation, glory, have been aggrandised, I cannot deny. They have been proudly and nobly aggrandised. I have also heard much of a charming notion of keeping our place in India and our tranquillity by a new system of generosity, moderation, and innocence.

This system, literally pursued, would be to give away as much as we can, to keep as little as we can, and to be as weak as we can. This is nonsense. To trust for tranquillity not to our power and influence, but to our moderation and innocence, is pretty in theory, but would be very foolish in practice, particularly applied to Mahrattas. To meet their ambition and enterprise with the language of peace, would be to preach to the roaring ocean to be still. For our security, we must rest upon our strength. Leave us as we are, but do not, by false and new doctrines, diminish the strength which we possess. Let us not establish maxims which are condemned by the history of all ages. Our empire in India is vast, and must be managed in the way of other empires. We must exist as a great state. Without croaking, it may be observed that our government is upon a dangerous experiment, and we may have cause to repent of the operation of the new principles. They have done no good yet. The assertion that we have been immoderate and aggressive is very untrue. We have, I am sure, been more moderate than any state placed in the same circumstances ever was before. I will be content to have this question decided by the natives of this country.

I do not like, in the existing policy, the inclination evident in the Governor-General's despatches to reduce every question to the consideration of mere expediency, and to give no weight to character and honor; to put out of view our proud pre-eminence, and to act as a petty, weak, temporising state. This is carried so far, and all objections are made so trifling when immediate convenience directs, as to amount in some instances (*vide* the despatches which assume the right to dissolve our alliances with the Rana of Gohud and the Rajah of Jyepore, without the consent of those allies), in my opinion, to a positive breach of faith. This policy, at least, operates to the injury of our reputation. The native powers of India understand the law of nations on a broad scale, though they may not adhere to it; but they are not acquainted with the nice quirks upon which our finished casuists would draw up a paper to establish political rights.

Our name is high, but these acts must lower it. And a natural consequence is, that we shall not again be trusted with confidence.

I would wish to see our government feelingly alive to points of honor, and less tenacious of questions of argumentative right. I would wish it to act in cases, such as the two mentioned, more according to the expectations which the native states are authorized to form, than to the letter of our own law. We may find a justification on such questions in some corner of our own books, but for the important purpose of reputation it is requisite that we should be justified in the mind of India. In the cases, however, which I have mentioned, we are justified, I think, nowhere. The arguments adduced are false (particularly on the Gohud question), and it would not be difficult to overthrow them by a plain statement of fact.

The Governor-General, in some of his despatches, distinctly says that he contemplates in the discord of the native powers an additional source of strength, and, if I am not mistaken, some of his plans go directly, and *are designed* to foment discord among those states. To foment discord seems to me barbarous, unwarrantable, and monstrous; and even to contemplate in it any source of strength is unworthy of our preeminent station. Such a policy at best can only be suited to petty estates. Applied to our empire in India it is extremely filthy[1]. Lord Wellesley's desire was to unite the tranquillity of all the powers of India with our own. How fair, how beautiful, how virtuous, does this system seem; how tenfold fair, beautiful, and virtuous when compared with the other ugly, nasty, abominable one.

But I can contemplate no source of strength in the discord of contiguous powers. It appears to me that in our advanced state of power no great contentions can arise which will not soon reach and entangle us. It is impossible completely to insulate ourselves, and we must be subject to the same chances which work upon states situated as we are. It is matter of astonishment that any person can think that it is in our power to draw in our arms and separate ourselves entirely from the affairs of India—that we can exist, great as we are, without dependent friend or foe—that wars are to kindle and rage on every part of our extensive frontier, and that we shall not be moved by them. This is a new and, I think, mistaken notion. It is our interest, I am sure (leaving out the question of morality and virtue, things not always admitted into politics), to promote the general peace. It is the only sure way of preserving tranquillity to ourselves. The acts of the last six months not only deprive us of the power of preserving peace in India, but must operate to cause and encourage dissension. I am very sorry for it.

---

[1] Lord Wellesley has censured this by anticipation. *Vide* his elegant reply to the Calcutta address in 1804. [Author's note.]

Our present motion is retrograde; I shall be happy when our governors will halt. This study to decrease our influence is funny. I cannot understand it. For my part, I wish to have our influence increased. It is generally sought for, and I am certain in its operation it gives the most real and essential benefit to all chiefs and states, and to the subjects of all chiefs and states over which it is exercised. There is a loud cry that we are in danger from extended dominion. For my part I can contemplate universal dominion in India without much fear.

I do not like the determined spirit of penury which is evident in this administration. Economy in a government is one of the greatest political virtues, but let the directors think what they will there may be too much of it if it is too parsimonious. It ceases then to be a virtue, and becomes one of the most absurd political follies, and one of the worst political vices. There is, I think, too much of it when it appears to be the ruling and sole principle of government; when it is displayed in every public advertisement and introduced into every secret despatch; when deductions of pence and farthings are considered more important than the fate of empires; in a word, when the government entirely discards liberality.

'Mere parsimony is not economy; it is separable in theory from it, and in *fact* it may, or it may not, be a part of economy, according to circumstances. Expense, and great expense, may be an essential part in true economy. If parsimony were to be considered as one of the kinds of that virtue, there is, however, another and a higher economy. Economy is a distributive virtue, and consists not in saving but in selection. Parsimony requires no providence, no sagacity, no powers of combination, no comparison, no judgment. Mere instinct, and that not an instinct of the noblest kind, may produce this false economy in perfection. The other economy has larger views.'

In a service like this, which is pursued for an independence, and to which the wealthy never have recourse, and in which services cannot be rewarded with honors, merit must be rewarded by situations uniting credit with emolument. It is in the nature of the human character to look to a reward. Without this hope there would be much less of zeal and public spirit than there now is. Self-love plays its part in our most disinterested acts. Every government of the world has instituted rewards as well as punishment for the encouragement of public virtue among its citizens; and when a government loses sight of this principle, it will soon lose the power of rewarding any public virtue, for all virtue will be extinguished. When a man's conscience tells him that he has worked hard and merited well, he expects reward.

I look on the consideration of public service or public ornament to be real and very justice; and I ever held a scanty and penurious justice to partake of the nature of a wrong. I hold it to be in its consequences the worst economy in the world. In saving money I soon can count up all the good I do; but when, by a cold penury, I blast the abilities of a nation, the ill I may do is beyond all calculation.

Indeed, no man knows, when he cuts off the incitements to a virtuous ambition, and the just rewards of public service, what infinite mischief he may do his country through all generations. Such saving to the public may prove the worst mode of robbing it.

Individuals may repeatedly be disappointed, as in all states some must be, without any extensive injury to the public interests, because the hope which is the incitement remains for all; but when to withhold reward and distinction comes to be a system of administration, then the public interests will suffer injury, incalculable injury. There is reason to think that this is the case, from the apparent system of this administration. Its inflexible adherence to its principles of parsimony, and its boasting display of them, leads us to believe that liberality is excluded from its vocabulary.

If this is the case, we may take the liberty of observing, that the present government will not excite zeal, will not encourage ability, and is no friend to enterprise, but a sure check to all public energies and spirit, and the consequences must be bad.

Distinct from the faults of parsimony, but operating with the same effect, is the coldness and want of feeling of the government. It does nothing with warmth and heart. This may appear to be a foolish objection, but will not prove to be so. Something more than cold approbation is required to foster great minds—the approbation should be hearty. Men who perform great actions want to be admired, and are not content with being approved. Men may serve under such a government correctly, but the good of the state requires that they should serve zealously. Men will not serve zealously unless their government is zealous to do them honor. I venture to pronounce that this administration will be coldly served. Lord Wellesley, from the fire of patriotism which blazed in his own breast, emitted sparks which animated the breasts of all who came within the reach of his notice.

Our present Governor is too cold in his own character to give any warmth to others; and this characteristic of his private life seems to be a feature of his public administration. If the case could be supposed of a state in which public spirit and the whole train of public virtues should be persecuted, condemned, and punished, it is not difficult to conceive that public virtues would, in that state, cease to exist. And by the same rule it appears that if these virtues are slighted and neglected, they will not flourish with the strength and beauty which is given to them by culture and attention.

There are truly great patriots, who, under any circumstances, will zealously labor for the interests of their country; but some uncommon greatness is required to keep them in their righteous course under such obstacles as have been alluded to. Such, then, there are; but general arguments are applied to the generality, and these do certainly require the stimulants of Hope and Ambition.

These loose, unconnected notes may serve to convey to my father, some of my ideas on the present administration. The subject is so extensive, that if I continued my observations, I should swell my paper to an enormous size. I am too lazy to put what I have said into any decent form; and after all, my thoughts can be of no importance.

I respect Sir George Barlow, and wish him well; but I cannot approve the principles which he professes and acts upon.

Lord Wellesley's system was abandoned at an unfortunate period, when its success was nearly completed. If that system had been carried into complete operation, permanent peace and consequent wealth would have been in our hands. The abandonment of that system, in an unlucky moment, throws India back into its former state of confusion and uncertainty. Our tranquillity will again depend upon the will of either Sindhiah, Holkar, or Bhoonsla; and our only hope of the continuance of it rests upon the notion that those chiefs, singly or united, will never dare to risk a war with us. I hope, as much as any man can, that the dread of our valor will always operate upon them; but I am convinced that an increase of their strength and influence, and a diminution of our own, are not the best means of keeping alive their consciousness of our superiority[1].

20. The same Writer.

Extension of Territory, and its Results.

(Extract.) December, 1814.

According to the system prescribed for our conduct in India, we are bound to be horror-struck at the bare idea of an increase of territory. Yet, unless we can raise additional resources in our present dominions, it is only by an extension of territory that we can obtain an increase of revenue for the support of our necessary expenses.

It may be objected to an increase of territory, that it is often attended with an extension of embarrassments, leading to an increase of expense beyond the amount of the additional revenue. It is sometimes so, and sometimes otherwise, according to circumstances. If by the extension of territory a State extend its frontiers, and come in contact with warlike powers with whom it never clashed before, then an increase of territory may become a source of such expense as will absorb more than the additional revenue derived from the addition of territory.

---

[1] *Selections from the Papers of Lord Metcalfe*, by John William Kaye, pp. 1–11.

But if the extension of territory improve the frontier—that is, render it more defensible—if it make dominions less divided and more compact—if it unite distant parts of territories and relations, and establish communications between points before unconnected—if it make the whole of the forces and resources of a State more available and more easily to be brought together to any given point, then an increase of territory, so far from being attended necessarily with an increase of expense, might enable a State to reduce its former expenses, and would, at all events, give an accession of strength, and afford payment for an addition of military force, without bringing on any concomitant source of weakness.

The preceding observations apply retrospectively and prospectively to our situation in India. We have made acquisitions of territory, such as those described under the first supposition, as the present extent of our frontier, combined with the multiplicity and perplexity of our foreign relations, will show.

21. Colonel George Chesney.

Result of Lord Wellesley's administration.

The administration of Lord Wellesley may be regarded as the third great epoch in the formation of the British Indian Empire. The acquisition of Bengal, Behar, and Orissa was in a great measure accidental. The managers of the Company's affairs at that time, both in England and India, would have been quite satisfied with maintaining the state of things under which the Nawab had the appearance, and they the reality, of power. That he should be driven to try conclusions with them was quite unexpected, and Clive, opportunely returning to India, discerned the advantage of the acquisition offered. The era of Lord Cornwallis was marked chiefly by administrative reforms, the territorial extension effected by him having been comparatively small; while, as has been already observed, his foreign policy was directed to maintain the *status quo* he found existing in India, and especially to cultivate friendly relations with the Mahrattas. Lord Wellesley was the first to perceive that in India a political equilibrium was impossible; that peace was only to be ensured by establishing the preponderance of British power; and that the task of breaking down the Mahratta Confederacy was as practicable as, sooner or later, it must have been necessary to be undertaken. The result of the contest was never for a moment doubtful, and from this time the Company became beyond all question the paramount power in India, even the states which remained independent submitting to receive a supervising British agent at their courts, and a subsidiary garrison of British troops. Henceforward the only country which could measure swords against it with any chance of success lay beyond the Sutlej; and from this time it may be said that the duties of territorial government took the place of buying and selling as the leading pursuit of the Company's servants in India.

His policy reversed by successors.

This policy was worked out by Lord Wellesley, not under the guidance of, but in direct opposition to, the wishes of his masters in England. The Directors, although they had from the first carried on their trade at a loss, still clung to trade as the only means of squaring their balance-sheet, and regarded with distrust every addition of territory, as productive of debt and financial embarrassment. Very much the same view appears to have been held by the English ministry; while the question has been much debated, whether Lord Wellesley's measures were not so far voluntary, rather than forced upon him by circumstances, as to constitute an infraction of the Acts of Parliament of 1784 and 1793, which enjoined a defensive and neutral policy, and distinctly prohibited territorial aggrandisement. However that may have been, the course pursued by Lord Wellesley, once entered on, could not be retraced; but the Court notwithstanding vainly desired to return to the former state of non-intervention and political equality with the Mahratta powers; and the influence of their sentiments so far affected the policy of Lord Wellesley's immediate successors, that the complete pacification of Central India, contemplated by him, was suspended on the eve of its accomplishment, and deferred till twelve years later. The Mahratta war of 1817–18 was the fruit of the timid policy of non-intervention pursued from 1805 until that time, and was forced on Lord Hastings' administration by the state of lawlessness which had grown up in Central India.[1]

[1] *Indian Polity*, pp. 32–33, 1st edition.

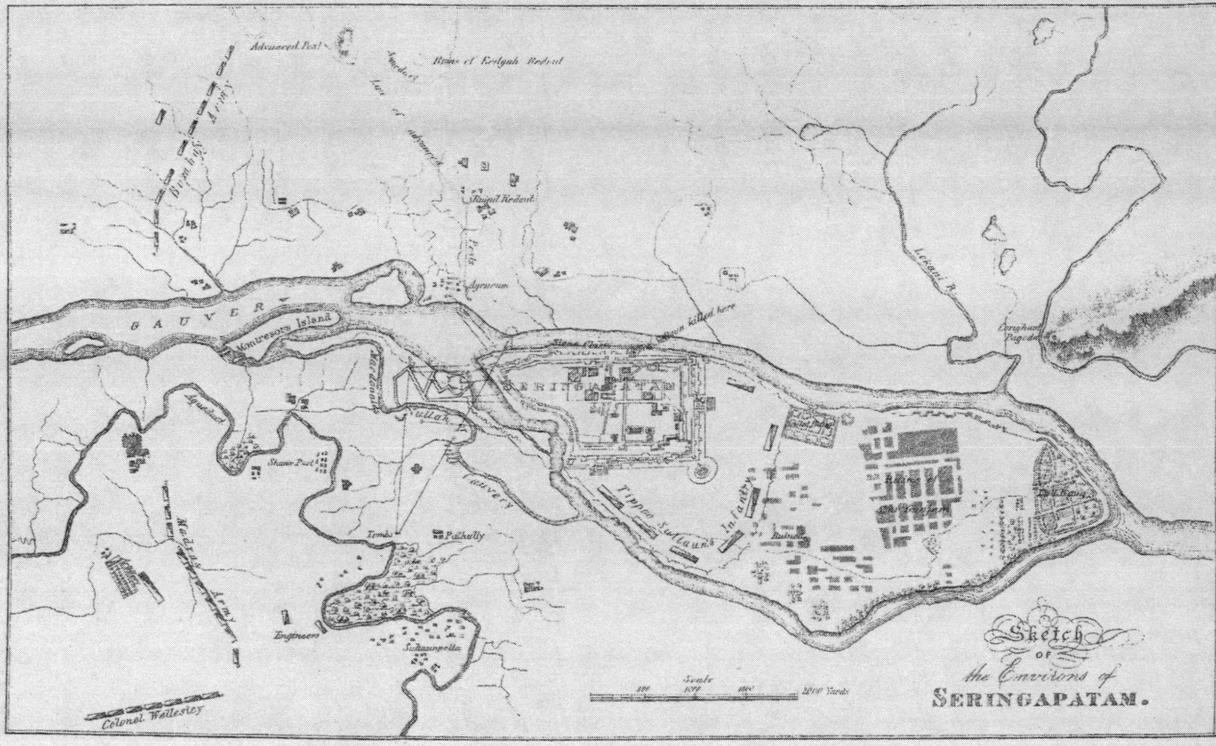
Sketch
OF
the Environs of
SERINGAPATAM.
Advanced Post
Ruins of Eedgah Redout
Line of advance
Bombay Army
Round Redout
Agrarum
GAUVERY
Montresors Island
Stone Chan
Lokani R.
Aqueduct
Shaw Post
Nullah
Cauvery
Tombs
Pachally
Tippoo Sultauns
Infantry
Madras Army
Engineers
Sultaunpetta
Colonel Wellesley
Scale
2000 Yards

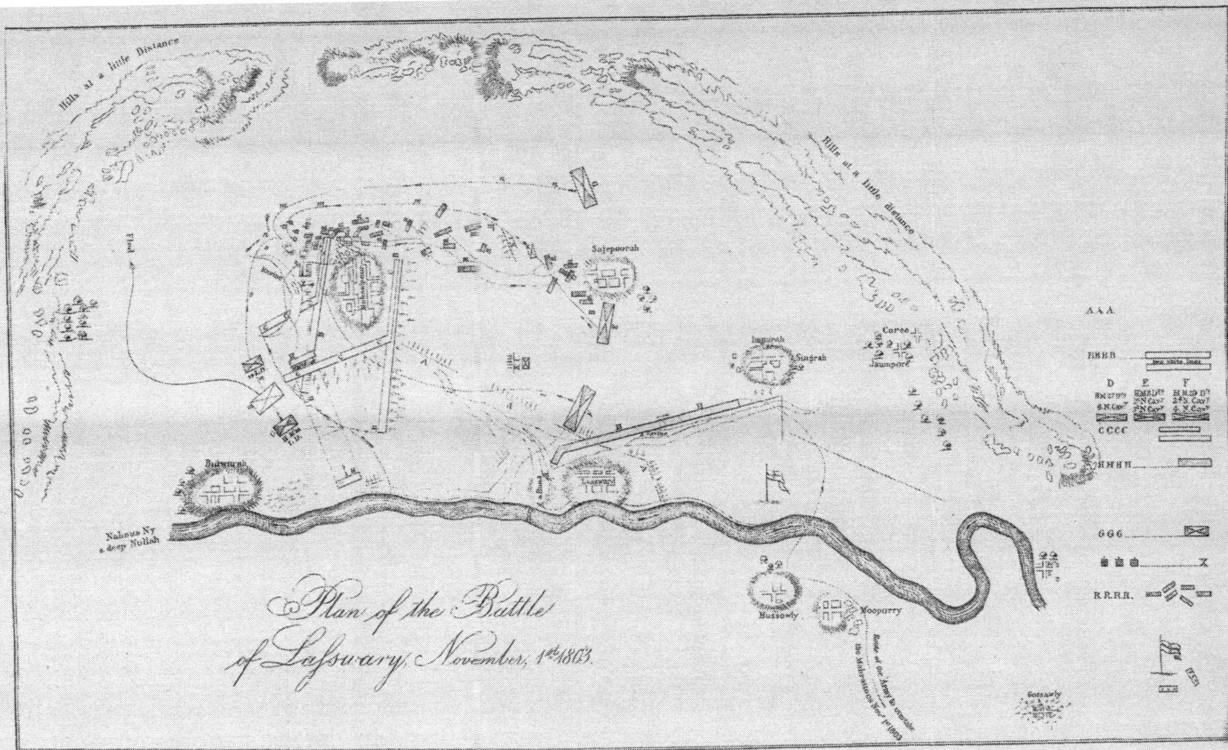

Plan of the Battle of Lafswary, November, 1st 1803.